NTC's ROMANIAN and ENGLISH Dictionary

Andrei Bantaş

NTC Publishing Group

Library of Congress Cataloging-in-Publication Data
is available from the United States Library of Congress.

First published in 1995 by NTC Publishing Group
A division of NTC/Contemporary Publishing Group, Inc.
4255 West Touhy Avenue, Lincolnwood (Chicago), Illinois 60646-1975 U.S.A.
Copyright © 1993 by TEORA Publishers, Romania
Printed in the United States of America
International Standard Book Number: 0-8442-4976-9
99 00 01 02 03 04 BC 21 20 19 18 17 16 15 14 13 12 11 10 9 8 7 6 5 4 3

CONTENTS

PREFACE

NTC's Romanian and English Dictionary is a two-way bilingual dictionary covering about 15,000 entries in each section. Each entry has an indication of its part of speech and, where appropriate, an indication of the
domain of the entry word. Many entries contain sub-entries showing
common compounds or other collocations. The word list includes scientific, medical, literary, and legal terms. The definitions and explanatory
material are concise and understandable, having been prepared by
Professor Andrei Bantaş, an internationally recognized scholar and lexi-
cographer of the Romanian language.

The English entries are equipped with a pronunciation aid using the phonetic symbols of the International Phonetic Association. Students of the
Romanian language will find that this dictionary will serve their needs
extremely well. English-speaking travelers in Romania, as well as Romanian-
speaking visitors in the English-speaking world, will find this volume useful,
up-to-date, and of the highest level of precision and scholarship.

Romanian-English

LIST OF ABBREVIATIONS

adj.	=	adjective	geom.	=	geometry
adv.	=	adverb	gram.	=	grammar
agr.	=	agriculture	impers.	=	impersonal
amer.	=	American	iht.	=	ichthyology
anat.	=	anatomy	interj.	=	interjection
aprox.	=	approximate	interog.	=	interrogative
arhit.	=	architecture	iron.	=	ironic
art.	=	article	ist.	=	history
astr.	=	astronomy	înv.	=	old-fashioned
auto.	=	automobiles	jur.	=	law
av.	=	aviation	lingv.	=	linguistics
bot.	=	botany	lit.	=	literary
c.f.	=	railways	mar.	=	navy
chim.	=	chemistry	mat.	=	mathmatics
com.	=	commerce	meta.	=	metalurgy
conj.	=	conjunction	med.	=	medicine
constr.	=	engineering	milt.	=	military
d.	=	about	muz.	=	music
dat.	=	dative	neg.	=	negative
econ.	=	economics	num.	=	numeral
el.	=	electricity	opt.	=	optics
entom.	=	entomology	ornit.	=	ornithology
fem.	=	feminine	part.	=	participle
fig.	=	figurative	peior.	=	derogatory
fin.	=	finance	pl.	=	plural
foto.	=	photography	poet.	=	poetic
gen.	=	genitive	pol.	=	politics
geog.	=	geography	poligr.	=	printing

prep.	=	preposition	tehn.	=	technology
pron.	=	pronoun	tel.	=	telecommunications
pt.	=	for	text.	=	textiles
rad.	=	radio	univ.	=	university
rel.	=	religion	v.	=	see
sf.	=	substantive feminine	v. aux.	=	auxiliary verb
sing.	=	singular	vi.	=	intransitive verb
sm.	=	substantive masculine	viit.	=	future
smb.	=	somebody	v. mod.	=	modal verb
smth.	=	something	vr.	=	reflexive verb
sn.	=	substantive neuter	vt.	=	transitive verb
superl.	=	superlative	zool.	=	zoology

A

a *art. hot. fem.* the. *art. pos.* of; ~ *lui Petru* Peter's; ~ *lui* his. *v aux.* has. *prep.* like; of. *interj.* a(h)! o(h)! *particulă infinitivală* to.

abajur *sn.* (lamp) shade.

abandon *sn.* abandonment.

abandona *vt., vi.* to abandon.

abandonare *sf.* renunciation; *(părăsire)* desertion.

abanos *sm.* ebony (tree).

abataj *sn. min.* working.

abate *sm.* abbot. *vt.* to divert; to turn; *a ~ de la drumul drept* to lead astray. *vr.* to swerve; to stray; *a se ~ asupra* to swoop upon; *a i se ~* to occur to one.

abatere *sf.* deviation; *(disciplinară)* misbehaviour.

abator *sn.* slaughter-house.

abătut *adj.* depressed.

abces *sn.* abscess.

abdica *vi.* to abdicate (smth.).

abecedar *sn.* primer.

abia *adv.* hardly.

abil *adj.* skilful; *(şiret)* sly.

abilitate *sf.* skill.

abis *sn.* abyss.

abitir *adv.: mai ~* better; harder.

abnegaţie *sf.* abnegation.

aboli *vt.* to abolish.

abona *vr.* to subscribe (to a newspaper etc.).

abonament *sn.* *(la ziar* etc.) subscription; *(foaie* sau *carnet)* season ticket.

abonat *sm.* subscriber.

aborda *vt.* to approach.

abrevia *vt.* to abbreviate.

abroga *vt.* to repeal.

abrupt *adj.* steep; *fig.* abrupt.

absent *sm.* absentee. *adj.* absent; *fig.* absent-minded.

absenţă *sf.* absence; *(lipsă)* want.

absolut *adj.* absolute. *adv.* absolutely.

absolvent *sm.* graduate.

absolvi *vt.* to graduate; *fig.* to absolve.

absorbi *vt.* to absorb; *fig.* to engross.

abstract *adj.* abstract.

absurd *sn., adj.* absurd.

abţibild *sn.* transfer picture.

abţine *vr.* to refrain.

abţinere *sf.* abstention.

abundent *adj.* abundant.

abundenţă *sf.* plenty.

abur *sm.* steam; *fig.* fume.

aburi *vt., vi., vr.* to steam.

abuz *sn.* abuse; *~ de încredere* breach of trust.

abuza *vt.: a ~ de* to misuse; to abuse.

ac *sn.* needle; *(bold)* pin; *(de viespe* etc.*)* sting; *~ de păr* hairpin; *~ de siguranţă* safety pin.

acadea *sf.* lollipop.
academician *sm.* academician.
academie *sf.* academy.
acapara *vt.* to monopolize.
acear *sm.* pointsman.
aceareturi *sn. pl.* outhouses; *(lucruri)* chattels; *(unelte)* implements.
acasă *adv.* at home; in; *(spre casă)* home.
accelera *vt.* to speed (up). *vi. auto.* to step on the gas.
accelerat *sn.* fast train. *adj.* accelerated; *c.f.* fast.
accent *sn.* stress; *(străin* etc.) accent.
accentua *vt.* to stress. *vr.* to increase.
accepta *vt.* to accept.
acces *sn.* access; *(de furie* etc.) fit.
accesibil *adj.* easy of access.
accesoriu *sn., adj.* accessory.
accident *sn.* accident.
aceu *adj.* that.
aceasta *adj.* this. *pron.* this (one).
această *adj.* this.
aceea *adj.* that. *pron.* that (one); *după* ~ then.
aceeași *adj., pron.* the same.
același *adj., pron.* the same.
aceea *adj.* that. *pron.* that (one).
același *adj., pron.* the same.
aceleași *adj., pron.* the same.
acest *adj.* this.
acesta *adj.* this. *pron.* this (one).
acestea *adj.* these; *toate* ~ all this; all these. *pron.* these (ones); *cu toate* ~ nevertheless.
aceștia *adj.* these. *pron.* these (ones).
achita *vt.* to pay (off); *jur.* to acquit. *vr. a se* ~ *de* to discharge *(a duty,* etc.).

achiziție *sf.* acquisition.
acid *sm., adj.* acid.
aclama *vt., vi.* to cheer.
aclamație *sf.* ovation.
acolo *adv.* there.
acomoda *vr.* to put up (with).
acompania *vt.* to accompany.
acompaniament *sn.* accompaniment.
acont *sn.* advance (money).
aconta *vt.* to pay an instalment on.
acoperi *vt.* to cover; to hide; *fig* to screen. *vr.* to cover oneself; to put on one's hat *sau* clothes.
acoperire *sf.* cover(ing); *fin.* security.
acoperiș *sn.* roof.
acord *sn.* agreement; *mus.* chord; *de* ~ *!* all right.
acorda *vt.* to grant; to concede; *muz., radio* to tune.
acordeon *sn.* accordion.
acosta *vt.* to accost. *vi.* to land.
acreală *sf.* sourness.
acri *vt.* to (make) sour. *vr.* to (turn) sour; *a i se* ~ *(de ceva)* to be fed up (with smth.).
acrobat *sm.* acrobat.
acrobație *sf.* acrobatics.
acru *sm.* acre *(0,4 ha). adj.* sour.
act *sn.* document, paper; *(acțiune)* action, deed, act; *(teatru)* act.
activ *sn., adj.* active.
activa *vt.* to hasten. *vi.* to work.
activist *sm.* militant.
activitate *sf.* activity.
actor *sm.* actor.
actriță *sf.* actress.
actual *adj.* present(-day); *(interesant)* topical.

actualitate *sf.* present; topical interest.

actualmente *adv.* now(adays).

acţiona *vt.* to sue. *vi.* to act.

acţionar *sm.* shareholder; *mare ~* stockholder.

acţiune *sf.* act(ion); *lit.* plot, story; *fin.* share; *jur.* (law)suit.

acuarelă *sf.* watercolour(s).

acum *adv.* now(adays); at once; *~ doi ani* two years ago.

acumulator *sn.* accumulator.

acustică *sf.* acoustics.

acut *adj.* acute.

acuza *vt.* to accuse.

acuzare *sf.* indictment.

acuzat *sm.* accused.

acuzativ *sn.*, *adj.* accusative.

acuzaţie *sf.* charge.

acvariu *sn.* aquarium.

adaos *sn.* addition; annex.

adapta *vt.*, *vr.* to adapt (oneself).

adăpa *vi.* to water. *vr.* to drink.

adăpost *sn.* shelter; *~ antiaerian* air-raid shelter; *la ~* safe(ly).

adăposti *vt.* to shelter; *(a găzdui)* to lodge. *vr.* to take shelter.

adăuga *vt.* to add. *vr.* to be added.

adecvat *adj.* suitable.

ademeni *vt.* to lure; to seduce.

adept *sm.* advocate, supporter.

adera *vi.* to adhere.

adesea, adeseori *adv.* often.

adevăr *sn.* truth(fulness); fact(s).

adevărat *adj.* true; real. *adv.* truly; really, actually.

adeveri *vt.* to certify. *vr.* to prove true.

adeverinţă *sf.* certificate; *(de primire)* receipt.

adeziune *sf.* adhesion.

adia *vi.* to breeze.

adică *adv.* that is; viz; *(şi anume)* namely; *la o ~* at a pinch.

adiere *sf.* breath of wind.

adineauri *adv.* just now.

adio *interj.* farewell!; good-bye!

adînc *sn.* depth; *fig.* bottom. *adj.* deep; *(temeinic)* thorough(going); *~i bătrîneţe* advanced years. *adv.* deeply; *(temeinic)* thoroughly.

adînci *vt.* to deepen; *fig.* to analyse profoundly. *vr.* to deepen; *(a se afunda, şi fig.)* to plunge.

adîncime *sf.* depth.

adjectiv *sn.* adjective.

adjunct *sm.* deputy; assistant.

administra *vt.* to administer.

administrator *sm.* administrator.

administraţie *sf.* administration; *mil.* commissariat.

admira *vt.* to admire.

admirabil *adj.* admirable. *adv.* admirably.

admirativ *adj.* admiring. *adv.* admiringly.

admirator *sm.* admirer.

admiraţie *sf.* admiration.

admis *adj.* accepted.

admite *vt.* to admit (of).

admitere *sf.* admission; *(la facultate)* matriculation.

admonesta *vt.* to reprimand.

adnota *vt.* to annotate.

adolescent *sm.*, **adolescentă** *sf.* teen-ager.

adolescenţă *sf.* adolescence; teens.

adopta *vt.* to adopt.

adoptare *sf.* adoption; *(aprobare)* endorsement.

adoptiv *adj.* adoptive.

adora *vt.* to love, to worship.

adorabil *adj.* adorable.

adorator *sm.* worshipper; *(al unei femei)* beau, suitor.

adormi *vt.* to lull (to sleep). *vi.* to fall asleep; to go to sleep.

adormit *adj.* asleep; sleepy.

adresa *vt.* to address. *vr.: a se ~ la* to appeal to; to address.

adresă *sf.* address; *la adresa cuiva fig.* against *sau* about smb.

aduce *vt.* to bring (in); to fetch; *(a produce)* to bring about; *(a conduce)* to take; *a(-i) ~ aminte* to remind; *a ~ la îndeplinire* to fulfil. *vi.: a ~ a sau cu* to look like.

aducere *sf.* bringing; *~ aminte* recollection; *~ la îndeplinire* fulfilment.

adula *vt.* to lionize.

adulmeca *vt.* to sniff; to smell.

adult *sm., adj.* grown-up.

adulter *sn.* adultery. *adj.* unfaithful.

aduna *vt.* to add; *(a strînge)* to gather (in); *(oameni)* to rally; *a-și ~ mințile* to collect oneself. *vi.* to add. *vr.* to rally.

adunare *sf.* addition; *pol.* assembly, meeting; *Marea Adunare Națională a R.S.R.* the Grand National Assembly of the Socialist Republic of Romania.

adunătură *sf.* gathering; *(amestec)* heap; *(gloată)* mob.

adus *adj.* brought; *~ de spate* stooping.

adverb *sn.* adverb.

advers *adj.* adverse.

adversar *sm.* opponent.

aer *sn.* air; *(înfățișare)* look(s); aspect; *în ~ liber* in the open (air).

aerian *adj.* air(y); aerial.

aerisi *vt., vr.* to air (oneself).

aerodinamic *adj.* aerodynamic.

aerodrom *sn.* airport.

aeromodel *sn.* plane model.

aeroplan *sn.* (air)plane.

aeroport *sn.* airport.

afabil *adj.* courteous.

afacere *sf.* affair; *fin.* business; *jur. și* case; *(chestiune)* matter; *afaceri externe* foreign affairs; *afaceri interne* home *sau* domestic affairs.

afacerist *sm.* racketeer.

afară *adv.* out(side); *~ de* except; *~ de asta* moreover.

afecta *vt.* to affect; to simulate; *(a preocupa)* to concern.

afectare *sf.* affectation; *(simulare)* pretence; *(destinare)* earmarking.

afectiv *adj.* emotional.

afectuos *adj.* affectionate. *adv.* lovingly.

afecțiune *sf.* affection.

afemeiat *sm.* ladies' man. *adj.* intemperate.

aferat *adj.* fussy.

afilia *vt., vr.* to affiliate.

afiliere *sf.* affiliation.

afin *sm.,* **afină** *sf. bot.* bilberry.

afinitate *sf.* affinity.

afirma *vt., vr.* to assert (oneself).

afirmativ *adj.* affirmative. *adv.* in the affirmative.

afirmație *sf.* assertion; *(neîntemeiată)* allegation.

afiș *sn.* poster; (play) bill.

afișa *vt.* to post; *fig.* to display. *vr.: a se ~ cu* to go out with.

afișier *sn.* bill *sau* notice board.

afîna *vt.* to break up.

afla *vt.* to learn (of), to hear. *vi.* to hear. *vr.* to be (present);

(a se răspîndi) to get abroad;
se află ceva cărţi pe acolo? are
there any books there?; *a
se ~ în treabă* to poke one's
nose (somewhere).

aflător *adj.* available.

afluent *sm.* tributary.

afluenţă *sf.* affluence.

aflux *sn.* rush.

afon *adj.* having no ear for
music.

african *sm., adj.,* **africană** *sf.,
adj.* African.

afront *sn.* outrage.

afuma *vt., vi.* to smoke.

afumat *adj.* smoked; *(beat)* tipsy.

afunda *vt., vr.* to plunge.

afurisit *adj.* accursed; *fig.* mischievous.

agale *adv.* leisurely; idly.

agasa *vt.* to annoy.

agat *sm.,* **agată** *sf.* agate.

agăţa *vt.* to hang (up); *(pe cineva)* to accost. *vr.: a se ~ de*
to catch at; *fig.* to cavil at.

agăţătoare *sf.* hanger; *bot.* climber.

ageamiu *sm.* greenhorn.

agendă *sf.* agenda; *(de buzunar)* pocket book.

agent *sm.* agent; policeman;
fin. broker.

agenţie *sf.* agency.

ager *adj.* keen.

agerime *sf.* keenness.

agheasmă *sf.* holy water.

aghiotant *sm.* aide (de camp).

agil *adj.* nimble.

agita *vt.* to stir. *vr.* to fret.

agitat *adj.* restless.

agitator *sm.* agitator.

agitatoric *adj.* propaganda.

agitaţie *sf.* agitation; *fig.* excitement.

aglomera *vt., vr.* to crowd.

aglomeraţie *sf.* crowd, throng.

agonie *sf.* agony.

agonisi *vt.* to earn; *(a aduna)*
to save.

agrafă *sf.* clip; safety *sau*
hair pin.

agrar *adj.* agricultural; agrarian.

agrava *vt., vr.* to worsen, to
aggravate.

agravare *sf.* worsening.

agrea *vt.* to like.

agreabil *adj.* agreeable.

agrement *sn.* pleasure; *(încuviinţare)* consent.

agresiune *sf.* aggression.

agresiv *adj.* aggressive; *(bătăios)* truculent.

agresor *sm.* aggressor.

agricol *adj.* agricultural.

agricultor *sm.* farmer.

agricultură *sf.* agriculture; farming.

agriş *sm.,* **agrişă** *sf.* gooseberry.

agronom *sm.* agronomist.

agronomic *adj.* agronomic(al).

agronomie *sf.* agronomy.

ah *interj.* ah (me)!

aha *interj.* oh (I see)!

ahtiat *adj.* dead set (on).

ai *art.* of; *~ mei* my folk(s).

aia *adj., pron.* that.

aici *adv.* here; *de ~* hence;
de ~ înainte from now on;
pe ~ this way; *(prin împrejurimi)* here (abouts); *pînă ~*
so far; enough!

aidoma *adj.* (quite) alike.

aievea *adj.* virtual. *adv.* virtually.

ailaltă *adj.* the other. *pron.*
the other (one).

aisberg *sn.* iceberg.

aiura *vi.* to rant.

aiurea *adv.* foolishly; *(în altă*

parte) elsewhere. *interj.* nonsense!

aiureală *sf.* raving; *(prostii)* nonsense; *(zăpăceală)* confusion.

aiurit *sm.* zany. *adj.* moony.

ajun *sn.* eve; *~ul Anului nou* New Year's Eve; *în ~ (ul acelei zile)* on the eve (of that day).

ajunge *vt.* to overtake; *(a atinge)* to reach. *vi.* to arrive; *(a deveni)* to (be)come; *(a fi suficient)* to be enough; *~!* that will do! enough! *a nu ~* to fall short. *vr.* to be enough, to do; *(a parveni)* to get on (in the world).

ajuns *sn.: de ~* sufficient; enough. *adj.* successful.

ajusta *vt., vr.* to fit; to adjust.

ajuta *vt., vi.* to help; to assist. *vr.* to help each other; *c se ~ cu* to make use of.

ajutător *adj.* auxiliary.

ajutor *sm.* assistant. *sn.* help; assistance; *(material)* relief; aid; *(sprijin)* support; *(de boală etc.)* benefit; *de ~* helpful.

al *art.* of; *~ mamei* mother's; *~ meu* mine.

alai *sn.* procession; *(pompă)* pomp.

alaltăieri *adv.* the day before yesterday.

alaltăseară *adv.* the night before last.

alamă *sf. (și pl.)* brass.

alambic *sn.* still.

alambicat *adj.* (over) elaborate.

alandala *adv.* at random; *(pe dos)* topsy-turvy.

alarma *vt.* to alarm. *vr.* to be alarmed.

alarmant *adj.* alarming; *(amenințător)* ominous.

alarmă *sf.* alarm.

alăpta *vt.* to suckle.

alătura *vt.* to juxtapose; *(a atașa)* to enclose. *vr.* to come near; *a se ~ la* to join.

alăturat *adi.* adjoining; *(atașat)* enclosed. *adv.* (here) enclosed.

alături *adv.* (close) by; *(umăr la umăr)* side by side; *(în vecini)* next door; *~ de* alongside (of).

alb *sm.* white (man). *sn.* white. *adj.* white; *(gol)* blank.

albanez *sm., adj.,* **albaneză** *sf., adj.* Albanian.

albastru *sn.* blue (sky). *adj.* blue; *fig.* hard.

albatros *sm.* albatross.

albă *sf.* white woman; *Albă ca zăpada* Snow-White.

albăstrea *sf.* cornflower.

albeață *sf.* white (spot).

albi *vt.* to whiten. *vi., vr.* to turn white *sau* grey.

albicios *adj.* whitish.

albie *sf.* riverbed; *(copaie)* trough.

albină *sf.* bee.

album *sn.* album.

albuș *sn.* white (of egg).

alcătui *vt.* to make (up). *vr.: a se ~ din* to consist of.

alcătuire *sf.* structure.

alchimie *sf.* alchemy.

alchimist *sm.* alchemist.

alcool *sn.* alcohol; spirit(s).

alcoolic *sm.* alcohol addict. *adj.* alcoholic.

aldămaș *sn.: a bea ~ul* to wet the bargain.

alde *art.* the. *prep.* like, such as; *de ~ astea* such things.

alea *adj., pron.* those.
alee *sf.* alley; *(pt. trăsuri* etc.) drive; *(pt. plimbare)* walk.
alegător *sm.* elector, voter.
alege *vt., vi.* to choose, to select; *pol.* to elect. *vr.* to be chosen *sau* elected; *a se ~ cu* to be left with.
alegere *sf.* choice; selection; *pol. (și pl.)* election.
alegorie *adj.* allegoric(al).
alegorie *sf.* allegory.
alene *adv.* idly.
alerga *vi.* to run to race; *(a se grăbi)* to rush.
alergare *sf.* race, run.
alergător *sm.* runner. *adj.* running.
alergătură *sf.* running (to and fro); *fig.* trouble.
ales *sm.* person of one's choice. *sn.* choice; *pe ~e* at choice. *adj.* select(ed); choice.
alfabet *sn.* alphabet.
alfabetic *adj.* alphabetic.
alfabetiza *vt.* to teach (smb.) the three r's.
algă *sf.* alga.
algebră *sf.* algebra.
algebric *adj.* algebraic(al).
alia *vt.* to ally; *tehn.* to alloy. *vr.* to become allied.
aliaj *sn.* alloy.
alianță *sf.* alliance.
aliat *sm.* ally. *adj.* allied.
alibi *sn.* alibi.
alice *sf. pl.* small shot.
alifie *sf.* ointment, salve.
aligator *sm.* alligator.
aliment *sn. (și pl.)* food.
alimenta *vt., vr.* to feed; to supply.
alimentar *adj.* food...
alimentară *sf.* food shop.
alimentație *sf.* nourishment.

alina *vt.* to soothe.
alineat *sn.* paragraph.
alinia *vt., vr.* to line (up); to fall into line.
alinta *vt.* to spoil; *(a mîngîia)* to caress. *vr.* to simper.
alipi *vt.* to join. *vr.: a se ~ la* to join.
almanah *sn.* almanac(k).
alo *interj.* hullo!
aloca *vt.* to allot, to earmark.
alocație *sf.* allocation.
alocuri *adv.: pe ~* here and there.
alpaca *sf.* alpaca; (aliaj) argentan.
alpin *adj.* Alpine.
alpinism *sn.* mountaineering.
alpinist *sm.* mountaineer.
alt *adj.* (an)other; further; *pron. un ~ul, o altă* another (one); *alții, altele* others.
altar *sn.* altar; *arhit.* chancel.
altădată *adv.* another time; *(de mult)* formerly; *de ~* former.
altceva *pron.* something else; *interog. sau neg.* anything.
altcineva *pron.* another; somebody else; *interog. sau neg.* anybody else.
alteori *adv.* (at) other times.
altera *vt.* to adulterate. *vr.* to go bad.
alterna *vt., vi.* to alternate.
alternativ *adj.* alternative; *el.* alternating.
alternativă *sf.* alternative.
alteță *sf.* Highness.
altfel *adv.* otherwise; or (else).
altist *sm.,* **altistă** *sf.* alto.
altitudine *sf.* height.
altminteri *adv.* otherwise; or else.

altòi[1] *sn.* graft(ing).
altoi[2] *vt.* to (en)graft.
altoire *sf.* grafting.
altruist *sm.* altruist. *adj.* selfless.
altundeva *adv.* elsewhere.
aluat *sn.* dough.
aluminiu *sn.* aluminium.
alun *sm.* filbert.
alună *sf.* hazel(nut); *(arahi-dă)* ground-nut.
aluneca *vi.* to slide; *(a cădea)* to slip.
alunecare *sf.* slip; slide.
alunecos *adj.* slippery.
alunga *vt.* to drive (away).
aluniţă *sf.* beauty spot; *(neg)* mole.
aluzie *sf.* hint; *(răutăcioasă)* innuendo.
aluziv *adj.* allusive.
alviţă *sf.* nougat.
amabil *adj.* kind(ly). *adv.* kindly.
amalgam *sn.* amalgam.
amanet *sn.* pawn.
amaneta *vt.* to pawn.
amant *sm.* lover.
amantă *sf.* mistress.
amar *sn.* bitterness. *adj.* bitter. *adv.* bitterly.
amarnic *adj., adv.* hard.
amator *sm.* fan; *(diletant)* amateur. *adj.* amateur.
amăgeală *sf.* mystification.
amăgi *vt.* to mistify; *(a momi)* to lure. *vr.* to indulge in illusions.
amăgire *sf.* delusion.
amăgitor *adj.* (d)elusive.
amănunt *sn.* detail; *cu ~ul* (by) retail.
amănunţit *adj.* detailed, minute. *adv.* in (great) detail.
amărăciune, amăreală *sf.* bitterness.

amărî *vt.* to embitter. *vr.* to become bitter *sau* embittered.
amărît *sm.* poor devil. *adj.* embittered.
ambala *vt.* to pack. *vr.* to warm up.
ambalaj *sn.*, ambalare *sf.* packing.
ambasadă *sf.* embassy.
ambasador *sm.* ambassador; *fig.* messenger.
ambianţă *sf.* environment, milieu.
ambiguitate *sf.* ambiguity.
ambiguu *adj.* ambiguous.
ambii *pron., num.* both.
ambiţie *sf.* ambition.
ambiţios *adj.* ambitious.
ambulant *adj.* itinerant.
ambulanţă *sf.* ambulance.
ameliora *vt., vr.* to improve.
amenaja *vt.* to arrange; *(a utila)* to equip.
amenda *vt.* *(pe cineva)* to fine; *(o lege* etc.) to amend.
amendament *sn.* amendment.
amendă *sf.* fine.
ameninţa *vt., vi.* to threaten.
ameninţare *sf.* threat(ening).
ameninţător *adj.* threatening; ominous. *adv.* menacingly.
american *sm., adj.*, americană *sf., adj.* American.
ameriza *vi.* to alight.
amestec *sn.* mixture; *(interven-ţie)* interference.
amesteca *vt.* to mix (up); *(a implica)* to involve. *vr.* to mix; *(a interveni)* to meddle.
amestecat *adj.* mixed (up); *(variat)* sundry.
amestecătură *sf.* medley.
ametist *sn.* amethyst.
ameţeală *sf.* dizziness.
ameţi *vt.* to giddy; *(a îmbăta)*

to intoxicate. *vi.* to be(come) dizzy. *vr.* to become giddy; *(cu alcool)* to get tipsy.

ameţit *adj.* dizzy; *(de băutură)* fuddled.

ameţitor *adj.* giddy; *(uluitor)* astounding.

amfiteatru *sn.* amphitheatre; *univ.* lecture room.

amiază, amiazi *sf.* noon; *după ~* (in the) afternoon; *înainte de ~* in the morning.

amic *sm.* friend.

amical *adj.* friendly. *adv.* in a friendly way.

amigdală *sf.* tonsil.

amigdalită *sf.* tonsilitis.

amin *interj.* amen! *(gata)* napoo!

aminti *vt., vi.* to recall; *a-şi ~ (de)* to remember; *a ~ cuiva (ceva)* to remind smb. (of smth.).

amintire *sf.* memory; *(suvenir)* keepsake.

amiral *sm.* admiral.

amîna *vt., vi.* to postpone; *jur., pol.* to adjourn.

amînare *sf.* postponement; *jur., pol.* adjournment.

amîndoi *pron., adv.* both.

amnistia *vt.* to amnesty.

amnistie *sf.* amnesty.

amor *sn.* love (affair); *~ propriu* vanity.

amoral *adj.* non-moral.

amoreza *vr.: a se ~ de* to fall in love with, to fall for; to be infatuated with.

amorezat *adj.* infatuated (with smb.).

amoros *adj.* love; amorous.

amortisment *sn.* payment.

amortiza *vt.* to (re)pay; *tehn.* to deaden.

amorţeală *sf.* numbness; *fig.* torpor.

amorţi *vt.* to (be)numb. *vi.* to be(come) benumbed *sau* stiff.

amploare *sf.* scope: *de (mare) ~* vast in scope; ample.

amplu *adj.* ample.

amprentă *sf.* stamp; *(digitală)* fingerprint.

amputa *vt.* to amputate.

amuletă *sf.* amulet.

amurg *sn.* dusk, twilight.

amuţi *vt.* to silence. *vi.* to be(come) silent.

amuza *vt.* to amuse, to entertain. *vr.* to have a good time.

amuzament *sn.* amusement, merriment.

amuzant *adj.* amusing.

amvon *sn.* pulpit.

an *sm.* year; *~ bisect* leap year; *~ul curent* this year; *Anul nou* the New Year; *~ul trecut* last year; *de ~i de zile* for years on end; *din ~ în Paşte* once in a blue moon; *la mulţi ~i!* many happy returns of the day! *(la Anul nou)* A Happy New Year!; *tot ~ul* throughout the year.

anacronic *adj.* superannuated.

anale *sf. pl.* annals.

analfabet *sm., adj.* illiterate.

analfabetism *sn.* illiteracy.

analitic *adj.* analytic.

analiza *vt.* to analyse.

analiză *sf.* analysis.

analog *adj.* analogous.

analogie *sf.* analogy.

ananas *sm.* pine-apple.

ananghie *sf.* predicament; *la ~* up a tree.

anarhic *adj.* anarchical. *adv.* anarchically.

anarhie *sf.* anarchy.
anarhist *sm.* anarchist.
anason *sm.* anise.
anatomie *sf.* anatomy.
ancheta *vt., vi.* to investigate.
anchetă *sf.* inquiry; inquest.
ancora *vt., vr.* to (cast) anchor.
ancorare *sf.* anchorage.
ancoră *sf.* anchor.
andivă *sf.* endive.
andrea *sf.* (knitting) needle.
anecdotă *sf.* anecdote.
anemie *adj.* feeble; *med.* a-
naemic. *adv.* feebly.
anemie *sf.* anaemia.
anemonă *sf.* anemone.
anevoie *adv.* painstakingly.
anevoios *adj.* hard.
anexa *vt.* to annex; *(a alătura)*
to enclose.
anexă *sf.* annex(e).
angaja *vt.* to engage; to hire;
vr. to commit oneself; *(în
slujbă)* to take a job; *mil.*
to enlist.
angajament *sn.* pledge.
angajat *sm.* employee.
angarale *sf. pl.* troubles.
angină *sf.* quinsy; ~ *difterică*
diphtheritis; ~ *pectorală* angina
pectoris.
anglican *sm., adj.* Anglican.
angrena *vt.* to (throw into)
gear. *vr.* to (get into) gear.
angrenaj *sn.* gearing.
angrosist *sm.* wholesale dealer.
anihila *vt.* to annihilate.
anima *vt.* to animate. *vr.* to
be enlivened.
animal *sn.* animal; ~ *de povară*
beast of burden; ~ *de pradă*
predator; ~ *de tracțiune* beast
of draught; ~ *sălbatic* wild
beast. *adj.* animal...

animalic *adj.* animal.
animat *adj.* animated; *(vioi)*
lively; ~ *de* imbued *sau* pervad-
ed with.
animator *sn.* animator.
animație *sf.* liveliness.
anin *sm.* alder-tree.
anina *vt.* to hang (up).
aniversa *vt.* to celebrate.
aniversare *sf.* anniversary.
anomalie *sf.* anomaly.
anonim *sm.* anonymous person.
adj. anonymous.
anonimă *sf.* anonymous letter.
anormal *adj.* anomalous. *adv.*
abnormally.
anost *adj.* vapid, dull.
anotimp *sn.* season.
ansamblu *sn.* ensemble; *arhit.*
project; *de* ~ general; *în* ~
generally (speaking).
antagonism *sn.* antagonism.
antarctic *adj.* Antarctic.
antebelic *adj.* pre-war.
antebraț *sn.* forearm.
antecedente *sn. pl.* record.
antenă *sf.* antenna; *radio și*
aerial.
anterior *adj.* previous; *anat.*
fore-. *adv.* previously.
anteriu *sn.* surplice.
antet *sn.* heading.
antiaerian *adj.* anti-aircraft.
antialcoolic *sm.* teetotaller. *adj.*
antialcoholic.
antibiotic *sn., adj.* antibiotic.
antic *adj.* ancient.
anticameră *sf.* anteroom.
anticar *sm.* secondhand book-
seller; *(și pt. obiecte)* antiquary.
adj. anti-tank.
anticariat *sn.*, anticărie *sf.* secondhand bookshop.
antichitate *sf.* antiquity.

anticipa *vt.*, *vi.* to anticipate.
anticipat *adj.* anticipated. *adv.* in advance.
antidemocratic *adj.* antidemocratic.
antidot *sn.* antidote.
antifascist *sm.*, *adj.* antifascist.
antilopă *sf.* antelope; *(piele)* shammy.
antimuncitoresc *adj.* anti-labour.
antinevralgic *sn.* head pill. *adj.* antineuralgic.
antipartinic *adj.* anti-Party.
antipatic *adj.* repugnant.
antipatie *sf.* dislike.
antipod *sm.* antipode.
antirăzboinic *adj.* anti-war.
antisemit *sm.* Jew-baiter. *adj.* anti-Semitic.
antisemitism *sn.* Jew-baiting.
antistatal *adj.* anti-State.
antiteză *sf.* antithesis.
antologie *sf.* anthology.
antract *sn.* interval.
antren *sn.* pep.
antrena *vt.* to rally; *sport* to train. *vr.* to warm up; *sport* to train.
antrenament *sn.* training, practice.
antrenant *adj.* thrilling.
antrenor *sm.* coach.
antreprenor *sm.* contractor; ~ de pompe funebre undertaker.
antreu *sn.* vestibule.
antricot *sn.* spare rib, steak.
antropofag *sm.* man-eater. *adj.* man-eating.
anual *adj.*, *adv.* yearly.
anuar *sn.* year-book.
anula *vt.* to cancel.
anume *adj.* special; *un sau o* ~ a certain. *adv.* deliberately; *şi* ~ namely.

anumit *adj.* certain.
anunţ *sn.* notice; *(reclamă)* advertisement.
anunţa *vt.* to announce. *vr.* to promise.
anvelopă *sf. auto.* tyre.
anvergură *sf. av.* span; *fig.* scope.
aoleu *interj.* ah !; oh (my) !
apanaj *sn.* privilege.
aparat *sn.* apparatus; *(dispozitiv)* device; *(avion)* (air)plane; ~ de fotografiat camera; ~ de radio radio; ~ de ras safety razor.
aparent *adj.* apparent; sham. *adv.* apparently.
aparenţă *sf.* appearance; *în* ~ apparently.
apariţie *sf.* appearance; *(fantomă)* apparition.
apartament *sn.* flat.
aparte *adj.* particular; apart. *adv.* apart; *teatru* aside.
apartenenţă *sf.* affiliation; *(proprietate)* ownership.
aparţine *vi.:* a ~ *(cu dat.)* to belong to.
apaş *sm.* ruffian; *(indian)* Apache.
apatic *adj.* listless. *adv.* listlessly.
apatie *sf.* apathy.
apă *sf.* water; *(curs de* ~*)* water-course; ~ *dulce sau de băut* fresh *sau* drinking water; ~ de colonie eau de Cologne; ~ oxigenată peroxide; *ca apa, ca pe* ~ glibly; *pe* ~ by water.
apăra *vt.*, *vr.* to defend (oneself).
apărare *sf.* defence; protection; *fără* ~ defenceless; *legitimă* ~ self-defence.

apărătoare *sf.* (mud)guard.

apărător *sm.* defender. *jur.* counsel (for the defence).

apărea *vi.* to appear; *(a veni)* to turn up; *(a părea)* to seem.

apăsa *vt.* to press; to push; *fig.* to oppress. *vi.* to weigh; *a ~ pe* to press.

apăsare *sf.* pressing; *fig.* pressure; *(împilare)* oppression.

apăsat *adj.* (com)pressed; *fig.* emphatic. *adv.* thickly; *fig.* emphatically.

apăsător *adj.* oppressive.

apel *sn.* appeal; *mil.*, *şcoală* roll call; *tel.*, *fig.* call.

apela *vi.* to appeal.

apendice *sn.* appendix.

apendicită *sf.* appendicitis.

aperitiv *sn.* appetizer.

apetisant *adj.* appetizing

apicultor *sm.* beekeeper.

apicultură *sf.* beekeeping.

aplana *vt.* to appease.

aplauda *vt.*, *vi.* to applaud, to cheer.

aplauze *sf. pl.* applause.

apleca *vt.* to bend, to incline; *(a pleca)* to lower. *vr.* to bend; *a ţi se ~* to feel sick.

aplecare *sf.* bending, lean(ing); inclination.

aplica *vt.* to apply; *(a executa)* to carry out. *vr.* to be applied; to apply.

aplicare *sf.* application.

aplicat *adj.* applied; *text.* appliqué.

aplicaţie *sf.* application; *(înclinaţie)* skill; bent.

apogeu *sn.* apogee; *fig.* acme.

apoi *adv.* then.

apolitic *sm.* non-politician. *adj.* apolitical.

apolitism *sn.* indifference to politics.

apologet *sm.* extoller.

apologetic *adj.* eulogistic.

apologie *sf.* eulogy, extolling.

apoplexie *sf.* stroke.

aport *sn.* contribution.

apos *adj.* watery.

apostol- *sm.* apostle.

apostrof *sn.* apostrophe.

apostrofa *vt.* to apostrophize.

aprecia *vt.* to estimate; *(favorabil)* to appreciate.

apreciabil *adj.* considerable. *adv.* palpably.

apreciat *adj.* praised; successful.

apreciere *sf.* estimation; *(favorabilă)* appreciation.

aprig *adj.* fiery; *(îndîrjit)* grim; *(aspru)* harsh. *adv.* passionately; *(îndîrjit)* grimly; *(aspru)* harshly.

april(ie) *sm.* April.

aprinde *vt.* to kindle; *(lampa etc.)* to put on; *a ~ un chibrit* to strike a match. *vr.* to catch fire.

aprindere *sf.* kindling; *fig.* passion; *cu ~* passionately.

aprins *adj.* alight; *(strălucitor)* bright; *~ la faţă* red in the face.

aproape *sm.* neighbour. *adv.* near(by); *(circa)* nearly; *~ de* near (to); *~ să* about to *(cu inf.)*.

aproba *vt.*, *vi.* to approve (of). *vr.* to be carried.

aprobare *sf.* approval.

aprod *sm.* usher; *jur.* bailiff.

aprofunda *vt.* to study thoroughly.

apropia *vt.* to draw near(er). *vr.* to approach; *a se ~ de sfîrşit* to draw to a close.

apropiat *adj.* near; *fig.* intimate; *(din viitor)* forthcoming.

apropiere *sf.* *(vecinătate)* proximity; *(venire)* approach(ing); *fig.* rapprochement; în sau prin ~ hereabouts.

apropo *sn.* innuendo. *adv., interj.* by the way.

aproviziona *vt.* to supply (to). *vr.* to make one's stock.

aprovizionare *sf.* supply.

aproximativ *adj.* approximate. *adv.* roughly (speaking).

aproximație *sf.* approximation; *cu* ~ approximately.

apt *adj.* (cap)able.

aptitudine *sf.* ability, bent.

apuca *vt.* to catch; *(a lua, a cuprinde)* to seize; *(a surprinde)* to overtake; *(a găsi)* to find; *(în timp)* to have known; *a nu* ~ *să* not to have the time to; *n-am* ~*t filmele mute* silent films were (much sau well) before my time; *ce te-a* ~*t?* what's come over you?. *vi.* to start. *vr.: a se* ~ *de* to set about.

apucat *sm.* (mono)maniac. *sn.: pe* ~*e* by fits and starts. *adj.* seized; *(nebun)* mad.

apucătură *sf.* grasp; *(obicei)* habit.

apune *vi.* to set.

apus *sn.* west; *(asfințit)* sunset. *adj.* dead.

apusean *sm., adj.* western.

ar *sm.* are.

ara *vt., vi.* to plough.

arab *sm., adj.,* arabă *sf., adj.* Arab(ian); *lingv.* Arabic.

arabil *adj.* arable.

arac *sm.* vine prop.

aragaz *sn.* blaugas; *(plită)* gas stove.

arahidă *sf.* ground-nut.

aramă *sf.* copper.

aranja *vt.* to (ar)range; *(a găti)* to trim (up); *(a rezolva)* to settle; *a* ~ *pe cineva* to cook smb.'s goose. *vr.* to be arranged; *(a se rezolva)* to be settled; *(a se găti)* to get up.

aranjament *sn.* arrangement.

arareori *adv.* seldom.

arat *sn.* ploughing.

arăbesc *adj.* Arabian.

arămiu *adj.* copper(-coloured).

arăta *vt.* to show; *(a etala)* to display; *(a dezvălui)* to reveal. *vi.* to point; *(a părea)* to look. *vr.* to appear.

arătare *sf.* showing; *(nălucă)* phantom.

arătător *sn.* forefinger.

arătos *adj.* good-looking.

arătură *sf.* ploughing; *(ogor)* ploughland.

arbitra *vt., vi.* to arbitrate; *sport* to umpire.

arbitrar *adj.* arbitrary. *adv.* arbitrarily.

arbitru *sm.* arbitrator; *sport* ref(eree), umpire; *(de tușă)* linesman; *fig.* arbiter.

arbora *vt.* to hoist; *fig.* to put on.

arbore *sm.* tree.

arbust *sm.* shrub.

are *sn.* bow; *.(boltă)* arch; *(resort)* spring; *el., geom.* arc; ~ *de triumf* triumphal arch.

arcadă *sf.* archway; *anat.* arch.

arcaș *sm.* archer.

arcă *sf.* ark.

arctic *adj.* arctic.

arcui *vr.* to bend; to arch.

arcuș *sn.* bow.

arde *vt.* to burn (down); *(a frige)* to scorch; *fig.* to cou-sume. to urge. *vi*. to burn ; to be on fire ; *(moonit)* to smoulder ; *(a lumina)* to light ; *fig.* to die (with desire, etc.) ; *nu-mi ~ de glume* I'm in no mood for jokes. *vr.* to be *sau* get burnt ; to be sunburnt ; *fig.* to be cheated.

ardei *sm.* (mild) pepper ; *(iute)* paprika.

ardelat *adj.* highly seasoned.

ardelean *sm., adj.* Transylvanian.

ardere *sf.* burning.

ardoare *sf.* ardour ; *cu ~* zealously.

arenă *sf.* arena ; *pe ~* in the arena.

arenda *vt.* to lease.

arendaş *sm.* leaseholder.

arendă *sf.* rent.

arest *sn.* custody.

aresta *vt.* to arrest.

arestare *sf.* arrest.

arestat *sm.* prisoner.

argat *sm.* (farm) hand.

argilă *sf.* clay.

argint *sm.* (silver) coin ; *fig.* lucre. *sn.* silver ; *~ viu* quick silver.

arginta *vt.* to silver.

argintărie *sf.* silver ware ; *(tacîmuri)* silver plate.

argintiu *adj.* silver(y).

argou *sn.* slang ; *(interlop)* cant.

argument *sn.* reason.

argumenta *vt.* to motivate.

arhaie *adj.* archaic ; *(demodat)* obsolete.

arhaism *sn.* archaism.

arheolog *sm.* archaeologist.

arheologic *adj.* archaeological.

arhiepiscop *sm.* archbishop.

arhipelag *sn.* archipelago.

arhiplin *adj.* chock-full.

arhitect *sm.* architect.

arhitectonic, arhitectural *adj.* architectural.

arhitectură *sf.* architecture.

arhivar *sm.* keeper of public records.

arhivă *sf.* archives.

arici *sm.* hedgehog.

arid *adj.* barren.

arie *sf.* area ; *(de treier)* threshing floor ; *muz.* aria.

arin *sm.* alder tree.

aripă *sf.* wing ; *iht.* fin ; *auto.* mudguard.

aripioară *sf.* little wing ; *iht.* fin.

aristocrat *sm.* aristocrat.

aristocratic *adj.* aristocratic.

aristocraţie *sf.* aristocracy.

aritmetic *adj.* arithmetical.

aritmetică *sf.* arithmetics.

arivist *sm.* pusher.

armament *sn.* armament.

armat *adj.* armed ; *mil.* cocked ; *constr.* reinforced.

armată *sf.* army ; *fig.* host.

armator *sm.* shipowner.

armă *sf.* weapon ; *pl. şi* arms ; *(puşcă)* gun ; *(specialitate militară)* branch ; *arme de foc* fire arms.

armăsar *sm.* stallion.

armean *sm., adj*, **armeancă** *sf.*, **armenesc** *adj.* Armenian.

armistiţiu *sn.* truce.

armonic *adj.* harmonious.

armonică *sf.* concertina ; *(muzicuţă)* mouth organ.

armonie *sf.* harmony.

armonios *adj.* harmonious. *adv.* harmoniously.

armoniza *vt., vr.* to harmonize.

armură *sf.* armour.

arogant *adj.* arrogant.

aroganţă *sf.* haughtiness.
aromat *adj.* flavoured.
aromă *sf.* aroma.
arpacaş *sn.* pearl barley.
ars *adj.* (sun)burnt.
arsenal *sn.* arsenal.
arsenic *sn.* arsenic.
arsură *sf.* burn; *(pl., la stomac)* heartburn.
arşiţă *sf.* dog-days.
artă *sf.* art; *(măiestrie)* skill, craft(smanship); *arte frumoase* fine arts; ～ *pentru* ～ art for art's sake.
arteră *sf.* artery; *(drum)* thoroughfare.
artezian *adj.* artesian.
articol *sn.* article; *(obiect)* item; *pl. com.* goods.
articula *vt.* to articulate; *gram.* to use with the article. *vr. gram.* to require the article.
articulaţie *sf.* joint.
artificial *adj.* artificial. *adv.* artificially.
artificiu *sn.* artifice; *pl.* fireworks.
artilerie *sf.* artillery.
artist *sm.* artist; *(dramatic)* actor.
artistic *adj.* art(istic). *adv.* artistically.
artizanat *sn.* handicraft.
arţar *sm.* maple(tree).
arţăgos *adj.* petulant.
arunca *vt.* to throw, to cast; *(un proiectil etc.)* to hurl; *(jos)* to drop; *a ～ în aer* to blow up. *vi.: a ～ cu ceva în cineva* to throw smth. at smb. *vr.* to throw oneself; to plunge.
aruncare *sf.* throw(ing).
aruncătură *sf.* throw; ～*de ochi* glance.
arvună *sf.* earnest (money).

arzător *sn.* burner. *adj.* burning.
as *sm.* ace.
asalt *sn.* attack; *(la scrimă)* bout; *cu* ～ by storm.
asalta *vt.* to storm; to beset.
asasin *sm.* murderer.
asasina *vt.* to murder.
asasinare *sf.*, asasinat *sn.* murder.
ascendent *sn.* influence, pull. *adj.* upward.
ascendenţă *sf.* parentage, descent.
ascensiune *sf.* climb(ing); *în* ～ rising.
ascensor *sn.* lift.
ascet *sm.*, ascetic *adj.* ascetic.
asculta *vt.* to listen to; *(a se supune)* to obey. *vi.* to listen; *a* ～ *de* to obey.
ascultare *sf.* listening; *(supunere)* obedience.
ascultător *sm.* listener. *adj.* submissive.
ascunde *vt., vr.* to hide (oneself).
ascunzătoare *sf.* hiding place.
ascunziş *sn.* cache; *fig.* secret.
ascuţi *vt.* to sharpen; *fig.* to enhance. *vr.* to sharpen; *fig.* to be enhanced.
ascuţime *sf.* sharpness.
ascuţiş *sn.* point; edge.
ascuţit *adj.* sharp(ened); pointed; *fig.* keen.
ascuţitoare *sf.* sharpener.
aseară *adv.* last night.
asedia *vt.* to besiege.
asediu *sn.* siege.
asemăna *vt.* to liken. *vr.* to be alike; *a se* ～ *cu* to resemble.
asemănare *sf.* similitude; *(asemuire)* comparison; *fără* ～ peerless.
asemănător *adj.* similar. *adv.* likewise.

asemenea *adj.* alike. *adv.:* de ~ also.

asemui *v.* asemăna.

asentiment *sn.* assent.

aservi *vt.* to enthral.

aservire *sf.* enslavement.

asesor *sm.* assessor.

asfalt *sn.* asphalt.

asfaltat *adj.* asphalt(ed)

asfinţi *vi.* to set.

asfinţit *sn.* sunset.

asfixia *vt., vr.* to stifle.

asfixiant *adj.* suffocating.

asiatic *sm., adj.,* asiatică *sf., adj.* Asian, Asiatic.

asiduu *adj.* assiduous. *adv.* assid-uously.

asigura *vt.* to ensure ; *(prin vorbe)* to assure ; *(pe viaţă* etc.*)* to insure ; *(a procura)* to secure. *vr.* to make sure ; *(contra incendiului* etc.*)* to open an insurance.

asigurare *sf.* ensurance ; *(în vorbe)* assurance ; *(garantare)* guarantee ; *(poliţă)* insurance.

asimetric *adj.* lop-sided.

asimetrie *sf.* asymmetry.

asimila *vt.* to assimilate. *vr.* to be assimilated.

asimilare, asimilaţie *sf.* assimilation.

asin *sm.* asine.

asirian *sm., adj.,* asiriană *sf., adj.* Assyrian.

asista *vt.* to assist. *vi.* to be present ; *a* ~ *la* to attend.

asistent *sm., adj.* assistant.

asistenţă *sf. (ajutor)* assistance ; *(spectatori)* audience.

asmuţi *vt.* to set (on smb.).

asocia *vt., vr.* to associate.

asociat *sm.* associate.

asociaţie *sf.* association ; *com.* partnership.

asorta *vt., vr.* to match.

asortat *adj.* assorted ; *bine* ~ well-matched; *com.* well-stocked.

aspect *sn.* aspect ; *(privinţă)* respect.

asperitate *sf.* roughness.

aspira *vt., vi.* to inhale ; *a* ~ *la* to aspire after.

aspirant *sm. mar.* midshipman ; *univ.* post-graduate student.

aspirator *sn.* vacuum cleaner.

aspiraţie *sf.* aspiration ; *(năzuinţă şi)* endeavour.

aspirină *sf.* aspirin.

aspri *vt., vr.* to harden.

asprime *sf.* roughness.

aspru *adj.* rough ; *fig.* harsh. *adv.* roughly ; *fig.* harshly.

asta *adj.* this. *pron.* this (one) ; ~ *e!* that's it.

astăzi *adv.* today ; *(acum)* now-(adays) ; ~ *după amiază* this afternoon.

astea *adj.* these ; *toate* ~ all this ; all these. *pron.* these (ones) ; *cu toate* ~ in spite of all this.

astfel *adv.* thus ; ~ *de* such.

astîmpăr *sn.* quiet(ness) ; *fără* ~ restless(ly).

astîmpăra *vt.* to quiet ; *(setea)* to quench ; *(foamea)* to stay. *vr.* to (become) quiet.

astronaut *sm.* spaceman, astronaut.

astronom *sm.* astronomer.

astronomic *adj.* astronomical.

astronomie *sf.* astronomy.

astru *sm.* star.

astupa *vt.* to stop (up) ; *(cu un dop)* to plug. *vr.* to fill (up).

asuda *vi.* to sweat; *fig.* to drudge.

asudat *adj.* all in a sweat.

asuma *vt.* to assume.

asupra *prep.* about, on; ~ *nopţii* at night.

asupri *vt.* to oppress; to exploit.

asuprire *sf.* oppression; exploitation.

asupritor *sm.* oppressor, exploiter.

asurzi *vt.* to deafen. *vi.* to grow deaf.

asurzitor *adj.* deafening.

aş *v aux.* should, would. *interj.* not at all!

aşa *adj.* such; ~-şi ~ middling. *adv.* so, thus; ~ ? really ?; ~ e ? isn't it ?; ~ şi ~ so-so; ~ că so that; ~-zis so-called. *interj.* there!

aşadar *adv.* therefore.

aşchie *sf.* splinter.

aşeza *vt.* to lay; *(a aranja)* to order; *(pe cineva)* to seat. *vr.* to sit down; *fig.* to set in.

aşezare *sf.* laying, setting; *(opoziţie)* situation; *(omenească)* settlement.

aşezat *adj.* seated; *fig.* settled; *(serios şi)* quiet; *(aflător)* situated.

aşezămînt *sn.* establishment.

aşijderea *adj.* likewise.

aştepta *vt.* to wait for; *(în viitor)* to expect; *(cu nerăbdare)* to be looking forward to (smth.). *vi.* to wait. *vr. a se* ~ *la* to expect.

aşteptare *sf.* expectation.

aşterne *vt., vr.* to spread.

aşternut *sn.* bed clothes.

atac *sn.* attack; *med.* stroke; ~ *banditesc* hold-up.

ataca *vt., vi.* to attack.

atare *adj.* such; *ca* ~ as such.

ataş *sn.* side car.

ataşa *vt.* to attach. *vr. a se* ~ *de* to be(come) attached to.

ataşament *sn.* attachment.

ataşat *sm.* attaché.

ateism *sn.* atheism.

atelier *sn.* (work)shop; *artă* studio.

atent *adj.* attentive. *adv.* attentively.

atenta *vi.. a* ~ *la viaţa cuiva* to make an attempt on smb.'s life.

atentat *sn.* attempt (on smb.'s life).

atenţie *sf.* attention; *(grijă)* care(fulness); *(cadou)* present; *cu* ~ carefully. *interj.* mind!

atenua *vt.* to mitigate.

atenuant *adj.: circumstanţe* ~*e* extenuating circumstances.

ateriza *vi.* to land.

aterizare *sf.* landing; ~ *forţată* crash landing.

atesta *vt.* to certify.

ateu *sm.* atheist.

atinge *vt.* to touch (upon); *(a ajunge la)* to reach; *(a afecta)* to affect; *(a jigni)* to hurt. *vr.* to be in touch *sau* contact; *a se* ~ *de* to attack.

atingere *sf.* touch(ing); *(jignire)* hurt; *(încălcare)* encroachment.

atins *adj.* touched; *fig.* hurt; *(realizat)* reached.

atitudine *sf.* attitude; *fig. şi* stand.

atîrna *vt., vi.* to hang.

atît *adj., adv.* so (much); ~ *timp* so long; ~ *că* ... only (that) ...; ~ *el cît şi Ion* both he and John;

~ *de drag* so dear; *cu ~ mai mult (cu cît)* all the more so (as).

atîta *adj.* so much; ~ *vreme (cît)* so long (as); ~ *pagubă* good riddance (to a bad bargain). *pron.* so much; ~ *tot* that's (about) all. *adv.* so much.

atîtea, atîţia *adj., pron.* so many.

atlas *sn.* atlas.

atlet *sm.*, **atletă** *sf.* athlete.

atletic *adj.* athletic.

atmosferă *sf.* atmosphere.

atom *sm.* atom.

atomic *adj.* atom(ic).

atomist *sm.* nuclear expert.

atonal *adj.* atonal.

atotbiruitor *adj.* all-conquering.

atoteuprinzător *adj.* all-embracing.

atotputernic *adj.* almighty, all-powerful.

atotputernicie *sf.* almightiness.

atotştiutor *adj.* omniscient.

atractiv *adj.* attractive.

atracţie *sf.* attraction.

atrage *vt.* to attract, to draw; *(a ispiti)* to (al)lure; *(după sine)* to bring about, to involve.

atrăgător *adj.* attractive; *(frumos)* winsome; *(ispititor)* tantalizing. *adv.* attractively.

atribui *vt.* to attribute; *(a repartiza)* to assign.

atribut *sn.* attribute.

atribuţie *sf.* duty; *(putere)* prerogative.

atroce *adj.* atrocious.

atrocitate *sf.* atrocity.

atu *sn.* trump (card).

atunci *adv.* then; ~ *cînd* when(ever); *de ~* since (then); *pe ~* at the time; *pînd ~* till then: *tot ~* concomitantly.

aţă *sf.* thread.

aţine *vt.:* *a ~ calea cuiva* to waylay smb.

aţinti *vt.* to focus.

aţipeală *sf.* doze.

aţipi *vi.* to doze off.

aţîţa *vt.* to rouse.

aţîţător • *sm.* instigator; ~ *la război* warmonger. *adj.* rousing.

au *interj.* ouch!

audia *vt.* to hear; *(lecţii etc.)* to attend.

audienţă *sf.* audience.

audiere *sf.* hearing.

audio-vizual *adj.* audio-visual.

auditor *sm.* listener.

auditoriu *sn.* audience; *(sală)* auditorium.

audiţie *sf.* hearing.

augur *sn.* augury; *de bun ~* auspicious; *de rău ~* portentous.

august[1] *sm.* august.

august[2] *adj.* august.

aulă *sf.* lecture room.

aur *sn.* gold; *de ~* gold(en).

aureolă *sf.* halo.

auri *vt.* to gild.

aurit *adj.* gilt.

auriu *adj.* golden.

auroră *sf.* daybreak; ~ *boreală* northern lights.

auspicii *sn. pl.* auspices.

auster *adj.* austere.

austeritate *sf.* austerity.

australian *sm., adj.*, **australiană** *sf., adj.* Australian.

austriac *sm., adj.*, **austriacă** *sf., adj.* Austrian. *sn. (pariu ~)* cumulator.

autentic *adj.* authentic.

autenticitate *sf.* authenticity.

autentifica *vt.* to certify.

auto *adj.* motor ..., self....

auto-admiraţie *sf.* self-admiration.

autobiografie *adj.* autobiograaphical.

autobiografie *sf.* autobiography.

autobuz *sn.* (motor) bus.

autocamion *sn.* (motor) lorry.

autocar *sn.* (motor) coach.

autocritic *adj.* self-critical. *adv.* self-critically.

autocritică *sf.* self-criticism.

autodemascare *sf.* self-exposure.

autodeservire *sf. v.* **autoservire**.

autodeterminare *sf.* self-determination.

autodidact *sm.* self-educated man.

autoflagelare *sf.* self-chastising.

autogară *sf.* bus terminal.

autograf *sn., adj.* autograph.

autoguvernare *sf.* self-government.

autoliniștire *sf.* complacency.

automat *sn.* automat ; *mil.* Tommy gun. *adj.* automatic.

automatism *sn.* automatism.

automatiza *vt., vr.* to automm(at)ize.

automatizare *sf.* automa(tiza)tion.

automobil *sn.* (motor) car. *adj.* self-propelled.

automobilism *sn.* motoring.

automotor *sn.* motorailer.

autonom *adj.* autonomous.

autonomie *sf.* autonomy.

autoportret *sn.* portrait of the artist, self-portrait.

autopsie *sf.* post-mortem (examination).

autor *sm.* author ; *(scriitor și)* writer ; *(al unei crime etc.)* perpetrator.

autoritar *adj.* authoritative.

autoritate *sf.* authority.

autoriza *vt.* to authorize.

autorizație *sf.* permit.

autoservire *sf.* self-service ; *cu ~* self-servicing.

autostradă *sf.* speedway.

autosugestie *sf.* self-suggestion.

autoturism *sn.* (motor) car.

autovehicul *sn.* motor vehicle.

auxiliar *sn., adj.* auxiliary.

auz *sn.* hearing ; *la ~ul acestei vești* (on) hearing the news.

auzi *vt., vi.* to hear ; *(a afla și)* to learn (of). *vr.* to be heard ; *fig.* to get abroad.

auzit *sn. : din ~e* from hearsay.

avalanșă *sf.* avalanche.

avangardă *sf.* vanguard ; *în ~* in the van.

avanpost *sn.* outpost.

avanpremieră *sf.* pre-view.

avans *sn.* advance ; *fig.* advantage.

avansa *vt.* to pay in advance ; to promote. *vi.* to make headway, to advance.

avansare *sf.* promotion.

avansat *sm.* advanced pupil. *adj.* advanced.

avantaj *sn.* advantage.

avantaja *vt.* to put to advantage ; *(a proteja)* to favour.

avantajos *adj.* advantageous. *adv.* advantageously.

avar *sm.* miser. *adj.* stingy.

avaria *vt.* to damage.

avarie *sf.* damage.

avea *v aux.* to have. *vt.* to have (got), to possess ; *(a se bucura de)* to enjoy. *vr.* to stand ; *a se ~ bine cu cineva* to be on the best of terms with smb. ; *a se ~ ca frații* to get on like a house on fire.

aventura *vr.* to venture (recklessly).

aventură *sf.* (ad)venture ; *(sentimentală)* love affair.

aventurier *sm.* adventurer.

avere *sf.* fortune ; *(proprietate)* property.

aversă *sf.* shower.

aversiune *sf.* dislike.

avertisment *sn.* warning.

avertiza *vt.* to warn.

aviatic *adj.* air(craft).

aviator *sm.* pilot, airman.

aviaţie *sf.* aviation ; *(militară)* air force.

avid *adj.* grasping ; *(curios)* eager.

avion *sn.* (air)plane, aircraft ; ~ *cu reacţie* jet plane ; ~ *de bombardament* bomber ; ~ *de pasageri* liner ; ~ *de recunoaştere* reconnaissance plane ; ~ *de şcoală* training plane ; ~ *de vînătoare* fighter (plane).

aviz *sn.* notice ; note ; warning ; *(părere)* opinion ; approval.

aviza *vt.* to let know ; to warn ; *(a referi asupra)* to sanction. *vi.* to advise.

avizier *sn.* notice board.

avînt *sn.* élan, upsurge ; *în plin* ~ in full swing.

avînta *vr.* to soar.

avîntat *adj.* dashing.

avocat *sm.* *(pledant)* barrister ; *(jurisconsult)* solicitor ; *(al statului)* attorney ; *(mai ales fig.)* advocate ; ~*ul apărării* counsel for the defence.

avocatură *sf.* the Bar.

avort *sn.* abortion ; *(spontan)* miscarriage.

avut *sn.* wealth. *adj.* well-off.

avuţie *sf.* riches.

ax *sn.* axle.

axa *vt., vr.* to centre.

axă *sf.* axis ; *tehn.* axle.

axiomă *sf.* axiom.

azbest *sn.* asbestos.

azi *adv.* today ; ~ *mîine* one of these days ; *de* ~ *înainte* from now on ; *de* ~ *într-o lună* today month.

azil *sn.* asylum ; *fig. şi* shelter, harbour ; ~ *de nebuni* lunatic asylum, madhouse ; ~ *de noapte* night shelter, flop house.

azot *sn.* nitrogen.

azotic *adj.* nitric.

azur *sn.* azure.

azuriu *adj.* azure (blue).

azvîrli *vt.* to fling. *vi.:* *a* ~ *cu ceva în cineva* to throw smth. at smb.

Ă

ăl *art.* the. *adj., pron.* that (one).

ăla *adj.* that. *pron.* that (one).

ălălalt *adj.* the other. *pron.* the other (one).

ăsta, ăstălalt *adj.* this. *pron.* this (one).

ăştia *adj.* these. *pron.* these (ones).

B

ba *adv.* (oh) no ; ~ *aşa*, ~ *aşa* now this way, now that ; ~ *da* oh yes.

babă *sf.* old woman ; *(rea)* hag, harridan ; *de-a baba oarba* blind-man's buff.

bac *sn.* ferry.

bacalaureat *sm.* school graduate. *sn.* school-leaving examination.

baci *sm.* (head) shepherd.

bacil *sn.* bacillus.

baclava *sf.* nut ánd syrup pastry.

bacşiş *sn.* tip.

bacterie *sf.* bacterium.

bacteriologie *sf.* bacteriology.

bade *sm.* (elder) brother ; *(iubit)* sweetheart.

bagaj *sn.* luggage.

bagatelă *sf.* trifle ; *muz.* baga-telle.

bagateliza *vt.* to minimize.

baghetă *sf.* wand ; *muz.* baton.

baiaderă *sf.* bayadère.

baie *sf.* bath ; *(cameră)* bath-room ; *(cadă)* (bath) tub ; *(scăl-dat)* bathe ; *pl.* watering place.

baieră *sf.* string.

baionetă *sf.* bayonet.

bal *sn.* ball, party ; ~ *costumat* fancy-dress ball ; ~ *mascat* masked ball.

baladă *sf.* ballad.

balama *sf.* hinge; *pl. fig.* strength.

balamuc *sn.* madhouse.

balans *sn.* poise.

balansa *vt.* to balance. *vr.* to swing.

balansoar *sn.* rocking chair.

balanţă *sf.* balance, *(cîntar şi)* scales ; ~ *romană* steel yard.

balast *sn.* ballast ; *fig.* lumber.

balaur *sm.* dragon.

balcanic *adj.* Balkan.

balcon *sn.* balcony ; ~*ul întîi* the dress circle ; ~*ul doi* the upper circle.

bale *sf. pl.* slobber.

balenă *sf.* whale ; *(de guler* etc.) whalebone.

balercă *sf.* keg.

balerin *sm.*, **balerină** *sf.* (ballet) dancer.

balet *sn.* ballet.

baliverne *sf. pl.* tall tale(s).

balnear *adj.* watering.

balon *sn.* balloon ; *(minge)* ball ; ~ *de săpun* soap bubble.

balot *sn.* bale.

balotaj *sn.* ballotage.

balsam *sn.* balm.

baltag *sn.* hatchet.

baltă *sf.* pool ; *(mică)* plash ; *(lac)* pond ; *(mlaştină)* marsh ; *a lăsa* ~ to drop.

balustradă *sf.* railing ; *(la scară)* banisters.

bamă *sf.* gumbo.

bambus *sm.* bamboo.

ban *sm. ist.* ban ; *(monedă)* ban, coin (1/100 of a leu) ; *pl.* money ; ~*i de buzunar* pocket money ; ~*i gheaţă* hard cash ; ~*i mărunţi* (small) change ; *cu* ~*i* well-to-do ; *fără* ~*i* short of money ; *(gratuit)* free(ly).

banal *adj.* commonplace.

banalitate *sf.* triviality.

banaliza *vt.* to hackney. *vr.* to become commonplace.

banan *sm.* banana tree.

banană *sf. bot.* banana ; *el.* banana plug.

banc *sn.* sand bank; *(glumă)* joke; *tehn.* bed.

bancar *adj.* bank(ing).

bancă *sf. (în parc)* bench; *(de şcoală)* form; *(pupitru)* desk; *com.* bank.

bancher *sm.* banker.

banchet *sn.* banquet.

banchetă *sf.* bench.

banchiză *sf.* ice pack.

bancnotă *sf.* (bank-)note.

bandaja *vt.* to bandage.

bandă *sf.* gang; *fig.* clique; *(fîşie)* band; *tehn.* belt; ~ *de magnetofon* (recording) tape; ~ *rulantă* running belt.

banderolă *sf.* banderole.

bandit *sm.* bandit.

banditesc *adj.* criminal.

baniţă *sf.* (half) bushel.

bar *sn.* night club; bar.

bara *vt.* to bar; *fig.* to curb; *(a şterge)* to cross out.

baracă *sf.* hut(ment); *(dugheană)* booth.

baraj *sn.* dam; *mil., fig.* barrage.

bară *sf.* bar; *(drug)* crowbar *(tijă)* rod.

barbar *sm., adj.* barbarian. *adv.* cruelly.

barbă *sf.* beard; *(bărbie)* chin; *(minciună)* lie.

barbişon *sn.* goatee.

barcagiu *sm.* boatman.

barcă *sf.* boat; *(lată)* punt; *pl. (la moşi)* swinging chairs; ~ *cu motor* motor boat; ~ *de salvare* life boat.

bard *sm.* bard.

bardă *sf.* hatchet.

barem[1] *sn.* standard.

barem[2] *adv.* leastways.

baretă *sf.* strap.

baricada *vt., vr.* to barricade (oneself).

baricadă *sf.* barricade.

barieră *sf.* barrier.

bariton *sm.* barytone.

baroc *sm., adj.* baroque.

barometru *sn.* barometer.

baron *sm.* baron.

baroneasă *sf.* baroness.

baronet *sm.* baronet.

baros *sn.* sledge (hammer).

barou *sn.* bar (association).

barză *sf.* stork.

bas *sm.* bass (singer *sau* voice).

basc *sm., adj.* Basque. *sn.* beret.

baschet *sn.* basket-ball.

basculă *sf.* weighing machine.

basm *sn.* (fairy) tale, story.

basma *sf.* (head)kerchief.

basorelief *sn.* bas-relief.

basta *adv.* no more.

bastard *sm., adj.* bastard.

baston *sn.* (walking-)stick, cane.

başca *adv., prep.* besides.

baştină *sf.: de* ~ native.

batalion *sn.* battalion.

bate *vt.* to beat; *(a învinge şi)* to defeat; *(cu băţul şi)* to cane; *(cu biciul)* to whip; *(a pălmui)* to box; *(rău)* to drub; *(uşor)* to pat; *(a lovi)* to strike; *(oudle)* to whisk; *(un record)* to break; *a* ~ *apa-n piuă* to saw wood; *a-şi* ~ *joc de* to mock, to flout. *vi.* to knock; *(ritmic)* to beat, to throb; *(uşor)* to rap; *(d. ceas)* to strike (the hours, etc.); *(d. clopot)* to toll; *(d. ploaie, grindină)* to patter; *(d. vînt)* to blow; *a* ~ *din palme* to slap (one's) hands; *a* ~ *în (altă culoare)* to have a shade of (another colour) ; *a ~ în lemn* to touch wood ; *a ~ în retragere* to beat a retreat ; *a ~ la cap* to pester ; *a ~ la ochi* to strike the eye ; *fig.* to be blatant. *vr.* to fight.

baterie *sf.* battery ; *(frapieră)* cooler.

batic *sn.* (head)kerchief.

batistă *sf.* handkerchief.

batjocori *vt.* to mock (at) ; *fig.* to violate.

batjocorire *sf.* mockery ; *(parodie)* travesty.

batjocoritor *adj.* derisive. *adv.* mockingly.

batjocură *sf.* ridicule ; *în ~* mockingly.

batog *sn.* haddock.

baton *sn.* stick.

batoză *sf.* threshing machine.

bau *interj.* wow !

baza *vr. : a se ~ pe* to rely on ; *(o idee etc.)* to proceed from.

bazaconie *sf.* maggot.

bazar *sn.* bazaar.

bază *sf.* base ; *fig.* basis ; *pl.* fundamentals; *~ sportivă* sports grounds ; *de ~* essential.

bazin *sn.* piscine, (swimming) pool ; *geogr., geol.* area ; *anat.* pelvis ; *~ carbonifer* coal field.

bă *interj.* (hey) you ! old man !

băbesc *adj.* old woman's ...

băbește *adv.* empirically.

băcan *sm.* grocer.

băcănie *sf.* grocer's (shop) ; grocery (trade).

bădăran *sm.* churl, boor.

bădărănie *sf.* boorishness.

băga *vt.* to thrust, to shove ; to introduce ; *a ~ ață în ac* to thread a needle ; *a ~ de seamă*

to notice ; *a ~ în buzunar* to pocket ; *a-și ~ nasul (unde nu-i fierbe oala)* to poke one's nose (where it's not wanted). *vr.* to pop in ; *(nepoftit)* to intrude ; *(a se amesteca)* to meddle ; *a nu se ~* to keep off ; *a se ~ pe sub pielea cuiva* to ingratiate oneself with smb.

băgare *sf.* shoving ; thrusting ; *~ de seamă* attention ; *cu ~ de seamă* carefully.

băgăreț *adj.* pushing ; *(curios)* inquisitive.

băiat *sm.* boy ; *(fiu)* son ; *(flăcău)* lad ; *(om)* chap ; *~ de prăvălie* shopboy ; *~ de viață* good sport ; *~ de zahăr* brick.

băiețandru *sm.* youngster.

băiețaș, băiețel *sm.* urchin.

băiețoi *sm.* hobbledehoy ; *(fată băiețoasă)* romp.

băiețos *adj.* boyish.

bălai, bălan *adj.* fair.

bălăbăni *vt., vr.* to dangle.

bălăci *vr.* to wallow.

bălăngăni *vr.* to dangle.

bălării *sf. pl.* weeds, thistles.

bălegar, băligar *sn.* manure.

bălmăji *vt.* to mix (up) ; *(a îndruga)* to mumble.

băltăreț *sn.* warm (marsh) wind. *adj.* marsh(y).

băltoacă *sf.* puddle.

bălțat *adj.* motley.

bănățean *sm.* inhabitant of the Banat. *adj.* from *sau* of the Banat.

bănesc *adj.* money...

bănește *adv.* in cash.

bănos *adj.* lucrative.

bănui *vt.* to suppose; *(a suspecta)* to suspect.

bănuială *sf. (presupunere)* supposition; *(gînd)* hunch; *(suspiciune)* doubt.

bănuit *sn.*: *a da de* ~ to arouse suspicion.

bănuitor *adj.* suspicious.

bănuţ *sm.* small coin; *(al oului)* cock's treadle.

bărăgan *sn.* moor(land).

bărbat *sm.* man, *pl.* men; *(soţ)* husband; *(mascul)* male. *adj.* manly.

bărbătesc *adj.* manly, man's.

bărbăteşte *adv.* like a man.

bărbăţie *sf.* manhood; virility; *(bravură)* bravery.

bărbie *sf.* chin.

bărbier *sm.* barber.

bărbieri *vt.* to shave. *vr.* to shave; *(la bărbier)* to get a shave.

bărbierit *sn.* shave. *adj.* shaved.

bărbos *adj.* bearded; *(neras)* unshaven.

băşica *vt., vr.* to blister.

băşicat *adj.* blistered.

băşică *sf. anat., zool.* bladder; *(rană)* blister; *(de săpun etc.)* bubble.

băştinaş *sm., adj.* native.

bătaie *sf.* beating; *(ciocănitură)* knock; *(uşoară)* tap(ping); *(pe umăr* etc.*)* pat(ting); *(din picior)* stamping; *(puls)* throb(bing); *(a ploii etc.)* pattering; *(luptă)* fight; *muz.* beat; *(a puştii etc.)* range; ~ *de cap* (care and) trouble; ~ *de joc* mockery; *în bătaia puştii* within (gun)-shot; *în bătaia soarelui* in the sun.

bătăios *adj.* pugnacious.

bătălie *sf.* battle.

bătător *sn.* carpet beater. *adj.*: ~ *la ochi* blatant; *(izbitor)* striking.

bătători *vt.* to tread.

bătătorit *adj.* trodden; *(d. mîini)* callous(ed).

bătătură *sf. (la picior)* corn; *(la mînă)* callosity; *(la casă)* trodden patch.

bătăuş *sm.* brawler. *adj.* pugnacious.

bătrîn *sm.* old man; *pl.* old folk; *din* ~*i* of yore. *adj.* old (-aged).

bătrînă *sf.* old woman.

bătrînesc *adj. (demodat)* old (-fashioned).

bătrîneţe *sf.* old age.

bătut *adj.* beaten; *(învins şi)* defeated; ~ *de soare* sun scorched; ~ *de vînturi* weather--beaten; ~ *în cap* dense, narrow-minded.

băţ *sn.* (walking) stick; *(pt. arătat pe hartă etc.)* pointer.

băţos *adj.* rigid; *(ceremonios)* formal; *(înţepat)* touchy. *adv.* stiffly; *(înţepat)* testily.

băut *sn.* drinking. *adj.* drunk(en).

băutor *sm.* (heavy) drinker; *(beţiv)* drunkard.

băutură *sf.* drink; *(fermentată)* beverage; *(beţie)* drinking; *băuturi spirtoase* spirits, liquor.

bea *vt.* to drink; *(a consuma)* to take; *(pînă la fund)* to drink up; *(a sorbi)* to sip; *(mult)* to swill. *vi.* to drink; *(mult)* to booze; *a* ~ *în sănătatea cuiva* to drink smb.'s health.

beat *adj.* drunk; ~ *mort sau ca un porc* as drunk as a lord.

bec *sn.* (electric) light bulb; *(de gaz)* gas burner.

becar *sm., adj.* natural.

becaţă *sf.* snipe.

beci *sn.* cellar.
becisnic *sm.* weakling. *adj.* weak.
behăi *vi.* to baa.
behăit *sn.* bleating.
bej *sn.*, *adj.* beige.
belciug *sn.* hook.
belea *sf.* trouble.
beletristică *sf.* fiction, belles lettres.
belgian *sm.*, *adj.*, **belgiană** *sf.*, *adj.* Belgian.
belicos *adj.* warlike.
beligerant *sm.*, *adj.* belligerent.
belşug *sn.* plenty; *din* ~ copiously.
bemol *sm.*, *adj.* flat.
benchetui *vi.* to feast.
beneficia *vi.* to benefit (by).
beneficiar *sm.* beneficiary.
beneficiu *sn.* benefit; profit; *în* ~*l cuiva* to smb.'s advantage.
benevol *adj.* voluntary. *adv.* at will.
benzină *sf.* auto. petrol; *amer.* gas(oline); *(neofalină)* benzine.
berar *sm.* brewer.
berărie *sf.* beer-house.
berbec *sm.* ram; *(batal)* wether; *ist.* battering ram.
berbeleacul *sn.: de-a* ~ head over heels.
bere *sf.* beer; ale; ~ *neagră* brown beer.
berechet *adj.*, *adv.* galore.
beregată *sf.* throat.
beretă *sf.* beret.
berlinez *sm.* Berliner. *adj.* Berlin.
bestial *adj.* savage. *adv.* bestially.
bestialitate *sf.* brutishness.
bestie *sf.* brute.
beteag *adj.* crippled.
beteală *sf.* tinsel.

beteşug *sn.* infirmity.
beton *sn.* concrete; ~ *armat* ferro-concrete.
beţie *sf.* *(ameţeală)* drunkenness, intoxication; *(chef)* drinking bout; *(obicei)* drink(ing); ~ *de cuvinte* verbosity.
beţiv *sm.* drunkard. *adj.* fond of the bottle.
beţivan *sm.* tippler.
bezea *sf.* meringue; *a face bezele cuiva* to blow smb. a kiss.
bezmetic *sm.* madman. *adj.* crazy.
beznă *sf.* (pitch) dark.
biban *sm.* perch.
bibelou *sn.* curio.
biberon *sn.* (feeding) bottle; *cu* ~*ul* at the bottle.
biblic *adj.* biblical.
biblie *sf.* Bible, the Book.
bibliofil *sm.* bibliophile.
bibliografie *sf.* bibliography.
biblioraft *sn.* ring-book.
bibliotecar *sm.*, **bibliotecară** *sf.* librarian.
bibliotecă *sf.* library; *(ca mobilă)* bookcase; ~ *de împrumut* lending library; ~ *documentară* reference library; ~ *volantă* circulating library.
bici *sn.* (horse) whip.
bicicletă *sf.* (push) bicycle, bike; ~ *cu motor* moped.
biciclist *sm.* (bi)cyclist.
biciui *vt.* to flog.
biciuitor *adj.* lashing.
bidinea *sf.* whitewashing brush.
bidon *sn.* can(teen).
bienală *sf.* biennial exhibition.
biet *adj.* poor; ~*ul de mine!* poor me!
biftec *sn.* (beef)steak; ~ *tocat* minced meat.
bifurca *vr.* to fork.

bigam *sm.* bigamist. *adj.* biga-
mous.
bigamie *sf.* bigamy.
bigot *sm.* bigot. *adj.* bigoted.
bigotism *sn.* bigotry.
bigudiu *sn.* (hair)curler.
bijuterie *sf.* jewel; *pl.* jewel-
(le)ry; *fig.* gem; *bijuterii false*
costume jewelry.
bijutier *sm.* jeweller.
bilanţ *sn. com.* balance sheet;
fig. survey.
bilateral *adj.* bilateral.
bilă *sf.* ball; *pl.* *(pietricele)*
marbles; *med.* bile.
bilet *sn.* ticket; *(scrisoare)* note;
~ *de bancă* bank-note; ~ *de
favoare* guest-ticket; ~ *de
peron* platform ticket; ~ *dus
şi întors* return ticket.
bileţel *sn.* note; *(de amor)* billet
doux.
biliard *sn.* billiards.
bilunar *adj.* bimonthly.
bimotor *sn.* bimotor aircraft.
adj. twin-engined.
bine *sn.* good; benefit; profit;
(noroc) fortune; *cu* ~ safely;
successfully; *(la revedere!)*
good-bye! so long! *de* ~ *de
rău* after all, in a way; *de-a
~lea* thoroughly; indeed. *adj.*
good-looking; nice; respectable.
adv. well; (all) right; O.K.;
properly; ~ *câ* ... it's a good
thing that ... ; ~ *dispus* cheerful; ~ *intenţionat* well-mean-
ing; *ce* ~*!* how fine! *cel mai*
~ best; *ei* ~ *(?)* well (?);
mai ~ better; *mai* ~ *de* over;
interj. good; OK!
binecrescut *adj.* well-bred.
binecuvînta *vt.* to bless.
binecuvîntare *sf.* blessing.

binefacere *sf.* charity; *(fericire)*
boon.
binefăcător *sm.* benefactor. *adj.*
beneficial.
bineînţeles *adv.* naturally.
bineţe *sf. pl.* greetings.
binevenit *adj.* welcome.
binevoi *vi.* to condescend.
binevoitor *sm.* well-wisher. *adj.*
benevolent.
binişor *sn.: cu* ~*ul* gently. *adv.*
well enough; *(uşurel)* gingerly.
interj. not so fast!
binoclu *sn.* binoculars; *(de teatru)* opera glasses.
biochimie *sf.* biochemistry.
biograf *sm.* biographer.
biografic *adj.* biographical.
biografie *sf.* biography.
biolog *sm.* biologist.
biologic *adj.* biological.
biologie *sf.* biology.
bir *sn.* tax, tribute.
birjar *sm.* cab man.
birjă *sf.* (hansom) cab.
birocrat *sm.* bureaucrat.
birocratic *adj.* bureaucratic.
birocraţie *sf.* red tape.
birou *sn.* bureau; *(cameră)* study;
(public) office; *(mobilă)* desk.
birt *sn.* eating house.
birtaş *sm.* innkeeper.
birui *vt.* to conquer. *vi.* to triumph.
biruinţă *sf.* victory.
biruitor *sm.* victor. *adj.* victorious. *adv.* triumphantly.
bis *sn., adv., interj.* encore.
bisa *vt., vi.* to encore.
biscuit *sm.* biscuit.
bisect *adj.* leap.
biserică *sf.* church; *biserica an-
glicană* the Church of England.
bisericesc *adj.* church.

bisericos *adj.* church-going.
bisericuţă *sf.* chapel; *fig.* coterie.
bisturiu *sn.* lancet.
bivol *sm.* buffalo; *fig.* stodgy person.
bivoliţă *sf.* buffalo (cow).
bivuac *sn.* bivouac.
bizantin *adj.* Byzantine.
bizar *adj.* quaint.
bizon *sm.* bison.
bizui *vr.: a se ~ pe* to depend on.
bîlgui *vt., vi.* to stammer, to mumble.
bîjbîi *vi.* to grope (about).
bîjbîială *sf.*, **bîjbîit** *sn.* groping; *pe bîjbîite* groping.
bîlbîi *vt., vr.* to stutter.
bîlbîială *sf.* stammer(ing).
bîlbîit *sm.* stammering person. *adj.* stammering.
bîlci *sn.* fair; *fig.* jumble.
bîntui *vt.* to haunt; *(a face ravagii în)* to play havoc in. *vi.* to rage.
bîrfă *sf.* gossip.
bîrfeală *sf.* gossip; *(calomnie)* scandal.
bîrfi *vt.* to talk about; *(calomnios)* to slander. *vi.* to gossip; *(a calomnia)* to talk scandal.
bîrfitor *sm.* scandalmonger; *(calomniator)* slanderer. *adj.* slanderous.
bîrlog *sn.* lair.
bîrnă *sf.* beam.
bîtă *sf.* club.
bîtlan *sm.* heron.
bîţîi *vi., vr.* to jitter.
bîţîială *sf.* jitters.
bîzîi *vi.* to buzz.
blacheu *sn.* toe-plate.
blajin *adj.* soft-hearted; soft--tongued. *adv.* mildly.

blam *sn.* (public) censure.
blama *vt.* to blame.
blană *sf.* fur (coat).
blaza *vt.* to be(come) blasé.
blazare *sf.* surfeit.
blazat *adj.* blasé.
blazon *sn.* coat of arms.
blănar *sm.* furrier.
blănărie *sf.* furrier's shop *sau* trade.
bleg *sm.* dolt. *adj.* soft(-minded); *(prost)* dull.
blegi *vt., vi., vr.* to droop; *fig.* to grow weak-minded.
blestem *sn.* curse.
blestema *vt., vi.* to curse.
blestemat *adj.* damned, accursed.
blestemăţie *sf.* foul trick.
bleumarin *sn., adj.* navy blue.
blid *sn.* dish.
blindaj *sn.* armour.
bliţ *sn.* flash-gun.
blînd *adj.* mild; *(domesticit)* tame; *(supus)* gentle; *(dulce)* sweet; *(liniştit)* peaceable. *adv.* mildly, gingerly.
blîndeţe *sf.* gentleness; *(bunătate)* kind(li)ness; *cu ~* gingerly.
bloc *sn.* block; *(clădire)* apartment-house; *pol.* bloc; *~ de desen* drawing tablet; *~ turn* tower house; *în ~* in the lump.
bloca *vt.* to block. *vr.* to be blocked.
blocadă *sf.* blockade.
blocaj *sn.*, **blocare** *sf.* blocking, stopping (up).
blocnotes *sn.* jotter.
blond *sm., adj.* blond(e).
blond(in)ă *sf.* blonde.
bluf *sn.* bluff.
bluză *sf.* blouse.

boa *sm.* boa.

boabă *sf.* berry; *(bob)* grain; *(de strugure)* grape; *fig.* whit. *adv.* (not) at all.

boacănă *sf.* blunder. *adj.* stupid, abominable.

boală *sf.* sickness; *(grea)* illness; *(mai ales infecţioasă)* disease; *(organică)* complaint; *(tulburare)* disorder; ~ *infecţioasă sau molipsitoare* infectious *sau* catching disease.

boare *sf.* breeze.

boarfă *sf.* rag; *pl.* old clothes.

bob *sm.* bean; *(plantă)* horse bean. *sn.* grain; *(de strugure)* grape; *(sanie)* bobsleigh.

bobină *sf.* reel; *el.* coil.

bobiţă *sf.* berry.

bobîrnac *sn.* fillip.

boboc *sm.* *bot.* bud; *(de raţă)* duckling; *(de gîscă)* gosling; *(student)* fresher.

bobot *sn.:* în ~e blindly, gropingly.

boboteazză *sf.* Epiphany.

bocanc *sm.* (hobnailed) boot.

bocăni *vi.* to hammer; to knock.

boccea *sf.* bundle.

bocet *sn.* keen; *(plînset)* wailing.

boci *vt.* to keen. *vi.*, *vr.* to lament.

bocitoare *sf.* (hired) mourner.

bocnă *adv.* frozen (stiff).

bodegă *sf.* pub.

bodogăni *vi.* to grumble.

boem *sm.*, *adj.* Bohemian.

boemă *sf.* Bohemianism.

bogat *sm.* rich man; *pl.* the rich. *adj.* rich, wealthy. *adv.* richly, amply.

bogătaş *sm.* wealthy man.

bogăţie *sf.* wealth; *(abundenţă)* profusion.

bogdaproste *sn.*, *interj.* many thanks!

boi *vt.* to dye; *(cu pensula, ruj* etc.*)* to paint. *vr.* to paint one's face.

boia *sf.* dye; *(de ardei)* paprika.

boiangiu *sm.* dyer.

boicot *sn.* boycott.

boicota *vt.* to boycott.

boier *sm.* *ist.* boyar(d).

boieresc *sn.* *ist.* corvée. *adj.* boyar's.

boiereşte *adv.* leisurely; grandly.

boieri *vt.* to ennoble. *vr.* to do the grand.

boierie *sf.* nobility.

boierime *sf.* (landed) gentry.

boiernaş *sm.* country squire.

boieros *adj.* haughty; *(leneş)* idle.

bojdeucă *sf.* hovel.

bojoci *sm. pl.* lights.

bol *sn.* bowl.

bolborosi *vt.* to mumble. *vi.* to babble; *(d. apă)* to bubble.

bolborosire *sf.* mumbling.

bold *sn.* pin.

bolid *sm.* meteor.

bolnav *sm.* invalid; *med.* patient. *adj.* ill (with).

bolnăvicios *adj.* weedy; *(plăpînd)* seedy.

bolovan *sm.* boulder.

bolşevic *sm.*, *adj.* Bolshevik.

boltă *sf.* vault; *(de verdeaţă)* bower; *bolta cerului* the canopy of heaven.

bolti *vt.*, *vr.* to arch.

boltit *adj.* vaulted; *(d. frunte)* domed.

bombarda *vt.* *(din avion)* to bomb; *(cu artileria)* to shell.

bombardament *sn.* air raid; *(de artilerie)* strafe.

bombardier *sn.* bomber.
bombastic *adj.* fustian. *adv.* bombastically.
bombat *adj.* bulging.
bombă *sf.* (air) bomb; *(obuz)* shell; ~ *atomică* A-bomb; ~ *cu hidrogen* H-bomb; ~ *cu întîrziere* time bomb.
bombăni *vt.* to nag. *vi.* to grumble.
bombeu *sn.* toe cap.
bomboană *sf.* sweet; *(de ciocolată)* chocolate; *o* ~ *de fată* a sweet girl.
bon *sn. com.* bill; *(de casă)* sales slip.
bonă *sf.* governess.
bondar *sm.* bumble bee.
bondoc *sm.* stumpy man. *adj.* thickset.
bonetă *sf.* bonnet; *(de baie)* bathing cap.
bonier *sn.* bill book.
bonjur *interj.* hello !
bont *adj.* blunt.
bor *sn.* brim.
borangic *sn.* floss silk.
borcan *sn.* (glass) jar.
borcănat *adj.* swollen.
bord *sn.* board; *(margine)* edge.
bordei *sn.* (mud) hut.
bordel *sn.* bawdy house.
borderou *sn.* bordereau.
bordură *sf.* street curb.
boreal *adj.* northern.
borfaş *sm.* thief.
bornă *sf.* landmark; *el.* terminal.
boroboaţă *sf.* blunder.
borş *sn.* bortsch.
borviz *sn.* table waters.
bosă *sf.* bump; *fig.* boss.
boschet *sn.* arbour.
boscorodi *vt.* to nag. *vi.* to grumble.

bostan *sm.* pumpkin.
bostănărie *sf.* pumpkin field.
bosumfla *vr.* to pout.
bosumflat *adj.* pouting.
bot *sn.* muzzle; *(rît)* snout; ~ *de deal* brow (of a hill); ~ *în* ~ cheek by jowl.
botanic *adj.* botanic(al).
botanică *sf.* botany.
botanist *sm.* botanist.
botez *sn.* christening.
boteza *vt.* to name; *rel.* to christen. *vr.* to be baptized.
botniţă *sf.* muzzle.
botos *adj.* pouting.
boţ *sn.* ball.
boţi *vt., vr.* to crumple.
bou *sm.* ox, *pl.* oxen; *fig.* dolt.
bour *sm.* aurochs.
bovin *adj.* ox, bovine.
bovine *sf. pl.* horned cattle.
box *sn.* boxing; *(piele)* box calf; *(pumnar)* knuckle duster; *de* ~ boxing.
boxa *vt., vi., vr.* to box.
boxă *sf.* dock.
boxer *sm.* boxer.
braconaj *sn.* poaching.
braconier *sm.* poacher.
brad *sm.* fir (tree).
bragagiu *sm.* millet beer vendor.
bragă *sf.* millet beer.
brambura *adv.* aimlessly; *(în dezordine)* topsy-turvy.
brancardă *sf.* stretcher.
brancardier *sm.* stretcher bearer.
branhii *sf. pl.* gills.
branşa *vt., vr.* to plug in.
branşament *sn.* branching, connection.
branşă *sf.* line; *(domeniu)* field.
bras *sn.* breast stroke.
braserie *sf.* brasserie; beer saloon.

braşoavă *sf.* crammer.

braţ *sn.* arm; *(dè rîu şi)* branch; *(de lemne* etc.*)* armful; ~*e de muncă* manpower; ~*ele de muncă* labour exchange; *(~) la* ~ arm in arm; *cu* ~*ele* by hand.

brav *sm.* hero. *adj.* brave.

brava *vt.* to defy.

bravo *interj.* bravo !

bravură *sf.* bravery.

brazdă *sf. (şanţ)* furrow; *(de iarbă)* sward; windrow.

brazilian *sm., adj.,* **braziliană** *sf., adj.* Brazilian.

brădet, brădiş *sn.* fir wood; *(buruieni)* water milfoil.

brăţară *sf.* bracelet.

brăzda *vt.* to furrow.

bre *interj.* (hey) you !

breaslă *sf.* guild.

breaz *adj.* piebald; *mai* ~ (any) better.

breloc *sn.* trinket.

breşă *sf.* breach.

bretea *sf.* (shoulder) strap; *pl.* braces.

breton *sm., adj.* Breton. *sn.* bang.

brevet *sn.* licence; *(de invenţie)* (letters) patent.

breveta *vt.* to patent.

briantină *sf.* brilliantine.

briceag *sn.* (pen)knife.

brichetă *sf.* (cigarette) lighter; *(de cărbuni)* briquette.

brici *sn.* razor.

bridă *sf.* strap.

brigadă *sf.* brigade; crew.

brigadier *sm.* brigade member; *(şef)* team leader; *(silvic)* forest keeper.

briliant *sn.* brilliant.

brio *sn.* brio.

brioşă *sf.* brioche.

brişcă *sf.* gig.

britanic *sm.* Englishman, Briton. *adj.* British.

briză *sf.* breeze.

brîncă *sf.* erysipelas; *pe brînci* on all fours; *fig.* hammer and tongs.

brînduşă *sf.* crocus.

brînză *sf.* cheese; ~ *de oaie* ewe's cheese; ~ *de vaci* cream cheese; ~ *telemea* (spiced) cottage cheese; *n-a făcut nici o* ~ what he did cuts no ice.

brînzeturi *sf. pl.* cheese.

brînzi *vr.* to curdle.

brîu *sn.* belt, girdle; *(talie)* waist.

broască *sf.* frog; *(rîioasă)* toad; *(de uşă)* lock; ~ *iale* safety lock; ~ *ţestoasă* turtle, tortoise.

broboadă *sf.* headkerchief.

broboană *sf.* bead.

brobonit *adj.* sweaty.

brocart *sn.* brocade.

broda *vt., vi.* to embroider.

broderie *sf.* embroidery.

brodeză *sf.* embroideress.

bromură *sf.* bromide.

bronhii *sf. pl.* bronchi.

bronşită *sf.* bronchitis.

bronz *sn.* bronz.

bronza *vt.* to tan. *vr.* to get a sun tan.

bronzat *adj.* sun-tanned.

broscoi *sm.* big frog; *fig.* urchin.

broşa *vt.* to stitch.

broşat *sn.* stitching. *adj.* paper (-covered).

broşură *sf.* booklet.

brotac, brotăcel *sm.* green frog.

bruftui *vt.* to treat harshly.

brumat *adj.* frosted.

brumă *sf.* hoarfrost; *fig.* smattering.
brumăriu *adj.* grey.
brun *adj.* brown; *(d. oameni)* dark (-haired).
brunet *sm.* swarthy man. *adj.* dark (-haired).
brunetă *sf.* brunette.
brusc *adj.* abrupt. *adv.* suddenly.
brusca *vt.* *(pe cineva)* to speak harshly to; *(lucrurile)* to press.
brusture *sm.* bur.
brut *adj.* raw; *com.* gross; *chim.*, *geol.* crude.
brutal *adj.* brutal. *adv.* brutally.
brutalitate *sf.* brutality.
brutaliza *vt.* to handle roughly.
brutar *sm.* baker.
brută *sf.* brute.
brutărie *sf.* bakery, baker's.
bruto *adv.* in the gross.
bubă *sf.* boil; *fig.* trouble.
buboi *sn.* boil.
bubos *adj.* scabby.
bubui *vi.* to thunder; *(d. tun)* to roar.
bubuit *sn.*, **bubuitură** *sf.* peal (of thunder); roar (of cannon).
bubuitor *adj.* thundering.
buburuză *sf.* lady bird.
bucal *adj.* oral.
bucată *sf.* piece; fragment, *(îmbucătură)* morsel; *(felie)* slice; *(de zahăr* etc.*)* lump; *(de drum)* distance; ~ *aleasă* tidbit; *(literară)* choice passage; *cu bucata* (by) retail; *dintr-o* ~ adamant.
bucate *sf. pl.* food; *(merinde)* victuals.
bucălat *adj.* chubby.
bucătar *sm.* cook; chef.

bucătăreasă *sf.* cook.
bucătărie *sf.* kitchen; *(artă culinară)* cookery; cuisine.
bucățică *sf.* bit *(de mîncare și)* morsel; *(capăt)* end.
bucher *sm.* swot.
buchet *sn.* bouquet.
bucium *sn.* alphorn.
buclat *adj.* curly.
buclă *sf.* curl; *fig.* loop.
bucluc *sn.* trouble.
buclucaș *adj.* troublesome; *(certăreț)* captious.
bucovinean *sm.* inhabitant of the Bucovina. *adj.* from *sau* of the Bucovina.
bucura *vt.* to fill with joy. *vr.* to rejoice; *a se* ~ *de* to rejoice (at smth.); *(drepturi* etc.*)* to enjoy.
bucureștean *sm.* Bucharester. *adj.* Bucharest.
bucurie *sf.* joy; *(veselie)* mirth; *(plăcere)* pleasure; *cu multă* ~ gladly.
bucuros *adj.* glad; *(vesel)* merry. *adv.* gladly.
budincă *sf.* pudding.
budism *sn.* Buddhism.
budist *sm.*, *adj.* Buddhist.
budoar *sn.* lady's closet.
buf *adj.* slapstick. *interj.* bang!
bufant *adj.* baggy.
bufet *sn.* buffet; *(mobilă)* sideboard; *(la teatru* etc.*)* refreshment room; *(restaurant și)* refreshment bar; ~ *expres* snack bar.
bufetier *sm.*, **bufetieră** *sf.* bartender.
bufnitură *sf.* thud.
bufniță *sf.* owl.
bufon *sm.* fool; *ist. și* jester.
bufonerie *sf.* slapstick (humour)

buget *sn.* budget.
bugetar *adj.* budgetary.
buhai *sm.* bull; ~ *de baltă (pasăre)* bittern; *(broască)* toad. *sn.* booming drum used on New Year's Eve.
buhă *sf.* owl.
buhăi *vr.* to swell (in the face).
buhăit *adj.* bloated.
buimac *adj.* sleepy; *(zăpăcit)* dizzy.
buimăci *vt.* to dumbfound. *vr.* to be taken aback.
bujie *sf.* sparking plug.
bujor *sm.*, peony; *un* ~ *de fată* a flower of a girl.
bulb *sm.* bulb.
bulboană *sf.* whirlpool.
bulbuca *vt.: a* ~ *ochii* to stare wide-eyed. *vr.* to bulge; *(d. ochi)* to start (from their sockets).
bulbucat *adj.* bulging.
buldog *sm.* bulldog.
buleandră *sf.* rag.
buletin *sn.* bulletin; ~ *de identitate* sau *populație* identity card, papers; ~ *de știri* news (bulletin); ~ *de vot* ballot; ~ *meteorologic* weather forecast; ~ *oficial* official gazette.
bulevard *sn.* avenue.
bulevardier *adj.* frivolous.
bulgar *sm.*, *adj.*, **bulgară** *sf.*, *adj.* Bulgarian.
bulgăre *sm.* ball; *(de pămînt)* clod.
bulgăresc *adj.* Bulgarian.
bulgăroaică *sf.* Bulgarian (woman).
bulin *sn.* pill; *pl. (picățele)* (polka) dots.
bulion *sn.* tomato sauce; *(supă)* broth.

buluc *adv.* in a jumble.
bum *interj.* bang!
bumb *sm.* button.
bumbac *sm.*, *sn.* cotton (plant); *de* ~ cotton.
bumbăcărie *sf.* cotton mill.
bumerang *sn.* boomerang.
bun *sm.* grandfather. *sn.* property; *pl.* goods; *și fig.* assets; ~ *de tipar* imprimatur; ~*uri funciare* landed property; ~*uri imobiliare* real estate; ~*uri mobile* personal estate, chattels. *adj.* good, fine; *(de treabă și)* kind(ly); *(potrivit și)* fit; *(veritabil)* genuine; *(nestricat)* in good repair; *(norocos)* auspicious; ~*ă ziua!* hello!; *(vă salut!)* how do you do!; ~ *de gură* glib; ~ *de plată* honest; *mai* ~ better, finer, etc.
bună-credință *sf.* good will.
bună-cuviință *sf.* decorum; *(politețe)* politeness.
bunăoară *adv.* for example.
bunăseamă *sf.: de* ~ (as a matter) of course.
bunăstare *sf.* welfare.
bunătate *sf.* goodness; *(suflet bun)* kind(li)ness; *pl.* tidbits, delikatessen.
bunăvoie *sf.: de* ~ voluntarily.
bunăvoință *sf.* goodwill.
bun-gust *sn.* refinement; *de* ~ in good taste.
bunic *sm.* grandfather, grandpa.
bunică *sf.* grandmother, granny.
bura *vi. impers.* to drizzle.
buratic *sm.* tree frog.
bură *sf.* drizzle.
burduf *sn. (bășică)* bladder; *(sac)* skin; *(foale)* bellows; ~ *de carte* crammed with knowledge. *adv.* fast.

burete *sm.* sponge ; *(ciupercă)* mushroom.

burghez *sm., adj.* bourgeois ; ~-o-moşieresc bourgeois-landlord ; *mic-~* petty bourgeois.

burghezie *sf.* middle classes, bourgeoisie ; *marea* ~ the upper bourgeoisie ; *mica* ~ the petty bourgeoisie.

burghiu *sn.* gimlet.

buric *sn.* navel ; *(la deget)* tip ; ~-*ul pămîntului* the hub of the universe.

burlac *sm.* bachelor.

burlan *sn.* (drain)pipe.

burlesc *adj.* burlesque.

burniţa *vi.* *impers.* to drizzle.

burniţă *sf.* drizzle.

bursă *sf.* scholarship ; *fin.* (stock) exchange ; ~ *neagră* black market.

bursier *sm.* stipended student *sau* pupil.

bursuc *sm.* badger.

burtă *sf.* belly ; *(mare)* paunch ; *(ca mîncare)* tripe ; *pe* ~ prone.

burtos *adj.* big-bellied.

buruiană *sf.* weed ; *(de leac)* simple.

burzului *vr.* to bristle up.

burzuluit *adj.* furious.

busolă *sf.* compass ; *fig.* guide.

bust *sn.* bust.

busuioc *sn.* (sweet) basil.

buşi *vt.* to push (down).

buşon *sn.* stopper.

buştean *sm.* log ; *(ciot)* (tree-)stump. *adv.* asleep.

butadă *sf.* quip.

butaforie *sf.* papier-mâché (set pieces).

butaş *sm.* cutting, slip.

bute *sf.* hogshead.

butelie *sf.* bottle ; ~ *de aragaz* gas cylinder.

butoi *sn.* cask.

butoiaş *sn.* keg ; *(de revolver)* cylinder.

buton *sm.* cuff link; *(de guler)* collar stud. *sn.* push (button); *(la radio)* etc. knob; *(şalter)* switch.

butonieră *sf.* buttonhole.

butuc *sm.* log ; *(de viţă)* vine ; *(la măcelar)* (chopping)block ; *pl. (obezi)* stocks ; *pe* ~*i* under repair.

buturugă *sf.* tree-stump.

buzat *adj.* thick-lipped.

buză *sf.* lip ; *med.* labium.

buzdugan *sn.* mace.

buzna *adv.* unawares ; *(direct)* pop.

buzunar *sn.* pocket ; *zool.* pouch ; *de* ~ pocket ...

buzunări *vt.* to pick *sau* search smb.'s pockets.

C

ca *conj.* as, (so...) as ; *(decît)* than ; *(în chip de)* for ; *(în privinţa)* as to ; ~ *de pildă* such as ; ~ *la vreo* ... about... ; ~ *nu cumva (să)* lest ... ; ~ *să* for ; ~ *şi* as well as ; ~ *şi cum* as if.

cabană *sf.* hut ; *(în munţi)* chalet.

cabaret *sn.* cabaret.

cabină *sf.* cabin ; *(cuşetă)* berth ; *(de camion)* cab ; *(de lift)* cage ; ~ *telefonică* telephone booth.

cabinet *sn.* cabinet ; *(birou şi)* office ; ~ *medical* surgery.

cablu *sn.* cable.

cabotin *sm.* ham actor. *adj.* hammy.

cacao *sf.* cocoa (tree).

cacialma *sf.* bluff.

cacofonie *sf.* cacophony.

cactus *sm.* cactus.

cadastru *sn.* survey.

cadaveric *adj.* cadaverous.

cadavru *sn.* corpse.

cadă *sf.* tub.

cadenţat *adj.* rhythmic. *adv.* rhythmically.

cadenţă *sf.* cadence.

cadet *sm.* cadet.

cadînă *sf.* odalisque.

cadou *sn.* gift, present.

cadra *vi.:* *a* ~ *cu* to fit.

cadran *sn.* dial ; ~ *solar* sun dial.

cadre *sn. pl.* personnel (office).

cadrilat *adj.* chequered.

cadru *sn.* frame ; *(persoană)* worker ; *fig.* background ; *pl.* staff ; ~ *didactic* teacher ; *în* ~*l...* as part of ...

cafea *sf.* coffee ; ~ *filtru* filter (coffee).

cafeină *sf.* caffeine.

cafenea *sf.* café.

cafeniu *adj.* brown.

caiac *sn.* kayak.

caier *sn.* bundle, flock.

caiet *sn.* (copy) book ; *(de note)* (rough) note book ; ~ *de sarcini com.* conditions of contract.

caimac *sn.* cream ; skin (of milk).

cais *sm.* apricot tree.

caisă *sf.* apricot.

cal *sm.* horse ; *(la şah)* knight ; ~ *de bătaie* hobby horse ; ~ *de paradă* palfrey ; ~ *năravaş* balky *sau* restive horse ; ~*ul popii* dragon fly ; ~*-putere* horse power ; *cai verzi (pe pereţi)* a mare's nest.

calabalîc *sn.* caboodle.

calambur *sn.* pun.

calamitate *sf.* calamity.

calapod *sn.* last ; *fig.* pattern.

cală *sf.* hold ; *(doc)* slip(way) ; *bot.* calla.

calc *sn.* tracing paper ; ~ *lingvistic* loan translation.

calcan *sm.* turbot. *sn.* blind *sau* blank wall.

calcar *sn.* limestone.

calcaros *adj.* limestone ...

calchia *vt.* to trace ; *fig.* to copy.

calchiere *sf.* decal(comania).

calciu *sn.* calcium.

calcul *sm.* gravel. *sn.* calculation ; *pl. fig.* plans.

calcula *vt.* to calculate ; *fig.* to speculate on.

calculat *adj.* cautious ; *(econ.)* thrifty.

cald *adj.* warm ; *(fierbinte)* hot ; *(d. pîine etc.)* fresh.

caldarîm *sn.* pavement.

cale *sf.* road ; *şi fig.* way, path ; ~*a de mijloc* the golden mean ; *Calea laptelui* the Milky Way ; ~ *ferată* railway ; *căi maritime* water-ways ; *din* ~ *afară (de)* extremely ; *pe căi ocolite* in a devious way.

caleaşcă *sf.* carriage.

caleidoscop *sn.* kaleidoscope.

calendar *sn.* calendar.

calende *sf. pl.* calends.

calfă *sf.* journeyman.

calibru *sn.* calibre.

calic *sm.* pauper; *(avar)* curmudgeon. *adj.* beggarly; *(avar)*
niggardly.

califica *vt., vr.* ,to qualify.

calificare *sf.* skill; training;
sport etc. qualification.

calificat *adj.* skilled.

calificativ *sn.* epithet. *adj.* qual-
ifying.

caligrafic *adj.* calligraphic. *adv.*
calligraphically.

caligrafie *sf.* penmanship.

calitate *sf.* (fine) quality; *(în-
sușire)* feature; *(situație)* capacity; *de (bună)* ~ fine;
în ~ *de* ... as a ...

calitativ *adj.* qualitative.

calm *sn., adj.* calm. *adv.* quietly.

calma *vt.* to quiet(en); *(a alina)*
to soothe. *vr.* to calm down.

calomnia *vt.* to slander.

calomnie *sf.* calumny; *(publică)*
libel.

calomnios *adj.* defamatory; *jur.*
libellous.

calorie *sf.* calorie.

calorifer *sn.* central heating (radiator).

calvar *sn.* ordeal.

calvin *sm., adj.* Calvinist.

calvinism *sn.* Calvinism.

cam *adv.* about; *(oarecum)*
rather; ~ *așa* approximately;
~ *o oră* an hour or so.

camarad *sm.* comrade; *(coleg)*
mate.

camaraderie *sf.* comradeship.

camătă *sf.* usury.

cameo *sf.* cameo.

cameleon *sm.* chameleon.

camelie *sf.* camellia.

cameră *sf.* room; *(mobilată)*
chamber; *pol.* house; *(de bi-*

cicletă etc.) tube; *(de minge)*
bladder; *Camera Comunelor* the
House of Commons; *Camera
de Comerț* the Chamber of Commerce; *Camera Lorzilor* the
House of Lords; *Camera Re-
prezentanților* the House of Representatives; ~ *de zi* sitting
room.

cameristă *sf.* chamber-maid.

camfor *sn.* camphor.

camion *sn.* (motor) lorry; *(pt.
mobilă)* van.

campanie *sf.* campaign; *fig. și*
drive.

campion *sm.* champion.

campionat *sn.* championship(s).

camufla *vt., vr.* to black out;
(a masca) to camouflage.

camuflaj *sn.* blackout; *(mascare)* camouflage.

canadian *sm., adj.* Canadian.

canadiană *sf.* Canadian (woman);
(jachetă) wind jacket. *adj.* Canadian.

canal *sn.* *(de la canalizare)*
sewer; *(pentru ape de ploaie)*
drain; *(navigabil)* channel; *(artificial)* canal; *anat.* duct, tube;
el. channel; *Canalul Mînecii*
the English Channel.

canalie *sf.* rascal.

canaliza *vt.* to sewer; *fig.* to
channel.

canalizare *sf.* sewerage.

canar *sm.* canary (bird).

canava *sf.* canvas.

cană *sf.* decanter; *(cu capac)*
tankard.

cancan *sn.* scandal.

cancelar *sm.* chancellor.

cancelarie *sf.* office; *(la școală)*
teachers' room.

cancer *sn.* cancer.

candelabru *sn.* chandelier.
candelă *sf.* votive light.
candid *adj.* candid. *adv.* candidly.
candida *vi.: a ~ la . . . pol.* to stand for ...; *fig.* to aspire to.
candidat *sm.* candidate.
candidatură *sf.* candidateship.
candoare *sf.* candour.
cange *sf.* harpoon.
cangur *sm.* kangaroo.
canibal *sm.* cannibal.
canibalic *adj.* man-eating.
canibalism *sn.* cannibalism.
canicular *adj.* sultry.
caniculă *sf.* dog days.
canin *sm.* holder. *adj.* canine.
canion *sn.* canyon.
canoe *sf.* canoe.
canon *sn. (chin)* ordeal; *(pedeapsă)* punishment; *(regulă)* canon.
canotaj *sn.* boating; *~ academic* rowing.
canotor *sm.* rower.
cantalup *sm.* melon.
cantată *sf.* cantata.
cantină *sf.* canteen.
cantitate *sf.* quantity, amount; *mat. şi* number.
cantitativ *adj.* quantitative. *adv.* quantitatively.
canto *sn.* singing.
canton *sn. geogr.* canton; *c.f.* block station; *(de şosea)* gate keeper's cabin.
cantona *vt.* to billet.
cantonament *sn.* cantonment; *(sportiv)* training camp.
cantonier *sm.* line inspector.
canţonetă *sf.* canzonet.
cap *sm.* chief. *sn. anat.* head; *(minte)* mind; *(început)* start; *(capăt)* end; *(vîrf)* top; *geogr.* cape; *~ de acuzare* count of

indictment; *~ de pod* bridgehead; *~ul răutăţilor* ring leader; *~ sau pajură?* heads or tails? *cu ~ul gol* bareheaded; *din ~ pînă în picioare* from top to toe; *din .~ul locului* from the outstart; *din ~ul lui* off his bat; *în ~* exactly; *în ~ul mesei* at the head of the table; *în ~ul oaselor* sitting up; *peste ~ul cuiva* în spite of smb.'s will; *pînă peste ~* up to the teeth.
capabil *adj.* (cap)able; *~ de orice* unscrupulous.
capac *sn.* lid.
capacitate *sf.* capacity; *fig. şi* ability; *(om)* authority.
capăt *sn.* end; *de la un ~ la altul* throughout.
capcană *sf.* trap.
capelă *sf.* chapel; *mil.* (peaked) cap.
capişon *sn.* hood.
capital *sn., adj.* capital; *~ social* registered capital.
capitală *sf.* capital.
capitalism *sn.* capitalism.
capitalist *sm., adj.* capitalist.
capitaliza *vt.* to capitalize.
capitol *sn.* chapter.
capitona *vt.* to upholster.
capitula *vi.* to surrender.
capitulant *sm.* capitulator. *adj.* capitulating.
capitulare *sf.* surrender.
capodoperă *sf.* masterpiece.
caporal *sm.* corporal.
capot *sn.* dressing gown.
capră *sf.* (she-)goat; *(de trăsură)* dicky; *(de lemn)* (sawing-)-trestle; *(pt. gimnastică)* vaulting horse; *~ neagră* chamois; *(jocul) de-a capra* leap frog.

capricios adj. ' freakish.
capriciu sn. whim; muz. capriccio.
capsa vt. to staple.
capsă sf. mil. percussion cap;
(pt. hîrtie) staple.
capsulă sf. capsule.
capta vt. to capture; (apă etc.)
to collect.
captiv sm., adj. captive.
captiva vt. to captivate; (d.
cărţi etc.) to thrill.
captivant adj. thrilling.
captivitate sf. captivity.
captura vt. to seize.
captură sf. capture.
car sm. entom. silver fish; sn.
cart; (încărcătură) cartful; ~
funebru hearse; Carul mare the
Great Bear; Carul mic the
Lesser Bear; cu ~ul in plenty.
carabină sf. rifle.
caracatiţă sf. octopus.
caracter sn. nature.
caracteristic adj. characteristic
(of).
caracteristică sf. specific feature.
caracteriza vt. to characterize.
vr. to be characterized.
caracterizare sf. character(iza-
tion).
carafă sf. carafe.
caraghios sm. fool. adj. funny.
adv. comically.
caraghioslîc sn. funny thing.
caramelă sf. caramel.
carantină sf. quarantine.
carapace sf. shell.
caras sm. crucian.
carat sn. carat.
caravană sf. caravan; ~ cinematografică mobile cinema.
carbon sn. carbon (paper).
carbonic adj. carbonic.
carbonifer adj. coal-bearing.

carbonizu vt., vr. to burn.
carburator sn. carburetter.
carcasă sf. carcasse.
carceră sf. lock-up.
cardiac sm. cardiac patient. adj.
cardiac, heart.
cardinal sm., adj. cardinal.
cardiolog sm. cardiologist.
care adj. what. pron. (pt. persoane) who; (unii) some; (pt.
lucruri) which; (relativ, pt. persoane şi lucruri) that; ~ dintre
ei? which of them? ~ mai
de ~ vying with each other.
careu sn. square.
careva pron. somebody.
cargobot sn. cargoboat.
caricatural adj. caricatural.
caricatură sf. cartoon; fig. caricature.
caricaturist sm. cartoonist.
caricaturiza vt. to caricature.
carie sf. (dental) decay.
carieră sf. career; (de piatră
etc.) quarry; de ~ professional.
carierism sn. self-seeking.
carierist sm. self-seeker. adj. self-
seeking.
caritabil adj. charitable.
caritate sf. charity.
carîmb sm. top of the boot.
carlingă sf. cock-pit.
carmin sn., adj. carmine.
carnaţie sf. carnation.
carnaval sn. carnival.
carne sf. (vie) flesh; (tăiată)
meat; fig. flesh, body; ~ de
berbec sau oaie mutton; ~ de
miel lamb; ~ de pasăre fowl;
~de porc pork; ~ de vacă
beef; ~ de viţel veal; ~ friptă
roast; ~ de tun cannon fodder; in ~ şi oase alive.
carnet sn. (legitimaţie) card; (de

note) notebook; ~ *de membru* membership card; ~ *de şofer* driving licence.

carnivor *sn.* carnivore. *adj.* carnivorous.

caro *sn.* diamonds.

carosabil *adj.*: *partea* ~*ă* carriage road.

caroserie *sf.* body (of a car).

carou *sn.* square; *în*~*ri* check-(ered).

carpen *sm.* hornbeam.

carpetă *sf.* rug.

cartă *sf.* charter.

carte *sf.* book; *(de joc)* playing card; *(cunoştinţe)* schooling; *(legitimaţie)* card; *pol.* paper; ~ *albă* white paper; ~ *de bucate* cookery book; ~ *de citire* reader; ~ *de impresii* guest book; ~ *de vizită* visiting card; ~ *poştală (ilustrată)* (picture) post card.

cartel *sn.* cartel.

cartelă *sf.* ration book; *(de îmbrăcăminte)* clothing coupons.

cartier *sn.* quarter; ~ *general* headquarters; ~ *sărac* slum; *în* ~ in the neighbourhood.

cartof *sm.* potato (plant); ~*i prăjiţi* chips.

cartofor *sm.* gambler.

carton *sn.* cardboard; *(de prăjituri)* carton.

cartonat *adj.* in boards.

cartotecă *sf.* card index (drawers).

cartuş *sn.* cartridge; *(de ţigări)* carton.

cartuşieră *sf.* cartridge box.

casa *vt.* to quash.

casată *sf.* combined icecream.

casaţie *sf.* (court of) cassation.

casă *sf.* house; *(locuinţă)* dwell-ing; *(cămin)* home; *(pt. plată)* pay desk; ~ *de ajutor reciproc* Mutual Aid Fund; ~ *de amanet* pawn shop; ~ *de bani* strongbox; ~ *de bilete* booking office, *teatru şi* box office; ~ *de economii* savings bank; ~ *de naşteri* maternity house; ~ *de odihnă* rest home; ~ *de raport* tenement house; ~ *de toleranţă* bawdy house; *ai casei* one's folk; *în* ~ indoors.

cascadă *sf.* waterfall.

cască *sf.* helmet; *(de radio)* headphones.

casetă *sf.* casket; *(pt. bani)* money box; *poligr.* font.

casier *sm.* cashier.

casierie *sf.* pay office.

casieriţă *sf.* cashier.

casnic *adj.* domestic.

casnică *sf.* housewife.

cast *adj.* chaste.

castan *sm.* chestnut tree.

castană *sf. (sălbatică)* (horse) chestnut; *(dulce)* sweet chestnut.

castaniete *sf. pl.* castanets.

castaniu *adj.* chestnut.

castă *sf.* caste.

castel *sn.* castle.

castitate *sf.* chastity.

castor *sm.* beaver.

castra *vt.* to geld.

castravecior *sm.* gherkin.

castravete *sm.* cucumber.

castron *sn.* tureen.

castronaş *sn.* porringer.

caş *sn.* green ewe cheese.

caşalot *sm.* sperm whale.

caşcaval *sn.* pressed cheese.

caşmir *sn.* cashmere.

cat *sn.* storey; *(pe dinăuntru)* floor.

cataclism sn. disaster.
catacombă sf. catacomb.
catalige sf. pl. stilts.
catalog sn. catalogue ; (la şcoală) roll.
catapeteazmă sf. iconostasis.
cataplasmă sf. cataplasm.
catapultă sf. catapult.
cataractă sf. cataract.
cataramă sf. buckle ; la ~ close-(ly).
catarg sn. mast.
catarsis sn. catharsis.
catartic adj. cathartic.
catastrofal adj. catastrophic.
catastrofă sf. catastrophe.
catedrală sf. cathedral.
catedră sf. chair ; (secţie şi) department.
categoric adj. categorical. adv. pointblank.
categorie sf. category.
catifea sf. velvet.
catifelat adj. velvety.
catîr sm. mule.
catolic sm., adj. Catholic.
catolicism sn. Catholicism.
catrafuse sf. pl. caboodle.
catran sn. tar.
catren sn. quatrain.
catrinţă sf. peasant skirt.
caţă sf. scold.
cauciuc sn. rubber ; (de automobil) tyre ; ~ spongios foam rubber.
cauciuca vt. to rubberize.
caudin adj. Caudine.
caustic adj. caustic.
causticitate sf. causticity.
cauţiune sf. bail.
cauza vt. to cause.
cauzal adj. causative.
cauză sf. cause ; o ~ dreaptă a right(ful) cause ; din această ~,

din cauza asta on that account ; din cauza ... because of ...
cavalcadă sf. cavalcade.
cavaler sm. ist. knight ; fig. gallant ; sport. adj. gallant.
cavaleresc adj. chivalrous.
cavalerism sn. gallantry.
cavalerie sf. cavalry.
cavalerist sm. cavalry man ; pl. cavalry.
cavernă sf. cave(rn) ; med. cavity.
cavernos adj. hollow.
caviar sn. caviar.
cavitate sf. cavity.
cavou sn. tomb, vault.
caz sn. case ; instance ; (zarvă) fuss ; (problemă) issue, matter ; ~ fortuit accident ; în ~ de... in the event of ...
caza vt. to accommodate.
cazac sm., adj. cazacă sf., adj. Cossack.
cazan sn. boiler ; (de rufe) copper ; (de ţuică'etc.) still.
cazangiu sm. boiler maker.
cazanie sf. homily.
cazare sf. accommodation.
cazarmă sf. barrack(s).
cazemată sf. pill box.
cazier sn. (criminal sau identification) record.
cazinou sn. casino.
cazma sf. spade.
cazna sf. torture ; (strădanie) effort.
cazon adj. soldierly.
că conj. that ; (întrucît) for ; ~ altfel or else ; cum ~ to the effect that.
căci conj. for.
căciulă sf. fur cap ; de ~ per head.
căciuliţă sf. bonnet.

cădea *vi.* to fall (down), to drop; *(la examen* etc.*)* to fail (in an examination); *(d. evenimente* etc.*)* to happen; *a ~ (în) baltă* to go to pot; *a-i ~ cu tronc* to grow fond of; *a ~ de acord* to reach an agreement; *a ~ în greşeală* to err; *a ~ la pat* to fall ill; *a ~ pe gînduri* to grow thoughtful. *vr.* to be fit; *a i se ~* to be one's due.

cădelniţă *sf.* censer.

cădere *sf.* fall; *(insucces)* failure; *(pricepere)* competence; *la ~a nopţii* at nightfall.

căi *vr.* to repent.

căina *vt.* to pity. *vr.* to lament.

căinţă *sf.* contriteness; *cu ~* contritely.

călare *adj., adv.* on horseback; *~ pe* astride of; *fig.* master of.

călăreţ *sm.* horseman.

călări *vi.* to ride.

călărie *sf.* riding.

călător *sm.* traveller; *(pasager)* passenger. *adj.* travelling; *(migrator)* migratory.

călători *vi.* to travel; *(pe uscat şi)* to journey; *(a naviga şi)* to voyage.

călătorie *sf.* travel; *(scurtă)* trip; *(pe uscat)* journey; *(pe mare)* voyage; *(cu maşina)* drive; *(cu tramvaiul* etc.*)* ride.

călău *sm.* executioner.

călăuză *sf.* guide(-book).

călăuzi *vt.* to guide. *vr.*: *a se ~ după* to take as a guide.

călca *vt.* to tread; *(d. hoţi)* to rob; *(cu fierul)* to iron; *a ~ în picioare* to trample (under foot); *a ~ legea* to break the law; *a ~ porunca cuiva* to interfere with smb.'s orders. *vi.* to tread; *(cu fierul)* to press linen.

călcat *sn.* ironing.

călcîi *sn.* heel.

căldare *sf.* bucket.

căldură *sf.* warmth; *pl.* dogdays; *zool.* heat; *cu ~* heartily.

călduros *adj.* warm. *adv.* warmly.

călduţ *adj.* lukewarm.

căli *vt.* to temper. *vr.* to be tempered.

călimară *sf.* ink-pot.

călugăr *sm.* monk.

călugăresc *adj.* monastic.

călugări *vt.* *(d. bărbaţi)* to enter a monastery; *(d. femei)* to take the veil.

călugărie *sf.* monasticism; *(mănăstire)* monastery; *(de maici)* convent.

călugăriţă *sf.* nun.

căluş *sn.* gag.

căluşari *sm. pl.* *aprox.* morris dance.

căluşei *sm. pl.* merry-go-round.

căluţ *sm.* poney.

cămară *sf.* pantry.

cămaşă *sf.* shirt; *(pt. femei)* chemise; *~ de forţă* strait jacket; *~ de noapte* night shirt; *(de damă)* nightie, nightgown; *în ~* in one's shirt sleeves.

cămătar *sm.* usurer.

cămătăresc *adj.* usurious.

cămătărie *sf.* usury.

cămilă *sf.* camel.

cămin *sn.* hearth; *(casă)* home; *~ cultural* house of culture; *~ de studenţi* student hostel; *~ de zi* day nursery.

căpăstru *sn.* bridle.

căpăta *vt.* to get, to obtain; *(a cîştiga)* to earn; *a ~ curaj* to take heart.

căpătîi *sn.* head of the bed; *(suport)* trestle; *(fig.)* shelter; *de ~* basic; *fără ~* vagrant.

căpătuială *sf.* money (making).

căpăţînă *sf.* head; *(ţeastă)* skull; *bot.* bulb; *(de zahăr)* sugar loaf.

căpcăun *sm.* ogre.

căpetenie *sf.* chief(tain); *de ~* cardinal.

căpitan *sm.* captain; *sport, mar. şi* skipper.

căpiţă *sf.* hayrick.

căprar *sm.* corporal.

căprioară *sf.* roe, deer.

căprior *sm. zool.* roebuck; *arhit.* rafter.

căpriţă *sf.* kid.

căprui *adj.* hazel.

căpşun *sm.* strawberry plànt.

căpşună *sf.* strawberry.

căptuşeală *sf.* lining.

căptuşi *vt.* to line.

căpuşă *sf.* tick.

căra *vt.* to carry; *(cu sine)* to take. *vr.* to skedaddle.

cărare *sf.* path; *(în păr)* parting.

cărăbăni *vt.* to move. *vr.* to skip.

cărăbuş *sm.* cock chafer.

cărămidă *sf.* brick; *~ aparentă* face brick.

cărămidărie *sf.* brickyard.

cărămiziu *adj.* brick-coloured.

cărăuş *sm.* carter.

cărăuşie *sf.* carting.

cărbune *sm.* coal; *(tăciune)* ember; *bot.* smut; *el.* carbon; *artă* charcoal.

cărnos *adj.* fleshy.

cărpănos *adj.* dingy.

cărticică *sf.* booklet.

cărturar *sm.* scholar.

cărturăresc *adj.* scholarly.

cărucior *sn.* tub; *~ de copil* pram.

cărunt *adj.* grizzled.

căruţ *sn.* truck; *(de copil)* perambulator.

căruţaş *sm.* waggoner.

căruţă *sf.* waggon; *(încărcătură)* cartful.

căsăpi *vt.* to butcher.

căsători *vt.* to marry (away). *vr.:* *a se ~ (cu cineva)* to marry (smb.).

căsătorie *sf.* marriage; *(căsnicie)* wedlock; *(religioasă)* wedding.

căsătorit *adj.* married; *tineri căsătoriţi* newly-weds.

căsca *vt.* to open (wide); *a ~ gura la ceva* to gaze at something. *vi., vr.* to yawn.

căscat *sn.* yawn(ing). *adj.* (wide) open; *fig.* scatter-brained.

căsnicie *sf.* wedlock.

căsuţă *sf.* little house; *~ poştală* P.O.B.

cătănie *sf.* conscription.

cătrăni *vt.* to embitter. *vr.* to grow sad.

cătrănit *adj.* embittered; *(posomorît)* sulky.

către *prep.* towards.

cătun *sn.* hamlet.

cătuşe *sf. pl.* hand-cuffs.

căţăra *vr.* to clamber; *(d. plante)* to creep.

căţărător *adj.* climbing.

căţea *sf.* bitch.

căţel *sm.* little dog; *(pui)* puppy; *~ de usturoi* clove of garlic.

căuş *sn.* dipper; *(pt. apă)* bailer.

căuta *vt.* to seek (for); to look for; *(în dicţionar* etc.*)* to look up; *(a îngriji)* to look after; *a ~ să* to try to. *vi.* to seek; *a-şi ~ de* to mind. *vr.* to be in demand; *(a se îngriji)* to look after one's health; *se caută muncitori* hands are wanted.

căutare *sf.* search; *fig.* demand; *pl.* seekings, gropings; *în ~ de* on the look-out for.

căutat *adj.* in great demand; *(artificial)* recherché.

căutător *sm.* seeker; *~ de aur* gold-digger.

căutătură *sf.* glance; *(urîtă)* glare.

căzătură *sf.* fall; *(persoană)* wreck.

căzni *vr.* to strive (hard).

ce *sm.* something. *adj.* what; *(care)* which; *din ~ cauză?* why? *pron.* what; *~ spui!* you don't say so!; *adv.* how (much); *~ de oameni!* how many people!

cea *art.* the; *~ care* she who; *(d. lucruri)* that which. *interj.* ho!

ceafă *sf.* nape (of the neck); *de ~* by the scruff of smb's neck.

ceai *sn.* tea; *bot.* tea shrub; *(petrecere)* (tea-)party.

ceainic *sn.* tea-pot.

cealaltă *adj., pron.* the other.

ceangău *sm.* Csango.

ceapă *sf.* onion.

ceară *sf.* (bee's) wax; *(din urechi)* cerumen; *(de parchet)* floor polish; *~ roşie* sealing wax; *de ~* wax(en).

cearcăn *sn.* dark ring.

ceardaş *sn.* czardas.

cearşaf *sn.* bed-sheet; *(de plapumă)* quilt cover, turn-down sheet.

ceartă *sf.* quarrel.

ceas *sn.* hour; *(de buzunar* etc.*)* watch; *(de perete* etc.*)* clock; *~ bun* propitious hour; *~ cu cuc* cuckoo clock; *~ de ~* every hour; *~ de mînă* (wrist) watch; *~ de nisip* sand glass; *~ de soare* sun-dial; *~ deşteptător* alarm clock; *~uri întregi* for hours on end.

ceasornic *sn.* clock; *bot.* passion flower.

ceasornicar *sm.* watchmaker.

ceasornicărie *sf.* watchmaker's (shop); *(ca meserie)* watchmaking.

ceaşcă *sf.* cup; *(conţinut)* cupful.

ceată *sf.* band.

ceaţă *sf.* mist; *(deasă)* fog; *(uşoară)* haze.

ceaun *sn.* cast-iron kettle.

cec *sn.* cheque.

ceda *vt., vi.* to yield.

cedare *sf.* yielding.

cedru *sm.* cedar.

ceea *adj., pron.* that; *~ ce* which.

ceferist *sm.* Romanian railwayman.

cegă *sf.* sterlet.

ceh *sm., adj.,* **cehă** *sf., adj.* Czech.

cehoslovac *sm., adj.* **cehoslovacă** *sf., adj.* Czechoslovak.

cei *art.* the. *adj., pron.* those.

cel *art.* the; *~ mai bun* the best. *adj., pron.* that; *~ de sus* God; *~ mult* at (the) most; *~ puţin* at least; *~ mai tîrziu* at the latest.

celălalt *adj., pron.* the other.

cele *art.* the. *adj.* those. *pron.* those.

celebra *vt.* to celebrate; *(o căsătorie)* to solemnize.

celebritate *sf.* celebrity.

celebru *adj.* famous, celebrated.

celibatar *sm.* bachelor. *adj.* single.

celibatară *sf.* spinster.

celofan *sn.* cellophane.

celofibră *sf.* staple fibre.

celt *sm.* Celt.

celtic *adj.* Celtic.

celular *adj.* cell(ular).

celulă *sf.* cell; *anat. și* corpuscle.

celuloid *sm.* celluloid.

celuloză *sf.* cellulose.

cenaclu *sn.* literary circle.

cent *sm.* cent.

centaur *sm.* centaur.

centenar *sm.* centenarian. *sn., adj.* centenary.

centimă *sf.* penny; farthing.

centimetru *sm.* centimetre; *sn.* measuring tape.

centra *vt., vi.* to centre.

central *adj.* central. *adv.* in the centre.

centrală *sf.* headquarters; ~ *electrică* power station; ~ *telefonică* telephone exchange.

centraliza *vt.* to centralize.

centrifug *adj.* centrifugal.

centru *sm., sn.* centre; middle; *centre populate* populous centres; ~ *muncitoresc* industrial centre; ~ *înaintaș* centre forward.

centură *sf.* girdle; ~ *de salvare* life belt.

cenușă *sf.* ash(es); cinders.

Cenușăreasa *sf.* Cinderella.

cenușiu *sn., adj.* grey.

cenzor *sm.* censor; *fin.* auditor; *de* ~*i* auditing.

cenzura *vt.* to censor.

cenzură *sf.* censorship.

cep *sn.* spigot.

cer *sm. bot.* Turkey oak. *sn.* sky; *fig.* heaven; ~*ul gurii* the palate; *spre* ~ skywards.

ceramică *sf.* pottery.

cerb *sm.* stag.

cerbice *sf.* nape of the neck; *fig.* pride; *cu* ~*a groasă* obstinate.

cerbicie *sf.* obstinacy.

cerc *sn.* circle; *(de butoi, pt. copii)* hoop; *fig.* sphere; *(grup)* group.

cercel *sm.* ear ring.

cerceta *vt.* to examine, to study; *(a sonda)* to fathom.

cercetare *sf.* investigation, research; *mil.* reconnaissance.

cercetaș *sm.* (boy) scout.

cercetășie *sf.* boy scouting.

cercetător *sm.* researcher, research worker. *adj.* searching; *(curios)* inquisitive. *adv.* inquisitively.

cercevea *sf.* frame.

cerdac *sn.* balcony.

cere *vt.* to ask (for); *(imperios)* to claim; *(a îndemna)* to urge; *(a cerși)* to beg; *a (-și)* ~ *iertare* to apologize; *a* ~ *pe cineva în căsătorie* to propose to smb.; *cît ceri?* how much do you charge? *vr.* to be demanded.

cereală *sf.* cereal.

cerebral *adj.* cerebral.

ceremonial *sn., adj.* ceremonial.

ceremonie *sf.* ceremony; *(politețe)* formalism; *fără* ~ informally.

ceremonios *adj.* formal. *adv.* punctiliously.

cerere *sf.* demand; *(petiţie)* petition; *(de numire, admitere)* application; ~ *în căsătorie* marriage proposal; *la* ~ on demand.

ceresc *adj.* heavenly.

cerne *vt., vi., vr.* to sift.

cerneală *sf.* ink; ~ *simpatică* invisible ink.

cernit *adj.* mourning.

cerşetor *sm.* beggar.

cerşetorie *sf.* beggary.

cerşi *vt., vi.* to beg.

cert *adj.* doubtless. *adv.* surely.

certa *vt.* to reprimand. *vr.* to quarrel; *fig.* to fall out.

certat *adj.* reprimanded; *pl.* at loggerheads.

certăreţ *sm.* caviller. *adj.* quarrelsome.

certifica *vt.* to certify.

certificat *sn.* certificate.

certitudine *sf.* certainty; *cu* ~ for certain.

cetate *sf.* citadel.

cetăţean *sm.* citizen.

cetăţenesc *adj.* civic.

cetăţenie *sf.* citizenship.

cetăţuie *sf.* citadel.

cetină *sf.* fir-tree needles.

ceţos *adj.* misty.

ceva *adj.* a little, some. *pron.* something; *interog.* anything; *aşa* ~ such a thing; *un ceas şi* ~ (about) an hour or so.

cheag *sn.* rennet; *(de sînge)* clot; *fig.* money.

chef *sn.* carousal; *(dispoziţie)* desire.

chefliu *sm.* boozer. *adj.* gay.

chefui *vi.* to go on the spree.

chei *sn.* quay; *(de mărfuri)* wharf.

cheie *sf.* key; *muz. şi* clef; *pl. geogr.* gorge(s); ~ *de boltă* keystone; ~ *falsă* sau *potrivită* masterkey. *adj.* key.

chel *sm.* bald-headed man. *adj.* bald(-headed).

chelălăi *vi.* to yelp.

cheli *vi.* to grow bald.

chelie *sf.* baldness.

chelner *sm.* waiter.

chelneriţă *sf.* waitress.

cheltui *vt., vi.* to spend. *vr.* to be spent; *fig.* to work one's head off.

cheltuială *sf.* expense; *fin.* expenditure.

cheltuitor *sm.* squanderer. *adj.* extravagant.

chema *vt.* to call (for); *(la telefon)* to ring up; *mă cheamă Nicolaie* my name is Nicholas; *a* ~ *în ajutor* to appeal to. *vr.* to be called; *(a însemna)* to mean.

chemare *sf.* call(ing); *(provocare)* challenge.

chenar *sn.* border; *text.* festoon, list.

chenzină *sf.* fortnight(ly wages).

cheotoare *sf.* button-hole; *(copcă)* clasp.

cherem *sn.: la* ~*ul cuiva* at smb.'s beck and call.

cherestea *sf.* timber.

chermesă *sf.* kermis.

chestie *sf.* affair.

chestionar *sn.* questionnaire.

chestiune *sf.* matter; ~ *de onoare* point of honour; ~ *litigioasă* outstanding question; *în* ~ at issue.

chetă *sf.* collection.

chezaş *sm.* guarantor.
chezăşie *sf.* guarantee, surety.
chiabur *sm.* kulak. *adj.* wealthy.
chiaburime *sf.* kulaks.
chiar *adv.* even ; *(personal)* oneself ; *(tocmai)* precisely ; ~ *acum* right now ; ~ *aşa* just like that ; ~ *el* the very man ; *ba* ~*!* oh yes !
chibiţa *vi.* to kibitz.
chibrit *sn.* match.
chibzui *vt., vi.* to consider.
chibzuială *sf.* consideration ; *cu* ~ considerate(ly).
chibzuinţă *sf.* wisdom ; *(economie)* thrift.
chibzuit *adj.* considerate ; *(econom)* chary.
chică *sf.* long hair.
chichiţă *sf.* subtlety.
chicinetă *sf.* kitchenette.
chiciură *sf.* hoar frost.
chicot *sn.* snigger.
chicoti *vi.* to giggle.
chiflă *sf.* (French) roll.
chiftea *sf.* minced-meat ball.
chihli(m)bar *sn.* amber.
chilipir *sn..* good bargain.
chiloţi *sm. pl.* drawers ; (bathing) trunks.
chimen *sn.* caraway.
chimic *adj.* chemical. *adv.* chemically.
chimicale *sf. pl.* chemicals.
chimie *sf.* chemistry.
chimion *sn.* cumin.
chimir *sn.* (money) belt.
chimist *sm.* chemist.
chin *sn.* torment ; *(trudă)* labour(s) ; ~*urile facerii* throes (of childbirth).
chinez *sm., adj.,* **chineză** *adj.* Chinese.
chinezesc *adj.* Chinese.

chinezeşte *adv.* (like a) Chinese.
chinezoaică *sf.* Chinawoman.
chingă *sf.* girth.
chinină *sf.* quinine.
chintal *sn.* quintal.
chintă *sf. (de tuse)* coughing fit.
chintesenţă *sf.* quintessence.
chinui *vt., vr.* to torment (oneself).
chinuitor *adj.* tormenting.
chior *sm.* boss-eyed person. *adj.* one-eyed.
chioriş *adv.* askance.
chioşc *sn.* kiosk ; *(de ziare)* news stand ; *(gheretă)* booth.
chiot *sn.* shout.
chip *sn.* face ; *(imagine)* image ; *(fel)* manner ; ~ *cioplit* graven image ; *cu orice* ~ at all costs.
chiparoasă *sf.* tuberose.
chiparos *sm.* cypress.
chipeş *adj.* good-looking.
chipiu *sn.* peaked cap.
chipurile *adv.* as it were.
chirci *vr.* to cower.
chiriaş *sm.* lodger.
chirie *sf.* rent ; *(pt. obiecte)* hire.
chirilic *adj.* Cyrillic.
chirpici *sn.* adobe.
chirurg *sm.* surgeon.
chirurgical *adj.* surgical.
chirurgie *sf.* surgery.
chit *sn.* putty. *adj.: a fi* ~ to be quits.
chitanţă *sf.* receipt.
chitară *sf.* guitar.
chitic *sm.: a tăcea* ~ to keep mum.
chiţ *interj.* eek !
chiţăi *vi.* to squeak.
chiţăit *sn.* squeak(ing).

chițibuș *sn.* cavil.

chițibușar *sm.* pettifogger. *adj.* cavillous.

chiu *sn.: cu ~ cu vai* at great pains.

chiui *vi.* to shout.

chiuit *sn.* shriek.

chiul *sn.* shifting; *(absență)* truancy.

chiulangiu *sm. (la școală)* truant; *fig.* slacker, lagger.

chiuli *vi.* to play truant.

chiuvetă *sf.* wash-hand basin; *(de bucătărie)* sink.

ci *conj.* but.

cicatrice *sf.* scar.

cicatriza *vr.* to heal.

cică *adv.* as the story goes

cicăleală *sf.* nagging.

cicăli *vt.* to bicker.

ciclism *sn.* cycling.

ciclist *sm.* cyclist.

ciclon *sn.* cyclone.

ciclu *sn.* cycle.

cicoare *sf.* chicory.

cifra *vt.* to cipher. *vr.: a se ~ la* to amount to.

cifră *sf.* figure.

cifru *sn.* cipher.

cilindru *sm.* cylinder; *cu patru cilindri* four-cylindered.

cimbru *sn.* savory.

ciment *sn.* cement.

cimenta *vt.* to cement. *vr.* to be cemented.

cimitir *sn.* graveyard.

cimpanzeu *sm.* chimpanzee.

cimpoi *sn.* bagpipe.

cina *vi.* to eat supper.

cină *sf.* supper; *Cina cea de taină* The Last Supper.

cinci *sm., adj., num.* five.

cincilea *adj., num.* (the) fifth.

cincime *sf.* fifth.

cincinal *adj.* five-year.

cincisprezece *sm., adj., num.* fifteen.

cincisprezecelea *adj., num.* (the) fifteenth.

cincizeci *sm., adj., num.* fifty.

cincizecilea *adj., num.* (the) fiftieth.

cine *pron.* who; ~ *din voi?* which of you? *cu ~ ?* with whom? *pe ~ ?* who(m)?

cineast *sm.* film-maker.

cineclub *sn.* film-fan club.

cinema *sn.* cinema.

cinemascop *sn.* cinemascope.

cinematograf *sn.* pictures.

cinematografic *adj.* film.

cinematografie *sf.* cinema(tography).

cineva *pron.* somebody; *interog. și neg.* anybody.

cingătoare *sf.* girdle.

cinic *sm.* cynic. *adj.* cynical.

cinism *sn.* cynicism.

cinste *sf.* honour; *(onestitate)* honesty; *(virtute)* virtue; *(glorie și)* glory; *(cu ~)* creditably; *în ~a cuiva* for smb.'s health; *pe ~* greatly, capital(ly); *pe ~a mea* upon my word of honour.

cinsti *vt.* to honour.

cinstire *sf.* veneration.

cinstit *adj.* honest; *(credincios)* true; *(virtuos)* chaste; *(onorat)* venerated. *adv.* honestly.

cintezoi *sm.* chaffinch.

cioară *sf.* crow.

ciob *sn.* potsherd.

cioban *sm.* shepherd.

ciobănesc *adj.* shepherd's ...

cioc *sn.* beak, bill; *(barbă)* goatee; *(minciună)* shave. *interj.* knock!

ciocan *sn.* hammer; *(de lemn)* gavel; ~ *de lipit* soldering gun; ~ *pneumatic* air hammer.

ciocăni *vt., vi.* to hammer (away); *(d. păsări)* to peck.

ciocănitoare *sf.* wood-pecker.

ciocănitură *sf.* knock.

ciocîrlie *sf.* skylark.

cioclu *sm.* undertaker; *(gropar)* grave digger.

ciocni *vt.* to clink. *vi.* to clink glasses. *vr.* to collide.

ciocnire *sf.* clash.

ciocnit *adj.* broken.

ciocoi *sm.* boyar; *(parvenit)* upstart, pusher.

ciocoiesc *adj.* boyar's; *(de parvenit)* upstart.

ciocolată *sf.* chocolate.

ciolan *sn.* bone.

ciolănos *adj.* bony.

ciomag *sn.* cudgel.

ciomăgi *vt.* to cudgel.

ciondăneală *sf.* bickering.

ciondăni *vr.* to squabble.

ciopîrți *vt.* to hack.

ciopli *vt.* to carve. *vr.* to improve one's manners.

ciorap *sm.* *(lung)* stocking; *(scurt)* sock; *com. pl.* hose; ~*i trei sferturi* knee-length stockings.

ciorbă *sf.* (sour) soup.

ciorchine *sm.* bunch.

ciornă *sf.* draft.

ciorovăi *vr.* to haggle.

ciot *sn.* gnarl; *(buturugă)* stump.

cioturos *adj.* gnarled.

ciozvîrtă *sf.* hunk.

cirac *sm.* disciple; *peior.* lickspittle.

circ *sn.* circus; *fig.* mockery.

circa *adv.* about.

circă *sf.* militia station; *med.* circuit.

circuit *sn.* circuit.

circula *vi.* to circulate; *(a face naveta)* to ply; *(d. zvonuri)* to be about; ~*ți !* move on !

circulară *sf.* circular *sau* form letter.

circulație *sf.* circulation; *(trafic)* traffic; *de mare* ~ widespread.

circumcis *adj.* circumcised.

circumcizie *sf.* circumcision.

circumlocuțiune *sf.* circumlocution.

circumscripție *sf.* *(de miliție)* militia station; *med.* circuit; *pol.* constituency.

circumspect *adj.* cautious.

circumspecție *sf.* wariness.

circumstanță *sf.* circumstance; *circumstanțe atenuante* extenuating *sau* palliating circumstances; *de* ~ for the nonce.

circumstanțial *adj.* circumstantial; *gram.* adverbial.

cireadă *sf.* herd.

cireașă *sf.* (sweet) cherry.

cireș *sm.* (sweet) cherry tree.

ciripi *vt., vi.* to twitter, to chirp.

ciripit *sn.* chirping, twittering.

cisternă *sf.* tank.

cișmea *sf.* (water)pump; *(robinet)* tap.

cita *vt.* to quote; *(un exemplu)* to cite; *jur.* to summon.

citadelă *sf.* citadel.

citadin *adj.* city...

citat *sn.* quotation.

citație *sf.* subpoena.

citeț *adj.* legible. *adv.* legibly.

citi *vt.* to read; *(atent)* to peruse; *(neatent)* to skim over.

vi. to read; *(tare)* to read out. *vr.* to read, to be read.

citire *sf.* reading.

citit *sn.* reading. *adj.* (well-) read.

cititor *sm.* reader.

citric *sn.* citrus fruit. *adj.* citric.

ciubotă *sf.* boot.

ciuboţică *sf.* bootee; *ciuboţica cucului* cowslip.

ciubuc *sn.* hookah; *fig.* tip.

ciucure *sm.* tassel.

ciudat *adj.* odd; *(original)* peculiar. *adv.* oddly.

ciudă *sf.* anger; *(pică)* spite; *cu sau în ~* out of spite; *în ciuda ...* despite...

ciudăţenie *sf.* oddity, queerness.

ciuf *sn.* tuft.

ciufulit *adj.* ruffled; *(d. o persoană)* dishevelled.

ciufut *sm.* hedgehog. *adj.* peevish.

ciuguli *vt.* to peck.

ciulama *sf.* white sauce stew.

ciuli *vt.* to prick up.

ciulin *sm.* thistle.

ciumat *sm.* plague-stricken man. *adj.* plague-stricken.

ciumă *sf.* plague; *fig.* fright.

ciumăfaie *sf.* Jimson weed.

ciung *adj.* one-armed.

ciunt *adj.* crippled.

ciunti *vt.* to maim; *fig.* curtail.

ciupercă *sf.* mushroom; *(mică)* fungus; *(pt. ciorapi)* darning egg.

ciupi *vt.* to pinch; *(a fura)* to filch.

ciupit *adj.* *(de vărsat)* pockmarked.

ciupitură *sf.* pinch; *(de vărsat)* pockmark.

ciur *sn.* sieve; *(mare)* riddle.

ciuruc *sn.* wretch; *pl.* refuse.

ciurui *vt.* to riddle.

ciută *sf.* hind.

ciutură *sf.* well bucket.

civic *adj.* civil.

civil *sm.* civilian; *în ~* in civvies. *adj.* civilian; *jur.* civil; *(d. haine)* plain. *adv.* in plain clothes.

civiliza *vt.* to civilize. *vr.* to become civilized.

civilizat *adj.* civilized; refined. *adv.* in a civilized way.

civilizaţie *sf.* civilization.

cizela *vt., vr.* to polish (oneself).

cizmar *sm.* shoemaker; *(cîrpaci)* cobbler.

cizmă *sf.* (top)boot; *fig.* dolt.

cizmărie *sf.* bootmaking; shoemaker's (shop).

cîine *sm.* dog; *(de vînătoare)* hound; *fig.* cur; *~ ciobănesc* shepherd dog; *~le grădinarului* a dog in the manger; *~ lup* wolf hound; *~ poliţist* sleuth hound; *~ turbat* mad dog.

cîlţi *sm. pl.* tow.

cîmp *sm.:* *a bate ~ii* to rant; to saw wood; *a-şi lua ~ii* to run away. *sn.* field; *(cîmpie)* plain; *~ de bătaie* battle field; *în ~ul muncii* employed.

cîmpenesc *adj.* field...

cîmpie *sf.* plain.

cînd *adv.* when(ever); *~ aici, ~ acolo* here today and gone tomorrow; *~ şi ~, din ~ în ~* occasionally; *de ~?* since when? *de ~ cu* since; *pe ~* while.

cîndva *adv.* some day; *(în trecut)* one day.

cînepă *sf.* hemp; *de* ~ hemp(en).
cînt *sn.* song; *(canto)* singing.
cînta *vt.* to sing; *(la un instrument)* to play; *fig.* to extol, to glorify, to praise. *vi.* to sing; *(la un instrument)* to play; *(la un instrument de suflat)* to blow.
cîntar *sn.* scales; *(mare)* weighing machine.
cîntăreţ *sm.* singer.
cîntări *vt., vi., vr.* to weigh.
cîntec *sn.* song; *rel.* hymn; ~ *bătrînesc* traditional; ~ *de leagăn* lullaby; ~*ul lebedei* swan song; *cu* ~ intricate.
cîrcă *sf.:* în ~ on one's back.
cîrcel *sm. bot.* tendril; *med.* cramp.
cîrciumar *sm.* publican.
cîrciumă *sf.* pub(lic house).
cîrciumăreasă *sf.* innkeeper; *bot.* zinnia.
cîrcotaş *adj.* cavilling.
cîrdăşie *sf.* collusion.
cîrîi *vt., vr.* to bicker. *vi.* to croak.
cîrjă *sf.* crutch; *(de păstor)* staff; *rel.* crozier.
cîrlig *sn.* hook; *(pt. rufe)* peg; *fig.* appeal.
cîrlionţ *sm.* ringlet; *(pe frunte)* kiss-me-quick.
cîrlionţat *adj.* curled.
cîrmaci *sm.* helmsman; *sport* cox(swain).
cîrmă *sf.* rudder; *(roata şi fig.)* helm.
cîrmi *vt., vi.* to steer.
cîrmui *vt., vi.* to rule.
cîrmuire *sf.* government.
cîrmuitor *sm.* ruler. *adj.* ruling.
cîrn *adj.* snub(-nosed).

cîrnat *sm.* sausage.
cîrpaci *sm.* cobbler; *fig.* bungler.
cîrpă *sf.* rag; *(de praf)* duster; *pl. (scutece)* swaddling clothes; *fig.* weakling.
cîrpi *vt.* to mend; *(a peteci)* to patch (up); *(ciorapi şi)* to darn; *(prost)* to bungle; *a* ~ *o minciună* to fib; *a* ~ *cuiva o palmă* to box smb.'s ears.
cîrteală *sf.* grumbling.
cîrti *vi.* to grumble.
cîrtiţă *sf.* mole.
cîştig *sn.* gain; *(prin muncă)* earnings; *(venit)* income; *(profit)* profit; *(la loterie)* prize.
cîştiga *vt.* to win; *(bani, experienţă)* to gain; *(prin muncă)* to earn; *(a căpăta)* to get. *vi.* to win; to earn; *fig.* to profit.
cîştigător *sm.* winner. *adj.* winning.
cît *sn.* quotient. *adj., pron., num.* how much; what; *(de)* ~ *timp?* how long? *al* ~ *elea?* which? *adv.* how (much); ~ *de* ~ at all; ~ *mai bine* as well as possible; ~ *pe ce* almost; *cu* ~ ... *cu atît* the (more) ... the (better); ~ *ai bate din palme* in a jiffy; ~ *e ceasul?* what is the time? ~ *vezi cu ochii* as far as the eye can reach. *prep.* as (much as), like. *conj.* as long as; however (good, etc.); ~ *despre* as to; *atît* ... ~ *şi* ... both ... and ...
cîtăva *adj.* a little.
cîte *adj., pron.* all; *(interog.)* how many? ~ *şi mai* ~ and

what not. *prep.: ~ doi* by
twos.
cîteodată *adv.* sometimes.
cîteva *adj., pron.* some.
cîtuşi *adv.: ~ de puţin* not at
all.
cîtva *adj., pron., adv.* a little.
cîţ *interj.* boo !
cîţi *adj., pron.* all; *(interog.)*
how many ?
cîţiva *adj., pron.* some.
clac *sn.* crush hat.
clacă *sf.* group work. *ist.* statute labour.
claie *sf.* hayrick; *o ~ de păr*
a shock of hair; *~ peste grămadă* pell-mell.
clamă *sf.* paper clip.
clan *sn.* clan.
clandestin *adj.* surreptitious. *adv.*
surreptitiously.
clanţă *sf.* door handle.
clapă *sf. muz.* key; *(la buzunar)*
flap.
clapon *sm.* capon.
clar *sn.: ~ de lună* moonlight
(night). *adj.* clear; *(evident)*
obvious. *adv.* clearly, evidently.
clarifica *vt.* to elucidate. *vr.* to
become clear.
clarinet *sn.* clarinet.
claritate *sf.* clarity.
clarvăzător *adj.* clear-sighted.
clasa *vt.* to classify; *jur.* to stop.
vr. to be classified; *sport* to
place.
clasament *sn.* classification.
clasă *sf.* class; *(sală)* class-
room; *~ conducătoare* ruling
class; *clasa muncitoare* the
working class.
clasic *sm.* classic (author). *adj.*
classic; *(tradiţional)* classical.

clasicism *sn.* classicism.
clasifica *vt.* to classify.
clasificare, clasificaţie *sf.* classification; *(la şcoală)* ratings.
clauză *sf.* clause.
clavecin *sn.* clavichord.
claviatură *sf.* keyboard.
claxon *sn.* horn.
claxona *vi.* to toot one's horn.
clăbuc *sm.* (soap)sud.
clăcaş *sm.* bondsman.
clădi *vt.* to build.
clădire *sf.* building; *(publică
şi)* edifice.
clănţăni *vi.* to chatter.
clăti *vt., vr.* to rinse.
clătina *vt.* to shake; *(a zdruncina)* to shatter. *vi. a ~ din
cap* to shake one's head. *vr.*
to shake; *(pe picioare)* to
stagger.
clătită *sf.* pancake.
clei *sn.* glue; *~ de peşte* isinglass. *adj.* ignorant.
cleios *adj.* sticky; *fig.* ignorant.
cleptoman *sm., adj.* kleptoma-
niac.
cler *sn.* clergy.
clerical *adj.* clerical.
cleştar *sn.* crystal; *ca ~ul*
crystal clear.
cleşte *sm.* tongs; pliers; *(mic)*
pincers; *(de perforat)* punch;
zool. claw.
cleveti *vi.* to backbite.
clică *sf.* clique.
client *sm. com.* customer; *jur.*
client; *med.* patient.
clientelă *sf. com.* custom(ers);
jur., med. practice.
climat *sn.* climate.
climateric *adj.* climatic.
climă *sf.* climate.
clin *sm.* gusset.

clinchet *sn.* tinkling.

clinic *adj.* clinical.

clinică *sf.* clinic.

clinti *vt.* to move. *vr.* to budge.

clipă *sf.* moment.

clipi *vt.* to blink; *(ca semn)* to wink.

clipită *sf.* moment.

clipoci *vi.* to ripple.

clismă *sf.* enema.

clișeu *sn.* negative; *fig.* cliché.

cloacă *sf.* cloaca.

cloci *vt.* to hatch. *vi.* to brood.

clocit *sn.* hatching. *adj.* bad; *(d. apă)* foul.

clocitoare *sf.* incubator.

clocot *sn.* bubbling.

clocoti *vi.* to seethe.

clocotit *adj.* boiling (hot).

cloncăni *vi.* to cluck, to cackle.

clopot *sn.* bell.

clopotar *sm.* bell ringer.

clopotniță *sf.* belfry.

clopoțel *sm.* bell; *bot.* bellflower; *pl. (ghiocei)* snow-drops.

clor *sn.* chlorine.

closet *sn.* lavatory; water closet; ~ *public* public convenience.

closcă *sf.* hatching hen.

clovn *sm.* clown; *fig.* buffoon.

clovnerie *sf.* clownery.

club *sn.* club (house).

coacăză *sf.* gooseberry.

coace *vt.* to bake; *(d. soare)* to ripen; *fig.* to hatch; *a i-o* ~ *cuiva* to cook somebody's goose. *vi.* to gather (to a head). *vr.* to ripen; *(la cuptor)* to be baking; *med.* to gather.

coadă *sf.* tail; *(pieptănătură)* pigtail; plait; *bot.* stalk; *(de unealtă)* handle; *(de rochie)* train; *(șir)* queue; *coada șori-*

celului milfoil; ~ *de topor fig.* decoy.

coafa *vt.* to dress (smb.'s hair). *vr.* to have a hairdo.

coafeză *sf.*, coafor *sm.* hairdresser.

coafură *sf.* hairdo.

coagula *vt.*, *vr.* to coagulate, to curdle.

coajă *sf.* *(de copac)* bark; *(crustă)* crust; *(de fruct)* skin; *(de ou* etc.*)* shell.

coală *sf.* sheet.

coaliție *sf.* coalition.

coaliza *vt.*, *vr.* to confederate.

coamă *sf.* *zool.* mane; *(de zid)* coping.

coapsă *sf.* thigh.

coardă *sf.* cord; *muz. și* string; *(pt. copii)* skipping rope.

coarnă *sf.* cornel.

coasă *sf.* scythe; *(cosit)* haymaking.

coase *vt.*, *vi.* to sew.

coastă *sf.* *anat.* rib; *(latură)* side; *(de deal)* slope; *(de mare)* coast.

coautor *sm.* joint author; *jur.* accomplice.

cobai *sm.* guinea pig.

cobalt *sn.* cobalt.

cobe *sf.* croaker; *(la găină)* pip.

cobi *vi.* to forebode evil.

cobiliță *sf.* yoke.

coborî *vt.* to lower; *(a înjosi)* to debase. *vi.*, *vr.* to go down *sau* off; *(a descăleca)* to dismount.

coborîre *sf.* descent; lowering; *(dintr-un vehicul)* coming off.

coborîș *sn.* descent; *(pantă)* slope.

coborîtor *sm.* descendant. *adj.* downward.

cobră *sf.* cobra.

cobză *sf.* kobsa. *adv.* tightly, hand and foot.

coc *sn.* loop of hair.

cocaină *sf.* cocaine.

cocă *sf.* dough.

cocean *sm.* (corn) cob.

cochet *adj.* coquettish. *adv.* smartly.

cocheta *vi.* to flirt.

cochetă *sf.* coquette.

cochetărie *sf.* coquetry.

cocină *sf.* pigsty.

cocioabă *sf.* shanty.

cocleală *sf.* verdigris; *(gust rău)* foul taste, dry mouth.

cocoașă *sf.* hump.

cocoli *vt.* to mollycoddle.

cocoloș *sn.* ball; *(mic)* pellet.

cocoloși *vt.* to crumple; *fig.* to hush up.

cocon *sm.* cocoon.

cocor *sm.* crane.

cocos *sm.* coconut tree; *nucă de ~* coconut.

cocostîrc *sm.* stork.

cocoș *sm.* cock; *~ de munte, ~ sălbatic* capercaillie.

cocoșat *sm.* hunchback. *adj.* hunchbacked.

cocoșel *sm.* cockerel; *(ban)* gold coin; *pl.* (floricele) popcorn.

cocotă *sf.* cocotte, demirep.

cocotier *sm.* coconut tree.

cocoța *vt., vr.* to perch.

cocs *sn.* coke.

cod *sm. iht.* cod(fish). *sn.* code; *~ penal* criminal code.

codaș *sm.* slacker, lagger. *adj.* lagging.

codi *vr.* to hesitate; *a se ~ să* to shrink from.

codicil *sm.* rider.

codiță *sf.* (short) tail.

codobatură *sf.* wagtail.

codru *sm.* forest; *un ~ de pîine* a hunk of bread; *ca în ~* recklessly.

coerent *adj.* coherent. *adv.* coherently.

coerență *sf.* coherence.

coexista *vi.* to coexist.

coexistență *sf.* coexistence.

coeziune *sf.* cohesion.

cofă *sf.* wooden pail.

cofetar *sm.* confectioner.

cofetărie *sf.* confectionery.

cogeamite *adj.* huge.

coif *sn.* helmet.

coincide *vi.* to dovetail.

coincidență *sf.* coincidence.

cointeresa *vt.* to offer an incentive to.

cointeresare *sf.* (providing) incentives.

cointeresat *adj.* jointly interested.

coji *vt.* to skin, to peel; *(copaci)* to bark. *vr.* to peel (off).

cojoc *sn.* sheepskin coat.

cojocar *sm.* furrier.

colabora *vi.* to co-operate; *(la o publicație)* to contribute (to a magazine, etc.).

colaborare *sf.* co-operation; *(la o publicație)* contribution.

colaborator *sm.* co-worker; *(la o publicație)* contributor.

colac *sm.* knot-shaped bread; *(cerc)* ring; *~ de salvare* life-buoy; *~ peste pupăză* to crown it all.

colant *adj.* clinging.

colateral *adj.* collateral.

colcăi *vi. a ~ de* to be alive with.

colea *adv.* (over) there, not far from here.
colecta *vt.*, *vi.* to gather.
colectare *sf.* gathering.
colectă *sf.* collection.
colectiv *sn.* community; *(de muncă)* staff. *adj.* collective.
colectivitate *sf.* collectivity.
colecţie *sf.* collection; *(de ziare)* file.
colecţiona *vt.* to collect.
colecţionar *sm.* collector; *(de antichităţi)* antiquary.
coleg *sm.* fellow; mate; *(de clasă)* classmate; *(de şcoală)* schoolmate; ∼ *de cameră* roommate.
colegial *adj.* fellow-like. *adv.* in a friendly way.
colegiu *sn.* college; *(colectiv)* collegium; ∼ *de avocaţi* bar association.
colet *sn.* parcel.
colhoz *sn.* kolkhoz.
colhoznic *sm.* kolkhoznik. *adj.* kolkhoz...
colibă *sf.* hovel.
colibri *sm.* humming bird.
colică *sf.* colic.
colier *sn.* necklace.
colină *sf.* hill(ock).
colind *sn.* (Christmas) carol.
colinda *vt.* to scour. *vi.* to go carol-singing.
colindător *sm.* wait.
colivă *sf.* funeral wheat porridge.
colivie *sf.* cage.
colo *adv.* (over) there; *de ∼ pînă ∼* up and down.
coloană *sf.* column.
colocatar *sm.* inmate.
colocviu *sn.* viva-voce (examination).
colonel *sm.* colonel.

colonial *adj.* colonial.
coloniale *sf. pl.* colonial goods.
colonialism *sn.* colonialism.
colonialist *sm.*, *adj.* colonialist.
colonie[1] *sf.* colony; *(de copii etc.)* holiday camp.
colònie[2] *sf.* eau-de-Cologne.
colonist *sm.* colonist.
coloniza *vt.* to colonize.
colonizator *sm.* colonizer. *adj.* colonizing.
colontitlu *sn.* column head.
colora *vt.* to colour; *(a vopsi)* to dye. *vr.* to colour; *(a roşi)* to blush.
colorant *sm.* dye(stuff). *adj.* colouring.
colorat *adj.* coloured; *fig.* vivid.
colorit *sn.* colours.
colos *sm.* colossus.
colosal *adj.* colossal; *(straşnic)* capital. *adv.* enormously.
colporta *vt.* to spread; *(a vinde)* to peddle.
colţ *sm.* (eye)tooth; *zool.* fang; *(de stîncă)* crag. *sn.* corner; *(cotlon)* nook.
colţunaş *sm.* dumpling.
colţuros *adj.* angular; *(d. stînci)* craggy.
comanda *vt.*, *vi.* to command; *şi com.* to order.
comandament *sn.* headquarters; *fig.* command(ment).
comandant *sn.* commander.
comandă *sf.* command; *şi com.* order; *tehn.* control; *de ∼* made to order *sau* to measure.
comandor *sm.* colonel.
comasa *vt.* to merge.
comasare *sf.* fusion.
comă *sf.* coma.
combatant *sm.* fighter; *fost ∼* ex-service man. *adj.* fighting.

combate *vt.* to control.
combatere *sf.* fighting.
combativ *adj.* militant.
combativitate *sf.* militancy.
combina *vt., vr.* to combine.
combinat *sn.* combine(d works).
combinație *sf.* combination.
combină *sf.* combine.
combinezon *sn.* slip; *(de avia-tor)* overalls.
combustibil *sm.* fuel. *adj.* com-bustible.
comediant *sm.* comedian.
comedie[1] *sf.* comedy; ~ *de moravuri* comedy of manners.
comedie[2] *sf.* farce; *fig.* trick; *ce* ~ *l* the idea of it l
comemora *vt.* to commemorate.
comemorativ *adj.* memorial.
comenta *vt.* to comment upon.
comentariu *sn.* comment(ary).
comentator *sm.* commentator; *(la ziar și)* columnist.
comercial *adj.* commercial.
comercializa *vt.* to market.
comerciant *sm.* merchant; *(mic)* shopkeeper.
comerț *sn.* trade; ~ *angro sau cu ridicata* wholesale trade; ~ *cu amănuntul* retail trade; ~ *exterior* foreign trade.
comesean *sm.* companion at table; *pl.* company.
comestibil *adj.* edible.
cometă *sf.* comet.
comic *sm.* comic actor. *sn.* comic character. *adj.* comical. *adv.* comically.
comicărie *sf.* buffoonery.
comis *sm.:* ~-*voiajor* commercial traveller; *amer.* salesman.
comisar *sm.* police inspector.
comisariat *sn.* police station.
comisie *sf.* committee, commis-

sion; ~ *de redactare* editing panel; ~ *de revizie* auditing committee.
comision *sn.* commission; *(ser-viciu)* errand.
comisionar *sm.* errand boy.
comitat *sn.* county.
comite *vt.* to perpetrate.
comitet *sn.* committee; ~ *de partid* Party committee; ~ *de întreprindere* shop-stewards' committee.
comoară *sf.* treasure; wealth.
comod *adj.* comfortable; conve-nient; *(la îndemînă)* handy; *(indolent)* indolent. *adv.* com-fortably, conveniently.
comoditate *sf.* snugness.
comoție *sf.* commotion.
compact *adj.* dense. *adv.* densely.
companie[1] *sf.* company.
companie[2] *sf. mil.* company.
compara *vt., vr.* to compare.
comparabil *adj.* comparable.
comparat *adj.* comparative.
comparativ *sn., adj.* compara-tive. *adv.* comparatively.
comparație *sf.* comparison; *(lite-rară)* simile.
compartiment *sn.* compartment.
compas *sn.* compasses; *(pt. mă-surat distanțe)* divider; *mar.* compass.
compasiune *sf.* sympathy, pity.
compatibil *adj.* compatible.
compatriot *sm.* fellow country-man.
compătimi[1] *vt.* to commiserate.
compătimire *sf.* sympathy.
compensa *vt.* to compensate for. *vr.* to be compensated.
compensator *adj.* compensatory.
compensație *sf.* compensation.
competent *adj.* competent.

competență *sf.* competence.
competiție *sf.* competition.
compila *vt.* to plagiarize.
compilație *sf.* plagiarism.
complăcea *vr.* to indulge (in).
complement *sn.* complement;
gram. object; ~ *circumstanțial*
adverbial (modifier).
complementar *adj.* complementary.
complet *sn.* panel (of judges). *adj.*
complete; *(profund)* thorough;
(plin) full (up). *adv.* entirely;
thoroughly.
completa *vt.* to complete; *(un
formular)* to fill in; *(a întregi)*
to round up. *vr.* to complete
(each other).
completare *sf.* completion.
completiv *adj.* object.
complex *sn.* complex; ~ *sportiv*
sports grounds.
complexitate *sf.* intricacy.
complezență *sf.* obligingness; *de*
~ perfunctory.
complica *vt.* to complicate. *vr.*
to become intricate.
complicat *adj.* intricate.
complicație *sf.* complication.
complice *sm.* accomplice.
complicitate *sf.* complicity.
compliment *sn.* compliment.
complimentar *adj.* complementary.
complot *sn.* plot.
complota *vt.* to conspire.
complotist *sm.* plotter.
component *sn., adj.* component.
componență *sf.* make-up.
comporta *vt.* to involve. *vr.* to
behave.
comportament *sn.,* **comportare**
sf. behaviour.
compot *sn.* stewed fruit.

compozitor *sm.* composer.
compoziție *sf.* composition;
(structură și) make-up, lay-
-out; *(tablou)* subject painting;
actor de ~ character actor.
compresă *sf.* compress.
compresor *sn.* steam roller;
auto. supercharger.
comprima *vt.* to (com)press.
comprimat *sn.* tablet. *adj.* com-
pressed.
compromis *sn.* compromise. *adj.*
discredited.
compromite *vt.* to compromise.
vr. to be compromised.
compromițător *adj.* disreputable.
compune *vt., vi.* to compose.
vr. to consist (of).
compunere *sf.* composition.
compus *sm., adj.* compound.
comun *sn., adj.* common.
comunal *adj.* communal.
comună *sf.* commune; *comuna
primitivă* the primitive communal system.
comunica *vt., vi.* to communicate.
vr. to be transmitted.
comunicabilitate *sf.* communica-
bility.
comunicare *sf.* communication;
(științifică) paper.
comunicat *sn.* communiqué.
comunicativ *adj.* communica-
tive.
comunicație *sf.* communication.
comunism *sn.* communism.
comunist *sm., adj.* communist.
comunitate *sf.* community.
comutator *sn.* switch.
con *sn.* cone.
conac *sn.* manor.
concav *adj.* concave.
concedia *vt.* to dismiss.
concediere *sf.* dismissal.

concediu *sn.* leave, holidays; ~ *de boală* sick leave.

concentra *vt.* to concentrate; *mil.* to call up. *vr.* to concentrate.

concentrare *sf.* concentration; *mil.* call-up.

concentrat *sn.* concentrate. *adj.* concentrated; *fig. și* intent.

concepe *vt., vi.* to conceive.

concept *sn.* draft; *(concepție)* notion; *(hîrtie)* scribbling paper.

concepție *sf.* conception; *(generală)* outlook; ~ *despre lume* world outlook.

concern *sn.* concern.

concert *sn.* *(spectacol)* concert; *(bucată)* concerto.

concesie *sf.* concession.

concesiona *vt.* to lease.

concesiune *sf.* concession.

concetățean *sm.* fellow citizen.

conciliant *adj.* conciliatory.

concis *adj.* lapidary.

concizie *sf.* concision.

concludent *adj.* conclusive.

concluzie *sf.* conclusion.

concomitent *adj.* concomitant. *adv.* simultaneously.

concorda *vi.* to agree.

concordanță *sf.* concordance; *gram.* sequence.

concordie *sf.* concord.

concret *adj.* concrete. *adv.* definitely.

concretiza *vt., vr.* to materialize.

concura *vt.* to compete with. *vi.* to compete.

concurent *sm.* rival; *sport* competitor. *adj.* rival.

concurență *sf.* competition; *pînă la concurența sumei de* up to the amount of.

concurs *sn.* competition; con-test; *(ajutor)* support; ~ *de împrejurări* concourse of events.

condamna *vt.* to condemn.

condamnabil *adj.* blamable.

condamnare *sf.* sentencing; *fig. și* condemnation.

condamnat *sm.* convict.

condei *sn.* pen(holder); *fig.* pen (-manship); *dintr-un* ~ at one stroke of the pen.

condensa *vt., vr.* to condense.

condescendent *adj.* condescending.

condescendență *sf.* condescension.

condică *sf.* register.

condiment *sn.* spice.

condimenta *vt.* to season.

condiție *sf.* condition; *(clauză)* provision; *condiții de muncă* working conditions; *condiții de trai* living conditions; *cu condiția ca* provided that; *fără condiții* unconditional(ly).

condițional *sn., adj.* conditional.

condoleanțe *sf. pl.* sympathy.

conducător *sm.* leader. *adj.* leading, ruling.

conduce *vt.* to lead, to conduct; *(a călăuzi)* to guide; *(mașina etc.)* to drive; *(a dirija)* to manage; *(a stăpîni)* to rule; *(a însoți)* to accompany; *(la plecare)* to see off; *muz.* to conduct; *mil.* to command; *(dezbaterile etc.)* to chair; *auto.* to drive. *vr.: a se* ~ *după* to take as a guide.

conducere *sf.* leadership; management; *(călăuzire)* guidance.

conductă *sf.* pipe.

conductor *sm., sn.* conductor.

conduită *sf.* conduct.

condúr *sm.* pointed shoe ; ∼*ul*
doamnei nasturtium.
confecţie *sf.* manufacture ; *pl.*
ready-made clothes.
confecţiona *vt.* to make.
confederaţie *sf.* (con)federation.
conferenţia *vi.* to lecture.
conferenţiar *sm.* lecturer.
conferi *vt.* to award. *vi.: a* ∼
asupra to confer úpon.
conferinţă *sf.* lecture ; *(consfătuire)* conference ; ∼ *de presă*
press conference.
confesiune *sf.* confession ; *(sectă)*
denomination.
confidentă *sf.* confidante.
confidenţă *sf.* secret.
confidenţial *adj.* confidential.
adv. in private.
confirma *vt.* to confirm ; *(primire etc.)* to acknowledge. *vr.*
to be confirmed.
confirmare *sf.* confirmation ; *(de
primire)* acknowledgement.
confisca *vt.* to confiscate.
conflagraţie *sf.* conflagration.
conflict *sn.* strife ; ∼ *armat*
war ; *în* ∼ at variance.
confluenţă *sf.* confluence.
conform *adj.* concordant ; *prep. :*
∼ *cu* in accordance with.
conforma *vr.: a se* ∼ *unei
cereri* etc. to comply with a
request, etc.
conformism *sn.* conformism.
conformist *sm.* conformist. *adj.*
time serving.
conformitate *sf.* concord(ance).
confort *sn.* convenience(s).
confortabil *adj.* comfortable. *adv.*
comfortably.
confrate *sm.* brother, *pl.* brethren.
confrunta *vt.* to confront ; *(o
traducere)* to collate.

confunda *vt.* to mix up. *vr.* to
be mixed up.
confuz *adj.* confused ; *(d. stil)*
prolix. *adv.* confusedly.
confuzie *sf.* confusion.
congela *vt., vr.* to freeze.
congestie *sf.* congestion ; *(cerebrală)* stroke.
congestiona *vt.* to congest. *vr.*
to be congested.
conglomerat *sn.* conglomerate.
congres *sn.* congress, conference ;
amer. pol. convention.
coniac *sn.* cognac, brandy.
conic *adj.* conic(al).
conifer *sn.* coniferous tree. *adj.*
coniferous.
conivenţă *sf.: a fi de* ∼ *cu*
to abet.
conjuga *vt.* to conjugate. *vr.* to
be conjugated.
conjugal *adj.* conjugal.
conjugare *sf.* conjugation.
conjunctiv *sn.* subjunctive. *adj.*
conjunctive ; *gram.* subjunctive.
conjunctură *sf.* juncture.
conjuncţie *sf.* conjunction.
conjura *vt.* to conjure.
conjuraţie *sf.* conspiracy.
conlucra *vi.* to co-operate.
conlucrare *sf.* co-operation.
conopidă *sf.* cauliflower.
consacra *vt.* to devote ; *(a consfinţi)* to sanction. *vr.* to devote
oneself.
consacrare *sf.* devotion ; *(a re-
numelui)* recognition, acknowledgement.
consacrat *adj.* established ; *(d.
un lucru)* (universally) accepted.
consecinţă *sf.* result ; *în* ∼ consequently.

consecutiv *adj.* running; consecutive; *gram.* of result. *adv.* in succession.

consecvent *adj.* consistent. *adv.* consistently.

consecvenţă *sf.* consistency.

consemn *sn.* order; *(parolă)* password.

consemna *vt.* to record; *mil.* to confine; *(un elev)* to keep after hours.

conserva *vt.* to preserve. *vr.* to keep.

conservat *adj.* preserved; *(în cutii)* tinned.

conservator *sm.* conservative; *(în Anglia şi)* Tory. *sn.* music academy. *adj.* conservative; *(în Anglia)* Tory.

conservă *sf.* tin(ned food).

consfătui *vr.* to confer.

consfătuire *sf.* conference.

consfinţi *vt.* to sanction.

considera *vt.* to consider. *vr.* to consider oneself; *se consideră că* it is thought that.

considerabil *adj.* considerable. *adv.* appreciably.

considerare, consideraţie *sf.* consideration.

considerent *sn.* reason.

consignaţie *sf.* junk shop.

consilier *sm.* advisor.

consiliu *sn.* council; *~ de administraţie* board of directors; *Consiliu de Securitate* Security Council; *Consiliu de Stat* State Council.

consimţămînt *sn.* agreement.

consimţi *vt.* to accept. *vi.* to consent.

consistent *adj.* substantial.

consistenţă *sf.* firmness.

consoană *sf.* consonant.

consola *vt.* to solace. *vr.: a se ~ cu* to find comfort in.

consolare *sf.* consolation.

consolida *vt., vr.* to strengthen.

consorţiu *sn.* corporation.

conspect *sn.* epitome.

conspecta *vt.* to summarize.

conspira *vt.* to plot.

conspirativ *adj.* underground.

conspiraţie *sf.* conspiracy.

consta *vi.: (din mai multe elemente)* to consist of; *(în ceva)* to consist in.

constant *adj.* constant.

constanţă *sf.* steadfastness.

constata *vt.* to ascertain; *(a afla)* to find. *vr.* to be found.

constatare *sf.* finding.

constelaţie *sf.* constellation.

consterna *vt.* to perplex.

constipa *vt.* to constipate. *vr.* to become costive.

constipat *adj.* costive; *fig.* narrow-minded.

constitui *vt.* to constitute.

constituţie *sf.* constitution; *(fizică)* build.

constituţional *adj.* constitutional.

constrînge *vt.* to force.

constrîngere *sf.* compulsion; *jur.* coercion.

constructiv *adj.* constructive.

constructor *sm.* builder.

construcţie *sf.* construction; *(de maşini etc.)* engineering; *(de locuinţe)* housing.

construi *vt.* to construct; *(drumuri)* to lay (out). *vi.* to build. *vr.* to be built.

construire *sf.* construction; *~a socialismului* socialist construction.

consul *sm.* consul.

consulat *sn.* consulate.
consult *sn.* consultation.
consulta *vt.* to consult. *vr.* to confer.
consultant *sm.* counsellor. *adj.* consulting.
consultaţie *sf.* consultation.
consum *sn.* consumption; *de larg* ~ mass consumption.
consuma *vt.* to consume; *(a minca)* to eat. *vr.* to be consumed; *fig.* to fret.
consumator *sm.* consumer.
consumaţie *sf.* consumption; *(plată)* reckoning.
conştient *adj.* conscious. *adv.* consciously.
conştienţă *sf.* awareness.
conştiincios *adj.* conscientious; thorough(going). *adv.* conscientiously.
conştiinţă *sf.* consciousness; *(etică)* conscience.
cont *sn.* account.
conta *vi.* to count (on).
contabil *sm.* book-keeper. *adj.* book-keeping.
contabilitate *sf.* book-keeping.
contact *sn.* contact; *(legătură)* connection; *auto.* ignition.
contagios *adj.* catching.
contamina *vt.* to contaminate. *vr.* to become contaminated.
conte *sm.* count; *(în Anglia)* earl.
contempla *vt.* to watch.
contemporan *sm., adj.* contemporary.
contemporaneitate *sf.* the present day.
contesă *sf.* countess.
contesta *vt.* to dispute.
contestaţie *sf.* appeal.
context *sn.* context.

continent *sn.* continent.
continental *adj.* continental.
contingent *sn.* levy.
contingenţă *sf.* affinity.
continua *vt., vi., vr.* to continue.
continuare *sf.* continuation; *(la un roman* etc.*)* sequel.
continuator *sm.* continuer.
continuitate *sf.* continuity.
continuu *adj.* continuous. *adv.* continuously.
contopi *vt., vr.* to merge.
contor *sn.* meter.
contra *adj., adv.* counter. *prep.* against; *jur., sport* şi versus; *(în schimbul a)* in exchange for.
contraamiral *sm.* rear-admiral.
contrabalansa *vt.* to counterbalance.
contrabandă *sf.* smuggling; *de* ~ smuggled.
contrabandist *sm.* smuggler.
contrabas *sm.* double bass.
contracara *vt.* to counteract.
contract *sn.* contract; ~ *colectiv* collective (bargaining) agreement.
contracta *vt., vr.* to contract.
contradictoriu *adj.* contradictory.
contradicţie *sf.* contradiction.
contrafăcut *adj.* counterfeit.
contraindicat *adj.* unadvisable.
contramaistru *sm.* foreman.
contramanda *vt.* to call off.
contramarcă *sf.* check.
contrapunct *sn.* counterpoint.
contrar *sn., adj.* contrary. *prep.* contrary to.
contrarevoluţie *sf.* counter-revolution.
contrarevoluţionar *sm., adj.* counter-revolutionary.
contraria *vt.* to vex.
contrariu *sn.* opposite.

contrasens *sn.* misinterpretation.
contrast *sn.* contrast; *în ~ cu* unlike.
contrasta *vt., vi.* to contrast.
contratimp *sm. în ~* out of time.
contravaloare *sf.* equivalent.
contraveni *vi.* to run counter (to).
contravenient *sm.* offender.
contravenţie *sf.* trespass.
contrazice *vt., vr.* to contradict (oneself).
contribuabil *sm.* tax payer.
contribui *vi.* to contribute.
contribuţie *sf.* contribution.
control *sn.* control; *fin.* auditing.
controla *vt.* to check; *fin.* to audit.
controlor *sm.* controller; *fin.* auditor; *(de bilete)* ticket collector.
controversat *adj.* disputed.
controversă *sf.* controversy.
contur *sn.* contour, outline.
contura *vt.* to outline. *vr.* to be outlined.
conţine *vt.* to contain.
conţinut *sn.* content(s).
conţopist *sm.* clerk.
convalescent *sm., adj.* convalescent.
convalescenţă *sf.* convalescence.
convenabil *adj.* convenient; *(ieftin)* cheap. *adv.* conveniently; *(ieftin)* cheaply.
conveni *vi.* to agree; *(a fi convenabil)* to be convenient.
convenţie *sf.* convention.
convenţional *adj.* conventional. *adv.* conventionally.
conversa *vi.* to talk.
conversaţie *sf.* talk, conversation.

converti *vt.* to convert *vr.* to become converted.
convex *adj.* convex.
convieţui *vi.* to live together.
convingător *adj.* convincing.
convinge *vt.* to convince; *a ~ pe cineva să facă ceva* to persuade smb. to do smth. *vr.* to see for oneself.
convingere *sf.* conviction; persuasion.
convins *adj.* convinced; inveterate.
convoca *vt.* to convene.
convocare *sf.* convocation.
convocator *sn.* summons.
convoi *sn.* convoy; *(alai)* procession; *~ de maşini* autocade.
convorbire *sf.* talk; *(telefonică)* (telephone) call; *(interurbană)* trunk call.
convulsie *sf.* convulsion.
coopera *vi.* to co-operate.
cooperatist *adj.* co-operative.
cooperativă *sf.* co-op(erative society); *~ agricolă de producţie* co-operative farm; *~ de consum* consumers' co-op(erative).
cooperativiza *vt., vr.* to turn co-operative.
cooperator *sm.* co-operator; co-operative farmer. *adj.* co-operative.
cooperaţie *sf.* co-operation; *~ agricolă* co-operative agriculture *sau* farming.
coopta *vt.* to co-opt.
coordona *vt.* to coordinate.
coordonator *adj.* coordinating.
copac *sm.* tree.
copcă *sf.* clasp; *med.* wound clip; *(gaură)* (ice)hole.
copertă *sf.* cover.

copia *vt.* to copy (out) ; *(la şcoală)* to crib. *vi.* to crib.

copie *sf.* copy ; *(a unei statui etc.)* replica.

copil *sm.* child, *pl.* children ; kid ; *(mic)* baby ; *(fiu)* boy ; son ; *(fiică)* girl ; daughter ; *pl.* şi family ; ~ *din flori* love child ; ~ *găsit* foundling ; *de* ~ child('s), children('s) ; *(din copilărie)* from *sau* since a child.

copilă *sf.* (little) girl.

copilăresc *adj.* childish.

copilări *vi.* to spend one's childhood.

copilărie *sf.* childhood ; *(prostie)* stupidity ; *din* ~ since a child.

copilăros *adj.* childish ; *fig.* foolish.

copios *adj.* plentiful. *adv.* abundantly.

copist *sm.* clerk.

copită *sf.* hoof ; *(lovitură)* kick ; *(urmă)* hoof mark.

copleşi *vt.* to overwhelm.

copoi *sm.* sleuth-hound.

coproprietar *sm.* joint owner.

copt *sn.* ripening ; *(la cuptor)* baking. *adj.* ripe ; *(în cuptor)* baked.

cor *sn.* chorus ; *rel.* choir ; quire.

corabie *sf.* (sailing) ship.

coral *sm.* coral. *adj.* choral.

corb *sm.* raven ; *fig.* vulture.

corcitură *sf.* crossbreed ; *(javră)* mongrel.

corcoduş *sm.* wax cherry tree.

corcoduşă *sf.* wax cherry.

cord *sn.* heart.

cordial *adj.* cordial. *adv.* wholeheartedly.

cordon *sn.* girdle ; *(şnur)* cord ; ~ *sanitar* (sanitary) cordon.

corect *adj.* correct ; *(cinstit)* fair. *adv.* accurately ; *(cinstit)* fairly.

corecta *vt.* to correct ; *(a îndrepta)* to rectify ; *(şpalturi etc.)* to revise. *vr.* to mend ; *(a reveni)* to correct oneself.

corectare *sf.* correction.

corectitudine *sf.* correctness ; *(cinste)* uprightness.

corector *sm.* proof reader.

corectură *sf.* proof (reading).

corean *sm., adj.,* **coreană** *sf., adj.* Korean.

coregrafic *adj.* dancing.

coregrafie *sf.* choreography.

corelaţie *sf.* correlation.

coresponda *vi.* to write (to each other).

corespondent *sm.* correspondent.

corespondenţă *sf.* correspondence ; *(poştă)* mail ; *bilet de* ~ transfer ticket.

corespunde *vi.* to correspond ; *a* ~ *unei situaţii* etc. to suit a situation.

corespunzător *adj.* adequate. *adv.* accordingly.

coridor *sn.* corridor.

corifeu *sm.* leader (of the chorus).

corigent *sm.* pupil ploughed in an examination.

corigenţă *sf.* second examination.

corija *vt., vr.* to improve.

corist *sm.* chorus singer.

corn *sm.* cornel tree. *sn.* horn ; *(de cerb)* antler ; *(de vînătoare şi)* bugle ; *(pîine)* roll, croissant ; ~*ul abundenţei* cornu copia.

cornet *sn.* cornet ; ~ *acustic* ear trumpet.

cornist *sm.* bugler.

cornut *adj.* horned.

coroană *sf.* crown; *(de flori etc.)* wreath.

coroiat *adj.* hooked.

coroniță *sf.* coronet.

corosiv *adj.* corrosive.

corp *sn.* body; *(mort)* corpse; *mil., pol.* corps; *(literă)* size of type; ~ *de balet* corps de ballet; ~ *de casă* house; ~ *delict* material evidence; ~ *didactic* teaching staff; *(universitar)* professoriate; ~ *la* ~ bodily.

corpolent *adj.* stout.

corporație *sf.* guild.

corsaj *sn.* bodice.

corsar *sm.* corsair.

corset *sn.* stays.

cort *sn.* tent.

cortegiu *sn.* train.

cortină *sf.* curtain.

corupător *sm.* seducer; *(mituitor)* briber. *adj.* corrupting.

corupe *vt.* to corrupt.

corupere *sf.* corruption; ~ *de minori* debauchery of youth.

corupt *adj.* corrupt.

corupție *sf.* corruption.

corvadă *sf.* drudgery; *ist.* corvée.

cosaş *sm.* mower; *(insectă)* grig.

cosciug *sn.* coffin.

cosi *vt.* to mow.

cosit *sn.* haymaking. *adj.* mown.

cositor *sn.* tin.

cositori *vt.* to tin.

cosmonaut *sm.* spaceman, cosmonaut.

cosmos *sn.* outer space, cosmos.

cost *sn.* cost; price.

costa *vi.* to cost; *(a valora)* to be worth; *cît costă?* how much is it?

costisitor *adj.* expensive.

costum *sn.* suit (of clothes); *(îmbrăcăminte)* costume; ~ *de baie* swimsuit, swimbriefs; ~ *de gata* reach-me-down.

costumat *adj.* fancy-dress.

coş *sn.* *(pe faţă)* pimple; *(paner)* basket; *(mic)* hamper; *(horn)* stove-pipe, chimney; ~ *de hîrtii* waste paper basket; ~*ul pieptului* chest.

coşar *sm.* chimney sweep.

coşcogeamite *adj.* huge.

coşmar *sn.* nightmare.

coşniţă *sf.* basket; *fig.* (money for) food.

coşuleţ *sn.* hamper; *(pt. lucru de mînă)* work-basket.

cot *sm.* ell. *sn.* elbow; *(ghiont)* nudge; *(cotitură)* bend, turn; ~*la* ~ *cu* shoulder to shoulder with.

cota *vt.* to quote, to rate; *a fi* ~*t* to be considered (as), to pass (for).

cotă *sf.* share, quota; *com.* quotation; *geogr.* height; *(la curse)* odds.

coteţ *sn.* (hen) coop; *(cocină)* pigsty.

coti *vi.* to turn (right *sau* left).

cotidian *sn., adj., adv.* daily

cotit *adj.* tortuous.

cotitură *sf.* turn(ing); *fig.* turning point.

cotiza *vi.* to pay one's dues.

cotizaţie *sf.* due.

cotlet *sn.* cutlet.

cotlon *sn.* nook.

cotoi *sm.* tom-cat.

cotor *sn.* stub; *(de varză)* stump; *(de bilet* etc.) counterfoil.

cotrobăi *vi.* to search.

cotropi *vt.* to overrun.
cotropitor *sm.* invader.
coţofană *sf.* magpie.
coviltir *sn.* tilt.
covîrşi *vt.* to overcome.
covîrşitor *adj.* overwhelming.
covor *sn.* carpet ; *(carpetă)* rug.
covrig *sm.* bretzel ; *fig.* coil.
cozonac *sm.* sponge cake.
cozoroc *sn.* peak.
crab *sm.* crab.
crac *sm.* leg.
cracare *sf.* cracking.
cracă *sf.* limb ; branch.
crah *sn.* crash.
crai *sm.* king ; *(don juan)* philanderer ; ~*i de la răsărit* the three Magi ; ~ *nou* new moon.
crainic *sm.* announcer ; *ist.* town crier.
cramă *sf.* wine cellar.
crampă *sf.* cramp.
crampon *sn.* cramp(iron) ; *(la bocanc)* spike ; *(de fotbal)* stud ; *fig.* cling.
crampona *vr.:* a se ~ *de* to cling to.
craniu *sn.* skull.
crap *sm.* carp.
cratiţă *sf.* (frying) pan.
craul *sn.* crawl.
cravaşă *sf.* horse whip.
cravată *sf.* (neck) tie ; *(de pionier* etc.*)* red scarf.
crăcăna *vt., vr.* to straddle (one's legs).
crăcănat *adj.* bandy-legged.
Crăciun *sn.* Christmas.
crănţăni *vi.* to crunch.
crăpa *vt.* to split ; *(uşa* etc.*)* to half open ; *(a mînca)* to wolf. *vi.* to cleave ; *(a se sparge)* to burst ; *a ~ de ruşine* to die with shame. *vr.* to

crack ; *(d. piele)* to be chapped ; *se crapă de ziuă* it dawns.
crăpat *adj.* cracked ; *(d. piele)* chapped.
crăpătură *sf.* crack.
crea *vt., vi.* to create. *vr.* to be created.
creangă *sf.* branch.
creare *sf.* creation ; *(întemeiere)* setting up.
creastă *sf.* crest ; *(de cocoş şi)* comb ; *geogr.* ridge.
creator *sm.* creator. *adj.* creative.
creatură *sf.* creature.
creaţie *sf.* creation.
crede *vt.* to think ; *(a socoti adevărat)* to believe ; *(a-şi închipui)* to imagine. *vi.* to believe. *vr.* to think oneself (important, etc.) ; *se ~ că nu e în oraş* he is thought to be out of town.
credincios *sm.* believer. *adj.* faithful ; *(cuiva şi)* loyal.
credinţă *sf.* faith ; *(părere)* belief ; *(încredere)* trust ; *rea-~* dishonesty.
credit *sn.* credit ; *(împrumut şi)* loan ; *pe ~* on tick.
credita *vt.* to credit.
creditor *sm.* creditor. *adj.* credit...
credul *adj.* credulous.
creier *sm.* brain(s) ; *(minte)* reason ; *în ~ii munţilor* in the heart of the mountains.
creion *sn.* pencil ; ~ *chimic* indelible pencil ; ~ *automat* propelling pencil.
creiona *vt.* to pencil.
crem *adj.* cream-coloured.
crematoriu *sn.* crematorium.
cremă *sf.* cream ; *(de ghete)* shoe polish.

cremene *sf.* flint.
crenel *sn.* crenel.
crenvurşt *sm.* frankfurter.
creol *sm., adj.* creole.
crep *sn.* crape (rubber).
crepuscul *sn.* twilight.
crescător *sm.* breeder.
crescătorie *sf.* nursery.
crescînd *adj.* growing.
crescut *adj.* grown; *bine* ~ well-bred.
cresta *vt.* to notch; *(a tăia)* to cut.
crestătură *sf.* cut.
creşă *sf.* crèche, nursery.
creşte *vt.* to bring up; *(animale)* to breed; *(plante)* to grow (up); *(d. ape şi fig.)* to swell.
creştere *sf.* growth; *(dezvoltare)* rise; *(educaţie)* upbringing; ~a *albinelor* bee-keeping; *bună* ~ good breeding.
creştet *sn.* top.
creştin *sm., adj.* Christian.
creştina *vt.* to christianize. *vr.* to become Christian.
creştinism *sn.* Christianity.
cretă *sf.* chalk.
cretin *sm.* moron.
cretinism *sn.* imbecility.
creton *sn.* cretonne.
creţ *sn.* crease; *(rid)* wrinkle. *adj.* curly; *(plisat)* pleated.
crez *sn.* creed.
crezare *sf.* credit.
crichet *sn.* cricket.
crimă *sf.* crime.
criminal *sm., adj.* criminal.
criminalitate *sf.* delinquency.
crin *sm.* lily.
criptă *sf.* vault.
criptic *adj.* criptic; abstruse.
crispa *vt., vr.* to contract.
cristal *sn.* crystal.

cristalin *sn.* crystalline lens. *adj.* crystalline.
cristaliza *vt., vr.* to crystallize.
cristelniţă *sf.* font.
criteriu *sn.* criterion.
critic *sm.* critic. *adj.* critical
critica *vt.* to criticize.
critică *sf.* criticism; *(literară şi)* critique; ~ *apologetică* puffing.
crivăţ *sn.* north wind.
crizantemă *sf.* chrysanthemum.
criză *sf.* crisis; *(economică şi)* slump; *med.* attack, fit; *(lipsă)* shortage.
crîcni *vi.* to protest, to grumble.
crîmpei *sn.* fragment.
crîncen *adj.* grim. *adv.* grimly.
crîng *sn.* spinney.
croat *sm.* Croat. *adj.* Croatian.
croazieră *sf.* cruise.
crocant *adj.* crisp.
crocodil *sm.* crocodile.
croi *vt.* to cut (to measure); *(un drum etc.)* to open.
croială *sf.* cut.
croitor *sm.* tailor.
croitoreasă *sf.* dressmaker.
croncăni *vt., vi.* to croak.
cronic *adj.* chronic. *adv.* chronically.
cronicar *sm.* chronicler.
cronică *sf.* chronicle; *(recenzie)* book review; ~ *dramatică* etc. critique.
cronologic *adj.* chronological.
cronometra *vt.* to time.
cronometru *sn.* chronometer.
cros *sn.* cross-country race.
crosă *sf.* stick.
croşeta *vt., vi.* to crochet.
cruce *sf.* cross; *(încrucişare)* crossroads; *în* ~ crossways.
cruci *vr.* to cross oneself.
cruciadă *sf.* crusade.

crucial *adj.* crucial.

cruciat *sm.* crusader.

cruciş *adj.* squint(ing). *adv.* cross-ways.

crucişător *sn.* cruiser.

crud *adj.* raw; *(necopt)* green; *(sălbatic)* cruel.

crunt *adj.* savage; *(aspru)* ter-rible. *adv.* terribly, cruelly.

crustă *sf.* crust.

cruţa *vt.* to spare; *(viaţa* etc. *şi)* to pardon. *vr.* to take it easy.

cruţare *sf.* sparing; *(milă)* ruth; *fără* ~ relentlessly.

cruzime *sf.* cruelty.

ctitor *sm.* founder.

ctitorie *sf.* foundation.

cu *prep.* with, by; *(şi)* and.

cub *sn.* cube; *(pl. jucării)* (toy) bricks. *adj.* cubic.

cubic *adj.* cubic; *(d. zahăr)* lump.

cubist *sm., adj.* cubist.

cuc *sm.* cuckoo.

cuceri *vt.* to conquer; *(a cîş-tiga)* to win (over).

cucerire *sf.* conquest; *fig.* gain, achievement.

cuceritor *sm.* conqueror. *adj.* conquering. *adv.* victoriously.

cucernic *adj.* devout. *adv.* piously.

cucoană *sf.* lady; *(vocativ)* mad-am, ma'am; *(consoartă)* spouse.

cucu *interj.* bo-peep !

cucui *sn.* bump.

cucurigu *sn.* attic; *teatru* gods; *interj.* cock-a-doodle-doo !

cucută *sf.* hemlock.

cucuvaie *sf.* owl.

cufăr *sn.* chest.

cufunda *vt.* to plunge. *vr.* to duck.

cuget *sn.* thought; *(conştiinţă)* soul.

cugeta *vi.* to think.

cugetare *sf.* reflection.

cugetător *sm.* thinker.

cui *sn.* nail.

cuib *sn.* nest; *(de vipere* etc.*)* den; *agr.* hole; ~ *de cuvinte* word cluster.

cuibar *sn.* nest.

cuibări *vr.* to nestle.

cuier *sn.* peg; *(mare)* hallstand.

cuirasat *sn.* man-of-war.

cuirasă *sf.* armour.

cuişoare *sn. pl. bot.* clove.

culant *adj.* generous.

culca *vt.* to put to bed; *(a doborî)* to fell. *vr.* to go to bed; *(a se întinde)* to lie down.

culcat *adj.* recumbent.

culcuş *sn.* bed.

culege *vt.* to gather; *(a alege)* to cull.

culegere *sf.* gathering; *(de texte* etc.*)* collection.

cules *sn.* harvest; ~*ul viilor* vintage

culinar *adj.* culinary.

culisă *sf.* side-scenes; *în culise* behind the scenes.

culme *sf.* summit; *fig.* acme.

culmina *vi.* to culminate.

culoar *sn.* corridor.

culoare *sf.* colour; *(vopsea)* dye; *de* ~ coloured.

cult *sn.* worship. *adj.* cultured.

cultiva *vt.* to cultivate. *vr.* to improve one's mind.

cultivare *sf.* cultivation.

cultural *adj.* cultural.

culturalizare *sf.* dissemination of culture.

cultură *sf.* culture; *agr. şi* crop; ~ *generală* all-round education.

cum *adv.* how (much) ? *(poftim?)* beg your pardon ? ~ *e noul profesor?* what is the new teacher like?; ~ *aşa?* how is it possible?; ~ *de nu!* oh yes, indeed!; ~ *te cheamă?* what is your name?; ~ *o mai duci?* how are you? *conj.* as. *interj.* why!

cuminte *adj.* quiet; *(înţelept)* wise. *adv.* obediently, quietly.

cuminţenie *sf.* obedience; *(înţelepciune)* wisdom.

cumnat *sm.* brother-in-law.

cumnată *sf.* sister-in-law.

cumpănă *sf.* balance; *(de fîntînă)* sweep; *fig. (şovăială)* prevarication.

cumpăni *vt.* to weigh. *vr.* to find one's balance.

cumpănit *adj.* moderate.

cumpăra *vt.* to buy; *(a mitui)* to bribe; *(martori)* to suborn.

cumpărare *sf.* purchasing; *(mituire)* corruption.

cumpărător *sm.* buyer.

cumpărătură *sf.* purchase; *pl. (tîrguieli)* shopping.

cumpăt *sn.* balance.

cumpătare *sf.* temperance.

cumpătat *adj.* moderate.

cumplit *adj.* grim. *adv.* terribly.

cumsecade *adj.* decent. *adv.* properly.

cumul *sn.* plurality of offices.

cumula *vt.* to (ac)cumulate.

cumulard *sm.* pooh-bah.

cumva *adv.* somehow; *(poate)* perhaps.

cunoaşte *vt.* to know; *(a recunoaşte)* to recognize. *vr.* to be acquainted; *(a se observa)* to be perceptible; *vă ~ţi?* have you met?

cunoaştere *sf.* knowledge; cognition.

cunoscător *sm., adj.* expert.

cunoscut *sm.* acquaintance. *adj.* (well-)known, familiar.

cunoştinţă *sf.* acquaintance; *fig.* şi information; *(trezie)* consciousness.

cununa *vt., vr.* to wed.

cunună *sf.* coronet, wreath.

cununie *sf.* wedding; *cu ~* legally.

cupă *sf.* cup; *tehn.* bucket; *(la cărţi)* hearts.

cuplet *sn.* couplet.

cuplu *sn.* couple.

cupolă *sf.* cupola.

cupon *sn.* coupon.

cuprinde *vt.* to include; *(a conţine)* to contain; *(a cuceri)* to conquer. *vr.:* *a se ~ în* to be included in.

cuprins *sn.* (table of) contents; *(întindere)* expanse; *pe tot ~ul ţării* throughout the country. *adj.* comprised; *fig.* seized with (remorse, etc.).

cuprinzător *adj.* comprehensive.

cupru *sn.* copper.

cuptor *sn.* oven; *tehn.* furnace; *(de var* etc.) kiln.

curaj *sn.* courage; *(tupeu)* nerve.

curajos *adj.* courageous. *adv.* courageously.

curat *adj.* clean; *(pur)* pure; *(d. aer)* fresh. *adv.* cleanly; *(de-a dreptul)* really.

cură *sf.* cure; *(de slăbire)* banting.

curăţa *vt.* to (wash) clean. *vr.* to clean; *(de bani)* to be ruined.

curăţel *adj.* neat.

curăţenie *sf.* cleanliness; *(puritate)* purity; *(acţiunea)* cleaning; *(purgativ)* purge.

curb *adj.* curved.

curcan *sm.* turkey (cock).

curcă *sf.* turkey hen.

curcubeu *sn.* rainbow.

curea *sf.* belt.

curent *sm.* current; *(între ferestre)* draught; ~ *electric* (electric) power; *contra ~ului* against the stream. *sn.* current; *fig. și* tendency; *la* ~ posted. *adj.* current; obtaining; *(fluent)* glib; *(d. lună* etc.) instant. *adv.* currently, usually; *(fluent)* fluently.

curgător *adj.* running; *(fluent)* fluent, glib. *adv.* fluently.

curge *vi.* to flow, to run; *(d. un vas* etc.) to leak.

curier *sm.* courier; *(corespondență)* mail.

curios *sm.* busy-body. *adj.* curious; *(băgăreț)* inquisitive. *adv.* curiously.

curiozitate *sf.* curiosity; *(exagerată)* inquisitiveness; *(obiect)* curio; *de* ~ out of curiosity.

curînd *adv.* soon (afterwards); *de* ~ recently.

curma *vt., vr.* to stop.

curmal *sm.* date tree.

curmală *sf.* date.

curmeziș *adv.* crossways; *în* ~ crossways; *de-a ~ul* across.

curs *sn.* course; *(oră)* lecture; *fin.* rate of exchange; *~ul pieții* market prices; *~ seral* evening classes; *în* ~ under way; *în ~ul a* during.

cursant *sm.* student.

cursă *sf. (întrecere)* race; *(drum)* run; *(tren)* local; *(capcană)* snare.

cursiv *adj.* fluent; *tipogr.* italic. *adv.* fluently.

cursive *sf. pl.* italics.

curte *sf.* court.

curtenitor *adj.* courteous.

curtoazie *sf.* courtesy.

cusătoreasă *sf.* seamstress.

cusătură *sf.* seam.

cuscri *sm. pl.* in-laws.

custode *sm.* custodian.

cusur *sn.* defect, flaw.

cusut *sn.* sewing. *adj.* sewn; ~ *cu ață albă fig.* obvious, clumsy.

cușcă *sf.* cage; *(de cîine)* kennel; *(pt. sufler* etc.) box.

cutare *adj.* (this or) that. *pron.* so and so.

cută *sf.* fold; *(rid)* wrinkle.

cuteza *vt., vi.* to dare.

cutezător *adj.* audacious.

cutie *sf.* box; *ca (scos) din* ~ (just) out of the bandbox.

cutră *sf.* weathercock.

cutreiera *vt.* to scour.

cutremur *sn.* earthquake.

cutremura *vt., vr.* to shake (with fear, etc.).

cuțit *sn.* knife; *la ~e* at loggerheads.

cuțitaș *sn.* penknife.

cuțu *interj.* come on!

cuveni *vr.* to be fit(ting); to be due; *nu se cuvenea să vorbească astfel* he oughtn't to have spoken like that.

cuvenit *adj.* proper.

cuvertură *sf.* counterpane.

cuviincios *adj.* civil; *(decent)* decorous. *adv.* decently.

cuviință *sf.* decency.

cuvios *adj.* pious.

cuvioșie *sf.* piety.

cuvînt *sn.* word; *(cuvîntare)* speech; *(la ședință* etc.) floor; *cuvinte încrucișate* crossword (puzzle); ~ *cu* ~ word for word; ~ *de ordine* watchword; ~ *înainte* foreword; ~ *urît* four-letter word; *sub* ~ *că* under colour of.

cuvînta *vt.*, *vi.* to speak.
cuvîntare *sf.* speech; *(scurtă)* address.
evartet *sn.* quartet.
evintet *sn.* quintet.

D

da *vt.* to give; to offer; *(a acorda)* to grant; *(a furniza)* to supply; *(a înmîna)* to hand; *(a produce)* to yield; *a-și* ~ *aere* to put on airs; *a* ~ *afară* to kick out; *(a concedia)* to cashier; *a* ~ *atenție (la)* to pay attention (to); *a* ~ *cărțile* to deal the cards; *a* ~ *cuiva cu împrumut* to lend to smb.; *a* ~ *de gol* to give away; *a* ~ *de rușine* to shame; *a* ~ *dreptate cuiva* to acknowledge smb.'s right; *a* ~ *înapoi* to restore; *a* ~ *la o parte* to remove; *a* ~ *o lovitură* to deal a blow (at smb., etc.); *a* ~ *mîna cu* to shake hands with; *îmi dă mîna* I can (well) afford it; *a* ~ *pace cuiva* to let smb. alone. *vi.* to strike; *a* ~ *cu piciorul (la)* to kick (away); *a* ~ *de belea* sau *de bucluc* to get into trouble; *a* ~ *de bine* to find a good place, etc.; *a* ~ *de cineva* to run into smb.; *a-i* ~ *înainte* to carry on; *a* ~ *înapoi* to withdraw; *a* ~ *să* to start (doing smth.). *vr.* to yield; *a se* ~ *drept* ... to pretend to be ...; *a se* ~ *în* leagăn etc. to swing; *a se* ~ *la cineva* to have at smb.; *a se* ~ *pe brazdă* to improve. *adv.* yes; *interog.* really? *ba* ~ oh yes. *conj.* but.

dac *sm.*, *adj.* **dacă** *sf.*, *adj.* Dacian.

dacă *conj.* *(condiţional)* if; *(în alte propoziţii şi)* whether; *(pe cînd)* while; *(cînd)* when; ~ *cumva* should ...; ~ *nu* unless.

dactilografă *sf.* typist.
dactilografia *vt.* to type.
dactilografie *sf.* typewriting.
dafin *sm.* laurel.
dală *sf.* flagstone.
dalie *sf.* dahlia.
daltă *sf.* chisel.
damă *sf.* tart; *(doamnă)* lady; *(la şah şi cărţi)* queen; *(pl. jocul)* draughts.
damblá *sf.* palsy; *(obsesie)* fad; *(nebunie)* fury.
damigeană *sf.* demijohn.
dandana *sf.* mess.
dandy *sm.* dandy.
danez *sm.* Dane. *adj.* Danish.
daneză *sf.* Danish (woman).
dangăt *sn.* toll.
dans *sn.* dance.
dansa *vt.*, *vi.* to dance.

dansant *adj.* dancing.
dansatoare *sf.* dancer; *(de varie-teu)* chorus *sau* pep girl.
dansator *sm.* (ballet) dancer.
dantelă *sf.* lace; *fig.* tracery.
dantură *sf.* teeth; ~ *falsă* store teeth.
danubian *adj.* Danubian.
dar *sn.* gift; *(cadou și)* present; *(obicei)* habit. *adv.* then. *conj.* but; ~ *mi-te* ... let alone ...
dara *sf.* tare.
darabană *sf.* drum.
dare *sf.* tax; ~ *de mînă* wealth; ~ *de seamă* account.
darnic *adj.* generous.
dascăl *sm.* schoolmaster.
dat *sn.* donnée, datum. *adj.* given; ~ *fiind că* as; ~ *uitării* forgotten.
data *vt., vi.* to date.
datat *adj.* dated; *fig.* și superannuated.
dată *sf.* date; *(oară)* time; *(în știință)* datum, *pl.* data; *pe* ~ immediately; *o (singură)* ~ (just) once; *o* ~ *cu capul* in no case.
datină *sf.* custom.
dativ *sn.* dative.
dator *adj.* indebted.
datora *vt.* to owe. *vr.* to be due (to smb., etc.).
datorie *sf.* debt; *fig.* duty; *(credit)* credit; *la* ~ on duty.
datorită *prep.* thanks to; *(din cauza)* because of, owing to.
datornic *sm.* debtor.
daună *sf.* damage; *(plată)* damages.
dădacă *sf.* (dry) nurse.
dădăci *vt.* to nurse.
dăinui *vi.* to last.
dăltui *vt.* to chisel.

dărăpănat *adj.* ramshackle.
dărîma *vt.* to demolish.
dărîmare *sf.* demolition.
dărîmătură *sf.* ruin.
dărnicie *sf.* generosity.
dărui *vt.* to present (smb. with smth.).
dăruire *sf.:* ~ *de sine* abnegation.
dătător *sm.* giver. *adj.* giving.
dăuna *vi.:* *a* ~ *cuiva* to harm smb.
dăunător *sm.* pest. *adj.* injurious, deleterious (to smb.'s health, etc.).
de *adv.:* ~ *prost ce era* (as) he was so stupid. *prep.* of; *(de la)* from; *(în timp)* for; *(lipit* ~*)* against; *(din pricina)* out of; ~ *aceea* that is why; ~ *atunci* since (then); ~ *azi într-o lună* today month; ~ *ce?* why? ~ *curînd* recently; ~ *la* from; *(din)* of, at, in; *(temporal)* since; ~ *la o vreme* after a time; ~ *loc* not at all; ~ *mult* long ago; ~ *pe* from; *(static)* on; *conj.* if. *interj.* well!
de-a binelea *adv.* thoroughly.
de-a bușilea *adv.* on all fours.
de-a curmezișul *adv., prep.* across.
de-a dreptul *adv.* directly.
deal *sn.* hill; *la* ~ up hill.
de-a lungul *adv.* lengthways.
de-a pururi *adv.* for ever.
de asemenea *adv.* also.
deasupra *adv.* above; *(peste)* over; *pe* ~ moreover. *prep.* above; *(peste)* over.
de-a valma *adv.* pell-mell.
debarca *vt., vi.* to land; *fig.* to overthrow.
debarcader *sn.* jetty.

debarcare *sf.* landing.

debil *sm.:* ~ *mintal* non compos mentis. *adj.* feeble.

debilita *vt.* to debilitate. *vr.* to grow weak.

debilitate *sf.* debility.

debit *sn.* *(de tutun)* tobacconist's; *(chioşc de ziare)* newsstand; *com.* debit.

deborda *vi.* to overflow; *(a vărsa)* to vomit; *a ~ de bucurie* to exult.

debordant *adj.* overflowing.

debuşeu *sn.* outlet.

debut *sn.* début.

debuta *vi.* to make one's début.

debutant *sm.* débutant.

decadă *sf.* ten days.

decadent *sm., adj.* decadent.

decadenţă *sf.* decadence.

decalaj *sn.* disparity; *(rămînere în urmă)* lag(ging) behind.

decan *sm.* dean; *(de vîrstă etc.)* doyen.

decanat *sn.* dean's office.

decapita *vt.* to behead.

decădea *vi.* to decline.

decădere *sf.* decline; *(degradare)* debasement.

decăzut *adj.* degenerate.

deceda *vi.* to die.

decembrie *sm.* December.

deceniu *sn.* decade; *~l al 7-lea* the sixties.

decent *adj.* decorous. *adv.* decorously.

decenţă *sf.* propriety.

decepţie *sf.* disappointment.

decepţiona *vt.* to disappoint.

decerna *vt.* to award.

decernare *sf.* award(ing).

deces *sn.* decease.

deci *conj.* therefore.

decide *vt., vi., vr.* to decide.

decima *vt.* to decimate.

decimal *adj.* decimal.

decis *adj.* resolute.

decisiv *adj.* decisive.

decizie *sf.* decision.

decît *adv.:* *n-ai* ~ *!* as you please! *prep., conj.* than.

declama *vt., vi.* to recite.

declamaţie *sf.* declamation.

declanşa *vt.* to unleash.

declara *vt.* to declare; *jur.* to pronounce. *vr.* to declare (oneself).

declarat *adj.* avowed.

declarativ *adj.* declarative.

declaraţie *sf.* declaration.

declin *sn.* decline; *în* ~ on the wane.

declina *vt.* to decline. *vr.* to be declined.

declinare *sf.* *gram.* declension.

decola *vt.* to take off.

decolare *sf.* take-off.

decolora *vt.* to discolour. *vr.* to lose colour.

decoltat *adj.* low-cut; *(d. femei)* bare-shouldered; *fig.* blue.

decolteu *sn.* décolletage.

decor *sn.* décor; *(natural)* scenery; *(faţadă)* pretence.

decora *vt.* to decorate.

decorator *sm.* decorator. *adj.:* *pictor* ~ stage designer.

decoraţie *sf.* decoration.

decovil *sn.* mountain railway.

decret *sn.* decree.

decreta *vt.* to decree.

decupa *vi.* to cut up.

decurge *vi.* to devolve; *(a se desfăşura)* to unfold.

decurs *sn.* course.

deda *vr.* to indulge (in,.

dedesubt *sn.* secret. *adv.* below, under.

dedesubtul *prep.* under.
dedica *vt.*, *vr.* to devote (oneself).
dedicaţie *sf.* dedication.
dediţel *sm.* campana.
deduce *vt.* to infer; *(a scădea)* to deduct.
deductiv *adj.* deductive.
deducţie *sf.* deduction.
defalca *vt.* to deduct.
defavoare *sf.* detriment.
defavorabil *adj.* unfavourable.
defăima *vt.* to defame.
defăimare *sf.* defamation.
defăimător *sm.* slanderer. *adj.* defamatory.
defect *sn.* flaw; *(deficienţă)* deficiency; ~ *fizic* infirmity. *adj.* in bad repair.
defecta *vt.* to spoil. *vr.* to go out of order.
defectuos *adj.* faulty. *adv.* defectively.
defecţiune *sf.* desertion.
defensivă *sf.* defensive.
deficient *adj.* deficient.
deficienţă *sf.* deficiency.
deficit *sn.* deficit.
defila *vi.* to parade.
defileu *sn.* narrow path.
defini *vt.* to define.
definit *adj.* definite.
definitiv *adj.* definitive; *în* ~ after all. *adv.* for good and all.
definitiva *vt.* to finalize.
definiţie *sf.* definition.
deforma *vt.* to deform; *fig.* to distort. *vr.* to become deformed.
deformare, deformaţie *sf.* deformation.
defrauda *vt.* to embezzle.
defunct *sm.*, *adj.* late.
degaja *vt.* to give off; *(a curăţa)* to clear (up); *sport* to clear. *vr.* to get rid.

degajare *sf.* casualness.
degajat *adj.* free (and easy). *adv.* casually.
degeaba *adv.* gratis; *(inutil)* vainly; *pe* ~ for a song.
degenera *vi.* to degenerate.
degenerat *sm.*, *adj.* degenerate.
degera *vi.* to be frozen.
degerat *adj.* benumbed.
degerătură *sf.* chilblain.
deget *sn.* finger; *(de la picior)* toe; *(măsură)* inch; ~*ul arătător* forefinger; ~*ul inelar* ring finger; ~*ul mijlociu* middle finger; ~*ul mare* thumb; ~*ul mic* little finger.
degetar *sn.* thimble.
deghiza *vt.*, *vr.* to disguise.
degrabă *adv.* quickly; *mai* ~ rather.
degrada *vt.*, *vr.* to degrade (oneself).
deja *adv.* already.
dejuca *vt.* to foil.
dejun *sn.* lunch (time); *micul* ~ breakfast.
dejuna *vi.* to lunch; *(dimineaţa)* to breakfast.
delapida *vt.* to defalcate.
delapidare *sf.* embezzlement.
delapidator *sm.* peculator.
delăsa *vr.* to lag.
delecta *vt.* to delight. *vr.* to indulge (in a pleasure, etc.).
delegat *sm.* delegate.
delegaţie *sf.* deputation.
delfin *sm.* dolphin.
delibera *vi.* to confer.
deliberare *sf.* consultation.
delicat *adj.* delicate; *(dificil)* ticklish. *adv.* delicately.
delicios *adj.* delicious.
deliciu *sn.* relish.
delict *sn.* offence.

delimita vt. to (de)limit.
delincvent sm. offender.
delir sn. delirium.
delira vi. to rave.
deltă sf. delta.
deluros adj. hilly.
demagog sm. demagogue.
demagogie sf. demagogy.
demasca vt., vr. to expose (one-self).
demascare sf. exposure.
dement sm. lunatic. adj. de-mented.
demenţă sf. madness.
demers sn. step.
demilitariza vt. to demilitarize.
demisie sf. resignation.
demisiona vi. to resign.
demn adj. dignified; ~ de worthy of. adv. in a dignified manner.
demnitar sm. statesman.
demnitate sf. dignity.
demobiliza vt. to demob(ilize); fig. to discourage.
demobilizat sm. demobee.
democrat sm. democrat. adj. democratic.
democratic adj. democratic. adv. democratically.
democraţie sf. democracy.
demoda vr. to become old-fa-shioned.
demodat adj. old-fashioned.
demon sm. demon.
demonetiza vt. to become hack-neyed.
demonstra vt. to demonstrate.
demonstrativ adj. demonstra-tive.
demonstraţie sf. demonstration.
demonta vt. to dismantle.
demoraliza vt. to dishearten. vr. to lose heart.

demult adv. long ago; de ~ former.
denatura vt. to falsify.
denaturat adj. monstrous; (d. alcool) methylated.
dens adj. dense.
densitate sf. density.
dentar adj. dental.
dentist sm. dentist.
denuclearizat adj. atom-free.
denumi vt. to name.
denunţ sn. denunciation.
denunţa vt. to denounce.
deoarece conj. because.
deocamdată adv. for the time being.
deochea vt. to hoodoo, to jinx.
deocheat adj. spoilt by the evil eye; fig. ill-famed.
deochi sn. the evil eye.
deodată adv. suddenly; (îm-preună) at once.
deoparte adv. aside.
deopotrivă adj., adv. alike.
deosebi vt. to tell (one from the other). vr. to differ.
deosebire sf. difference; fără ~ indiscriminately; fără ~ de irrespective of; spre ~ de unlike.
deosebit adj. diverse; (distinct) distinct; (ciudat) peculiar; (ales) choice. adv.: ~ de aceasta besides; ~ de bun etc. extremely good, etc.
deparazitare sf. disinfestation.
departament sn. department.
departe adv. far (away); fig. ~ de mine ... not that I should... ; de ~ remote(ly); (superior) by far; mai ~ further (down); (în spaţiu) farther; pe ~ deviously.
depăna vt. to reel; a ~ o poveste to spin a yarn.

depărta *vt., vr.* to remove; *a se ~ de la ceva* to deviate from smth.

depărtare *sf.* distance.

depărtat *adj.* remote.

depăşi *vt.* to outrun; *fig. şi* to surpass; *a ~ norma* etc. to exceed the quota, etc.

depăşire *sf.* outrunning; *(a planului* etc.*)* overfulfilment; *~a interzisă* no overtaking.

depăşit *adj.* overfulfilled; *fig.* superannuated.

dependent *adj.* dependent (on).

dependenţă *sf.* dependence (on).

dependinţe *sf. pl.* outbuildings.

depinde *vi.* to depend (on).

deplasa *vt.* to remove. *vr.* to move; *(departe)* to travel.

deplasare *sf.* removal; official trip.

deplasat *adj.* out of place.

deplin *adj.* complete, thorough (going); *fig.* absolute. *adv.* thoroughly; *pe ~* entirely.

deplinge *vt.* to deplore.

deplorabil *adj.* lamentable.

deporta *vt.* to transport.

deportat *sm.* deported person.

depou *sn.* depot.

depozit *sn.* warehouse; *mil.* dump.

depozita *vt.* to store.

depoziţie *sf.* testimony.

depravat *sm.* debauchee. *adj.* depraved.

deprecia *vt.* to belittle. *vr.* to lose its value.

depresiune *sf.* depression.

deprima *vt.* to dishearten.

deprimare *sf.* depression.

deprimat *adj.* downcast.

deprinde *vt.* to adopt; *a ~ cu* to accustom to. *vr.: a se ~ cu* to become accustomed to.

deprindere *sf.* habit; *(abilitate)* skill.

deprins *adj.* accustomed.

depunător *sm.* depositor.

depune *vt.* to deposit; *a ~ jurămîntul* to be sworn in; *a ~ mărturie* to give evidence. *vr.* to fall.

depunere *sf.* deposition.

deputat *sm. (în Anglia)* M.P., Member of Parliament; *(în S.U.A.)* representative; *(în Europa)* deputy.

deraia *vi.* to run off the rails.

deranj *sn.* disorder; *fig.* trouble.

deranja *vt.* to disturb; *(hainele* etc.*)* to put awry. *vr.* to get out of one's way.

deranjat *adj.* disturbed; *(stricat)* in bad repair.

derbedeu *sm.* guttersnipe.

deretica *vi.* to tidy up.

deriva *vt.* to derive. *vi.: a ~ din* to derive *sau* arise from.

derivat *sn.* derivative. *adj.* derived.

derizoriu *adj.* ridiculous.

deridere *sf.* derision.

deroga *vi.: a ~ de la* to depart from.

deruta *vt.* to mislead.

derută *sf.* rout.

des *adj.* dense; *(frecvent)* frequent; *(stufos)* bushy. *adv.* often; *(dens)* thickly.

desagă *sf.* wallet.

desărcina *vt.* to dismiss.

desăvîrşi *vt.* to perfect. *vr.* to be perfected.

desăvîrşire *sf.* consummation; *(terminare)* completion; *cu ~* totally.

desăvîrşit *adj.* consummate; *(terminat)* finished. *adv.* perfectly.

descalifiea *vt.* to disqualify.

descăleca *vi.* to dismount.

descălţa *vr.* to take off one's shoes.

descărca *vt.* to unload; *fig.* to unburden; *(mînia etc.)* to vent. *vr.* to be unloaded; *(d. armă)* to go off.

descătuşa *vt.* to unfetter. *vr.* to free oneself.

descendent *sm.* descendant. *adj.* downward.

descheia *vt.* to unbutton; *(un nasture)* to undo. *vr.* to unbutton one's clothes; *(d. nasture)* to come undone.

deschide *vt., vi., vr.* to open.

deschidere *sf.* opening.

deschis *adj.* open; *fig.* open-hearted; *(d. culori)* light. *adv.* openly; *(limpede)* plainly.

deschizător *sm.:* ~ *de drumuri* pioneer, trail blazer.

deschizătură *sf.* opening; *(lungă)* slit.

descifra *vt.* to decipher.

descinde *vi.* to alight.

descindere *sf.* raid; *(percheziţie)* search.

descîlci *vt.* to disentangle.

descînta *vt.* to exorcise.

descîntec *sn.* exorcism.

descleşta *vt.* to open.

descoase *vt.* to undo; *fig.* to pump. *vr.* to come undone.

descompleta *vt.* to curtail. *vr.* to be curtailed.

descompune *vt.* to decompose. *vr.* to disintegrate; *(a putrezi)* to decay.

descompunere *sf.* decomposition; *(putrezire)* decay.

descongestiona *vt.* to release; to relieve.

desconsidera *vt.* to ignore.

desconsiderare *sf.* disdain.

descoperi *vt.* to uncover; *fig.* to discover. *vr.* to uncover (one's head).

descoperire *sf.* discovery.

descoperit *adj.* uncovered; *(fără pălărie)* bareheaded.

descotorosi *vr.:* *a se* ~ *de* to get rid of.

descreierat *sm.* demented person. *adj.* reckless.

descreşte *vi.* to decrease.

descreştere *sf.* decrease.

descreţi *vt.* to smooth out.

descrie *vt.* to describe.

descriere *sf.* description.

descriptiv *adj.* descriptive.

descuia *vt.* to unlock. *vr.* *fig.* to become broad-minded.

descuiat *adj.* unlocked; *fig.* liberal.

descult *adj.* barefooted. *adv.* barefoot.

descumpăni *vt.* to upset.

descuraja *vt.* to dishearten. *vr.* to lose heart.

descurca *vt.* to unravel. *vr.* to fend for oneself.

descurcăreţ *adj.* efficient.

desemna *vt.* to appoint; *(un candidat)* to nominate; *(a indica)* to designate.

desen *sn.* drawing; *(model)* design; ~*e animate* (animated) cartoons.

desena *vt.* to draw. *vr.* to take shape.

desenator *sm.* drawer; *(tehnic)* draughtsman.

deseori *adv.* often.

desert *sn.* dessert.

deservi *vt.* to harm; *(a sluji)* to cater for.

deservire *sf.* catering.

desface *vt.* to unbind; *(a deschide)* to open; *(a desfăşura)* to unfurl; *(a vinde)* to sell. *vr.* to come apart; *(d. şiret etc.)* to come undone; *(a se deschide)* to open.

desfacere *sf.* unbinding; *(vînzare)* sale; *(anulare)* cancellation.

desfăşura *vt.* to unfold; *(a duce)* to carry on. *vr.* to unfold; *(a avea loc)* to proceed.

desfăşurare *sf.* unfolding; *(etalare)* display.

desfăşurat *adj.* unfolded; *fig.* large-scale.

desfăta *vt., vr.* to delight.

desfătare *sf.* relish.

desfigura *vt.* to maim.

desfiinţa *vt.* to abolish; *(a anula)* to cancel; *(a lichida)* to eliminate.

desfiinţare *sf.* abolition.

desfrînat *sm.* profligate. *adj.* debauched.

desfriu *sn.* dissipation.

desfunda *vt.* to open; *(un butoi)* to broach.

desfundat *adj.* bottomless; *(d: drum)* impracticable.

deshăma *vt.* to unharness.

desigur *adv.* certainly, by all means.

desiş *sn.* thicket.

desluşi *vt.* to discern; *(a lămuri)* to elucidate. *vr.* to become clear.

desluşit *adj.* distinct. *adv.* clearly.

desolidariza *vr.* to dissociate oneself (from).

despacheta *vt.* to unpack.

despăduri *vt.* to deforest.

despăgubi *vt.* to compensate. *vr.* to make up for a loss.

despăgubire *sf.* damages.

despărţi *vt.* to separate; *(a dezbina)* to divide. *vr.* to separate; to (get a) divorce.

despărţire *sf.* separation; parting.

despături *vt.* to unfold.

despera *vt.* to render desperate. *vi.* to despair.

desperare *sf.* despondency.

desperat *adj.* hopeless. *adv.* desperately.

desperecheat *adj.* odd.

despersonaliza *vt.* to depersonalize.

despica *vt.* to cleave; *(lemne)* to chop.

despletit *adj.* dishevelled.

despre *prep.* about.

desprinde *vt.* to detach; *fig.* to infer. *vr.* to come off, to be torn (away); *fig.* to devolve.

desprindere *sf.* detachment.

despuia *vt., vr.* to strip.

despuiat *adj.* naked; *(d. arbori)* bare.

despuiere *sf.* stripping; ~*a scrutinului* vote count.

destăinui *vt.* to disclose. *vr.* to open one's heart.

destăinuire *sf.* confession.

destin *sn.* destiny.

destina *vt.* to destine.

destinatar *sm.* addressee; *com.* consignee.

destinaţie *sf.* destination.

destinde *vt.* to loosen. *vr.* to relax.

destindere *sf.* relaxation.

destitui *vt.* to discharge.

destoinic *adj.* efficient.

destrăbălare *sf.* dissipation; fornication.

destrăbălat *sm.* debauchee. *adj.* licentious.

destrăma vt. to tear; fig. to shatter. vr. to be torn; fig. to come to nought.

destul adj. enough; ~ zahăr enough sugar. adv. enough; ~! that will do!; ~ de tîrziu late enough; ~ să pomenim că... suffice it to mention that ...

destupa vt. to uncork.

desţeleni vt. to break up.

desuet adj. obsolescent.

deşănţat adj. indecent.

deşert sn. desert; (gol) vacuum; în ~ vainly. adj. empty; geogr. waste; (inutil) useless.

deşerta vt. to empty; (a bea) to drink (up).

deşertăciune sf. vanity; (inutilitate) wantonness, uselessness.

deşeuri sn. pl. offals.

deşi conj. (al)though.

deşira vt. to unwind. vr. to come off; (d. ciorapi) to ladder.

deşirat adj. unwound; (slab) lanky.

deştept sm. clever man; iron. dolt. adj. clever; (treaz) wide awake. adv. cleverly.

deştepta vt. to wake; fig. to arouse. vr. to grow wise; (a se trezi) to awake.

deşteptare sf. awakening; mil. reveille.

deşteptăciune sf. cleverness.

deşteptător sn. alarm clock.

deşucheat sm. libertine. adj. gay; (d. glumă) smutty.

detaliu sn. detail.

detaşa vt. to detach; (pe cineva) to transfer temporarily. vr. to come off; (a se distinge) to stand out.

detaşament sn. detachment.

detaşare sf. (a cuiva) transfer; (a unui obiect) detaching.

detaşat adj. detached; fig. aloof.

detectiv sm. detective.

detenţiune sf. imprisonment.

deteriora vt. to spoil. vr. to get out of order, to be damaged.

determina vt. to establish; (a hotărî) to determine.

determinant sm. determinative. adj. decisive.

detesta vt. to loathe.

detestabil adj. hateful.

detriment sn. detriment; în ~ul cuiva to smb.'s detriment.

detrona vt. to depose.

detunătură sf. blast; (de puşcă) report.

deturna vt. to embezzle.

deţinător sm. holder.

deţine vt. to own.

deunăzi adv. the other day.

devaliza vt. to loot.

devasta vt. to lay waste.

deveni vt. to become.

devenire sf. formation; în ~ in the making.

devia vi. to deviate.

deviaţie, deviere sf. deviation.

deviz sn. estimate.

deviză sf. motto.

devize sf. pl. foreign currency.

devora vt. to devour.

devota vr. to dedicate oneself.

devotament sn. loyalty.

devotat adj. devoted.

devreme adv. early; ~ ce since.

dexteritate sf. deftness.

dezacord sn. discord.

dezacorda vt. to put out of tune. vr. to get out of tune.

dezacordat adj. out of tune.

dezagreabil adj. unpleasant.

dezagrega vt., vr. to disintegrate.

dezamăgi *vt.* to disappoint.
dezaproba *vt.* to disapprove of.
dezaprobare *sf.* disapproval.
dezarma *vt.*, *vi.* to disarm.
dezastru *sn.* disaster.
dezastruos *adj.* disastrous.
dezavantaj *sn.* disadvantage.
dezavantaja *vt.* to hamper.
dezavantajos *adj.* unfavourable.
dezbate *vt.* to debate.
dezbatere *sf.* discussion.
dezbăra *vt.* to rid. *vr.: a se ~ de* to give up.
dezbina *vt.* to split.
dezbinare *sf.* scission; *(dușmănie)* feud.
dezbrăca *vt.*, *vr.* to undress.
dezbrăcat *adj.* un(der)dressed; *(gol)* naked.
dezdoi *vt.*, *vr.* to unbend.
dezechilibra *vt.* to unbalance. *vr.* to lose one's poise.
dezechilibru *sn.* lack of poise.
dezerta *vi.* to desert.
dezertare *sf.* desertion.
dezertor *sm.* deserter.
dezgheț *sn.* thaw.
dezgheța *vt.*, *vr.* to thaw.
dezghețat *adj.* thawed; *fig.* quick.
dezgoli *vt.*, *vr.* to bare (oneself).
dezgolit *adj.* naked.
dezgropa *vt.* to dig up.
dezgust *sn.* disgust.
dezgusta *vt.* to disgust.
dezgustat *adj.* disgusted (at, with); *~ de* sick with.
deziderat *sn.* desideratum.
deziluzie *sf.* deception.
deziluziona *vt.* to disappoint.
dezinfecta *vt.* to disinfect.
dezintegra *vt.*, *vr.* to disintegrate.
dezinteres *sn.* carelessness.
dezinteresa *vr.* to pay no heed (to)

dezinteresat *adj.* disinterested.
dezinvoltură *sf.* ease.
dezlănțui *vt.* to unleash. *vr.* to burst
dezlănțuit *adj.* reckless.
dezlega *vt.* to untie; *(a absolvi)* to forgive; *(a rezolva)* to solve. *vr.* to come undone; *(a se elibera)* to wrest oneself free.
dezlegare *sf.* unbinding; *(absolvire)* absolution.
dezlipi *vt.*, *vr.* to detach (oneself).
dezlînat *adj.* unstrung.
dezmăț *sn.* shamelessness.
dezmățat *sm.* profligate. *adj.* slatternly; *(destrăbălat)* wanton; *(neglijent)* untidy.
dezmetici *vt.* to waken. *vr.* to wake up.
dezmierda *vt.* to caress.
dezmierdare *sf.* caress.
dezminți *vt.* to deny. *vr.* to contradict oneself.
dezmințire *sf.* denial.
dezmorți *vt.* to revive. *vr.* to stretch oneself.
dezmoșteni *vt.* to disown.
dezmoștenit *sm.* poor devil.
deznădăjdui *vi.* to despair.
deznădăjduit *adj.* hopeless.
deznădejde *sf.* despair.
deznoda *vt.* to undo.
deznodămînt *sn.* dénouement, resolution.
dezobișnui *vt.*, *vr.* to break (from a habit).
dezolant *adj.* sad(dening).
dezolat *adj.* (ag)grieved.
dezonora *vt.* to disgrace.
dezordine *sf.* disorder.
dezordonat *adj.* untidy.
dezorganiza *vt.* to disorganize.
dezorienta *vt.* to bewilder.
dezrădăcina *vt.* to uproot.

dezrobi *vt.* to set free.
dezrobire *sf.* abolition of slavery.
dezumaniza *vt.* to dehumanize.
dezumfla *vt., vr.* to deflate.
dezvălui *vt.* to disclose. *vr.* to come out.
dezvăluire *sf.* revelation.
dezvăţa *vt.* to wean (from a habit). *vr.* to get rid (of a habit, etc.).
dezveli *vt., vr.* to uncover (oneself).
dezvinovăţi *vt., vr.* to exculpate (oneself).
dezvolta *vt., vr.* to develop (oneself).
dezvoltare *sf.* development; *(creştere)* increase.
dezvoltat *adj.* advanced; *(amănunţit)* ample.
diabolic *adj.* devilish.
diademă *sf.* tiara.
diafan *adj.* diaphanous; *fig.* delicate.
diafilm *sn.* film strip.
diagnostic *sn.* diagnosis.
diagonal *adj.* diagonal.
diagonală *sf.* diagonal; *(la uniformă)* baldric.
diagramă *sf.* diagram.
dialect *sn.* dialect.
dialectal *adj.* dialectal.
dialectic *adj.* dialectical.
dialectică *sf.* dialectics.
dialog *sn.* dialogue.
diamant *sn.* diamond; *fig.* gem.
diametral *adv.* diametrically.
diametru *sn.* diameter.
diapazon *sn.* *(instrument)* tuning fork; *(înălţime)* pitch.
diapozitiv *sn.* lantern slide.
diateză *sf. gram.* voice.
diavol *sm.* fiend, devil.

dibaci *adj.* skilful.
dibăcie *sf.* deftness.
dibui *vt.* to seize.
dibuit *sn.*: *pe ~e* groping(ly).
dichis *sn.* trimmings.
dichisi *vt.* to trim (up). *vr.* to tit(t)ivate.
dicta *vt.* to dictate.
dictare *sf.* dictation; *după sau sub ~* to dictation.
dictat *sn.* dictate.
dictator *sm.* dictator.
dictatură *sf.* dictatorship; *dictatura proletariatului* proletarian dictatorship.
dicton *sn.* adage.
dicţionar *sn.* dictionary.
dicţiune *sf.* diction.
didactic *adj.* didactic.
dietă *sf.* diet.
dietetic *adj.* diet.
diez *sm., adj.* sharp.
diferend *sn.* dispute.
diferenţă *sf.* difference; *la o ~ de trei puncte* by a three point margin.
diferenţia *vt., vr.* to differentiate.
diferit *adj.* different; *(variat)* varied; *în ~e rînduri* several times.
dificil *adj.* difficult; *(mofturos)* fastidious.
dificultate *sf.* difficulty; *dificultăţi băneşti* straitened circumstances.
diform *adj.* misshapen.
diftină *sf.* moleskin.
diftong *sm.* diphthong.
difuz *adj.* diffuse.
difuza *vt.* to spread; *(prin radio)* to broadcast. *vr.* to be spread *sau* broadcast.
difuzare *sf.* spread(ing).

difuzor *sn.* loudspeaker ; *(persoană)* distributor.

dig *sn.* dyke.

digera *vt.* to digest.

digestie *sf.* digestion.

digresiune *sf.* digression.

dihor *sm.* polecat, fitch(ew).

dijmaş *sm.* sharecropper.

dijmă *sf.* tithe.

dilata *vt., vr.* to dilate.

dilatare *sf.* dila(ta)tion.

dilemă *sf.* quandary.

diletant *sm.* dilettante.

dilua *vt.* to dilute.

dimensiune *sf.* size.

dimineaţa *adv.* in the morning.

dimineaţă *sf.* morning ; *(zori)* dawn ; *azi* ~ this morning ; *dis de* ~ in the early morning ; *în dimineaţa acelei zile* on that morning. *adv.* in the morning.

diminua *vt., vr.* to decrease.

diminutiv *sn.* diminutive.

dimpotrivă *adv.* on the contrary.

din *prep.* *(static)* in, of, at ; *(dinamic)* from ; *(dinăuntrul)* out of ; *(cauzal)* out of ; *(ca material)* of, from ; ~ *afară* from without ; ~ *cauza (asta)* because of (this) ; ~ *ce în ce* more and more ; ~ *întîmplare* by chance.

dinadins *adv.* purposely.

dinafară *adv.* from without ; *pe* ~ outwardly ; *(pe de rost)* by heart.

dinainte *adv.* before ; *de* ~ fore-.

dinaintea *prep.* before.

dinam *sn.* dynamo.

dinamic *adj.* dynamic.

dinamită *sf.* dynamite.

dinamiza *vt.* to activize.

dinapoi *adj., adv.* behind ; *de* ~ hind.

dinapoia *prep.* behind.

dinastie *sf.* dynasty.

dinăuntru *adj.* inner(most). *adv.* (from) within ; *pe* ~ (from) within.

dincoace *adv.* (over) here ; ~ *de* on this side of ; *pe* ~ this way.

dincolo *adj.* beyond ; *(alături)* in the next room ; *pe* ~ the other way.

dineu *sn.* dinner (party).

dinspre *prep.* from.

dinte *sm.* tooth, *pl.* teeth ; *(colţ)* fang ; *(de elefant)* tusk ; *(de roată)* sprocket ; *(de pieptene)* cog ; *(de furcă)* prong.

dintîi *adj.* first.

dintotdeauna *adv.* always.

dintre *prep.* between ; *(selectiv)* from among.

dintr-o dată *adv.* at once.

dinţat *adj.* toothed.

diplomat *sm.* diplomat. *adj.* certificated ; *fig.* tactful.

diplomatic *adj.* diplomatic. *adv.* diplomatically.

diplomaţie *sf.* diplomacy.

diplomă *sf.* diploma.

direct *adj.* direct ; *(deschis)* open. *adv.* straightly ; *(deschis)* frankly ; *(de-a dreptul)* entirely.

directivă *sf.* directive.

directoare *sf.* manageress ; *(de şcoală)* headmistress.

director[1] *sm.* manager ; *(de şcoală)* headmaster ; ~ *de scenă* producer ; ~*ul filmului* producer.

director[2] *adj.* directing.

direcţie *sf.* direction ; *(birou)* manager's office ; *(la scoală)* headmaster's office; *(conducere)* management; în ce ~? whither?

diriginte *sm.* form master; *(la poştă)* postmaster.

dirija *vt., vi.* to conduct.

dirijor *sm.* conductor.

disc *sn.* disc; *(de patefon şi)* record; *sport.* discus.

discernămînt *sn.* discernment.

discerne *vt.* to distinguish.

disciplina *vt.* to discipline.

disciplinar *adj.* disciplinary. *adv.* as a penalty.

disciplină *sf.* discipline; *(materie de studiu şi)* subject.

discipol *sm.* disciple.

discordant *adj.* discordant.

discordanţă *sf.* disagreement.

discordie *sf.* discord.

discotecă *sf.* record library.

discredita *vt.* to discredit. *vr.* to compromise oneself.

discrepanţă *sf.* discrepancy.

discret *adj.* discreet; *(modest)* unobtrusive. *adv.* discreetly; *(modest)* modestly.

discreţie *sf.* discretion.

discriminare *sf.* discrimination; ~ rasială colour bar.

discurs *sn.* speech.

discuta *vt., vi.* to discuss; *(în contradictoriu)* to argue. *vr.* to be discussed.

discutabil *adj.* questionable.

discutat *adj.* mooted.

discuţie *sf.* discussion; *(aprinsă)* argument; *fără* ~ undoubtedly.

dis-de-dimineaţă *adv.* at dawn.

diseară *adv.* tonight.

disertaţie *sf.* dissertation, paper.

disloca *vt.* to dislocate.

disonanţă *sf.* dissonance.

disparat *adj.* disconnected.

dispariţie *sf.* disappearance; *(moarte)* demise; *(pierdere)* lose.

dispărea *vi.* to disappear; *(a muri)* to pass away.

dispărut *sm.* the late; *pl.* the missing. *adj.* missing; *(specie etc.).* extinct.

dispecer *sm.* dispatcher.

dispensa *vt.* to exempt from. *vr.* to do without.

dispensar *sn.* health unit.

dispensă *sf.* exemption.

displăcea *vi.* to displease.

disponibil *sn.* available assets. *adj.* available.

dispozitiv *sn.* device.

dispoziţie *sf.* disposal; *(legală etc.)* provision; *(aşezare)* arrangement; *(sufletească)* mood; *(ordin)* order; *la* ~ available.

dispreţ *sn.* scorn.

dispreţui *vt.* to disdain; *de* ~t contemptible, mean.

dispreţuitor *adj.* contemptuous. *adv.* scornfully.

disproporţie *sf.* incongruousness.

dispune *vt.* to dispose; *(a înveseli)* to cheer. *vi.* to dispose; *a* ~ *de ceva* to have; *sport* to defeat.

dispus *adj.* ready, willing; *(vesel)* cheerful; *bine* ~ in high spirits; *prost* ~ in low spirits.

disputa *vt.* to dispute. *vr.* to be fought.

dispută *sf.* contest.

distant *adj.* aloof.

distanţa *vt.* to outdistance. *vr.* to move away.

distanţare *sf.* detachment.

distanţă *sf.* distance.

distinct *adj.* distinct. *adv.* clearly

distinctiv *adj.* specific.

distincţie *sf.* distinction.
distinge *vt.* to distinguish. *vi.*:
a ~ între to tell (one from the other). *vr.* to stand out.
distins *adj.* refined.
distra *vt.* to amuse. *vr.* to have a good time.
distractiv *adj.* amusing.
distracţie *sf.* entertainment ; *fig.* absent-mindedness.
distrage *vt.* to divert ; *(a abate)* to side-track.
distrat *adj.* absent-minded ; *(neatent)* pie-eyed. *adv.* absently.
distribui *vt.* to distribute ; *(într-un rol)* to cast.
distribuţie *sf.* distribution ; *teatru* cast.
district *sn.* district.
distrugător *sm., sn.* destroyer. *adj.* destructive.
distruge *vt.* to destroy ; *(cameni)* to exterminate ; *fig.* to shatter.
distrugere *sf.* destruction.
distrus *adj.* destroyed ; *(ruinat)* ruined ; *fig.* down-hearted.
diurnă *sf.* (daily) allowance.
divagaţie *sf.* digression.
divan *sn.* divan ; *(mobilă şi)* sofa.
divergent *adj.* divergent.
divers *adj.* diverse.
diverse *sf. pl.* miscellaneous news ; points, etc. ; *(cheltuieli)* sundries.
diversifica *vt., vr.* to diversify.
diversionist *sm.* wrecker.
diversitate *sf.* diversity.
diversiune *sf.* diversion ; *(amuzament)* entertainment.
divertisment *sn.* entertainment ; *muz.* divertimento.
dividend *sn.* dividend.
divin *adj.* divine.

diviza *vt., vr.* to divide.
divizibil *adj.* divisible.
divizi(un)e *sf.* division.
divorţ *sn.* divorce.
divorţa *vt.* to divorce. *vi.* to (get a) divorce.
divulga *vt.* to give away.
dizeur *sm.,* **dizeuză** *sf.* vocalist.
dizgraţie *sf.* disgrace.
dizgraţios *adj.* disgraceful ; *(diform)* ungainly.
dizolva *vt., vr.* to dissolve.
dizolvant *adj.* dissolvent ; *fig.* negative, dissociating.
dîmb *sn.* hillock, mount.
dînsa *pron.* she.
dînsele *pron.* they.
dînsul *pron.* he.
dînşii *pron.* they.
diră *sf.* trail.
dîrdîi *vi.* to tremble.
dîrz *adj.* firm.
dîrzenie *sf.* staunchness.
do *sm.* do, C.
doagă *sf.* stave.
doamnă *sf.* lady ; *(în scris)* Mrs. ; *(vocativ)* madam, ma'am.
doar *adv.* only, just ; *fără ~ şi poate* beyond any doubt.
doară *sf.*: *într-o ~* tentatively ; meaninglessly.
dobitoc *sm.* blockhead. *sn.* animal.
dobitocie *sf.* stupidity.
dobîndă *sf.* interest ; *(cămătărească)* usury ; *cu ~* at interest.
dobîndi *vt.* to get, to obtain. *vr.* to be obtained *sau* got.
doborî *vt.* to fell ; *fig.* to overthrow.
doborîre *sf.* felling ; *fig.* overthrow.

dobrogean *sm.* inhabitant of the Dobrudja. *adj.* of *sau* from the Dobrudja.

doc *sn. mar.* dock; *text.* duck.

docar *sn.* dog-cart.

docher *sm.* docker.

docil *adj.* docile.

docilitate *sf.* tameness.

doct *adj.* erudite.

doctor *sm.* doctor; *(clinician şi)* physician; *(chirurg)* surgeon; *fig.* expert, adept; *(în ştiinţă* etc.) master; ∼ *în litere* master of arts.

doctorat *sn.* doctor's *sau* master's degree.

doctorie *sf.* drug; *(lichidă)* medicine.

doctoriţă *sf.* doctoress.

doctrină *sf.* doctrine.

document *sn.* document.

documenta *vr.* to gather evidence.

documentar *sn., adj.* documentary.

documentare *sf.* reference material.

documentat *adj.* well-informed.

dogar *sm.* cooper.

doge *sm.* doge.

dogi *vr.* to crack.

dogit *adj.* broken.

dogmatic *adj.* dogmatic.

dogmatism *sn.* dogmatism.

dogmă *sf.* dogma.

dogoare *sf.* heat.

dogori *vt., vi.* to burn.

dogoritor *adj.* scorching.

doi *sm., adj., num.* two; ∼ *cîte* ∼ by twos, in couples.

doică *sf.* (wet) nurse.

doilea *adj., num.* (the) second; *în al* ∼ *rînd* secondly.

doime *sf.* half; *muz.* minim.

doină *sf.* melancholy Romanian folk song.

doisprezece *sm., adj., num.* twelve.

doisprezecelea *adj., num.* (the) twelfth.

dojana *sf.* reproach.

dojeni *vt.* to rebuke.

dolar *sm.* dollar.

doldora *adj.* chock-full.

doleanţă *sf.* grievance, request.

doliu *sn.* mourning; *(de văduvă şi)* weeds.

dolofan *adj.* plump.

dom *sn.* dome.

domeniu *sn.* domain; area.

domestic *adj.* domestic; *(d. animale şi)* tame.

domestici *vt.* to tame. *vr.* to become tame.

domesticit *adj.* tame(d).

domicilia *vi.* to reside.

domiciliu *sn.* (place of) residence.

domina *vt.* to dominate; *(d. clădire* etc.) to tower over. *vi.* to prevail.

dominant *adj.* ruling; *(predominant)* (pre)dominant.

dominaţie *sf.,* **dominion** *sn.* dominion.

domino *sn.* domino; *(joc)* dominoes.

domn *sm.* (gentle)man; *ist. şi rel.* lord; *(în ţările româneşti)* hospodar; *(stăpîn)* master; ∼*ul Ionescu* Mr. Ionescu; ∼*le Ionescu* Sir; Mr. Ionescu; *doamne fereşte!* not at all!

domnesc *adj.* princely.

domni *vi.* to reign; *fig.* to live in clover.

domnie *sf.* reign; *domnia sa* he; *domnia voastră* you.

domnişoară *sf.* young lady; ~ *bătrînă* spinster; ~ *de onoare* bridesmaid; *domnişoara Maria (Ionescu)* Miss Mary (Ionescu).

domnitor *sm.* hospodar. *adj.* reigning.

domol *adj.* slow; *(liniştit)* quiet. *adv.* gently; *(treptat)* gradually.

domoli *vt.* to comfort; *(a împăca)* to appease; *(setea)* to quench; *(foamea)* to stay; *(durerea)* to allay. *vr.* to calm *sau* quiet down; *(d. furtună* etc.*)* to abate.

dona *vt.* to donate.

donator *sm.* donor.

donaţie *sf.* donation.

doniţă *sf.* pail.

dop *sn.* cork; *(astupuş)* plug.

dor *sn.* longing; *(tristeţe)* melancholy; ~ *de casă sau ţară* homesickness.

dori *vt.* to desire; *(a ura)* to wish; *de* ~*t* desirable; *aş* ~ *să merg la plimbare* I should like to go for a walk; *ce doriţi?* what can I do for you?

dorinţă *sf.* desire, wish; *după* ~ at one's choice *sau* request.

dorit *adj.* long-expected.

doritor *adj.* eager (for).

dormi *vi.* to sleep; *(a aţipi)* to snooze; *a* ~ *buştean* to sleep like a log.

dormitor *sn.* bedroom; *(la internat* etc.*)* dormitory.

dornic *adj.* desirous; *(nerăbdător)* keen (on).

dos *sn.* back(side); *(şezut)* behind; *din* ~ (at the) back; *în* ~*ul* ... behind; *pe* ~ upside down; *(îmbrăcăminte)* inside out.

dosar *sn.* folder, file; *(personal)* record; *jur.* case.

dosi *vt., vr.* to hide.

dota *vt.* to endow.

dotă *sf.* dowry.

doua *adj., num.* (the) second; *a* ~ *zi* the next day.

două *adj., num.* two; *din* ~ *în* ~ *zile* every other day; *de* ~ *ori* twice; *de* ~ *ori şi jumătate* two and a half times; *pe din* ~ fifty fifty.

douăzeci *sm., adj., num.* twenty, a score.

douăzecilea *adj., num.* (the) twentieth.

dovadă *sf.* proof; *pl.* evidence; *(certificat)* certificate.

dovedi *vt.* to prove; *(a arăta)* to demonstrate; *(a atesta)* to certify. *vr.* to prove.

dovleac *sm.* pumpkin.

dovlecel *sm.* vegetable marrow.

doza *vt.* to measure.

doză *sf.* doze; *el.* pick-up cartridge.

drac *sm.* devil; ~*e!* hell!; *al* ~*ului* wicked; *la* ~*u!* hang it all!; *pe* ~*u* not in the least.

drag *sm.* sweetheart; ~*ul meu* my dear. *sn.* love; *cu tot* ~*ul* eagerly; *de* ~*ul cuiva* for smb.'s sake. *adj.* dear; *(preferat)* pet; *cu* ~*ă inimă* gladly.

dragă *sf.* sweetheart; *tehn.* dredger.

dragon *sm.* dragon; *mil.* dragoon.

dragoste *sf.* love; *de sau din* ~ love...; *din* ~ *pentru cineva* out of love for smb.

drajeu *sn.* dragée.

dramatic *adj.* dramatic. *adv.* dramatically.

dramatism *sn.* dramatic nature.

dramatiza *vt.* to adapt.

dramatizare *sf.* stage version.

dramaturg *sm.* playwright.

dramaturgie *sf.* drama.

dramă *sf.* tragedy.

drapel *sn.* flag.

draperie *sf.* hangings.

drastic *adj.* drastic. *adv.* drastically.

drăcesc *adj.* fiendish.

drăcie *sf.* devillish trick; *fig.* device.

drăgălaş *adj.* lovely.

drăgălăşenie *sf.* grace; *(amabilitate)* kindliness.

drăgăstos *adj.* affectionate. *adv.* lovingly.

drăguţ *sm.* beloved. *adj.* nice.

dreaptă *sf.* straight (line); *(mînă)* right hand; *pol.* right wing; *la dreapta* on the right (hand side).

drege *vt.* to mend, to repair; *fig.* to rectify; *(vinul)* to doctor; *a-şi ~ glasul* to clear one's throat. *vr.* to improve.

drept *sn.* right; *(legi)* law; *(dreptate)* justice; right foot *sau* leg; *~ civil* etc. civil, etc. law; *~ de autor* copyright; *pl.* royalties; *~ penal* criminal law; *~ul la muncă* the right to work; *de ~* by right; *pe ~* rightly. *adj.* right; *(just şi)* fair; *geom.* straight; *(direct)* direct; *(ţeapăn)* erect; *(adevărat)* true; *(cinstit)* righteous; *cu ~ cuvînt* for good reason (too). *adv.* straight; *(exact)* precisely. *prep.* for.

dreptate *sf.* justice; *(justeţe)* fairness.

dreptunghi *sn.* rectangle.

dresa *vt.* to train; *(a domestici)* to tame; *(a alcătui)* to write.

dresaj *sn.* training.

drie *sn.* hearse.

dril *sn. text.* tick.

droaie *sf.* legion.

drogherie *sf.* druggist's shop

drojdie *sf.* dregs; *(de bere)* yeast; *(de cafea)* grounds.

dromader *sm.* dromedary.

dropie *sf.* bustard.

drug *sm.* (crow)bar.

drum *sn.* road; *fig.* (path)way; *(călătorie)* travel; *~ bun* farewell; *de sau la ~ul mare* highway; *în ~ spre (casă* etc.*)* on the way (home, etc.).

drumeţ *sm.* traveller.

dubă *sf.* (police) van.

dubios *adj.* doubtful.

dubiu *sn.* doubt.

dubla *vt.* to (re)double; *(un actor)* to understudy; *(un film)* to dub. *vr.* to double.

dublu *sm., adj.* double. *adv.* twice (as much).

ducat *sm.* ducat. *sn.* duchy.

ducă *sf.* going; *pe ~ running* short *sau* out.

duce *sm.* duke. *vt.* to take; *(o activitate* etc.*)* to carry on; *(o viaţă)* to live; *(un război)* to wage; *(a călăuzi)* to guide; *(a căra)* to carry; *(a păcăli)* to diddle; *a o ~* to get on; *cum o (mai) duci?* how are you? *vi.* to resist; *(a conduce)* to lead. *vr.* to go; *(a pleca)* to leave; *(a dispărea)* to die; *a se ~ pe copcă sau de rîpă* to go to the dogs; *du-te vino* comings and goings.

ducere *sf.* going; *la* ~ **on the** journey out.

ducesă *sf.* duchess.

dud *sm.*, **dudă** *sf.* mulberry (tree).

duel *sn.* duel.

duela *vi.*, *vr.* to fight a duel; *fig.* to spar.

duet *sn.* duet.

dugheană *sf.* booth; *(prăvălie)* shop.

duh *sn.* spirit; *(haz)* wit; *cu* ~*ul blîndeţii* kindly.

duhni *vi.* to reek (of wine, etc.).

duhovnic *sm.* confessor.

duios *adj.* tender; *(înduioşător)* sad. *adv.* lovingly.

duioşie *sf.* fondness.

duium *sn.*: *cu* ~*ul* (in) heaps.

dulap *sn.* cupboard; *(pt. haine)* wardrobe; *(bufet)* sideboard.

dulău *sm.* mastiff.

dulce *sn.* dessert; *pl.* sweets; *de* ~ meat. *adj.* sweet. *adv.* sweetly; *(drăgăstos)* lovingly.

dulceag *adj.* fulsome; *fig.* mawkish.

dulceaţă *sf.* sweetness; *(gem)* jam; *(de citrice)* marmalade.

dulcegărie *sf.* sloppiness.

dulgher *sm.* carpenter.

dulgherie *sf.* joinery.

dumbravă *sf.* grove.

dumeri *vt.* to enlighten. *vr.* to see.

duminica *adv.* on Sunday(s).

duminical *adj.* Sunday...

duminică *sf.* Sunday; *adv.* on Sunday.

dumitale *adj.* your; *al* ~ yours.

dumneaei *adj.* her; *al* ~ hers. *pron.* she; *(ei)* to her; *pe* ~ her.

dumnealor *adj.* their; *al* ~ theirs. *pron.* they; (to) them; *pe* ~ them.

dumnealui *adj.* his; *al* ~ his. *pron.* he.

dumneata *pron.* you; *pe* ~ you.

dumneavoastră *adj.* your; *al* ~ yours. *pron.* you; *(dativ)* (to) you; *pe* ~ you.

dumnezeiesc *adj.* divine.

dumnezeieşte *adv.* divinely.

Dumnezeu *sm.* (the Lord) God; *pentru* ~*!* for goodness' sake !

dună *sf.* dune.

dunărean *adj.* Danubian.

dungă *sf.* stripe; *(la pantaloni)* crease; *în dungi* striped.

după *prep.* after; ~ *spusele* according to; ~ *toate aparenţele* in all likelihood; ~ *mine* to my mind.

dur *adj.* hard; *(sever)* dour.

dura¹ *vt.* to build. *vi.* **to** last.

dura² *adv.*: *de-a* ~ head over heels.

durabil *adj.* durable.

durată *sf.* length; *de lungă* ~ of long standing.

durduliu *adj.* plump; *fem. şi* buxom.

durea *vt.* to hurt, to pain; *(d. dinţi, inimă)* to ache; *(d. ochi, picioare)* to be sore; *mă doare capul* my head aches, I have a headache; *mă doare gîtul* I have a sore throat.

durere *sf.* ache, pain; *(suferinţă)* suffering; *(sufletească)* sorrow; ~ *de dinţi* toothache; ~ *de cap* headache; ~ *de inimă* heartache; *durerile facerii* throes *sau* labours of childbirth; *cu* ~ sorrowfully.

dureros *adj.* painful ; *(d. un punct)* sore.

dus *sn.* going ; ～ *şi întors* return (ticket) ; out and in journey. *adj.* led, taken ; *(d. ochi)* wistful ; ～ *pe gînduri* wrapped up in thoughts ; *a dormi* ～ to be fast asleep.

duş *sn.* shower (bath) ; *fig.* cold water.

duşcă *sf.* draught ; *o* ～ *la botul calului* a stirrup cup ; *dintr-o* ～ at one gulp.

duşman *sm.* enemy ; *(adversar)* opponent ; ～ *de moarte* deadly foe.

duşmăni *vt.* to hate. *vr.* to be on bad terms.

duşmănie *sf.* enmity ; *(pică)* rancour.

duşmănos *adj.* inimical. *adv.* hostilely.

duşumea *sf.* floor(ing).

duzină *sf.* dozen ; *de* ～ ordinary ; *(prost)* poor.

E

ea *pron.* she ; *pe* ～ *(acuzativ)* her.

ebraic *sm.*, *adj.*, **ebraică** *sf.*, *adj.* Hebrew.

ebrietate *sf.* intoxication.

echer *sn.* (set) square.

echilibra *vt.*, *vr.* to balance.

echilibru *sn.* balance.

echipa *vt.*, *vr.* to equip (oneself).

echipaj *sn.* crew.

echipament *sn.* equipment ; *mil.* şi kit ; *tehn.*, *sport* outfit.

echipă *sf.* team ; *(de muncitori şi)* crew.

echitabil *adj.* fair. *adv.* justly.

echitate *sf.* equity, fairness.

echivala *vt.* to equalize. *vi.:* *a* ～ *cu* to be tantamount to.

echivalent *sm.*, *adj.* equivalent.

echivoc *sn.* ambiguity. *adj.* equivocal ; *(obscen)* smutty.

eclipsa *vt.* to eclipse ; *fig. şi* to outshine. *vr.* to disappear.

eclipsă *sf.* eclipse ; ～ *de lună* lunar eclipse ; ～ *de soare* solar eclipse.

ecluză *sf.* sluice.

econom *sm.* treasurer. *adj.* economical.

economie *adj.* *(din domeniul economiei)* economic ; *(econ.)* thrifty ; *(ieftin)* cheap. *adv.* economically.

economicos *adj.* economical.

economie *sf.* economy ; *(ştiinţă şi)* economics ; *(la mîncare etc.)* thrift ; *pl.* savings ; *(administraţie)* husbandry ; *cu* ～ sparingly.

economisi *vt.* to save.

ecou *sn.* echo.

ecran *sn.* screen ; ～ *lat* wide screen.

ecraniza *vt.* to film.

ecuator *sn.* the equator.

ecuaţie *sf.* equation.

edifica *vt.* to enlighten. *vr.* to be enlightened.

edificator *adj.* illustrating, enlightening.

edificiu *sn.* building.

edilitar *adj.* town..., (of) public utility.

edita *vt.* to publish; *(a îngriji)* to edit.

editor *sm.* publisher; *(îngrijitor de ediţie)* editor.

editorial *sn.*, *adj.* editorial.

editură *sf.* publishing house.

ediţie *sf.* edition.

educa *vt.* to bring up.

educat *adj.* educated.

educativ *adj.* instructive.

educator *sm.* pedagogue.

educaţie *sf.* upbringing; *(maniere)* good breeding; ~ *fizic* physical training.

efect *sn.* effect; *pl.* clothes; *mil.* equipment; *de* ~ effective; *fără* ~ without issue.

efectiv *sn.*, *adj.* effective. *adv.* actually.

efectua *vt.* to effect. *vr.* to be done.

efemer *adj.* ephemeral.

efervescenţă *sf.* effervescence.

eficace *adj.* efficient.

eficacitate *sf.* efficiency.

eficient *adj.* efficacious.

efigie *sf.* effigy.

efort *sn.* effort.

efuziune *sf.* effusion.

egal *sm.* equal; *fără* ~ matchless. *adj.* equal; *fig.* even.

egala *vt.* to equal(ize). *vi. sport* to tie.

egalitate *sf.* equality; *(uniformitate)* regularity; *(ca re-*

zultat) tie; ~ *în drepturi* equal rights *sau* opportunities; *la* ~ at a draw.

egaliza *vt.* to equalize.

egidă *sf.* aegis.

egiptean *sm.*, *adj.*, **egipteană** *sf.*, *adj.* Egyptian.

egoism *sn.* selfishness.

egoist *sm.* egotist. *adj.* selfish.

eh *interj.* well !

ei *adj.* her; *al* ~ hers; *(pt. lucruri)* its. *pron.* they; *(dativ)* (to) her; *pe* ~ *(acuzativ)* them. *interj.* hey! well! what ?; ~ *bine?* well ?; ~ *şi?* and what of that ?

el *pron.* he; *(d. lucruri)* it; ~ *însuşi* he himself *sau* personally; *pe* ~ *(acuzativ)* him.

elabora *vt.* to elaborate; to evolve.

elan *sm. zool.* elk. *sn.* élan; *(avînt)* upsurge.

elastic *sn.*, *adj.* elastic. *adv.* elastically.

elasticitate *sf.* resilience.

ele *pron.* they; *pe* ~ *(acuzativ)* them.

elector *sm.* elector.

electoral *adj.* electoral.

electric *adj.* electric(al). *adv.* electrically.

electrician *sm.* electrician.

electricitate *sf.* electricity; *(curent)* (electric) power.

electrifica *vt.* to electrify.

electronic *adj.* electronic.

electronică *sf.* electronics.

elefant *sm.* elephant.

elegant *adj.* elegant; *(la modă)* fashionable. *adv.* elegantly.

eleganţă *sf.* elegance; *(modă)* fashionabless; *cu* ~ elegantly.

elegie *sf.* elegy.

element *sn.* element. *el.* cell.
elementar *adj.* elementary; *(la
şcoală şi)* lower.
elen *sm.* Hellene. *adj.* Hellenic.
eleşteu *sn.* (fish)pond.
elev *sm.* schoolboy; *(în general)*
pupil; ~ *extern* day-pupil.
elevă *sf.* schoolgirl, pupil.
elibera *vt.* to (set) free; *(un
act)* to deliver. *vr.* to liberate
oneself.
eliberare *sf.* liberation; ~ *con-
diţionată* parole.
elice *sf.* propeller.
elicopter *sn.* helicopter.
elimina *vt.* to eliminate; *(de
la şcoală)* to expel.
elipsă *sf. geom.* ellipse; *lingv.*
ellipsis.
eliptic *adj.* elliptical.
elită *sf.* élite; *de* ~ topnotch.
elixir *sn.* elixir.
elocvent *adj.* eloquent.
elocvenţă *sf.* rhetoric.
elogia *vt.* to extol.
elogios *adj.* eulogistic.
elogiu *sn.* praise.
elucida *vt.* to elucidate.
eluda *vt.* to evade.
elveţian *sm., adj.,* **elveţiancă**
sf. Swiss.
email *sn.* enamel.
emaila *vt.* to enamel.
emana *vt.* to give off. *vi.* to
emanate.
emanaţie *sf.* emanation.
emancipa *vt.* to emancipate. *vr.*
to become emancipated.
emblemă *sf.* emblem.
embrion *sn.* embryo.
emerit *adj.* merited.
emfatic *adj.* pompous.
emfază *sf.* grandiloquence.
emigra *vi.* to emigrate.

emigrant *sm.* emigrant.
eminent *adj.* eminent.
eminenţă *sf.* eminence.
emisferă *sf.* hemisphere.
emisune *sf.* emission; *(de bani
etc.)* issue; *(radio)* broadcast.
emite *vt.* to emit; *(sunete,
bani şi)* to utter; *fiz. şi* to
send forth; *(o teorie etc.)* to
advance.
emiţător *sn.* transmitter. *adj.*
transmitting.
emotiv *adj.* shy.
emoţie *sf.* emotion; *(tulburare
şi)* excitement; *emoţii tari*
thrills.
emoţiona *vt.* to move. *vr.* to
be excited *sau* touched.
emoţional *adj.* emotional.
emoţionant *adj.* touching.
emoţionat *adj.* excited.
enciclopedic *adj.* encyclopae-
dic.
enciclopedie *sf.* encyclopaedia.
energetic *adj.* power...
energic *adj.* energetic. *adv.* strongly.
energie *sf.* energy; ~ *electrică* (electric) power.
enerva *vt.* to irritate. *vr.* to be
impatient.
englez *sm.* Englishman; ~*ii*
the English. *adj.* English.
engleză *sf.* English, the English
language.
englezesc *adj.* English.
englezeşte *adv.* English; like
an Englishman; *(pe furiş)*
by stealth.
englezoaică *sf.* English woman.
enigmatic *adj.* quizzical.
enigmă *sf.* enigma.

enorm *adj.* enormous ; *(înspăimîntător)* tremendous. *adv.* im-
mensely.
enormitate *sf.* enormity ; *(prostie)* stupid thing.
entomologie *sf.* entomology.
entuziasm *sn.* enthusiasm ; *(încîntare)* rapture(s) ; *cu* ~ enthu-
siastically.
entuziasma *vt.* to enthuse. *vr.*
to be enraptured.
enumera *vt.* to enumerate.
enunț *sn.* enunciation.
enunța *vt.* to enunciate, to state.
epavă *sf.* wreck.
epic *adj.* epic.
epidemie *sf.* epidemic.
epidiascop *sn.* epidiascope.
epigon *sm.* epigone, imitator.
epigramă ·*sf.* epigram.
epilepsie *sf.* epilepsy.
epilog *sn.* epilogue.
episcop *sm.* bishop.
episcopie *sf.* bishopric.
episod *sn.* episode.
epistolă *sf.* letter.
epitaf *sn.* epitaph.
epitet *sn.* epithet.
epocal *adj.* epochmaking.
epocă *sf.* epoch ; *de* ~ period...
epolet *sm.* epaulette.
epopee *sf.* epic, saga.
eprubetă *sf.* test tube.
epuiza *vt.* to exhaust. *vr.* to be
exhausted ; *(d. cărți)* to get
out of print.
epuizare *sf.* exhaustion.
epuizat *adj.* exhausted ; *(d.
carte)* out of print.
epura *vt.* to purge ; *(un text)*
to bowdlerize.
erată *sf.* erratum.
eră *sf.* era ; *al erei noastre* A.D. ;
înaintea erei noastre B.C.

ereditar *adj.* hereditary.
erete *sm.* merlin.
ermetic *adj.* (air) tight ; *fig.*
hermetic. *adv.* hermetically,
tight.
ermetism *sn.* abstruseness.
ermină *sf.* sable.
ermit *sm.* hermit.
eroare *sf.* error.
eroic *adj.* heroic(al). *adv.* brave-
ly.
eroicomic *adj.* mock-heroic.
eroină *sf.* heroine.
eroism *sn.* heroism.
eronat *adj.* erroneous.
erotic *adj.* erotic.
erou *sm.* hero.
erudit *sm.* scholar. *adj.* erudite
erudiție *sf.* erudition.
erupe *vi.* to erupt ; *med.* to
break out.
erupție *sf.* eruption ; *(urticarie)*
rash.
escalada *vt.* to climb ; *mil.* to
escalate.
escală *sf.* stop(over) ; *fără* ~
non-stop.
eschimos *sm.*, *adj.* Eskimo.
eschiva *vr.* to shirk (from).
escorta *vt.* to escort.
escortă *sf.* escort.
escroc *sm.* swindler.
escroca *vt.* to fleece.
escrocherie *sf.* swindle.
eseist *sm.* essay-writer.
eseistic *adj.* essay-like.
eseistică *sf.* essay-writing.
esență *sf.* essence ; *în* ~ essentially.
esențial *sn.* pith (and marrow)
adj. essential.
esențialmente *adv.* essentially.
eseu *sn.* essay.
esperanto *sn.* Esperanto.

est *sn.* East; *de* ~ east(ern); *la* ~ east (of).

estet *sm.* aesthete.

estetic *adj.* aesthetic. *adv.* aesthetically.

estetică *sf.* aesthetics.

estetism *sn.* art for art's sake.

estic *adj.* eastern.

estimativ *adj.* estimated.

estompa *vt.* to blur; *(artă)* to stump. *vr.* to grow dim.

eston *sm., adj.* **estonă** *sf., adj.* Estonian.

estradă *sf.* platform; *(revistă)* music hall; *de* ~ promenade.

estuar *sn.* estuary.

eşafod *sn.* scaffold.

eşalona *vt.* to space; to phase.

eşantion *sn.* sample.

eşarfă *sf.* scarf; *med.* arm sling.

eşec *sn.* failure.

eşua *vi.* to be stranded; *fig.* to fail.

etaj *sn.* *(pe dinăuntru)* floor; *(pe dinafară)* stor(e)y; *la* ~ upstairs; *la* ~*ul* întîi on the first floor; *cu două* ~*e* two-storeyed.

etajeră *sf.* bookstand; *(poliţă)* shelf.

etala *vt.* to display. *vr.* to show off.

etalare *sf.* display.

etalon *sn.* standard.

etanş *adj.* (air)tight.

etapă *sf.* stage.

etate *sf.* age; *în* ~ elderly.

etc(etera) *adv.* etc(etera), a.s.o. (and so on).

eter *sn.* ether.

etern *sn., adj.* eternal. *adv.* for ever.

eternitate *sf.* eternity.

etic *adj.* moral.

etică *sf.* ethics.

etichetă *sf.* label; *(politeţe)* etiquette; *fără* ~ *fig.* informally.

etimologie *sf.* etymology.

etiopian *sm., adj.* Ethiopian.

eu *sn.* ego. *pron.* I, myself.

eucalipt *sm.* eucalyptus.

eufemism *sn.* euphemism.

european *sm., adj.*, **europeană** *sf., adj.*, **europenesc** *adj.* European.

ev *sn.* century; *(eră)* age; ~*ul mediu* the Middle Ages.

evacua *vt.* to evacuate; *(aburul)* to exhaust.

evada *vi.* to escape.

evadare *sf.* escape; *fig.* escapism.

evadat *sm.* fugitive.

evalua *vt.* to assess.

evaluare *sf.* estimate.

evanghelic *adj.* Evangelic.

evanghelie *sf.* Gospel.

evantai *sn.* fan.

evapora *vt., vr.* to evaporate.

evazionism *sn.* escapism.

evazionist *sm.* escapist; ~ *fiscal* tax dodger.

evaziv *adj.* evasive. *adv.* vaguely.

eveniment *sn.* event; development; *plin de* ~*e* eventful.

eventual *adj.* likely. *adv.* possibly; *(la nevoie)* if need be.

eventualitate *sf.* contingency; *pentru orice* ~ just in case.

evident *adj.* obvious. *adv.* evidently.

evidenţă *sf.* evidence; *(situaţie)* record; ~ *contabilă* bookkeeping.

evidenţia *vt.* to distinguish; *(a sublinia)* to point out. *vr.* to make oneself conspicuous.

evita *vt.* to avoid; *(a ocoli)* to dodge.

evlavie *sf.* devoutness; *cu ~* piously.

evlavios *adj.* pious.

evoca *vt.* to recall.

evocare *sf.* evocation.

evocator *adj.* reminiscent (of).

evolua *vi.* to evolve; *(în public)* to perform.

evoluat *adj.* advanced.

evoluţie *sf.* evolution; *(mişcare)* act(ing).

evreică *sf.* Jewess.

evreiesc *adj.* Jewish; *(idiş)* Yiddish.

evreieşte *adv.* Yiddish; in the Jewish fashion.

evreu *sm.* Jew.

exact *adj.* accurate; *(punctual)* punctual; *(minuţios)* minute; *(adevărat)* true. *adv.* precisely; *(punctual)* punctually; *(îngrijit)* accurately; *(minuţios)* minutely; *(ca exclamaţie)* that's it! *~ ca şi* just like; *~ la ora cinci* at five o'clock sharp.

exactitate *sf.* accuracy; *(punctualitate)* punctuality.

exagera *vt., vi.* to exaggerate.

exagerat *adj.* exaggerate(d).

exalta *vt., vr.* to warm up.

exaltat *sm.* enthusiast. *adj.* enthusiastic.

examen *sn.* examination; *(la şcoală şi)* exam.

examina *vt.* to examine.

exaspera *vt.* to exasperate.

excavator *sn.* steam navvy *sau* shovel.

excedent *sn.* surplus.

excela *vi.* to excel.

excelent *adj.* excellent. *adv.* excellently.

excelenţă *sf.* excellency; *prin ~* above all.

excentric *sm., adj.* eccentric.

excepta *vt.* to except, to bar.

excepţie *sf.* exception; *cu excepţia* except(ing); *fără ~* to a man; without exception.

excepţional *adj.* exceptional. *adv.* exceptionally.

exces *sn.* excess; *(lipsă de cumpătare)* intemperance.

excesiv *adj.* excessive; *(violent)* violent. *adv.* excessively.

excita *vt.* to rouse. *vr.* to be roused.

exclama *vt.* to exclaim, to ejaculate.

exclude *vt.* to exclude; *(a da afară)* to expel; *(a împiedica şi)* to preclude.

excludere *sf.* exclusion; *(dintr-o organizaţie)* expulsion.

exclus *adj.* excluded; *(imposibil)* out of the question.

exclusiv *adj.* exclusive. *adv.* exclusively.

excursie *sf.* trip; *fig.* investigation.

excursionist *sm.* excursionist.

execrabil *adj.* abominable.

executa *vt.* to perform; *(a ucide)* to execute. *vr.* to obey.

executiv *adj.* executive.

execuţie *sf.* execution; *(îndeplinire)* implementation.

exemplar *sn.* copy; *fig.* instance; *adj.* exemplary. *adv.* exemplarily.

exemplifica *vt.* to illustrate (with examples).

exemplu *sn.* example; *de ~* for instance; *după ~l lui* taking his example.

exercita *vt.* to exert; *(a practica)* to practise.

exercițiu *sn.* exercise; *(rutină și)* practice; *pl.* homework; *în ~l funcțiunii* (while) discharging one's duties.

exersa *vt., vi., vr.* to practise.

ex(h)iba *vt., vr.* to make a show of (oneself).

ex(h)ibiție *sf.* ostentation.

exigent *adj.* exacting.

exigență *sf.* exactingness, exigency.

exil *sn.* exile.

exila *vt., vr.* to exile (oneself).

exista *vi.* to be, to exist; *există* there is; there are.

existent *adj.* extant.

existență *sf.* existence; *(trai)* livelihood.

exmatricula *vt.* to expel.

exorbitant *adj.* exorbitant.

exotic *adj.* exotic.

expansiune *sf.* expansion.

expansiv *sf.* expansive.

expatria *vr.* to go into exile.

expedia *vt.* to dispatch; *(prin poștă)* to post; *com.* to ship.

expedient *sn.* makeshift.

expediere *sf.* sending.

expeditiv *adj.* expeditious. *adv.* promptly.

expeditor *sm.* sender; *com.* shipper.

expediție *sf.* dispatch(ing); *(călătorie)* expedition.

experiență *sf.* *(de laborator* etc.) experiment; *(întîmplare)* experience(s); *(înțelepciune)* experience; *experiențe nucleare* nuclear tests; *cu ~* experienced.

experimenta *vt.* to test.

experimental *adj.* experimental.

experimentat *adj.* expert.

expert *sm.* specialist.

expertiză *sf.* (expert) examination; *~ contabilă* auditing.

expira *vt., vi.* to expire.

explica *vt.* to explain; *(a justifica)* to explain away. *vr.* to be explained *sau* justified.

explicabil *adj.* accountable.

explicativ *adj.* explanatory.

explicație *sf.* explanation; *(justificare)* justification; *(discuție)* showdown.

explicit *adj.* explicit. *adv.* explicitly.

exploata *vt.* to exploit; *(oameni și)* to sweat; *(o mină* etc.) to work.

exploatare *sf.* exploitation; *com.* running; *(mină* etc.) mine; working; *(forestieră)* lumber station.

exploatat *sm.* exploited person; *pl.* the exploited. *adj.* exploited; *(d. mină* etc.) worked.

exploatator *sm.* exploiter. *adj.* exploiting.

exploda *vi.* to burst out.

explora *vt.* to explore.

explorator *sm.* explorer.

explozibil *sn., adj.* explosive.

explozie *sf.* blast.

exploziv *sn., adj.* explosive.

exponat *sn.* exhibit.

exponent *sm.* exponent; *fig.* spokesman.

export *sn.* exportation; *(marfă)* export(s); *de ~* export.

exporta *vt.* to export.

exportator *sm.* exporter. *adj.* exporting.

expozeu *sn.* exposé.

expoziție *sf.* exhibition; *(sală)* gallery; *~ personală* one--man show.

expres *sn.* express train. *adj.* express. *adv.* purpose(ful)ly.

expresie *sf.* expression : *(lo-cuţiune şi)* idiom.

expresiv *adj.* expressive. *adv.* graphically.

expresivitate *sf.* expressiveness.

exprima *vt.* to express ; *(a formula)* to couch ; *(a manifesta)* to manifest. *vr.* to express oneself.

exprimare *sf.* expression.

expropria *vt.* to expropriate.

expulza *vt.* to expel.

expulzare *sf.* expulsion.

expune *vt.* to exhibit ; *(la neplăceri etc.)* to expose ; *(o teorie etc.)* to expound. *vr.* to incur a risk.

expunere *sf.* exposition ; *(discurs)* exposé.

expus *adj.* exposed ; ~ *la...* liable to...

extaz *sn.* ecstasy.

extazia *vr.* to go into ecstasies.

extemporal *sn.* offhand paper.

extenua *vt., vi., vr.* to exhaust (oneself).

exterior *sn.* exterior ; *(înfăţişare)* appearance ; *în* ~ outwardly ; *(în străinătate)* abroad. *adj.* outside ; *pol.* foreign.

extermina *vt.* to exterminate.

exterminare *sf.* extermination ; ~ *în masă* mass destruction.

extern *sm.* extern ; *(elev)* day--pupil. *adj.* external, outside.

externe *sn. pl.* (ministry of) foreign affairs.

extinde *vt., vr.* to extend.

extindere *sf.* spreading.

extra *adj.* extra(fine).

extract *sn.* extract ; certificate.

extrage *vt.* to extract ; *(un dinte)* to pull out.

extraordinar *sn.* extraordinary (event). *adj.* extraordinary ; *(remarcabil)* remarkable. *adv.* uncommonly ; ~ *de repede* exceedingly quick.

extras *sn.* extract ; *(pasaj şi)* excerpt.

extravagant *adj.* eccentric ; *(nebunesc)* crazy.

extravaganţă *sf.* extravagance.

extrem *sn.* extreme ; *la* ~ to the utmost. *adj.* excessive ; *(îndepărtat)* far(thest) ; ~ *de* extremely. *adv.* exceedingly.

extremă *sf.* extreme ; *sport* outside (forward) ; ~ *stîngă sport* left outside.

extremitate *sf.* extremity ; *(vîrf)* tip.

exuberant *adj.* buoyant.

exuberanţă *sf.* exuberance.

exulta *vi.* to exult.

ezita *vi.* to waver.

ezitare *sf.* hesitation.

F

fa *sm.* F, fa.

fabrica *vt.* to manufacture ; *fig.* to concoct. *vr.* to be made.

fabricant *sm.* mill-owner, manufacturer.

fabricaţie *sf.* make.

fabrică *sf.* factory; *(uzină)* works; *(mai ales în industrie ușoară)* mill; *(de cărămizi, cherestea)* yard.

fabulă *sf.* fable.

fabulos *adj.* fabulous.

face *vt.* *(a crea)* to make; *(a se ocupa cu)* to do; *(a comite)* to perpetrate; *(a da naștere la)* to bear; *(a produce)* to yield; *(mîncare)* to cook; *(prăjituri)* to bake; *(a clădi)* to build; *(a alcătui)* to make up; *(un desen)* to draw; *(a încheia)* to conclude; *(a scrie)* to write; *(a preface)* to turn; *(a numi)* to appoint; *a ~ o aluzie* to drop a hint; *a ~ armata* to serve under the colours; *a ~ baie* to take a bath; *(în mare etc.)* to bathe; *a ~ bilanțul* to draw the balance-sheet; *fig.* to survey; *a ~ față la* to cope with; *a-și ~ o haină* to have a coat made; *a ~ pe grozavul* to preen (oneself); *a ~ pe nebunul* to play the giddy goat; *a-ți ~ rău* to sicken one; *a-și ~ toaleta* to trim up; *a ~ tot ce poate* to do one's best *sau* worst; *ce ~ ?* what ?. *vi.* *(a valora)* to be (worth); *(a acționa)* to do; *a-și ~ de cap* to have one's fling; to sow one's wild oats. *vr.* to be made *sau* done; *(a deveni)* to become; *(a se preface)* to pretend; *s-a făcut!* OK! all right! *se făcea că...* it seemed that...; *a i se ~ de...* to feel like...; *a se ~ bine* to recover; *a se ~ de rîs* to make a fool of oneself; to

become everybody's laughing stock; *a i se ~ foame, sete* etc. to be(come) hungry, thirsty etc. *se ~ frumos* it is clearing up; *a se ~ mare* to grow up; *a se ~ nevăzut* to vanish; *se ~ tîrziu* it is getting late; *se ~ ziuă* day is breaking; *așa se ~ că* and so...; *nu se ~* such things are simply not done.

facere *sf.* making; *(naștere)* childbirth.

facilita *vt.* to facilitate.

facilitate *sf.* facility.

faclă *sf.* torch.

factor *sm.* factor; *(poștaș)* postman.

factură *sf.* invoice; *fig.* structure.

facultate *sf.* faculty.

facultativ *adj.* optional. *adv.* at will.

fad *adj.* vapid.

fag *sm.* beech.

fagot *sn.* bassoon.

fagure *sm.* honeycomb.

faianță *sf.* faience.

faimă *sf.* fame.

faimos *adj.* famous; *peior.* precious.

falangă *sf.* phalanx.

fală *sf.* glory.

falcă *sf.* jaw.

fald *sn.* fold.

faleză *sf.* cliff.

faliment *sn.* bankruptcy.

falimentar *adj.*, **falit** *sm.*, *adj.* bankrupt.

falnic *adj.* lofty. *adv.* proudly.

fals *sn.* false(hood). *adj.* false; *(greșit)* fallacious; *(prefăcut)* phon(e)y; *(d. bani etc.)* counterfeit; *(artificial)* imitation.

adv. falsely ; *muz.* out of tune ; *(greşit)* mistakenly.

falsifica *vt.* to falsify ; *(băuturile şi)* to doctor ; *(bani etc.)* to forge.

falsificat *adj.* counterfeit, specious.

familial *adj.* family.

familiar *adj.* familiar. *adv.* informally.

familiaritate *sf.* intimacy ; *peior.* liberties.

familiariza *vt.* to make familiar. *vr.* to be inured (to smth.).

familie *sf.* family.

familist *sm.* family man.

fanatic *sm.* fan(atic). *adj.* fanatical.

fandosi *vr.* to do the grand.

fanfară *sf.* fanfare.

fanfaron *sm.* braggart. *adj.* boastful.

fantastic *adj.* fantastical ; *(straşnic)* capital. *adv.* fantastically.

fante *sm.* ladykiller ; *(valet)* knave.

fantezie *sf.* fancy ; *(imaginaţie şi)* fantasy.

fantezist *adj.* fanciful ; *(neadevărat)* fabricated.

fantomatic *adj.* ghostlike.

fantomă *sf.* phantom.

fapt *sn.* fact ; *(acţiune)* deed ; *(întîmplare)* event ; *~e diverse* news in brief ; *~ împlinit* accomplished fact ; *de ~* actually ; *(la urma urmei)* in fact ; *în ~ul zilei* at break of day ; *asupra ~ului* redhanded.

faptă *sf.* deed ; *(eroică)* exploit ; *(performanţă)* stunt.

far *sn.* lighthouse ; *şi fig.* beacon ; *auto.* headlight.

faraon *sm.* Pharaoh.

fard *sn.* make-up.

farda *vt., vr.* to paint (one's face).

farfurie *sf.* plate ; *(conţinutul)* plateful ; *~ adîncă* soup plate ; *~ întinsă* dinner plate.

farfurioară *sf.* saucer.

farmaceutic *adj.* pharmaceutical.

farmacie *sf.* pharmacy

farmacist *sm.* chemist.

farmec *sn.* charm ; *(vrajă şi)* spell ; *ca prin ~* as if by magic.

farsă *sf.* farce ; *(festă)* practical joke.

farsor *sm.* humbug.

fascina *vt.* to fascinate.

fascism *sn.* fascism.

fascist *sm., adj.* fascist.

fasole *sf.* bean(s).

fast *sn.* pomp.

fastuos *adj.* luxurious.

faşă *sf.* dressing ; *pl. (pt. copii)* swaddling clothes.

fatal *adj.* fatal. *adv.* inevitably ; *(din nenorocire)* fatally.

fatalitate *sf.* fatality.

fată *sf.* girl ; *(fecioară)* maiden ; *(fiică)* daughter ; *~ bătrînă* spinster ; *~ în casă* maid (-servant).

faţadă *sf.* façade ; *fig.* show ; *de ~ fig.* sham.

faţă *sf.* face *(înfăţişare)* appearance ; *(aer)* mien ; *(ten)* complexion ; *(expresie)* countenance ; *(suprafaţă)* surface ; *(parte din faţă)* front ; *(pagină)* page ; *~ de masă* table cloth ; *~ de pernă* pillow case ; *~ în ~* face to face ; *~ de (situaţie etc.)* given (the situation, etc.) ; *de ~*

present ; *de ~cu* in the presence of ; *din ~* fore ; *în ~* in front ; *în ~a mea* before my (very) eyes ; *pe ~* openly.

favoare *sf.* favour ; *(cadou* etc.*)* handout ; *de ~* complimentary ; *în ~a cuiva* to smb.'s advantage.

favorabil *adj.* favourable ; *(propice)* propitious ; *(binevoitor)* kind. *adv.* propitiously.

favorit *sm.* pet.

favoriţi *sm. pl.* (side) whiskers.

favoriza *vt.* to favour.

fazan *sm.* pheasant ; *fig.* dupe.

fază *sf.* phase ; *(la faruri)* beam.

făclie *sf.* torch.

făcut *sn.: parcă e un ~* it seems to be fated. *adj.* made (up) ; *(artificial)* artificial.

făgaş *sn.* rut ; *fig.* routine.

făgădui *vt.* to promise.

făgăduială *sf.* pledge.

făină *sf.* flour ; meal.

făinos *adj.* mealy.

făli *vr.* to brag ; *a se ~ cu* to boast (of).

făptaş *sm.* perpetrator.

făptui *vt.* to commit.

făptură *sf.* creature ; *(trup)* body ; *(fire)* nature.

făraş *sn.* dust pan ; *(pt. sobă)* fire shovel.

fără *prep.* without ; *(minus)* but ; *(cu excepţia)* except(ing) ; *~ ajutorul tău* but for you ; *~ dinţi* toothless ; *~ inimă* callous(ly) ; *~ veste* unawares ; *~voie* involuntary; unwillingly. *conj.* without.

fărîmă *sf.* bit.

fărîmicios *adj.* brittle.

fărîmiţa *vt.* to crumb.

făt *sm.* foetus ; *Făt Frumos* Prince Charming.

făta *vt.* to bring forth.

făţarnic *sm.* hypocrite. *adj.* double-faced.

făţărnicie *sf.* double-dealing.

făţiş *adj.* open ; *(neruşinat)* shameless. *adv.* above board ; *(fără ruşine)* shamelessly.

făuri *vt.* to create.

făuritor *sm.* maker.

febră *sf.* fever ; *~ tifoidă* typhoid.

febril *adj.* feverish. *adv.* feverishly.

februarie *sm.* February.

fecioară *sf.* virgin.

fecior *sm.* boy ; *(fiu)* son ; *~ de bani gata* white-headed boy.

feciorelnic *adj.* maiden(ly).

feciorie *sf.* virginity.

fecund *adj.* fertile ; *fig. şi* prolific.

federal *adj.* federal.

federaţie *sf.* (con)federation.

feerie *adj.* fairy(-like).

feerie *sf.* romance.

fel *sn.* *(cale)* way ; *(tip)* kind ; *(mîncare)* dish ; *(al doilea, al treilea)* course ; *fig.* disposition ; *~ de ~* all kinds *sau* sorts ; *în ~ul acesta* thus ; *la ~* identical(ly).

felcer *sm.* feldsher.

felicita *vt.* to congratulate (smb. on an event, etc.). *vr.* to be gratified ; *(reciproc)* to congratulate each other.

felicitare *sf.* congratulation ; *(carte de vizită)* greeting.

felie *sf.* slice ; *(de carne şi)* cut ; *(de slănină)* rasher.

felinar *sn.* street lamp ; *(de mină)* lantern.

felurit *adj.* sundry, different.

femeie *sf.* woman, *pl.* women ; *(soție)* wife ; ~ *afurisită* shrew.

femeiesc *adj.* womanly ; *(d. sex)* female.

feminin *sn.*, *adj.* feminine.

feminitate *sf.* womanhood.

fenomen *sn.* phenomenon.

fenomenal *adj.* phenomenal. *adv.* remarkably.

ferat *adj.* : *cale* ~*ă* railway.

ferăstrău *sn.* saw.

fercheş *adj.* spruce.

ferchezui *vt.*, *vr.* to dress up.

fereastră *sf.* window ; *(geam și)* window pane ; *(gol)* gap.

fereca *vt.* to lock (up) ; *(a înlănțui)* to chain.

ferfeniță *sf.* tatter(s).

feri *vt.* to shelter ; *a* ~ *de* to keep from. *vi.* : *ferească Dumnezeu!* God forbid! *vr.* to step aside ; *a se* ~ *de* to avoid.

fericire *sf.* happiness ; *din* ~ fortunately.

fericit *adj.* happy ; *(norocos)* lucky ; *(favorabil)* propitious. *adv.* happily.

ferigă *sf.* fern.

ferit *adj.* safe.

ferm *adj.* firm. *adv.* steadfastly.

fermă *sf.* farm ; ~ *de animale* cattle farm ; ~ *de lapte* dairy farm ; ~ *de stat* state farm.

fermeca *vt.* to charm.

fermecat *adj.* bewitched.

fermecător *adj.* enchanting.

fermier *sm.* farmer.

fermitate *sf.* firmness.

fermoar *sn.* zip (fastener).

feroce *adj.* ferocious ; *(nemilos)* grim. *adv.* savagely.

feroviar *sm.* railway worker *sau* man. *adj.* rail(way).

fertil *adj.* fertile.

fertilitate *sf.* fruitfulness.

fervent *adj.* fervent. *adv.* hotly.

festă *sf.* (nasty) trick.

festiv *adj.* festive.

festival *sn.* festival.

festivitate *sf.* solemnity.

fetiş *sn.* fetish.

fetişcană *sf.* flapper.

fetiță *sf.* little girl ; *(fiică)* daughter.

fetru *sn.* felt.

feudal *sm.* feudal lord. *adj.* feudal.

feudalism *sn.* feudalism.

feudă *sf.* feoff.

fi *v aux.* to be. *v mod.* to ~ to; *a urma să.* *vi.* to be, to exist ; *(a se afla)* to be found ; *(a consta)* to consist (in) ; *(a aparține)* to belong (to) ; *(a costa)* to cost ; *este* there is ; *sînt destui* there are (enough) ; *este?* isn't it? *o* ~ maybe ; *a-i fi bine* to feel well ; *e bine așa?* all right? *a fi cît peaci să* to be about to ; *fie ce-o fi* come what may ; *să-ți fie de bine* to your pleasure ; *peior.* serve you right ; *cum îți este?* how are you? are you all right?

fiară *sf.* (wild) beast.

ficat *sm.* liver.

fictiv *adj.* fictitious.

ficțiune *sf.* imagination.

fidea *sf.* vermicelli.

fidel *adj.* faithful. *adv.* loyally.

fidelitate *sf.* fidelity ; *(exactitate)* accuracy.

fie *conj.* : *fie* ... *fie* ... either ... or ...

fiecare *adj.* *(separat)* each ; *(toți)* every ; ~ *față a paginii* either side of the page. *pron.* *(sepa-*

rat) each (one) ; *(toţi)* everybody ; ~ *din ei* each of them ; ~ *dintre doi* either (of the two).

fier *sn.* iron ; *(de călcat şi)* flat iron ; ~ *de plug* ploughshare ; ~ *vechi* scrap iron ; *de ~* (made of) iron.

fierar *sm.* (black)smith, ironsmith.

fierărie *sf.* smith's trade ; *(atelier)* forge ; *(magazin)* ironmonger's shop ; *(fiare)* hardware.

fierbe *vt.* to boil. *vi.* to boil ; *(la foc mic)* to simmer ; *a ~ de minie* to seethe with rage.

fierbinte *adj.* hot ; scorching, burning.

fiere *sf.* gall.

fiert *sn.* boiling. *adj.* boiled ; *fig.* downcast ; ~ *tare* hard boiled.

figura *vi.* to be present.

figurant *sm. teatru* super ; *cinema* extra.

figurantă *sf. (varieteu)* chorus girl ; *(balet)* figurante ; *cinema* extra.

figurat *adj.* figurative.

figură *sf.* face ; *(mutră)* countenance ; *(chip)* image ; *geom., fig.* figure ; *(la cărţi)* face card ; *(la şah)* piece ; *(farsă)* (nasty) trick ; ~ *de stil* figure of speech ; *o ~ istorică* an historical character.

fiică *sf.* daughter.

fiindcă *conj.* because.

fiinţă being ; *(existenţă)* existence ; *(fire)* nature ; *în ~* extant.

filantrop *sm.* philanthropist.

filantropic *adj.* charitable.

filantropie *sf.* philanthropy.

filarmonică *sf.* philharmonic (orchestra).

filatelic *adj.* philatelic.

filatelie *sf.* philately.

filatelist *sm.* stamp collector.

filă *sf.* leaf.

fildeş *sm.* tusk. *sn.* ivory.

filfizon *sm.* coxcomb.

filială *sf.* branch.

film *sn.* film ; *(de lung metraj)* feature film ; *(de scurt metraj)* short ; *(documentar)* documentary ; ~ *în culori* colour film ; ~ *sonor* talking picture.

filma *vt.* to film.

filmare *sf.* shot.

filodormă *sf.* key money.

filolog *sm.* philologist.

filologic *adj.* philological.

filologie *sf.* philology.

filon *sn.* vein.

filozof *sm.* philosopher.

filozofic *adj.* philosophical.

filozofie *sf.* philosophy ; *fig.* difficulty.

filtra *vt.* to filter.

filtru *sn.* filter.

fin *sm.* godson. *adj.* fine ; *(graţios)* slender ; *(ales)* choice ; *(rafinat)* refined. *adv.* finely ; *(subţire)* thinly ; *(delicat)* delicately.

final *sn.* finale ; *(sfîrşit)* end. *adj.* final.

finală *sf.* final(s).

financiar *adj.* financial ; *(fiscal)* fiscal.

finanţa *vt.* to finance.

finanţe *sf. pl.* finance(s).

fine *sn.* end ; *în ~* at last.

fineţe *sf.* fineness ; *(subţirime)* thinness ; *(delicateţe)* delicacy.

finisa *vt.* to finish.

finisaj *sn.* finishing.

finlandez *sm.* Finn. *adj.* Finnish.

finlandeză *sf.* Finn(ish woman);
(limba) Finnish.

fiolă *sf.* ampoule.

fior *sm.* shiver; *(plăcut)* thrill.

fiord *sn.* fjord.

fioros *adj.* terrible; *(sălbatic)*
savage. *adv.* fiercely.

fir *sn.* thread; *(de păr)* hair;
(de sîrmă) wire; *(de iarbă)*
blade; *(grăunte și fig.)* grain;
~ul apei current.

firav *adj.* feeble.

fire *sf.* nature; *din* ~ naturally;
în toată ~a mature.

firesc *adj.* natural.

firește *adv.* (as a matter) of
course, naturally.

firimitură *sf.* crumb; *fig.* bit.

firmament *sn.* firmament.

firmă *sf.* sign; *(întreprindere)*
firm.

fisă *sf.* coin; *(pt. joc)* counter.

fisc *sn.* fisc.

fistic *sm., sn.* pistachio.

fistichiu *adj.* peculiar; crazy.

fisură *sf.* fissure, crack.

fișa *vt.* to card.

fișă *sf.* slip; library card; *el.*
jack; plug.

fișic *sn.* roll (of money).

fișier *sn.* card index; *fig.* refer-
ences.

fit *sn.: a trage la* ~ to play
truant.

fitil *sn.* wick; *fig.* intrigue.

fițuică *sf.* slip (of paper); *(la
școală)* crib; *peior. (ziar)* rag.

fiu *sm.* son.

fix *adj.* fixed; *(constant)* steady;
(neschimbat) unchanged; *(exact)*
sharp. *adv.* fixedly; *(în gol)*
vacantly.

fixa *vt.* to fix; *(a stabili)* to

settle; *(a preciza)* to determine; *(a măsura)* to measure;
(cu privirea) to stare (fixedly)
at. *vr.* to be fixed; *(a se
stabili)* to settle.

fizic *sn.* looks; *(trup)* frame.
adj. physical.

fizică *sf.* physics; ~ *atomică*
nuclear physics.

fizician *sm.* physicist.

fiziologie *sf.* physiology.

fizionomie *sf.* physiognomy.

fîlfîi *vi.* to flutter.

fîn *sn.* hay.

fîneață *sf.* hay field.

fîntînă *sf.* (draw) well; ~ *arte-
ziană* artesian well.

fîsîi *vi.* to fizz.

fîstîci *vr.* to be taken aback.

fîșie *sf.* strip; *(de lumină)*
streak.

fîșîi *vi.* to swish.

fîțîi *vr.* to fidget; *(a se fandosi)*
to put on airs.

flacără *sf.* flame; *în flăcări*
ablaze.

flagel *sn.* scourge.

flagrant *adj.* glaring; *în* ~
delict flagrante delicto.

flamand *sm.* Fleming. *adj.* Flemish.

flamandă *sf.* Flemish woman;
(limba) Flemish.

flamură *sf.* banner.

flanc *sn.* flank.

flanelă *sf.* flannel.

flașnetar *sm.* organ grinder.

flașnetă *sf.* barrel organ.

flata *vt.* to flatter.

flaut *sn.* flute.

flautist *sm.* flute player.

flăcău *sm.* lad; *(holtei)* bachelor.

flămînd *adj.* hungry; *(înfome-
tat)* famished.

flămînzi *vi.* to starve.
fleac *sn.* trifle.
flecar *sm.* windbag. *adj.* talkative.
flecări *vi.* to blab.
flegmatic *adj.* phlegmatic. *adv.* phlegmatically.
flegmă *sf.* phlegm.
fler *sn.* flair.
flexibil *adj.* flexible.
flexiune *sf.* flexion.
flirt *sn.* flirtation.
flirta *vi.* to flirt.
floare *sf.* flower; *(de arbore)* blossom; *(mucegai)* mould; ~ *de cîmp* wild flower; ~ *de colţ* edelweiss; *din flori* born under the rose; *în* ~ in bloom.
florăreasă *sf.* flower girl.
florărie *sf.* flowershop.
floretă *sf.* foil.
florii *sf. pl.* Palm Sunday.
flotă *sf.* fleet.
fluctua *vi.* to fluctuate.
fluctuaţie *sf.* fluctuation.
fluent *adj.* fluent. *adv.* fluently.
fluenţă *sf.* fluency.
fluier *sn.* whistle; *(de păstor)* pipe.
fluiera *vt.* to whistle; *(a huidui)* to hiss. *vi.* to whistle; *(a vîjîi)* to whiz.
fluierat *sn.*, **fluierătură** *sf.* whistle.
fluorescent *adj.* fluorescent.
fluşturatic *sm.* madcap. *adj.* fickle.
flutura *vt.* to wave; *(ameninţător)* to brandish. *vi.* to flutter.
fluture *sm.* butterfly.
fluvial *adj.* river ...
fluviu *sn.* river; *fig.* stream.

flux *sn.* tide; *fig.* wave; ~ *şi reflux* ebb and flow.
foaie *sf.* leaf; *(coală, pînză)* sheet; *(pagină)* page; *pl.* skirt; ~ *de cort* tarpaulin; ~ *volantă* loose leaf.
foaier *sn.* foyer.
foame *sf.* hunger.
foamete *sf.* starvation.
foarfece *sn.* scissors; *(mare)* shears; *(la rac)* claws.
foarte *adv.* very.
fobie *sf.* abhorrence.
foc *sn.* fire; *(vîlvătaie)* blaze; *jur.* arson; *(împuşcătură)* shot; *(tir)* firing; *fig.* passion; *(durere)* sorrow; *(minie)* anger; ~ *(uri) de artificii* fire works; *în* ~*ul luptei* at the height of the battle.
focar *sn.* focus; *med. şi fig.* hotbed.
focă *sf.* seal.
fochist *sm.* stoker.
focos *sn.* fuse. *adj.* ardent.
fofila *vr.* to slink; *fig.* to dodge.
foileton *sn.* feuilleton; *(roman)* serial. *adj.* published serially.
foiletonist *sm.* lampoonist.
foişor *sn.* (watch) tower.
foiţă *sf.* thin paper.
folclor *sn.* folklore.
folcloric *adj.* folk(lore).
folclorist *sm.* folklorist.
folos *sn.* use; *(profit)* profit; *ce* ~ *?* to what purpose? *cu* ~ usefully; *de (mare)* ~ useful; *fără* ~ vainly.
folosi *vt.* to use. *vi.* to be useful. *vr.* to be used; *a se* ~ *de* to take advantage of.
folosinţă, folosire *sf.* utilization.
folositor *adj.* useful.
fond *sn.* *fin.* fund; *fig.* stock;

(caracter) natuŗe; *(bază)* fundamentals; *artă* background; *sport* long distance; *în ~* after all.

fonda *vt.* to found.

fondator *sm.* founder. *adj.* founding.

fonetic *adj.* phonetical.

fonetică *sf.* phonetics.

fonograf *sn.* phonograph.

fontă *sf.* cast iron; *(brută)* pig iron.

for *sn.* forum.

foraj *sn.* drilling.

forestier *adj.* forest(ry); *(de cherestea)* timber.

forfeca *vt.* to cut (with the scissors); *fig.* to shred.

forfecuță *sf.* nail scissors.

forfotă *sf.* agitation.

forfoti *vi.* to bustle; *(a mișuna)* to teem.

forma *vt.* to form; *(a alcătui și)* to make up; *(a educa și)* to train; *(un număr de telefon)* to dial. *vr.* to be moulded; *(a se înființa)* to be set up.

formal *adj.* formal. *adv.* formally; specifically; *(de formă)* perfunctorily.

formalism *sn.* form(alism).

formalitate *sf.* formality.

formare *sf.* forming; *(înființare)* foundation.

format *sn.* size; *(de carte)* format. *adj.* moulded; *(matur)* full-fledged.

formați(un)e *sf.* formation; *(orînduire)* system; *(echipă)* team.

formă *sf. (geometrică* etc.*)* shape; *fig.* form; *(înfățișare)* aspect; *(ceremonie)* form(ality); *gram.* voice; *(calapod)* last; *(mod)* manner; *sport* mettle; *de ~*

perfunctorily; *de ~ pătrată* square.

fomidabil *adj.* formidable. *adv.* wonderfully. *interj.* you don t say so!

formula *vt.* to formulate; *(a exprima)* to couch.

formular *sn.* form.

formulare *sf.* wording.

formulă *sf.* formula.

fort *sn.* fort.

fortăreață *sf.* fortress.

forte *adj.: a se face ~ să* to try hard to, to pledge (oneself) to do. *adv.* forte.

fortifica *vt.* to fortify.

fortificație *sf.* earth *sau* defence works.

forța *vt.* to compel; *(a sparge)* to break open. *vr.* to try hard.

forțat *adj.* forced; *(nesincer)* affected.

forță *sf.* force; *(putere)* power; *(intensitate)* energy; *mil.* (armed) forces; *(~a argumentelor* etc.*)* cogency; *~ de muncă* manpower; *~ majoră* emergency; *de ~* excellent.

fosfor *sn.* phosphorus.

fosforescent *adj.* phosphorescent.

fosilă *sf.* fossil; *fig.* old crock.

fost *sm.* has been. *adj.* former; *(defunct)* late.

foșnet *sn.* rustle, swish.

foșni *vi.* to rustle.

fotă *sf.* peasant skirt.

fotbal *sn.* soccer.

fotbalist *sm.* footballer.

fotogenic *adj.* photogenic.

fotograf *sm.* cameraman; *(la atelier)* photographer.

fotografia *vt.* to photograph. *vr.* to have a photo taken.

fotografic *adj.* photographic.

fotografie *sf.* photo(graph) ; *(artă)* photography.

fotoliu *sn.* armchair ; *teatru (*orchestra)stall ; ~-*pat* chairbed.

fotoreporter *sm.* photographer.

fox(trot) *sn.* fox-trot.

frac *sn.* tail coat.

fractura *vt.* to break.

fractură *sf.* fracture.

fracţie *sf.* faction.

fracţionist *adj.* factional.

fracţiune *sf.* faction.

frag *sm.*, **fragă** *sf.* wild strawberry.

fraged *adj.* tender.

fragil *adj.* brittle, fragile.

fragilitate *sf.* fragility.

fragment *sn.* fragment ; *(pasaj)* excerpt.

fragmenta *vt.* to break up.

fragmentar *adj.* fragmental. *adv.* by bits.

franc *sm. ist.* Frank ; *(monedă)* franc ; *(gologan)* copper. *adj. ist.* Frankish ; *(deschis)* frank. *adv.* frankly.

franca *vt.* to stamp.

francez *sm.* Frenchman ; ~*ii* the French. *adj.* French.

franceză *sf. (limba)* French.

francmason *sm.* freemason.

franctiror *sm.* gunman.

franj *sn.* fringe.

franţuzesc *adj.* French.

franţuzeşte *adv.* French ; in the French style.

franţuzoaică *sf.* French woman.

franzelă *sf.* (long) loaf.

frapa *vt.* to strike.

frapant *adj.* glaring.

frasin *sm.* ash(-tree).

frate *sm.* brother ; *(confrate)* brother, *pl.* brethren ; ~ *de cruce* sworn brother ; ~ *de lapte* foster brother ; ~ *vitreg* step--brother.

fraternitate *sf.* brotherhood.

fraterniza *vt.* to fraternize.

fraudă *sf.* defalcation ; *(înşelăciune)* swindle.

fraudulos *adj.* fraudulent.

frază *sf. gram.* (compound *sau* complex) sentence ; *muz.* phrase.

frazeologic *adj.* idiomatic.

frămînta *vt.* to knead ; *fig.* to worry ; *(a discuta)* to debate ; *a-şi* ~ *creierii* to rack one's brain; *a-şi* ~ *mîinile* to wring one's hands. *vr.* to fret.

frămîntare *sf.* kneading ; *fig.* unrest ; stir ; *frămîntările epocii* the challenges of the time.

frăţesc *adj.* fraternal.

frăţeşte *adv.* fraternally ; equally.

frăţie *sf.* fraternity ; ~ *de arme* brotherhood at arms.

freamăt *sn.* rustling ; *(murmur)* murmur; *(agitaţie)* stir ; *(fior)* thrill.

freca *vt.* to rub ; *(cu peria)* to scrub ; *fig.* to criticize. *vr.* to rub oneself ; to rub one's eyes, etc.

frecare *sf.* friction.

frecuş *sn.* friction ; *fig. şi* disagreement.

frecvent *adj.* frequent. *adv.* often.

frecventa *vt.* to frequent; *(cursuri etc.)* to attend.

frecvenţă *sf.* frequency ; *(participare)* attendance.

fredona *vt.* to hum.

fremăta *vi.* to fret ; *(a foşni)* to rustle.

frenetic *adj.* frantic. *adv.* passionately.

frenezie *sf.* frenzy.

frescă *sf.* fresco; *fig. şi* cross-section.

freză *sf.* haircut; *tehn.* milling machine; *(a dentistului)* drill.

frezor *sm.* milling-machine operator.

frică *sf.* fear; *(panică)* panic; *fără* ~ dauntless(ly).

fricos *sm.* coward. *adj.* cowardly.

fricţiune *sf.* friction.

frig *sn.* cold; *(mare)* frost; *pl.* the ague.

friganea *sf.* sippet.

frigare *sf.* spit; *la* ~ spitted.

frige *vt.* to roast; *(la grătar)* to grill; *(a arde)* to burn. *vi.* to burn; *(a avea febră)* to be feverish. *vr.* to be burnt.

frigid *adj.* frigid.

frigider *sn.* refrigerator, fridge.

frigorifer *sn.* deep freeze. *adj.* refrigerating.

friguros *adj.* cold.

fripta *sf.* hot cockles.

friptură *sf.* roast (meat); ~ *de porc* roast pork; ~ *de vacă* roastbeef.

frişcă *sf.* whip(ped) cream.

frivol *adj.* wanton.

frivolitate *sf.* frivolousness; *(neseriozitate)* shallowness.

friza *vt.* to curl; *fig.* to approach (madness, etc.). *vr.* to curl one's hair.

frizer *sm.* barber.

frizerie *sf.* barber's (shop).

frizură *sf.* haircut.

frîna *vt.* to brake; *fig.* to curb. *vi.* to put on the brake.

frînar *sm.* brakesman.

frînă *sf.* brake; *(la căruţă)* drag; *fig.* hindrance.

frînge *vt.* to break (up); *(mîinile)* to wring. *vr.* to break.

frînghie *sf.* rope.

frînt *adj.* broken; *(obosit)* exhausted.

frîntură *sf.* bit.

frîu *sn.* rein.

front *sn.* front.

frontieră *sf.* frontier.

frontispiciu *sn.* frontispiece; *(la carte)* title page.

fronton *sn.* gable.

fruct *sn.* fruit.

fructărie *sf.* fruiterer's.

fructifer *adj.* fruit(-bearing).

fructifica *vt.* to fructify.

fructuos *adj.* fruitful.

frugal *adj.* frugal.

frumos *sn.* the beautiful. *adj.* beautiful; *(arătos şi)* good-looking. *adv.* beautifully; *(uşurel)* nicely; ~ *îţi şade!* for shame!

frumuseţe *sf.* beauty; *de toată* ~*a* as fine as one could wish.

frumuşel *adj.* pretty. *adv.* gingerly.

fruntaş *sm.* frontranker; *pol.* leader; ~ *a ,vieţii publice* public man; ~ *în producţie* top-ranking worker. *adj.* top-ranking; *(la învăţătură)* proficient.

frunte *sf.* forehead; *fig.* (pick and) flower; ~*a sus!* keep your pecker up!; *de* ~ prominent; *în* ~ *cu* headed by.

frunză *sf.* leaf.

frunzări *vt.* to skim through.

frunziş *sn.* foliage.

frustra *vt.: a* ~ *de* to deprive of.

frustraţie *sf.* frustration.

fudul *adj.* conceited; ~ *de o ureche* hard of hearing. *adv.* haughtily.

fuduli *vr.* to strut; *a se ~ cu* to take pride in.

fudulie *sf.* haughtiness; *fudulii de berbec* lamb fries.

fugar *sm.*, *adj.* fugitive.

fugă *sf.* run; *(evadare)* escape; *fuga* at a run; *din ~* in passing; *în fuga mare* at full speed; *în ~* casually; *pe ~* in a hurry.

fugări *vt.* to chase.

fugi *vi.* to run (away); *(a se grăbi)* to rush (along); *(a se refugia)* to flee; *(cu cineva)* to elope; *a ~ ca din pușcă* to run for one's life; *fugi de-aici!* get along (with you)!

fugitiv *adj.* fleeting.

fuior *sn.* bundle.

fular *sn.* muffler.

fulg *sm.* flake; *pl.* down; *~i de ovăz* porridge; *ca ~ul* as light as a feather.

fulger *sn.* (flash of) lightning; *fig.* flash; *ca ~ul* at lightning speed. *adj.*, *adv.* express.

fulgera *vt.* to thunder; *(cu privirea)* to look daggers at (smb.). *vi.* to flash (with anger, etc.); *fulgeră impers.* it lightens.

fulgerător *adj.* flashing. *adv.* at lightning speed.

fulgui *vi. impers.* to snow lightly.

fum *sn.* smoke; *(într-o sobă)* flue; *pl. fig.* conceit.

fuma *vt.*, *vi.* to smoke.

fumat *sn.* smoking; *~ul oprit* no smoking.

fumător *sm.* smoker.

fumega *vi.* to smoke.

fumoar *sn.* smoking room.

fumuriu *adj.* dim.

funciar *adj.* land(ed); *(fundamental)* fundamental.

funcție *sf.* function; *~ de* varying with; *în ~ de* in accordance with, in terms of ...

funcționa *vi.* to work; *a nu ~* to be out of order.

funcționar *sm.* office worker; *(înalt)* official; *~ public* civil servant.

funcționare *sf.* work(ing).

funcțiune *sf.* function(ing).

fund *sn.* bottom; *(spate și)* back(side); *(de lemn)* trencher; *(la pantaloni)* seat; *din ~*, *în ~* (at the) back; *fără ~* bottomless.

fundal *sn.* background.

fundament *sn.* foundation.

fundamenta *vt.* to ground.

fundamental *adj.* basic.

fundaș *sm.* (full) back.

fundație *sf.* foundation.

fundă *sf.* bow.

fundătură *sf.* dead end.

funebru *adj.* funereal.

funeralii *sn. pl.* obsequies.

funerar *adj.* funeral.

funest *adj.* ill-fated.

funicular *sn.* rope-way.

funie *sf.* rope.

funingine *sf.* soot.

fura *vt.* to steal; *(a șterpeli)* to filch; *(o persoană)* to kidnap; *(a delapida)* to embezzle; *m-a furat somnul* I fell asleep; *îți fură ochii* it dazzles one. *vi.* to steal.

furaj *sn.* fodder.

furat *sn.* stealing; *de ~* stolen; *pe ~e* off and on.

furcă *sf.* (pitch)fork; *(de tors)* distaff; *(la telefon)* cradle.

furculiță *sf.* fork.

furie *sf.* fury; *(nebunie)* madness.

furios *adj.* furious. *adv.* angrily.
furiş *adj.* stealthy. *adv.:* *pe* ~
surreptitiously.
furişa *vr.* to slink (in *sau* away).
furnal *sn.* furnace; ~ *înalt*
blast furnace.
furnica *vt.* to tingle. *vi.* to
teem (with).
furnicar *sm.* *(animal)* ant-eater.
sn. ant-hill; *fig.* throng.
furnică *sf.* ant.
furnicătură *sf.* itch.
furnituri *sf.. pl.* supplies; *(de
croitor)* furnishings.
furniza *vt.* to supply.
furnizor *sm.* purveyor; *pl.*
trades folk *sau* people.

furori *sf. pl.:* *a face* ~ to be
quite a sensation.
fursecuri *sn. pl.* fancy cakes.
furt *sn.* theft; *(mărunt)* larceny; *(prin efracţie)* burglary.
furtişag *sn.* filching.
furtun *sn.* (water) hose.
furtună *sf.* (thunder) storm;
(vînt) gale.
furtunos *adj.* tempestuous.
furuncul *sn.* boil.
fus *sn.* spindle; ~ *orar* meantime
zone.
fustă *sf.* skirt; *(jupon)* petticoat.
fuziona *vi.* to merge.
fuziune *sf.* fusion; *fig.* merging.

G

gabardină *sf.* gaberdine.
gabarit *sn.* gauge.
gafă *sf.* blunder.
gaică *sf.* (back) strap.
gaiţă *sf.* jay(bird).
gaj *sn.* pledge; *pl. (joc)* forfeit(s).
gal *sm.* Gaul.
galant *adj.* gallant; *(generos)*
generous.
galantar *sn.* shop-window.
galanterie *sf.* gallantry; *(prăvălie)* haberdashery; *(de damă)*
hosiery.
galanton *adj.* large-handed.
gală *sf.* gala; *de* ~ festive.
galben *sm. ist.* ducat. *sn. (culoare)* yellow. *adj.* yellow; *(palid)* pale; *(hepatic)* jaundiced;
(blond) fair.

galerie *sf.* gallery; *(la sport* etc.*)*
supporters; *(la sobă)* fireguard.
galeş *adj.* loving. *adv.* languidly.
galon *sn.* braid; *pl.* stripes.
galop *sn.* gallop; *în* ~ at a
gallop.
galopa *vi.* to gallop.
galoş *sm.* galosh.
gamă *sf.* scale, gamut; *fig. şi*
range.
gambetă *sf.* pot hat.
gamelă *sf.* mess kettle.
gang *sn.* passage.
gangster *sm.* gangster.
gara *vt.* to garage.
garafă *sf.* carafe.
garaj *sn.* garage.
garanta *vt., vi.* to guarantee.
garantat *adj.* sure, vouchsafed

garanţie *sf.* guarantee; *(gaj şi)* collateral; *(cauţiune)* bail.
gară *sf.* (railway) station.
gard *sn.* fence; *(zid)* wall; *(viu)* hedge; *(uluci)* paling; *sport* hurdle.
gardă *sf.* guard; *de ∼* on duty; *în ∼* on guard.
garderob *sn.* wardrobe.
garderobă *sf.* cloakroom; *(haine)* wardrobe.
gardian *sm.* guard(ian); *(poliţist)* policeman.
garnitură *sf.* *(de unelte* etc.*)* set; *(culinară)* garnish(ing); *(podoabe)* trimmings; *c.f.* train; *tehn.* fittings; *∼ de mobilă* furniture set.
garoafă *sf.* carnation.
garsonieră *sf.* one-room *sau* studio flat.
gata *adj., adv.* ready; *de ∼* ready-made, off the hook.
gater *sn.* frame saw.
gaură *sf.* hole; *(loc gol)* gap; *gaura cheii* keyhole.
gaz *sn.* gas; *med.* wind; *text.* gauze; *(petrol)* kerosene.
gazdă *sf.* host; *(femeie)* hostess.
gazetar *sm.* journalist.
gazetă *sf.* (news)paper; *∼ de perete* wall gazette.
gazetăresc *adj.* journalistic.
gazetărie *sf.* journalism.
gazon *sn.* sod.
gazos *adj.* gaseous.
găină *sf.* hen.
găinărie *sf.* pilfering.
gălăgie *sf.* noise; *(scandal)* racket.
gălăgios *adj.* noisy.
gălbeneală *sf.* pallor.
gălbenele *sf. pl.* marigold.
gălbenuş *sn.* yolk of (an) egg.

gălbui *adj.* yellowish.
găleată *sf.* pail.
găluşcă *sf.* dumpling; *(de carne şi)* meat ball.
gămălie *sf.* (pin) head.
găoace *sf.* (egg) shell.
gărgăriţă *sf.* ladybird.
gărgăun *sm.* hornet; *pl. fig.* maggots.
găsi *vt.* to find (out); *(a gîndi)* to consider; *(a întîmpina)* to meet with; *fig.* to come upon smb.; *bine te-am ∼t* I am glad to see you well. *vr.* to lie; *(a se pomeni)* to find oneself; *(a fi disponibil)* to be found; *se găseşte destul* there is enough; *de ∼t* available.
găteală *sf.* ornament.
găti *vt.* to cook; *(a îmbrăca)* to trim; *(a termina)* to finish. *vi.* to cook. *vr.* to get ready; to dress (up).
gătit *sn.* cooking. *adj.* trimmed.
găunos *adj.* hollow.
găuri *vt.* to bore (holes into); *(a perfora)* to punch. *vr.* to be torn *sau* pierced.
găzdui *vt.* to house; *fig.* to play host to.
găzduire *sf.* accommodation.
geam *sn.* window (pane); *pe ∼* at the window; out of the window.
geamandură *sf.* buoy.
geamantan *sn.* suitcase; *(cufăr)* trunk.
geamăn *sm.* twin brother. *adj.* twin.
geamăt *sn.* groan.
geamgiu *sm.* glazier.
geană *sf.* eyelash; *(de lumină)* streak.

geantă *sf.* bag ; *(de damă și)* handbag ; *(servietă și)* porto- folio ; *auto.* rim ; *pe ~ fig.* on the rocks.

gelatină *sf.* gelatine.

gelos *adj.* jealous (of smb.) ; envious (of smb.).

gelozie *sf.* jealousy.

gem *sm.* jam.

geme *vi.* to groan ; *a ~ de lume* etc. to be packed with people, etc.

gen *sn.* kind, sort ; *(manieră)* manner ; *gram.* gender ; *(ra- mură)* genre ; *~ul dramatic* the drama ; *de ~* genre ; *în ~ul ăsta* like this. *prep.* like *(și ca sufix) : în ~ul Watteau* Watteau-like.

genealogie *sf.* genealogical table.

genera *vt.* to generate.

general *sm., sn.* general ; *în ~* as a rule. *adj.* general ; *(șef)* chief.

generaliza *vt., vi.* to generalize. *vr.* to become general.

generator *sn.* generator. *adj.* generating.

generație *sf.* generation ; lifetime.

genere *sn. :* în ~ generally, roughly speaking.

generos *adj.* generous. *adv.* libe- rally.

generozitate *sf.* generosity.

geneză *sf.* creation.

genial *adj.* brilliant. *adv.* brilli- antly.

genitiv *sn.* genitive.

geniu *sn.* genius ; *mil.* engineers.

gentil *adj.* kind ; *(drăguț)* nice, gentle. *adv.* courteously.

gentilețe *sf.* kindness.

genunchi *sm.* knee ; *în ~* on one's bended knees.

geograf *sm.* geographer.

geografic *adj.* geographical.

geografie *sf.* geography.

geolog *sm.* geologist.

geologie *sf.* geology.

geometrie *sf.* geometry.

ger *sn.* frost.

german *sm., adj.,* **germană** *sf., adj.* German.

germanic *adj.* Germanic.

germen *sm.* embryo.

gerunziu *sn.* present participle.

gest *sn.* gesture.

gesticula *vi.* to gesticulate.

gestionar *sm.* administrator.

get *sm.* Geta.

get-beget *adj.* true-born.

gheară *sf.* claw ; *pl.* clutches.

gheată *sf.* boot ; *(pantof)* shoe.

gheață *sf.* ice ; *(grindină)* hail ; *la ~* iced ; *ca gheața* icy.

gheb *sn.* hump.

gheizer *sn.* geyser.

ghem *sn.* ball.

ghemotoc *sn.* crumpled paper.

ghemui *vt.* to roll up. *vr.* to crouch.

ghepard *sm.* sheetah.

gheretă *sf.* lodge ; *mil.* sentry box ; *com.* booth.

gherghină *sf.* dahlia.

ghes *sn. : a da ~ (cu dat.)* to goad *(cu ac.).*

ghetou *sn.* ghetto.

ghetre *sf. pl.* gaiters.

ghețar *sm.* glacier ; *(aisberg)* iceberg. *sn.* ice box.

ghețărie *sf.* ice house.

ghețuș *sn.* ice.

ghici *vt.* to guess ; *(a prevedea)* to forecast ; *(gîndurile etc.)* to read. *vi.* to tell fortunes. *vr.* to be sensed.

ghicit *sn.* guessing ; *pe* ~*e* by guesswork.

ghicitoare *sf.* riddle ; *(prezicătoare)* fortune teller.

ghid *sm.* guide. *sn.* guide(-book).

ghida *vt.* to guide. *vr.* to be guided (by smth.).

ghidon *sn.* handlebar.

ghiduş *sm.* wag. *adj.* merry.

ghiftui *vt.* to cloy. *vr.* to gormandize.

ghilimele *sf. pl.* inverted commas, quotation marks.

ghilotină *sf.* guillotine.

ghimpat *adj.* spiked ; *(d. sîrmă)* barbed.

ghimpe *sm.* thorn ; *fig. şi* sting ; *zool.* spine ; *bot.* thistle.

ghindă *sf.* acorn.

ghinion *sn.* bad luck.

ghinionist *sm.* unlucky man.

ghioagă *sf.* mace.

ghiocel *sm.* snowdrop.

ghiol *sn.* lake.

ghiont *sn.* nudge.

ghionti *vt.* to nudge.

ghiozdan *sn.* satchel.

ghips *sn.* plaster (of Paris), gypsum.

ghirlandă *sf.* garland.

ghişeu *sn.* window ; *(casă)* pay-office.

ghitară *sf.* guitar ; *(havaiană)* ukulele.

ghiulea *sf.* cannon ball.

ghiveci *sn.* flower pot ; *(mîncare şi fig.)* hotchpotch.

gigant *sm.* colossus.

gigantic *adj.* mammoth.

gimnastică *sf.* gym(nastics).

gimnaziu *sn.* gymnasium.

gin *sn.* gin.

ginecologie *sf.* gynaecology.

ginere *sm.* son-in-law.

gingaş *adj.* tender; *(dulce)* sweet; *(plăpînd)* frail ; *(dificil)* ticklish. *adv.* gingerly, delicately.

gingăşie *sf.* gentleness.

gingie *sf.* gum.

gir *sn.* endorsement.

gira *vt.* to guarantee ; *(a suplini)* to manage.

girafă *sf.* giraffe.

giugiuli *vt.* to pet. *vr.* to bill and coo.

giumbuşlue *sn.* antic.

giuvaer *sn.* jewel ; *şi fig.* gem.

giuvaergiu *sm.* jeweller.

gîdila *vt.* tickle. *vr.* to be ticklish.

gîdilătură *sf.* tickling.

gîfîi *vi.* to pant.

gîgîi *vi.* to gaggle.

gîlceavă *sf.* discord.

gîlcevitor *adj.* quarrelsome.

gîlgîi *vi.* to gurgle.

gînd *sn.* thought ; *(idee)* idea ; *(intenţie)* intention ; *(părere)* opinion ; *(gîndire)* thinking ; *pl. (griji)* worry ; *un* ~ *bun* a fine thought; a brainwave; ~*uri negre* low spirits; *în* ~ in one's mind ; *nici* ~ nothing of the sort.

gîndac *sm.* beetle ; *(de bucătărie)* cockroach.

gîndi *vt.* to think. *vi., vr.* to think (over smth.) ; *(a medita)* to ponder (over smth.) ; *a se* ~ *să* to intend to ; *a se* ~ *bine* to think hard.

gîndire *sf.* thinking ; *(gînd)* thought.

gînditor *sm.* thinker. *adj.* pensive.

gînganie *sf.* insect.

gîngav *adj.* stammering.

gînguri *vi.* to babble ; *(d. porumbei)* to coo.

gînsac sm. gander.
gîrbov(it) adj. stooping.
gîrbovi vr. to stoop.
gîrlă sf. stream. adv. galore.
gîscan sm. gander.
gîscar sm. gooseherd.
gîscă sf. goose, pl. geese.
gîsculiţă sf. gosling ; fig. silly girl.
gît sn. neck; (beregată) throat; (duşcă) draught ; pînă în ~ up to the teeth.
gîtlej sn. throat.
gîtui vt. to throttle.
gîză sf. mite.
glaciar adj. glacial.
gladiolă sf. gladiolus.
glandă sf. gland.
glas sn. voice; fig. sound.
glaspapir sn. emery paper.
glastră sf. flower pot.
glasvand sn. French window.
glazură sf. glaze.
glăsui vi. to say.
gleznă sf. ankle.
glicerină sf. glycerine.
glisant adj. gliding.
gloabă sf. jade.
gloată sf. mob.
glob sn. globe.
global adj. aggregate.
globulă sf. (blood) corpuscle.
glod sn. mud.
glonţ sn. bullet. adv. plum.
glorie sf. glory.
glorios adj. glorious.
glosar sn. glossary.
glugă sf. hood.
glumă sf. joke ; (farsă) practical joke ; ~ răsuflată stale joke ; în ~ joking(ly) ; nu ~ regular(ly).
glumeţ sm. wit. adj. joking; witty.

glumi vi. to joke ; fig. to trifle.
goană sf. race ; (urmărire) chase ; (viteză) speed.
gofra vt. to goffer.
gogoaşă sf. doughnut ; (cocon) cocoon; pl. shaves.
gogoman sm. fool. adj. foolish.
gogoriţă sf. bugbear.
gogoşar sm. bell pepper.
gol sn. gap ; (vid) vacuum ; (într-un text) blank; sport goal ; în ~ idly. adj. naked, nude ; (pustiu) desert ; (descoperit) bare ; (fără conţinut) empty.
golan sm. street arab ; (ticălos) ruffian ; (mitocan) cad.
golănie sf. caddishness.
golănime sf. riff-raff.
golf sn. geogr. gulf ; sport golf.
goli vt. to empty. vr. to grow empty.
goliciune sf. nakedness ; fig. shallowness.
golire sf. evacuation.
gologan sm. copper (coin).
gondolă sf. gondola.
gong sn. gong.
goni vt. to drive (away) ; fig. to banish. vi. to race.
gorilă sf. gorilla.
gornist sm. bugler.
gospodar sm. householder ; (administrator) good manager. adj. thrifty.
gospodăresc adj. household ; (econ.) thrifty.
gospodări vt. to manage. vi. to manage the house.
gospodărie sf. farm(stead) ; (casă) household ; (menaj) housekeeping ; ~ agricolă de stat state farm ; ~ chibzuită self management ; ~ comunală communal equipment.

gospodărire sf. administration.
gospodină sf. housewife; (menajeră) housekeeper.
got sm. Goth.
gotic adj. Gothic.
grabă sf. hurry; în ~ in a hurry; mai de ~ rather.
grabnic adj. speedy; (urgent) urgent; ~ă însănătoşire speedy recovery. adv. speedily, urgently.
grad sn. degree; (mil.) rank; 20 ~e Celsius 20 degrees centigrade.
grada vt. to graduate.
gradat sm. non-com, NCO. adj. graduated; (treptat) gradual. adv. gradually.
grafic sn. graph; (orar) time-table. adj. graphic.
grafică sf. graphics.
grafician sm. drawer.
grai sn. speech; (limbă) language; ~ popular vernacular; prin viu ~ by word of mouth.
grajd sn. stable; fig. pigsty.
gram sn. gram.
gramatical adj. grammatical. adv. grammatically.
gramatică sf. grammar(-book).
grandios adj. grand(iose). adv. impressively.
grangur sm. (ornit.) oriole; fig. toff.
granit sn. granite; fig. monolith.
graniţă sf. border; fig. confines; de ~ frontier.
grapă sf. harrow.
gras adj. fat(ty); (d. mîncare şi) rich; (unsuros şi) greasy. adv. well, liberally, much.
gratie sf. bar.
gratificaţie sf. gratuity.

gratis adv. gratuitously.
gratuit adj. free (of charge); (nejustificat) groundless. adv. gratis; (nejustificat) groundlessly.
gratuitate sf. gratuitousness.
graţia vt. to pardon.
graţie sf. grace(fulness); de ~ deadly. prep. thanks to.
graţiere sf. pardon.
graţios adj. graceful. adv. gracefully.
graur sm. starling.
grav adj. serious; (sever) stern. muz. deep, low. adv. gravely.
grava vt. to engrave.
gravidă sf. pregnant woman. adj. with child.
graviditate sf. pregnancy.
gravitate sf. seriousness; (severitate) solemnity.
gravor sm. engraver.
gravură sf. engraving; (în lemn) woodcut; (cu apă tare) etching.
grăbi vt. to quicken up; (pe cineva) to hurry; a ~ pasul to make haste. vr. to hurry (up).
grăbit adj. hurried; (pripit) rash. adv. in a hurry.
grădinar sm. gardener.
grădină sf. garden; (de zarzavat) kitchen garden; (livadă) orchard; (publică) park.
grădiniţă sf. (de copii) kindergarten.
grăi vt. to say. vi. to speak.
grăitor adj. telling. adv. eloquently.
grăjdar sm. stable man; mil. farrier.

grămadă *sf.* pile ; *(morman)* cluster ; *(mulţime)* crowd ; *pl.* lots. *adv.* in a lump.

grănicer *sm.* frontier guard.

grăpa *vt., vi.* to harrow.

grăsime *sf.* fat ; *(corpolenţă)* burliness.

grăsuţ *adj.* plump.

grătar *sn.* grill ; *(în sobă)* grate ; *la* ~ grilled.

grăunte *sm.* grain.

greacă *sf.* Greek.

greaţă *sf.* nausea ; *(scîrbă)* disgust.

grebla *vt., vi.* to rake.

greblă *sf.* rake.

grec *sm., adj.* Greek ; *ist.* Hellene.

grecesc *adj.* Greek ; *ist.* Hellenic.

greceşte *adv.* Greek.

grecoaică *sf.* Greek woman.

greco-catolic *sm., adj.* Greek-Catholic.

greco-roman *adj.* Gr(a)eco-Roman.

grefă *sf. med.* grafting ; *jur.* court clerk's office.

grefier *sm.* court clerk.

greier *sm.* cricket.

grenadă *sf.* (hand) grenade.

greoi *adj.* heavy ; *(neîndemî-natic)* clumsy ; *(d. cap)* dull. *adv.* heavily ; clumsily.

grep(frut) *sn.* grapefruit.

gresa *vt.* to grease.

gresie *sf.* gritstone ; *(de ascu-ţit)* whetstone.

greş *sn.* failure ; *fără* ~ faultlessly ; *(negreşit)* without fail.

greşeală *sf.* mistake ; *(vină)* fault ; *(lipsă)* shortcoming ; ~ *boacănă* glaring mistake ; ~ *de calcul* miscalculation ; ~ *de ortografie* misspelling ; ~ *de*

tipar misprint ; *din* ~ by mistake, erroneously ; *fără* ~ faultless(ly).

greşi *vt.* to mistake ; *(ţinta)* to miss ; *(drumul)* to lose one's way ; *a* ~ *adresa* to go to the wrong house, man, etc. *vi.* to be mistaken ; *(a cădea în gre-şeală)* to err, to trespass ; *(a fi vinovat)* to be guilty ; *(a nu nimeri)* to be wide of the mark.

greşit *adj.* mistaken ; *(nedrept)* unjust. *adv.* wrongly.

greţos *adj.* fulsome ; *(dezgustă-tor)* disgusting.

greu *sn.* weight ; *fig.* brunt ; *cu* ~ at great pains ; *din* ~ hard. *adj.* heavy ; *(greoi)* clumsy ; *(apăsător)* burdensome ; *(dificil)* hard ; *(obositor)* tiresome ; *(complicat)* involved ; *(as-pru)* severe ; *(d. somn şi)* deep ; ~ *de mulţumit* hard to please. *adv.* heavily ; *(difi-cil)* with difficulty ; *(abia)* scarcely.

greutate *sf.* weight ; *(încărcătu-ră)* load ; *(povară)* burden ; *(dificultate)* hardness ; *(influ-enţă şi)* influence ; *greutăţi financiare sau pecuniare* straitened circumstances ; *cu* ~ important, weighty ; with difficulty ; *fără (nici o)* ~ easily.

grevă *sf.* strike ; *greva foamei* hunger strike.

grevist *sm.* striker. *adj.* strike.

gri *sn., adj.* grey.

grijă *sf.* care ; *(îngrijorare)* concern, worry ; *cu* ~ careful(ly) ; *fără* ~ careless(ly) ; *prin grija cuiva* thanks to smb.

grijuliu *adj.* careful.

grilaj *sf.* lattice work.

grindă *sf.* girder.

grindină *sf.* hail.

gripă *sf.* flu.

griș *sn.* semolina.

grînar *sn.* granary.

grîne *sf. pl.* grain(s).

grîu *sn.* wheat; ~ *de toamnă* winter wheat; *de* ~ wheaten.

groapă *sf.* pit; *(mormînt)* grave.

groază *sf.* horror; *o* ~ *de* no end of.

groaznic *adj.* awful. *adv.* frightfully.

grohăi *vi.* to grunt.

gropar *sm.* gravedigger.

gropiță *sf.* dimple.

gros *sn.* bulk; *(închisoare)* stone jug. *adj.* thick; *(gras)* fat; *(dens)* dense; ~ *la pungă* rich; *din* ~ abundantly. *adv.* thickly; warmly.

grosime *sf.* thickness; *(lățime)* breadth; *(adîncime)* depth.

grosolan *adj.* gross; *(nepoliticos)* rude; *(vulgar)* coarse; *(d. greșeală)* glaring. *adv.* coarsely.

grosolănie *sf.* rudeness.

grotă *sf.* grotto.

grotesc *sn., adj.* grotesque.

grozav *sm.*: *a face pe* ~*ul* to ride the high horse. *adj.* terrible; *(uriaș)* colossal. *adv.* extremely; *(foarte)* awfully.

grozăvie *sf.* horror; *(minune)* marvel.

grumaz *sm.* neck.

grup *sn.* group; *(pîlc)* cluster.

grupa *vt., vr.* to group (together), to rally.

grupare *sf.* group(ing).

grupă *sf.* group.

guașă *sf.* gouache.

gudura *vr.* to fawn (upon smb.).

guița *vi.* to squeak.

guler *sn.* collar; *(la bere)* head.

gulie *sf.* kohlrabi.

gumă *sf.* rubber; *(de șters)* india rubber ; ~ *arabică* gum arabic.

gunguri *vt., vi.* to babble; *(d. porumbei)* to coo.

gunoi *sn.* garbage.

gunoier *sm.* scavenger.

guraliv *adj.* talkative.

gură *sf.* mouth; *(buze)* lips; *(îmbucătură)* mouthful; *tehn. și* muzzle; *(deschizătură)* opening; *(vorbire)* gab(b)le; *(scandal)* row; *(sărutare)* kiss; *(de băutură)* sip; *gura leului* snap dragon; *gura lumii* the talk of the town; ~ *de apă* hydrant; ~ *rea* idle tongue; *bun de* ~ with a glib tongue; *cu jumătate de* ~ half-heartedly; reluctantly; *de-ale gurii* victuals; *în gura mare* from the housetops; *la gura sobei* at the fire side.

gură-cască *sm.* dupe; *(pierde-vară)* lounger, loafer.

gurmand *sm.* glutton. *adj.* greedy.

gust *sn.* taste; *(savoare)* relish; *(aromă)* flavour; *(poftă)* desire; *cu* ~ tasteful(ly); *fără* ~ tasteless; *de prost* ~ in bad taste; *pe* ~*ul meu* to my liking.

gusta *vt.* to taste; *(a sorbi)* to sip; *(a savura)* to enjoy; *(a trece prin)* to experience.

gustare *sf.* snack; *(de dimineață)* breakfast.

gustat *adj.* appreciated.

gustos *adj.* tasteful.

guşat *sm.* man with a goitre. *adj.* goitrous.

guşă *sf.* double chin; *med.* goitre; *ornit.* crop.

gutui *sm.* quince tree.

gutuie *sf.* quince.

gutural *sn.* cold (in the head), coryza.

guvern *sn.* government.

guverna *vt.* to govern. *vi.* to rule.

guvernamental *adj.* government.

guvernantă *sf.* governess.

guvernator *sm.* governor.

guvernămînt *sn.* government.

guzgan *sm.* rat.

H

ha *interj.* ha!

habar *sn.* idea; *(grijă)* care.

hac *sn.: a veni de ~ cuiva* to get the better of smb.

hai(de) *interj.* come on!

haiduc *sm.* outlaw.

haiducesc *adj.* of outlawry.

haiducie *sf.* outlawry.

haihui *adv.* aimlessly.

haimana *sf.* vagabond. *adv.* roamingly.

hain *adj.* heinous; *(aspru)* cruel. *adv.* cruelly.

haină *sf.* coat; *pl.* clothes; *(sacou)* jacket; *(palton)* top-coat; *haine de seară* evening dress; *~ de ploaie* mac(kin-tosh); *haine civile* mufti; *~ (de) gata* reach-me-downs.

hait *interj.* well (I never)!.

haită *sf.* pack.

hal *sn.* bad plight.

halal *interj.* good for you! *peior.* serve you right!

halat *sn.* overall; *(de casă)* dressing gown; *(de baie)* bath-gown.

hală *sf.* hall; *(piață)* market (place).

halbă *sf.* mug; *(cantitate)* pint.

haltă *sf.* c.f. flag station; *(oprire)* halt; *~ de ajustare mil.* bait.

haltere *sf. pl.* dumb bells; *(ca sport)* weight lifting.

halterofil *sm.* weight lifter.

halucinație *sf.* hallucination.

halva *sf.* khalva.

ham *sn.* harness. *interj.* bow-wow!

hamac *sn.* hammock.

hamal *sm.* porter.

hambar *sn.* barn.

hamei *sn.* hops.

hamsie *sf.* anchovy.

han *sm. ist.* khan. *sn.* inn.

handbal *sn.* handball.

handicap *sn.* handicap; *fig.* hin-drance.

handicapa *vt.* to handicap.

hangar *sn.* hangar.

hangiță *sf.*, **hangiu** *sm.* innkeep-er.

haos *sn.* chaos.

haotic *adj.* chaotic. *adv.* in a jumble.

hap *sn.* pill.

hapcă *sf.: cu hapca* forcibly.

hapeiu *interj.* at-cha !

hapsîn *adj.* greedy ; *(hain)* hard-
-hearted.

har *sn.* gift ; *rel.* grace.

harababură *sf.* jumble ; *(zarvă)*
hullabaloo.

haram *sn.* nag ; *de* ~ ill-got.

harapnic *sn.* whip.

harcea-parcea *adv.: a face* ~
to play ducks and drakes
with.

hardughie *sf.* ramshackle house.

harem *sn.* harem.

harnaşament *sn.* harness.

harnic *adj.* hardworking. *adv.*
industriously.

harpă *sf.* harp.

harpistă *sf.* harpplayer.

harpon *sn.* harpoon.

hartă *sf.* map ; *mar. şi* chart.

harţă *sf.* quarrel.

hat *sn.* ba(u)lk.

hatîr *sn.* favour ; *de* ~*ul meu*
for my sake.

havană *sf.* cigar.

havuz *sn.* artesian fountain.

haz *sn.* humour ; *(veselie)* sport ;
(farmec) charm ; *fără* ~ stale.

hazard *sn.* hazard, chance.

hazardat *adj.* venturesome.

hazliu *adj.* funny ; *(spiritual)*
witty.

hăis *interj.* right !

hăitui *vt.* to hunt.

hămesit *adj.* starving.

hărăzi *vt.* to bestow (upon smb.) ;
(a sorti) to destine.

hărmălaie *sf.* hubbub ; *(învălmăşeală)* harum-scarum.

hărnicie *sf.* diligence.

hărţui *vt.* to harass.

hărţuială *sf.* harassing. *mil.* attrition.

hăt *adv.:* ~ *departe* very far.

hăţ *sn.* bridle ; *pl.* reins.

hăţiş *sn.* thicket.

hău *sn.* chasm.

hectar *sn.* hectare.

hei *interj.* heigh !

hemoragie *sf.* h(a)emorrhage.

hemoroizi *sm. pl.* piles.

henţ *sn.* hands.

herghelie *sf.* stud.

hering *sm.* herring.

hermină *sf.* hermine.

hernie *sf.* rupture.

heruvim *sm.* cherub.

hexametru *sm.* hexameter.

hiat *sn.* hiatus.

hiberna *vi.* to hibernate.

hibrid *sm., adj.* hybrid.

hidos *adj.* hideous.

hidoşenie *sf.* repulsiveness.

hidraulic *adj.* hydraulic.

hidră *sf.* hydra.

hidroavion *sn.* hydroplane.

hidrobuz *sn.* water-bus.

hidrogen *sn.* hydrogen.

hienă *sf.* hyena ; *fig.* vulture.

hieroglifă *sf.* hieroglyph.

himeră *sf.* chimera.

himeric *adj.* chimeric.

hindus *sm., adj.* Hindoo.

hindusă *sf.* Hindoo ; *(limba)*
Hindi.

hingher *sm.* knacker.

hiperbolă *sf.* hyperbole.

hipic *adj.* horse...

hipnotiza *vt.* to hypnotize.

hipodrom *sn.* race course.

hipopotam *sm.* hippo(potamus).

hirsut *adj.* hirsute ; *fig.* uncouth.

hitlerism *sn.* Hitlerism.

hitlerist *sm.* Hitlerite. *adj.* Hit-
ler's, Hitlerite.

hîd *adj.* ugly.

hîrb *sn.* crock.

hîrcă sf. skull; (fig.) harridan.

hîrciog sm. hamster.

hîrdău sn. tub.

hîrîi vi. to rattle.

hîrîit sn. rattle. adj. rattling.

hîrjoni vr. to frisk.

hîrleţ sn. spade.

hîrtie sf. paper; (bancnotă) (bank)note; ~ igienică toilet paper.

hîrţoage sf. pl. old papers.

hlamidă sf. mantle.

ho interj. stop !

hoardă sf. horde.

hochei sn. (ice) hockey; (pe iarbă) field hockey.

hodorogit adj. broken; fig. decrepit.

hodoronc tronc adv. unawares.

hohot sn. (de rîs) guffaw; (de plîns) burst of tears.

hohoti vi. (de rîs) to guffaw; (de plîns) to sob.

hoinar sm. tramp. adj. transient.

hoinări vi. to roam.

hoit sn. corpse; (de animal) carcase.

hol sn. (entrance) hall.

holba vt. to open wide. vr. to stare.

holbat adj. starting (out of their sockets); (d. cineva) with bulging eyes.

holdă sf. crop.

holeră sf. cholera.

holtei sm. bachelor.

homar sm. lobster.

homeric adj. Homeric.

homosexual sm., adj. homosexual, queer.

homosexualitate sf. homoism.

hop sn. jerk; fig. obstacle. interj. hop !

horă sf. hora, Romanian round dance.

horcăi vi. to snort.

horcăit sn. (death) rattle.

hormon sm. hormone.

horn sn. chimney.

horoscop sn. horoscope.

horticultor sm. horticulturist.

horticultură sf. horticulture.

hotar sn. boundary.

hotărî vt. to decide; (a convinge) to persuade; (a stabili) to settle. vi., vr. to decide.

hotărîre sf. decision; (scrisă şi) resolution; (siguranţă) resolve; (ordin) decree; cu ~ firmly.

hotărît adj. definite; (decis) resolute; (stabilit) settled; (sigur) sure; (ferm) firm. adv. definitely, positively; (ferm) resolutely.

hotărîtor adj. decisive.

hotel sn. hotel; (pt. automobilişti) motel.

hoţ sm. thief; (de buzunar) pickpocket; (spărgător) burglar; fig. rogue.

hoţie sf. theft; (escrocherie) swindle.

hrană sf. food; (pt. vite) forage; (întreţinere) upkeep; ~ sufletească spiritual assets.

hrăni vt. to feed; fig. to harbour; (a întreţine) to provide for. vi. to feed (on something); a se ~ cu iluzii to indulge in illusions.

hrănitor adj. nourishing.

hrăpăreţ adj. grasping.

hrean sm. horse radish.

hrişcă sf. buckwheat.

huhurez sm. eagle owl; fig. noctambulist.

huidui *vt.* to boo.
huligan *sm.* hooligan.
huliganism *sn.* hooliganism.
hulpav *adj.* ravenous. *adv.* ravenously.
humă *sf.* clay.

hun *sm.* Hun.
hurui *vi.* to rumble.
husă *sf.* (slip) cover.
huțul *sm.* Guzul.
huzur *sn.* (life of) leisure.
huzuri *vi.* to live in clover.

I

ia *interj.* come! now! ; ~ *să vedem* let us see.
iaca *interj.* well! why! here is!
iad *sn.* hell.
iaht *sn.* yacht.
iama *sf.:* *a da* ~ *prin* to play havoc in *sau* among.
iamb *sm.* iambus.
iancheu *sm., adj.* yankee.
ianuarie *sm.* January.
iapă *sf.* mare.
iar *adv.* (once) again. *conj.* while.
iarăşi *adv.* (once) again.
iarbă *sf.* grass; *pl.* herbs; *(medicinale)* simple.
iarmaroc *sn.* fair.
iarna *adv.* in winter.
iarnă *sf.* winter; *astă-* ~ last winter.
iască *sf.* tinder.
iasomie *sf.* jasmine.
iatagan *sn.* yataghan.
iată *interj.* look! here is! here are!
iaz *sn.* (fish) pond.
ibric *sn.* coffee pot; tea kettle.
ici *adv.* here; ~-*colo* here and there.
icni *vi.* to gasp; *(a geme)* to groan.

icoană *sf.* icon; *fig.* picture.
iconoclast *sm.* iconoclast, debunker. *adj.* iconoclastic.
icre *sf. pl.* spawn; *(ca mîncare)* (salted) roe; ~ *negre* caviar(e).
icter *sn.* jaundice.
ideal *sn., adj.* ideal.
idealist *sm.* idealist. *adj.* idealistic.
idealiza *vt.* to idealize.
idee *sf.* idea; *(concepţie)* notion; *(gînd, nuanţă)* thought; *(plan)* plan; ~ *fixă* crotchet; ~ *genială* brain wave.
idem *adv.* id(em).
identic *adj.* identical. *adv.* likewise.
identifica *vt., vr.* to identify.
identitate *sf.* identity.
ideolog *sm.* ideologist.
ideologic *adj.* ideological.
ideologie *sf.* ideology.
idilă *sf.* idyll; love affair.
idilic *adj.* idyllic.
idiot *sm.* idiot; *med.* half-wit. *adj.* idiotic; *med.* idiot.
idiş *sn.* Yiddish.
idol *sm.* idol, graven image.
idolatrie *sf.* idolatry.
idolatriza *vt.* to lionize.
idolatru *sm.* votary.

ie *sf.* peasant woman's embroidered blouse.

ied *sm.* kid.

iederă *sf.* ivy.

ieftin *adj.* cheap; ~ *ca braga* dirt cheap. *adv.* cheap(ly); *fig.* unscathed.

ieftini *vt., vr.* to cheapen.

iele *sf. pl.* pixies.

ienibahar *sn.* juniper.

ienupăr *sm.* juniper tree.

iepuraş *sm.* leveret; bunny.

iepure *sm.* hare; *(de casă)* rabbit; bunny.

ierarhic *adj.* hierarchical. *adv.* hierarchically.

ierarhie *sf.* hierarchy.

ierbar *sn.* herbarium.

ierbos *adj.* grassy.

ieri *adv.* yesterday; *(în trecut)* formerly; *de ~ de alaltăieri* recent; *mai ~* the other day.

ierna *vi.* to hibernate.

ierta *vt.* to forgive; *a ~ de* to exempt from.

iertare *sf.* forgiveness; *rel. şi* absolution; *(scutire)* exemption.

iertător *adj.* forgiving.

iesle *sf.* manger.

ieşi *vi.* to go out (of doors); *(la lumină, la suprafaţă)* to emerge; *(a apărea)* to appear; *(de soare)* to fade; *a ~ bine* to turn out well; *(a reuşi)* to do well; *a ~ în afară* to stand out; *a ~ la pensie* to retire.

ieşire *sf.* emergence; *(izbucnire)* outburst; *(din impas)* way out.

iezuit *sm.* Jesuit. *adj.* Jesuitic.

ifose *sn. pl.* airs (and graces).

igienă *sf.* hygiene.

igienic *adj.* hygienic; toilet.

ignora *vt.* to ignore; *(pe cineva)* to cut.

ignorant *sm.* ignoramus. *adj.* ignorant.

ignoranţă *sf.* ignorance.

igrasie *sf.* dampness.

ilar *adj.* hilarious.

ilaritate *sf.* laughter.

ilegal *adj.* illegal; *(clandestin)* underground. *adv.* illegally; *(clandestin)* underground.

ilegalist *sm.* underground militant.

ilegalitate *sf.* illegality; unlawfulness; *pol.* underground activity; *în ~* underground.

ilicit *adj.* illicit.

ilizibil *adj.* illegible.

ilumina *vt., vr.* to light (up).

iluminat *sn.* lighting. *adj.* illuminated.

iluminism *sn.* the Enlightenment.

iluminist *sm.* illuminist.

ilustra *vt.* to illustrate. *vr.* to become illustrious.

ilustrat *adj.* illustrated.

ilustrată *sf.* picture postcard.

ilustraţie *sf.* illustration.

ilustru *adj.* brilliant.

iluzie *sf.* illusion.

iluzoriu *adj.* illusory.

imaculat *adj.* spotless.

imagina *vt.* to imagine.

imaginabil *adj.* conceivable.

imaginar *adj.* fancy.

imaginaţie *sf.* imagination.

imagine *sf.* image.

imaş *sn.* common.

imbecil *sm.* imbecile. *adj.* idiotic.

imbold *sn.* fillip; *(material)* incentive.

imediat *adj.* immediate; direct. *adv.* directly.

imemorial *adj.* immemorial.
imens *adj.* immense. *adv.* tremendously.
imensitate *sf.* vastness.
iminent *adj.* imminent.
imita *vt.* to imitate ; *(a mima)* to ape.
imitativ *adj.* onomatopeic.
imitator *sm.* imitator.
imitaţie *sf.* counterfeit ; *(d. bijuterii şi)* rhinestone.
imn *sn.* anthem ; *rel. şi fig.* hymn.
imòbil[1] *sn.* building.
imobil[2] *adj.* immobile ; *jur.* real (estate).
imobilitate *sf.* immobility.
imobiliza *vt.* to immobilize.
imoral *adj.* immoral.
imoralitate *sf.* immorality.
imortaliza *vt.* to immortalize.
impar *adj.* odd.
imparţial *adj.* impartial, unbiassed.
imparţialitate *sf.* fairness.
impas *sn.* deadlock.
impasibil *adj.* impassive.
impecabil *adj.* faultless. *adv.* faultlessly.
impediment *sn.* obstacle.
impenetrabil *adj.* impenetrable.
imperativ *sn., adj.* imperative.
impereeptibil *adj.* imperceptible. *adv.* imperceptibly.
imperfect *sn., adj.* imperfect.
imperial *adj.* imperial.
imperialism *sn.* imperialism.
imperialist *sm., adj.* imperialist.
imperios *adj.* imperious. *adv.* peremptorily.
imperiu *sn.* empire ; *fig.* dominion.
impermeabil *sn., adj.* waterproof.

impersonal *adj.* impersonal.
impertinent *adj.* saucy.
imperturbabil *adj.* unruffled.
impetuos *adj.* impetuous. *adv.* impetuously.
impietate *sf.* impiety.
implacabil *adj.* implacable.
implica *vt.* to involve ; *(a presupune)* to imply.
implicaţie *sf.* implication ; *(subtext)* overtone.
implicit *adj.* implicit. *adv.* implicitly.
implora *vt.* to beseech.
imponderabil *sn.* inscrutable destiny. *adj.* imponderable, weightless.
imponderabilitate *sf.* weightlessness.
import *sn.* importation ; *pl.* imports.
importa *vt.* to import. *vi.* to matter.
important *adj.* important; weighty ; *(istoric)* momentous ; *puţin ~* immaterial.
importanţă *sf.* importance, consequence ; *fără ~* unimportant ; *plin de ~, care-şi dă ~* consequential.
imposibil *sn., adj., interj.* impossible.
imposibilitate *sf.* impossibility.
impostor *sm.* humbug.
impostură *sf.* imposture.
impozant *adj.* stately.
impozit *sn.* tax ; *~ pe salariu sau venit* income tax.
imprecis *adj.* vague.
impresar *sm.* impresario.
impresie *sf.* impression ; *(greşită)* delusion.
impresiona *vt.* to impress.
impresionant *adj.* impressive.

impresionism *sn.* impressionism.

imprima *vt.* to print; *(a da)* to lend. *vr.* to be printed; *(cuiva)* to linger (in one's memory).

imprimat *sn.* form.; *pl.* printed matter. *adj.* printed.

imprimerie *sf.* printing works.

imprimeuri *sn. pl.* prints.

improbabil *adj.* unlikely.

impropriu *adj.* improper.

improviza *vt., vi.* to improvise.

improvizație *sf.* improvisation.

imprudent *adj.* uncautious.

imprudență *sf.* imprudence.

impuls *sn.* impulse.

impulsiona *vt.* to impel, to promote.

impulsiv *adj.* hot-blooded.

impunător *adj.* commanding.

impune *vt.* to impose; *(a obliga la)* to entail; *(un impozit)* to tax. *vi.* to be impressive. *vr.* to be(come) established; *(d. scriitor etc.)* to compel recognition; *(a fi necesar)* to be necessary.

imputa *vt.* to charge. *vr.* to be charged with smth.

imputare *sf.* imputation; *(reproș)* reproach.

imun *adj.* immune (from disease, etc.).

in *sn. bot.* flax; *(sămînță)* linseed; *de ~ text.* linen.

inacceptabil *adj.* unacceptable.

inaccesibil *adj.* inaccessible.

inadaptabil *adj.* misfit.

inadmisibil *adj.* inadmissible.

inalienabil *adj.* inalienable, indefeasible.

inalterabil *adj.* free from tainting.

inamic *sm., adj.* enemy.

inapt *adj.* unfit.

inaugura *vt.* to inaugurate.

incalculabil *adj.* incalculable.

incapabil *adj.* incapable.

incapacitate *sf.* incapacity; *(invaliditate)* disability.

incasabil *adj.* unbreakable.

incendia *vt.* to set on fire.

incendiere *sf.* arson.

incendiu *sn.* fire.

incertitudine *sf.* uncertainty.

incest *sn.* incest.

inchiziție *sf.* inquisition.

incident *sn., adj.* incident.

incidental *adj.* incidental. *adv.* accidentally.

incinera *vt.* to cremate.

incintă *sf.* precincts.

incisiv *sm.* incisor. *adj.* incisive.

include *vt.* to include.

inclusiv *adv.* inclusive(ly).

incoerent *adj.* incoherent.

incolor *adj.* colourless.

incomod *adj.* uncomfortable; *fig.* embarrassing; *(greoi)* clumsy; *(d. cineva)* unmanageable.

incomoda *vt.* to disturb.

incomparabil *adj.* peerless. *adv.* incomparably.

incompatibil *adj.* incompatible.

incompetent *adj.* incompetent.

incomplet *adj.* incomplete.

incomprehensiune *sf.* incomprehension.

incomunicabilitate *sf.* incommunicability.

inconsecvent *adj.* inconsistent.

inconsecvență *sf.* inconsistency.

inconsistent *adj.* loose.

inconstant *adj.* unsteady.

inconștient *sm., adj.* unconscious.

inconștiență *sf.* unconsciousness; *(nebunie)* recklessness.

incontestabil *adj.* indisputable. *adv.* indisputably.

inconvenient sn. difficulty.
incorect adv. incorrect.
incorigibil adj. incorrigible.
incoruptibil adj. incorruptible.
incredibil adj. incredible, unbelievable.
inculpat sm. accused.
incult adj. uneducated.
incultură sf. ignorance.
incurabil adj. incurable.
incursiune sf. foray.
indecent adj. indecent, immodest.
indefinit adj. indefinite.
indemnizaţie sf. pay; allowance.
independent sm., adj. independent; ~ de irrespective of. adv. independently (of smth.).
independenţă sf. independence.
indescifrabil adj. undecipherable.
index sn. index.
indezirabil sm. intruder. adj. undesirable.
indian sm., adj., indiană sf., adj. Indian.
indica vt. to indicate.
indicat adj. advisable.
indicativ sn., adj. indicative.
indicator sn. indicator; econ. index; (rutier) trafficator.
indicaţie sf. indication.
indice sm., sn. index.
indiciu sn. sign; trace.
indiferent adj. indifferent; (apatic) listless. adv. indifferently.
indiferenţă sf. indifference; (pasivitate) passivity.
indigen sm. aboriginal; pl. aborigines. adj. native.
indigna vt., vr. to revolt.
indignare sf. indignation.
indignat adj. indignant (at smth.).

indigo sn. indigo; (carbon) carbon paper.
indirect adj. indirect; (ocolit) devious. adv. indirectly.
indiscret adj. inquisitive.
indiscreţie sf. indiscretion.
indiscutabil adj. unquestionable. adv. unquestionably.
indispensabil adj. indispensable.
indispensabili sm. pl. drawers, unmentionables.
indispoziţie sf. indisposition; fig. dumps.
indispune vt. to upset. vr. to be upset.
indispus adj. out of sorts; (bolnav) unwell.
indistinct adj. dim. adv. indistinctly.
individ sm. individual; peior. person.
individual adj. individual. adv. individually.
indolent adj. indolent.
indonezian sm., adj., indoneziană sf., adj. Indonesian.
induce vt. to induce; (în eroare) to mislead.
indulgent adj. lenient.
indulgenţă sf. indulgence.
industrial adj. industrial.
industrializare sf. industrialization.
industriaş sm. manufacturer.
industrie sf. industry.
inechitabil adj. unjust, unfair.
inedit adj. unpublished; (nou) new(-fangled).
inefabil adj. ineffable.
inegal adj. unequal. adv. unfairly.
inegalabil adj. inimitable.
inegalitate sf. inequality.
inel sn. ring; (verighetă) wedding ring.

inelar *sn.* ring finger. *adj.* ring-
-shaped.
inepuizabil *adj.* inexhaustible.
inerent *adj.* inherent.
inert *adj.* inert ; indolent.
inerţie *sf.* inertness ; *fiz.* inertia.
inevitabil *adj.* inevitable. *adv.*
inevitably.
inexact *adj.* inaccurate. *adv.*
inaccurately.
inexistenţă *sf.* absence.
inexplicabil *adj.*| unaccountable.
inexprimabil *adj.* inexpressible.
infailibil *adj.* unfailing.
infamie *sf.* infamy.
infanterie *sf.* infantry, foot.
infanterist *sm.* infantryman.
infantil *adj.* infant(ile), child ...
infect *adj.* awful.
infecta *vt.* to infect. *vr.* to become infected.
infecţie *sf.* infection ; *(porcărie)*
awful thing.
infecţios *adj.* catching.
inferior *sm.* underling. *adj.* inferior.
inferioritate *sf.* inferiority.
infern *sn.* hell.
infernal *adj.* infernal ; *(rău)*
diabolical.
infidel *adj.* unfaithful.
infim *adj.* infinitesimal.
infinit *sm., sn., adj.* infinite. *adv.*
greatly.
infinitate *sf.* infinity.
infinitiv *sn., adj.* infinitive.
infirm *sm.* cripple. *adj.* disabled.
infirmerie *sf.* sick room.
infirmieră *sf.* (sick) nurse.
infirmitate *sf.* infirmity.
inflaţie *sf.* inflation.
inflexibil *adj.* inflexible.
influent *adj.* influential, weighty.
influenţa *vt.* to influence.

influenţabil *adj.* subject to in-
fluence(s).
influenţă *sf.* influence; *fig. şi* pull.
inform *adj.* shapeless.
informa *vt.* to inform. *vr.* to
inquire {into smth.).
informare *sf.* report.
informat *adj.* well-informed, posted.
informativ *adj.* informative.
informator *sm.* informer.
informaţie *sf.* (piece of) information. *pl.* information.
infractor *sm.* offender.
infracţiune *sf.* offence.
ingenios *adj.* clever.
ingeniozitate *sf.* ingenuousness.
ingenuă *sf.* ingenue.
inginer *sm.* engineer ; ~ *agronom* agronomist ; ~ *chimist*
industrial, chemist; ~ *constructor* civil engineer ; ~ *silvic* forestry expert.
inginerie *sf.* engineering.
ingrat *adj.* ungrateful ; *(dificil)*
unrewarded.
ingratitudine *sf.* ingratitude.
inhiba *vt.* to inhibit.
inimă *sf.* heart ; *(suflet)* soul ;
~ *albastră* the blues ; ~ *de
piatră* callousness ; ~ *rea* grief
cu dragă ~ willingly ; *cu* ~
energetically ; *pe inima goală* on
an empty stomach.
inimos *adj.* large-hearted.
ininteligibil *adj.* unintelligible.
iniţia *vt.* to initiate. *vr.* to learn.
iniţial *adj.* initial. *adv.* initially.
iniţială *sf.* initial.
iniţiat *sm.* adept. *adj.* conversant (with smth).
iniţiativă *sf.* initiative ; *plin de*
~ resourceful ; *lipsit de* ~
shiftless.

initiator *sm.* initiator.
injectat *adj.* injected; *(d. ochi)* bloodshot.
injecţie *sf.* injection; *med. şi* shot, hypodermic.
injurie *sf.* insult.
injurios *adj.* outrageous.
inocent *adj.* guiltless.
inocenţă *sf.* innocence.
inofensiv *adj.* harmless.
inoportun *adj.* unseasonable.
inova *vi.* to innovate.
inovator *sm.* innovator.
inovaţie *sf.* innovation.
inoxidabil *adj.* stainless.
ins *sm.* bloke.
insalubru *adj.* insanitary; unwholesome.
inscripţie *sf.* inscription.
insectă *sf.* insect.
insecticid *sn., adj.* insecticide.
insensibil *adj.* insensible.
inseparabil *adj.* inseparable.
insidios *adj.* insidious.
insignă *sf.* badge.
insignifiant *adj.* unimportant.
insinua *vt.* to insinuate. *vr.* to slink (in).
insinuant *adj.* insinuating.
insipid *adj.* insipid.
insista *vi.* to insist (on); to argue (a point).
insistent *adj.* insistent. *adv.* insistently.
insistenţă *sf.* insistence; *cu ~* insistently.
insolaţie *sf.* sunstroke.
insolent *adj.* saucy.
insolenţă *sf.* cheek(iness).
insomnie *sf.* sleeplessness.
inspecta *vt.* to inspect.
inspector *sm.* inspector.
inspecţie *sf.* inspection.

inspira *vt.* to inspire (with smth.). *vr.: a se inspira din* to draw upon.
inspirat *adj.* (well-)inspired.
inspiraţie *sf.* inspiration.
instabil *adj.* unsteady.
instala *vt.* to install. *vr.* to settle (down).
instalator *sm.* plumber.
instalaţie *sf.* installation; *(de apă)* plumbing; *(de canalizare)* sewerage; *instalaţii sanitare* sanitation.
instantaneu *sn.* snapshot. *adj.* momentary.
instanţă *sf.* instance; *în ultimă ~* eventually.
instaura *vt.* to set up.
instaurare *sf.* establishment.
instiga *vt.* to incite.
instinct *sn.* instinct.
instinctiv *adj.* instinctive. *adv.* naturally.
institut *sn.* institute; *~ de proiectări* design office.
institutor *sm.* school-teacher.
instituţie *sf.* office, institution.
instructaj *sn.* briefing.
instructiv *adj.* instructive.
instructoare *sf.*, **instructor** *sm.* instructor.
instrucţi(un)e *sf.* instruction; *mil.* drill.
instrui *vt.* to brief; *mil.* to train; *jur.* to investigate. *vr.* to learn.
instruit *adj.* well-read; *mil.* trained.
instrument *sn.* instrument.
instrumental *adj.* instrumental.
insucces *sn.* failure.
insuficient *adj.* insufficient.
insufla *vt.* to inspire with.

insulă *sf.* island ; *(ca nume geo-grafic și)* isle.
insulta *vt.* to abuse.
insultă *sf.* insult, abuse, outrage.
insuportabil *adj.* unbearable. *adv.* unbearably.
insurecție *sf.* insurrection.
intact *adv.* intact.
integra *vt.* to bring in. *vr.* : *a se ~ în* to fit in.
integral *adj.* integral ; *(d. pîine)* whole-meal. *adv.* totally.
integrant *adj.* constitutive.
integritate *sf.* integrity.
integru *adj.* honest.
intelect *sn.* brains.
intelectual *sm.*, *adj.* intellectual.
intelectualitate *sf.* intellectuals.
inteligent *adj.* intelligent. *adv.* wisely.
inteligență *sf.* intelligence ; *~ naturală* mother wit.
inteligibil *adj.* intelligible. *adv.* intelligibly.
intemperie *sf.* (bad) weather.
intendent *sm.* administrator.
intens *adj.* intense. *adv.* intensely.
intensifica *vt.* to enhance. *vr.* to intensify.
intensitate *sf.* intensity.
intenta *vt.* : *a ~ un proces cuiva* to sue smb. (at law).
intenție *sf.* intention ; *(plan)* plan ; *cu ~* deliberately ; *fără ~* unwillingly.
intenționa *vt.* to intend.
intenționat *adj.* purposeful ; *jur.* prepense.
interdicție *sf.* interdiction.
interes *sn.* interest(s).
interesa *vt.* to concern ; *nu mă interesează* it is not my funeral. *vi.* to matter. *vr.* to be inter-

ested (in smth., etc.) ; to inquire (for smb., etc.) ; *a se ~ la* to apply to.
interesant *adj.* interesting.
interesat *adj.* concerned ; *(lacom)* grasping.
interior *sn.* interior ; *(la telefon)* extension. *adj.* internal ; *(d. comerț)* home.
interjecție *sf.* interjection.
interlocutor *sm.* interlocutor.
interlop *adj.* underworld.
intermediar *sm.* wangler, interloper. *adj.* intermediate.
intermediu *sn.* agency.
interminabil *adj.* endless.
intern *sm.* *(elev)* boarder ; *med.* intern. *adj.* internal ; home.
interna *vt.* to hospitalize ; *(a închide)* to confine. *vr.* to go to hospital.
internat *sn.* boarding school. *adj.* interned ; hospitalized.
internațional *adj.* international ; world ...
internaționala *sf.* international ; *(cîntecul)* the Internationale.
internaționalism *sn.* internationalism.
interoga *vt.* to examine.
interogativ *adj.* interrogative.
interogatoriu *sn.* examination.
interpela *vt.* to interpellate.
interpret *sm.* interpreter.
interpreta *vt.* to interpret ; *(muzică etc.)* to perform ; *a ~ greșit* to misinterpret.
interpretare *sf.* interpretation ; *muz. și* rendition ; *teatru și* acting.
intersecție *sf.* crossing.
interurban *adj.* interurban ; *(la telefon)* trunk...
interval *sn.* interval ; *(gol)* gap.

interveni *vi.* to intervene; *(a se amesteca)* to interfere; *a ~ pentru cineva* to intercede in smb.'s favour.

intervenţie *sf.* intervention; *(cuvîntare)* speech; *(pilă)* wangle; *(tehnică)* repair; *de ~* emergency ...

interviu *sn.* interview.

interzice *vt.* to ban.

interzicere *sf.* prohibition.

interzis *adj.* forbidden.

intestin *sn.* bowel; *~ul gros* the large intestine; *~ul subţire* the small intestine.

intim *sm.* bosom friend. *adj.* intimate; *(retras)* private. *adv.* intimately; *(retras)* privately; *(îndeaproape)* well.

intimida *vt.* to brow beat. *vr.* to grow shy.

intimidat *adj.* self-conscious.

intimitate *sf.* intimacy; *pl.* secrets.

intitula *vt.* to entitle. *vr.* to be entitled.

intolerant *adj.* illiberal

intona *vt.* to tune.

intonaţie *sf.* intonation.

intoxica *vt.* to intoxicate. *vr.* to become intoxicated.

intoxicaţie *sf.* intoxication; *~ alimentară* food poisoning.

intra *vi.* to enter; *a ~ într-o organizaţie* etc. to join an organization, etc.; *intră!* come in!

intransigent *adj.* intransigent.

intranzitiv *adj.* intransitive.

intrare *sf.* entrance; *(fundătură)* (blind) alley; *~a oprită* private.

intriga *vt.* to puzzle.

intrigant *sm.* intriguer. *adj.* designing.

intrigă *sf.* intrigue; *(acţiune)* plot.

introduce *vt.* to introduce. *vr.* to elbow one's way; *(a fi introdus)* to be introduced.

introducere *sf.* introduction; *(la o scrisoare)* salutation.

introductiv *adj.* introductory.

intrus *sm.* intruder.

intui *vt.* to infer.

intuiţie *sf.* intuition.

inuman *adj.* inhuman.

inunda *vt.* to flood.

inundaţie *sf.* flood.

inutil *adj.* useless. *adv.* needlessly.

inutilitate *sf.* futility.

inutilizabil *adj.* useless.

invada *vt.* to invade.

invadator *sm.* invader.

invalid *sm.* cripple, invalid. *adj.* crippled, invalid.

invariabil *adj.* invariable.

invazie *sf.* invasion.

inventa *vt.* to invent.

inventar *sn.* inventory; *~ mort* implements; *~ viu* livestock.

inventator *sm.* inventor.

inventiv *adj.* resourceful.

invenţie *sf.* invention; *(minciună)* fabrication.

invers *adj.* reverse. *adv.* upside down; conversely.

inversa *vt.* to invert.

inversiune *sf.* inversion.

investi *vt.* to invest.

investiţie *sf.* investment.

invidia *vt.* to envy.

invidie *sf.* envy.

invidios *adj.* envious; *(pizmaş)* covetous.

invincibil *adj.* unconquerable.

invita *vt.* to invite, to ask.

invitat *sm.* guest.

invitație *sf.* invitation.
invizibil *adj.* invisible.
invoca *vt.* to invoke.
involuntar *adj.* involuntary. *adv.* unwillingly.
invulnerabil *adj.* invulnerable.
iobag *sm.* serf.
iobăgie *sf.* serfdom.
iod *sn.* iodine.
iolă *sf.* yawl.
iotă *sf.* jot.
ipocrit *sm.* pharisee. *adj.* hypocritical.
ipocrizie *sf.* hypocrisy.
ipotecă *sf.* mortgage.
ipotetic *adj.* hypothetical.
ipoteză *sf.* assumption.
ipsos *sn.* plaster.
irascibil *adj.* bad-tempered.
irațional *adj.* irrational.
ireal *adj.* unreal.
irecuperabil *adj.* irreparable, unredeemable.
iremediabil *adj.* irreparable. *adv.* irretrievably.
ireproșabil *adj.* faultless. *adv.* perfectly.
iresponsabil *adj.* irresponsible.
ireversibil *adj.* irreversible.
irevocabil *adj.* irrevocable. *adv.* irrevocably.
irezistibil *adj.* irresistible.
iriga *vt.* to irrigate.
irigație *sf.* irrigation.
iris *sm.*, *sn.* iris.
irita *vt.* to irritate. *vr.* to become irritated.
iritare *sf.* irritation.
irlandez *sm.* Irishman. *adj.* Irish.
irlandeză *sf.* Irishwoman; *(limba)* Irish.
irod *sm.* Herod (in a folk minstrel show); *pl.* minstrel show.

ironic *adj.* ironical. *adv.* ironically.
ironie *sf.* irony.
ironiza *vt.* to banter.
irosi *vt.* to squander; to fritter (away).
isca *vt.* to arouse. *vr.* to arise.
iscăli *vt.*, *vi.*, *vr.* to sign.
iscălitură *sf.* signature.
iscodi *vt.* to probe, to investigate; *(cu privirea)* to peer into *sau* at.
iscusință *sf.* skill.
iscusit *adj.* apt.
ispăși *vt.* to expiate.
ispășitor *adj.*: *țap* ~ scapegoat.
ispită *sf.* temptation.
ispititor *adj.* (al)luring.
ispravă *sf.* deed; *(realizare)* achievement; *de* ~ reliable.
isprăvi *vt.* to finish; *(un discurs)* to wind up; *(a epuiza)* to run out of. *vr.* to be (all) over.
isteric *adj.* hysterical. *adv.* hysterically.
isterie *sf.* hysteria.
isteț *adj.* keen.
istm *sn.* isthmus.
istoric *sm.* historian. *adj.* historical; *(important)* historic.
istorie *sf.* history; *(poveste)* story; *(încurcătură)* sad tale.
istorioară *sf.* anecdote.
istorisi *vt.* to tell.
istovi *vt.*, *vr.* to exhaust oneself.
istovit *adj.* worn out.
italian *sm.*, *adj.*, italiană *sf.*, *adj.* Italian.
italienește *adv.* (like an) Italian.
itinerar *sn.* itinerary.
iță *sf.* thread.

iubi *vt., vr.* to love (each other).
iubire *sf.* fondness.
iubit *sm.* lover. *adj.* (be)loved.
iubită *sf.* sweetheart.
iubitor *adj.* loving.
iugoslav *sm., adj.,* **iugoslavă** *sf., adj.* Yugoslav.
iulie *sm.* July.
iunie *sm.* June.
iureş *sn.* rush.
iută *sf.* jute.
iute *adj.* quick, swift; *(agil)* nimble; *(pripit)* rash; *(nervos)* quick-tempered; *(la gust)* hot; ~ *de picior* swift-footed; ~ *de mînă* deft. *adv.* fast.
iuţeală *sf.* speed.
iuţi *vt.* to quicken; *(o mîncare)* to pepper. *vr.* to pick up speed; *(la gust)* to turn acrid.
iveală *sf.: a scoate la* ~ to bring out, to produce.
ivi *vt.* to appear; to turn up.
iz *sn.* reek.
izbăvi *vt.* to deliver.

izbi *vt.* to hit. *vr.* to strike (against); *a se* ~ *de* to come up against.
izbitor *adj.* striking.
izbîndă *sf.* victory.
izbîndi *vi.* to succeed (in doing smth.).
izbucni *vi.* to break out; *(d. cineva)* to burst (into tears, etc.).
izbucnire *sf.* outbreak; *(de mînie, etc.)* outburst.
izbuti *vt., vi.* to manage (to do smth.).
izbutit *vt.* accomplished.
izgoni *vt.* to banish.
izlaz *sn.* common.
izmă *sf.* (pepper)mint.
izmene *sf. pl.* pants; small clothes.
izola *vt.* to isolate; *el.* to insulate. *vr.* to live in seclusion.
izvor *sn.* spring.
izvorî *vi.* to rise. *fig.* to arise (from).

Î

îmbarca *vt., vr.* to embark.
îmbălsăma *vt.* to embalm.
îmbărbăta *vt.* to hearten.
îmbăta *vt.* to intoxicate. *vr.* to get drunk.
îmbătător *adj.* inebriating.
îmbătrîni *vt., vi.* to age.
îmbelşugat *adj.* abundant.
îmbia *vt.* to prompt; *(a ispiti)* to draw.
îmbiba *vt.* to imbue. *vr.* to be imbued.

îmbietor *adj.* inviting.
îmbina *vt., vr.* to blend; to combine; *(a (se) potrivi)* to dovetail.
îmbinare *sf.* joining.
îmbîcsi *vt., vr.* to stuff; to fill.
îmblănit *adj.* fur-lined.
îmblînzi *vt.* to tame; *(a dresa)* to train. *vr.* to become tame.
îmblînzitor *sm.* tamer.
îmboboci *vi.* to bud.

îmbogăţi *vt.* to enrich. *vr.* to grow rich(er) ; to make a fortune.

îmbogăţire *sf.* enrichment.

îmboldi *vt.* to spur.

îmbolnăvi *vt.* to render sick. *vr.* to fall ill.

îmbrăca *vt.* to put on ; *(pe cineva)* to dress ; *(a înveli)* to cover. *vr.* to dress (oneself).

îmbrăcăminte *sf.* clothes ; *(veşmînt)* garment.

îmbrăţişa *vt., vr.* to embrace.

îmbrăţişare *sf.* embrace.

îmbrînci *vt.* to push. *vr.* to jostle each other.

îmbrobodi *vt.* to wrap up (one's head) ; *fig.* to hoodwink.

îmbuca *vt.* to swallow ; *(a înfuleca)* to gobble. *vr.* to join.

îmbucătură *sf.* mouthful.

îmbucurător *adj.* rejoicing.

îmbufna *vr.* to sulk.

îmbufnat *adj.* scowling.

îmbuiba *vt., vr.* to gorge.

îmbuibat *adj.* surfeited.

îmbujora *vr.* to flush.

îmbulzeală *sf.* throng.

îmbulzi *vr.* to crush (into each other) ; *(a se repezi)* to rush.

îmbuna *vt.* to placate.

îmbunătăţi *vt., vr.* to improve.

împacheta *vt.* to pack up.

împăca *vt.* to conciliate ; *(a mîngîia)* to soothe. *vr.* to reconcile ; *(a se înţelege)* to agree.

împăcare *sf.* reconciliation.

împăciui *vt.* to appease.

împăciuire *sf.*, **împăciuitorism** *sn.* appeasement.

împăciuitor *adj.* placatory.

împădurit *adj.* wood-clad.

împăia *vt.* to stuff.

împăienjeni *vr.* to grow dim.

împămînteni *vr.* to take roots.

împărat *sm.* emperor.

împărăteasă *sf.* empress.

împărătesc *adj.* imperial.

împărăţie *sf.* empire.

împărtăşi *vt.* to impart ; *rel.* to give (smb.) the eucharist. *vr.* to receive the eucharist ; *a se ~ din* to share.

împărţeală *sf.* repartition.

împărţi *vt.* to divide ; *(a distribui)* to deliver ; *(cărţile de joc)* to deal (out) ; *(dreptate)* to mete out. *vr.* to be divided.

împărţire *sf.* division ; *(distribuţie)* distribution.

împătrit *adj., adv.* fourfold.

împături *vt.* to fold.

împăuna *vr.: a se ~ cu* to plume oneself on.

împerechea *vt., vr.* to pair.

împestriţa *vt.* to mottle.

împiedica *vt.* to hinder. *vr.* to stumble (over smth.).

împietri *vi.* to turn to stone. *vr.* to harden.

împietrit *adj.* turned to stone ; *fig.* callous ; *(încremenit)* dumbfounded.

împila *vt.* to oppress.

împinge *vt.* to push ; *fig.* to goad.

împînzi *vt.* to stud.

împleti *vt.* to knit ; *(a ţese)* to weave ; *(părul)* to plait. *vr.* to be knitted ; *fig.* to interweave.

împletici *vr.* to stagger.

împletitură *sf.* knitting ; *(de nuiele)* wickerwork.

împlini *vt.* to complete ; *(a îndeplini)* to carry out ; *(o dorinţă)* to comply with ; *(o vîrstă)* to reach (an age) ; *a ~i*

20 *de ani* she has turned twenty. *vr.* to come true; *(a se scurge)* to elapse; *(la trup)* to fill out; *se împlinesc zece ani de atunci* it is ten years since (then).

împlinire *sf.* completion; *(îndeplinire)* fulfilment.

împodobi *vt.* to adorn. *vr.* to smarten up.

împopoţona *vt.* to adorn (heavily). *vr.* to titivate.

împotmoli *vr.* to get stuck.

împotriva *prep.* against; *jur., sport.* versus, vs.

împotrivă *adv.* counter.

împotrivi *vr.* to oppose (smth.).

împotrivire *sf.* resistance.

împovăra *vt.* to burden.

împrăştia *vt., vr.* to scatter.

împrăştiat *adj.* scattered; *(distrat)* hare-brained.

împrejmui *vt.* to enclose.

împrejur *adv. (mai ales static)* around; *(mai ales cu verbe de mişcare)* round.

împrejurare *sf.* occurrence.

împrejurimi *sf. pl.* environs.

împrejurul *prep. (mai ales static)* around; *(mai ales cu verbe de mişcare)* round.

împresura *vt.* to encircle.

împreuna *vt., vr.* to unite; *(a împerechea)* to couple.

împreunare *sf.* union; *(împerechere)* copulation.

împreună *adv.* together.

împrieteni *vr.* to make *sau* become friends.

împroprietărire *sf.* appropriation of land.

împrospăta *vt.* to refresh.

împroşca *vt.* to splash; *(cu noroi)* to sling mud at.

împrumut *sn.* loan; *de ∼* lending; borrowed.

împrumuta *vt. (cuiva)* to lend (to smb.); *(de la)* to borrow (from). *vr.* to borrow (from smb.).

împuia *vt.: a ∼ capul cuiva* to make smb.'s head swim.

împunge *vt.* to prick; *(a înţepa)* to sting; *fig. şi* to nettle. *vr.* to prick oneself.

împunsătură *sf.* prick; *(de ac)* stitch.

împuşca *vt.* to shoot (dead). *vi.* to shoot. *vr.* to blow out one's brains.

împuşcătură *sf.* shot.

împuternici *vt.* to authorize.

împuternicire *sf.* mandate.

împuţina *vt., vr.* to lessen.

în *prep. (static)* in, at; *(indicînd mişcarea)* into; *(într-un spaţiu (de))* within; *(ca dată)* on; *(pt. lună, an etc.)* in; *într-o (bună) zi* once, one day; *(în viitor)* some day (or other); *∼ săptămîna aceea* that week.

înainta *vt.* to advance; *(o cerere etc.)* to put forward. *vi.* to advance.

înaintare *sf.* advance(ment).

înaintaş *sm.* precursor; *sport* forward.

înaintat *adj.* advanced; *(progresist)* forward-looking.

înainte *adv.* forward; *(mai de mult)* before; *(în faţă şi)* ahead; *∼ de* before; *de azi ∼* from now on.

înaintea *prep.* before; *(în faţa şi)* in front of; *(în avans faţă de)* ahead of.

înalt *sn.: în ∼ul cerului* on high. *adj.* tall; high; *fig. şi* lofty; *muz., el., tehn.* high;

~ *de zece metri* thirty-five feet high.

inapoi *adv.* back(wards).

înapoià[1] *vt., vr.* to return.

înapòia[2] *prep.* behind.

înapoiat *adj.* backward.

înapoiere *sf.* return ; *fig.* backwardness.

înaripa *vt.* to wing.

înarma *vt.* to arm ; *fig.* to equip. *vr.* to arm (oneself).

înarmare *sf.* armament.

înavuţire *sf.* enrichment.

înăbuşi etc. *v.* **înnăbuşi** etc.

înălţa *vt.* to raise ; *(steagul)* to hoist. *vr.* to rise.

înălţare *sf.* raising ; *(a steagului)* hoisting ; *rel.* Ascension.

înălţător *sn. mil.* backsight. *adj.* uplifting.

înălţime *sf.* height ; *geogr.* elevation; *fig.* loftiness; *muz.* pitch; *(ca titlu)* Highness ; *la* ~ *(fig.)* up to the mark.

înăspri *vt., vr.* to harden.

înăuntru *adv.,* **înăuntrul** *prep.* in(side).

încadra *vt.* to frame ; *(pe cineva)* to surround ; *(în slujbă)* to appoint. *vr.* to join (a collective), to harmonize (with smb. *sau* smth.) ; to take a job.

încadrare *sf.* framing ; *(numire)* appointment ; *(categorie)* wage- -class ; *(salariu)* wages.

încasa *vt.* to cash ; *(a strînge)* to collect ; *(o lovitură)* to get.

încă *adv. (afirmativ)* still ; *(negativ)* yet ; *(pînă acum)* so far ; *(mai mult)* some *sau* any more ; *(chiar)* even ; ~ *din* ... as early as ... ; ~ *unul* another ; ~ *doi* another two ; *şi* ~ *cum!* with a vengeance ! you bet !

încăiera *vr.* to come to grips.

încăierare *sf.* brawl.

încălca *vt.* to encroach upon.

încăleca *vt., vi.* to mount. *vr.* to overlap.

încălţa *vt., vr.* to put on (one's shoes, etc.).

încălţăminte *sf.* footwear.

încălzi *vt.* to warm (up) ; *(a înfierbînta)* to heat ; *fig.* to encourage ; *ce mă încălzeşte pe mine?* what is that to me ! *vr.* to warm oneself ; *(a se însufleţi)* to warm up ; *(a se înfierbînta)* to grow hot.

încălzire *sf.* heating.

încăpător *adj.* roomy.

încăpăţîna *vr.* to persist (in smth.).

încăpăţînare *sf.* stubbornness.

încăpăţînat *sm.* mule. *adj.* obstinate, stubborn.

încăpea *vi.* to go in ; *fig.* to fall (into smb.'s hands).

încăpere *sf.* room.

încărca *vt.* to load ; *(prea mult)* to over-load ; *el.* to charge ; *fin.* to overcharge. *vi., vr.* to load.

încărcătură *sf.* load ; *tehn.* charge; *mar.* freight.

încărunţi *vt., vi.* to turn grey.

încătuşa *vt.* to shackle.

începător *sm., adj.* beginner.

începe *vt., vi.* to begin, to start.

începere *sf.* beginning ; *cu* ~ *din ...* beginning on ...

început *sn.* beginning ; *pl.* inception, origin ; *la* ~ in the beginning ; *la* ~*ul cărţii* etc. at the beginning of the book, etc. ; *de la (bun)* ~ from the outset.

încerca *vt.* to try ; to attempt ; *(o haină)* to try on ; *(a simţi)* to experience.

încercare *sf.* trial; *(strădanie)* endeavour; *(probă)* test; *(greutate)* hardship.

încercat *adj.* (hard-)tried.

încercui *vt.* to encircle.

încet *adj.* slow; *(greoi)* dull; *(slab)* faint. *adv.* slowly; *(greoi)* idly.

înceta *vt., vi.* to cease; *a ~ din viață* to pass away.

încetare *sf.* cessation; *~ din viață* decease; death; *fără ~* ceaselessly.

încetățeni *vt.* to naturalize. *vr.* to be established.

încetineală *sf.* slowness.

încetini *vt., vi.* to slow down.

încețoșa *vr.* to grow foggy.

închega *vt., vr.* to coagulate; *fig.* to unite.

închegat *adj.* close-knit *sau* woven.

încheia *vt.* to finish; *(o înțelegere etc.)* to conclude; *(nasturii)* to button up; *(a îmbina)* to fix. *vr.* to close; *(la haine)* to button oneself up.

încheiere *sf.* conclusion; *(sfîrșit și)* end.

încheietură *sf.* joint.

închide *vt.* to close, to shut; *(cu zăvorul)* to bolt; *(cu cheia)* to lock; *(a întemnița)* to imprison; *(un aparat)* to switch *sau* turn off. *vr.* to close, to shut; *(în odaie)* to lock oneself up; *(d. o rană)* to heal.

închidere *sf.* closing; *(cu cheia)* locking.

închina *vt.* to devote. *vi.* to propose a toast. *vr.* to cross oneself; *(a se pleca)* to bow down; *a se ~ la* to worship.

închipui *vt.* to imagine; *(a reprezenta)* to symbolize.

închipuire *sf.* fancy.

închipuit *sm.* coxcomb. *adj.* imaginary; *(încrezut)* vain.

închiria *vt.* *(a da cu chirie)* to let, to rent; *(obiecte)* to hire out; *(a lua cu chirie)* to rent; *(obiecte)* to hire; *de ~t* to let.

închis *adj.* closed, shut (up); *(la caracter)* as close as an oyster; *(d. aer)* stale; *(apăsător)* close; *(la culoare)* dark.

închisoare *sf.* prison.

închista *vr.* to be anchylosed.

închizătoare *sf.* fastener.

încinge *vt.* to gird(le); *(a înconjura)* to surround; *(a încălzi)* to heat. *vr.* to girdle oneself; *(a se înfierbînta)* to heat; *(a începe)* to start.

încludat *adj.* spiteful.

încîlci *vt.* to tangle. *vr.* to be (come) entangled.

încîlcit *adj.* tangled (up); *fig.* intricate.

încînta *vt.* to delight.

încîntare *sf.* relish.

încîntat *adj.* glad; *~ de* delighted with; *~ de cunoștință!* glad to meet you!

încîntător *adj.* charming.

încît *conj.* so (much) that.

înclesta *vt., vr.* to clench.

înclina *vt.* to bend. *vi.* to incline (towards). *vr.* to bend; *(a saluta)* to bow.

înclinare, înclinație *sf.* inclination; *fig.* ply.

încoace *adv.* hither, here; *~ și încolo* back and forth; *ce mai ~ și încolo?* let us go straight

to the point; *mai* ~ closer;
later on.

încolăci *vt.*, *vr.* to coil (up), to
wind.

încolo *adv.* (far) away; *mai* ~
further on.

încolona *vr.* to fall into a column.

încolţi *vt.* to corner; *(a muşca)*
to bite. *vi.* to germinate.

înconjur *sn.* detour; *fără* ~
without beating about the
bush.

înconjura *vt.* to surround; *(a
asedia)* to besiege; *(a da ocol
la)* to go round. *vr.* to rally
around (oneself).

înconjurător *adj.* environing.

încorda *vt.*, *vr.* to strain (oneself).

încordare *sf.* tension.

încorona *vt.* to crown. *vr.* to be
crowned.

încorpora *vt.* to incorporate;
mil. to conscript.

încotro *adv.* whither, where(ver).

încovoia *vt.*, *vr.* to bend.

încrede *vr.* to confide (in smb.).

încredere *sf.* trust; *(bizuire)*
reliance; *de* ~ reliable.

încredinţa *vt.* to entrust; *(a
asigura)* to assure (smb. of
smth.). *vr.* to make sure (that).

încredinţare *sf. (asigurare)* assur-
ance(s); *(înmînare)* entrust-
ing; *(convingere)* conviction.

încremeni *vi.* to turn to stone.

încreţi *vt.* to wave; *(a undui)*
to ripple; *(a zbîrci)* to wrinkle.
vi.: a ~ *din sprîncene* to frown.
vr. to be wrinkled; *(d. păr)*
to wave.

încrezător *adj.* confident.

încrezut *adj.* conceited.

încropi *vt. fig.* to knock together.

încrucişa *vt.*, *vr.* to cross.

încrucişare *sf.* crossing; *(de
drumuri)* crossroads.

încrucişat *adj.* crossed; *biol. şi*
crossbred; *(zbanghiu)* cross-
-eyed.

încrunta *vt.* to knit. *vr.* to frown.

încruntat *adj.* scowling.

încuia *vt.* to lock.

încuiat *adj.* locked; *fig.* narrow-
-minded.

încuietoare *sf.* bolt; *fig.* puz-
zling question.

încumeta *vr.* to venture.

încunoştinţa *vt.* to inform.

încununa *vt.* to crown.

încuraja *vt.* to encourage.

încurajare *sf.* support.

încurajator *adj.* encouraging.

încurca *vt.* to mix up; *fig. şi*
to confuse; *(a împiedica)* to
hinder; *(a deranja)* to trouble;
(a pune în încurcătură) to
flummox. *vr.* to get entangled; *(a se zăpăci)* to be per-
plexed.

încurcătură *sf.* confusion; *(necaz)* trouble; *(zăpăceală)* flounder; *în* ~ embarrassed.

încuviinţa *vt.* to consent.

îndată *adv.* immediately; *(de)*
~ *ce* as soon as.

îndatora *vt.* to oblige. *vr.* to be
obliged (to smb.).

îndatorire *sf.* duty.

îndatoritor *adj.* obliging.

îndărăt *adv.* back(wards).

îndărătnic *adj.* strong-headed.

îndărătul *prep.* behind.

îndeajuns *adv.* enough.

îndeaproape *adv.* closely.

îndelete *adv.: pe* ~ at leisure.

îndeletnici *vr.: a se* ~ *cu* to
deal with.

îndeletnicire *sf.* occupation.

îndelung *adv.* for long.

îndelungat *adj.* long.

îndemînare *sf.* ability.

îndemînatic *adj.* skilful; *(capabil)* able, clever.

îndemînă *adv.*: *la* ~ at hand.

îndemn *sn.* stimulus; *(apel)* call.

îndemna *vt.* to urge; *(a sfătui)* to advise.

îndeobşte *adv.* generally.

îndeosebi *adv.* especially.

îndepărta *vt.* to remove; *fig.* to estrange (from smb.). *vr.* to go away; *(de la subiect)* to wander.

îndepărtat *adj.* distant.

îndeplini *vt.* to carry out; *(îndatoririle)* to discharge. *vr.* to come true.

îndeplinire *sf.* fulfilment.

îndesa *vt., vr.* to cluster.

îndesat *adj.* crowded; *(ca fizic)* stodgy.

îndesi *vt.* to thicken; to render more frequent. *vr.* to become more frequent.

îndestula *vt.* to satiate. *vr.* to eat one's fill.

îndestulător *adj.* ample.

îndîrji *vt.* to render grim. *vr.* to be embittered.

îndîrjire *sf.* grimness.

îndîrjit *adj.* grim.

îndobitoci *vt.* to besot. *vr.* to grow stupid.

îndoi *vt.* to bend; *(o hîrtie* etc.*)* to fold; *(colţurile)* to dog-ear; *(a dubla)* to redouble. *vr.* to stoop; *(a spori)* to double; *(de un lucru)* to doubt.

îndoială *sf.* doubt; *fără* ~ undoubtedly.

îndoielnic *adj.* dubious.

îndolia *vt.* to cause to mourn.

îndopa *vt.* to cram. *vr.* to gormandize.

îndrăcit *adj.* devilish; *(nebunesc)* frenzied.

îndrăgi *vt.* to grow fond of.

îndrăgosti *vr.* to fall in love.

îndrăgostit *sm.* lover. *adj.* infatuated, in love (with smb.).

îndrăzneală *sf.* daring.

îndrăzneţ *adj.* bold.

îndrăzni *vt.* to dare.

îndrepta *vt.* to straighten; *fig.* to correct, to rectify; *(către)* to point; *(a îndruma)* to direct. *vr.* to straighten oneself; *fig.* to improve; *(după boală)* to recover; *(de năravuri)* to mend one's ways; *a se* ~ *spre* to make for.

îndreptar *sn.* guide(-book).

îndreptăţi *vt.* to entitle.

îndruga *vt.* to stammer; *(a trăncăni)* to chatter.

îndruma *vt.* to guide.

îndrumare *sf.* direction.

înduioşa *vt.* to move. *vr.* to take pity (on smb.).

înduioşător *adj.* touching.

îndulci *vt., vr.* to sweeten.

îndupleca *vt.* to make smb. relent. *vr.* to relent.

îndura *vt.* to suffer. *vr.* to yield; to take pity on (smb.); *a nu se* ~ *să* not to find it in oneself to.

îndurare *sf.* mercy.

îndurător *adj.* merciful.

îndurera *vt.* to aggrieve.

înec *sn.* drowning.

îneca *vt.* to drown. *vr.* to get drowned; *(a se sinucide)* to drown oneself; *(cu mîncarea)* to choke.

înecat *sm.* drowned man, etc. *adj.* drowned.

înfăptui *vt.* to achieve. *vr.* to materialize.

înfășa *vt.* to swaddle.

înfășura *vt., vr.* to wrap up.

înfățișa *vt.* to (re)present; *(a arăta)* to produce; *(a închipui)* to imagine. *vr.* to turn up; *mil.* to report (to smb.); *jur.* to appear.

înfățișare *sf.* appearance.

înfia *vt.* to adopt.

înfiera *vt.* to brand.

înfierbînta *vt.* to heat. *vr.* to get heated.

înfige *vt.* to stick. *vr.* to. thrust oneself forward.

înființa *vt.* to set up. *vr.* to be set up.

înfiora *vt.* to frighten. *vr.* to shiver.

înfiorător *adj.* terrible.

înfipt *adj.* stuck; *fig.* pushing.

înfiripa *vr.* to take shape.

înflăcăra *vt.* to fire. *vr.* to warm up.

înflăcărare *sf.* ardour.

înflăcărat *adj.* fiery.

înflori *vi.* to blossom.

înflorire *sf.* blossoming; *fig. și* prosperity.

înflorit *adj.* in bloom.

înfloritor *adj.* blossoming; *fig. și* thriving.

înfoeare *sf.* passion.

înfometa *vt.* to starve.

înfrăți *vt., vr.* to unite.

înfrățire *sf.* fraternity.

înfricoșa *vt.* to scare. *vr.* to take fright.

înfricoșător *adj.* frightful.

înfrigurat *adj.* shivering; *fig.* feverish.

înfrînge *vt.* to defeat.

înfrîngere *sf.* defeat.

înfrumuseța *vt.* to embellish.

înfrunta *vt.* to face.

înfrunzit *adj.* in leaf.

înfrupta *vr.* to partake (of smth.).

înfuleca *vt., vi.* to wolf (down).

înfumurat *adj.* self-important.

înfunda *vt.* to stop up. *vr.* to be stopped; *(a se îngloda)* to get stuck.

înfundat *adj.* plugged; *(ascuns)* hidden; *(d. sunet)* stifled; *(d. băuturi)* bottled.

înfuria *vt.* to anger. *vr.* to grow angry.

înfuriat *adj.* angry.

îngădui *vt.* to admit (of); *(a păsui)* to brook. *vr.* to be permitted.

îngăduință *sf.* permission.

îngăduitor *adj.* tolerant.

îngăima *vt.* to mumble.

îngălbeni *vt.* to yellow. *vi., vr.* to turn yellow; to grow pale.

îngenunchea *vt.* to bring down to one's knees. *vi.* to kneel.

înger *sm.* angel.

înghesui *vt., vr.* to throng.

înghesuială *sf.* crush.

înghet *sn.* frost.

îngheța *vt., vi.* to freeze (with cold).

înghețare *sf.* freezing; ~*a salariilor* wage-freeze.

înghețată *sf.* ice(cream); *(populară)* hokey-pokey.

înghionti *vt., vr.* to nudge.

înghiți *vt.* to swallow; *fig.* to stomach (smb.).

înghițitură *sf.* mouthful; *(de lichid)* sip.

îngîmfa *vr.* to put on airs.

îngîmfare *sf.* conceit(edness).

îngimfat sm. peacock. adj. vain.

îngîna vt. to echo (smb.'s words) ; (a murmura) to murmur.

îngîndurat adj. thoughtful; (îngrijorat) worried.

îngloba vt. to include.

îngloda vr. to stick in the mud; fig. to plunge into debts.

îngrădi vt. to fence (in); fig. to restrict.

îngrădire sf. enclosure ; fig. restriction.

îngrămădi vt. to crowd ; (unul peste altul) to pile up. vr. to throng ; (a se acumula) to accumulate.

îngrăşa vt. to fatten ; agr. to fertilize ; (cu bălegar) to manure. vr. to put on weight.

îngrăşămînt sn. fertilizer ; (natural) manure.

îngreţoşa vt. to disgust. vr. to be nauseated.

îngreuna vt. to burden; (a agrava) to worsen. vr. to grow heavier ; to become more difficult.

îngriji vt. to look after. vr. to take care (of smth., smb.).

îngrijire sf. care ; sub ~a cuiva under smb.'s care ; edited by.

îngrijit adj. dapper ; (corect) accurate ; (minuţios) minute. adv. neatly, accurately.

îngrijitoare sf. servant ; (menajerd) housekeeper.

îngrijora vt., vr. to worry.

îngrijorare sf. worry.

îngrijorat adj. anxious, care-worn.

îngrijorător adj. alarming.

îngropa vt., vr. to bury.

îngroşa vt., vr. to thicken ; fig. to worsen.

îngrozi vt. to frighten. vr. to be scared.

îngrozitor adj. dreadful. adv. terribly.

îngust adj. narrow ; (strîmt) tight ; (la minte) narrow-minded.

îngusta vt. to narrow ; (a strîmta) to tighten. vr. to grow narrow(er).

înhăma vt., vr. to harness (oneself).

înhăţa vt. to seize.

înjgheba vt. to knock together : (a aduna) to gather.

înjosi vt., vr. to abase.

înjosire sf. humiliation.

înjuga vt. to yoke.

înjumătăţi vt. to halve.

înjunghea vt. to stab.

înjura vt. to swear (at). vi. to swear (like a trooper).

înjurătură sf. oath, curse.

înlănţui vt. to link ; (pe cineva) to chain ; (cu braţele) to hug ; to fold. vr. to be linked, to concatenate.

înlănţuire sf. concatenation.

înlătura vt. to remove.

înlemni vi. to remain stock-still.

înlesni vt. to ease.

înlesnire sf. facility.

înlocui vt. to replace.

înlocuitor sm. substitute.

înmărmuri vi. to be flabbergasted.

înmiit adj., adv. thousandfold.

înmîna vt. to hand.

înmormînta vt. to bury.

înmormîntare sf. burial.

înmuguri vi. to bud.

înmuia vt. (a face mai moale) to soften ; (într-un lichid) to dip.

înmulţi vt., vr. to multiply.

înmulțire *sf.* multiplication; *(spor)* increase.

înnăbuși *vt.* to smother; *(a îneca)* to choke; *(sunetele)* to muffle; *(o răscoală)* to suppress. *vr.* to choke.

înnăbușitor *adj.* stifling.

înnădi *vt.* to sew together. *vr.:* *a se ~ la* to develop the habit of.

înnăscut *adj.* innate.

înnebuni *vt.* to drive mad. *vi.* to lose one's mind.

înnebunit *adj.* mad (with pain, etc.).

înnegri *vt.*, *vr.* to blacken.

înnegura *vt.* to dim (with mist). *vr.* to grow misty.

înnobila *vt.* to ennoble.

înnoda *vt.* to knot; *(șireturi)* to lace. *vr.* to knot.

înnoi *vt.* to renew. *vi.* to be renewed.

înnopta *vi.* to stay overnight. *vr.:* *se înnoptează* night is setting in.

înnora *vt.* to darken. *vr.* to cloud over.

înot *sn.*, *adv.* swimming.

înota *vi.* to swim.

înotător *sm.* swimmer. *adj.* swimming.

înrădăcinat *adj.* (deeply) rooted.

înrăi *vt.* to embitter. *vr.* to become ill-natured.

înrăit *adj.* inveterate.

înrăma *vt.* to frame.

înrăutăți *vt.*, *vr.* to worsen.

înregistra *vt.* to record.

înregistrare *sf.* recording.

înrîuri *vt.* to influence.

înrîurire *sf.* impact.

înrobi *vt.* to enslave.

înrola *vt.*, *vr.* to enrol.

înroși *vt.* to redden. *vr.* to flush; *(a roși)* to blush.

înrudi *vr.* to be related (to smb., etc.).

înrudire *sf.* relation(ship).

însă *conj.* but, yet.

însămi *pron.* myself.

însămînța *vt.* to sow.

însănătoși *vt.* to heal. *vr.* to recover.

însărcina *vt.* to charge.

însărcinat *sm.* chargé d'affaires.

însărcinată *adj.* pregnant.

însăși *pron.* herself.

însăți *pron.* yourself.

înscăuna *vt.* to establish. *vr.* to become established.

înscena *vt.* to stage.

înscenare *sf.* staging; *~ judiciară* frame-up.

înscrie *vt.* to write down. *vr.* to put one's name down; *a se ~ în* to join.

înscriere *sf.* registration.

însele *pron.* themselves.

însemna *vt.* to note down; *(a constitui)* to be. *vi.* to mean.

însemnare *sf.* note.

însemnat *adj.* noteworthy; *(considerabil)* considerable.

însemnătate *sf.* importance.

însenina *vr.* to brighten up.

însera *vr.:* *se înserează* night is falling.

înserare *sf.*, **înserat** *sn.* nightfall.

însetat *adj.* thirsty.

însîngerat *adj.* gory; blood-thirsty.

însorit *adj.* sunlit.

însoți *vt.* to accompany.

însoțitor *sm.* companion.

înspăimînta *vt.* to terrify. *vr.* to be frightened.

înspăimîntat *adj.* panic-stricken.
înspăimîntător *adj.* frightful.
înspre *prep.* towards; against.
înstărit *adj.* well-to-do.
înstelat *adj.* starlit, starry.
înstrăina *vt.* to alienate; *fig.* to
estrange. *vr.* to become est-
ranged (from smb.).
însufleţi *vt.* to animate. *vr.* to
grow more animated.
însufleţire *sf.* enthusiasm; *(vioiciune)* liveliness.
însufleţit *adj.* alive; *fig.* animated; ~ *de* inspired with.
însumi *pron.* myself.
însura *vr.* to marry (smb.).
însurătoare *sf.* marriage.
însuşi[1] *pron.* himself; *(d. lucruri* etc.*)* itself.
însuşi[2] *vt.* to appropriate; *fig.*
to assimilate.
însuşire *sf.* quality; *(preluare)*
appropriation.
însutit *adj., adv.* hundredfold.
însuţi *pron.* yourself.
înşela *vt.* to cheat; *(a trăda)*
to betray. *vi.* to cheat. *vr.* to
be wrong.
înşelăciune *sf.* fraud; *fig.* hoax.
înşelător *sm.* swindler. *adj.* delusive.
înşelătorie *sf.* deception.
înşine *pron.* ourselves.
înşira *vt.* to string; *(a enumera)*
to list. *vr.* to stretch.
înşişi *pron.* themselves.
înşivă *pron.* yourselves.
înştiinţa *vt.* to notify.
înştiinţare *sf.* notice.
întări *vt.* to strengthen; *(a fortifica)* to fortify; *(cu autoritate)* to sanction; *(sănătatea)*
to invigorate; *(a accentua)* to
stress. *vr.* to consolidate.

întăritor *sn.* physic. *adj.* bracing.
întărîta *vt.* to incite.
întemeia *vt.* to found; *a* ~ *pe*
to base on. *vr.* to rely; to
proceed (from smth.).
întemeiat *adj.* (well-)grounded.
întemeiere *sf.* foundation.
întemeietor *sm.* founder.
întemniţa *vt.* to jail.
înteţi *vt., vr.* to intensify.
întinde *vt.* to draw, to stretch;
(mîna etc.*)* to offer; *(a aşterne)*
to lay; *a o* ~ to take to one's
legs. *vr.* to stretch; *(a se culca)*
to lie down; *(a se tolăni)* to
sprawl; *(a dura)* to last.
întindere *sf.* extent; *(suprafaţă)* surface.
întineri *vt.* to rejuvenate. *vi.*
to grow younger.
întins *adj.* stretched; *(încordat)*
tense; *(vast)* extensive. *adv.*
straight.
întipări *vt., vr.* to imprint (upon
smth.).
întîi *num.* the first. *adv.* at
first; ~ *şi* ~ firstly.
întîietate *sf.* priority.
întîlni *vt.* to meet (with); *(întîmplător)* to run into. *vr.* to
meet (with smb.); to have an
appointment (with smb.).
întîlnire *sf.* appointment; *(sportivă* etc.*)* meet, encounter.
întîmpina *vt.* to meet; to welcome; *(greutăţi)* to face.
întîmpla *vr.* to occur; *ce s-a* ~*t?*
what is the matter? *orice s-ar*
~ come what may.
întîmplare *sf.* occurrence; *(soartă)* chance; *din* ~ accidentally;
la ~ at random.
întîmplător *adj.* fortuitous. *adv.*
accidentally.

întîrzia *vt.* to delay. *vi.* to be late (for the classes, etc.) ; to be behindhand (with the rent, etc.).

întîrziere *sf.* delay ; *(la ore* etc.*)* coming late ; *în* ~ behind-hand.

întoarce *vt.* to (re)turn ; *(pe dos)* to reverse ; *(ceasul)* to wind up. *vr.* to (re)turn ; *(a se răsuci)* to twist, to swing.

întoarcere *sf.* (re)turn ; ~*a interzisă* no U-turn.

întocmai *adv.* exactly ; *(desigur)* of course ; ~ *ca* just like.

întocmi *vt.* to draw up ; to write down, to prepare.

întocmire *sf.* elaboration ; *(structură)* structure.

întors *sn.* return. *adj.* (re)turned ; ~ *pe dos* upset.

întorsătură *sf.* turn.

întortocheat *adj.* winding ; *(complicat)* intricate.

întotdeauna *adv.* always.

întovărăşi *vt.* to see (home, etc.). *vr.* to join hands.

între *prep.* between ; *(*~ *mai mulţi)* among.

întreba *vt., vi.* to ask.

întrebare *sf.* question.

întrebuinţa *vt.* to use ; to resort to. *vr.* to be in usage.

întrebuinţare *sf.* utilization.

întrebuinţat *adj.* used ; *(uzat)* worn.

întrece *vt.* to outrun ; *(a depăşi)* to exceed. *vr.* to compete.

întrecere *sf.* competition ; *sport* contest ; ~ *socialistă* socialíst emulation.

întredeschis *adj.* half-open ; *(d. uşă şi)* ajar.

întreg *sm.* whole. *adj.* whole.

întregi *vt.* to complete. *vr.* to be rounded off.

întregime *sf.* entirety ; *în* ~ fully.

întreit *adj., adv.* threefold.

întrema *vr.* to pick up (strength).

întreprinde *vt.* to undertake, to begin.

întreprindere *sf.* industrial unit ; factory ; enterprise.

întreprinzător *adj.* enterprising.

întrerupător *sn.* switch.

întrerupe *vt.* to interrupt ; *(a opri)* to stop. *vr.* to break off.

întrerupere *sf.* interruption ; *(oprire)* stop.

întretăia *vt., vr.* to cross.

întretăiat *adj.* criss-crossed ; *(d. respiraţie)* panting.

întreţine *vt.* to keep (up). *vr.* to earn one's living ; *(a vorbi)* to talk (with smb.).

întreţinere *sf.* maintenance ; *(la bloc* etc.*)* rates.

întrevedea *vt.* to catch a glimpse of ; *(a prevedea)* to foresee. *vr.* to be in the offing.

întrevedere *sf.* meeting.

întrezări *vt.* to discern. *vr.* to loom.

întrista *vt.* to (ag)grieve. *vr.* to grow sad.

întristare *sf.* sadness.

întrona *vt.* to enthrone.

întru *prep.* in(to) ; *într-atît* ... *încît* so (much) ... that ; *într-una* incessantly.

întruchipa *vt.* to embody.

întrucît *conj.* as, since.

întrucîtva *adv.* somewhat.

întruni *vt.* to combine ; to meet. *vr.* to meet.

întrunire *sf.* rally.

întuneca *vt.* to darken. *vr.* to

cloud over; *se întunecă* it is getting dark.

întunecat *adj.* dark; *(posomorît)* gloomy; *(sinistru)* grim, sinister.

întunecime *sf.* obscurity.

întunecos *adj.* gloomy.

întuneric *sn.* dark(ness).

înțărca *vt.* to wean.

înțelegător *adj.* sympathetic. *adv.* sympathetically.

înțelege *vt.* to understand; *(a-și da seama de)* to realize; *(o aluzie)* to take (the hint); *(a distinge)* to distinguish; *a ~ greșit* to misunderstand. *vr.* to get on (together), to agree; *(a fi de înțeles)* to be understandable; *se ~ de la sine* it goes without saying.

înțelegere *sf.* agreement; *(compătimire)* sympathy.

înțelepciune *sf.* wisdom.

înțelept *adj.* wise, sagacious.

înțeles *sn.* meaning; *de ~* understandable; *(d. oameni)* pliant.

înțepa *vt.*, *vi.* to sting; *(a mușca)* to bite. *vr.* to prick (one's finger, etc.).

înțepat *adj.* pricked; *fig.* stuck-up.

înțepător *adj.* sharp; *(d. gust)* pungent.

înțepătură *sf.* sting.

înțepeni *vt.* to fasten. *vi.* to become stiff. *vr.* to get stuck.

înțesa *vt.* to pack.

învălmăși *vr.* to jumble (together).

învălmășit *adj.* confused.

învălui *vt.* to wrap; *(a înconjura)* to surround.

învăța *vt.*, *vi.* to learn; *(a preda)* to teach.

învățat *sm.* scholar. *adj.* learned; *(deprins)* accustomed (to smth.).

învățămînt *sn.* education; *~ profesional* vocational education.

învățător *sm.* school teacher; *fig.* teacher.

învățătură *sf.* learning; *(învățămînt)* education; *(morală)* teaching; *(cunoștințe)* knowledge.

învechi *vr.* to age; *(a se uza)* to be worn out.

învechit *adj.* old(-fashioned).

învecina *vr.* to be contiguous.

învecinat *adj.* neighbouring.

înveli *vt.*, *vr.* to wrap (oneself) up.

înveliș *sn.*, **învelitoare** *sf.* cover.

învenina *vt.* to envenom.

înverșuna *vr.* to become stubborn.

înverșunare *sf.* acrimony; *(îndîrjire)* grimness.

înverșunat *adj.* grim.

înverzi *vi.*, *vr.* to turn green.

înveseli *vt.*, *vr.* to cheer up.

înveșmînta *vt.*, *vr.* to clothe.

învia *vt.*, *vi.* to revive.

înviere *sf.* resurrection; *fig.* revival.

învineți *vt.* to render purple. *vr.* to turn purple.

învinețit *adj.* purple, blue; *(de bătăi)* black and blue.

învingător *sm.* victor. *adj.* triumphant.

învinge *vt.* to conquer; to worst, to beat; *(dificultăți etc.)* to overcome. *vi.* to carry the day.

învinovăți *vt.* to charge (with smth.).

învins *adj.* defeated.

învinui *vt.* to accuse (of smth.), to charge (with smth.).

înviora vt. to enliven. vr. to take heart.

înviorător adj. invigorating.

învîrti vt. to turn; (o armă etc.) to brandish. vr. to turn; fig. to get on in the world; mi se învîrteşte capul my head swims.

învîrtire, învîrtitură sf. turn; rotation.

învoi vt. to give (smb.) leave of absence. vr. to agree; (a accepta) to accept.

învoială sf. agreement.

învrăjbi vt. to set against each other. vr. to quarrel.

învrednici vr. to be(come) able (to do).

înzăpezi vt. to snow up. vr. to be snowed up.

înzdrăveni vr. to pick up (strength).

înzeci vt. to increase tenfold; to redouble.

înzestra vt. to endow; (o fată) to dower.

înzestrat adj. gifted, endowed (with).

J

jachetă sf. jacket.

jad sn. jade.

jaf sn. plunder.

jaguar sm. jaguar.

jale sf. grief; (jelanie) lament; (doliu) mourning; cu ~ sadly; de ~ sad.

jalnic adj. sorry; (deplorabil) lamentable. adv. grievously.

jalon sn. stake; fig. landmark.

jaluzele sf. pl. (Venetian) blind.

jambiere sf. pl. leggings.

jambon sn. ham.

jandarm sm. gendarme.

jandarmerie sf. gendarmerie; (în Anglia) constabulary.

japonez sm., adj. Japanese.

japoneză sf. Japanese (woman).

jar sn. embers.

jargon sn. jargon.

jartieră sf. garter.

javră sf. cur; fig. rip.

jaz sn. jazz.

jăratic sn. hot embers; ca pe ~ on tenter-hooks.

jder sm. marten.

jecmăni vt. to fleece.

jefui vt. to plunder.

jeg sn. filth.

jegos adj. filthy.

jeli vt. to mourn for; (a deplînge) to deplore. vi., vr. to lament.

jelui vr. to complain; (a se lamenta) to lament.

jena vt. to hinder; (a deranja) to disturb; (d. pantofi) to pinch. vr. to be self-conscious sau bashful; to shrink (from doing smth.).

jenant adj. embarrassing; (penibil) awkward.

jenat adj. embarrassed; self-conscious.

jenă sf. uneasinness; (sfială) self-consciousness; fără ~ shamelessly.

jerbă *sf.* wreath.
jerpelit *adj.* threadbare.
jerseu *sn.* jersey.
jertfă *sf.* sacrifice.
jertfi *vt., vr.* to sacrifice (oneself).
jeţ *sn.* armchair.
jgheab *sn.* pipe; *(la moară)* mill race.
jigărit *adj.* skinny.
jigni *vt.* to offend.
jignire *sf.* offence.
jignitor *adj.* outrageous.
jilav *adj.* moist.
jind *sn.* hankering; *cu* ~ covetously.
jindui *vt.* to covet.
jir *sn.* beech nut.
jneapăn *sm.* juniper tree.
joacă *sf.* play; *în* ~ in jest, jokingly.
joben *sn.* opera hat.
joc *sn.* game, play; *(sport)* sport; *(distracţie)* pastime; *fig.* trifle; *(dans)* dance; *teatru* acting; ~ *de cărţi* card game; ~ *de cuvinte* pun; ~*uri de salon* parlour tricks.
jocheu *sm.* jockey.
joi *sf.* Thursday. *adv.* (on) Thursday.
joia *adv.* on Thursday(s).
jongla *vi.* to juggle.
jongler *sm.* conjurer.
jos *sn.* bottom; *de* ~ lower; from below; *în* ~ down(wards); *(pe rîu)* downstream; *pe* ~ on foot. *adj.* low. *adv.* down; *(dedesubt)* below; *(la pămînt)* to *sau* on the ground; *(la parter)* downstairs; *(la fund)* at the bottom; ~ *mîinile!* hands off!; *mai* ~ lower down. *interj.* down!
josnic *adj.* base. *adv.* meanly.

josnicie *sf.* baseness.
jovial *adj.* cheerful. *adv.* cheerfully.
jubila *vi.* to exult.
jubileu *sn.* jubilee.
jubiliar *adj.* jubilee.
juca *vt.* to play (at); *(a face o mişcare)* to move; *teatru* to act; *(a dansa)* to dance; *(jocuri de noroc)* to gamble. *vi.* to play (games); *(a zburda)* to gambol; *teatru* to act; *(a dansa)* to dance; *(a mişca)* to move; *(la loterie)* to put in the lottery; *a* ~ *pe bani* to play for money. *vr.* to play; *(a zburda)* to gambol; *(a glumi)* to play tricks; *(d. o piesă* etc.*)* to be acted, to be on.
jucărie *sf.* toy, plaything; *fig.* trifle, a child's play.
jucător *sm.* player.
jucăuş *adj.* playful; *(vioi)* sprightly.
judeca *vt.* to judge; *jur.* to try; *(a critica)* to blame; *(a cîntări)* to consider. *vi.* to judge (by appearances, etc.). *vr.* to go to law.
judecată *sf.* judg(e)ment; ~ *penală* trial; *judecata de apoi* doomsday; *cu* ~ wise, reasonable; *la* ~ in court.
judecător *sm.* judge.
judecătoresc *adj.* judicial.
judecătorie *sf.* court (of law).
judeţ *sn.* district.
judeţean *adj.* county.
judiciar *adj.* judicial; *(d. medicină)* forensic.
judicios *adj.* judicious. *adv.* reasonably.
jug *sn.* yoke.

juli *vt.* to scratch. *vr.* to hurt oneself.

jumări *sf. pl.* scraps ; *(de ouă)* scrambled eggs.

jumătate *sf.* half ; *pe ~* fifty--fifty ; *pe ~ închis* half closed.

jumuli *vt.* to pluck ; *fig.* to bleed.

june *sm.* youth ; *~ prim* male lead.

junghi *sn.* stitch.

junglă *sf.* jungle.

jupon *sn.* underskirt.

jupui *vt.* to skin. *vr.* to peel.

jur *sn. : în ~, de ~ împrejur* all (a)round.

jura *vt.* to swear. *vi., vr.* to swear (by smth.) ; *a ~ strîmb* to commit perjury.

jurat *sm.* jury man. *adj.* sworn.

jurămînt *sn.* oath ; *fig.* vow ; *~ fals sau strîmb* perjury ; *sub ~* on oath.

juridic *adj.* law..., juridical.

jurisconsult *sm.* lawyer.

jurist *sm.* jurist.

juriu *sn.* jury.

jurnal *sn.* journal ; *(ziar)* newspaper ; *(personal)* diary ; *(de actualități)* news reel ; *~ de bord* log (book) ; *~ de călătorie* travelling log ; *~ de modă* fashion magazine ; *~ sonor* radio news reel.

jurnalist *sm.* newspaperman.

just *adj.* just, fair ; *(corect)* correct. *adv.* correctly. *interj.* hear ! hear !

justețe *sf.* correctness ; *(dreptate)* justice.

justifica *vt., vr.* to justify (oneself).

justificare *sf.* justification ; *(dovadă)* proof.

justiție *sf.* justice ; *jur.* law.

K

kaki *adj.* khaki.

kilo(gram) *sn.* kilo(gram).

kilometric *adj.* kilometric ; *fig.* endless.

kilometru *sm.* kilometre, two thirds of a mile.

kilovat *sm.* kilowatt.

L

la *sm.* A, la. *prep. (static)* at, in ; *(dinamic)* to ; *(către)* towards ; *(lipit de)* against ; *(temporal)* at ; *(ca zi)* on ; *~ noi* with us ; *~ oameni* in man ; *pe ~* (at) about, roundabout ; *pînă ~* (up) to.

labă *sf.* paw ; *(mînă)* hand,

fist; *(a piciorului)* foot; *în patru labe* on all fours.
labirint *sn.* labyrinth.
laborator *sn.* laboratory.
lac *sn. geogr.* lake; *(mic)* pond; *(baltă)* pool; *(lustru)* lacquer; *de ~* patent leather (shoes, etc.).
lacăt *sn.* padlock.
lacheu *sm.* lackey; *fig.* flunkey.
lacom *adj.* greedy. *adv.* greedily; *fig.* avidly.
laconic *adj.* laconic. *adv.* tersely.
lacrimă *sf.* tear.
lacună *sf.* gap.
ladă *sf.* case; *(pt. ambalaj)* crate; *(cufăr)* trunk; *~ de gunoi* garbage can.
lagăr *sn.* camp.
lagună *sf.* lagoon.
laic *adj.* lay.
lalea *sf.* tulip.
lamă *sf. zool.* llama; *(tăiş)* blade; *(de ras)* razor blade.
lamenta *vr.* to wail.
lamentabil *adj.* lamentable. *adv.* sadly.
lampă *sf.* lamp; *(bec)* light bulb; *~ de birou* gooseneck lamp.
lan *sn.* field.
lance *sf.* lance; spear.
languros *adj.* sentimental; *(d. priviri)* sheep's (eyes, etc.).
langustă *sf.* spiny lobster.
lansa *vt.* to launch; *(a răspîndi)* to spread; *(a iniţia)* to initiate. *vr.* to rush (headlong); *(a se aventura)* to venture; to be successful.
lanternă *sf.* flash light.
lanţ *sn.* chain; *pl. şi* fetters; *în ~* chain ... *adv.* in succession.

laolaltă *adv.* together.
lapidar *adj.* lapidary.
lapon *sm., adj.* Lapp.
laponă *sf., adj.* Lapp; *(limba)* Lapponic.
lapoviţă *sf.* sleet.
lapsus *sn.* slip (of the mind, etc.).
lapte *sn.* milk; *~ bătut* butter milk; *~ praf* powder milk.
lapţi *sm. pl.* soft roe.
larg *sn.* open (sea); *în ~* in the offing; *la ~ul său* at one's ease; *pe ~* in great detail. *adj.* wide; *(spaţios)* spacious; *(d. haine)* loose.
larmă *sf.* hubbub.
larvă *sf.* larva.
lasciv *adj.* randy; *(d. persoane)* lecherous.
laş *sm.* coward. *adj.* cowardly.
laşitate *sf.* poltroonery.
lat *sn.* broad (side); breadth; *(al săbiei)* flat; *de-a ~ul* across. *adj.* broad; *(d. farfurii)* flat; *~ în spate* broad-shouldered.
latent *adj.* latent. *adv.* latently.
lateral *adj.* lateral. *adv.* laterally.
latifundiar *sm.* great landowner.
latin *sm., adj.,* **latină** *sf., adj.* Latin.
latitudine *sf.* latitude; *fig.* freedom; *e la ~a ta* it is up to you.
latură *sf.* side; *în lături* laterally.
laţ *sn.* loop.
laudă *sf.* praise; *~ de sine* boastfulness.
laur *sm.* laurel.
laureat *sm.* laureate.
lavabou *sn.* wash-stand; *(spălător)* lavatory.
lavalieră *sf.* four-in-hand tie.
lavandă *sf.* lavender.

lavă *sf.* lava.

lavoar *sn.* washstand.

lăbărțat *adj.* out of shape.

lăcătuș *sm.* locksmith.

lăcomi *vr.* to be greedy ; *a se ~ la* to covet.

lăcomie *sf.* greed ; *(la mîncare)* gluttony ; *cu ~* eagerly.

lăcrima *vi.* to shed tears.

lăcrimioară *sf.* lily-of-the-valley.

lăcustă *sf.* locust ; *(cosaș)* grasshoper.

lăfăi *vr.* to sprawl ; *fig.* to live on the fat of the land.

lămîi *sm.* lemon-tree.

lămîie *sf.* lemon.

lămîiță *sf.* aloysia.

lămuri *vt.* to clear up ; *(pe cineva)* to enlighten. *vr.* to grow clear ; *(d. cineva)* to be(comc) enlightened.

lămurire *sf.* explanation.

lămurit *adj.* clear ; *(distinct)* distinct. *adv.* clearly ; *(distinct)* distinctly.

lămuritor *adj.* explanatory ; enlightening.

lăptar *sm.* milkman.

lăptăreasă *sf.* dairy maid.

lăptișor *sn.:* ~ *de matcă* royal jelly.

lăptos *adj.* milky.

lăptucă *sf.* lettuce.

lărgi *vt.* to broaden ; *(o haină)* to let out. *vr.* to widen ; *(d. haină* etc.*)* to grow loose.

lărgime *sf.* width.

lăsa *vt.* to let (loose) ; *(jos)* to drop ; *(a slobozi)* to set free ; *(a îngădui)* to allow ; *(a părăsi)* to leave ; *(a înceta)* to leave off ; *a-și ~ barbă* etc. to grow a beard, etc. ; *a ~ în urmă* to outstrip ; *a ~ la o parte*

to say nothing of ; *a ~ în pace* to let alone ; *las' pe mine* leave it to me. *vi.* not to mind ; *lasă, lasă!* take care ! *vr.* to allow (oneself) ; *(în jos)* to drop ; *(a se întinde)* to lie down ; *(a ceda)* to give way ; *(d. noapte* etc.*)* to set in ; *a nu se ~* not to let go ; *a se ~ de* to give up ; *a se ~ în voia* ... to indulge in ... ; *a se ~ greu* not to yield ; *a nu se ~ mai prejos* to keep up with smb., etc.

lăsător *adj.* indolent.

lăstar *sm.* offshoot ; *pl.* copse.

lătra *vi.* to bark.

lătrat *sn.* barking.

lăturalnic *adj.* side ; *(d. străzi* etc.*)* by-... , back.

lături[1] *sf. pl.* slops. *fig.* offal.

lături[2] *sf. pl.:* în ~, pe de ~ aside.

lăți *vt., vr.* to widen.

lățime *sf.* breadth.

lăuda *vt.* to praise. *vr.* to boast.

lăudabil *adj.* commendable.

lăudăros *sm.* windbag. *adj.* bragging.

lăudăroșenie *sf.* boastfulness.

lăuntric *adj.* inner(most). *adv.* inwardly.

lăutar *sm.* fiddler, musician.

leac *sn.* remedy ; *~uri băbești* quack medicine ; *de ~* medicinal ; *fără ~* incurable.

leafă *sf.* wages ; *(a funcționarilor)* salary.

leagăn *sn.* cradle ; *(azil)* nursery ; *(scrînciob)* swing.

leal *adj.* loyal.

lealitate *sf.* honesty.

lebădă *sf.* swan.

lebervurșt *sm.* liver sausage.

lector *sm.* (university) lecturer.
lectură *sf.* reading.
lecţie *sf.* lesson *(oră)* class ; *pl.* *(teme)* homework ; ~ *particulară* private lesson.
lecui *vt.* to heal. *vr.* to be healed ; *fig.* to get sick (of smth.).
lefter *adj.* penniless.
lega *vt.* to tie ; *(strîns)* to fasten ; *(de ceva)* to attach ; *(o rană)* to dress ; *(a înnoda)* to knot ; *fig.* to connect ; *a ~ prietenie* to make friends. *vr.* to be tied ; *a se ~ de* to be bound up with ; *(a pisa)* to importune ; *(a acosta)* to accost ; *(a ataca)* to cavil at.
legal *adj.* lawful. *adv.* legally.
legalitate *sf.* legality.
legat *adj.* bound ; *(închegat)* connected ; *bine ~* strong(ly built). *adv.* coherently.
legaţie *sf.* legation.
legămînt *sn.* pledge ; *(jurămînt)* vow.
legăna *vt.* to rock. *vr.* to swing.
legător *sm.* bookbinder.
legătorie *sf.* bookbinding.
legătură *sf.* bundle ; *(mănunchi)* bunch ; *(basma)* (head)kerchief ; *(de carte)* binding ; *(relaţie)* relation(ship) ; *(amoroasă şi mil.)* liaison ; *în ~ cu* as regards ; *(din pricina)* on account of.
lege *sf.* law ; *(în Anglia, S.U.A. şi)* act ; *(proiect)* bill.
legendar *adj.* legendary.
legendă *sf.* myth ; *(poveste)* tale ; *(a hărţii)* legendum ; *(la o fotografie etc.)* caption.
legionar *sm. pol.* iron guard(ist).
legislatură *sf.* legislature ; *(perioadă)* term (of office).

legitim *adj.* legitimate.
legitima *vt.* to identify ; *(a recunoaşte)* to legitimate. *vr.* to prove one's identity.
legitimaţie *sf.* identity card ; (personal) paper.
legiune *sf.* legion.
legumă *sf.* vegetable.
leguminoase *sf. pl.* vegetables, pulse.
lehuză *sf.* lying-in woman.
leit *adj.* exact ; ~ *taică-său* the dead spit of his father.
lejer *adj.* light. *adv.* easily.
lele *sf.* sister ; aunt; light woman.
lemn *sn.* (piece of) wood ; *(butuc)* log ; *pl.* (fire) wood ; *(netăiate)* lumber ; *(cherestea)* timber ; ~ *de rezonanţă* sounding board ; *de ~* wood(en) ; *fig.* insensible. *adj., adv.* unmoved.
lemnărie *sf.* wood ; *(cherestea)* timber.
lemnos *adj.* wooden.
lene *sf.* laziness.
leneş *sm.* lazybones. *adj.* slothful. *adv.* idly.
lenevi *vi.* to laze.
lenevie *sf.* laziness.
leninism *sn.* Leninism.
leninist *sm.* Leninist. *adj.* Lenin's, Lenin(ist).
lenjereasă *sf.* seamstress.
lenjerie *sf.*, **lenjuri** *sn. pl.* (under) linen ; *(de pat)* bed clothes.
lent *adj.* slow. *adv.* slowly.
lentilă *sf.* lens.
leoaică *sf.* lioness.
leoarcă *adj.* wringing wet.
leopard *sm.* leopard.
lepăda *vt.* to drop ; *(d. animale)* to shed. *vr.: a se ~ de* to disavow ; *(un obicei)* to leave off.

lepră *sf.* leprosy ; *fig.* villain.
lepros *sm.* leper. *adj.* leprous.
lesne *adv.* easily.
lesnicios *adj.* easy.
lespede *sf.* slab ; *(de mormînt)* tombstone.
leș *sn.* carrion ; *(de animal)* carcase.
leșie *sf.* lye.
leșin *sn.* swoon.
leșina *vi.* to faint.
leton *sm.* Lett. *adj.* Lettish, Latvian.
letonă *sf., adj.* Lettish.
leu *sm.* *(zool.)* lion ; *(monedă)* leu.
leuștean *sm.* lovage.
levănțică *sf.* lavender.
lexic *sn.* vocabulary.
lexicon *sn.* dictionary.
leza *vt.* to harm, to wrong.
leziune *sf.* lesion, wound.
libelulă *sf.* dragon fly.
liber *adj.* free (from) ; *(disponibil)* vacant ; *(independent)* independent ; *(deschis)* open ; *(d. ochi)* naked ; *(nesilit)* voluntary ; *(d. taxi)* for hire. *adv.* freely ; *(improvizat)* offhand.
libera *vt.* to liberate ; *mil.* to discharge. *vr.* to be discharged.
liberal *sm., adj.* liberal.
libertate *sf.* freedom ; *(îndrăzneală)* liberties ; *(permisiune)* leave ; ~*a cuvîntului* freedom of speech ; ~*a presei* freedom of the press ; *în* ~ at large.
libertin *sm.* libertine. *adj.* dissolute.
libidinos *adj.* lewd, lusty
librar *sm.* bookseller.
librărie *sf.* bookshop.

libret *sn.* *muz.* libretto ; ~ *de economii* savings book.
licări *vi.* to sparkle ; *(slab)* to flicker.
licărire *sf.* flicker.
licență *sf.* university degree *(brevet)* license ; ~ *în litere* B.A. (degree) ; ~ *poetică* poetic licence.
licențiat *sm.* bachelor (of law, arts, etc.).
licențios *adj.* bawdy.
liceu *sn.* secondary school.
lichea *sf.* lick-spittle ; *(ticălos)* ne'er-do-well.
lichid *sn.* liquid. *adj.* liquid ; *(d. bani)* ready.
lichida *vt.* to liquidate ; *(a încheia)* to settle (a debt).
lichidare *sf.* abolition.
lichior *sn.* liqueur.
licitație *sf.* auction.
licurici *sm.* glow-worm.
lider *sm.* leader.
lied *sn.* lied.
lift *sn.* lift.
liftier *sm.* liftboy.
ligă *sf.* league.
lighean *sn.* basin.
lighioană *sf.* (wild) beast.
lihnit *adj.* starving, hungry.
liliac *sm.* *bot.* lilac ; *zool.* bat
liman *sn.* *geogr.* liman ; *fig.* harbour.
limbaj *sn.* language.
limbă *sf.* tongue ; *(națională)* language ; *(vorbire)* speech ; *(de ceas)* hand ; *(încălțător)* shoehorn ; *(de pămînt)* strip ; ~ *maternă* mother tongue ; ~ *vorbită* colloquial speech ; *cu limba scoasă* breathlessly; thirsty ; *cu* ~ *de moarte* on one's deathbed.

limbric sm. belly worm.

limbut sm. loquacious fellow. adj. loquacious.

limita vt., vr. to limit (oneself).

limitat adj. limited; (redus) reduced; fig. obtuse.

limită sf. limit; fără ~ illimited; în limita posibilităților according to our possibilities; la ~ just on the line.

limonadă sf. lemonade.

limpede adj. clear; (deslușit) distinct; (transparent) transparent; (evident) obvious. adv. clearly.

limpezi vt. to clarify; (a clăti) to rinse. vr. to clear (up).

limuzină sf. sedan.

liu sm. iht. tench. adj. gentle; (neted) smooth. adv. quietly.

linge vt. to lick. vr.: a se ~ pe bot to whistle for it.

lingură sf. spoon; (polonic) ladle; (conținutul) spoonful.

lingurița sf. teaspoon; (conținutul) teaspoonful.

linguși vt. to flatter.

lingușire sf. flattery.

lingușitor sm. toad-eater; sycophant. adj. flattering.

lingvist sm. linguist.

lingvistică sf. linguistics.

linia vt. to rule.

linie sf. line; (riglă) ruler; ~ ferată railway (line); ~ de conduită behaviour; ~ interurbană toll line; în linii mari on the whole, roughly (speaking).

linioară sf. hyphen.

liniște sf. silence; (tihnă) peace, quiet. interj. silence!

liniști vt. to quiet(en); (a alina) to comfort. vr. to grow calm; (d. furtună etc.) to abate.

liniștit adj. quiet, calm; (tăcut) silent; (tihnit) peaceful. adv. quietly, calmly.

liniuță sf. dash; ~ de unire hyphen.

linoleum sn. linoleum; artă linocut.

lins adj. licked; (d. păr) sleek.

linșa vt. to lynch.

linșaj sn. lynching; Lynch Law.

linte sf. lentil.

lințoliu sn. pall.

linx sm. lynx.

lipi vt. to stick (together); to glue (on); (a suda) to solder. vr. to stick (to smth.); to cling (to smb.).

lipici sn. glue; fig. glamour.

lipicios adj. sticky; fig. affectionate.

lipie sf. flat round loaf.

lipit adj. stuck, glued; ~ de perete against the wall; sărac ~ in dire poverty.

lipitoare sf. leech.

lipitură sf. soldering.

lipsă sf. absence; (deficiență) shortcoming; (sărăcie) lack; (criză) shortage; ~ de grijă carelessness; ~ la cîntar short weight; în ~ jur. by default.

lipsi vt. to deprive. vi. to be absent; (a nu se găsi) to be wanting; a-i ~ (un lucru) to lack smth. vr. to give (it) up; mă lipsesc de el I'll do without it.

liră sf. fin. pound (sterling); (italiană) lira; muz. lyre.

liric adj. lyrical.

lirică sf. (lyrical) poetry.

listă sf. list.

literal adj. word for word.

literalmente adv. literally.

literar *adj.* literary.
literatură *sf.* literature ; *(biblio-grafie)* reference material ; ~ *universală* world literature.
literă *sf.* letter ; *(de tipar)* type ; *litere cursive* italics ; ~ *mare* capital ; ~ *mică* small letter.
litigios *adj.* litigious.
litigiu *sn.* disputed issue.
litoral *sn.* seacoast ; *pe* ~ at the sea side.
litră *sf.* *(capacitate)* half pint ; *(greutate)* half pound.
litru *sm.* litre ; quart.
liturghie *sf.* mass.
livadă *sf.* orchard.
livid *adj.* livid.
livra *vt.* to deliver.
livră *sf.* pound.
livret *sn.* (small) book ; ~ *mili-tar* soldier's record.
lînă *sf.* wool ; *lîna de aur* the Golden Fleece ; ~ *pură* all wool ; *de* ~ wool(len).
lîncezeală *sf.* torpor.
lîncezi *vi.* to stagnate.
lîngă *prep.* (close) by ; *(lipit de)* against ; ~ *geam* at the win-dow ; *de* ~ next to ; *de pe* ~ with ; *pe* ~ about ; *pe* ~ *că* besides.
lobodă *sf.* orach(e).
loc *sn.* place ; *(spaţiu)* room ; *(scaun)* seat ; *(teren)* (p)lot ; *(pămînt)* land ; *(post)* job ; ~ *comun* truism ; ~ *de casă* house lot ; *de* ~ not at all ; *de pe* ~ standing ; *din* ~ *în* ~ here and there ; *în* ~*ul* *cuiva* in smb.'s stead ; *în* ~*ul* *lui* if I were he ; *la* ~ again ; *la* ~*ul lui* modest ; *pe* ~ on the spot.
local *sn.* building ; premises ;

(restaurant etc.*)* restaurant ; ~ *de dans* hop. *adj.* local.
localitate *sf.* place ; locality.
localiza *vt.* to localize ; *(un in-cendiu* etc.*)* to bring under control.
localnic *sm.*, *adj.* native.
locatar *sm.* lodger.
locomotivă *sf.* railway engine.
locotenent *sm.* lieutenant ; ~*-colonel* lieutenant colonel ; ~ *major* senior lieutenant.
locţiitor *sm.* deputy.
locui *vi.* to live.
locuinţă *sf.* dwelling.
locuit *adj.* inhabited.
locuitor *sm.* inhabitant.
locvace *adj.* loquacious.
logaritm *sm.* logarithm.
logic *adj.* logical ; reasonable. *adv.* logically.
logică *sf.* logic.
logodi *vt.* to betroth. *vr.* to become engaged (to smb.).
logodnă *sf.* engagement ; *(cere-monie şi)* betrothal.
logodnic *sm.* fiancé.
logodnică *sf.* fiancée.
loial *adj.* loyal. *adv.* loyally.
lojă *sf.* box ; *(masonică)* lodge.
lopată *sf.* shovel ; *(vîslă)* oar.
lor *adj.* their. *al* ~ theirs. *pron.* (to) them.
lord *sm.* lord.
lot *sn.* (p)lot (of land) ; *(grup)* batch.
lovi *vt.* to strike ; *(a bate)* to knock ; *(cu cotul)* to nudge ; *(uşurel)* to pat ; *(cu pumnul şi fig.)* to deal a blow at ; *(cu piciorul)* to kick ; *(a răni)* to hurt ; *(a dăuna)* to harm. *vi.* to strike. *vr.* to bump into each other ; to hurt oneself.

to get hurt; *a se* ~ *de* to come up against.

lovitură *sf.* blow; *(de picior)* kick; *(în uşă)* knock; *(atac)* attack; *(la fotbal)* shot; *pol.* coup (d'Etat); *(spargere)* burglary; ~ *de graţie* finishing stroke; ~ *de pedeapsă* penalty (shot); ~ *de teatru* sensational turn of events; ~ *de trăsnet* thunderbolt; ~ *joasă*, ~ *sub centură* foul *sau* deep hit; *dintr-o* ~ at a stroke (of the pen).

loz *sn.* lottery ticket.

lozincă *sf.* slogan, catchword.

lua *vt.* to take; *(a apuca)* to seize; *(a prelua)* to assume; *(a răpi)* to deprive of; *(trenul etc.)* to go by; *(a cumpăra)* to buy; *(a consuma)* to eat; *(masa şi)* to have; *(a închiria)* to hire; *(a căpăta)* to catch; *(a cuceri)* to conquer; *(a minui)* to manage; *(greşit)* to mistake for; *a o* ~ *către ...* to go to ...; *a* ~ *cu împrumut* to borrow; *a* ~ *pe cineva pe departe* to beat about the bush. *vr.* to be taken; *(a fi molipsitor)* to be catching; *a se* ~ *de cineva* to cavil at smb.; *a se* ~ *după* to follow smb.'s example *sau* advice.

luare *sf.* taking; ~-*aminte* care(fulness); attention.

luceafăr *sm.* evening *sau* morning star.

lucernă *sf.* alfalfa.

luci *vi.* to glisten.

lucid *adj.* lucid.

luciditate *sf.* lucidity.

lucios *adj.* glowing.

lucitor *adj.* shining.

luciu *sn.* lustre. *adj.* glistening; *(lunecos)* slippery; *(neted)* smooth; *(d. sărăcie)* dire.

lucra *vt.* to process; *(pămîntul)* to till, *(pe cineva)* to sap. *vi.* to work; *(din greu)* to toil; *(a funcţiona şi)* to function. *vr.* to be worked; *(d. pămînt)* to be tilled.

lucrare *sf.* work; *(acţiune)* working; *(carte şi)* book; *(teză etc.)* paper, thesis; *(pl. dezbateri)* debates; *lucrări edilitare* urban equipment.

lucrătoare *sf.* working woman.

lucrător *sm.* worker; *(necalificat)* labourer. *adj.* work(ing).

lucru *sn.* thing; *(obiect şi)* object; *(muncă)* work; *(trudă)* toil; *(acţiune)* act(ion); *(chestiune)* matter; *pl.* belongings; ~ *cu bucata sau în acord* piecework; ~ *de mînă* needlework, knitting; *de* ~ working; *la* ~ at work.

lugubru *adj.* lugubrious. *adv.* sinisterly.

lui *adj.* his; its; *al* ~ his; *pron.* (to) him; (to) it.

lulea *sf.* (tobacco) pipe. *adv.* head over ears.

lume *sf.* world; *(univers)* universe; *(pămînt şi)* earth; *(omenire şi)* mankind; *(societate)* society; *(oameni şi)* people; ~*a mare* the wide world; high society; *ca* ~*a* proper(ly); *de cînd* ~*a* as old as the hills; *de* ~ wordly; *de ochii lumii* perfunctorily; *în* ~*a întreagă* everywhere, throughout the world; *pe* ~ on earth; *toată* ~*a* everybody.

lumesc *adj.* worldly ; *med.* vene-real.

lumina *vt.* to light(en) ; *(a lă-muri)* to enlighten ; *(a clari-fica)* to explain (away) ; *(a instrui)* to educate. *vi.* to shine. *vr.* to dawn; *(la față)* to bright-en ; *(d. vreme)* to clear up ; *(a înțelege)* to understand; *se lu-mineazd de ziud* day is breaking.

luminat *sn.* lighting. *adj.* light-ed ; *fig.* enlightened.

lumină *sf.* light ; *el.* lumen ; *fig.* learning ; *lumina lunii* moon-light ; *lumina soarelui* sunlight, daylight ; *lumina zilei* day-light ; *luminile ochilor* the apple of one's eye ; *(vedere)* eye-sight ; *luminile rampei* floats ; *fig.* limelight.

luminiș *sn.* clearing.

luminos *adj.* bright ; *(d. cameră* etc.) light.

luminare *sf.* candle.

lunar *adj.* monthly ; *astr.* lunar. *adv.* every month.

lună *sf.* month ; *astr.* moon ; *(lumină)* moonlight ; *~ de miere* honeymoon; *acum o ~* a month ago.

luncă *sf.* meadow.

lunea *adv.* on Monday(s).

luneca *vi.* to slip; *(a pluti)* to glide; *(a fi lunecos)* to be slippery.

lunecos *adj.* slippery.

lunetă *sf.* field glass ; *astr.* small telescope.

lung *sn.* length. *adj.* long ; *(pre-lung)* prolonged. *adv.* long.

lungi *vt.* to lengthen. *vr.* to stretch ; *(a se culca)* to lie down.

lungime *sf.* length ; *~ de undă* wave length.

luni *sf.* Monday. *adv.* (on) Monday.

luntraș *sm.* boatman.

luntre *sf.* boat.

lup *sm.* wolf ; *~ de mare* jack tar.

lupă *sf.* magnifying glass.

lupoaică *sf.* bitch wolf.

lupta *vt.*, *vr.* to fight.

luptă *sf.* struggle ; *(bătălie)* bat-tle ; *(încăierare)* fight ; *(răz-boi)* war(fare) ; *(sport)* wrest-ling ; *~ de clasă* class struggle ; *~ pentru pace* fight for peace.

luptător *sm.* fighter ; *sport* wrest-ler.

lustragiu *sm.* shoeblack.

lustru *sn.* lustre ; *(candelabru)* chandelier.

lustrui *vt.* to polish. *vr.* to brush up.

lut *sn.* clay, earth.

luteran *sm.*, *adj.* Lutheran.

lux *sn.* luxury ; *(abundență)* profusion ; *de ~* luxury.

luxa *vt.* to sprain.

luxos *adj.* luxurious.

M

mac *sn.* poppy. *interj.* quack !

macabru *adj.* grizzly, grue-some.

macara *sf.* crane.

macaroane *sf.*, *pl.* macaroni.

macaz *sn.* switch.

macedonean *sm.*, *adj.*, **macedo-neană** *sf.*, *adj.* Macedonian.

machetă *sf.* model; *(de carte etc.)* upmaking.

machia *vt., vr.* to make up.

machiaj *sn.* make up.

machiavelic *adj.* Machiavellian.

maculator *sn.* rough notebook.

maculatură *sf.* waste (sheets); *fig.* pulp.

madonă *sf.* Madonna.

madrigal *sn.* madrigal.

maestru *sm.* master; *muz.* maestro; *(specialist)* specialist, expert; ~ *emerit* merited master (in art, of sports, etc.).

mag *sm.* wise man.

magazie *sf.* ware-house.

magazin *sn.* shop; *(universal)* department store; *(cu sucursale)* multiple shop; *(revistă)* (illustrated) magazine.

magherniţă *sf.* hovel.

maghiar *sm., adj.*, **maghiară** *sf., adj.* Magyar, Hungarian.

magic *adj.* magic.

magie *sf.* magic.

magistral *adj.* masterly. *adv.* marvellously.

magistrală *sf.* thoroughfare.

magistrat *sm.* magistrate.

magnat *sm.* tycoon.

magnet *sm.* magnet.

magnetofon *sn.* tape recorder.

magneziu *sn.* magnesium.

magnific *adj.* magnificent.

mahala *sf.* suburb; *(în Anglia, aprox.)* slum; *de* ~ low.

mahalagiu *sm.* scandalmonger.

mahmur *adj.* seedy (with a hangover).

mahmureală *sf.* hangover; vapours.

mahomedan *sm., adj.* Moslem, Mohammedan.

mai *sm.* May; *Întîi Mai* May Day. *sn.* rammer. *adv.* another; (some) more; *(din nou)* (once) again; *(în continuare)* (further) on; *(încă)* still; ~ - ~ almost; ~ *ales* especially; ~ *bine* etc. better, etc.; ~ *deunăzi* the other day; ~ *înainte* before; ~ *întîi (de toate)* first of all; *şi* ~ *şi* one better (than...).

maia *sf.* leaven.

maică *sf.* mother; *(călugăriţă)* nun.

maidan *sn.* waste ground.

maiestate *sf.* Majesty; *fig.* stateliness.

maiestuos *adj.* majestic. *adv.* magnificently.

maimuţă *sf.* monkey; *şi fig.* ape.

maimuţări *vt.* to ape. *vr.* to play the giddy goat.

maimuţoi *sm.* missing link.

maioneză *sf.* mayonnaise.

maior *sm.* major.

maiou *sn.* undershirt; *(de balerin)* fleshings.

maistru *sm.* foreman; *fig.* expert.

major *adj.* major; *(matur şi)* of age; *(superior* etc.) greater.

majora *vt.* to increase; *(preţurile şi)* to up.

majorat *sn.* coming of age; *la* ~ of age.

majoritate *sf.* majority; most (people, cases, etc.).

majusculă *sf.* capital (letter).

mal *sn.* bank; *(de mare)* shore; *(de rîu, lac)* bank; *(coastă)* coast; *(rîpă)* cliff.

malaiez *sm., adj.*, **malaieză** *sf., adj.* Malay.

malarie *sf.* malaria.

maldăr *sn.* heap, lot.

maleabil *adj.* malleable.

maliţie *sf.* malice, acrimony.

maliţios *adj.* acrimonious. *adv.* maliciously.

maltrata *vt.* to illtreat.

malţ *sn.* malt.

mamă *sf.* mother; *zool.* dam; ~ *vitregă* step mother; *de* ~ maternal.

mamifer *sn.* mammal.

mamoş *sm.* obstetrician.

mamut *sm.* mammoth.

mană *sf.* manna.

mandarin *sm.* Mandarin.

mandarină *sf.* mandarine.

mandat *sn.* mandate; *(poştal)* money order; *(de arestare)* warrant (for arrest); *(de deputat)* seat; *sub* ~ mandated.

mandolină *sf.* mandoline.

manechin *sn.* dummy; *(persoană)* mannequin.

manevra *vt., vi.* to manoeuvre; *c.f.* ţr. shunt.

manevră *sf.* manoeuvre; *mil. şi* exercise. *c.f.* shunting.

mangal *sn.* charcoal.

maniac *sm.* (mono)maniac. *adj.* maniac.

manichiură *sf.* manicure.

manie *sf.* (mono)manie; *(pasiune)* hobby.

manierat *adj.* well-mannered.

manieră *sf.* manner.

manierism *sn.* mannerism.

manifest *sn.* manifesto; *(foaie)* leaflet. *adj.* manifest, obvious.

manifesta *vt.* to show. *vi.* to manifest. *vr.* to be(come) manifest.

manifestare *sf.* manifestation.

manifestaţie *sf.* demonstration.

manipula *vt.* to handle.

manipulant *sm.* tram-driver.

manivelă *sf.* crank.

mansardă *sf.* attic.

manşă *sf.* control column.

manşetă *sf.* cuff; *(la pantaloni)* turn-up; *(de ziar)* imprint.

manşon *sn.* muff.

manta *sf.* cloak; *(de ploaie)* waterproof.

manual *sn.* text book. *adj.* manual, hand.

manuscris *sn.* manuscript.

mapă *sf.* portfolio.

maramă *sf.* raw silk headdress.

marasm *sn.* morass.

maraton *sn.* marathon.

marea *vt.* to mark; *fin.* to hallmark; *sport* to score. *vi.* to score.

marcaj *sn.* marking; *fin.* hallmark.

marcant *adj.* prominent.

marcă *sf.* mark; *(tip)* type; *(timbru)* postage stamp; *marca fabricii* trade mark.

marchiz *sm.* marquis.

marchiză *sf.* marchioness; *arhit.* marquis.

mare *sf.* sea; *la* ~ at the seaside; *pe* ~ at sea. *adj.* great; *(întins, vast)* large, vast; *(voluminos, substanţial)* big; *(înalt)* tall, high; *(uriaş)* huge; *(grandios)* grand(iose); *(puternic)* mighty; *(matur)* grown up; *în* ~ by and large.

mareşal *sm.* marshal.

marfă *sf.* ware(s).

margaretă *sf.* ox-eye daisy.

margarină *sf.* margarine.

margine *sf.* edge; *(a paharului)* brim; *(graniţă)* border; *(capăt)* end; *(limită)* limit; *(de pră-*

pastie) verge; *la ~a oraşu-lui* on the outskirts; *fără margini* boundless.

marin *adj.* sea.

marinar *sm.* sailor.

marină *sf. mil.* navy; *(comercială)* merchant marine; *(pictură)* seascape.

marinăresc *adj.* sailor's.

marionetă *sf.* marionette; *fig. şi* puppet.

maritim *adj.* sea(going).

marmeladă *sf.* jam.

marmură *sf.* marble.

maro *adj.* brown.

marochinărie *sf.* (Morocco) leather goods.

marotă *sf.* hobby (horse),

marş *sn.* march; *~ nuptial* wedding march. *interj. mil.* forward! get out!

marşarier *sn.* reverse; *în ~ on* the reverse.

Marte *sn.* Mars.

martie *sm.* March.

martir *sm.* martyr.

martor *sm.* witness; *(în ştiinţă)* control; *~ ocular* eye witness.

marţ *sm.* gammon.

marţea *adv.* on Tuesday(s).

marţi *sf.* Tuesday. *adv.* (on) Tuesday; *marţea viitoare* next Tuesday.

marţial *adj.* martial.

marţian *sm.* Martian.

marxism *sn.* Marxism; *~-leninism* Marxism Leninism.

marxist *sm., adj.* Marxist; *~-leninist* Marxist Leninist.

masa *vt.* to massage; *(a îngrămădi)* to mass. *vr.* to throng.

masacra *vt.* to massacre; *fig.* to mangle.

masacru *sn.* massacre.

masaj *sn.* massage.

masă *sf.* table; *(mîncare)* meal, fare; *(întreţinere)* board, upkeep; *(prînz)* lunch, dinner; *(micul dejun)* breakfast; *(mulţime şi fiz.)* mass; *~ de scris* desk; *~ de seară* dinner, supper; *masele largi* the masses; *mase plastice* plastics; *după ~* in the afternoon; *de ~ mass*; *în ~* en masse; *(în serie)* serial.

masca *vt.* to mask; *fig.* to hide; *mil.* to camouflage.

mascaradă *sf.* masquerade.

mascat *adj.* masked; *mil.* camouflaged.

mască *sf.* mask; *fig. şi* cloak; *~ de gaze* gas mask.

mascotă *sf.* mascot.

mascul *sm.* male.

masculin *sn., adj.* masculine.

masiv *sn.* massif. *adj.* massive; *(corpolent)* burly, portly. *adv.* massively.

mason *sm.* freemason.

masonerie *sf.* freemasonry.

mastică *sf.* anisette, mastic.

maşinal *adj.* mechanical. *adv.* mechanically.

maşinaţie *sf.* machination.

maşină *sf.* machine; *(automobil)* (motor) car; *(maşinărie)* machinery; *(locomotivă)* locomotive; *~ agricolă* farming machine; *~ cu aburi* steam engine; *~ de calculat* computer; *~ de călcat* flat iron; *(de croitor)* goose, *pl.* gooses; *~ de cusut* sewing machine; *~ de gătit* cooking stove; *~ de scris* typewriter; *~ de spălat rufe* washing machine; *~ de tocat* meat mincing machine; ~ *de tricotat* knitting machine.

maşinărie *sf.* machinery.

mat *sn.* checkmate. *adj.* mat-(ted); *(d. sticlă și)* frosted.

mata *pron.* you.

matale *adj.* your; *al* ~ yours.

matahală *sf.* giant.

mateă *sf. zool.* queen; *(albie)* river bed; *(cotor)* stub.

matelot *sm.* sailor.

matematic *adj.* mathematical. *adv.* precisely.

matematică *sf.* mathematics.

material *sn.* material; ~ *didactic* teaching aid(s). *adj.* material; *(palpabil)* substantial.

materialism *sn.* materialism; ~ *dialectic (și istoric)* dialectical (and historical) materialism.

materialist *sm.* materialist. *adj.* materialist(ic); ~ *dialectic* dialectical materialistic.

materie *sf.* matter; *(de studiu)* subject (matter); *(material)* material; ~ *primă* raw material.

matern *adj.* maternal; *(d. limbă)* mother...

maternitate *sf.* maternity (hospital).

matineu *sn.* matinée (performance).

matriță *sf.* stencil; *metal.* die, mould.

matroz *sm.* seaman.

matur *adj.* mature; *(adult)* grown-up.

maturitate *sf.* maturity.

maturiza *vt., vr.* to mature.

maț *sn.* gut.

maur *sm.* Moor. *adj.* Moorish.

mausoleu *sn.* mausoleum.

maxilar *sn.* jaw.

maxim *sn., adj.* maximum; *fig.* utmost.

maximă *sf.* maxim.

maximum *sn.* maximum. *adv.* at (the) most.

mazagran *sn.* iced coffee.

mazăre *sf.* pea; *(boabele)* peas.

mazurcă *sf.* mazurka.

mă *pron.* me; you; *(reflexiv)* myself. *interj.* you! mister.

măcar *adv.* at least; ~ *că* although; ~ *dacă* if at least.

măcăi *vi.* to quack.

măcel *sn.* massacre.

măcelar *sm.* butcher.

măcelări *vt.* to slaughter.

măcelărie *sf.* butcher's (shop).

măceș *sm.* hip(rose).

măcina *vt.* to grind. *vr.* to crumble.

măcinat *sn.* grinding. *adj.* ground.

măciucă *sf.* bludgeon; *i s-a făcut părul* ~ his hair stood on end.

mădular *sn.* limb.

măduvă *sf.* marrow; *pînă în măduva oaselor* to the backbone.

măgar *sm.* donkey; *fig.* swine.

măgărie *sf.* caddishness.

măguli *vt.* to flatter. *vr.* to congratulate oneself.

măgulire *sf.* flattery.

măgulitor *adj.* complimentary.

măgură *sf.* knoll.

măi *interj.* hey you!

măiestrie *sf.* art.; ~ *literară* penmanship.

mălai *sn.* maize flour; *(turtă)* maize cake.

mămăligă *sf.* atole, corn mush; *fig.* milksop.

mămică *sf.* mummy.

mănăstire *sf.* monastery ; *(de maici)* nunnery.

mănos *adj.* profitable.

mănunchi *sn.* bunch.

mănuşă *sf.* glove ; *(de protecţie)* gauntlet ; *(fără degete)* mitten ; *cu mănuşi (fig.)* gently ; *fără mănuşi (fig.)* roughly.

măr *sm.* apple tree ; *(pădureţ)* crab tree. *sn.* apple ; *(pădureţ)* crab apple ; ~ *copt* baked apple ; ~*ul discordiei* the apple of discord. *adv.* soundly.

mărar *sm.* dill.

mărăcine *sm.* bramble.

măreţ *adj.* magnificent. *adv.* gloriously.

măreţie *sf.* stateliness.

mărfar *sn.* goods train.

mărgăritar *sn.* pearl ; *bot.* lily-of-the-valley.

mărgea *sf.* bead.

mărgean *sn.* coral.

mărgică *sf.* bead.

mărginaş *adj.* peripheral.

mărgini *vt.* to limit. *vr.* : *a se ~ cu* to border upon ; *a se ~ la sau să* to confine oneself to.

mărginit *adj.* limited ; *fig. şi* narrow-minded.

mări *vt.* to enlarge ; *opt.* to magnify. *vr.* to increase.

mărime *sf.* size; *(proporţii)* scope.

mărinimie *sf.* magnanimity.

mărinimos *adj.* large-hearted. *adv.* generously.

mărire *sf.* enlargement ; *fig.* splendour.

mărita *vt.* to marry (away). *vr.* to get married (to smb.).

măritat *sn.* marriage ; *de ~* marriageable.

mărturie *sf.* evidence : *fig.* token.

mărturisi *vt., vi., vr.* to confess.

mărturisire *sf.* avowal.

mărţişor *sn.* amulet.

mărunt *adj.* small ; *(meschin)* mean.

măruntaie *sf. pl.* entrails.

mărunţi *vt.* to break up.

mărunţiş *sn.* (small) change ; *pl.* trifles ; *pl. com.* haberdashery.

măscărici *sm.* fool.

măsea *sf.* molar ; ~ *de minte* wisdom tooth.

măslin *sm.* olive tree.

măslină *sf.* olive.

măsliniu *adj.* olive(-coloured).

măslui *vt.* to load (the dice) ; to mark (the cards).

măsura *vt.* to measure ; *(a cîntări)* to weigh. *vi.* to be (three inches, etc.) long, etc. *vr.* to measure one's strength (against smb.).

măsurat *adj.* measured ; *fig.* moderate.

măsură *sf.* measure ; *(cantitate)* quantity ; *muz.* bar ; *(la versuri)* foot ; *fig. (valoare)* value ; ~ *de capacitate* liquid measure ; ~ *de volum* cubic measure ; *cu ~* moderately ; *în egală ~* equally ; *în mare ~* in a large measure ; *în oarecare ~* to a certain extent ; *pe ~* made to measure *sau* order ; *pe ~ ce* according as ; *peste ~* exceedingly.

măsurătoare *sf.* measurement ; *(de teren)* survey.

mătanie *sf.* genuflexion ; *pl.* rosary.

mătase *sf.* silk ; ~*a broaştei* water weed.

mătăsos *adj.* silky.

mătrăgună *sf.* laurel.
mătreaţă *sf.* dandruff.
mătura *vt.* to sweep.
mătură *sf.* broom ; *(tîrn)* besom.
măturător *sm.* scavenger.
mătuşă *sf.* aunt.
măzăriche *sf. bot.* vetch ; *(lapo-viţă)* sleet.
mea *adj.* my ; *a ~* mine.
meandru *sn.* meander ; *cu mean-dre* winding.
mecanic *sm.* mechanic ; *(de lo-comotivă)* engine driver. *adj.* mechanical. *adv.* mechanically.
mecanică *sf.* mechanics.
mecanism *sn.* mechanism, de-vice.
meci *sn.* match ; *~ nul* tie ; *~ în nocturnă* floodlit match.
medaliat *sm.* medallist.
medalie *sf.* medal ; *~ de aur* gold medal.
medalion *sn.* medallion ; *(ar-ticol)* personal.
media *vi.* to mediate.
mediat *adj.* indirect.
medic *sm.* physician ; *~ legist* forensic expert ; *~ veterinar* veterinary surgeon.
medical *adj.* medical ; health...
medicament *sn.* medicine.
medicină *sf.* medicine ; *~ lega-lă* forensic medicine.
medie *sf.* average ; mean ; *în ~* on an average.
medieval *adj.* medi(a)eval.
mediocritate *sf.* mediocrity.
mediocru *adj.* mediocre ; *(slab)* poor.
medita *vt.* to coach. *vi.* to me-ditate (upon smth.).
meditator *sm.* coach.
meditaţie *sf.* meditation ; *(lec-ţie)* coaching.

mediu *sm.* medium. *sn.* milieu ; *(în ştiinţă)* medium. *adj.* aver-age ; *(d. şcoală)* middle.
megafon *sn.* loudspeaker.
mei *sn.* millet. *adj.* my ; *ai ~* mine ; my folk(s).
melancolic *adj.* melancholy.
melancolie *sf.* melancholy.
melasă *sf.* molasses.
mele *sm.* snail ; *ca ~ul* at a snail's pace.
mele *adj.* my ; *ale ~* mine.
meleaguri *sn. pl.* regions.
melodie *sf.* melody, tune.
melodios *adj.* melodious. *adv.* melodiously.
melodramatic *adj.* melodrama-tic.
melodramă *sf.* melodrama.
meloman *sm.* music fan.
membrană *sf.* membrane ; *tehn.* diaphragm.
membru *sm.* member ; *(element)* part ; *~ coresp ndent* cores-ponding member ; *~ de partid* party member ; *~ de sindicat* trade union member; *~ onorific, ~ de onoare* honorary member. *sn. anat.* limb.
memora *vt.* to memorize.
memorabil *adj.* unforgettable.
memorie *sf.* memory ; *din ~* by rote.
memoriu *sn.* memorial ; *(plîn-gere)* grievance ; *pl.* memoirs.
menaj *sn.* house(keeping) ; *(căs-nicie)* marriage ; *(pereche)* cou-ple.
menaja *vt., vr.* to spare (oneself).
menajament *sn.* sparing ; *cu ~e* gently ; *fără ~e* ruthlessly.
menajerie *sf.* menagerie.
mendre *sf. pl.* *a- i face ~le* to lord it.

meni *vt.* to destine.

meningită *sf.* meningitis.

menire *sf.* mission.

meniu *sn.* bill of fare; ~ *fix* ordinary.

menstruaţie *sf.* catamenia, turns.

mentalitate *sf.* outlook.

mentă *sf.* peppermint.

menţine *vt.* to maintain. *vr.* to continue.

menţiona *vt.* to mention.

menţiune *sf.* mention; *(premiu)* honourable mention.

menuet *sn.* minuet.

mercantil *adj.* mercantile.

mercenar *sm., adj.* mercenary.

mercerie *sf.* small ware (shop).

merceriza *vt.* to mercerize.

mercur *sn.* mercury.

mereu *adj.* always, (for) ever.

merge *vi.* to go; *(pe jos)* to walk; *(d. mecanism)* to work; *(a se mişca)* to move; *(a acţiona)* to act; *(cu un vehicul)* to ride; *a-i ~ (bine)* to get on (well); *nu-ţi ~ cu mine* you can't have me at that; *~ pe 20 de ani* he is rising *sau* coming 20; *aşa nu ~* that won't do; *cum îţi ~ ?* how are things with you?; *pe unde ~m?* which way do we take?

meridian *sn.* meridian.

meridional *sm., adj.* meridional.

merinde *sf. pl.* victuals.

merit *sn.* merit, desert; *de ~* praiseworthy.

merita *vt.* to deserve; *(d. lucruri şi)* to be worth (reading, etc.). *vi.* to be worthwhile.

meritoriu *adj.* laudable.

merituos *adj.* deserving.

mers *sn.* going; *(al cuiva)* gait; *~ înainte* progress; *~ul trenurilor* time-table; *(ghid)* ABC.

mesager *sm.* messenger.

mesaj *sn.* message; *(apel)* appeal.

meschin *adj.* petty; *(zgîrcit)* stingy.

meschinărie *sf.* meanness; *(zgîrcenie)* niggardliness.

meseriaş *sm.* handicraftsman.

meserie *sf.* trade; *(profesie)* calling; *şcoală de meserii* vocational school.

mesteacăn *sm.* birch tree.

mesteca *vt.* to chew; *(a amesteca)* to stir. *vi.* to chew.

meşter *sm.* master; *(meseriaş)* craftsman. *adj.* expert.

meşteri *vt.* to arrange. *vi.: a ~ la* to potter about.

meşteşug *sn.* trade; *(pricepere)* art; *(mijloc)* method.

meşteşugăresc *adj.* handicraft.

metafizică *sf.* metaphysics.

metaforă *sf.* metaphor.

metal *sn.* metal.

metalic *adj.* metallic.

metalurgic *adj.* metal(lurgic).

metamorfoză· *sf.* metamorphosis.

metan *sm., adj.* methane.

meteahnă *sf.* flow; *(boală)* complaint; *(nărav)* habit.

meteor *sm.* meteor.

meteorologic *adj.* weather.

meteorologie *sf.* meteorology.

meticulos *adj.* minute. *adv.* meticulously.

metodă *sf.* method; *fără ~* desultory; at random.

metodic *adj.* methodical. *adv.* methodically.

metonimie *sf.* metonymy.

metraj *sn.* length (of cloth);
de lung ~ full length; *de scurt* ~ short reel.

metro *sn.* underground, tube.

metropolă *sf.* metropolis; *(capitală)* capital.

metru *sm.* metre; *(de croitor)* tape measure.

meu *adj.* my; *al* ~ mine.

mexican *sm., adj.,* **mexicană** *sf., adj.* Mexican.

mezelărie *sf.* sausage factory *sau* shop.

mezeluri *sm. pl.* sausages.

mezin *sm.* youngest (child).

mi *sm.* E, mi. *pron.* (to) me.

miazănoapte *sf.* north; *de* ~ north(ern).

miazăzi *sf.* south; *de* ~ south(ern).

mie *sm.* grilled minced meat roll. *adj.* little, tiny; *(necorespunzător)* small; *(scund)* short; *(pitic)* midget; *(îndesat)* dumpy; *(nedezvoltat)* stunted; *(strîmt)* tight; *(slab)* feeble; *(jos)* low; *(ca vîrstă)* young; *(mărunt fig.)* minor, petty; *(ușor)* light; ~*a burghezie* the petty bourgeoisie; ~ *burghez* petty bourgeois; *de* ~ *copil* from early childhood.

micime *sf.* smallness; *fig.* pettiness.

microb *sm.* microbe.

microbuz *sn.* minibus, baby bus.

microfon *sn.* microphone.

microporos *sn.* mipor.

microscop *sn.* microscope; ~ *electronic* electron microscope.

micsandră *sf.* gillyflower.

micșora *vt.* to reduce. *vr.* to dwindle; *(a scădea)* to decrease.

micșunea *sf.* stock.

mie *sf., adj., num.* thousand; *O* ~ *și una de nopți* the Arabian Nights; *trei mii* three thousand. *pron.* (to) me.

miel *sm.* lamb.

miercurea *adv.* on Wednesday(s).

miercuri *sf.* Wednesday. *adv.* (on) Wednesday.

miere *sf.* honey.

mierlă *sf.* blackbird.

mieros *adj.* honeyed. *adv.* unctuously.

mieuna *vi.* to mew.

miez *sn.* heart; *(de nucă etc.)* kernel; *fig. și* depth; *(substanță)* pith (and marrow); ~*ul nopții* midnight; *cu* ~ substanțial.

migală *sf.* meticulousness.

migdal *sm.* almond tree.

migdalat *adj.* almond-shaped.

migdală *sf.* almond.

migrație *sf.* migration.

miime *sf.* thousandth.

miji *vi.* to appear; *(d. ochi)* to blink. *vr.: a se* ~ *de ziuă* to dawn.

mijloc *sn.* middle; *(talie)* waist; *(metodă)* means; *(de transport)* vehicle; *(posibilitate)* possibility; *pl.* means; *la* ~ in the middle.

mijlocaș *sm.* middle peasant; *sport* halfback. *adj.* middle.

mijloci *vt.* to mediate; *(o afacere)* to negotiate.

mijlocitor *sm.* go-between.

mijlociu *adj.* middle; *(moderat)* moderate; *(mediu)* average, mean.

milă *sf. (măsură)* mile; *(caritate)* pity; *(bunătate)* kindness; *(compătimire)* compassion; *(pomană)* alms; ~ *ma-*

rină sea mile; *de* ~ out of pity; *fără* ~ pitiless(ly).

milenar *adj.* millenary; age-old.

mileniu *sm.* chiliad.

miliard *sn., num.* a thousand million; *amer.* billion.

miliardar *sm.* multi-millionaire; *amer.* billionaire.

miligram *sn.* miligram.

milimetru *sm.* millimeter.

milion *sn., num.* million.

milionar *sm.* millionaire.

milita *vi.* to militate.

militant *sm., adj.* militant.

militar *sm.* soldier; *pl.* the millitary. *adj.* military.

militărie *sf.* military service; *la* ~ under the colours.

milițian *sm.* militia man.

miliție *sf.* militia.

milogi *vr.* to cadge.

milos *adj.* sympathetic.

milostiv *adj.* charitable; *rel.* pitiful.

milostivi *vt.* to take pity (on smb.).

milui *vt.* to give alms to.

mim *sm.* mime.

mima *vt.* to mimic.

mimă *sf.* mime.

mimică *sf.* mimicry.

mimoză *sf.* sensitive plant.

mina *vt.* to mine; *fig.* to undermine.

mină *sf.* mine; *(puț și)* pit; *(de creion)* lead; *(pt. pix)* refill; *(față etc.)* mien; *(expresie)* countenance.

mincinos *sm.* liar. *adj.* lying.

minciună *sf.* lie; *(născocire)* concoction, fabrication; *(prăjitură)* cruller; ~ *gogonată* whopper; ~ *nevinovată* white lie.

miner *sm.* miner.

mineral *sn. adj.* mineral.

minereu *sn.* ore.

minge *sf.* ball; ~ *de fotbal* football.

miniatură *sf.* miniature.

minier *adj.* mining.

minim *sn., adj.* minimum.

minimaliza *vt.* to minimize.

minister *sn.* ministry; *(în Anglia și)* office, board; *(în S.U.A.)* department.

ministerial *adj.* ministerial; *coală* ~*ă* petition paper.

ministeriabil *adj.* cabinetable.

ministru *sm.* (cabinet) minister, secretary of State; *(ambasador)* envoy, minister; ~ *adjunct* deputy minister; *(în Anglia)* undersecretary; ~ *plenipotențiar* minister plenipotentiary.

minor *sm.* minor. *adj.* minor; *(ca vîrstă și)* under age; *(ca importanță și)* lesser.

minoritate *sf.* minority.

mintal *adj.* mental. *adv.* mentally

minte *sf.* mind; *(înțelepciune)* brains; *(memorie)* memory; *cu* ~ wise; *fără* ~ unreasonable.; *(prostesc)* foolish.

minți *vt.* to deceive. *vi.* to lie.

minuna *vt.* to astonish. *vr.* to marvel (at).

minunăție *sf.* marvel.

minune *sf.* wonder; *de* ~ perfectly.

minus *sn., adv.* minus.

minuscul *adj.* tiny.

minut *sn.* minute.

minutar *sn.* minute hand.

minută *sf.* minute(s).

minuțios *adj.* thorough(going). *adv.* minutely.

miop *sm.* short-sighted person. *adj.* short-sighted.

miopie *sf.* short-sightedness.

mioriţă *sf.* ewe (lamb).

miorlăi *vi., vr.* to mew; *fig.* to whine.

mira *vt.* to surprise. *vr.* to wonder; *te miri ce* almost nothing.

miracol *sn.* miracle.

miraculos *adj.* miraculous.

miraj *sn.* mirage.

mirare *sf.* surprise; *de ~* extraordinary.

mirat *adj.* astonished.

mire *sm.* bridegroom.

mireasă *sf.* bride.

mireasmă *sf.* fragrance, scent.

mirodenie *sf.* spice.

miros *sn.* smell; *(plăcut)* scent; *(urît)* stench.

mirosi *vt.* to smell, to scent. *vi.* to smell (of smth.); *(urît)* to stink (of smth.).

misionar *sm.* missionary.

misit *sm.* agent.

misiune *sf.* mission; *mil.* sortie.

misogin *sm.* woman hater.

mister *sn.* mystery.

misterios *adj.* mysterious. *adv.* mysteriously.

mistic *sm.* mystical person. *adj.* mystical.

mistreţ *sm.* wild boar.

mistui *vt.* to digest; *(a arde)* to consume. *vr.* to be digested; *fig.* to yearn.

mistuitor *adj.* consuming.

mişca *vt., vi., vr.* to move.

mişcare *sf.* movement; *(activitate)* activity; *(la şah şi fig.)* move; *(revoluţie)* rising; *~ de eliberare naţională* national liberation movement.

mişcător *adj.* moving.

mişel *sm.* rascal; *(laş)* coward. *adj.* knavish; *(laş)* faint-hearted.

mişelesc *adj.* base; *(laş)* dastardly.

mişuna *vi.* to swarm (with).

mit *sn.* myth.

mită *sf.* bribe(ry).

miting *sn.* meeting.

mititei *sm. pl.* grilled minced meat balls.

mitiza *vt.* to lionize.

mitocan *sm.* cad.

mitocănie *sf.* boorishness.

mitologic *adj.* mythological.

mitologie *sf.* mythology.

mitoman *sm.* airmonger, braggart.

mitralia *vt.* to machine-gun.

mitralieră *sf.* machine-gun.

mitră *sf. rel.* mitre; *anat.* womb.

mitropolie *sf.* metropolitan seat *sau* church.

mitropolit *sm.* metropolitan (bishop).

mitui *vt.* to bribe.

mixt *adj.* joint.

miza *vt.* to stake. *vi.* to bank.

mizantrop *sm.* misanthrope.

miză *sf.* stake.

mizerabil *adj.* miserable. *adv.* poorly.

mizerie *sf.* misery.

mîhni *vt.* to (ag)grieve. *vr.* to grow sorry.

mîhnire *sf.* grief.

mîine *adv.* tomorrow.

mîl *sn.* silt.

mîna *vt., vi.* to drive.

mînă *sf.* hand; *(pumn)* fist; *o ~ de ajutor* a helping hand; *de ~* hand(icraft); *pe sub ~* underhand.

mînca *vt.* to eat; *(a irita)* to itch. *vr.* to be eaten; *fig.* to disparage each other. .

mîncare *sf.* food; *(fel)* dish.

mîncăcios *sm.* glutton. *adj.* gluttonous.

mîncărime *sf.* rash.

mîndră *sf.* beauty; sweetheart.

mîndrețe *sf.* splendour.

mîndri *vr.* to take pride (in smth.)

mîndrie *sf.* pride; *(deşartă)* vanity.

mîndru *adj.* proud; *fig.* lofty; *(frumos)* splendid.

mînecă *sf.* sleeve.

mîner *sn.* handle; *(de sabie etc.)* hilt.

mîngîia *vt.* to caress; *fig.* to comfort. *vr.* to console oneself (with a thought, etc.).

mîngîiere *sf.* caress; *fig.* consolation.

mînia *vt.* to vex. *vr.* to grow angry.

mînie *sf.* wrath; *(furie)* fury.

mînios *adj.* wrathful; *(furios)* furious. *adv.* wrathfully; *(furios)* furious.

mînji *vt., vr.* to sully.

mîntui *vt.* to save; *(a isprăvi)* to end. *vr.* to be saved; *(a se sfîrşi)* to end.

mîntuială *sf.*: *de* ~ scamped.

mîntuire *sf.* salvation.

mîntuitor *sm.* saviour.

mînui *vt.* to handle; to manipulate.

mînuitor *sm.* operator, manipulator.

mînz *sm.* colt.

mînzeşte *adv.*. *a ríde* ~ to put on a forced smile.

mîrîi *vi.* to snarl.

mîrlan *sm.* boor.

mîrşav *adj., adv.* base.

mîrşăvie *sf.* meanness.

mîrţoagă *sf.* jade.

mîţă *sf.* cat; ~ *blîndă* lip worshipper; sanctimonious person.

mîţişori *sm. pl.* catkins.

mîzgă *sf.* slime.

mîzgăli *vt.* to daub; *(cuvinte)* to scribble.

mîzgălitură *sf.* scribbling.

mlaştină *sf.* marsh; *fig.* morass.

mlădia *vt., vr.* to twist.

mlădios *adj.* lithe.

mlădiţă *sf.* shoot; *fig.* offspring.

mlăştinos *adj.* swampy. .

moale *sn.*: ~*le capului* fontanelle. *adj.* soft; *(prea* ~ *)* flabby, flaccid; *(mlădios)* pliant, flexible; *(dulce)* low; *(uşor)* light; *(d. ouă)* softboiled; *fig.* weak(ly). *adv.* softly.

moară *sf.* mill; *(ţintar)* nine--men's morris; ~ *stricată* chatterbox.

moarte *sf.* death; *(deces)* demise; ~ *bună* natural death; *cu* ~*a în suflet* with one's heart in one's mouth; *de* ~ mortal(ly); *fără* ~ immortal; *pînă la* ~ to one's dying day.

moaşă *sf.* midwife.

mobil *sn.* motive; *fig.* body in motion. *adj.* mobile; *(schimbător)* versatile; *(vioi)* agile; *jur.* personal.

mobila *vt.* to furnish.

mobilă *sf.* (piece of) furniture; ~ *stil* period furniture.

mobilier *sn.* furniture.

mobiliza *vt., mil.* to mobilize; *fig.* to rally.

mocăi *vr.* to (dilly-)dally, to lag.

mocîrlă *sf.* marsh ; *fig.* mire.

mocni *vi.* to smoulder.

mocnit *adj.* smouldering ; *fig.* hidden.

mod *sn.* mode ; *(fel)* manner ; *gram.* mood ; ~ *de întrebuinţare* usage (instructions) ; ~ *de viaţă* way of life.

modal *adj.* modal.

modalitate *sf.* modality.

modă *sf.* fashion ; *(obicei)* custom ; *de* ~ fashion ; *la* ~ fashionable.

model *sn.* model ; *(tipar şi)* pattern; *după* ~*ul lui . . .* following the example of. . . *adj.* model.

modela *vt.* to model ; *(a da formă la)* to mould. *vr.* to be modelled.

modera *vt.* to moderate.

moderat *adj.* temperate.

modern *adj.* modern ; *(la zi)* up-to-date ; *(la modă)* fashionable.

modernism *sn.* modernism.

moderniza *vt.* to modernize.

modest *adj.* modest ; *(simplu)* simple. *adv.* in a small way.

modestie *sf.* modesty.

modifica *vt.* to alter ; to amend.

modificare *sf.* modification.

modistă *sf.* milliner.

modula *vt., vr.* to modulate.

moft *sn.* whim ; *(fleac)* trifle.

mofturos *adj.* finical.

mohorît *adj.* dark ; *(d. vreme şi)* overcast.

moină *sf.* thaw.

mojic *sm.* churl. *adj.* boorish.

mojicie *sf.* coarseness.

molcom *adj.* mild ; *(tăcut)* silent.

moldovean *sm., adj.* **moldoveancă** *sf.* Moldavian.

moldovenesc *adj.* Moldavian.

moleculă *sf.* molecule.

molestare *sf.* assault (and battery).

moleşeală *sf.* torpor ; *(toropeală)* drowsiness.

moleşi *vt.* to enervate. *vr.* to become torpid.

moliciune *sf.* softness.

molid *sm.* spruce fir.

molie *sf.* moth.

molimă *sf.* epidemic.

molipsi *vt.* to contaminate ; *fig.* to honeycomb. *vr.* to be infected (by smth.).

molipsire *sf.* contagion.

molipsitor *adj.* catching.

moloz *sn.* debris.

moluscă *sf.* mollusc, jellyfish.

momeală *sf.* lure, bait.

moment *sn.* moment ; *de* ~ momentary ; *din* ~ *ce* as ; *din* ~ *în* ~ any minute now ; *la* ~ at once ; *la un* ~ *dat* after a time ; *pentru* ~ for the time being.

momentan *adj.* momentary. *adv.* right now.

momi *vt.* to (al)lure.

monarch *sm.* monarch.

monarhic *adj.* monarchic.

monarhie *sf.* monarchy ; *fig.* crown.

monden *adj.* fashionable.

mondial *adj.* world (wide).

monedă *sf.* currency, legal tender ; *(gologan)* coin ; ~ *măruntă* change ; ~ *cu curs forţat* fiat money.

monetar *sn.* account(s). *adj.* monetary.

mongol *sm., adj.,* **mongolă** *sf., adj.* Mongolian.

monitor *sm.* monitor. *sn.* (Official) Gazette ; *mar.* monitor.

monoclu *sn.* monocle.
monografie *sf.* monograph.
monogramă *sf.* monogram.
monolog *sn.* soliloquy.
monopol *sn.* monopoly.
monopolist *sm.* monopolist. *adj.* monopoly.
monopoliza *vt.* to monopolize.
monoton *adj.* monotonous; tedious. *adv.* monotonously.
monotonie *sf.* monotony.
monstru *sm.* monster. *adj.* monstrous.
monstruos *adj.* monstrous.
monta *vt.* to mount; *(a înrăma)* to frame; *(a potrivi)* to set; *teatru* to stage; *tehn.* to assemble; *fig.* to set. *vr.* to be mounted; *fig.* to warm up.
montaj *sn.* mounting; *tehn.* assembly; *(radiofonic etc.)* montage; *cinema* editing.
montare *sf.* assembly.
montor *sm.* fitter; *cinema* editor.
monument *sn.* monument.
monumental *adj.* monumental.
mops *sm.* pug dog.
moral *sn.* morale; ~ *ridicat* high spirits. *adj.* ethical.
morală *sf.* *(etică)* morality; *(învăţătură)* moral; *(reproşuri)* sermon.
moralitate *sf.* morals, morality. (play).
morar *sm.* miller.
moravuri *sn. pl.* manners.
morbid *adj.* morbid.
morcov *sm.* carrot.
morfină *sf.* morphia.
morfinoman *sm.* dope fiend.
morfologic *adj.* morphological.
morfologie *sf.* morphology.
morgă *sf.* morgue; *(trufie)* pride.

morişcă *sf.* handmill; *(de vînt)* weather cock; *(gură)* chatterbox.
morman *sn.* heap.
mormăi *vt., vi.* to grumble.
mormînt *sn.* grave; *(monument)* tomb.
mormoloc *sm.* tadpole; *(copil)* kid; *(om moale)* mollycoddle.
morocănos *adj.* sullen.
morsă *sf.* walrus.
morse *sn.* Morse; the Morse alphabet.
mort *sm.* dead person; *pl.* the dead. *adj.* dead; *(defunct)* late; *fig.* still; ~ *copt* at all costs; ~ *de oboseală* dead tired; *născut* ~ still-born; *nici* ~ on no account.
mortal *adj.* fatal. *adv.* mortally.
mortalitate *sf.* death rate.
mortar *sn.* mortar.
mortuar *adj.* mortuary.
morţiş *adv.* obstinately.
morun *sm.* sturgeon.
mosc *sm., sn.* musk; *de* ~ musk.
moschee *sf.* mosque.
mosor *sn.* reel.
mostră *sf.* sample; *fig.* foretaste.
moş *sm.* old man; *(strămoş)* forefather; ancestor; *pl.* fair; *Moş Ene* the dustman.
moşie *sf.* estate.
moşier *sm.*, moşieresc *adj.* landowner.
moşierime *sf.* landed gentry.
moşneag *sm.* old man.
moşteni *vt.* to inherit. *vr.* to be inherited.
moştenire *sf.* legacy.
moştenitoare *sf.* heiress.
moştenitor *sm.* heir.
motan *sm.* tomcat; *Motanul încălţat* Puss-in-boots.

motel *sn.* motel.
motiv *sn.* motive ; *artă* motif ; *muz.* theme ; *fără* ~ grounless-ly.
motiva *vt.* to justify.
moto *sn.* motto.
motocicletă *sf.* motor-cycle.
motociclist *sm.* motor-cyclist.
motonavă *sf.* motorship.
motor *sn.* engine, motor. *adj.* motive.
motoretă *sf.* motor bicycle, mo-ped.
motorină *sf.* diesel oil.
motorizat *adj.* motorized.
mototoli *vt.* to crumple.
motrice *adj.* motive.
moț *sn.* crest ; *pl.* curl papers ; *(ciucure)* tassel.
moțat *adj.* tufted ; *fig.* excep-tional.
moțăi *vi.* to doze (away).
moțiune *sf.* motion.
mov *adj.* mauve, lavender.
movilă *sf.* hillock ; *(morman)* pile.
mozaic[1] *sn.* mosaic.
mozàic[2] *adj.* Mosaic.
mreană *sf.* barbel.
muc *sn.* wick ; *(de luminare)* candle end ; *(de țigară)* butt.
mucalit *sm.* wit. *adj.* waggish.
mucegai *sn.* mould.
mucegăi *vi., vr.* to get mouldy.
mucegăit *adj.* musty ; *fig. şi* stale.
mucenic *sm.* martyr ; *pl. rel. aprox.* All Saints' Day.
mucezi *vi., vr.* to mould.
muchie *sf.* edge ; *pe* ~ *de cuțit* on a razor's edge.
mucoasă *sf.* mucous membrane.
mucos *sm.* sniveller. *adj.* snotty ; *fig.* unfledged.

muget *sn.* (bel)lowing.
mugi *vi.* to (bel)low ; *(d. mare etc.)* to roar.
mugur *sm.* bud.
muia *vt., vr.* to dip ; *(ca tărie)* to soften.
mujdei *sn.* garlic juice.
mula *vt.* to mould. *vr.* to fit closely.
mulaj *sn.* cast(ing).
mulatru *sm.* mulatto.
mulgătoare *sf.* milkmaid.
mulge *vt.* to milk.
muls *sn.* milking.
mult *adj.* much. a lot of ✦ ~ *timp* a long time ; *de* ~*e ori* often. *pron.* much, a lot. *adv.* much ; *(îndelung)* long ; ~ *mai* ... far greater ... ; ~ *şi bine* for a long time ; *cel* ~ at the most ; *mai* ~ *sau mai puțin* more or less.
multilateral *adj.* multilateral.
mulți *pron.* many, a lot of people.
mulțime *sf.* crowd ; *(de obiecte)* lots (of).
mulțumi *vt.* to satisfy. *vi.* to thank. *vr.* to be content (with smth.).
mulțumire *sf.* satisfaction ; *(răs-plată)* reward ; *pl.* thanks.
mulțumit *adj.* content(ed).
mulțumită *prep.* thanks to.
mulțumitor *adj.* satisfactory.
mumie *sf.* mummy.
muncă *sf.* work ; *(efort)* labour ; *(trudă)* toil ; *(osteneală)* pains ; *(activitate)* activity ; *munca cîmpului* field work ; ~ *fizică* manual labour ; ~ *în acord* piecework ; ~ *obştească* public work.
munci *vt.* to till (the ground) ;

fig. to torment. *vi.* to work; *(a trudi)* to toil. *vr.* to try hard; *(a se frăminta)* to worry.

muncit *adj.* tired; *(de gînduri)* tormented.

muncitor *sm.* worker, working man; *(necalificat)* labourer; ~ *agricol* farm hand; ~ *calificat* skilled worker. *adj.* (hard) working.

muncitoresc *adj.* workers', working (class).

muncitorime *sf.* workers, labour.

municipal *adj.* city ...

municipalitate *sf.* local authorities.

municipiu *sn.* city.

muniţie *sf. şi pl.* ammunition.

munte *sm.* mountain; *(ca nume)* Mount; *fig.* pile; ~ *de gheaţă* iceberg; *un* ~ *de om* a hulking fellow; ~ *de pietate* pawn shop *sau* broker.

muntean *sm.* Wallachian; mountaineer. *adj.* Wallachian.

muntenesc *adj.* Wallachian; mountain.

muntos *adj.* mountainous.

mura *vt.* to pickle.

mural *adj.* wall.

mură *sf.* blackberry; ~ *în gură* like a windfall.

murătură *sf.* pickle.

murdar *adj.* dirty; *fig. şi* foul; *(obscen)* obscene. *adv.* basely.

murdări *vt.* to (make) dirty; *(a păta)* to stain; *fig.* to sully. *vr.* to get dirty; *fig.* to be defiled.

murdărie *sf.* dirt, filth(iness); *(stricăciune)* bawdiness; *(meschinărie)* niggardliness.

murg *sm., adj.* dark bay (horse).

muri *vi.* to die, to depart (this life); *mil.* to get the chopper; *fig.* to die down; *a* ~ *de bătrîneţe* to die of old age; *a* ~ *de boală* to die of illness; *a* ~ *de dorinţa de a* ... to die with desire, to die to ..., *a* ~ *de foame* to starve; *a* ~ *de frig* to die with cold; *a* ~ *de mîna lui* to die by one's own hand; *a* ~ *de moarte bună* to die in one's bed; *a* ~ *de pe urma unei răni* to die from a wound; *a* ~ *pe cîmpul de luptă* to die in battle; *a nu* ~ *de moarte bună* to die in one's shoes.

muribund *sm.* dying man. *adj.* dying.

muritor *sm., adj.* mortal.

murmur *sn.* murmur.

murmura *vt., vi.* to murmur; *(împotriva)* to grumble (at smth.).

musafir *sm.* guest; *pl.* company.

muscă *sf.* fly; *(momeală)* lure.

muscular *adj.* muscular.

musculos *adj.* brawny.

muson *sm.* monsoon.

must *sn.* must.

mustaţă *sf.* moustache; *zool.* whiskers.

mustăcios *adj.* mustachioed.

musti *vi.* to ooze.

mustra *vt.* to reprimand; *(d. conştiinţă)* to torture.

mustrare *sf.* reprimand; *mustrări de conştiinţă* qualms.

mustrător *adj.* reproachful.

musulman *sm., adj.* Moslem.

muşama *sf.* oil cloth.

muşamaliza *vt.* to hush up.

muşca *vt., vi.* to bite; *(d. insecte)* to sting.

muşcată *sf.* geranium.

muşcător *adj.* biting.
muşcătură *sf.* bite ; *(de insectă)* sting.
muşchi *sm. anat.* muscle ; *(aliment)* sirloin ; *bot.* moss.
muşeţel *sn.* camomile.
muştar *sn.* mustard.
muşteriu *sm.* customer.
muşuroi *sn.* hill ; *(de cîrtiţă)* mole hill ; *(de furnici)* ant hill.
mut *sm.* dumb person. *adj.* dumb; mute ; *(d. film)* silent.
muta *vt., vr.* to move (into a new house).
mutare *sf.* removal ; *(mişcare)* move.

mutila *vt.* to maim.
mutră *sf.* mug ; *(strîmbătură)* long face.
mutual *adj.* mutual.
muţenie *sf.* dumbness.
muză *sf.* muse.
muzeu *sn.* museum.
muzical *adj.* musical.
muzicant *sm.* musician.
muzică *sf.* music ; *(orchestră)* band ; ~ *de cameră* chamber music ; ~ *populară* folk music ; ~ *de dans* dance music.
muzician *sm.* composer; performer.
muzicuţă *sf.* mouth-organ.

N

na *interj.* here (you are) !
nabab *sm.* nabob.
nacelă *sf.* gondola.
nadă *sf.* bait.
naftalină *sf.* moth balls ; *la* ~ *fig.* on the shelf.
nai *sn.* Pan's pipe.
naiba *sf.* the devil ; *la* ~ ! oh hell !
nailon *sn.* nylon.
naiv *sm.* simpleton. *adj.* naïve.
naivitate *.sf.* naïveté.
nalbă *sf.* mallow.
namilă *sf.* strapping person.
naos *sn.* nave.
nap *sm.* turnip (-rooted cabbage).
nară *sf.* nostril.
narcisă *sf.* narcissus ; *(galbenă)* daffodil.
narval *sm.* narwhale.

nas *sn.* nose ; ~ *borcănat* bottle nose.
nasture *sm.* button.
naş *sm.* godfather ; *(la cununie)* best man.
naşă *sf.* godmother ; *(la cununie)* sponsor.
naşte *vt.* to give birth to. *vr.* to be born ; *fig.* to originate (in smth).
naştere *sf.* birth ; *(lăuzie)* delivery ; *de* ~ birth...
natal *adj.* native.
natalitate *sf.* birth rate.
nataţie *sf.* swimming.
natural *adj.* natural ; *(veritabil)* genuine ; *(pur)* pure ; *(ca mărime)* full-size. *adv.* (as a matter) of course. *interj.* certainly.

naturalist *sm.*, *adj.* naturalist.
natură *sf.* nature ; ~ *moartă* still-life ; *în* ~ in kind.
naţional *adj.* national.
naţionalism *sn.* jingo(ism); nationalism.
naţionalist *sm.* nationalist. *adj.* jingoistic.
naţionalitate *sf.* nationality.
naţiune *sf.* nation.
naufragia *vi.* to be shipwrecked.
naufragiu *sn.* shipwreck.
nautic *adj.* nautical; *sport* aquatic.
naval *adj.* naval.
navă *sf.* vessel, ship ; ~ *cosmică* space ship.
navetă *sf.* commutation.
navetist *sm.* commuter.
naviga *vi.* to sail.
navigabil *adj.* navigable.
navigaţie *sf.* navigation.
nazal *adj.* nasal.
nazuri *sn. pl.* whims.
nădăjdui *vt.*, *vi.* to hope (for).
nădejde *sf.* hope; *cu* ~ vigorously ; *de* ~ reliable.
năduşeală *sf.* sweat.
năduşi *vi.* to perspire.
năimi *vt.* to hire.
nălucă *sf.* phantom.
nălucire *sf.* hallucination.
nămete *sm.* snow drift.
nămol *sn* (medicinal) mud.
năpastă *sf.* calamity ; *(nedreptate)* injustice.
năpădi *vt.* to invade.
năpăstui *vt.* to wrong.
năpăstuit *sm.* victim. *adj.* unfortunate.
năpîrcă *sf.* viper.
năpîrli *vi.* to shed one's hair.
năprasnic *adj.* unexpected ; *(violent)* violent. *adv.* suddenly.

năpusti *vr.* to swoop (upon smb., etc.).
nărav *sn.* vice.
nărăvaş *adj.* vicious ; *(d. cal)* balky, restive.
nărăvit *adj.* inveterate.
nărui *vt.* to shatter. *vr.* to crumble.
năsălie *sf.* bier.
născoci *vt.* to invent ; *(minciuni* etc.*)* to concoct.
născocire *sf.* invention ; *(minciună şi)* lie.
născut *adj.* born ; ~*ă Ionescu* née Ionescu ; *nou-*~ new-born child.
năstruşnic *adj.* extraordinary ; *(ciudat)* extravagant.
nătăfleţ *sm.* blockhead. *adj.* stupid, dolt.
nătărău *sm.* ninny.
nătîng *sm.* dolt. *adj.* dull ; *(stîngaci)* lubberly.
năuc *sm.* addle-brained fellow. *adj.* giddy.
năuci *vt.* to dumbfound.
năut *sn.* chick pea.
năvalnic *adj.* tempestuous. *adv.* impetuously.
năvăli *vi.* to rush ; *a* ~ *în* to overrun.
năvălire *sf.* invasion.
năvod *sn.* trawl.
năzări *vr.: a i se* ~ *(că)* to fancy (that).
năzbîtie *sf.* prank.
năzdrăvan *adj.* uncanny ; *(vrăjit)* enchanted.
năzdrăvănie *sf.* prodigy ; *(năzbîtie)* frisk.
năzui *vi.* to aspire (after).
năzuinţă *sf.* aspiration (after).
ne *pron.* us ; *(refelexiv)* oneself.
nea *sf.* snow.

neabătut *adj.* unflinching.

neadevăr *sn.* untruth.

neadormit *adj.* vigilant ; *(neobosit)* untiring.

neagresiune *sf.* non-aggression.

neajuns *sn.* shortcoming ; *(supărare)* trouble.

neajutorat *adj.* helpless ; *(nevoiaş)* needy.

neam *sn.* people ; *(familie)* family ; *(origine)* descent ; *(rudă)* relative ; ~ *prost* churl.

neamţ *sm.* German.

neant *sn.* nothingness.

neaoş *adj.* true-born.

neapărat *adj.* indispensable. *adv.* by all means.

nearticulat *adj.* inarticulate ; *gram.* without an article.

neascultare *sf.* disobedience.

neascultător *adj.* naughty.

neasemuit *adj.* incomparable.

neastîmpăr *sn.* fretting.

neastîmpărat *adj.* unruly ; *(d. copii)* naughty.

neaşteptat *sn.* : *pe* ~*e* out of the blue. *adj.* unexpected.

neatent *adj.* inattentive. *adv.* absent-mindedly.

neatenţie *sf.* listlessness.

neatins *adj.* untouched.

neatîrnare *sf.* independence.

neatîrnat *adj.* free.

nebăgare *s.f.* : ~ *de seamă* oversight.

nebun *sm.* lunatic, madman ; *(la şah)* bishop ; *ca un* ~ madly. *adj.* mad ; *(prostesc)* reckless ; *(turbat)* distraught ; ~ *de bucurie* beside oneself with joy ; ~ *de legat* raving mad.

nebunatic *adj.* playful.

nebunese *adj.* crazy.

nebuneşte *adv.* madly.

nebunie *sf.* lunacy ; *fig.* folly ; *la* ~ to distraction.

necalifieat *adj.* unskilled.

necaz *sn.* trouble ; *(ciudă)* spite.

necăji *vt.* to annoy ; *(a bate la cap)* to bother. *vr.* to be angry *sau* sorrowful.

necăjit *adj.* worried ; *(trist)* depressed.

necăsătorit *adj.* unmarried, single.

necesar *sn., adj.* necessary.

necesita *vt.* to require.

necesitate *sf.* necessity.

nechemat *sm.* intruder.

necheza *vi.* to neigh.

nechibzuit *adj.* reckless ; *(la bani)* thriftless.

necinsti *vt.* to dishonour ; *(a viola)* to rape

necinstit *adj.* shady. *adv.* dishonestly.

necioplit *adj.* churlish.

neciteţ *adj.* illegible.

neclar *adj.* dim, obscure. *adv.* indistinctly.

neclintit *adj.* unflinching.

neconceput *adj.* . *de* ~ inconceivable.

necondiţionat *adj.* unconditional. *adv.* unconditionally.

necontenit *adj.* ceaseless. *adv.* permanently.

necontestat *adj.* unquestionable.

necopt *adj.* raw ; *(d. alimente)* half-baked.

necorespunzător *adj.* unsuitable.

necredincios *sm.* atheist ; *(păgîn)* heathen. *adj.* faithless ; *(neîncrezător)* doubting.

necredinţă *sf.* disloyalty.

necrezut *adj.* : *de* ~ unbelievable.

necrolog *sn.* obituary.

necruţător *adj.* merciless.

nectar *sn.* nectar.

necugetat *adj.* thoughtless.

necumpătat *adj.* intemperate.

necunoscut *sm.* stranger. *sn.* the unknown. *adj.* unknown; *(obscur)* obscure.

necuviincios *adj.* disrespectful; *(indecent)* scurrilous. *adv.* disrespectfully.

nedemn *adj.* unworthy (of).

nedescris *adj.: de ~* indescribable.

nedescurcăreţ *adj.* shiftless.

nedesluşit *adj., adv.* indistinct (ly).

nedespărţit *adj.* inseparable.

nedezminţit *adj.* never-failing.

nedisciplinat *adj.* unruly.

nedorit *adj.* uncalled for.

nedormit *adj.* sleepless.

nedrept *sn.* injustice; *pe ~* wrongly. *adj.* unjust.

nedreptate *sf.* injustice.

nedreptăţi *vt.* to wrong.

nedumerire *sf.* bewilderment.

nedumerit *adj.* puzzled.

neexpresiv *adj.* inexpressive.

nefast *adj.* ill-fated.

nefavorabil *adj.* inauspicious.

nefericire *sf.* calamity; *din* unfortunately.

nefericit *adj.* unhappy; *(nenorocos)* unfortunate.

nefiresc *adj.* unnatural.

nefolositor *adj.* useless.

neg *sm.* wart.

nega *vt., vi.* to deny.

negativ *sn., adj.* negative. *adv.* in the negative.

negaţie *sf.* negation.

neghină *sf.* corncockle.

neghiob *sm.* lout. *adj.* clumsy.

neghiobie *sf.* foolishness.

negîndit *sn.: pe ~e* out of the blue.

neglija *vt.* to neglect.

neglijabil *adj.* negligible.

neglijent *adj.* neglijent.

neglijenţă *sf.* negligence.

negocia *vt.* to negotiate.

negociere *sf.* negotiation; *pl.* şi talks.

negoţ *sn.* trade.

negresă *sf.* Negro woman, Negress.

negreşit *adv.* without fail.

negricios *adj.* swarthy.

negru *sm.* Negro. *fig.* ghost; hack writer. *sn.* black. *adj.* black; *(referitor la negri)* Negro; *(negricios)* dark; *(bronzat)* sunburnt; *(întunecat)* dark, gloomy.

negură *sf.* fog; *fig.* darkness

negustor *sm.* merchant; *(mic)* shopkeeper; *(angrosist)* (wholesale) dealer; *(ambulant)* pedlar, *(de zarzavaturi* etc.*)* costermonger.

negustoresc *adj.* mercantile.

negustorie *sf.* trade.

neguvernamental *adj.* non-government.

nehotărîre *sf.* hesitation.

nehotărît *adj.* irresolute; *gram.* indefinite.

neiertat *adj.: de ~* impardonable.

neiertător *adj.* unforgiving; *fig.* implacable.

neimpozabil *adj.* tax-free.

neintervenţie *sf.* non-interference.

neisprăvit *sm.* good-for-nothing; half-wit. *adj.* unfinished; *(necopt)* immature.

neizbutit *adj.* unsuccessful.

neîmblînzit *adj.* wild.
neîmpăcat *adj.* irreconcilable.
neîmplinit *adj.* unfulfilled ; *(d.
ani)* not yet reached.
neîncăpător *adj.* narrow.
neînceput *adj.* whole.
neîncetat *adj.* permanent. *adv.*
ceaselessly.
neînchipuit *adj.* inconceivable.
adv. ∼ *de* ... inconceivably...,
very ; *de* ∼ unthinkable.
neîncredere *sf.* distrust.
neîncrezător *adj.* doubting; doubtful (of). *adv.* tentatively.
neîndeminatic *adj.* clumsy.
neîndoielnic, neîndoios *adj.* doubtless.
neînduplecat *adj.* adamant.
neîndurător *adj.* ruthless.
neînfricat *adj.* dauntless.
neînfrînt *adj.* unvanquished ; *de*
∼ invincible.
neîngăduit *adj.* inadmissible.
neîngrijit *adj.* neglected ; *(ca
aspect)* uncouth.
neînlăturat *adj.: de* ∼ unavoidable.
neînsemnat *adj.* insignificant.
neînsufleţit *adj.* inanimate.
neîntemeiat *adj.* groundless.
neîntîrziat *adj.* urgent. *adv.* immediately.
ńeîntrecut *adj.* unsurpassed.
neîntrerupt *adj.* uninterrupted.
adv. permanently.
neînţelegere *sf.* misunderstanding.
neînţeles *adj.* misunderstood ; *de*
∼ incomprehensible ; *(inexplicabil)* unaccountable.
neînvins *adj.* unvanquished ; *de*
∼ invincible.
nejustificat *adj.* unjustified.
nelămurire *sf.* doubt.

nelămurit *adj.* obscure ; *(d. cineva)* doubtful. *adv.* indistinctly.
nelegitim *adj.* illegitimate.
nelegiuire *sf.* wrongdoing.
nelegiuit *sm.* evildoer. *adj.* criminal.
nelimitat *adj.* illimited.
nelinişte *sf.* restlessness.
nelinişti *vt.* to trouble ; to worry.
vr. to be worried.
neliniştit *adj.* troubled ; *(îngrijorat)* anxious.
nelipsit *adj.* unfailing.
nelocuit *adj.* uninhabited.
nemaiauzit, nemaipomenit, ne-
maivăzut *adj.* unprecedented.
nemărginit *adj.* boundless.
nemăsurat *adj.* measureless.
nemernic *sm.* rascal.
nemijlocit *adj.* immediate. *adv.*
directly.
nemilos *adj.* pitiless.
nemiluita *sf.: cu* ∼ in plenty.
nemişcare *sf.* immobility.
nemişcat *adj.* motionless.
nemîncat *sm.* starveling. *sn.:
pe* ∼ on an empty stomach.
adj. starved.
nemîngîiat *adj.* unsolaced.
nemotivat *adj.* without leave ;
(neîntemeiat) groundless.
nemţesc *adj.* German.
nemţeşte *adv.* (like a) German.
nemţoaică *sf.* German (woman).
nemulţumi *vt.* to displease.
nemulţumire *sf.* discontent ;
(plîngere) grievance.
nemulţumit *sm.* discontented
person. *adj.* dissatisfied.
nemurire *sf.* immortality.
nemuritor *adj.* undying.
nene *sm.* uncle.
nenoroc *sn.* ill-luck.
nenoroci *vt.* to ruin.

nenorocire *sf.* misfortune; *din*
~ unfortunately.
nenorocit *sm.* wretch. *adj.* unlucky; miserable.
nenorocos *adj.* ill-fated.
nenumărat *adj.* countless.
neobişnuit *adj.* unusual; *(lipsit de rutină)* unaccustomed
(to smth.).
neobosit *adj.* tireless. *adv.* untiringly.
neobrăzare *sf.* impudence.
neobservat *sn.:* *pe* ~*e* unnoticed, stealthily. *adj.* unnoticed.
neocupat *adj.* vacant.
neodihnit *adj.* tireless.
neofalină *sf.* benzine.
neoficial *adj.* unofficial; off the
record.
neologism *sn.* neologism.
neomenesc *adj.* inhuman.
neomenos *adj.* cruel.
neon *sn.* neon.
necrealist *sf.* neo-realistic.
neorînduială *sf.* untidiness.
nepărtinitor *adj.* fair(-minded).
nepăsare *sf.* indifference.
nepăsător *adj.* listless. *adv.* indifferently.
nepătat *adj.* spotless.
nepătruns *adj.* impenetrable.
nepedepsit *adj.* unpunished.
nepermis *adj.* impermissible.
nepieritor *adj.* immortal.
neplată *sf.* failure to pay.
neplăcere *sf.* nuisance; *(silă)*
reluctance.
nepoată *sf.* niece; *(de bunic)*
grand-daughter.
nepoftit *sm.* intruder. *adj.* unin-
vited.
nepopular *adj.* unpopular.
nepot *sm.* nephew; *(de bunic)*
grandson; *pl. şi* grand-children.

nepotolit *adj.* unabated.
nepotrivire *sf.* discrepancy.
nepotrivit *adj.* unfit; out of
place.
nepractic *adj.* unpractical.
neprecupeţit *adj.* unstinted, unselfish; ungrudging.
nepregătit *sn.:* *pe* ~*e* unawares.
adj. unprepared; ignorant.
nepreţuit *adj.* invaluable.
neprevăzut *sn.* unforeseen situation. *adj.* unexpected.
nepriceput *sm.* blunderer. *adj.*
inexpert.
neprielnic *adj.* unpropitious.
neprihănit *adj.* immaculate.
neproductiv *adj.* unproductive.
nepublicat *adj.* unpublished.
neputincios *adj.* helpless.
neputinţă *sf.* impotence; *cu* ~
out of the question.
nerăbdare *sf.* impatience; *(zel)*
eagerness; *cu* ~ impatiently.
nerăbdător *adj.* eager.
nerecunoscător *adj.* ungrateful.
nerecunoştinţă *sf.* ingratitude.
neregulat *adj.* irregular; *(dezordonat)* disorderly.
neregulă *sf.* disorder; *(financia-
ră)* defalcation.
nereuşit *adj.* unsuccessful.
nerezolvat *adj.* unsettled; *de* ~
insoluble.
nerod *sm.* dullard. *adj.* stupid.
neroditor *adj.* barren.
nerozie *sf.* foolishness.
neruşinare *sf.* brazenness.
neruşinat *adj.* shameless.
nerv *sm.* nerve; *(energie)* go,
pep; *pl.* (conniption) fit.
nervos *adj.* irritable; impatient. *adv.* impatiently.
nervozitate *sf.* nervousness.
nesaţ *sn.* relish; *cu* ~ lustily.

nesăbuit *adj.* reckless.

nesănătos *adj.* unwholesome.

nesărat *adj.* unsalted ; *fig.* insipid.

nesătul *adj.* hungry ; unsatisfied.

nesăţios *adj.* insatiable.

nesecat *adj.* inexhaustible.

nesfîrşit *sn.* infinity ; *la* ~ endlessly. *adj.* boundless.

nesigur *adj.* uncertain ; *(şovăielnic)* unsteady.

nesiguranţă *sf.* uncertainty.

nesilit *adj.* free.

nesimţire *sf.* insensitiveness ; *(leşin)* unconsciousness.

nesimţit *sm.* cad. *sn.: pe* ~*e* imperceptibly. *adj.* thick-skinned.

nesimţitor *adj.* unfeeling.

nesincer *adj.* insincere. *adv.* insincerely.

nesocoti *vt.* to overlook, to ignore.

nesocotit *adj.* unreasonable.

nesomn *sn.* sleeplessness.

nespălat *sm.* country bumpkin. *adj.* unwashed ; *fig.* boorish.

nespus *adj.* unutterable ; ~ *de* very.

nestabil *adj.* unstable.

nestatornic *adj.* fickle.

nestăpînit *adj.* unrestrained.

nestăvilit *adj.* irresistible.

nestemată *sf.* gem.

nestingherit *adj.* unhampered, unhindered.

nestins *adj.* unextinguished; *(d. var)* quick.

nestînjenit *adj.* at ease ; unruffled, untroubled.

nestrămutat *adj.* unshaken.

nesuferit *sm.* public nuisance. *adj.* unbearable.

nesupunere *sf.* insubordination.

nesupus *adj.* disobedient.

neştiinţă *sf.* ignorance ; ~ *de carte* illiteracy.

neştire *sf.: în* ~ greedily ; unconsciously.

neştiut *adj.* unknown.

neştiutor *adj.* ignorant ; ~ *de carte* illiterate.

net *adj.* clear (cut) ; *(d. un răspuns)* flat ; *com.* net. *adv.* plainly.

netăgăduit *adj.* undeniable.

neted *adj.* smooth. *adv.* evenly.

netemeinicie *sf.* wantonness.

neterminat *adj.* unfinished.

netezi *vt.* to (make) smooth.

netot *sm.* dolt. *adj.* silly.

netrebnic *sm.* ne'er-do-well. *adj.* worthless.

netulburat *adj.* unruffled.

neţărmurit *adj.* illimited.

neuitat *adj.* unforgotten ; *de* ~ unforgettable.

neurolog *sm.* neurologist.

neutralitate *sf.* neutrality.

neutraliza *vt., vr.* to neutralize.

neutru *sn.* neuter. *adj.* neutral ; *gram.* neuter.

nevastă *sf.* wife ; married woman.

nevăstuică *sf.* ferret, weasel.

nevătămat *adj., adv.* unscathed, scot-free.

nevăzut *adj.* unseen.

neverosimil *adj.* (highly) improbable.

nevindecat *adj.* unhealed.

nevinovat *adj.* innocent ; *(blînd)* harmless.

nevinovăţie *sf.* innocence.

nevoiaş *sm.* pauper. *adj.* needy ; in want.

nevoie *sf.* need; *(necesitate și)* necessity; *(lipsă)* want; *la ~* in case of need.

nevoit *adj.* forced.

nevralgie *sf.* neuralgia.

nevrednic *adj.* unworthy.

nezdruncinat *adj.* unshaken.

nicăieri *adv.* nowhere, not ... anywhere.

nichel *sn.* nickel.

nici *adv.* not even; *~ un, ~ o* none; *~ unul (din doi)* neither. *conj.* neither, nor; *~ ...* *~* neither ... nor ...

nicicind *adv.* never.

nicideeum *adv.* not in the least.

nieiodată *adv.* never (more).

nicovală *sf.* anvil; *anat.* incus.

nimb *sn.* halo.

nimeni *pron.* nobody, not ... anybody.

nimereală *sf.* guess(work), hazard; *la ~* at random.

nimeri *vt.* to hit (upon); to find; *(a ghici)* to guess. *vi.* to reach; to get; to find oneself; *a ~ alături* to miss the mark. *vr.* to be; to find oneself; *(a se întîmpla)* to happen.

nimerit *adj.* adequate, good.

nimfă *sf. mit.* nymph; *entom.* nympha.

nimic *sn.* trifle; *(podoabă)* trinket. *pron.* nothing, not ... anything; *de ~* worthless; *cu ~* by no means; *mai ~* next to nothing; *pe ~* dirt cheap; *pentru ~ în lume* not for the world.

nimica *sf.* trifle.

nimici *vt.* to annihilate.

nimicitor *adj.* destructive.

nimicnicie *sf.* nothing(ness).

ninge *vi. impers.* to snow.

ninsoare *sf.* snow (fall).

nisetru *sm.* sturgeon.

nisip *sn.* sand; *~uri mișcătoare* quick sands.

nisipos *adj.* sandy.

nișă *sf.* niche.

niște *adj.* some; *(în prop. interog.)* any.

nit *sn.* rivet.

nitui *vt.* to rivet.

nițel *num.* a little.

nivel *sn.* level; *fig. și* standard; *~ de trai* living standard(s); *la ~ înalt* summit, top-level.

nivela *vt.* to level; *fig. și* to equalize.

nivelă *sf.* (water) level.

niznai *sm.*: *a face pe ~ul* to feign innocence.

noapte *sf.* night; *(întuneric)* gloom.; *(căderea nopții)* nightfall; *~ cu lună* moonlight night; *astă-~* last night; *la ~* tonight.

noaptea *adv.* at *sau* by night; *(frecventativ)* nights.

noastră *adj.* our; *a ~* ours.

noastre *adj.* our; *ale ~* ours.

nobil *sm.* nobleman, aristocrat. *adj.* noble; aristocratic.

nobilime *sf.* aristocracy.

noblețe *sf.* nobility.

nocturn *adj.* night...

nocturnă *sf.* nocturne; *în ~* floodlit (match, etc.).

nod *sn.* knot; *c.f.* junction; *~ul gordian* the Gordian knot.

noi *pron.* we; *la ~* with us; in this country; *pe ~ (acuzativ)* us.

noian *sn.* heap.

noiembrie *sm.* November.

noimă *sf.* sense; *fără ~* without rhyme or reason.

nomad *sm.* nomad. *adj.* nomadic.

nominativ *sn.*, *adj.* nominative.

nonsens *sn.* absurdity.

nonşalanţă *sf.* nonchalance.

noptieră *sf.* bedside table.

nor *sm.* cloud; *fără ~i* cloudless, clear.

noră *sf.* daughter-in-law.

nord *sn.* North; *de ~* north(ern); *în ~ul ţării* in the north of the country; *la ~ de* (to the) north of; *spre ~* northwards.

nord-est *sn.* North-East.

nordic *sm.* northerner; Scandinavian. *adj.* north(ern); *(d. vînt)* northerly.

nord-vest *sn.* North-West.

norma *vt.* to standardize.

normal *sn.*, *adj.* normal. *adv.* normally.

normă *sf.* norm; standard; *(de producţie şi)* rate.

noroc *sn.* luck; *(şansă)* chance; *~ că ...* fortunately; *la ~* at hazard. *interj.* good luck! *(la toasturi)* your health!

norocos *adj.* lucky; *(fericit)* happy.

noroi *sm.* mud.

noros *adj.* cloudy.

norvegian *sm.*, *adj.*, **norvegiană** *sf.*, *adj.* Norwegian.

nostalgie *sf.* homesickness; *(melancolie)* melancholy.

nostim *adj.* droll; *(atrăgător)* comely.

nostimadă *sf.* funny thing.

nostru *adj.* our; *al ~* ours.

noştri *adj.* our; *ai ~* ours; our folk(s).

nota *vt.* to note; *(a observa)* to remark.

notar *sm.* notary.

notare *sf.* noting; *(la şcoală)* marking.

notariat *sn.* public notary (office).

notă *sf.* note; *(la şcoală)* mark; *~ de plată* bill; *~ în josul paginii* footnote; *~ marginală* marginal (note); *note de călătorie* travel notes.

notes *sn.* jotter.

notiţe *sf. pl.* notes.

notoriu *adj.* notorious.

noţiune *sf.* notion.

nou *sn.* the new (elements). *adj.* new; *(recent)* recent; *(suplimentar)* further; *(inedit)* novel; *~-născut* new-born (child); *~-nouţ* brand-new; *~-venit* newcomer; *din ~* again, once more; new(ly).

nouă *sm.*, *adj.*, *num.* nine. *pron.* (to) us.

nouălea *adj.*, *num.* (the) ninth.

nouăsprezece *sm.*, *adj.*, *num.* nineteen.

nouăsprezecelea *adj.*, *num.* (the) nineteenth.

nouăzeci *sm.*, *adj.*, *num.* ninety.

nouăzecilea *adj.*, *num.* (the) ninetieth.

noutate *sf.* novelty; *(ştire)* (piece of) news.

nu *adv.* no; *(cu predicat)* not; *(de loc)* never; *~ chiar* not exactly; *~ numai ... ci şi* not only... but also.

nuanţat *adj.* nuancé.

nuanţă *sf.* shade.

nuc *sm.* walnut tree.

nucă *sf.* (wal)nut; *~ de cocos* coconut.

nuclear *adj.* nuclear; atom.

nucleu *sn.* nucleus.

nud *sn.*, *adj.* nude.

nufăr *sm.* water lily.

nuga *sf.* nougat.

nuia *sf.* twig, rod; *pl. (împletitură)* wattle.

nul *adj.* null (and void); *(prost)* stupid; *sport* draw.

nulitate *sf.* nullity; *(persoană)* non-entity.

numai *adv.* only; ~ *că* but.

numaidecît *adv.* directly; by all means.

număr *sn.* number; *(cifră şi)* figure; *(de ziar* etc.*)* issue; *(mulţime)* group; *(într-un spectacol)* act; *(măsură)* size; ~ *cu soţ* even number; ~ *de atracţie* sensational act; ~ *fără soţ* odd number; *în* ~ *mare* in force; *un mare* ~ *de* many.

număra *vt., vi., vr.* to count.

numărătoare *sf.* reckoning; *(abac)* abacus.

nu-mă-uita *sf.* forget-me-not.

nume *sn.* name; ~ *de botez* Christian name; ~ *de familie* surname; ~ *de fată* maiden name; ~ *propriu* proper name; *în* ~*le* ... in the name of..., on behalf of...; *pentru* ~*le lui Dumnezeu!* for God's sake!

numeral *sn.* numeral.

numerar *sn.* (hard) cash, specie.

numeros *adj.* numerous.

numerota *vt.* to number.

numi *vt.* to name, to call; *(într-o funcţie)* to appoint. *vr.* to be named; *cum te numeşti?* what is your name?

numire *sf. (nume)* term; *(într-un post)* appointment.

numit *sm.:* ~*ul* the said. *adj.* named.

nuntaş *sm.* wedding guest.

nuntă *sf.* wedding (party).

nuri *sm. pl.* sex appeal.

nurcă *sf.* mink.

nutreţ *sn.* fodder.

nutri *vt.* to feed; *fig.* to harbour. *vr.* to feed.

nuvelă *sf.* short story.

nuvelist *sm.* story-teller.

O

o *art* a, an. *num.* one; a, an. *interj.* oh!

oacheş *adj.* swarthy; *(d. animal)* spectacled.

oaie *sf.* sheep; *fem. şi* ewe; *(carne)* mutton; *(blana)* sheepskin; *de oi* sheep; ewe's.

oală *sf.* pot; *(conţinutul)* potful.

oară *sf.* time; *de cîte ori?* how many times?

oare *adv.* really?

oarecare *sm.* nobody. *adj.* certain; *într-o* ~ *măsură* to a certain extent.

oarecum *adv.* somehow.

oaspete *sf.* guest.

oaste *sf.* army; *fig.* host.

oază *sf.* oasis.

oberliht *sn.* transom(-window).

obez *adj.* obese.

obială *sf.* foot wrap.

obicei *sn.* habit; *(datină)* custom; *~ul pămîntului* local custom; *de ~* usually, as a rule; *ca de ~* as usual.

obiect *sn.* object; *(materie)* subject (matter); *(articol)* item; *fără ~* objectless; *la ~* relevant.

obiecta *vt., vi.* to object; *a ~ la* to oppose.

obiectiv *sn.* objective; *opt.* object lens; *~ turistic* sightseeing spot; *adj.* objective; *(imparţial şi)* unbiassed. *adv.* fairly.

obiectivitate *sf.* objectiveness.

obiecţie *sf.* objection.

obişnui *vt.* to accustom (to); *a ~ să* to be wont to. *vr.* to become inured (to); *se obişnuieşte să* ... it is usual to...

obişnuinţă *sf.* usage; *din ~* out of habit.

obişnuit *sm.* habitué. *adj.* usual; *(de rînd)* ordinary; *(curent)* obtaining; *~ cu* accustomed to. *adv.* usually, as a rule.

obîrşie *sf.* origin.

oblic *adj.* oblique; *(pieziş)* slanting.

obliga *vt.* to compel; *fig.* to oblige. *vr.* to commit oneself.

obligatoriu *adj.* compulsory.

obligaţie *sf.* obligation; *fin.* bond.

oblon *sn.* (window) shutter.

oboi *sn.* oboe.

obol *sn.* mite.

obor *sn.* (cattle) market.

oboseală *sf.* tiredness.

obosi *vt., vi., vr.* to tire (oneself).

obosit *adj.* tired; *(istovit)* fatigued.

obositor *adj.* wearisome.

obraz *sm.* cheek; *(faţă)* face.

obraznic *sm.* daring fellow. *adj.* cheeky; *(neastîmpărat)* naughty.

obrăznici *vr.* to become naughty *sau* cheeky.

obrăznicie *sf.* (piece of) impudence; *(poznă)* mischief.

obscen *adj.* lewd.

obscur *adj.* obscure.

obscuritate *sf.* obscurity; *(întunecime şi)* dark; *(neclaritate şi)* dimness.

obseda *vt.* to obsess.

obsedant *adj.* haunting.

observa *vt.* to observe; *(a remarca şi)* to notice. *vr.* to control oneself; *(impersonal)* to be noticed.

observator *sm.* observer. *sn.* observatory.

observaţie *sf.* observation; *pl.* reproof.

obsesie *sf.* obsession.

obsesiv *adj.* obsessive.

obstacol *sn.* obstacle; *sport* steeple.

obşte *sf.* community; *în de ~* as a rule.

obştesc *adj.* public.

obtuz *adj.* obtuse; *fig.* dull.

obţine *vt.* to obtain.

obuz *sn.* shell.

ocară *sf.* insult.

ocazie *sf.* occasion; *(favorabilă)* opportunity; *cu altă ~* some other time; *de ~* secondhand; *(ocazional)* circumstantial.

ocări *vt.* to reproach; *(a insulta)* to abuse. *vi.* to curse.

occident *sn.* West.

occidental *adj.* West(ern).

ocean *sn.* ocean.

ocheadă *sf.* sidelong glance.

ochean *sn.* field glass; *mar.* spy glass.

ochelari *sm. pl.* spectacles, glasses; ~ *de soare* sun glasses; ~ *de cal* blinkers; *fig.* narrow-mindedness; ~ *de protecție* goggles.

ochi[1] *sm.* eye; *pl.* eyesight; *(priviri)* glances; ~ *bulbucați* bulging eyes; ~ *căprui* hazel *sau* brown eyes; ~ *de pisică* cat's eye; ~*ul boului* aster; *cu* ~*i închiși* blindly; *cu* ~*i în gol* staring; *cu* ~ *și cu sprincene* glaring; *cu* ~*ul liber* with the naked eye; *de* ~ eye...; *între patru* ~ between you and me (and the bedpost). *sn. (fereastră)* window *sau* glass pane; *(de apă)* puddle; *(de plasă)* loop, mesh; *(de lanț)* link; *(de aragaz etc.)* ring; *pl.* fried eggs. *adv.* (full) to the brim.

ochi[2] *vt.* to shoot *sau* aim at. *vi.* to take aim (at smth., etc.).

ochire *sf.* sighting; *(privire)* glance.

ocnaș *sm.* gaol-bird.

ocnă *sf.* jail; *(de sare)* salt mine.

ocol *sn.* detour; *(îngrăditură)* enclosure; *(circumscripție)* circuit; *fără* ~ straight to the point.

ocoli *vt.* to avoid; *(a înconjura)* to side step. *vi.* to go round.

ocoliș *sn.* roundabout way; *fără* ~*uri* directly.

ocolit *sn.* detour; *pe* ~*e* beating about the bush. *adj.* devious.

ocroti *vt.* to protect.

ocrotire *sf.* defence; ~*a sănătății* health assistance.

ocrotitor *adj.* protective.

octombrie *sm.* October.

ocular *sn., adj.* ocular; *martor* ~ eye witness.

ocupa *vt.* to occupy; *(a cuceri și)* to conquer; *fig. și* to absorb; *(o locuință)* to live *sau* dwell in. *vr.* to deal (with)

ocupare *sf.* occupation.

ocupat *adj.* busy; engaged; *(cotropit)* seized.

ocupație *sf.* occupation.

odaie *sf.* room.

odată *adj.* true(born). *adv.* once (upon a time); *(în viitor)* some day; *(în același timp)* at once; *(laolaltă)* together.

odă *sf.* ode.

odgon *sn.* cable.

odihnă *sf.* rest; *(răgaz)* leisure; *fără* ~ restless(ly).

odihni *vt.* to rest. *vi., vr.* to rest; *(a dormi)* to sleep; *(a zăcea)* to lie.

odihnitor *adj.* restful.

odinioară *adv.* formerly.

odios *adj.* hateful.

odisee *sf.* odyssey.

odor *sn.* jewel.

odraslă *sf.* offspring.

of *sn.* sigh; *fig.* grief; *interj.* oh! alas.

ofensa *vt.* to offend; *(a jigni)* to hurt. *vr.* to take offence.

ofensă *sf.* insult.

ofensivă *sf.* offensive.

oferi *vt., vr.* to offer (oneself).

ofertă *sf.* offer; *com.* tender; *econ.* supply.

oficia *vt.* to celebrate. *vi.* to officiate.

oficial *adj.* official ; *(ceremonios)* ceremonial. *adv.* officially.

oficiu *sn.* office ; agency ; ~*ul stării civile* registrar's office ; *din* ~ ex officio ; appointed by the court.

ofili *vt.* to wither. *vr.* to fade.

ofiţer *sm.* (commissioned) officer ; ~ *al stării civile* registrar ; ~ *superior* senior officer.

ofrandă *sf.* offering.

ofta *vi.* to sigh ; *fig.* to yearn (for smth.).

oftat *sn.* sigh.

ogar *sm.* greyhound ; *ca un* ~ fast ; *(slab)* lanky.

oglindă *sf.* mirror, looking glass ; *ca oglinda* smooth.

oglindi *vt.* to mirror. *vr.* to look at oneself in a mirror ; *fig.* to be mirrored.

oglindire *sf.* reflection.

ogor *sn.* cultivated field.

oh *interj.* oh !

oho *interj.* quite ! I see !

oină *sf.* (the game of) rounders.

oişte *sf.* shaft.

olan *sn.* tile.

olandă *sf.* Holland ; Dutch cheese.

olandez *sm.* Dutchman ; *pl.* the Dutch. *adj.* Dutch.

olandeză *sf.* Dutch(woman).

olar *sm.* potter.

olărie *sf.* pottery ; crockery.

oligarhie *sf.* oligarchy.

olimpiadă *sf.* Olympiad.

olimpic *adj.* Olympic.

olog *sm.* lame man. *adj.* lame, crippled.

oltean *sm., adj.,* **olteancă** *sf.* Oltenian. **oltenesc** *adj.* Oltenian.

om *sm.* man ; *(fiinţă)* human being ; *(bărbat)* man, *pl.* men ; *(cineva)* somebody ; *(muritor)* mortal ; *pl.* people ; ~-*afiş* sandwichman ; ~ *cu cap* reasonable man ; ~ *cu stare* man of substance ; ~ *cu vază* great man ; ~ *cu ziua* day labourer ; ~ *de afaceri* business man ; ~ *de bine* doer of good ; ~ *de cuvînt* a man as good as his word ; ~ *de ispravă* worthy *sau* efficient man ; ~ *de încredere* confidential man ; ~ *de litere* writer ; ~ *de lume* a good mixer ; *un* ~ *de nimic* a cipher ; a skunk ; ~ *de onoare* honest *sau* honorable man ; ~ *de paie* dummy ; ~*ul de rînd* the man in the street ; ~ *de stat* statesman ; ~ *de ştiinţă* scientist ; *un* ~ *dintr-o bucată* an honest-minded fellow ; an intransigent character ; ~ *mare* grown-up ; *fig.* a great man ; *ca* ~*ul* as is but natural. *interj. :* ~*le !* my man !

omagiu *sn.* homage ; *pl.* respects.

omenesc *adj.* human ; *(ca lumea)* decent.

omeneşte *adv.* humanly (possible) ; *(ca lumea)* properly.

omenie *sf.* kind(li)ness ; *de* ~ kind(-hearted), kindly ; *lipsit de* ~ inhuman.

omenire *sf.* humanity ; mankind ; *(mulţime)* crowd.

omenos *adj.* humane.

omidă *sf.* caterpillar.

omisiune *sf.* omission ; *(lipsă)* flaw.

omite *vt.* to omit ; *a* ~ *să* to fail to.

omletă *sf.* omelette.

omogen *adj.* homogeneous.

omonim *sm. (tiz)* namesake. *sn.* homonym. *adj.* homonymous.

omoplat *sm.* shoulder blade.

omor *sn.* murder; *(crimă şi)* manslaughter.

omorî *vt.* to kill; *(a pisa)* to bother; *a ~ vremea* to while the time; *mă omori cu zile* you will be the death of me; *a ~ în bătăi* to pound to a jelly. *vi.* to be lethal. *vr.* to kill oneself.

omuşor *sm.* mannikin; *anat.* uvula.

ondula *vt., vi.* to wave.

ondulaţie *sf.* wave; *ondulaţii permanente* perm(anent wave).

onest *adj.* honest(-minded).

onoare *sf.* honour; *de ~* honour(able); *pe ~a mea* upon my word of honour.

onor *sn.* salute; *pl.* honours.

onora *vt.* to honour.

onorabil *adj.* honourable; *adv.* respectably.

onorariu *sn.* fee; charge.

opac *adj.* opaque.

opaiţ *sn.* earthen lamp, rushlight.

opări *vt.* to scald.

opărit *adj.* scalded; *fig.* downhearted.

opera *vt.* to operate; *(a face)* to make; *med.* to operate upon (smb.). *vi.* to operate; *(a acţiona şi)* to work; *(d. hoţi)* to steal. *vr.* to undergo an operation; to be effected.

operativ *adj.* expeditious; prompt. *adv.* efficiently.

operator *sm.* operator; *(de film)* cameraman.

operaţie *sf.* operation.

operă *sf.* work; *(acţiune şi)* action; *muz.* opera; *(teatru)* opera house; *~ bufă* comic opera; *~e de binefacere* charity.

operetă *sf. (clasică)* operetta; *(modernă)* musical comedy.

opincă *sf. aprox.* laced moccasin.

opinie *sf.* opinion; *~ publică* public opinion.

opiu *sn.* opium; *fig.* dope.

oportun *adj.* timely, seasonable.

oportunism *sn.* opportunism.

oportunist *sm.* time-server. *adj.* time-serving.

oportunitate *sf.* convenience.

opoziţie *sf.* opposition.

oprelişte *sf.* obstacle, prohibition.

opri *vt.* to stop, *(a face să înceteze)* to cease; *(a împiedica)* to curb, to stem; *(a reţine)* to retain; *(bilete etc.)* to book; *(a interzice)* to ban. *vi.* to stop; *(d. trăsură etc.)* to draw up. *vr.* to stop, to halt; *(a înceta)* to cease; *(a se reţine)* to refrain (from); *(a insista)* to dwell (upon smth., smb.); *nu mă pot ~* I can't help it.

oprima *vt.* to grind down.

oprire *sf.* stop(ping); *(escală)* stopover; *(încetare)* cease; *(interdicţie)* interdiction; *~a interzisă* no stopping; *fără ~* non-stop; ceaselessly.

oprit *adj.* banned; no (smoking, etc.).

opt *sm., adj., num.* eight. *sn.* curve, eight.

opta *vi.* to choose.

optic *adj.* optic.

optică *sf.* optics; *fig.* perspective.

optimism *sn.* optimism; high spirits.

optimist *sm.* optimist. *adj.* sanguine.

optsprezece *sm., adj., num.* eighteen.

optsprezecelea *adj., num.* (the) eighteenth.

optulea *adj., num.* (the) eighth.

optzeci *sm., adj., num.* eighty.

optzecilea *adj., num.* (the) eightieth.

opțiune *sf.* option.

opune *vt., vr.* to oppose (smth., etc.).

òpus¹ *sn.* opus.

opùs² *sm., adj.* opposite.

or *conj.* but; on the other hand.

oracol *sn.* oracle.

oral *sn.* viva voce. *adj.* oral; *(verbal și)* verbal; *(d. examene)* viva voce. *adv.* by word of mouth.

oranjadă *sf.* orangeade.

orar *sn.* time-table; *(ac)* hour hand. *adj.* hour(ly).

oraș *sn.* town; *(municipiu)* city; *de ~* city.

orator *sm.* orator.

oratoriu *sn.* oratorio.

oră *sf.* hour; *(ca cifră și)* o'clock; *(lecție și)* class; *ora închiderii* closing time; *ora mesei* lunch time; *ore de serviciu* office hours; *ore particulare* private lessons; *cu ora* by the hour; *din ~ în ~* every hour; *la ce ~ ?* at what time? *la ora trei precis* at three o'clock (sharp); *ultima ~ (la ziar)* stop news.

orăcăi *vi.* to croak; *(d. copii)* to pule.

orăcăit *sn.* croak(ing).

orășean *sm.* townsman; *pl.* townsfolk.

orășel *sn.* borough.

orășenesc *adj.* town..., city..., municipal.

orătănii *sf. pl.* poultry.

orb *sm.* blind man; *pl.* the blind. *sn.:* ~*ul găinilor* blindness. *adj.* blind; *(d. cartuș)* dummy.

orbește *adv.* blindly; *(nebunește)* madly.

orbi *vt.* to blind; *fig.* to dazzle; *(a înșela)* to blindfold. *vi.* to grow blind.

orbire *sf.* blindness.

orbită *sf.* orbit; *anat. și* (eye) socket.

orbitor *adj.* dazzling.

orchestral *adj.* orchestra(l).

orchestră *sf.* orchestra; *(mică)* (jazz-)band.

ordin *sn.* order; ~ *de zi* order of the day; citation for a medal.

ordinal *adj.* ordinal.

ordinar *adj.* common(place); *(grosolan și)* coarse.

ordine *sf.* order; discipline; ~ *de zi* agenda; *în aceeași ~ de idei* in the same connection; *la ~a zilei* topical.

ordona *vt.* to order; ~*ți!* orders!

ordonanță *sf.* ordinance; *(soldat)* orderly.

ordonat *adj.* tidy.

oreion *sn.* mumps.

orez *sn.* rice.

orezărie *sf.* rice field.

orfan *sm.* orphan.

orfelinat *sn.* orphanage.

organ *sn.* organ; *(de stat* etc. *și)* body.

organic *adj.* organic. *adv.* organically.

organism *sn.* organism.

organiza *vt.* to organize. *vr.* to be(come) organized.

organizare *sf.* organization; make-up.

organizație *sf.* organization; ~ *de bază* party branch.

orgă *sf.* organ.

orgie *sf.* orgy.

orgolios *adj.* vain.

orgoliu *sn.* pride.

orhidee *sf.* orchid.

ori *conj.* or; ~...~! it's now or never; ~ *e așa* ~ *e așa* either this way or another.

oribil *adj.* horrible. *adv.* terribly.

oricare *adj.* any. *pron.* any(body), anyone.

orice *adj.* any; *în* ~ *caz* anyhow; *cu* ~ *chip* at any rate *sau* price. *pron.* anything.

oricine *pron.* anybody, anyone; whoever...

oricît *adv.* however much, etc., as much *sau* long as (one likes, etc.); ~ *de* ... however (much, etc.). *conj.* however much.

oricum *adv.* anyhow; *(totuși și)* nevertheless, yet.

orient *sn.* East; ~*ul apropiat* the Near East; ~*ul mijlociu* the Middle East; *extremul* ~ the Far East.

orienta *vt.* to orientate; *(a îndruma)* to direct; *casa e* ~*tă spre răsărit* the house fronts east. *vr.* to find one's way (about); *fig.* to get one's bear-

ings; *a se* ~ *după ceva* to take smth. as a guide.

oriental *sm.* Eastern.

orientare *sf.* orientation; *pol.* look, deal; *(a unei case și)* aspect.

original *sm.* eccentric person, a (peculiar) character. *sn.* original; model; *în* ~ in the original. *adj.* original; *(ingenios)* ingenious; *(ciudat)* peculiar.

originar *adj.* native; *(înnăscut)* inborn; *(inițial și)* initial.

origine *sf.* origin; *(neam și)* descent; *la* ~ at the outset.

oriunde *adv.* anywhere. *conj.* wherever.

orizont *sn.* horizon; *la* ~ on the horizon; *fig.* in the offing.

orizontal *adj.* horizontal. *adv.* horizontally; *(la cuvinte încrucișate)* across.

orîndui *vt.* to order.

orînduire *sf.* system.

ornament *sn.* ornament.

ornamental *adj.* decorative.

ornitorinc *sm.* ornithorhyncus.

oroare *sf.* horror; *(urîțenie)* eyesore.

oropsi *vt.* to oppress.

ortodox *adj.* orthodox; *rel. și* Eastern.

ortografie *sf.* spelling; ~ *greșită* misspelling.

orz *sn.* barley.

os *sn.* bone; ~ *de balenă* whalebone; ~ *de pește* fishbone; ~ *domnesc* (crown) prince; *de* ~ bone.

oscila *vi.* to pendulate; *fig.* to vacillate.

oscilație *sf.* oscillation; *(șovăială)* hesitation.

oseminte *sn. pl.* bones.

osie *sf.* axle.

osîndă *sf.* punishment.

sîndi *vt.* to sentence; *fig.* to odoom; *(a condamna)* to blame.

osos *adj.* bony.

ospăta *vt.*, *vi.*, *vr.* to dine.

ospătar *sm.* waiter.

ospătărie *sf.* eating-house.

ospăţ *sn.* feast.

ospiciu *sn.* lunatic asylum.

ospitalier *adj.* hospitable.

ospitalitate *sf.* hospitality.

ostaş *sm.* soldier, man; *(ca grad)* private.

ostatic *sm.* hostage.

osteneală *sf.* effort(s); *(oboseală)* fatigue.

osteni *vt.* to tire. *vi.* to be(come) weary. *vr.* to take the trouble (to do smth.).

ostenit *adj.* tired.

ostentativ *adj.* ostentatious; *(formal)* perfunctory. *adv.* for form's sake.

ostentaţie *sf.* ostentation.

ostil *adj.* inimical.

ostilitate *sf.* hostility; *pl.* şi warfare.

ostrov *sn.* ait, eyot.

oştean *sm.* soldier, man.

oştire *sf.* army.

otoman *sm.*, *adj.* Ottoman.

otova *adj.* uniform; flat. *adv.* evenly; flatly.

otravă *sf.* poison.

otrăvi *vt.* to poison; *fig.* şi to envenom. *vr.* to take poison.

otrăvire *sf.* poisoning.

otrăvit *adj.* poisoned; *(veninos)* poisonous.

otrăvitor *adj.* poisonous.

oţări *vr.* to scowl; to sulk.

oţel *sn.* steel; *de* ~ steel; *fig.* steely, (as) hard as steel.

oţelărie *sf.* steelworks.

oţeli *vt.* to steel. *vr.* to be tempered.

oţet *sn.* vinegar.

oţetar *sm.* sumach.

oţeti *vr.* to turn sour.

ou *sn.* egg; ~*ă clocite* addled eggs; ~*ă jumări* scrambled eggs; ~*ă moi* soft-boiled eggs; ~*ă răscoapte* hard-boiled eggs.

oua *vt.*, *vi.*, *vr.* to lay (eggs).

oval *sn.*, *adj.* oval.

ovar *sn.* ovary.

ovaţii *sf. pl.* ovations.

ovaţiona *vt.*, *vr.* to cheer.

ovăz *sn.* oat(s).

oxid *sm.* oxide.

oxida *vt.*, *vr.* to oxidize.

oxigen *sn.* oxygen.

oxigena *vt.* to oxygenate; *(a decolora)* to peroxide. *vr.* to peroxide one's hair.

oxigenat *adj.* oxygenated; *(d. păr)* peroxide(d).

P

pace *sf.* peace; *(linişte şi)* quiet; *(nimic)* nothing; *în* ~ at peace; *de* ~ peace.

pachet *sn.* package; *(ambalaj)* parcel.

pacient *sm.* patient.

pacific adj. pacific.

pacoste sf. misfortune ; fig. nuisance.

pact sn. pact ; treaty.

pagină sf. page.

pagubă sf. damage ; (leziune) harm ; atîta ~, ~-n ciuperci good riddance (to a bad bargain).

pahar sn. glass ; (fără picior) tumbler ; (conținutul) glassful ; pl. (ventuze) cupping glasses ; un ~ la botul calului a doch and dorris.

pai sn. straw ; acoperiș de ~e thatched roof.

paiață sf. harlequin.

paisprezece sm., adj., num. fourteen.

paisprezecelea adj., num. (the) fourteenth.

paj sm. page.

pajiște sf. grassland ; lawn.

pajură sf. royal eagle ; (la o monedă) tails.

palat sn. palace ; anat. palate.

palavre sf. pl. idle talk, gas, babble ; (bîrfă) gossip.

paletă sf. palette ; sport bat.

palid adj. pale.

palier sn. landing ; (etaj) floor.

palmă sf. anat. palm ; (lovitură) slap ; o ~ de pămînt a plot of land ; fig. (not) an inch ; ~ de bătut covoare carpet beater.

palmier sm. palm tree.

paloare sf. pallor.

palpabil adj. palpable.

palpita vi. to throb.

paltin sm. sycamore maple tree.

palton sn. (over)coat.

pamflet sn. lampoon, skit.

pamfletar sm. lampoonist.

panama sf. Panama hat.

pană sf. feather ; (de gîscă) pen ; (de lemn) wedge ; (stricăciune) breakdown ; (a săbiei) flat (of the sword) ; ~ de cauciuc puncture ; ~ de curent power failure ; în ~ broken down ; fig. up a tree.

pancartă sf. placard.

pandur sm. pandour.

panglicar sm. windbag.

panglică sf. ribbon ; (de pălărie) hatband ; tehn. tape.

panică sf. panic.

panoramă sf. panorama.

panou sn. panel ; poster (of honour, etc.).

pansa vt. to dress.

pansament sn. dressing.

pansea, panseluță sf. pansy.

pantaloni sm. pl. trousers ; (izmene) pants ; (de călărie) breeches; (scurți) shorts; (lungi și largi) bell-bottoms ; ~ de golf plusfours ; ~ pescărești pedalpushers, Capri pants.

pantă sf. slope.

panteră sf. panther.

pantof sm. shoe ; (de casă) slipper.

pantofar sm. shoemaker.

pantomimă sf. dumbshow.

pap sn. glue, paste.

papagal sm. parrot ; fig. glib tongue.

papanaș sm. cheese dumpling ; apple fritter.

papară sf. bread pudding ; fig. thrashing.

paparudă sf. rainmaker.

papă sm. Pope.

papă-lapte sm. milksop.

papetărie sf. stationery.

papion sn. butterfly bow.

papirus sn. papyrus.

papuc *sm.* slipper; *(pantof)* shoe; *sub* ~ henpecked.
papură *sf.* bulrush.
par *sm.* stake; *(bîtă)* bludgeon. *adj.* even.
para *sf.* penny, little coin; *pl.* spondulicks. *vt.* to parry.
parabolă *sf.* parable; *geom.* parabola.
paradă *sf.* parade; *parada modei* fashion show; *de* ~ full (dress, etc.); *fig.* showy.
paradis *sn.* paradise.
paradox *sn.* paradox.
paradoxal *adj.* paradoxical. *adv.* paradoxically.
parafraza *vt.* to paraphrase.
parafrază *sf.* paraphrase.
paragină *sf.* dereliction.
paragraf *sn.* paragraph.
paralel *adj.* parallel. *adv.* concomitantly.
paralelă *sf.* parallel (line *sau* bar).
paralelism *sn.* parallelism; *econ.* duplication (of work).
paraliza *vt.* to paralyse. *vi., vr.* to be paralysed *sau* palsied.
paralizie *sf.* paralysis.
paranteză *sf.* bracket; *şi fig.* parenthesis.
parapet *sn.* parapet; *mar.* bulwark.
parastas *sn.* requiem.
paraşută *sf.* parachute.
paraşutism *sn.* parachutism.
paraşutist *sm.* parachutist; *mil.* paratrooper.
paratrăsnet *sn.* lightning rod.
paravan *sn.* screen.
parazit *sm.* parasite; *fig. şi* sponger; *el. pl.* statics. *adj.* parasitical.

pară *sf. bot.* pear; *(foc)* flame; *ca para focului* red-hot.
parbriz *sn.* windscreen.
parc *sn.* park; *(grădină)* garden; *(de maşini, tractoare)* fleet.
parca *vt.* to park.
parcare *sf.* parking; ~*a interzisă* no parking.
parcă *adv.* seemingly.
parcelă *sf.* house lot; plot of land.
parchet *sn.* parquet(ry); *jur.* prosecutor's office; *(în Anglia)* coroner's office.
parcurge *vt.* to traverse; *(cu ochii)* to skim over.
parcurs *sn.* route.
pardesiu *sn.* topcoat; *(de ploaie)* raincoat.
pardon *interj.* pardon!
pardoseală *sf.* floor.
parfum *sn.* perfume.
parfuma *vt., vr.* to perfume (oneself).
parfumerie *sf.* perfumery; *(magazin)* perfumer's shop.
paria[1] *sm.* pariah.
paria[2] *vt., vi.* to bet.
pariu *sn.* wager; ~*ul austriac* cumulator.
parizian *sm., adj.* Parisian.
parlament *sn.* Parliament; *(în S.U.A.)* Congress.
parlamenta *vi.* to negotiate.
parlamentar *sm.* Member of Parliament; *(în S.U.A.)* Congressman; *(delegat)* deputy. *adj.* parliamentary.
parodia *vt.* to parody.
parodie *sf.* parody; *fig.* travesty.
paroh *sm.* vicar.
parohie *sf.* parish; *(enoriaşi)* flock.

parolă *sf* watchword.
parolist *sm.* a man as good as his word.
parşiv *adj.* lousy.
parte *sf.* part; *(cotă)* share; *(loc)* place; *(latură)* side; *(soartă)* lot; *(la discuţii, afaceri)* party; ~ *integrantă* integral part; ~*a leului* the lion's share; *cea mai mare* ~ most; *de o* ~ aside; *din* ~*a mea* on my behalf; as for me; *în altă* ~ elsewhere; *în ce parte?* where? *în* ~ partly; *într-o* ~ mistaken(ly); *la o* ~ aside; *pe de o* ~ ... *pe de altă* ~ on the one hand ... on the other hand.
partener *sm.* partner.
parter *sn.* ground floor; *teatru* stalls, *(în fund)* pit; *la* ~ on the ground floor; downstairs.
participa *vi.* to participate (in).
participant *sm.* participant (in).
participare *sf.* participation (in); *(cotă)* share; *fig.* feeling; *cu* ~ warmly.
participiu *sn.* participle.
particular *sm.* private person. *adj.* private'; *(deosebit)* peculiar; *în* ~ particularly; *(între patru ochi)* privately.
particularitate *sf.* peculiarity.
particulariza *vt.* to particularize.
particulă *sf.* particle.
partid *sn.* party; *Partidul Comunist Român* the Romanian Communist Party; ~ *muncitoresc* workers' party; ~*e istorice* traditional parties; *de* ~ party; *fără (de)* ~ non-party.
partidă *sf.* match; *(de şah)* game; *(persoană şi)* partie.

partinic *adj.* party ...
partinitate *sf.* party spirit.
partitură *sf.* score.
partizan *sm.* partisan; *(susţinător)* advocate; *lupte de* ~*i* guerrilla fights.
parveni *vt.* to manage. *vi.* to arrive; *(în viaţă)* to succeed (in life).
parvenit *sm.* parvenu, mushroom.
pas *sm.* step; *(mare)* stride; *(mers)* pace; *(zgomot)* footstep; *tehn.* pitch; ~ *alergător* double time; ~ *cu* ~ step by step; closely; *un* ~ *greşit* a false step; *cu paşi mari* quickly; *la doi paşi* close by; *la fiecare* ~ at every turning; *la* ~ slowly. *sn.* gorge; *(defileu)* defile.
pasa *vt.* to pass; *(a strecura)* to strain.
pasager *sm.* passenger.
pasaj *sn.* passage; ~ *denivelat* fly over; ~ *de sau la nivel* level crossing.
pasarelă *sf.* foot bridge; *mar.* gangway.
pasă *sf.* pass; *în* ~ *bună* in luck; *în* ~ *proastă* in a nice fix.
pasăre *sf.* bird; ~*a furtunii* stormy petrel; ~*a muscă* humming bird; ~ *călătoare* bird of passage; ~ *cîntătoare* singing bird; ~ *de pradă* bird of prey; *păsări de curte* fowls, poultry.
pasibil *adj.* liable.
pasienţă *sf.* patience.
pasiona *vt.* to captivate. *vr.: a se* ~ *de* to become a fan of.
pasional *adj.* jealousy ....

pasionant *adj.* thrilling.
pasionat *sm.* fan(atic). *adj.* keen.
pasiune *sf.* passion; *(dragoste)* infatuation; *cu* ~ passionately; *fără* ~ reasonably.
pasiv *sn. com.* liabilities; *gram.* passive voice. *adj.* passive; *(apatic și)* apathetic. *adv.* listlessly.
pasivitate *sf.* passivity.
pastă *sf.* paste; ~ *de dinți* tooth paste; *paste făinoase* (Italian) pastes; macaroni.
pastel *sn. artă* crayon (picture); *lit.* poem of nature. *adj.* pastel.
pastilă *sf.* tablet.
pastișă *sf.* skit.
pastor *sm.* pastor.
pastoral *adi.*, **pastorală** *sf.* pastoral.
pastramă *sf.* pemmican.
pașaport *sn.* passport.
pașă *sm.* pasha.
pașnic *adj.* peaceful. *adv.* peaceably.
paște *vt.*, *vi.* to graze; *fig.* to wait (for).
Paști *sf. pl.* Easter.
pat *sn.* bed; *(mic)* cot; *(culcuș)* bedstead; *(de pușcă)* butt; *(strat)* mulch; *(la șah)* stalemate; ~ *de campanie* camp bed; *cu două* ~*uri* double-bedded.
pată *sf.* stain; *fără* ~ spotless.
patefon *sn.* gramophone.
patent *sn.* licence. *adj.* patent.
paternitate *sf.* paternity.
patetic *adj.* touching. *adv.* pathetically.
pateu *sn.* pie.
patimă *sf.* passion; *(părtinire)* bias.

patina *vi.* to skate; *(a aluneca)* to skid.
patinaj *sn.* skating; ~ *artistic* figure skating.
patină *sf.* skate; *(de vechime)* patina; *patine cu rotile* roller skates.
patinoar *sn.* skating rink.
patiserie *sf.* pastry (shop); *de* ~ pastry.
patos *sn.* pathos.
patrafir *sn.* stole.
patriarh *sm.* Patriarch.
patriarhal *adj.* patriarchal.
patriarhie *sf.* patriarchate.
patrician *sm.* patrician; *(cîrnat)* hot dog.
patrie *sf.* homeland.
patriot *sm.* patriot.
patriotic *adj.* patriotic.
patriotism *sn.* patriotism.
patron *sm.* employer; *(protector)* patron (saint).
patru *sm.*, *adj.*, *num.* four.
patrulă *sf.* patrol.
patrulea *adj.*, *num.* (the) fourth.
patruped *sn.* quadruped. *adj.* four-footed.
patrusprezece *sm.*, *adj.*, *num.* fourteen.
patrusprezecelea *adj.*, *num.* (the) fourteenth.
patruzeci *sm.*, *adj.*, *num.* forty.
patruzecilea *adj.*, *num.* (the) fortieth.
pauperiza *vt.* to impoverish.
pauză *sf.* pause; *(recreație și)* break.
pava *vt.* to pave; *(a pietrui)* to metal.
pavaj *sn.* pavement.
pavăză *sf.* shield.
pavilion *sn.* pavilion; *(chioșc)* summer house; *(steag)* colours;

sub ~ *românesc* under Romanian colours.

pavoaza *vt.* to decorate.

pază *sf.* guard.

paznic *sm.* watchman.

păcală *sm.* dupe.

păcat *sn.* sin; *(nenorocire)* pity; *(vină)* guilt, blame; ~ *capital* deadly sin; ~ *că* (it's) a pity that; *din* ~*e* unfortunately. *interj.* pity !

păcăleală *sf.* hoax; ~ *de 1 aprilie* April fool.

păcăli *vt.* to deceive. *vr.* to be mistaken.

păcătos *sm.* sinner. *adj.* sinful; *(prăpădit)* miserable.

păcătui *vi.* to sin, to trespass.

păcură *sf.* fuel oil.

păduche *sm.* louse, *pl.* lice; ~ *de lemn* bed bug.

păduchios *adj.* lousy.

pădurar *sm.* forester.

pădure *sf.* wood.

pădureţ *adj.* wild; *(d. măr)* crab.

păgîn *sm., adj.* heathen.

păgubaş *sm.* loser.

păgubi *vt.* to harm. *vi.* to be out of pocket.

păi *adv., interj.* well, why; ~ *de!* what did I tell you?

păianjen *sm.* spider.

păienjeniş *sn.* cobweb.

pălămidă *sf.* tunny fish.

pălărie *sf.* hat, *(de damă şi)* cap; *(de paie)* boater; *(melon)* billycock; *(de cowboy)* slouch hat.

pălărier *sm.* hatter.

pălăvrăgi *vi.* to babble.

păli *vt.* to strike. *vi.* to grow pale.

pălmui *vt.* to box (smb. s ears).

pămătuf *sn.* (shaving) brush.

pămînt *sn.* earth; *(teren uscat)* land; *(sol)* soil; *astr.* Terra; *de* ~ earthen; *la* ~ on *sau* to the ground.

pămîntean *sm.* earthling; *(băştinaş)* native. *adj.* earthly; *(băştinaş)* autochthonous.

pămîntese *adj.* earthly.

păpădie *sf.* dandelion.

păpuşar *sm.* puppetteer.

păpuşă *sf.* *(jucărie)* doll; *teatru* puppet; *(marionetă şi)* marionette; *fig.* tool.

păr *sm. şi pl.* hair; *bot.* pear tree; ~ *de porc* bristles; *în* ~ every man jack; *în doi peri* ambiguous(ly); *tras de* ~ preposterous.

părăgini *vr.* to lie fallow; to be ruined.

părăsi *vt.* to leave; to abandon.

părăsire *sf.* neglect.

părea *vi.* to seem; *îmi pare bine (de cunoştinţă)* I am glad (to meet you); *îmi pare rău* I am sorry. *vr.* to appear; *după cum mi se pare* as I see it; *mi s-a părut că* it seemed to me that.

părere *sf.* opinion; *(convingere)* belief; *(nălucire)* fancy; ~ *de rău* regret; *după* ~*a mea* in my opinion.

părinte *sm.* father; *pl.* parents.

părintese *adj.* parental.

păros *adj.* hairy.

părtaş *sm.* accomplice.

părtinire *sf.* partiality.

părtinitor *adj.* biassed.

păs *sn.* grievance.

păsa *vi.:* a-i ~ to care (for smth.); *ce-ţi pasă?* never mind.

păsăreşte *adv.:* a vorbi ~ to gobbledegook.

păsărică sf. little bird; fig. hobby horse.

păstaie sf. pod.

păstîrnac sm. parsnip.

păstor sm. shepherd.

păstori vt. to shepherd. vi. to be a shepherd.

păstra vt to keep. vr. to be kept; to reserve oneself.

păstrare sf. custody.

păstrăv sm. trout.

păsui vt. to allow (smb. a respite).

păşi vt. to cross. vi. to step; fig. to embark (upon a road).

păşune sf. pasture (land).

păta vt. to stain.

pătimaş adj. passionate. adv. ardently.

pătimi vt., vi. to suffer.

pătlăgea sf. tomato; (vînătă) egg-plant, egg-fruit.

pătrat sn., adj. square.

pătrime sf. fourth; muz. crotchet.

pătrunde vt., vi. to penetrate. vr.: a se ~ de to realize (fully).

pătrundere sf. penetration; fig. insight.

pătrunjel sm. parsley.

pătrunzător adj. piercing; fig. sharp.

pătură sf. blanket; fig. layer; pături sociale sections of the population.

păţanie sf. experience.

păţi vt. to suffer; a o¯ ~ to land into trouble; ce ai ~t? what's wrong with you?

păun sm. peacock.

păuniţă sf. peahen.

păzea interj. nix! beware!

păzi vt. watch; (a apăra) to defend; (a păstra) to treas-

ure. vr. to be cautious; a se ~ de to beware of.

păzitor sm., adj. guardian.

pe prep. on; (peste) over; (temporal) for; (în schimbul a) in exchange for; ~ aici this way; ~ alocuri occasionally; ~ atunci then; ~ cînd while; ~ englezeşte etc. in English, etc.; ~ jos on foot; ~ urmă later; ~ viaţă şi pe moarte tooth and nail.

pecete sf. seal.

pecetlui vt. to seal.

pedagog sm. pedagogue.

pedagogic adj. pedagogic.

pedală sf. pedal.

pedant sm. prig. adj. pedantic.

pedanterie sf. pedantry.

pedeapsă sf. penalty.

pedepsi vt. to punish.

pedepsire sf. punishment; de ~ punitive.

pedestru sm., adj. pedestrian.

pediatru sm. pediatrist.

pedicură sf. pedicure.

peiorativ adj. derogatory.

peisaj sn. landscape; (marin) seascape; (urban) townscape.

pelerină sf. mantle.

pelican sm. pelican.

peliculă sf. film; (de vopsea) coat.

pelin sn. wormwood (wine).

peltea sf. fruit jelly; fig. cock and bull story.

peltic adj. lisping.

peluză sf. lawn; sport grounds.

penal adj. criminal.

penar sn. pencil case.

pendulă sf. grandfather clock.

penel sn. (painter's) brush.

penibil adj. unpleasant.

penicilină sf. penicillin.

peninsulă *sf.* half-isle.
peniţă *sf.* nib; pen.
pensetă *sf.* tweezers.
pensie *sf.* pension; ~ *alimen-tară* alimony; ~ *viageră* life annuity; *la* ~ retired; *fig.* on the shelf.
pension *sn.* academy for young ladies.
pensiona *vt.* to pension off. *vr.* to retire.
pensionar *sm.* pensioner.
pensiune *sf.* board and lodging; *(localul)* pension.
pensulă *sf.* brush.
pentru *prep.* for. (in order) to; in favour of; *(de dragul)* for smb.'s sake; *(în loc de)* instead of; ~ *ca* in order that; ~ *că* because; ~ *ce?* why? ~ *puţin* don't mention it; ~ *zile negre* against a rainy day.
penultim *adj.* last but one.
pepene *sm.* melon; *(verde)* water melon.
pepinieră *sf.* nursery.
percepe *vt.* to perceive; *(a stringe)* to levy. *vr.* to be perceptible.
perceptor *sn.* tax collector.
percheziţie *sf.* search; ~ *corporală* bodily search.
percuţie *sf.* percussion; *de* ~ percussion.
perdea *sf.* curtain; *cu* ~ decorous; *fără* ~ obscene, blue.
pereche *sf.* pair; couple; *(corespondent)* match; *o* ~ *de boi* a yoke of oxen; *o* ~ *de găini* a brace of hens; *fără* ~ peerless. *adj.* even.
perete *sm.* wall.
perfect *sn.* perfect; ~ *ul simplu aprox.* past tense. *adj.*

perfect, consummate. *adv.* perfectly. *interj.* capital!
perfecta *vt.* to conclude.
perfecţie *sf.* perfection; consummation; *la* ~ wonderfully.
perfecţiona *vt., vr.* to improve.
perfid *adj.* perfidious. *adv.* perfidiously.
perfidie *sf.* deceit(fulness).
perfora *vt.* to punch; to clip (a ticket, etc.).
performanţă *sf.* performance; *de* ~ performance.
pergament *sn.* parchment.
peria *vt.* to brush; *fig.* to flatter. *vr.* to brush one's clothes.
pericol *sn.* peril; ~ *de moarte* fatal danger.
periculos *adj.* dangerous.
perie *sf.* brush.
periferie *sf.* suburb(s); *la* ~ on the outskirts, in the purlieus.
perima *vr.* to be(come) superannuated.
perimat *adj.* obsolete.
perimetru *sn.* perimeter.
perinda *vr.* to come by turns.
periniţa *sf.* kissing dance.
perioadă *sf.* period.
periodic *sn., adj.* periodical. *adv.* recurrently.
peripeţie *sf.* adventure.
perişoare *sf. pl.* minced meat balls (in soup).
periuţă *sf.* (tooth-)brush; *fig.* flatterer.
perlă *sf.* pearl; *fig.* gem; wit.
permanent *sn.* perm(anent wave). *adj.* permanent. *adv.* perpetually.
permanenţă *sf.* permanence; people on duty; *în* ~ ceaselessly.

permis *sn.* licence ; ~ *de conducere* driving licence. *adj.* permitted.

permisiune *sf.* permission.

permite *vt.* to allow ; *fig,* to enable (to do smth.) ; *își poate* ~ he can afford it.

pernă *sf. (de dormit)* pillow, *(ornament* etc.*)* cushion.

peron *sn.* platform.

perpeli *vr.* to fret.

perpendicular *adj.* perpendicular. *adv.* perpendicularly.

perpetua *vt.* to perpetuate. *vr.* to linger.

persan *sm., adj.,* **persană** *sf., adj.* Persian.

persecuta *vt.* to bait.

persecuție *sf.* persecution.

persevera *vi.* to persevere.

perseverent *adj.* persevering. *adv.* tenaciously.

persista *vi.* to persist ; to insist ; to continue.

persistent *adj.* persistent.

persoană *sf.* human being ; ~ *juridică* legal entity ; *in* ~ personally.

personaj *sn.* personage, character.

personal *sn.* personnel ; *c.f.* slow train. *adj.* personal ; private. *adv.* in person.

personalitate *sf.* personality.

perspectivă *sf.* prospect ; *(vedere)* vista ; *artă* perspective ; *de* ~ long-term.

perspicace *adj.* perspicacious.

perucă *sf.* wig ; *ist.* periwig.

peruzea *sf.* turquoise.

pervaz *sn.* (window) frame, sash.

pervers *adj.* perverse.

perversitate, perversiune *sf.* perversity.

perverti *vt.* to pervert.

pescar *sm.* fisher(man) ; *(amator)* angler.

pescăresc *adj.* fishing.

pescărie *sf.* fishing ; *(magazin)* fishmonger's.

pescăruș *sm.* sea-gull.

pescui *vt., vi.* to fish ; *(cu undița)* to angle ; *(cu mina)* to tickle (trout).

pescuit *sn.* fishing ; *(sportiv)* angling.

pesemne *adv.* probably.

pesimism *sn.* pessimism ; low spirits.

pesimist *sm.* pessimist. *adj.* pessimistic, dispirited, sad.

pesmet *sm.* biscuit ; *(din pîine uscată)* bread crumbs.

peste *prep.* over, above ; *(dincolo)* across ; *mai presus de* beyond ; ~ *tot* everywhere.

pestriț *adj.* variegated, motley.

peșin *adj.* hard (cash), ready (money).

pește *sm.* fish ; *ca* ~*le pe uscat* ill at ease.

peșteră *sf.* cave.

petală *sf.* petal.

petic *sn.* patch ; *(de hîrtie)* scrap.

petiție *sf.* petition.

petrece *vt.* to spend. *vi.* to have a good time. *vr.* to occur.

petrecere *sf.* merrymaking ; *(chef)* carousal.

petrol *sn.* petroleum ; ~ *lampant* kerosene.

petrolier *sn.* tanker. *adj.* oil.

petrolier *adj.* oil (field) . . .

petunie *sf.* petunia.

peți *vt.* to woo.

pețitoare *sf.* match-maker.

pețitor *sm.* suitor.

pian *sn.* piano; ~ *cu coadă* concert grand.

pianină *sf.* cottage piano.

pianist *sm.* pianist.

piatră *sf.* stone; *(tartru)* tartar; *(mică)* gravel; *med.* calculus; ~ *acră* alun; ~ *de hotar* landmark; ~ *de încercare* shibboleth; acid test; ~ *de moară* millstone; ~ *de mormînt* tombstone; ~ *de temelie* cornerstone; ~ *de var* limestone; ~ *filozofală* philosopher's stone; ~ *fundamentală* foundation stone; ~ *kilometrică* milestone; ~ *ponce* pumice stone; ~ *prețioasă* gem, jewel; ~ *unghiulară* cornerstone; ~ *vînătă* blue vitriol; *ca piatra* stone hard; *de* ~ stony.

piață *sf.* market; *arhit.* square; *pe* ~ *sau la* ~ in the market.

piază-rea *sf.* ill omen.

pic *sn.* bit.

pica *vt.* to spin. *vi.* to fall; *(a veni)* to pop in; *(la examen)* to fail (in an examination).

picant *adj.* pungent; *(decoltat)* racy; *(fascinant)* attractive.

pică *sf.* *(dușmănie)* spite; *(la cărți)* spades.

picătură *sf.* drop; *printre picături* in between.

pichet *sn.* picket; *text.* piqué.

pici *sm.* urchin.

picior *sn.* leg; *(labă)* foot, *pl.* feet; ~ *peste* ~ crosslegged; *cu picioarele goale* barefoot(ed); *cu* ~*ul* on foot; *în picioare* upright; *pe* ~ *de egalitate* on the same footing.

picnic *sn.* garden party, picnic.

picolo *sm.* young waiter.

pieromigdală *sf.* macaroon.

picta *vt.*, *vi.* to paint.

pictor *sm.* painter; ~ *decorator* scene painter; ~ *de firme* sign painter.

pictoriță *sf.* paintress.

pictură *sf.* painting; *(tablou și)* picture; ~ *în ulei* oil painting.

piculină *sf.* piccolo.

picup *sn.* (electric) gramophone, record-player.

picura *vt.* to let drop. *vi.* to drip, to drop.

piedestal *sn.* pedestal.

piedică *sf.* hindrance; *(pusă cuiva)* trip.

pieire *sf.* destruction.

pielar *sm.* leather dresser *sau* merchant.

pielărie *sf.* leather goods.

piele *sf.* skin; *(de animale)* hide; *(lucrată)* leather; ~ *de lac* patent leather; ~ *de drac* velvet leather; *de* ~ leather...; *în* ~*a goală* naked, in buff.

pieliță *sf.* peel, film.

piept *sn.* chest; *(sîn)* breast; *pl. și* bosom.

pieptăna *vt.* to comb; *fig.* to brush up. *vr.* to comb one's hair.

pieptănătură *sf.* hairdo.

pieptene *sm.* comb.

pierde *vt.* to lose; *(a scăpa)* to miss; *(a irosi)* to waste; *(a ruina)* to destroy; *(o ființă dragă)* to be bereft of; *a* ~ *din vedere* to overlook; *(pe cineva)* to lose sight of. *vi.* to lose. *vr.* to be lost.

pierdere *sf.* loss: *pl.* damage; *mil.* casualties; *în* ~ losing.

pierde-vară *sm.* loafer.

pierdut *adj.* lost (in thoughts, etc.).

pieri *vi.* to perish; *(a dispărea)* to vanish; *a ~ de sabie* to die by the sword.

pierit *adj.* frightened.

piersic *sm.* peach tree.

piersică *sf.* peach.

piesă *sf.* piece; *(la şah şi)* chessman; *(de teatru)* play; *pl.* drama; *(de maşină)* machine part; *~ bulevardieră* low brow drama; *~ de muzeu* curio; *~ de rezervă* spare (part); *~ de rezistenţă* pièce de résistance; *~ de schimb* spare (part).

pietate *sf.* piety.

pieton *sm.* pedestrian; *~ distrat* jay walker.

pietriş *sn.* gravel.

pietroi *sn.* stone, boulder.

pietrui *vt.* to pave.

pieziş *adj.* slanting; *(strîmb)* wry; *(d. privire)* hostile. *adv.* obliquely; *fig.* hostilely.

piftie *sf.* meat jelly.

pigmeu *sm.* pigmy.

pilaf *sn.* pilaff; *fig.* jelly.

pilă *sf.* file; *el.* battery; *fig.* wangler, intercession; *~ atomică* atomic pile.

pildă *sf.* model; *de ~* for example.

pili *vi.* to file. *vr.* to get drunk.

pilon *sm.* pillar; *(de pod)* pier.

pilot *sm.* pilot; *~ de încercare* test pilot. *adj.* pilot.

pilota *vt.* to pilot.

pilulă *sf.* pill.

pin *sm.* pine.

ping-pong *sn.* ping-pong.

pinguin *sm.* penguin.

pinten *sm.* spur.

pion *sm.* pawn.

pionier *sm.* pioneer.

pios *adj.* pious.

pipă *sf.* pipe.

pipăi *vt.* to feel; *(a mîngîia)* to fondle.

pipăit *sn.* touch.

piper *sm.* pepper.

pipera *vt.* to pepper.

piperat *adj.* (highly) seasoned; *fig. (d. preţ)* stiff; *(obscen)* ribald.

pipernicit *adj.* stunted.

pipotă *sf.* gizzard.

piramidă *sf.* pyramid.

piramidon *sn.* amidopyrin; head pill.

pirat *sm.* pirate.

piraterie *sf.* piracy.

pire *sn.* potato mash.

pironi *vt.* to nail (down); **to** rivet.

pirpiriu *adj.* frail.

pisa *vt.* to pound; *fig.* to pester.

pisălog *sm.* bore. *sn.* pestle. *adj.* bothering.

pisc *sn.* peak.

piscină *sf.* (indoor) swimming pool.

pisic, pisoi *sm.* kitten.

pisică *sf.* cat; *~ sălbatică* wild cat.

pistă *sf.* track; *av.* runway.

pistol *sn.* pistol; *~-mitralieră* Bren *sau* Tommy gun.

pistrui *sm.* freckle.

pişca *vt.* to pinch; *(a înţepa)* to sting. *vi.* to be sharp.

pitic *sm., adj.* dwarf; Lilliputian.

piton *sm. zool.* python. *sn.* piton.

pitoresc *sn.* picturesqueness; *adj.* picturesque.

pitula *vr.* to crouch.

pituliee *sf.* wren.

pițigăiat *adj.* shrill.

pițigoi *sm.* titmouse.

piuă *sf.* fulling mill; *piua în-tîi!* I bag!

piui *vi.* to peep.

piuneză *sf.* drawing-pin.

pivniță *sf.* (wine) cellar.

pix *sn.* clutch pencil.

pizmaș *adj.* covetous.

pizmă *sf.* envy.

pizmui *vt.* to envy.

piine *sf.* bread; *(franzelă)* (white) loaf; *fig. și* food; livelihood; ~ *caldă sau proaspătă* newly baked bread; ~ *cu unt* bread and butter; ~ *integrală* wholemeal bread; ~ *neagră* brown bread; ~ *rece* stale bread; *ea* ~*a caldă (bun)* good natured; *(repede)* like hot cakes.

pile *sn.* group, cluster.

pilnie *sf.* funnel.

pîlpîi *vi.* to flicker.

pînă *prep., conj.* till, until; ~ *la* until; *(în spațiu)* as far as; ~ *la urmă* in the end; ~ *și* even; ~ *una alta* in the meantime.

pîndă *sf.* watch; *(la vînătoare)* still-hunting.

pîndi *vt., vi.* to lie in wait (for).

pîngări *vt.* to defile; *(a viola)* to ravish.

pîntece *sn.* belly; *(al mamei)* womb; *fig.* entrails.

pînteeos *adj.* pot-bellied.

pînză *sf.* cloth; tissue; *(groasă, artă)* canvas; *mar.* mail; ~ *de păianjen* cobweb.

pînzeturi *sn. pl.* drapery.

pîrîu *sn.* brook.

pîrghie *sf.* lever.

pîrgui *vr.* to ripen.

pîrî *vt.* to tell on.

pîrîi *vi.* to crack.

pîrjoală *sf.* minced meat roll.

pîrjoli *vt.* to burn (down).

pîrleaz *sn.* stile.

pîrli *vt.* to singe. *vr.* to get burned.

pîrlit *sm.* pauper. *adj.* singed; poor.

pîrtie *sf.* path; *sport* track.

pîslă *sf.* felt.

plae *sn.* pleasure; *după bunul său* ~ at one's will.

placardă *sf.* placard.

placă *sf.* plate; *(disc)* (gramophone) record; *(pt. școală)* slate; *(comemorativă)* plaque.

plachetă *sf.* booklet.

placid *adj.* placid. *adv.* listlessly.

placiditate *sf.* apathy.

plafon *sn.* ceiling; *fig. și* limit.

plafona *vt.* to limit.

plagă *sf.* wound; *fig.* scourge.

plagia *vt.* to plagiarize.

plagiat *sn.* plagiarism.

plagiator *sm.* plagiarist.

plajă *sf.* beach, sands.

plan *sn.* *(suprafață)* plane; *(proiect)* plan; *(punctaj)* outline; ~ *de învățămînt* syllabus; ~ *de perspectivă* long term plan; *fig.* far-reaching plan; ~ *cincinal* five-year plan; *pe* ~*ul al doilea* in the middle ground; *fig.* secondly; *în prim* ~ in the fore-ground; *fig.* first and foremost. *adj.* plane, even; *(neted)* flat, level.

planetă *sf.* planet; *planeta noastră* the earth.

planifica *vt.* to plan.

planificare *sf.* planning.

planor *sn.* glider.

planșă *sf.* drawing; *(poză)* plate.

planşetă *sf.* draughtsman's board.

planta *vt.* to plant.

plantaţie *sf.* plantation.

plantă *sf.* plant; ~ *medicinală* simple; ~ *industrială* technical crop.

plapumă *sf.* counterpane; *(pilotă)* eiderdown.

plasa *vt.* to place; *(bani)* to sink, to invest; *(mărfuri)* to sell; *n-am putut* ~ *nici două vorbe* I could not put in a word edgeways. *vr.* to take (a stand); *(a se vinde)* to sell.

plasatoare *sf.* usherette.

plasator *sm.* usher.

plasă *sf.* (fishing) net; *c.f.* rack.

plastic *adj.* plastic; *fig.* graphic; *(d. artă)* fine. *adv.* eloquently.

plastică *sf.* plastic(ity); *(arte)* fine arts.

plastilină *sf.* plasticine.

plastură *sm.* plaster.

plat *adj.* flat.

platan *sm.* plane-tree. *sn.* scale; *(de picup)* turn table.

plată *sf.* pay(ment); *fig.* reward; ~ *în natură* payment in kind; *bun de* ~ as good as his word; *cu* ~ paid; *fără* ~ free.

platformă *sf.* platform.

platină *sf.* platinum.

platitudine *sf.* platitude.

platou *sn.* plateau; *(tavă)* tray; *(cinema)* stage, floor.

plauzibil *adj.* plausible.

plăcea *vt.* to like. *vi.* to be pleasant; *îi* ~ he liked it; *îmi plac prăjiturile* I like cakes; *îmi place să citesc* I enjoy reading.

plăcere *sf.* pleasure; *cu* ~ gladly; *fără* ~ reluctantly.

plăcintă *sf.* pie.

plăcintărie *sf.* pastry-cook's (shop).

plăcut *adj.* agreeable; *(simpatic)* nice. *adv.* pleasantly.

plămădi *vt.* to leaven; *(a modela)* to mould.

plămîn *sm.* lung.

plănui *vt.* to plan.

plăpînd *adj.* feeble.

plăsmui *vt.* to create; *(a inventa)* to concoct; *(a falsifica)* to fake.

plăsmuire *sf.* creation; *(invenţie)* fabrication; *(fals)* fake.

plăti *vt.* to pay; *(a răsplăti)* to repay, to pay back; *(bine)* to reward. *vi.* to pay. *vr.* to get rid of one's debts.

plătică *sf.* bream.

plebiscit *sn.* plebiscite.

pleca *vt.* to bend; *(ochii)* to lower. *vi.* to leave (for a place). *vr.* to bend, to bow; *(mult)* to stoop; *fig.* to yield.

plecare *sf.* departure.

plecat *adj.* absent, away; *(încovoiat)* bent; *fig.* submissive.

plecăciune *sf.* bow.

pled *sn.* plaid; *(pătură)* blanket.

pleda *vt., vi.* to plead.

pledoarie *sf.* pleading.

pleiadă *sf.* pleiad.

plenar *adj.* plenary.

plenară *sf.* plenary meeting; ~ *lărgită* enlarged plenum.

plenipotenţiar *adj.* plenipotentiary.

pleoapă *sf.* (eye)lid.

pleonasm *sn.* pleonasm.

pleoştit *adj.* sagging; *(ofilit)* withered; *fig.* downcast.

pleseăi vi. to splash ; (din buze) to champ.

plesni vt. to hit. vi. to burst.

plete sf. pl. locks.

pletos adj. long-haired ; (d. salcie) weeping.

plexiglas sn. plexiglass.

pliant sn. folder. adj. folding.

plic sn. envelope.

plicticos adj. tedious.

plictiseală sf. boredom ; (necaz) trouble.

plictisi vt. to bore (to death) ; fig. to bother. vr. to be bored.

plictisit adj. bored, sick (with smth., etc.) ; (supărat) annoyed.

plictisitor adj. boring.

plimba vt. to take for a walk sau drive ; (a muta) to shift. vr. to (take a) walk ; (cu mașina) to drive ; (cu bicicletă) to go for a ride.

plimbare sf. stroll ; (cu un vehicul) drive ; ride.

plin sn. full (supply) ; din ~ fully ; în ~ like greased lightning. adj. full (of), packed (with) ; (complet) complete ; ~ de praf dusty ; ~ ochi brimful ; ~ pînă la refuz full to capacity ; în ~ sezon at the height of the season.

plise sn. beak ; fig. mouth.

pliță sf. kitchen range.

pliu sn. fold.

plivi vt. to weed.

plîngăreț adj. whining.

plînge vt. to deplore ; fig. to pity. vi. to weep ; (a se lamenta) to lament ; . a ~ de bucurie to cry with joy. vr. to complain.

plîngere sf. grievance.

plîns sn. weeping. adj. tear-stained.

ploaie sf. rain ; (torențială) downpour ; (aversă) shower ; (măruntă) drizzle ; ca o ~ in a shower ; pe ~ in the rain.

ploconi vr. kow-tow (to smb.).

ploios adj. rainy.

plombă sf. stopping.

plop sm. poplar ; (tremurător) asp(en tree).

ploscă sf. gourd ; (pt. bolnavi) bedpan.

ploșniță sf. bed bug, B flat.

ploua vi. impers. to rain ; (mărunt) to drizzle.

plouat adj. wet with rain ; fig. crestfallen.

plug sn. plough ; (la ski) stem.

plugar sm. ploughman.

plumb sm. lead.

plumbui vt. to seal.

plural sn., adj. plural.

plus sn. plus ; (adaos) surplus ; în ~ moreover. conj. plus, and.

plusprodus sn. surplus product.

plusvaloare sf. surplus value.

pluș sn. plush.

plutaș sm. rafter.

plută sf. raft ; bot. cork (tree).

plutărit sn. rafting.

pluti vi. to float ; (a naviga) to sail.

plutire sf. sailing.

plutitor adj. floating.

pluton sn. platoon ; sport bunch.

plutonier sm. N.C.O. ; sergeant.

pneumatic adj. pneumatic ; air..

pneumonie sf. pneumonia.

poală sf. hem ; pl. lap ; la poalele dealului at the foot of the hill.

poamă sf. fruit.

poantă *sf.* gist (of a story) ; *(la balet)* toe-dancing.

poartă *sf.* gate(way) ; *sport* goal ; *ist.* the (Sublime) Porte.

pocăi *vr.* to repent.

pocăinţă *sf.* regrets.

pocăit *sm., adj.* penitent.

pocher *sn.* poker.

poci *vt.* to maim.

pocit *adj.* disfigured.

pocnet *sn.* crack ; *(împuşcătură)* shot.

pocni *vt.* to hit. *vi.* to burst.

pocnitoare *sf.* cracker.

pod *sn.* *(punte)* bridge ; *(al casei)* garret ; *(la şură* etc.*)* loft ; ~ *de vase* pontoon bridge; ~ *rulant* travelling crane ; ~*ul palmei* the palm of one's hand.

podea *sf.* floor(ing).

podgorie *sf.* vineyard.

podidi *vt.* to overcome ; *m-au* ~*t lacrimile* tears welled from my eyes.

podiş *sn.* tableland, plateau.

podium *sn.* dais.

podoabă *sf.* ornament ; *şi fig.* jewel.

poem *sn.,* **poemă** *sf.* poem ; *fig.* gem.

poet *sm.* poet.

poetă *sf.* poetess.

poetic *adj.* poetic(al). *adv.* poetically.

poezie *sf.* poem ; *(artă şi fig.)* poetry.

pofidă *sf.:* *în pofida...* in spite of ...

poftă *sf.* appetite ; *(puternică)* lust (for) ; *(chef)* (half a) mind ; ~ *bună* bon appétit ; *cu* ~ heartily ; *după pofta inimii* to one's heart content ; *fără* ~ spiritlessly.

pofti *vt.* to invite ; *(a dori)* to wish ; *(a îndrăzni)* to dare. *vi.:* *a* ~ *la* to covet.

pofticios *adj.* greedy ; *(lasciv)* randy. *adv.* covetously.

poftim *interj.* please (come in) ; *(cum?)* beg your pardon? sorry? *(ţine)* here you are! ; *(supărat)* that's the limit!

pogon *sn.* acre.

poiană *sf.* glade.

poimîine *adv.* the day after tomorrow.

pojar *sn.* measles.

pojghiţă *sf.* (thin) crust.

pol *sm.* pole ; *(bani)* twenty lei.

polar *adj.* polar ; *(d. stea)* north.

polca *sf.* polka.

polei[1] *sn.* glazed frost.

polei[2] *vt.* to gild.

polemic *adj.* contentious.

polemică *sf.* polemic.

polen *sn.* pollen.

policlinică *sf.* polyclinic.

poliglot *sm., adj.* polyglot.

poligon *sn.* *geom.* polygon ; *(de tragere)* shooting range.

poligrafie *sf.* printing.

poliomielită *sf.* polio(myelitis).

polip *sm.* *zool.* polyp ; *med.* polypus.

politehnic *adj.* polytechnic.

politehnică *sf.* polytechnic.

politeţe *sf.* politeness.

politic *adj.* political.

politică *sf.* politics ; *(atitudine* etc.*)* policy ; ~ *de pace* peace(ful) policy ; ~ *externă* foreign policy.

politician *sm.* statesman.

politicos *adj.* polite. *adv.* courteously.

poliţă *sf.* *(raft)* shelf ; *com.* promissory note.

poliţie *sf.* police (station).
poliţist *sm.* policeman; *(pe stradă)* constable. *adj.* police... *(d. romane* etc.*)* detective.
polo *sn.* polo; ~ *pe apă* water polo.
polon *adj.,* **polonă** *sf., adj.* Polish.
polonez *sm.* Pole. *adj.* Polish.
poloneză *sf.* Polish (woman); *muz.* polonaise.
polonic *sn.* ladle.
pom *sm.* (fruit) tree.
pomadă *sf.* pomade.
pomană *sf.* alms; *de* ~ gratis; *(inutil)* useless(ly).
pomeneală *sf.: nici* ~ nothing of the kind.
pomeni *vt.* to mention; *(a cunoaşte)* to know; *(a întîlni)* to see. *vi.: a* ~ *de* to cite. *vr.* to be known; *(a se întîmpla)* to happen; *(a se trezi)* to find oneself.
pomenire *sf.* mentioning; *rel.* prayer (for the dead); *veşnica* ~ may he rest in peace.
pomeţi *sm. pl.* cheek bones.
pomină *sf.* fame; *de* ~ famous; *(extraordinar)* unforgettable; *(ridicol)* ridiculous.
pompa *vt.* to pump (in *sau* out).
pompă *sf.* pump; *(ceremonie)* pomp; ~*e funebre* funeral furnishers; *cu toată pompa* with all due respect; in full attire.
pompier *sm.* fireman; *pl.* fire brigade.
pompos *adj.* pompous.
ponderat *adj.* well-balanced.
ponegri *vt.* to backbite.
ponei *sm.* poney.
ponos *sn.* blame.
ponosit *adj.* worn-out.

ponta *vt.* to clock. *vi.* to clock in *sau* out; *(la cărţi)* to stake.
popas *sn.* halt, stop (over).
popă *sm.* parson, pope; *(la jocuri)* king.
popic *sn.* skittle; *pl. şi* ninepins; *amer.* bowls.
popicărie *sf.* bowling alley.
popîndău *sm.* ground squirrel.
poplin *sn.* poplin.
popor *sn.* people; *(mulţime)* crowd; ~*ul muncitor* the working people; *din* ~ of the people; folk...
poporanism *sn.* populism.
poposi *vi.* to halt; to put up (at an inn, etc.).
popotă *sf.* officers' mess; canteen.
poprire *sf.* keeping back.
popula *vt.* to people.
popular *adj. (din popor)* folk..., popular; *(al poporului)* people's; *(simpatizat)* popular (with the public).
popularitate *sf.* popularity.
populariza *vt.* to popularize; *(a răspîndi)* to spread.
popularizare *sf.* vulgarization; *(răspîndire)* dissemination.
populat *adj.* populated; *(aglomerat)* populous.
populaţie *sf.* population.
por *sm.* pore.
porc *sm.* pig; *(îngrăşat)* hog (ger); *pl.* swine; *(vier)* boar; *(carne)* pork; ~ *mistreţ* wild boar.
porcărie *sf. (murdărie)* filth; *(ticăloşie)* foul trick; *pl. (pornografie)* bawdy; four-letter words; *(lături)* pigwash.
porcesc *adj.* piggish; *(d. noroc)* blind.

porcos *adj.* smutty, blue; foul-mouthed.
poreclă *sf.* nickname.
porecli *vt.* to nickname.
porni *vt.* to set (moving *sau* going); *(a dezlănţui)* to unleash. *vi., vr.* to start; *(a se pune în mişcare)* to be set moving.
pornire *sf.* starting; *(înclinaţie)* bent, ply; *(părtinire)* bias.
pornografic *adj.* scurrilous.
pornografie *sf.* bawdy.
port *sn.* port, harbour; *(costum)* costume; *(purtare)* conduct.
portabil *adj.* portable.
portar *sm.* janitor; *sport* goalkeeper.
portativ *sn.* stave. *adj.* portable.
portavion *sn.* aircraft carrier.
portăreasă *sf.* janitress.
portbagaj *sn.* carrier.
portiţă *sf.* (wicket) gate; *(de la sobă)* damper; *fig.* way out, issue.
portjartier *sn.* (suspender) girdle.
portmoneu *sn.* wallet.
portocal *sm.* orange tree.
portocală *sf.* orange; ~ *roşie* blood orange.
portocaliu *adj.* orange.
portofel *sn.* pocket-book.
portofoliu *sn.* portfolio.
portret *sn.* portrait.
portţigaret *sn.* cigarette-holder; *(tabacheră)* cigarette-box.
portughez *sn., adj.,* **portugheză** *sf., adj.* Portuguese.
portvizit *sn.* pocket-book.
porţelan *sn.* china.
porţie *sf.* helping; *şi fig.* portion.
porţiune *sf.* section.

porumb *sm.* maize, Indian corn.
porumbel *sm.* pigeon; ~ *călător* homer; ~ *mesager* homing pigeon.
porumbiţă *sf.* (turtle)dove.
poruncă *sf.* order; *rel.* commandment.
porunci *vt.* to command. *vi.* to order people about.
posac *adj.* sullen.
poseda· *vt.* to possess.
posesie *sf.* possession; *(proprietate)* ownership.
posesiune *sf.* possession.
posesiv *sn., adj.* possessive.
posesor *sm.* owner.
posibil *sn., adj.* possible; feasible. *adv.* possibly.
posibilitate *sf.* possibility.
posomori *vr.* to cloud over.
posomorit *adj.* gloomy.
post *sn.* post; *rel.* fast; ~*ul mare* Lent.
postament *sn.* pedestal.
postav *sn.* (thick) cloth.
postbelic *adj.* post-war...
posterior *adj.* hind(er); *(ulterior)* later; *anat. şi* posterior.
posti *vi.* to fast.
post restant *sn.* poste restante.
postscriptum *sn.* postscript.
postum *adj.* posthumous. *adv.* posthumously.
poşetă *sf.* (hand)bag.
poştal *adj.* post(al).
poştaş *sm.* postman.
poştă *sf.* post (office); *(curier şi)* mail; *prin poşta aeriană* via airmail.
potabil *adj.* drinking.
potasiu *sn.* potassium.
potcoavă *sf.* horseshoe; *(de bocanc)* clout.
potcovar *sm.* smith.

potcovi *vt.* to shoe.
potecă *sf.* path.
poticni *vr.* to stumble (over smth.).
potîrniche *sf.* partridge.
potoli *vt.* to soothe; *(setea)* to quench; *vr.* to quiet (down); *(d. furtună* etc.*)* to abate.
potolit *adj.* quiet; *(cuminte)* equable.
potop *sn.* flood. *adv.* in·a torrent.
potou *sn.* winning post, home.
potpuriu *sn.* medley.
potrivă *sf.* likeness; *de o* ~ to match.
potrivi *vt.* to arrange; *(a pune la punct)* to adjust; *(a pune de acord)* to match; *(a armoniza)* to harmonize; *(ceasul)* to set; *(bine)* to hit·it off. *vr.* to agree; *(a corespunde pentru)* to suit, to be suited; *a se* ~ *la vorbele cuiva* to obey smb.
potrivire *sf.* concord; harmony.
potrivit *adj.* adequate; *(moderat)* moderate. *adv.* moderately; ~ *cu* in keeping with.
potrivnic *sm.* opponent. *adj.* hostile.
povară *sf.* burden.
povață *sf.* counsel; *pl.* advice.
povățui *vt.* to advise.
poveste *sf.* story; *(basm)* fairy tale; *(minciună)* fabrication; *nici* ~ nothing of the kind.
povesti *vt.* to tell. *vr.* to be said.
povestire *sf.* story.
povestitor *sm.* narrator; *(scriitor)* story-teller.
povîrniș *sn.* slope.
poza *vi.* to pose (as).

poză *sf.* picture; *(fotografie)* photo(graph); *fig.* pose.
pozitiv *sn., adj.* positive.
poziție *sf.* position; *(așezare)* situation; *(atitudine și)* stand (point).
poznaș *sm.* wag. *adj.* tricky.
poznă *sf.* prank; blunder; *(farsă)* practical joke.
practic *adj.* practical; *fig. și* matter-of-fact. *adv.* virtually.
practica *vt.* to practise; *(a aplica și)* to apply.
practică *sf.* practice; *(a studenților* etc.*)* practical (period).
pradă *sf.* prey; *(prin jaf)* booty; *(de război)* spoils.
praf *sn.* dust; *(pudră)* powder; ~ *de copt* baking soda, saleratus; ~ *de pușcă* gunpowder. *adj.* powder.
prag *sn.* threshold; *fig. și* limit; *în* ~*ul*... on the brink of...
praștie *sf.* sling.
praz *sm.* leek.
praznic *sn.* *(funeral)* feast; *(hram)* wake.
prăbuși *vr.* to fall, to crumble.
prăbușire *sf.* collapse; *(a unei clădiri)* cave-in.
prăda *vt.* to plunder.
prăfui *vt., vr.* to cover with dust.
prăfuit *adj.* dusty; *fig.* stale, dated.
prăji *vt., vr.* to fry; *(la soare)* to bask in the sun.
prăjină *sf.* pole.
prăjitură *sf.* cake.
prăpastie *sf.* precipice.
prăpăd *sn.* disaster.
prăpădi *vt.* to destroy. *vr.* to be destroyed; *(a pieri)* to perish.
prăpădit *adj.* wretched.

prăşi *vt.* to weed.

prăvăli *vt.* to upset. *vr.* to crumble down.

prăvălie *sf.* shop.

prea *adj.* too; quite; ~ de tot too much.

preajmă *sf.* vicinity; *în preajma cuiva* close to smb.; *în preajma unui eveniment* on the eve of an avent.

prealabil *adj.* preliminary; *în* ~ beforehand.

preamări *vt.* to extol.

preaviz *sn.* notice (to quit).

precar *adj.* precarious.

precaut *adj.* cautious.

precauţie *sf.* prudence; *ca* ~ for better safety; *cu* ~ cautiously.

precădere *sf.* priority; *cu* ~ priority...; pre-eminently.

preceda *vt.* to precede.

precedent *sn.* precedent; *fără* ~ unprecedented. *adj.* (*ultimul dinainte*) preceding; (*de demult*) previous.

precept *sn.* precept.

precipita *vt.* to hasten. *vr.* to rush.

precipitat *adj.* hurried.

precipitaţii *sf. pl.* rainfall; (*radioactive*) fall-out.

precis *adj.* precise, accurate. *adv.* accurately; (*sigur*) definitely; (*d. oră*) sharp.

preciza *vt.* to specify. *vr.* to become precise.

precizare *sf.* explanation; (*declaraţie*) statement.

precizie *sf.* accuracy.

precoce *adj.* precocious.

preconceput *adj.* preconceived; cut and dried; (*nejustificat*) unwarranted.

preconiza *vt.* to contemplate; (*a propune*) to suggest.

precum *conj.* as; ~ şi as well as; ~ urmează as follows.

precumpăni *vi.* to prevail.

precupeţi *vt.* to stint.

precursor *sm.* forerunner.

preda *vt.* to deliver; (*în învăţământ*) to teach. *vr.* to surrender.

predare *sf.* delivery; (*în învăţământ*) teaching; (*capitulare*) capitulation.

predecesor *sm.* forerunner.

predestinat *adj.* fated.

predica *vt.*, *vi.* to preach.

predicat *sn.* predicate.

predicativ *adj.* predicative.

predică *sf.* sermon.

predilecţie.*sf.* predilection; *de* ~ favourite.

predispune *vt.* to predispose.

predispus *adj.* liable (to).

predomina *vi.* to prevail.

predominant *adj.* prevalent.

prefabricat *sn.* prefab.

preface *vt.* to change (into smth.). *vr.* to turn (into smth.); (*a simula*) to feign; *a se* ~ *bolnav* to malinger.

prefacere *sf.* transformation.

prefaţă *sf.* preface.

prefăcătorie *sf.* simulation; (*ipocrizie*) cant.

prefăcut *adj.* adulterated; (*ipocrit*) hypocritical.

prefera *vt.* to prefer; *aş* ~ *să plec* I'd rather go.

preferabil *adj.* preferable. *adv.* rather.

preferat *sm.*, *adj.* pet.

preferinţă *sf.* preference; *de* ~ preferably.

pregăti *vt.* to prepare; (*a in-*

strui) to train; (masa) to cook; a ~ terenul pentru to pave the way for. vr. to make ready; (pentru un examen) to study.

pregătire sf. preparation; (predare) teaching; (nivel) information.

pregătit adj. prepared; (gata) ready; (instruit) well-trained.

pregătitor adj. preparatory.

pregeta vi. to shrink.

pregnant adj. pithy.

preistorie sf. pre-history.

preîntîmpina vt. to forestall.

prejos adv.: mai ~ de below, behind.

prejudecată sf. prejudice; fără prejudecăți unprejudiced.

prejudicia vt. to harm.

prejudiciu vt. damage.

prelegere sf. university lecture.

preliminar adj. preliminary; tentative.

prelinge vr. to trickle.

prelua vt. to assume; to take over.

prelucra vt. to process; (o problemă) to analyse; (pe cineva) to brief.

prelucrare sf. manufacture; (instructaj) briefing.

preludiu sn. prelude.

prelungi vt. to prolong. vr. to last.

prematur adj. premature.

premeditare sf. premeditation; cu ~ deliberate(ly).

premeditat adj. intentional.

premergător sm. forerunner. adj. previous.

premia vt. to award a prize to.

premier sm. premier.

premieră sf. première.

premisă sf. premise; pl. pre--requisites.

premiu sn. prize.

prenume sn. Christian sau given name.

preocupa vt. to concern. vr. to concern oneself (with).

preocupare sf. preoccupation.

preocupat adj. wrapped up in thought; ~ de concerned in sau with.

preot sm. priest; (popă) pope.

prepara vt. to prepare; (mîncarea) to cook.

preparator sm. tutor.

prepeliță sf. quail.

preponderent adj. preponderant.

preponderență sf. prevalence.

prepoziție sf. preposition.

prerie sf. prairie.

presa vt. to press; (a zori) to urge.

presă sf. press.

presăra vt. to (be)sprinkle.

preschimba vt. to (ex)change. vr. to turn (into).

preschimbare sf. transformation.

prescurta vt., vr. to abbreviate.

prescurtare sf. abbreviation.

presimți vt. to get a foreboding of.

presimțire sf. misgiving.

presiune sf. pressure.

prespapier sn. paper weight.

presta vt. to perform; a ~ jurămînt to be sworn in.

prestabilit adj. pre-established, cut and dried.

prestanță sf. stateliness.

prestare sf. performance; sub ~ de jurămînt under oath.

prestație sf. catering.

prestigiu sn. prestige; de ~ creditable.

presupune *vt.* to suppose ; *(a necesita)* to require.

presupunere *sf.* supposition.

presus *adj.*: *mai ~ de* above.

preş *sn.* door mat.

preşcolar *adj.* preschool...

preşedintă *sf.* chairwoman.

preşedinte *sm.* chairman ; *(de republică* etc.*)* president ; *(în Camera Comunelor)* speaker.

preşedinţie *sf.* presidency.

preta *vr.* to lend oneself (to smth.).

pretendeut *sm.* claimant ; *(peţitor)* suitor.

pretenţie *sf.* pretension ; *(revendicare şi)* claim ; *cu pretenţii* pretentious ; *(afectat)* miminy-piminy ; *fără pretenţii* unassuming.

pretenţios *adj.* exacting ; fastidious.

pretext *sn.* pretext ; *sub ~ul că* under colour of.

pretexta *vt.* to pretend.

pretinde *vt.* to claim ; *(a susţine şi)* to allege.

pretins *adj.* so-called.

pretutindeni *adj.* everywhere.

preţ *sn.* price ; *~ de cost* cost price ; *cu ~ul vieţii* at the risk of one's life ; *cu orice ~* by hook or by crook ; *de ~* valuable ; *fără ~* priceless.

preţios *adj.* (in)valuable ; *(afectat)* stilted.

preţui *vt.* to value. *vi.* to cost.

preţuire *sf.* appreciation.

prevala *vi.* to prevail. *vr.* to avail oneself (of an opportunity, etc.).

prevăzător *adj.* cautious.

prevedea *vt.* to foresee ; *(fonduri)* to earmark ; *a ~ că* to stipulate that ; *a ~ cu* to endow with. *vr.* to be forecast.

prevedere *sf.* foresight ; *pl.* stipulations.

preveni *vt.* to (fore)warn ; *(a preîntîmpina)* to forestall.

prevesti *vt.* to forebode.

previziune *sf.* foreseeing.

prezbit *adj.* long-sighted.

prezent *sn.*, *adj.* present ; *în ~* now ; *pînă în ~* so far.

prezenta *vt.* to present ; *(a arăta)* to show ; *(pe cineva cuiva)* to introduce (smb. to smb. else). *vr.* to offer *sau* present oneself ; *(cuiva)* to introduce oneself (to smb.) ; *(d. un candidat)* to stand (for an examination, elections, etc.) ; *(a se ivi)* to appear.

prezentabil *adj.* engaging.

prezentare *sf.* presentation ; introduction ; *~ grafică* make-up.

prezenţă *sf.* presence ; *(a elevilor* etc.*)* attendance ; *~ de spirit* presence of mind.

prezicător *sm.* soothsayer.

prezice *vt.* to forecast ; *a ~ viitorul* to tell fortunes.

prezida *vt.* to chair. *vi.* to be in the chair.

prezidiu *sn.* presidium.

preziuă *sf.* eve ; *în preziua* on the eve of.

pribeag *sm.* exile. *adj.* vagrant.

pribegie *sf.* exile ; *(rătăcire)* wandering.

pricepe *vt.* to understand. *vr.* *(a se înţelege)* to be clear ; to be competent ; *a se ~ la ceva* to be conversant with a subject ; to be an expert hand at smth.

pricepere *sf.* know-how; *(înde-minare)* skill.

priceput *adj.* skilled.

prichici *sn.* window sill.

prichindel *sm.* midget; *(copil)* chit.

pricină *sf.* reason; *(rîcă)* grudge; *din pricina cuiva* because of smb.

pricinui *vt.* to cause.

prididi *vi.* to cope (with).

pridvor *sn.* porch.

prielnic *adj.* favourable.

prieten *sm.* friend; ~ *bun* bosom friend.

prietenesc *adj.* friendly.

prietenie *sf.* friendship.

prietenos *adj.* friendly.

prigoană *sf.* victimization, persecution.

prigoni *vt.* to persecute.

prihană *sf.* blemish; *fără* ~ unblemished.

prii *vi.: a* ~ *cuiva* to agree with smb.

prilej *sn.* (favourable) occasion, *(fericit)* opportunity.

prilejui *vt.* to occasion.

prim *adj., num.* first; *mat., pol.* prime.

primar *sm.* mayor. *adj.* elementary, primary.

primă *sf.* bonus, premium.

primărie *sf.* mayoralty; *(local)* town hall.

primăvara *adv.* in spring.

primăvară *sf.* spring; *la* ~ next spring.

primejdie *sf.* danger, peril; ~ *de moarte* mortal danger.

primejdios *adj.* perilous.

primejdui *vt.* to jeopardize.

primeni *vt.* to renew. *vr.* to change (one's linen).

primi *vt.* to receive; *(a accepta)* to accept. *vi.* to consent.

primire *sf.* reception.

primitiv *sm., adj.* primitive; crude.

primitor *adj.* hospitable.

primordialitate *sf.* priority.

primus *sn.* primus (stove).

prin *prep.* through; *(pe la)* about; *(în)* in; ~ *urmare* therefore.

principal *adj.* main; outstanding; *(predominant)* staple.

principat *sn.* principality.

principial *adj.* principled; of principle. *adv.* in principle.

principiu *sn.* principle; (basic) element; *din* ~ on principle; principle; *în* ~ theoretically.

prinde *vt.* to catch; *(a apuca)* to grasp; *(repede)* to snatch. *(prizonieri* etc.) to capture; *(din urmă)* to catch up with; *(a cuprinde)* to embrace; *(a înțelege și)* to understand: *(a fixa)* to fasten; *(a lega)* to tie; *(a căpăta)* to acquire; *a* ~ *asupra faptului* to catch red-handed; *a* ~ *curaj* to take heart; *a* ~ *pește* to fish; to tickle (trout); *a* ~ *puteri* to pick up strength; *a* ~ *rădăcini* to strike root(s); *a* ~ *o vorbă din zbor* to overhear a conversation. *vi.* to work off; *(d. plante)* to strike root; *a* ~ *de veste* to learn (of *sau* that). *vr.* to catch (at); *fig.* to pledge; *(a paria)* to bet; *(a se întări)* to set; *(d. lapte)* to catch; *nu se* ~ *(la mine)!* it won't go down (with me)!

prinsoare *sf.* wager,

printre *prep.* among; ∼ *altele* among other things.

prinţ *sm.* prince.

prinţesă *sf.* princess.

prioritate *sf.* priority; *(la circulaţie)* right of way.

pripă *sf.* rashness; *în* ∼ hastily.

pripi *vr.* to be rash.

pripit *adj.* hasty.

prismă *sf.* prism; *fig.* angle.

prisos *sn.* redundance; *de* ∼ useless.

prisosi *vi.* to be in excess.

prisosinţă *sf.*: *cu* ∼ abundantly; *fig.* with a vengeance.

prispă *sf.* porch.

priva *vt.* to deprive (of). *vr.*: *a se* ∼ *de* to go without.

privaţiune *sf.* (de)privation.

privelişte *sf.* view.

privi *vt.* to watch; *(a interesa)* to concern; *în ceea ce mă priveşte* as for me; *nu te priveşte* it is none of your business; *nu mă priveşte pe mine* it's not my funeral. *vi.* to look; *(fix)* to stare; *(atent)* to peer; *a* ∼ *la* to watch. *vr.* to look at each other; *(în oglindă)* to (take a) look at oneself in the mirror.

privighetoare *sf.* nightingale.

privilegiat *adj.* privileged.

privilegiu *sn.* privilege.

privinţă *sf.* respect; *în privinţa* as regards.

privire *sf.* look; *cu* ∼ *la* as regards.

privitor *sm.* onlooker. *adj.*: ∼ *la* regarding.

priză *sf.* plug; *fig.* hold (on the public, etc.); *în* ∼ plugged (in); *scos din* ∼ unplugged.

prizonier *sm.* prisoner (of war).

prînz *sn.* lunch; *(substanţial)* dinner; *(amiază)* noon.

prînzi *vi.* to lunch; to dine.

proaspăt *adj.* fresh; *(d. pîine)* newly-baked.

proba *vt.* *(a dovedi)* to prove; *(a încerca)* to test; *(o rochie etc.)* to try on.

probabil *adj.* probable; *puţin* ∼ unlikely. *adv.* probably; *foarte* ∼ most likely.

probabilitate *sf.* probability; *după toate probabilităţile* in all likelihood.

probă *sf.* test; *(dovadă)* proof; *(verificare şi)* verification; *(mostră)* specimen; *(examen)* exam(ination); *(la croitor)* fitting; *sport* event; *de* ∼ trial.

problematic *adj.* problematical.

problemă *sf.* problem; *fig.* challenge, issue.

proceda *vi.* to proceed (to).

procedeu *sn.* method.

procedură *sf.* procedure.

procent(aj) *sn.* percentage.

proces *sn.* process; *(curs)* course; *jur.* *(penal)* trial; *(civil)* lawsuit; ∼ *de conştiinţă* remorse; ∼ *de divorţ* divorce suit; ∼*-verbal* report; *(al unei şedinţe)* minute.

procesiune *sf.* procession.

proclama *vt.* to proclaim.

proclamare, proclamaţie *sf.* proclamation.

procopsi *vt.* to provide. *vr.* to enrich oneself.

procura *vt.* to secure.

procuratură *sf.* prosecutor's office.

procură *sf.*, **procurist** *sm.* proxy.

procuror *sm.* public prosecutor; *(în Anglia şi S.U.A.)* attorney; ~ *general* Attorney General.

prodecan *sm.* deputy dean.

prodigios *adj.* prodigious.

producător *sm.* producer.

produce *vt.* to yield; to cause. *vi.* to be profitable. *vr.* to take place; *(în public)* to perform in public.

productiv *adj.* productive.

productivitate *sf.* productivity.

producție *sf.* production; *(produse)* output; yield; ~ în serie serial manufacture; ~ la hectar yield per hectare.

produs *sn.* product; *(natural)* produce; ~e agricole farm produce.

proeminent *adj.* prominent; *fig.* remarkable.

profan *sm.* tyro. *adj.* profane; *(laic)* lay.

profana *vt.* to profane.

profesie *sf.* calling; *de* ~ professional; by profession.

profesional *adj.* professional; *(d. învățămînt)* vocational; *(d. boală)* occupational.

profesionist *sm., adj.* professional; *liberii profesioniști* the professional people.

profesiune *sf.* profession.

profesoară *sf.* teacher; *(învățătoare)* schoolmistress.

profesor *sm.* teacher; *(universitar și)* professor; *(învățător)* schoolmaster.

profet *sm.* prophet.

profetic *adj.* prophetic(al).

profeție *sf.* prophecy.

profil *sn.* profile; *fig.* structure; *din* ~ in profile.

profila *vr.* to loom; *fig.* to specialize (in).

profit *sn.* profit; ~ *net* clear profit.

profita *vi.* to benefit; *a* ~ *de prilej* to improve the occasion.

profund *adj.* profound; *(d. somn și)* sound; *(serios și)* thorough (going). *adv.* deeply; thoroughly.

profunzime *sf.* depth.

prognoză *sf.* forecast.

program *sn.* programme; *(afiș)* playbill; *pol. și* platform; *(orar)* time table; *(de studii)* syllabus.

programa *vt.* to schedule; *și mat.* to programme.

progres *sn.* progress.

progresa *vi.* to make headway.

progresist *sm., adj.* progressive, radical.

progresiv *adj.* gradual. *adv.* gradually.

prohibiție *sf.* prohibition.

proiect *sn.* plan; *tehn.* design; *(ciornă etc.)* draft; ~ *de lege* bill; ~ *de rezoluție* draft resolution.

proiecta *vt.* to project; to design. *vr.* to be projected.

proiectant *sm.* designer.

proiectil *sn.* missile; *(glonte)* bullet; *(obuz)* shell; ~ *teleghidat* guided missile.

proiecție *sf.* projection.

proletar *sm., adj.* proletarian; ~*i din toate țările uniți-vă!* Workers of the world, unite!

proletariat *sn.* proletariat; labour.

prolog *sn.* prologue.

promisiune *sf.* promise.

promite *vt., vi.* to promise.

promițător *adj.* promising.

promoroacă *sf.* white frost.

promoție *sf.* graduates (of one year) ; enrolment.
promova *vt.* to promote. *vi.* to be promoted (to the next class, etc.).
promovare *sf.* promotion.
prompt *adj.* quick. *adv.* promptly.
promptitudine *sf.* promptness.
pronosport *sn.* football pool, coupons.
pronostic *sn.* forecast.
pronume *sn.* pronoun.
pronunța *vt.* to pronounce ; *jur.* to pass. *vr.* to declare.
pronunțare *sf.* pronunciation ; *(a sentinței)* passing.
propagandă *sf.* propaganda.
propagandist *sm.* propagandist.
propăși *vi.* to thrive.
propășire *sf.* advance(ment).
proporție *sf.* proportion ; *pl.* scope ; *de proporții* ample.
proporțional *adj.* proportional (to) ; *adv.* in proportion (as).
proporționat *adj.* well-balanced.
propovădui *vt.* to preach ; to spread.
propoziție *sf.* sentence ; *(într-o frază)* clause.
proprietar *sm.* owner ; *(de casă sau de teren)* landlord; *(moșier)* landowner.
proprietate *sf.* property ; *(drept)* ownership.
proprietăreasă *sf.* landlady.
propriu *adj.* one's own ; *(potrivit)* proper ; ~-*zis* proper.
propti *vt.* to prop up. *vr.* to take a fixed stand.
propune *vt.* to suggest.
propunere *sf.* proposal.
proră *sf.* prow.
prorector *sm.* pro-rector.

proroc *sm.* prophet.
proroci *vt.* to prophesy.
prosop *sn.* towel.
prospect *sf.* prospectus.
prosper *adj.* prosperous.
prospera *vi.* to thrive.
prosperitate *sf.* flowering.
prospețime *sf.* freshness.
prost *sm.* fool. *adj.* silly ; *(de proastă calitate)* bad. *adv.* badly ; poorly.
prostănac *sm.* ninny. *adj.* stupid.
prostesc *adj.* foolish.
prosti *vt.* to brutify ; *fig.* to hoodwink. *vr.* to become foolish.
prostie *sf.* folly ; *pl.* rubbish.
prostituată *sf.* prostitute.
prostituție *sf.* prostitution.
protagonist *sm.* lead(ing actor).
protector *sm.* protector. *adj.* protective.
protecție *sf.* protection ; *de* ~ protective.
proteja *vt.* to protect.
protest *sn.* protest.
protesta *vt., vi.* to protest.
protestant *sm., adj.* Protestant.
proteză *sf.* prosthesis ; *(dentară)* denture ; store teeth.
protocol *sn.* protocol ; *(etichetă)* etiquette.
proveni *vi.* to proceed (from).
proveniență *sf.* origin.
proverb *sn.* proverb.
providență *sf.* providence.
provincial *sm., adj.* provincial.
provincie *sf.* province ; *de* ~ country ; *în* ~ in the country (side).
provizie *sf.* provision.
provizoriu *adj.* provisional. *adv.* for the time being.

provoca *vt.* to challenge ; *(a cauza)* to bring about ; *(a instiga)* to incite.

provocare *sf.* provocation ; *(la întrecere, duel)* challenge.

provocator *m.* agent provocateur. *adj.* provocative.

proxenet *sm.* pander.

prozaic *adj.* prosaic.

prozator *sm.* prose writer.

proză *sf.* prose ; *(epică și)* fiction.

prudent *adj.* wary.

prudență *sf.* prudence.

prun *sm.* plum tree.

prună *sf.* plum.

prunc *sm.* baby.

prundiș *sn.* gravel.

prusac *sm., adj.,* **prusacă** *sf., adj.* Prussian.

psalm *sm.* psalm.

pseudonim *sn.* pseudonym ; pen-name.

psihiatru *sm.* psychiatrist.

psihic *sn.* mind. *adj.* psychic.

psiholog *sm.* psychologist.

psihologie *sf.* psychology.

pst *interj.* hey !

public *sn.* public ; *marele* ~ the public at large. *adj.* public. *adv.* publicly.

publica *vt.* to publish.

publicare *sf.* publication.

publicație *sf.* publication, work ; *(periodic)* periodical.

publicist *sm.* journalist.

publicitate *sf.* publicity ; *mica* ~ classified ads.

pudra *vt., vr.* to powder (oneself).

pudră *sf.* powder. *adj.* powdered.

pudrieră *sf.* powder case.

puf *sn.* down ; *(pt. pudră)* puff.

pufăi *vi.* to puff.

pufni *vi.* to snort ; *a* ~ *în rîs* to burst out laughing.

puhav *adj.* flabby.

pui *sm.* young one ; *(de găină)* chicken ; *(de pasăre mică)* chick ; *(de animal)* cub, whelp ; *(de gîscă)* gosling ; *(de rață)* duckling ; ~ *de somn* nap ; ~*ule !* my son !

pulbere *sf.* powder.

pulover *sn.* pull-over.

pulpă *sf.* pulp ; *anat.* calf ; *(coapsă)* thigh ; *(mîncare)* joint.

puls *sn.* pulse.

pulsa *vi.* to throb.

pumn *sm.* (blow with the) fist ; *(conținutul)* handful.

pumnal *sn.* dagger.

punct *sn.* point ; *(pe i)* dot ; *(oprire)* full stop ; *(chestiune și)* item ; *(pe program)* act ; ~ *cu* ~ in great detail ; ~ *culminant* climax ; ~ *de plecare* starting point ; ~ *de sprijin* fulcrum ; ~ *de vedere* standpoint ; ~*e cardinale* points of the compass ; ~*e* ~*e* dots ; ~ *mort* deadlock ; ~ *și virgulă* semicolon ; *din* ~ *de vedere al* in point of ; *două* ~*e* colon ; *la* ~ perfect ; *pe* ~*ul de a* about to ; *pînă la un* ~ to a certain extent. *adv.* sharp, exactly.

punctaj *sn.* skeleton ; *sport* score.

punctual *adj.* punctual. *adv.* on time.

punctualitate *sf.* punctuality.

punctuație *sf.* punctuation.

pune *vt.* to put ; to set ; *(a așterne)* to lay ; *(a aplica)* to apply ; *(o haină)* to put on ; *(a sili)* to make ; *a* ~ *bine*

to lay by; *a ~ în discuţie*
to raise; *a ~ în scenă* to stage;
a ~ o întrebare to ask a question,
a-şi ~ amprenta pe to leave its
mark on; *a ~ un disc, muzică,
o placă* to play a record. *vr.* to
be put, laid *sau* set; *(a se aşeza)*
to sit down; *a se ~ bine cu
cineva* to appease smb.; *a se
~ rău cu cineva* to incur smb.'s
displeasure.

pungaş *sm.* thief; *(de buzunare)*
pickpocket; *fig.* villain.

pungă *sf.* purse; *(sac)* pouch;
(de hîrtie) paper bag.

pungăşie *sf.* theft; *(înşelăciune)* swindle.

punte *sf.* bridge; *mar.* deck.

pupă *sf. mar.* poop; *entom.* pupa.

pupăză *sf.* hoopoe.

pupilă *sf. anat.* pupil; *jur.* ward.

pupitru *sn.* desk.

pur *adj.* pure; *(original şi)*
genuine; *(simplu şi)* mere.

purcede *vi.* to set out.

purcel *sm.* porkling.

purgativ *sn.* purgative.

purica *vt.* to flea; *fig.* to examine minutely.

purice *sm.* flea.

purifica *vt.* to purify. *vr.* to be
cleansed.

puroi *sn.* pus.

purpură *sf.* purple.

purta *vt.* to carry; *(a mîna)*
to drive; *(îmbrăcăminte etc.)*
to wear. *vr.* to behave; *(d.
haine)* to wear (well); to
be en vogue.

purtare *sf.* behaviour.

purtat *adj.* carried, borne; *(d.
haine)* worn; *(uzat)* shabby.

purtător *sm.* bearer; *~ de
cuvînt* spokesman. *adj.* carrier.

pustietate *sf.* desert.

pustii *vt.* to lay waste.

pustiitor *adj.* devastating.

pustiu *sn.* desert.

pustnic *sm.* hermit.

puşcaş *sm.* gunman.

puşcă *sf.* gun; *(carabină)* rifle
(de vînătoare) shotgun; *~-mi-
tralieră* sub-machine-gun.

puşcărie *sf.* prison.

puşculiţă *sf.* piggy bank.

puşlama *sf.* rogue.

puşti *sm.* kid.

putea *vt.* can; to be able (to);
(a avea posibilitatea) to be in
a position (to); can afford;
(a avea voie) may; to be permitted *sau* allowed (to); *a nu
~ să* to be unable to; *nu pot
să nu rîd* I can't help laughing;
a nu mai ~ de oboseală to be
fagged out. *vr.* may; can, to
be possible; *se (prea) poate*
it may be, quite possibly.

putere *sf.* strength; *(energie şi)*
pol. power; *(forţă)* force; *(vigoare)* vigour; *~ de cumpărare* purchasing power; *cu toată ~a* with might and main;
în ~a nopţii in the dead of
night.

puternic *adj.* strong; *(energic)*
powerful; *(intens)* intense;
(mare) important; *(robust)* re-
sistant. *adv.* strongly, violently.

putinţă *sf.* possibility.

putred *adj.* rotten; *~ de bogat*
rolling (in money).

putregai *sn.* rot(tenness).

putrezi *vi.* to rot; *(d. cînepă)*
to ret.

putreziciune *sf.* decay.

puţ *sn.* well; *min. şi* shaft; *~
petrolifer* oil well *sau* derrick.

puți *vi.* to stink (of smth.).
puțin *sn.* little. *adj.* a little.
pl. (a) few; *(insuficient)* (too)
little; *(slab)* poor, small; *mai*
~*i* fewer. *adv.* a little; *(cam)*
rather, somehow; *(insuficient)*
(too) little; ~ *cîte* ~ gradually; *cel* ~ at least; *mai* ~
less; *peste* ~ before long.
puzderie *sf.* dust; *fig.* lots (of).

R

rabat *sn.* rebate.
rabatabil *adj.*, rabatare *sf.* folding.
rabin *sm.* Rabbi.
rablă *sf.* jalopy.
rac *sm.* crayfish.
rachetă *sf.* rocket; *(pt. zăpadă*
sau sport) racket.
rachiu *sn.* brandy.
racilă *sf.* evil.
radar *sn.* radar.
rade *vt.* to scrape *sau* rub out;
(de la pămînt) to raze (from
the ground); *(a bărbieri)* to
shave. *vr.* to (get a) shave.
radia *vt.* to erase; *(a iradia)*
to radiate. *vi.* to beam.
radiator *sn.* radiator.
radical *sm.*, *sn.*, *adj.* radical.
adv. thoroughly.
radio *sn.* radio (set), wireless set;
broadcasting; ~ *cu picup* radiogram; ~ *cu tranzistori* transistor radio; *la* ~ on the radio;
prin ~ by radio.
radioactiv *adj.* radioactive.
radioamator *sm.* radio amateur.
radiodifuza *vt.* to broadcast.
radiodifuziune *sf.* radio *sau* broadcasting stations.
radioficare *sf.* wire broadcasting.

radiofonic *adj.* radio ..., broadcasting.
radiografie *sf.* radiography; *(pla-*
că) X-ray photograph.
radiojurnal *sn.* news (on the
radio).
radios *adj.* radiant. *adv.* in rap-
tures.
radioscopie *sf.* X-ray (examination).
radiu *sn.* radium.
rafală *sf.* squall; *(de mitra-*
lieră) volley of shots.
rafie *sf.* raffia.
rafina *vt.* to refine; *fig. și* to
polish. *vr.* to polish oneself.
rafinament *sn.* refinement.
rafinat *adj.* refined.
raft *sn.* shelf.
rage *vi.* to (bel)low; *(furios)* to
roar.
rahat *sn.* rahat lakoum, Turkish delight.
rai *sn.* eden, paradise.
raid *sn.* (air) raid.
raion *sn.* district; *com.* department; ~ *de partid* district
party committee.
raional *adj.* district.
raită *sf.* round; *(rond)* beat.
ralia *vr.: a se* ~ *la* to join.

ramă *sf.* frame ; *(de tablou şi)* mat ; *(de pantofi)* welt ; *(vîslă)* oar.

ramburs *sn.* (re)payment ; *(contra* ~ cash on delivery.

ramifica *vr.* to branch out.

ramoli *vr.* to dodder.

ramolit *sm.* old dotard. *adj.* soft-minded.

rampă *sf.* platform ; ramp ; *teatru* floats.

ramură *sf.* branch ; *(crenguţă)* twig.

rană *sf.* wound.

randament *sn.* efficiency.

rang *sn.* rank.

raniţă *sf.* knapsack ; *mil.* pack.

rapace *adj.* rapacious.

rapid *sn.* fast train. *adj.* rapid. *adv.* rapidly.

rapiditate *sf.* quickness.

rapiţă *sf.* colza.

raport *sn.* report ; *(dare de seamă şi)* account ; *(legătură)* relation ; *(proporţie)* ratio ; *(comparaţie)* comparison ; *(privinţă)* respect.

raporta *vt.* to report ; *(a aduce)* to bring in. *vr.* to refer.

raportor *sm.* speaker (who delivers a report), rapporteur. *sn.* *geom.* protractor.

rapsodie *sf.* rhapsody.

rar *adj.* rare ; *(neîndestulător)* scarce ; *(neobişnuit şi)* uncommon ; *(lent)* slow. *adv.* rarely ; *(lent)* slowly.

rareori *adv.* seldom.

ras *sn.* shave. *adj.* shaven ; *(d. linguriţă etc.)* brimful.

rasă *sf.* race ; *zool.* breed ; *(de călugăr)* frock ; *de* ~ thoroughbred ; *fig.* remarkable.

rasial *adj.* racial ; Jim Crow.

rasist *sm.* racist.

rasol *sn.* boiled meat ; *fig.* scamping.

rata *vt.* to miss. *vi.* to miss fire ; to fail. *vr.* to become a human failure.

ratat *sm.* cropper. *adj.* failing.

rată *sf.* instalment ; *în rate* by instalments.

raţă *sf.* duck.

raţie *sf.* ration.

raţiona *vt.* to ration. *vi.* to reason.

raţional *adj.* rational.

raţionament *sn.* judgement.

raţiune *sf.* reason.

ravagiu *sn.* (*i pl.*) havoc.

rază *sf.* ray, beam ; *(licărire)* gleam ; *geom.* radius ; ~ *de soare* sunray ; ~ *de lună* moonbeam ; *pl.* moonshine.

razie *sf.* (police) raid.

razna *adv.* : *a o lua* ~ to go astray ; *(în vorbire)* to ramble.

răbda *vt., vi.* to endure ; *a* ~ *de foame* to hunger.

răbdare *sf.* patience.

răbdător *adj.* suffering. *adv.* patiently.

răbufni *vi.* to break out.

răceală *sf.* cold ; *fig.* coldness.

răchită *sf.* osier ; *(împletitură şi)* wickerwork.

răci *vt.* to cool. *vi.* to catch (a) cold. *vr.* to grow cold.

răcire *sf.* cooling.

răcitor *sn.* ice-box.

răcituri *sf. pl.* meat jelly.

răcnet *sn.* yell, shriek.

răcni *vt., vi.* to yell, to roar.

răcoare *sf.* coolness ; *pl.* shiver.

răcori *vt., vr.* to cool (down).

răcoritoare *sf. pl.* cooling drinks.

răcoritor *adj.* cooling.

răcoros *adj.* cool.

rădăcină *sf.* root.

răfui *vr.* to settle accounts.

răgaz *sn.* respite.

răget *sn.* roar.

răguşeală *sf.* hoarseness.

răguşi *vi.* to get hoarse.

răguşit *adj.* hoarse.

rămas *sn.* staying ; ~-*bun* fare-well. *adj.* left.

rămăşag *sn.* wager.

rămăşiţă *sf.* remnant ; *pl.* re-mains.

rămîne *vi.* to remain ; *(a sta)* to stay ; *(a continua)* to conti-nue ; *a* ~ *dator* to get into debt.

rămînere *sf.* remaining ; ~ *în urmă* lag(ging behind).

răni *vt.* to wound.

răpăi *vi.* to rattle.

răpi *vt.* to ravish ; *(pt. răscum-părare)* to kidnap ; *a* ~ *drep-turile cuiva* to deprive smb. of his rights.

răpire *sf.* kidnapping.

răpitor *sm.* abductor. *adj.* pre-datory ; *(d. frumuseţe)* enthrall-ing.

răposat *sm.* the deceased. *adj.* late.

răpune *vt.* to worst.

rări *vt.* to space out. *vr.* to grow rarer.

răsări *vi.* to rise ; *(a se ivi şi)* to turn up ; *agr.* to spring.

răsărit *sn.* sunrise ; *(punct car-dinal)* east ; *adj.* risen ; *(mare)* tall(ish) ; *(deosebit)* outstanding.

răsăritean *adj.* East(ern), Ori-ental.

răscoală *sf.* (up)rising ; revolt ; mutiny.

răscoli *vt.* to rummage ; *fig.* to (a)rouse.

răscopt *adj.* overripe ; *(d. ou)* hard-boiled.

răscruce *sf.* crossroad(s) ; *fig.* moment of choice.

răscula *vr.* to revolt.

răsculat *sm.* rebel.

răscumpăra *vt.* to redeem ; *fig.* to expiate ; *(un captiv)* to ransom.

răscumpărare *sf.* redemption ; *(plată)* ransom.

răsfăţa *vt.* to pamper. *vr.* to play the spoilt child.

răsfăţat *adj.* spoilt.

răsfira *vt., vr.* to spread (out).

răsfoi *vt.* to skim through.

răsfrînge *vt.* to reflect. *vr.* to be reflected.

răsfrînt *adj.* reflected ; *(d. guler etc.)* turned up.

răspăr *sn.* : *în* ~ against the hair ; *fig.* against the grain.

răspicat *adj.* outspoken. *adv.* plainly.

răspîndi *vt.* to spread ; *(a îm-prăştia)* to scatter ; *(a pro-paga şi)* to circulate. *vr.* to spread.

răspîndire *sf.* spreading ; *(arie)* expanse.

răspîndit *adj.* (wide)spread.

răspîntie *sf.* crossroads ; *fig. şi* turning point.

răsplată *sf.* reward.

răsplăti *vt.* to reward.

răspoimîine *adv.* in three days.

răspunde *vt.* to answer ; *(a riposta)* to retort. *vi.* to answer ; *(cuiva şi)* to reply (to).

răspundere *sf.* responsibility.

răspuns *sn.* answer ; *(replică)* repartee ; *(la examen şi)* script.

răspunzător *adj.* responsible.

răsputeri *sf. pl.* : *din* ~ mightily.

răstălmăci *vt.* to misconstrue.
răsti *vr.* to bluster; *a se ~ la*
to give (smb.) rough-house.
răstigni *vt.* to crucify.
răstimp *sn.* (lapse of) time.
răsturna *vt.* to upset; *pol.* to
overthrow. *vt.* to capsize.
răsuci *vt., vr.* to twist; *(a rula)*
to roll.
răsufla *vi.* to breathe (freely);
(a ofta) to heave a sigh; *(a
se afla)* to leak (out).
răsuflare *sf.* breath(ing); *cu ~a*
întretăiată excitedly.
răsuna *vi.* to (re)sound.
răsunător *adj.* sonorous; *fig.*
thundering.
răsunet *sn.* echo; *fig.* response.
răşină *sf.* resin.
rătăci *vt.* to lose (one's way,
etc.); *(un lucru)* to mislay.
vi. to ramble. *vr.* to get lost.
rătăcire *sf.* straying; *fig.* error;
(nebunie) madness.
rătăcit *adj.* stray; *fig.* wild.
rătăcitor *adj.* wandering; *(d.
cavaler)* errant.
rățoi¹ *sm.* drake.
rățoi² *vr.* to swashbuckle; *a se ~
la* to jaw.
rățușcă *sf.* duckling.
rău *sn.* evil; *(necaz)* harm;
(boală) sickness; *~ de aer*
airsickness; *~ de mare* seasickness; *atîta ~* never mind. *adj.*
bad; poor; *(ticălos)* wicked; *(neastîmpărat)* naughty; *(stricat)*
perverse; *cel mai ~* the worst;
mai ~ worse. *adv.* badly;
wickedly; *(prost)* poorly.
răufăcător *sm.* malefactor.
răutate *sf.* ill nature; *(faptă)*
misdeed, wrong; *cu ~* vici-
ously.

răutăcios *adj.* malicious, acrimonious.
răuvoitor *adj.* malevolent. *adv.*
unkindly.
răvăşit *adj.* helter-skelter; *fig.*
uspet; *(d. păr)* dishevelled.
răzătoare *sf.* shredder.
răzbate *vi.* to penetrate; to
succeed.
răzbi *vt.* to overcome. *vi.* to
penetrate.
război¹ *sn.* war; *(ostilități)*
warfare; *(de țesut)* loom; *~ de
partizani* guerilla war; *~ mondial* world war.
război² *vr.* to (be at) war.
războinic *sm.* warrior. *adj.* war-
(like).
răzbuna *vt.* to avenge. *vr.* to
take one's revenge (on smb.).
răzbunare *sf.* revenge.
răzbunător *sm.* avenger. *adj.*
vindictive.
răzeş *sm.* yeoman; *pl.* yeomanry.
răzgîndi *vr.* to change one's
mind.
răzleț *adj.* stray.
răzvrăti *vr.* to rebel.
re *sm.* D, re.
rea-credință *sf.* dishonesty; *de ~*
unprincipled.
reactor *sn.* reactor; *(avion)*
jet(-plane).
reacție *sf.* reaction; *fig. și* response;
cu ~ jet.
reacționa *vi.* to react (upon
smth.).
reacționar *sm., adj.* reactionary.
reacțiune *sf.* reaction.
real *adj.* actual.
realism *sn.* realism.
realist *sm.* realist. *adj.* realistic.
realitate *sf.* reality; *în ~* in
(actual) fact.

realiza *vt.* to achieve. *vr.* to materialize; *fig.* to make one's mark.

realizare *sf.* achievement.

realmente *adv.* actually.

reaminti *vt., vi.* to recall; *(cuiva)* to remind smb. (of smth.); *a-și* ~ to remember.

rea-voință *sf.* ill-will.

reazem *sn.* (main)stay.

rebel *sm.* rebel. *adj.* rebellious; *(dificil)* obstinate.

rebeliune *sf.* rebellion; subversion.

rebus *sn.* rebus.

rebut *sn.* reject; *pl. și* waste.

recalcitrant *adj.* refractory.

recapitula *vt.* to summarize.

recăpăta *vt.* to recover.

rece *sn.* chill; *la* ~ in a cool place; *fig.* calmly. *adj.* cold; *(răcoros)* cool; *(și umed)* chill(y); *fig.* unresponsive; *(glacial)* icy; *(d. pîine)* stale. *adv.* coldly; *(calm)* coolly; *(glacial)* icily.

recensămînt *sn.* census.

recent *adj.* latest. *adv.* recently.

recenza *vt.* to review (a book).

recenzie *sf.* (book) review.

receptiv *adj.* responsive.

recepție *sf.* reception; *com.* check (on delivery).

rechin *sm.* shark.

rechizite *sf. pl.* writing materials, stationery; *(școlare)* school supplies.

recipient *sn.* container.

recipisă *sf.* receipt.

reciproc *adj.* mutual. *adv.* reciprocally; each other.

reciprocitate *sf.* reciprocity.

recita *vt.* to recite.

recital *sn.* recital.

reciti *vt.* to read again.

reclama *vt.* to complain against; *(în justiție)* to sue at law; *(a cere)* to claim; *(a necesita)* to require; to necessitate.

reclamant *sm.* plaintiff.

reclamație *sf.* complaint.

reclamă *sf.* advertising; *(desănțată)* puffing; *(anunț)* advertisment; *ad; (firmă)* (neon) sign.

recolta *vt.* to harvest.

recoltă *sf.* harvest; *(la hectar)* yield (per hectare).

recomanda *vt.* to recommend; *(a prezenta)* to introduce. *vr.* to introduce oneself.

recomandabil *adj.* advisable.

recomandare *sf.* recommendation.

recomandat *adj.* recommended; *(d. scrisoare)* registered.

recomandată *sf.* registered letter.

recomandație *sf.* (letter of) introduction.

recompensă *sf.* reward; *drept* ~ as a reward.

reconsidera *vt.* to reappraise; to reconsider.

reconstitui *vt.* to reconstitute.

reconstrucție *sf.* reconstruction; urban renewal.

record *sn., adj.* record.

recrea *vt.* to recreate. *vr.* to amuse oneself.

recreativ *adj.* entertaining.

recreație *sf.* break; *(odihnă)* rest.

recruta *vt.* to recruit; *fig.* to enlist.

rector *sm.* rector.

rectorat *sn.* rector's office.

reculegere *sf.* (solitary) meditation ; *a păstra un minut de ~* to mark one's regret by standing silently for a minute.

recunoaşte *vt. (pe cineva)* to recognize ; *(meritele etc. şi)* to acknowledge ; *(a mărturisi)* to admit ; *mil.* to reconnoitre. *vr.* to acknowledge (defeat, etc.).

recunoaştere *sf.* recognition; *(mărturisire)* confession.; *mil.* reconnaissance.

recunoscător *adj.* grateful.

recunoscut *adj.* acknowledged.

recunoştinţă *sf.* gratitude ; *cu ~* gratefully.

recurge *vi.* to resort (to).

recurs *sn.* appeal.

reda *vt.* to restore ; *fig.* to render.

redacta *vt.* draw up; *(a formula)* to word.

redactor *sm.* (sub-)editor ; *(de editură)* reader (for the publisher) ; *~ şef* editor (in chief).

redacţie *sf.* editorial staff ; *(local)* editorial office.

redare *sf.* restoration ; *muz.* rendition ; *artă etc.* expression.

redobîndi *vt.* to retrieve.

reduce *vt.* to reduce. *vr.* to diminish ; *a se ~ la* to boil down to.

reducere *sf.* reduction ; cut (in prices, etc.).

redus *adj.* reduced ; *(mărginit)* narrow-minded.

redutabil *adj.* formidable, redoubtable.

reedita *vt.* to republish ; *fig.* to repeat.

reface *vt.* to remake, to re--write. *vr.* to recover (one's health).

refacere *sf.* improvement ; *(însănătoşire)* recovery; *econ.* rehabilitation.

referat *sn.* essay ; paper ; *(raport)* report.

referent *sm.* reviewer ; *(raportor)* adviser ; *~ tehnic* expert.

referi *vi.* to report (on). *vr.* to refer (to) ; to dwell (on).

referinţă *sf.* reference ; *(recomandaţie)* (letter of) introduction.

referire *sf.* reference ; *cu ~ la* regarding.

referitor *adj.: ~ la* concerning.

reflecta *vt.* to reflect. *vi.* to consider. *vr.* to be mirrored.

reflectare *sf.* reflection.

reflector *sn.* searchlight ; *teatru etc. şi fig.* spotlight.

reflecţie *sf.* reflection ; *(gînd)* thought.

reflex *sn., adj.* reflex ; *~ condiţionat* conditioned reflex.

reflexiv *sn.* reflexive voice. *adj.* reflexive.

reflux *sn.* ebb(ing).

reforma *vt.* to reform.

reformat *sm. rel.* Protestant. *adj.* reformed.

reformator *sm.* reformer. *adj.* reforming.

reformă *sf.* reform ; *rel.* Reformation ; *~ agrară* land reform ; *~ bănească* currency reform.

refractar *adj.* refractory.

refren *sn.* refrain ; *fig.* tag.

refugia *vr.* to take refuge.

refugiat *sm.* refugee.

refugiu *sn.* refuge.

refuz *sn.* refusal.

refuza *vt.* to refuse.

regalist *sm., adj.* royalist.

regat *sn.* realm ; kingdom.

regăsi vt. to recover. vr. to be oneself again.

rege sm. king.

regie sf. administration; (cheltuieli) overhead; teatru direction.

regim sn. pol. system; (guvern) government; (condiţii) conditions; (dietă) diet; gram. regimen, rection; vechiul ~ the former regime.

regiment sn. regiment.

regină sf. queen; regina balului the reine of the ball; regina nopţii nicotiana.

regional adj. region(al).

registru sn. register; (mare) ledger.

regiune sf. region.

regiza vt. to direct; teatru şi to stage.

regizor sm. director; teatru stage manager.

regla vt. to regulate; to adjust.

reglementa vt. to settle.

reglementar adj. regular.

regres sn. regress.

regresa vi. to regress.

regret sn. regret; (remuşcare) compunction; pl. searchings of the heart; cu ~ regretfully.

regreta vt., vi. to regret.

regretabil adj. unfortunate.

regulament sn. rules.

regulat adj. regular; (armonios) harmonious. adv. steadily.

regulă sf. rule; de ~ as a rule; în ~ all right, O.K.

reieşi vi. to result.

reintegra vt. to reinstate.

reînarma vt., vr. to rearm.

reîncepe vt. to resume.

reînnoi vt. to renew.

reînvia vt., vi. to revive.

reînviere sf. resurgence.

relaş sn. day off; (afiş) no performance.

relata vt. to relate.

relatare sf. narration.

relativ adj. relative. adv. comparatively.

relaţie sf. relation(ship); pl. intercourse; (proptele) props; (informaţii) information.

relaxare sf. relaxation.

releva vt. to point out; to remark.

relievă sf. relic.

relief sn. relief.

reliefa vt. to underline. vr. to be outlined.

religie sf. religion; (credinţă) faith; (confesiune) persuasion.

religios adj. religious.

relua vt. to resume.

reluare sf. resumption.

remaia vt. to ladder (up).

remarca vt. to notice. vr. to become conspicuous.

remarcabil adj. remarkable (for).

remedia vt. to remedy. vr. to be mended.

remediu sn. remedy.

remi sn. rummy.

reminiscenţă sf. reminiscence.

remiză sf. com. commission; sport drawn game.

remorca vt. to tow.

remorcă sf. trailer; (remorcare) towing.

remorcher sn. tug(-boat).

remunera vt. to pay.

remuneraţie sf. pay; fig. emolument.

remuşcare sf. remorse; pl. repentance.

ren sm. reindeer.

renaşte vi. to rise (again).

renaştere sf. revival ; lit. Renaissance.
renăscut adj. reborn.
renega vt. to deny.
renovă vt. to renovate.
renta vi. to be profitable.
rentabil adj. lucrative ; com. profitable.
rentă sf. rent ; (viageră) life annuity ; ~ în natură rent in kind.
rentier sm. rentier, annuitant.
renume sn. renown.
renumit adj. famous.
renunţa vi.: a ~ la to renounce.
renunţare sf. renunciation.
reorganiza vt. to reorganize.
repara vt. to repair ; (o greşeală) to set to rights ; (a compensa) to redress ; (a cîrpi) to darn.
reparaţie sf. repair ; (revizie) overhauling.
repartiţie sf. repartition (deed).
repartiza vt. to distribute ; (a aloca) to earmark.
repartizare sf. distribution.
repatria vt., vr. to repatriate (oneself).
repaus sn. rest ; (răgaz) respite ; în ~ at rest ; pe loc ~ ! place, rest !
repede adj. quick ; (ager şi) nimble ; (furtunos) tempestuous. adv. fast ; (curînd) shortly (afterwards).
repercusiune sf. repercussion.
repertoriu sn. repertory ; (catalog) catalogue.
repeta vt., vi. to repeat ; teatru etc. to rehearse. vr. to be recurrent ; (în vorbe) to repeat oneself.
repetent sm. non-promoted pupil.

repetiţie sf. repetition ; teatru etc. rehearsal ; ~ generală dress rehearsal ; (la şcoală) general revision.
repezeală sf. haste ; la ~ in a hurry.
repezi vt. to thrust ; (pe cineva) to snub ; to shout at (smb.). vr. to hurry ; a se ~ la to swoop upon.
repeziciune sf. swiftness.
repezit adj. rash.
replică sf. retort ; teatru speech ; cue ; fig. rebuff ; artă replica.
reportaj sn. (feature) report, reportage.
reporter sm. reporter.
represalii sf. pl. reprisals.
represiune sf. repression.
reprezenta vt. to (re)present ; teatru to perform ; (pe cineva) to act for ; (a însemna şi) to mean ; (grafic) to plot. vr. to be represented ; teatru to be performed.
reprezentant sm. representative ; fig. spokesman.
reprezentare sf. representation ; (grafică) plotting.
reprezentaţie sf. performance ; a juca în ~ to be a guest star.
reprima vt. to repress.
reprimi vt. to take back.
repriză sf. half (of match) ; (la box) round.
reproduce vt., vr. to reproduce.
reproducere, reproducţie sf. reproduction.
reprofila vt. to reshape ; to streamline.
reproş sn. reproach.
reproşa vt. to reproach (smb. with smth.).
reptilă sf. reptile.

republican *sm.* republican. *adj.* republican; all-country.

republică *sf.* republic; ~ *populară* people's republic; *Republica Socialistă România* the Socialist Republic of Romania; ~ *autonomă* autonomous republic.

repugna *vi.*: *îmi repugnă* I abhor it, etc.

repulsie *sf.* repellence.

repune *vt.* to restore.

reputaţie *sf.* reputation.

resemna *vr.* to resign oneself.

resemnare *sf.* resignation.

resimţi *vt.* to feel. *vr.* to be felt; *a se* ~ *de pe urma* to suffer from.

resort *sn.* (main)spring; *(sector)* department; *de ~ul cuiva* within smb.'s province.

respect *sn.* respect; *pl.* compliments; *cu* ~ reverently.

respecta *vt.* *(pe cineva)* to revere; *(ceva)* to observe. *vr.* to respect (oneself, each other).

respectabil *adj.* honourable.

respectiv *adj.* respective. *adv.* respectively.

respectuos *adj.* respectful. *adv.* courteously.

respingător *adj.* repulsive.

respinge *vt.* to repel; *(a refuza)* to reject, to decline, to refuse; *(cu dispreţ)* to spurn.

respira *vt.*, *vi.* to breathe (in).

respiraţie *sf.* breathing.

responsabil *sm.* chief; *com.* manager. *adj.* responsible.

responsabilitate *sf.* responsibility.

rest *sn.* rest; *(la o bancnotă etc.)* change.

restabili *vt.* to restore. *vr.* to recover.

restabilire *sf.* re-establishment; *(a unui bolnav)* recovery.

restant *adj.* overdue; outstanding.

restanţă *sf.* arrears; *în* ~ behind(hand).

restaura *vt.* to restore.

restaurant *sn.* restaurant.

restitui *vt.* to return.

restricţie *sf.* restriction.

restrînge *vt.* to restrict. *vr.* to scrounge, to skimp.

restrîns *adj.* limited.

resursă • *sf.* resource; *pl.* şi means.

reşedinţă *sf.* residence.

reşou *sn.* electric boiling ring.

reteza *vt.* to cut (off).

reticenţă *sf.* reticence.

retipări *vt.* to reprint.

retoric *adj.* rhetorical. *adv.* oratorically.

retracta *vt.* to retract.

retrage *vt.*, *vr.* to withdraw.

retragere *sf.* withdrawal; *mil.* şi retreat; ~ *cu torţe* torch procession.

retras *adj.* retired; solitary. *adv.* in loneliness.

retrăi *vt.* to live again.

retribui *vt.* to remunerate.

retribuţie *sf.* wages; *econ.* distribution (according to work, etc.).

retrograd *sm.*, *adj.* retrograde.

retrospectiv *adj.* retrospective. *adv.* retrospectively.

retroversiune *sf.* version.

retur *sn.* return. *adv.* back.

reţea *sf.* net(work).

reţetă *sf. med.* prescription. *(culinară etc.)* recipe; *(încasări)* (box office) returns.

reţine *vt.* to hold (back), to arrest; *(a întîrzia)* to keep;

(a opri) to stop ; *(a împiedica)* to hamper ; *(a memora)* to memorize ; *(dinainte)* to book ; to subscribe. *vr.* to control oneself.

reţinere *sf.* restraint ; *(bani etc.)* money, etc. held back.

reţinut *adj.* restrained.

reumatism *sn.* rheumatism.

reuni *vt.* to (re)unite. *vr.* to gather.

reuniune *sf.* reunion ; *(adunare)* gathering ; *(petrecere)* party ; *sport* meet.

reuşi *vt., vi.* to succeed (in doing smth.) ; *a nu* ~ to fail (to do smth).

reuşit *adj.* successful ; *(minunat)* wonderful ; *(potrivit)* apt.

revanşă *sf.* revenge ; *sport* return match.

revărsa *vt.* to discharge ; *a-şi* ~ *mînia asupra cuiva* to vent one's fury on smb. *vr.* to overflow.

revărsare *sf.* flood.

revedea *vt.* to meet again ; *(a revizui)* to revise. *vr.* to meet again.

revedere *sf.* seeing (each other) again ; *(revizie)* revision ; *la* ~ *!* good-bye ! see you later !

revelaţie *sf.* revelation.

revelion *sn.* New Year's Eve (party).

revendica *vt.* to claim.

revendicare *sf.* claim.

reveni *vi.* to come back ; *(a se întîmpla)* to occur (again) ; *(a reapărea)* to re-appear ; *a-şi* ~ to come to (one's senses); *a* ~ *asupra unei păreri* to go back on one's opinion ; *a* ~ *la* to revert to ; to amount to (a sum) ; *ne revine sarcina de a scrie* the task of writing is incumbent on us.

revenire *sf.* return.

rever *sn.* lapel ; *sport* backhand (stroke).

reverenţios *adj.* respectful.

revistă *sf.* review ; *(ilustrată)* magazine ; *teatru* revue ; *(inspecţie)* review ; *fig. şi* survey.

revizie *sf.* revision ; *tehn. şi* overhauling.

revizor *sm.* inspector (general) ; *(contabil)* auditor.

revizui *vt.* to revise ; *(conturi)* to audit.

revolta *vt., vr.* to revolt.

revoltat *adj.* indignant. *adv.* in revolt.

revoltă *sf.* revolt.

revoltător *adj.* shocking.

revoluţie *sf.* revolution.

revoluţionar *sm.* revolutionist. *adj.* revolutionary.

revolver *sn.* revolver.

rezema *vt., vr.* to lean (against smth.).

rezerva *vt.* to reserve ; *(bilete etc.)* to book ; *(d. viitor)* to have in store.

rezervat *adj.* reserved.

rezervă *sf.* reserve ; *(de spital)* side-room ; *sport* spare ; *de* ~ spare ; *sub rezerva ratificării* etc. pending ratification, etc.

rezervor *sn.* reservoir.

rezilia *vt.* to cancel.

rezista *vi.: a* ~ *la* to resist (smth.).

rezistent *adj.* resisting ; *(tare)* strong, hardy ; *(durabil)* lasting.

rezistenţă *sf.* resistance; *fig. şi* stamina.

rezoluţie *sf.* resolution.

rezolva *vt.* to solve.

rezolvare *sf.* settlement; *(cheie)* key.

rezonabil *adj.* reasonable.

rezulta *vi.* to result.

rezultat *sn.* result; *fără ~* useless(ly).

rezuma *vt.* to sum up. *vr.: a se ~ la* to confine oneself to.

rezumat *sn.* epitome; abstract.

rezumativ *adj.* summarizing.

ricin *sm.* castor-oil plant.

ricină *sf.* castor oil.

rid *sn.* wrinkle; *(cută)* furrow.

ridica *vt.* to raise; *(a desprinde de pe o suprafaţă)* to lift; *(steagul)* to hoist; *(a aresta)* to arrest; *(o pedeapsă)* to quash; *(bani)* to cash; *(a spori)* to increase; *fig.* to enhance; *(o clădire)* to erect. *vr.* to rise; *(în picioare)* to stand up; *(la luptă)* to rise in arms; *(a creşte)* to grow; *a se ~ la* to amount to (the sum of).

ridicare *sf.* raising; *(creştere)* growth; *prin ~ de mîini* by show of hands.

ridicat *adj.* raised; *(înalt)* lofty; *(d. voce)* loud; *fig.* advanced.

ridicata *sf.: cu ~* wholesale.

ridicătură *sf.* elevation.

ridiche *sf.* radish.

ridicol *sn.* ridicule. *adj.* ridiculous.

ridiculiza *vt.* to ridicule.

rigid *adj.* rigid; *fig.* stern.

rigiditate *sf.* rigidity.

riglă *sf.* rule(r); *~ de calcul* sliding rule.

rigoare *sf.* rigour; *la ~* at a pinch.

riguros *adj.* rigorous; *(exact)* accurate. *adv.* strictly; *(exact)* accurately.

rima *vt., vi.* to rhyme.

rimă *sf.* rhyme.

ring *sn.* ring; *(de dans)* dancing floor.

rinichi *sm.* kidney.

rinocer *sm.* rhinoceros.

riposta *vt., vi.* to retort; to give a rebuff (to smb.).

risc *sn.* risk; *cu ~ul de a* at the risk of.

risca *vt.* to risk. *vi.* to take risks.

riscant *adj.* hazardous.

risipă *sf.* waste.

risipi *vt.* to squander; *(a împrăştia)* to scatter; *fig.* to dispel. *vr.* to dispel.

risipitor *sm.* squanderer. *adj.* wasteful.

rit *sn.* rite; *(credinţă)* persuasion.

ritm *sn.* rhythm; *(viteză şi)* rate; *într-un ~ rapid* at a rapid pace.

ritmat, ritmic *adj.* rhythmic.

ritual *sn., adj.* ritual.

rival *sm., adj.* rival.

rivalitate *sf.* rivalry.

rivaliza *vi.* to vie.

rîde *vi.* to laugh; *(în sinea lui)* to chuckle; *(a chicoti)* to titter; *(de cineva şi)* to scoff (at smb.).

rîie *sf.* scab.

rîios *adj.* mangy; *fig.* haughty.

rînced *adj.* rancid.

rînd *sn. (de scaune* etc.) row; *şi fig.* rank; *(şir)* file; *(serie)* range; *(ordine)* turn; *(dată)* time; *(de litere)* line; *(de haine)* suit; *de ~* common;

în primul ~ first of all;
la ~ in succession; *pe* ~
in turn; *la* ~*ul lui* in his
turn; ~ *pe* ~ one after the
other.
rîndui *vt.* to arrange.
rîndunea. rîndunică *sf.* swallow.
rînjet *sn.* grin.
rînji *vi.* to grin; *(agresiv)*
to snarl.
rîpă *sf.* steep ravine.
rîs *sm. zool.* lynx. *sn.* laugh(ter);
(satisfăcut) chuckle; *(chicot)*
snigger; *(hohot)* peal of laughter.
rîşni *vt.* to grind.
rîşniţă *sf.* hand mill.
rît *sn.* snout.
rîu *sn.* river.
rîvnă *sf.* zeal.
rîvni *vi.:* *a* ~ *la* to covet.
roabă *sf.* slave; *(tărăboanţă)*
wheelbarrow.
roade *vt.* to gnaw; *(a mînca
şi)* to nibble; *(a uza)* to eat
away. *vr.* to wear (out).
roată *sf.* wheel; *(cerc)* circle;
~ *de rezervă* spare wheel.
adv. roundabout.
rob *sm.* slave.
robi *vt.* to enslave. *vi.* to drudge.
robie *sf.* thraldom; slavery.
robinet *sn.* tap.
robot *sm.* robot.
roboti *vi.* to toil and moil.
robust *adj.* robust.
rochie *sf.* dress; ~ *de bal*
ball dress; ~ *de casă* tea-
-gown; ~ *(decoltată)* low-necked
dress; ~ *de oraş sau de stradă*
walking dress; *(de vară)* frock.
rochiţă *sf.* frock; *rochiţa rîn-
dunelei* bindweed.
rod *sn.* fruit; *fig. şi pl.* fruit(s);
pe ~ in bearing.

roda *vt.* tu run in.
rodaj *sn.* running in.
rodi *vi.* to bear fruit.
rodie *sf.* pomegranate.
roditor *adj.* fruit-bearing; *fig.*
fruitful.
rodnic *adj.* productive.
rogojină *sf.* mat.
roi [1] *sn.* swarm; *fig. şi* bevy.
roi [2] *vi.* to swarm.
roib *sm.* sorrel horse. *adj.* sorrel.
rol *sn.* role, part; ~ *de compoziţie* character part; ~ *principal* lead(ing part); ~ *secundar* minor part; *fig.* second
fiddle.
rolă *sf.* roll; *(de magnetofon etc.)*
reel.
rom *sm.* Rom(any), gypsy. *sn.*
rum.
roman *sm.* Roman. *sn.* novel;
~ *de aventuri* romance, tale
of adventure; ~ *foileton* serial
(story); ~ *poliţist* whodunit.
adj. Roman; Latin.
romancier *sm.* novelist.
romanic *adj.* Romance, Romanic.
romantic *sm.* romanticist. *adj.*
romantic.
romantism *sn.* romanticism.
romanţat *adj.* fictionalized.
romanţă *sf.* drawing-room ballad.
român *sm.* Romanian; *(ist.,
iobag)* serf. *adj.* Romanian.
română *sf., adj.* Romanian.
româncă *sf.* Romanian (woman).
românesc *adj.* Romanian.
româneşte *adv.* (like a) Romanian.
(răspicat) clearly.
romb *sn.* rhombus.
rond *sn.* flower bed; *(al poli-
ţistului etc.)* beat.
ronţăi *vt.* to crunch.
ropot *sn.* clatter (of hoofs);

(de ploaie) shower ; *(de aplauze)* peal (of applause).

ros *adj.* gnawed ; *(d. haine)* threadbare.

rost *sn.* sense ; *(scop)* purpose ; *(utilitate)* use(fulness) ; *fără ~* useless(ly).

rosti *vt.* to utter.

rostire *sf.* pronunciation.

rostogol *sn.: de-a ~ul* turning somersaults.

rostogoli *vt., vr.* to turn.

roșcat *adj.* reddish.

roșcovă *sf.* carob (beans).

roși *vt.* to redden. *vi.* to redden ; *(de emoție etc.)* to blush.

roșiatic *adj.* reddish.

roșie *sf.* tomato.

roșu *sn.* red ; *(de buze)* lipstick, rouge. *adj.* red ; *(aprins)* scarlet ; *(emoționat)* flushed.

rotație *sf.* rotation ; *prin ~* by turns.

roti *vt., vr.* to turn (round).

rotocol *sn.* roll.

rotofei *adj.* dumpy.

rotulă *sf.* knee pan.

rotund *adj.* round.

rotunji *vt.* to round off. *vr.* to be rounded.

rotunjime *sf.* roundness.

rouă *sf.* dew.

roz *sn., adj.* pink.

rozător *sn., adj.* rodent.

rozmarin *sm.* rosemary.

rubeolă *sf.* German measles.

rubin *sn.* ruby.

rublă *sf.* rouble.

rubrică *sf* heading.

rucsac *sn.* knapsack.

rudă *sf.* relative ; *pl. și* kin(sfolk) ; *(prin alianță)* in-law.

rudenie *sf.* relationship.

rudimentar *adj.* rudimentary.

rufă *sf.* underwear ; *pl.* (under)-clothes.

rug *sn.* stake.

ruga *vt.* to ask, to implore ; *(a pofti)* to invite. *vr.* to pray ; *a se ~ de cineva* to entreat smb.

rugă *sf.* prayer ; *(rugăminte)* request.

rugăciune *sf.* prayer.

rugăminte *sf.* entreaty.

rugător *adj.* beseeching.

rugbi *sn.* rugby ; *amer.* football.

rugină *sf.* rust ; *bot.* blight.

rugini *vi., vr.* to rust.

ruginit *adj.* rusty ; *fig.* stick--in-the-mud.

ruina *vt.* to ruin. *vr.* to be ruined.

ruinat *adj.* ruined ; *(d. case și)* dilapidated.

ruină *sf.* ruin.

ruj *sn.* rouge ; *(de buze și)* lipstick.

ruja *vr.* to rouge.

rula *vt.* to roll (up) ; *(bani)* to use ; *cinema* to show. *vi.* to roll ; *cinema* to be on.

ruletă *sf.* roulette ; *(pt. măsurat)* tape measure.

rulotă *sf.* trailer.

rulou *sn.* roll ; *(oblon)* roller blind.

rumega *vt., vi.* to chew.

rumeguș *sn.* sawdust.

rumen *adj.* ruddy ; *(fript)* well roasted.

rumeni *vt.* to redden ; *(a frige)* to roast to a turn. *vr.* to redden ; *(a se frige)* to be done to a turn.

rumoare *sf.* hubbub.

rundă *sf.* round.

rupe *vt.* to break ; *(a sfîșia)* to tear ; *(a culege)* to pluck ;

(a întrerupe) to break off ;
(a vorbi) to speak ; *a o ~ cu*
to break away from ; *(cu
cineva)* to part company with
smb. *vr.* to break ; *(a se
sfîşia)* to tear ; to wear out.
rupere *sf.* breaking ; *(sfîşiere)*
tearing ; *~ de nori* cloud burst.
rupt *sn.*: *nici în ~ul capului*
on no account ; *pe ~e* with
a vengeance. *adj.* broken ; *(sfî-
şiat)* torn ; *(zdrenţuit)* tattered ;
~ în coate out at elbows.
ruptură *sf.* break ; *(sfîşiere)*
tear ; *fig.* breaking off.
rural *adj.* rural.

rus *sm.*, *adj.* Russian.
rusalii *sf. pl.* Whitsuntide ; *duminica ~lor* Whit Sunday.
rusesc *adj.* Russian.
ruseşte *adv.* (like a) Russian.
rusoaică *sf.* Russian (woman).
rustic *adj.* rustic.
ruşina *vt.* to shame. *vr.* to be
ashamed.
ruşine *sf.* shame ; *(timiditate)*
bashfulness ; *fără ~* shame-
less(ly).
ruşinos *adj.* shameful ; *(timid)*
shy.
rută *sf.* route.
rutină *sf.* experience ; practice.

S

sa *adj. (pt. masc.)* his ; *(pt. fem.)*
her ; *(pt. lucruri)* its ; *a ~* his ;
her.
sabie *sf.* sword ; *fig.* battle.
sabota *vt.* to sabotage.
sabotaj *sn.* sabotage.
sabotor *sm.* saboteur.
sac *sm.* bag ; *(desagă)* knapsack ;
(conţinutul) sackful ; *~ fără
fund* glutton.
saca *sf.* water-cart.
sacadat *adj.* jerky.
sacagiu *sm.* water-carrier.
sacîz *sn.* rosin.
sacoşă *sf.* (shopping) bag.
sacou *sn.* (sack) coat.
sacramental *adj.* sacramental.
sacrifica *vt.*, *vr.* to sacrifice (oneself).
sacrificiu *sn.* sacrifice ; *(ucidere
şi)* immolation,

sacrilegiu *sn.* sacrilege.
sacru *adj.* sacred.
sadea *adj.* sheer. *adv.* truly.
sadic *sm.* sadist. *adj.* sadistic.
sadism *sn.* sadism.
safir *sn.* sapphire.
salahor *sm.* day labourer.
salam *sn.* salame.
salamandră *sf.* salamander.
salariat *sm.* wage-earner. *adj.*
paid ; *(angajat)* employed.
salariu *sn.* wage(s) ; *(lunar şi)*
salary.
salariza *vt.* to pay.
salarizare *sf.* wages, pay, re-
muneration.
salată *sf.* salad ; *bot.* (cos) lettuce.
sală *sf.* hall ; room ; *(de spectacol)*
house ; *(publicul)* audience ; *(coridor)* corridor ; *~ de aşteptare*
waiting-room ; *~ de sport* gym.

salbă *sf.* necklace.

salcie *sf.* willow(tree) ; ~ *plîngă-toare* weeping willow.

salcîm *sm.* acacia.

sale *adj.* (*pt. masc.*) his ; (*pt. fem.*) her ; (*pt. lucruri*) its ; *ale* ~ his ; hers.

salină *sf.* salt works.

salivă *sf.* saliva.

salon *sn.* drawing-room ; (*de spital*) ward ; (*expoziţie*) show room ; (*de dans, coafură*) saloon ; *de* ~ fashionable.

salonaş *sn.* morning-room.

salopetă *sf.* overall(s).

salt *sn.* jump ; (*de pe loc*) leap ; (*ţopăială*) hop ; *triplu* ~ hop--step-and-jump; ~ *calitativ* qualitative leap.

saltea *sf.* mattress.

saltimbanc *sm.* rope walker ; *fig.* mountebank.

salubritate *sf.* sanitation (service).

salubru *adj.* wholesome.

salut *sn.* greeting(s) ; *interj.* hallo ! (*la revedere*) good bye !

saluta *vt.* to greet ; (*a se înclina*) to bow to (smb.) ; (*din cap*) to nod ; (*cu mîna*) to wave to (smb.); *fig.* to hail. *vi.* to salute. *vr.* to be on nodding terms.

salutar *adj.* beneficial ; salutary.

salutare *sf.* greeting.

salva *vt.* to save ; *a* ~ *aparenţele* to keep up appearances.

salvare *sf.* rescue ; *med.* emergency service.

salvator *sm.* rescuer. *adj.* saving.

salvă *sf.* salvo.

samavolnic *adj.* arbitrary.

samsar *sm.* jobber.

sanatoriu *sn.* sanatorium.

sanctuar *sn.* sanctuary.

sancţiona *vt.* to sanction ; (*a aproba şi*) to approve.

sancţiune *sf.* sanction ; (*pedeapsă şi*) penalty.

sandală *sf.* sandal.

sandviş *sn.* sandwich.

sanie *sf.* sledge.

sanitar *sm.* medical orderly. *adj.* sanitary.

sanscrit *adj.* **sanscrită** *sf., adj.* Sanskrit.

santinelă *sf.* sentry, sentinel.

sapă *sf.* hoe ; *min.* bit ; (*săpare*) hoeing.

sarabandă *sf.* saraband ; *fig.* devilish dance.

saraille *sf.* almond cake dipped in syrup.

saramură *sf.* (pickling) brine ; pickled fish.

sarcasm *sn.* sarcasm.

sarcastic *adj.* sarcastic.

sarcină *sf.* load ; (*de lemne*) faggot ; *fig.* task ; (*graviditate*) pregnancy.

sarcofag *sn.* sarcophagus.

sardea *sf.* sardine.

sare *sf.* salt ; *fig.* pep ; *pl.* smelling salts.

sarică *sf.* long-haired shepherd's coat.

sarmale *sf. pl.* force-meat rolls in cabbage *sau* vine leaves.

sas *sm.* Saxon.

saşiu *adj.* cross-eyed. *adv.* asquint.

sat *sn.* village ; villagers.

satană *sf.* fiend.

satelit *sm.* satellite.

satin *sn.* satin.

satir *sm. şi fig.* satyr.

satiră *sf.* satire.

satiric *sm.* satirist. *adj.* satiric(al).

satiriza *vt*. to satirize.
satisface *vt*. to satisfy; *(necesităţi)* to meet.
satisfacere, satisfacţie *sf*. satisfaction.
satisfăcător *adj*. satisfactory.
satisfăcut *adj*. content(ed).
satîr *sn*. (meat) chopper.
saturaţie *sf*. saturation; *fig. şi* surfeit; *pînă la_* ~ *fig.* up to the teeth.
saţ *sn*. satiety; *(greaţă)* cloying; *fără* ~ insatiable.
sau *conj.* or; ~ ... ~ either ... or.
savant *sm*. scientist. *adj*. scholarly. *adv*. skilfully.
savarină *sf*. savarin.
savoare *sf*. savour.
savura *vt*. to relish.
savuros *adj*. savoury; *fig.* racy.
saxofon *sn.* saxophone.
saxon *sm., adj.* Saxon.
să *conj.* (so) that, *(dacă)* if; *(pt. imperativ)* let; *(particulă)* to; *măcar* ~ if at least; *numai* ~ if only; *pînă* ~ until.
săculeţ *sn.* satchel.
sădi *vt.* to plant; *fig.* to implant.
săgeată *sf.* arrow.
săgeta *vt.* to shoot (with an arrow).
săi *adj.* his; *fem.* her; *pt. lucruri* its; *ai săi* his *sau* her folk(s); his, hers.
sălăşlui *vi.* to live.
sălbatic *sm.* savage; wild *sau* uncouth man. *adj.* wild; *(d. animale şi)* untamed; *(d. oameni şi)* savage; *(crud şi)* cruel.
sălbătici *vt., vr.* to turn wild.
sălbăticie *sf.* savagery; *(pustiu)* wilderness; *cu* ~ cruelly.

sălbăticit *adj.* (grown) wild.
sălciu *adj.* brackish; *fig.* vapid.
sălta *vt.* to heave (up); to help (smb.) up. *vi., vr.* to jump, to hop; to rise.
săltăreţ *adj.* jaunty; *(d. muzică)* lively.
sămînţă *sf.* seed; *(neam)* kind.
sănătate *sf.* health; *(caracter normal)* soundness.
sănătoasă *sf.*: *a o lua la sănătoasa* to take to one's heels.
sănătos *adj.* sound; *(la trup şi)* healthy; *(voinic şi)* strong; *(salubru şi)* wholesome. *adv.* healthily.
săniuş *sn.* sleigh-riding.
săpa *vt.* to dig (up); *(a grava)* to engrave; *(d. animale)* to burrow; *(a excava)* to excavate; *(a submina)* to sap.
săptămînal *sn., adj., adv.* weekly.
săptămînă *sf.* week; ~ *de lucru* working week; *săptămîni întregi* for weeks on end; *două săptămîni* a fortnight.
săpun *sn.* (cake of) soap; ~ *de ras* shaving soap.
săpuneală *sf.* lathering; *fig.* dressing-down, reprimand.
săpuni *vt.* to soap; to lather; *fig.* to haul smb. over the coals. *vr.* to soap oneself; *(pt. bărbierit)* to lather one's face.
săra *vt.* to salt; *(în saramură)* to brine.
sărac *sm.* pauper, poor man; *pl.* the poor; ~*ul de mine!* poor me! *adj.* poor; *(nevoiaş şi)* needy; *(arid şi)* unproductive; *fig.* meagre; *(biet şi)* wretched; ~ *lipit pămîntului*

as poor as a church mouse; ~ *cu duhul* poor in spirit.

sărat *adj.* salt(y); *fig.* pungent; *(d. preţuri)* stiff.

sărăcăcios *adj.* poor(ly); *(d. hra-nă)* meagre; *(d. pămînt)* barren; *fig.* stinted.

sărăci *vt.* to impoverish. *vi.* to grow poor.

sărăcie *sf.* poverty; *(lipsă)* penury; ~ *cu lustru* shabby gentility.

sărăcime *sf.* the paupers.

sărbătoare *sf.* holiday; *(petrecere şi)* festivity; de ~ festive; ~a, *sărbătorile* on holidays.

sărbătoresc *adj.* solemn.

sărbătoreşte *adv.* festively.

sărbători *vt.* to celebrate, to fête.

sări *vt.* to clear; to jump (over); *(a omite)* to skip. *vi.* to jump; to leap; to vault; *(a ţopăi)* to hop; *(în sus)* to spring; *(în apă)* to dive; *fig.* to overlook; a ~ *cu gura pe (cineva)* to jaw (smb.); *a-i* ~ *cuiva de gît* to fling one's arms around smb.; a ~ *în aer* to blow up; a ~ *în ajutor* to come to rescue (smb.); a ~ *în ochi* to be striking; *a-i* ~ *muştarul* sau *ţandăra* to lose patience.

sărit *sn.*: pe ~e by hops and skips. *adj.* dotty.

săritor *adj.* obliging.

săritură *sf.* jump, leap; ~ *cu prăjina* pole vault; ~ *în înălţime* high jump; ~ *în lungime* long jump.

sărman *sm.* pauper; *adj.* poor, needy; ~*ul!* poor thing!

sărut *sn.* kiss.

săruta *vt.* to kiss; *sărut mîna* how do you do! *vi., vr.* to kiss (one another).

sărutare *sf.*, **sărutat** *sn.* kiss(ing).

săsesc *adj.* Saxon.

săsoaică *sf.* Saxon woman.

sătean *sm.* villager.

săteancă *sf.* peasant-woman.

sătesc *adj.* rural.

sătul *adj.* (chock)full; *fig.* (sick and) tired.

sătura *vt.* to satiate. *vr.* to eat one's fill; *fig.* to have enough (of smth.).

săturat *sn.*: pe ~e to one's heart's content.

său *adj.* his, her; *pt. lucruri* its; al ~ his, hers.

săvîrşi *vt.* to commit; *(a executa)* to implement. *vr.* to be done; a se ~ *din viaţă* to depart this life.

scabros *adj.* indecorous.

scadent *adj.* (falling) due.

scadenţă *sf.* settling day.

scafandru *sm.* diver; *sn.* *(costum)* diving-suit.

scalpa *vt.* to scalp.

scamator *sm.* juggler.

scamatorie *sf.* jugglery.

scamă *sf.* lint; *fig.* fluff.

scanda *vt.* to scan; to shout (slogans).

scandal *sn.* *(gălăgie)* row; *fig.* scandal.

scandalagiu *sm.* tough.

scandaliza *vt.* to scandalize. *vr.* to be indignant (at smth.).

scandalos *adj.* disgraceful.

scandinav *sm., adj.* **scandinavă** *sf., adj.* Scandinavian.

scară *sf.* staircase; (flight of) stairs; *(treaptă)* step; *(mobilă)* ladder; *(rulantă)* escalator; *(de frînghie)* rope ladder; *(pt. căld-*

rie) stirrup ; *(de maşină)* footboard ; *(de vagon)* running-board ; *muz., geogr.* scale ; *pe ~ mare* (on a) large scale.

scarlatină *sf.* scarlet fever.

scatiu *sm.* siskin.

scaun *sn.* chair ; *(fără spetează)* stool ; *med.* stool ; *~ pliant* camp stool ; *cu ~ la cap* wise ; *sfîntul ~* the Holy See.

scădea *vt.* to subtract ; *(a coborî)* to lower. *vi.* to diminish, to recede ; *fig.* to abate.

scădere *sf.* subtraction ; diminution ; *fig.* defect.

scăfîrlie *sf.* skull.

scălda *vt.* to bathe ; *a o ~ to* give an elusive answer. *vr.* to bathe.

scălîmbăia *vr.* to contort.

scămoşa *vt., vi* to shred. *vr.* to fray.

scăpa *vt.* to save ; *(din mînă etc.)* to drop ; *(a pierde)* to miss ; *(a omite)* to omit ; *a ~ din vedere* to overlook ; *a ~ o vorbă* to let slip a word. *vi.* to escape ; *a ~ de* to get rid of ; *a ~ teafăr* to get away safe and sound ; *a ~ ca prin urechile acului* to make a hairbreadth escape.

scăpare *sf.* escape ; *(omisiune)* omission.

scăpăra *vt.* to strike *(a match etc.).* *vi.* to flash ; *(a scînteia)* to sparkle.

scăpăta *vi.* to set ; *fig.* to go down in the world.

scăriţă *sf.* small ladder *sau* staircase ; *anat.* stirrup, stapes.

scărmăna *vt.* to card ; *fig.* to thrash.

scărpina *vt., vr.* to scratch ; *a se* *~ în cap* to scratch one's head.

scăunaş, scăunel *sn.* stool.

scăzut *adj.* low.

scelerat *sm.* scoundrel. *adj.* criminal.

scenarist *sm.* script-writer.

scenariu *sn.* (film) script ; *~ radiofonic* radio play.

scenă *sf.* scene ; *(estradă)* stage.

scenetă *sf.* sketch ; one-act play.

scenograf *sm.* stage *sau* set designer.

scenografie *sf.* stage designing.

sceptic *sm., adj.* sceptic. *adv.* sceptically.

scepticism *sn.* scepticism.

sceptru *sn.* sceptre.

scheci *sn.* sketch.

schelă *sf.* scaffolding ; *min.* oilfield ; *(sondă)* oil-well.

schelet *sn.* skeleton.

schematic *adj.* diagrammatic ; *peior.* over-simplified.

schematism *sn.* over-simplification.

schemă *sf.* scheme ; staff list : *pe ~* on the staff.

scheuna *vi.* to yelp.

schi *sn.* ski(ing) ; *(pe apă)* aquaplane.

schia *vi.* to ski.

schif *sn.* skiff.

schijă *sf.* (shell) splinter.

schilod *sm.* cripple. *adj.* maimed.

schilodi *vt.* to mutilate.

schimb *sn.* exchange; *(schimbare)* change, alteration ; *(într-o uzină)* shift ; *cu ~ul* by turns ; *în ~* (in exchange) for ; instead.

schimba *vt. (a înnoi)* to change ; *(a modifica)* to alter ; *(unul* *cu altul)* to exchange; *(a înlocui)* to replace; *a ~ vorba* to switch to another subject. *vr.* to change; to be altered; *(în bine)* to change for the better.

schimbare *sf.* change; *(schimb)* exchange.

schimbător *sn. tehn.* switch; *auto.* gearshift.

schimonoseală *sf.* grimace.

schimonosi *vt.* to disfigure. *vr.* to grimace.

schingiui *vt.* to torture.

schingiuire *sf.* torture.

schit *sn.* hermitage.

schița *vt.* to sketch, to outline; *a ~ un zîmbet* to give the ghost of a smile.

schiță *sf.* sketch; *(proiect și)* outline.

scinda *vt., vr.* to split (up).

scindare *sf.* scission.

scit *sm., adj.* Scythian.

sciziune *sf.* split.

scîlcia *vt., vr.* to wear down.

scîlciat *adj.* down at heel.

scîncet *sn.* whimper(ing).

scînci *vi., vr.* to whine.

scîndură *sf.* board; *(de brad)* deal board.

scînteia *vi.* to sparkle.

scînteie *sf.* spark.

scînteietor *adj.* scintillating.

scîrbă *sf.* aversion; *(om)* nasty man.

scîrbi *vt.* to disgust. *vr.* to be sickened (by).

scîrbit *adj.* disgusted (at).

scîrbos *adj.* fulsome, repulsive.

scîrții *vi.* to creak; *(d. peniță* etc.*)* to scratch.

scîrțîială *sf.*, **scîrțîit** *sn.* creaking.

sclav *sm.* slave; *fig. și* thrall.

sclavagism *sn.* slave system.

sclavă *sf.* slave (woman).

sclavie *sf.* slavery.

scliîosi *vr. (a se miorlăi)* to snivel; *(a se preface)* to gush.

sclipi *vi.* to twinkle.

sclipire *sf.* sparkle.

sclipitor *adj.* brilliant.

sclivisi *vt.* to polish. *vr.* to titivate.

sclivisit *adj.* squoo; *(elegant)* dapper.

scoarță *sf. bot.* bark; *anat.* cortex; *geogr.* etc. crust; *(covor)* rug; *din ~ în ~* from A to Izzard.

scoate *vt.* to pull *sau* draw out; *(a îndepărta)* to take out; *(la iveală)* to reveal; *(a dezbrăca)* to take off; *fig.* to get; *(a izgoni)* to drive away; *(a concedia)* to dismiss; *(a scăpa)* to get out; *(a publica)* to publish; *(a arunca)* to throw out; *(a rosti)* to utter; *(pui)* to hatch; *(d. plante)* to put out (shoots, etc.); *a ~ ochii cuiva* to put out smb.'s eyes; *fig.* to reproach smb. (with smth.).

scobi *vt.* to hollow (out); *(dinții)* to pick. *vi.* to dig. *vr.: a se ~ în dinți* etc. to pick one's teeth, etc.

scobitoare *sf.* tooth-pick.

scobitură *sf.* hollow; groove.

scofală *sf.* deed; *mare ~!* nothing to write home about.

scofîlci *vr.* to become emaciated *sau* wasted.

scofîlcit *adj.* gaunt; *(d. obraji)* sunken.

scoică *sf.* shell; *(stridie)* oyster; icecream cone.

scolastic *adj.* scholastic.

sconta *vt.* to discount; *fig.* to expect.

scop *sn.* purpose; *în ~ul* ...
with a view to (doing, etc.)...

scor *sn.* score; *~ alb* love all;
~ egal draw.

scorburǎ *sf.*, **scorburos** *adj.* hollow.

scorbut *sn.* scurvy.

scormoni *vt.*, *vi.* to rummage;
fig. to stir up.

scornealǎ *sf.* concoction.

scorni *vt.* to invent.

scoroji *vr.* to shrivel; to be dried.

scorpie *sf. zool.* scorpion. *fig.*
shrew.

scorpion *sm.* scorpion.

scorţişoarǎ *sf.* cinnamon.

scotoci *vt.* to rummage. *vi.*, *vr.*
to rummage; to fumble (in
one's pocket, etc.).

scoţian *sm.* Scot(sman). *adj.* Scottish.

scoţianǎ *sf.* Scot(woman).

scrie *vt.*, *vi.* to write; *a ~ cu*
creionul to (write in) pencil;
a ~ la maşinǎ to type. *vr.*
to be spelt.

scriere *sf.* writing.

scriitor *sm.* writer.

scrimǎ *sf.* fencing.

scrin *sn.* chest-of-drawers.

scripete *sm.* pulley.

scripturǎ *sf.* the Holy Scriptures.

scris *sn.* (hand)writing; *(cali-*
grafie şi) hand.

scrisoare *sf.* letter; *scrisori de*
acreditare credentials.

scrînti *vt.* to sprain; *a o ~* to
make a blunder. *vr.* to grow
potty.

scrîntit *adj.* sprained; *(nebun)*
crazy.

scrîşni *vi.* to gnash one's teeth.

scroafǎ *sf.* sow.

scrobealǎ *sf.* starch.

scrobi *vt.* to starch.

scrum *sn.* ashes.

scrumbie *sf.* mackerel; *(afumatǎ*
şi) bloater; *(sǎratǎ şi)* kipper.

scrumierǎ *sf.* ash tray.

scrupul *sn.* scruple; *fǎrǎ ~e*
unscrupulous(ly).

scrupulos *adj.* scrupulous. *adv.*
carefully.

scruta *vt.* to scan.

scrutǎtor *adi.* searching.

scrutin *sn.* ballot (count).

scuar *sn.* square.

scufiţǎ *sf.* cap; *Scufiţa Roşie*
Little Red Riding Hood.

scufunda *vt.*, *vr.* to sink.

scuipa *vt.*, *vi.* to spit.

scuipat *sn.* spit(tle).

scuipǎtoare *sf.* spittoon.

scula *vt.* to wake. *vr.* to rise;
(în picioare) to stand up.

sculǎ *sf.* tool.

sculpta *vt.* to sculpture.

sculptor *sm.* sculptor.

sculptural *adj.* sculptural.

sculpturǎ *sf.* sculpture.

scump *adj.* dear; *(costisitor şi)*
expensive; *(preţios)* valuable;
(zgîrcit) miserly. *adv.* dearly.

scumpete *sf.* dearness; *(persoa-*
nǎ) jewel.

scumpi *vt.* to (put) up the price
of. *vr.* to grow dearer; to
grudge the expense of a thing.

scund *adj.* dumpy.

scurge *vt.* to drain; *(a filtra)*
to strain. *vr.* to flow; *(cîte puţin)*
to trickle; *(picǎturǎ cu picǎ-*
turǎ) to drip; *(d. vreme)* to
elapse.

scurgere *sf.* trickling; *(a timpu-*
lui) lapse.

scurma *vt.* to (g)rout.

scurt *adj.* short; *fig. şi* brief;

(redus) little; *(d. fustă* etc.*)* skimpy; *din* ～ tightly; *în ～ă vreme* soon afterwards; *pe ～* tersely. *adv.* briefly.

scurta *vt., vr.* to shorten.

scut *sn.* shield.

scutec *sn.* swaddling band; *pl. și* swaddling clothes.

scuter *sn.* (motor) scooter.

scuti *vt.* to spare (from).

scutire *sf.* sparing; exemption (from taxes, etc.).

scutura *vt.* to shake; *(covoare și)* tò dust; *(a critica)* to censure. *vi.* to tidy up. *vr.* to be shaken.

scuturătură *sf.* shake.

scuza *vt.* to excuse; *scuzați(-mă)!* I beg your pardon! *vr.* to apologize.

scuzabil *adj.* pardonable.

scuză *sf.* excuse.

se *pron.* oneself; himself, etc.; *(impersonal)* it; *(reciproc)* each other.

seamă *sf.* account; *(cantitate)* lot; *o ～ de* many; *de bună ～* of course; *de o ～* of the same age; *de ～* remarkable.

seamăn *sm.* neighbour; *fără ～* matchless.

seara *adv.* in the evening.

seară *sf.* evening; *(tîrzie)* night; *(înserare)* nightfall; *într-o ～* one evening.

searbăd *adv.* flat, vapid.

sec *adj.* dry; *(arid)* barren; *(gol)* empty. *adv.* drily.

seca *vt.* to drain; *(a usca)* to dry. *vi.* to run dry; *fig.* to be exhausted.

secară *sf.* rye.

secătui *vt.* to drain.

secătură *sf.* good-for-nothing.

seceră *sf.* sickle.

secerător *sm.* reaper.

seceriș *sn.* reaping; *(recoltare și)* harvest.

secesiune *sf.* secession.

secetă *sf.* drought.

secetos *adj.* droughty.

sechestra *vt.* to sequester.

sechestru *sn.* distraint.

secol *sn.* century; *(epocă)* age.

secret *sn.* secret; *în ～* secretly. *adj.* secret. *adv.* secretly.

secretar *sm.,* **secretară** *sf.* secretary; *～ general* secretary general.

secretariat *sn.* secretariate.

sectar *sm.* illiberal person. *adj.* illiberal. *adv.* in a sectarian way.

sectă *sf.* sect.

sector *sn.* sector; *fig. și* province.

secție *sf.* section; *(de miliție)* militia station.

secțiune *sf.* section.

secui *sm.,* **secuiesc** *adj.* Szekler.

secular *adj.* secular; *(vechi și)* century old.

seculariza *vt.* to secularize.

secund *sm.* second; *mar.* first mate. *adj.* second(ary).

secundar *sn.* second hand. *adj.* secondary.

secundă *sf.* second.

secure *sf.* axe.

securit *sm.* safety glass.

securitate *sf.* security; *(siguranță și)* safety; *～a muncii* labour safety.

sediu *sn.* headquarters.

seducător *sm.* seducer. *adj.* seductive. *adv.* seductively.

seduce *vt.* to seduce.

seducție *sf.* seduction.

segment *sm. tehn.* piston ring. *sn.* segment.

segrega *vt.* to segregate.

segregare, segregaţie *sf.* segregation; *(în Africa de Sud)* apartheid. '

select *adj.* select, choice.

selecta *vt.* to select.

selecţie *sf.* choice.

selecţiona *vt.* to select; to pick; *sport* to spot.

semafor *sn.* semaphore; *(pe stradă)* traffic light(s).

semantic *adj.* semantic.

semantică *sf.* semantics.

semăna *vt.* to sow; *fig. şi* to spread. *vi.* to sow; *(cu cineva)* to be alike; to resemble *(smb.)*.

semănat *sn.* sowing (time).

semănătoare *sf.* seeder.

semănător *sm.* sower.

semănătură *sf.* sown field; *pl.* crops.

semestrial *adj., adv.* half-yearly.

semestru *sn.* half-year, term.

semeţ *adj.* haughty. *adv.* haughtily.

semeţie *sf.* haughtiness.

semicerc *sn.* semicircle.

semilună *sf.* half moon.

seminar *sn.* seminar; *rel.* seminary.

semit *sm., adj.* Semite.

semiton *sn.* semitone.

semn *sn.* sign; *(simbol)* token; *(urmă şi)* mark, trace; *(semnal)* signal; ~ *bun* good omen *sau* auspices; ~ *de exclamaţie* exclamation mark; ~*e de punctuaţie* punctuation marks; ~ *de întrebare* note of interrogation; ~*e particulare* peculiarities; ~ *rău* bad omen; *în* ~ *de*

(protest etc.*)* in (protest. etc.); *pe* ~*e* probably.

semna *vt.* to sign.

semnal *sn.* signal; *(semn)* sign; ~ *de alarmă* emergency signal.

semnala *vt.* to point out. *vr.* to be recorded.

semnaliza *vi.* to signal.

semnalmente *sn. pl.* personal description.

semnare *sf.* conclusion (of a treaty, etc.).

semnatar *sm.* signatory (to a treaty).

semnătură *sf.* signature.

semnificativ *adj.* meaningful; *(important)* important. *adv.* significantly.

semnificaţie *sf.* significance; *(înţeles şi)* signification.

senat *sn.* senate (house).

senator *sm.* senator.

senil *sm.* dodderer. *adj.* senile.

senin *sn.* clear sky; *fig.* serenity; *din* ~ out of the blue. *adj.* serene; *(fără nori şi)* clear.

seninătate *sf.* serenity.

senior *sm.* feudal lord. *adj.* senior.

sens *sn.* meaning; sense; *(direcţie)* direction; ~ *giratoriu* rotary, merry-go-round; ~ *interzis* no entry; ~ *propriu* literal sense; ~ *unic* one-way traffic; *fără* ~ useless; *în* ~*ul acelor de ceasornic* clockwise; *în* ~ *invers acelor de ceasornic* counter-clockwise.

sensibil *adj.* sensitive; *(considerabil)* palpable; ~ *la* alive to. *adv.* appreciably.

sensibilitate *sf.* sensitiveness.

sentiment *sn.* feeling, sentiment; *fără* ~*(e)* callous.

sentimental *sm.* sentimentalist;

peior. milksop. *adj.* sentimental; *(dulceag)* soppy. *adv.* sentimentally.

sentimentalism *sn.* sentimentalism ; *peior.* mawkishness.

sentinţă *sf.* sentence.

senzaţie *sf.* sensation ; ·*de* ~ sensational.

senzaţional *adj.* sensational.

senzual *sm.* sensualist. *adj.* sensual.

separa *vt., vr.* to separate (from).

separat *adj.* separate(d). *adv.* separately.

separaţie *sf.* separation.

sepie *sf. zool.* cuttle-fish.

septembrie *sm.* September.

ser *sn.* serum.

serafim *sm.* seraph.

serai *sn.* seraglio.

seral *adj.* evening.

serată *sf.* soirée.

seră *sf.* green house ; hot house.

serba *vt.* to celebrate. *vr.* to be celebrated.

serenadă *sf.* serenade.

sergent *sm.* non-com ; policeman ; ~-*major* senior sergeant.

sericicultură *sf.* seri(ci)culture.

serial *sn.* serial story.

serie *sf.* series ; *cinema* part ; *în* ~ serial(ly).

seringă *sf.* syringe.

serios *sn.* seriousness ; *în* ~ seriously. *adj.* earnest ; *(grav)* serious ; *(adevărat)* real. *adv.* earnestly ; *(grav)* seriously.

seriozitate *sf.* earnestness ; *(gravitate)* seriousness.

serpentină *sf.* winding (road) ; *tehn.* coil ; *în* ~ winding, meandering.

sertar *sn.* drawer.

servantă *sf.* sideboard ; *(pe roa-*

te) dumb waiter ; *(servitoare)* maid (servant).

servi *vt.* to serve (for) ; *(la masă)* to wait on ; to help (to a dish) ; *(un client şi)* to attend to. *vi.* to serve. *vr.* to help oneself ; *a se* ~ *de* to use.

serviabil *adj.* obliging.

serviciu *sn.* service ; *(slujbă şi)* job ; *(chelner* etc.*)* attendance ; *(adus cuiva)* (good) turn ; *(birou)* department ; *de* ~ on duty ; *(d. scară* etc.*)* back ; *fig.* routine, perfunctory ; *în* ~*l cuiva* at smb.'s service.

servietă *sf.* brief case.

servil *adj.* servile. *adv.* servilely.

servitoare *sf.* maid (servant) ; *şi pl.* help ; *(cu ziua)* daily ; *(la toate* char.

servitor *sm.* (man) servant.

sesiune *sf.* session.

sesiza *vt.* to grasp ; *(a remarca)* to note ; *(pe cineva)* to inform. *vr.* to take notice ; *(de ceva)* to realize.

sesizare *sf.* understanding ; *(informare)* intimation.

set *sn.* set ; *(de pulovere)* twin set.

sete *sf.* thirst ; *fig. şi* craving (for) ; *cu* ~ thirstily ; *fig.* eagerly ; spitefully.

setos *adj.* thirsty ; *fig. şi* eager ; ~ *de sînge* bloodthirsty.

seu *sn.* suet, tallow.

sevă *sf.* sap.

sever *adj.* hard ; *(ca atitudine şi)* severe ; *(rigid şi)* austere. *adv.* hard ; sternly.

severitate *sf.* severity ; *(stricteţe)* strictness ; *(asprime)* sternness.

sex *sn.* sex ; ~*ul frumos* sau *slab* the fair *sau* gentle sex.

sexual *adj.* sexual.

sexualitate *sf.* sex.

sezon *sn.* season; ~ *mort* slack time; *de* ~ in season.

sezonier *adj.* seasonal.

sfadă *sf.* quarrel.

sfat *sn.* counsel; *(consfătuire)* conference; ~ *popular* people's council.

sfărîma *vt.* to crush. *vr.* to break (into pieces).

sfărîmătură *sf.* fragment; *pl.* débris.

sfărîmicios *adj.* brittle.

sfătui *vt.* to advise. *vr.* to put heads together; *a se* ~ *cu* to consult.

sfătuitor *sm.* adviser.

sfeclă *sf.* beet; ~ *de zahăr* sugar beet.

sfecli *vt.*: *a o* ~ to be in a blue funk.

sferă *sf.* sphere.

sfert *sn.* quarter.

sfeşnic *sn.* candlestick.

sfetnic *sm.* counsellor.

sfială *sf.* shyness.

sfida *vt.* to defy. *vi.* to be defiant.

sfidare *sf.* defiance.

sfidător *adj.* challenging.

sfii *vr.* to be timid; *a se* ~ *să* not to find it in oneself to (do smth.).

sfinţenie *sf.* holiness; *cu* ~ piously; *(exact)* scrupulously.

sfinţi *vt.* to hallow.

sfinx *sm.* sphinx.

sfios *adj.* bashful.

sfînt *sm.* saint. *adj.* holy.

sfîrc *sn.* nipple, teat; *(al urechii)* lobe; *(al biciului)* lash.

sfîrîi *vi.* to sizzle.

sfîrşeală *sf.* exhaustion.

sfîrşi *vt.* to (bring to an) end. *vi.* to cease; *a* ~ *cu ceva* to put an end to smth.; *a* ~ *cu cineva* to break off with smb. *vr.* to run short; to cease.

sfîrşit *sn.* end(ing); *(moarte)* death; *fără* ~ endless(ly); *în* ~ at last; *la* ~ in the end; *la* ~*ul* ... at the close of ... ; *pe* ~*e* nearly over. *adj.* exhausted.

sfîrtica *vt.* to mangle.

sfîşia *vt.* to tear; *a* ~ *inima cuiva* to break smb.' s heart.

sfîşietor *adj.* (heart-)rending.

sfoară *sf.* string; ~ *de moşie* a plot of land.

sforăi *vi.* to snore; *(d. cai)* to snort.

sforăială *sf.*, **sforăit** *sn.* snoring, snore.

sforăitor *adj.* snor(t)ing; *fig.* blatant.

sforărie *sf.* plot(ting).

sforţa *vr.* to strain (oneself).

sforţare *sf.* exertion.

sfredel *sn.* gimlet; *(mare)* auger.

sfredeli *vt.* to drill.

sfredelitor *adj.* piercing; *(d. ochi şi)* gimlet.

sfrijit *adj.* scrawny.

sfruntat *adj.* shameless.

si *sm. muz.* B sau H, si.

siamez *sm., adj.*, **siameză** *sf., adj.* Siamese.

sicilian *sm., adj.*, **siciliană** *sf., adj.* Sicilian.

sicriu *sn.* coffin; *amer.* casket.

sidef *sn.* mother-of-pearl.

siderurgic *adj.* iron-and-steel.

siderurgie *sf.* metallurgy.

sieşi *pron.* to oneself.

sifilis *sn.* syphilis; pox.

sifon *sn.* siphon (bottle); *(apă gazoasă)* soda (water).

sigila *vt.* to seal (up).

sigiliu *sn.* seal; *(la inel)* signet; *fig.* stamp.

sigur *adj.* sure; positive; *(convins)* convinced; *(de încredere)* reliable, trustworthy; *(în afară de pericol)* safe; secure. *adv.* certainly, for sure.

siguranţă *sf.* safety, security; *(convingere)* certitude; *ist.* security police; *el.* fuse; *cu ~* doubtlessly; *de ~* safety; *în ~* safe(ly).

sihastru *sm.* hermit. *adj.* recondite.

sihăstrie *sf.* hermitage.

silabă *sf.* syllable.

silabisi *vt.* to syllabify; *(în engleză)* to spell.

silă *sf.* loathing; force; *cu de-a sila* forcibly; *în ~* reluctantly.

sili *vt.* to compel. *vr.* to take pains.

silinţă *sf.* effort, assiduity.

silit *adj.* constrained.

silitor *adj.* hard-working.

silnic *adj.* forced; *muncă ~ă* hard labour.

siloz *sn.* silo.

siluetă *sf.* outline; *(corp)* figure.

silui *vt.* to rape.

silvic *adj.* forest.

silvicultură *sf.* forestry.

simbol *sn.* symbol.

simbolic *adj.* symbolic(al). *adv.* symbolically.

simbolism *sn.* symbolism.

simboliza *vt.* to signify.

simbrie *sf.* pay.

simetric *adj.* symmetrical.

simetrie *sf.* symmetry.

simfonic *adj.* symphonic.

simfonie *sf.* symphony.

similar *adj.* similar (to).

simpatic *adj.* nice; *anat., chim* sympathetic. *adv.* agreeably

simpatie *sf.* liking; *(înţelegere)* understanding; *(persoană)* sweetheart.

simpatiza *vt.* to like.

simplifica *vt.* to simplify. *vr.* to become simple.

simplist *adj.* over-simplified.

simplitate *sf.* simplicity; *(naivitate)* simple-mindedness.

simplu *adj.* simple; elementary; *(obişnuit)* common; *(fără altceva)* mere; *(modest)* plain; *(uşor)* easy. *adv.* simply, plainly; merely; naturally.

simpozion *sn.* symposium.

simptom *sn.* symptom.

simptomatic *adj.* symptomatic (of).

simţ *sn.* sense; *~ul ridicolului* sense of humour; *bun-~* common sense, mother wit.

simţămînt *sn.* feeling; sensation.

simţi *vt.* to feel; *(a adulmeca)* to scent. *vr.* to feel; to be (felt); *a se ~ bine* to feel all right; *cum te mai ~?* how are you?

simţire *sf.* feeling; *(conştienţă)* consciousness; *fără ~* unconscious.

simţit *adj.* felt; *(manierat)* well--bred.

simţitor *adj.* sensitive.

simula *vt., vi.* to feign.

simulacru *sn.* semblance.

simultan *adj.* simultaneous. *adv.* concomitantly.

simultaneitate *sf.* concomitance.

simun *sn.* simoom.

sinagogă *sf.* synagogue.

sincer *adj.* sincere, frank, open-
-hearted; *(adevărat)* heart-
-felt, cordial, genuine. *adv.* sin-
cerely, frankly.

sinceritate *sf.* sincerity, frank-
ness.

sinchisi *vr.* to care; *a se ~ de*
to mind, to heed.

sincroniza *vt.* to synchronize.

sindical *adj.* trade union.

sindicat *sn.* (trade) union; *~*
patronal syndicate.

sine *pron.* oneself; *de la ~*
naturally.

sinea *sf.: în ~ mea* to myself,
inwardly.

sinecură *sf.* sinecure.

singular *sn., adj.* singular; *la*
~ in the singular.

singur *adj.* only; lonely; *(unic)*
single; *(folosit predicativ)* alone;
(însumi etc.) (by) myself, yourself, etc.

singuratic *adj.* lonely.

singurătate *sf.* solitude.

sinistrat *sm.* victim (of calamity). *adj.* suffering from calamity.

sinistru *sn.* catastrophe. *adj.*
sinister; *(înfiorător)* gruesome
adv. lugubriously.

sinonim *sn.* synonym. *adj.* synon-
ymous.

sintactic *adj.* syntactical. *adv.*
syntactically.

sintaxă *sf.* syntax.

sintetic *adj.* synthetic. *adv.*
synthetically.

sintetiza *vt.* to synthesize.

sinucide *vr.* to commit suicide.

sinucidere *sf.* self-slaughter.

sinucigaş *sm.* suicide.

sionism *sn.* Zionism.

sirenă *sf.* siren; *mit. şi* mermaid; *(fluier şi)* hooter.

sirop *sn.* syrup; *~ de tuse*
linctus.

siropos *adj.* syrupy; *fig.* mawkish.

sista *vt.* to cease.

sistem *sn.* system.

sistematic *adj.* systematic. *adv.*
methodically.

sistematiza *vt.* to system(at)ize.

sitar *sm.* woodcock.

sită *sf.* sieve; *(mare)* screen.

sitronadă *sf.* lemon squash.

situa *vt.* to place. *vr.* to take a
place *sau* stand.

situat *adj.* situated; *bine ~*
well located; *fig.* in easy
circumstances.

situaţie *sf.* situation; *(stare*
şi) condition; *(raport)* account;
~ dificilă sau *proastă* sorry
plight.

sîcîi *vt.* to pester.

sîmbăta *adv.* on Saturday(s).

sîmbătă *sf.* Saturday. *adv.* on
Saturday.

sîmbure *sm.* kernel; *(mare)*
stone; *(mic)* pip; *(miez şi)*
core; *un ~ de adevăr* a grain
of truth.

sîn *sm.* breast; *pl. fig. şi* bosom;
în ~ in one's bosom.

sînge *sn.* blood; *(închegat)* gore;
cu ~ rece cold-blooded; in
cold blood.

sîngera *vi.* to bleed.

sîngeros *adj.* sanguinary; *(cri-*
minal şi) bloodthirsty.

sîrb *sm., adj.* Serbian.

sîrbă *sf.* lively Romanian folk
dance.

sîrg sn.: cu ~ industriously.
sîrguincios adj. diligent, hard--working. adv. sedulously.
sîrguinţă sf. diligence.
sîrmă sf. wire.
sîrmos adj. wiry.
sîsîi vi. to hiss; (a vorbi peltic) to lisp.
slab adj. weak; (fără grăsime) lean; (subţire) thin; (fără vlagă şi) feeble; (prost) poor; ~ de înger faint-hearted. adv. weakly; poorly.
slalom sn. slalom; ~ uriaş giant slalom.
slav sm., adj., slavă sf., adj. Slav; (d. limbă şi) Slavonic.
slavă sf. glory; ~ Domnului! thank God! în slava cerului in the heights.
slavon adj. Slavonic; (d. alfabet) Cyrillic.
slăbănog sm. weakling. adj. weedy.
slăbi vt. to loosen; (pe cineva) to leave alone, not to bother; a nu ~ din ochi to watch closely. vi. to lose flesh; (prin tratament) to reduce; (a scădea) to abate, to decrease.
slăbiciune sf. weakness; (debilitate şi) feebleness; (lipsă şi) shortcoming; (punct nevralgic) raw spot.
slăbire sf. weakening; (cură) reducing.
slăbit adj. weak(ened).
slănină sf. (grasă) lard; (slabă) bacon.
slăvi vt. to extol.
slăvit adj. exalted.
slei vt. to freeze; (de puteri) to drain. vr. to freeze; (a se epuiza) to be exhausted.

sleit adj. frozen; (îngroşat) thickened; (istovit) drained.
slip sn. slips.
slobod adj. free.
slobozi vt. to release; (a elibera) to free; (a arunca) to throw; (o exclamaţie) to utter.
sloi sn. ice floe.
slovac sm., adj., slovacă sf., adj. Slovak(ian).
slovă sf. letter; word.
slugarnic adj. cringing.
slugă sf. servant; peior. flunkey.
slugări vi. to serve.
slugărnicie sf. obsequiousness.
sluj sn.: a sta sau face ~ to sit up (on one's hind legs); fig. to cringe.
slujbaş sm. clerk.
slujbă sf. service; (funcţie şi) job; fără ~ out of a job
sluji vt., vi. to serve. vr.: a se ~ de to use.
slut adj. ugly.
sluţi vt. to make ugly; (a mutila) to disfigure. vr. to make grimaces.
smalţ sn. enamel.
smaragd sn. emerald.
smălţui vt. to enamel; fig. to fleck (with flowers, etc.).
smead adj. swarthy.
smerenie sf. meekness; (evlavie) piety.
smerit adj. humble. adv. meekly.
sminteală sf. lunacy; (pagubă) harm.
sminti vt. to trouble; a ~ în bătaie to beat (smb.) to pulp. vr. to run mad.
smintit adj. potty.
smiorcăi vr. to snivel; (a plinge) to whimper.

smirna *adv.* rigidly ; *mil.* to attention.

smirnă *sf.* myrrh.

smîntînă *sf.* cream.

smîrc *sn.* swamp.

smoală *sf.* tar ; *ca smoala* as dark as pitch.

smoc *sn.* tuft.

smochin *sm.* fig(-tree).

smochină *sf.* fig.

smoching *sn.* smoking jacket.

smuci *vt.* to jerk. *vr.* to struggle.

smucitură *sf.* jerk.

smulge *vt.* to pull out ; *(a smuci)* to snatch ; *fig. vr.* to wrest away ; *(a se elibera)* to break loose.

snoavă *sf.* anecdote.

snob *sm.* snob.

snobism *sn.* snobbery.

snop *sm.* sheaf.

snopi *vt.* to thrash.

soacră *sf.* mother-in-law.

soare *sm.* sun ; ~ *apune* West ; sunset ; ~ *răsare* East ; sunrise.

soartă *sf.* fate ; *(fatalitate)* Fatum.

sobă *sf.* stove ; *(cuptor)* oven ; *(cămin)* fireplace.

sobrietate *sf.* sobriety ; *(cumpătare)* temperance.

sobru *adj.* austere ; *(solemn)* solemn. *adv.* temperately.

soc *sm.* elder tree.

sociabil *adj.* sociable.

social *adj.* social ; ~ *-cultural* socio-cultural ; ~ *-democrat* social democrat(ic).

socialism *sn.* socialism.

socialist *sm., adj.* socialist.

socializa *vt.* to socialize.

societate *sf.* society ; *pol. şi* (social) system ; *(asociaţie şi)* association ; *com.* company.

sociolog *sm.* sociologist.

sociologie *sf.* sociology.

soclu *sn.* socle.

socoteală *sf.* reckoning ; *com.* addition ; *(chibzuinţă)* consideration ; *(economie)* thrift ; *cu* ~ thoughtful(ly) ; *după socotelile mele* in my opinion ; *fără* ~ inconsiderate(ly) ; *pe socoteala cuiva* at smb.'s expense.

socoti *vt.* to reckon ; *fig.* to consider ; *a* ~ *greşit* to miscalculate. *vi.* to reckon. *vr.* to think oneself (better, etc.) ; to settle accounts (with smb.).

socotit *adj.* reckoned ; *(econom)* thrifty ; *(chibzuit)* moderate.

socru *sm.* father-in-law ; *pl.* parents-in-law.

sodă *sf.* (washing) soda ; ~ *caustică* sodium hydroxide.

sodiu *sn.* sodium.

sofa *sf.* sofa.

soi *sn.* kind ; *(rasă)* race ; ~ *bun* a fine character ; ~ *rău* a bad lot *sau* egg ; *de* ~ fine.

soia *sf.* soy(beans).

soios *adj.* filthy.

sol *sm. (mesager)* messenger ; *muz.* G, sol. *sn.* soil ; *(pămînt şi)* earth.

solar *sn.* solarium. *adj.* solar.

sold *sn.* balance ; *(vînzare)* clearance sale.

solda *vt.* to sell off. *vr.: a se* ~ *cu* to end *sau* result in.

soldat *sm.* soldier ; *(ca grad)* private ; *fig.* champion.

soldă *sf.* pay.

solemn *adj.* solemn ; *(grav)* serious. *adv.* solemnly.

solemnitate *sf.* solemnity.

solfegiu *sn.* sol-fa.

solicita *vt.* to require; *fig.* to challenge; *(a necesita)* to entail.

solicitant *sm.* applicant.

solicitare *sf.* challenge.

solicitudine *sf.* sòlicitude.

solid *sn.* solid (body); *pl.* solid food. *adj.* solid; *fig. și* sound. *adv.* solidly; *fig.* thoroughly.

solidar *adj.* solid(ary). *adv.* jointly.

solidaritate *sf.* solidarity.

solidariza *vr.: a se ~ cu* to declare solidary with, to make common cause with.

soliditate *sf.* solidity; *(înțelepciune)* soundness.

solie *sf.* deputation; message.

solist *sm.* soloist.

solitar *sm.* anchorite. *sn.* solitaire (diamond). *adj.* solitary.

solniță *sf.* salt cellar.

solo *sn.* solo.

soluție *sf.* solution.

soluționa *vt.* to solve. *vr.* to be settled.

solz *sm.* scale.

soma *vt.* to summon.

somieră *sf.* spring *sau* box mattress.

somitate *sf.* authority.

somn *sm. iht.* sheat fish. *sn.* sleep; *(odihnă)* rest; *(scurt)* nap; *(toropeală)* slumber; *~ul de veci* the sleep of the brave; *~ ușor!* sweet dreams!

somnambul *sm.* somnambulist.

somnifer *sn.* soporific; sleep pill. *adj.* soporific.

somnolență *sf.* slumber.

somnoros *sm.* sleepy person. *adj.* sleepy, drowsy. *adv.* in a sleepy voice.

somon *sm.* salmon.

somptuos *adj.* sumptuous.

sonată *sf.* sonata.

sonda *vt.* to sound; *mar. fig. și* to fathom.

sondă *sf. (de petrol)* well; *mar.* sounding lead; *med.* probe.

sondaj *sn.* test.

sonerie *sf.* (electric) bell.

sonet *sn.* sonnet.

sonor *adj.* sonorous; *(tare)* loud; *(d. consoane și)* voiced. *adv.* sonorously.

sonoritate *sf.* sonorousness.

soprană *sf.* soprano.

soră *sf.* sister; *(călugăriță și)* nun; *(de caritate)* (medical) nurse; *~ de lapte* foster sister; *~ vitregă* step *sau* half sister.

sorbi *vt.* to drink; *(cîte o gură)* to sip; *a ~ cuvintele cuiva* to hang on smb.'s lips; *a ~ din ochi* to feast one's eyes upon.

sorbitură *sf.* draught.

sorcovă *sf.* bouquet used for New Year's wishes.

sorcovi *vt.* to wish (smb.) a Happy New Year.

sordid *adj.* squalid.

soroc *sn.* term.

sort *sn.* sort.

sorta *vt.* to sort.

sorti *vt.* to (pre)destine.

sortiment *sn.* assortment.

sorți *sm. pl.* odds.

sos *sn.* sauce; *(de friptură)* gravy; *~ picant* ketchup.

sosi *vi.* to arrive.

sosire *sf.* arrival; *sport* finish.

soț *sm. (bărbat)* husband; *(unul din parteneri)* spouse; *pl.* couple; *cu ~* even; *fără ~* odd.

soție *sf*. wife.
soviet *sn*. Soviet.
sovietic *sm*. Soviet citizen. *adj*.
Soviet...
sovîrf *sm*. common marjoram.
spadasin *sm*. swordsman; *(uci-gaș)* desperado.
spadă *sf*. sword.
spaghete *sf*. *pl*. spaghetti.
spaimă *sf*. fear.
spanac *sn*. spinach; *fig*. rubbish.
spaniol *sm*. Spaniard. *adj*. Span-ish.
spaniolă *sf*. Spanish (woman).
sparanghel *sm*. asparagus.
sparge *vt*. to break; *(a zdrobi)*
to smash; *(lemne)* to chop;
(nuci etc.*)* to crack; *a-și ~*
capul to get one's head bro-ken; *fig*. to rack one's brains
(about smth.); *a ~ casa*
cuiva to break into smb's
house; *fig*. to wreck smb.'s
marriage; *a-și ~ pieptul* to
waste one's breath. *vi*. to
break open. *vr*. to break, to
burst.
spargere *sf*. breaking; *(furt)*
burglary.
spart *sn*. breaking; *la ~ul*
tîrgului after the fair. *adj*.
broken; *(răgușit și)* hoarse.
spate *sn*. back; *(umeri)* shoul-ders; *mil*. *(tehnica ~lui)* log-istics; *fig*. prop; *~ în ~*
back to back; *în ~le...* at
the back of...
spațial *adj*. space...
spațios *adj*. roomy.
spațiu *sn*. space; *(gol)* gap;
~ locativ floor space; hous-ing office; *~ cosmic* outer
space; *~ verde* open space,
lung (of the town).

spăla *vt*. to wash; *(vasele)* to
wash up; *(rufe și)* to launder.
vi. to wash. *vr*. to wash
(oneself); *(d. rufe* etc.*)* to
launder (well, etc.); *a se ~*
pe mîini etc. to wash one's
hands, etc.
spălat *sn*. washing; laundering.
adj. washed; *fig*. civilized.
spălăcit *adj*. watery; *fig*. dull.
spălător *sn*. washstand; *(ca-meră)* lavatory.
spălătoreasă *sf*. laundress.
spălătorie *sf*. wash-house.
spărgător *sm*. burglar; *~ de*
grevă scab, knobstick. *sn*. break-er; *~ de gheață* icebreaker;
~ de nuci nutcracker.
spărtură *sf*. breach.
spătar *sm*. sword bearer. *sn*. back.
spătos *adj*. broad-shouldered.
special *adj*. special; *în ~* es-pecially. *adv*. purpose(ful)ly.
specialist *sm*., *adj*. expert.
specialitate *sf*. specialty; *(bran-șă)* speciality.
specializa *vt*., *vr*. to specialize.
specie *sf*. species.
specific *sn*. specific nature. *adj*.
typical (of). *adv*. specifically.
specifica *vt*. to specify.
specimen *sn*. specimen.
specios *adj*. dubious, spurious.
spectacol *sn*. performance; show.
spectaculos *adj*. spectacular.
spectator *sm*. spectator; *pl*.
audience.
specula *vt*. to speculate.
speculant *sm*. speculator.
speculă *sf*. speculation.
spera *vt*., *vi*. to hope (for).
speranță *sf*. hope; expectation;
(încredere) confidence; *fără ~*
desperate(ly).

speria *vt.* to frighten. *vr.* to be scared.

sperietoare *sf.* scarecrow.

sperios *adj.* cowardly.

sperjur *sm.* perjurer. *sn.* perjury.

spetează *sf.* back (of a chair); *text.* crossbeam.

speti *vt.* to break the back of; to exhaust. *vr.* to break one's back; to be penniless.

speţă *sf.* case.

spic *sn.* ear.

spicher *sm.* announcer.

spicui *vt.* to glean; *fig. şi* to cull.

spilcuit *adj.* titivated, dressed to kill.

spin *sm.* thorn.

spinare *sf.* back.

spinos *adj.* thorny; *fig.* ticklish.

spinteca *vt.* to rip.

spion *sm.* spy.

spiona *vt.* to spy upon. *vi.* to spy.

spionaj *sn.* espionage.

spirală *sf.* spiral; în ~ winding.

spiriduş *sm.* elf.

spirit *sn.* spirit; *(minte)* mind; *(glumă)* witticism; *(geniu)* genius; *plin de* ~ ingenious; *(amuzant)* witty, brilliant.

spiritism *m.* spiritism.

spiritual *adj.* spiritual; *(nostim)* witty; *(deştept)* bright.

spirt *sn.* alcohol; ~ *denaturat* methylated spirits. *adj.* quick.

spirtos *adj.* alcoholic.

spital *sn.* hospital.

spiţă *sf.* spoke; *(neam)* relation.

spîn *sm.* glabrous man. *adj.* glabrous.

spînzura *vt.* to hang. *vi.* to hang (from). *vr.* to hang oneself.

spînzurat *sm.* gallows bird; *fig.* scapegrace. *adj.* hanged.

spînzurătoare *sf.* gallows.

splai *sn.* embankment.

splendid *adj.* splendid; *(strălucitor)* glorious. *adv.* splendidly.

splendoare *sf.* splendour.

splină *sf.* spleen.

spoi *vt.* to paint; *(a vărui)* to whitewash; *(a cositori)* to tin.

spoială *sf.* painting; *fig.* smattering.

spontan *adj.* spontaneous. *adv.* spontaneously.

spontaneitate *sf.* spontaneity.

spor *sm. bot.* spore. *sn.* efficiency; *(progres)* headway; *(folos)* use.

sporadic *adj.* sporadic. *adv.* sporadically.

spori *vt., vi.* to increase.

sporire *sf.* increase.

spornic *adj.* efficient; *(economic)* economical.

sporovăi *vi.* to prate.

sport *sn.* sport(s); ~*uri de iarnă* winter sports; ~*uri nautice* aquatic sports.

sportiv *sm.* sportsman. *adj.* sports; sporting.

sportivă *sf.* sportswoman.

spovedanie *sf.* confession.

spovedi *vr.* to confess (oneself).

spre *prep.* to(wards); *(temporal şi)* against; *(pe la)* about; *(pentru)* with a view to.

sprijin *sn.* support; *(ajutor şi)* help.

sprijini *vt.* to support; *(a propti şi)* to prop up. *vr.* to support (each other); *a se ~ pe* to lean upon; *fig.* to rely on.

sprinten *adj.* nimble. *adv.* quickly.

sprinţar *adj.* sprightly.

sprînceană *sf.* (eye)brow; *pe ~* partially; *ales pe ~* choice; selected.

spulbera *vt.* to sweep (away); *fig.* to dispel; *(visuri)* to shatter. *vr.* to end in smoke.

spumă *sf.* foam; *(albă şi)* froth; *(de supă)* scum; *~ de mare* meerschaum; *~ de săpun* soap suds; *(pt. bărbierit)* lather.

spumega *vi.* to foam.

spumos *adj.* foamy; *(d. vin)* frothy.

spune *vt.* to say; *(a relata)* to tell; *a ~ baliverne* to draw the long bow; *a ~ bazaconii* to talk through one's hat. *vi.* to say, to speak. *vr.* to be said; *se ~ că e plecat* he is said to be out of town; *mi s-a spus că...* I was told that...

spurcat *adj.* filthy; *(blestemat)* accursed.

spusă *sf.* statement; *după spusele lui* according to him.

sst *interj.* hush! hist!

sta *vi.* to stand; *(pe scaun)* to sit; *(a zăcea)* to lie; *(a locui)* to live; *(a se opri)* to stop; *a ~ bine cuiva* to sit well (to smb.); *cum stai cu sănătatea?* how are you?; *a ~ la baza (cu gen.)* to lie at the basis of...

stabil *adj.* stable; *(durabil şi)* lasting; *fig. şi* settled.

stabili *vt.* to establish; *(a afla)* to find out. *vr.* to settle (down); to establish oneself.

stabilit *adj.* settled.

stabilitate *sf.* stability.

stabilizare *sf.* stabilization; *fin.* currency reform.

stacojiu *adj.* scarlet.

stadion *sn.* stadium.

stadiu *sn.* stage.

stafidă *sf.* sultana; *(mică)* currant.

stafie *sf.* phantom.

stagiu *sn.* probation (period); *(vechime)* seniority.

stagiune *sf.* (theatrical) season.

stagna *vi.* to stagnate; *fig.* to flag.

stagnare *sf.* stagnation.

stal *sn.* stalls; *~ul doi* pit.

stalactită *sf.* stalactite.

stalagmită *sf.* stalagmite.

stambă *sf.* (printed) calico.

stampă *sf.* print.

stand *sn.* stall.

standard *sn., adj.* standard.

staniol *sn.* tinfoil.

stare *sf.* state; *(avere)* circumstances; *(şedere)* stay; *~ civilă* civil status; *(ca serviciu)* registrar's; *~ de asediu* state of emergency; *~ de spirit* frame of mind; *~ pe loc* immobility; *~ proastă* bad condition; *~ sufletească* mood; *în ~ bună* in good repair.

stareţ *sm.* abbot.

stareţă *sf.* abbess.

start *sn.* start.

stat *sn. pol.* state; *(listă)* list; *(statură)* stature; *~ de plată* pay roll; *~-major* general staff; *~ul bunăstării* the welfare state; *de ~* state; *mic de ~* small.

statistică *sf.* statistics.

statornic *adj.* steadfast; *(stabil și)* lasting. *adv.* steadily.
statuetă *sf.* statuette.
statuie *sf.* statue.
statură *sf.* stature.
statut *sn.* statute.
stație *sf.* station; *(de tramvai etc.)* stop; *(de taxiuri)* taxi rank.
staționa *vi.* to be stationed.
staționare *sf.* waiting; *mil.* stationing; *~a interzisă* no waiting.
stațiune *sf.* station; *~ balneară* spa; *~ climaterică sau ~ de odihnă* health resort; *~ de mașini și tractoare* machine and tractor station.
staul *sn.* stable.
stavilă *sf.* obstacle.
stăpîn *sm.* master; *(proprietar și)* owner.
stăpînă *sf.* mistress (of the house).
stăpîni *vt.* to master; *(a conduce)* to rule; *(a domina)* to dominate; *(a avea)* to own; *(a stăvili)* to restrain. *vi.* to sway. *vr.* to master one's temper, etc.
stăpînire *sf.* mastery; power; *(posesiune)* ownership; *(de sine)* self-possession *sau* control.
stăpînit *adj.* self-controlled; *~ de un gînd* thought-ridden.
stăpînitor *sm.* ruler. *adj.* ruling.
stărui *vi.* to insist; *(a rămîne)* to persist; *(asupra unui lucru și)* to dwell (on a thing); *(a dăinui și)* to linger.
stăruință *sf.* insistence; perseverance; *(proptea)* intercession.

stăruitor *adj.* persevering. *adv.* persistently.
stătător *adj.* stagnant; *de sine ~* independent.
stăvilar *sn.* weir.
stăvili *vt.* to dam; *fig.* to stem.
stea *sf.* star; *(asterisc)* asterisk; *mil. și* pip; *~ călăuzitoare* lode star; *~ua polară* the pole star; *fig.* one's lodestar; *cu ~ în frunte* remarkable.
steag *sn.* *(național)* flag; *mil. și* colours; *(stindard și fig.)* banner.
stejar *sm.* oak tree.
stelaj *sn.* shelves.
steluță *sf.* little star; *(asterisc)* asterisk.
stemă *sf.* (coat of) arms.
stenodactilografă *sf.* stenotypist.
stenograf *sm.*, **stenografă** *sf.* stenographer.
stenografia *vt.* to take down in shorthand.
stenografie *sf.* shorthand (writing).
stenogramă *sf.* minutes.
stepă *sf.* steppe.
stereofonic *adj.* stereophonic.
stereotip *adj.* stereotype(d); *fig. și* corny.
steril *sn.* barren gangue. *adj.* sterile.
sterlină *adj.*: *liră ~* pound sterling.
sterp *adj.* barren.
sticlă *sf.* glass; *(de geam)* window pane; *(clondir)* bottle; *(mică)* phial; *(de lampă)* chimney; *~ cu apă* bottle of water; *~ de ceas* watch glass; *~ de vin* wine bottle; *~ mată* matted glass; *de ~* glass(y).

sticlărie *sf.* glassware.
sticlete *sm.* thistlefinch.
stieli *vi.* to glitter.
sticlos *adj.* glassy.
sticluţă *sf.* vial.
stil *sn.* style; ~ *familiar* collo-quial style; *de* ~ period; *în* ~ *mare* grandly.
stilistic *adj.* stylistic.
stiliza *vt.* to brush up, to edit; *artă* to stylize.
stilou *sn.* fountain pen; *(cu pastă)* ball pen, byro.
stima *vt.* to esteem.
stimabil *sm., adj.* honourable.
stimat *adj.* respected; ~*e domn* dear sir.
stimă *sf.* esteem; *cu* ~ yours respectfully.
stimula *vt.* to stimulate.
stimulent *sn.* stimulent.
stingător *sn.* fire extinguisher.
stinge *vt.* *(focul, lumina)* to put out; *(de la întrerupător)* to switch off; *(o datorie)* to pay off; *(varul)* to slake. *vr.* to die (out).
stingere *sf.* extinction; *mil.* taps.
stingher *adj.* alien; *(singuratic)* lonely.
stinghereală *sf.* embarrassment.
stingheri *vt.* to embarrass.
stins *adj.* extinguished; *(slab)* faint. *adv.* faintly.
stipula *vt.* to stipulate.
stivă *sf.* stack.
stîlci *vt.* *(a bate)* to pommel; *(a schilodi)* to cripple; *(o limbă)* to mangle; *(un cuvînt)* to corrupt.
stîlp *sm.* pillar; post; ~ *de cafenea* a man about town; ~*ul bătrîneţilor cuiva* smb.'s support in old age.

stînă *sf.* sheepfold.
stîncă *sf.* rock; *(colţuroasă)* crag; *(faleză)* cliff; *(recif)* reef.
stîncos *adj.* rocky.
stîng *sn.* left leg; *fig.* wrong leg. *adj.* left; *pol. şi* left wing.
stînga *sf.* left hand; *pol.* the left; ~ *împrejur mil.* left about!
stîngaci *sm.* left-handed person. *adj.* left-handed; *fig. şi* clumsy. *adv.* clumsily.
stîngăcie *sf.* clumsiness.
stîngism *sn.* left-wing commu-nism.
stîngist *sm., adj.* leftist.
stînjen *sm.* fathom; *bot.* iris.
stînjeneală *sf.* uneasiness.
stînjenel *sm.* iris.
stînjeni *vt.* to inconvenience.
stîrc *sm.* heron.
stîrni *vt.* to (a)rouse. *vr.* to break out.
stîrpitură *sf.* midget.
stoarce *vt.* to squeeze; *(rufe)* to wring; *fig.* to drain; *(bani)* to extort; *(pe cineva)* to fleece; *a* ~ *lacrimi* to bring tears (in) to smb.'s eyes.
stoc *sn.* stock.
stoca *vt.* to stock(pile).
stofă *sf.* stuff; *(ţesătură şi)* material; ~ *ecosez* tartan-cloth, plaid.
stoic *sm.* stoic. *adj.* stoical. *adv.* stoically.
stoicism *sn.* stoicism.
stol *sn.* flock, flight, bevy.
stomac *sn.* stomach; *zool. şi fig.* paunch.
stomatologie *sf.* stomatology.
stop *sn.* traffic light(s). *interj.* stop!

stopa *vt.* to stop; *(ciorapi* etc.*)* to close-darn.

stor *sn.* (roller) blind.

stors *sn.* wringing (of washing). *adj.* wrung out; *(istovit)* drained.

strachină *sf.* bowl, dish.

stradă *sf.* street; ~ *dosnică* sau *laterală* by-street; ~ *mare* main street; *pe* ~ in the street.

strajă *sf.* watch.

strană *sf.* pew; *(a dascălilor)* lectern.

strangula *vt.* to strangle.

straniu *adj.* strange. *adv.* queerly.

strapontin *sn.* bracket seat.

stras *sn.* rhinestone; *pl.* costume jewelry.

straşnic *adj.* terrible; *(oribil)* dreadful; *(minunat)* excellent. *adv.* awfully; wonderfully. *interj.* capital!

strat *sn.* stratum, layer; *(de vopsea)* coat (of paint); *(de flori)* bed; plot; ~*uri sociale* walks of life.

stratagemă *sf.* stratagem.

strateg *sm.* strategist.

strategic *adj.* strategical. *adv.* strategically.

strategie *sf.* strategy.

străbate *vt.* to traverse; *(a străpunge)* to pierce.

străbun *sm.* ancestor. *adj.* traditional.

străbunic *sm.* great grandfather.

străbunică *sf.* great grandmother.

străbunici *sm. pl.* great grandparents.

strădanie *sf.* endeavour.

strădui *vr.* to strive.

străfulgera *vi.* to flash (through one's mind).

străfulgerare *sf.* flash (of lightning); *fig.* brainwave.

străfund *sn.* in(ner)most depths.

străin *sm.* foreigner; *(necunoscut)* stranger; *(oaspete)* guest; *prin* ~*i* abroad. *adj.* foreign; *(necunoscut)* strange; *(al altcuiva)* somebody else's.

străinătate *sf.* foreign countries; *din* ~ from abroad; *în* ~ abroad.

strájui *vt.* to guard. *vi.* to tower.

străluci *vi.* to shine; *(a fulgera)* to flash; *(a scînteia)* to sparkle; *(slab)* to glow.

strălucire *sf.* brilliance; *(a unui metal)* glint.

strălucit *adj.* bright. *adv.* wonderfully.

strălucitor *adj.* radiant.

strămoş *sm.* ancestor; *pl.* forbears.

strămoşesc *adj.* traditional.

strămuta *vt.* to displace.

strănepoată *sf.* great granddaughter.

strănepot *sm.* great grandson; *pl.* great grandchildren.

strănut *sn.* sneeze.

strănuta *vi.* to sneeze.

străpunge *vt.* to pierce; *(a înjunghia)* to stab.

străşnicie *sf.* sternness.

strávechi *adj.* ancient.

străveziu *adj.* transparent; *fig.* obvious.

streaşină *sf.* eaves.

streche *sf.* gadfly.

strecura *vt.* to strain; *(a introduce)* to smuggle. *vr.* to slink in *sau* out.

strecurătoare *sf.* collander.

strepezi *vt.* to set on edge. *vr.* to be set on edge.

streptomicină *sf.* streptomycin.
strica *vt.* to spoil; *(a sparge)* to break; *fig. și* to blast; *(a corupe)* to pervert. *vi.* to be harmful; *n-ar ~ să pleci* you'd better go. *vr.* to go bad *sau* wrong.
stricat *sm.* debauchee. *adj.* spoilt; *(putred)* decayed; *(pervers)* perverse; *(d. aer)* foul, stale. *adv.* badly.
stricată *sf.* harlot.
stricăciune *sf.* harm; *(corupție)* corruption.
strict *sn.:* ~*ul necesar* the essential. *adj.* strict. *adv.* strictly.
stricteţe *sf.* strictness.
strident *adj.* shrill; *fig. și* jarring. *adv.* stridently.
stridenţă *sf.* harshness; *fig.* jarring note.
stridie *sf.* oyster.
striga *vt.* to call. *vi.* to call (out); *(strident)* to yell; *a ~ catalogul* to call the roll.
strigăt *sn.* call.
strigător *adj.* crying; *~ la cer* revolting.
strigătură *sf.* witty couplet (accompanying a folk dance).
strigoi *sm.* ghost.
strivi *vt.* to crush.
strîmb *adj.* wry; *(înclinat)* slanting; *fig.* false. *adv.* awry; *fig.* wrongly.
strîmba *vt.* to twist; *și fig.* to distort. *vi.: a ~ din nas* to turn up one's nose (at smth.). *vr.* to twist; *(a face strîmbături)* to make wry faces.
strîmbătură *sf.* grimace.
strîmt *adj.* narrow; tight.

strîmta *vt.* to (make) narrow; *(hainele)* to take in. *vr.* to (get) narrow.
strîmtoare *sf.* straits; *(între munţi)* pass, gorges; *fig.* tight spot; *la ~* at a pinch.
strîmtora *vt.* to hamper.
strîmtorat *adj.* under straitened circumstances.
stringător *adj.* sparing.
strînge *vt.* to tighten; *(a restrînge)* to limit; *(a împături)* to fold; *(d. pantofi)* to pinch; *(a aduna)* to gather; *(a culege)* to pick up; *(a acumula)* to hoard; *(a colecţiona)* to collect; *(impozite)* to levy; *a ~ masa* to clear the table; *a ~ rîndurile* to rally. *vi.* to press; *(d. pantofi)* to pinch. *vr.* to gather; *(a se ghemui)* to crouch.
strîngere *sf.* pressing; *~ de inimă* pang; *~ de mînă* handshake.
strîns *sn.* pressing; *~ul recoltei* gathering in. *adj.* tight; close; (com)pressed; *(d. rînduri)* serried; *~ pe corp* tight-fitting. *adv.* closely, rightly.
strînsoare *sf.* tight grip; pressure.
strînsură *sf.* gathering; *de ~* of sorts.
strofă *sf.* stanza.
strop *sm.* drop; *fig.* bit.
stropi *vt.* to sprinkle; *(a păta)* to (be)smear. *vi.* to sputter. *vr.* to make oneself dirty.
stropitoare *sf.* watering can.
structural *adj.* structural.
structură *sf.* structure.
strugure *sm.* (bunch of) grapes.
strună *sf.* string. *adv.* perfectly.

strung *sn.* lathe.
strungar *sm.* turner.
struni *vt.* to bridle; *fig. şi* to curb.
struţ *sm.* ostrich.
structură *sf.* moulding.
student *sm.* student; *(boboc)* freshman; *(mare)* undergraduate; ~ *în medicină* medical student.
studenţesc *adj.* student(s') ...
studia *vt., vi.* to study.
studiat *adj.* studied; *(afectat şi)* affected; *(laborious)* elaborate.
studio *sn.* studio; *(pat)* couch bed.
studios *adj.* studious.
studiu *sn.* study; *muz. şi* étude; *în* ~ under consideration.
stuf *sn.* reed; rush.
stufat *sn.* onion stew.
stufos *adj.* bushy; *(des)* thick.
stup *sm.* beehive.
stupefiant *sn.* intoxicant, dope. *adj.* stupefying.
stupefiat *adj.* dumbfounded.
stupid *adj.* stupid; *(monoton)* dull. *adv.* foolishly.
stupiditate *sf.* stupidity.
stupoare *sf.* stupor.
sturz *sm.* thrush.
suav *adj.* suave.
sub *prep.* under; *(mai jos de)* below; ~ *pămînt* underground; ~ *zero* below zero.
subaltern *sm.* underling. *adj.* subaltern.
subconştient *sn., adj.* subconscious.
subdirector *sm.* deputy manager; *(de coală)* deputy headmaster.
subestima *ve.* to underrate.

subiect *sn.* subject; *(conţinut şi)* matter; *(povestire şi)* plot; *(temă)* theme; *(de conversaţie)* topic; *(obiect)* object.
subiectiv *adj.* subjective; *(părtinitor)* biassed. *adv.* subjectively.
subit *adj.* sudden. *adv.* unexpectedly.
subînchiria *vt.* to sublet.
subînţelege *vr.: se* ~ it goes without saying.
subînţeles *sn.* connotation; *cu* ~ meaningful(ly). *adj.* implied.
subjonctiv *sn.* subjunctive.
subjuga *vt.* to subjugate.
sublim *sn., adj.* sublime. *adv.* wonderfully.
sublinia *vt.* to underline.
sublocotenent *sm.* second lieutenant.
submarin *sn., adj.* submarine.
submina *vt.* to undermine.
subofiţer *sm.* non-com(missioned officer).
subordona *vt.* to subordinate.
subordonat *adj.* subordinate.
subscrie *vt.* to sign; *(o sumă)* to subscribe. *vi.* to subscribe (to an opinion, for a collection).
subscripţie *sf.* subscription (list).
subsecretar *sm.* under-secretary.
subsemnatul *sm.* the undersigned.
subsidiar *adj.* subsidiary.
subsol *sn. agr.* subsoil; *arhit.* basement; *(al paginii)* foot.
substantiv *sn.* noun.
substanţă *sf.* substance; *(esenţă şi)* gist.
substanţial *adj.* substantial. *adv.* substantially.
substitui *vt.* to substitute (a new thing for the old one). *vr.*

to take the place of (smb else).

substrat *sn.* substratum.

subsuoară *sf.* armpit; *la ~* under one's arm.

subteran *sn., adj.* underground.

subterfugiu *sn.* subterfuge.

subtext *sn.* overtones; implications.

subtil *adj.* subtle. *adv.* subtly.

subtilitate *sf.* subtlety.

subtitlu *sn.* subtitle.

subţia *vt.* to (make) thin; *(a dilua)* to dilute; *fig.* to refine. *vr.* to grow thinner; *fig.* to brush up.

subţire *adj.* thin; *(fin)* fine; *(zvelt)* slender. *adv.* thinly; *(uşor)* finely.

subunitate *sf. mil.* element.

suburbie *sf.* suburb; purlieus.

subvenţie *sf.* subvention.

subvenţiona *vt.* to subsidize.

subversiv *adj.* seditious.

sue *sn.* juice; *~ de fructe* sherbet.

succeda *vi., vr.* to succeed.

succes *sn.* success; *pl.* victorics; *(d. un cîntec., o piesă)* hit; *cu ~* successfully; *de ~* successful.

succesiune *sf.* succession; *jur. şi* inheritance.

succesiv *adj.* successive. *adv.* successively.

succesor *sm.* successor; heir.

succint *adj.* concise, terse.

suci *vt.* to twist; *(a scrînti)* to sprain; *(gîtul, mîna)* to wring. *vr.* to twist.

sucit *sm.* erratic fellow. *adj.* twisted; *(ciudat)* crotchety.

sucursală *sf.* branch.

sud *sn.* south; *de ~* south(ern); *la ~* in the south; *la ~ de* south of; *spre ~* southwards.

suda *vt., vr.* to weld.

sud-est *sn.* South-East.

sudic *adj.* South(ern).

sudoare *sf.* sweat.

sudor *sm.* welder.

sud-vest *sn.* South-West.

suedez *sm.* Swede. *adj.* Swedish.

suedeză *sf.* Swede, Swedish woman; *(limbă)* Swedish.

suferi *vt.* to suffer; *a nu ~ întîrziere* to brook no delay. *vi.* to suffer (from).

suferind *sm.* invalid. *adj.* ailing.

suferinţă *sf.* suffering.

sufertaş *sn.* lunch pail.

suficient *adj.* sufficient; *(încrezut)* self-sufficient. *adv.* enough.

sufix *sn.* suffix.

sufla *vt.* to blow (off *sau* away); *(cuiva)* to prompt; *(a lua)* to steal; *a nu ~ un cuvînt* not to breathe a word. *vi.* to blow; *(a respira, a adia)* to breathe; *(cuiva)* to prompt; *a ~ din greu* to pant.

suflare *sf.* breath(ing); *fără ~* breathless; *(mort)* dead.

suflător *sm.* wind instrument-(alist); *pl.* winds.

sufleca *vt.* to roll *sau* turn up.

sufler *sm.* prompter.

suflet *sn.* soul; heart; *(viaţă şi)* life; *(conştiinţă)* conscience; *(suflare)* breath(ing); *(gîfîit)* panting; *(om)* man; *cu ~ul la gură* out of breath; *de ~* adopted; *din ~* heartfelt; *fără ~* heartless(ly); *într-un ~* in a hurry.

sufletesc *adj.* soul; spiritual.

suflu *sn.* blast (of an explosion); *(suflare)* breath.

sufoca *vt., vr.* to stifle.

sufragerie *sf.* dining-room (furniture).

sugaci, sugar *sm., adj.* suckling.

sugativă, sugătoare *sf.* blotting paper.

suge *vt., vi.* to suck; *(a bea)* to booze.

sugera *vt.* to suggest; *(a insinua)* to insinuate.

sugestie *sf.* suggestion; hypnosis.

sugestiv *adj.* eloquent. *adv.* graphically.

sughiţ *sn.* hiccup; *(de plîns)* sob.

sughiţa *vi.* to hiccup; *(de plîns)* to sob.

sugruma *vt.* to smother.

sui *vt., vi., vr.* to climb up.

suită *sf.* suite.

suitor *adj.* rising.

sul *sn.* roll.

sulf *sn.* sulphur.

sulfamidă *sf.* sulphamid.

suliţă *sf.* javelin; *ist.* spear.

sultan *sm.* sultan.

suman *sn.* thick long coat.

sumar *sn., adj.* summary. *adv.* scantily.

sumă *sf.* sum; *(număr)* number; o ~ *de* a lot of.

sumbru *adj.* gloomy.

sumedenie *sf.* lot; a great deal (of).

suna *vt.* to ring; *(la telefon)* to ring up; *(d. ceas)* to strike. *vi.* to ring; to sound; *(d. clopote şi)* to toll; *(d. zurgălăi)* to chime; *(a răsuna)* to resound; *(d. ceas)* to strike the hours; *(a glăsui)* to read; a ~ *din (corn etc.)* to blow (the horn, etc.).

sunătoare *sf.* rattle; *bot.* all--saints'-wort.

sunet *sn.* sound; *(de clopote şi)* ring; în ~ *de* to the sound of.

supă *sf.* soup; *(de pui etc.)* broth.

supăra *vt.* to annoy; *(a deranja)* to trouble. *vr.* to be angry; *(a se certa)* to fall out; *(a se întrista)* to grieve.

supărare *sf.* anger; *(necaz)* trouble; *(pierdere)* bereavement.

supărat *adj.* cross (with smb., at a thing); *(trist)* aggrieved.

supărăcios *adj.* ill-tempered, grumpy.

supărător *adj.* annoying.

superb *adj.* superb; *(admirabil)* admirable.

superficial *adj.* superficial; *fig.* shallow. *adv.* wantonly.

superior *sm.* superior. *adj.* superior (to); *(mai înalt)* high(er); *(de sus)* upper.

superioritate *sf.* superiority.

superlativ *sn., adj.* superlative.

superstiţie *sf.* superstition.

supleant *sm.* deputy. *adj.* alternate.

supliciu *sn.* torture; *fig. şi* torment.

supliment *sn.* supplement; extra dish *sau* ticket *sau* payment.

suplimentar *adj.* supplementary; *(d. muncă etc.)* overtime.

suplini *vt.* to replace; *(o lipsă etc.)* to compensate.

suplinitor *sm.* substitute.

suplu *adj.* supple.

suport *sn.* support.

suporta *vt.* to bear; *(a suferi)* to tolerate.

suportabil *adj.* bearable. *adv.* tolerably.

supracopertă *sf.* jacket, wrapper.

suprafață *sf.* surface; *(întindere)* area; *(spațiu)* space; *de* ~ shallow; *la* ~ on the surface.

supranatural *sn., adj.* preternatural.

supranumi *vt.* to (nick)name, to call.

supraom *sm.* superman.

supraomenese *adj.* superhuman.

suprapune *vt., vr.* to overlap.

suprapunere *sf.* superposition.

suprarealism *sn.* surrealism.

suprarealist *sm., adj.* surrealist.

suprasolicita *vt.* to overtax.

suprastructură *sf.* superstructure.

supraveghea *vt.* to oversee; *(a păzi)* to watch. *vr.* to keep oneself in hand.

supraveghere *sf.* supervision.

supraveghetor *sm.* overseer.

supraviețui *vi.* to outlive (smb.); to survive (smth.).

supraviețuitor *sm.* survivor. *adj.* surviving.

suprem *adj.* supreme.

supremație *sf.* supremacy.

suprima *vt.* to suppress; *(un cuvînt)* to cross out; *(pe cineva)* to kill.

supt *sn.* sucking. *adj.* wasted; *(d. obraji)* sunken.

supune *vt.* to subjugate; *(cercetării)* to examine; *(a prezenta)* to submit. *vr.* to submit; *(unei rugăminți)* to comply (with a request, etc.).

supunere *sf.* obedience.

supus *sm.* subject. *adj.* submissive; ~ *la* liable to. *adv.* dutifully.

sur *adj.* grey.

surcea *sf.* chip.

surd *sm.* deaf person. *adj.* deaf; *(d. consoane)* mute, voiceless;

(d. zgomot) muffled; *(ascuns)* hidden.

surdină *sf.* mute; *în* ~ in an undertone.

surdomut *sm.* deaf-mute. *adj.* deaf and dumb.

surescita *vt.* to (over)excite, to agitate.

surghiun *sn.* exile, banishment.

surghiuni *vt.* to banish.

suride *vi.* to smile (at smb.).

surîs *sn.* smile; *(ironic)* sneer.

surîzător *adj.* smiling.

surmena *vt.* to overwork. *vr.* to strain too hard.

surmenaj *sn.* overworking.

surmenat *adj.* overwrought.

surogat *sn.* ersatz; *fig.* imitation.

surpa *vt.* to ruin. *vr.* to crumble.

surplus *sn.* surplus.

surprinde *vt.* to surprise; to catch unawares; *(a auzi)* to overhear.

surprindere *sf.* surprise; *prin* ~ by surprise.

surprinzător *adj.* surprising. *adv.* amazingly.

surpriză *sf.* surprise.

sursă *sf.* source.

surveni *vi.* to occur.

surzenie *sf.* deafness.

surzi *vt.* to deafen. *vi.* to grow deaf.

sus *sn.* upper part; *cu* ~*ul în jos* upset; *în* ~*ul rîului* upstream. *adv.* up, above; on top; *sus mîinile!* hands up!; ~ *și tare* loudly; *de* ~ (on) high; *în* ~ upward; *pe* ~ high; *(cu de-a sila)* bodily. *interj.* up!

susan *sm.* sesame.

susceptibil *adj.* susceptible; tetchy; ~ *de* liable to.

susceptibilitate *sf.* susceptibility.

suspect *sm.* suspect. *adj.* doubtful.

suspecta *vt.* to suspect.

suspenda *vt.* to suspend; *(şedinţa etc.)* to ajourn; *(a a-tîrna)*· to hang.

suspensie *sf.* suspension.

suspiciune *sf.* suspicion.

suspin *sn.* sigh; sob.

suspina *vi.* to sob; *a ~ după* to hanker after.

suspus *adj.* highly placed.

sustrage *vt.* to subtract; *(a fura)* to defalcate. *vr.: a se ~ de la* to shirk.

susţinător *sm.* upholder; *(al familiei)* breadwinner.

susţine *vt.* to uphold; *(a încuraja)* to countenance; *(o părere etc. şi)* to maintain; *(a pretinde)* to allege. *vr.* to hold (one's ground); *(materialiceşte)* to earn one's living.

susţinut *adj.* constant.

susur *sn.* purl(ing).

susura *vi.* to purl.

sută *sf., adj., num.* hundred; *la ~* per cent.

sutălea *adj., num.* (the) one hundredth.

sutien *sn.* bra(ssière).

suveică *sf.* shuttle.

suvenir *sn.* keepsake; *(amintire)* memory.

suveran *sm., adj.* sovereign.

suveranitate *sf.* sovereignty.

Ş

şa *sf.* saddle.

şablon *sn.* pattern. *adj.* staple; standardized; routine...

şacal *sm.* jackal.

şah *sm.* shah. *sn.* chess; *(atac)* check; *~-mat* checkmate; *în ~* in check. *interj.* check!

şahist *sm.* chess player.

şaisprezece *sm., adj., num.* sixteen.

şaisprezecelea *adj., num.* (the) sixteenth.

şaizeci *sm., adj., num.,* sixty.

şaizecilea *adj., num.* (the) sixtieth.

şal *sn.* shawl.

şalău *sm.* pike perch, zander.

şale *sf. pl.* loins.

şalupă *sf.* (motor) boat.

şalvari *sm. pl.* shalwars.

şampanie *sf.* champagne.

şampon *sn.* shampoo.

şandrama *sf.* jerrybuilt house.

şanjant *adj.* shot silk.

şansă *sf.* chance.

şantaj *sn.* (piece of) blackmail.

şantaja *vt.* to blackmail.

şantier *sn.* (building) site; *mar.* shipyard.

şanţ *sn.* ditch; *tehn.* groove.

şapcă *sf.* peaked cap.

şapte *sm., adj., num.* seven.

şaptelea *adj., num.* (the) seventh.

şaptesprezece *sm., adj., num.* seventeen.

şaptesprezecelea *adj., num.* (the) seventeenth.

şaptezeci *sm., adj., num.* seventy ; three score and ten.

şaptezecilea *adj., num.* (the) seventeeth.

şaradă *sf.* puzzle, enigma.

şarja *vt.* to charge. *vi.* to play up.

şarlatan *sm.* quack.

şarpe *sm.* snake ; ~ *cu clopoţei* rattlesnake ; ~ *cu ochelari* naja.

şase *sm., adj., num.* six. *interj.* nix ! jiggers !

şaselea *adj., num.* (the) sixth.

şasiu *sn.* chassis.

şaten *adj.* brown.

şatră *sf.* Gipsy camp *sau* tribe.

şchioapă *sf.* span ; *de o* ~ knee-high to a grasshopper.

şchiop *sm.* lame man. *adj.* lame.

şchiopăta *vi.* to limp ; *fig.* to be deficient.

şcoală *sf.* school ; *(învăţătură)* schooling ; ~ *elementară* elementary school ; ~ *medie* secondary school ; ~ *profesională* vocational school ; ~ *primară* elementary school ; *cu* ~ educated.

şcolar *sm.* school boy ; *pl.* school-children. *adj.* school.

şedea *vi.* to sit (down) ; *(a locui)* to live ; *(a se odihni)* to (take) rest ; *a-i* ~ *(bine, rău* etc.*)* to sit smb. (well, badly, etc.) ; *a-i* ~ *bine să* to become smb., to.

şedere *sf.* stay(ing).

şedinţă *sf.* meeting.

şef *sm.* chief, head ; ~ *de cabinet* secretary ; ~ *de gară* station master. *adj.* chief.

şeptel *sn.* livestock.

şeptime *sf.* seventh (part).

şerb *sm.* serf.

şerbet *sn.* fruit syrup boiled hard.

şerpui *vi.* to wind.

şerpuitor *adj.* meandering.

şervet *sn.* napkin ; *(prosop)* towel.

şerveţel *sn.* napkin.

şes *sn.* plain. *adj.* flat, even.

şesime *sf.* sixth (part).

şevalet *sn.* easel.

şezătoare *sf.* (literary) social.

şezlong *sn.* deck chair.

şezut *sn.* bottom.

şfichiui *vt.* to lash.

şi *conj.* and. *adv.* also, too ; *(deja)* already ; *(chiar)* even ; *şi tu* you too, also you ; ~ *mai* ~ even better.

şic *sn.* fashionableness. *adj.* smart. *adv.* elegantly.

şicana *vt.* to hamper.

şicană *sf.* pettifoggery.

şifona *vt.* to rumple. *vr.* to crease ; *fig.* to take offence.

şifonier *sn.* wardrobe.

şiling *sm.* shilling.

şină *sf.* rail ; *(de sanie)* runner.

şindrilă *sf.* shingle.

şipcă *sf.* slat.

şir *sn.* row ; *geogr.* range ; *(serie)* series ; *(legătură)* link ; *în* ~ in a file.

şirag *sn.* necklace ; chain ; *(de mărgele)* a string of beads.

şiră *sf. (de paie)* hayrick ; *şira spinării* backbone, spinal cord.

şiret *sn.* (shoe) lace. *adj.* cunning, sly, artful. *adv.* cunningly, artfully.

şiretenie *sf.* cunning, art(fulness).

şiretlic *sn.* trick, dodge.

şiròi[1] *sn.* flow ; stream, torrent

şiroi[2] *vi.* to stream ; *(a se pre-linge)* to trickle.

şleau *sn.* road ; *pe* ~ openly.

şleful *vt.* to polish.

şlep *sn.* barge.

şmecher *sm.* slyboots. *adj.* sly.

şmecherie *sf.* art(fulness) ; *(arti-ficiu)* dodge.

şniţel *sn.* breaded steak.

şnur *sn.* cord.

şoaptă *sf.* whisper ; *în* ~ whispering.

şoarece *sm.* mouse, *pl.* mioe ; ~ *de bibliotecă* bookworm.

şobolan *sm.* rat.

şoc *sn.* shock ; *de* ~ shock...

şoca *vt.* to shock.

şofer *sm.* (car) driver ; *(al cuiva)* chauffeur.

şoim *sm.* falcon.

şold *sn.* hip.

şoma *vi.* to be unemployed.

şomaj *sn.* unemployment.

şomer *sm.* unemployed worker ; *pl.* the unemployed ; ~·*par-ţial* worker on short hours. *adj.* unemployed.

şopîrlă *sf.* lizard.

şopron *sn.* shed.

şopti *vt., vi.* to whisper.

şort *sn.* shorts.

şorţ *sn.* apron ; *(de fetiţă şi)* pinafore.

şosea *sf.* highway.

şosetă *sf.* sock.

şoşon *sm.* overshoe.

şotie *sf.* prank.

şovăi *vi.* to waver, to dilly-dally.

şovăială, şovăire *sf.* hesitation, vacillation ; *fără* ~ unhesitatingly.

şovăitor *adj.* halting ; *(d. glas)* faltering.

şovin *adj.* chauvinistic.

şovinism *sn.* jingoism.

şpalt *sn.* galleyproof.

şperaclu *sn.* skeleton *sau* master key.

şpriţ *sn.* soda wine.

ştafetă *sf.* relay race.

ştampila *vt.* to stamp.

ştampilat *adj.* stamped ; *(d. tim-bre)* obliterated, used.

ştampilă *sf.* stamp ; *fig.* tag.

şterge *vt.* to wipe (up) ; *(a usca)* to dry ; *(praful)* to dust ; *(a curăţa)* to clean ; *(cu guma etc.)* to erase, to rub out ; *(un text)* to strike out ; *fig.* to wipe off ; *a* ~ *cu buretele* to let bygones be bygones. *vr.* to wipe oneself (dry) ; *fig.* to dissolve ; *a se* ~ *pe mîini* to wipe one's hands.

şterpeli *vt.* to purloin.

şters *sn.* wiping. *adj.* dull, drab.

ştevie *sf.* patience.

şti *vt.* to know ; ~*i să dansezi ?* can you dance ? ; *a nu* ~ *ce să facă* to be at a loss (what to do). *vi.* to know. *vr.* to be known.

ştiinţă *sf.* science ; *(cunoaştere)* knowledge, acquaintance ; *cu (bună)* ~ deliberately.

ştiinţific *adj.* scientific. *adv.* scientifically.

ştirb *adj.* gap-toothed.

ştirbi *vt.* to notch ; *fig.* to encroach upon ; *(a micşora)* to diminish.

ştire *sf.* (piece of) news ; *pl.* tidings ; *cu* ~*a cuiva* with smb.'s knowledge.

ştiucă *sf.* pike.

ştiulete *sm.* corn cob.

ştrand *sn.* swimming pool.

ștreang *sn.* halter.
ștrengar *sm.* scapegrace. *adj.* roguish.
ștrengărie *sf.* merry prank.
șubred *adj.* frail; *(bolnăvicios)* sickly; *(subțire)* flimsy; *(d. case)* tottering.
șubrezi *vt., vr.* to weaken.
șuiera *vi.* to whistle.
șuierat *sn.* whistling.
șuierător *adj.* whistling; *(d. consoană și)* sibilant.

șuncă *sf.* ham.
șurub *sn.* screw.
șurubelniță *sf.* screwdriver.
șușoteală *sf.* whispering.
șușoti *vi.* to whisper.
șut *sn.* shot; *min.* shift.
șuta *vi.* to shoot.
șuviță *sf.* tress; *(fîșie)* stripe.
șuvoi *sn.* stream.
șvab *sm., adj.* Swabian.
șvaițer *sn.* Swiss cheese.

T

ta *adj.* your; *a ~* yours.
tabachera *sf.* cigarette box; snuff-box.
tabără *sf.* camp; *mil.* și bivouac; *~ de vară* holiday camp.
tabel *sn.* table.
tablă *sf.* tin *sau* iron plate; *(la școală)* blackboard; *(tabel)* table; *pl. (joc)* backgammon; *tabla înmulțirii* multiplication table; *~ ondulată* corrugated iron.
tabletă *sf.* tablet.
tablou *sn.* picture; *(pînză și)* canvas; *teatru* scene; *(tabel)* table; *tehn.* board.
tabu *sn.* taboo.
taburet *sn.* ottoman.
tachina *vt.* to tease.
tacit *adj.* tacit. *adv.* tacitly.
taciturn *adj.* silent.
tacîm *sn.* cover (for one, for two, etc.); *pl.* (silver) plate.

tact *sn. muz.* rhythm; *fig.* tact; *fără ~* tactless; *cu ~* tactful
tactic *adj.* tactic.
tactică *sf.* tactic(s).
tacticos *adj., adv.* leisurely.
tafta *sf.* taffeta.
taifas *sn.* chat.
taifun *sn.* typhoon.
tain *sn.* ration, quota.
taină *sf.* mystery; *în ~* secretly.
tainic *adj.* mysterious; hidden.
taior *sn.* costume.
talaz *sn.* breaker.
talc *sn.* talc (powder).
tale *adj.* your; *ale ~* yours.
talent *sn.* talent.
talentat *adj.* talented.
taler *sn.* thaler; *(blid)* plate; *pl. (de balanță)* scales; *sport* skeet, clay pigeons.
talger *sn.* dish; *pl. muz.* cymbals.

talie *sf.* waist (line); *(mărime)* size.

talisman *sn.* talisman.

talmeş-balmeş *sn.* hotch-potch. *adv.* helter-skelter.

talon *sn.* heel (of stocking); *(tichet)* counterfoil.

talpă *sf.* sole (leather); runner (of a sledge); *talpa iadului* the devil's dam; *talpa ţării* the common people, the rank and file.

taman *adv.* precisely; *(numai)* only.

tamburină *sf.* tambourine.

tampon *sn.* c *f.* buffer; *(de vată* etc.*)* swab.

tampona *vt.* to collide with; *med.* to tampon. *vr.* to collide.

tanc *sn.* tank; *(petrolier)* tanker.

tandreţe *sf.* tenderness.

tandru *adj.* affectionate.

tangenţial *adj.* tangent; *fig.* indirect.

tangou *sn.* tango.

tanti *sf.* aunt.

tapaj *sn.* fuss.

tapet *sn.* tapestry; *pe* ~ on the carpet.

tapir *sm.* tapir.

tapisa *vt.* to upholster.

tapiserie *sf.* tapestry.

tapiţer *sm.* upholsterer.

tapiţerie *sf.* upholstery.

tarabă *sf.* stall; *(gheretă)* booth.

taraf *sn.* folk music band.

tară *sf.* tare; *fig.* defect.

tardiv *adj.* belated. *adv.* too late in the day.

tare *adj.* hard; *(puternic)* strong; *(durabil)* lasting; *(d. pînză)* starched; *(d. fiinţe)* robust; *(împietrit)* steeled; *(pregătit)* well-informed; *(convingător)* convincing; *(sonor)* loud; *(d. aer)* bracing; *(d. culori)* vivid; ~ *de cap* dull; ~ *de ureche* hard of hearing. *adv.* very (much); *(sonor)* loudly; *(intens)* strongly.

targă *sf.* stretcher.

tarhon *sm.* tarragon.

tarif *sn.* tariff; *(taxă, curs)* rate.

tartă *sf.* tart.

tartină *sf.* sandwich.

tartor *sm.* devil; *fig.* ring leader.

tată *sm.* father; *(străbun)* forefather; ~ *de familie* head of the family; *din* ~ *în fiu* from generation to generation.

tatona *vt.* to probe *vi.* to grope.

tatua *vt.*, *vr.* to tattoo (oneself).

tatuaj *sn.* tattoo(ing).

taur *sm.* bull.

tavan *sn.* ceiling.

tavă *sf.* tray; *(de copt)* griddle.

tavernă *sf.* low drinking-house.

taxa *vt.* to tax; *fig.* to consider.

taxator *sm.* conductor.

taxă *sf.* com., jur. duty; *(de intrare, şcolară* etc.*)* fee; *(cotizaţie)* due; *(la electricitate* etc.*)* rate(s); *(la poştă* etc.*)* charge.

taxi(metru) *sn.* taxi(cab).

tăbăcar *sm.* tanner.

tăbăcărie *sf.* tannery.

tăbăci *vt.* to tan.

tăbărî *vi.* to swoop.

tăbliţă *sf.* plate; slate; ~ *indicatoare* finger post.

tăcea *vi.* to be silent; to stop talking, singing, etc.; *tacă-ţi gura!* sau *taci (din gură)!* shut up!

tăcere *sf.* silence; *(liniște)* stillness; în ~ silently.

tăciune *sm.* ember; *bot.* mildew.

tăcut *sn.:* pe ~e quietly. *adj.* silent.

tăgădui *vt.* to deny.

tăi *adj.* your; ai ~ yours.

tăia *vt.* to cut; *(a despica)* to split; *(a șterge)* to cross out; *(un drum)* to open; *(a săpa)* to dig; *(a brăzda)* to furrow; *(a străbate)* to traverse, to cross; *(a ucide)* to kill; *(un animal)* to butcher; *(a cresta)* to notch; *(a spinteca)* to rip; *fig. (a reteza)* to suppress; nu mă taie capul ce să fac I don't know what to do. *vi.* to cut; to use a short cut; el taie și spînzură he is the boss. *vr.* to get cut; *(d. țesături)* to rend; *(d. lapte)* to curdle; m-am ~t la deget I cut my finger.

tăiere *sf.* cutting.

tăietor *sm.* cutter; ~ de lemne woodcutter.

tăietură *sf.* cut; *(rană și)* wound; tăieturi din presă press clippings.

tăinui *vt.* to hide.

tăinuitor *sm.* fence.

tăios *adj.* cutting; *(pătrunzător)* piercing. *adv.* sharply.

tăiș *sn.* edge; cu două ~uri double-edged.

tăiței *sm. pl.* noodles.

tălmăci *vt.* to translate; to explain.

tămădui *vt.* to heal; *(suferințe)* to allay. *vr.* to recover (from).

tămăduitor *adj.* curing.

tămbălău *sn.* uproar; *(chef)* junket.

tămîia *vt. rel.* to incense; *fig.*

to extol; to flatter. *vr.* se ~ză reciproc it's scratch my back and I'll scratch yours.

tămîie *sf.* (frank)incense.

tămîios *adj.* muscadine; *(d. vin)* muscat(el).

tărăgăna *vt.* to protract; *(vorba)* to drawl. *vi.* to shilly-shally.

tărăgănare *sf.* tergiversation; *(la vorbă)* drawl.

tărbacă *sf.:* a lua în ~ to tar and feather.

tărcat *adj.* striped.

tărie *sf.* power; *(rezistență)* resistance; *(insistență și)* emphasis; *(alcoolică)* concentration.

tărîm *sn.* realm; *(lume)* world; *fig.* sphere.

tărîțe *sf. pl.* husk; *(fine)* bran; *(de lemn)* saw-dust.

tătar *sm., adj.,* **tătăresc** *adj.* Tartar.

tău *sn.* lake. *adj.* your; al ~ yours.

tăun *sm.* gadfly.

tăvăleală *sf.* rolling; *fig.* wear and tear.

tăvăli *vt.* to roll; *fig.* to besmirch. *vr.* to roll; *fig.* to wallow; a se ~ de rîs to split one's sides with laughter.

tăvălug *sn.* (steam-)roller.

te *pron.* you; *(reflexiv)* yourself.

teacă *sf.* sheath.

teafăr *adj.* healthy; *(la minte)* sane; *(nepedepsit)* scotfree.

teamă *sf.* fright; din ~ de for fear of.

teanc *sn.* pile.

teapă *sf.* kind; de aceeași ~ of the same kidney.

teatral *adj.* theatrical; *fig. și* affected.

teatru *sn.* theatre; *(sală şi)* house; *(gen dramatic)* drama; *fig.* circus; ~ *de marionete* puppet show; ~ *de păpuşi* Punch and Judy show; ~ *de revistă* revue, burlesque; ~ *de vară* open-air theatre.

tehnic *adj.* technical; technological.

tehnică *sf.* technique(s); technology.

tehnician *sm.* technician.

tehnologie *sf.* technology.

tei *sm.* lime *sau* linden tree.

tejghea *sf.* counter.

teleferic *sn.* funicular; ski-lift.

telefon *sn.* telephone (set); *(convorbire)* (phone-)call; *(interurbană)* toll call.

telefona *vi.* to (tele)phone; *(cuiva)* to ring smb. up; *(cu taxa inversă)* to reverse charges.

telefonic *adj.* telephone. *adv.* by telephone.

telegraf *sn.* telegraph(y); Morse telegraph.

telegrafia *vt.* to wire.

telegrafic *adj.* telegraph(ic); *fig.* lapidary. *adv.* by telegraph.

telegrafie *sf.* telegraph(y); ~ *fără fir* radio-telegraph(y).

telegramă *sf.* telegram.

telepatie *sf.* telepathy.

telescop *sn.* telescope.

telespectator *sm.* (tele)viewer, TV spectator.

televiziune *sf.* television, TV; *la* ~ on TV.

televizor *sn.* TV-set; telly; *la* ~ on TV.

temă *sf.* theme; *pl.* homework; *(rădăcină)* radical; *pe tema...* around ...

temător *adj.* distrustful.

tembel *sm.* dawdler. *adj.* indolent.

tembelism *sn.* indolence.

teme *vr.* to be afraid (of), to fear (smth.); *(a se îngrijora)* to worry; *se* ~ *şi de umbra lui* he is a coward.

temei *sn.* foundation, ground; *de* ~ thorough; *fără* ~ groundless; *cu* ~ earnestly.

temeinic *adj.* solid; thorough (going); *(d. raţionament etc.)* cogent.

temeinicie *sf.* solidity; *(seriozitate)* thoroughness.

temelie *sf.* foundation(s).

temere *sf.* fear.

temnicer *sm.* jailer.

temniţă *sf.* jail.

tempera *vt.* to moderate. *vr.* to abate.

temperament *sn.* temperament; *(vigoare)* pep.

temperat *adj.* temperate. *adv.* temperately.

temperatură *sf.* temperature.

templu *sn.* temple.

temporar *adj.* transient. *adv.* temporarily.

temut *adj.* dreaded.

ten *sn.* complexion.

tenace *adj.* tenacious.

tenacitate *sf.* tenaciousness.

tencui *vt.* to plaster (up).

tencuială *sf.* mortar.

tendenţios *adj.* tendentious.

tendinţă *sf.* tendency; *(înclinaţie)* ply; *(părtinire)* bias.

tendon *sn.* tendon.

tenie *sf.* tape-worm.

tenis *sn.* tennis; ~ *de masă* table tennis.

tenor *sm.* tenor.

tensiune *sf.* tension; blood pressure.

tenta *vt.* to tempt.
tentativă *sf.* attempt.
tentaţie *sf.* temptation.
teolog *sm.* theologian.
teologie *sf.* divinity.
teoremă *sf.* theorem.
teoretic *adj.* theoretical.
teoretician *sm.* theorist.
teorie *sf.* theory.
teracotă *sf.* terracotta.
terasă *sf.* terrace.
terci *sn.* gruel; porridge; *(terciuială)* squash.
teren *sn.* ground; *(loc)* (house) lot; *(de sport)* sportsground; *(mic)* court; *(de golf)* links; *fig.* setting, venue.
terestru *adj.* land; terrestrial.
terfeli *vt.* to soil.
tergal *sn.* terylene, tergal.
tergiversa *vt.* to tergiversate.
teribil *adj.* terrible. *adv.* terribly.
teritorial *adj.* territorial.
teritoriu *sn.* territory.
termal *adj.* thermal; hot.
termen *sm.* term. *sn.* term; date; deadline; în ~ in due time; *mil.* conscripted; *ultimul* ~ time limit.
termina *vt.* to finish. *vr.* to end; s-a ~t cu el he is lost.
terminare *sf.* end.
terminat *sn.:* pe ~e running short; nearly over.
terminaţie *sf.* ending.
terminologie *sf.* nomenclature; vocabulary.
termocentrală *sf.* thermo-electric power station.
termoficare *sf.* district heating.
termometru *sn.* thermometer.
termos *sn.* thermos(-bottle).
teroare *sf.* terror.

terorist *sm., adj.* terrorist.
teroriza *vt.* to terrorize; to bully.
tertip *sn.* trick.
teşcovină *sf.* husks of grapes; marc brandy.
testament *sn.* will; şi *rel.* testament.
teşi *vt.* to blunt.
tevatură *sf.* fret.
text *sn.* text; *muz.* lyrics.
textil *adj.* textile.
textilă *sf.* textile plant; *pl.* fabrics.
textual *adj.* textual. *adv.* to the letter.
tezaur *sn.* treasure; *(de monede şi)* hoard; *fig.* thesaurus; *fin.* treasury.
teză *sf.* written work; *(idee)* thesis; ~ de licenţă graduation paper.
ti *interj.* gee! why! o! oh! alas!
tic *sn.* tic.
ticăi *vi.* *(d. inimă)* to go pit-a-pat; *(d. ceasornice)* to tick. *vr.* to dally.
ticăit *sn.* pit-a-pat; *(al ceasului)* tick. *adj.* slow.
ticălos *sm.* miscreant. *adj.* wicked.
ticăloşie *sf.* wickedness.
tichet *sn.* ticket.
ticlui *vt.* to arrange; *fig.* to devise.
ticsit *adj.* thronged.
tictac *interj.* tick!
tiflă *sf.* snook.
tifoid *adj.* typhoid.
tifon *sn.* gauze; *med.* lint.
tifos *sn.* typhoid fever; ~ exantematic exanthemum fever, typhus.
tigaie *sf.* (frying-)pan.
tigroaică *sf.* tigress.

tigru *sm.* tiger.
tigvă *sf.* pate ; *bot.* gourd.
tihnă *sf.* rest ; *în* ~ at leisure ; *fără* ~ untiringly.
tihnit *adj.* peaceable.
tijă *sf.* rod ; *bot.* stem.
timbra *vt.* to stamp.
timbru *sn.* stamp ; *muz.* timbre.
timid *adj.* timid.
timiditate *sf.* shyness.
timp *sm.* time. *sn.* time ; *(vreme)* weather ; *(răgaz)* respite ; *(epocă)* age ; *muz.* beat ; *gram.* tense ; ~ *liber* leisure ; *cu* ~*ul* in the long run ; *cîtva* ~ for some time ; *la* ~ ; *din* ~ in due time.
timpan *sn.* ear drum ; *muz. pl.* timpani.
timpuriu *adj.* early ; forward ; *de* ~ (too) early.
tindă *sf.* entry.
tinde *vi.* to tend.
tine *pron.* you.
tineresc *adj.* youth(ful).
tineret *sf.* youth, young people ; *de* ~ youth(ful).
tinereţe *sf.* youth.
tinerime *sf.* young people.
tinichea *sf.* tin (box *sau* plate). *adj. fig.* not in tin.
tinichigiu *sm.* tinker.
tip *sm.* cove. *sn.* (arche)type.
tipar *sn.* print(ing) ; *(şablon)* pattern ; *(mulaj)* cast ; *sub* ~ in press.
tipări *vt.* to print. *vr.* to be printed.
tipăritură *sf.* publication ; *pl.* printed matter.
tipic[1] *sn.* (quint)essence. *adj.* typical (of), specific (to).
tipic[2] *sn.* pattern ; custom.

tipicar *sm.* fastidious person. *adj.* finical.
tipiza *vt.* to typify.
tipizare *sf.* typification ; *arhit.* type design.
tipograf *sm.* printer.
tipografie *sf.* printing press.
tiptil *adv.* on tiptoe.
tir *sn. mil.* fire ; *sport* target shooting.
tiradă *sf.* tirade.
tiraj *sn.* circulation ; *(la sobă)* draught.
tiran *sm.* tyrant.
tiranic *adj.* tyrannical.
tiranie *sf.* tyranny.
tirbuşon *sn.* corkscrew.
tirolez *sm.*, *adj.*, tiroleză *sf.*, *adj.* Tirolese.
tisă *sf.* yew tree.
titan *sm.* titan.
titanic *adj.* titanic.
titirez *sn.* (spinning) top.
titlu *sn.* title ; *fig.* claim ; *chim.* titre ; ~ *de glorie* desert ; ~ *de proprietate* property deed ; *cu* ~ *de împrumut* as a loan ; *cu* ~ *de încercare* tentatively.
titular *sm.* holder. *adj.* permanent ; *(d. profesor)* in ordinary.
titulatură *sf.* title.
tiv *sn.* hem(-stitch), selvedge.
tivi *vt.* to hem-stitch.
tiz *sm.* namesake.
tîlc *sn.* sense, interpretation ; *cu* ~ meaningful(ly).
tîlhar *sm.* robber ; *fig.* scoundrel ; ~ *de drumul mare* highwayman ; footpad.
tîlhăresc *adj.* predatory.
tîlhărie *sf.* robbery ; hold-up.
tîmpenie *sf.* stupidity.
tîmpi *vt.* to stultify. *vr.* to grow dull.

tîmpit sm. nitwit. adj. idiotic.

tîmplar sm. carpenter; (de mobilă) joiner.

tîmplă sf. temple.

tîmplărie sf. carpentry; (de mobilă) joinery.

tînăr sm. youth, youngster. adj. young; (tineresc) juvenile; de ~ from an early age.

tînără sf. young girl.

tîngui vr. to wail.

tînguială sf. lament(ation).

tînguios, tînguitor adj. mournful.

tînjală sf.: a se lăsa pe ~ to slack work.

tînji vi. to languish; (d. plante) to wilt.

tîrcol sn.: a da tîrcoale to hover about.

tîrfă sf. whore.

tîrg sn. (bîlci) fair; (tranzacţie) bargain; (oraş) borough, market town.

tîrgui vt. to shop. vr. to haggle.

tîrguială sf. shopping; (tocmeală) bargaining.

tîrî vt. to drag (along). vr. to creep; (d. obiecte) to hang low.

tîrîş adv. crawling; ~-grăpiş at great pains.

tîrîtoare sf. reptile.

tîrnăcop sn. pick-axe.

tîrziu sn.: într-un ~ after a long time. adj. late, belated. adv. late; cel mai ~ at the latest; mai ~ later, further on, afterwards.

toacă sf. bell board; fig. vesper.

toaletă sf. toilet; (closet) lavatory.

toamna adv. in autumn.

toamnă sf. autumn; ~ tîrzie Indian summer; la ~ next autumn; astă ~ last autumn.

toană sf. caprice; mood; cu toane moody.

toarce vt., vi. to spin; (d. pisici) to purr.

toartă sf. ear (of a vessel); la ~ intimate.

toast sn. toast.

toasta vi. to toast (smb.'s health, etc.).

toată, toate adj., pron. v. tot.

tobă sf. drum; mosaic salame; (la cărţi) diamonds; toba mare kettle drum; ~ de ... full of...

tobogan sn. slide, chute.

toc sn. (de scris) pen(holder); (de pantof) heel; (teacă) scabbard; (de uşă etc.) jamb; ~ cui stiletto heel; ~ cu pastă ball point, byro; ~ rezervor fountain pen. interj. knock.

toca vt. to hash; (cu maşina) to mince; (a creşte) to notch; fig. to squander. vi. to rattle; rel. to hammer on the bellboard.

tocană sf. goulash.

tocat adj. hashed.

tocătură sf. forcemeat.

toceală sf. swotting.

toci vt. to blunt; fig. to dull; (a învăţa) to swot. vi. fig. to cram. vr. to be blunted.

tocilar sm. whetstone grinder; fig. swot.

tocilă sf. grindstone; (piatră) whetstone.

tocit adj. blunted.

tocmai adv. precisely; (de curînd) recently; ~ acum now of all times; nu ~ not exactly;

e ~ *cine ne trebuie* he is the very man.

tocmeală *sf.* bargaining; *(înțelegere)* convention.

tocmi *vt.* to hire; *(a închiria și)* to book. *vr.* to bargain, to pledge (to do).

togă *sf.* toga.

toi *sn.* climax; *în* ~*ul luptei* in the thick of the battle.

tolăni *vr.* to sprawl.

toiag *sn.* staff; (walking) stick.

tolera *vt.* to tolerate.

tolerant *adj.* tolerant.

toleranță *sf.* tolerance.

tombolă *sf.* tombola.

tomnatic *adj.* autumn(al); *fig.* middle-aged.

ton *sm.* tunny (fish). *sn. muz.* tone; tune; *(nuanță)* shade.

tonalitate *sf. muz.* tune, tonality; *(culoare)* hue.

tonă *sf.* (metric) ton.

tonic *sn., adj.* tonic, cordial.

tonomat *sn.* juke-box.

tont *sm.* booby; *(neîndemînatic)* gawk. *adj.* dull; *(neîndeminatic)* gawky.

topi *vt.* to melt; *(zăpada)* to thaw; *(cînepa etc.)* to ret. *vr.* to melt; *se topește* it thaws.

topire *sf.* melting; *(a zăpezii)* thaw(ing); *(a cînepii)* retting.

topografie *sf.* topography; *(așezare)* lie (of the land).

topor *sn.* axe; *din* ~ coarse.

toporaș *sm.* violet.

toptan *sn.: cu* ~*ul* wholesale.

toreador *sm.* bull-fighter.

torent *sn.* torrent.

torențial *adj.* pouring. *adv.* cats and dogs.

torid *adj.* torrid.

toropeală *sf.* torpor.

toropi *vt.* to enervate.

toropit *adj.* drowsy.

torpila *vt.* (sink by a) torpedo; *fig.* to wreck.

torpilă *sf.* torpedo.

torpilor *sn.* torpedo boat.

tors *sn.* spinning; purring (of a cat); *anat.* torso. *adj.* spun.

tort *sn.* spun yarn; spool; *(prăjitură)* iced cake; birth-day *sau* wedding cake.

tortura *vt.* to torture; *(mai ales fig.)* to torment.

tortură *sf.* torture.

torță *sf.* torch.

tos *adj.: zahăr* ~ castor sugar.

tot *sn.* whole; the pith (and marrow). *adj.* all; *(întreg)* whole; *(fiecare)* every; *toate acestea* all this *sau* these; *toată lumea* everybody; *toată ziua* all day long; ~ *anul* throughout the year; ~ *omul* every man (Jack); ~ *timpul* always; *de toate zilele* everyday . . . ; *peste* ~ *locul* everywhere; *în* ~ *cazul* anyhow; *în toate părțile* everywhere; *cu toate acestea* however; *cu toată*. . . in spite of . . . ; *toate celea* everything. *pron. (și pl.) toate* everything (else); all (things); *(toți)* everybody (else), all (people); *de toate* all and sundry; *după toate* after all; *înainte de toate* first of all; above all; *toate ca toate dar* . . . all right but . . . . *adv. (temporal)* still; even now; *(negativ)* not yet, not even now; *(în continuare)* further; *(mereu)* always; *(cam)* about; *(invariabil)* invariably; *(repetat)* repeatedly; *(crescînd)* more; *(la fel)* likewise;

(tocmai) precisely ; *(iar)* again ;
(numai) only; *(complet)* wholly;
(în orice caz) in any case ;
~ *de atîtea ori* as many times.
total *sn.* (sum)total ; *în* ~
in all. *adj.* total, absolute ;
econ. all-out.
totaliza *vt.* to tote (up); *(a se ridica
la)* to amount to.
totdeauna *adv.* always ; *pentru*
~ for good (and all) ; *rel.*
şi poetic for ever (and ever).
totodată *adv.* concomitantly, at
the same time.
totuna *adv.* all the same.
totuşi *conj.* yet ; *şi* ~ for all
that.
toţi *adj., pron.* all ; every(body).
tovarăş *sm.,* **tovarăşă** *sf.* comrade ; mate ; ~ *de cameră*
room-mate ; ~ *de drum* fellow-
-traveller ; ~ *de suferinţă* fellow sufferer ; ~ *de viaţă* life-
-mate.
tovărăşesc *adv.* comradely.
tovărăşie *sf.* comradeliness ; *(societate)* company ; *com.* partnership.
trabuc *sn.* cigar.
trac *sm.* Thracian. *sn.* (stage-)
fright. *adj.* Thracian.
tracic *adj.* Thracian.
tractor *sn.* tractor ; ~ *pe şenile*
caterpillar tractor.
tractorist *sm.* tractor-driver.
tradiţie *sf.* tradition.
tradiţional *adj.* traditional.
traducător *sm.* translator.
traduce *vt.* to translate ; *a* ~ *în
viaţă* to materialize.
traducere *sf.* translation ; ~ *în
viaţă* materialization.
trafic *sn.* trade ; traffic.
trafica *vi.* to traffic (in).

traficant *sm.* racketeer ; ~ *de
stupefiante* dope dealer ; ~ *de
carne vie* slave dealer.
traforaj *sn.* fret-saw.
trage *vt.* to draw ; *(puternic)*
to pull ; to haul ; *(a scoate)*
to pull out ; *(clopotele)* to
ring ; *(zăvorul)* to shoot ; *(a
tîrî)* to drag ; *(a suferi)* to
suffer ; *(concluzii şi)* to infer ;
a ~ *mîţa de coadă* to live
from hand to mouth ; *a* ~
pe roată to break on the
wheel ; *a* ~ *pe sfoară* to
diddle ; *a* ~ *la răspundere*
to haul smb. over the coals ;
a ~ *la sorţi* to draw lots (for) ;
a ~ *palme cuiva* to box smb.'s
ears ; *a* ~ *un somn* to get
forty winks ; *a* ~ *chiulul
(la şcoală)* to play truant ;
fig. to idle. *vi.* to pull ; *(cu
arma)* to shoot ; *(a cîntări)* to
weigh ; *(a poposi)* to put up (at
a house, etc.) ; *(a tinde)* to
tend (towards) ; *(d. curent,
sobă etc.)* to draw ; *a* ~ *cu
urechea* to eavesdrop ; *a* ~
cu ochiul to cast glances at ;
a ~ *la măsea* to booze ; ~
să moară he breathes his last.
vr. to move ; *(dintr-o familie)* to
descend (from) ; *(dintr-un loc)*
to come ; *(a fi provocat)* to
originate (in) ; *se* ~ *dintr-o
familie muncitorească* he was
born into the working class.
tragedian *sm.* tragedian.
tragedie *sf.* tragedy.
tragere *sf.* drawing ; *(tir)* shooting ; ~ *de inimă* zeal, enthusiasm ; ~ *la sorţi* drawing
of lots ; ~ *la ţintă* target
shooting.

tragic *sn.* tragic (aspect, etc.) ; în ~ tragically. *adj.* tragic. *adv.* sadly.

trai *sn.* living ; *(material şi)* livelihood ; bread.

trainic *adj.* lasting. *adv.* solidly.

traistă *sf.* wallet, bagful ; *traista-ciobanului bot.* shepherd's purse.

trambulină *sf.* springboard ; *(la înot)* diving board.

tramvai *sn.* tram(way) ; *cu ~ul* by tram.

trandafir *sm.* rose (flower) ; thin, spiced pork sausage ; ~ *bătut* moss rose ; ~ *sălbatic* dog-rose ; *lemn de ~* rose-wood.

trandafiriu *adj.* rosy.

transatlantic *sn.* liner. *adj.* transatlantic.

transborda *vt.* to transship.

transcrie *vt.* to transcribe.

transcriere *sf.* transcription.

transfer *sn.* transfer.

transfera *vt.* to transfer. *vr.* to change one's job.

transfigura *vr.* to be transfigured.

transforma *vt.* to transform. *vr.* to turn (into).

transformare *sf.* transformation.

transfuzie *sf.* transfusion.

transilvan *adj.*, **transilvănean** *sm.*, **transilvăneancă** *sf.*, **transilvănesc** *adj.* Transylvanian.

transistor *sn.* transistor ; *cu ~ i* transistor(ed).

translator *sm.* interpreter.

transmisi(un)e *sf.* transmission ; *radio şi* broadcast.

transmite *vt.* to transmit ; *(a preda şi)* to convey; *(la radio şi)* to broadcast. *vi.* to transmit. *vr.* to spread ; to be handed

down (from one generation to another) ; *(a se moşteni)* to run in the family.

transparent *sn.* (Venetian) blind ; *(pt. scris)* black lines. *adj.* transparent; pellucid; *(d. ţesături şi)* flimsy.

transparenţă *sf.* transparence.

transperant *sn.* (Venetian) blind.

transpira *vi.* to perspire ; *fig.* to leak.

transpiraţie *sf.* perspiration.

transport *sn.* transport(ation) ; *pl.* transports ; *(cantitate)* consignment.

transporta *vt.* to transport.

transportor *sm.*, *adj.* conveyor.

transpune *vt.* to transpose. *vr. fig.* to imagine oneself.

tranşa *vt.* to solve ; to carve (meat).

tranşă *sf.* portion.

tranşee *sf.* trench.

tranzacţie *sf.* transaction, compact, convention.

tranzit *sn.* transit.

tranzitiv *adj.* transitive.

tranziţie *sf.* transition ; *de ~* provisional.

trap *sn.* trot ; *la ~* at a trot.

trapez *sn.* trapeze ; *geom.* trapezium. *anat.* trapezius.

tras *adj.* drawn ; *(d. faţă)* worn, haggard.

trasa *vt.* to draw ; to outline ; *(o sarcină)* to assign.

traseu *sn.* route.

trata *vt.* to treat ; *(oaspeţi)* to entertain ; *(un bolnav şi)* to cure ; *(o temă)* to deal with ; *(a numi)* to call. *vi.* to negotiate.

tratament *sn.* treatment ; *med. şi* cure.

tratare *sf.* treatment.

tratat *sn.* treaty; *(carte)* treatise.

tratative *sf. pl.* talks.

traversa *vt.* to traverse. *vi.* to cross (over).

traversă *sf.* sleeper.

travesti *sn.* disguise. *vr.* to disguise oneself.

trăda *vt., vr.* to betray (oneself).

trădare *sf.* betrayal; *(de țară)* treason.

trădător *sm.* traitor. *adj.* treacherous.

trăgaci *sn.* trigger.

trăi *vi.* to live; *Trăiască R.S.R.!* Long live the Socialist Republic of Romania! *să trăiești!* your health! *a ~ ca în sînul lui Avram* to live in clover.

trăinicie *sf.* durability.

trăncăneală *sf.* prattle.

trăncăni *vt.* to prattle. *vi.* to gas.

trăsătură *sf.* line; *(caracteristică)* feature; *dintr-o ~ de condei* at one stroke of the pen.

trăsnaie *sf.* odd freak.

trăsnet *sn.* thunder(bolt).

trăsni *vt.* to thunder; *(a lovi)* to strike. *vi. impers.* to thunder; *fig.* to occur.

trăsnit *sm.* loony. *adj.* thunderstruck; *fig.* barmy on the crumpet.

trăsură *sf.* carriage; *(birjă)* cab; *~ de unire* hyphen.

treabă *sf.* business; *(muncă)* work; *(slujbă)* job; *(chestiune)* problem; *(situație)* condition; *de ~* reliable.

treacăt *sn.* passing; *în ~* incidentally, fugitively; offhandedly.

treaptă *sf.* step; *pl.* flight (of steps); *fig.* degree, level; stage, phase.

treaz *adj.* (wide) awake; *(nebăut)* sober; *(atent)* watchful.

trebui *vi.* must, to have to; *(moralmente)* ought to; *(indicînd o obligație mai slabă)* should; *(a avea nevoie de)* to need; *(a fi necesar)* to be necessary; *~e să mă duc* I must go; *~e neapărat să mă duc* I must needs go; *~e să fi sosit (deja)* he must have arrived (already).

trebuință *sf.* need; *de ~* needful.

trecătoare *sf.* (mountain) pass.

trecător *sm.* passer-by. *adj.* transient.

trece *vt.* to pass (through); *(a traversa)* to cross; *(a înscrie)* to register; *a ~ sub tăcere* to hush. *vi.* to pass; *(pe lîngă)* to pass by, to go past; *(d. proiectile)* to shoot past; *(d. vînt)* to blow; *(înainte)* to go forward *sau* along; *(prin) fig.* to experience; *(pe la cineva etc.)* to call (at smb's house); *(de un punct)* to pass.; *fig. (prin minte etc.)* to occur; *(a străpunge)* to break through; *(d. timp și)* to elapse; *(d. boli și)* to heal; *(a depăși)* to exceed; *a ~ drept ceva sau cineva* to be held as ...; *a ~ în istorie* to go down in history; *a ~ la fapte* to take action; *a ~ peste* to ignore; *a ~ peste capul cuiva* to act in defiance of smb. *vr.* to wither; *(d. fructe)* to grow overripe; *(a se sfîrși)* to be spent; *(a depăși)* to go beyond the limits; *a se ~ cu firea* to exaggerate.

trecere *sf.* passage; *fig.* pull; ~ *de nivel* level crossing; *în* ~ off-handedly.

trecut *sm.* past (tense); ~*ul apropiat* the recent past; ~*ul de luptă al poporului* the people's past struggles; *în* ~ formerly; *din* ~ of yore. *adj.* past; previous; *(ca vîrstă)* old; *(ofilit)* wilted.

treflă *sf.* clubs.

trei *sm., adj., num.* three; *cîte* ~ by threes.

treier *sn.* threshing.

treiera *vt.* to thresh.

treierat, treieriş *sn.* threshing (-time).

treilea *adj., num.* (the) third.

treime *sf.* one third; *rel.* trinity.

treisprezece *sm., adj., num.* thirteen.

treisprezecelea *adj., num.* (the) thirteenth.

treizeci *sm., adj., num.* thirty.

treizecilea *adj., num.* (the) thirtieth.

tremur *sn.* trembling; shiver; *(de aripi, frunze* etc.) quiver.

tremura *vi.* to tremble; *(uşor)* to quiver; *(de frig)* to shiver; *(a se înfiora)* to shudder.

tremurat *sn.* tremble, trembling. *adj.* quivering; *(nesigur)* shaky.

tremurător *adj.* trembling; *(nesigur)* hesitant.

tren *sn.* train; ~ *accelerat* fast train; ~ *de marfă* goods train; ~ *expres* express train; ~ *personal* slow train; ~ *rapid* through train.

trenă *sf.* train.

trenci *sn.* mackintosh.

trening *sn.* training suit.

trepida *vi.* to vibrate.

trepied *sn.* tripod.

treptat *adj.* gradual. *adv.* step by step.

tresă *sf.* braid.

tresări *vi.* to start.

tresărire *sf.* start(ing).

trestie *sf.* reed; ~ *de zahăr* sugar cane.

trezi *vt.* to wake; *fig.* to (a)rouse. *vr.* to awake; *(din beţie)* to be sobered; *(din leşin)* to come to; *(cu cineva)* to find oneself (face to face with smb.); *(d. băuturi* etc.*)* to grow stale.

tria *vt.* to sort.

triaj *sn.* selection; *c.f.* marshalling *sau* shunting (yard).

trib *sn.* tribe.

tribunal *sn.* law court; *(judecătorii)* the bench; ~ *suprem* Supreme Court.

tribună *sf.* (grand) stand; *(pt. discursuri)* rostrum; *(ziar)* tribune.

tribut *sn.* tribute.

tricolor *sn., adj.* tricolour.

tricota *vt., vi.* to knit.

tricotaje *sn. pl.* knitwear.

tricou *sn.* jersey.

triere *sf.* picking.

trifoi *sn.* trefoil.

trigonometrie *sf.* trigonometry.

tril *sn.* trill.

trilogie *sf.* trilogy.

trimestrial *adj.* quarterly.

trimestru *sn.* quarter; *(la şcoală)* term.

trimis *sm.* envoy.

trimite *vt.* to send; *(prin poştă)* to post; *(a expedia)* to ship;

(a transmite) to convey; *a ~ pe cineva în judecată* to sue smb. at law. *vi.* to send (for the doctor, etc.).

trimitere *sf.* reference.

trio *sn., muz.* trio.

tripla *vt.* to treble.

triplu *adj.* treble.

tripou *sn.* gambling-house.

trist *adj.* sad; *de ~ă amintire* odious.

tristețe *sf.* sadness.

trișa *vi.* to trick (in card playing).

triumf *sn.* triumph; *fig.* success; *în ~* triumphantly.

triumfa *vi.* to triumph; *fig.* to succeed.

triumfal *adj.* triumphal.

triumfător *adj.* triumphant.

triunghi *sn.* triangle.

triunghiular *adj.* triangular.

trivial *adj.* coarse.

trîmbiță *sf.* bugle; *trîmbița judecății de apoi* the last trump.

trîndav *adj.* slothful.

trîndăvi *vi.* to idle.

trîntă *sf.* wrestle.

trînti *vt.* to fling; *(a doborî)* to fell; *(a izbi)* to slam; *(a scăpa)* to drop; *(la examen)* to pluck. *vi.* to fling things about, to vent one's anger. *vr.* to fling oneself (down).

trîntor *sm.* drone.

troacă *sf.* trough.

troc *sn.* truck.

trofeu *sn.* trophy.

troglodit *sm.* cave-dweller.

troheu *sm.* trochee.

troian *sn.* snowdrift; welter (of things). *adj.* Trojan.

troieni *vt.* to bury in snow.

troienit *adj.* snowbound.

troiță *sf.* crucifix.

troleibuz *sn.* trolley-bus.

troleu *sn.* trolley.

trombă *sf.* water-spout; *(vîrtej)* whirlwind.

trombon *sn.* trombone.

trompă *sf.* trunk; *(la insecte)* proboscis; *anat.* tube.

trompetă *sf.* trumpet.

trompetist *sm.* trumpet-player.

tron *sn.* throne.

trona *vi.* to rule; *fig.* to dominate.

tropăi *vi.* to trample.

tropăit *sn.* trampling; clatter (of hoofs).

tropic *sn.* tropic.

tropical *adj.* tropical.

tropot *sn.* clatter of hoofs.

trosnet *sn.* crash.

trosni *vt., vi.* to crack.

trosnitură *sf.* crack.

trotinetă *sf.* (child's) scooter.

trotuar *sn.* side walk, pavement.

trubadur *sm.* troubadour.

truc *sn.* trick.

trudă *sf.* toil; *(osteneală)* trouble; *cu multă ~* at great pains.

trudi *vi., vr.* to toil (and moil).

trufanda *sf.* early fruit *sau* vegetable.

trufaș *adj.* haughty. *adv.* arrogantly.

trufie *sf.* conceit.

trunchi *sn.* trunk; (chopping) log; *(ciot)* stump; *geom.* frustum.

trunchia *vt.* to mutilate; *(un text și)* to distort.

trup *sn.* body; *(trunchi)* trunk.

trupă *sf. mil.* troop, rank and file; *(teatru)* company; *trupe de șoc* commando(s); rangers.

trupese *adj.* bodily; sexual.

trusă *sf.* (surgeon's, etc.) case.

trusou *sn.* trousseau.

trust *sn.* *(capitalist)* corpora tion ; *(socialist)* group of industries.

tu *pron.* you ; *înv.* thou.

tub *sn.* tube ; *(ţeavă şi)* pipe.

tuberculos *sm.* consumptive patient. *adj.* consumptive.

tuberculoză *sf.* tuberculosis, tb.

tuciuriu *sm.* blackamoor. *adj.* swarthy.

tufă *sf.* shrub ; ~ *de Veneţia* nothing ; nobody.

tufiş *sn.* shrub(bery).

tulbura *vt.* to trouble ; *(pe cineva şi)* to move ; *(a zăpăci)* to confuse. *vr.* *(d. ape)* to be troubled ; *(d. oameni)* to be flurried ; *(a se emoţiona)* to lose countenance.

tulburare *sf.* trouble ; *fig.* unrest ; *(emoţie)* worry ; *pol.* riot.

tulburat *adj.* troubled ; *(d. oameni şi)* moved.

tulburător *adj.* troubling ; exciting ; *(d. frumuseţe)* tantalizing.

tulbure *adj.* troubled ; *(d. apă)* muddy ; *(neclar)* *fig.* dim.

tulpină *sf.* stem ; *(de copac)* trunk ; *med.* strain.

tumbă *sf.* summersault, dido.

tumult *sn.* tumult ; *(zarvă)* hubbub.

tumultuos *adj.* tumultuous.

tun *sn.* cannon ; ~ *antiaerian* anti-aircraft gun ; ~ *anticar* anti-tank gun. *adv.* soundly.

tuna *vi.* *impers.* to thunder ; *a ~t şi i-a adunat* they are a nicely assorted set.

tunător *adj.* thunderous.

tunde *vt.* to cut (the hair of) ; to shear (animals) ; to mow (the grass). *vr.* to get a haircut.

tunel *sn.* tunnel.

tunet *sn.* thunder.

tunică *sf.* tunic.

tuns *sn.* hair-cut ; *(al animalelor)* shearing. *adj.* cut ; trimmed, *(d. mustaţă şi)* clipped ; *(d. animale)* shorn ; *(d. iarbă)* mown.

tunsoare *sf.* haircut.

tupeu *sn.* pluck.

tupila *vr.* to cower, to slink.

tur *sn.* tour ; *sport* lap (of the route) ; seat (of the trousers); ~ *de orizont* general survey ; ~ *de forţă* tour de force ; *~ul oraşului* seeing *sau* showing the lions (of the town).

tură *sf.* shift ; *(la şah)* castle, rook ; *în tura de noapte* on the night shift.

turba *vi.* to grow rabid ; *fig.* to grow mad.

turban *sn.* turban.

turbare *sf.* rabies ; *fig.* fury.

turbat *adj.* *med.* rabid ; *fig.* furious. *adv.* rabidly.

turbă *sf.* peat.

turbină *sf.* turbine.

turbopropulsor *sn.* turbo-prop (plane).

turboreactor *sn.* turbojet.

turbulent *adj.* riotous; *(nesupus)* mutinous.

turc *sm.* Turk. *adj.* Turkish ; Ottoman.

turcesc *adj.* Turkish.

turceşte *adj.* like the Turks. *adv.* Turkish ; cross-legged.

turcoaică *sf.* Turk(ish woman).

turism *sn.* tourism ; motor-car.

turist *sm.* tourist.

turistic *adj.* touristic.

turlă *sf.* tower ; spire (of a church) ; *(la sondă)* oil-derrick.

turmă *sf.* flock ; *fig.* rabble.

turn *sn.* tower ; *(la șah)* rook, castle.

turna *vt.* to pour ; *(fontă* etc.*)* to cast ; *(în forme)* to mould ; *(a denunța)* to denounce ; *(un film)* to shoot. *vi.* to pour ; *fig.* to squeak.

turnare *sf.* casting; *cinema* shooting.

turnător *sn.* foundry-worker ; *fig.* squeak.

turnătorie *sf.* foundry (works).

turneu *sn.* tour.

turtă *sf.* cake ; ~ *dulce* ginger bread. *adv.* dead (drunk).

turti *vt.* to flatten. *vr.* to be battered.

turtit *adj.* flat(tened) ; *(d. nas)* bashed in.

turturică *sf.* turtle dove.

tuse *sf.* cough(ing) ; ~ *convulsivă* whooping cough.

tuș *sn.* China ink ; *sport* touch.

tușă *sf.* touch (line).

tuși *vi.* to cough.

tutelă *sf.* guardianship ; *pol.* trusteeship.

tutore *sm.* guardian.

tutui *vt., vr.* to thou and thee (each other).

tutun *sn.* tobacco.

tutungerie *sf.* tobacconist's.

tutungiu *sm.* tobacconist.

Ț

țambal *sn.* dulcimer.

țanc *sn.* crag ; *la* ~ on the dot.

țandără *sf.* splinter.

țap *sm.* he-goat ; mug (of beer) ; ~ *ispășitor* scapegoat.

țar *sm.* czar.

țară *sf.* country ; land ; *(patrie)* homeland; *(regiune rurală)* country(side) ; villages ; *Țara Românească* Wallachia ; *Țările de Jos* the Low Countries.

țarc *sn.* pen ; reservation.

țarină[1] *sf.* upturned land.

țarină[2] *sf.* czarevna.

țarist *adj.* czarist.

țață *sf.* aunt ; *(mahalagioaică)* dowdy.

țăcăni *vi.* to rattle.

țăran *sm.* peasant ; villager ; *(în alte țări)* farmer ; ~ *co-operator* co-operative farmer ; ~ *mijlocaș* middle peasant.

țărancă *sf.* peasant woman.

țărănesc *adj.* peasant...

țărănime *sf.* peasantry, **pea**sants ; ~ *cooperatistă* co-operative farmers.

țărînă *sf.* dust ; *(pămînt)* earth.

țărm *sn.* shore ; *(de rîu)* bank.

țăruș *sm.* stake.

țeapă *sf.* sliver ; *(spin)* thorn ; *(de animal)* spine ; *(pt. tortură)* stake.

țeapăn *adj.* stiff ; *(de durere)* benumbed. *adv.* stiffly.

țeastă *sf.* skull ; *(cap)* head.

țeavă *sf.* pipe ; *(de armă)* barrel.

țel *sn.* aim.

țelină *sf.* celery ; *agr.* fallow land.

ţep *sm.* prick ; *(de animal)* spike.

ţesală *sf.* currycomb.

ţesăla *vt.* to currycomb.

ţesător *sm.* weaver.

ţesătorie *sf.* weaving ; *(fabrică)* weaving mill.

ţesătură *sf.* texture.

ţese *vt.* to weave ; *(ciorapi)* to darn ; *fig.* to hatch. *vi.* to weave.

ţesut *sn.* tissue. *adj.* woven.

ţiceneală *sf.* craze.

ţiceni *vr.* to go mad.

ţicnit *adj.* batty.

ţie *pron.* (to) you.

ţigan *sm.* Gipsy ; *(rom)* Rom(any).

ţigancă *sf.* Gipsy woman.

ţigară *sf.* cig(arette) ; ~ *de foi* cigar.

ţigaret *sn.* cigarette holder.

ţigaretă *sf.* cigarette.

ţigănesc *adj.* gipsy (like) ; *(d. limbă)* Romany.

ţigăneşte *adv.* (in) Romany.

ţigăni *vr.* to cadge ; *(a se tocmi)* to squabble.

ţigănie *sf.* haggling.

ţigănos *adj.* swarthy.

ţiglă *sf.* tile.

ţine *vt.* to hold ; *(a păstra)* to keep ; *(a reţine şi)* to retain, to stop ; *(a conserva şi)* to preserve ; *(a întreţine şi)* to keep up ; *(a purta)* to carry ; *a* ~ *să* to insist on (doing smth.) ; *a* ~ *casa* to be the breadwinner ; *a* ~ *o cuvîntare* to make a speech ; *a-şi* ~ *firea* to keep oneself in check ; *a* ~ *o lecţie* to give a lesson ; *a* ~ *o conferinţă* to lecture. *vi.* to last, to keep ; *(a rezista)* to endure ; *a* ~ *cu cineva* to side with smb. ;

a ~ *de* to belong to ; *a* ~ *la cineva* to be fond of smb. *vr.* to hold (oneself) (erect, etc.) ; *(a se stăpîni)* to refrain oneself; *(a avea loc)* to take place ; *a se* ~ *de* to lean against ; *a se* ~ *de cuvînt* to be as good as one's word ; *nu m-am putut* ~ *de rîs* I could not help laughing ; *a se* ~ *de treabă* to stick to one's job

ţinere *sf.* keeping ; ~ *de minte* memory.

ţintar *sn.* nine men's morris.

ţintaş *sm.* marksman.

ţintă *sf.* target ; *fig. şi* goal ; *(a unui atac)* receiving end ; *(cui)* tack ; *(de bocanc)* spike ; *(pt. alpinism)* clinker ; ~ *a batjocurii* laughing stock ; *fără* ~ aimless(ly).

ţinti *vt.* to aim at. *vi.* to aim (at smth.) ; *(a năzui la)* to strive (for).

ţintui *vt.* to fasten ; to rivet ; *a fi* ~*t la pat* to be bed-ridden.

ţinut *sn.* region. *adj.* kept.

ţinută *sf.* carriage ; *(mers)* gait ; *(purtare)* conduct ; *(haine)* clothes ; *mil.* uniform ; ~ *de gală* evening suit ; *de* ~ lofty.

ţipa *vt., vi.* to shout ; *(tare)* to yell ; *(sinistru)* to screech.

ţipar *sm.* grig ; *(anghilă şi fig.)* eel.

ţipăt *sn.* shout ; *(puternic)* yell ; *(sinistru)* screech.

ţipător *adj.* blatant.

ţipenie *sf.* person ; *nici* ~ not the shadow of a ghost.

ţiţei *sn.* crude oil.

ţiui *vi.* to whizz ; *(d. glonţ şi)* to ping ; *îmi* ~*e urechile* my ears tingle.

ţiuit *sn.* whizz(ing sound) ; *(de glonţ)* ping ; *(al urechilor)* tingle.

ţîfnă *sf.* pip ; *fig.* petulance.

ţîfnos *adj.* tetchy.

ţînţar *sm.* gnat, mosquito ; ~ *anofel* anopheles.

ţîr *sm.* dried herring.

ţîrîi *vi.* to ring ; *(d. greier)* to chirp ; *(d. ploaie)* to mizzle.

ţîrîită *sf.* : *cu ţîrîita* by drops.

ţîşni *vi.* to gush ; *fig.* to spring (out).

ţîşnitoare *sf.* drinking fountain.

ţiţă *sf.* teat ; *pl. (sîni)* bubs.

ţoapă *sf.* cad ; *(femeie)* dowdy.

ţoi *sn.* brandy glass.

ţol *sm.* inch. *sn.* carpet.

ţopăi *vi.* to hop.

ţugui *vt.* to taper ; *a-şi* ~ *buzele* to purse one's lips. *vr.* to taper.

ţuguiat *adj.* tapering.

ţuică *sf.* plum brandy.

ţurcă *sf.* *(joc)* tipcat ; *(căciulă)* fur bonnet.

ţurţure *sm.* icicle.

U

ucenic *sm.* apprentice ; *fig.* disciple.

ucenicie *sf.* apprenticeship ; *(contract)* indenture.

ucide *vt.* to kill ; *(a asasina)* to murder.

ucigaş *sm.* assassin. *adj.* murderous.

ucigător *adj.* terrible.

ucrainian *sm.*, *adj.*, **ucrainiană** *sf.*, *adj.* Ukrainian.

ud *sn.* water. *adj.* wet ; *(umed)* damp ; moist ; ~ *leoarcă* drenched.

uda *vt.* to wet ; *(a umezi)* to moisten ; *(d. un rîu)* to flow through ; *(florile)* to water. *vr.* to get soaked ; to wet one's clothes.

uger *sn.* udder.

uimi *vt.* to stagger.

uimire *sf.* amazement.

uimit *adj.* thunderstruck.

uimitor *adj.* perplexing.

uita *vt.* to forget ; *(a neglija)* to overlook ; *nu* ~ remember. *vi.* to forget. *vr.* to look (at) ; *(a fi* ~*t)* to be forgotten ; *a se* ~ *la* to watch ; *fig.* to mind.

uitare *sf.* oblivion ; ~ *de sine* self-denial.

uituc *sm.* scatterbrain. *adj.* absent-minded.

ulcer *sn.* ulcer.

ulei *sn.* (edible) oil ; *(tablou şi)* oil painting.

uleios *adj.* oily.

uliu *sm.* kite.

ulm *sm.* elm (tree).

ulterior *adj.* subsequent. *adv.* later (on).

ultim *adj.* last ; *(cel mai recent)* latest.

ultimatum *sn.* ultimatum.
ultrascurt *adj.* ultra-short.
ultrasecret *adj.* top secret.
ultrasunet *sn.* ultra-sound.
ului *vt.* to amaze.
uluit *adj.* taken aback.
uman *adj.* human, man's ; *(ome-nos)* humane. *adv.* decently.
umanism *sn.* humanism.
umanist *sm.* humanist.
umanistică *sf.* humanities.
umanitar *adj.* humanitarian.
umanitate *sf.* humanity ; *(ome-nie şi)* humanenness ; *(ome-nire şi)* mankind.
umaniza *vt.* to humanize. *vr.* to become human *sau* humane.
umăr *sm.* shoulder ; ~ *la* ~ shoulder to shoulder.
umbla *vt.* to scour. *vi.* to go ; *(pe jos şi)* to walk ; *(a călă-tori)* to travel ; *(cu un vehicul public* sau *călare)* to ride ; *(cu automobilul)* to drive ; *(a rătăci)* to wander ; *a* ~ *cu* to handle ; *fig.* to use ; *(o maşină)* to use ; to drive ; *a* ~ *după* to seek.
umbră *sf.* *(răcoare, întuneric)* shade ; *(a unei persoane etc.)* shadow ; *(frig)* coolness ; *fig.* aspersions ; *umbre chinezeşti* galanty show.
umbrelă *sf.* umbrella ; *(de soare)* sunshade.
umbri *vt.* to shade ; *fig.* to eclipse.
umbros *adj.* shady ; cool.
umed *adj.* damp ; *(ud)* wet.
umeraş *sn.* coat hanger.
umezeală *sf.* moisture.
umezi *vt.* to moisten ; *(tare)* to drench. *vr.* to become damp.
umfla *vt.* to fill ; *(tare)* to (cause to) swell ; *(a exagera)*

to exaggerate ; *(a lua)* to seize ; *l-a* ~*t rîsul* he could not help laughing. *vr.* to be swollen.
umflat *adj.* swollen ; *fig.* high-flown ; pompous.
umflătură *sf.* swelling.
umil *adj.* humble, low(ly) ; unob-trusive. *.adv.* humbly.
umili *vt.* to humble. *vr.* to humiliate oneself.
umilinţă *sf.* humility ; *(ruşine)* shame.
umilit *adj.* humble(d).
umilitor *adj.* degrading.
umor *sn.* humour ; *(scris şi)* facetiae ; ~ *ieftin* slapstick.
umorist *sm.* humorist
umoristic *adj.* humorous.
umple *vt.* to fill (up) ; *(a ghiftui)* to stuff ; *a* ~ *de o boală* to infect with a disease. *vr.* to fill.
umplut *adj.* filled ; *(îndesat)* stuffed.
umplutură *sf.* filling ; forcemeat ; *fig.* rubbish.
un *adj.* one ; *pl.* some ; *pron.,* *num.* somebody ; one ; *pl.* some ; ~*ul altuia* (to) each other ; ~*ul după altul* one after another ; *nici* ~*ul* none (of them), nobody ; *nici* ~*ul din doi* neither.
unanim *adj.* unanimous. *adv.* unanimously.
unanimitate *sf.* unanimity.
unchi *sm.* uncle.
undă *sf.* wave.
unde *adv.* where ; *(încotro şi)* whither ; *(cînd)* when ; then ; *acolo* ~ where ; *de* ~ whence ; *pe* ~ where ? which way ?
undeva *adv.* somewhere (or else) ; *interog. şi neg.* anywhere.

undiţă *sf.* fishing rod.
unealtă *sf.* tool; *(agricolă)* implement.
unelti *vt., vi.* to plot.
uneltire *sf.* machination.
uneori *adv.* sometimes.
ungar *sm., adj.,* **ungară** *sf., adj.* Hungarian.
unge *vt.* to lubricate; *(o rană* etc.*)* to salve; *(a vopsi)* to paint; *(domn* etc.) to anoint.
ungher *sn.* nook.
unghi *sn.* angle.
unghie *sf.* nail.
unguent *sn.* ointment.
ungur *sm.* Hungarian.
unguresc *adj.* Hungarian.
ungureşte *adv.* (in) Hungarian.
unguroaică *sf.* Hungarian (woman).
uni *sn.* plain (colour). *adj.* plain. *vt., vr.* to unite, to join; *fig. şi* to rally.
unic *adj.* single; *(deosebit)* unique; *pol.* united.
unicitate *sf.* oneness.
unifica *vt.* to unify. *vr.* to amalgamate.
unificare *sf.* unification; *pol.* merger.
uniform *adj.* uniform; *(neted)* even. *adv.* homogeneously; *(neted)* evenly.
uniformă *sf.* uniform.
uniformitate *sf.* uniformity.
uniformiza *vt.* to homogenize.
unilateral *adj.* unilateral.
unilateralitate *sf.* one-sidedness.
unional *adj.* union.
unire *sf.* union; harmony; alliance.
unison *sn.* unison.
unit *adj.* united; joint; *fig.* close-knit.

unitate *sf. (element)* unit; *(unire)* unity; ~ *de măsură* measure.
uniune *sf.* union; *(unire şi)* alliance; *Uniunea Tineretului Comunist* the Union of Communist Youth.
univers *sn.* universe.
universal *adj.* universal. *adv.* universally.
universitar *sm.* member of the professoriate. *adj.* university ...
universitate *sf.* university.
unsoare *sf.* grease; *(alifie)* ointment.
unsprezece *sm., adj., num.* eleven.
unsprezecelea *adj., num.* (the) eleventh.
unsuros *adj.* greasy; *(murdar)* filthy; sticky; *(uleios)* oily.
unt *sn.* butter; *(ulei)* oil; ~ *de ricin* castor oil.
untdelemn *sn.* (edible) oil.
untură *sf.* grease; ~ *de peşte* cod-liver oil.
ura[1] *sn.* cheer; *pl. şi* applause. *interj.* hurrah!
ura[2] *vt.* to wish.
uragan *sn.* hurricane.
uraniu *sn.* uranium.
urare *sf.* wish; *pl.* good wishes.
ură *sf.* hatred.
urban *adj.* town...
urca *vt.* to climb; *(a înălţa)* to put up. *vi.* to rise; *(a creşte)* to grow; *(într-un vehicul)* to get up. *vr.* to climb (up), to ascend; *(a se înălţa)* to rise; *(într-un vehicul)* to get up.
urcare *sf.* climbing; rise; *(uşă)* entrance.
urcior *sn.* pitcher; *(la ochi)* sty.
urcuş *sn.* climb.

urdă *sf.* soft cottage cheese (incorporating whey).

ureche *sf.* ear (for music); *(de ac)* eye (of a needle).

uree *sf.* urea.

urgent *adj.* pressing; *adv.* urgently.

urgenţă *sf.* urgency; *de ~* immediately.

urgie *sf.* wrath; *(a soartei)* scourge.

uriaş *sm., adj.* giant.

urina *vi.* to pass water.

urină *sf.* urine.

urî *vt.* to hate. *vr.* to hate each other; *a i se ~ cu* to be fed up with (smth.).

urîcios *adj.* hateful; *(urît)* ungainly; *(rău)* wicked; *(scîrbos)* disgusting, repulsive.

urît *sn.* spleen. *adj.* ugly; *(imoral)* odious; *(d. miros)* foul. *adv.* unfairly.

urîţenie *sf.* ugliness, ungainliness.

urîţi *vt.* to render ugly. *vr.* to grow plain.

urla *vi.* to roar.

urlet *sn.* howl.

urma *vt.* to follow (close); *(cursuri)* to attend; *(a continua)* to continue; *a ~ să* to be (supposed) to; *urmînd politica* etc. in pursuance of the policy, etc. *vi.* to follow; *(a continua)* to continue; *(la facultate* etc.*)* to attend courses; *va ~* to be continued; *după cum urmează* as follows.

urmare *sf.* sequel; *(rezultat)* consequence; *ca ~* as a result; *prin ~* therefore.

urmaş *sm.* successor; *(moştenitor)* heir; *pl.* progeny.

urmă *sf.* trace; *(de picior)* footprint; *(semn)* sign; *(de vînat)* trail; *cel din ~* the last; *(cel din ~ din doi)* the latter; *din ~* from behind; *în cele din ~* eventually; *în urma* following; *cu doi ani în ~* two years ago; *pe ~* then, afterwards.

urmări *vt.* to follow; *(a fila)* to shadow; *(a persecuta şi)* to persecute; *(a goni)* to chase; *(în justiţie)* to sue (at law); *(un scop şi)* to have in view; *(o expunere* etc.*)* to be with (smb., etc.).

urmărire *sf.* pursuit; *(goană)* chase.

următor *adj.* next; *(ulterior)* subsequent.

urnă *sf.* urn; *(electorală)* ballot box; *la urne* at the polls.

urni *vt., vr.* to budge.

urs *sm.* bear; *~ alb* polar bear.

ursă *sf.: Ursa Mare* the Great Bear; *Ursa Mică* the Lesser Bear.

ursită *sf.* lot.

ursitoare *sf.* Fate, Parca.

ursoaică *sf.* she-bear; skylight.

ursuleţ *sm.* bear's cub *sau* whelp; *(jucărie)* Teddy bear.

ursuz *sm.* morose person. *adj.* surly. *adv.* grumpily.

urticarie *sf.* rash.

urzeală *sf.* warp; *(maşinaţie)* machination.

urzi *vt.* to warp; *fig.* to hatch.

urzica *vt., vi., vr.* to nettle (oneself).

urzică *sf.* (stinging) nettle; *(moartă)* dead nettle.

usca *vt.* to dry; *(fînul şi)* to ted; *(a şterge)* to wipe (dry). *vr.* to (become) dry; *(a seca)* to run dry; *(d. flori)* to droop.

uscare *sf.* drying; *(a fînului și)* tedding.

uscat *sn.* drying; *(pămînt)* land; *(continent)* mainland; *de ~* land. *adj.* dry; *(ofilit)* withered; *(ars)* parched.

uscăciune *sf.* dryness; *(secetă)* drought.

ustensile *sf. pl.* utensils.

ustura *vt.* to smart; *fig. și* to sting.

usturător *adj.* smarting; *fig.* lashing.

usturime *sf.* smarting pain.

usturoi *sm.* garlic.

ușă *sf.* door; *(prag)* threshold; *(deschiderea)* doorway; *fig. și* gate; *~ de sticlă* French window.

ușier *sm.* usher.

ușor *sm.* (door) jamb. *adj.* light; *(de făcut)* easy; *(mic)* slight. *adv.* easily; *(fără apăsare* etc.*)* lightly.

ușura *vt.* to lighten; *(a slăbi)* to relieve; *(a alina)* to soothe; *(o povară și)* to alleviate. *vr.* to relieve oneself; *(a-și face nevoile)* to relieve nature.

ușurare *sf.* relief; facilitation.

ușuratic *adj.* flippant. *adv.* wantonly.

ușurel *adv.* gently.

ușurință *sf.* facility; *(nechibzuință)* carelessness; *cu ~* easily; *(neserios)* recklessly.

utecist *sm.* young communist.

util *adj.* useful.

utila *vt.* to equip.

utilaj *sn.* equipment.

utilitar *sm., adj.* utilitarian.

utilitate *sf.* utility.

utiliza *vt.* to use.

utopic *adj.* Utopian.

utopie *sf.* Utopia.

uvertură *sf.* overture.

uz *sn.* usage; *(obicei și)* custom.

uza *vt.* to use; *(a roade* etc.*)* to wear out. *vi.: a ~ de* to resort to. *vr.* to wear out.

uzat *adj.* worn out; *(d. haine)* threadbare.

uzină *sf.* works. *~ de apă* water works; *~ de gaz* gas works; *~ electrică* power station.

uzitat *adj.* in (current) usage.

uzual *adj.* usual. *adv.* usually.

uzură *sf.* wear (and tear); *fig. și* attrition.

uzurpa *vt.* to usurp.

uzurpator *sm.* usurper.

V

va *v aux.* will. *vi.: mai ~* just wait; *~ să zică* therefore, then.

vacant *adj.* vacant.

vacanță *sf.* holiday(s); *jur., pol.* recess; *(slujbă)* vacancy; *vacanța mare* the summer holidays, the long.

vacarm *sn.* uproar.

vacă *sf.* cow; *fig.* goose; ~ *cu lapte* milch cow; ~ *de muls fig.* pigeon.

vaccin *sn.* vaccine; *(vaccinare)* vaccination.

vaccina *vt.* to vaccinate.

vacs *sn.* blacking; *fig.* trifle. *interj.* (tommy) rot!

vad *sn.* ford; *com.* (shop of) good custom.

vag *adj.* vague; *fig.* dim. *adv.* vaguely.

vagabond *sm.* tramp. *adj.* vagrant.

vagabonda *vi.* to loaf.

vagabondaj *sn.* vagrancy.

vagin *sn.* vagina.

vagon *sn.* waggon; *(de pasageri)* carriage; *(de marfă)* truck; ~ *cisternă* tank waggon; ~ *de bagaje* luggage van; ~ *de dormit* sleeping car; ~ *restaurant* dining car, diner.

vagonet *sn.* truck; tub.

vai *interj.* oh dear! poor me!; ~ *de tine!* I pity you!

vaiet *sn.* lament(ation).

vajnic *adj.* dauntless.

val *sn.* wave; *(mare)* billow; *(de apărare)* wall; ~ *de căldură* heat wave; ~ *de greve* strike wave; ~*urile vieții* the ups and downs of life; ~ *vîrtej* quickly, fast.

valabil *adj.* valid; *(curent și)* available; *(îndreptățit)* legitimate.

valabilitate *sf.* validity.

valah *sm., adj.* Vlach, Wallachian.

vale *sf.* valley; *în sau la* ~ down (hill); *(pe rîu)* downstream; *mai la* ~ *fig.* below.

valet *sm.* valet; *(la cărți)* knave.

valiză *sf.* valise; *(mare)* suitcase; ~ *diplomatică* diplomatic mail.

valoare *sf.* value; *și fig.* worth; *de* ~ valuable; *fără* ~ worthless; *în* ~ *de* to the sum of.

valora *vi.* to be worth.

valorifica *vt.* to turn to (good) account.

valorificare *sf.* capitalization.

valoros *adj.* valuable.

vals *sn.* waltz, valse.

valută *sf.* (foreign) currency.

vamal *adj.* custom(-house).

vamă *sf.* customs; *(taxă)* (custom) duty.

vameș *sm.* custom-house officer.

vampă *sf.* vamp; gold-digger.

vampir *sm.* vampire.

van *adj.* vain; *în* ~ vainly.

vandabil *adj.* saleable, marketable.

vandal *sm.* vandal.

vandalism *sn.* vandalism.

vanilie *sf.* vanilia (flavour).

vanitate *sf.* vanity.

vanitos *adj.* vain.

vapor *sm.* vapour. *sn.* steamer; (steam)ship.

vaporos *adj.* vaporous.

var *sn.* lime; ~ *nestins* quick lime; ~ *stins* slaked lime.

vara *adv.* in summer.

vară *sf.* (girl) cousin; *(anotimp)* summer; ~ *primară* cousin german; *astă* ~ last summer; *de* ~ summer (time); *la* ~ next summer.

varia *vt., vi.* to vary.

variabil *adj.* variable; *(nestabil)* inconstant.

variantă *sf.* variant.

variat *adj.* varied.

variaţie *sf.* variation.

varietate *sf.* variety.

varieteu *sn.* variety show.

varză *sf.* cabbage ; ∼ *acră* sau *murată* sauerkraut.

vas *sn.* vessel ; *(oală şi)* receptacle ; *mar.* şi ship ; ∼ *de flori* flower vase ; ∼ *de lut* sau *pămînt* earthen pot ; ∼ *de război* man-of-war.

vasal *sm., adj.* vassal.

vaselină *sf.* pertrolatum.

vast *adj.* vast.

vată *sf.* (absorbent) cotton ; *(de croitorie)* wadding ; ∼ *de sticlă* glasswool.

vatră *sf.* fireplace.

vază *sf.* (flower) vase ; *(renume)* renown ; *(autoritate)* influence ; *cu* ∼ famous.

vă *pron.* you *(reflexiv)* yourself ; *pl.* yourselves.

văcar *sm.* cowherd.

vădi *vt.* to show. *vr.* to turn out.

vădit *adj.* obvious.

văduv *sm.* widower.

văduvă *sf.* widow ; ∼ *de paie* grass widow.

văduvi *vt.* to deprive (of).

văduvie *sf.* widowhood.

văgăună *sf.* gully.

văicăreală *sf.* lamentation.

văita *vr.* to wail.

văl *sn.* veil ; ∼*ul palatului* soft palate.

vămui *vt.* to make (smth.) clear customs.

văpaie *sf.* blaze.

văr *sm.* cousin ; ∼ *primar* cousin german ; ∼ *de-al doilea* cousin twice removed.

vărgat *adj.* striped.

vărsa *vt.* to spill ; *(a turna)* to pour (out) , *(sînge, lacrimi)* to shed ; *(bani)* to pay ; *(a voma)* to throw up ; *(a răsturna)* to upset. *vi.* to cast forth. *vr.* to be spilled ; *(d. rîu)* to flow (into the sea, etc.).

vărsare *sf.* pouring ; *geogr.* river mouth ; ∼ *de sînge* bloodshed.

vărsat *sn.* smallpox ; *(vărsătură)* vomit(ing) ; ∼ *de vînt* chickenpox ; ∼ *negru* cow pox.

vărui *vt.* to whitewash.

văruit *sn.* whitewashing.

vătaf *sm.* bailiff ; *(administrator)* manager.

vătăma *vt.* to harm ; *(a răni)* to wound.

vătămare *sf.* harm.

vătămător *adj.* harmful ; *fig.* detrimental (to).

vătrai *sn.* poker.

văz *sn.* (eye)sight.

văzduh *sn.* air.

veac *sn.* century ; *fig.* şi age ; *în veci* for ever.

vecernie *sf.* vespers.

vechi *adj.* old; *(demodat)* obsolete.

vechime *sf.* age ; *(în slujbă)* seniority ; length of service ; *din* ∼ (from days) of yore.

vechitură *sf.* old thing ; *pl.* old clothes ; *(mobile)* lumber.

vecie *sf.* eternity ; *pe* ∼ for ever.

vecin *sm.* neighbour ; *prin* ∼*i* in the neighbourhood. *adj.* neighbouring.

vecinătate *sf.* neighbourhood ; *bună* ∼ neighbourliness.

vedea *vt.* to see ; *(a observa)* to notice ; *(a vizita)* to visit ; *vezi să nu* don't fear ; *vezi să nu cazi* mind your step. *vi.* to see ; *a* ∼ *de* to look after ; *ca să vezi* just imagine. *vr* to be seen *sau* visible; *(a se pomeni)* to find oneself; *(a se ivi)* to show.

vedenie *sf.* apparition, phantom.

vedere *sf.* (eye)sight; *(privelişte)* view; *(părere)* opinion; *(întîlnire)* meeting; *în ~a acestui eveniment* etc. with a view to this event, etc.

vedetă *sf.* star; *mar.* vedette; *~ rapidă* speed boat.

vegeta *vi.* to vegetate.

vegetal *adj.* vegetable.

vegetarian *sm., adj.* vegetarian.

vegetaţie *sf.* vegetation; *pl. med.* adenoids.

veghe *sf.* wakefulness; *de ~* vigilant.

veghea *vt., vi.* to watch.

vehement *adj.* vehement. *adv.* vehemently.

vehicul *sn.* vehicle.

vehicula *vt.* to spread, to circulate.

velă *sf.* sail.

veleitate *sf.* ambition.

velodrom *sm.* cycling track.

venera *vt.* to worship.

venerabil *adj.* venerable.

veneraţie *sf.* veneration.

veni *vi.* to come; *(a intra)* to drop; *(a apărea)* to turn up; *a-i ~ (bine, rău* etc.*)* to fit (smb.) well, badly, etc.; *a-i ~ să* to feel like (smoking, etc.); *a ~ din (o cauză)* to result from (a cause); *ce i-a ~t?* what made him do it?; *a ~ pe lume* to be born; *a ~ acasă* to come home; *bine aţi ~t!* welcome!

venin *sn.* venom; *(fiere)* gall.

veninos *adj.* venomous; *(rău)* pernicious.

venire *sf.* coming.

venit *sn.* income, revenue; *bun- ~* welcome. *adj.: nou- ~* newcomer.

ventilator *sn.* fan.

ventilaţie *sf.* ventilation.

ventuză *sf.* cupping glass; *zool* sucker.

verandă *sf.* veranda.

verb *sn.* verb.

verbal *adj.* verbal. *adv.* orally.

verde *sn.* green (colour); *(verdeaţă)* verdure. *adj.* green; *(verzui şi)* greenish; *(proaspăt şi)* fresh. *adv.* openly.

verdeaţă *sf.* green; *(plante şi)* verdure; *pl.* greens, greengrocery.

verdict *sn.* verdict.

vergea *sf.* rod.

veridic *adj.* truthful. *adv.* veridically.

verifica *vt.* to check (up).

verificare *sf.* check(ing).

verigă *sf.* link.

verighetă *sf.* wedding ring.

verişoară *sf., verişor* *sm.* cousin (german).

veritabil *adj.* genuine; *(autentic şi)* authentic; *(pur)* sterling.

vermut *sn.* vermouth.

vernisaj *sn.* varnishing (day).

verosimil *adj.* truthlike.

vers *sn. (şi pl.)* verse; *pl. şi* poetry; *(rînd)* line; *~uri albe* blank verse.

versifica *vt., vi.* to versify.

versiune *sf.* version.

vertebrat *sn., adj.* vertebrate.

vertebră *sf.* vertebra.

vertical *adj.* vertical. *adv.* vertically; *(la cuvinte încrucişate)* down.

verticală *sf.* vertical (line).
vertiginos *adj.* breathtaking, soaring. *adv.* dizzily.
vervă *sf.* verve.
vesel *adj.* merry. *adv.* joyfully.
veseli *vr.* to rejoice (at smth.).
veselie *sf.* mirth.
vest *sn.* West ; *de* ~ West(ern).
vestă *sf.* waistcoat.
veste *sf.* (piece of) news ; *pl.* tidings ; *fără* ~ unexpectedly.
vesti *vt.* to herald ; to announce.
vestiar *sn.* cloakroom ; *(cu dulăpioare)* locker room.
vestibul *sn.* entrance hall.
vestit *adj.* famous.
vestitor *sm.* herald.
veston *sn.* jacket.
veşmînt *sn.* attire ; *rel.* vestment.
veşnic *adj.* eternal ; *(neîntrerupt)* endless. *adv.* always.
veşnicie *sf.* eternity ; *fig.* ages.
veşted *adj.* faded.
veşteji *vt.* to wither ; *(a înfiera)* to brand. *vr.* to wilt.
veteran *sm.* ex-serviceman ; *şi fig.* veteran.
veterinar *sm.* vet(erinary surgeon) ; *mil. şi* farrier. *adj.* veterinary.
veto *sn.* veto.
veveriţă *sf.* squirrel.
via *prep.* via.
viabil *adj.* viable.
viaţă *sf.* life ; *(realitate)* reality ; *(ca durată)* lifetime ; *viaţa la ţară* country life ; *de* ~ life ; *fig.* gay ; *în* ~ above ground.
vibra *vi.* to vibrate.
vibrant *adj.* vibrating.
vibraţie *sf.* vibration.
vicepreşedinte *sm.* vice-chairman ; *prim* ~ first vice-chairman.

viceversa *adv.* vice versa.
vicia *vt.* to vitiate ; *(aerul etc.)* to pollute.
viciat *adj.* corrupt(ed) ; *(d.' aer etc.)* foul.
vicios *adj.* vicious.
vicisitudine *sf.* hardship.
viciu *sn.* vice.
viclean *adj.* cunning ; *cel* ~ the evil one. *adv.* slyly.
vicleim *sn.* nativity drama.
viclenie *sf.* slyness.
vicleşug *sn.* fraud.
victimă *sf.* victim ; prey.
victorie *sf.* victory.
victorios *adj.* victorious. *adv.* triumphantly.
vid *sn.* vacuum.
vidră *sf.* otter.
vie *sf.* vineyard.
vier *sm.* wine grower ; *zool.* boar.
vierme *sm.* worm ; ~ *de mătase* silk worm.
viespar *sn.* hornets' nest.
viespe *sf.* wasp ; *fig.* scold.
vietate *sf.* creature.
vieţuitoare *sf.* living being.
viezure *sm.* badger.
vifor *sn. sf.* gale ; snowstorm.
viforos *adj.* wintry.
vigilent *adj.* vigilant.
vigilenţă *sf.* watchfulness ; *lipsit de* ~ easy gullible.
vigoare *sf.* vigour ; *în* ~ in force.
viguros *adj.* vigorous.
viitor *sn.* future ; *de* ~ promising ; *în* ~ in (the) future ; *pe* ~ from now on. *adj.* future ; *(următor)* following ; to come.
vijelie *sf.* gale.
vijelios *adj.* stormy.
vilă *sf.* villa ; *(mică)* cottage.
vileag *sn.* common knowledge ; *în* ~ publicly.

vilegiatură *sf.* villeggiatura ; *în* ~ on holiday(s).

vilegiaturist *sm.* holiday maker.

vin *sn.* wine ; ~ *fiert* mulled wine ; ~ *gol* plain wine.

vină *sf.* guilt(iness) ; *de* ~ guilty ; *fără vina cuiva* without anybody being to blame.

vinde *vt.* to sell ; *(a trăda)* to sell out ; *a* ~ *angro sau cu ridicata* to sell wholesale ; *a* ~ *cu amănuntul* to retail. *vi.* to sell. *vr.* to sell (oneself) ; *(d. marfă)* to sell (like hot cakes, etc.).

vindeca *vt.* to heal. *vr.* to get over (an illness).

vindecare *sf.* recovery.

vinerea *adv.* on Friday(s).

vineri *sf.* Friday ; *Vinerea Mare* Good Friday. *adv.* (on) Friday.

vinicultură *sf.* wine growing.

vinovat *sm.* culprit. *adj.* guilty.

vinovăţie *sf.* guilt(iness).

vioară *sf.* violin.

vioi *adj.* lively ; *(vesel)* sprightly ; *(rapid)* brisk. *adv.* briskly.

vioiciune *sf.* liveliness.

viol *sn.* rape.

viola *vt.* to violate.

violă *sf.* viola.

violent *adj.* violent ; hot(-blooded) ; *(vehement)* vehement. *adv.* violently.

violenţă *sf.* violence.

violet *sm.*, *adj.* violet.

violetă *sf.* violet.

violoncel *sn.* cello.

violoncelist *sm.* cellist.

violonist *sm.* violinist.

viperă *sf.* viper.

vira *vt.* to transfer. *vi.* to steer.

viraj *sn.* turning.

virament *sn.* transfer.

viran *adj.* waste.

virgin *adj.* virgin.

virgulă *sf.* comma; *(punct)* point.

viril *adj.* virile.

virilitate *sf.* manliness.

virtual *adj.* virtual.

virtuos *sm.* virtuoso; *adj.* virtuos.

virtuozitate *sf.* virtuosity.

virtute *sf.* virtue ; *în* ~*a* ... by virtue of ...

virus *sn.* virus.

vis *sn.* dream ; *(visare şi)* wistfulness ; *(fantezie)* chimera ; illusion ; ~*uri plăcute* sweet dreams ; *de* ~ fairy (like).

visa *vt.* to dream (of smb., etc.). *vi.* to dream (of).

visare *sf.* dreaminess.

visător *sm.* dreamer. *adj.* dreamy.

viscol *sn.* snowstorm, blizzard.

viscoli *vi. impers.* : *viscoleşte* a blizzard is raging.

vistierie *sf.* treasury.

vişin *sm.* (morello) cherry tree.

vişinată *sf.* cherry brandy.

vişină *sf.* (morello) cherry.

vişiniu *adj.* purple.

vital *adj.* vital.

vitalitate *sf.* vitality.

vitamină *sf.* vitamin.

vită *sf.* ox ; cow ; *pl.* cattle ; *fig.* blockhead ; *vite cornute* horned cattle ; *vite de prăsilă sau rasă* breeding stock ; *vite de muncă* draught cattle ; *fig.* hacks, drudges.

viteaz *sm.* brave man. *adj.* valiant.

vitejese *adj.* gallant.

vitejie *sf.* bravery.

viteză *sf.* speed ; *(rapiditate)* rapidity ; *cu o* ~ *de* at a rate of ; *cu* ~ *maximă* (at) top speed.

viticol *adj.* viticultural.
viticultură *sf.* viticulture.
vitraliu *sn.* stained glass window.
vitreg *adj.* step, half(brother, etc.) ; *fig.* unfair ; *(nefavorabil)* inauspicious. *adv.* harshly.
vitregie *sf.* hostility.
vitrină *sf.* shop window ; *(în casă* etc.*)* show *sau* glass case.
viță *sf. bot.* vine ; *(neam)* stock ; ~ *de vie* vine ; ~ *sălbatică* creeper.
vițel *sm.* calf ; *(carne)* veal.
viu *sm.* living person ; *pl.* the living ; *rel.* the quick ; *viii cu viii și morții cu morții* let the dead bury the dead and the quick live with the quick. *adj.* living ; alive ; *(puternic)* strong ; *(vioi)* vivid ; *(d. lumină, culori)* bright ; *rel.* quick ; *(d. argint)* quick ; *de* ~ alive. *adv.* vividly.
vivace *adj.* lively ; *muz.* vivace.
vivacitate *sf.* liveliness.
viza *vt.* to vise ; *(a tinți la)* to aim at ; *(pe cineva)* to hint at.
vizavi *sn.* counterpart ; *de* ~ opposite. *adv.* across the street.
viză *sf.* visé, visa ; ~ *turistică* tourist visa.
vizibil *adj.* visible. *adv.* perceptibly.
vizibilitate *sf.* visibility.
viziona *vt.* to see.
vizita *vt.* to visit ; to call on (smb.).
vizitator *sm.* caller.
vizită *sf.* call ; *(lungă)* visit ; ~ *de etichetă* duty call ; ~ *medicală* medical inspection ; *în* ~ on a visit (to smb.).
vizitiu *sm.* coachman.
viziune *sf.* vision.

vizon *sm.* vison.
vizual *adj.* of view.
vizuină *sf.* lair ; *(gaură)* burrow.
vîjîi *vi.* to whistle ; *(d. urechi)* to buzz.
vîjîit *sn.* whizz(ing).
vîlcea *sf.* dale, glen.
vîltoare *sf.* eddy.
vîlvă *sf.* commotion.
vîlvătaie *sf.* blaze.
vîlvoi *adj.* dishevelled.
vîna *vt., vi.* to hunt.
vînat *sn.* game ; *(mîncare)* venison ; *(vînătoare)* hunting.
vînă *sf.* vein ; *anat. și* vena ; *min.* lode ; ~ *cavă* vena cavă ; ~ *de bou* bull's pizzle ; *pe vine* squatting, hunching.
vînăt *adj.* blueish.
vînătaie *sf.* bruise ; black eye, etc.
vînătă *sf.* egg-plant, aubergine.
vînătoare *sf.* hunt(ing) ; *(goană)* chase ; ~ *de balene* whaling ; ~ *de păsări* fowling ; *de* ~ hunting ; sporting.
vînător *sm.* hunter ; ~*i de munte* mountain troops.
vînătoresc *adj.* hunter's.
vîndut *sm.* traitor. *adj.* sold (out).
vînjos *adj.* sturdy.
vînt *sn.* wind ; *(adiere)* breeze ; *(puternic)* gale ; hurricane ; *ca* ~*ul* (as) quick as lightning ; *de* ~ wind ; *în* ~ uselessly.
vîntos *adj.* windy.
vîntura *vt.* to winnow ; *(o idee* etc.*)* to ventilate ; *(lumea)* to scour. *vr.* to wander.
vînzare *sf.* sale ; *(trădare)* treachery ; ~ *la licitație* sale by auction.

vînzătoare *sf.* shop assistant.

vînzător *sm.* shop assistant, vendor ; ~ *ambulant* pedlar.

vîrf *sn.* tip ; top ; *(pisc)* peak ; *fig. și* climax, acme ; *(ascuțiș)* point ; *geom.* vertex ; *în ~ul degetelor* on tip-toe ; *cu ~* full to the brim ; *cu ~ și îndesat fig.* with a vengeance.

vîrî *vt.* to shove ; *(implica)* to involve ; *(a investi)* to invest ; *(adînc)* to bury. *vr.* to intrude ; *a se ~ sub pielea cuiva* to curry favour with smb.

vîrstă *sf.* age ; *în ~* elderly ; *în ~ de șapte ani* seven years old ; *între două ~e* middle--aged ; *cu vîrsta* with the years.

vîrstnic *adj.* mature.

vîrtej *sn.* whirlpool ; *(de vînt)* whirlwind ; *fig.* whirl.

vîrtos *adj.* vigorous ; *(țeapăn)* rigid ; *și fig.* tough. *adv.* firmly ; *cu atît mai ~ cu cît* .. (all) the more so as ...

vîsc *sn.* mistletoe.

vîscos *adj.* viscous.

vîslaș *sm.* oarsman.

vîslă *sf.* oar ; *(padelă)* paddle.

vîsli *vi.* to row ; *(cu padela)* to paddle.

vlagă *sf.* vitality.

vlăgui *vt.* to drain ; *fig. și* to deplete.

vlăguit *adj.* exhausted.

vlăstar *sn.* offspring ; *bot. și* offshoot.

voal *sn.* veil.

voala *vt.* to veil ; *(sunete)* to muffle ; *foto* to fog. *vr.* to become fogged.

voastră *adj.* your ; *a ~* yours.

voastre *adj.* your ; *ale ~* yours.

vocabular *sn.* vocabulary.

vocal *adj.* vocal.

vocală *sf.* vowel.

vocativ *sn., adj.* vocative.

vocație *sf.* vocation ; *(înclinație)* proclivity.

voce *sf.* voice ; *cu ~ scăzută* in a low voice ; *cu ~ tare* aloud.

vocifera *vi.* to bawl.

vodă *sm.* hospodar.

vodevil *sn.* vaudeville.

vogă *sf.* fashion, vogue.

voi¹ *pron.* you ; yourselves ; ~ *ăștia* you all.

voi² *vi.* will, to want ; to be willing.

voiaj *sn.* travel ; *(pe mare)* voyage.

voiaja *vi.* to travel ; *(pe mare)* to voyage.

voiajor *sm.* traveller ; ~ *comercial* commercial traveller.

voie *sf.* will ; *(plăcere)* content ; *(permisiune)* consent ; ~ *bună* mirth ; *de bună ~* of one's own accord ; *de ~! mil.* at ease ; *fără ~* unwillingly ; *în voia soartei* at the mercy of fate.

voievod *sm.* hospodar.

voinic *sm.* hero ; prince charming. *adj.* robust ; *(sănătos)* sound.

voință *sf.* will.

voios *adj.* cheerful. *adv.* mirthfully.

voioșie *sf.* joyousness.

voit *adj.* intentional. *adv.* deliberately.

volan *sn.* steering-wheel ; *(la rochie)* flounce.

volant *adj.* flying ; *(d. hîrtie)* loose ; *foaie ~ă* leaflet.

volbură *sf.* whirlwind ; *(bulboană)* eddy ; *bot.* bindweed.

volei *sn.* volley-ball.

volieră *sf.* aviary; *(de fazani)* pheasant preserve.

volt *sm.* volt.

voltaj *sn.* voltage.

volubil *adj.* talkative.

volubilitate *sf.* loquaciousness.

volum *sn.* volume.

voluminos *adj.* bulky.

voluntar *sm.* volunteer. *adj.* voluntary; *(neascultător)* self--willed.

voluptate *sf.* delight; voluptuousness.

voluptos *adj.* voluptuous.

voma *vt:, vi.,* **vomita** *vt., vi.* to vomit.

vopsea *sf. (de ulei)* paint; *(chimică)* dye.

vopsi *vt.* to dye; *(cu pensula)* to paint; *(a vărui)* to whitewash. *vr.* to paint- (one's face, etc.).

vopsitor *sm.* painter.

vopsitorie *sf.* dye works.

vorbă *sf.* word; *(vorbărie)* gossip; *(ceartă)* quarrel; *(proverb)* saying; *(promisiune și)* promise; *(obiecție)* opposition; *vorba aceea* as the saying goes; ~ *cu* ~ word for word; ~ *lungă* rigmarole; *(persoană)* chatterbox; *din* ~ *în* ~ by the way; *auzi* ~! a likely story!

vorbăreț *sm.* chatterbox. *adj.* talkative.

vorbărie *sf.* idle talk.

vorbi *vt.* to speak; to talk; *a* ~ *pe cineva (de rău* etc.) to speak (evil, etc.) of smb. *vi.* to speak (to smb.); *(a discuta)* to talk; *(în public și)* to make a speech; *a* ~ *deschis* to speak one's mind; *a* ~ *în vînt* to

waste one's breath; *a* ~ *în fața unei adunări* to address a meeting; *a* ~ *într-aiurea* to talk nonsense; *a* ~ *pe nas* to twang; *a* ~ *liber* to speak off-hand; *a* ~ *peltic* to lallate, to lisp; *la drept* ~nd in fact. *vr.* to agree *sau* be to.

vorbire *sf.* speech.

vorbitor *sm.* speaker; lecturer. *sn.* receiving room. *adj.* talking, speaking.

vostru *adj.* your; *al* ~ yours.

voștri *adj.* your; *ai* ~ yours.

vot *sn.* vote; *(drept de vot și)* franchise; *(votare)* polling; ~ *anulat* invalid vote; ~ *deschis* show of hands; ~ *secret* vote by ballot.

vota *vt.* to vote; *(o lege* etc.*)* to carry. *vi.* to vote; to poll.

votare *sf.* poll(ing).

vrabie *sf.* sparrow.

vraf *sn.* heap.

vrajă *sf.* spell; *(magie)* magic.

vrajbă *sf.* feud; *în* ~ at variance.

vrăji *vt.* to bewitch.

vrăjit *adj.* charmed; *fig. și* entranced.

vrăjitoare *sf.* witch.

vrăjitor *sm.* wizard.

vrăjitorie *sf.* witchcraft.

vrăjmaș *sm.* enemy. *adj.* hostile; *(d. natură* etc.*)* inhospitable.

vrăjmășie *sf.* hostility; feud.

vrea *vt.* to want. *vi.* will, to be willing.

vreascuri *sn. pl.* brushwood.

vrednic *adj.* worthy; *(harnic)* hardworking; *(potrivit)* fit; ~ *de cinste* honourable.

vrednicie *sf.* merit; *(hărnicie)* industry.

vreme *sf.* *(meteorologic)* **weather**; *(cronologic)* time; *pl.* times; ~ *bună* fine weather; ~ *frumoasă* glorious weather; *cu* ~*a* in the long run; *de la o* ~ after a time; *de* ~ *ce* since, because; *din vremuri de demult* from times of yore; *în* ~*a acéea* at that time; *pe* ~*a mea* in my time; *pe vremuri* formerly.

vremelnic *adj.* temporary; *(trecător)* transient. *adv.* provisionally.

vreo *adj.* some; *interog.* any.

vreodată *adv.* ever.

vreun *adj.* some; *interog.* any.

vreuna, vreunul *pron.* some (of them); somebody; *interog.* any (-body).

vrută *sf.*: *vrute și nevrute* idle talk.

vui *vi.* to din; *(a mugi)* to roar; *(d. urechi)* to buzz.

vuiet *sn.* din; *(muget)* roaring.

vulcan *sm.* volcano.

vulcanic *adj.* volcanic.

vulgar *adj.* vulgar; *(ordinar)* coarse. *adv.* coarsely.

vulgaritate *sf.* vulgarity; *(în îmbrăcăminte* etc.*)* dowdiness.

vulnerabil *adj.* vulnerable.

vulpe *sf.* (she-)fox.

vulpoi *sm.* (he-)fox.

vultur *sm.* eagle; vulture; *de* ~ eagle's ...

W

whisky *sn.* whisky.

X

xilofon *sn.* xylophone.

xilogravură *sf.* wood cut.

xilon *sn.* xylenol.

Z

za *sf.* link; *pl.* coat of mail.

zacuscă *sf.* (pickled fish) snack.

zadar *sn.*: *în* ~ uselessly.

zadarnic *adj.* useless. *adv.* in vain.

zadă *sf.* larch tree.

zahana *sf.* slaughter house ; *(specialități)* choice meat cuts.

zaharisi *vt.* to sugar. *vr.* to candy ; *fig.* to dodder.

zahăr *sn.* sugar ; ~ *candel* candy ; ~ *cubic* lump sugar ; ~ *de trestie* cane sugar ; ~ *praf* sau *pudră* glazing sugar ; ~ *tos* castor *sau* granulated sugar ; *de* ~ sugar(y) ; *fig.* wonderful.

zambilă *sf.* hyacinth.

zar *sn.* die, *pl.* dice.

zare *sf.* horizon ; streak (of light) ; *în* ~ in the distance.

zarvă *sf.* tumult ; *(scandal)* row ; *(agitație)* bustle.

zarzavagiu *sm.* greengrocer ; *(ambulant)* costermonger.

zarzavat *sn.* vegetables.

zarzăr *sm.* ungrafted apricot tree.

zarzără *sf.* ungrafted apricot.

zaț *sn.* matter ; *(de cafea)* lees.

zăbală *sf.* (curb) bit.

zăbavă *sf.* delay ; *fără* ~ prompt
(ly).

zăbovi *vi.* to tarry, to linger.

zăbrea *sf.* iron bar.

zăbreli *vt.* to lattice.

zăcămînt *sn.* deposits.

zăcea *vi.* to lie ; *(a se afla și)* to be (found).

zădărnici *vt.* to foil, to frustrate ; to baffle.

zădărnicie *sf.* uselessness.

zăgaz *sn.* dam ; *(ecluză)* weir.

zăgăzui *vt.* to dam up ; *fig. și* to stem.

zămisli *vt.* to conceive.

zăngăni *vt.* to clang ; *fig. și* to brandish. *vi.* to clatter.

zăngănit *sn.* clatter.

zăpadă *sf.* snow ; *ca zăpada* snow-white.

zăpăceală *sf.* flurry ; *(nedumerire)* bewilderment.

zăpăci *vt.* to dumbfound. *vr.* to lose one's head.

zăpăcit *sm.* scatter-brains. *adj.* hare-brained ; *(nebun)* crazy ; *(amețit)* bewildered.

zăpușeală *sf.* sultry heat.

zăpușitor *adj.* sultry.

zări *vt.* to catch sight of ; *(a percepe)* to discern. *vr.* to heave in sight.

zău *interj.* honest !

zăvor *sn.* bolt.

zăvorî *vt.* to bolt. *vr.* to shut oneself up.

zbate *vr.* to struggle.

zbengui *vr.* to cut capers.

zbenguială *sf.* frolic.

zbiera *vi.* to yell ; *(d. măgar)* to bray.

zbieret *sn.* yell ; *(de măgar)* bray.

zbir *sm.* sbirro.

zbîrci *vt.* to wrinkle. ; *a o* ~ to fail. *vr.* to be wrinkled.

zbîrcit *adj.* wrinkled.

zbîrcitură *sf.* wrinkle.

zbîrli *vt.* to ruffle. *vr.* to bristle up.

zbîrlit *adj.* tousled.

zbîrnîi *vi.* to buzz.

zbîrnîit *sn.* buzz.

zbor *sn.* flying ; *(drum)* flight ; *(înălțare)* soar(ing) ; ~*ul omului în cosmos* manned space flight ; *în* ~ upon the wing.

zbucium *sn.* turmoil ; anxiety, worry.

zbuciuma *vr.* to toss ; *fig.* to fret.

zbuciumat *adj.* agitated ; eventful.

zbughi *vt.: a o* ~ to fly (away).

zbura *vt.* to blow out. *vi.* to fly; *(a se înălţa)* to soar; *fig.* to dash; *(a dispărea)* to vanish.

zburătoare *sf.* bird; *fig.* feather.

zburător *sm.* airman; *(duh)* harpy. *adj.* flying.

zburda *vi.* to frisk.

zburdalnic *adj.* playful.

zdravăn *adj.* sturdy; *(sănătos)* healthy.; *(la minte)* sane; *(tare)* terrible. *adv.* awfully; heavily.

zdrăngăni *vt., vi.* to thrum.

zdreanţă *sf.* rag.

zdreli *vt., vr.* to scratch (oneself).

zdrenţăros *sm.* ragamuffin. *adj.* tattered.

zdrenţuit *adj.* ragged.

zdrobi *vt.* to crush; *fig. şi* to destroy. *vr.* to be crushed.

zdrobit *adj.* crushed; *(istovit)* exhausted; *(de durere)* overwhelmed.

zdrobitor *adj.* crushing; *(numeros)* overwhelming.

zdruncina *vt.* to shake; *(d. căruţă)* to jolt; *(convingerile etc.)* to shatter; *(a slăbi)* to sap. *vi.* to jolt.

zeamă *sf.* juice; *(de carne şi)* gravy; *(supă)* soup; *(lungă)* skilly.

zebră *sf.* zebra.

zece *sn., adj., num.* ten; *de ~ ori* ten times.

zecelea *adj., num.* (the) tenth.

zecimal *adj.* decimal.

zecime *sf.* tenth.

zefir *sm., sn.* zephyr.

zeflemea *sf.* mockery.

zeflemitor *adj.* bantering.

zeflemisi *vt.* to scoff (at).

zeiţă *sf.* goddess.

zel *sn.* zeal.

zelos *adj.* zealous.

zemos *adj.* juicy.

zepelin *sn.* zeppelin.

zer *sn.* whey.

zero *sm., sn., num.* nought; *(la termometru)* zero; *sport* nil; *(la telefon)* O; *(nimic şi)* nothing; *(persoană şi)* cipher; *~ la ~* love (all).

zestre *sf.* dowry.

zeu *sm.* god.

zevzec *sm.* nincompoop. *adj.* empty-headed.

zgardă *sf.* collar.

zgîi *vr.* to stare.

zgîlţîi *vt.* to jerk; *(a scutura)* to shake. *vr.* to shake.

zgîndări *vt.* to rake; *fig.* to revive; *(a aţîţa)* to incite.

zgîrcenie *sf.* avarice.

zgîrci[1] *sn.* cartilage.

zgîrci[2] *vt.* to contract. *vr.* to contract; *(la ceva)* to stint; to grudge (the expense of).

zgîrcit *sm.* miser. *adj.* stingy; skimpy; *~ la vorbă* chary of words.

zgîria *vt.* to scratch. *vr.* to get a scratch.

zgîrie-nori *sm.* sky-scraper.

zgîrietură *sf.* scratch.

zglobiu *adj.* sprightly.

zgomot *sn.* noise; *(scandal)* row.

zgomotos *adj.* noisy. *adv.* blatantly.

zgribuli *vr.* to huddle; to tremble (with cold).

zgrunţuros *adj.* rough.

zgudui *vt., vr.* to shake.

zguduire *sf.* shock.

zguduitor *adj.* terrible.

zguduitură *sf.* commotion.

zgură *sf.* slag ; *şi fig.* dross ; *sport* cinder.

zi *sf.* day ; *(lumină şi)* daylight ; *(dată)* date ; *pl.* times ; ~ *de lucru* week *sau* working day ; ~ *de muncă* workday ; ~ *de naştere* birthday ; ~ *de sărbătoare* red-letter day ; ~ *de* ~ everyday ; ~*lele acestea* (one of) these days ; ~*lele trecute* a few days ago ; ~*ua* by day(light) ; ~*ua numelui* one's name day ; *acum cîteva* ~*le* a few days ago ; *bună* ~*ua* good morning ; good afternoon ; *(la revedere)* good bye ; *de* ~ day ; *din* ~ *în* ~ from one day to another ; *într-o* ~ once ; *(în viitor)* someday ; *în* ~*ua aceea* on that day ; *la* ~ up to day ; *toată* ~*ua* all day (long).

ziar *sn.* (news)paper, daily ; *(publicaţie)* journal.

ziarist *sm.* journalist ; *(comentator)* columnist ; *(vînzător)* newspaper boy.

zicală, zicătoare *sf.* saying.

zice *vt.* to say ; *(a rosti şi)* to utter ; *(a relata şi)* to tell. *vi.* to say ; *(a cînta)* to sing ; *(dintr-un instrument)* to play ; *ca să* ~*m aşa* so to speak, as it were ; *zis şi făcut* no sooner said than done. *vr.: se* ~ *că* it is said that ; *se* ~ *că e plecat* he is said to be away ; *s-a zis cu tine* you are done for.

zid *sn.* wall.

zidar *sm.* bricklayer.

zidărie *sf.* masonry ; *(construcţie şi)* brickwork.

zidi *vt.* to build ; *(a închide)* to wall in *sau* up.

zigzag *sn.* zigzag.

zilier *sm.* day-labourer.

zilnic *adj., adv.* daily.

zimbru *sm.* aurochs.

zimţ *sm.* dent ; tooth.

zinc *sn.* zinc.

zis *adj.* styled ; *aşa-* ~ so-called ; would-be.

zîmbăreţ *adj.* smiling.

zîmbet *sn.* smile ; *(rînjet)* grin ; *(afectat)* simper.

zîmbi *vi.* to smile ; *a* ~ *mînzeşte* to grin.

zîmbitor *adj.* smiling. *adv.* smilingly.

zînă *sf.* fairy ; *(zeiţă)* goddess.

zît *interj.* shut up ! *(pt. pisici)* scot !

zizanie *sf.* discord.

zloată *sf.* sleet.

zmeu *sm.* dragon. *sn.* *(jucărie)* kite.

zmeură *sf.* raspberry.

zodie *sf.* sign (of the zodiac).

zonare *sf.* zoning.

zonă *sf.* zone ; ~ *denuclearizată* atom-free zone.

zoolog *sm.* zoologist.

zoologic *adj.* zoological.

zoologie *sf.* zoology.

zootehnic *adj.* zootechnical.

zootehnie *sf.* livestock breeding.

zor *sn.* hurry ; *de* ~ hastily.

zorele *sf. pl.* morning glory.

zori[1] *sf. pl.* dawn ; *în* ~ at daybreak.

zori[2] *vt.* to goad. *vr.* to hurry.

zornăi *vt., vi.* to jingle.

zorzoane *sf. pl.* gewgaws.

zugrav *sm.* house painter.

zugrăvi *vt.* to paint ; *fig.* to depict.

zuluf *sm.* ringlet.

zumzet *sn.* buzz(ing).

zurgălău *sm.* little bell.

zurliu *adj.* crazy, dotty.

zvastică *sf.* swastika, fylfot, ha-
kenkreuz.

zvăpăiat *adj.* frolicsome; *(zăpăcit)* giddy.

zvelt *adj.* slender, lithe.

zvieni *vi.* to throb; *(a sări)* to
dash.

zvienire *sf.* throb.

zvînta *vt.* to air; *fig.* to beat.
vr. to dry (in the air).

zvîrcoli *vr.* to writhe.

zvîrcolire *sf.* convulsion.

zvîrli *vt.* to cast, to toss.

zvîrlugă *sf. iht.* groundling; *fig.*
eel.

zvon *sn.* rumour; *(zgomot)* din;
(de clopote) ringing.

zvoni *vr.* to get about; *se zvo-
nește că* it is rumoured that.

English-
Romanian

LIST OF ABBREVIATIONS

adj. = adjectiv
adv. = adverb
agr. = agronomie
amer. = termen folosit în S.U.A.
anat. = anatomie
aprox. = aproximativ
arhit. = arhitectură
art. nehot. = articol nehotărît
aux. = auxiliar
auto. = automobilism
bot. = botanică
cin. = cinematografie
chim. = chimie
com. = comerţ
compar. = comparativ
cond. = condiţional
conj. = conjuncţie
constr. = construcţii
d. = despre
dat. = dativ
el. — electricitate
econ. = economie
fig. = figurat
fin. = finanţe
foto. = fotografie
geom. = geometrie
gram. = gramatică
geogr. = geografie
iht. = ihtiologie
ind. prez. = indicativ prezent
inf. = infinitiv
interj. = interjecţie
interog. = interogativ
iron. = ironic
ist. = istorie
înv. = învechit

jur. = juridic
mar. = marină
mat. = matematică
med. = medicină
mil. = militar
mine. = minerit
muz. = muzică
neg. = negativ
num. = numeral
ornit. = ornitologie
part. = participiu
peior. = peiorativ
pers. = persoană
pl. = plural
poet. = poetic
poligr. = poligrafie
prep. = prepoziţie
pron. = pronume
rad. = radiotehnică
rel. = religie
s. = substantiv
sing. = singular
smb. = *somebody* = cineva
smth. = *something* = ceva
superl. = superlativ
tehn. = tehnică
text. = textile
trec. = trecut
v. = vezi
v. aux. = verb auxiliar
vi. = verb intranzitiv
viit. = viitor
v. mod. = verb modal
vr. = verb reflexiv
vt. = verb tranzitiv
zool. = zoologie

3

4

Simboluri fonetice utilizate în volumul de faţă
Extrase din lista semnelor fonetice pentru sistemul IPA
(International Phonetic Association)

Nr. din sistemul IPA	Simbol	Explicaţii	Exemple	Transcriere	Corespondent (aproximativ) în româneşte
VOCALISMUL					
a) Vocale					
1	[i:]	*i* foarte lung	**feeler**	['fi:lɔ]	„filă" (cu *i* mai prelung)
2	[i]	*i* scurt, foarte deschis, aproape de *e*	**fit**	[fit]	„fit" (cu *i* foarte scurt, nepalatalizat)
3	[e]	*e* puţin mai deschis ca în româneşte	**set**	[set]	„set" (cu *e* mai deschis, nepalatalizat)
4	[æ]	*e* foarte deschis spre *a*, ca în graiul ardelenesc	**Sam**	[sæm]	„seamă" (dar cu diftongul îmbinat)
5	[u:]	*a* foarte deschis ; format în fundul gurii	**bar**	[bɑ:]	„bar" (cu *a* prelung şi fără *r*)
6	[ɔ]	*o* scurt, deschis spre *a*, rostit cu buzele trase în jos, ca în graiul ardelenesc	**tot** **cod**	[tɔt] [kɔd]	„tot" (dar mai aproape de sunetul din „toată") „cod" (dar mai asemănător cu „coadă")
7	[ɔ:]	*o* lung, deschis, şi cu buzele trase în jos	**door** **lord**	[dɔ:] [lɔ:d]	„dor" (cu *o* lung, deschis, fără *r*) „lord" (fără *r*, cu *o* lung, deschis)
8	[u]	*u* foarte scurt	**cook**	[kuk]	„cuc" (cu *u* scurtat)
9	[u:]	*u* foarte lung	**boon**	[bu:n]	„bun" (cu *u* foarte lung, ca în „iulie")
10	[ʌ]	*a* foarte scurt şi închis, rostit în centrul gurii	**supper**	['sʌpɔ]	„sapă" (cu *a* foarte scurt, retezat)

(continuarea tabelului)

Nr. din sistemul IPA	Simbol	Explicații	Exemple	Transcriere	Corespondent (aproximativ) în românește
11	[ɔ:]	vocală centrală, un fel de *ă* foarte lung, rostit cu dinții apropiați și buzele întinse lateral	**Sir**	[sə:]	„să" (cu vocala foarte lungă și închisă)
12	[ə]	vocală centrală neaccentuată, un fel de *ă* foarte scurt	**sitter**	['sitə]	„sită" (cu vocala finală închisă și retezată)

b) Diftongi

Nr.	Simbol	Explicații	Exemple	Transcriere	Corespondent
13	[ei]	similar cu diftongul românesc, dar mai deschis și fără palatalizare	**lay** **hey**	[lei] [hei]	„lei" (cu vocale mai deschise, fără palatalizare) „hei" (idem)
14	[ou]	ca *ău* din română, dar cu buzele rotunjite, cea de jos ieșită înainte	**tow**	[tou]	„tău" (cu vocală *ă* rotunjită)
15	[ai]	ca *ai* din românește, dar mai deschis	**sky**	[skai]	„scai" (cu *a* mai deschis, mai lung, ușor nazalizat, și *i* foarte scurt)
16	[au]	ca *au* din românește, dar mai deschis	**how**	[hau]	„hau" (cu *a* mai deschis, ușor nazalizat)
17	[ɔi]	cu *o* deschis — nr. 6 — ardelenesc, urmat de un *i* foarte scurt	**boy**	[bɔi]	„boi" (dar cu *o* foarte deschis — nr. 6 — nerotunjit, cu buzele trase în jos)
18	[iə]	*i* deschis, urmat de *ă* scurt	**fear**	[fiə]	
19	[ɛə]	*e* foarte deschis, urmat de *ă* scurt	**Mary**	['mɛəri]	
20	[uə]	*u* scurt, urmat de *ă* scurt, închis	**continuer**	[kon'tinjuə]	„continuă" cu *ă* mai scurt, coborîtor

(continuarea tabelului)

Nr. din sistemul IPA	Sim-bol	Explicații	Exem-ple	Tran-scriere	Corespondent (aproxi-mativ) în românește

CONSONATISMUL

a) ocluzive (explozive)

	[p]	*p* urmat de obicei de o mică explozie, ca un *h* scurt	**part**	[pɑ:t]	„pat" (cu *p* foarte tare și *a* lung)
	[b]	ca *b* românesc, dar mai sonor	**bun**	[bʌn]	„ban" (cu *b* foarte vi-brat și *a* foarte scurt)
	[t]	*t* rostit cu limba la rădăcina dinților, urmat de obicei de o mică explozie, ca un *h* scurt	**Tom**	[tɔm]	„tom" (cu *t* foarte tare, post-dental și cu *o* foarte deschis)
	[d]	*d* foarte sonor, ros-tit cu limba la rădăcina dinților	**din** / **dun**	[din] / [dʌn]	„din" cu (consoanele foarte sonore și voca-la foarte scurtă) „Dan" (idem)
	[k]	*c* foarte tare, nepa-latalizat, urmat de o mică explozie de aer ca un *h* scurt	**cut**	[kʌt]	„cat" (cu *c* foarte tare, urmat de un fel de *h* și de *a* scurt)
	[g]	ca *g* românesc, foarte sonor	**gum-mer**	['gʌmɔ]	„gamă" (cu *a* scurt, — nr. 10 — și *ă* scurt — nr. 12)

b) semi-ocluzive (africate)

| | [tʃ] | *t* îmbinat cu *ș*, ca în *ci* românesc (nepalatalizat) | **touch** / **much** | [tʌtʃ] / [mʌtʃ] | „taci" (cu *i* foarte scurt, nepalatalizat, și *a* scurt — nr. 10) „maci" (idem) |
| | [dʒ] | *d* îmbinat cu *j*, ca în *gi* românesc (nepalatalizat) | **jam** | [dʒæm] | „geam" (cu consoana nepalatalizată, și dif-tongul *ea* îmbinat) |

(continuarea tabelului)

Nr. din sistemul IPA	Simbol	Explicații	Exemple	Transcriere	Corespondent (aproximativ) în românește

c) nazale

	[m]	ca *m* românesc	**moot**	[muːt]	„mut" (cu *u* lung)
	[n]	ca *n* românesc	**nod**	[nɔd]	„nod" (cu *o* foarte deschis — nr. 6)
	[ʊ]	*n* velar (realizat prin lipirea dosului limbii de vălul palatului ca în rom. „lîngă", „crîng", „pungă")	**bunker**	[ˈbʌnkɔ]	„bancă" (cu *n* mai nazalizat, și *a* și *ă* scurte)

d) laterale

	[l]	ca *l* românesc (cu limba mai retrasă, cînd consoana apare la sfîrșitul cuvîntului)	**luck**	[lʌk]	„lac" (cu *a* scurt — nr. 10)

e) fricative (șuierătoare)

	[f]	ca *f* românesc	**fin**	[fin]	„fin" (cu *i* scurt)
	[v]	ca *v* românesc (dar mai sonor)	**vie**	[vai]	„vai" (cu diftongul ușor nazalizat)
	[θ]	consoană surdă, pronunțată cu limba ținută între dinți (ca un *s* foarte peltic)	**thick**	[θik]	
	[ð]	consoană foarte sonoră, pronunțată cu limba ținută între dinți (ca un *s* foarte peltic)	**without**	[wiˈðaut]	
	[s]	ca *s* românesc	**sauce**	[sɔːs]	„sos" (cu *o* deschis, lung — nr. 7)
	[z]	ca *z* românesc, foarte sonor	**zinc**	[zink]	„zinc" (cu *i* deschis, scurt și *n* velar)

8

(continuarea tabelului)

Nr. din sistemul IPA	Simbol	Explicaţii	Exemple	Transcriere	Corespondent (aproximativ) în româneşte
[ʃ]	ca ş românesc	shock	[ʃɔk]	„şoc" (cu *o* deschis — nr. 6)
[ʒ]	ca *j* românesc, foarte sonor	rouge	[ru:ʒ]	„ruj" (cu *r* lichid şi *u* lung)
[r]	consoană lichidă, aproape fără fricţiune, fără vibraţia limbii	bravo	['brɑ:-'vou]	„bravo" (cu *r* foarte moale, lichid, fără vibraţia limbii; la sfîrşit diftongul [ou])
[h]	un *h* pronunţat mai în fundul gîtului decît în româneşte	high	[hai]	„hai" (cu un *h* mai aspru, gutural)

f) semiconsoane (semivocale)

[w]	*u* foarte scurt, cu buzele făcute pungă, folosit înaintea vocalelor	oner	['wʌnɔ]	„Oană" (cu *a* scurtat — nr. 10 — şi *ă* scurt — nr. 12)
[j]	*i* tare, foarte palatalizat (iot), folosit înaintea vocalelor	yod	[jɔd]	„iod" (cu *o* foarte deschis — nr. 6)

A

A¹ [ei] *s.* A, a; (nota) la; *A1* grozav.

a² [ə,ei] *art. nehot.* un, o.

aback [ə'bæk] *adv.* înapoi; *taken* ~ surprins.

abandon [ə'bændən] *vt.* a abandona; a ceda.

abandoned [ə'bændənd] *adj.* părăsit; destrăbălat.

abate [ə'beit] *vt.* a micșora. *vi.* a scădea, a slăbi.

abbey ['æbi] *s.* mănăstire.

abbot ['æbət] *s.* stareț.

abbreviate [ə'bri:vieit] *vt.* a (pre)scurta.

ABC ['eibi:'si:] *s.* alfabet; rudimente.

abdicate ['æbdikeit] *vt.* a renunța la.

abdomen ['æbdəmen] *s.* abdomen.

abet [ə'bet] *vt.* a încuraja; a fi complice cu.

abide [ə'baid] *vt.* a aștepta. *vi.* a sta; a locui; *to* ~ *by* a respecta.

ability [ə'biliti] *s.* capacitate; abilitate.

abject ['æbdʒekt] *adj.* josnic, meschin.

able ['eibl] *adj.* capabil; *to be* ~ *to* a putea.

abnormal [æb'nɔ:ml] *adj.* anormal; excepțional.

aboard [ə'bɔ:d] *adv.* pe bord; *amer.* în vagoane.

abode [ə'boud] *s.* locuință. *vt., vi. trec. și part. trec. de la* **abide.**

abolish [ə'bɔliʃ] *vt.* a desființa.

A-bomb ['eibɔm] *s.* bombă atomică.

abominable [ə'bɔminəbl] *adj.* groaznic; odios.

abound [ə'baund] *vi.* a abunda.

about [ə'baut] *adj.* treaz; pe picioare. *adv.* (de jur) împrejur; pe aproape; *to be* ~ *to* a fi pe punctul de a. *prep.* în jurul; aproape de.

above [ə'bʌv] *prep.* deasupra, mai (pre)sus de; ~ *all* mai presus de orice; mai ales.

abreast [ə'brest] *adv.*: ~ *of* în pas cu.

abridge [ə'bridʒ] *vt.* a (pre)scurta.

abroad [ə'brɔ:d] *adv.* în străinătate; peste tot.

abscess ['æbsis] *s.* abces, bubă.

absence ['æbsns] *s.* absență; ~ *of mind* neatenție, distracție.

absent ['æbsnt] *adj.* absent; distrat.

absent-minded ['æbsnt 'maindid] *adj.* distrat; zăpăcit.

absolute ['æbsəlu:t] *adj.* absolut.

absolutism ['æbsəlu:tizəm] *s.* absolutism.

absolve [əb'zɔlv] *vt.* a ierta; a scuti.

absorb [əb'sɔːb] *vt.* a absorbi.

abstain [əb'stein] *vi.* a se abține.

abstract ['æbstrækt] *s.* rezumat; esență. *adj.* abstract.

absurd [əb'səːd] *adj.* absurd.

abundant [ə'bʌndənt] *adj.* abundent.

abuse¹ [ə'bjuːs] *s.* abuz; batjocură, insultă.

abuse² [ə'bjuːz] *vt.* a abuza de; a insulta.

abut [ə'bʌt] *vi.* a se învecina.

abyss [ə'bis] *s.* prăpastie.

acacia [ə'keiʃə] *s.* salcîm.

academy [ə'kædəmi] *s.* academie.

accede [æk'siːd] *vi.* a consimți; *to ~ to* a ajunge la *sau* pe; a intra în.

accelerate [æk'seləreit] *vt., vi.* a (se) grăbi.

accent¹ ['æksnt] *s.* accent.

accent² [æk'sent] *vt.* a accentua, a sublinia.

accept [ək'sept] *vt.* a accepta.

accident ['æksidnt] *s.* accident; întîmplare; *by ~* întîmplător.

acclaim [ə'kleim] *vt.* a aclama.

accommodate [ə'kɔmədeit] *vt.* a potrivi; a împăca; a găzdui.

accommodation [ə,kɔmə'deiʃn] *s.* acomodare; locuință.

accompany [ə'kʌmpəni] *vt.* a acompania, a însoți.

accomplice [ə'kɔmplis] *s.* complice.

accomplish [ə'kɔmpliʃ] *vt.* a realiza; a (de)săvîrși.

accomplishment [ə'kɔmpliʃmənt] *s.* îndeplinire; (de)săvîrșire; pricepere.

accord [ə'kɔːd] *s.* acord; armonie; *of one's own ~* de bună voie. *vt., vi.* a (se) armoniza.

accordance [ə'kɔːdns] *s.: in ~ with* după, conform cu.

according [ə'kɔːdiŋ] *adv.: ~ as* pe măsură ce; *~ to* după, conform cu.

accordingly [ə'kɔːdiŋli] *adv.* ca atare; deci.

accordion [ə'kɔːdjən] *s.* acordeon.

account [ə'kaunt] *s.* socoteală; bilanț; cont; relatare; *on ~ of* din pricina. *vi.: to ~ for* a explica; a justifica.

accountant [ə'kauntənt] *s.* contabil.

accumulate [ə'kjuːmjuleit] *vt., vi.* a (se) acumula.

accurate ['ækjurit] *adj.* exact; precis; corect.

accursed [ə'kəːsid] *adj.* blestemat.

accusation [ækju'zeiʃn] *s.* acuzație.

accusative [ə'kjuːzətiv] *s.* acuzativ.

accuse [ə'kjuːz] *vt.* a acuza.

accustom [ə'kʌstəm] *vt.* a deprinde; *to be ~ed to* a fi obișnuit să.

ace [eis] *s.* as.

ache [eik] *s.* durere.

achieve [ə'tʃiːv] *vt.* a îndeplini; a obține.

achievement [ə'tʃiːvmənt] *s.* succes; realizare.

acid ['æsid] *s., adj.* acid.

acknowledge [ək'nɔlidʒ] *vt.* a recunoaște; a confirma.

acorn ['eikɔːn] *s.* ghindă.

acquaint [ə'kweint] *vt.* a familiariza; a face să cunoască.

acquaintance [ə'kweintns] s. cunoştinţă; cunoaştere.

acquiesce [,ækwi'es] vi. a fi de acord; a încuviinţa.

acquire [ə'kwaiə] vt. a căpăta; a cîştiga.

acquit [ə'kwit] vt. a achita.

acre ['eikə] s. pogon.

across [ə'krɔs] adv. în curmeziş; orizontal; vizavi; în faţă. prep. în faţa; peste.

act [ækt] s. acţiune; act; (proiect de) lege. vt. a juca (un rol). vi. a acţiona; a juca teatru; a servi.

acting ['æktiŋ] s. joc (al actorilor). adj. provizoriu.

action ['ækʃn] s. acţiune; luptă.

active ['æktiv] adj. activ; energic.

activity [æk'tiviti] s. activitate.

actor ['æktə] s. actor.

actress ['æktris] s. actriţă.

actual ['æktjuəl] adj. real; existent; curent.

actuality [,æktju'æliti] s. realitate.

actually ['æktjuəli] adv. în realitate; de fapt.

A.D. ['ei'di:] adj. al erei noastre.

adage ['ædidʒ] s. proverb; maximă.

adamant ['ædəmənt] s. diamant; fig. piatră.

adapt [ə'dæpt] vt. a adapta; a modifica.

add [æd] vt. a adăuga; a aduna. vi. a (se) adăuga.

adder ['ædə] s. viperă.

addition [ə'diʃn] s. adăugare; adaos; mat. adunare; in ~ to pe lîngă.

addle ['ædl] adj. stricat.

addle-brained ['ædl,breind],
addle-headed ['ædl,hedid] adj. zevzec; zăpăcit.

address [ə'dres] s. adresă; pricepere; discurs; pl. omagii. vt., vr. a (se) adresa.

adept ['ædept] s. specialist, expert.

adequate ['ædikwit] adj. potrivit.

adhere [əd'hiə] vi. a se lipi; a adera.

adhesion [əd'hi:ʒn] s. adeziune.

adieu [ə'dju:] s., interj. adio.

adjective ['ædʒiktiv] s. adjectiv.

adjoining [ə'dʒɔiniŋ] adj. alăturat.

adjourn [ə'dʒə:n] vt. a amîna; a suspenda.

adjunct ['ædʒʌŋkt] s. adjunct; ajutor. adj. auxiliar.

adjust [ə'dʒʌst] vt. a aranja; a adapta; a ajusta.

administration [əd,minis'treiʃn] s. administraţie; guvern.

admirable ['ædmərəbl] adj. admirabil.

admiral ['ædmərəl] s. amiral.

admiralty ['ædmərəlti] s. amiralitate; ministerul marinei.

admire [əd'maiə] vt. a admira.

admission [əd'miʃn] s. admitere; mărturisire.

admit [əd'mit] vt. a primi; a mărturisi; a permite.

admittance [əd'mitns] s. intrare.

admonish [əd'mɔniʃ] vt. a sfătui; a avertiza.

ado [ə'du:] s. zarvă; încurcătură.

adolescent [ædə'lesnt] s., adj. adolescent(ă).

adopt [ə'dɔpt] vt. a adopta; a alege.

adoption [ə'dɔpʃn] s. adoptare.

adore [ə'dɔ:] vt. a adora.

adorn [ə'dɔ:n] vt. a împodobi.

adult ['ædʌlt] s., adj. adult; matur.

adulterate [ə'dʌltəreit] vt. a preface.

adultery [ə'dʌltəri] s. adulter.

advance [əd'vɑ:ns] s. propăşire; avans. vt., vi. a avansa.

advantage [əd'vɑ:ntidʒ] s. avantaj.

advantageous [ˌædvən'teidʒəs] adj. avantajos.

adventure [əd'ventʃə] s. aventură; risc.

adventurer [əd'ventʃrə] s. aventurier.

adverb ['ædvə:b] s. adverb.

adverse ['ædvə:s] adj. opus; contrar.

adversity [əd'və:siti] s. nenorocire; ghinion.

advertise ['ædvətaiz] vt. a anunţa. vi. a face reclamă.

advertisment [əd'və:tismənt] s. anunţ; reclamă.

advice [əd'vais] s. sfaturi; pl. informaţii.

advisable [əd'vaizəbl] adj. recomandabil.

advise [əd'vaiz] vt. a sfătui; a recomanda.

adviser [əd'vaizə] s. consilier; sfetnic.

advocate[1] ['ædvəkit] s. susţinător; apărător.

advocate[2] ['ædvəkeit] vt. a sprijini; a apăra.

aerial ['ɛəriəl] s. antenă. adj. aerian; eteric.

aeroplane ['ɛərəplein] s. avion.

aesthetic [i:s'θetik] adj. estetic.

aesthetics [i:s'θetiks] s. pl. estetică.

affable ['æfəbl] adj. politicos, amabil.

affair [ə'fɛə] s. afacere, treabă; grijă; idilă, legătură amoroasă.

affect [ə'fekt] vt. a afecta.

affection [ə'fekʃn] s. afecţiune.

affectionate [ə'fekʃnit] adj. drăgăstos.

affidavit [ˌæfi'deivit] s. declaraţie sub jurămînt.

affiliate [ə'filieit] vt. a afilia.

affinity [ə'finiti] s. înrudire; atracţie.

affirm [ə'fə:m] vt. a afirma.

afflict [ə'flikt] vt. a chinui; a necăji.

affliction [ə'flikʃn] s. mizerie; chin.

afford [ə'fɔ:d] vt. a oferi; I can ~ it îmi dă mîna (s-o fac etc.).

affront [ə'frʌnt] s. insultă. vt. a insulta.

afraid [ə'freid] adj. speriat; I'm ~ mi-e teamă, mă tem.

African ['æfrikən] s., adj. african(ă).

after ['ɑ:ftə] adv. ulterior. prep. după. conj. după ce.

afternoon ['ɑ:ftə'nu:n] s. după-amiază.

afterwards ['ɑ:ftəwədz] adv. după aceea.

again [ə'gen] adv. iar(ăşi).

against [ə'genst] prep. împotriva, contra; lipit de.

age [eidʒ] s. vîrstă; epocă; of ~ major.

aged ['eidʒid] adj. bătrîn; he is ~ [eidʒd] ten are zece ani.

agency ['eidʒnsi] s. mijloc; agenţie.

agenda [ə'dʒendə] s. ordine de zi.

agent ['eidʒnt] s. agent; factor.

aggravate ['ægrəveit] vt. a agrava; a enerva.

aggregate ['ægrigit] s. total; agregat.

aggression [ə'greʃn] s. agresiune; atac.

aggressive [ə'gresiv] adj. agresiv.

aggrieve [ə'gri:v] vt. a mîhni; a chinui.

aghast [ə'gɑ:st] adj. înspăimîntat.

agile ['ædʒail] adj. agil; activ.

agitate ['ædʒiteit] vt., vi. a (se) agita.

agitation [ˌædʒi'teiʃn] s. mişcare; agitaţie; tulburare.

ago [ə'gou] adv. în urmă; five days ~ acum cinci zile; long ~ de mult.

agony ['ægəni] s. chin; agonie.

agrarian [ə'grɛəriən] adj. agrar; agricol.

agree [ə'gri:] vi. a se înţelege; a fi în armonie.

agreeable [ə'griəbl] adj. plăcut; amabil.

agreement [ə'gri:mənt] s. acord; înţelegere.

agricultural [ˌægri'kʌltʃrl] adj. agricol.

agriculture ['ægrikʌltʃə] s. agricultură.

agronomy [ə'grɔnəmi] s. agronomie.

ague ['eigju:] s. malarie, friguri.

ahead [ə'hed] adv. înainte; în faţă.

ahem [hm] interj. hm.

aid [eid] s. ajutor; complice. vt. a ajuta.

ailment ['eilmənt] s. boală.

aim [eim] s. ţel. vt., vi. a ţinti.

air [ɛə] s. aer; pl. aere. vt., vr. a (se) aerisi.

airborne ['ɛəbɔ:n] adj. aeropurtat.

aircraft ['ɛəkrɑ:ft] s. avion; aviaţie.

airfield ['ɛəfi:ld] s. aerodrom.

air force ['ɛəfɔ:s] s. aviaţie.

airman ['ɛənˌæn] s. aviator.

airport ['ɛəpɔ:t] s. aeroport.

airscrew ['ɛəskru:] s. elice.

airy ['ɛəri] adj. aerian; delicat; superficial.

aisle [ail] s. interval (între scaune la biserică; amer. la teatru etc.); pasaj.

ajar [ə'dʒɑ:] adj. întredeschis.

akimbo [ə'kimbou] adv.: with arms ~ cu mîinile în şolduri.

akin [ə'kin] adj. înrudit; asemănător.

alarm [ə'lɑ:m] s. alarmă. vt. a alarma.

alarm clock [ə'lɑ:mˌklɔk] s. ceas deşteptător.

alas [ə'lɑ:s] interj. ah; vai; din păcate.

Albanian [æl'beinjən] s., adj. albanez(ă).

album ['ælbəm] s. album.

alchemy ['ælkimi] s. alchimie.

alcohol ['ælkəhɔl] s. alcool.

alder ['ɔ:ldə] s. arin.

alderman ['ɔ:ldəmən] s. consilier (municipal etc.).

ale [eil] s. bere.

ale-house ['eilhaus] s. berărie.

alert [ə'lə:t] adj. atent; vioi.

algebra ['ældʒibrə] s. algebră.

alien ['eiljən] s., adj. străin.

alienation [ˌeiljə'neiʃn] s. înstrăinare; alienaţie (mintală).

alight [ə'lait] *adj.* aprins. *vi.* a descăleca ; a coborî.

alike [ə'laik] *adj.* asemenea, asemănător. *adv.* la fel.

alimony ['æliməni] *s.* pensie alimentară.

alive [ə'laiv] *adj.* viu ; vioi ; activ ; *look ~* (mișcă-te) mai repede.

alkali ['ælkəlai] *s. chim.* bază.

all [ɔ:l] *adj.* tot, toți ; întreg ; orice. *pron.* toți, toată lumea ; totul ; toate. *~ right* bine ; în regulă ; *not at ~* de loc, cîtuși de puțin ; n-aveți pentru ce! ; *~ the same* totuși. *adv.* complet ; foarte ; în întregime, tot.

allay [ə'lei] *vt.* a potoli ; a alina.

allege [ə'ledʒ] *vt.* a pretinde, a susține.

allegedly [ə'ledʒədli] *adv.* chipurile.

allegiance [ə'li:dʒns] *s.* supunere ; credință.

alleviate [ə'li:vieit] *vt.* a ușura.

alley ['æli] *s.* alee ; popicărie.

alliance [ə'laiəns] *s.* alianță ; rudenie.

allot [ə'lɔt] *vt.* a aloca ; a distribui, a repartiza.

all-out ['ɔ:l‚aut] *adj.* global.

allow [ə'lau] *vt.* a permite ; a acorda ; a recunoaște. *vi. to ~ of* a permite ; *to ~ for* a ține seamă de. *vr.* a-și permite ; a se lăsa.

allowance [ə'lauəns] *s.* permisiune ; alocație ; stipendiu ; reducere ; *to make ~(s) for* a ține seama de.

alloy ['ælɔi] *s.* aliaj ; amestec.

all-round ['ɔ:lraund] *adj.* multilateral ; general.

allude [ə'lu:d] *vt.* a face aluzie ; a se referi.

allure [ə'ljuə] *vt.* a ispiti.

allusion [ə'lu:ʒn] *s.* aluzie.

ally[1] ['ælai] *s.* aliat.

ally[2] [ə'lai] *vt., vr.* a (se) alia ; a (se) uni.

almanac(k) ['ɔ:lmənæk] *s.* almanah ; calendar.

almighty [ɔ:l'maiti] *adj.* atotputernic.

almond ['a:mənd] *s.* migdal(ă).

almost ['ɔ:lmoust] *adv.* aproape ; cît pe-aci să.

alms [a:mz] *s.* pomană.

alone [ə'loun] *adj.* singur(atic) ; izolat ; *leave* sau *let me ~* lasă-mă în pace ; *let ~...* ca să nu mai vorbim de ... *adv.* numai.

along [ə'lɔŋ] *adv.* înainte ; *all ~* tot timpul. *prep.* de-a lungul.

alongside [ə'lɔŋsaid] *prep.* pe lîngă.

aloof [ə'lu:f] *adj.* distant ; *adv.* departe, la distanță *(mai ales fig.)* ; de o parte ; *~ from* departe de.

aloud [ə'laud] *adv.* tare ; răspicat.

alphabet ['ælfəbit] *s.* alfabet.

already [ɔ:l'redi] *adv.* deja.

also ['ɔ:lsou] *adv.* și, de asemenea.

altar ['ɔ:ltə] *s.* altar.

alter ['ɔ:ltə] *vt., vi.* a (se) schimba ; a (se) modifica.

alternate[1] [ɔ:l'tə:nit] *adj.* altern(ativ).

alternate[2] ['ɔ:ltə:neit] *vt., vi.* a alterna.

alternate member [ɔ:l'tə:nit 'membə] *s.* membru supleant.

alternative [ɔ:l'tə:nətiv] *s.* alternativă. *adj.* alternativ.

although [ɔ:l'ðou] *conj.* deși.

altitude ['æltitju:d] *s.* altitudine.

altogether [ˌɔ:ltə'geðə] *adv.* cu totul.

aluminium [ˌælju'minjəm] *s.* aluminiu.

always [ˌɔ:lwəz] *adv.* întotdeauna.

am [əm, æm] *v. aux., vi. pers. I sg. ind. prez. de la* **be**.

amalgamate [ə'mælgəmeit] *vt., vi.* a (se) amesteca; a (se) uni.

amass [ə'mæs] *vt.* a aduna.

amateur ['æmətə:] *s.* amator.

amaze [ə'meiz] *vt.* a ului.

ambassador [æm'bæsədə] *s.* ambasador; sol.

amber ['æmbə] *s.* chihlimbar.

ambiguous [æm'bigjuəs] *adj.* echivoc.

ambition [æm'biʃn] *s.* ambiție; țel.

ambitious [æm'biʃəs] *adj.* ambițios; îndrăzneț.

ambulance ['æmbjuləns] *s.* ambulanță; salvare.

ambush ['æmbuʃ] *s.* ambuscadă. *vt. mil.* a hărțui.

ameliorate [ə'mi:ljəreit] *vt., vi.* a (se) îmbunătăți.

amen ['ɑ:'men] *interj.* amin.

amend [ə'mend] *vt., vi.* a (se) îndrepta.

amendment [ə'mendmənt] *s.* amendament; îmbunătățire.

amends [ə'mendz] *s.* compensație.

American [ə'merikən] *s., adj.* american(ă).

amiable ['eimjəbl] *adj.* prietenos; drăguț.

amicable ['æmikəbl] *adj.* prietenos.

amid(st) [ə'mid(st)] *prep.* în mijlocul.

amiss [ə'mis] *adj., adv.* greșit; rău.

ammunition [ˌæmju'niʃn] *s.* muniții.

amnesty ['æmnesti] *s.* amnistie.

among(st) [ə'mʌŋ(st)] *prep.* printre; între.

amount [ə'maunt] *s.* cantitate; valoare. *vi.* to ~ to a se ridica la.

ample ['æmpl] *adj.* amplu; suficient.

amplitude ['æmplitju:d] *s.* proporții; amploare.

amuck [ə'mʌk] *adv.: to run ~* a înnebuni.

amuse [ə'mju:z] *vt.* a distra.

an [ən, æn] *art. nehot.* un, o (*înaintea vocalelor*).

analogous [ə'næləgəs] *adj.* similar.

analyse ['ænəlaiz] *vt.* a analiza.

analyses [ə'næləsi:z] *s. pl. de la* **analysis.**

analysis [ə'næləsis] *s.* analiză.

anarchy ['ænəki] *s.* anarhie; dezordine.

anatomy [ə'nætəmi] *s.* anatomie; disecție.

ancestor ['ænsistə] *s.* strămoș.

anchor ['æŋkə] *s.* ancoră; *at ~* ancorat. *vt., vi.* a ancora; a (se) fixa.

anchovy ['æntʃəvi] *s.* hamsie; anșoa.

anchylose ['æŋkilouz] *vt., vi.* a (se) anchiloza.

ancient ['einʃnt] *s.: the ~s* popoarele antice. *adj.* antic; vechi.

and [ənd, ænd] *conj.* și.

anecdote ['ænikdout] *s.* anecdotă.

anemone [ə'neməni] s. anemonă.

anew [ə'nju:] adv. iarăşi; altfel.

angel ['eindʒl] s. înger; sol.

anger ['æŋgə] s. furie; mînie. vt. a supăra.

angina [æn'dʒainə] s. anghină.

angle ['æŋgl] s. unghi; vîrf; punct de vedere; undiţă. vi. a pescui cu undiţa.

angler ['æŋglə] s. pescar cu undiţa.

angry ['æŋgri] adj. supărat; furios; ţîfnos; to be ~ with smb. a se supăra pe cineva.

anguish ['æŋgwiʃ] s. chin; durere.

angular ['æŋgjulə] adj. ascuţit; colţuros.

animal ['æniml] s. animal; fiinţă. adj. trupesc.

animal husbandry ['æniməl 'hʌzbəndri] s. creşterea vitelor; zootehnie.

animate ['ænimeit] vt. a însufleţi; a inspira.

animosity [,æni'mɔsiti] s. duşmănie.

anise ['ænis] s. anason.

aniseed ['ænisi:d] s. sămînţă de anason.

ankle ['æŋkl] s. gleznă.

annals ['ænlz] s. pl. anale; cronică.

annex [ə'neks] vt. a anexa; a ataşa.

annex(e) ['æneks] s. (clădire) anexă.

annihilate [ə'naiəleit] vt. a nimici.

annihilation [ə,naiə'leiʃn] s. nimicire.

anniversary [,æni'və:sri] s. aniversare; sărbătorire.

annotate ['ænoteit] vt. a adnota.

announce [ə'nauns] vt. a anunţa.

announcer [ə'naunsə] s. crainic (de radio).

annoy [ə'nɔi] vt. a supăra, a deranja.

annoyance [ə'nɔiəns] s. supărare.

annual ['ænjuəl] s. plantă anuală; anuar. adj. anual.

annuity [ə'njuiti] s. cotă anuală; pensie.

annul [ə'nʌl] vt. a anula.

annular ['ænjulə] adj. inelar.

annunciation [ə,nʌnsi'eiʃn] s. (buna)vestire.

anoint [ə'nɔint] vt. a unge; a numi.

anomalous [ə'nɔmələs] adj. neregulat; anormal.

anon [ə'nɔn] adv. curînd; iarăşi.

anonymous [ə'nɔniməs] adj. anonim.

another [ə'nʌðə] adj. alt; încă (un). pron. un altul; încă unul.

answer ['a:nsə] s. răspuns. vt. a răspunde la sau cuiva; a corespunde la. vi. a răspunde.

answerable ['a:nsrəbl] adj. răspunzător.

ant [ænt] s. furnică.

antagonist [æn'tægənist] s. adversar.

antarctic [ænt'a:ktik] s.: the A ~ Antarctica. adj. antarctic.

ant-eater ['ænt i:tə] s. zool. furnicar, pangolin.

antecedent [,ænti'si:dnt] s. antecedent.

antechamber ['ænti,tʃeimbə] s. anticameră.

antedate ['ænti'deit] vt. a antedata.

antelope ['æntiloup] s. antilopă.

ante-room ['æntirum] s. anti-cameră.

anthem ['ænθəm] s. imn.

ant-hill ['ænthil] s. mușuroi de furnici.

anthology [æn'θɔlədʒi] s. anto-logie ; selecție.

anthrax ['ænθræks] s. dalac ; bot. cărbune.

anti-aircraft ['ænti'ɛəkrɑːft] adj. antiaerian.

antic ['æntik] s. clovn ; scama-tor ; pl. clovnerii ; capricii. adj. grotesc ; ciudat.

anticipate [æn'tisipeit] vt. a anticipa.

anticipation [æn,tisi'peiʃn] s. an-ticipare ; așteptare.

anticlimax ['ænti'klaimæks] s. efect contrar ; cădere, declin.

antidote ['æntidout] s. antidot.

anti-Party ['ænti'pɑːti] adj. anti-partinic.

antiquarian [,ænti'kwɛəriən] s. anticar ; arheolog.

antiquary ['æntikwəri] s. cerce-tător al antichităților.

antiquated ['æntikweitid] adj. demodat.

antique [æn'tiːk] s. obiect sau stil antic. adj. antic.

antithesis [æn'tiθisis] s. anti-teză ; contrast.

antithetic [,ænti'θetik] adj. ba-zat pe contrast ; opus.

antitrade ['ænti'treid] s. con-traalizeu.

antlers ['æntləz] s. pl. coarne de cerb.

antonym ['æntənim] s. anto-nim.

anvil ['ænvil] s. nicovală.

anxiety [æŋ'zaiəti] s. neliniș-te.

anxious ['æŋʃəs] adj. nerăbdă-tor ; neliniștit(or).

any ['eni-] adj. oric(ar)e ; cu (inte-rog.) vreun ; (cu neg.) nici un. pron. oricare ; vreunul. adv. de loc.

anybody ['eni,bɔdi] s. un oare-care. pron. oricine ; (cu neg.) nimeni ; (cu interog.) cineva.

anyhow ['enihau] adv. oricum.

anyone ['eniwʌn] pron. oricine ; (cu neg.) nimeni ; (cu interog.) cineva.

anything ['eniθiŋ] pron. orice ; (cu neg.) nimic ; (cu interog.) ceva.

anyway ['eniwei] adv. oricum.

anywhere ['eniwɛə] adv. oriunde.

anywise ['eniwaiz] adv. oricum.

apart [ə'pɑːt] adv. separat ; jesting ~ lăsînd gluma la o parte.

apartment [ə'pɑːtmənt] s. ca-meră ; amer. apartament.

apartment-house [ə'pɑːtmənt-,haus] bloc (de locuințe).

apathetic [,æpə'θetik] adj. apa-tic.

apathy ['æpəθi] s. apatie.

ape [eip] s. maimuță. vt. a maimuțări.

aperture ['æpətjuə] s. deschiză-tură ; gaură.

apex ['eipeks] s. vîrf ; culme.

apiary ['eipjəri] s. prisacă.

apiece [ə'piːs] adv. de fiecare.

apish ['eipiʃ] adj. de maimuță ; grotesc.

apogee ['æpodʒiː] s. apogeu ; culme.

apologetic(al) [ə,pɔlə'dʒetik(l)] adj. spus sau prezentat ca o scuză ; umil ; plin de regret.

apologize [ə'pɔlədʒaiz] vi. a-și cere iertare.

apology [ə'pɔlədʒi] s. scuze; explicaţie; simulacru.

apostle [ə'pɔsl] s. apostol.

apostrophe [ə'pɔstrəfi] s. apostrof(ă).

appal [ə'pɔ:l] vt. a îngrozi.

apparatus [ˌæpə'reitəs] s. aparat(e).

apparel [ə'pærl] s. veşminte.

apparent [ə'pærnt] adj. aparent; vizibil.

apparition [ˌæpə'riʃn] s. vedenie.

appeal [ə'pi:l] s. apel; atracţie. vi. a apela; a ispiti.

appear [ə'piə] vi. a (a)părea.

appearance [ə'piərns] s. apariţie; înfăţişare; aparenţă.

appease [ə'pi:z] vt. a linişti; a mulţumi.

appellation [ˌæpe'leiʃn] s. num(ir)e.

append [ə'pend] vt. a adăuga.

appendicitis [əˌpendi'saitis] s. apendicită.

appendix [ə'pendiks] s. apendice; anexă.

appetite ['æpitait] s. poftă.

appetizing ['æpitaiziŋ] adj. îmbietor.

applaud [ə'plɔ:d] vt., vi. a aplauda.

applause [ə'plɔ:z] s. aplauze.

apple ['æpl] s. măr.

appliance [ə'plaiəns] s. dispozitiv; unealtă; articol.

applicant ['æplikənt] s. solicitant; petiţionar.

application [ˌæpli'keiʃn] s. cerere; aplicare.

apply [ə'plai] vt. a aplica. vi. a se aplica; a corespunde; to ~ for a solicita.

appoint [ə'pɔint] vt. a numi; a alege.

appointment [ə'pɔintmənt] s. numire; slujbă; întîlnire.

appraise [ə'preiz] vt. a evalua, a aprecia.

appreciate [ə'pri:ʃieit] vt. a aprecia.

apprehension [ˌæpri'henʃn] s. teamă.

apprentice [ə'prentis] s. ucenic.

approach [ə'proutʃ] s. apropiere; acces; concepţie, (mod de) abordare. vt. a se apropia de; a aborda.

appropriate¹ [ə'proupriit] adj. potrivit.

appropriate² [ə'prouprieit] vt. a-şi însuşi; a aloca.

approval [ə'pru:vl] s. aprobare.

approve [ə'pru:v] vt. a aproba. vi.: to ~ of a privi cu ochi buni; a aproba.

approximate [ə'prɔksimit] adj. aproximativ.

apricot ['eiprikɔt] s. cais(ă).

April ['eiprl] s. aprilie.

apron ['eiprn] s. şorţ.

apt [æpt] adj. potrivit; ager.

aptitude ['æptitju:d] s. aptitudine.

aquarium [ə'kwεəriəm] s. acvariu.

Arab ['ærəb] s. arab. adj. arab(ă).

arable ['ærəbl] adj. arabil.

arbitrary ['ɑ:bitrəri] adj. arbitrar.

arbour ['ɑ:bə] s. boschet.

arc [ɑ:k] s. tehn. arc.

arcade [ɑ:'keid] s. arcadă; gang.

arch [ɑ:tʃ] s. arhit. arc.

archaeology [ˌɑ:ki'ɔlədʒi] s. arheologie.

archaic [ɑ:'keiik] adj. arhaic.

archbishop ['ɑ:tʃ'biʃəp] s. arhiepiscop ; mitropolit.

archer ['ɑ:tʃə] s. arcaş.

architect ['ɑ:kitekt] s. arhitect ; constructor.

architecture ['ɑ:kitektʃə] s. arhitectură ; structură.

archives ['ɑ:kaivz] s. arhivă.

ardent ['ɑ:dnt] adj. arzător ; entuziast.

arduous ['ɑ:djuəs] adj. dificil ; aspru.

are [ə, ɑ:] v. aux., vi. pers. a II-a sg. şi pers. I, a II-a şi a III-a pl. ind. prez. de la be.

area ['ɛəriə] s. suprafaţă, întindere.

argue ['ɑ:gju:] vt. a susţine ; a dovedi. vi. a se certa.

argument ['ɑ:gjumənt] s. controversă ; discuţie, ceartă ; argument.

arid ['ærid] adj. arid.

arise [ə'raiz] vi. a apărea ; a se naşte.

arisen [ə'rizn] vi. part. trec. de la arise.

aristocracy [,æris'tɔkrəsi] s. aristocraţie.

arithmetic(s) [ə'riθmətik(s)] s. aritmetică.

ark [ɑ:k] s. arcă.

arm [ɑ:m] s. armă ; braţ ; stemă. vt., vi. a (se) înarma.

armament ['ɑ:məmənt] s. armament ; înarmare.

armchair ['ɑ:m'tʃɛə] s. fotoliu.

Armenian [ɑ:'mi:njən] s., adj. armean(ă).

armistice ['ɑ:mistis] s. armistiţiu.

armour ['ɑ:mə] s. armură.

armoured car ['ɑ:məd,kɑ:] s. car blindat.

arm-pit ['ɑ:mpit] s. subsuoară.

army [ɑ:mi] s. armată.

arose [ə'rouz] vi. trec. de la arise.

around [ə'raund] adv. (de jur) împrejur. prep. în jurul.

arouse [ə'rauz] vt. a trezi ; a stîrni.

arrangement [ə'reindʒmənt] s. aranjament ; acord.

arrears [ə'riəz] s. pl. restanţe.

arrest [ə'rest] s. arestare. vt. a aresta ; a opri.

arrival [ə'raivl] s. sosire.

arrive [ə'raiv] vi. a sosi.

arrogant ['ærəgənt] adj. trufaş.

arrow ['ærou] s. săgeată.

arson ['ɑ:sn] s. incendiere.

art [ɑ:t] s. artă ; litere ; umanistică. v. aux., vi. formă arhaică pentru pers. a II-a sg. are eşti.

artery ['ɑ:təri] s. arteră.

artful ['ɑ:tfl] adj. viclean; dibaci.

artichoke ['ɑ:titʃouk] s. anghinare.

article ['ɑ:tikl] s. articol.

articulate¹ [ɑ:'tikjulit] adj. distinct, clar.

articulate² [ɑ:'tikjuleit] vt. a articula ; a rosti.

artifice ['ɑ:tifis] s. şmecherie.

artillery [ɑ:'tiləri] s. artilerie.

artisan [,ɑ:ti'zæn] s. meşteşugar.

artist ['ɑ:tist] s. artist (plastic).

as [əz, æz] pron. care ; such ~ ca. conj. ca (şi) ; deoarece ; pe cînd ; (după) cum ; ~ a rule de obicei ; ~ far ~ pînă la ; în măsura în care ; ~ if, ~ though ca şi cum ; ~ it were parcă ; chipurile ; ~ long ~ atîta vreme cît ; cu condiţia ca ; ~ much aşa ; ~ soon mai degrabă ; ~ *well* şi ; ~ *well* ~ precum şi ; ~ *yet* deocamdată ; *so* ~ *to* pentru ca ; ~ *to*, ~ *for* în privinţa.

ascend [ə'send] *vt., vi.* a (se) urca.

ascent [ə'sent] *s.* urcuş.

ascertain [ˌæsə'tein] *vt.* a descoperi, a stabili.

ascribe [ə'skraib] *vt.* a atríbui.

ash [æʃ] *s.* cenuşă ; *pl.* scrum.

ashamed [ə'ʃeimd] *adj.* ruşinat.

ash-can ['æʃkæn] *s. amer.* ladă *sau* coş de gunoi.

ashore [ə'ʃɔ:] *adv.* pe ţărm ; pe uscat.

ash-tray ['æʃtrei] *s.* scrumieră.

ash-tree ['æʃtri:] *s.* frasin.

Ash Wednesday ['æʃ'wenzdi] *s.* lăsata secului.

Asian ['eiʃn] *s., adj.* asiatic(ă).

aside [ə'said] *adv.* la o parte, de o parte.

ask [ɑ:sk] *vt.* a întreba ; a cere ; a ruga. *vi.* a întreba ; *to* ~ *for* a cere.

asleep [ə'sli:p] *adj.* adormit ; *to be* ~ a dormi ; *to fall* ~ a adormi.

asparagus [əs'pærəgəs] *s.* sparanghel ; *bot.* umbra-iepurelui.

aspect ['æspekt] *s.* aspect ; înfăţişare.

asperity [æs'periti] *s.* asprime ; asperitate.

aspire [əs'paiə] *vi.* a năzui.

ass [æs] *s.* măgar ; *fig.* tîmpit.

assail [ə'seil] *vt.* a ataca.

assault [ə'sɔ:lt] *s.* atac ; atentat la pudoare, viol. *vt.* a ataca ; a viola.

assemble [ə'sembl] *vt., vi.* a (se) aduna.

assembly [ə'sembli] *s.* adunare ; montaj.

assent [ə'sent] *s.* încuviinţare. *vi.* a încuviinţa.

assert [ə'sə:t] *vt., vr.* a (se) afirma.

assertion [ə'sə:ʃn] *s.* afirmaţie ; afirmare.

assess [ə'ses] *vt.* a evalua.

assessor [ə'sesə] *s.* asesor ; portărel.

asset ['æset] *s.* bun ; *pl.* avere.

assiduous [ə'sidjuəs] *adj.* harnic.

assign [ə'sain] *vt.* a repartiza ; a încredinţa.

assignment [ə'sainmənt] *s.* sarcină.

assimilate [ə'simileit] *vt.* a asimila. *vi.* a (se) asimila.

assist [ə'sist] *vt., vi.* a ajuta.

assistance [ə'sistns] *s.* ajutor.

assistant [ə'sistnt] *s.* ajutor ; asistent.

assizes [ə'saiziz] *s. pl.* sesiune a tribunalului.

associate[1] [ə'souʃiit] *s.* tovarăş ; asociat.

associate[2] [ə'souʃieit] *vt., vi.* a (se) asocia.

association [əˌsousi'eiʃn] *s.* asociaţie ; asociere.

assort [ə'sɔ:t] *vt., vi.* a (se) asorta.

assortment [ə'sɔ:tmənt] *s.* sortiment.

assuage [ə'sweidʒ] *vt.* a alina.

assume [ə'sju:m] *vt.* a-şi asuma ; a presupune.

assumption [ə'sʌmʃn] *s.* asumare ; presupunere.

assurance [ə'ʃuərns] *s.* asigurare ; siguranţă.

assure [ə'ʃuə] *vt.* a asigura.

aster ['ɑ:stə] *s. bot.* ochiul-boului.

astern [ə'stə:n] *adv.* la pupă.

asthma ['æsmə] *s.* astmă.

astir [ə'stə:] *adj.* agitat, în miscare.

astonish [əs'tɔniʃ] *vt.* a uimi.

astray [ə'strei] *adv.* aiurea; *to lead* ~ a corupe.

astronomer [əs'trɔnəmə] *s.* astronom.

astronomy [əs'trɔnəmi] *s.* astronomie.

astute [əs'tju:t] *adj.* isteţ.

asunder [ə'sʌndə] *adv.* separat; în două.

asylum [ə'sailəm] *s.* azil.

at [ət, æt] *prep.* la; în; ~ *once* de îndată; ~ *that* astfel; pe deasupra.

ate [et] *vt., vi. trec. de la* **eat.**

atheism ['eiθiizəm] *s.* ateism.

athlete ['æθli:t] *s.* atlet.

athletics [æθ'letiks] *s. pl.* atletism.

atmosphere ['ætməsfiə] *s.* atmosferă.

atom ['ætəm] *s.* atom; părticică.

atone [ə'toun] *vt.: to* ~ *for* a compensa.

atrocious [ə'trouʃəs] *adj.* atroce.

attach [ə'tætʃ] *vt., vi.* a (se) ataşa.

attack [ə'tæk] *s.* atac. *vt.* a ataca; a începe.

attain [ə'tein] *vt.* a atinge.

attempt [ə'temt] *s.* încercare; efort; atentat. *vt.* a încerca.

attend [ə'tend] *vt.* a îngriji; a asista la; a urma (şcoala etc.); a însoţi. *vi. to* ~ *to* a se ocupa de; *to* ~ *upon* a servi.

attendance [ə'tendəns] *s.* îngrijire; însoţire; public.

attendant [ə'tendənt] *s.* ajutor. *adj.* însoţitor.

attention [ə'tenʃn] *s.* atenţie; *pl.* complimente. *interj. mil.* drepţi.

attentive [ə'tentiv] *adj.* atent.

attest [ə'test] *vt.* a dovedi. *vi.* a depune mărturie.

attic ['ætik] *s.* mansardă.

attire [ə'taiə] *s.* îmbrăcăminte. *vt.* a îmbrăca.

attitude ['ætitju:d] *s.* atitudine.

attorney [ə'tə:ni] *s.* prepus; reprezentant; avocat.

attorney-general [ə'tə:ni 'dʒenrl] *s.* procuror general; *amer.* ministru de justiţie.

attract [ə'trækt] *vt.* a atrage.

attractive [ə'træktiv] *adj.* atrăgător.

attribute[1] ['ætribju:t] *s.* atribut.

attribute[2] [ə'tribjut] *vt.* a atribui.

auburn ['ɔ:bən] *adj.* roşcat.

auction ['ɔ:kʃn] *s.* licitaţie.

audacious [ɔ:'deiʃəs] *adj.* îndrăzneţ.

audacity [ɔ:'dæsiti] *s.* îndrăzneală.

audience ['ɔ:djəns] *s.* public; audienţă.

audit ['ɔ:dit] *s.* revizie (contabilă). *vt.* a revizui (conturi).

auditor ['ɔ:ditə] *s.* revizor contabil; ascultător.

auditorium [,ɔ:di'tɔ:riəm] *s.* sală de spectacol.

augment [ɔ:g'ment] *vt., vi.* a (se) mări.

August[1] ['ɔ:gəst] *s.* august.

august[2] [ɔ:'gʌst] *adj.* maiestuos; nobil.

aunt [ɑ:nt] *s.* mătuşă.

auspices ['ɔ:spisiz] *s. pl.* auspicii.

auspicious [ɔ:s'piʃəs] *adj.* norocos; favorabil.

austere [ɔs'tiə] *adj.* aspru ; auster.

austerity [ɔs'teriti] *s.* strictețe ;
privațiune.

Austrian ['ɔstriən] *s., adj.* aus-
triac(ă).

author ['ɔ:θə] *s.* autor.

authoress ['ɔ:θəris] *s.* autoare.

authoritative [ɔ:'θɔritətiv] *adj.*
autoritar ; valabil.

authorize ['ɔ:θəraiz] *vt.* a autoriza.

authorship ['ɔ:θəʃip] *s.* origine ;
paternitate ; scris ; calitatea de
scriitor.

autobiography [,ɔ:tobai'ɔgrəfi]
s. autobiografie.

autocrat ['ɔ:təkræt] *s.* autocrat ;
tiran.

autograph ['ɔ:təgrɑ:f] *s.* autograf.

automatic [,ɔ:tə'mætik] *adj.* automat.

automation [,ɔ:tə'meiʃn] *s.* automatizare.

automobile ['ɔ:təməbi:l] *s. (mai
ales amer.)* automobil.

autonomous [ɔ:'tɔnəməs] *adj.*
autonom.

autumn ['ɔ:təm] *s.* toamnă.

avail [ə'veil] *s.* folos ; avantaj. *vi.*
a folosi ; a ajuta. *vr.* a profita.

available [ə'veiləbl] *adj.* folositor ; disponibil ; de găsit.

avalanche ['ævəlɑ:nʃ] *s.* avalanșă.

avarice ['ævəris] *s.* zgîrcenie.

avaricious [,ævə'riʃəs] *adj.* zgîrcit ; lacom.

avenge [ə'vendʒ] *vt., vr.* a (se)
răzbuna.

avenue ['ævinju:] *s.* bulevard ;
fig. cale.

average ['ævəridʒ] *s.* medie.

adj. mediu ; obișnuit. *vt.* a da
o medie de.

averse [ə'və:s] *adj.* potrivnic ;
refractar.

aversion [ə'və:ʃn] *s.* aversiune.

avert [ə'və:t] *vt.* a abate; a evita.

avoid [ə'vɔid] *vt.* a evita.

avoidance [ə'vɔidns] *s.* evitare.

avoirdupois [,ævədə'pɔiz] *s.* sistem de greutăți folosit în țările
de limbă engleză *(un funt =
= 16 uncii)*.

avow [ə'vau] *vt.* a mărturisi ; a
recunoaște, a declara.

avowal [ə'vauəl] *s.* mărturisire
(publică).

await [ə'weit] *vt.* a aștepta.

awake [ə'weik] *adj.* treaz ; conștient. *vt., vi.* a (se) trezi.

awaken [ə'weikn] *vt., vi.* a (se)
trezi.

award [ə'wɔ:d] *s.* premiu; primă;
distincție ; sentință. *vt.* a acorda.

aware [ə'wɛə] *adj.* conștient.

away [ə'wei] *adv.* departe.

awe [ɔ:] *s.* respect ; teamă. *vt.*
a înspăimînta.

awfully ['ɔ:f(u)li] *adv.* teribil ;
foarte.

awkward ['ɔ:kwəd] *adj.* stîngaci ; dificil ; penibil.

awl [ɔ:l] *s.* sulă.

awning ['ɔ:niŋ] *s.* acoperiș de
pînză ; marchiză.

awoke [ə'wouk] *vt., vi.* trec. și
part. trec. de la awake.

awry [ə'rai] *adj., adv.* strîmb.

ax(e) [æks] *s.* topor.

axiom ['æksiəm] *s.* axiomă.

axis ['æksis] *s.* axă.

axle ['æksl] *s.* osie.

ay(e) [ai] *s., adv.* da ; *the ~s
have it* majoritatea este pentru.

azure ['æʒə] *s.* azur. *adj.* azuriu.

B

B [bi:] *s.* B, b; (nota) si; si bemol.

babble ['bæbl] *s.* bolboroseală. *vi.* a flecări; a gînguri.

babe [beib] *s.* prunc.

baby ['beibi] *s.* copilaş, prunc; pitic; om copilăros; miniatură (*fig.*).

baby sitter ['beibi,sitə] *s* persoană angajată să stea cu copilul în absenţa părinţilor.

bachelor ['bætʃlə] *s.* celibatar; licenţiat.

bacilli [bə'silai] *s. pl. de la* **bacillus.**

bacillus [bə'siləs] *s.* bacil.

back [bæk] *s.* spate; dos; spetează (de scaun); *sport* fundaş. *adj.* din spate; din fund; posterior. *vt.* a sprijini; a face să dea înapoi. *vi.* a da înapoi. *adv.* înapoi, în spate; în fund; ~ *and forth* înainte şi înapoi.

backbite ['bækbait]. *vt.* a bîrfi, a defăima.

backbone ['bækboun] *s.* şira spinării.

backer ['bækə] *s.* sprijinitor; parior (la curse).

backgammon [bæk'gæmən] *s.* (joc de) table.

background ['bækgraund] *s.* fundal; fond; cadru; pregătire.

back number ['bæk,nʌmbə] *s.* ziar vechi; lucru *sau* om demodat.

backward ['bækwəd] *adj.* din spate; înapoiat; întîrziat. *adv.* înapoi.

backwater ['bæk,wɔ:tə] *s.* japşă; bulboană; impas; stagnare.

bacon ['beikn] *s.* slănină; costiţă.

bacteria [bæk'tiəriə] *s. pl. de la* **bacterium.**

bacterium [bæk'tiəriəm] *s.* bacterie.

bad [bæd] *adj.* rău; urît; stricat; nepriceput; *not half* ~ bun; satisfăcător.

bade [beid] *vt., vi. trec. de la* **bid.**

badge [bædʒ] *s.* insignă; semn.

badger ['bædʒə] *s.* bursuc.

bad lot ['bæd'lɔt] *s.* soartă rea; păcătos; stricată.

badly ['bædli] *adv.* rău, teribil.

badly off ['bædli 'ɔ:f] *adj.* sărac.

bad-tempered [,bæd'tempəd] *adj.* supărăcios.

baffle ['bæfl] *vt.* a zădărnici; a nedumeri.

bag [bæg] *s.* sac; pungă; tolbă. *vt.* a prinde; a lua.

baggage ['bægidʒ] *s.* bagaj; echipament.

baggy ['bægi] *adj.* larg, care atîrnă.

bagpipe(s) ['bægpaip(s)] *s.* cimpoi.

bail [beil] *s.* cauţiune; chezăşie. *vt.* a elibera pe cauţiune. *vi.* a goli apa (din barcă).

bailiff ['beilif] *s.* portărel; aprod; vechil; arendaş.

bait [beit] *s.* momeală; furaj. *vt.* a momi.

bake [beik] *vt., vi.* a (se) coace.

baker ['beikə] *s.* brutar.

baker's dozen ['beikəz'dʌzn] s. treisprezece.

bakery ['beikəri] s. brutărie.

balance ['bæləns] s. balanţă, cîntar; echilibru; bilanţ. vt. a cîntări; a echilibra.

balance sheet ['bælənsʃi:t] s. bilanţ.

balcony ['bælkəni] s. balcon.

bald [bɔ:ld] adj. chel, pleşuv.

balderdash ['bɔ:ldədæʃ] s. prostii.

bale [beil] s. balot.

baleful ['beilfl] adj. rău; veninos.

balk [bɔ:k] s. piedică; hat. vt., vi. a (se) opri; a (se) împiedica.

ball [bɔ:l] s. minge; ghem; bilă; glontc.

ballad ['bæləd] s. baladă.

ballast ['bæləst] s. balast.

ball bearing ['bɔ:l'bɛəriŋ] s. rulment.

ballet ['bælei] s. balet.

balloon [bə'lu:n] s. balon.

ballot ['bælət] s. (buletin de) vot.

ballot-box ['bælət,bɔks] s. urnă.

ball pen ['bɔ:l,pen] s. stilou cu pastă.

ball-room [,bɔ:lrum] s. sală de bal.

balm [bɑ:m], **balsam** ['bɔ:lsəm] s. balsam.

baluster ['bæləstə] s. stîlp de balustradă.

bamboo [bæm'bu:] s. bambus.

ban [bæn] s. interdicţie. vt. a interzice.

banal [bə'næl] adj. banal.

banana [bə'nɑ:nə] s. bananier; banană.

band [bænd] s. fîşie; bandă; grup; ceată; orchestră de muzică uşoară; fanfară. vt., vi. a (se) strînge.

bandage ['bændidʒ] s. bandaj. vt. a bandaja.

bandbox ['bænbɔks] s. cutie de pălării.

bandit ['bændit] s. bandit, tîlhar.

bandmaster ['bæn,mɑ:stə] s. capelmaistru.

bandy ['bændi] adj. crăcănat. vt.: to ~ words a se certa.

bane [bein] s. nenorocire; otravă.

baneful ['beinfl] adj. rău, dăunător.

bang [bæŋ] s. lovitură; pocnitură. vt., vi. a pocni; a trînti. interj. poc.

banish ['bæniʃ] vt. a surghiuni; a izgoni.

banister(s) ['bænistə(z)] s. balustradă.

bank [bæŋk] s. mal; banc; hat; bancă.

bank-book ['bæŋkbuk] s. livret de economii; carnet de cecuri.

banker ['bæŋkə] s. bancher.

bank-holiday ['bæŋk'hɔlədi] s. sărbătoare; prima luni din august.

banking ['bæŋkiŋ] s. finanţe; operaţii bancare.

bank-note ['bæŋknout] s. bancnotă.

bankrupt ['bæŋkrəpt] s., adj. falit.

bankruptcy ['bæŋkrəpsi] s. faliment.

banner ['bænə] s. steag, stindard.

banns [bænz] s. pl. publicaţii de căsătorie.

banquet ['bæŋkwit] s. banchet.

banter ['bæntə] s. glumă; ironie. vt., vi. a tachina.

baptism ['bæptizəm] s. botez.
baptize ['bæptaiz] vt. a boteza.
bar [bɑ:] s. bară; barieră; banc de nisip; dungă; decorație; tresă; muz. măsură; jur. bară; boxa acuzaților sau martorilor; the Bar barou; avocatură. vt. a zăvorî; a bara.
barbarian [bɑ:'bɛəriən] s., adj. barbar; necioplit.
barbed [bɑ:bd] adj. ghimpat.
barber ['bɑ:bə] s. bărbier, frizer.
bare [bɛə] adj. gol; pleșuv; simplu; infim. vt. a dezgoli; a dezvălui.
bare-faced ['bɛəfeist] adj. nerușinat; obraznic.
bare-foot(ed) ['bɛəfut(id)] adj. desculț.
barely ['bɛəli] adv. abia, doar; (pur și) simplu.
bargain ['bɑ:gin] s. tocmeală; afacere; chilipir; into the ~ pe deasupra. vi. a se tocmi; to ~ for a se aștepta la.
barge [bɑ:dʒ] s. șlep; vas de agrement.
bark [bɑ:k] s. lătrat; scoarță (de copac). vt. a coji. vi. a lătra.
barley ['bɑ:li] s. orz(oaică).
barmaid ['bɑ:meid] s. chelneriță.
barman ['bɑ:mən] s. barman; cîrciumar.
barn [bɑ:n] s. hambar; magazie.
barnacle ['bɑ:nəkl] s. scoică de mare.
barometer [bə'rɔmitə] s. barometru.
baron ['bærən] s. baron.
barracks ['bærəks] s. pl. cazarmă.
barrel ['bærl] s. butoi; baril; țeavă (de armă).

barrel-organ ['bærl‚ɔ:gən] s. flașnetă.
barren ['bærn] adj. sterp, steril.
barricade ['bærikeid] s. baricadă. vt. a baricada.
barrier ['bæriə] s. barieră; obstacol.
barring ['bɑ:riŋ] prep. fără, în afară de.
barrister ['bæristə] s. avocat pledant.
barrow ['bærou] s. cărucioară; roabă.
barter ['bɑ:tə] s. troc. vt. a face troc.
basalt ['bæsɔ:lt] s. bazalt.
base [beis] s. fund; bază. adj. josnic; meschin; ticălos; inferior. vt. a baza.
baseball ['beisbɔ:l] s. baseball.
baseless ['beislis] adj. neîntemeiat.
basement ['beismənt] s. pivniță; subsol.
bashful ['bæʃfl] adj. timid; rușinos.
basic ['beisik] adj. fundamental.
basin ['beisn] s. lighean; bol; bazin.
basis ['beisis] s. fig. bază.
bask [bɑ:sk] vi. a sta (la soare, la căldură).
basket ['bɑ:skit] s. coș.
basket ball ['bɑ:skitbɔ:l] s. baschet.
bass [beis] s., adj. bas.
bassoon [‚bə'su:n] s. fagot.
bastard ['bæstəd] s. copil nelegitim; ticălos.
bat [bæt] s. zool. liliac; sport băț, bîtă.
batch [bætʃ] s. grup; număr; încărcătură.

bated ['beitid] *adj.* întretăiat (*d. răsuflare*).

bath [bɑ:θ] *s.* (cameră de) baie; *pl.* băi. *vt.*, *vi.* a (se) îmbăia.

bathe [beiỏ] *s.* scăldat. *vt.*, *vi.* a (se) scălda; a (se) spăla.

baton ['bætn] *s.* baghetă.

battalion [bə'tæljən] *s.* batalion.

bathing trunks ['beiỏiŋ‚trʌnks] *s.* chiloți de baie.

batter ['bætə] *vt.* a lovi; a turti.

battery ['bætəri] *s.* baterie.

battle ['bætl] *s.* bătălie; luptă. *vi.* a se lupta.

battleship ['bætlʃip] *s.* cuirasat.

bauble ['bɔ:bl] *s.* jucărie; podoabă fără valoare.

baulk [bɔ:k] *v.* balk.

bawl [bɔ:l] *s.* urlet. *vt.*, *vi.* a urla.

bay [bei] *s.* golf; geamlîc; laur; roib; lătrat; *at* ~ la ananghie. *vi.* a lătra.

bayonet ['beiənit] *s.* baionetă.

bazaar [bə'zɑ:] *s.* bazar; magazin.

be [bi(:)] *v. aux. pentru diateza pasivă și aspectul continuu, v. mod.* a trebui, a urma să. *vi.* a fi, a exista; a se întîmpla; a costa.

beach [bi:tʃ] *s.* plajă.

beacon ['bi:kn] *s.* far.

beads [bi:dz] *s. pl.* mărgele; mătănii; picături.

beak [bi:k] *s.* cioc (de pasăre).

beam [bi:m] *s.* grindă; drug; rază; zîmbet. *vi.* a zîmbi; a străluci.

bean(s) [bi:n(z)] *s.* fasole; bob(i).

bear [bɛə] *s.* urs. *vt.* a căra, a purta; (a pro)duce; a îndura; a naște; *to* ~ *in mind* a ține minte.

beard [biəd] *s.* barbă.

beardless ['biədlis] *adj.* spîn; fără barbă.

bearer ['bɛərə] *s.* purtător; producător; mesager.

bearing ['bɛəriŋ] *s.* legătură; poziție; purtare.

beast [bi:st] *s.* animal; fiară; vită; bestie.

beastly ['bi:stli] *adj.* nesuferit; scîrbos.

beat [bi:t] *s.* lovitură; rond; cartier; *muz.* bătaie, măsură. *vt. inf. și trec.* a bate; a lovi; a pedepsi; a învinge; a izgoni; *to* ~ *time* a bate măsura; *fig.* a bate pasul pe loc. *vi.* a bate; a face gălăgie; *to* ~ *about the bush* a vorbi pe ocolite; a bate apa în piuă.

beaten ['bi:tn] *adj.* bătut; bătătorit. *vt.*, *vi. part. trec. de la* beat.

beater ['bi:tə] *s.* bătător.

beatitude [bi'ætitju:d] *s.* fericire; beatitudine.

beautiful ['bju:təfl] *s.*, *adj.* frumos.

beautify ['bju:tifai] *vt.* a înfrumuseța.

beauty ['bju:ti] *s.* frumusețe; frumos.

beaver ['bi:və] *s.* castor.

became [bi'keim] *trec. de la* become.

because [bi'kɔz] *conj.* fiindcă; pentru că; ~ *of* din pricina; din cauza.

beck [bek] *s.: to be at smb.'s* ~ *and call* a fi la cheremul cuiva.

beckon ['bekn] *vt.*, *vi.* a face semn cu mîna (cuiva).

become [bi'kʌm] *inf. și part*

trec. a deveni. *vt.* a şedea, a veni (bine, rău).

bed [bed] *s.* pat; albie (de rîu); strat.

bedclothes ['bedklouðz] *s. pl.* aşternut.

bedding ['bediŋ] *s.* aşternut; culcuş.

bedeck [bi'dek] *vt.* a împodobi; a pavoaza.

bedlam ['bedləm] *s.* ospiciu.

bed-rid(den) ['bed‚ridn] *adj.* ţintuit la pat.

bed-rock ['bed'rɔk] *s.* temelie.

bedroom ['bedrum] *s.* dormitor.

bedside ['bedsaid] *s.* marginea patului.

bedstead ['bedsted] *s.* cadru de pat; pat (masiv).

bedtime ['bedtaim] *s.* ora culcării.

bee [bi:] *s.* albină.

beech [bi:tʃ] *s.* fag.

beef [bi:f] *s.* carne de vacă.

beef-steak ['bi:f'steik] *s.* fleică.

beef tea [bi:f'ti:] *s.* supă de vacă.

beehive ['bi:haiv] *s.* stup.

bee-line ['bi:lain] *s.* linie dreaptă.

been [bi(:)n] *vi. part. trec. de la* **be.**

beer [biə] *s.* bere.

beet [bi:t] *s.* sfeclă.

beetle ['bi:tl] *s.* gîndac; insectă.

beetroot ['bi:tru:t] *s.* sfeclă.

befit [bi'fit] *vt.* a fi potrivit pentru.

before [bi'fɔ:] *adv.* înainte; *long ~* demult. *prep.* înaintea; în faţa; mai degrabă decît; *~ long* curînd. *conj.* înainte de a; mai degrabă ... decît să.

beforehand [bi'fɔ:hænd] *adv.* dinainte.

beg [beg] *vt.* a cerşi; a cere; *I ~ your pardon* scuzaţi! poftim? *vi.* a se ruga; a cerşi.

began [bi'gæn] *vt., vi. trec. de la* **begin.**

beggar ['begə] *s.* cerşetor.

beggarly ['begəli] *adj.* sărăcăcios.

begin [bi'gin] *vt., vi.* a începe; a porni.

beginner [bi'ginə] *s.* începător.

beginning [bi'giniŋ] *s.* început.

beguile [bi'gail] *vt.* a păcăli; a face să treacă (timpul).

begun [bi'gʌn] *vt., vi. part. trec. de la* **begin.**

behalf [bi'hɑ:f] *s.: on ~ of* din partea; în numele.

behave [bi'heiv] *vi.* a se purta; a funcţiona. *vr.* a se purta; *~ yourself* poartă-te frumos.

behaviour [bi'heivjə] *s.* purtare; maniere.

behead [bi'hed] *vt.* a decapita.

behind [bi'haind] *s.* spate; dos. *adv.* în urmă; înapoi; în restanţă. *prep.* în urma; în spatele; dinapoia; *~ time* tîrziu; *~ the scenes* în culise.

behindhand [bi'haindhænd] *adj., adv.* în urmă.

being ['bi:iŋ] *s.* fiinţă (omenească); existenţă.

belabour [bi'leibə] *vt.* a bate.

belated [bi'leitid] *adj.* întîrziat.

belch [beltʃ] *vi.* a rîgîi.

belfry ['belfri] *s.* clopotniţă.

Belgian ['beldʒn] *s., adj.* belgian(ă).

belie [bi'lai] *vt.* a dezminţi; a dezamăgi.

belief [bi'li:f] *s.* credinţă; încredere.

believe [bi'li:v] *vt., vi.* a crede.

believer [bi'li:və] s. credincios.

belittle [bi'litl] vt. a diminua; a deprecia.

bell [bel] s. (sunet de) clopot; sonerie.

bellow ['belou] s. muget. vi. a mugi; a urla.

bellows ['belouz] s. pl. foale.

belly ['beli] s. pîntec(e).

belong [bi'lɔŋ] vi.: to ~ to a (apar)ţine; a face parte.

belongings [bi'lɔŋiŋz] s. lucruri; avere.

beloved [bi'lʌvd] s., adj. iubit(ă).

below [bi'lou] adv. dedesubt; la fund. prep. sub.

belt [belt] s. curea; centură.

bench [bentʃ] s. bancă; laviţă; judecător; tribunal.

bend [bend] s. curbă, cotitură. vt. a îndoi. vi. a coti; a se îndoi.

beneath [bi'ni:θ] adv. dedesubt, mai jos. prep. dedesubtul, sub; mai prejos de.

benediction [ˌbeni'dikʃu] s. binecuvîntare.

benefactor ['beniˌfæktə] s. binefăcător.

beneficial [ˌbeni'fiʃl] adj. folositor.

benefit ['benifit] s. ajutor; avantaj. vt. a ajuta. vi. a profita.

benevolence [bi'nevələns] s. bunăvoinţă.

bent [bent] s. înclinaţie, tendinţă. vt., vi. trec. şi part. trec. de la bend.

benumb [bi'nʌm] vt. a amorţi; a înţepeni.

benzine ['benzi:n] s. neofalină.

bequeath [bi'kwi:ð] vt. a lăsa (moştenire).

bereave [bi'ri:v] vt. a răpi; to ~ of a priva de.

bereft [bi'reft] vt. trec. şi part. trec. de la bereave.

berry ['beri] s. bacă; fruct (sălbatic).

berth [bə:θ] s. cuşetă; compartiment; dană; slujbă.

beseech [bi'si:tʃ] vt. a implora.

beset [bi'set] vt. inf., trec. şi part. trec. a asedia.

beside [bi'said] prep. alături de; pe lîngă; în comparaţie cu; ~ oneself înnebunit.

besides [bi'saidz] adv. pe lîngă asta; de asemenea. prep. pe lîngă, în afară de.

besiege [bi'si:dʒ] vt. a asedia; a asalta.

besought [bi'sɔ:t] vt. trec. şi part. trec. de la beseech.

bespeak [bi'spi:k] vt. a angaja, a reţine (dinainte); a dovedi.

bespoke [bi'spouk] vt. trec. (şi part. trec.) de la bespeak.

bespoken [bi'spoukn] vt. part. trec. de la bespeak.

best [best] adj. superl. de la good cel mai bun; perfect; for the ~ part în cea mai mare măsură. adv. superl. de la well cel mai bine; cel mai mult.

best man ['best'mæn] s. cavaler de onoare; aprox. naş.

bestow [bi'stou] vt. a (acor)da.

best-seller ['best'selə] s. carte sau autor de mare popularitate.

bet [bet] s. pariu. vt., vi. a paria.

betray [bi'trei] vt., vr. a (se) trăda.

betrayal [bi'treiəl] s. trădare.

betrothal [bi'trouðl] s. logodnă.

better ['betə] s.: our ~s mai

marii noştri. *adj. compar. de la*
good mai bun ; ~ *off* (mai)
înstărit ; *the* ~ *half* mai mult
de jumătate ; soţie. *adv. compar.*
de la **well** mai bine ; *you had* ~
go ai face mai bine să pleci.
vt. a îmbunătăţi ; a depăşi, a
întrece.

betterment ['betəmənt] *s.* îmbunătăţire.

between [bi'twi:n] *prep.* între.

beverage ['bevəridʒ] *s.* băutură
(nealcoolică).

bevy ['bevi] *s.* grup ; stol ; *fig.*
buchet.

bewail [bi'weil] *vt.* a (de)plînge.

beware [bi'wɛə] *vt., vi.* a se
păzi (de).

bewilder [bi'wildə] *vt.* a zăpăci ;
a tulbura.

bewitch [bi'witʃ] *vt.* a vrăji.

beyond [bi'jɔnd] *adv.* dincolo ;
departe. *prep.* dincolo de ; ~
compare fără seamăn.

bias ['baiəs] *s.* înclinaţie ; părtinire.

Bible ['baibl] *s.* Biblie.

bibliography [ˌbibli'ɔgrəfi] *s.*
bibliografie.

bicker ['bikə] *vi.* a se ciondăni.

bicycle ['baisikl] *s.* bicicletă.

bid [bid] *s.* ofertă ; licitare. *vt.*
a oferi (un preţ) ; a porunci ;
a spune. *vi.* a licita.

bidden ['bidn] *vt., vi. part. trec.*
de la **bid.**

bidder ['bidə] *s.* licitator ; ofertant.

bide [baid] *vt.* a aştepta.

bier [biə] *s.* catafalc, năsălie.

big [big] *adj.* mare ; voluminos ;
important ; măreţ ; generos.

bigamist ['bigəmist] *s.* bigam.

bigoted ['bigətid] *adj.* habotnic ;
obtuz.

bigotry ['bigətri] *s.* bigotism.

bike [baik] *s.* bicicletă.

bile [bail] *s.* fiere ; supărare.

bilge [bildʒ] *s. mar.* fundul vasu-
lui ; apă stătută.

bilious ['biljəs] *adj.* supărăcios.

bill [bil] *s.* cioc (de pasăre) ;
notă de plată ; poliţă ; afiş ;
(proiect de) lege ; *amer.* bancnotă. *vi.: to* ~ *and coo* a se
giuguli.

billet ['bilit] *s.* încartiruire. *vt.*
a încartirui.

billiards ['biljədz] *s. pl.* biliard.

billion ['biljən] *s.* bilion ; *amer.*
miliard.

bill of fare ['bil əv 'fɛə] *s.* meniu.

bill of indictment ['bil əv in'dait-
mənt] *s.* act de acuzare.

billow ['bilou] *s.* talaz ; *fig.* mare.
vi. a undui.

bi-monthly ['bai'mʌnθli] *adj.,*
adv. bilunar.

bin [bin] *s.* cutie ; ladă ; benă.

bind [baind] *vt.* a lega ; a lipi ;
a întări ; a obliga. *vr.* a se
obliga.

binder ['baində] *s.* legător.

binding ['baindiŋ] *s.* legătură.
adj. obligatoriu.

binoculars [bi'nɔkjuləz] *s. pl.*
binoclu.

biographer [bai'ɔgrəfə] *s.* biograf.

biography [bai'ɔgrəfi] *s.* biografie.

biologist [bai'ɔlədʒist] *s.* biolog.

biology [bai'ɔlədʒi] *s.* biologie.

birch [bə:tʃ] *s.* mesteacăn ; nuia.

bird [bə:d] *s.* pasăre.

bird's-eye view ['bə:dzai 'vju:]
s. privire *sau* vedere generală.

birth [bə:θ] s. naştere ; origine.

birthday ['bə:θdei] s. zi de naştere.

birth-place ['bə:θpleis] s. loc natal.

birth-rate ['bə:θreit] s. natalitate.

bishop ['biʃəp] s. episcop.

bison ['baisn] s. bizon, zimbru.

bit [bit] s. bucăţică ; firimitură ; sfredel ; zăbală. vt., vi. trec. şi part. trec. de la bite.

bitch [bitʃ] s. căţea.

bite [bait] s. muşcătură ; îmbucătură ; bucată. vt. a muşca ; a reteza ; a tăia ; a răni ; a înţepa.

biting ['baitiŋ] adj. muşcător ; tăios ; sarcastic.

bitten ['bitn] vt., vi. part. trec. de la bite.

bitter ['bitə] adj. amar ; dureros ; aspru ; înverşunat ; to the ~ end pînă în pînzele albe.

bizarre [bi'za:] adj. ciudat, bizar ; grotesc.

blab [blæb] vt. a trăda (un secret). vi. a pălăvrăgi.

black [blæk] s. negru ; murdărie ; funingine ; doliu. adj. negru ; oacheş ; întunecat, sumbru.

black-beetle ['blæk'bi:tl] s. gîndac de bucătărie.

blackberry ['blækbri] s. mură.

blackbird ['blækbə:d] s. mierlă.

blackboard ['blækbɔ:d] s. tablă (la şcoală).

blacken ['blækn] vt. a înnegri ; a ponegri.

black-eye ['blæk'ai] s. ochi negru ; vînătaie la ochi.

blackguard ['blæga:d] s. ticălos.

blacking ['blækiŋ] s. cremă (neagră) de ghete.

blacklead ['blæk'led] s. grafit.

blackleg ['blækleg] s. spărgător de grevă.

blacklist ['blæklist] s. listă neagră.

blackmail ['blækmeil] s. şantaj. vt. a şantaja.

blackout ['blækaut] s. camuflaj.

blacksmith ['blæksmiθ] s. potcovar ; fierar.

bladder ['blædə] s. băşică ; cameră de minge.

blade [bleid] s. lamă, tăiş ; fir de iarbă ; frunză ascuţită.

blame [bleim] s. blam, dezaprobare ; critică ; răspundere. vt. a blama ; who is to ~ ? cine e de vină ?

bland [blænd] adj. amabil.

blank [blæŋk] s. (loc) gol ; formular. adj. gol ; cu spaţii goale ; în alb ; stupid ; (d. vers) alb.

blank cartridge ['blæŋk₁ka:tridʒ] s. cartuş orb.

blanket ['blæŋkit] s. pătură.

blankly ['blæŋkli] adv. fără expresie.

blare [blɛə] vt., vi. a trîmbiţa.

blaspheme [blæs'fi:m] vt., vi. a huli ; a blestema.

blasphemy ['blæsfimi] s. hulă ; insulte.

blast [bla:st] s. explozie ; curent. vt. a distruge.

blatant ['bleitnt] adj. sforăitor ; ţipător.

blaze [bleiz] s. vîlvătaie ; izbucnire. vt. a aprinde ; a însemna (copaci etc.) ; to ~ a trail a deschide un drum (nou).

blazer ['bleizə] s. jerseu.

blazing ['bleiziŋ] adj. strălucitor.

bleach [bli:tʃ] vt., vi. a (se) albi.

bleak [bli:k] *adj.* sterp ; rece ; lugubru ; bătut de vînturi.

blear [bliə] *adj.* întunecat ; ceţos.

bleat [bli:t] *s.* behăit. *vi.* a behăi.

bled [bled] *vt.*, *vi. trec. şi part. trec. de la* **bleed**.

bleed [bli:d] *vt.* a lua sînge (cuiva) ; a jecmăni. *vi.* a sîngera ; a suferi.

blemish ['blemiʃ] *s.* pată ; defect. *vt.* a strica ; a păta.

blend [blend] *s.* amestec ; îmbinare. *vt.*, *vi.* a (se) îmbina ; a (se) amesteca.

blent [blent] *vt.*, *vi. trec. şi part. trec. de la* **blend**.

bless [bles] *vt.* a binecuvînta ; a ferici ; a sfinţi.

blessed ['blesid] *adj.* fericit ; norocos.

blessing ['blesiŋ] *s.* binecuvîntare.

blew [blu:] *vt.*, *vi. trec. de la* **blow**.

blight [blait] *s.* mălură. *vt.* a distruge ; a strica.

blind [blaind] *s.* jaluzea, stor. *adj.* orb ; chior ; obtuz ; absurd ; închis. *vt.* a orbi.

blind alley ['blaind'æli] *s.* fundătură.

blindfold ['blainfould] *adj.* legat la ochi ; *fig.* orb(it). *vt.* a lega la ochi. *adv.* orbeşte.

blind-man's-buff ['blainmænz-'bʌf] *s.* baba-oarba.

blindness ['blaindnis] *s.* orbire.

blink [bliŋk] *vi.* a clipi.

bliss [blis] *s.* fericire.

blister ['blistə] *s.* băşicuţă. *vi.* a se umfla.

blithe [blaið] *adj.* vesel ; fericit.

blizzard ['blizəd] *s.* viscol

bloated ['bloutid] *adj.* umflat.

bloater ['bloutə] *s.* scrumbie sărată *sau* afumată.

blob [blɔb] *s.* pată ; picătură.

bloc [blɔk] *s. pol.* bloc.

block [blɔk] *s.* butuc ; pietroi ; ansamblu de locuinţe ; *amer.* cvartal, distanţa dintre două străzi ; calapod. *vt.* a bloca ; a opri.

blockade [blɔ'keid] *s.* blocadă.

blockhead ['blɔkhed] *s.* tîmpit.

blood [blʌd] *s.* sînge ; rudenie ; origine, familie ; dispoziţie ; temperament ; patimă.

bloodhound ['blʌdhaund] *s.* copoi.

bloodless ['blʌdlis] *adj.* fără (vărsare de) sînge.

bloodshed ['blʌdʃed] *s.* vărsare de sînge.

bloodshot ['blʌdʃɔt] *adj.* injectat, congestionat.

blood-sucker ['blʌd,sʌkə] *s.* lipitoare ; exploatator.

bloodthirsty ['blʌd,θə:sti] *adj.* sălbatic ; criminal.

bloody ['blʌdi] *adj.* sîngeros, însîngerat ; scîrbos.

bloom [blu:m] *s.* floare ; puf ; strălucire ; *in* ~ înflorit. *vi.* a înflori.

bloomers ['blu:məz] *s. pl.* chiloţi (de sport).

blossom ['blɔsəm] *s.* floare (a unui pom) ; inflorescenţă. *vi.* a înflori.

blot [blɔt] *s.* pată ; defect. *vt.* a păta ; a şterge ; a estompa.

blotch [blɔtʃ] *s.* pată. *vt.* a păta.

blotter ['blɔtə] *s.* sugativă ; tampon ; mapă de birou.

blotting-paper ['blɔtiŋ,peipə] *s.* sugativă.

blouse [blauz] *s.* bluză.
blow [blou] *s.* lovitură ; pumn.
vt. a sufla ; a cînta la (trompetă etc.) ; a fluiera ; a anunța ;
a umfla ; *to ~ out* a stinge ;
a arunca în aer ; a zbura (creierii) ; *to ~ up* a umfla ; a
arunca în aer. *vi.* a (ră)sufla ;
to ~ out a exploda.
blower ['blouə] *s.* foale ; suflător ; suflai.
blown [bloun] *vt., vi. part. trec.*
de la **blow.**
blow-out ['blou'aut] *s.* explozie.
bludgeon ['blʌdʒn] *s.* măciucă.
vt. a ciomăgi.
blue [blu:] *s., adj.* albastru ;
out of the ~ din senin ; *in*
the ~s melancolic, trist.
bluebell ['blu:bel] *s.* campanulă.
blue-print ['blu:'print] *s.* proiect.
blue vitriol ['blu:'vitriəl] *s.* piatră vînătă.
bluff [blʌf] *s.* creastă (de deal) ;
mal abrupt ; cacialma, bluf.
adj. deschis ; entuziast. *vt.* a
păcăli.
bluish ['bluiʃ] *adj.* albăstrui.
blunder ['blʌndə] *s.* greșeală ;
gafă. *vt.* a greși ; a face gafe.
blunt [blʌnt] *adj.* tocit ; teșit ;
necioplit. *vt.* a toci ; a teși.
blur [blə:] *s.* obscuritate ; pată.
vt. a întuneca ; a încețoșa.
blurt [blə:t] *vt.: to ~ out* a
scăpa (o vorbă etc.).
blush [blʌʃ] *s.* roșeață. *vi.* a
roși.
bluster ['blʌstə] *s.* izbucnire. *vi.*
a izbucni.
boa [boə] *s.* boa.
boar [bɔ:] *s.* vier ; porc mistreț.
board [bɔ:d] *s.* bord ; scîndură ;

tablă ; carton ; masă ; mîncare ;
întreținere, pensiune ; consiliu ;
minister. *vt.* a podi ; a hrăni ;
a se îmbarca pe. *vi.* a lua masa.
boarder ['bɔ:də] *s.* (elev) intern ;
chiriaș.
boarding ['bɔ:diŋ] *s.* scînduri ;
podea ; întreținere.
boarding-house ['bɔ:diŋhaus] *s.*
pensiune.
boarding-school ['bɔ:diŋsku:l] *s.*
școală cu internat.
boast [boust] *s.* laudă de sine ;
(prilej de) mîndrie. *vt.* a se
lăuda cu ; a avea.
boastful ['boustfl] *adj.* laudă-
ros.
boat [bout] *s.* vas, ambarca-
țiune ; barcă ; castron. *vi.* a
naviga.
boating ['boutiŋ] *s.* canotaj ;
sporturi nautice.
boatman ['boutmən] *s.* barcagiu.
boatswain ['bousn] *s.* șeful echi-
pajului.
bob [bɔb] *s.* bob ; zdruncinătură ; șiling ; păr tuns scurt.
vt. a scurta.
bobbin ['bɔbin] *s.* bobină.
bobby-soxer ['bɔbi,sɔksə] *s.* puș-
tancă, codană.
bode [boud] *vt. trec. de la* **bide.**
bodice ['bɔdis] *s.* corsaj ; sutien ; pieptar.
bodily ['bodili] *adj.* trupesc. *adv.*
în întregime, cu totul.
body ['bɔdi] *s.* corp ; cadavru ;
om ; esență ; grup ; organ(iza-
ție) ; caroserie.
body-guard ['bɔdiga:d] *s.* gardă
personală.
Boer ['boə] *s.* bur.
bog [bɔg] *s.* mlaștină.
bogus ['bougəs] *adj.* fals.

boil [bɔil] s. fierbere; bubă.
vt., vi. a fierbe.
boiler ['bɔilə] s. cazan.
boisterous ['bɔistərəs] adj. zgomotos.
bold [bould] adj. curajos;
obraznic; izbitor.
bolster ['boulstə] s. pernă (de
canapea). vt. a sprijini.
bolt [boult] s. zăvor; foraibăr;
bulon; bolţ; săgeată; izbucnire. vt. a zăvorî. vi. a fugi.
bomb [bɔm] s. bombă. vt. a
bombarda.
bombard [bɔm'bɑ:d] vt. a bombarda (cu artileria).
bombardment [bɔm'bɑ:dmənt]
s. bombardament.
bombastic [bɔm'bæstik] adj.
bombastic.
bomber ['bɔmə] s. bombardier.
bond [bɔnd] s. angajament; fin.
titlu; contract; legătură; lanţ.
bondage ['bɔndidʒ] s. sclavie.
bond(s)man ['bɔn(z)mən] s. rob.
bone [boun] s. os; ~ of contention mărul discordiei.
bonfire ['bɔnfaiə] s. foc; rug.
bonnet ['bɔnit] s. bonetă; husă.
bonny ['bɔni] adj. drăguţ; a
trăgător.
bonus ['bounəs] s. primă.
bony ['bouni] adj. osos.
boo [bu:] interj. huo!
booby ['bu:bi] s. prostănac.
book [buk] s. carte; parte a
unei cărţi; capitol; registru;
caiet; carnet; agendă; the
Book Biblia. vt. a înregistra;
a înscrie; a reţine (bilete etc.).
book-case ['bukkeis] s. (dulap
de) bibliotecă.
booking-office ['bukiŋ,ɔfis] s.
casă de bilete.

bookish ['bukiʃ] adj. livresc,
cărturăresc.
book-keeper ['buk,ki:pə] s. contabil.
book-keeping ['buk,ki:piŋ] s.
contabilitate.
booklet ['buklit] s. broşură, cărticică.
book-maker ['buk,meikə] s. a-
gent de pariuri la curse.
book-seller ['buk,selə] s. librar.
bookstall ['bukstɔ:l] s. stand de
cărţi.
bookworm ['bukwə:m] s. zool.
car; fig. şoarece de bibliotecă.
boom [bu:m] s. prăjină; bubuit; avînt economic. vi. a bubui; a prospera.
boon [bu:n] s. avantaj; bine;
favoare. adj. plăcut.
boor [buə] s. ţopîrlan
boorish ['buəriʃ] adj. necioplit.
boot [bu:t] s. gheată; cizmă;
bocanc.
bootblack ['bu:tblæk] s. lustragiu.
booth [bu:ð] s. tarabă; cabină
(telefonică etc.).
booty ['bu:ti] s. pradă (de război).
border ['bɔ:də] s. margine; chenar; frontieră; limită. vt., vi.
a (se) mărgini; a se învecina
(cu).
bore¹ [bɔ:] s. om plicticos. vt.
a sfredeli; a plictisi.
bore² [bɔ:] vt., vi. trec. de la
bear.
boredom ['bɔ:dəm] s. plictiseală.
born [bɔ:n] vt., vi. part. trec.
de la bear născut; to be ~
a se naşte.
borne [bɔ:n] vt., vi. part. trec.
de la bear purtat etc.

borough ['bʌrə] s. tîrg; orăşel.
borrow ['bɔrou] vt. a lua cu împrumut.
bosom ['buzəm] s. sîn.
boss [bɔs] s. şef; patron. vt., vi. a porunci, a comanda.
botany ['bɔtəni] s. botanică.
botch [bɔtʃ] vt. a cîrpăci.
both [bouθ] adj., pron. amîndoi. conj. ~... and atît ... cît şi; şi ... şi.
bother ['bɔðə] s. pacoste; bătaie de cap. vt. a necăji; a pisa. vi. a se necăji; a se deranja.
bottle ['bɔtl] s. sticlă; garafă. vt. a pune la sticle; a închide.
bottleneck ['bɔtlnek] s. gît de sticlă; strîmtoare; încurcătură de circulaţie.
bottom ['bɔtəm] s. fund; dos; temelie; fig. străfund(uri). adj. ultimul; cel mai de jos
bough [bau] s. ramură.
bought [bɔ:t] vt., vi. trec. şi part. trec. de la buy.
boulder ['bouldə] s. bolovan.
boulevard ['bu:lvɑ:] s. bulevard.
bounce [bauns] vi. a sări; a ţopăi.
bound¹ [baund] s. margine, limită; graniţă; săritură. adj.: to be ~ for a se îndrepta către. vt. a limita; a stăpîni. vi. a sări; a ţopăi.
bound² [baund] vt., vi. trec. şi part. trec. de la bind; to be ~ to a fi obligat sau menit să.
boundary ['baundri] s. graniţă; limită.
boundless ['baundlis] adj. nelimitat.

bounteous ['bauntiəs] adj. copios; generos.
bounty ['baunti] s. mărinimie; cadou.
bouquet ['bukei] s. buchet.
bourgeois ['buəʒwɑ:] s., adj. burghez(ă).
bout [baut] s. luptă; atac; acces; perioadă; chef, beţie.
bow¹ [bou] s. arc(uş); curcubeu; nod; fundă; papion.
bow² [bau] s. plecăciune; salut; proră. vt. a îndoi, a (a)pleca. vi. a face o plecăciune, a saluta.
bowels ['bauəlz] s. pl. intestine; centru.
bower ['bauə] s. boltă de verdeaţă; chioşc.
bowl [boul] s. bol, castronaş; scobitură; bilă de popice; pl. popice. vi. a juca popice.
bow-legged ['boulegd] adj. crăcănat.
bowler ['boulə] s. jucător de popice sau de crichet; gambetă.
box [bɔks] s. cutie; ladă; lojă; boxă; colibă; cabină; palmă, lovitură. vt. to ~ smb.'s ears a pălmui pe cineva. vi. a boxa.
boxer ['bɔksə] s. boxer.
boxing ['bɔksiŋ] s. box.
Boxing-day ['bɔksiŋdei] s. ziua cadourilor (26 decembrie).
box-office ['bɔks,ɔfis] s. casă de bilete.
boy [bɔi] s. băiat.
boycott ['bɔikət] s. boicot. vt. a boicota.
boyhood ['bɔihud] s. copilărie: adolescenţă.
boyish ['bɔiiʃ] adj. băieţos; copilăros.
brace [breis] s. legătură; aco-

ladă ; pereche ; *pl.* bretele. *vt.* a învora.

bracelet ['breislit] *s.* brăţară.

bracket ['brækit] *s.* consolă paranteză.

brackish ['brækiʃ] *adj.* sălciu.

brag [bræg] *vi.* a se lăuda.

braggart ['brægət] *s.* lăudăros.

braid [breid] *s.* găitan ; panglică ; cosiţă.

brain [brein] *s.* creier ; minte ; capacitate.

brainless ['breinlis] *adj.* zevzec.

brain(s) trust ['brein(z)'trʌst] *s.* experţi ; „cine ştie cîştigă".

brake [breik] *s.* frînă. *vt., vi.* a frîna.

bran [bræn] *s.* tărîţe.

branch [brɑːntʃ] *s.* ramură ; despărţitură ; filială, sucursală ; organizaţie (de partid etc.). *vi.* a se despărţi ; a se ramifica.

brand [brænd] *s.* stigmat ; semn ; sort ; marcă. *vt.* a înfiera.

brandish ['brændiʃ] *vt.* a agita.

brand-new ['bræn'njuː] *adj.* nou-nouţ.

brandy ['brændi] *s.* rachiu.

brass [brɑːs] *s.* alamă ; alămuri ; obrăznicie ; bani.

brat [bræt] *s.* ţînc, copil.

brave [breiv] *adj.* curajos, viteaz ; temerar. *vt.* a brava.

bravery ['breivri] *s.* curaj.

brawl [brɔːl] *s.* scandal ; bătaie. *vi.* a se bate ; a se certa.

brawny ['brɔːni] *adj.* musculos.

bray [brei] *vi. (d. măgar)* a rage.

brazen ['breizn] *adj.* de alamă ; obraznic.

brazier ['breiziə] *s.* grătar ; sobiţă pentru jeratec.

breach [briːtʃ] *s.* încălcare ; abuz ; spărtură.

bread [bred] *s.* pîine.

breadth [bredθ] *s.* lăţime.

break [breik] *s.* ruptură ; întrerupere ; ocazie ; distracţie ; recreaţie ; schimbare. *vt.* a sparge ; a rupe ; a strica ; a crăpa ; a zdrobi ; a frînge ; a încălca ; a slăbi ; a bate (un record) ; a supune, a îmblînzi ; *to ~ down* a (s)fărîma ; a nimici ; *to ~ up* a (s)fărîma ; a despărţi ; a dezbina. *vi.* a se sparge, a se sfărîma ; a se desface ; a se revărsa ; a izbucni ; a începe ; *(d. vreme)* a se strica ; *to ~ away* a fugi ; *to ~ down* a se strica ; a se prăbuşi ; *to ~ off* a se întrerupe ; *to ~ up* a se desface ; a se destrăma ; a se despărţi.

breakdown ['breikdaun] *s.* **pană** ; accident ; criză (de nervi).

breaker ['breikə] *s.* talaz.

breakfast ['brekfəst] *s.* gustarea de dimineaţă.

breakwater ['breik,wɔːtə] *s.* dig.

breast [brest] *s.* sîn ; piept ; inimă.

breath [breθ] *s.* (ră)suflare ; aer, adiere ; *out of ~* fără suflu.

breathe [briːð] *vt., vi.* a (ră)sufla.

breathless ['breθlis] *adj.* fără suflare ; mort.

bred [bred] *vt., vi. trec. şi part. trec. de la* **breed**.

breech [briːtʃ] *s.* închizător (de armă).

breeches ['britʃiz] *s. pl.* pantaloni (de călărie etc.).

breed [briːd] *s.* rasă, specie. *vt.* a naşte ; a creşte. *vi.* a se înmulţi.

breeding ['bri:diŋ] s. creştere.

breeze [bri:z] s. briză.

breezy ['bri:zi] adj. uşor ; vesel.

brethren ['breðrin] s. pl. de la brother confraţi.

breviary ['bri:vjəri] s. breviar.

brevity ['breviti] s. concizie ; scurtime.

brew [bru:] s. băutură ; bere. vt. a fierbe ; fig. a cloci.

brewer ['bruə] s. berar.

brewery ['bruəri] s. fabrică de bere.

briar ['braiə] s. măceş ; iarbăneagră.

bribe [braib] s. mită. vt. a mitui.

bribery ['braibəri] s. mită ; corupţie.

brick [brik] s. cărămidă ; bucată. vt. a zidi.

bricklayer ['brik,leiə] s. zidar.

brickwork ['brikwə:k] s. zidărie.

bride [braid] s. mireasă.

bridegroom ['braidgrum] s. mire.

bridesmaid ['braidzmeid] s. domnişoară de onoare.

bridge [bridʒ] s. pod ; punte ; (jocul de) bridge. vt. a traversa.

bridle ['braidl] s. căpăstru. vt. a ţine în frîu.

brief [bri:f] s. jur. dosar ; instructaj ; caz ; pl. chiloţi. adj. scurt.

briefcase ['bri:fkeis] s. servietă.

briefly ['bri:fli] adv. curînd ; pe scurt.

brigade [bri'geid] s. brigadă.

brigand ['brigənd] s. tîlhar.

bright [brait] adj. strălucitor ; isteţ.

brighten ['braitn] vt., vi. a (se) lumina.

brightness ['braitnis] s. strălucire.

brilliance ['briljəns] s. strălucire.

brilliant ['briljənt] adj. strălucit(or).

brim [brim] s. margine ; bor.

brimful(l) ['brim'ful] adj. plin ochi.

brine [brain] s. saramură ; (apă de) mare.

bring [briŋ] vt. a aduce ; a produce ; a determina ; to ~ down a dărîma ; to ~ home a lămuri ; to ~ up a creşte, a educa.

brink [briŋk] s. margine.

brisk [brisk] adj. rapid ; ager.

bristle ['brisl] s. păr ţepos. vi. a se ridica ; to ~ with a fi plin de.

British ['britiʃ] adj. britanic, englezesc.

Briton ['britn] s. britanic, englez.

brittle ['britl] adj. fragil.

broach [broutʃ] vt. a da cep la ; a aborda (un subiect etc.).

broad [brɔ:d] adj. larg ; lat ; vag ; limpede.

broadcast ['brɔ:dkɑ:st] s. emisiune (radiofonică etc.). vt., vi. a emite.

broaden ['brɔ:dn] vt., vi. a (se) lărgi, a (se) lăţi.

broad-minded ['brɔ:d'maindid] adj. înţelept ; descuiat.

brocade [brə'keid] s. brocart.

broke [brouk] adj. falit. vt., vi. trec. de la break.

broken ['broukn] vt., vi. part. trec. de la break.

broker ['broukə] s. agent de schimb.

bronze [brɔnz] s. bronz.

brooch [broutʃ] s. broşă.

brood [bru:d] s. pui ieşiţi din ou. vi. a cloci.

brook [bruk] *s.* pîriu. *vt.* a tolera.
broom [bru:m] *s.* mătură.
broth [brɔθ] *s.* supă.
brother ['brʌðə] *s.* (con)frate.
brotherhood ['brʌðəhud] *s.* frăţie.
brother-in-law ['brʌðrinlɔ:] *s.*
cumnat.
brought [brɔ:t] *vt. trec. şi part.
trec. de la* **bring.**
brow [brau] *s.* frunte; bot (de
deal etc.).
browbeat ['braubi:t] *vt.* a teroriza.
brown [braun] *s., adj.* maro,
cafeniu. *vt., vi.* a (se) rumeni.
bruise [bru:z] *s.* contuzie; rană;
lovitură. *vt., vi.* a (se) lovi;
a (se) juli.
brunt [brʌnt] *s.* greul (luptei etc.).
brush [brʌʃ] *s.* perie; pensulă;
bidinea; (trăsătură de) penel.
vt. a peria; a lustrui; a atinge;
a spăla; a curăţa; *to ~ up*
a revizui; a pune la punct.
brushwood ['brʌʃwud] *s.* tufişuri; cătină.
brutal ['bru:tl] *adj.* sălbatic;
inuman; brutal.
brutality [bru:'tæliti] *s.* sălbăticie; brutalitate.
brute [bru:t] *s.* brută; fiară.
adj. brut.
brutish ['bru:tiʃ] *adj.* animalic;
primitiv; brutal.
bubble ['bʌbl] *s.* băşică; balon
(de săpun etc.). *vi.* a face
băşici; a bolborosi.
buccaneer [,bʌkə'niə] *s.* pirat.
buck [bʌk] *s.* cerb; dolar. *vi.:*
to ~ up a prinde puteri *sau*
curaj.
bucket ['bʌkit] *s.* găleată; doniţă.

buckle ['bʌkl] *s.* cataramă. *vt.*
a încătărăma; a încuia.
buckram ['bʌkrəm] *s.* pînză
aspră.
buckwheat ['bʌkwi:t] *s.* hrişcă.
bud [bʌd] *s.* boboc; mugure.
vi. a înmuguri.
Buddhism ['budizəm] *s.* budism.
budge [bʌdʒ] *vi.* a se clinti.
budget ['bʌdʒit] *s.* buget.
buff [bʌf] *s.* piele (de bivol);
in ~ gol.
buffalo ['bʌfəlou] *s.* bivol.
buffer ['bʌfə] *s. tehn.* tampon.
buffet¹ ['bʌfit] *s.* lovitură. *vt.*
a pocni.
buffet² ['bufei] *s.* bufet.
buffoon [bʌ'fu:n] *s.* bufon;
clovn.
buffoonery [bʌ'fu:nəri] *s.* bufonerie; clovnerie.
bug [bʌg] *s.* ploşniţă; *amer.*
insectă.
bugbear ['bʌgbɛə] *s.* gogoriţă.
bugle ['bju:gl] *s.* trîmbiţă, goarnă.
build [bild] *s.* formă, structură;
construcţie. *vt.* a clădi; a construi; a făuri. *vi.* a clădi.
builder ['bildə] *s.* constructor.
building ['bildiŋ] *s.* clădire; construcţii; construire.
built [bilt] *vt., vi. trec. şi part.
trec. de la* **build.**
bulb [bʌlb] *s.* bulb; bec electric.
Bulgarian [bʌl'gɛəriən] *s., adj.*
bulgar(ă).
bulge [bʌldʒ] *s.* umflătură. *vt.,
vi.* a (se) umfla.
bulk [bʌlk] *s.* cantitate; volum; majoritate; gros.
bulky ['bʌlki] *adj.* voluminos;
greoi.
bull [bul] *s.* taur; bulă (pa-
pală etc.).

bulldog ['buldɔg] s. buldog.

bullet ['bulit] s. glonte.

bull-fight ['bulfait] s. coridă.

bullock ['bulək] s. tăuraş; boulean.

bully ['buli] s. terorist. vt. a teroriza.

bulwark ['bulwək] s. bastion.

bump [bʌmp] s. umflătură; cucui. vt. a ciocni; a lovi.

bumper ['bʌmpə] s. pahar plin. adj. abundent.

bumpkin ['bʌmkin] s. ţărănoi.

bumptious ['bʌmʃəs] adj. încrezut.

bun [bʌn] s. aprox. brioşă.

bunch [bʌntʃ] s. mănunchi; buchet; pîlc.

bundle ['bʌndl] s. boccea. vt. a lega.

bungalow ['bʌŋgəlou] s. căsuţă fără etaj.

bungle ['bʌŋgl] s. cîrpăceală. vt. a rasoli.

bunk [bʌŋk] s. pătuţ; prici; prostii; minciuni.

bunker ['bʌŋkə] s. mar. cală, magazie de cărbuni; buncăr.

bunny ['bʌni] s. iepuraş.

buoy [bɔi] s. geamandură. vt. a baliza.

buoyancy ['bɔiənsi] s. capacitate de plutire; rezistenţă.

burden ['bə:dn] s. povară; refren. vt. a încărca; a împovăra.

burdensome ['bə:dnsəm] adj. împovărător; obositor; dificil.

bureau [bju'rou] s. birou; departament.

bureaucracy [bju'rɔkrəsi] s. birocraţie; aparat de stat.

bureaucrat ['bjuərokræt] s. birocrat.

burglar ['bə:glə] s. spărgător, hoţ.

burglary ['bə:gləri] s. spargere, furt.

burial ['beriəl] s. înmormîntare.

burlesque [bə:'lesk] s. comedie bufă; revistă, varieteu. adj. burlesc.

burly ['bə:li] adj. corpolent, masiv.

Burmese [bə:'mi:z] s., adj. birman(ă).

burn [bə:n] s. arsură. vt. a arde; a frige; a distruge; a ataca. vi. a arde; a frige.

burner ['bə:nə] s. arzător; lampă; ochi (de aragaz etc.).

burnish ['bə:niʃ] vt. a lustrui.

burnt [bə:nt] vt., vi. trec. şi part. trec. de la burn.

burr [bə:] s. brusture; scai.

burrow ['bʌrou] s. vizuină. vt. a săpa. vi. a se ascunde.

burst [bə:st] s. izbucnire; explozie. vt. inf., trec. şi part. trec. a sparge; a arunca în aer. vi. izbucni; a exploda; a crăpa; to ~ open a se deschide; to ~ in a intra cu de-a sila.

bury 'beri] vt. a îngropa; a ascunde.

bus [bʌs] s. autobuz.

bush [buʃ] s. tufiş; arbust.

bushel ['buʃl] s. buşel (circa 2 baniţe).

bushy ['buʃi] adj. stufos.

business ['biz(i)nis] s. ocupaţie; afacere, afaceri; întreprindere; treabă.

business-like ['biznislaik] adj. practic.

bust [bʌst] s. bust.

bustle ['bʌsl] s. agitaţie; zarvă. vt. a zori. vi. a se agita; a se grăbi.

busy ['bizi] *adj.* ocupat; activ; harnic. *vr.* a se ocupa.

busybody ['bizi͵bɔdi] *s.* om băgăreţ.

but [bət, bʌt] *s.* obiecţie. *pron.* care (să) nu. *adv.* numai; *all ~* aproape. *prep.* fără; *the last ~ cne* penultimul; *~ for* fără (ajutorul etc.). *conj.* dar; totuşi; decît.

butcher ['butʃə] *s.* măcelar; *fig.* călău. *vt.* a măcelări; a tăia (vite etc.).

butler ['bʌtlə] *s.* majordom; lacheu.

butt [bʌt] *s.* pat (de puşcă etc.); ţintă (a batjocurii etc.). *vt., vi.* a se lovi.

butter ['bʌtə] *s.* unt. *vt.* a unge cu unt.

butterfly ['bʌtəflai] *s.* fluture.

buttocks ['bʌtəks] *s. pl.* fese, fund.

button ['bʌtn] *s.* nasture; buton. *vt.* a încheia (la nasturi).

buttonhole ['bʌtnhoul] *s.* butonieră. *vt.* a pisa, a ţine de vorbă.

buxom ['bʌksəm] *adj.* dolofană; atrăgătoare.

busy ['bizi] *adj.* ocupat; activ; harnic. *vr.* a se ocupa.

buy [bai] *vt.* a cumpăra; a mitui; a obţine; *to ~ up* a cumpăra tot.

buzz [bʌz] *s.* bîzîit. *vi.* a bîzîi.

buzzer ['bʌzə] *s.* sonerie, buzer; sirenă.

by [bai] *adj.* local; lateral; secundar. *adv.* alături; aproape; prin apropiére; în; *in days gone ~* în vremuri de demult; *~ and ~* curînd; după aceea. *prep.* lîngă; prin; peste; dincolo de; pe (lîngă); pînă la; cu (ajutorul); cu (bucata); pe (bucată etc.); după; *~ day* ziua; *~ myself* singur; *~ the ~, ~ the way* apropo.

bye-bye ['bai'bai] *interj.* la revedere, pa.

bygone ['baigɔn] *adj.* trecut.

by-road ['bairoud] *s.* drum secundar; drum lateral.

bystander ['bai͵stændə] *s.* spectator.

byway ['baiwei] *s.* drum secundar; drum lateral.

byword ['baiwə:d] *s.* zicătoare; lucru *sau* om proverbial.

C

C [si:] *s.* C, c; (nota) do; C 3 de rang inferior; de proastă calitate.

cab [kæb] *s.* birjă; taxi; cabină.

cabbage ['kæbidʒ] *s.* varză.

cabin ['kæbin] *s.* colibă; cabină.

cabinet ['kæbinit] *s.* dulap; cabinet; guvern.

cabinet-maker ['kæbinit͵ meikə] *s.* tîmplar (de mobilă).

cable ['keibl] *s.* odgon; cablu, telegramă. *vt., vi.* a telegrafia.

cablegram ['keiblgræm] *s.* telegramă.

cabman ['kæbmən] *s.* birjar; şofer de taxi.

cacao [kə'ka:ou] *s.* (arbore de) cacao.

cache [kæʃ] *s.* ascunzătoare; depozit.

cackle ['kækl] *s.* cloncănit; cotcodăcit. *vi.* a cotcodăci; a cloncăni.

cad [kæd] *s.* mitocan; ticălos.

caddish ['kædiʃ] *adj.* mitocănesc; mojic; rău.

cadet [kə'det] *s. mar.* cadet; fiu mai mic.

cadge [kædʒ] *vt., vi.* a cerşi.

café ['kæfei] *s.* cafenea.

cafeteria [ˌkæfi'tiəriə] *s. amer.* bufet-expres.

cage [keidʒ] *s.* colivie; *(în mină)* lift.

cajole [kə'dʒoul] *vt.* a linguşi; a trage pe sfoară.

cake [keik] *s.* prăjitură; cozonac; chec; turtă; bucată (de săpun etc.).

calamity [kə'læmiti] *s.* nenorocire; calamitate.

calcium ['kælsiəm] *s.* calciu.

calculate ['kælkjuleit] *vt., vi.* a socoti; a plănui.

calculation [ˌkælkju'leiʃn] *s.* socoteală.

calendar ['kælində] *s.* calendar.

calf [ka:f] *s.* (piele de) viţel; gambă.

calibre ['kælibə] *s.* calibru; valoare.

calico ['kælikou] *s.* stambă; pînză albă.

call [kɔ:l] *s.* strigăt; chemare; convorbire telefonică; mesaj; vizită; atracţie. *vt.* a chema; a striga; a numi; a atrage; *to ~ off* a opri; a anula; *to ~ a strike* a declara grevă; *to ~ the roll* a face apelul; *to ~ up* a chema la telefon; a încorpora; a reaminti. *vi.* a striga, a ţipa; a face o vizită; *to ~ for* a necesita; *to ~ out* a striga.

caller ['kɔ:lə] *s.* vizitator.

calling ['kɔ:liŋ] *s.* profesiune, meserie; vocaţie.

callous ['kæləs] *adj.* aspru; nesimţitor.

calm [ka:m] *s., adj.* calm. *vt., vi.* a (se) linişti.

calumniate [kə'lʌmnieit] *vt.* a defăima.

calumny ['kæləmni] *s.* calomnie.

calvary ['kælvəri] *s.* calvar.

cambric ['keimbrik] *s.* chembrică.

came [keim] *vi. trec. de la* come.

camel ['kæml] *s.* cămilă.

camera ['kæmrə] *s.* aparat de fotografiat, de cinema *sau* de televiziune.

cameraman ['kæmrəmæn] *s.* fotograf; operator.

camouflage ['kæmufla:ʒ] *s.* camuflaj; mascare. *vt.* a camufla.

camp [kæmp] *s.* tabără; lagăr. *vi.* a campa; a aşeza tabăra.

campaign [kæm'pein] *s.* campanie.

camp-bed ['kæmp'bed] *s.* pat de campanie.

camphor ['kæmfə] *s.* camfor.

camping ['kæmpiŋ] *s.* camping; turism.

campus ['kæmpəs] *s. amer.* localul *sau* incinta unei universităţi; universitate.

can [kæn] *s.* cutie de tinichea; bidon; conservă. *vt.* a conserva. *v. mod. defectiv* [kən, kæn] a putea, a şti să; a fi posibil.

Canadian [kə'neidjən] *s., adj.* canadian(ă).

canal [kə'næl] s. canal artificial; *anat.* tub, canal.

canary [kə'nɛəri] s. canar.

cancel ['kænsl] *vt.* a anula; a şterge.

candid ['kændid] *adj.* cinstit; sincer; naiv.

candidate ['kændidit] s. candidat.

candle ['kændl] s. lumînare.

candle stick ['kændlstik] s. sfeşnic.

candour ['kændə] s. candoare; sinceritate.

candy ['kændi] s. zahăr candel; *amer.* dulciuri; bomboane.

candy store ['kændistɔ:] s. bombonerie.

cane [kein] s. trestie; bambus; baston. *vt.* a bate.

cane-sugar ['kein'ʃugə] s. zahăr de trestie.

canine ['keinain] *adj.* canin.

canister ['kænistə] s. canistră, bidon; cutie de metal.

canker ['kæŋkə] s. aftă; rană; *bot.* cărbune; putreziciune.

cannibal ['kænibl] s. canibal.

cannon ['kænən] s. tun.

cannon-ball ['kænənbɔ:l] s. ghiulea.

cannot ['kænɔt] *v. mod. neg.* de la can.

canny ['kæni] *adj.* viclean; prudent.

canon ['kænən] s. canon; principiu; preot.

canopy ['kænəpi] s. baldachin.

cant [kænt] s. minciuni; argo.

cantankerous [kən'tæŋkrəs] *adj.* certăreţ.

canteen [kæn'ti:n] s. cantină; bufet; bidon.

canter ['kæntə] s. galop uşor.

canto ['kæntou] s. cînt.

canvas ['kænvəs] s. canava; pînză; tablou.

canvass ['kænvəs] *vt.* a dezbate. *vi.* a face propagandă (electorală etc.).

cap [kæp] s. şapcă; bască; bonetă.

capability [,keipə'biliti] s. capacitate.

capable ['keipəbl] *adj.* capabil.

capacious [kə'peiʃəs] *adj.* încăpător.

capacity [kə'pæsiti] s. capacitate; calitate.

cape [keip] s. capă; *geogr.* cap.

caper ['keipə] s. giumbuşluc. *vi.* a zburda.

capital ['kæpitl] s. capitală; majusculă; *fin.* capital. *adj.* capital; excelent; esenţial.

capitalism ['kæpitəlizəm] s. capitalism.

capitalist ['kæpitəlist] s. capitalist.

Capitol ['kæpitl] s. Capitoliu; Parlamentul american.

capitulate [kə'pitjuleit] *vi.* a capitula.

caprice [kə'pri:s] s. capriciu, fantezie.

capsize [kæp'saiz] *vt., vi.* a (se) răsturna.

capsule ['kæpsju:l] s. capsulă.

captain ['kæptin] s. căpitan; şef.

caption ['kæpʃn] s. titlu; legendă (de ilustraţie).

captious ['kæpʃəs] *adj.* şicanator.

captivate ['kæptiveit] *vt.* a captiva, a vrăji.

captive ['kæptiv] s. deţinut, prizonier. *adj.* captiv. *vt.* a captura; a atrage.

car [kɑ:] s. vagon; automobil; tramvai; nacelă.

caramel ['kærəmel] s. caramel(ă).

carat ['kærət] s. carat.

caravan [ˌkærə'væn] s. caravană; căruţă cu coviltir.

carbon ['kɑ:bən] s. carbon, cărbune.

carbon-paper ['kɑ:bənˌpeipə] s. indigo.

carbuncle ['kɑ:bʌŋkl] s. antrax; umflătură; rubin.

carburettor ['kɑ:bjuretə] s. carburator.

carcase, carcass ['kɑ:kəs] s. stîrv (de animal).

card [kɑ:d] s. carte (de joc, de vizită); carton; legitimaţie; one's best ~ atu.

cardboard ['kɑ:dbɔ:d] s. carton.

cardinal ['kɑ:dinl] s. cardinal. adj. cardinal; fundamental.

care [kɛə] s. grijă; răspundere. vt. (cu inf.) a dori să. vi. a se îngriji; to ~ for smb. a ţine la cineva; a-i păsa de cineva; a îngriji; to ~ for smth. a-i plăcea ceva.

career [kə'riə] s. carieră; înaintare. vi. a înainta; a goni.

careful ['kɛəfl] adj. atent, grijuliu.

careless ['kɛəlis] adj. neatent; nepăsător; neserios.

caress [kə'res] s. mîngîiere; sărutare. vt. a mîngîia.

caressing [kə'resiŋ] adj. mîngîietor.

caretaker ['kɛəˌteikə] s. îngrijitor; custode.

cargo ['kɑ:gou] s. încărcătură.

cargo boat ['kɑ:gouˌbout] s. cargobot.

caricature [ˌkærikə'tjuə] s. caricatură; şarjă. vt. a caricaturiza.

carload ['kɑ:loud] s. încărcătură.

carnage ['kɑ:nidʒ] s. măcel.

carnal ['kɑ:nl] adj. trupesc.

carnation [kɑ:'neiʃn] s. garoafă.

carnival ['kɑ:nivl] s. carnaval.

carnivorous [kɑ:'nivrəs] adj. carnivor.

carol ['kærl] s. colindă. vi. a cînta colinde.

carousal [kə'rauzl] s. chef.

carouse [kə'rauz] vi. a chefui.

carp [kɑ:p] s. crap. vi. a fi nemulţumit; to ~ at a pisa.

carpenter ['kɑ:pintə] s. dulgher.

carpet ['kɑ:pit] s. covor. vt. a acoperi cu covoare.

carriage ['kæridʒ] s. trăsură; vagon de pasageri; cărăuşie; tehn. car; afet; ţinută (a corpului).

carriage-way ['kæridʒˌwei] s. parte carosabilă.

carrier ['kæriə] s. cărăuş; mesager.

carrion ['kæriən] s. leş.

carrot ['kærət] s. morcov.

carry ['kæri] vt. a duce, a căra; a prelungi, a continua; a răpi; a cîştiga; a ţine; to ~ off a răpi; a cîştiga; to ~ on a desfăşura; to ~ out a îndeplini; to ~ through a înfăptui. vi. a ajunge; to ~ on a continua.

cart [kɑ:t] s. docar, şaretă; car, căruţă.

carter ['kɑ:tə] s. căruţaş.

carton ['kɑ:tn] s. cutie de carton.

cartoon [kɑ:'tu:n] s. caricatură; desen animat.

cartridge ['kɑ:tridʒ] s. cartuş; el. doză; foto. casetă.

carve [ka:v] *vt.* a ciopli ; a tăia ; a sculpta ; a dăltui.

carving ['ka:viŋ] *s.* sculptură ; cioplire.

case [keis] *s.* caz ; situaţie ; pacient ; proces ; pledoarie ; ladă.

casement (window) ['keismənt ('windou)] *s.* fereastră batantă.

cash [kæʃ] *s.* bani (gheaţă) ; capital ; ~ *down* cu bani peşin ; ~ *on delivery* contra ramburs. *vt.* a încasa.

cash-book ['kæʃbuk] *s.* registru de încasări.

cashier [kæ'ʃiə] *s.* casier. *vt.* a concedia.

cashmere [kæʃ'miə] *s.* caşmir.

casing ['keisiŋ] *s.* înveliş ; *tehn.* lagăr.

casino [kə'si:nou] *s.* cazino.

cask [ka:sk] *s.* butoi.

casket ['ka:skit] *s.* cutie ; *amer.* sicriu.

cast [ka:st] *s.* aruncare ; mulaj ; *teatru* distribuţie. *vt. inf., trec. şi part. trec.* a arunca ; *tehn.* a turna, a mula ; *to* ~ *a vote* a vota ; *to* ~ *lots* a trage la sorţi ; *to* ~ *about for* a căuta din ochi.

castaway ['ka:stəwei] *s.* naufragiat ; părăsit.

caste [ka:st] *s.* castă.

caster ['ka:stə] *s. v.* **castor.**

castigate ['kæstigeit] *vt.* a pedepsi ; a bate ; a critica.

casting ['ka:stiŋ] *s.* mulaj ; turnare.

casting-vote ['ka:stiŋ'vout] *s.* vot decisiv.

cast iron ['ka:st'aiən] *s.* fontă. *adj.* fix, neclintit ; de fier.

castle ['ka:sl] *s.* castel ; cetate.

castor ['ka:stə] *s.* rotilă ; solniţă ; presărătoare.

castor bean ['ka:stə̗bi:n] *s.* (boabă de) ricin.

castor oil [ka:stər'ɔil] *s.* unt de ricin.

castor-oil plant ['ka:stər̗ɔil 'pla:nt] *s.* ricin.

castor sugar ['ka:stə'ʃugə] *s.* zahăr tos *sau* granulat.

castrate [kæs'treit] *vt.* a castra.

casual ['kæʒjuəl] *s. pl.* haine de fiecare zi. *adj.* întîmplător ; neglijent ; sporadic.

casualty ['kæʒjuəlti] *s.* victimă ; *pl.* pierderi.

cat [kæt] *s.* pisică ; felină ; bici, pisica cu nouă cozi.

cataclysm ['kætəklizəm] *s.* cataclism.

catapult ['kætəpʌlt] *s.* praştie ; catapultă.

catalogue ['kætəlɔg] *s.* catalog.

catarrh [kə'ta:] *s.* guturai, răceală ; catar.

catastrophe [kə'tæstrəfi] *s.* catastrofă.

catch [kætʃ] *s.* captură ; opritoare ; încuietoare. *vt.* a prinde (din urmă) ; a opri ; a se molipsi de ; a înţelege ; *to* ~ *sight of* a zări ; a distinge ; *to* ~ *fire* a se aprinde ; ˙*to* ~ *up with* a ajunge din urmă. *vi.* a se fixa ; a se apuca.

catching ['kætʃiŋ] *adj.* molipsitor.

catechism ['kætikizəm] *s.* catehism ; interogatoriu.

category ['kætigəri] *s.* categorie, grup.

cater ['keitə] *vi.: to* ~ *for* a aproviziona, a alimenta ; *to* ~ *to* a se ocupa de.

caterer ['keitərə] s. furnizor.

caterpillar ['kætəpilə] s. omidă; şenilă.

catgut ['kætgʌt] s. catgut.

cathedral [kə'θi:drl] s. catedrală.

cathode ['kæθoud] s. catod.

Catholic ['kæθəlik] s., adj. catolic(ă).

catkin ['kætkin] s. bot. mîţişor.

cattle ['kætl] s. pl. vite (cornute).

caucus ['kɔ:kəs] s. nucleu al unui partid; întrunire (electorală).

caught [kɔ:t] vt., vi. trec. şi part. trec. de la catch.

cauldron ['kɔ:ldrn] s. ceaun; cazan.

cauliflower ['kɔliflauə] s. conopidă.

caulk [kɔ:k] vt. a călăfătui; a etanşa.

causative ['kɔ:zətiv] adj. cauzal.

cause [kɔ:z] s. cauză; justificare. vt. a pricinui.

causeway ['kɔ:zwei] s. potecă.

caution ['kɔ:ʃn] s. grijă, precauţie; avertisment. vt. a avertiza.

cautious ['kɔ:ʃəs] adj. atent, precaut.

cavalier [,kævə'liə] s. cavaler. adj. uşuratic.

cavalry ['kævlri] s. cavalerie.

cave [keiv] s. peşteră. vi.: to ~ in a se prăbuşi.

cavil ['kævil] vi.: to ~ at a obiecta; a critica.

cavity ['kæviti] s. cavitate, scobitură.

cease [si:s] vt., vi. a înceta.

ceaseless ['si:slis] adj. neîncetat.

cedar ['si:də] s. cedru.

ceiling ['si:liŋ] s. tavan, plafon.

celebrate ['selibreit] vt. a sărbă-

tori; a lăuda. vi. a se veseli; a chefui.

celebrated ['selibreitid] adj. celebru.

celebration [,seli'breiʃn] s. sărbătorire; petrecere.

celerity [si'leriti] s. iuţeală.

celery ['seləri] s. ţelină.

celibacy ['selibəsi] s. celibat.

celibate ['selibit] s., adj. celibatar.

cell [sel] s. celulă; element galvanic.

cellar ['selə] s. pivniţă.

cello ['tʃelou] s. violoncel.

cellophane ['seləfein] s. celofan.

celluloid ['seljulɔid] s. celuloid.

cellulose ['seljulous] s. celuloză.

Celt [kelt] s. celt.

cement [si'ment] s. ciment. vt. a cimenta.

censer ['sensə] s. cădelniţă.

censor ['sensə] s. cenzor. vt. a cenzura.

censorship ['sensəʃip] s. cenzură.

censure ['senʃə] s. critică; blam. vt. a blama; a critica.

census ['sensəs] s. recensămînt.

cent [sent] s. cent; per~la sută.

centenary [sen'ti:nəri] s., adj. centenar.

centennial [sen'tenjəl] adj. centenar.

center ['sentə] s. v. centre.

centigrade ['sentigreid] adj. centigrad (Celsius).

centimetre ['sentimi:tə] s. centimetru.

central ['sentrl] adj. central; principal.

centralize ['sentrəlaiz] vt. a concentra.

centre ['sentə] s. centru, nucleu. vt., vi. a (se) concentra.

century ['sentʃuri] s. secol.

ceremonious [ˌseri'mounjəs] adj. ceremonios.

ceremony ['seriməni] s. ceremonie ; politeţe; caracter oficial.

certain ['sə:tn] adj. sigur ; anumit, oarecare ; for ~ fără doar şi poate.

certainly ['sə:tnli] adv. bineînţeles ; cu plăcere.

certainty ['sə:tnti] s. certitudine.

certificate [sə'tifikit] s. certificat.

certify ['sə:tifai] vt. a atesta.

certitude ['sə:titju:d] s. siguranţă.

cessation [se'seiʃn] s. încetare.

cession ['seʃn] s. cedare.

cess-pit ['sespit], cess-pool ['sespu:l] s. hazna ; fig. cloacă.

chafe [tʃeif] vt. a freca ; a încălzi ; a aţîţa. vi. a se încălzi ; a se enerva.

chaff [tʃa:f] s. pleavă, tărîţe ; tachinărie. vt. a tachina.

chaffinch ['tʃæfintʃ] s. cintezoi.

chain [tʃein] s. lanţ ; serie. vt. a înlănţui, a lega.

chair [tʃɛə] s. scaun ; fotoliu (prezidenţial) ; catedră ; preşedinte ; prezidiu. vt. a prezida.

chairman ['tʃɛəmən] s. preşedinte.

chalet ['ʃælei] s. cabană.

chalk [tʃɔ:k] s. cretă ; calcar.

challenge ['tʃælindʒ] s. provocare ; fig. (semn de) întrebare ; problemă ; interogatoriu. vt. a provoca.

chamber ['tʃéimbə] s. cameră.

chamberlain ['tʃeinbəlin] s. şambelan.

chambermaid ['tʃeimbəmeid] s. fată în casă.

chameleon [kə'mi:ljən] s. cameleon.

chamois ['ʃæmwa:] s. capră neagră ; piele de antilopă.

champagne [ʃæm'pein] s. şampanie.

champion ['tʃæmpjən] s. campion ; apărător ; susţinător. vt. a apăra ; a susţine.

championship ['tʃæmpjənʃip] s. campionat ; titlu de campion ; apărare.

chance [tʃa:ns] s. întîmplare ; şansă. adj. întîmplător. vt. a încerca, a risca. vi. a se întîmpla ; a surveni ; to ~ upon smb. a da peste cineva.

chancellor ['tʃa:nsələ] s. cancelar ; dregător ; decan ; preşedinte, prim-ministru.

chancery ['tʃa:nsri] s. tribunal ; curtea cancelarului ; notariat ; arhivă ; in ~ la judecată.

chandelier [ˌʃændi'liə] s. candelabru.

chandler ['tʃa:ndlə] s. băcan ; furnizor.

change [tʃeindʒ] s. schimbare ; trecere ; variaţie ; mărunţiş ; rest ; for a ~ pentru a evita monotonia. vt. a (pre)schimba ; to ~ one's mind a se răzgîndi ; to ~ colour a se schimba la faţă. vi. a se schimba.

changeable ['tʃeindʒəbl] adj. schimbător.

channel ['tʃænl] s. canal (natural) ; braţ de rîu etc. ; fig. sursă ; mijloc. vt. a canaliza ; a îndrepta (către).

chant [tʃa:nt] s. cîntec. vt. a cînta ; a scanda.

chaos ['keiɔs] s. haos.

chaotic [kei'ɔtik] adj. haotic.

chap [tʃæp] s. om ; băiat ; individ. vt., vi. a (se) crăpa.

chapel ['tʃæpl] s. paraclis; capelă.

chaplain ['tʃæplin] s. capelan; preot militar.

chapter ['ʃtæptə] s. capitol; serie, lanț.

char [tʃɑ:] s. mangal; cărbune; femeie cu ziua; curățenie generală; treabă. vt., vi. a (se) preface în mangal.

character ['kæriktə] s. (tărie de) caracter; personalitate; specific; caracterizare.; recomandație; reputație.

characteristic [ˌkæriktə'ristik] s. caracteristică. adj. caracteristic; înnăscut.

characterize ['kæriktəraiz] vt. a caracteriza.

charcoal ['tʃɑ:koul] s. mangal.

charge [tʃɑ:dʒ] s. acuzație; sarcină; poruncă; responsabilitate; persoană dată în grija cuiva; mil. șarjă; com. preț, cost; to be in ~ of a avea în grijă. vt. a acuza; a ataca, a șarja; a cere (preț, onorariu); a încărca; a însărcina.

chargé d'affaires ['ʃɑ:ʒeidæ'fɛə] s. însărcinat cu afaceri.

charitable ['tʃæritəbl] adj. caritabil.

charity ['tʃæriti] s. pomană; caritate.

Charles's Wain ['tʃɑ:lziz'wein] s. Carul Mare

charm [tʃɑ:m] s. farmec; atracție; vrajă, descîntec; amuletă. vt. a vrăji; a încînta; a descînta.

chart [tʃɑ:t] s. hartă (marină); tabel, grafic. vt. a trasa; a plănui.

charter ['tʃɑ:tə] s. cartă; hrisov.

charming ['tʃɑ:miŋ] adj. încîntător, fermecător; simpatic

charwoman [['tʃɑ:,wumən] s. femeie cu ziua.

chary ['tʃɛəri] adj. prudent; timid; zgîrcit.

chase [tʃeis] s. goană. vt. a goni; a urmări; a izgoni.

chasm ['kæzəm] s. spărtură; prăpastie.

chassis ['ʃæsi] s. șasiu.

chaste [tʃeist] adj. cast, cuminte; simplu.

chasten ['tʃeisn], **chastise** [tʃæs'taiz] vt. a pedepsi.

chastity ['tʃæstiti] s. castitate, puritate.

chat [tʃæt] s. conversație; șuetă. vi. a flecări, a conversa.

chattels ['tʃætlz] s. pl. lucruri, avere mobilă.

chatter ['tʃætə] s. flecăreală; clănțănit; zgomot. vi. a trăncăni; a clănțăni; a face zgomot.

chatter-box ['tʃætəbɔks] s. fig. moară stricată.

chauffeur ['ʃoufə] s. șofer particular.

cheap [tʃi:p] adj., adv. ieftin.

cheapen ['tʃi:pn] vt. a ieftini.

cheat [tʃi:t] s. pungaș, escroc. vt., vi. a înșela.

check [tʃek] s. verificare, control; oprire; piedică; bifare; contramarcă; carou; amer. cec. vt. a verifica; a opri; a preda.

checkers ['tʃekəz] s. pl. amer. (jocul de) dame; carouri.

checkmate ['tʃek'meit] s. șah mat. vt. a face șah mat.

cheek [tʃi:k] s. obraz; obrăznicie, nerușinare.

cheeky ['tʃi:ki] adj. obraznic, nerușinat.

cheer [tʃiə] s. ovaţie, ura; veselie. vt. a înveseli; a îmbăta; a ovaţiona. vi. a se înveseli; to ~ up a se lumina.

cheerful ['tʃiəfl] adj. vesel; optimist; plăcut.

cheerio(h) ['tʃiəri'ou] interj. la revedere; noroc.

cheerless ['tʃiəlis] adj. trist, nenorocit; întunecat.

cheese [tʃi:z] s. brînză.

chemical ['kemikl] adj. chimic.

chemist ['kemist] s. chimist; farmacist; droghist.

chemistry ['kemistri] s. chimie.

cheque [tʃek] s. cec.

cheque book ['tʃekbuk] s. carnet de cecuri.

cherish ['tʃeriʃ] vt. a păstra (cu grijă); a nutri; a iubi.

cherry ['tʃeri] s. vişin(ă); cireş; cireaşă. adj. roşu.

cherub ['tʃerəb] s. heruvim; îngeraş.

chess [tʃes] s. (jocul de) şah.

chessboard ['tʃesbɔ:d] s. tablă de şah.

chessman ['tʃesmən] s. piesă de şah.

chest [tʃest] s. cufăr; ladă; piept.

chestnut ['tʃesnət] s. castan(ă); roib. adj. castaniu, şaten; roib.

chest-of-drawers ['tʃestəv'drɔ:z] s. scrin.

chew [tʃu:] vt., vi. a mesteca.

chewing-gum ['tʃuiŋɡʌm] s. gumă de mestecat.

chick(en) ['tʃik(in)] s. pui; păsărică.

chicken pox ['tʃikin'pɔks] s. vărsat de vînt.

chid [tʃid] vt. trec. şi part. trec. de la chide.

chide [tʃaid] vt. a ocărî.

chief [tʃi:f] s. şef; conducător. adj. principal; suprem; şef.

chiefly ['tʃi:fli] adv. mai ales.

chieftain ['tʃi:ftən] s. căpetenie.

chilblain ['tʃilblein] s. degerătură.

child [tʃaild] s. copil.

childbed ['tʃaildbed] s. naştere, lăuzie.

childbirth ['tʃaildbə:θ] s. naştere.

childhood ['tʃaildhud] s. copilărie.

childish ['tʃaildiʃ] adj. copilăresc; copilăros.

childless ['tʃaildlis] adj. fără copii.

childlike ['tʃaildlaik] adj. copilăresc; nevinovat.

children ['tʃildrn] s. pl. de la child.

child's play ['tʃaildzplei] s. fleac, jucărie (fig.).

Chilean ['tʃiliən] s., adj. chilian(ă).

chill [tʃil] s. răceală; răcoare. adj. răcoros; rece; glacial. vt., vi. a (se) răc(or)i.

chime [tʃaim] s. (sunet de) clopot. vt., vi. a suna; to ~ in a se amesteca în conversaţie; a se armoniza.

chimera [kai'miərə] s. himeră.

chimney ['tʃimni] s. coş, horn.

chimney-sweep(er) ['tʃimni‚swi:-p(ə)] s. coşar.

chimpanzee [‚tʃimpən'zi:] s. cimpanzeu.

chin [tʃin] s. bărbie.

china ['tʃainə] s. porţelan(uri).

china ware ['tʃainə‚wɛə] s. porţelanuri.

Chinese [tʃai'ni:z] s. chinez(oaică); limba chineză. adj. chinez(ă).

chink [tʃiŋk] s. crăpătură; clin-

chet (de pahare etc.). *vt.*, *vi.*
a zornăi; a (se) ciocni,
chintz [tʃints] *s.* creton.
chip [tʃip] *s.* aşchie; ciob;
ciupitură; felie; *pl.* cartofi
prăjiţi; *a ~ of the old block*
leit taică-su. *vt.* a aşchia;
a ciobi; a tăia subţire. *vi.* a
se ciobi, a se strica.
chirp [tʃəːp] *s.* ciripit. *vt.*, *vi.*
a ciripi.
chisel ['tʃizl] *s.* daltă. *vt.* a cizela;
a dăltui.
chivalrous ['ʃivlrəs] *adj.* viteaz;
politicos; cavaler.
chivalry ['ʃivlri] *s.* cavalerism;
echitate.
chloride ['klɔːraid] *s.* clorură.
chlorine ['klɔːriːn] *s.* clor.
chlorophyll ['klɔrəfil] *s.* clorofilă.
chock [tʃɔk] *s.* piedică, opritoare.
chock-full ['tʃɔkful] *adj.* plin ochi.
chocolate ['tʃɔklit] *s.* (bomboană
de)-ciocolată; (lapte cu) cacao.
choice [tʃɔis] *s.* (posibilitate de)
alegere; ales; sortiment. *adj.*
ales; remarcabil.
choir [kwaiə] *s.* cor; galeria
corului la biserică.
choke [tʃouk] *s. auto.* accelerator.
vt., *vi.* a (se) înăbuşi; a (se)
îneca.
choler ['kɔlə] *s.* furie.
cholera ['kɔlərə] *s.* holeră.
choleric ['kɔlərik] *adj.* nervos.
choose [tʃuːz] *vt.* a alege;֊ a
hotărî; a dori.
chop [tʃɔp] *s.* friptură; fleică;
cotlet; falcă; bucată. *vt.* a
tăia, a ciopli; *to ~ off* a
reteza.
chopsticks ['tʃɔpstiks] *s. pl.*
beţişoare de mîncat (orez etc.).
choral ['kɔːrl] *adj.* coral.

chord [kɔːd] *s.* coardă; *muz.*
acord.
chore [tʃɔː] *s.* treabă; muncă
casnică; corvoadă.
chorister ['kɔristə] *s.* corist.
chorus ['kɔrəs] *s.* cor; refren.
chorus girl ['kɔrəsˌgəːl] *s.* balerină; figurantă (la revistă).
chose [tʃouz] *vt.*, *vi. trec. de la*
choose.
chosen ['tʃouzn] *vt.*, *vi. part.*
trec. de la **choose.**
Christ [kraist] *s.* Cristos. *interj.*
doamne.
christen ['krisn] *vt.* a boteza.
Christendom ['krisndəm] *s.* creştinătate.
Christian ['kristjən] *s.*, *adj.* creştin.
Christianity [kristi'æniti] *s.*
creştinătate; creştinism.
Christian name ['kristjən'neim]
nume de botez.
Christmas ['krisməs] *s.* Crăciun.
chrome [kroum], **chromium**
['kroumjəm] *s. chim.* crom.
chronicle ['krɔnikl] *s.* cronică.
chronologic(al) [ˌkrɔnə'lɔdʒik(l)]
adj. cronologic.
chrysanthemum [kri'sænθməm]
s. crizantemă.
chubby ['tʃʌbi] *adj.* bucălat;
durduliu.
chuck [tʃʌk] *vt.* a arunca; a
părăsi.
chuckle ['tʃʌkl] *s.* chicot. *vi.* a
ride pe înfundate; a chicoti.
chum [tʃʌm] *s.* prieten; tovarăş.
chunk [tʃʌŋk] *s.* bucată.
church [tʃəːtʃ] *s.* biserică; liturghie.
church-goer ['tʃəːtʃˌgouə] *s.*
credincios.

churchyard ['tʃə:tʃ'jɑ:d] *s.* cimitir.

churl [tʃə:l] *s.* bădăran.

churlish -['tʃə:liʃ] *adj.* bădăran.

churn [tʃə:n] *s.* putinei. *vt.* a bate (untul etc.).

cider ['saidə] *s.* cidru.

cigar [si'gɑ:] *s.* trabuc.

cigarette [ˌsigə'ret] *s.* ţigar(et)ă.

cigarette case [ˌsigə'retˌkeis] *s.* tabacheră.

cigarette holder [ˌsigə'ret'houldə] *s.* portţigaret.

cinder ['sinˌdə] *s. pl.* zgură; cenuşă.

Cinderella [ˌsində'relə] *s.* Cenuşăreasa.

cinema(tograph) [ˌsini'mætəgrɑ:f] *s.* cinema(tograf).

cinnamon ['sinəmən] *s.* scorţişoară.

cipher ['saifə] *s.* zero; nimic; cifră; nulitate; cifru. *vt.* a socoti; a cifra.

circle ['sə:kl] *s.* cerc; inel; serie, lanţ; *teatru* balcon. *vt.* a înconjura. *vi.* a se învîrti în cerc.

circuit ['sə:kit] *s.* circuit; tur (neu); circumscripţie.

circuitous [sə'kjuitəs] *adj.* indirect; pe ocolite.

circular ['sə:kjulə] *s.* circulară. *adj.* rotund; circular.

circulate ['sə:kjuleit] *vt.* a răspîndi. *vi.* a circula; a merge în cerc.

circulating ['sə:kjuleitiŋ] *adj.* ambulant; volant.

circulation [ˌsə:kju'leiʃn] *s.* circulaţie; răspîndire; tiraj.

circumference [s'kʌmfrns] *s.* circumferinţă.

circumlocution [ˌsə:kəmlɔ'kju:ʃn] *s.* vorbărie; circumlocuţie.

circumscribe ['sə:kəmskraib] *vt.* a circumscrie, a limita.

circumscription [ˌsə:kəm'skripʃn] *s.* inscripţie; circumscriere.

circumstance ['sə:kəmstəns] *s.* împrejurare, condiţie; eveniment; amănunt; *pl.* avere; *in the* ~s dată fiind situaţia.

circumstantial [ˌsə:kəm'stænʃl] *adj.* amănunţit.

circumvent [ˌsə:kəm'vent] *vt.* a împiedica.

circus ['sə:kəs] *s.* circ; piaţă.

citadel ['sitədl] *s.* fortăreaţă.

cite [sait] *vt.* a cita.

citizen ['sitizn] *s.* cetăţean; locuitor.

citizenship ['sitiznʃip] *s.* cetăţenie; îndatoriri cetăţeneşti.

city ['siti] *s.* oraş; *the City* cartierul comercial al Londrei.

civil ['sivl] *adj.* cetăţenesc; civil; politicos; oficial.

civil servant ['sivl 'sə:vnt] *s.* funcţionar de stat.

civilian [si'viljən] *s., adj.* civil.

civility [si'viliti] *s.* politeţe.

civilization [ˌsivilai'zeiʃn] *s.* civilizaţie; civilizare.

clad [klæd] *adj.* îmbrăcat; împădurit.

claim [kleim] *s.* pretenţie; revendicare; drept. *vt.* a pretinde, a revendica.

claimant ['kleimənt] *s.* pretendent.

clam [klæm] *s.* scoică.

clamber ['klæmbə] *vi.* a se căţăra.

clammy ['klæmi] *adj.* jilav; lipicios.

clamo(u)r ['klæmə] *s.* gălăgie, zarvă; plîngere. *vi.* a face gălăgie; a protesta.

clan [klæn] s. clan; neam; clică.

clang [klæŋ] s. dangăt. vt., vi. a suna.

clango(u)r ['klæŋgə] s. dangăt; sunet metalic.

clannishness ['klæniʃnis] s. spirit de gaşcă.

clap [klæp] s. pocnet, bubuit(ură); pl. aplauze. vt. a pocni; a lovi (uşurel). vi. a trosni; a aplauda.

claret ['klærət] s. vin roşu (de Bordeaux).

clarify ['klærifai] vt., vi, a (se) clarifica.

clarion ['klæriən] s. trîmbiţă.

clarity ['klæriti] s. claritate.

clash [klæʃ] s. ciocnire; discordie. vt. a ciocni, a izbi. vi. a se ciocni; a zăngăni.

clasp [klɑ:sp] s. scoabă; strîngere de mînă; îmbrăţişare. vt. a strînge, a apuca bine; a fixa.

class [klɑ:s] s. (oră de) clasă; lecţie; categorie; grup(ă).

classic ['klæsik] s. clasic; operă clasică. adj. clasic; binecunoscut.

classical ['klæsikl] adj. clasic; antic; excelent.

classification [,klæsfi'keiʃn] s. clasificare.

classify ['klæsifai] vt. a clasifica.

class-mate ['klɑ:smeit] s. coleg (de clasă).

class-room ['klɑ:srum] s. clasă.

clatter ['klætə] s. tropot; zarvă. vt. a zăngăni. vi. a tropoti; a zăngăni.

clause [klɔ:z] s. clauză; propoziţie (dintr-o frază).

claw [klɔ:] s. gheară. vt. a apuca; a zgîria.

clay [klei] s. lut, argilă; pămînt.

clayey ['kleii] adj. argilos.

clean [kli:n] adj. curat; proaspăt; neîntrebuinţat; pur; corect; îndemînatic. vt. a spăla; a curăţa (de bani); a înlătura. adv. curat; total.

clean-cut ['kli:n'kʌt] adj. clar; drept; bine făcut.

cleanliness ['klenlinis] s. curăţenie.

cleanly ['klenli] adj., adv. curat.

cleanse [klenz] vt. a curăţa; a purifica.

clean-shaven ['kli:n'ʃeivn] adj. ras; fără barbă sau mustaţă.

clear [kliə] adj. clar; curat; ferit; slobod, com. total. vt. a curăţa; a clarifica; a trece; a elibera; a scăpa de; a curăţa de bani; to ~ away a strînge (masa); to ~ one's throat a-şi drege glasul; to ~ customs a fi vămuit. vi. a se limpezi; a se însenina; to ~ off sau out a pleca.

clearance ['kliərns] s. eliberare; spaţiu.

clear-cut ['kliə'kʌt] adj. clar, limpede; drept.

clearing ['kliəriŋ] s. poiană; fin. cliring.

clearly ['kliəli] adv. limpede; evident.

cleavage ['kli:vidʒ] s. crăpătură; despărţire; sciziune.

cleave [kli:v] vt. a despica; a separa. vi. a se desface.

clef [klef] s. muz. cheie.

cleft [kleft] s. crăpătură, despicătură. vt., vi. trec. şi part. trec. de la cleave.

clemency ['klemənsi] s. îndurare.

clement ['klemənt] *adj.* îndurător.

clench [klentʃ] *vt.* a strînge; a rezolva.

clergy ['klə:dʒi] *s.* cler.

clergyman ['klə:dʒimən] *s.* preot (anglican).

clerical ['klerikl] *adj.* bisericesc; funcţionăresc.

clerk[1] [kla:k] *s.* funcţionar comercial; conţopist; notar; grefier.

clerk[2] [klə:k] *s. amer.* vînzător de prăvălie.

clever ['klevə] *adj.* deştept; isteţ; iscusit.

click [klik] *s.* pocnitură. *vt., vi.* a pocni.

cliff [klif] *s.* faleză; buză de deal; stîncă.

climate ['klaimit] *s.* climă; climat.

climax ['klaimæks] *s.* culme.

climb [klaim] *s.* urcuş; pantă. *vt.* a urca, a se căţăra pe. *vi.* a se (ab)urca; a parveni (în viaţă); *to ~ down* a coborî; a fi în declin.

climber ['klaimə] *s.* plantă agăţătoare; alpinist; parvenit.

clime [klaim] *s. poet.* climă; ţinut; meleaguri.

cling [kliŋ] *vi.* a se lipi; a se agăţa.

clinic ['klinik] *s.* clinică.

clink [kliŋk] *s.* clinchet. *vt., vi.* a ciocni; a zornăi.

clip [klip] *s.* clamă; agrafă. *vt.* a reteza; a prinde cu o agrafă etc.

clipper ['klipə] *s.* goeletă; (avion) transatlantic; *pl.* foarfece (de tuns).

clipping ['klipiŋ] *s.* tăietură (de ziar).

clique [kli:k] *s.* clică.

cloak [klouk] *s.* manta; mantie; *fig.* paravan. *vt.* a tăinui.

cloak-room *s.* ['kloukrum] vestiar; garderobă; casă de bagaje (la gară).

clock [klɔk] *s.* orologiu, ceas. *vt., vi.* a ponta.

clockwise ['klɔkwaiz] *adj., adv.* în sensul acelor unui ceasornic.

clockwork ['klɔkwə:k] *s.* mecanism de ceasornic.

clod [klɔd] *s.* bulgăre (de pămînt).

clog [klɔg] *s.* sabot. *vt., vi.* a (se) năclăi; a (se) bloca.

cloister ['klɔistə] *s.* mănăstire; galerie.

close[1] [klouz] *s.* sfîrşit, încheiere. *vt.* a închide; a încheia; a strînge. *vi.* a se apropia; a se învoi.

close[2] [klous] *s.* împrejmuire; curte. *adj.* apropiat; la îndemînă; înghesuit; ascuns; închis.

close call ['klous ˌkɔ:l] *s.* mare primejdie.

closely ['klousli] *adv.* îndeaproape; strîns.

closeshave ['klousʃeiv] *s.* primejdie de moarte; salvare miraculoasă.

closet ['klɔzit] *s.* cămăruţă; dulap; closet.

close-up ['klousʌp] *s. foto.* prim-plan.

clot [klɔt] *s.* cheag. *vi.* a se închega; a se năclăi.

cloth [klɔθ] *s.* postav; pînză; cîrpă.

clothe [klouð] *vt.* a îmbrăca; a acoperi.

clothes [klouðz] s. pl. haine; lenjerie (de pat etc.).

clothes-line ['klouðzlain] s. funie de rufe.

clothes peg ['klouðzpeg] s. cîrlig de rufe.

clothing ['klouðiŋ] s. îmbrăcăminte.

cloud [klaud] s. nor; ceață; hoardă; stol; pl. cer; to be in the ~s a fi cu capul în nori. vt., vi. a (se) înnora.

cloudless ['klaudlis] adj. senin.

cloudy ['klaudi] adj. înnorat; cețos.

clout [klaut] s. cîrpă; palmă; dupac. vt. a pocni.

clove [klouv] s. bot. cuişoare; cățel de usturoi. vt., vi. trec. de la cleave.

cloven ['klouvn] vt., vi. part. trec. de la cleave.

clover ['klouvə] s. trifoi; in ~ în sînul lui Avram.

clown [klaun] s. clovn; mîrlan.

clownish ['klauniʃ] adj. de bufon.

cloy [kloi] vt. a sătura; a scîrbi.

club [klʌb] s. bîtă; crosă; băț de golf etc.; treflă; club. vt. a ciomăgi. vi. a se asocia.

clue [klu:] s. cheie; rezolvare.

clump [klʌmp] s. pîlc; bulgăre.

clumsy ['klʌmzi] adj. stîngaci; greoi.

clung [klʌŋ] vi. trec. şi part. trec. de la cling.

cluster ['klʌstə] s. ciorchine. vi. a se aduna.

clutch [klʌtʃ] s. apucare; gheară; ambreiaj. vt. a apuca, a prinde.

coach [koutʃ] s. trăsură; diligență; vagon; autobuz; antrenor; meditator. vt. a prepara, a medita; a antrena.

coachman ['koutʃmən] s. vizitiu.

coal [koul] s. cărbune; pl. cărbuni, jar.

coal-field ['koulfi:ld] s. bazin carbonifer.

coalition [,kouə'liʃn] s. coaliție; unire.

coal-pit ['koulpit] s. mină de cărbuni.

coal-tar ['koulta:] s. gudron de huilă.

coarse [ko:s] adj. aspru; grosolan; ordinar; mitocan.

coarseness ['ko:snis] s. grosolănie.

coast [koust] s. coastă, țărm. vi. a merge de-a lungul coastei; a coborî o pantă.

coast-guard ['kousga:d] s. grănicer.

coat [kout] s. haină; înveliş; strat (de vopsea etc.). vt. a înveli; a îmbrăca; a vopsi.

coating ['koutiŋ] s. înveliş.

coat-of-arms ['koutəv'a:mz] s. blazon; stemă.

coax [kouks] vt. a îndupleca.

cob [kob] s. ştiulete.

cobble ['kobl] s. piatră de rîu. vt. a pietrui; a cîrpăci.

cobbler ['koblə] s. cîrpaci, cizmar.

cobweb ['kobweb] s. pînză de păianjen.

coca-cola ['koukə'koulə] s. coca-cola, limonadă.

cock [kok] s. cocoş; robinet. vt. a ciuli (urechile).

cockade [ko'keid] s. cocardă.

cockney ['kokni] s. (dialect) londonez. adj. din mahalalele londoneze.

cockpit ['kokpit] s. carlingă; arenă.

cockroach ['kɔkroutʃ] s. gîndac de bucătărie.

cockscomb ['kɔkskoum] s. creastă de cocoş.

cocksure ['kɔkʃuə] adj. încrezut.

cocktail ['kɔkteil] s. cocteil.

cocoa ['koukou] s. cacao.

coconut ['koukənʌt] s. nucă de cocos.

cocoon [kə'ku:n] s. cocon (de vierme de mătase).

cocopalm ['koukəpɑ:m] s. cocotier.

cod [kɔd] s. iht. cod.

coddle ['kɔdl] vt. a cocoli.

code [koud] s. cod(ice).

codify ['kɔdifai] vt. a codifica.

cod-liver oil ['kɔdlivər'ɔil] s. untură de peşte.

co-ed ['kou'ed] s. elevă la o şcoală mixtă.

co-education ['kou,edju'keiʃn] s. învăţămînt mixt.

coerce [kou'ə:s] vt. a sili.

coercion [kou'ə:ʃn] s. constrîngere.

co-exist ['kouig'zist] vi. a co-exista.

co-existence ['kouig'zistns] s. co-existenţă.

coffee ['kɔfi] s. ˉcafea.

coffee-house ['kɔfihaus] s. cafenea.

coffer ['kɔfə] s. cufăr; ladă; tezaur.

coffin ['kɔfin] s. sicriu.

cogent ['koudʒnt] adj. convingător.

cogitation [,kɔdʒi'teiʃn] s. cugetare.

cognate ['kɔgneit] adj. înrudit; similar.

cognizance ['kɔgnizns] s. cunoştinţă.

cog-wheel ['kɔgwi:l] s. roată dinţată.

coherent [ko'hiərnt] adj. coerent; clar; inteligibil.

coil [kɔil] s. serpentină; bobină. vt. a răsuci, a face ghem. vi., vr. a se răsuci, a se încolăci.

coin [kɔin] s. monedă. vt. a fabrica; a bate (monedă).

coinage ['kɔinidʒ] s. baterea monezilor; sistem monetar; cuvînt nou.

coincide [,koin'said] vi. a coincide.

coincidence [ko'insidns] s. coincidenţă.

coke [kouk] s. cocs.; coca cola. vt. a cocsifica.

cold [kould] s. frig; ger; răceală. adj. rece; îngheţat; neatrăgător; calm; glacial.

cold-blooded ['kould'blʌdid] adj. cu sînge rece; calm; împietrit.

cold-hearted ['kould'hɑ:tid] adj. nesimţitor; cu inima împietrită.

collaborate [kə'læbəreit] vi. a conlucra.

collapse [kə'læps] s. prăbuşire; eşec; leşin. vi. a se nărui; a eşua.

collapsible [kə'læpsəbl] adj. pliant, rabatabil; decapotabil.

collar ['kɔlə] s. guler; garnitură; zgardă. vt. a apuca (de guler).

collar-bone ['kɔləboun] s. claviculă.

collar-stud ['kɔləstʌd] s. buton de guler.

collate [kɔ'leit] vt. aˊcolaţiona; a compara.

colleague ['kɔli:g] s. coleg.

collect [kə'lekt] vt. a strînge; a(-şi) aduna (gîndurile etc.). vi. a se aduna.

collection [kə'lekʃn] *s.* strîngere ; colecţi(onar)e ; colectă.

collective [kə'lektiv] *s., adj.* colectiv.

collector [kə'lektə] *s.* colecţionar ; controlor de bilete ; perceptor ; colector.

college ['kɔlidʒ] *s.* colegiu ; universitate ; liceu superior.

collide [kə'laid] *vi.* a se ciocni.

collie ['kɔli] *s.* cîine ciobănesc (scoţian).

collier ['kɔliə] *s.* miner (într-o mină de cărbuni).

colliery ['kɔljəri] *s.* mină de cărbuni.

collision [kə'liʒn] *s.* ciocnire.

collocation [ˌkɔlə'keiʃn] *s.* expresie.

colloquial [kə'loukwiəl] *adj.* de conversaţie ; familiar.

colloquy ['kɔləkwi] *s.* conversaţie.

collusion [kə'lu:ʒn] *s.* cîrdăşie.

colon ['koulən] *s.* două puncte (:).

colonel ['kə:nl] *s.* colonel.

colonization [ˌkɔlənai'zeiʃn] *s.* colonizare ; colonialism.

colonizer ['kɔlənaizə] *s.* colon(ial)ist.

colony ['kɔləni] *s.* colonie.

color ['kʌlə] *s. amer. v.* **colour.**

colossus [kə'lɔsəs] *s.* colos.

colour ['kʌlə] *s.* culoare ; nuanţă ; înfăţişare, *pl.* drapel, *under ~ of* sub pretext că. *vt.* a colora ; a vopsi ; a schimba ; *fig.* a înflori. *vi.* a se colora ; a se îmbujora.

colour-bar ['kʌləba:] *s.* discriminare rasială.

colour-blind ['kʌləblaind] *adj.* insensibil la culori ; suferind de daltonism.

coloured ['kʌləd] *adj.* colorat ; de culoare, negru.

colouring ['kʌləriŋ] *s.* culoare ; colorit ; vopsea.

colourless ['kʌləlis] *adj.* incolor ; palid ; şters.

colt [koult] *s.* mînz.

column ['kɔləm] *s.* coloană ; comentariu ; reportaj.

columnist ['kɔləmnist] *s.* comentator.

coma ['koumə] *s.* comă.

comb [koum] *s.* pieptene ; darac ; fagure. *vt.* a pieptăna ; a perchezіţiona.

combat ['kɔmbət] *s.* luptă. *vt.* a combate. *vi.* a (se) lupta.

combination [ˌkɔmbi'neiʃn] *s.* combinaţie ; afacere ; asociaţie ; *pl.* combinezon.

combine[1] ['kɔmbain] *s.* asociaţie ; cartel ; combină ; combinat.

combine[2] [kəm'bain] *vt., vi.* a (se) combina.

combustible [kəm'bʌstəbl] *s.* combustibil. *adj.* combustibil ; iritabil.

combustion [kəm'bʌstʃn] *s.* combustie.

come [kʌm] *vi. inf. şi part trec.* a veni ; a se apropia ; a ajunge ; a deveni ; a se ridica ; a se petrece ; *~ along!* haide ! ; *~ on!* grăbeşte-te ! ; *~ in!* intră ! poftim ! ; *to ~ by* a obţine ; *to ~ to an end* a se sfîrşi ; *to ~ to an agreement* a se înţelege ; *to ~ to (oneself)* a-şi veni în fire ; *to ~ sau round* a-şi reveni ; a se învoi ; *to ~ of age* a ajunge la majorat ; *to ~ out* a apărea, a ieşi la iveală ; *to ~ down* a coborî ; a scăpăta ; *to ~*

off a se produce ; *to ~ up* a creşte, a progresa ; *to ~ to blows* a ajunge la bătaie ; *to ~ to nothing* a da greş ; *to ~ to pass* sau *to ~ about* a se întîmpla ; *to ~ across* sau *upon* a întîlni din întîmplare.

come-back ['kʌmbæk] *s.* revenire.

comedian [kə'mi:djən] *s.* (actor) comic.

come-down ['kʌmdaun] *s.* decădere ; înrăutăţire.

comedy ['kɔmidi] *s.* comedie ; întîmplare hazlie.

comely ['kʌmli] *adj.* atrăgător ; arătos.

comfort ['kʌmfət] *s.* consolare ; uşurare ; confort ; mulţumire. *vt.* a consola ; a împăca.

comfortable ['kʌmftəbl] *adj.* confortabil ; tihnit.

comfortably ['kʌmftəbli] *adv.* confortabil ; *~ off* înstărit.

comforter ['kʌmfətə] *s.* consolator ; fular.

comic(al) ['kɔmik(l)] *adj.* comic.

coming ['kʌmiŋ] *adj.* (de) viitor ; cu perspective.

comity ['kɔmiti] *s.* amabilitate.

comma ['kɔmə] *s.* virgulă.

command [kə'ma:nd] *s.* poruncă; comandă ; autoritate ; conducere ; *in ~ of* stăpîn pe. *vt.* a porunci ; a stăpîni ; a deţine ; a impune ; a domina.

commandeer [ˌkɔmən'diə] *vt.* a rechiziţiona.

commander [kə'ma:ndə] *s.* comandant ; *mar.* comandor.

commander-in-chief [kə'ma:ndrin'tʃi:f] *s.* comandant suprem.

commanding [kə'ma:ndiŋ] *adj.* impunător ; poruncitor ; comandant.

commandment [kə'ma:ndmənt] *s.* poruncă ; ordin.

commando [kə'ma:ndou] *s.* detaşament de asalt.

commemoration [kəˌmemə'reiʃn] *s.* comemorare ; amintire.

commence [kə'mens] *vt., vi.* a începe.

commend [kə'mend] *vt.* a lăuda ; a trimite.

commensurate [kə'menʃrit] *adj.* proporţional ; potrivit.

comment ['kɔment] *s.* comentariu. *vi.* a face comentarii.

commerce ['kɔməs] *s.* comerţ (cu ridicata).

commercial traveller [kə'mə.ʃl'trævlə] *s.* comis voiajor.

commiseration [kəˌmizə'reiʃn] *s.* milă ; înţelegere.

commissariat [ˌkɔmi'sɛəriət] *s.* intendenţă ; *mil.* administraţie ; *pol.* comisariat.

commissary ['kɔmisəri] *s.* intendent ; reprezentant ; comisar.

commission [kə'miʃn] *s.* grad de ofiţer ; comision ; comitet ; însărcinare ; *in ~* gata (de luptă). *vt.* a însărcina ; a inaugura.

commissioned [kə'miʃnd] *adj.* autorizat ; confirmat.

commissioner [kə'miʃnə] *s.* membru al unei comisii ; comisar, reprezentant guvernamental.

commit [kə'mit] *vt.* a comite ; a încredinţa ; a angaja. *vr.* a se angaja.

commitment [kə'mitmənt] *s.* angajament ; obligaţie.

committee [kə'miti] *s.* comitet ; comisie.

commodious [kə'moudjəs] *adj.* spaţios.

commodity [kə'mɔditi] *s.* marfă.

commodore ['kɔmədɔ:] *s.* comandor.

common ['kɔmən] *s.* izlaz; comunitate; *pl.* popor; *out of the ~* neobişnuit; *the (House of) Commons* Camera Comunelor. *adj.* comun; de rînd; răspîndit; frecvent; grosolan.

common law ['kɔmənlɔ:] *s.* cutumă.

commonly ['kɔmənli] *adv.* de obicei, în general.

commoner ['kɔmənə] *s.* om de rînd; deputat.

commonplace ['kɔmənpleis] *s.* platitudine. *adj.* banal, plat.

common sense ['kɔmən,sens] *s.* înţelepciune; scaun la cap; simţ al realităţii.

commonwealth ['kɔmənwelθ] *s.* avere comună; naţiune; republică; *the Commonwealth* Comunitatea Britanică de Naţiuni; Imperiul Britanic.

commotion [kə'mouʃn] *s.* agitaţie; încurcătură.

communal ['kɔmju:nl] *adj.* comunal; obştesc.

commune¹ ['kɔmju:n] *s.* comună.

commune² [kə'mju:n] *vi.* a comunica, a se înţelege.

communicable [kə'mju:nikəbl] *adj.* transmisibil; molipsitor.

communicate [kə'mju:nikeit] *vt., vi.* a comunica.

communication [kə,mju:ni'keiʃn] *s.* comunicare; comunicat; informaţie; comunicaţii.

communion [kə'mju:njən] *s.* comunitate; *rel.* împărtăşanie; discuţie.

communiqué [kə'mju:nikei] *s.* comunicat.

communism ['kɔmjunizəm] *s.* comunism.

communist ['kɔmjunist] *s., adj.* comunist.

community [kə'mju:niti] *s.* colectiv; societate; proprietate obştească.

commutation ticket [kɔmju'teiʃn tikit] *s. amer.* abonament (la tren etc.).

commutator ['kɔmjuteitə] *s.* şaltăr.

commute [kə'mju:t] *vt.* a comuta; a schimba. *vi. amer.* a face naveta.

commuter [kə'mju:tə] *s. amer.* navetist.

compact¹ ['kɔmpækt] *s.* pact; pudrieră.

compact² [kəm'pækt] *adj.* compact; solid; unit.

companion [kəm'pænjən] *s.* tovarăş; prieten; om de lume; însoţitor; damă de companie; pereche; manual.

companionship [kəm'pænjənʃip] *s.* tovărăşie.

company ['kʌmpni] *s.* companie; trupă; societate; musafir(i); tovarăşi.

company manners ['kʌmpəni mænəz] *s.* maniere alese; maniere afectate.

comparable ['kɔmprəbl] *adj.* comparabil.

comparative [kəm'pærətiv] *s., adj.* comparativ.

compare [kəm'pɛə] *s.* comparaţie; *beyond* sau *past ~* fără egal. *vt.* a compara; a asemui.

comparison [kəm'pærisn] *s.* comparaţie.

compass ['kʌmpəs] s. busolă; pl. compas.

compassion [kəm'pæʃn] s. milă; înţelegere.

compatible [kəm'pætəbl] adj. compatibil.

compel [kəm'pel] vt. a sili; a stoarce.

compensate ['kɔmpenseit] vt., vi. a (se) compensa.

compensation [ˌkɔmpen'seiʃn] s. compensaţie; despăgubire; consolare.

compete [kəm'piːt] vi. a concura; a rivaliza.

competence ['kɔmpitns] s. competenţă; avere.

competent ['kɔmpitnt] adj. competent; calificat.

competition [ˌkɔmpi'tiʃn] s. întrecere; concurenţă.

competitive [kəm'petitiv] adj. de concurenţă; competitiv.

competitor [kəm'petitə] s. concurent.

compilation [ˌkɔmpi'leiʃn] s. compilaţie; selecţie.

compile [kəm'pail] vt. a compila; a alcătui, a redacta.

compiler [kəm'pailə] s. redactor.

complacency [kəm'pleisnsi] s. mulţumire (de sine).

complain [kəm'plein] vi. a se plînge.

complaint [kəm'pleint] s. plîngere; boală.

complaisance [kəm'pleizns] s. complezenţă.

complement ['kɔmplimənt] s. complinire; complement.

complementary [ˌkɔmpli'mentri] adj. complementar.

complete [kəm'pliːt] adj. întreg;

perfect. vt. a desăvîrşi; a completa.

completion [kəm'pliːʃn] s. completare; desăvîrşire.

complex ['kɔmpleks] s. întreg; complex. adj. complex; complicat.

complexion [kəm'plekʃn] s. ten; înfăţişare.

complex sentence ['kɔmpleks 'sentəns] s. frază compusă prin subordonare.

complexity [kəm'pleksiti] s. complex(itate).

compliance [kəm'plaiəns] s. încuviinţare; bunăvoinţă; in ~ with conform (cu dat.).

compliant [kəm'plaiənt] adj. binevoitor.

complication [ˌkɔmpli'keiʃn] s. complicaţie.

complicity [kəm'plisiti] s. complicitate.

compliment[1] ['kɔmplimənt] s. compliment; omagiu; salut; pl. felicitări.

compliment[2] ['kɔmpliment] vt. a omagia; a lăuda; a felicita.

complimentary [ˌkɔmpli'mentri] adj. admirativ; de favoare.

comply [kəm'plai] vi.: to ~ with a satisface; a se supune la.

compose [kəm'pouz] vt. a compune; poligr. a culege; a linişti; a împăca.

composed [kəm'pouzd] adj. liniştit.

composer [kəm'pouzə] s. compozitor.

composite ['kɔmpəzit] adj. compus.

composition [ˌkɔmpə'ziʃn] s. compunere; compoziţie.

compositor [kəm'pɔzitə] s. zeţar.

compost ['kɔmpɔst] s. bălegar.

composure [kəm'pouʒə] s. calm.

compound¹ ['kɔmpaund] s. compus; împrejmuire. adj. compus.

compound² [kəm'paund] vt. a compune; a prepara.

compound sentence ['kɔmpaund 'sentəns] s. frază compusă prin coordonare.

comprehend [ˌkɔmpri'hend] vt. á înţelege; a cuprinde.

comprehensible [ˌkɔmpri'hensəbl] adj. de înţeles.

comprehension [ˌkɔmpri'henʃn] s. înţelegere; cuprindere.

comprehensive [ˌkɔmpri'hensiv] adj. cuprinzător.

compress¹ ['kɔmpres] s. compresă.

compress² [kəm'pres] vt. a comprima.

compression [kəm'preʃn] s. comprimare.

comprise [kəm'praiz] vt. a cuprinde; a fi alcătuit din.

compromise ['kɔmprəmaiz] s. compromis; împăcare. vt. a împăca; a compromite. vi. a face un compromis.

compulsion [kəm'pʌlʃn] s. constrîngere; strîmtoare (fig.).

compulsory [kəm'pʌlsri] adj. obligatoriu.

compunction [kəm'pʌŋkʃn] s. scrupul.

computation [ˌkɔmpju'teiʃn] s. socoteală.

compute [kəm'pju:t] vt., vi. a calcula.

comrade ['kɔmrid] s. tovarăş.

con [kɔn] s. argument sau vot potrivnic. vt. a studia. adv. împotrivă.

conceal [kən'si:l] vt. a ascunde, a tăinui.

concede [kən'si:d] vt. a ceda; a acorda.

conceit [kən'si:t] s. îngîmfare; concepţie; noţiune.

conceited [kən'si:tid] adj. încrezut.

conceivable [kən'si:vəbl] adj. de conceput; posibil.

conceive [kən'si:v] vt., vi. a concepe.

concentrate ['kɔnsentreit] vt., vi. a (se) concentra.

concentration [ˌkɔnsen'treiʃn] s. concentrare; aglomeraţie.

concept ['kɔnsept] s. noţiune.

conception [kən'sepʃn] s. concepţie; plan.

concern [kən'sə:n] s. grijă; interes; întreprindere: trust. vt. a interesa; a afecta; a îngrijora; as ~s ... cît despre, în ce priveşte... vr. to ~ oneself with a se ocupa de.

concerned [kən'sə:nd] adj. îngrijit; preocupat; interesat.

concerning [kən'sə:niŋ] prep. cu privire la.

concert ['kɔnsət] s. concert; spectacol; in ~ împreună; de comun acord.

concerted [kən'sə:tid] adj. comun; concertat.

concertina [ˌkɔnsə'ti:nə] s. armonică.

concerto [kən'tʃə:tou] s. concert (instrumental).

concession [kən'seʃn] s. cedare; concesi(un)e.

conciliate [kən'silieit] vt. a împăca.

conciliatory [kən'siliətri] adj. împăciuitor(ist).

conclude [kən'klu:d] *vt.* a încheia ; a rezolva ; a desăvîrși ; a conchide. *vi.* a se încheia.

concise [kən'sais] *adj.* concis ; lapidar ; succint.

conclusion [kən'klu:ʒn] *s.* concluzie ; încheiere ; rezolvare.

conclusive [kən'klu:siv] *adj.* concludent ; hotărîtor.

concoct [kən'kɔkt] *vt.* a pregăti ; a născoci.

concoction [kən'kɔkʃn] *s.* născocire.

concord ['kɔŋkɔ:d] *s.* armonie.

concordance [kən'kɔ:dns] *s.* acord ; index ; glosar.

concourse ['kɔŋkɔ:s] *s.* conjunctură ; adunare.

concrete¹ ['kɔnkri:t] *s.* beton. *adj.* concret. *vt.* a betona.

concrete² [kən'kri:t] *vi.* a se aglomera.

concur [kən'kə:] *vi.* a fi de acord ; a se uni ; a coincide.

concurrence [kən'kʌrns] *s.* acord ; concurs (de împrejurări etc.).

concurrent [kən'kʌrnt] *adj.* paralel ; concomitent.

concussion [kən'kʌʃn] *s.* lovitură ; comoție.

condemn [kən'dem] *vt.* a condamna ; a confisca.

condense [kən'dens] *vt.* a condensa ; a concentra. *vi.* a se condensa.

condenser [kən'densə] *s.* condensator.

condescend [ˌkɔndi'send] *vi.* a catadicsi.

condescension [ˌkɔndi'senʃn] *s.* condescendență.

condign [kən'dain] *adj.* meritat.

condition [kən'diʃn] *s.* condiție ; stare ; rang ; *pl.* împrejurări. *vt.* a determina ; a condiționa.

condole [kən'doul] *vi.* a exprima condoleanțe.

condolence [kən'doulans] *s.* condoleanțe.

condone [kən'doun] *vt.* a trece cu vederea ; a accepta.

conducive [kən'dju:siv] *adj.: to be ~ to* a determina.

conduct¹ ['kɔndʌkt] *s.* purtare ; conducere.

conduct² [kən'dʌkt] *vt.* a (con)duce ; a stăpîni ; a îndeplini ; a transmite. *vi. muz.* a dirija. *vr.* a se purta.

conductor [kən'dʌktə] *s.* conduc(ă)tor ; dirijor ; taxator.

conduit ['kɔndit] *s.* conductă.

cone [koun] *s.* con.

confection [kən'fekʃn] *s.* prăjitură ; *pl.* dulciuri ; *pl.* confecții.

confectioner [kən'fekʃnə] *s.* cofetar.

confectionery [kən'fekʃnəri] *s.* cofetărie ; dulciuri.

confederacy [kən'fedrəsi] *s.* (con)federație.

confederate¹ [kən'fedrit] *s.* aliat ; federat. *adj.* federal.

confederate² [kən'fedəreit] *vt., vi.* a (se) federaliza.

confer [kən'fə:] *vt.* a conferi. *vi.* a se consulta.

conference ['kɔnfrns] *s.* schimb de vederi, conferință ; congres ; adunare.

confess [kən'fes] *vt., vi.* a (se) mărturisi.

confession [kən'feʃn] *s.* spovedanie ; mărturisire.

confessor [kən'fesə] *s.* duhovnic.

confide [kən'faid] *vt.* a mărturisi; a încredinţa. *vi.* a se încrede.

confidence ['kɔnfidns] *s.* credinţă; încredere; confidenţă.

confident ['kɔnfidnt] *adj.* încrezător.

confine [kən'fain] *vt.* a limita; a îngrădi; a ţine închis.

confined [kən'faind] *adj.* limitat; îngust; strîmt; *she is* ~ naşte; e lăuză.

confinement [kən'fainmənt] *s.* captivitate; închisoare; naştere; lăuzie.

confines ['kɔnfainz] *s. fig. pl.* graniţă.

confirm [kən'fə:m] *vt.* a confirma; a întări.

confirmation [ˌkɔnfə'meiʃn] *s.* confirmare; întărire.

confirmed [kən'fə:md] *adj.* înrăit, inveterat; confirmat.

confiscate ['kɔnfiskeit] *vt.* a confisca.

conflict ['kɔnflikt] *s.* conflict.

confluence ['kɔnfluəns] *s.* confluenţă; întîlnire.

conform [kən'fɔ:m] *vt.* a pune de acord. *vi.* a se conforma.

conformist [kən'fɔ:mist] *s.* conformist.

conformity [kən'fɔ:miti] *s.* conformitate; supunere.

confound [kən'faund] *vt.* a buimăci; a încurca; a înfrînge; ~ *it!* dracul să-l ia!

confront [kən'frʌnt] *vt.* a confrunta; a opune; a înfrunta.

confuse [kən'fju:z] *vt.* a încurca.

confusion [kən'fju:ʒn] *s.* încurcătură; ruşine.

congeal [kən'dʒi:l] *vt., vi.* a îngheţa; a congela.

congenial [kən'dʒi:njəl] *adj.* plăcut; potrivit.

congestion [kən'dʒestʃn] *s.* congestie; congestionare; aglomeraţie.

conglomerate [kən'glɔmərit] *s.* aglomeraţie; conglomerat. *adj.* conglomerat. *vt., vi.* a (se) aglomera.

congratulate [kən'grætjuleit] *vt., vr.* a (se) felicita.

congratulations [kənˌgrætju'leiʃnz] *s. pl.* felicitări.

congregate ['kɔŋgrigeit] *vt., vi.* a (se) aduna.

congregation [ˌkɔŋgri'geiʃn] *s.* parohie; enoriaşi.

congress ['kɔŋgres] *s.* congres; conferinţă; *amer. the Congress* Congresul (Parlamentul) S.U.A.

Congressman ['kɔŋgresmən] *s. amer.* membru al Camerei Reprezentanţilor.

conjecture [kən'dʒektʃə] *s.* ipoteză; presupunere. *vt., vi.* a presupune.

conjoint ['kɔndʒɔint] *adj.* unit; comun.

conjugate ['kɔndʒugeit] *vt.* a conjuga; a uni.

conjunction [kən'dʒʌŋkʃn] *s.* conjuncţie; unire; legătură.

conjure[1] ['kʌndʒə], *vt.* a jongla; a invoca; a evoca.

conjure[2] [kən'dʒuə] *vt.* a implora.

conjurer ['kʌndʒərə] *s.* scamator.

connect [kə'nekt] *vt.* a lega; a uni. *vi.* a se lega; a se uni; a se înrudi.

connection [kə'nekʃn] *s.* unire; legătură; *pl.* relaţii; clientelă.

connective [kə'nektiv] *adj.* de legătură.

connexion [kə'nekʃn] *s. v.* **connection.**

connive [kə'naiv] *vi.: to ~ at* a trece cu vederea ; a fi de coniventă cu.

connivance [kə'naivns] *s.* conivență ; complicitate.

connoisseur [ˌkɔni'sə:] *s.* cunoscător.

connotation [ˌkɔno'teiʃn] *s.* implicație.

connote [kɔ'nout] *vt.* a implica.

conquer ['kɔŋkə] *vt.* a cuceri ; a ocupa ; a înfrînge ; a stăpîni.

conqueror ['kɔŋkrə] *s.* cuceritor ; învingător.

conquest ['kɔŋkwest] *s.* cucerire.

consanguinity [ˌkɔnsæŋ'gwiniti] *s.* rudenie de sînge.

conscience ['kɔnʃns] *s.* simț etic ; conştiință.

conscientious [ˌkɔnʃi'enʃəs] *adj.* conştiincios.

conscientious objector [ˌkɔnʃi'enʃəs əb'dʒektə] *s.* adversar al omuciderii *sau* violenței.

conscious ['kɔnʃəs] *adj.* conştient ; ştiutor.

consciousness ['kɔnʃəsnis] *s.* conştiență ; conştiință.

conscript¹ ['kɔnskript] *s.* recrut.

conscript² [kən'skript] *vt.* a recruta, a încorpora.

conscription [kən'skripʃn] *s.* recrutare (obligatorie).

consecrate ['kɔnsikreit] *vt.* a sfinți ; a consacra.

consensus [kən'sensəs] *s.* consens.

consent [kən'sent] *s.* încuviințare. *vi.* a încuviința.

consequence ['kɔnskwəns] *s.* urmare ; importanță.

consequential [ˌkɔnsi'kwenʃl] *adj.* care-şi dă importanță ; firesc.

consequently ['kɔnskwəntli] *adv.* în consecință. *conj.* aşadar, prin urmare.

conservation [ˌkɔnsə'veiʃn] *s.* păstrare.

conservatism [kən'sə:vətizəm] *s.* caracter conservator.

conservative [kən'sə:vətiv] *s., adj.* conservator ; moderat.

conservatory [kən'sə:vətri] *s.* seră ; conservator.

conserve [kən'sə:v] *s.* dulceață ; gem. *vt.* a păstra ; a conserva.

consider [kən'sidə] *vt., vi.* a se gîndi ; a chibzui ; a considera.

considerable [kən'sidrəbl] *adj.* considerabil ; mare ; important.

considerably [kən'sidrəbli] *adv.* foarte.

considerate [kən'sidrit] *adj.* moderat ; grijuliu.

consideration [kənˌsidə'reiʃn] *s.* chibzuială ; considerent ; *under ~* în studiu ; *in ~ of* pe baza.

considering [kən'sidriŋ] *adv.* la urma urmei. *prep.* ținînd seama de (împrejurări etc.).

consign [kən'sain] *vt.* a expedia ; a încredința ; a înmîna.

consignee [ˌkɔnsai'ni:] *s.* destinatar.

consigner [kən'sainə] *s.* expeditor.

consignment [kən'sainmənt] *s.* expediere ; transport ; încredințare.

consist [kən'sist] *vi.: to ~ of*

a fi alcătuit din; *to ~ in* a consta în.

consistence [kən'sistns] *s.* consistență.

consistency [kən'sistnsi] *s.* consecvență; consistență.

consistent [kən'sistnt] *adj.* consecvent; *~ with* potrivit cu.

consolation [ˌkɔnsə'leiʃn] *s.* consolare.

consolatory [kən'sɔlətri] *adj.* de consolare.

console[1] ['kɔnsoul] *s.* consolă.

console[2] [kən'soul] *vt.* a consola.

consolidate [kən'sɔlideit] *vt.*, *vi.* a (se) întări; a (se) uni.

consonant ['kɔnsənənt] *s.* consoană. *adj.* armonios; corespunzător.

consort[1] ['kɔnsɔ:t] *s.* consort; consoartă; însoțitor.

consort[2] [kən'sɔ:t] *vi.* a se înțelege; a se potrivi a se înhăita.

conspicuous [kən'spikjuəs] *adj.* remarcabil; evident; izbitor.

conspiracy [kən'spirəsi] *s.* complot.

conspirator [kən'spirətə] *s.* complotist.

conspire [kən'spaiə] *vt.*, *vi.* a unelti.

constable ['kʌnstəbl] *s.* polițist.

constabulary [kən'stæbjuləіi] *s.* jandarmerie; poliție.

constancy ['kɔnstnsi] *s.* constanță.

constant ['kɔnstnt] *s.* constantă. *adj.* constant.

constantly ['kɔnstntli] *adv.* mereu; adeseori.

constellation [ˌkɔnstə'leiʃn] *s.* constelație.

consternate ['kɔnstəneit] *vt.* a consterna.

consternation [ˌkɔnstə'neiʃn] *s.* consternare.

constituency [kən'stitjuənsi] *s.* circumscripție electorală; alegători.

constituent [kən'stitjuənt] *s.* element constitutiv; alegător. *adj.* constituant.

constitute ['kɔnstitju:t] *vt.* a constitui; a înființa; a numi; a promulga.

constitution [ˌkɔnsti'tju:ʃn] *s.* constituție; structură (psihică).

constitutional [ˌkɔnsti'tju:ʃənl] *s.* plimbare. *adj.* constituțional; structural.

constrain [kən'strein] *vt.* a constrînge.

constrained [kən'streind] *adj.* chinuit.

constraint [kən'streint] *s.* constrîngere.

construct [kən'strʌkt] *vt.* a construi; a alcătui.

construction [kən'strʌkʃn] *s.* construcție; interpretare; explicație; *under ~* în construcție.

construe [kən'stru:] *vt.* a analiza gramatical; a traduce; a interpreta.

consul ['kɔnsl] *s.* consul.

consult [kən'sʌlt] *vt.* a consulta; a chibzui asupra. *vi.* a se consulta.

consume [kən'sju:m] *vt.* a distruge; a consuma; a epuiza; a irosi. *vi.* a se consuma; a se chinui.

consumer [kən'sju:mə] *s.* consumator.

consumer goods [kən'sju:mə-ˌgudz] *s.* bunuri de larg consum.

consummate¹ [ken'sʌmit] *adj.* desăvîrşit ; complet.

consummate² ['kɔnsəmeit] *vt.* a consuma ; a desăvîrşi ; a realiza.

consummation [ˌkɔnsʌ'meiʃn] *s.* desăvîrşire ; împlinire ; încoronare.

consumption [kən'sʌmʃn] *s.* consum(aţie) ; oftică.

consumptive [kən'sʌmtiv] *s.*, *adj.* tuberculos.

contact¹ ['kɔntækt] *s.* contact ; comunicaţie ; comunicare ; înţelegere ; discuţie ; relaţie ; legătură.

contact² [kən'tækt] *vt.* a lua legătura cu.

contagion [kən'teidჳn] *s.* molipsire ; răspîndire.

contagious [kən'teidჳəs] *adj.* contagios.

contain [kən'tein] *vt.* a conţine ; a reţine ; a limita.

container [kən'teinə] *s.* cutie ; borcan ; vas.

contaminate [kən'tæmineit] *vt.* a contamina ; a murdări.

contemplate ['kɔntempleit] *vt.* a contempla ; a întrezări ; a plănui.

contemplation [ˌkɔntem'pleiʃn] *s.* contemplaţie ; plan.

contemporaneous [kənˌtempə-ˌreinjəs] *adj.* contemporan ; concomitent.

contemporary [kən'temprəri] *s.*, *adj.* contemporan.

contempt [kən'temt] *s.* dispreţ ; sfidare.

contemptible [kən'temtibl] *adj.* nevrednic ; ruşinos.

contemptuous [kən'temtjuəs] *adj.* dispreţuitor.

contend [kən'tend] *vt.* a susţine ; a argumenta. *vi.* a se lupta ; a se întrece ; a se certa.

content¹ [kən'tent] *s.* mulţumire ; tihnă ; *to one's heart's* ~ după pofta inimii. *adj.* mulţumit ; doritor ; dispus. *vt.* a satisface.

content² ['kɔntent] *s.* conţinut ; sens ; *pl.* cuprins ; tablă de materii.

contention [kən'tenʃn] *s.* discordie ; dezbatere.

contentious [kən'tenʃəs] *adj.* certăreţ ; discutabil.

contest¹ ['kɔntest] *s.* luptă ; concurs.

contest² [kən'test] *vt.* a contesta ; a(-şi) disputa.

contestant [kən'testnt] *s.* concurent.

context ['kɔntekst] *s.* context.

contiguity [ˌkɔnti'gjuiti] *s.* învecinare, alăturare ; atingere.

contiguous [kən'tigjuəs] *adj.* învecinat, alăturat.

continence ['kɔntinəns] *s.* stăpînire ; abstinenţă.

continent ['kɔntinənt] *s.* continent ; *the C* ~ Europa. *adj.* stăpînit ; cumpătat.

continental [ˌkɔnti'nentl] *s.* european. *adj.* continental ; european.

contingency [kən'tindჳnsi] *s.* posibilitate ; probabilitate ; eventualitate.

contingent [kən'tindჳnt] *s.* contingent ; detaşament. *adj.* probabil ; eventual.

continual [kən'tinjuəl] *adj.* repetat ; necontenit.

continually [kən'tinjuəli] *adv.* repetat.

continuance [kən'tinjuəns] *s.* durată; permanenţă.

continuation [kənˌtinju'eiʃn] *s.* continuare; adaos; anexă.

continue [kən'tinju] *vt.* a continua; *to be ~d* va urma. *vi.* a merge mai departe; a rămîne mai departe.

continuity [ˌkɔnti'njuiti] *s.* continuitate; continuare; comperaj; *cin.* listă de titluri *sau* de montaj.

continuous [kən'tinjuəs] *adj.* permanent; continuu.

contort [kən'tɔːt] *vt.* a suci; a deforma.

contortion [kən'tɔːʃn] *s.* contorsiune; schimă.

contortionist [kən'tɔːʃnist] *s.* caricaturist; contorsionist.

contour ['kɔntuə] *s.* contur.

contract¹ ['kɔntrækt] *s.* contract; acord.

contract² [kən'trækt] *vt.* a contracta; a limita; a deprinde. *vi.* a se (re)strînge.

contraction [kən'trækʃn] *s.* contracţie; formă contrasă.

contractor [kən'træktə] *s.* antreprenor; furnizor.

contradict [ˌkɔntrə'dikt] *vt.* a contrazice; a încălca.

contradiction [ˌkɔntrə'dikʃn] *s.* contradicţie; contrazicere; negare; neînţelegere.

contradictory [ˌkɔntrə'diktri] *adj.* contradictoriu.

contraption [kən'træpʃn] *s.* dispozitiv; rablă.

contrariety [ˌkɔntrə'raiəti] *s.* contradicţie; antagonism.

contrarily ['kɔntrərili] *adv.* invers.

contrariwise ['kɔntrəriwaiz] *adv.* dimpotrivă; invers; în caz contrar.

contrary ['kɔntrəri] *adj.* contrar; nefavorabil; încăpăţînat; *on the ~* dimpotrivă.

contrast¹ ['kɔntræst] *s.* contrast; opoziţie.

contrast² [kən'træst] *vt., vi.* a contrasta; a (se) compara.

contravene [ˌkɔntrə'viːn] *vt.* a încălca; a contrazice.

contribute [kən'tribjut] *vt.* a contribui cu; a da; a trimite (colaborări). *vi.* a-şi aduce contribuţia; a colabora la o publicaţie.

contribution [ˌkɔntri'bjuːʃn] *s.* contribuţie; colaborare.

contributor [kən'tribjutə] *s.* colaborator.

contributory [kən'tribjutri] *adj.* auxiliar; folositor.

contrite ['kɔntrait] *adj.* pocăit.

contrition [kən'triʃn] *s.* (po-)căinţă.

contrivance [kən'traivns] *s.* născocire; dispozitiv.

contrive [kən'traiv] *vt.* a născoci; a izbuti să. *vi.* a izbuti.

control [kən'troul] *s.* control; stăpînire; autoritate; comandă; influenţă; combatere; *beyond ~* de nestăpînit. *vt.* a stăpîni; a verifica; a combate.

controller [kən'troulə] *s.* controlor; regulator.

controversial [ˌkɔntrə'vəːʃl] *adj.* controversat.

controversy ['kɔntrəvəːsi] *s.* controversă.

contumely ['kɔntjumli] *s.* dispreţ; obrăznicie; insultă.

contusion [kən'tjuːʒn] s. contuzie.

conundrum [kə'nʌndrəm] s. joc de cuvinte ; enigmă.

convalescence [ˌkɔnvə'lesns] s. convalescenţă.

convene [kən'viːn] vt. a convoca. vi. a se aduna.

convenience [kən'viːnjəns] s. convenienţă ; avantaj ; pl. confort.

convenient [kən'viːnjənt] adj. convenabil.

convent ['kɔnvnt] s. mănăstire de maici.

convention [kən'venʃn] s. convenţie ; congres.

conventional [kən'venʃənl] adj. conventional ; banal ; tradiţional.

converge [kən'vəːdʒ] vt., vi. a (se) concentra.

conversant [kən'vəːsnt] adj. : to be ~ with a cunoaşte bine.

conversation [ˌkɔnvə'seiʃn] s. conversaţie ; discuţie.

conversational [ˌkɔnvə'seiʃənl] adj. de conversaţie ; flecar.

converse[1] ['kɔnvəːs] adj. opus.

converse[2] [kən'vəːs] vi. a conversa.

conversely ['kɔnvəːsli] adj. invers.

conversion [ˌkən'vəːʃn] s. (pre)-schimbare ; conversi(un)e.

convert[1] ['kɔnvəːt] s. convertit.

convert[2] [kən'vəːt] vt. a (pre)-schimba ; a converti.

convertible [kən'vəːtəbl] adj. transformabil ; decapotabil.

convey [kən'vei] vt. a transmite.

conveyance [kən'veiəns] s. transmitere ; transfer ; vehicul.

conveyer [kən'veiə] s. mesager ; curier ; tehn. conveier.

convict[1] ['kɔnvikt] s. condamnat ; ocnaş.

convict[2] [kən'vikt] vt. a condamna ; a declara vinovat.

conviction [kən'vikʃn] s. convingere ; condamnare ; declarare a vinovăţiei.

convince [kən'vins] vt. a convinge.

convincing [kən'vinsiŋ] adj. convingător.

convivial [kən'viviəl] adj. vesel ; amabil.

conviviality [kənˌvivi'æliti] s. veselie ; amabilitate.

convocation [ˌkɔnvə'keiʃn] s. convocare ; întrunire.

convoke [kən'vouk] vt. a convoca.

convolvulus [kən'vɔlvjuləs] s. rochiţa-rîndunelei.

convoy ['kɔnvɔi] s. convoi ; alai. vt. a escorta.

convulse [kən'vʌls] vt. a zgudui.

convulsion [kən'vʌlʃn] s. convulsie ; zguduire.

coo [kuː] s. gungurit. vt., vi. a gunguri.

cook [kuk] s. bucătar, bucătăreasă. vt. a găti ; a falsifica ; a născoci. vi. a (se) găti.

cooker ['kukə] s. maşină de gătit.

cookery ['kukəri] s. artă culinară.

cookery book ['kukəribuk] s. carte de bucate.

cookie, cooky ['kuki] s. pişcot ; prăjitură.

cool [kuːl] adj. răcoros ; calm ; liniştit ; fig. glacial ; a ~ thousand nici mai mult nici mai puţin decît o mie. *vt.*, *vi.* a (se) răci ; *to ~ down* sau *off* a se linişti.

cooler ['ku:lə] *s.* vas de răcire.

cool-headed ['ku:l'hedid] *s.* calm.

coolness ['ku:lnis] *s.* răcoare ; *fig.* răceală ; calm.

coop [ku:p] *s.* coteţ. *vt.* a închide.

cooper ['ku:pə] *s.* dogar.

co-operate [ko'ɔpəreit] *vi.* a colabora ; a se uni.

co-operation [ko,ɔpə'reiʃn] *s.* colaborare.

co-operative [ko'ɔprətiv] *adj.* cooperatist.

co-operative farm [ko'ɔprətiv ,fa:m] *s.* cooperativă agricolă de producţie.

co-operative farmer [ko'ɔprətiv ,fa:mə] *s.* ţăran cooperator.

co-operative society [ko'ɔprətiv sə,saiəti] *s.* cooperativă.

co-opt [ko'ɔpt] *vt.* a coopta.

co-ordinate¹ [ko'ɔ:dnit] *adj.* coordonat.

co-ordinate² [ko'ɔ:dineit] *vt.* a coordona.

cop [kɔp] *s.* poliţai ; detectiv.

co-partner ['kou'pa:tnə] *s.* tovarăş, asociat.

cope [koup] *vi.* : *to ~ with* a face faţă la.

copious ['koupjəs] *adj.* abundent ; fecund.

copper ['kɔpə] *s.* aramă ; bănuţ ; cazan ; poliţai. *vt.* a arămi.

copperplate ['kɔpəpleit] *s.* zinc ; clişeu pe metal ; caligrafie.

coppice ['kɔpis] *s.* pădure tînără ; tufişuri.

copse [kɔps] *s.* *v.* **coppice.**

copy ['kɔpi] *s.* copie ; exemplar ; model ; manuscris pentru tipar ; subiect. *vt.*, *vi.* a copia ; a imita.

copy-book ['kɔpibuk] *s.* caiet.

copyhold ['kɔpihould] *s.* (drept de) proprietate.

copyright ['kɔpirait] *s.* drept de autor. *adj.* apărat de legea drepturilor de autor.

coquettish [ko'ketiʃ] *adj.* cochet.

coral ['kɔrl] *s.*, *adj.* coral.

cord [kɔ:d] *s.* funie ; coardă.

cordial ['kɔ:djəl] *s.* tonic. *adj.* cald ; prietenos ; întăritor.

cordiality [,kɔ:dj'æliti] *s.* cordialitate ; sinceritate.

cordon ['kɔ:dn] *s.* cordon.

corduroy ['kɔ:dərɔi] *s.* pluşcord ; (pantaloni de) catifea reiată.

core [kɔ:] *s.* miez ; inimă.

cork [kɔ:k] *s.* dop ; plută. *vt.* a astupa cu un dop.

corkscrew ['kɔ:kskru:] *s.* tirbuşon.

corn [kɔ:n] *s.* (bob de) cereale ; grîu ; *amer.* porumb ; *anat.* bătătură. *vt.* a săra.

corncob ['kɔ:nkɔb] *s.* ştiulete.

corner ['kɔ:nə] , *s.* colţ ; cotlon. *vi.* a înghesui ; a încolţi.

corner-stone ['kɔ:nəstoun] *s.* piatră unghiulară ; temelie (*fig.*).

cornet ['kɔ:nit] *s.* cornet ; *muz.* corn.

cornflour ['kɔ:nflauə] *s.* mălai.

coronation [,kɔrə'neiʃn] *s.* încoronare.

coroner ['kɔrənə] *s.* procuror.

coronet ['kɔrənit] *s.* coroniţă.

corporal ['kɔ:prl] *s.* caporal. *adj.* corporal.

corporate ['kɔ:prit] *adj.* unit ; comun.

corporation [ˌkɔːpəˈreiʃn] s. municipalitate; societate (pe acţiuni).

corporeal [kɔːˈpɔːriəl] adj. trupesc; fizic.

corps [kɔː] s. corp (de armată).

corpse [kɔːps] s. cadavru.

corpuscle [ˈkɔːpʌsl] s. globulă; corpuscul.

corral [kɔˈrɑːl] s. împrejmuire. vt. a împrejmui.

correct [kəˈrekt] adj. just; exact; corespunzător. vt. a corecta.

correction [kəˈrekʃn] s. corectură; corectiv.

correspond [ˌkɔrisˈpɔnd] vi. a corespunde; a coresponda.

correspondence [ˌkɔrisˈpɔndəns] s. acord; armonie; corespondenţă.

correspondent [ˌkɔrisˈpɔndənt] s. corespondent. adj. corespunzător.

corresponding [ˌkɔrisˈpɔndiŋ] adj. corespunzător; corespondent; în corespondenţă.

corroborate [kəˈrɔbəreit] vt. a confirma; a întări; a verifica.

corrode [kəˈroud] vt., vi. a (se) roade; a (se) rugini.

corrosion [kəˈrouʒn] s. coroziune; ruginire.

corrosive [kəˈrousiv] s., adj. corosiv.

corrugate [ˈkɔrugeit] vt., vi. a (se) încreţi.

corrugated iron [ˈkɔrugeitid ˈaiən] s. tablă ondulată.

corrupt [kəˈrʌpt] adj. putred, stricat; corupt; stîlcit; pocit. vt. a corupe; a mitui; a stîlci; a poci. vi. a fi corupt; a se strica.

corruption [kəˈrʌpʃn] s. putreziciune, descompunere; corupţie; stîlcire.

corrupt practices [kəˈrʌpt ˈpræktisiz] s. mită; corupţie.

corsair [ˈkɔːsɛə] s. pirat.

cosine [ˈkousain] s. cosinus.

cosmonaut [ˈkɔzmonɔːt] s. cosmonaut.

cosmopolitan [ˌkɔzməˈpɔlitən] s., adj. cosmopolit.

Cossack [ˈkɔsæk] s. cazac. adj. căzăcesc.

cost [kɔst] s. cost; preţ; pl. cheltuieli (de judecată). vi. inf., trec. şi part. trec. a costa.

coster(monger) [ˈkɔstə(mʌŋgə)] s. vînzător ambulant de zarzavaturi (şi fructe).

costive [ˈkɔstiv] adj. constipat.

costly [ˈkɔstli] adj. costisitor.

costume [ˈkɔstjuːm] s. costum; taior.

cosy [ˈkouzi] adj. cald; plăcut; confortabil.

cot [kɔt] s. pătuţ; pat de campanie; colibă; căsuţă.

cottage [ˈkɔtidʒ] s. căsuţă; vilă mică.

cotton [ˈkɔtn] s. (ţesături de) bumbac; aţă.

cotton-wool [ˈkɔtnˈwul] s. vată; tifon.

couch [kautʃ] s. divan; pat. vt. a exprima; a înclina; a culca.

cough [kɔf] s. tuse; răceală. vt., vi. a tuşi.

cough-drop [ˈkɔfˌdrɔp] s. pastilă sau bomboană contra tusei.

could [kəd, kud] v. mod. trec. de la can.

council ['kaunsl] *s.* sfat.

councillor ['kaunsilə] *s.* consilier.

counsel ['kaunsl] *s.* sfat; consilier; avocat. *vt.* a sfătui.

counsellor ['kaunslə] *s.* sfetnic; avocat.

count [kaunt] *s.* socoteală; cont; conte (în afara teritoriului Angliei). *vt.* a socoti, a considera. *vi.* a conta; a numără.

countenance ['kauntinəns] *s.* înfățișare; expresie; încurajare. *vt.* a sprijini.

counter ['kauntə] *s.* tejghea; fisă; jeton. *adj.* opus. *vt., vi.* a (se) opune. *adv.* împotrivă.

counteract [,kauntə'rækt] *vt.* a contracara.

counterfeit ['kauntəfit] *s.* fals; fals(ificator); impostor. *adj.* fals; falsificat. *vt.* a falsifica; a imita.

counterfoil ['kauntəfɔil] *s.* contramarcă; cotor.

countermand [,kauntə'mɑ:nd] *s.* (ordin de) revocare. *vt.* a contramanda, a revoca.

counter-offensive ['kauntərɔ'fensiv] *s.* contraofensivă.

counterpane ['kauntəpein] *s.* cuvertură.

counterpart ['kauntəpɑ:t] *s.* corespondent.

counterpoint ['kauntəpoint] *s.* contrapunct.

counterpoise ['kauntəpoiz] *s.* contragreutate; contrapondere. *vt.* a contrabalansa.

counter-revolution ['kauntərevə,lu:ʃn] *s.* contrarevoluție.

countersign ['kauntəsain] *s.* parolă; contrasemnătură. *vt.* a contrasemna.

countess ['kauntis] *s.* contesă.

countless ['kauntlis] *adj.* nenumărat; infinit.

country ['kʌntri] *s.* țară; stat; patrie; națiune; provincie; sat; *in the* ~ la țară.

country dance ['kʌntri,dɑ:ns] *s.* dans popular; contradanț.

countryman ['kʌntrimən] *s.* țăran; conațional.

countryside ['kʌntri'said] *s.* țară; provincie; peisaj.

county ['kaunti] *s.* district; comitat.

county town ['kaunti,taun] *s.* capitală de comitat *sau* de ținut.

coup (d'état) ['ku:(dei'tɑ:)] *s.* lovitură de stat.

couple ['kʌpl] *s.* pereche; cuplu. *vt.* a cupla; a uni.

couplet ['kʌplit] *s.* cuplet.

coupon ['ku:pɔn] *s.* cupon; bon de cartelă.

courage ['kʌridʒ] *s.* curaj.

courageous [kə'reidʒəs] *adj.* curajos.

courier ['kuriə] *s.* curier.

course [kɔ:s] *s.* înaintare; rută; curs; teren; conduită; fel de mîncare; șir; rînd; durată; *pl.* obiceiuri; menstruație; *in due* ~ la timpul său; *of* ~ bineînțeles. *vt.* a fugări. *vi.* a fugi; a curge.

court [kɔ:t] *s.* tribunal; curte; teren sportiv. *vt.* a curta; a urmări.

courteous ['kə:tjəs] *adj.* curtenitor.

courtesy ['kə:tisi] *s.* curtoazie; favoare.

courtier ['kɔ:tjə] *s.* curtean.

courtly ['kɔ:tli] *adj.* politicos.

court-martial ['kɔ:t'mɑ:ʃl] *s.* curte marţială.

courtship ['kɔ:tʃip] *s.* curte; peţire.

courtyard ['kɔ:t'jɑ:d] *s.* curtea casei.

cousin ['kʌzn] *s.* văr; vară; rudă.

cousin german ['kʌzn'dʒə:mən] *s.* văr primar; vară primară.

cover ['kʌvə] *s.* învelitoare; capac; copertă; plic; adăpost; acoperiş; paravan; mască; tacîm. *vt.* a acoperi; a adăposti; a proteja; a ascunde; a parcurge; a relata.

covering ['kʌvəriŋ] *s.* acoperiş; învelitoare; protecţie; relatare (în presă); montă.

covert ['kʌvət] *s.* adăpost. *adj.* ascuns; camuflat.

covet ['kʌvit] *vt.* a rîvni la; a pizmui.

covetous ['kʌvitəs] *adj.* pizmaş; lacom.

cow [kau] *s.* vacă; femelă (de balenă etc.). *vt.* a înfricoşa; a intimida.

coward ['kauəd] *s., adj.* fricos, laş.

cowardice ['kauədis] *s.* frică, laşitate.

cowboy ['kaubɔi] *s.* cowboy; văcar.

cower ['kauə] *vi.* a se chirci.

cowherd ['kauhə:d] *s.* văcar.

cowl [kaul] *s.* glugă.

cowpox ['kaupɔks] *s.* vaccină, vărsat negru.

cowslip ['kauslip] *s.* ciuboţica-cucului.

cox [kɔks] *s.* cîrmaci.

coxcomb ['kɔkskoum] *s.* scufie (de bufon); filfizon; îngîmfat.

coxswain ['kɔks(wei)n] *s.* cîrmaci.

coy [kɔi] *adj.* timid; modest.

crab [kræb] *s.* crab; măr pădureţ.

crabbed ['kræbid] *adj.* certăreţ; dificil; mîzgălit.

crack [kræk] *s.* spărtură; crăpătură; pocnitură; lovitură. *adj.* grozav; de prima calitate. *vt.* a crăpa; a pocni; a plesni din (bici etc.); *to* ~ *a joke* a face o glumă. *vi.* a crăpa; a se sparge; a pocni; (*d. voce*) a suna spart.

crack-brained ['krækbreind] *adj.* trăsnit; nebunesc.

cracker ['krækə] *s.* biscuit; foc de artificii, *pl.* spărgător de nuci.

cradle ['kreidl] *s.* leagăn. *vt.* a legăna; a educa; *mine.* a spăla.

craft [krɑ:ft] *s.* meserie; breaslă; viclenie; vrăjitorie; ambarcaţiune; vase; avion; aviaţie.

craftsman ['krɑ:ftsmən] *s.* meşteşugar, meseriaş.

craftsmanship ['krɑ:ftsmənʃip] *s.* artizanat.

crafty ['krɑ:fti] *adj.* viclean; înşelător.

crag [kræg] *s.* colţ de stîncă.

cram [kræm] *vt.* a îndopa; a înfunda; a învăţa; a toci (*fig.*).

cramp [kræmp] *s.* crampă; cîrcel; *tehn.* scoabă. *vt.* a înţepeni; a paraliza.

cramped [kræmpt] *adj.* strîmt; împiedicat; îmbîcsit.

crane [krein] *s.* cocor; macara.

vt. a întinde (gîtul). *vi.* a se apleca.

crank [kræŋk] *s.* manivelă; vinci; maniac.

cranky ['kræŋki] *adj.* stricat; firav; excentric.

crape [kreip] *s.* crêpe-de-Chine.

crash [kræʃ] *s.* pocnitură; trosnet; tunet; prăbuşire; crah. *vt.* a zdrobi; a turti; a dărîma. *vi.* a trosni; a se zdrobi; a se prăbuşi; a da faliment.

crass [kræs] *adj.* cras.

crate [kreit] *s.* ladă; cuşcă.

crave [kreiv] *vt.* a cere; a cerşi; a dori. *vi.* a tînji.

craving ['kreiviŋ] *s.* dor; dorinţă.

crawfish ['krɔ:fiʃ] *s.* rac.

crawl [krɔ:l] *s.* tîrîre; (înot) craul. *vi.* a se tîrî.

crayfish ['kreifiʃ] *s.* rac.

crayon ['kreiən] *s. artă* pastel; cărbune de desen.

craze [kreiz] *s.* entuziasm; nebunie; modă. *vt.* a înnebuni.

crazy ['kreizi] *adj.* nebun; entuziast; fantezist; şubred.

creak [kri:k] *s.* scîrţîit. *vi.* a scîrţîi.

cream [kri:m] *s.* caimac; smîntînă; frişcă; cremă.

crease [kri:s] *s.* dungă. *vt., vi.* a (se) îndoi; a (se) şifona.

create [kri'eit] *vt.* a crea; a produce; a bîrfi.

creation [kri'eiʃn] *s.* creaţie.

creative [kri'eitiv] *adj.* creator.

creator [kri'eitə] *s.* creator.

creature ['kri:tʃə] *s.* fiinţă; creatură.

crèche [kreiʃ] *s.* creşă.

credentials [kri'denʃlz] *s. pl.* scrisori de acreditare.

credible ['kredəbl] *adj.* demn de crezare *sau* încredere.

credit ['kredit] *s.* crezare; credinţă; încredere; reputaţie; mîndrie; credit; cont. *vt.* a crede; a acorda credit (cuiva).

creditable ['kreditəbl] *adj.* lăudabil.

credulous ['kredjuləs] *adj.* credul.

creed [kri:d] *s.* crez.

creek [kri:k] *s. geogr.* golf; *amer.* pîrîu.

creep [kri:p] *s.: to give smb. the ~s* a-ţi face piele de gîscă, a-ţi da fiori. *vi.* a se tîrî; a se scurge încet.

creeper ['kri:pə] *s.* plantă agăţătoare; insectă tîrîtoare.

crêpe [kreip] *s.* crep.

crept [krept] *vi. trec. şi part. trec. de la* **creep.**

crescent ['kresnt] *s.* semilună; crai-nou; corn. *adj.* în formă de semilună; crescînd.

crest [krest] *s.* creastă.

crest-fallen ['krest‚fɔ:ln] *adj.* dezamăgit; descurajat; necăjit.

cretonne [kre'tɔn] *s.* creton.

crevice ['krevis] *s.* crăpătură.

crew [kru:] *s.* echipaj; echipă; bandă. *vi. trec. de la* **crow.**

crib [krib] *s.* pat de copil; colibă; căsuţă; iesle; juxtă; fiţuică. *vt.* a înghesui; a copia; a plagia. *vi.* a copia; a folosi juxta.

cricket ['krikit] *s.* greiere; (jocul de) crichet; *it's not ~* nu e just *sau* frumos.

crier ['kraiə] *s. ist.* crainic.

crime [kraim] *s.* crimă; delict; ticăloşie.

criminal ['kriminl] *s.* criminal. *adj.* penal; criminal.

crimson ['krimzu] s., adj. staco-jiu. vt., vi. a (se) înroşi.

cringe [krindʒ] vi. a se face mic ; a se gudura.

cripple ['kripl] s. infirm ; invalid ; ciung ; şchiop. vt. a mutila ; a ciunti.

crises ['kraisi:z] s. pl. de la **crisis**.

crisis ['kraisis] s. criză.

crisp [krisp] adj. crocant ; tare ; creţ.

criss-cross ['kriskrɔs] adj., adv. în zigzag.

criterion [krai'tiəriən] s. criteriu.

critic ['kri˛tik] s. critic ; recenzie ; critică.

critical ['kritikl] adj. critic ; primejdios ; şicanator.

criticism ['kritisizəm] s. critică.

criticize ['kritisaiz] vt., vi. a critica.

critique [kri'ti:k] s. critică.

croak [krouk] s. orăcăit ; croncănit. vi. a orăcăi ; a croncăni ; a prevesti lucruri rele ; a muri.

crochet ['krouʃei] s. lucru de mînă. vt., vi. a croşeta.

crochet hook ['krouʃihuk] s. croşet.

crock [krɔk] s. oală ; ciob ; mîrţoagă ; infirm ; ratat.

crockery ['krɔkəri] s. oale ; olărit ; ceramică.

crocus ['kroukəs] s. brînduşă.

crony ['krouni] s. prieten la toartă.

crook [kruk] s. cîrjă ; îndoitură ; cot ; escroc. vt., vi. a (se) încovoia.

crooked ['krukid] adj. strîmb ; necinstit.

crop [krɔp] s. recoltă, cultură ; ornit. guşă ; cravaşă ; tunsoare. vt. a paşte ; a tunde ; agr. a cultiva. vi. a se ivi ; a produce ; a renta.

cropper ['krɔpə] s. plantă care dă mult rod ; cădere.

croquet ['kroukei] s. (jocul de) crochet.

cross [krɔs] s. cruce ; bara de la t ; încrucişare ; creştinism ; calvar ; corcitură. adj. supărat ; nervos ; încrucişat ; opus. vt. a traversa ; a trece ; a şterge ; a marca cu o cruce ; a încrucişa ; a se întîlni cu ; a împiedica ; to ~ smb.'s mind a trece prin mintea cuiva ; to ~ one's t's a pune punctul pe i. vi. a trece dincolo ; a se încrucişa. vr. a-şi face cruce.

cross-bar ['krɔsbɑ:] s. bară transversală.

cross-beam ['krɔsbi:m] s. grindă.

cross-bred ['krɔsbred] corcit.

cross-breed ['krɔsbri:d] s. corcitură.

cross-country ['krɔs'kʌntri] adj. pe teren variat.

cross-cut ['krɔskʌt] s. beschie ; ferăstrău.

cross-examination ['krɔsig˛zæmi-'neiʃn] s. interogatoriu (suplimentar).

cross-examine ['krɔsig'zæmin] vt. a interoga (suplimentar).

cross-eyed ['krɔsaid] adj. saşiu.

cross-fire ['krɔsfaiə] s. foc concentric.

cross-grained ['krɔsgreind] adj. neregulat ; ţîfnos.

crossing ['krɔsiŋ] s. trecere, traversare ; barieră ; pasaj de nivel.

cross-purposes ['krɔs'pə:pəsiz] s. pl. : to be at ~ a nu se înţelege.

cross-road ['krɔsroud] s. drum lateral; pl. răscruce.

cross-section ['krɔs͵sekʃn] s. tăietură transversală.

crosswise ['krɔswaiz] adv. cruciş; încrucişat.

cross-word (puzzle] ['krɔswə:d ('pʌzl)] s. cuvinte încrucişate.

crotch [krɔtʃ] s. crăcană.

crotchet ['krɔtʃit] s. muz. pătrime; capriciu; fantezie; pl. gărgăuni.

crouch [krautʃ] s. şedere pe vine. vi. a se ghemui; a şedea pe vine.

croup [kru:p] s. crup; tuse convulsivă.

crow [krou] s. cioară; cîntatul cocoşului, cucurigu. vi. a cîrîi; a cînta cucurigu.

crowbar ['kroubɑ:] s. bară de metal; gură de lup.

crowd [kraud] s. mulţime; aglomeraţie; grup. vt., vi. a (se) îngrămădi; a (se) aduna; a (se) aglomera; a (se) înghesui.

crown [kraun] s. coroană; încoronare; răsplată; (monedă de) cinci şilingi; vîrf. vt. a încorona; a încununa.

crow's-feet ['krouzfi:t] s. pl. riduri; semnele bătrîneţii.

crucial ['kru:ʃəl] adj. crucial; esenţial.

crucible ['kru:sibl] s. cazan; creuzet; calvar.

crucifix ['kru:sifiks] s. crucifix; troiţă.

crucifixion [͵kru:sifikʃn] s. răstignire.

crude [kru:d] adj. necopt; lipsit de rafinament.

cruel [kruəl] adj. sălbatic; chinuitor; crud.

cruelty ['kruəlti] s. cruzime; sălbăticie; asprime.

cruet ['kruit] s. sticluţă (pentru oţet, untdelemn); pl. serviciu de salată.

cruet stand ['kruitstænd] s. serviciu de salată.

cruise [kru:z] s. mar. croazieră; călătorie. vi. a face o croazieră; a naviga.

cruiser ['kru:zə] s. crucişător.

crumb [krʌm] s. firimitură.

crumble ['krʌmbl] vt. a fărîmiţa. vi. a se fărîmiţa; a se prăbuşi; a se ruina.

crumpet ['krʌmpit] s. gogoaşă.

crumple ['krʌmpl] vt. a îndoi; a mototoli. vi. a se mototoli; to ~ up a se prăbuşi.

crunch [krʌntʃ] s. crănţănit. vt., vi. a crănţăni; a strivi.

crusade [kru:'seid] s. cruciadă; campanie. vi. a face o cruciadă.

crusader [kru:'seidə] s. cruciat.

crush [krʌʃ] s. zdrobire; înghesuială; dragoste la prima vedere. vt. a zdrobi; a boţi. vi. a se zdrobi; a se şifona; a se înghesui.

crust [krʌst] s. crustă; scoarţă.

crustacean [krʌs'teiʃjən] s. crustaceu.

crusty ['krʌsti] adj. tare; scorţos; crocant.

crutch [krʌtʃ] s. cîrjă; sprijin.

crux [krʌks] s. miez (fig.); dificultate; cheie (fig.).

cry [krai] s. strigăt; plînset; a far ~ from cu totul altceva decît. vt. a striga; a anunţa;

to ~ *up* a lăuda. *vi.* a striga; a plînge; a țipa; *to* ~ *for* (*the moon*) a cere (imposibilul).

crying ['kraiiŋ] *adj.* urgent; strigător la cer.

cryptic ['kriptik] *adj.* tainic; obscur.

crystal ['kristl] *s.* cristal.

crystal-clear ['kristl͵kliə] *adj.* limpede ca lacrima.

cub [kʌb] *s.* pui de leu, de urs etc.

Cuban ['kju:bən] *s., adj.* cuban(ă); cubanez(ă).

cube [kju:b] *s.* cub. *adj.* cubic. *vt.* a ridica la cub.

cuckoo ['kuku:] *s.* cuc.

cucumber ['kju:kəmbə] *s.* castravete.

cud [kʌd] *s.* furaj rumegat; *to chew the* ~ *fig.* a rumega.

cuddle ['kʌdl] *vt.* a strînge în brațe; a cocoli. *vi.* a se cuibări.

cudgel ['kʌdʒl] *s.* măciucă. *vt.* a ciomăgi; *to* ~ *one's brains* a-și bate capul.

cue [kju:] *s.* replică; aluzie; indicație.

cuff [kʌf] *s.* manșetă; palmă; ghiont. *vt.* a pocni.

cuff-links ['kʌflinks] *s.* butoni de manșetă.

cull [kʌl] *vt.* a alege; a culege.

culminate ['kʌlmineit] *vi.* a culmina.

culpable ['kʌlpəbl] *adj.* vinovat.

culprit ['kʌlprit] *s.* vinovat; acuzat.

cultivate ['kʌltiveit] *vt.* a cultiva; a perfecționa.

cultivation [͵kʌlti'veiʃn] *s.* cultivare; cultură; rafinament.

cultivator ['kʌltiveitə] *s.* cultivator; mașină de plivit.

culture ['kʌltʃə] *s.* agricultură; cultură.

cultured ['kʌltʃəd] *adj.* cult; binecrescut; rafinat.

cumber ['kʌmbə] *vt.* a împovăra.

cumbersome ['kʌmbəsəm], **cumbrous** ['kʌmbrəs] *adj.* obositor; incomod; greoi.

cunning ['kʌniŋ] *s.* viclenie; abilitate. *adj.* viclean; abil; *amer.* atrăgător.

cup [kʌp] *s.* ceașcă; cupă; pahar; ventuză; *to be in one's* ~*s* a fi beat. *vt.* a face (mîinile) căuș.

cupbearer ['kʌp͵bɛərə] *s.* paharnic.

cupboard ['kʌbəd] *s.* dulap.

cupboard-love ['kʌbədlʌv] *s.* dragoste interesată.

cupful ['kʌpful] *s.* (cît încape într-o) ceașcă, cupă.

cupidity [kju'piditi] *s.* lăcomie.

cur [kə:] *s.* javră.

curable ['kjuərəbl] *adj.* vindecabil.

curate ['kjuərit] *s.* diacon.

curator [kjuə'reitə] *s.* custode; îngrijitor.

curb [kə:b] *s.* frîu; bordură. *vt.* a ține în frîu.

curd [kə:d] *s.* lapte bătut; *pl.* brînză de vaci.

curdle ['kə:dl] *vi.* (*d. lapte*) a se strica, a se tăia.

cure [kjuə] *s.* cură; remediu; vindecare. *vt.* a vindeca; a înlătura; a săra; a afuma (pește etc.).

curfew ['kə:fju:] *s.* stingerea focurilor; interzicerea circulației pe întuneric.

curio ['kjuəriou] *s.* bibelou; obiect de artă; *pl.* antichități; curiozități.

curiosity [ˌkjuəri'ɔsiti] s. curiozitate ; bibelou.

curious ['kjuəriəs] adj. curios.

curl [kə:l] s. buclă ; sul (de fum etc.). vt. a (ră)suci. vi. a se (ră)suci ; a se strîmba ; to ~ up a se încolăci.

curl-papers ['kə:lˌpeipəz] s. pl. moaţe, bigudiuri.

curmudgeon [kə:'mʌdʒn] s. zgîrie-brînză.

currant ['kʌrnt] s. stafidă.

currency ['kʌrnsi] s. răspîndire, frecvenţă ; universalitate ; monedă ; valută.

current ['kʌrnt] s. curent ; curs ; tendinţă ; drum. adj. curent.

curriculum [kə'rikjuləm] s. programă (analitică).

currish ['kə:riʃ] adj. laş ; mizerabil.

curry ['kʌri] s. condiment. vt. a găti cu sos picant ; a ţesăla ; to ~ favour with smb. a se băga pe sub pielea cuiva.

curse [kə:s] s. blestem ; înjurătură. vt. a blestema ; a înjura ; a nenoroci. vi. a blestema ; a înjura.

cursory ['kə:sri] adj. fugar.

curt [kə:t] adj. scurt ; repezit.

curtail [kə:'teil] vt. a ciunti ; a reduce.

curtailment [kə:'teilmənt] s. ciuntire ; limitare.

curtain ['kə:tn] s. perdea ; cortină ; paravan. vt. a acoperi cu perdele ; to ~ off a separa.

curtsey ['kə:tsi] s. reverenţă. vi. a face o plecăciune.

curvature ['kə:vətʃə] s. curbură.

curve [kə:v] s. curbă ; cot. vt., vi. a (se) îndoi.

cushion ['kuʃn] s. pernă de sprijin ; perniţă.

cuspidor ['kʌspidɔ:] s. amer. scuipătoare.

cuss [kʌs] s. înjurătură ; individ.

custard ['kʌstəd] s. cremă de ouă.

custodian [kʌs'toudjən] s. custode ; îngrijitor.

custody ['kʌstədi] s. pază ; închisoare.

custom ['kʌstəm] s. datină ; obicei ; clientelă ; pl. vamă.

customary ['kʌstəmri] adj. obişnuit.

customer ['kʌstəmə] s. client ; individ.

custom-house ['kʌstəmhaus] s. (post de) vamă.

cut [kʌt] s. tăietură ; reducere ; tunsoare ; scurtătură ; bucată de carne ; lovitură ; croială ; aluzie ; poligr. zinc. vt. inf., trec. şi part. trec. a tăia ; a împărţi ; a reduce ; a croi ; a cresta ; a ignora (pe cineva) ; a lipsi de la ; a micşora ; to ~ away a înlătura ; to ~ down a reteza ; a dărîma ; a reduce ; to ~ off a reteza ; to ~ out a decupa ; a zdrobi ; to be ~ out for a fi potrivit pentru ; to ~ up a împărţi ; a nimici ; a chinui ; a necăji ; to ~ short a scurta ; a întrerupe ; to ~ loose a separa ; to ~ a poor figure a face impresie proastă. vi. a (se) tăia ; a fugi ; to ~ in a se băga în vorbă ; to ~ up rough a face pe nebunul.

cute [kju:t] adj. isteţ ; amer. nostim, frumos.

cutlery ['kʌtləri] s. cuţite ; tacîmuri.

cutlet ['kʌtlit] *s.* cotlet.
cutter ['kʌtə] *s.* tăietor; croitor; *mar.* cuter; barcă.
cutthroat ['kʌtθrout] *s.* asasin. *adj.* fioros.
cutting ['kʌtiŋ] *s.* tăietură; canal; defileu; butaş.
cuttle-fish ['kʌtlfiʃ] *s.* sepie.
cycle ['saikl] *s.* ciclu; veac; bicicletă. *vi.* a merge pe bicicletă.
cycling ['saikliŋ] *s.* ciclism.
cyclist ['saiklist] *s.* (bi)ciclist.
cyclone ['saikloun] *s.* ciclon.

cyclop(a)edia [ˌsaiklə'pi:djə] *s.* enciclopedie.
cylinder ['silində] *s.* cilindru.
cymbals ['simblz] *s. pl. muz.* talgere.
cynic ['sinik] *s.* cinic.
cynical ['sinikl] *adj.* cinic.
cynicism ['sinisizəm] *s.* cinism; observaţie cinică.
cypher ['saifə] *s. v.* **cipher.**
cypress ['saipris] *s.* chiparos.
czar [zɑ:] *s.* ţar.
Czech [tʃek] *s., adj.* ceh(ă); cehoslovac(ă).

D

D [di:] *s.* D, d; (nota) re.
'd[d] *v. aux., v. mod. v.* **had** sau **would**; *I'd rather* aş prefera.
dab [dæb] *s.* atingere.
dabble ['dæbl] *vt.* a stropi. *vi.* a se bălăci; a se afla în treabă.
dad(dy) ['dæd(i)] *s.* tăticu.
daffodil ['dæfədil] *s.* narcisă galbenă.
dagger ['dægə] *s.* pumnal.
dahlia ['deiliə] *s.* dalie.
daily ['deili] *s., adj., adv.* cotidian.
dainty ['deinti] *s.* delicatese; *pl.* bunătăţi. *adj.* delicat; delicios.
dairy ['dɛəri] *s.* lăptărie.
dairy-farm ['dɛərifɑ:m] *s.* fermă de lapte.
dairy-maid ['dɛərimeid] *s.* mulgătoare; lăptăreasă.
dais [deiis] *s.* estradă.

daisy ['deizi] *s. bot.* părăluţă; bumbişor; margaretă.
dalliance ['dæliəns] *s.* neseriozitate.
dally ['dæli] *vi.* a se juca; a zăbovi.
dam [dæm] *s.* zăgaz; baraj. *vt.* a stăvili.
damage ['dæmidʒ] *s.* pagubă; *pl.* daune. *vt.* a strica.
dame [deim] *s.* baroneasă; artistă emerită; *amer.* damă.
damn [dæm] *vt.* a osîndi; a blestema.
damnation [dæm'neiʃn] *s.* osîndire. *interj. amer.* la naiba!
damp [dæmp] *s.* umezeală. *adj.* umed. *vt.* a umezi; a descuraja.
dampness ['dæmpnis] *s.* umezeală; climat ploios.

dance [dɑːns] s. dans; ceai dansant. vt., vi. a dansa.

dancer ['dɑːnsə] s. dansator; balerin(ă).

dancing ['dɑːnsiŋ] s. dans; balet.

dandelion ['dændilaiən] s. păpădie.

dandruff ['dændrəf] s. mătreaţă.

dandy ['dændi] s. filfizon.

Dane [dein] s. danez(ă).

danger ['deindʒə] s. primejdie; ameninţare.

dangerous ['deindʒrəs] adj. primejdios.

dangle ['dæŋgl] vt., vi. a (se) legăna; a (se) bălăbăni; to ~ after smb. a se ţine (scai) de cineva.

Danish ['deiniʃ] s. (limba) daneză. adj. danez(ă).

dank [dæŋk] adj. umed.

dapper ['dæpə] adj. îngrijit; sclivisit.

dappled ['dæpld] adj. bălţat.

dare [dɛə] vt. a îndrăzni; a desfide; I ~ say that cred că. vi. a fi îndrăzneţ, curajos.

dare-devil ['dɛə,devl] s. aventurier temerar. adj. foarte riscant, nesăbuit.

daring ['dɛəriŋ] adj. îndrăzneţ.

dark [dɑːk] s. întuneric; ignoranţă. adj. întunecat; oacheş; tainic.

darken ['dɑːkn] vt., vi. a (se) întuneca.

darling ['dɑːliŋ] s. iubit(ă). adj. drăguţ. interj. dragă!

darn [dɑːn] vt., vi. a ţese ciorapi etc.

dart [dɑːt] s. suliţă; săgeată; izbucnire. vt. a arunca; a scoate. vi. a ţîşni; a merge ca săgeata.

dash [dæʃ] s. izbucnire; ţîşnire; plescăit; izbitură; picătură; vioiciune; fugă; liniuţă. vt. a arunca; a face să ţîşnească; a nărui. vi. a ţîşni; a se repezi.

dashing ['dæʃiŋ] adj. îndrăzneţ; vioi; elegant; chipeş.

dastard ['dæstəd] s. laş; ticălos.

data ['deitə] s. pl. date; realităţi.

date [deit] s. dată; zi; perioadă; amer. întîlnire; curmală; out of ~ demodat. vt., vi. a data.

daub [dɔːb] s. strat; pictură proastă; mîzgăleală. vt., vi. a murdări; a picta prost; a mîzgăli.

daughter ['dɔːtə] s. fiică.

daughter-in-law ['dɔːtrinlɔː] s. noră.

daunt [dɔːnt] vt. a înfricoşa.

dauntless ['dɔːntlis] adj. neînfricat.

dawdle ['dɔːdl] vt.: to ~ away a irosi (timpul). vi. a pierde vremea.

dawn [dɔːn] s. zori; dimineaţă; fig. început; răsărit. vi. a se face ziuă, a se revărsa de ziuă; a apărea; it ~ed on me that mi-am dat seama că.

day [dei] s. zi; lumină; epocă; eveniment; luptă; by ~ ziua (pe lumină); all the ~ long toată ziua; the ~ before yesterday alaltăieri; the ~ after tomorrow poimîine; the other ~ deunăzi; one ~ odată (de mult); some ~ într-o bună zi (în viitor).

daybreak ['deibreik] s. revărsatul zorilor.

day-dream ['deidriːm] s. visare.

daylight ['deilait] s. lumina zilei.

day-nursery ['dei‚nə:sri] s. cămin de zi; creşă.

daze [deiz] s. uluire. vt. a orbi; a ameţi.

dazzle ['dæzl] vt. a orbi; a lua ochii.

deacon ['di:kn] s. diacon.

dead [ded] s.: the ~ morţii; the ~ of night miezul nopţii. adj. mort; stins; total nefolosit. adv. complet.

deaden ['dedn] vt. a amorţi; a alina; a amortiza.

deadlock ['dedlɔk] s. impas.

deadly ['dedli] adj., adv. mortal.

deaf [def] adj. surd.

deafen ['defn] vt. a asurzi.

deafness ['defnis] s. surzenie.

deal [di:l] s. cantitate (mare); afacere; învoială; împărţirea cărţilor de joc; scîndură; a great ~ mult. vt. a face (cărţile). vi.: to ~ with a se ocupa de; a trata (cu); to ~ in a face negoţ cu.

dealer ['di:lə] s. negustor; jucător care împarte cărţile.

dealing ['di:liŋ] s. atitudine; relaţie; afacere.

dealt [delt] vt., vi. trec. şi part. trec. de la deal.

dean [di:n] s. arhimandrit; decan.

dear [diə] s., adj., adv. scump; my ~ dragul meu; Dear Sir Stimate domn.

dearly ['diəli] adv. scump; foarte mult.

dearness ['diənis] s. scumpete; afecţiune.

dearth [də:θ] s. lipsă.

death [deθ] s. moarte; sfîrşit; on one's ~ bed pe patul de moarte.

death-rate ['deθreit] s. mortalitate.

debase [di'beis] vt. a înjosi; a strica.

debatable [di'beitəbl] adj. discutabil; în discuţie.

debate [di'beit] s. dezbatere; discuţie. vt., vi. a discuta.

debauch [di'bɔ:tʃ] s. desfrîu. vt. a corupe; a strica.

debauchery [di'bɔ:tʃri] s. desfrîu.

debility [di'biliti] s. debilitate.

debit ['debit] s. sold debitor, debit.

debonair [‚debə'nɛə] adj. vesel; plăcut; binevoitor.

débris ['debri:] s. moloz; dărîmătură.

debt [det] s. datorie (bănească).

debtor ['detə] s. datornic.

decade ['dekeid] s. deceniu.

decadence ['dekədns] s. decadenţă.

decamp [di'kæmp] vi. a pleca; a fugi.

decant [di'kænt] vt. a turna.

decanter [di'kæntə] s. garafă.

decay [di'kei] s. putreziciune; stricăciune; carie. vi. a se strica; a putrezi; a decădea.

decease [di'si:s] s. deces. vi. a deceda.

deceit [di'si:t] s. înşelăciune, prefăcătorie.

deceitful [di'si:tfl] adj. mincinos.

deceive [di'si:v] vt. a păcăli; a înşela.

December [di'sembə] s. decembrie.

decency ['di:snsi] s. decenţă; ruşine; modestie.

decent ['di:snt] adj. decent; potrivit; cumsecade; curat; bun; de treabă.

deception [di'sepʃn] s. decepţie; înşelăciune; impostură.

deceptive [di'septiv] adj. înşelător.

decide [di'said] vt., vi. a (ɜ:) hotărî.

decidedly [di'saididli] adv. fără doar şi poate.

deciduous [di'sidjuəs] adj. cu frunze căzătoare.

decimal ['desiml] adj. zecimal.

decipher [di'saifə] vt. a descifra.

decision [di'siʒn] s. hotărîre.

decisive [di'saisiv] adj. hotărît(or).

deck [dek] s. mar. punte. vt. a împodobi; a înveseli.

deck-chair ['dek'tʃɛə] s. şezlong.

declaim [di'kleim] vt., vi. a declama.

declamation [,deklə'meiʃn] s. declamaţie; cuvîntare.

declaration [,deklə'reiʃn] s. declaraţie.

declare [di'klɛə] vt., vi. a (se) declara.

declension [di'klenʃn] s. declinare.

decline [di'klain] s. declin; slăbire; oftică. vt. a refuza. vi. a slăbi.

declivity [di'kliviti] s. pantă.

declutch ['di:'klʌtʃ] vi. a debreia.

decompose [,di:kəm'pouz] vt., vi. a (se) descompune.

decorate ['dekəreit] vt. a zugrăvi (o casă); a decora.

decoration ['dekə'reiʃn] s. împodobire; podoabă; decoraţie.

decorous [,dekərəs] adj. decent; demn; de bun gust.

decorum [di'kɔ:rəm] s. decenţă; purtare aleasă: pl. conveniente.

decoy [di'kɔi] s. momeală; capcană; provocator. vi. a momi.

decrease¹ ['di:kri:s] s. scădere; declin.

decrease² [di:'kri:s] vt., vi. a scădea; a (se) împuţina.

decree [di'kri:] s. decret. vt. a decreta; a porunci.

decrepit [di'krepit] adj. îmbătrînit; ramolit.

dedicate ['dedikeit] vt. a dedica.

dedication [,dedi'keiʃn] s. dedicaţie.

deduce [di'dju:s] vt. a deduce.

deduct [di'dʌkt] vt. a scădea.

deduction [di'dʌkʃn] s. scădere; deducţie.

deed [di:d] s. acţiune; act, faptă.

deem [di:m] vt. a considera.

deep [di:p] adj. adînc, profund; întunecat.

deepen ['di:pn] vt., vi. a (se) adînci.

deep-rooted ['di:p'ru:tid], deep-seated ['di:p'si:tid] adj. (profund) înrădăcinat.

deer [diə] s. cerb(i); căprioară.

defalcate ['di:fælkeit] vi. a delapida.

defamation [,defə'meiʃn] s. defăimare.

defame [di'feim] vt. a defăima.

default [di'fɔ:lt] s. lipsă (de la o îndatorire); neplată (a unei datorii); absenţă, contumacie.

defeat [di'fi:t] s. înfrîngere; eşec. vt. a înfrînge.

defective [di'fektiv] adj. deficient; defectiv.

defence [di'fens] s. apărare; protecţie; pledoarie.

defenceless [di'fenslis] adj. fără apărare; neajutorat.

defend [di'fend] *vt.* a apăra;
a ocroti.

defendant [di'fendənt] *s.* acuzat.

defender [di'fendə] *s.* apărător.

defense [di'fens] *s. amer. v.*
defence.

defensive [di'fensiv] *s.* defensivă, apărare. *adj.* defensiv.

defer [di'fə:] *vt.* a amîna. *vi.*
a ceda.

deference ['defrns] *s.* respect;
cedare; ascultare.

deferential [,defə'renʃl] *adj.* respectuos.

defiance [di'faiəns] *s.* sfidare;
încălcare.

defiant [di'faiənt] *adj.* sfidător.

deficiency [di'fiʃnsi] *s.* lipsă.

defile [di'fail] *vt.* a pîngări; a
spurca; a murdări.

define [di'fain] *vt.* a defini.

definite ['definit] *adj.* hotărît; clar.

definition [,defi'niʃn] *s.* defini-
ție; definire.

deflate [di'fleit] *vt.* a dezumfla; a reduce.

deflect [di'flekt] *vt., vi.* a (se)
abate.

deform [di'fɔ:m] *vt.* a deforma;
a poci.

deformity [di'fɔ:miti] *s.* difor-
mitate.

deft [deft] *adj.* abil.

defy [di'fai] *vt.* a sfida; a înfrunta; a învinge.

degenerate[1] [di'dʒenrit] *adj.* decăzut; degenerat.

degenerate[2] [di'dʒenəreit] *vi.* a
degenera.

degrade [di'greid] *vt.* a degrada.

degradation [,degrə'deiʃn] *s.* degradare; decădere.

degree [di'gri:] *s.* grad; rang;
by ~*s* treptat.

deify ['di:ifai] *vt.* a venera.

deign [dein] *vt., vi.* a catadicsi.

deity ['di:iti] *s.* zeitate.

dejected [di'dʒektid] *adj.* trist.

dejection [di'dʒekʃn] *s.* tristețe;
deprimare.

delay [di'lei] *s.* întîrziere; răgaz.
vt. a întîrzia; a amîna.

delegate[1] ['deligit] *s.* delegat.

delegate[2] ['deligeit] *vt.* a delega;
a încredința.

delegation [,deli'geiʃn] *s.* dele-
gație; delegare.

delete [di'li:t] *vt.* a șterge (cuvinte).

deletion [di'li:ʃn] *s.* ștersătură;
ștergere.

deliberate[1] [di'librit] *adj.* intenționat; bine chibzuit.

deliberate[2] [di'libəreit] *vt., vi.*
a delibera; a (se) consulta.

deliberately [di'libritli] *adv.* a-
nume; cu grijă.

deliberation [di,libə'reiʃn] *s.* grijă; intenție; deliberare.

delicacy ['delikəsi] *s.* delicatețe;
slăbiciune; trufanda.

delicate ['delikit] *adj.* delicat;
fin; firav; mofturos.

delicious [di'liʃəs] *adj.* delicios.

delight [di'lait] *s.* încîntare;
plăcere; bucurie. *vt.* a încînta.
vi.: to ~ *in* a savura.

delightful [di'laitfl] *adj.* încîntător.

delimit [di:'limit] *vt.* a delimita.

delineate [di'linieit] *vt.* a descrie; a desena.

delinquency [di'liŋkwənsi] *s.* criminalitate.

delinquent [di'liŋkwənt] *s.* delincvent.

delirious [di'liriəs] *adj.* în delir.

deliver [di'livə] *vt.* a furniza;

a oferi; a preda; a da ; a elibera ;
a rosti. *vr.* a se preda.

deliverance [di'livrns] *s.* eliberare ; izbăvire ; declarație.

delivery [di'livri] *s.* predare ; fur-
nitură ; transport ; rostire ; dic-
țiune.

delude [di'lu:d] *vt.* a înșela.

delusion [di'lu:ʒn] *s.* înșelare,
iluzie.

delusive [di'lu:siv] *adj.* înșelă-
tor ; iluzoriu.

delve [delv] *vt., vi.* a săpa; a
cerceta.

demand [di'mɑ:nd] *s.* cerere ;
pretenție ; revendicare ; necesitate ; *in great* ~ foarte căutat.

demarcation [‚di:mɑ:'keiʃn] *s.*
demarcație.

demean [di'mi:n] *vr.* a se înjosi.

demeanour [di'mi:nə] *s.* comportare.

demented [di'mentid] *adj.* nebun ; înnebunit.

demigod ['demigɔd] *s.* semizeu.

demise [di'maiz] *s.* deces.

demi-semiquaver ['demi‚semi-
'kweivə] *s. muz.* treizecidoime.

democracy [di'mɔkrəsi] *s.* de-
mocrație.

democratic [‚demə'krætik] *adj.*
democrat.

demographic [‚di:mə'græfik] *adj.*
demografic.

demolish [di'mɔliʃ] *vt.* a dărîma ; a distruge.

demolition [‚demə'liʃn] *s.* dărîmare ; ruină.

demon ['di:mən] *s.* demon.

demonstrate ['demənstreit] *vt.,*
vi. a demonstra ; a manifesta.

demonstration [‚demən'streiʃn]
s. demonstrație ; manifestație.

demonstrative [di'mɔnstrətiv]

adj. demonstrativ ; expansiv ;
vizibil.

demur [di'mə:] *s.* obiecție ; ezitare. *vi.* a șovăi ; a obiecta.

demure [di'mjuə] *adj.* serios ;
cuminte ; prefăcut.

den [den] *s.* vizuină ; tavernă.

denial [di'nail] *s.* negare ; refuz.

denizen ['denizn] *s.* locuitor (al
pădurii etc.).

denomination [di‚nɔmi'neiʃn] *s.*
nume ; numire ; categorie ; sectă.

denote [di'nout] *vt.* a indica ;
a desemna.

denounce [di'nauns] *vt.* a denunța.

dense [dens] *adj.* des ; gros ;
greu de cap.

density ['densti] *s.* densitate.

dentist ['dentist] *s.* dentist.

dentistry ['dentistri] *s.* dentis-
tică.

denunciation [di‚nʌnsi'eiʃn] *s.*
denunț(are).

deny [di'nai] *vt.* a (re)nega ; a
refuza.

depart [di'pɑ:t] *vi.* a pleca ; a
se abate ; a răposa.

department [di'pɑ:tmənt] *s.* des-
părțitură ; departament ; facultate ; minister.

department store [di'pɑ:tmənt
‚stɔ:] *s.* magazin universal.

departure [di'pɑ:tʃə] *s.* plecare ;
abatere.

depend [di'pend] *vi.* a se bizui ;
a depinde.

dependable [di'pendəbl] *adj.* de
nădejde.

dependence [di'pendəns] *s.* de-
pendență ; încredere.

dependency [di'pendənsi] *s.* colonie.

dependent [di'pendənt] *s.* întreţinut. *adj.* dependent; subordonat.

depict [di'pikt] *vt.* a descrie.

deplete [di'pli:t] *vt.* a goli.

deplore [di'plɔ:] *vt.* a deplînge.

deploy [di'plɔi] *s.* desfăşurare. *vt., vi.* a (se) desfăşura.

deport [di'pɔ:t] *vt.* a deporta. *vr.* a se purta.

deportation [ˌdi:pɔ:'teiʃn] *s.* deportare.

deportment [di'pɔ:tmənt] *s.* comportare; ţinută.

depose [di'pouz] *vt.* a demite; a debarca; a detrona.

deposit [di'pɔzit] *s.* depunere; depozit. *vt.* a depune; a depozita.

deposition [ˌdepə'ziʃn] *s.* depunere; răsturnare de la putere; depoziţie.

depositor [di'pɔzitə] *s.* depunător.

depot ['depou] *s.* depozit; depou; *amer.* ['di:pou] gară.

depraved [di'preivd] *adj.* depravat.

depravity [di'præviti] *s.* depravare; ticăloşie.

deprecate ['deprikeit] *vt.* a dezaproba.

depreciate [di'pri:ʃieit] *vt., vi.* a (se) deprecia.

depredation [ˌdepri'deiʃn] *s.* prădăciune, jaf.

depress [di'pres] *vt.* a deprima.

depression [di'preʃn] *s.* depresiune.

deprive [di'praiv] *vt.* a priva.

depth [depθ] *s.* adîncime; înţelepciune; adînc.

deputation [ˌdepju'teiʃn] *s.* delegaţie.

deputy ['depjuti] *s.* adjunct;

delegat; deputat (în afara teritoriului Angliei).

derail [di'reil] *vt.* a face să deraieze. *vi.* a deraia.

derange [di'reindʒ] *vt.* a deranja; a tulbura.

derangement [di'reindʒmənt] *s.* deranj(ament); nebunie.

Derby[1] ['dɑ:bi] *s.* derbi, cursă de cai.

derby[2] ['dɑ:bi] *s.* gambetă.

derelict ['derilikt] *adj.* părăsit; părăginit.

derision [di'riʒn] *s.* batjocură.

derisive [di'raisiv] *adj.* batjocoritor.

derivation [ˌderi'veiʃn] *s.* derivare; origine.

derivative [di'rivətiv] *s.* derivat.

derive [di'raiv] *vt.* a obţine. *vi.* a proveni; a decurge.

derogatory [di'rɔgətri] *adj.* nefavorabil; peiorativ.

derrick ['derik] *s.* macara.

descend [di'send] *vt.* a coborî. *vi.* a coborî; a se trage; a se năpusti.

descendant [di'sendənt] *s.* urmaş.

descent [di'sent] *s.* coborîre; origine; atac.

describe [dis'kraib] *vt.* a descrie, a înfăţişa.

description [dis'kripʃn] *s.* descriere, relatare; fel.

desecrate ['desikreit] *vt.* a pîngări; a înjosi.

desert[1] ['dezət] *s., adj.* pustiu.

desert[2] [di'zə:t] *s.* merit; răsplată. *vt.* a părăsi, a abandona, a lăsa la ananghie. *vi.* a dezerta.

deserter [di'zə:tə] *s.* dezertor.

desertion [di'zə:ʃn] *s.* dezertare; părăsire.

deserve [di'zə:v] *vt.* a merita; a cîştiga prin trudă.

deservedly [di'zə:vidli] *adj.* pe merit.

design [di'zain] *s.* desen; plan. *vt.* a desena; a proiecta.

designate ['dezigneit] *vt.* a indica.

designation [,dezig'neiʃn] *s.* numire.

designer [di'zainə] *s.* desenator; proiectant.

designing [di'zainiŋ] *s.* proiectare; desen. *adj.* viclean; intrigant.

desirable [di'zaiərəbl] *adj.* de dorit.

desire [di'zaiə] *s.* dorinţă. *vt.* a dori; a cere.

desirous [di'zaiərəs] *adj.* doritor.

desist [di'zist] *vi.:* to ~ from a înceta (să).

desk [desk] *s.* pupitru; birou; catedră; *com.* casă.

desolate¹ ['desəlit] *adj.* pustiu; părăsit; deznădăjduit.

desolate² ['desəleit] *vt.* a pustii; a întrista.

despair [dis'pɛə] *s.* deznădejde; chin. *vi.* a fi deznădăjduit.

despatch [dis'pætʃ] *s. v.* **dispatch.**

desperado [,despə'ra:dou] *s.* om în stare de orice; criminal.

desperate ['desprit] *adj.* nesăbuit; fără speranţă.

despicable ['despikəbl] *adj.* mizerabil; vrednic de dispreţ.

despise [dis'paiz] *vt.* a dispreţui.

despite [dis'pait] *prep.* în ciuda.

despondence [dis'pondəns] *s.* deznădejde.

despondent [dis'pondənt] *adj.* desperat; nenorocit.

dessert [di'zə:t] *s.* fructe; desert; *amer.* prăjituri, dulce.

destination [,desti'neiʃn] *s.* destinaţie.

destine ['destin] *vt.* a destina.

destiny ['destini] *s.* destin.

destitute ['destitju:t] *adj.* nevoiaş; nenorocit.

destitution [,desti'tju:ʃn] *s.* sărăcie; lipsuri.

destroy [dis'troi] *vt.* a nimici; a ucide.

destroyer [dis'troiə] *s.* distrugător.

destruction [dis'trʌkʃn] *s.* distrugere; exterminare.

destructive [dis'trʌktiv] *adj.* distrugător.

desultory ['desəltri] *adj.* dezordonat; împrăştiat.

detach [di'tætʃ] *vt.* a desprinde; a detaşa.

detachable [di'tætʃəbl] *adj.* separabil.

detachment [di'tætʃmənt] *s.* detaşament; detaşare; independenţă.

detail ['di:teil] *s.* amănunt.

detain [di'tein] *vt.* a deţine; a reţine.

detect [di'tekt] *vt.* a descoperi; a detecta.

detective [di'tektiv] *s.* detectiv.

detective story [di'tektiv,stori] *s.* roman poliţist.

detention [di'tenʃn] *s.* reţinere; detenţiune.

deter [di'tə:] *vt.* a împiedica; a reţine; a opri.

deteriorate [di'tiəriəreit] *vt., vi.* a (se) înrăutăţi.

determinate [di'tə:mnit] *adj.* determinat; fix; limitat.

determination [di͵tə:mi'neiʃn] *s.*
hotărîre ; determinare.
determinative [di'tə:minətiv] *s.*,
adj. determinant.
determine [di'tə:min] *vt.* a hotărî ; a preciza ; a stabili. *vi.*
a se hotărî.
determined [di'tə:mind] *adj.* hotărît.
deterrent [di'ternt] *s.* piedică ;
disuadare ; *pol.* factor de reţinere.
detest [di'test] *vt.* a detesta.
detestation [͵di:tes'teiʃn] *s.* ură ;
oroare.
dethrone [di'θroun] *vt.* a detrona.
détour ['deituə] *s.* întoarcere ;
ocol.
detract [di'trækt] *vt.* a defăima.
detrimental [͵detri'mentl] *adj.*
dăunător.
deuce [dju:s] *s.* numărul doi ;
dracul ; *sport* egalitate.
devastate ['devəsteit] *vt.* a pustii.
develop [di'veləp] *vt.* a dezvolta ; a manifesta ; a produce.
vi. a se dezvolta ; a se transforma.
development [di'veləpmənt] *s.*
dezvoltare ; creştere ; schimbare ; eveniment.
deviate ['di:vieit] *vi.* a se abate.
device [di'vais] *s.* plan ; intenţie ; şmecherie ; dispozitiv ; deviză.
devil ['devl] *s.* drac ; ticălos ;
nenorocit.
devilish ['devliʃ] *adj.* drăcesc.
devious ['di:vjəs] *adj.* ocolit ;
necinstit.
devise [di'vaiz] *vt.* a născoci.
devoid [di'vɔid] *adj.:* ~ of
lipsit de.
devolve [di'vɔlv] *vt.* a trans-

fera. *vi.: to* ~ *upon* a reveni ;
a incumba.
devote [di'vout] *vt.* a dedica.
devoted [di'voutid] *adj.* devotat ; credincios.
devotion [di'vouʃn] *s.* dragoste ;
devotament ; *pl.* rugăciuni.
devour [di'vauə] *vt.* a devora ;
a chinui.
devout [di'vaut] *adj.* pios ; serios ; sincer.
dew [dju:] *s.* rouă.
dewy ['dju:i] *adj.* înrourat.
dexterous ['dekstrəs] *adj.* îndemînatic.
diabetes [͵daiə'bi:ti:z] *s.* diabet.
diadem ['daiədem] *s.* diademă ;
coroniţă.
diagnosis [͵daiəg'nousis] *s.* diagnostic.
dial ['daiəl] *s.* cadran ; disc *(la
telefon).* *vt.* a face un număr de
telefon.
dialectic(al) [͵daiə'lektik(l)] *adj.*
dialectic.
dialogue ['daiələg] *s.* dialog.
diameter [dai'æmitə] *s.* diametru.
diametrically [͵daiə'metrikəli]
adv. diametral ; total.
diamond ['daiəmənd] *s.* diamant ;
caro *(la cărţi).*
diarrhoea [͵daiə'riə] *s.* diaree.
diary ['daiəri] *s.* agendă ; jurnal (intim).
dice [dais] *s. pl.* zaruri. *vi.* a
juca zaruri.
dickens ['dikinz] *s.* aghiuţă ;
how goes the ~ *?* cît e ceasul ?
dictate¹ ['dikteit] *s.* dictat ; îndemn.
dictate² [dik'teit] *vt., vi.* a dicta.
dictation [dik'teiʃn] *s.* dictare.
dictator [dik'teitə] *s.* dictator.

dictatorship [dik'teitəʃip] s. dictatură.

diction ['dikʃn] s. dicţiune.

dictionary ['dikʃnri] s. dicţionar.

did [did] v. aux., vt., vi. trec. de la **do.**

die [dai] s. zar; matriţă; perforator. vi. a muri; a fi chinuit; a dispărea; never say ~! nu te lăsa; to ~ off a se stinge (pe rînd); to ~ out a se sfîrşi; to ~ away a se ofili; to ~ down a slăbi.

die-hard ['dai'hɑːd] s. încăpăţînat; conservator; retrograd.

diet ['daiət] s. dietă; (hrană de) regim.

differ ['difə] vi. a se deosebi; a nu se înţelege.

difference ['difrns] s. deosebire; dezacord.

different ['difrnt] adj. diferit; separat.

differentiate [ˌdifə'renʃieit] vt., vi. a (se) diferenţia, a (se) deosebi.

difficult ['difiklt] adj. dificil; neplăcut.

difficulty ['difiklti] s. dificultate; piedică.

diffident ['difidnt] adj. neîncrezător.

diffuse[1] [di'fjuːs] adj. difuz; neclar.

diffuse[2] [di'fjuːz] vt., vi. a (se) difuza; a (se) răspîndi.

dig [dig] s. ghiont; ironie; pl. locuinţă. vt. a săpa; a dezgropa; a cerceta; a înghionti. vi. a săpa; a studia.

digest[1] ['daidʒest] s. rezumat; prezentare trunchiată.

digest[2] [di'dʒest] vt. a digera; a înţelege; a suporta. vi. a mistui.

digestion [di'dʒestʃn] s. digestie.

digging ['digiŋ] s. mină; pl. locuinţă.

dignified ['dignifaid] adj. demn.

dignify ['dignifai] vt. a înnobila.

dignitary ['dignitri] s. demnitar.

dignity ['digniti] s. demnitate; comportare aleasă; demnitar.

digress [dai'gres] vi. a se abate.

digression [dai'greʃn] s. digresiune.

dike [daik] s. şanţ; dig.

dilapidated [di'læpideitid] adj. dărîmat.

dilapidation [diˌlæpi'deiʃn] s. dărîmare.

dilate [dai'leit] vt., vi. a (se) dilata.

dilatory ['dilətri] adj. încet; zăbavnic.

dilettante [ˌdili'tænti] s. diletant.

diligence ['dilidʒns] s. silinţă; seriozitate.

diligent ['dilidʒnt] adj. silitor; serios.

dill [dil] s. mărar.

dilly-dally ['dilidæli] vi. a zăbovi; a fi nehotărît.

dilute [dai'ljuːt] vt. a dilua.

dilution [dai'luːʃn] s. diluare.

dim [dim] adj. ceţos; întunecos; slab; neclar; vag. vt. a (se) întuneca; a (se) înceţoşa.

dimness ['dimnis] s. neclaritate; întunecare.

dime [daim] s. amer. zece cenţi.

dimension [di'menʃn] s. dimensiune; mărime; pl. proporţii; importanţă.

diminish [di'miniʃ] vt., vi. a diminua.

diminution [ˌdimi'nju:ʃn] s. diminuare.

diminutive [di'minjutiv] s. diminutiv. adj. mic(uț); diminutival.

dimple ['dimpl] s. gropiță. vi. a face gropițe (în obraji).

din [din] s. zgomot; zarvă. vt. a repeta (zgomotos); a țipa. vi. a face gălăgie.

dine [dain] vt., vi. a (se) ospăta.

diner ['dainə] s. persoană care ia masa; vagon-restaurant.

dingy ['dindʒi] adj. murdar; fără culoare; mizerabil.

dining-car ['daiɳka:] s. vagon-restaurant.

dining-room ['daiɳrum] s. sufragerie.

dinner ['dinə] s. masa principală; prînz; cină; dineu.

dinner-jacket ['dinəˌdʒækit] s. smoching.

dinner-party ['dinəˌpa:ti] s. dineu.

dint [dint] s. semn; by ~ of datorită; prin.

dip [dip] s. baie; scăldătoare; groapă; coborîre. vt. a cufunda; a coborî; a (în)muia. vi. a coborî; a se cufunda.

diphtheria [dif'θiəriə] s. difterie.

diphthong ['difθɔɳ] s. diftong.

diplomacy [di'plouməsi] s. diplomație.

diplomatic [ˌdiplə'mætik] adj. diplomat(ic).

diplomatist [di'ploumətist] s. diplomat.

dipper ['dipə] s. căuș; polonic.

dire ['daiə] adj. cumplit; extrem.

direct [di'rekt] adj. direct; apropiat; sincer. vt. a îndruma; a conduce. vi. a dirija. adv. direct.

direction [di'rekʃn] s. direcție; indicație; conducere; îndrumare; pl. instrucțiuni; pl. adresă.

directly [di'rektli] adv. direct; imediat; curînd. conj. de îndată ce.

directness [di'rektnis] s. sinceritate; caracter deschis, drept etc.

director [di'rektə] s. îndrumător; director; membru în consiliul de administrație.

directory [di'rektri] s. ghid; carte de telefon.

dirge [də:dʒ] s. bocet.

dirigible ['diridʒəbl] adj. dirijabil.

dirk [də:k] s. stilet.

dirt [də:t] s. murdărie; țărînă; noroi; obscenitate.

dirt-cheap ['də:t'tʃi:p] adj. ieftin ca braga; pe nimic.

dirt-track ['də:t træk] s. pistă de zgură; drum nepietruit.

dirty ['də:ti] adj. murdar; obscen; (d. vreme) proastă. vt. a murdări.

disability [ˌdisə'biliti] s. incapacitate; invaliditate.

disable [dis'eibl] vt. a mutila; a răni; a face neputincios.

disabuse [ˌdisə'bju:z] vt. a dezamăgi; a lămuri; a trezi la realitate.

disadvantage [ˌdisəd'va:ntidʒ] s. dezavantaj; daună.

disadvantageous [ˌdisædva:n'teidʒəs] adj. nefavorabil.

disagree [ˌdisə'gri:] vi. a nu fi

de acord; a se certa; a fi nepotrivit; a fi dăunător.

disagreeable [͵disə'griəbl] *adj*. dezagreabil, neplăcut; nesuferit.

disagreement [͵disə'gri:mənt] *s*. dezacord.

disappear [͵disə'piə] *vi*. a dispărea.

disappoint [͵disə'pɔint] *vt*. a dezamăgi.

disappointment [͵disə'pɔintmənt] *s*. dezamăgire; necaz.

disapproval [͵disə'pru:vl] *s*. dezaprobare; critică.

disapprove ['disə'pru:v] *vt*. a dezaproba; a condamna.

disarm [dis'ɑ:m] *vt., vi*. a dezarma.

disarmament [dis'ɑ:məmənt] *s*. dezarmare.

disaster [di'zɑ:stə] *s*. dezastru.

disastrous [di'zɑ:strəs] *adj*. dezastruos.

disavow ['disə'vau] *vt*. a nega; a dezaproba; a dezavua.

disband [dis'bænd] *vt*. a demobiliza.

disbelieve ['disbi'li:v] *vt., vi*. a nu crede.

disc [disk] *s*. disc.

discard [dis'kɑ:d] *vt*. a arunca (la o parte); a ignora; a se despărți de.

discern [di'sə:n] *vt., vi*. a distinge.

discernment [di'sə:nmənt] *s*. discernămînt; clarviziune.

discharge [dis'tʃɑ:dʒ] *s*. descărcare; foc (de armă); eliberare; achitare; scurgere. *vt*. a descărca; a scoate; a elimina; a trage (o săgeată, un foc); a concedia; a lăsa la vatră; a plăti; a îndeplini.

disciple [di'saipl] *s*. discipol.

disciplinary ['disiplinəri] *adj*. disciplinar.

discipline ['disiplin] *s*. disciplină; pedeapsă. *vt*. a disciplina; a pedepsi.

disclose [dis'klouz] *v*. a dezvălui.

disclosure [dis'klouʒə] *s*. dezvăluire; declarație.

discolo(u)r [dis'kʌlə] *vt., vi*. a (se) decolora; a (se) schimba.

discomfit [dis'kʌmfit] *vt*. a necăji; a șicana.

discomfort [dis'kʌmfət] *s*. neplăcere.

disconcert [͵diskən'sə:t] *vt*. a tulbura.

disconnect ['diskə'nekt] *vt*. a separa.

disconsolate [dis'kɔnslit] *adj*. trist; neconsolat.

discontent ['diskən'tent] *s*. nemulțumire. *vt*. a nemulțumi.

discontinue ['diskən'tinju] *vt., vi*. a înceta.

discord ['diskɔ:d] *s*. neînțelegere; dezacord.

discountenance [dis'kauntinəns] *vt*. a dezaproba; a împiedica.

discourage [dis'kʌridʒ] *vt*. a descuraja; a împiedica.

discourse [dis'kɔ:s] *s*. cuvîntare; cuvînt. *vi*. a vorbi pe larg.

discourteous [dis'kə:tjəs] *adj*. nepoliticos.

discourtesy [dis'kə:tisi] *s*. nepolitețe.

discover [dis'kʌvə] *vt*. a descoperi.

discoverer [dis'kʌvərə] *s*. descoperitor.

discovery [dis'kʌvri] *s.* descoperire.

discredit [dis'kredit] *vt.* a discredita ; a nu crede.

discreet [dis'kri:t] *adj.* prudent ; discret ; la locul lui.

discrepancy [dis'krepnsi] *s.* diferenţă ; contradicţie.

discretion [dis'kreʃn] *s.* discreţie ; înţelepciune.

discriminate [dis'krimineit] *vt., vi.* a discrimina ; a· distinge ; a diferenţia.

discrimination [dis,krimi'neiʃn] *s.* discriminare ; discernămînt.

discursive [dis'kə:siv] *adj.* discursiv ; haotic.

discus ['diskəs] *s. sport.* disc.

discuss [dis'kʌs] *vt.* a discuta.

discussion [dis'kʌʃn] *s.* discuţie.

disdain [dis'dein] *s.* dispreţ. *vt.* a dispreţui.

disdainful [dis'deinfl] *adj.* dispreţuitor.

disease [di'zi:z] *s.* boală.

disembark ['disim'ba:k] *vt., vi.* a debarca.

disengage ['disin'geidʒ] *vt.* a elibera ; a desface.

disengaged ['disin'geidʒd] *adj.* liber ; neocupat.

disentangle ['disin'tæŋgl] *vt.* a descurca.

disfavour ['dis'feivə] *s.* dizgraţie. *vt.* a dezaproba.

disfigure [dis'figə] *vt.* a desfigura.

disgrace [dis'greis] *s.* ruşine ; dizgraţie. *vt.* a dezonora.

disgraceful [dis'greisfl] *adj.* ruşinos.

disguise [dis'gaiz] *s.* travestire ; travestiu ; mască ; *fig.* paravan. *vt.* a deghiza ; a travesti ; a ascunde.

disgust [dis'gʌst] *s.* dezgust. *vt.* a dezgusta.

disgusting [dis'gʌstiŋ] *adj.* dezgustător.

dish [diʃ] *s.* farfurie ; (fel de) mîncare.

dish-cloth ['diʃklɔθ] *s.* cîrpă de vase.

dishearten [dis'ha:tn] *vt.* a descuraja.

dishevel(l)ed [di'ʃevld] *adj.* zburlit.

dishonest [dis'ɔnist] *adj.* necinstit.

dishonesty [dis'ɔnisti] *s.* necinste.

dishono(u)r [dis'ɔnə] *s.* ruşine. *vt.* a dezonora.

disillusion [,disi'lu:ʒn] *s.* deziluzie. *vt.* a deziluziona ; a trezi la realitate.

disinclination [,disinkli'neiʃn] *s.* împotrivire ; repulsie.

disinfect [,disin'fekt] *vt.* a dezinfecta.

disinherit ['disin'herit] *vt.* a dezmoşteni.

disintegrate [dis'intigreit] *vt., vi.* a (se) dezintegra.

disinterested [dis'intristid] *adj.* dezinteresat.

disk [disk] *s.* disc.

dislike [dis'laik] *s.* antipatie. *vt.* a nu putea suferi.

dislocate ['disləkeit] *vt.* a disloca ; a tulbura.

disloyal ['dis'lɔil] *adj.* necredincios ; nesincer.

dismal ['dizml] *adj.* trist ; sinistru.

dismantle [dis'mæntl] *vt.* a demonta.

dismay [dis'mei] *s.* spaimă. *vt.* a înspăiminta.

dismember [dis'membə] vt. a dezmembra.

dismiss dis'mis] vt. a lăsa liber ; a concedia ; a alunga.

dismissal [dis'misl] s. concediere ; izgonire.

dismount [dis'maunt] vt. a coborî ; a demonta. vi. a descăleca ; a coborî.

disobedient [ˌdisə'bi:djənt] adj. nesupus.

disobey ['disə'ḅei] vt. a nu asculta (de).

disorder [dis'ɔ:də] s. dezordine ; tulburare.

disorderly [dis'ɔ:dəli] adj. dezordonat ; turbulent ; învălmăşit.

disorganize [dis'ɔ:gənaiz] vt. a dezorganiza.

disown [dis'oun] vt. a renega ; a dezmoşteni.

disparage [dis'pæridʒ] vt. a discredita ; a bîrfi.

disparagingly [dis'pæridʒiŋli] adv. insultător ; cu duşmănie.

disparity [dis'pæriti] s. nepotrivire ; inegalitate.

dispatch [dis'pætʃ] s. expediere ; mesaj ; telegramă ; grabă. vt. a expedia ; a termina repede ; a ucide.

dispel [dis'pel] vt. a împrăştia.

dispensary [dis'pensri] s. farmacie (filantropică).

dispensation [ˌdispən'seiʃn] s. împărţire ; dispensă.

dispense [dis'pens] vt. a distribui ; a prepara (medicamente). vi. : to ~ with a se lipsi de.

disperse [dis'pə:s] vt., vi. a (se) dispersa ; a (se) împrăştia.

dispirited [di'spiritid] adj. trist ; descurajat.

displace [dis'pleis] vt. a deplasa ; a înlocui ; a dispersa.

display [dis'plei] s. expoziţie ; manifestare ; etalare (vulgară). vt. a expune ; a arăta ; a manifesta.

displease [dis'pli:z] vt. a displăcea (cu dat.) ; a nemulţumi.

displeasure [dis'pleʒə] s. nemulţumire.

disposal [dis'pouzl] s. dispoziţie ; dispunere ; înstrăinare ; eliminare.

dispose [dis'pouz] vt. a dispune ; a predispune ; a hotărî. vi. : to ~ of a scăpa de ; a vinde.

disposition [ˌdispə'ziʃn] s. mentalitate ; dispoziţie.

dispossess [ˌdispə'zes] vt. a deposeda.

disproportionate [ˌdisprə'pɔ:ʃnit] adj. disproporţionat.

disprove [dis'pru:v] vt. a respinge ; a infirma.

disputable [dis'pju:təbl] adj. discutabil.

dispute [dis'pju:t] s. dezbatere ; ceartă ; beyond ~ indiscutabil. vt. a discuta ; a disputa. vi. a se certa.

disqualify [dis'kwɔlifai] vt. a descalifica ; a împiedica.

disquiet [dis'kwaiət] s. nelinişte. vt. a nelinişti ; a tulbura.

disregard ['disri'gɑ:d] s. neglijare ; neglijenţă ; neatenţie. vt. a nesocoti.

disrepute ['disri'pju:t] s. faimă proastă.

disrespect [ˌdisris'pekt] s. nepoliteţe.

disrespectful [ˌdisris'pektfl] adj. lipsit de respect.

disrupt [dis'rʌpt] *vt.* a fărîmiţa ; a dezbina.

disruptive [dis'rʌptiv] *adj.* care dezbină ; diversionist.

dissatisfy [di'sætisfai] *vt.* a nemulţumi.

dissection [di'sekʃn] *s.* disecţie ; fragment ; bucăţică.

disseminate [di'semineit] *vt.* a răspîndi.

dissension [di'senʃn] *s.* neînţelegere.

dissent [di'sent] *s.* dezacord ; neconformism. *vi.* a fi în dezacord ; a nu se conforma.

dissenter [di'sentə] *s.* neconformist ; eretic.

dissever [di'sevə] *vt.* a despărţi.

dissimilar ['di'similə] *adj.* diferit.

dissimulate [di'simjuleit] *vt.*, *vi.* a (se) ascunde.

dissipate ['disipeit] *vt.*, *vi.* a (se) risipi, a (se) împrăştia.

dissipated ['disipeitid] *adj.* desfrînat.

dissipation [,disi'peiʃn] *s.* împrăştiere ; risipă ; desfrîu.

dissociate [di'souʃieit] *vt.* a separa. *vr.* a se desolidariza.

dissolute ['disəluːt] *adj.* destrăbălat.

dissolution [,disə'luːʃn] *s.* desfacere ; dizolvare ; imoralitate.

dissolve [di'zɔlv] *vt.*, *vi.* a (se) dizolva ; a (se) destrăma.

dissuade [di'sweid] *vt.* a disuada ; a opri ; a abate.

distaff ['distɑːf] *s.* furcă de tors.

distance ['distns] *s.* distanţă ; timp.

distant ['distnt] *adj.* îndepărtat ; vag.

distaste ['dis'teist] *s.* antipatie.

distasteful [dis'teistfl] *adj.* dezagreabil, neplăcut.

distemper [dis'tempə] *s.* răpciugă ; tentă. *vt.* a colora.

distend [dis'tend] *vt.*, *vi.* a (se) umfla.

distil [dis'til] *vt.*, *vi.* a (se) distila ; a picura.

distillery [dis'tiləri] *s.* distilerie.

distinct [dis'tiŋkt] *adj.* clar ; distinct.

distinction [dis'tiŋkʃn] *s.* distincţie.

distinctive [dis'tiŋktiv] *adj.* deosebit ; distinctiv.

distinctly [dis'tiŋktli] *adv.* clar ; fără îndoială.

distinguish [dis'tiŋgwiʃ] *vt.*, *vi.* a (se) distinge.

distinguished [dis'tiŋgwiʃt] *adj.* distins ; remarcabil.

distort [dis'tɔːt] *vt.* a deforma.

distortion [dis'tɔːʃn] *s.* deformare.

distract [dis'trækt] *vt.* a distrage ; a tulbura ; a înnebuni.

distraction [dis'trækʃn] *s.* distragere ; tulburare ; nebunie.

distraint [dis'treint] *s.* sechestru.

distraught [dis'trɔːt] *adj.* înnebunit.

distress [dis'tres] *s.* necaz ; mizerie ; primejdie. *vt.* a supăra.

distribute [dis'tribjut] *vt.* a distribui ; a repartiza.

distributive [dis'tribjutiv] *adj.* distributiv.

district ['distrikt] *s.* regiune ; raion ; cartier.

distrust [dis'trʌst] *s.* neîncredere. *vt.* a suspecta.

distrustful [dis'trʌstfl] *adj.* bănuitor.

disturb [dis'təːb] *vt.* a tulbura.

disturbance [dis'tə:bns] *s.* tulburare.

disunite ['disju:'nait] *vt.*, *vi.* a (se) dezbina.

disuse ['dis'ju:s] *s.* nefolosire; paragină.

ditch [ditʃ] *s.* şanţ.

ditto ['ditou] *adv.* idem.

ditty ['diti] *s.* cîntec(el).

dive [daiv] *s.* plonjon; săritură; picaj. *vi.* a plonja; a sări; a intra în picaj.

diver ['daivə] *s.* scafandru; săritor de la trambulină; *zool.* cufundar.

diverge [dai'və:dʒ] *vi.* a fi în divergenţă; a se separa; a se deosebi.

divergency [dai'və:dʒnsi] *s.* divergenţă; deosebire.

diversify [dai'və:sifai] *vt.* a diversifica.

diversion [dai'və:ʃn] *s.* distragere; diversiune; distracţie.

diversity [dai'və:siti] *s.* varietate.

divert [dai'və:t] *vt.* a distrage; a distra.

diverting [dai'və:tiŋ] *adj.* amuzant.

divest [dai'vest] *vt.* a scoate; a arunca.

divide [di'vaid] *s.* despărţire; creastă. *vt.*, *vi.* a despărţi; a (se) împărţi; a (se) dezbina.

dividend ['dividend] *s.* dividend; deîmpărţit.

divine [di'vain] *s.* teolog; cleric. *adj.* divin; minunat; splendid. *vt.* a ghici.

divinity [di'viniti] *s.* divinitate; teologie.

division [di'viʒn] *s.* împărţire; diviziune; graniţă; dezacord; votare.

divorce [di'vɔ:s] *s.* divorţ; *fig.* separaţie; dezacord. *vt.* a se despărţi de. *vi.* a divorţa.

divulge [dai'vʌldʒ] *vt.* a divulga.

dizziness ['dizinis] *s.* ameţeală.

dizzy ['dizi] *adj.* ameţit; ameţitor; zăpăcit.

do [du(:)] *v. aux. folosit la ind., interog. şi neg., prez. şi trec. al verbelor noţionale şi la imper. neg.; v. mod. arată insistenţa:* he did help me *într-adevăr m-a ajutat. vt.* a face; a săvîrşi; a păcăli; a strica; *to ~ duty as* a sluji de; *to ~ smb. in* a ucide pe cineva; *to be done for* a fi distrus. *vi.* a acţiona; a se ocupa; a o duce; a corespunde; a fi destul, a ajunge; *how ~ you ~* bună ziua; vă salut; îmi pare bine de cunoştinţă; *to have to ~ with* a avea de-a face cu; *to ~ for* a sluji; a ucide; *to ~ (well) by* a se purta (frumos) cu; *to ~ with smth.* a termina cu cineva; *can you ~ with a cup of tea?* ai vrea o ceaşcă de ceai? *to ~ without smth.* a se (putea) lipsi de; *to ~ away with* a desfiinţa; *nothing doing* nu e nimic de făcut. *ca înlocuitor: I like it. Do you?* îmi place. Zău? *I like it and so does he* îmi place şi mie şi lui; *so do I* şi mie la fel.

dock [dɔk] *s. mar.* doc; boxa acuzaţilor; măcriş.

docker ['dɔkə] *s.* docher.

doctor ['dɔktə] *s.* doctor. *vt.* a trata; a falsifica.

doctrine ['dɔktrin] *s.* doctrină; dogmă.

document ['dɔkjumənt] *s.* document.

documentary [ˌdɔkju'mentri] *s.,* *adj.* documentar.

dodder ['dɔdə] *s. bot.* cuscută. *vi.* a se bălăbăni; a vorbi în dodii.

dodge [dɔdʒ] *s.* eschivare; truc. *vt.* a evita. *vi.* a se eschiva.

dodger ['dɔdʒə] *s.* chiulangiu; evazionist.

doe [dou] *s.* căprioară; iepuroaică.

doer ['duə] *s.* om de acţiune; executant.

does [dəz, dʌz] *pers. a III-a sing. ind. prez. de la* **do.**

doeskin ['douskin] *s.* piele de căprioară.

doff [dɔf] *vt.* a-şi scoate (pălăria etc.).

dog [dɔg] *s.* cîine; javră.

dog-cart ['dɔgkɑːt] *s.* docar.

dog-days ['dɔgdeiz] *s.* zilele lui cuptor.

doge [doudʒ] *s.* doge.

dog-eared ['dɔg iəd] *adj. (d. cărţi)* rufos.

dogged ['dɔgid] *adj.* încăpăţînat; tenace.

doggerel ['dɔgrl] *s.* versuri proaste; *fig.* maculatură.

dog-tired ['dɔg 'taiəd] *adj.* istovit.

doings ['duiŋz] *s. pl.* acţiuni.

doldrums ['dɔldrəmz] *s. pl.* mare calmă; tristeţe.

dole [doul] *s.* pomană; plată; ajutor de şomaj. *vt.* a da cu ţîrîita.

doleful ['doulfl] *adj.* trist.

doll [dɔl] *s.* păpuşă.

dollar ['dɔlə] *s.* dolar.

dolphin ['dɔlfin] *s.* delfin.

dolt [doult] *s.* tîmpit.

domain [də'mein] *s.* domeniu.

dome [doum] *s.* dom.

domestic [də'mestik] *adj.* domestic; familial; intern.

dominant ['dɔminənt] *adj.* dominant.

dominate ['dɔmineit] *vt., vi.* a stăpîni.

domineering [ˌdɔmi'niəriŋ] *adj.* autoritar; arogant.

dominion [də'minjən] *s.* stăpînire; dominion.

don [dɔn] *s.* nobil; membru în conducerea unei universităţi. *vt.* a îmbrăca.

donate [do'neit] *vt.* a dona.

done [dʌn] *part. trec. de la* **do.**

donkey ['dɔŋki] *s.* măgar; *fig.* tîmpit.

donor ['dounə] *s.* donator.

doom [duːm] *s.* soartă (rea); judecata de apoi. *vt.* a osîndi, a sorti.

doomsday ['duːmzdei] *s.* ziua judecăţii de apoi.

door [dɔː] *s.* uşă; poartă; portiţă.

door-bell ['dɔːbel] *s.* sonerie.

door-frame ['dɔːfreim] *s.* cadrul uşii.

door-keeper ['dɔːˌkiːpə] *s.* portar.

door-step ['dɔːstep] *s.* prag.

door-way ['dɔːwei] *s.* intrare; cadrul uşii.

dope [doup] *s.* stupefiant; dopaj; tîmpit; *amer. pont. vt.* a dopa; a droga.

dope-fiend ['doupfiːnd] *s.* toxicoman.

dormer(-window) ['dɔːmə('windou)] *s.* lucarnă.

dormitory ['dɔːmitri] *s.* dormitor (comun).

dormouse ['dɔ:maus] s. zool. alunar, pîş.

dose [dous] s. doză. vt. a administra (o doctorie).

dot [dɔt] s. punct; picătură; dotă. vt. a pune punct la.

dotage ['doutidʒ] s. ramoleală.

dotard ['doutəd] s. ramolit.

dote [dout] vi.: to ~ on a iubi nebuneşte.

doth [dəθ, dʌθ] înv. pers. a III-a sing. prez. de la do.

double ['dʌbl] s. dublu; dublură; pas alergător; meci de dublu. adj. dublu. vt. a dubla; a îndoi; a trece (colţul etc.). vi. a se îndoi; a merge în pas alergător; to ~ up a se ghemui, a se încovoia. adv. dublu, de două ori; perechi, perechi.

double-barrelled ['dʌbl ˌbærld] adj. cu două ţevi; fig. echivoc.

double-bass ['dʌbl'beis] s. contrabas.

double-breasted ['dʌbl'brestid] adj. (d. haină) la două rînduri.

double-cross ['dʌbl'krɔs] vt. a înşela.

double-dealer ['dʌbl'di:lə] s. ipocrit.

double-Dutch ['dʌbl'dʌtʃ] s. limbă păsărească.

double-edged ['dʌbl'edʒd] adj. cu două tăişuri.

double-faced ['dʌbl'feist] adj. făţarnic.

doubly ['dʌbli] adv. de două ori.

doubt [daut] s. îndoială; dilemă; in ~ la îndoială; no ~, without (a) ~, beyond a ~ fără îndoială. vt. a pune la îndoială.

doubtful ['dautfl] adj. şovăielnic; dubios.

doubtfully ['dautfli] adv. cu inima îndoită.

doubtless ['dautlis] adv. sigur.

dough [dou] s. aluat; bani.

dough-nut ['dou nʌt] s. gogoaşă.

dove [dʌv] s. turturea; porumbel.

dove-cot ['dʌvkɔt] s. hulubărie.

dovetail ['dʌvteil] s. îmbinare. vt., vi. a (se) potrivi.

dowager ['dauədʒə] s. văduvă moştenitoare.

dowdy ['daudi] adj. împopoţonat; îmbrăcat fără gust.

down [daun] s. dună; luncă; puf; tristeţe. adj. coborîtor; trist; prăpădit; flămînd; bolnav; ~ and out distins; extremist. vt. a lăsa (în) jos; a trînti; a da pe gît; to ~ tools a intra în grevă. adv. (în) jos; vertical; ~ to pînă la. prep. în josul; de-a lungul.

downcast ['daunkɑ:st] adj. descurajat; trist.

downfall ['daunfɔ:l] s. cădere; precipitaţii.

down-hearted ['daun'hɑ:tid] adj. deprimat.

downhill ['daun'hil] adv. în jos.

Downing Street ['dauniŋ 'stri:t] s. reşedinţa primului ministru britanic.

downpour ['daunpɔ:] s. ploaie torenţială.

downright ['daunrait] adj., adv. cinstit; total.

downstairs ['daun'stɛəz] adv. jos; la parter.

downtown ['daun'taun] adv. cartierul comercial; amer. în centru.

down train ['daun'trein] s. tren care merge (de la Londra) în provincie

downtrodden ['daun‚trɔdn] *adj.* asuprit.

downward ['daunwəd] *adj.* descendent; scăpătat. *adv.* în jos.

dowry ['dauəri] *s.* zestre; talent.

doze [douz] *s.* aţipeală. *vi.* a aţipi; a dormita.

dozen ['dʌzn] *s.* duzină.

drab [dræb] *adj.* murdar; mizer; şters.

draft [drɑːft] *s.* schiţă; plan; proiect; recrutare obligatorie. *vt.* a schiţa; a proiecta; *amer.* a lua în armată.

draftsman ['drɑːftsmən] *s.* proiectant; redactor (al unui document).

drag [dræg] *s.* dîră; piedică. *vt.* a trage, a tîrî; a draga. *vi.* a se tîrî(i).

dragon ['drægn] *s.* balaur.

dragon-fly ['drægnflai] *s.* libelulă.

dragoon [drə'guːn] *s. mil.* dragon.

drain [drein] *s.* jgheab; ţeavă; scurgere; duşcă; picătură. *vt.* a scurge; a canaliza; a suge. *vi.* a se scurge; a slăbi.

drainage ['dreinidʒ] *s.* canalizare; (apă) de scurgere.

drain-pipe ['drein paip] *s.* conductă.

drake [dreik] *s.* răţoi.

dram [dræm] *s.* dram, picătură.

drama ['drɑːmə] *s.* genul dramatic; teatru; piesă; dramă.

dramatist ['dræmətist] *s.* dramaturg.

dramatize ['dræmətaiz] *vt.* a dramatiza; a lua în tragic.

drank [dræŋk] *vt., vi. trec. de la* **drink**.

drape [dreip] *vt.* a drapa.

draper ['dreipə] *s.* pînzar.

drapery ['dreipəri] *s.* (magazin de) pînzeturi.

drastic ['dræstik] *adj.* drastic.

draught [drɑːft] *s.* tracţiune; decantare; duşcă; pescaj; curent; *pl.* (jocul de) dame. *vt. v.* **draft**.

draughtsman ['drɑːftsmən] *s.* desenator (tehnic); proiectant; piesă la jocul de dame.

draughty ['drɑːfti] *adj.* în care trage curentul.

draw [drɔː] *s.* tragere; remiză; meci nul. *vt.* a tîrî; a (a)trage; a scoate; a desena; *to ~ back* a retrage; *to ~ up* a redacta, a elabora; *to ~ lots* a trage la sorţi. *vi.* a se apropia; a desena; *to ~ back* a se retrage; a şovăi; *to ~ off* a se îndepărta; *to ~ on* a se apropia; a se inspira din; *to ~ together* a se uni; *to ~ away* a se îndepărta; *to ~ up* a se alinia; a se opri; a trage la scară.

drawback ['drɔːbæk] *s.* piedică; dezavantaj.

drawbridge ['drɔːbridʒ] *s.* pod basculant.

drawer [drɔː] *s.* sertar; desenator; *pl.* chiloţi.

drawing ['drɔːiŋ] *s.* desen; grafică.

drawing-board ['drɔːiŋbɔːd] *s.* planşetă de desen.

drawing-pin ['drɔːiŋpin] *s.* pioneză.

drawing-room ['drɔːiŋrum] *s.* salon(aş).

drawl [drɔːl] *s.* vorbă tărăgănată. *vt.* a tărăgăna. *vi.* a vorbi tărăgănat.

drawn [drɔːn] *vt., vi. part. trec. de la* **draw**.

dray [drei] s. faeton, camion (cu cai).

dread [dred] vt., vi. a (se) înspăiminta. adj. grozav, temut.

dreadful ['dredfl] adj. înspăimîntător; neplăcut.

dreadfully ['dredfuli] adv. teribil.

dreadnought ['drednɔ:t] s. cuirasat.

dream [dri:m] s. vis; visare. vt. a visa; a-şi închipui. vi. a visa.

dreamer ['dri:mə] s. visător.

dreamt [dremt] vi. trec. şi part. trec. de la dream.

dreamy ['dri:mi] adj. visător; vag; de vis.

dreary ['driəri] adj. îngrozitor; sinistru; întunecos.

dredge [dredʒ] s. dragă. vt., vi. a draga.

dredger ['dredʒə] s. dragă.

dregs [dregz] s. pl. drojdie.

drench [drentʃ] vt. a uda leoarcă.

dress [dres] s. rochie; îmbrăcăminte. vt. a îmbrăca; a împodobi; a găti; a pregăti; to ~ up a îmbrăca elegant. vi. a se îmbrăca (elegant).

dress-circle ['dres'sə:kl] s. balconul I.

dress-coat ['dres'kout] s. frac; jachetă.

dresser ['dresə] s. infirmier; garderobieră; bufet, servantă.

dressing ['dresiŋ] s. îmbrăcare; preparare a mîncării; salată; sos; bandaj; scrobeală; ocară.

dressing-case ['dresiŋkeis] s. trusă medicală.

dressing-gown ['dresiŋgaun] s. halat, capot.

dressing-table ['dresiŋ,teibl] s. măsuţă de toaletă.

dressmaker ['dres,meikə] s. croitoreasă.

dress rehearsal ['dresri,hə:sl] s. repetiţie generală (în costume).

drew [dru:] vt., vi. trec de la draw.

dribble ['dribl] s. picurare; dribling. vt., vi. a picura; a dribla.

drift [drift] s. curent; troian; morman; alunecare. vt. a abate. vi. a fi luat de curent.

drill [dril] s. sfredel; freză; mil. instrucţie; exerciţii, repetiţie; dril. vt. a sfredeli; a instrui.

drink [driŋk] s. băutură (alcoolică); in ~ beat. vt. a bea; a toasta pentru; to ~ up sau off sau down a bea pînă la fund; to ~ in a sorbi; a absorbi. vi. a bea.

drinking bout ['driŋkiŋbaut] s. chef, beţie.

drip [drip] s. picătură; picurare. vt., vi. a picura.

dripping ['dripiŋ] adj. ud leoarcă.

drive [draiv] s. plimbare cu un vehicul; alee; lovitură (cu mingea); energie; campanie; efort; cursă. vt. a mîna (caii); a conduce; a duce cu un vehicul; a împinge; a determina; a bate (un cui); to ~ away a izgoni; to ~ home a duce la bun sfîrşit; a face să triumfe. vi. a mîna caii; a conduce maşina; a merge cu maşina; to ~ at a ţinti la.

drivel ['drivl] s. prostii, vorbe goale. vi. a spune prostii.

driven ['drivn] vt., vi. part. trec. de la drive.

driver ['draivə] s. şofer; vizitiu; păstor.

drizzle ['drizl] s. burniţă. vi. a bura.

droll [droul] adj. nostim.

dromedary ['drʌmədri] s. dromader.

drone [droun] s. trîntor; zumzet. vi. a zumzăi; a vorbi monoton.

droop [dru:p] s. cădere; ofilire. vi. a atîrna; a se ofili.

drop [drɔp] s. picătură; cădere. vt. a lăsa să cadă; a scăpa. vi. a cădea; a scădea; a coborî; a scăpăta; to ~ off a scădea; a aţipi; to ~ in a face o scurtă vizită.

dropsy ['drɔpsi] s. hidropizie.

dross [drɔs] s. zgură.

drossy ['drɔsi] adj. fără valoare.

drought [draut] s. secetă.

drove [drouv] s. turmă; ceată. vt., vi. trec. de la drive.

drown [draun] vt. a îneca; a acoperi. vi., vr. a se îneca.

drowse [drauz] vi. a moţăi.

drowsiness ['drauzinis] s. toropeală; piroteală.

drowsy ['drauzi] adj. adormitor; adormit.

drudge [drʌdʒ] s. rob (fig.). vi. a munci pe rupte; a robi.

drudgery ['drʌdʒri] s. robie; (fig.) trudă.

drug [drʌg] s. doctorie; drog; stupefiant. vt. a droga; a preface; a falsifica.

drugstore ['drʌgstɔ:] s. amer. drogherie; magazin universal; bufet-expres.

drum [drʌm] s. tobă; rezervor. vt. a bate toba pe.

drummer ['drʌmə] s. toboşar.

drunk [drʌŋk] vt., vi. part. trec. de la drink. adj. beat; ameţit.

drunkard ['drʌŋkəd] s. beţivan.

drunken ['drʌŋkn] adj. beat; ameţit.

dry [drai] adj. sec; secetos; antialcoolic. vt., vi. a (se) usca.

dub [dʌb] vt. a porecli; a dubla (un film).

dubious ['dju:bjəs] adj. şovăitor; dubios.

duchess ['dʌtʃis] s. ducesă.

duck [dʌk] s. raţă; pînză de doc; cufundare; plonjon. vt. a cufunda; a apleca. vi. a se apleca.

duckling ['dʌkliŋ] s. răţuşcă.

.duct [dʌkt] s. tub; canal.

ductile ['dʌktail] adj. ductil; docil.

due [dju:] s. datorie; pl. taxă, cotizaţie. adj. scadent; cuvenit; planificat. prep. ~ to datorit(ă).

duel ['djuəl] s. duel.

dug [dʌg] vt., vi. trec. şi part. trec. de la dig.

dug-out ['dʌgaut] s. antiaerian.

duke [dju:k] s. duce.

dukedom ['dju:kdəm] s. rangul de duce; ducat; principat.

dull [dʌl] adj. greoi; tîmpit; monoton; mohorît; tocit. vt. a atenua; a estompa; a toci.

dullard ['dʌləd] s. tîmpit.

duly ['dju:li] adv. cînd trebuie; cum trebuie.

dumb [dʌm] adj. mut.

dumb-bells ['dʌm,belz] s. pl. haltere.

dumbfound [dʌm'faund] vt. a ului; a amuţi.

dumb-show ['dʌm'ʃou] s. joc mut; mimă.

dummy ['dʌmi] s. manechin; înlocuitor; imitaţie; mînă moartă; martor mut.

dump [dʌmp] *vt.* a descărca; a arunca (pe piaţă).

dumping ['dʌmpiŋ] *s.* inundarea pieţii cu mărfuri ieftine.

dumpling ['dʌmpliŋ] *s.* găluşcă; gogoaşă.

dumps [dʌmps] *s.* indispoziţie.

dumpy ['dʌmpi] *adj.* îndesat.

dunce [dʌns] *s.* tîmpit.

dung [dʌŋ] *s.* bălegar.

dungeon ['dʌndʒn] *s.* temniţă.

dupe [dju:p] *s.* prost, gurăcască. *vt.* a păcăli; a escroca.

duplex ['dju:pleks] *adj.* dublu.

duplicate[1] ['dju:plikit] *s.* copie. *adj.* dublu; copiat.

duplicate[2] ['dju:plikeit] *vt.* a copia; a dubla.

duplicity [dju'plisiti] *s.* făţărnicie.

durable ['djuərəbl] *adj.* durabil.

duration [djuə'reiʃn] *s.* durată.

during ['djuəriŋ] *prep.* în timpul.

durst [də:st] *v. mod. trec. de la* **dare.**

dusk [dʌsk] *s.* amurg.

dusky ['dʌski] *adj.* întunecat; întunecos.

dust [dʌst] *s.* praf, pulbere; ţărînă. *vt.* a scutura de praf; a presăra; *to ~ smb.'s jacket* a bate pe cineva.

dust-bin ['dʌstbin] *s.* ladă de gunoi.

dust-cart ['dʌstkɑ:t] *s.* maşină a salubrităţii.

duster ['dʌstə] *s.* cîrpă de praf; cutie pentru presărat prafuri.

dustman ['dʌstmən] *s.* gunoier.

dusty ['dʌsti] *adj.* prăfuit; în praf.

Dutch [dʌtʃ] *s.* (limba) olandeză; *the ~* olandezii. *adj.* olandez(ă).

Dutchman ['dʌtʃmən] *s.* olandez.

duteous ['dju:tjəs] *adj.* conştiincios; ascultător.

dutiful ['dju:tifl] *adj.* respectuos; supus; pătruns de simţul datoriei.

duty ['dju:ti] *s.* îndatorire, datorie; sarcină; treabă; taxă (vamală); *on ~* de serviciu; *to be in ~ bound* a fi obligat.

duty-free ['dju:ti'fri:] *adj.* scutit de taxe vamale.

dwarf [dwɔ:f] *s.* pitic. *vt.* a micşora; a reduce.

dwell [dwel] *vi.* a locui; a rămîne; a insista.

dweller ['dwelə] *s.* locuitor.

dwelling(-house) ['dweliŋ(haus)] *s.* locuinţă.

dwelt [dwelt] *vt., vi. trec. şi part. trec. de la* **dwell.**

dwindle ['dwindl] *vi.* a se micşora; a scădea.

dye [dai] *s.* vopsea; *fig.* categorie. *vt., vi.* a (se) vopsi, a (se) colora.

dyeing ['daiiŋ] *part. prez. de la* **dye.**

dyestuff ['daistʌf] *s.* vopsea; colorant.

dying ['daiiŋ] *adj.* muribund. *vi. part. prez. de la* **die.**

dyke [daik] *s.* dig; şanţ.

dynamic [dai'næmik] *adj.* dinamic; energic.

dynamics [dai'næmiks] *s. pl.* dinamică.

dynamite ['dainəmait] *s.* dinamită. *vt.* a dinamita.

dynamo ['dainəmou] *s.* dinam.

dynasty ['dinəsti] *s.* dinastie.

dysentery ['disntri] *s.* dizenterie.

E

E [i:] *s.* E, e; (nota) mi.

each [i:tʃ] *adj., pron.* fiecare.

eager ['i:gə] *adj.* doritor; nerăbdător.

eagerness ['i:gənis] *s.* nerăbdare; dorință.

eagle ['i:gl] *s.* vultur.

ear [iə] *s.* ureche (muzicală); auz; spic.

earl [ə:l] *s.* conte.

early ['ə:li] *adj.* timpuriu; prim; prematur. *adv.* devreme; timpuriu.

earmark ['iəmɑ:k] *s.* stampilă; semn. *vt.* a marca; a aloca.

earn [ə:n] *vt.* a cîştiga; a merita.

earnest ['ə:nist] *s.* seriozitate. *adj.* serios.

earnings ['ə:niŋz] *s. pl.* salariu; cîştig.

earphone ['iəfoun] *s.* cască.

ear-ring ['iəriŋ] *s.* cercel.

earshot ['iəʃɔt] *s.* distanţă de la care se poate auzi.

earth [ə:θ] *s.* pămînt; lume; uscat.

earthen ['ə:θn] *adj.* (ca) de pămînt; argilos.

earthenware ['ə:θnwɛə] *s.* ceramică.

earthly ['ə:θli] *adj.* pămîntesc.

earthquake ['ə:θkweik] *s.* cutremur.

earthwork ['ə:θwə:k] *s.* fortificaţie.

earthworm ['ə:θwə:m] *s.* rîmă.

eartrumpet ['iə͵trʌmpit] *s.* cornet acustic.

earwig ['iəwig] *s.* urechelniţă.

ease [i:z] *s.* tihnă; huzur; *at* ∼ liniştit; *mil.* pe loc repaus. *vt., vi.* a slăbi; a (se) linişti.

easel ['i:zl] *s.* şevalet.

easily ['i:zili] *adv.* uşor.

east [i:st] *s.* răsărit. *adj.* de răsărit.

Easter ['i:stə] *s.* Paşti.

eastern ['i:stən] *adj.* răsăritean; oriental.

easy ['i:zi] *adj.* uşor, facil; liniştit; tihnit; plăcut; simpatic. *adv.* uşurel, uşor; încetişor.

eat [i:t] *vt., vi.* a mînca.

eatable ['i:təbl] *s.* mîncare. *adj.* comestibil.

eaten [i:tn] *vt., vi. part. trec. de la* .eat.

eating-house ['i:tiŋ͵haus] .*s.* ospătărie; restaurant.

eaves [i:vz] *s. pl.* streaşină.

eavesdrop ['i:vzdrɔp] *vi.* a trage cu urechea.

ebb [eb] *s.* reflux; declin; scădere. *vi.* a scădea; a decădea.

ebony ['ebəni] *s.* abanos.

eccentric [ik'sentrik] *s., adj.* excentric.

ecclesiastic [i͵kli:zi'æstik] *s.* cleric. *adj.* clerical.

echo ['ekou] *s.* ecou; răsunet; imitaţie. *vt.* a repeta (ca un ecou). *vi.* a răsuna.

eclipse [i'klips] *s.* eclipsă; întunecare. *vt.* a întuneca; a eclipsa.

economic [͵i:kə'nɔmik] *adj.* economic.

economical [͵i:kə'nɔmikl] *adj.* chibzuit; econom(ic).

economics [͵i:kə'nɔmiks] *s.* economie politică.

economize [i:'kɔnəmaiz] *vt.*, *vi.* a economisi.

economy [i:'kɔnəmi] *s.* economie (politică) ; administraţie.

ecstasy ['ekstəsi] *s.* extaz.

ecstatic [eks'tætik] *adj.* vesel ; îmbucurător.

eddy ['edi] *s.* vîrtej.

Eden ['i:dn] *s.* paradis.

edge [edʒ] muchie; margine. *vt.* a mărgini; a-şi face (loc, drum). *vi.* a se strecura.

edgeways ['edʒweiz] *adv.* pe muchie ; lateral.

edible ['edibl] *s.* aliment. *adj.* comestibil.

edifice ['edifis] *s.* clădire.

edify ['edifai] *vt. fig.* a lumina ; a îndrepta.

edit ['edit] *vt.* a pune la punct (un text) ; a redacta ; a conduce (un ziar) ; a monta (un film).

edition [i'diʃn] *s.* ediţie ; format ; tiraj.

editor ['editə] *s.* redactor (şef).

editorial [ˌedi'tɔ:riəl] *s.* articol de fond. *adj.* redacţional.

educate ['edjukeit] *vt.* a educa ; a învăţa.

education [ˌedju'keiʃn] *s.* învăţămînt ; educaţie.

educational [ˌedju'keiʃənl] *adj.* educativ.

eel [i:l] *s.* anghilă, ţipar.

eerie, eery ['iəri] *adj.* straniu.

efface [i'feis] *vt.* a şterge.

effect [i'fekt] *s.* efect; sens ; *in ~* în fapt; în vigoare. *vt.* a produce ; a efectua.

effective [i'fektiv] *adj.* efectiv ; eficace.

effectual [i'fektjuəl] *adj.* eficace ; în vigoare.

effete [e'fi:t] *adj.* istovit.

efficacious [ˌefi'keiʃəs] *adj.* eficace.

efficiency [i'fiʃnsi] *s.* randament.

efficient [i'fiʃnt] *adj.* eficace ; capabil ; activ.

effort ['efət] *s.* sforţare, efort ; încercare.

effusion [i'fju:ʒn] *s.* izbucnire ; ţîşnire.

egg [eg] *s.* ou. *vt. : to ~ on* a îndemna.

egg-plant ['egplɑ:nt] *s.* (pătlăgică) vînătă.

egotism ['egotizəm] *s.* egoism ; egocentrism.

egotist ['egotist] *s.* egoist ; egocentric.

Egyptian [i'dʒipʃn] *s.*, *adj.* egiptean(ă).

egress ['i:gres] *s.* ieşire.

eh [ei] *interj.* cum ? ei ?

eiderdown ['aidədaun] *s.* pilotă.

eight [eit] *s.*, *num.* opt.

eighteen [ei'ti:n] *s.*, *num.* optsprezece.

eighteenth ['ei'ti:nθ] *s.*, *num.* al optsprezecelea.

eighth [eitθ] *s.* optime. *num.* al optulea.

eightieth ['eitiiθ] *s.*, *num.* al optzecilea.

eighty ['eiti] *s.*, *num.* optzeci.

either ['aiðə] *adj.*, *pron.* fiecare, oricare (din doi). *adv.: not ~* nici. *conj. : ~ . . . or* fie . . . fie.

ejaculate [i'dʒækjuleit] *vt.*, *vi.* a exclama.

eject [i'dʒekt] *vt.* a scoate ; a izgoni.

eke [i:k] *vt. : to ~ out* a completa (lipsurile).

elaborate[1] [i'læbrit] *adj.* îngrijit ; elaborat cu grijă.

elaborate² [i'læbəreit] *vt.* a elabora ; a detalia.

elapse [i'læps] *vi.* a trece.

elated [i'leitid] *adj.* încîntat ; exaltat.

elation [i'leiʃn] *s.* încîntare ; exaltare.

elbow ['elbou] *s.* cot ; *out at* ~*s* rupte în coate. *vt.* a-şi croi (drum).

elder ['eldə] *s.* mai-mare, superior ; *bot. soc. adj. compar. de la* old mai vîrstnic.

elderly ['eldəli] *adj.* bătrîior.

eldest ['eldist] *adj. superl. de la* old cel mai vîrstnic.

elect [i'lekt] *adj.* ales. *vt.* a alege ; a hotărî.

election [i'lekʃn] *s.* alegere.

electioneering [i,lekʃə'niəriŋ] *s.* campanie electorală.

elective [i'lektiv] *adj.* electiv ; electoral ; facultativ.

elector [i'lektə] *s.* elector ; alegător.

electorate [i'lektrit] *s.* corp electoral.

electricity [i,lek'trisiti] *s.* electricitate.

electrify [i'lektrifai] *vt.* a electrifica ; a electriza.

element ['elimənt] *s.* element; aspect ; pic(ătură) ; *pl.* rudimente.

elemental [,eli'mentl] *adj.* natural ; elementar.

elementary [,eli'mentri] *adj.* elementar ; rudimentar.

elephant ['elifənt] *s.* elefant.

elevate ['eliveit] *vt.* a ridica ; a înălţa.

elevation [,eli'veiʃn] *s.* ridicare ; înălţime ; grandoare.

elevator [,eli'veitə] *s.* elevator ; *amer.* ascensor : **siloz**.

eleven [i'levn] *s.* unsprezece ; echipă de fotbal. *num.* unsprezece.

eleventh [i'levnθ] *s.* unsprezecime. *num.* al unsprezecelea.

elf [elf] *s.* spiriduş.

elicit [i'lisit] *vt.* a solicita ; a necesita ; a smulge.

eliminate [i'limineit] *vt.* a desfiinţa ; a elimina.

ell [el] *s.* cot *(unitate de măsură)*.

ellipse [i'lips] *s. geom.* elipsă.

ellipsis [i'lipsis] *s. gram.* elipsă.

elm [elm] *s.* ulm.

elocution [,elə'kju:ʃn] *s.* oratorie.

elope [i'loup] *vi.* a fugi (cu iubitul).

elopement [i'loupmənt] *s.* răpire ; fuga îndrăgostiţilor.

eloquence ['eləkwns] *s.* elocinţă ; oratorie.

eloquent ['eləkwnt] *adj.* grăitor ; elocvent.

else [els] *adj.* alt. *adv.* mai ; altfel.

elsewhere ['els'wɛə] *adv.* aiurea ; în altă parte.

elucidate [i'lu:sideit] *vt.* a lămuri.

elude [i'lu:d] *vt.* a evita ; a eluda.

elusive [i'lu:siv] *adj.* fugitiv ; inefabil ; lunecos *(fig.)*.

emaciate [i'meiʃieit] *vt.* a slăbi, a slei.

emanate ['eməneit] *vt.* a emana.

emancipate [i'mænsipeit] *vt.* a elibera ; a emancipa.

embalm [im'ba:m] *vt.* a îmbălsăma.

embankment [im'bæŋkmənt] *s.* taluz.

embark [im'ba:k] *vt., vi.* a (se) îmbarca.

embarrass [im'bærəs] *s.* a încurca ; a stînjeni.

embarassment [im'bærəsmənt] s. încurcătură ; necaz.

embassy ['embəsi] s. ambasadă ; misiune.

embed [im'bed] vt. a încrusta.

embellish [im'beliʃ] vt. a înfrumuseţa.

embers ['embəz] s. pl. jeratic.

embezzle [im'bezl] vt. a delapida.

embitter [im'bitə] vt. a amărî ; a acri.

embodiment [im'bɔdimənt] s. întruchipare.

embody [im'bɔdi] vt. a întru(chi)pa.

emboss [im'bɔs] vt. a gofra ; a ştanţa.

embrace [im'breis] s. îmbrăţişare. vt. a îmbrăţişa ; a lua.

embroider [im'brɔidə] vt., vi. a broda.

embroidery [im'brɔidri] s. broderie.

embryo ['embriou] s. embrion.

emend [i'mend] vt. a corecta ; a îmbunătăţi.

emerald ['emərld] s. smarald.

emerge [i'mə:dʒ] vi. a ieşi (la iveală) ; a se afla.

emergency [i'mə:dʒnsi] s. urgenţă ; pericol ; stare excepţională.

emery ['eməri] s. şmirghel.

emetic [i'metik] s. vomitiv.

emigrate ['emigreit] vi. a emigra.

eminence ['eminəns] s. faimă ; înălţime ; eminenţă.

emissary ['emisri] s. emisar.

emission [i'miʃn] s. emisiune.

emit [i'mit] vt. a emite.

emolument [i'mɔljumənt] s. onorariu ; cîştig.

emotion [i'mouʃn] s. emoţie.

emotional [i'mouʃənl] adj. afectiv.

emperor ['emprə] s. împărat.

emphasis ['emfəsis] s. subliniere ; accent.

emphasize ['emfəsaiz] vt. a sublinia ; a accentua.

emphatic [im'fætik] adj. apăsat ; pompos.

empire ['empaiə] s. imperiu ; stăpînire.

employ [im'plɔi] vt. a folosi ; a angaja.

employee [,emplɔi'i:] s. salariat ; funcţionar.

employer [im'plɔiə] s. patron.

employment [im'plɔimənt] s. slujbă ; angajare.

empress ['empris] s. împărăteasă.

empty ['emti] adj. gol ; liber. vt., vi. a (se) goli.

emulation [,emju'leiʃn] s. întrecere.

enable [i'neibl] vt. a face posibil ; a face capabil ; a permite.

enact [i'nækt] vt. a promulga ; a decreta ; a monta (o piesă) ; a juca (o piesă).

enamel [i'næml] s. smalţ. vt. a emaila.

encase [in'keis] vt. a închide ; a ambala.

enchant [in'tʃɑ:nt] vt. a vrăji.

enchantment [in'tʃɑ:ntmənt] s. vrajă ; încîntare.

encircle [in'sə:kl] vt. a înconjura.

enclose [in'klouz] vt. a împrejmui ; a închide (în plic).

enclosure [in'klouʒə] s. îngrădire.

encompass [in'kʌmpəs] vt. a cuprinde.

encore [ɔŋ'kɔ:] s., *interj*. bis. *vt*. a bisa.

encounter [in'kauntə] s. întîlnire ; luptă. *vt.*, *vi*. a (se) întîlni.

encourage [in'kʌridʒ] *vt*. a încuraja ; a stimula.

encouragement [in'kʌridʒmənt] s. încurajare.

encroach [in'kroutʃ] *vi. :* *to* ~ *(up) on* a încălca.

encroachment [in'kroutʃmənt] s. încălcare.

encumber [in'kʌmbə] *vt*. a împovăra ; a aglomera.

encumbrance [in'kʌmbrns] s. povară ; piedică.

encyclop(a)edia [en,saiklo'pi:djə] s. enciclopedie.

end [end] s. capăt ; moarte ; scop ; *at a loose* ~ neavînd ce face ; *no* ~ *of* o mulțime de. *vt.*, *vi*. a (se) sfîrși.

endanger [in'deindʒə] *vt*. a primejdui.

endear [in'diə] *vt*. a face să fie îndrăgit. *vr*. a se face iubit.

endearment [in'diəmənt] s. afecțiune.

endeavo(u)r [in'devə] s. efort ; strădanie. *vi*. a se strădui.

ending ['endiŋ] s. terminație ; sfîrșit.

endless ['endlis] *adj*. nesfîrșit.

endorse [in'dɔ:s] *vt*. a gira ; a sprijini.

endorsement [in'dɔ:smənt] s. aprobare ; gir.

endow [in'dau] *vt*. a înzestra ; a învesti.

endowment [in'daumənt] s. înzestrare ; alocare.

endurance [in'djuərns] s. rezistență.

endure [in'djuə] *vt*. a îndura. *vi*. a dura.

enemy ['enimi] s. inamic(i) ; diavol.

energetic [,enə'dʒetik] *adj*. energic ; activ.

energy ['enədʒi] s. energie.

enervate ['enə:veit] *vt*. a moleși ; a slăbi.

enfold [in'fould] *vt*. a înfășura ; a îmbrățișa.

enforce [in'fɔ:s] *vt*. a aplica ; a promulga.

enfranchise [in'fræntʃaiz] *vt*. a acorda drepturi electorale (cuiva) ; a emancipa.

engage [in'geidʒ] *vt*. a angaja ; a logodi ; a obliga. *vi*. a se ocupa ; a se prinde. *vr*. a se angaja.

engaged [in'geidʒd] *adj*. ocupat ; logodit.

engagement [in'geidʒmənt] s. angajament ; promisiune ; logodnă ; luptă.

engaging [in'geidʒiŋ] *adj*. atrăgător ; amabil.

engender [in'dʒendə] *vt*. a produce.

engine ['endʒin] s. motor ; mașină ; locomotivă.

engineer [,endʒi'niə] s. inginer ; mecanic (de locomotivă) ; *mil*. pionier. *vt*. a pune la cale.

engineering [,endʒi'niəriŋ] s. construcții (mecanice) ; inginerie.

English ['iŋgliʃ] s. (limba) engleză; *the* ~ englezii; *in plain* ~ pe șleau. *adj*. englezesc, britanic.

English Channel ['iŋgliʃ'tʃænl] s. (*the* ~) Canalul *sau* Marea Mînecii.

Englishman ['iŋgliʃmən] s. englez, britanic.

Englishwoman ['iŋgliʃˌwumən] s. englezoaică.

engrave [in'greiv] vt. a grava; a imprima; a impresiona.

engraving [in'greiviŋ] s. gravură.

engross [in'grous] vt. a absorbi; a ocupa.

engulf [in'gʌlf] vt. a înghiţi.

enhance [in'hɑːns] vt. a spori; a înălţa; a intensifica.

enjoin [in'dʒɔin] vt. a porunci; a cere (imperios).

enjoy [in'dʒɔi] vt. a se bucura de; a savura; a avea.

enjoyment [in'dʒɔimənt] s. plăcere.

enlarge [in'lɑːdʒ] vt. a mări. vi. a vorbi pe larg.

enlargement [in'lɑːdʒmənt] s. mărire; amplificare; adaos.

enlighten [in'laitn] vt. a lumina; a lămuri.

enlightenment [in'laitnmənt] s. luminare; iluminism.

enlist [in'list] vt. a înrola; a obţine. vi. a se înrola; a se angaja.

enliven [in'laivn] vt. a anima.

enmity ['enmiti] s. duşmănie; ură.

ennoble [i'noubl] vt. a înnobila.

enormity [i'nɔːmiti] s. enormitate; ticăloşie; crimă.

enormous [i'nɔːməs] adj. uriaş.

enough [i'nʌf] adj. suficient. adv. destul; foarte.

enrage [in'reidʒ] vt. a înfuria.

enrapture [in'ræptʃə] vt. a încînta; a vrăji.

enrich [in'ritʃ] vt., vr. a (se) îmbogăţi.

enrol(l) [in'roul] vt., vr. a (se) înregimenta; a (se) înrola.

enrolment [in'roulmənt] s. înrolare; promoţie.

ensign ['ensain] s. steag; insignă; semn; sublocotenent.

enslave [in'sleiv] vt. a înrobi.

ensnare [in'snɛə] vt. a prinde în capcană.

ensue [in'sjuː] vi. a urma.

ensure [in'ʃuə] vt., vr. a (se) asigura.

entail [in'teil] vt. a determina; a necesita; a lăsa moştenire.

entangle [in'tæŋgl] vt. a încurca.

enter ['entə] vt. a intra în; a înscrie. vi. a intra.

enterprise ['entəpraiz] s. curaj; aventură; antrepriză.

enterprising ['entəpraiziŋ] adj. întreprinzător; îndrăzneţ.

entertain [ˌentə'tein] vt. a primi, a ospăta; a distra; a întreţine.

entertaining [ˌentə'teiniŋ] adj. distractiv; încîntător.

entertainment [ˌentə'teinmənt] s. distracţie; spectacol; ospitalitate.

enthral(l) [in'θrɔːl] vt. a (în)robi; a vrăji.

enthusiasm [inˌθjuːziæzəm] s. entuziasm.

enthusiastic [inˌθjuːzi'æstik] adj. entuziast.

entice [in'tais] vt. a momi.

entire [in'taiə] adj. tot(al).

entitle [in'taitl] vt. a îndreptăţi; a justifica; a intitula.

entity ['entiti] s. fiinţă; entitate.

entrails ['entreilz] s. pl. măruntaie.

entrance[1] ['entrns] s. intrare.

entrance[2] [in'trɑːns] vt. a vrăji; a încînta.

entreat [in'triːt] vt. a implora.

entreaty [in'triːti] s. rugăminte.

entrench [in'trentʃ] vt. a fortifica.

entrust [in'trʌst] vt. a încredinţa.

entry ['entri] *s.* intrare ; înregistrare ; articol de dicţionar etc.

enumerate [i'nju:məreit] *vt.* a enumera.

envelop [in'veləp] *vt.* a cuprinde ; a învălui.

envelope ['enviloup] *s.* plic.

enviable ['enviəbl] *adj.* de invidiat.

envious ['envjəs] *adj.* invidios.

environment [in'vaiərnmənt] *s.* mediu ; cadru.

environs ['envirnz] *s. pl.* împrejurimi.

envoy ['envɔi] *s.* trimis.

envy ['envi] *s.* (subiect de) invidie. *vt.* a invidia.

ephemeral [i'femərl] *adj.* efemer.

epic ['epik] *s.* epopee ; poem epic. *adj.* epic.

epidemic [ˌepi'demik] *s.* epidemie. *adj.* epidemic.

epilogue ['epilɔg] *s.* epilog ; final.

episode ['episoud] *s.* episod.

epistle [i'pisl] *s.* epistolă.

epithet ['epiθet] *s.* epitet.

epitome [i'pitəmi] *s.* rezumat ; simbol.

epoch ['i:pɔk] *s.* epocă.

epoch-making ['i:pɔkˌmeikiŋ] *adj.* epocal.

equable ['ekwəbl] *adj.* liniştit ; regulat.

equal ['i:kwl] *s.* egal. *adj.* egal ; liniştit ; *to feel ~ to* a fi în stare de.

equality [i'kwɔliti] *s.* egalitate.

equalize ['i:kwəlaiz] *vt.* a egaliza.

equanimity [ˌi:kwə'nimiti] *s.* calm.

equation [iˌkweiʃn] *s.* ecuaţie.

equator [i'kweitə] *s.* ecuator.

equinox ['i:kwinɔks] *s.* echinocţiu.

equip [i'kwip] *vt.* a echipa ; a înzestra.

equipment [i'kwipmənt] *s.* echipament ; instalaţii ; utilaj.

equitable ['ekwitəbl] *adj.* just ; rezonabil.

equity ['ekwiti] *s.* dreptate ; *E ~* sindicatul actorilor.

equivalent [i'kwivələnt] *s., adj.* echivalent.

equivocal [i'kwivəkl] *adj.* echivoc ; dubios.

era ['iərə] *s.* eră.

eradicate [i'rædikeit] *vt.* a dezrădăcina.

erase [i'reiz] *vt.* a şterge ; a rade.

eraser [i'reizə] *s.* radieră.

erect [i'rekt] *adj.* vertical. *vt.* a înălţa.

ermine ['ə:min] *s.* (blană de) hermină.

err [ə:] *vi.* a greşi.

errand ['ernd] *s.* serviciu, comision ; ţintă.

errand-boy ['ernbɔi] *s.* comisionar.

erratic [i'rætik] *adj.* extravagant ; ciudat.

erratum [e'ra:təm] *s.* erată.

erroneous [i'rounjəs] *adj.* greşit.

error ['erə] *s.* greşeală.

eruption [i'rʌpʃn] *s.* erupţie ; izbucnire.

escalator ['eskəleitə] *s.* scară rulantă.

escape [is'keip] *s.* scăpare ; ieşire ; evadare. *vt.* a scăpa (de) ; a evita. *vi.* a fugi ; a scăpa ; a evada.

eschew [is'tʃu:] *vt.* a evita.

escort[1] ['eskɔ:t] *s.* escortă ; însoţitor.

escort[2] [is'kɔ:t] *vt.* a escorta.

escutcheon [is'kʌtʃn] *s.* blazon.

especially [i'speʃli] adv. mai ales.

espionage [ˌespiə'nɑːʒ] s. spionaj.

espouse [is'pauz] vt. a lua de nevastă ; fig. a adopta.

espy [is'pai] vt. a zări.

esquire [is'kwaiə] s. domnului. . . (în corespondenţă).

essay ['esei] s. eseu ; încercare.

essence ['esns] s. esenţă.

essential [i'senʃl] adj. fundamental.

establish [is'tæbliʃ] vt. a înfiinţa ; a stabili.

establishment [is'tæbliʃmənt] s. înfiinţare ; stabilire ; instituţie.

estate [is'teit] s. moşie ; proprietate ; avere.

esteem [is'tiːm] s. stimă. vt. a stima ; a considera.

estimate¹ ['estimit] s. deviz ; calcul ; apreciere.

estimate² ['esti'meit] vt. a aprecia ; a evalua. vi. a face un deviz.

estimation [ˌesti'meiʃn] s. apreciere ; părere ; stimă ; evaluare.

estrange [is'treindʒ] vt. a înstrăina.

estuary ['estjuəri] s. estuar.

etch [etʃ] vt., vi. a grava ; a schiţa.

etching ['etʃiŋ] s. gravură.

eternal [i'təːnl] adj. etern ; neîncetat.

eternity [i'təːniti] s. eternitate.

ether ['iːθə] s. eter.

ethereal [i:'θiəriəl] adj. eteric.

ethic(al) ['eθik(l)] adj. moral.

ethics ['eθiks] s. morală.

etiquette [ˌeti'ket] s. (reguli de) etichetă.

eulogize ['juːlədʒaiz] vt. a lăuda.

eulogy ['juːlədʒi] s. laudă.

euphemism ['juːfimizəm] s. eufemism.

European [juərə'piən] s., adj. european(ă).

evacuate [i'vækjueit] vt. a evacua.

evade [i'veidʒ] vt. a scăpa de ; a se sustrage de la.

evanescent [ˌiːvə'nesnt] adj. trecător ; disparent.

evaporate [i'væpəreit] vt., vi. a (se) evapora.

evasion [i'veiʒn] s. scăpare ; sustragere ; evaziune.

evasive [i'veisiv] adj. evaziv.

eve [iːv] s. ajun.

even ['iːvn] adj. neted ; egal ; par. vt. a egaliza. adv. chiar ; tocmai ; încă şi ; egal ; la fel.

evenly ['iːvnli] adv. liniştit ; egal ; regulat.

evening ['iːvniŋ] s. seară.

evening dress ['iːvniŋ dres] s. haine de seară ; mare ţinută.

event [i'vent] s. eveniment ; întîmplare ; sport probă.

eventful [i'ventfl] adj. bogat în întîmplări.

eventually [i'ventjuəli] adv. în cele din urmă.

ever ['evə] adv. oricînd ; mereu ; (cu neg.) niciodată ; (la interog.) vreodată ; foarte.

evergreen ['evəgriːn] s. plantă perenă. adj. veşnic verde ; peren.

everlasting [ˌevə'lɑːstiŋ] adj. veşnic.

evermore ['evə'mɔː] adv. mereu.

every ['evri] adj. fiecare ; toţi, toate.

everybody ['evribɔdi] pron. toată lumea ; toţi ; fiecare.

everyday ['evridei] adj., adv. zilnic ; obişnuit.

everyone ['evriwʌn] s. v. **everybody.**

everything ['evriθiŋ] pron. tot(ul).

everywhere ['evriwɛə] adv. pretutindeni.

evict [i'vikt] vt. a izgoni ; a evacua.

evidence ['evidns] s. dovadă ; mărturii.

evil ['i:vl] s. rău ; racilă ; păcat. adj. rău ; ticălos.

evil-doer ['i:vl'duə] s. răufăcător.

evince [i'vins] vt. a manifesta ; a indica.

evoke [i'vouk] vt. a evoca ; a stîrni ; a invoca.

evolution [,i:və'lu:ʃn] s. evoluție.

evolve [i'vɔlv] vt. a desfăşura ; a transforma. vi. a evolua.

ewe [ju:] s. oaie.

ewer ['ju:ə] s. urcior, chiup.

exact [ig'zækt] adj. exact ; corect ; precis. vt. a cere ; a solicita ; a impune ; a pretinde.

exacting [ig'zæktiŋ] adj. exigent.

exaggerate [ig'zædʒəreit] vt., vi. a exagera.

exalt [ig'zɔ:lt] vt. a înălţa ; a slăvi.

exaltation [,egzɔ:l'teiʃn] s. înălţare ; slăvire ; exaltare.

exam [ig'zæm] s. examen.

examination [ig,zæmi'neiʃn] s. examen ; cercetare ; interogatoriu.

examine [ig'zæmin] vt. a cerceta ; a interoga.

example [ig,zɑ:mpl] s. exemplu.

exasperate [ig'zɑ:spəreit] vt. a exaspera.

excavate ['ekskəveit] vt. a excava.

excavation [,ekskə'veiʃn] s. săpătură.

excavator [,ekskə'veitə] s. excavator.

exceed [ik'si:d] vt. a întrece.

exceedingly [ik'si:diŋli] adv. foarte (mult).

excel [ik'sel] vt. a depăşi. vi. a excela.

excellence ['eksləns] s. perfecţiune.

Excellency ['ekslənsi] s. excelenţă.

excellent ['ekslənt] s. excelent ; splendid.

except [ik'sept] vt. a excepta. prep. fără ; în afară de, cu excepţia a.

excepting [ik'septiŋ] prep. v. **except.**

exception [ik'sepʃn] s. excepţie ; obiecţie.

exceptional [ik'sepʃənl] adj. excepţional.

excerpt ['eksə:pt] s. fragment.

excess [ik'ses] s. exces ; depăşire ; in ~ of peste. adj. suplimentar ; excedentar.

exchange [iks'tʃeindʒ] s. schimb ; bursă. vt., vi. a (se) schimba.

exchequer [iks'tʃekə] s. (ministerul de) finanţe ; vistierie.

excise [ek'saiz] s. impozit ; taxă. vt. a taxa.

excite [ik'sait] vt. a emoţiona ; a agita ; a stîrni.

excitement [ik'saitmənt] s. emoţie ; tulburare ; senzaţie.

exclaim [iks'kleim] vt., vi. a exclama.

exclamation [,eksklə'meiʃn] s. exclamaţie.

exclude [iks'klu:d] vt. a exclude.

exclusion [iks'klu:ʒn] s. excludere.

exclusive [iks'klu:siv] adj. exclusiv; exclusivist; rezervat; select; snob; ~ of fără.

excrete [eks'kri:t] vt. a scoate.

excruciating [iks'kru:ʃieitiŋ] adj. chinuitor.

exculpate ['ekskʌlpeit] vt. a dezvinovăți; a reabilita.

excursion [iks'kə:ʃn] s. excursie.

excuse[1] [iks'kju:s] s. scuză.

excuse[2] [iks'kju:z] vt. a scuza.

execrable ['eksikrəbl] adj. groaznic.

execute ['eksikju:t] vt. a executa.

execution [ˌeksi'kju:ʃn] s. execuție.

executioner [ˌeksi'kju:ʃnə] s. călău.

executive [ig'zekjutiv] s. director; administrator; consiliu de conducere; ramură executivă. adj. executiv; de acțiune; eficace.

exemplary. [ig'zempləri] adj. exemplar.

exempt [ig'zemt] adj. scutit. vt. a scuti.

exercise ['eksəsaiz] s. exercițiu; mișcare; mil. manevră; pl. amer. ceremonie. vt. a exercita. vi. a face mișcare.

exert [ig'zə:t] vt. a exercita. vr. a se strădui.

exertion [ig'zə:ʃn] s. exercitare; efort.

exhale [eks'heil] vt., vi. a răsufla; a exala.

exhaust [ig'zɔst] s. evacuare. vt. a epuiza; a evacua.

exhaustion [ig'zɔ:stʃn] s. istovire.

exhaustive [ig'zɔ:stiv] adj. complet.

exhibit [ig'zibit] s. exponat; obiect. vt., vi. a (se) expune; a (se) manifesta.

exhibition [ˌeksi'biʃn] s. expoziție; manifestare.

exhilarate [ig'ziləreit] vt. a înveseli.

exhilaration [igˌzilə'reiʃn] s. veselie.

exhort [ig'zɔ:t] vt. a ruga.

exigency ['eksidʒənsi] s. necesitate; exigență.

exile ['eksail] s. exil; exilat. vt. a exila.

exist [ig'zist] vi. a exista.

existence [ig'zistns] s. existență; trai.

exit ['eksit] s. ieșire. vi. a ieși.

exodus ['eksədəs] s. exod.

exonerate [ig'zɔnəreit] vt. a dezvinovăți.

exotic [eg'zɔtik] adj. exotic; ciudat.

expand [iks'pænd] vt. a lărgi; a desfășura. vi. a se dezvolta; a înflori.

expanse [iks'pæns] s. întindere.

expansion [iks'pænʃn] s. expansiune.

expatiate [eks'peiʃieit] vi. a vorbi sau scrie pe larg.

expect [iks'pekt] vt. a se aștepta la; a necesita.

expectancy [iks'pektnsi] s. așteptare.

expectant [iks'pektnt] adj. în așteptare.

expectant mother [iks'pektnt 'mʌðə] s. (femeie) gravidă.

expectation [ˌekspek'teiʃn] s. așteptare; perspectivă.

expedience [iks'pi:djəns] s. convenabilitate; oportunitate.

expedient [iks'pi:djənt] s. expedient. adj. avantajos; eficient.

expedite ['ekspidait] vt. a grăbi.

expedition [ˌekspi'diʃn] s. expediție ; grabă.

expel [iks'pel] vt. a expulza ; a exclude.

expenditure [iks'penditʃə] s. cheltuială (bănească, de energie etc.).

expense [iks'pens] s. cheltuială ; socoteală.

expensive [iks'pensiv] adj. scump.

experience [iks'piəriəns] s. experiență ; pl. întîmplări. vt. a trece prin ; a cunoaște.

experienced [iks'piəriənst] adj. încercat; abil.

experiment [iks'perimənt] s. probă, experiență ; metodă experimentală.

expert ['ekspə:t] s. specialist. adj. expert.

expiate ['ekspieit] vt. a ispăși.

expire [iks'paiə] vi. a expira.

explain [iks'plein] vt., vi. a explica ; a (se) justifica.

explanation [ˌeksplə'neiʃn] s. explicație.

explanatory [iks'plænətri] adj. explicativ ; justificativ.

explode [iks'ploud] vt. a face să explodeze. vi. a exploda.

exploit¹ ['eksploit] s. faptă glorioasă.

exploit² [iks'ploit] vt. a exploata.

exploitation [ˌeksploi'teiʃn] s. exploatare.

exploiter [iks'ploitə] s. exploatator.

exploration [ˌeksplo:'reiʃn] s. explorare.

explore [iks'plo:] vt. a explora ; a cerceta.

explorer [iks'plo:rə] s. explorator ; cercetător.

explosion [iks'plouʒn] s. explozie ; izbucnire.

export¹ ['ekspo:t] s. (articol de) export.

export² [eks'po:t] vt. a exporta.

exportation [ˌekspo:'teiʃn] s. export.

expose [iks'pouz] vt. a demasca ; a expune ; a etala ; a dezgoli.

exposition [ˌekspə'ziʃn] s. expunere.

expostulate [iks'postjuleit] vi. a discuta ; a protesta.

exposure [iks'pouʒə] s. demascare ; expunere ; dezgolire.

expound [iks'paund] vt. a explica ; a clarifica.

express [iks'pres] adj. expres ; clar, exact. vt. a exprima. adv. (trimis) expres.

expression [iks'preʃn] s. exprimare ; expresie.

expressly [iks'presli] adv. clar; anume.

expulsion [iks'pʌlʃn] s. expulzare ; excludere.

expurgate ['ekspə:geit] vt. a expurga ; a cenzura.

exquisite ['ekskwizit] adj. excelent ; minunat ; teribil.

extant [eks'tænt] adj. existent.

extempore [eks'tempəri] adj., adv. fără pregătire ; spontan.

extend [iks'tend] vt. a extinde ; a întinde ; a răspîndi. vi. a se întinde ; a se mări ; a continua ; a ajunge.

extension [iks'tenʃn] s. întindere ; mărire ; prelungire ; anexă ; (la telefon) interior ; cuplaj ; derivație.

extensive [iks'tensiv] adj. întins ; larg ; vast ; de mari proporții.

extent [iks'tent] s. măsură; spațiu; grad.

extenuate [eks'tenjueit] vt. a scuza; a atenua.

exterior [eks'tiəriə] s., adj. exterior.

exterminate [eks'tə:mineit] vt. a nimici.

external [eks'tə:nl] adj. exterior.

extinct [iks'tiŋkt] adj. stins; mort.

extinguish [iks'tiŋgwiʃ] vt. a stinge.

extirpate ['ekstə:peit] vt. a extirpa.

extol [iks'toul] vt. a lăuda (mult).

extort [iks'tɔ:t] vt. a stoarce (bani etc.).

extortion [iks'tɔ:ʃn] s. escrocherie.

extortionate [iks'tɔ:ʃnit] adj. exagerat; cămătăresc.

extra ['ekstrə] s. supliment; figurant. adj., adv. suplimentar.

extract¹ ['ekstrækt] s. extras.

extract² [iks'trækt] vt. a extrage; a obține; a stoarce.

extraction [iks'trækʃn] s. extragere; origine; loc de baștină.

extraneous [eks'treinjəs] adj. fără legătură; exterior.

extraordinary [iks'trɔ:dnri] adj. remarcabil; extraordinar.

extravagance [iks'trævigəns] s. extravaganță; exagerare; nechibzuială.

extravagant [iks'trævigənt] adj. extravagant; risipitor; exagerat.

extreme [iks'tri:m] s. adj., extrem; extremă.

extremity [iks'tremiti] s. extremitate; măsură extremă; culme.

extricate ['ekstrikeit] vt., vr. a (se) elibera; a (se) descurca.

exuberant [ig'zjubrnt] adj. exuberant; abundent; fantastic.

exult [ig'zʌlt] vi. a se bucura mult.

exultation [ˌegzʌl'teiʃn] s. bucurie.

eye [ai] s. ochi; privire; vedere; ureche de ac.

eyeball ['aibɔ:l] s. globul ocular.

eyebrow ['aibrau] s. sprînceană.

eyeglass ['aiglɑ:s] s. lentilă; pl. ochelari.

eyelash ['ailæʃ] s. geană.

eyeless ['ailis] adj. orb.

eyelet ['ailit] s. gaură; inel; ochi.

eyelid ['ailid] s. pleoapă.

eyesight ['aisait] s. vedere.

eyesore ['aisɔ:] s. urîciune; muma pădurii.

eyewash ['aiwɔʃ] s. med. colir; prostii; mofturi.

eye-witness ['ai'witnis] s. martor ocular.

F

F [ef] s. F, f.; (nota) fa.

fable ['feibl] s. fabulă; legendă, poveste; mit(uri); minciuni, scorneli.

fabric ['fæbrik] s. țesătură.

fabricate ['fæbrikeit] vt. a născoci.

fabrication [ˌfæbri'keiʃn] s. născocire.

fabulous ['fæbjuləs] *adj.* fabulos.
façade [fə'sɑːd] *s.* faţadă.
face [feis] *s.* suprafaţă; chip; îndrăzneală; strîmbătură. *vt.* a înfrunta; a (se) îndrepta către.
facet ['fæsit] *s.* faţetă.
facetious [fə'siːʃəs] *adj.* glumeţ.
facilitate [fə'siliteit] *vt.* a uşura.
facility [fə'siliti] *s.* uşurinţă; *pl.* posibilităţi.
fact [fækt] *s.* fapt(ă); realitate; *in* ~ de fapt.
faction ['fækʃn] *s.* f(r)acţiune; dezbinare.
factitious [fæk'tiʃəs] *adj.* artificial
factor ['fæktə] *s.* element; factor; agent.
factory ['fæktri] *s.* fabrică.
faculty ['fæklti] *s.* facultate.
fad [fæd] *s.* capriciu; manie.
fade [feid] *vt.* a decolora. *vi.* a scădea; a se decolora; a se ofili.
fag [fæg] *s.* trudă; ţigară. *vt.* a istovi. *vi.* a trudi.
fag(g)ot ['fægət] *s.* sarcină de lemne.
fail [feil] *vt.* a trînti la examen; a nu ajuta. *vi.* a nu izbuti; a nu face; a cădea la examen; a slăbi; a lipsi.
failing ['feiliŋ] *s.* slăbiciune. *prep.* fără.
failure ['feiljə] *s.* insucces; omisiune; faliment.
faint [feint] *adj.* slab; vag. *vi.* a leşina; a slăbi.
faint-hearted ['feint'hɑːtid] *adj.* fricos.
fair [fɛə] *s.* bîlci; tîrg; bazar; expoziţie. *adj.* corect; drept; cinstit; frumos; moderat; blond; de culoare deschisă.

fairly ['fɛəli] *adv.* sincer; corect; moderat; complet; relativ.
fairy ['fɛəri] *adj.* de basm, ca în poveşti.
fairy-tale ['fɛəriteil] *s.* basm.
faith [feiθ] *s.* încredere; credinţă; promisiune.
faithful ['feiθfl] *adj.* credincios; exact.
faithless ['feiθlis] *adj.* necinstit; necredincios.
fake [feik] *s.* fals; imitaţie. *vt.* a falsifica; a imita.
falcon ['fɔː(l)kn] *s.* şoim.
fall [fɔːl] *s.* cădere; prăbuşire; *amer.* toamnă; *pl.* cascadă. *vi.* a cădea; a scădea; a se prăbuşi; a se ivi; a păcătui; a muri; a se sfărîma; a se împărţi; a deveni; *to* ~ *asleep* a adormi; *to* ~ *short* a nu ajunge; *to* ~ *due* a fi scadent; *to* ~ *behind* a rămîne în urmă; *to* ~ *(up)on* sau *to* a se năpusti (asupra); *to* ~ *back* a se retrage; *to* ~ *in with* a se întîlni cu; a accepta; *to* ~ *out* a se certa.
fallacious [fə'leiʃəs] *adj.* fals; înşelător; greşit.
fallacy ['fæləsi] *s.* fals.
fallen ['fɔːln] *vi. part. trec. de la* **fall.**
fall-out ['fɔːlaut] *s.* cădere radioactivă.
fallow ['fælou] *s.* ţarină. *adj.* necultivat; sterp.
false [fɔːls] *adj.* greşit; fals; falsificat.
falsehood ['fɔːlshud] *s.* minciună.
falsification ['fɔːlsifi'keiʃn] *s.* fals; falsificare.
falsify ['fɔːlsifai] *vt.* a falsifica.
falsity ['fɔːlsiti] *s.* fals; falsitate.

falter [ˈfɔːltə] *vt.* a îngăima. *vi.* a şovăi; a se bălăbăni; a bolborosi.

faltering [ˈfɔːltəriŋ] *adj.* şovăitor; tremurător.

fame [feim] *s.* celebritate; renume, faimă.

familiarity [fəˌmiliˈæriti] *s.* familiaritate; cunoaştere profundă.

family [ˈfæmili] *s.* familie; copii.

family tree [ˈfæmiliˈtriː] *s.* arbore genealogic.

famine [ˈfæmin] *s.* foamete; criză, lipsă.

famish [ˈfæmiʃ] *vt., vi.* a flămînzi.

famous [ˈfeiməs] *adj.* celebru; straşnic.

fan [fæn] *s.* evantai; amator; fanatic. *vt.* a ventila; a răcori; a face vînt.

fancier [ˈfænsiə] *s.* crescător de animale *sau* de plante.

fanciful [ˈfænsifl] *adj.* fantezist; aiurit.

fancy [ˈfænsi] *s.* fantezie; pasiune; capriciu. *adj.* fantezist; trăsnit; *amer.* luxos. *vt.* a-şi închipui; a îndrăgi; a savura.

fancy (dress) ball [ˈfænsi(ˌdres) ˈbɔːl] *s.* bal mascat *sau* costumat.

fancy work [ˈfænsiwəːk] *s.* dantelă; lucru de mînă.

fang [fæŋ] *s.* colţ, dinte.

fantastic(al) [fænˈtæstik(l)] *adj.* fantastic; grotesc.

fantasy [ˈfæntəsi] *s.* fantezie.

far [faː] *adj.* îndepărtat; extrem; celălalt. *adv.* departe; în mare măsură; foarte; cu nimic; *as ~ as* pînă la; *so ~* pînă acum; *in so ~ as* ... în măsura în care; *~ and wide* peste tot; *by ~* cu mult.

far-away [ˈfaːrəwei] *adj.* îndepărtat.

farce [faːs] *s.* farsă.

farcical [ˈfaːsikl] *adj.* grotesc; de farsă.

fare [fɛə] *s.* costul călătoriei; mîncare. *vi.* a o duce (bine *sau* rău).

Far East [ˈfaːrˈist] *s. (the ~)* Extremul Orient. *adj.* din Extremul Orient.

farewell [ˈfɛəˈwel] *s., interj.* adio.

far-fetched [ˈfaːˈfetʃt] *adj.* nefiresc, forţat.

farm [faːm] *s.* fermă; gospodărie. *vt.* a cultiva, a lucra. *vi.* a face agricultură.

farmer [ˈfaːmə] *s.* fermier; ţăran.

farmstead [ˈfaːmsted] *s.* fermă, gospodărie.

far-off [ˈfaːrˈɔːf] *adj.* îndepărtat.

far-reaching [ˈfaːˈriːtʃiŋ] *adj.* important; cu scadenţă întîrziată.

far-sighted [ˈfaːˈsaitid] *adj.* clarvăzător.

farther [ˈfaːðə] *compar. de la* **far** *adj.* mai îndepărtat; celălalt. *adv.* mai departe; în plus.

farthermost [ˈfaːðəmoust] *adj.* cel mai îndepărtat.

farthest [ˈfaːðist] *superl. de la* **far** *adj.* cel mai îndepărtat; *at (the) ~* cel mult; cel mai tîrziu. *adv.* cel mai departe.

farthing [ˈfaːðiŋ] *s.* bănuţ; sfert de penny.

fascinate [ˈfæsineit] *vt.* a fascina; a atrage.

fashion ['fæʃn] s. modă; stil; obicei; lumea bună; *in* ~ la modă; *out of* ~ demodat. *vt.* a fasona.

fashionable ['fæʃnəbl] *adj.* elegant; la modă.

fast [fɑːst] s. *rel.* post. *adj.* strîns; fix; ţeapăn; credincios; statornic; rapid; frivol; *my watch is (three minutes)* ~ ceasul meu a luat-o înainte (cu trei minute). *vi.* a posti. *adv.* strîns; fix; ţeapăn; repede; în grabă; *stand* ~ stai aici; ţine-te bine; *he is* ~ *asleep* doarme dus.

fasten ['fɑːsn] *vt.* a fixa; a ţintui; a lega; a închide.

fastener ['fɑːsnə] s. fixator; capsă; fermoar.

fastidious [fæs'tidiəs] *adj.* dificil; greu de mulţumit.

fat [fæt] s. grăsime; untură; ulei. *adj.* gras; gros; bogat; unsuros.

fatal ['feitl] *adj.* fatal; mortal.

fatality [fə'tæliti] s. nenorocire; fatalitate.

fate [feit] s. soartă; moarte; *the Fates* Parcele.

fated ['feitid] *adj.* fatal; destinat.

fateful ['feitfl] *adj.* vital; fatal.

fathead ['fæthed] s. cap sec.

father ['fɑ ðə] s. tată; părinte; strămoş; preot.

father-in-law ['fɑːðrinlɔː] s. socru.

fatherly ['fɑ ðəli] *adj.* părintesc.

fathom ['fæðəm] s. stînjen. *vt.* a măsura; a sonda; a înţelege.

fathomless ['fæðəmlis] *adj.* adînc; nepătruns.

fatigue [fə'tiːg] s. osteneală. *vt.* a istovi.

fatten ['fætn] *vt.*, *vi.* a (se) îngrăşa.

fatty ['fæti] *adj.* gras.

fatuous ['fætjuəs] *adj.* stupid.

faucet ['fɔːsit] s. *amer.* robinet.

fault [fɔːlt] s. greşeală; vină; vinovăţie; falie; *at* ~ vinovat.

faultless ['fɔːltlis] *adj.* ireproşabil.

faulty ['fɔːlti] *adj.* deficient.

favo(u)r ['feivə] s. favoare; graţie. *vt.* a favoriza; a sprijini.

favo(u)rable ['feivrəbl] *adj.* favorabil; potrivit.

favo(u)rite ['feivrit] s. favorit. *adj.* favorit, preferat.

fawn [fɔːn] s. căprioară. *adj.* castaniu. *vi.* a se gudura.

fawning ['fɔːniŋ] *adj.* linguşitor.

fear [fiə] s. teamă; risc; respect; *for* ~ *that* ca nu cumva să. *vt.* a se teme de; a respecta.

fearful ['fiəfl] *adj.* înspăimîntător.

fearless ['fiəlis] *adj.* neînfricat.

feasible ['fiːzəbl] *adj.* posibil; realizabil.

feast [fiːst] s. ospăţ; sărbătoare; încîntare. *vt.*, *vi.* a ospăta; a (se) hrăni; a (se) delecta.

feat [fiːt] s. faptă (măreaţă); trăsătură.

feather ['feðə] s. pană. *vt.* a împodobi.

feature ['fiːtʃə] s. trăsătură; film de lung metraj; punct din program; articol; reportaj literar. *vt.* a arăta; a sublinia; a prezenta.

February ['februəri] s. februarie.

fed [fed] *vt.*, *vi. trec. şi part.*

trec. de la **feed** : ~ *up* sau ~ *to the teeth* sătul (pînă-n gît).

federation [ˌfedə'reiʃn] *s.* (con-) federaţie.

fee [fi:] *s.* taxă; onorariu.

feeble ['fi:bl] *adj.* slab; plăpînd.

feed [fi:d] *s.* alimentare; furaj. *vt.* a alimenta; a aproviziona; a întreţine. *vi.* a mînca; a se hrăni.

feel [fi:l] *vt.* a simţi (din plin); a pipăi; a atinge; a considera; *to* ~ *one's way* a bîjbîi. *vi.* a se simţi; a fi sensibil, milos; a bîjbîi; *I* ~ *like (drinking) tea* am chef să beau ceai.

feeler ['fi:lə] *s.* zool., fig. antenă.

feeling ['fi:liŋ] *s.* sentiment; mentalitate; convingere; impresie; emoţie; sensibilitate. *adj.* înţelegător; sensibil; sentimental.

feet [fi:t] *s. pl. de la* **foot.**

feign [fein] *vt.* a simula; a născoci.

feint [feint] *s.* fentă; simulacru. *vi.* a fenta; a simula.

felicitous [fi'lisitəs] *adj.* nimerit.

felicity [fi'lisiti] *s.* fericire.

fell [fel] *adj.* criminal; ticălos. *vt.* a doborî. *vi. trec. de la* **fall.**

fellow ['felou] *s.* individ; tovarăş; membru; prieten; pereche.

fellow-countryman ['felou'kʌntrimən] *s.* compatriot.

fellowship ['felouʃip] *s.* tovărăşie; asociaţie.

felon ['felən] *s.* criminal.

felony ['feləni] *s.* crimă.

felt [felt] *s.* fetru; pîslă. *vt., vi. trec. şi part. trec. de la* **feel.**

female ['fi:meil] *s.* femelă; femeie. *adj.* feminin; femeiesc.

feminine ['feminin] *adj.* feminin; femeiesc.

fen [fen] *s.* mlaştină.

fence [fens] *s.* gard; scrimă; tăinuitor. *vt.* a îngrădi. *vi.* a face scrimă.

fencing ['fensiŋ] *s.* scrimă; gard.

fend [fend] *vt.* a feri. *vi.* a procura hrană; a se descurca.

fender ['fendə] *s.* galerie (dinaintea sobei); apărătoare.

ferment[1] ['fə:ment] *s.* ferment; agitaţie.

ferment[2] [fə'ment] *vt.* a face să fermenteze; a agita. *vi.* a fi în fierbere.

fermentation [ˌfə:men'teiʃn] *s.* fermentaţie; agitaţie, fierbere.

fern [fə:n] *s.* ferigă.

ferocious [fə'rouʃəs] *adj.* feroce; sălbatic.

ferocity [fə'rɔsiti] *s.* sălbăticie; asprime.

ferret ['ferit] *s.* nevăstuică. *vt.* a scoate la iveală; a căuta.

ferro-concrete ['ferou'kɔŋkri:t] *s.* beton armat.

ferry ['feri] *s.* bac. *vt., vi.* a traversa cu bacul.

ferry-boat ['feribout] *s.* feribot.

fertile ['fə:tail] *adj.* rodnic; productiv.

fertilizer ['fə:tilaizə] *s.* îngrăşăminte.

ferule ['feru:l] *s.* nuia.

fervent ['fə:vnt] *adj.* fierbinte.

fervid ['fə:vid] *adj.* strălucitor; fierbinte.

fervo(u)r ['fə:və] *s.* zel.

fester ['festə] *vi.* a se infecta.

festival ['festəvl] s. festival; sărbătoare.

festivity [fes'tiviti] s. festivitate; petrecere.

festoon [fes'tu:n] s. feston, chenar. vt. a festona.

fetch [fetʃ] vt. a se duce să aducă; a produce.

fête [feit] s. festival; sărbătoare. vt. a sărbători.

fetich(e), **fetish** ['fi:tiʃ] s. fetiş; amuletă.

fetter ['fetə] s. lanţ; pl. fig. cătuşe. vt. a înlănţui.

feud [fju:d] s. gîlceavă; feudă.

fever ['fi:və] s. friguri; febră.

feverish ['fi:vəriʃ] adj. febril; fierbinte.

few [fju:] adj., pron. (prea) puţini; a ~ cîţiva; destui.

fiancé [fi'a:nsei] s. logodnic.

fiancée [fi'a:nsei] s. logodnică.

fib [fib] s. minciună. vi. a minţi.

fiber, fibre ['faibə] s. fibră; caracter.

fickle ['fikl] adj. nestatornic.

fickleness ['fiklnis] s. neseriozitate; capriciu.

fiction ['fikʃn] s. beletristică; proză epică; ficţiune; plăsmuire.

fictitious [fik'tiʃəs] adj. fictiv.

fiddle ['fidl] s. scripcă.

fiddler ['fidlə] s. scripcar, lăutar; pierde-vară.

fiddlestick ['fidlstik] s. arcuş; ~s! prostii!

fidelity [fi'deliti] s. fidelitate.

fidget ['fidʒit] s. neastîmpăr. vi. a se agita.

fidgety ['fidʒiti] adj. nervos; neastîmpărat.

fie [fai] interj. ruşine!

field [fi:ld] s. cîmp (de luptă); teren (sportiv); lan; domeniu.

field-glass ['fi:ldgla:s] s. telemetru; pl. binoclu.

fiend [fi:nd] s. diavol; ticălos; toxicoman.

fiendish ['fi:ndiʃ] s. diabolic.

fierce [fiəs] adj. aspru; violent; rău; sălbatic.

fiery ['faiəri] adj. aprins; arzător.

fife [faif] s. fluier.

fifteen ['fif'ti:n] s. echipă de rugbi. num. cincisprezece.

fifteenth ['fif'ti:nθ] s., num. al cincisprezecelea.

fifth [fifθ] s. cincime. num. al cincilea.

fiftieth ['fiftiiθ] s. a cincizecea parte. num. al cincizecilea.

fifty ['fifti] s., num. cincizeci.

fig [fig] s. smochin(ă).

fight [fait] s. luptă; meci; combativitate. vt. a combate; a se lupta cu; to ~ off a respinge, a izgoni. vi. a se lupta; a se bate.

fighter ['faitə] s. luptător; boxer.

fighter-plane ['faitə,plein] s. avion de vînătoare.

fighting ['faitiŋ] s. luptă. adj. combativ; de luptă; certăreţ.

figment ['figmənt] s. plăsmuire.

figurative ['figjurətiv] adj. figurat.

figure ['figə] s. cifră; pl. aritmetică; siluetă; figură (de stil, geometrică); poză. vt. a închipui; a desena; a înţelege; a socoti. vi. a figura.

figurehead ['figəhed] s. galion; marionetă.

filch [filtʃ] vt. a şterpeli.

file [fail] s. dosar; colecţie; arhivă; fir; rînd; pilă. vt. a colecţiona; a depune; a înregistra ; a pili. *vi*. a pleca pe rînd.

filibuster ['filibʌstə] *s*. corsar ; obstrucţionist. *vi*. a face obstrucţie.

filigree ['filigri:] *s*. filigran.

filings ['failiŋz] *s. pl*. pilitură.

fill [fil] *s*. plin ; plinătate. *vt*. a umple ; a ocupa ; a exercita (o funcţie) ; a completa ; a executa ; *to ~ out* a umple ; a umfla ; *to ~ in* a completa. *vi*. a se umple ; a se umfla ; *to ~ out* a se umfla ; a se îngrăşa.

fillip ['filip] *s*. bobîrnac ; impuls.

filly ['fili] *s*. mînză.

film [film] *s*. pieliţă ; strat subţire ; văl ; film. *vt*. a ecraniza ; a acoperi cu o pieliţă etc.

filmy ['filmi] *adj*. ceţos.

filter ['filtə] *s*. filtru. *vt.*, *vi*. a (se) filtra ; a (se) strecura.

filth [filθ] *s*. murdărie.

filthy ['filθi] *adj*. murdar ; obscen.

fin [fin] *s*. aripioară de peşte.

final ['fainl] *s*. ultimul examen ; finală. *adj*. final ; hotărîtor.

finale [fi'nɑ:li] *s*. final.

finality [fai'næliti] *s*. hotărîre ; caracter definitiv.

finalize ['fainəlaiz] *vt*. a definitiva.

finally ['fainəli] *adv*. în sfîrşit ; definitiv.

finance [fai'næns] *s*. finanţe ; *pl*. bani. *vt*. a finanţa.

financial [fai'nænʃl] *adj*. financiar.

financier [fai'nænsiə] *s*. om de afaceri.

finch [fintʃ] *s*. cintez(ă).

find [faind] *s*. descoperire. *vt*. a (se) găsi ; a descoperi ; a constata ; a nimeri ; *to ~ fault with* a critica ; a reproşa. *vr*. a se afla ; a se trezi.

findings ['faindiŋz] *s. pl*. constatări.

fine [fain] *s*. amendă. *adj*. frumos ; senin ; plăcut ; bun ; minunat ; subţire ; fin ; ascuţit ; mărunt ; rafinat. *vt*. a amenda.

fineness ['fainnis] *s*. fineţe ; ascuţime ; subţirime.

finery ['fainəri] *s*. eleganţă ; *pl*. podoabe.

finger ['fiŋgə] *s*. deget. *vt*. a pipăi.

fingerprint ['fiŋgəprint] *s*. amprentă digitală.

finical ['finikl] *adj*. dificil, pretenţios.

finish ['finiʃ] *s*. capăt ; finiş ; finisaj. *vt*. a termina ; a finisa.

finite ['fainait] *adj*. limitat ; finit ; *gram*. predicativ.

Finn [fin] *s*. finlandez(ă).

Finnish ['finiʃ] *s*. (limba) finlandeză. *adj*. finlandez(ă).

fiord [fjɔ:d] *s*. fiord.

fir [fə:] *s*. brad ; pin.

fire ['faiə] *s*. foc ; incendiu ; tir. *vt*. a descărca o armă ; a aprinde ; a concedia. *vi*. a trage cu arma ; a se înflăcăra ; *~ away!* dă-i drumul ! spune odată !

fire-brigade ['faiəbri,geid] *s*. pompieri.

fire-damp ['faiədæmp] *s*. grizu, gaz de mină.

fire-engine ['faiər'endʒin] *s*. pompă de incendiu.

fire-escape ['faiər is,keip] *s*. scară de incendiu.

firefly ['faiɔflai] *s.* licurici.

fireman ['faiəmən] *s.* pompier; fochist.

fireplace ['faiəpleis] *s.* cămin, vatră.

fireproof ['faiəpru:f] *adj.* neinflamabil.

fireside ['faiəsaid] *s.* gura sobei; viaţă tihnită.

fireworks ['faiəwə:ks] *s. pl.* foc(uri) de artificii.

firing ['faiəriŋ] *s.* tir; focuri; concediere.

firm [fə:m] *s.* firmă. *adj., adv.* tare; ferm.

firmament ['fə:məmənt] *s.* firmament.

first [fə:st] *s.* început; primul; primii. *adj., num.* întîi; prim; primordial. *adv.* mai întîi; mai degrabă.

first-class ['fə:st'klɑ:s] *adj.* de primă calitate. *adv.* cu clasa întîi; perfect.

first-hand ['fə:st'hænd] *adj., adv.* direct.

firstly ['fə:stli] *adv.* întîi.

first-rate ['fə:st'reit] *adj., adv.* excelent.

fish [fiʃ] *s.* (mîncare de) peşte; peşti. *vt.* a pescui; a prinde; a scoate; a obţine; a căuta. *vi.* a pescui; *to ~ for* a umbla după.

fisherman ['fiʃəmən] *s.* pescar.

fishery ['fiʃəri] *s.* pescuit; cherhana.

fishing ['fiʃiŋ] *s.* pescuit.

fishing-line ['fiʃiŋlain] *s.* undiţă.

fishing-rod ['fiʃiŋrɔd] *s.* undiţă.

fishmonger ['fiʃ,mʌŋgə] *s.* negustor de peşte.

fishy ['fiʃi] *adj.* de peşte; dubios.

fission ['fiʃn] *s.* fisiune.

fist [fist] *s.* pumn.

fit [fit] *s.* acces, criză; potrivire; *by ~s and starts* pe apucate; în asalt. *adj.* potrivit; gata; corect; voinic. *vt.* a potrivi; a se potrivi (cu); a şedea bine (cuiva); *to ~ out* a aproviziona; *to ~ up* a echipa. *vi.* a se potrivi.

fitness ['fitnis] *s.* potrivire; sănătate; formă.

fitter ['fitə] *s.* ajustor; instalator; maistru croitor.

fitting ['fitiŋ] *s.* potrivire; probă; *pl.* accesorii; garnituri. *adj.* potrivit; decent; nimerit.

five [faiv] *s., num.* cinci.

fiver ['faivə] *s.* cinci (lire).

fix [fiks] *s.* situaţie grea. *vt.* a fixa; a repara; a (pre)găti; a definitiva; a ţinti; a atrage.

fixture ['fikstʃə] *s.* accesoriu fix; anexă; lucru imobil; om imobil.

fizz(le) ['fiz(l)] *vi.* a fîsîi.

fjord [fjɔ:d] *s.* fiord.

flabbergast ['flæbəgɑ:st] *vt.* a ului.

flabby ['flæbi], **flaccid** ['flæksid] *adj.* moale, flasc.

flag [flæg] *s.* steag; dală. *vt.* a semnaliza. *vi.* a se ofili.

flagon ['flægən] *s.* cană de vin; sticlă de vin.

flagrant ['fleigrnt] *adj.* flagrant.

flagship ['flægʃip] *s.* vas-amiral.

flagstaff ['flægstɑ:f] *s.* catarg de steag.

flail [fleil] *s.* îmblăciu.

flake [fleik] *s.* fulg.

flame [fleim] *s.* flacără; izbucnire; pasiune.

flank [flæŋk] *s.* flanc; coastă. *vt.* a flanca.

flannel ['flænl] s. (haină de) flanelă.

flap [flæp] s. clapă. vt., vi. a fîlfîi.

flare [flɛə] s. pîlpîit; flacără; izbucnire. vi. a pîlpîi; a izbucni.

flash [flæʃ] s. fulger; fulgerare; izbucnire; licărire. vt. a aprinde; a lumina. vi. a străluci; a (stră)fulgera; a izbucni.

flashlight ['flæʃlait] s. lanternă; reflector.

flask [flɑːsk] s. garafă.

flat [flæt] s. apartament; cîmpie; lat (de palmă etc.); muz. bemol. adj., adv. întins; plat; total; clar; ~ iron fier de călcat.

flatten ['flætn] vt., vi. a (se) turti; a (se) întinde.

flatter ['flætə] vt. a linguşi; a încînta; a felicita. vi. a fi linguşitor. vr. a se felicita; a se amăgi cu gîndul.

flattery ['flætəri] s. linguşire.

flaunt [flɔːnt] vt. a etala. vi. a se împăuna.

flavo(u)r ['fleivə] s. savoare; aromă. vt. a parfuma.

flavo(u)ring ['fleivəriŋ] s. mirodenie; aromatizare.

flaw [flɔː] s. slăbiciune; lipsă; defect.

flawless ['flɔːlis] adj. perfect.

flax [flæks] s. in.

flaxen ['flæksn] adj. de in; ca inul.

flay [flei] vt. a jupui.

flea [fliː] s. purice.

fleck [flek] s. pată; punct. vi. a păta; a stropi.

fled [fled] vt., vi. trec. şi part. trec. de la **flee** şi **fly** a fugi.

fledged [fledʒd] adj. matur.

fledg(e)ling ['fledʒliŋ] s. pasăre tînără; fig. ageamiu.

flee [fliː] vt. a fugi, a scăpa de. vi. a fugi.

fleece [fliːs] s. caer; lînă; nor. vt. a jefui; a escroca.

fleet [fliːt] s. flotă. adj. rapid.

Fleet Street ['fliːt 'striːt] s. strada ziarelor la Londra; presa.

Fleming ['flemiŋ] s. flamand(ă).

Flemish ['flemiʃ] s. (limba) flamandă. adj. flamand(ă).

flesh [fleʃ] s. carne; trup; instincte.

fleshly ['fleʃli] adj. senzual.

flesh-pots ['fleʃpɔts] s. pl. lux; huzur.

fleshy ['fleʃi] adj. cărnos; gras.

flew [fluː] vt., vi. trec. de la **fly**.

flexible ['fleksəbl] adj. flexibil.

flick [flik] s. plesnitură. vt. a plesni.

flicker ['flikə] s. licărire. vi. a licări.

flier ['flaiə] s. aviator.

flight [flait] s. zbor; stol; grup de scări; fugă.

flighty ['flaiti] adj. nestatornic.

flimsy ['flimzi] adj. subţirel; şubred; străveziu.

flinch [flintʃ] vi. a se clinti.

fling [fliŋ] vt., vi. a (se) arunca; a (se) trînti.

flint [flint] s. cremene.

flip [flip] vt. a pocni; a da un bobîrnac.

flippancy ['flipənsi] s. neseriozitate.

flippant ['flipənt] adj. neserios.

flirt [fləːt] s. cochetă; crai. vi. a cocheta.

flirtation [flə:'teiʃn] s. flirt.

flit [flit] vi. a zbura; a fugi.

float [flout] vt. a lansa. vi. a pluti.

flock [flɔk] s. turmă; stol; enoriaşi. vi. a se aduna.

floe [flou] s. sloi.

flog [flɔg] vt. a biciui; a bate; a vinde.

flood [flʌd] s. inundaţie; revărsare; potop; flux. vt., vi. a inunda.

flood-light ['flʌdlait] s. reflector.

floor [flɔ:] s. duşumea; pardoseală; etaj. vt. a pardosi; a doborî; a încurca.

flooring ['flɔ:riŋ] s. pardoseală.

flop [flɔp] s. cădere; eşec. vt. a trînti. vi. a cădea. adv. (hodoronc)tronc.

florid ['flɔrid] adj. înflorit; înfloritor; împopoţonat.

florist ['flɔrist] s. florăreasă.

flotsam ['flɔtsəm] s. obiecte purtate de valuri.

flounder ['flaundə] s. cambulă. vi. a se zbuciuma.

flour ['flauə] s. făină.

flourish ['flʌriʃ] s. fluturare; înflolitură; trîmbiţare. vt. a învîrti; a ameninţa cu. vi. a înflori.

flout [flaut] vt. a batjocori.

flow [flou] s. scurgere. vi. a curge; a se scurge.

flower ['flauə] s. floare; înflolitură. vi. a înflori.

flower-girl ['flauəgə:l] s. florăreasă.

flowery ['flauəri] adj. înflorit; înfloritor.

flown [floun] vt., vi. part. trec. de la **fly.**

flu [flu:] s. gripă.

fluctuate ['flʌktjueit] vi. a fluctua.

flue [flu:] s. fum; coş.

fluency ['fluənsi] s. fluenţă.

fluent ['fluənt] adj. curgător; fluent.

fluff [flʌf] s. puf. vt. a scămoşa.

fluffy ['flʌfi] adj. pufos; flocos.

fluid [fluid] s., adj. fluid.

flummox ['flʌməks] vt. a zăpăci.

flung [flʌŋ] vt., vi. trec. şi part. trec. de la **fling.**

flunkey ['flʌŋki] s. lacheu.

flurry ['flʌri] s. ropot; încurcătură. vt. a zăpăci; a încurca.

flush [flʌʃ] s. torent; îmbujorare; elan. adj. umflat. vt. a umple; a îmbujora. vi. a se scurge; a se îmbujora.

fluster ['flʌstə] s. nervozitate. vt. a tulbura.

flute [flu:t] s. fluturat; agitaţie. vt., vi. a flutura; a (se) tulbura.

flutter ['flʌtə] s. fluturat; agitaţie. vt., vi. a flutura; a (se) tulbura.

flux [flʌks] s. flux.

fly [flai] s. muscă; prohab. vt. a înălţa; a părăsi. vi. a zbura; a se înălţa; a flutura; a se întinde; a fugi; a se grăbi.

flyer ['flaiə] s. aviator.

flying ['flaiiŋ] s. zbor. adj. zburător; fulger(ător).

fly-leaf ['flaili:f] s. forzaţ.

fly-paper ['flai peipə] s. hîrtie de muşte.

foal [foul] s. mînz. vi. a făta.

foam [foum] s. spumă; mare. vi. a spumega.

focus ['foukəs] s. focar; centru. vt., vi. a se concentra.

fodder ['fɔdə] s. furaj (uscat).

foe [fou] s. duşman.

foetus ['fi:təs] s. făt.

fog [fɔg] s. ceaţă; pîclă; confuzie.

foggy ['fɔgi] adj. ceţos.

fogy ['fougi] s. babalîc; reacţionar.

foible [fɔibl] s. slăbiciune.

foil [fɔil] s. foiţă metalică; contrast, opus; floretă. vt. a zădărnici.

fold [fould] s. îndoitură; creţ; ţarc; stînă. vt. a îndoi; a împături; a încreţi; a îmbrăţişa; a închide. vi. a se îndoi; a se încreţi.

folder ['fouldə] s. pliant.

folding ['fouldiŋ] adj. pliant; rabatabil.

foliage ['fouliidʒ] s. frunziş.

folio ['fouliou] s. (volum in) folio; pagină dublă.

folk [fouk] s. oameni; public; popor; pl. neamuri, familie. adj. popular, folcloric.

folklore ['fouklɔ:] s. folclor; înţelepciune populară.

follow ['fɔlou] vt. a urma; a urmări; a înţelege; a asculta (de). vi. a urma; a se lămuri; a decurge.

follower ['fɔlouə] s. adept; însoţitor.

following ['fɔlouiŋ] adj. următor.

folly ['fɔli] s. prostie; nebunie.

foment [fo'ment] vt. a stîrni; a îngriji.

fond [fɔnd] adj. iubitor; tandru; drag; to be ~ of a ţine (mult) la.

fondly ['fɔndli] adv. din inimă.

fondness ['fɔndnis] s. dragoste; tandreţe.

fondle ['fɔndl] vt. a mîngîia; a pipăi.

food [fu:d] s. hrană.

food stuff ['fu:d stʌf] s. aliment(e).

fool [fu:l] s. prost; zevzec; bufon. vt. a-şi bate joc de. vi. a se purta prosteşte; a se juca.

foolery ['fu:ləri] s. prostie; aiureală.

foolhardy ['fu:l͵ha:di] adj. nesăbuit.

foolish ['fu:liʃ] adj. prostesc; aiurit.

foolscap ['fu:lzkæp] s. coală ministerială; tichie de bufon.

foot [fut] s. picior; laba piciorului; (măsură de) 30 cm; capăt; poale; mil. infanterie; on ~ pe jos. vt. a dansa; a pune capăt la.

football ['futbɔ:l] s. (minge de) fotbal; amer. rugbi.

foot-bridge ['futbridʒ] s. pod pentru pietoni.

footfall ['futfɔ:l] s. (zgomot de) pas.

foothold ['futhould] s. loc de pus piciorul; loc sigur.

footing ['futiŋ] s. poziţie; nivel; fig. picior.

footlights ['futlaits] s. pl. luminile rampei.

footman ['futmən] s. servitor.

footmark ['futma:k] s. urmă de picior.

footnote ['futnout] s. notă în josul paginii.

footprint ['futprint] s. urmă de picior.

footstep ['futstep] s. (úrmă de) pas.

footwear ['futwɛə] *s.* încălţăminte.

fop [fɔp] *s.* filfizon.

for [fɔ:, fə] *prep.* pentru ; timp de ; din (pricina) ; după ; în loc de ; ~ *all that* totuşi ; ~ *aught I know* după cîte ştiu ; ~ *ever* de-a pururi ; *what* ~? pentru ce ? ~ *that matter* cît despre asta ; la urma urmei. *conj.* căci.

forage ['fɔridʒ] *s.* furaj. *vi.* a furaja ; a scotoci ; a jefui.

foray ['fɔrei] *s.* atac ; incursiune. *vi.* a face o incursiune.

forbade [fə'beid] *vt., vi. trec.* de la **forbid.**

forbear[1] ['fɔ:bɛə] *s.* strămoş.

forbear[2] [fɔ:'bɛə] *vt.* a se abţine de la ; a renunţa.

forbearance [fɔ:'bɛərns] *s.* răbdare ; stăpînire de sine.

forbid [fə'bid] *vt.* a interzice ; a opri.

forbidden [fə'bidn] *vt. part. trec.* de la **forbid.**

forbidding [fə'bidiŋ] *adj.* sever ; ameninţător.

forbore [fɔ:'bɔ:] *vt. trec.* de la **forbear.**

forborne [fɔ:'bɔ:n] *vt. part. trec.* de la **forbear.**

force [fɔ:s] *s.* putere ; forţă ; armată ; *jur.* vigoare ; sens. *vt.* a forţa ; a scoate.

forceful ['fɔ:sfl] *adj.* puternic ; forţat.

forcible ['fɔ:səbl] *adj.* forţat ; puternic.

ford [fɔ:d] *s.* vad.

fore [fɔ:] *s.* parte din faţă. *adj.* din faţă.

forearm ['fɔ:rɑ:m] *s.* antebraţ.

forebode [fɔ:'boud] *vt.* a prevesti (rău).

forecast ['fɔ:kɑ:st] *s.* previziune. *vt. inf., trec. şi part. trec.* a prezice.

forefather ['fɔ:,fɑ ðə] *s.* strămoş.

forefinger ['fɔ:,fiŋgə] *s.* arătător.

forefront ['fɔ:frʌnt] *s.* partea din faţă ; *mil.* linia întîi.

foregoing [fɔ:'goiŋ] *adj.* (pomenit) anterior.

foregone [fɔ:'gɔn] *adj.* dinainte stabilit.

foregone conclusion ['fɔ:gɔn kən'klu:ʒn] *s.* rezultat inevitabil ; lucru de la sine înţeles.

foreground ['fɔ:graund] *s.* primplan.

forehead ['fɔrid] *s.* frunte.

foreign ['fɔrin] *adj.* străin ; extern ; exterior.

foreigner ['fɔrinə] *s.* străin.

Foreign Office ['fɔrin 'ɔfis] *s.* Ministerul de Externe (britanic).

foreleg ['fɔ:leg] *s.* picior dinainte.

forelock ['fɔ:lɔk] *s.* cîrlionţ.

foreman ['fɔ:mən] *s.* (contra)maistru ; şef de echipă ; primul jurat.

foremost ['fɔ:moust] *adj.* principal ; prim.

forerunner ['fɔ:,rʌnə] *s.* premergător ; predecesor.

foresaw [fɔ:'sɔ:] *vt. trec.* de la **foresee.**

foresee [fɔ:'si:] *vt.* a prevedea.

foreseen [fɔ:'si:n] *vt. part. trec.* de la **foresee.**

foreshadow [fɔ:'ʃædou] *vt.* a prevesti.

foresight ['fɔ:sait] *s.* prevedere.

forest ['fɔrist] *s.* codru.

forestall [fɔ:'stɔ:l] *vt.* a preveni ; a anticipa.

forester ['fɔristə] *s.* pădurar.

forestry ['fɔristri] *s.* silvicultură.

foretaste ['fɔ:teist] *s.* (de)gustare ; mostră.

foretell [fɔ:'tel] *vt.* a prezice.

foretold [fɔ:'tould] *vt. trec. și part. trec. de la* **foretell.**

forever [fə'revə] *adv.* de-a pururi.

forewarn [fɔ:'wɔ:n] *vt.* a avertiza.

foreword ['fɔ:wə:d] *s.* prefață.

forfeit ['fɔ:fit] *s.* pierdere ; pedeapsă ; *pl.* gajuri. *adj.* de pedeapsă. *vt.* a pierde (ca pedeapsă).

forgave [fə'geiv] *vi. trec. de la* **forgive.**

forge [fɔ:dʒ] *s.* forjă ; foale ; atelier de fierărie. *vt.* a forja ; a făuri ; a falsifica.

forgery ['fɔ:dʒri] *s.* fals ; falsificare ; plastografie.

forget [fə'get] *vt., vi.* a uita.

forgetful [fə'getfl] *adj.* uituc ; neglijent.

forget-me-not [fə'getminɔt] *s.* nu-mă-uita.

forgive [fə'giv] *vt., vi.* a ierta.

forgiven [fə'givn] *vt., vi. part. trec. de la* **forgive.**

forgiveness [fə'givnis] *s.* iertare.

forgo [fɔ:'gou] *vt.* a renunța la ; a da uitării.

forgot [fə'gɔt] *vt., vi. trec. de la* **forget** ; *amer. și part. trec.*

forgotten [fə'gɔtn] *vt., vi. part. trec. de la* **forget.**

fork [fɔ:k] *s.* furcă ; furculiță ; răscruce. *vt.* a lua cu furca. *vi.* a se bifurca.

forlorn [fə'lɔ:n] *adj.* nenorocit ; părăsit.

form [fɔ:m] *s.* formă ; înfățișare ; formular ; circulară ; ceremonie ; pompă ; bancă ; clasă. *vt.* a forma ; a alcătui. *vi.* a se naște ; a se forma.

formal ['fɔ:ml] *adj.* oficial ; formal ; superficial.

formality [fɔ:'mæliti] *s.* formalitate ; caracter oficial.

formation [fɔ:'meiʃn] *s.* formare ; formați(un)e.

former ['fɔ:mə] *adj.* de pe ·vremuri ; vechi ; fost ; anterior ; cel dintîi din doi.

formerly ['fɔ:məli] *adv.* pe vremuri.

formidable ['fɔ:midəbl] *adj.* teribil.

formula ['fɔ:mjulə] *s.* formulă.

formulate ['fɔ:mjuleit] *vt.* a formula.

fornication [,fɔ:ni'keiʃn] *s.* păcate trupești ; imoralitate, adulter.

forsake [fə'seik] *vt.* a părăsi.

forsaken [fə'seikn] *vt. part. trec. de la* **forsake.**

forsook [fə'suk] *vt. trec. de la* **forsake.**

forswear [fɔ:'swɛə] *vt.* a nega ; a renega. *vi., vr.* a jura strîmb.

forswore [fɔ:'swɔ:] *vt., vi., vr. trec. de la* **forswear.**

forsworn [fɔ:'swɔ:n] *vt., vi., vr. part. trec. de la* **forswear.**

forte [fɔ:t] *s.* specialitate ; punct tare.

forth [fɔ:θ] *adv.* înainte ; afară.

forthcoming [fɔ:θ'kʌmiŋ] *adj.* așteptat ; viitor ; gata.

forthright ['fɔ:θrait] *adj.* deschis ; sincer.

forthwith ['fɔ:θ'wið] *adv.* îndată.

fortieth ['fɔ:tiiθ] *s., num.* al patruzecilea.

fortification [ˌfɔːtifiˈkeiʃn] *s*. fortificaţie.

fortify [ˈfɔːtifai] *vt*. a întări.

fortitude [ˈfɔːtitjuːd] *s*. curaj.

fortnight [ˈfɔːtnait] *s*. două săptămîni.

fortnightly [ˈfɔːtˌnaitli] *adj., adv.* bilunar.

fortress [ˈfɔːtris] *s*. fortăreaţă.

fortuitous [fɔːˈtjuitəs] *adj.* întîmplător.

fortunate [ˈfɔːtʃnit] *adj.* norocos.

fortunately [ˈfɔːtʃnitli] *adv.* din fericire.

fortune [ˈfɔːtʃn] *s*. noroc; destin; avere.

forty [ˈfɔːti] *s., num.* patruzeci.

forum [ˈfɔːrəm] *s*. for.

forward [ˈfɔːwəd] *s. sport* înaintaş. *adj.* în înaintare; timpuriu; obraznic. *vt*. a înainta; a expedia. *adv.* înainte; spre viitor.

forwardness [ˈfɔːwədnis] *s*. promptitudine; bunăvoinţă; pripeală.

fossil [ˈfɔsl] *s*. fosilă. *adj.* fosilizat.

foster [ˈfɔstə] *vt*. a creşte; a alăpta; a nutri; a sprijini.

foster brother [ˈfɔstəˌbrʌðə] *s*. frate de lapte; frate adoptiv.

fought [fɔːt] *vt., vi. trec. şi part. trec. de la* **fight.**

foul [faul] *s*. rău; purtare incorectă; *sport* fault. *adj.* urît; murdar; rău (mirositor); incorect.

found[1] [faund] *vt., vi. trec. şi part. trec. de la* **find.**

found[2] [faund] *vt*. a întemeia.

foundation [faunˈdeiʃn] *s*. întemeiere; fundaţie; temelie.

founder [ˈfaundə] *s*. întemeietor; ctitor. *vt*. a scufunda. *vi*. a se scufunda; a cădea; a se împotmoli.

foundling [ˈfaundliŋ] *s*. copil găsit.

foundry [ˈfaundri] *s*. topitorie, turnătorie.

fount [faunt] *s*. fîntînă; izvor; casetă cu litere.

fountain [ˈfauntin] *s*. fîntînă; cişmea.

fountain-head [ˈfauntinˈhed] *s*. izvor.

fountain-pen [ˈfauntinˈpen] *s*. stilou.

four [fɔː] *s., num.* patru; *on all ~s* în patru labe.

fourfold [ˈfɔːfould] *adj., adv.* împătrit.

four-footed [ˈfɔːˈfutid] *adj.* patruped.

four-in-hand [ˈfɔːrinˈhænd] *s*. trăsură cu patru cai.

fourpence [ˈfɔːpns] *s*. patru penny.

fourteen [ˈfɔːˈtiːn] *s., num.* patrusprezece.

fourteenth [ˈfɔːˈtiːnθ] *s*. paisprezecime. *num.* al paisprezecelea.

fourth [fɔːθ] *s*. pătrime. *num.* al patrulea.

fowl [faul] *s*. găină; pasăre de curte; pasăre care se vînează.

fowler [ˈfaulə] *s*. vînător.

fowling [ˈfauliŋ] *s*. vînătoare (de păsări).

fowling-piece [ˈfauliŋpiːs] *s*. puşcă de vînătoare.

fox [fɔks] *s*. vulpe.

foxglove [ˈfɔksglʌv] *s. bot.* degeţel-roşu.

fox-terrier [ˈfɔksˌteriə] *s*. foxterier.

foxtrot [ˈfɔkstrɔt] *s*. foxtrot.

foxy [ˈfɔksi] *adj.* şiret.

foyer ['fɔiei] s. foaier.

fraction ['frækʃn] s. fracţiune; fracţie.

fracture ['fræktʃə] s. fractură.

fragile ['frædʒail] adj. fragil; delicat.

fragment ['frægmənt] s. fragment; bucată.

fragrance ['freigrns] s. aromă; parfum.

fragrant ['freigrnt] adj. parfumat; încîntător.

frail [freil] adj. slab; firav.

frailty ['freilti] s. uşurinţă; slăbiciune; greşeală.

frame [freim] s. cadru; ramă; construcţie. vt. a încadra; a pregăti; amer. a înscena un proces împotriva (cuiva).

frame-up ['freimʌp] s. înscenare judiciară.

framework ['freimwə:k] s. cadru.

franc [fræŋk] s. franc.

franchise ['fræntʃaiz] s. drepturi cetăţeneşti; autorizaţie.

frank [fræŋk] adj. sincer.

frankincense ['fræŋkin,sens] s. tămîie.

frantic ['fræntik] adj. nebunesc.

fraternal [frə'tə:nl] adj. frăţesc.

fraternity [frə'tə:niti] s. frăţie.

fraternize ['frætənaiz] vi. a fraterniza.

fraud [frɔ:d] s. înşelăciune.

fraudulent ['frɔ:djulənt] adj. necinstit; înşelător.

fraught [frɔ:t] adj.: ~ with plin de.

fray [frei] s. luptă. vt., vi. a (se) uza.

freak [fri:k] s. capriciu.

freakish ['fri:kiʃ] adj. capricios; ciudat.

freckle ['frekl] s. pistrui. vt., vi. a (se) pistruia.

free [fri:] adj. liber; gratuit; graţios; generos. vt. a elibera. adv. gratis.

freedom ['fri:dəm] s. libertate; familiaritate.

freemason ['fri:,meisn] s. francmason.

free speech ['fri:'spi:tʃ] s. libertatea cuvîntului.

free-thinker ['fri:'θiŋkə] s. libercugetător.

freeze [fri:z] vt. a îngheţa. vi. a îngheţa; a se slei.

freezing-point ['fri:ziŋ,pɔint] s. punct de îngheţare a apei.

freight [freit] s. marfă; transport. vt. a transporta.

freighter ['freitə] s. armator; vas comercial.

French [trentʃ] s. (limba) franceză; the ~ francezii. adj. francez, franţuzesc.

Frenchman ['trentʃmən] s. francez.

Frenchwoman ['frentʃ,wumən] s. franţuzoaică.

frenzied ['frenzid] adj. înnebunit; nebunesc.

frenzy ['frenzi] s. nebunie; frenezie.

frequency ['fri:kwənsi] s. frecvenţă; repetiţie.

frequent[1] ['fri:kwənt] adj. frecvent.

frequent[2] [fri'kwent] vt. a frecventa.

frequently ['fri:kwəntli] adv. adeseori.

fresco ['freskou] s. frescă.

fresh [freʃ] s. prospeţime; răcoare. adj. proaspăt; nou;

curat; înviorător; *(d. apă)*
dulce; *amer.* obraznic.

freshman ['freʃmən] *s.* student
în anul I, boboc.

fret [fret] *vt.* a agita; a necăji;
a ajura. *vi.* a se necăji; a se
agita; a fi nervos.

fretful ['fretfl] *adj.* nervos; agitat; nemulțumit.

fret-saw ['fretsɔ:] *s.* traforaj.

fretwork ['fretwə:k] *s.* ajur.

friar ['fraiə] *s.* călugăr.

friction ['frikʃn] *s.* frecare; neînțelegere.

Friday ['fraidi] *s.* vineri.

friend [frend] *s.* prieten(ă);
iubit(ă); rudă.

friendly ['frendli] *adj.* priete-
noș; amabil.

friendship ['frendʃip] *s.* prietenie.

frieze [fri:z] *s.* friză.

frigate ['frigit] *s.* fregată.

fright [frait] *s.* spaimă; sperie-
toare.

frighten ['fraitn] *vt.* a speria.

frightful ['fraitfl] *adj.* înspăimîntător.

frightfully ['fraitfli] *adv.* teribil;
foarte.

frigid ['fridʒid] *adj.* rece; frigid;
neprietenos.

frill [fril] *s.* jabou; volănaș;
pl. zorzoane; aere.

frilled [frild] *adj.* înzorzonat.

fringe [frindʒ] *s.* franjuri; breton; margine. *vt.* a mărgini;
a împodobi.

frisk [frisk] *vi.* a se zbengui.

frisky ['friski] *adj.* jucăuș.

frivolity [fri'vɔliti] *s.* neseriozitate.

frivolous ['frivələs] *adj.* neserios; fără importanță.

frock [frɔk] *s.* rochiță; halat.

frock-coat ['frɔk'kout] *s.* redin-
gotă.

frog [frɔg] *s.* broască; brotac.

frogman ['frɔgmən] *s.* scafandru.

frolic ['frɔlik] *s.* capriciu; năzbîtie. *vi.* a zburda; a se ține
de șotii.

frolicsome ['frɔliksəm] *adj.* jucăuș.

from [frəm, frɔm] *prep.* de la;
de (pe); din (pricina); față
de; ~ ... *to* între; de la pînă
la; ~ *time to time* din cînd
în cînd.

front [frʌnt] *s.* față; frunte;
fațadă; front; țărm.

frontier ['frʌntjə] *s.* frontieră;
limită. *adj.* de frontieră.

frontier-guard ['frʌntjəgɑ:d] *s.*
grănicer.

frontispiece ['frʌntispi:s] *s.* frontispiciu (la o carte etc.).

frost [frɔst] *s.* ger; frig; răceală.
vt. a îngheța. *vi.* a îngheța;
a degera.

frost-bite ['frɔsbait] *s.* degerătură.

frost-bitten ['frɔs,bitn] *adj.* degerat.

frosting ['frɔstiŋ] *s.* glazură;
jivraj.

frosty ['frɔsti] *adj.* geros; în-
ghețat.

froth [frɔθ] *s.* spumă.

frothy ['frɔθi] *adj.* spumos.

frown [fraun] *s.* încruntare. *vi.*
a se încrunta.

froze [frouz] *vt., vi.* trec. de la
freeze.

frozen ['frouzn] *vt., vi. part.
trec. de la* **freeze**.

frugal ['fru:gl] *adj.* redus; cumpătat.

fruit [fru:t] *s.* fruct(e); *pl.* roade. *vi.* a da roade.

fruitful ['fru:tfl] *adj.* rodnic.

fruitless ['fru tlis] *adj.* sterp; inutil.

frustrate [frʌs'treit] *vt.* a zădărnici; a nemulţumi.

frustration [frʌs'treiʃn] *s.* zădărnicire; nemulţumire.

fry [frai] *s.* peştişori mici. *vt., vi.* a (se) prăji.

frying-pan ['fraiiŋpæn] *s.* tigaie cu coadă.

fuchsia ['fju:ʃə] *s.* fucsie, cerceluş.

fuddle ['fʌdl] *vt.* a îmbăta; a ameţi.

fuel [fjuəl] *s.* combustibil. *vt., vi.* a (se) alimenta cu combustibil.

fuel oil ['fjuəl'ɔil] *s.* păcură.

fugitive ['fju:dʒitiv] *s., adj.* fugar.

fulfil [ful'fil] *vt.* a îndeplini; a desăvîrşi; a săvîrşi.

full [ful] *adj.* plin; deplin; matur.

full-blooded ['ful'blʌdid] *adj.* pasionat; de rasă pură.

full dress ['ful‚dres] *s.* haine de gală; mare ţinută.

full-fledged ['ful'fledʒd] *adj.* matur.

full house [‚ful'haus] *s.* sală arhiplină.

full-length ['ful'leŋθ] *adj.* în mărime naturală; plin; deplin.

ful(l)ness ['fulnis] *s.* plenitudine; mulţumire.

fulminate ['fʌlmineit] *vi.* a fulgera.

fulsome ['fulsəm] *adj.* excesiv; greţos.

fumble ['fʌmbl] *vt.* a mînui neîndeminatic. *vi.* a bîjbîi; a fi stîngaci.

fume [fju:m] *s.* abur; agitaţie. *vt.* a afuma. *vi.* a fumega.

fumigate ['fju:migeit] *vt.* a afuma.

fun [fʌn] *s.* distracţie; veselie; glumă.

function ['fʌŋʃn] *s.* funcţi(un)e; scop; *pl.* îndatoriri; ceremonie. *vi.* a funcţiona; a îndeplini o îndatorire.

functionary ['fʌŋʃnəri] *s.* funcţionar.

fund [fʌnd] *s.* fond; *pl.* resurse.

fundamental [‚fʌndə'mentl] *s.* bază. *adj.* fundamental; elementar.

funeral ['fju:nrl] *s.* înmormîntare. *adj.* funerar.

funeral-repast ['fjunrl ri'pa:st] *s.* praznic.

fungi ['fʌngai] *pl. de la* **fungus.**

fungus ['fʌŋgəs] *s.* ciupercă.

funk [fʌŋk] *s.* spaimă. *vt., vi.* a (se) speria.

funnel ['fʌnl] *s.* pîlnie; coş (de vapor, locomotivă).

funny ['fʌni] *adj.* nostim; ciudat.

funny story ['fʌni'stɔ:ri] *s.* anecdotă; glumă.

fur [fə:] *s.* (animale cu) blană. *vt.* a îmblăni.

furbish ['fə:biʃ] *vt.* a lustrui.

furious ['fjuəriəs] *adj.* violent; furios.

furlong ['fə:lɔŋ] *s.* optime de milă (*200 m*).

furlough ['fə:lou] *s. mil.* permisie; concediu.

furnace ['fə:nis] *s.* furnal; coş; cuptor.

furnish ['fə:niʃ] *vt.* a mobila; a aproviziona

furniture ⌐'tə.nitʃə] s. mobilă.
furrier [ˈfʌriə] s. blănar.
furrow [ˈfʌrou] s. brazdă *(şi fig.).* vi. a brăzda.
furry [ˈfəːri] adj. îmblănit; cu blană.
further [ˈfəːðə] comp. de la **far** adj. mai îndepărtat; nou; viitor; ulterior. vt. a promova; a continua; a ajuta. adv. în continuare; în plus; mai departe.
furtherance [ˈfəːðrns] s. promovare.
furthermore [ˈfəːðəˈmɔː] adv. pe deasupra.
furthest [ˈfəːðist] superl. de la **far** adj. cel mai îndepărtat; celălalt. adv. cel mai departe; cel mai tîrziu.
furtive [ˈfəːtiv] adj. (pe) furiş; secret.

fury [ˈfjuəri] s. furie; izbucnire.
fuse ⌐'fjuːz] s. fitil; el. siguranţă. vt., vi. a (se) topi; a fuziona.
fuselage [ˈfjuːzilaːʒ] s. fuzelaj.
fusion [ˈfjuːʒn] s. fuziune; unire; îmbinare.
fuss [fʌs] s. emoţie; zarvă. vt. a enerva. vi. a se agita; a se afera.
fussy [ˈfʌsi] adj. agitat; aferat; pisălog.
fustian [fʌstiən] s. sibir; palavre. adj. ordinar; bombastic.
fusty [ˈfʌsti] adj. mucegăit; cu iz.
futile [ˈfjuːtail] adj. zadarnic.
futility [fjuːˈtiliti] s. zădărnicie; lucru de prisos.
future [ˈfjuːtʃə] s., adj. viitor.
fuzzy [ˈfʌzi] adj. rufos; vag; flocos.

G

G [dʒiː] s. G, g; (nota) sol.
gabble [ˈgæbl] s. flecăreală. vi. a flecări.
gaberdine [ˈgæbədiːn] s. gabardină.
gable [ˈgeibl] s. fronton.
gadfly [ˈgædflai] s. tăun; streche.
gag [gæg] s. căluş; *teatru, cin.* gag, truc, idee năstruşnică. vt. a face să tacă.
gaiety [ˈgeiəti] s. veselie.
gaily [ˈgeili] adv. vesel; dezordonat; ţipător.
gain [gein] s. cîştig; spor. vt.

a cîştiga. vi. a cîştiga; *(d. ceas)* a o lua înainte.
gait [geit] s. mers.
gaiters [ˈgeitəz] s. jambiere; ghetre.
gale [geil] s. vînt puternic; furtună; izbucnire.
gall [gɔːl] s. fiere; rosătură. vt. a amărî; a roade.
gallant [ˈgælənt] s. dandi. adj. viteaz; elegant; galant.
gallantry [ˈgæləntri] s. vitejie; galanterie.
gallery [ˈgæləri] s. galerie.

galley ['gæli] s. galeră.

gallon ['gælən] s. măsură de capacitate (3,4 sau 4,34 l).

gallop ['gæləp] s. galop. vi. a galopa.

gallows ['gælouz] s. spînzurătoare.

gallows-bird ['gælouzbə:d] s. criminal; spînzurat.

galore [gə'lɔ:] adv. din belşug.

galosh [gə'lɔʃ] s. galoş; amer. şoşon.

galvanize ['gælvənaiz] vt. a galvaniza; fig. a electriza.

gamble ['gæmbl] s. aventură; joc de noroc. vt. a risca. vi. a juca cărţi (sau alte jocuri de noroc).

gambling ['gæmbliŋ] s. jocuri de noroc.

gambling-house ['gæmbliŋhaus] s. tripou.

gambol ['gæmbl]ˉ s. zburdălnicie; giumbuşluc. vi. a zburda.

game [geim] s. joc; partidă; glumă; plan; vînat. adj. brav; pregătit; invalid. vt., vi. a juca (jocuri de noroc).

gamut ['gæmət] s. gamă.

gander ['gændə] s. gîscan.

gang [gæŋ] s. grup; echipă; bandă.

gangrene ['gæŋgri:n] s. gangrenă. vt., vi. a (se) gangrena.

gangster ['gæŋstə] s. bandit.

gangway ['gæŋwei] s. pasarelă; interval.

gaol [dʒeil] s. temniţă. vt. a întemniţa.

gaol-bird ['dʒeilbə:d] s. ocnaş.

gaoler ['dʒeilə] s. temnicer.

gap [gæp] s. gol; prăpastie; pauză.

gape [geip] s. căscat; mirare. vi. a (se) căsca.

garage [gæ'rɑ:ʒ] s. garaj.

garb [gɑ:b] s. îmbrăcăminte. vt., vi. a (se) îmbrăca.

garbage ['gɑbidʒ] s. gunoi; lături.

garden ['gɑ:dn] s. grădină.

garden-party ['gɑ:dn͵pɑ:ti] s. picnic; chermeză.

gardener ['gɑ:dnə] s. grădinar.

gardening ['gɑ:dniŋ] s. grădinărit.

gargle ['gɑ:gl] s. gargară. vi. a gargarisi.

gargoyle ['gɑ:gɔil] s. arhit. cap de balaur, gargoil.

garland ['gɑlənd] s. ghirlandă.

garlic ['gɑ:lik] s. usturoi.

garment ['gɑ:mənt] s. îmbrăcăminte.

garnish ['gɑ:niʃ] s. garnitură. vt. a garnisi.

garret ['gærət] s. mansardă.

garrison ['gærisn] s. garnizoană.

garrulous ['gæruləs] adj. flecar.

garter ['gɑtə] s. jartieră.

gas [gæs] s. gaz (de iluminat); amer. benzină. vt. a gaza. vi. a trăncăni.

gaseous ['geizjəs] adj. gazos.

gash [gæʃ] s. tăietură; rană. vt. a tăia.

gasolene, gasoline ['gæsəli:n] s. gazolină; amer. benzină.

gasp [gɑ:sp] s. icnit; răsuflare întretăiată. vt. a bolborosi. vi. a-şi pierde răsuflarea; a se sufoca; a icni.

gate [geit] s. poartă.

gather ['gæðə] vt. a culege; a strînge; a înţelege. vi. a se aduna; med. a coace.

gathering ['gæðriŋ] s. adunare.

gaudy ['gɔːdi] *adj.* ţipător; arătos.

gauge [geidʒ] *s.* măsură; calibru; ecartament; gabarit. *vt.* a măsura.

gaunt [gɔːnt] *adj.* sfrijit.

gauze [gɔːz] *s.* voal, gaz.

gave [geiv] *vt., vi. trec. de la* **give.**

gawky ['gɔːki] *adj.* stîngaci.

gay [gei] *adj.* vesel; pitoresc; imoral.

gaze [geiz] *s.* privire insistentă. *vi.* a se uita lung.

gazette [gə'zet] *s.* Monitorul *sau* Buletinul Oficial; ziar.

gazetteer [ˌgæzi'tiə] *s.* dicţionar geografic.

gear [giə] *s.* angrenaj; viteză; echipament; mecanism; *out of* ◀ stricat. *vt.* a angrena; a adapta. *vi.* a se angrena.

gear-box ['giəbɔks] *s.* cutie de viteze.

geese [giːs] *s. pl. de la* **goose** gîşte.

gelatin(e) [ˌdʒelə'tiːn] *s.* gelatină.

geld [geld] *vt.* a jugăni, a castra.

gelding ['geldiŋ] *s.* jugănire, scopire; animal castrat.

gem [dʒem] *s.* giuvaer.

gendarme ['ʒɑːndɑm] *s.* jandarm.

gender ['dʒendə] *s. gram.* gen.

genealogy [ˌdʒiːni'ælədʒi] *s.* genealogie.

genera ['dʒenərə] *s. pl. de la* **genus.**

general ['dʒenrl] *s., adj.* general.

generality [ˌdʒenə'ræliti] *s.* generalitate; majoritate.

generalization [ˌdʒenrəlai'zeiʃn] *s.* generalizare.

generally ['dʒenrli] *adv.* în general.

generate ['dʒenəreit] *vt.* a genera; a produce.

generation [ˌdʒenə'reiʃn] *s.* generaţie; generare.

generous ['dʒenrəs] *adj.* generos; abundent.

genial ['dʒiːnjəl] *adj.* simpatic; favorabil; blînd.

geniality [ˌdʒiːni'æliti] *s.* blîndeţe; amabilitate.

genii ['dʒiːniai] *s. pl. de la* **genius** duhuri, spirite.

genitive ['dʒenitiv] *s., adj.* genitiv.

genius ['dʒiːnjəs] *s.* geniu; spirit, duh (rău *sau* bun).

genocide ['dʒenosaid] *s.* crimă împotriva umanităţii.

genre [ʒɑːŋr] *s.* stil; gen (literar); *artă* compoziţie.

genteel [dʒen'tiːl] *adj.* rafinat; (prea) politicos.

gentian ['dʒenʃiən] *s.* genţiană.

gentile ['dʒentail] *s.* arian.

gentility [dʒen'tiliti] *s.* rafinament (formal).

gentle [dʒentl] *adj.* blînd; prietenos; tandru; nobil.

gentlefolk ['dʒentlfouk] *s. pl.* aristocraţie.

gentleman ['dʒentlmən] *s.* domn; aristocrat.

gentlewoman ['dʒentlwumən] *s.* doamnă; aristocrată.

gentry ['dʒentri] *s.* (mică) nobilime.

genuine ['dʒenjuin] *adj.* autentic, veritabil, adevărat.

genus ['dʒiːnəs] *s.* gen (în ştiinţă).

geography [dʒi'ɔgrəfi] *s.* geografie.

geology [dʒi'ɔlədʒi] s. geologie.
geometry [dʒi'ɔmitri] s. geometrie.
geranium [dʒi'reinjəm] s. muşcată.
germ [dʒəːm] s. germene.
German ['dʒəːmən] s., adj. ger-
man(ă).
germinate ['dʒəːmineit] vi. a
încolţi.
gerund ['dʒernd] s. gram. gerund.
gesticulate [dʒes'tikjuleit] vi. a
gesticula.
gesture ['dʒestʃə] s. gest.
get [get] vt. a căpăta; a lua;
a procura; a învăţa; a face;
a găsi; a cîştiga; a păţi; a
înţelege; a cuceri; a prinde;
a enerva; a omorî; to ~ back
a recăpăta; a răzbuna; to ~
in a strînge; a recăpăta; a
plasa; a învăţa; to ~ off a
scoate; a scăpa de; a învăţa
pe de rost; to ~ out a scoate,
a smulge; to ~ through a duce
la bun sfîrşit; to ~ together
a aduna (laolaltă); to ~ under
a înfrînge; a subjuga; to ~ up
a ridica; a aţîţa; a îmbrăca;
a pregăti. vi. a ajunge; a
deveni; a începe (să); a veni;
a se duce; a creşte; a cîştiga;
to ~ about a umbla; a fi pe
picioare; a se răspîndi; to ~
abroad a se răspîndi; to ~
along a înainta; a izbuti; a se
înţelege; a pleca; to ~ angry
a se supăra; to ~ at a ajunge
sau a ţinti la; to ~ away a
pleca; to ~ back a se întoarce;
a se răzbuna; to ~ done a
isprăvi; to ~ down a coborî;
to ~ down to a se apuca; to
~ in a intra; a se urca;

to ~ into a pătrunde; a se
deprinde cu; to ~ off a se
da jos; a pleca; a scăpa (uşor);
to ~ on a înainta (în vîrstă);
a continua; a (se) înţelege;
to ~ out a ieşi (la iveală); a
coborî; a scăpa; to ~ over a
trece peste sau de; a învinge;
a-şi reveni; to ~ round a ocoli;
a eluda; a se răspîndi; a convinge; a momi; to ~ through
a trece; a o scoate la capăt; a
triumfa; a obţine legătura;
a termina; to ~ to a se apuca
de; a ajunge; to ~ together
a se aduna; a se înţelege; to
~ up a se scula; a se înălţa;
a se înteţi.
get-together ['gettə‚geðə] s. a-
dunare; petrecere.
get-up ['getʌp] s. înfăţişare.
gewgaw ['gjuːgɔː] s. fleac; podoabă.
ghastly ['gɑːstli] adj. înspăimîntător.
gherkin ['gəːkin] s. castravecior.
ghost [goust] s. duh; strigoi.
ghostly ['goustli] adj. spectral;
sufletesc.
giant ['dʒaiənt] s., adj. uriaş.
gibberish ['gibəriʃ] s. trăncăneală; bolboroseală.
gibbet ['dʒibit] s. spînzurătoare.
gibe [dʒaib] s. glumă; ironie.
vi. a glumi.
giblets ['dʒiblits] s. potroace;
măruntaie.
giddy ['gidi] adj. zăpăcit.
gift [gift] s. dar.
gig [gig] s. şaretă; barcă.
gigantic [dʒai'gæntik] adj. gigantic.
giggle ['gigl] s. chicot(it). vi.
a chicoti.

gild [gild] *vt.* a polei ; *to ~ the
pill* a îndulci hapul.

gill [gil] *s.* branhie.

gillyflower ['dʒili͵flauə] *s.* micsandră.

gilt [gilt] *vt. trec. şi part. trec.
de la* **gild.**

gimlet ['gimlit] *s.* sfredel.

gin [dʒin] *s.* gin ; darac (pentru
bumbac). *vt.* a egrena.

ginger ['dʒindʒə] *s.* ghimbir.
vt. a înviora.

gingerbread ['dʒindʒəbred] *s.*
turtă dulce.

gingerly ['dʒindʒəli] *adj., adv.*
delicat ; prudent.

gipsy ['dʒipsi] *s., adj.* ţigan(că).

giraffe [dʒi'rɑːf] *s.* girafă.

gird [gəːd] *vt.* a încinge.

girder ['gəːdə] *s.* grindă.

girdle ['gəːdl] *s.* cingătoare,
brîu. *vt.* a încinge ; a conjura.

girl [gəːl] *s.* fată ; domnişoară ;
iubită.

girlhood ['gəːlhud] *s.* copilărie ;
adolescenţă.

girt [gəːt] *s.* chingă. *vt. trec.
şi part. trec. de la* **gird.**

gist [dʒist] *s.* esenţă (*fig.*).

give [giv] *vt.* a (acor)da ; a
transmite ; a scăpa ; a lăsa
(moştenire) ; a oferi ; a hărăzi ;
a toasta pentru ; a face ; a
ceda ; a arăta ; *to ~ away* a
da (în căsătorie) ; a trăda ; a
emite ; a reflecta ; *to ~ forth*
sau *off* a produce ; a răspîndi ;
a scoate ; *to ~ out* a anunţa ;
to ~ over a abandona ; *to ~
up* a părăsi, a ceda ; a înmîna ;
a declara pierdut ; *to ~ way*
a ceda. *vi.* a fi generos ; a ceda ;
a slăbi ; *to ~ up* a renunţa.

given ['givn] *vt., vi. part. trec.
de la* **give.**

given name ['givn ͵neim] *s.*
nume de botez.

gizzard ['gizəd] *s.* pipotă ; gît.

glacier ['glæsjə] *s.* gheţar.

glad [glæd] *adj.* bucuros ; încîntător.

gladden ['glædn] *vt.* a bucura.

glade [gleid] *s.* luminiş.

gladiolus [͵glædi'ouləs] *s.* gladiolă.

glamorous ['glæmərəs] *adj.* fermecător.

glamour ['glæmə] *s.* farmec ;
vrajă.

glance [glɑːns] *s.* privire ; licărire. *vi.* a privi ; a scînteia.

gland [glænd] *s.* glandă.

glare [glɛə] *s.* strălucire ; privire aspră. *vi.* a străluci ; a se
uita fioros.

glaring ['glɛəriŋ] *adj.* orbitor ;
feroce ; izbitor.

glass [glɑːs] *s.* sticlă ; oglindă ;
lunetă ; barometru ; pahar ; *pl.*
ochelari ; binoclu.

glass case ['glɑːskeis] *s.* vitrină
(piesă de mobilier).

glassy ['glɑːsi] *adj.* sticlos.

glaze [gleiz] *s.* glazură ; smalţ ;
faianţă. *vt.* a pune geam la ;
a glasa. *vi.* a deveni sticlos.

glazier ['gleizjə] *s.* geamgiu.

gleam [gliːm] *s.* licărire. *vi.* a
licări.

glean [gliːn] *vt., vi.* a spicui.

glee [gliː] *s.* veselie.

glib [glib] *adj.* iute ; abil.

glide [glaid] *s.* alunecare ; gli-
sadă. *vi.* a aluneca.

glider (plane) ['glaidə (plein)] *s.*
planor.

glimmer ['glimə] *s.* licărire. *vi.* a licări.

glimpse [glims] *s.* privire; ocheadă.

glint [glint] *s.* scînteiere. *vi.* a scînteia.

glisten ['glisn] *vi.* a scînteia.

glitter ['glitə] *s.* strălucire; splendoare. *vi.* a străluci.

gloat [glout] *vi.: to ~ over* a sorbi din ochi; a privi cu lăcomie.

globe [gloub] *s.* glob.

globe-trotter ['gloub͵trɔtə] *s.* turist (pedestru).

gloom [glu:m] *s.* întunecime; tristeţe.

gloomy ['glu:mi] *adj.* întunecos; trist.

glorify ['glɔ:rifai] *vt.* a ridica în slăvi.

glorious ['glɔ:riəs] *adj.* glorios; splendid; încîntător.

glory ['glɔ:ri] *s.* glorie; strălucire; splendoare. *vi.: to ~ in* a se făli cu.

gloss [glɔs] *s.* luciu. *vt.* a lustrui.

glossary ['glɔsəri] *s.* glosar.

glossy ['glɔsi] *adj.* lucios.

glove [glʌv] *s.* mănuşă.

glow [glou] *s.* licărire; fierbinţeală; roşeaţă. *vi.* a fi fierbinte; a străluci; a se îmbujora.

glowing ['glouiŋ] *adj.* strălucitor; entuziast; îmbujorat.

glowworm ['glouwə:m] *s.* licurici.

glue [glu:] *s.* clei. *vt.* a lipi.

glum [glʌm] *adj.* posomorît.

glutton ['glʌtn] *s.* mîncău.

gnarled [nɑ:ld] *adj.* noduros; *fig.* aspru.

gnash [næʃ] *vt.* a scrîşni (din dinţi).

gnat [næt] *s.* ţînţar.

gnaw [nɔ:] *vt., vi.* a roade; a (se) chinui.

go [gou] *s.* energie; entuziasm; încercare; modă; *on the ~* în activitate; *all the ~* ultima modă. *vt.* a încerca; a străbate. *vi.* a merge; a (se) duce; a curge; a circula; a tinde; a acţiona; a se vinde; a scăpa; a deveni; *to ~ ahead* a merge; *to ~ at* a se năpusti asupra; *to ~ back* a da *sau* a veni înapoi; *to ~ before* a avea precădere; *to ~ between* a mijloci; *to ~ beyond* a depăşi; *to ~ by* a se scurge; a trece (pe lîngă); *to ~ down* a coborî; a se afunda; a merge; a slăbi; a apune; *to ~ fast* a o lua înainte; *to ~ for* a căuta; a ataca; a valora; a-i plăcea; *to ~ forward* a înainta; a progresa; *to ~ in* a intra; a sosi; *to ~ in for* a se apuca de; a se ocupa de; *to ~ off* a pleca; a leşina; a muri; a se produce; a se desfăşura; a exploda; a se descărca; a scădea; *to ~ on* a continua; a avea succes; a trece; a progresa; a se apropia; *to ~ out* a ieşi (în societate); a apărea; a se răspîndi; a se sfîrşi; *to ~ over* a trece dincolo; a examina; a reciti; a întrece; a birui; *to ~ through* a trece prin; a sfîrşi; a cerceta; *to ~ to* a recurge la; *to ~ together* a se potrivi; a merge împreună; *to ~ under* a se scufunda; a cădea; a decădea; *to ~ up* a se ridica; a creşte; a merge la Londra; *to ~ without* a fi lipsit de;

a se priva de; *it goes without saying* se înțelege de la sine; *as far as it goes* deocamdată.

goad [goud] *s.* strămurare; îndemn. *vt.* a îndemna.

goal [goul] *s.* țintă; *sport* poartă.

goal-keeper ['goul͵ki:pə] *s. sport* portar.

goat [gout] *s.* capră; țap.

goatee [gou'ti:] *s.* barbișon.

gobble ['gɔbl] *s.* bolboroseală. *vt., vi.* a înfuleca.

go-between ['goubi͵twi:n] *s.* mijlocitor; codoș.

goblet ['gɔblit] *s.* pahar; cupă.

goblin ['gɔblin] *s.* spiriduș.

God¹ [gɔd] *s.* Dumnezeu.

god²[gɔd] *s.* zeu; *teatru the* ~*s* galerie.

godchild ['gɔdtʃaild] *s.* fin.

goddess ['gɔdis] *s.* zeiță.

godfather ['gɔd͵fɑ:ðə] *s.* naș (la botez).

god-fearing ['gɔd͵fiəriŋ] *adj.* cu frica lui Dumnezeu; pios.

god-forsaken ['gɔdfə'seikn] *adj.* prăpădit; mizerabil.

godless ['gɔdlis] *adj.* nelegiuit.

godly ['gɔdli] *adj.* pios.

godmother ['gɔd͵mʌðə] *s.* nașă (la botez).

godparents ['gɔdpɛərnts] *s. pl.* nași; cumetri.

godsend ['gɔdsend] *s.* noroc; pomană.

god-speed ['gɔd'spi:d] *s.* succes; noroc.

goggles ['gɔglz] *s. pl.* ochelari (de protecție).

going ['goiŋ] *s.* plecare; viteză; drum. *adj.* activ; rentabil.

goings-on ['goiŋz'ɔn] *s. pl.* întîmplări; purtare.

goiter, goitre ['gɔitə] *s.* gușă.

gold [gould] *s.* aur. *adj.* de aur; auriu.

golden ['gouldn] *adj.* auriu; de aur.

gold fever ['gould fi:və] *s.* goana după aur.

goldfield ['gouldfi:ld] *s.* bazin aurifer.

gold rush ['gouldrʌʃ] *s.* goana după aur.

goldsmith ['gouldsmiθ] *s.* aurar.

golf [gɔlf] *s. sport* golf.

golf links ['gɔlf liŋks] *s.* teren de golf.

golosh [gə'lɔʃ] *s.* galoș; *amer.* șoșon.

gone [gɔn] *vt., vi. part. trec. de la* go.

gong [gɔŋ] *s.* gong.

good [gud] *s.* bun; proprietate; avantaj, folos; *pl.* mărfuri; avere; *for* ~ *(and all)* definitiv; ~*s and chattels* efecte personale. *adj.* bun; minunat; potrivit; capabil; cuminte; *as* ~ *as* aproape; *as* ~ *as his word* de cuvînt.

good-bye [gud'bai] *s., interj.* adio; rămas bun; la revedere.

good-for-nothing ['gudfə͵nʌθiŋ] *s.* neisprăvit; prăpădit.

good-humoured ['gud'hju:məd] *adj.* plăcut; vesel; binevoitor.

good-looking ['gud'lukiŋ] *adj.* chipeș; arătos; frumos.

goodly ['gudli] *adj.* frumușel; suficient.

good-natured ['gud'neitʃəd] *adj.* de treabă; amabil.

goodness ['gudnis] *s.* bunătate; *for* ~' *sake!* pentru numele lui Dumnezeu! *thank* ~*!* slavă Domnului!

good riddance ['gud'ridns] *s.*

bine c-am scăpat! călătorie sprîncenată!

good-tempered ['gud 'tempəd] *adj.* calm.

good-will ['gud'wil] *s.* bună-voinţă; conciliere.

goose [gu:s] *s.* gîscă; fier de călcat (de croitorie).

gooseberry ['guzbri] *s.* coacăz(ă).

gore [gɔ:] *s.* sînge (închegat).

gorge [gɔ:dʒ] *s.* strîmtoare; chei; gît. *vt., vi.* a (se) îndopa.

gorgeous ['gɔ:dʒəs] *adj.* strălu-citor; minunat; splendid.

gory ['gɔ:ri] *adj.* însîngerat.

gosling ['gɔzliŋ] *s.* boboc de gîscă.

gospel ['gɔspl] *s.* Evanghelie.

gospel truth ['gɔspltru:θ] *s.* adevărul adevărat.

gossamer ['gɔsəmə] *s.* borangic; voal; funigei.

gossip ['gɔsip] *s.* vorbe de clacă; bîrfă. *vi.* a flecări; a bîrfi.

got [gɔt] *vt., vi. trec. şi part. trec. de la* **get.** *particulă de întărire pentru verbul* **have.**

Goth [gɔθ] *s.* got.

Gothic ['gɔθik] *s., adj.* gotic(ă).

gotten ['gɔtn] *amer. vt. vi. part. trec de la* **get.**

gourd [guəd] *s.* dovleac; tigvă.

gout [gaut] *s.* gută.

govern ['gʌvn] *vt.* a guverna; a determina. *vi.* a guverna.

governess ['gʌvnis] *s.* guver-nantă.

government ['gʌvnmənt] *s.* gu-vern; guvernare; guvernămînt.

governor ['gʌvənə] *s.* guverna-tor; consilier; şef; tată.

gown [gaun] *s.* halat; rochie; robă.

grab [græb] *vt.* a apuca; a smulge.

grace [greis] *s.* graţie; har; rugăciune de mulţumire; îndu-rare. *vi.* a onora; a împodobi.

graceful ['greisfl] *adj.* graţios; amabil.

graceless ['greislis] *adj.* urît; ticălos; dizgraţios.

gracious ['greiʃəs] *adj.* plăcut; îndurător.

gradation [grə'deiʃn] *s.* gradaţie.

grade [greid] *s.* rang; grad; *amer.* notă; clasă (*la şcoală*); pantă. *vt.* a grada; a nota; a nivela.

gradient ['greidjənt] *s.* pantă.

gradual ['grædjuəl] *adj.* treptat.

graduate[1] ['grædjuit] *s.* absol-vent.

graduate[2] ['grædjueit] *vt.* a gra-da; a absolvi; *amer.* a da o diplomă (cuiva). *vi.* a absolvi.

graduation [,grædju'eiʃn] *s.* (ce-remonie de) absolvire; *pl.* gra-daţii.

graft [grɑ:ft] *s.* altoi; altoire; *med.* grefă; *amer.* corupţie, mită; escrocherie. *vt.* a altoi; a grefa; a mitui.

grain [grein] *s.* bob; fir; greu-tate de 0,065 gr; *pl.* grîne; *against the* ~ contra firii.

grammar ['græmə] *s.* gramatică.

grammarian [grə'mɛəriən] *s.* gramatician.

grammar-school ['græməsku:l] *s.* gimnaziu; şcoală secundară.

gram(me) [græm] *s.* gram.

gramophone ['græməfoun] *s.* gramofon; patefon; picup.

granary ['grænəri] *s.* hambar; grînar.

grand [grænd] *adj.* măreţ; no-bil; splendid; arogant; prin-cipal.

grandchild ['græntʃaild] s. nepot sau nepoată de bunic.

granddaughter ['græn‚dɔ:tə] s. nepoată de bunic.

grandeur ['grændʒə] s. grandoare; măreţie.

grandfather ['græn‚fɑ:ðə] s. bunic.

grandiloquent [græn'dïləkwənt] adj. pompos.

grandiose ['grændious] adj. grandios.

grandmother ['græn‚mʌðə] s. bunică.

grandparents ['græn‚pɛərnts] s. pl. bunici.

grandson ['grænsʌn] s. nepot de bunic.

grange [greindʒ] s. conac.

grannie, granny ['græni] s. bunicuţă.

grant [grɑ:nt] s. alocaţie; dar. vt. a acorda; a recunoaşte.

grape [greip] s. (boabă de) strugure.

grape fruit ['greipfru:t] s. grep(frut).

grape vine ['greipvain] s. viţă de vie.

graph [grɑ:f] s. grafic.

graphic ['græfik] adj. grafic; grăitor.

graphite ['græfait] s. grafit.

grapple ['græpl] vt., vi. a se lupta (cu).

grasp [grɑ:sp] s. strînsoare; putere. vt. a apuca; a strînge; a înţelege.

grasping ['grɑ:spiŋ] adj. apucător.

grass [grɑ:s] s. iarbă.

grasshopper ['grɑ:s‚hɔpə] s. zool. cosaş.

grassland ['grɑ:slænd] s. păşune.

grass-widow ['grɑ:s'widow] s. văduvă de paie.

grate [greit] s. grătar; galerie (în faţa sobei). vt. a zgîria; a rade; a pune gratii la. vi. a fi supărător sau discordant.

grateful ['greitfl] adj. recunoscător; agreabil.

gratify ['grætifai] vt. a gratifica; a încînta; a satisface.

grating ['greitiŋ] s. gratii.

gratitude ['grætitju:d] s. recunoştinţă.

gratuitous [grə'tjuitəs] adj. gratuit.

gratuity [grə'tjuiti] s. bacşiş.

grave [greiv] s. mormînt. adj. grav; solemn.

gravel ['grævl] s. pietriş.

grave stone ['greivstoun] s. piatră de mormînt.

grave yard ['greivjɑ:d] s. cimitir.

gravity ['græviti] s. gravitate; greutate (specifică etc.); solemnitate.

gravy ['greivi] s. sos; zeamă de carne.

gray [grei] s., adj. v. grey.

graze [greiz] s. rosătură; julitură. vt. a roade; a juli; a duce la păscut. vi. a paşte.

grease [gri:s] s. untură; grăsime; murdărie. vt. a unge.

greasy ['gri:zi] adj. unsuros; alunecos; murdar.

great [greit] adj. mare, important; măreţ; splendid; amuzant; drăguţ; nobil.

great coat ['greitkout] s. palton.

greatly ['greitli] adv. foarte.

greed [gri:d] s. lăcomie.

greedy ['gri:di] adj. lacom.

Greek [gri:k] s. grec, elen; (limba) greacă. adj. grec(esc).

green [gri:n] s. (spaţiu) verde; verdeaţă; imaş. adj. verde; inocent; proaspăt.

greenback ['gri:nbæk] s. amer. bancnotă.

greenery ['gri:nəri] s. verdeaţă.

greengrocer ['gri:n‚grousə] s. zarzavagiu.

greenhorn ['gri:nhɔ:n] s. ageamiu.

greenhouse ['gri:nhaus] s. seră.

greenish ['gri:niʃ] adj. verzui.

greet [gri:t] vt. a saluta; a întîmpina.

greeting ['gri:tiŋ] s. salut(are).

grenade [gri'neid] s. grenadă (de mînă).

grew [gru:] vt., vi. trec. de la grow.

grey [grei] s. cenuşiu. adj. cenuşiu; cărunt.

greybeard ['greibiəd] s. bătrîn.

greyhound ['greihaund] s. ogar.

grid [grid] s. grilă; grătar.

gridiron ['grid‚aiən] s. grătar de fript.

grief [gri:f] s. supărare; necaz.

grievance ['gri:vns] s. necaz; plîngere; revendicare.

grieve [gri:v] vt., vi. a (se) necăji.

grievous ['gri:vəs] adj. supărător; trist; dureros.

grill [gril] s. (friptură la) grătar. vt. a frige la grătar; fig. a chinui; a perpeli.

grim [grim] adj. aspru; sălbatic; sinistru; sever; întunecat.

grimace [gri'meis] s. strîmbătură. vi. a se strîmba.

grime [graim] s. murdărie. vt. a murdări.

grin [grin] s. rînjet (satisfăcut). vi. a rînji; a zîmbi.

grind [graind] s. trudă. vt. a măcina; a zdrobi; a tiraniza; a ascuţi; a trudi la; a scrîşni; to ~ down a împila. vi. a trudi; a se chinui; a se freca; a toci.

grinder ['graində] s. măsea; rîşniţă; moară; tocilar.

grindstone ['graindstoun] s. (piatră de) tocilă.

grip [grip] s. strînsoare; apucare. vt. a apuca; a captiva.

grippe [grip] s. gripă.

grisly ['grizli] adj. oribil; înspăimîntător; sinistru.

grist [grist] s. grine; fig. folos.

gristle ['grisl] s. zgîrci.

grit [grit] s. nisip; pietricele; cremene; tărie de caracter. vt., vi. a scrîşni (din dinţi).

grizzled ['grizld] adj. cărunt.

groan [groun] s. geamăt; murmur. vt. a murmura; a spune oftînd. vi. a geme.

grocer ['grousə] s. băcan.

grocery ['grousri] s. băcănie; pl. alimente.

grog [grɔg] s. rachiu cu apă şi lămîie, grog.

groggy ['grɔgi] adj. ameţit; slăbit.

groin [grɔin] s. arcadă; anat. stinghie.

groom [grum] s. grăjdar; servitor; mire. vt. a ţesăla; a îngriji (caii); a dichisi.

groove [gru:v] s. scobitură; şanţ; rilă. vt. a scobi.

grope [group] vt. a căuta pe bîjbîite. vi. a bîjbîi.

gross [grous] s. (măsură de) 12 duzini; toptan. adj. grosolan; greoi; total; strigător la cer.

grotesque [grou'tesk] adj. grotesc; ciudat.

grotto ['grɔtou] *s.* grotă.

ground[1] [graund] *s.* teren; domeniu; pămînt; sol; curte; motiv; temei; fundal; *pl.* drojdie. *vt.* a pune la pămînt; a bizui; a întemeia; a învăța esențialul. *vi.* a ateriza; a da de pămînt.

ground[2] [graund] *vt., vi. trec. și part. trec. de la* **grind.**

ground-floor ['graun'flɔ:] *s.* parter.

groundless ['graundlis] *adj.* neîntemeiat.

ground-nut ['graundnʌt] *s.* (alună) arahidă.

groundwork ['graundwə:k] *s.* bază; fond; fundament.

group [gru:p] *s.* grup. *vt., vi.* a (se) grupa.

grouse [graus] *s.* ieruncă, gotcă; plîngere. *vi.* a mormăi.

grove [grouv] *s.* crîng; dumbravă.

grovel ['grɔvl] *vi.* a se tîrî; a se ploconi.

grow [grou] *vt.* a crește; a cultiva. *vi.* a crește; a spori; a se dezvolta; a trăi; a deveni; *to ~ out of* a nu mai încăpea în; a se trage din; a se dezbăra de; *to ~ up* a se face mare.

growl [graul] *s.* mîrîit. *vt.* a mîrîi, a mormăi. *vi.* a mîrîi; a bubui.

grown [groun] *vt., vi. part. trec. de la* **grow.**

grown-up ['groun'ʌp] *s.* adult.

growth [grouθ] *s.* creștere; spor; sporire; excrescență.

grub [grʌb] *s.* mîncare.

grudge [grʌdʒ] *s.* ciudă, pică. *vt.* a nu voi să dea; a nu voi să recunoască; a-i părea rău de.

gruel [gruəl] *s.* fulgi de ovăz; terci.

gruesome ['gru:səm] *adj.* oribil, sinistru.

gruff [grʌf] *adj.* aspru; nepoliticos.

grumble ['grʌmbl] *s.* nemulțumire; mormăit. *vt.* a mormăi. *vi.* a protesta; a mormăi.

grumbler ['grʌmblə] *s.* nemulțumit.

grumpy ['grʌmpi] *adj.* țîfnos.

grunt [grʌnt] *vi.* a grohăi; a mormăi.

guarantee [ˌgærn'ti:] *s.* garanție; gir; chezășie; gaj. *vt.* a garanta; a gira; a promite.

guarantor ['gærntɔ:] *s.* girant.

guaranty ['gærnti] *s. jur.* garanție; gaj; gir.

guard [gɑ:d] *s.* pază; gardă; paznic; *pl.* trupe de gardă; apărătoare. *vt.* a păzi; a apăra. *vi.* a fi în gardă; a fi prudent.

guard house ['gɑ:dhaus] *s.* corp de gardă.

guardian ['gɑ:djən] *s.* tutore; epitrop; păzitor.

guardianship ['gɑ:djənʃip] *s.* tutelă.

gue(r)rilla [gə'rilə] *s.* (război de) partizani.

guess [ges] *s.* presupunere; ghiceală; *by ~* pe ghicite. *vt., vi.* a ghici. *amer.* a gîndi, a crede.

guess-work ['geswə:k] *s.* ghicit; ipoteze.

guest [gest] *s.* oaspete; client.

guffaw [gʌ'fɔ:] *s.* hohot. *vi.* a hohoti.

guidance ['gaidns] *s.* călăuzire.

guide [gaid] s. călăuză ; model. vt. a călăuzi ; a îndruma.

guided missiles ['gaidid'misailz] s. pl. proiectile teleghidate.

guild [gild] s. breaslă.

guile [gail] s. păcăleală.

guileless ['gaillis] adj. nevinovat.

guillotine [ˌgilə'tiːn] s. ghilotină. vt. a ghilotina.

guilt [gilt] s. vină.

guiltless ['giltlis] adj. nevinovat.

guilty ['gilti] adj. vinovat.

guinea ['gini] s. guinee (21 de şilingi).

guinea-pig ['ginipig] s. cobai.

guise [gaiz] s. veşmînt; înfăţişare ; mască.

guitar [gi'taː] s. chitară.

gulf [gʌlf] s. golf ; prăpastie.

gull [gʌl] s. pescăruş ; fraier. vt. a păcăli.

gullible ['gʌləbl] adj. credul, naiv.

gullet ['gʌlit] s. gîtlej.

gully ['gʌli] s. şanţ ; canal.

gulp [gʌlp] s. înghiţitură ; sorbitură. vt., vi. a înghiţi ; a sorbi.

gum [gʌm] s. gingie ; gumă ; cauciuc ; eucalipt. vt. a lipi ; a guma.

gumption ['gʌmʃn] s. simţ practic ; inventivitate ; eficienţă.

gun [gʌn] s. armă de foc; puşcă ; puşcaş ; amer. pistol ; mil. tun.

gunboat ['gʌnbout] s. canonieră ; monitor.

gunman ['gʌnmən] s. puşcaş ; bandit.

gunner ['gʌnə] s. tunar.

gunpowder ['gʌnˌpaudə] s. praf de puşcă.

gunshot ['gʌnʃot] s. împuşcătură ; bătaia puştii.

gunsmith ['gʌnsmiθ] s. armurier.

gunwale ['gʌnl] s. copastie, bord.

gurgle ['gəːgl] vi. a bolborosi.

gush [gʌʃ] s. izbucnire. vi. a ţîşni ; a izbucni ; to ~ over a se entuziasma de.

gusset ['gʌsit] s. clin.

gust [gʌst] s. rafală ; torent ; fig. izbucnire.

gusto ['gʌstou] s. entuziasm.

gut [gʌt] s. maţ ; catgut ; strună ; pl. esenţă ; pl. curaj. vt. a curăţi (de maţe) ; a distruge.

gutta-percha ['gʌtə'pəːtʃə] s. gutapercă.

gutter ['gʌtə] s. jgheab ; rigolă ; fig. mocirlă.

gutter-snipe ['gʌtəsnaip] s. golan.

guttural ['gʌtrl] adj. gutural.

guy [gai] s. persoană ; tip (ciudat).

guzzle ['gʌzl] vt., vi. a sorbi (cu lăcomie).

gym(nasium) [dʒim('neizjəm)] s. (sală de) gimnastică.

gymnastics [dʒim'næstiks] s. gimnastică.

gypsy ['dʒipsi] s. ţigan(că). adj. ţigănesc.

H

H [eitʃ] s. H, h ; (nota) si.

ha [haː] interj. ha ; aşi.

haberdashery ['hæbə'dæʃəri] s. mercerie ; galanterie.

habit ['hæbit] s. obicei; obişnuinţă; îmbrăcăminte.
habitual [hə'bitjuəl] adj. obişnuit.
habituate [hə'bitjueit] vt. a
deprinde.
hack [hæk] s. cal de povară;
fig. rob. vt. a ciopîrţi.
hackney ['hækni] s. cal · de
povară. vt. a banaliza.
hackney coach ['hækni‚koutʃ] s.
birjă.
had [həd, hæd] v. aux., vt.
trec. şi part. trec. de la **have.**
hag [hæg] s. vrăjitoare; babă
(rea).
haggard ['hægəd] adj. istovit;
stors.
haggle ['hægl] vi. a se tocmi;
a se certa.
hail [heil] s. grindină; lapoviţă;
salutare. vt. a saluta. vi. a
cădea ca o grindină; a veni.
interj. salut.
hair [hɛə] s. (fir de) păr; to a
~ exact.
haircut ['hɛəkʌt] s. tuns(oare).
hairdresser ['hɛə‚dresə] s. coafor;
frizer.
hairless ['hɛəlis] adj. pleşuv;
spîn.
hairpin ['hɛəpin] s. agrafă sau
ac de cap.
hair-splitting ['hɛə‚splitiŋ] s. des-
picarea firului în patru. adj.
extrem de fin; de amănunt.
hairy ['hɛəri] adj. păros.
halcyon ['hælsiən] adj. liniştit;
senin.
hale [heil] adj. sănătos; voinic.
half [hɑːf] s. jumătate; one's
better ~ soţie. adv. pe jumătate;
not ~ bad bun(icel).

half-back ['hɑːf'bæk] s. sport
mijlocaş.
half-baked ['hɑːf'beikt] adj. necopt.
half-blood ['hɑːfblʌd] s. frate
etc. vitreg.
half-breed ['hɑːfbriːd] s. corcitură.
half-brother ['hɑːf‚brʌðə] s. frate
vitreg.
half-caste ['hɑːfkɑːst] s. metis.
half-crown['hɑːf'kraun] s. (monedă de) doi şilingi şi şase penny.
half-hearted ['hɑːf'hɑːtid] adj.
indiferent; apatic.
half-holiday ['hɑːf'holədi] s. după
amiază liberă.
half-mast ['hɑːf'mɑːst] adj. în
bernă.
half-penny ['heipni] s. jumătate
de penny.
half-seas-over['hɑːfsiːz'ouvə] adj.
cherchelit.
half-sister ['hɑːf‚sistə] s. soră
vitregă.
half-time ['hɑːf'taim] s. jumătate de zi; sport repriză.
half-way ['hɑːf'wei] adj., adv.
la jumătatea drumului; incomplet.
half-witted ['hɑːf'witid] adj. imbecil.
hall [hɔːl] s. sală; hol; local;
conac; palat.
hall-mark ['hɔːl'mɑːk] s. marcaj (la bijuterii); marcă; fig.
ştampilă. vt. a marca; a însemna.
hallo [hə'lou] s. salut. interj.
alo; bună (ziua).
hallow ['hælou] s. sfînt. vt. a
sfinţi.
hallucination [hə‚luːsi'neiʃn] s.
halucinaţie.

halo ['heilou] *s.* nimb; halo.
halt [hɔ:lt] *s.* oprire; haltă. *vt.*
a opri. *vi.* a se opri; a şovăi;
a se poticni.
halter ['hɔ:ltə] *s.* laţ; ştreang;
căpăstru.
halting ['hɔ:ltiŋ] *adj.* şchiop;
şovăielnic.
halve [ha:v] *vt.* a înjumătăţi.
halves [ha:vz] *s. pl.* de la **half.**
ham [hæm] *s.* şuncă.
hamlet ['hæmlit] *s.* cătun.
hammer ['hæmə] *s.* ciocan. *vt.*,
vi. a ciocăni; a lovi.
hammer-and-tongs ['hæmərən-
tɔŋz] *adv.* pe brînci.
hammock ['hæmək] *s.* hamac.
hamper ['hæmpə] *s,* coşuleţ.
vt. a stînjeni.
hamstring ['hæmstriŋ] *s.* tendon.
vt. a paraliza.
hamstrung ['hæmstrʌŋ] *vt., trec.*
şi part. trec. de la **hamstring.**
hand [hænd] *s.* mînă; palmă;
pl. păstrare; influenţă; sursă;
muncitor; marinar; îndemînare;
manşă, levată (*la cărţi*); ac (de
ceasornic); scris; *at* ~ la
îndemînă; *by* ~ cu mîna;
in ~ la dispoziţie; *on* ~ disponibil; ~*s off!* jos mîna!;
~*s up!* mîinile sus! *vt.* a
înmîna; a **transmite.**
hand-bag ['hændbæg] *s.* sac de
voiaj; poşetă.
hand-barrow ['hænd,bærou] *s.*
targă (pt. brazde etc.).
handbill ['hænbil] *s.* manifest;
reclamă.
hand-book ['hænbuk] *s.* manual.
handcuff ['hænkʌf] *s.* cătuşă.
handful ['hænful] *s.* (cît încape
într-o) mînă; rebel.

handicap ['hændikæp] *s.* (cursă
cu) handicap; oprelişte. *vt.* a
handicapa.
handicraft ['hændikra:ft] *s.* meşteşug; artizanat.
handily ['hændili] *adv.* convenabil; uşor.
handiwork ['hændiwə:k] *s.* lucru
de mînă.
handkerchief ['hæŋkətʃif] *s.*
batistă; batic.
handle ['hændl] *s.* mîner; manivelă. *vt.* a mînui; a trata;
a conduce; a vinde.
hand-made ['hænmeid] *adj.*
lucrat manual.
hand-organ ['hænd,ɔ:gən] *s.* flaşnetă.
hand-out ['hændaut] *s.* cadou,
chilipir.
hand-rail ['hændreil] *s.* balustradă.
handsome ['hænsəm] *adj.* chipeş;
bine făcut; mărinimos.
handwriting ['hænd,raitiŋ] *s.*
scris; caligrafie.
handy ['hændi] *adj.* îndemînatic; convenabil; la îndemînă.
hang [hæŋ] *vt.* a atîrna; a
agăţa; a spînzura; *to* ~ *up*
a amîna; a întrerupe. *vi.*
a atîrna; a spînzura; a rămîne; a zăbovi; *to* ~ *on to*
a se ţine scai de; a persevera
în; *to* ~ *over* a ameninţa;
to ~ *together* a nu se despărţi.
hanged [hæŋd] *adj.* spînzurat.
hanger ['hæŋə] *s.* umăr de
haine; agăţătoare.
hanging ['hæŋiŋ] *s.* spînzurare;
spînzurătoare; *pl.* draperii. *adj.*
criminal.
hangman ['hæŋmən] *s.* călău.

hangover ['hæŋˌouvə] s. mahmureală.

hanker ['hæŋkə] vi. a tînji.

hansom(cab) ['hænsəm(ˌkæb)] s. birjă.

haphazard ['hæp'hæzəd] adj. întîmplător.

hapless ['hæplis] adj. nenorocos.

happen ['hæpn] vi. a se întîmpla; a se produce; a se nimeri.

happening ['hæpniŋ] s. întîmplare; eveniment.

happiness ['hæpinis] s. fericire; noroc.

happy ['hæpi] adj. fericit; nimerit.

happy-go-lucky ['hæpigou'lʌki] adj. vesel; fără grijă; nepăsător.

harangue [hə'ræŋ] s. discurs; fig. predică. vt., vi. a ține o predică (cuiva).

harass ['hærəs] vt. a hărțui.

harbinger ['hɑːbindʒə] s. vestitor.

harbo(u)r ['hɑːbə] s. port; fig. liman. vt. a ocroti; fig. a nutri. vi. a se adăposti.

hard [hɑːd] adj. tare; dificil; voinic; aspru; ~ and fast strict; ~ of hearing surd. adv. (din) greu; aspru; tare; aproape; ~ by curînd; aproape.

hard-boiled ['hɑːd'bɔild] adj. tare; (d. ou) răscopt.

hard cash ['hɑːd'kæʃ] s. bani gheață.

harden ['hɑːdn] vt., vi. a (se) întări; a (se) oțeli.

hard-headed ['hɑːd'hedid] adj. practic; interesat; amer. încăpățînat; împietrit.

hard-hearted ['hɑːd'hɑːtid] adj. fără inimă.

hardihood ['hɑːdihud] s. îndrăzneală; obrăznicie.

hard-labour ['hɑːd'leibə] s. muncă silnică.

hardly ['hɑːdli] adv. abia; cu greu(tate).

hardship ['hɑːdʃip] s. dificultate; privațiune.

hardware ['hɑːdwεə] s. articole de fierărie și menaj.

hardwood ['hɑːdwud] s. (lemn de) esență tare.

hard-working ['hɑːdˌwəːkiŋ] adj. harnic, sîrguincios.

hardy ['hɑːdi] adj. rezistent; călit.

hare [hεə] s. iepure (de cîmp).

hare-brained ['hεəˌbreind] adj. zăpăcit.

harlequin ['hɑːlikwin] s. arlechin, clovn.

harlot ['hɑːlət] s. prostituată.

harm [hɑːm] s. rău; stricăciune; atingere; pagubă. vt. a strica; a răni; a dăuna (cuiva).

harmful ['hɑːmfl] adj. dăunător; periculos.

harmless ['hɑːmlis] adj. inofensiv.

harmonic [hɑː'mɔnik] s. notă armonică. adj. armonic.

harmonica [hɑː'mɔnikə] s. muzicuță de gură.

harmonious [hɑː'mounjəs] adj. armonios; melodios, dulce.

harmonize ['hɑːmənaiz] vt., vi. a (se) potrivi.

harmony ['hɑːməni] s. armonie; potrivire; înțelegere.

harness ['hɑːnis] s. harnașament; hamuri. vt. a înhăma; fig. a exploata (un rîu etc.).

harp [hɑːp] s. harpă. vi. a insista.

harpoon [haː'puːn] s. harpon.
vt. a prinde cu harponul.

harpsichord ['haːpsikɔːd] s. clavecin.

harridan ['hæridn] s. baborniță.

harrow ['hærou] s. grapă. vt. a grăpa; fig. a chinui; a jefui; a necăji; a hărțui.

harsh [haːʃ] adj. aspru; supărător; sever.

hart [haːt] s. cerb.

harum-scarum ['hɛərəm'skɛərəm] adj. nesăbuit.

harvest ['haːvist] s. recoltă; seceriș. vt. a secera; a recolta.

harvester ['haːvistə] s. secerător; combină.

has [həz, hæz] v. aux., vt. pers. a III-a sg. ind. prez. de la have.

hash [hæʃ] s. tocană; tocătură; fig. rasol. vt. a toca; a rasoli.

haste [heist] s. grabă; pripă.

hasten ['heisn] vt., vi. a (se) grăbi.

hasty ['heisti] adj. pripit.

hat [hæt] s. pălărie.

hatch [hætʃ] s. tambuchi; trapă. vt. a cloci; a scoate (pui). vi. a cloci.

hatchet ['hætʃit] s. baltag.

hatchway ['hætʃwei] s. tambuchi.

hate [heit] s. ură; dușmănie. vt. a urî; a nu putea suferi.

hateful ['heitfl] adj. urîcios; dușmănos.

hath [hæθ] înv. v. aux. vt., vi. pers. a III-a ind. prez. de la have.

hatred ['heitrid] s. ură; ostilitate; antipatie.

hatter ['hætə] s. pălărier.

haughty ['hɔːti] adj. semeț; arogant.

haul [hɔːl] s. tragere; tracțiune; captură; pradă. vt., vi. a trage.

haunch [hɔːntʃ] s. sold; coapsă.

haunt [hɔːnt] s. loc vizitat adeseori; refugiu obișnuit. vt. a vizita adesea; a bîntui; a obseda; a reveni.

have [həv, hæv] v. aux., v. mod.: to ~ (got) to a trebui să. vt. a avea; a poseda; a manifesta; a dovedi; a permite; a suferi; a lua; a obține; a consuma; a se bucura de.

haven ['heivn] s. port; fig. liman.

havoc ['hævək] s. dezastru; ravagii.

hawk [hɔːk] s. șoim. vt. a vinde; a colporta (și fig.). vi. a vîna cu șoimi; a-și drege glasul.

hawker ['hɔːkə] s. vînzător ambulant.

hawthorn ['hɔːθɔːn] s. gherghin.

hay [hei] s. fîn.

haycock ['heikɔk] s. căpiță de fîn.

hayrick ['heirik] s. claie de fîn.

hazard ['hæzəd] s. șansă; risc; (joc de) noroc. vt. a risca; a îndrăzni să faci.

hazardous ['hæzədəs] adj. riscant; în voia soartei.

haze [heiz] s. aburul cîmpiei; ceață (ușoară).

hazel ['heizl] s. alun(ă); culoarea castanie. adj. castaniu; căprui.

hazel-nut ['heizlnʌt] s. alună.

hazy ['heizi] adj. cețos; vag.

H-bomb ['eitʃbɔm] s. bombă cu hidrogen.

he [hiː(ː)] pron. el; prefix masculin ex.: he-fox vulpoi; ~ who cel care.

head [hed] s. cap; conducător;

şef; vîrf; capitol; criză. *vt.* a conduce. *vi.* a se îndrepta.

headache ['hedeik] *s.* durere de cap.

head-dress ['heddres] *s.* pălărie; basma; bonetă.

heading ['hediŋ] *s.* titlu (de ziar, coloană).

headland ['hedlənd] *s.* promontoriu.

headlight ['hedlait] *s.* far (de automobil etc.).

headline ['hedlain] *s.* titlu de articol.

headlong ['hedlɔŋ] *adj.*, *adv.* cu capul înainte; *fig.* pripit.

headmaster ['hed'mɑ:stə] *s.* director de şcoală.

head-on ['hed'ɔn] *adj.*, *adv.* frontal.

head-phones ['hedfounz] *s. pl.* căşti.

head-piece ['hedpi:s] *s.* cap; minte; *radio.* cască.

headquarters ['hed'kwɔ:təz] *s.* cartier general; sediu (central).

headstrong ['hedstrɔŋ] *adj.* încăpăţînat; voluntar.

headway ['hedwei] *s.* progres.

heal [hi:l] *vt.*, *vi.* a (se) vindeca.

health [helθ] *s.* sănătate.

healthy ['helθi] *adj.* sănătos; voinic.

heap [hi:p] *s.* morman; amestecătură; mulţime; ~s of *times* adeseori. *vt.* a acumula; a îngrămădi; a încărca. *adv.* ~s foarte; mult.

hear [hiə] *vt.* a auzi; a asculta; a distinge; a afla de. *vi.* a auzi (bine); ~ *!* ~ *!* bravo !

heard [hə:d] *vt.*, *vi. trec. şi part. trec. de la* **hear.**

hearing ['hiəriŋ] *s.* auz; ascultare; audiţie; şedinţă (a tribunalului etc.); *out of* ~ prea departe ca să poată auzi.

hearsay ['hiəsei] *s.* bîrfă; zvon; *from* ~ din auzite.

hearse [hə:s] *s.* dric.

heart [hɑ:t] *s.* inimă; curaj; cupă (*la cărţi*).

heart-ache ['hɑ:teik] *s.* durere de inimă; tristeţe profundă.

heart-breaking ['hɑ:t,breikiŋ] *adj.* sfîşietor.

heart-broken ['hɑ:t,broukn] *adj.* întristat; cu inima frîntă.

heart-burn ['hɑ:tbə:n] *s.* arsură la stomac.

hearten ['hɑ:tn] *vt.* a încuraja; a înveseli.

heartfelt ['hɑ:tfelt] *adj.* sincer; profund.

hearth [hɑ:θ] *s.* vatră; cămin.

hearth-rug ['hɑ:θrʌg] *s.* carpeta din faţa căminului.

heartily ['hɑ:tili] *adv.* din inimă; cu poftă.

heartless ['hɑ:tlis] *adj.* împietrit; fără inimă.

heart-rending ['hɑ:t,rendiŋ] *adj.* sfîşietor.

heart-strings ['hɑ:tstriŋz] *s.* adîncul inimii; sentimente profunde.

hearty ['hɑ:ti] *adj.* sincer; entuziast; pofticios; solid.

heat [hi:t] *s.* căldură; zel; *sport* serie. *vt.*, *vi.* a (se) încălzi.

heater ['hi:tə] *s.* sobă; radiator; boiler.

heath [hi:θ] *s.* ierburi; băragan; şes acoperit cu iarbă neagră.

heathen ['hi:ðn] *s.*, *adj.* păgîn.

heather ['heðə] *s.* iarbă neagră.

heave [hi:v] vt. a ridica; a aburca; a scoate. vi. a se ridica; a undui; a fi agitat; a apărea.

heaven ['hevn] s. cer; paradis.

heavenly ['hevnli] adj. ceresc; divin.

heavy ['hevi] adj. greu; greoi; abundent; încărcat; (d. ploaie) torenţială. adv. apăsător; greu.

heavy-weight ['heviweit] s. om greoi; (boxer de) categoria grea.

Hebrew ['hi:bru:] s. evreu; (limba) ebraică.

hecatomb ['hekətoum] s. măcel.

heckle ['hekl] vt. a hărţui cu întrebări.

hectare ['hektɑ:] s. hectar.

hectic ['hektik] adj. aprins; înfierbîntat.

hedge [hedʒ] s. gard viu. vt. a înconjura (cu un gard); a împrejmui. vi. a face un gard; fig. a se ascunde; a se eschiva.

hedgehog ['hedʒɔg] s. arici.

heed [hi:d] s. atenţie; importanţă. vt. a lua în seamă. vi. a fi atent.

heel [hi:l] s. călcîi; toc (de pantofi); ticălos; to cool one's ~s a face anticameră; ~s over head cu susul în jos; în mare grabă; down at ~ scîlciat; neglijent.

hefty ['hefti] adj. voinic; viguros; mare.

hegemony [hi'gemani] s. hegemonie.

he-goat ['hi:'gout] s. ţap.

heifer ['hefə] s. juncă.

heigh-ho ['hei'hou] interj. hai(t)!

height [hait] s. înălţime; culme.

heighten ['haitn] vt. a înălţa; a spori.

heinous ['heinəs] adj. ticălos.

heir [ɛə] s. moştenitor.

heiress ['ɛəris] s. moştenitoare.

heirloom ['ɛəlu:m] s. amintire de familie.

held [held] vt., vi. trec. şi part. trec. de la hold.

helicopter ['helikɔptə] s. elicopter.

hell [hel] s. iad; go to ~! du-te naibii!. interj. drace.

hellish ['heliʃ] adj. îngrozitor; drăcesc.

hello ['he'lou] s., interj. (bună) ziua!; alo!

helm [helm] s. cîrmă.

helmet ['helmit] s. coif; cască.

helmsman ['helmzmən] s. cîrmaci.

help [help] s. ajutor; soluţie. vt. a ajuta; a sprijini; a servi (cu mîncare etc.); a împiedica; I can't ~ it n-am încotro. vi. a fi folositor.

helpful ['helpfl] adj. util; preţios.

helping ['helpiŋ] s. porţie (de mîncare).

helpless ['helplis] adj. neputincios; imobilizat; lipsit de ajutor.

helpmate ['helpmeit] s. tovarăş; ajutor.

helter-skelter ['heltə'skeltə] adv. în dezordine.

hem [hem] s. tiv. vt. a tivi; a înconjura. vi. a tuşi (cu înţeles); a se bîlbîi. interj. [hm] hm!

hemlock ['hemlɔk] s. cucută.

hemp [hemp] s. cînepă.

hemstitch ['hemstitʃ] s. tiv. vt. a tivi.

hen [hen] s. găină; femela unor păsări.

hence [hens] *adv.* de aici (înainte); deci.

henceforth ['hens'fɔ:θ] *adv.* pe viitor.

henchman ['hentʃmən] *s.* agent.

henpecked ['henpekt] *adj.* sub papuc.

her [hə:] *adj.* ei. *pron.* pe ea, o; îi, ei.

herald ['herld] *s.* vestitor. *vt.* a vesti.

heraldry ['herldri] *s.* heraldică.

herb [hə:b] *s.* iarbă (medicinală).

herd [hə:d] *s.* turmă; păstor.

herdsman ['hə:dzmən] *s.* păstor.

here [hiə] *adj.* de aici; local. *adv.* aici; iată; acum.

hereabout(s) ['hiərəˌbaut(s)] *adv.* pe aici.

hereafter [hiər'ɑ:ftə] *adv.* în viitor.

hereditary [hi'reditri] *adj.* ereditar; moştenit.

heredity [hi'rediti] *s.* ereditate.

heresy ['herəsi] *s.* erezie.

heretic ['herətik] *s.* eretic.

hereupon ['hiərə'pɔn] *adv.* la care; imediat după aceea.

herewith ['hiə'wið] *adv.* alăturat; cu această ocazie.

heritage ['heritidʒ] *s.* moştenire.

hermetic [hə'metik] *adj.* ermetic.

hermit ['hə:mit] *s.* pustnic.

hermitage ['hə:mitidʒ] *s.* schit.

hero ['hiərou] *s.* erou.

heroic [hi'rouik] *adj.* eroic.

heroine ['heroin] *s.* eroină; *chim.* heroină.

heroism ['heroizəm] *s.* eroism.

heron ['herən] *s.* bîtlan.

herring ['heriŋ] *s.* scrumbie.

hers [hə:z] *pron.* al ei.

herself [hə:'self] *pron.* se; însăşi; ea; *she hurt* ~ s-a lovit; *by* ~ singură.

hesitate ['heziteit] *vi.* a şovăi.

heterogeneous ['hetəro'dʒi:njəs] *adj.* eterogen.

hew [hju:] *vt.* a ciopli; a tăia.

hewn [hju:n] *vt. part. trec. de la* **hew.**

hey [hei] *interj.* hei.

heyday ['heidei] *s.* toi; *fig.* floare.

hiatus [hai'eitəs] *s.* hiat; lipsă.

hiccough, hiccup ['hikʌp] *s.* sughiţ. *vi.* a sughiţa.

hid [hid] *vt., vi. trec. şi part. trec. de la* **hide.**

hidden ['hidn] *vt., vi. part. trec. de la* **hide.**

hide [haid] *s.* piele (netăbăcită); blană. *vt.* a ascunde; a bate. *vi.* a se ascunde.

hide-and-seek ['haidən'si:k] *s.* (de-a) v-aţi ascunselea.

hidebound ['haidbaund] *adj.* îngust; închistat; dogmatic.

hideous ['hidjəs] *adj.* hidos.

hiding ['haidiŋ] *s.* ascunzătoare; bătaie.

hiding-place ['haidiŋpleis] *s.* ascunzătoare.

hierarchy ['haiərɑ:ki] *s.* ierarhie.

higgledy-piggledy ['higldi 'pigldi] *adj., adv.* cu susul în jos.

high [hai] *s.* cer. *adj.* înalt; acut; nobil; important; mare; (*d. timp*) înaintat. *adv.* sus; la înălţime.

high-born ['haibɔ:n] *adj.* nobil.

high-brow ['haibrau] *s., adj.* snob (intelectual).

high-flown ['haifloun] *adj.* pompos.

high-handed ['hai'hændid] *adj.* arogant; arbitrar.

high jump ['hai'dʒʌmp] s. săritură în înălţime.

highland ['hailənd] s. regiune muntoasă.

highly ['haili] adv. extrem de; foarte (mult).

high-minded ['hai'maindid] adj. cu suflet nobil.

highness ['hainis] s. înălţime; alteţă.

high-pitched ['hai'pitʃt] adj. ascuţit.

highroad ['hairoud] s. şosea.

high seas ['hai 'si:z] s. pl. largul mării.

high spirits ['hai'spirits] s. pl. bună dispoziţie; optimism.

high-strung ['hai'strʌŋ] adj. sensibil; nervos.

high tide ['hai 'taid] s. maximul fluxului.

highway ['haiwei] s. şosea; cale.

highwayman ['haiweimən] s. tilhar.

hike [haik] s. plimbare; excursie; spor (de salariu etc.). vi. a se plimba; a face o excursie.

hilarious [hi'lɛəriəs] adj. vesel; ilariant.

hill [hil] s. deal; munte; movilă; muşuroi.

hillock ['hilək] s. movilă; deal.

hilt [hilt] s. mîner (de sabie etc.).

him [him] pron. pe el, îl; lui, îi.

himself [him'self] pron. se; însuşi; el; he cut ~ s-a tăiat; by ~ singur.

hind [haind] s. căprioară. adj. din spate.

hinder ['hində] vt. a împiedica; a stînjeni.

hindmost ['hainmoust] adj. cel mai din spate, ultimul.

hindrance ['hindrns] s. oprelişte.

hinge [hindʒ] s. balama; fig. esenţă. vi. a atîrna; a se învîrti (şi fig.).

hint [hint] s. aluzie; sugestie. vt. a face aluzie; a sugera.

hip [hip] s. şold.

hippo(potamus)[ˌhipə('pɔtəməs)] s. hipopotam.

hire ['haiə] s. închiriere; angajare; salariu. vt. a închiria; a angaja; to ~ out a da cu chirie.

hireling ['haiəliŋ] s. salariat; servitor; lacheu.

his [hiz] adj. lui, său. pron. al lui.

hiss [his] s. şuierat. vt., vi. a şuiera.

historian [his'tɔ:riən] s. istoric.

historic [his'tɔrik] adj. de importanţă istorică; istoric.

historical [his'tɔrikl] adj. din istorie; istoric.

history ['histri] s. istorie.

histrionic [ˌhistri'ɔnik] adj. teatral, actoricesc.

hit s. lovitură; atac; pocnitură; succes; şlagăr. inf., trec. şi part. trec. vt. a lovi; a jigni; a nimeri. vi. a lovi; a da o lovitură; to ~ (up)on a nimeri; a găsi.

hitch [hitʃ] s. hop; salt; obstacol; încurcătură. vt. a ridica; a sălta; a lega. vi. a se agăţa; a se încurca.

hither ['hiðə] adv. încoace.

hitherto ['hiðə'tu:] adv. pînă acum.

hive [haiv] s. stup; pl. urticarie.

ho [hou] interj. o! ho!

hoard [hɔ:d] s. comoară; tezaur. vt. a aduna.

hoar-frost ['hɔ:'frɔst] s. promoroacă.

hoarse [hɔːs] *adj.* răguşit.

hoary ['hɔːri] *adj.* cărunt; coliliu; bătrîn.

hoax [houks] *s.* păcăleală. *vt.* a păcăli.

hobble ['hɔbl] *s.* şchiopătat; pripon. *vt.* a priponi. *vi.* a şchiopăta.

hobbledehoy ['hɔbldi'hɔi] *s.* matahală; lungan.

hobby ['hɔbi] *s.* distracţie; obsesie; marotă; pasiune.

hobby-horse ['hɔbihɔːs] *s.* cal de lemn; pasiune; cal de bătaie, marotă.

hobgoblin ['hɔbˌgɔblin] *s.* duh rău; strigoi; aghiuţă.

hobnail ['hɔbneil] *s.* ţintă (de bocanc).

hobnob ['hɔbnɔb] *vi.* a se bate pe burtă.

hock [hɔk] *s.* risling.

hockey ['hɔki] *s.* hochei.

hocus-pocus ['houkəs'poukəs] *s.* păcăleală; diversiune.

hoe [hou] *s.* sapă. *vt., vi.* a săpa; a plivi.

hog [hɔg] *s.* porc (îngrăşat).

hogshead ['hɔgzhed] *s.* butoi.

hoist [hɔist] *s.* macara; ridicare. *vt.* a ridica.

hold [hould] *s. mar.* cală; magazie; ţinere; păstrare; stăpînire; putere. *vt.* a ţine; a susţine; a menţine; a stăpîni; a avea; a ocupa; a cuprinde; *to ~ back* a reţine; a ascunde; *to ~ forth* sau *out* a oferi; *to ~ off* a ţine la distanţă; *to ~ over* a amîna; a ameninţa cu; *to ~ together* a uni; *to ~ up* a arăta; a opri; a întîrzia; a jefui. *vi.* a se ţine; a continua; a dăinui; *to ~ forth*

a predica; *to ~ off* sau *aloof* a sta de o parte; *~ on!* ţine-te bine!; stai un moment!; *to ~ out* a rezista; *to ~ together* a rămîne uniţi.

holder ['houldə] *s.* deţinător; cutie.

holding ['houldiŋ] *s.* proprietate.

hold-up ['houldʌp] *s.* atac banditesc; jaf; încurcătură de circulaţie.

hole [houl] *s.* gaură; scobitură; hop; încurcătură.

holiday ['hɔlədi] *s.* sărbătoare; *(mai ales la pl.)* vacanţă.

holiness ['houlinis] *s.* sfinţenie.

hollow ['hɔlou] *s.* scobitură; depresiune; vîlcea. *adj.* scobit; supt; gol; găunos; nesincer. *vt.* a scobi; a goli.

holly ['hɔli] *s.* ilice.

hollyhock ['hɔlihɔk] *s.* nalbă.

holm(-oak) ['houm('ouk)] *s.* gorun.

holocaust ['hɔləkɔːst] *s.* nimicire; masacru.

holy ['houli] *adj.* sfînt; pios.

homage ['hɔmidʒ] *s.* omagiu.

home [houm] *s.* casă; cămin; domiciliu; (viaţă de) familie; azil; *at ~* acasă; în ţară; nestînjenit. *adj.* intern; domestic. *adv.* acasă; în ţară; la ţintă.

homeless ['houmlis] *adv.* fără adăpost.

homely ['houmli] *adj.* simplu; plat; familiar; *amer.* urît.

home-made [ˌhoum'meid] *adj.* făcut în casă *sau* în ţară.

Home Office ['houm ˌɔfis] *s.* Minister de Interne.

Home Secretary ['houm ˌsekrətri] *s.* ministru de interne.

homesick ['houmsik] adj. plin de nostalgie.

homesickness ['houmsiknis] s. nostalgie.

homespun ['houmspʌn] s. stofă de casă (aspră). adj. de casă; simplu; obișnuit.

homestead ['houmsted] s. gospodărie, fermă.

homeward ['houmwəd] adj., adv. spre casă.

homework ['houmwə:k] s. teme, lecții (pentru acasă).

homicide ['hɔmisaid] s. omucidere; criminal.

homily ['hɔmili] s. predică.

hominy ['hɔmini] s. mămăligă.

homogeneous [ˌhɔmə'dʒi:njəs] adj. omogen.

homonym ['hɔmənim] s. omonim.

hone [houn] s. piatră de ascuțit; cute. vt. a ascuți.

honest ['ɔnist] adj. cinstit; sincer; curat.

honesty ['ɔnisti] s. cinste; sinceritate.

honey ['hʌni] s. miere; iubit(ă).

honeycomb ['hʌnikoum] s. fagure.

honeyed ['hʌnid] adj. mieros.

honeymoon ['hʌnimu:n] s. lună de miere.

honeysuckle ['hʌnisʌkl] s. caprifoi.

honk [hɔŋk] s. claxon. vi. a claxona.

honorary ['ɔnrəri] adj. onorific.

hono(u)r ['ɔnə] s. cinste; reputație; distincție; pl. onoruri. vt. a onora; a respecta.

hono(u)rable ['ɔnrəbl] adj. cinstit.

hood [hud] s. glugă; acoperiș; capotă.

hoodwink ['hudwiŋk] vt. a păcăli.

hoof [hu:f] s. copită.

hook [huk] s. cîrlig. vt. a agăța; a prinde.

hooked ['hukt] adj. încîrligat; acvilin.

hooligan ['hu:ligən] s. huligan.

hoop [hu:p] s. cerc; inel. vt. a prinde cu un cerc.

hooping-cough ['hu:piŋ kɔf] s. tuse măgărească.

hoot [hu:t] s. huiduială; vuiet. vi. a striga; a huidui.

hooter ['hu:tə] s. sirenă.

hooves [hu:vz] s. pl. de la hoof.

hop [hɔp] s. hamei; țopăială; escală. vt. a sări (peste); a evita. vi. a sări; a țopăi; a pleca.

hope [houp] s. speranță; beyond ~ deznădăjduit; irealizabil. vt., vi. a spera; a aștepta.

hopeful ['houpfl] adj. încrezător; promițător.

hopeless ['houplis] adj. desperat.

horde [hɔ:d] s. hoardă.

horizon [hə'raizən] s. orizont.

horn [hɔ:n] s. corn.

horned [hɔ:nd] adj. cu coarne; cornut.

hornet ['hɔ:nit] s. gărgăun.

horrible ['hɔrəbl] adj. groaznic.

horrid ['hɔrid] adj. scîrbos; insuportabil.

horrify ['hɔrifai] vt. a îngrozi.

horror ['hɔrə] s. groază; oroare.

horror-stricken ['hɔrəˌstrikn], horror-struck ['hɔrəstrʌk] adj. îngrozit.

horse [hɔ:s] s. cal; cavalerie; sport capră.

horseback ['hɔ:sbæk] s.: on ~ călare.

horse-chestnut ['hɔ:s'tʃesnət] s. castan (obişnuit); castană (porcească).

horseflesh ['hɔ:sfleʃ] s. carne de cal; cai.

horseman ['hɔ:smən] s. călăreţ.

horsemanship ['hɔ:smənʃip] s. echitaţie.

horse-power ['hɔ:s,pauə] s. cal--putere.

horse-radish ['hɔ:s,rædiʃ]s. hrean.

horse-shoe ['hɔ:sʃu:] s. potcoavă.

horsewhip ['hɔ:swip] s. cravaşă. vt. a cravaşa.

horsewoman ['hɔ:s,wumən] s. amazoană; călăreaţă.

hosanna [ho'zænə] s. osana.

hose [houz] s. furtun; tub; ciorapi lungi. vt. a stropi (cu furtunul).

hosier ['houʒə] s. negustor de galanterie.

hosiery ['houʒəri] s. galanterie (de damă); ciorapi (de damă).

hospitable ['hɔspitəbl] adj. ospitalier.

hospital ['hɔspitl] s. spital.

host [houst] s. gazdă; proprietar; hangiu.

hostage ['hɔstidʒ] s. ostatic.

hostel ['hɔstl] s. cămin (studenţesc).

hostess ['houstis] s. (femeie) gazdă; hangiţă.

hostile ['hɔstail] adj. duşman; duşmănos.

hostility [hɔs'tiliti] s. duşmănie; ostilitate.

hot [hɔt] adj. fierbinte; foarte cald; arzător; iute; violent; proaspăt. adv. fierbinte; arzător; to blow ~ and cold a fi

schimbător; give it him ~ trage-i o săpuneală.

hotbed ['hɔtbed] s. agr. pat cald; fig. focar.

hot-blooded ['hɔt'blʌdid] adj. pasionat; nerăbdător.

hotel [(h)ou'tel] s. hotel.

hotel keeper [(h)ou'tel,ki:pə] s. hotelier.

hothead ['hɔthed] s. om pripit; pl. capete înfierbîntate.

hothouse ['hɔthaus] s. seră.

hot water ['hɔt'wɔ:tə] s. apă fierbinte; bucluc.

hound [haund] s. cîine (de vînătoare).

hour ['auə] s. oră; pl. orar; ocazie.

hour-glass ['auəglɑ:s] s. ceas de nisip, clepsidră.

hour-hand ['auəhænd] s. acul orar.

hourly ['auəli] adj. orar; din oră în oră. adv. din oră în oră.

house¹ [haus] s. casă (de comerţ); locuinţă; clădire; cămin; sală de spectacol; pol. cameră.

house² [hauz] vt. a găzdui; a adăposti; a da case la.

house-agent ['haus,eidʒnt] s. misit de locuinţe.

house-breaker ['haus,breikə] s. spărgător.

household ['hausould] s. gospodărie; familie.

housekeeper ['haus,ki:pə] s. gospodină; menajeră.

housemaid ['hausmeid] s. servitoare.

House of Commons ['hausəv 'kɔmənz] s. Camera Comunelor.

House of Lords sau **Peers** ['hausəv'lɔ:dz sau 'piəz] s. Camera Lorzilor.

House of Representatives ['haus-əv ˌrepri'zentətivz] s. Camera Reprezentanţilor.

house-top ['haustɔp] s. acoperişul casei; *from the* ~(s) în gura mare.

housewife[1] ['hauswaif] s. gospodină; stăpîna casei.

housewife[2] ['hʌzif] s. cutie de lucru.

housework ['hauswə:k] s. treburi casnice.

hove [houv] vt., vi. trec. şi part. trec. de la **heave**.

hovel ['hɔvl] s. cocioabă.

hover ['hɔvə] vi. a pluti în aer.

how [hau] adv. cum (se poate); cît (de); ~ *do you do?* bună ziua; îmi pare bine de cunoştinţă; ~ *are you?* ce mai faci?

however [hau'evə] adv. oricît de. conj. totuşi; în orice caz.

howl [haul] s. urlet. vt., vi. a urla.

hub [hʌb] s. butucul roţii; centru; *the* ~ *of the earth* buricul pămîntului.

hubbub ['hʌbʌb] s. zarvă.

hubby ['hʌbi] s. bărbăţel.

huckleberry ['hʌklberi] s. amer. afin(ă).

huckster ['hʌkstə] s. negustor (ambulant) de mărunţişuri.

huddle ['hʌdl] s. învălmăşeală. vt., vi. a (se) învălmăşi; a (se) strînge.

hue [hju:] s. nuanţă; culoare.

hue-and-cry ['hju:ən'krai] s. zarvă; alarmă; hărţuială.

huffy ['hʌfi] adj. ţîfnos; nervos.

hug [hʌg] s. îmbrăţişare. vt. a îmbrăţişa; a strînge.

huge [hju:dʒ] adj. uriaş.

hulk [hʌlk] s. matahală.

hulking ['hʌlkiŋ] adj. mătăhălos; greoi.

hull [hʌl] s. coajă, păstaie; carenă. vt. a coji.

hullabaloo [ˌhʌləbə'lu:] s. zarvă.

hullo ['hʌ'lou] interj. alo! hei!

hum [hʌm] s. zumzet; fredonare; murmur. vi. a zumzăi; a fi agitat; a fredona; a tuşi; a-şi drege glasul; *to* ~ *and haw* a şovăi; a se bîlbîi.

human ['hju:mən] adj. uman.

humane [hju'mein] adj. omenos.

humanism ['hju:mənizəm] s. umanism.

humanitarian [hju:ˌmæni'tɛəriən] s. filantrop. adj. umanitar.

humanity [hju'mæniti] s. omenire; omenie; pl. umanistică.

humanize ['hju:mənaiz] vt., vi. a (se) umaniza.

humankind ['hju:mən'kaind] s. omenire.

humble ['hʌmbl] adj. umil. vt. a umili; *to eat* ~ *pie* a-şi cere scuze; a se umili.

humbug ['hʌmbʌg] s. mistificare; farsă; impostură; impostor. vt. a înşela. interj. prostii.

humdrum ['hʌmdrʌm] adj. monoton; banal.

humid ['hju:mid] adj. umed.

humiliate [hju'milieit] vt. a umili.

humility [hju'militi] s. modestie.

humming-bird ['hʌmiŋbə:d] s. colibri.

hummock ['hʌmək] s. movilă; deal.

humorist ['hju:mərist] s. umorist.

humorous ['hju:mrəs] adj. comic.

humo(u)r ['hju:mə] s. umor; dispoziţie. vt. a face pe plac (cuiva); a mulţumi (pe cineva).

hump [hʌmp] s. umflătură; cocoaşă.

humpback ['hʌmpbæk] s. cocoşat.

humph [hʌmf] interj. aşi.

hunch [hʌntʃ] s. cocoaşă; bucată; bănuială. vt. a cocoşa.

hunchback ['hʌntʃbæk] s. cocoşat.

hundred ['hʌndrəd] s., num. sută.

hundredfold ['hʌndrədfould] adv. însutit.

hundredth ['hʌndrədθ] s. sutime. num. al o sutălea.

hundredweight ['hʌndrədweit] s. măsură de 50 sau 45 kg.

hung [hʌŋ] vt., vi. trec. şi part. trec. de la hang a atîrna; a agăţa.

Hungarian [hʌŋ'gɛəriən] s., adj. maghiar(ă).

hunger ['hʌŋgə] s. foame; poftă; fig. dorinţă; dor. vi. a flămînzi; a tînji.

hungry ['hʌŋgri] adj. flămînd; fig. însetat.

hunk [hʌŋk] s. bucată mare.

hunt [hʌnt] s. vînătoare. vt. a vîna; a hăitui. vi. a vîna.

hunter ['hʌntə] s. vînător.

hunting ['hʌntiŋ] s. vînătoare.

huntsman ['hʌntsmən] s. vînător.

hurdle ['hə:dl] s. sport obstacol.

hurdy-gurdy ['hə:di,gə:di] s. flaşnetă.

hurl [hə:l] vt. a arunca.

hurrah [hu'rɑ:], hurray [hu'rei] vi. a ovaţiona. interj. ura.

hurricane ['hʌrikən] s. uragan.

hurried ['hʌrid] adj. grăbit.

hurry ['hʌri] s. grabă; in a ~ grăbit; uşor. vt., vi. a (se) grăbi.

hurt [hə:t] s. rană; lovitură; durere; jignire. vt. inf., trec. şi part. trec. a răni; a strica; a jigni. vi. a-l durea; a suferi.

hurtful ['hə:tfl] adj. dureros; dăunător.

husband ['hʌzbənd] s. soţ. vt. a chibzui; a economisi.

husbandry ['hʌzbəndri] s. administrare; administraţie; economie.

hush [hʌʃ] s. tăcere. vt. a face să tacă; to ~ up a tăinui; a muşamaliza. vi. a tăcea. interj. sst.

husk [hʌsk] s. coajă; pleavă. vt. a coji.

husky ['hʌski] adj. voinic; plin de coji; (d. glas) aspru, răguşit.

hussy ['hʌsi] s. ticăloasă; obrăznicătură; tîrîtură.

hustle ['hʌstl] s. învălmăşeală. vt. a lua pe sus. vi. a se grăbi.

hut [hʌt] s. colibă; baracă.

hyacinth ['haiəsnθ] s. zambilă.

hydraulic [hai'drɔ:lik] adj. hidraulic.

hydro-chloric ['haidrə'klɔrik] adj. clorhidric.

hydroplane ['haidroplein] s. hidroavion; barcă cu motor.

hyena [hai'i:nə] s. hienă.

hymn [him] s. imn religios.

hyphen ['haifn] s. liniuţă; cratimă.

hypocrisy [hi'pɔkrəsi] s. făţărnicie.

hypocrite ['hipəkrit] s. ipocrit(ă); mironosiţă.

hypodermic [,haipə'də:mik] s. injecţie. adj. subcutanat.

hypothesis [hai'pɔθisis] s. ipoteză.

hysterics [his'teriks] s. pl. istericale.

I

I [ai] s. I, i. *pron.* eu.
iambic [ai'æmbik] s. iamb. *adj.*
iambic.
ice [ais] s. gheaţă; îngheţată.
vt. a îngheţa; a răci; a glasa.
ice-box ['aisbɔks] s. răcitor.
ice-breaker ['ais breikə] s. spărgător de gheaţă.
ice-cream ['ais'kri:m] s. îngheţată.
icicle ['aisikl] s. ţurţure.
icing ['aisiŋ] s. glazură.
icon ['aikɔn] s. icoană.
icy ['aisi] *adj.* îngheţat; glacial.
idea [ai'diə] s. idee; *pl.* gărgăuni.
ideal [ai'diəl] s., *adj.* ideal.
idealism [ai'diəlizəm] s. idealism.
identic(al) [ai'dentik(l)] *adj.* i-
dentic.
identify [ai'dentifai] *vt.* a identifica.
identity [ai'dentiti] s. identitate.
ideological [ˌaidiə'lɔdʒikl] *adj.*
ideologic.
ideologist [ˌaidi'ɔlədʒist] s. ideolog.
ideology [ˌaidi'ɔlədʒi] s. ideologie.
ides [aidz] s. *pl.* ide.
id est ['id'est] *conj.* şi anume,
adică.
idiocy ['idiəsi] s. tîmpenie.
idiom ['idiəm] s. expresie; dialect; limbaj.
idiomatic(al) [ˌidiə'mætik(l)]
adj. frazeologic; de conversaţie.
idiot ['idiət] s. tîmpit; cretin.

idle ['aidl] *adj.* trîndav; nefolosit; şomer; inutil; prostesc. *vi.*
a pierde vremea; a şoma.
idler ['aidlə] s. pierde-vară.
idol ['aidl] s. idol.
idolize ['aidəlaiz] *vt.* a idolatriza.
i.e. ['ai'i:] *conj.* şi anume; adică.
if [if] *conj.* (chiar) dacă; (ori)-
cînd; *as* ~ ca şi cum.
ignite [ig'nait] *vt.*, *vi.* a (se)
aprinde.
ignoble [ig'noubl] *adj.* ruşinos.
ignominious [ˌignə'miniəs] *adj.*
ruşinos; necinstit.
ignorance ['ignərns] s. ignoranţă;
nesocotire.
ignore [ig'nɔ:] *vt.* a nesocoti;
a nu lua în seamă.
ill [il] s. rău; racilă. *adj.* rău;
bolnav; ticălos; ~ *at ease*
stînjenit. *adv.* rău; nefavorabil.
ill-blood ['il'blʌd] s. duşmănie;
ură.
illegal [i'li:gl] *adj.* ilegal.
illegible [i'ledʒəbl] *adj.* neciteţ.
illegitimate [ˌili'dʒitimit] *adj.*
nelegitim; ilicit; nejustificat.
ill-fated ['il'feitid] *adj.* nenorocit.
ill-gotten ['il'gɔtn] *adj.* de haram.
ill-humoured ['il'hju:məd] *adj.*
ţîfnos; prost .dispus.
illiberal [i'librl] *adj.* intolerant;
meschin.
illiteracy [i'litrəsi] s. analfabetism.
illiterate [i'litrit] s., *adj.* analfabet; ignorant.

ill-natured ['il'neitʃəd] adj. antipatic; nesuferit; nervos.

illness ['ilnis] s. boală.

ill-temper ['il'tempə] s. nervozitate; caracter antipatic sau dificil.

ill-tempered ['il'tempəd] adj. ţifnos; dificil; antipatic.

ill-timed ['il'taimd] adj. inoportun.

ill-treat ['il'tri:t] vt. a maltrata.

illumin(at)e [i'lju:min(eit)] vt. a (i)lumina; a împodobi.

ill-use ['il'ju:z] vt. a maltrata; a batjocori.

illusion [i'lu:ʒn] s. iluzie.

illusive [i'lu:siv] adj. iluzoriu.

illustrate ['iləstreit] vt. a ilustra; a explica.

illustration [ˌiləs'treiʃn] s. ilustraţie.

illustrious [i'lʌstriəs] adj. ilustru.

ill-will ['il'wil] s. duşmănie; ură; răutate.

image ['imidʒ] s. imagine; chip. vt. a imagina; a oglindi.

imagery ['imidʒri] s. imagini; figuri de stil.

imaginary [i'mædʒinri] adj. închipuit.

imagination [iˌmædʒi'neiʃn] s. închipuire; imaginaţie; fantezie.

imagine [i'mædʒin] vt. a(-şi) imagina.

imbecile ['imbisi:l] s., adj. imbecil.

imbibe [im'baib] vt. a îmbiba.

imbroglio [im'brouliou] s. încurcătură.

imbue [im'bju:] vt. a umple; a îmbiba.

imitate ['imiteit] vt. a imita.

imitation [ˌimi'teiʃn] s. imitaţie; copie. adj. fals.

immaterial [ˌimə'tiəriəl] adj. neimportant; fără legătură; imaterial.

immeasurable [i'meʒrəbl] adj. nemăsurat.

immediate [i'mi:djət] adj. imediat; direct.

immemorial [ˌimi'mɔ:riəl] adj. străvechi; uitat.

immerse [i'mə:s] vt. a (în)muia; a absorbi.

immoderate [i'mɔdrit] adj. excesiv; necumpătat.

immodest [i'mɔdist] adj. neruşinat; obscen.

immortal [i'mɔ:tl] s., adj. nemuritor.

immovable [i'mu:vəbl] s. bun imobiliar. adj. imobil; fix; neclintit.

immutable [i'mju:təbl] adj. imuabil, neschimbător.

imp [imp] s. drăcuşor.

impact ['impækt] s. influenţă; ciocnire.

impair [im'pɛə] vt. a slăbi; a strica.

impart [im'pɑ:t] vt. a împărtăşi.

impassable [im'pɑ:səbl] adj. de netrecut; impracticabil.

impassioned [im'pæʃnd] adj. pasionat.

impassive [im'pæsiv] adj. impasibil.

impatient [im'peiʃnt] adj. nerăbdător; nervos.

impeach [im'pi:tʃ] vt. a acuza (de trădare etc.).

impede [im'pi:d] vt. a împiedica; a stînjeni.

impediment [im'pedimənt] s. impediment, piedică.

impel [im'pel] vt. a împinge; a îndemna.

impend [im'pend] vi. a ameninţa; a fi iminent.

impending [im'pendiŋ] adj. iminent; ameninţător.

impenetrable [im'penitrəbl] adj. impenetrabil.

imperative [im'perətiv] s. imperativ; poruncă. adj. imperativ; imperios; obligatoriu.

imperfect [im'pə:fikt] s., adj. imperfect.

imperial [im'piəriəl] s. barbişon. adj. imperial.

imperialism [im'piəriəlizəm] s. imperialism.

imperil [im'peril] vt. a primejdui.

imperishable [im'periʃəbl] adj. nepieritor.

impersonate [im'pə:səneit] vt. a personifica; a întruchipa; a juca (un rol).

impervious [im'pə:vjəs] adj. impenetrabil; neinfluenţabil.

impetus ['impitəs] s. imbold, impuls.

impiety [im'paiəti] s. lipsă de pietate sau respect.

impinge [im'pindʒ] vi.: to ~ upon a influenţa; a încălca.

impious ['impiəs] adj. lipsit de pietate; lipsă de respect.

impish ['impiʃ] adj. drăcesc; răutăcios.

implement¹ ['implimənt] s. unealtă.

implement² ['impliment] vt. a aplica; a traduce în viaţă.

implicit [im'plisit] adj. implicit; total; absolut.

implore [im'plɔ:] vt. a implora.

imply [im'plai] vt. a implica; a sugera; a face aluzie la.

impolite [ˌimpə'lait] adj. nepoliticos.

import¹ ['impɔ:t] s. (marfă de) import; semnificaţie.

import² [im'pɔ:t] vt. a importa; a însemna.

importance [im'pɔ:tns] s. importanţă.

important [im'pɔ:tnt] adj. important; care-şi dă importanţă.

importation [ˌimpɔ:'teiʃn] s. import.

importunate [im'pɔ:tjunit] vt. a importuna; a pisa.

importune [im'pɔ:tju:n] vt. a importuna, a pisa.

impose [im'pouz] vt. a impune; a solicita. vi. to ~ upon a înşela.

imposing [im'pouziŋ] adj. impunător.

imposition [ˌimpə'ziʃn] s. impunere; impozit; înşelătorie.

impossible [im'pɔsəbl] adj. imposibil; supărător; dificil.

impotent ['impətnt] adj. neputincios.

impoverish [im'pɔvriʃ] vt. a sărăci.

impracticable [im'præktikəbl] adj. dificil, nerezonabil; inaplicabil.

imprecate ['imprikeit] vt. a blestema.

impregnable [im'pregnəbl] adj. de necucerit.

impress [im'pres] vt. a imprima; a impresiona.

impression [im'preʃn] s. impresie; imprimare; ediţie.

impressive [im'presiv] adj. impresionant.

imprint¹ ['imprint] s. urmă.

imprint² [im'print] *vt.* a (în)-tipări; a lipi.

imprison [im'prizn] *vt.* a întemniţa.

improbable [im'prɔbəbl] *adj.* puţin probabil; de necrezut.

improper [im'prɔpə] *adj.* nepotrivit; indecent.

improve [im'pru:v] *vt.* a îmbunătăţi; a valorifica. *vi.* a se îmbunătăţi; a se face bine.

improvement [im'pru:vmənt] *s.* îmbunătăţire; progres.

improvident [im'prɔvidnt] *adj.* nechibzuit.

improvise ['imprəvaiz] *vt., vi.* a improviza.

impudent ['impjudnt] *adj.* neruşinat; obraznic.

impulse ['impʌls] *s.* impuls; îndemn.

impure [im'pjuə] *adj.* impur; imoral.

in [in] *adv.* înăuntru; acasă; la destinaţie; la putere; la modă; de găsit. *prep.* în; la; cu; ~ that întrucît; ~ so far as în măsura în care; ~ fact de fapt.

inability [inə'biliti] *s.* neputinţă.

inaccuracy [in'ækjurəsi] *s.* inexactitate; greşeală.

inadequate [in'ædikwit] *adj.* necorespunzător; insuficient.

inane [i'nein] *adj.* stupid; prostesc.

inanimate [in'ænimit] *adj.* mort; fără viaţă; stupid.

inanity [i'næniti] *s.* stupiditate.

inappropriate [inə'proupriit] *adj.* nepotrivit.

inarticulate [inɑ:'tikjulit] *adj.* neclar; mut; nearticulat.

inasmuch [inəz'mʌtʃ] *conj.:* ~ as întrucît.

inaudible [in'ɔ:dəbl] *adj.* (de) neauzit.

inaugurate [i'nɔ:gjureit] *vt.* a inaugura; a instala; a instaura; a deschide.

inauspicious [inɔ:s'piʃəs] *adj.* nefericit; de rău augur.

inborn ['in'bɔ:n] *adj.* înnăscut.

inbred ['in'bred] *adj.* înnăscut; natural; din familie.

inbreeding ['in'bri:diŋ] *s.* endogamie.

incalculable [in'kælkjuləbl] *adj.* nemăsurat; nesigur; capricios.

incantation [inkæn'teiʃn] *s.* incantaţie; vrajă.

incapable [in'keipəbl] *adj.* incapabil.

incapacitate [inkə'pæsiteit] *vt.* a scoate din uz.

incapacity [inkə'pæsiti] *s.* neputinţă; incapacitate; *jur.* interdicţie.

incarnate¹ [in'kɑ:nit] *adj.* întruchipat; materializat.

incarnate² ['inkɑ:neit] *vt.* a întru(chi)pa; a concretiza.

incendiary [in'sendjəri] *s.* incendiator; agitator. *adj.* incendiar; aţîţător.

incense¹ ['insens] *s.* tămîie.

incense² [in'sens] *vt.* a înfuria.

incentive [in'sentiv] *s.* stimulent.

inception [in'sepʃn] *s.* început.

incessant [in'sesnt] *adj.* neîncetat; repetat.

inch [intʃ] *s.* (măsură de un) ţol (2,54 cm); firimitură; by ~es treptat; every ~ total.

incidence ['insidns] *s.* frecvenţă; incidenţă.

incident ['insidnt] s. incident;
episod. adj. întîmplător; ~ to
legat de.

incision [in'siʒn] s. tăietură.

incisive [in'saisiv] adj. muşcător; vioi; ascuţit.

incite [in'sait] vt. a aţîţa; a
stîrni.

inclement [in'klemənt] adj. aspru.

inclination [,inkli'neiʃn] s. înclinaţie; înclinare.

incline [in'klain] vt., vi. a (se)
înclina; a atrage.

include [in'klu:d] ,vt. a cuprinde.

inclusive [in'klu:siv] adj. cuprinzător; ~ of inclusiv.

income ['inkəm] s. venit.

incoming ['in,kʌmiŋ] adj. care
intră; viitor.

incommensurate [,inkə'menʃrit]
adj. nemăsurat; incomparabil;
disproporţionat.

incomparable [in'kɔmprəbl] adj.
incomparabil; fără pereche.

incomprehensible [in,kɔmpri hen-
səbl] adj. de neînţeles.

inconceivable [,inkən'si:vəbl]
adj. de neconceput; uluitor.

inconclusive [,inkən'klu:siv] adj.
neconvingător; neconcludent.

incongruous [in'kɔŋgruəs] adj.
nepotrivit; nefiresc.

inconsequent [in'kɔnsikwənt]
adj. incoerent; nelogic.

inconsiderable [,inkən'sidrəbl]
adj. infim.

inconsiderate [,inkən'sidrit] adj.
nechibzuit; neatent.

inconsistency [,inkən'sistnsi] s.
nepotrivire; inconsecvenţă.

inconsistent [,inkən'sistnt] adj.
inconsecvent; nepotrivit.

inconsolable [,inkən'souləbl] adj.
neconsolat.

inconspicuous [,inkən'spikjuəs]
adj. modest; retras; minuscul.

incontinent [in'kɔntinənt] adj.
nestăpînit.

incontrovertible ['inkɔntrə'və:-
təbl] adj. indiscutabil.

inconvenience [,inkən'vi:njəns]
s. lipsă de confort; necaz; in-
convenienţă. vt. a supăra; a
deranja.

inconvenient [,inkən'vi:njənt]
adj. supărător; nepotrivit.

incorporate[1] [in'kɔ:prit] adj. unit.

incorporate[2] [in'kɔ:pəreit] vt.,
vi. a (se) încorpora; a (se)
uni.

incorporeal [,inkɔ:'pɔ:riəl] adj.
imaterial.

incorrect [,inkə'rekt] adj. ne-
just; nepotrivit.

incorrigible [in'kɔridʒəbl] adj.
incorigibil.

incorruptible [,inkə'rʌptəbl] adj.
incoruptibil; cinstit; nepieritor; inalterabil.

increase[1] ['inkri:s] s. creştere;
spor.

increase[2] [in'kri:s] vt., vi. a
spori.

incredibly [in'kredəbli] adv. nemaipomenit de.

incredulous [in'kredjuləs] adj.
neîncrezător.

increment ['inkrimənt] s. spor-
(ire).

incriminate [in'krimineit] vt. a
acuza.

inculcate ['inkʌlkeit] vt. a inculca; a imprima.

incumbent [in'kʌmbənt] s. paroh. adj. datorat; it is ~
(up)on you e de datoria ta.

incur [in'kə:] vt. a înfrunta; a stîrni.

incurable [in'kjuərəbl] adj. nevindecabil.

indebted [in'detid] adj. îndatorat.

indecent [in'di:snt] adj. neruşinat; imoral; nepoliticos.

indecision [indi'siʒn] s. nehotărîre.

indecorous [in'dekərəs] adj. indecent; de prost gust.

indeed [in'di:d] adv. într-adevăr; foarte. interj. aşa e; nu zău.

indefatigable [,indi'fætigəbl] adj. neobosit.

indefeasible [,indi'fi:zəbl] adj. inalienabil.

indefinite [in'definit] adj. indefinit; neprecis; nehotărît.

indelible [in'delibl] adj. de neşters.

indelible pencil [in'delibl 'pensl] s. creion chimic.

indelicate [in'delikit] adj. neruşinat; ordinar.

indemnify [in'demnifai] vt. a compensa.

indemnity [in'demniti] s. asigurare; despăgubire.

indent [in'dent] vt. a dinţa; a cresta.

indenture [in'dentʃə] s. contract de ucenicie. vt. a da la meserie.

independence [indi'pendəns] s. independenţă.

independent [,indi'pendənt] s., adj. independent.

indescribable [,indis'kraibəbl] adj. de nedescris.

index ['indeks] s. indice; index; semn.

Indian ['indjən] s., adj. indian(ă).

Indian corn ['indjən'kɔ:n] s. porumb.

Indian file ['indjən'fail] s. şir indian.

Indian ink ['indjən'iŋk] s. tuş.

Indian summer ['indjən'sʌmə] s. toamnă lungă sau tîrzie.

india-rubber ['indjə'rʌbə] s. gumă (de şters).

indicate ['indikeit] vt. a indica; a prescrie; a sugera.

indicative [in'dikətiv] s. indicativ. adj. caracteristic; indicator; grăitor.

indices ['indisi:z] s. pl. de la index.

indict [in'dait] vt. a pune sub acuzaţie.

indictment [in'daitmənt] s. (act de) acuzaţie.

indifferent [in'difrnt] adj. indiferent; neutru; banal.

indigence ['indidʒns] s. sărăcie.

indigenous [in'didʒinəs] adj. indigen; specific.

indigent ['indidʒnt] adj. sărac.

indignant [in'dignənt] adj. indignat.

indignity [in'digniti] s. insultă; umilinţă.

indirect [,indi'rekt] adj. indirect; ocolit.

indiscreet [,indis'kri:t] adj. imprudent; neatent; neglijent.

indiscretion [,indis'kreʃn] s. indiscreţie; nechibzuială; nepoliteţe.

indiscriminate [,indis'kriminit] adj. la întîmplare; amestecat.

indisposition [,indispə'ziʃn] s. indispoziţie; ostilitate.

indisputable [,indis'pju:təbl] adj. indiscutabil.

indistinct [,indis'tiŋt] adj. neclar.

indite [in'dait] vt. a compune, a redacta, a crea.

individual [‚indi'vidjuəl] s. individ. adj. individual; specific.

individuality [‚indi‚vidju'æliti] s. individualitate; personalitate.

indomitable [in'dɔmitəbl] adj. nestăpînit; neînfrînt.

indoor ['indɔ:] adj. (din, de) interior.

indoors ['in'dɔ:z] adv. în casă.

indubitable [in'dju:bitəbl] adj. neîndoios.

induce [in'dju:s] vt. a determina; a influenţa.

inducement [in'dju:smənt] s. stimulent.

induction [in'dʌkʃn] s. inducţie.

indulge [in'dʌldʒ] vt. a lăsa liber; a răsfăţa. vi. a-şi permite; a se lăsa (dus de pasiuni, iluzii etc.).

indulgence [in dʌldʒns] s. indulgenţă; libertate; imoralitate; plăcere.

industrious [in'dʌstriəs] adj. muncitor, harnic.

industry ['indəstri] s. industrie; întreprindere; hărnicie.

inebriate¹ [i'ni:briit] s. beţiv. adj. beat.

inebriate² [i'ni:brieit] vt. a îmbăta.

ineffable [in'efəbl] adj. inefabil.

ineffective [‚ini'fektiv] adj. ineficace.

ineffectual [‚ini'fektjuəl] adj. ineficace; nereuşit.

inefficient [‚ini'fiʃnt] adj. ineficace; incapabil.

inelegant [in'eligənt] adj. de prost gust.

inept [i'nept] adj. stupid.

inequality [‚ini'kwɔliti] s. inegalitate; neregularitate.

inequity [in'ekwiti] s. nedreptate.

inescapable [‚inis'keipəbl] adj. inevitabil; ineluctabil.

inestimable [in'estiməbl] adj. nepreţuit.

inexcusable [‚iniks'kju:zəbl] adj. de neiertat.

inexhaustible [‚inig'zɔ:stəbl] adj. inepuizabil.

inexorable [in'eksərəbl] adj. necruţător; implacabil.

inexpedient [‚iniks'pi:djənt] adj. nepotrivit.

inexpensive [‚iniks'pensiv] adj. ieftin.

inexperience [‚iniks'piəriəns] s. lipsă de experienţă.

inexpert [‚ineks'pə:t] adj. nepriceput; stîngaci.

inexpressible [‚iniks'presəbl] adj. inexprimabil.

inextricable [in'ekstrikəbl] adj. de nerezolvat.

infallible [in'fæləbl] adj. infailibil.

infamous ['infəməs] adj. ticălos; ruşinos.

infamy ['infəmi] s. ticăloşie.

infancy ['infənsi] s. copilărie.

infant ['infənt] s. copil mic; minor. adj. de (pentru) copii; infantil.

infantry ['infəntri] s. infanterie.

infantry-man ['infəntrimən] s. infanterist; pedestraş.

infatuate [in'fætjueit] vt. a înnebuni; a prosti.

infatuated [in'fætjueitid] adj. îndrăgostit.

infatuation [in͵fætju'eiʃn] *s.* nebunie; dragoste nebună.

infect [in'fekt] *vt.* a infecta.

infection [in'fekʃn] *s.* infecţie; influenţă.

infectious [in'fekʃəs] *adj.* molipsitor.

infer [in'fə:] *vt.* a deduce; a sugera.

inference ['infrns] *s.* deducţie; concluzie.

inferior [in'fiəriə] *adj.* inferior.

infest [in'fest] *vt.* a infesta; a umple.

infidel ['infidl] *s.*, *adj.* necredincios; păgîn.

infidelity [͵infi'deliti] *s.* păgînism; infidelitate.

infinite ['infinit] *adj.* infinit.

infinitude [in'finitju:d] *s.* infinitate.

infirm [in'fə:m] *adj.* slab; bolnav.

infirmary [in'fə:məri] *s.* infirmerie.

infirmity [in'fə:miti] *s.* infirmitate; boală; slăbiciune.

inflame [in'fleim] *vt.*, *vi.* a (se) aprinde.

inflammable [in'flæməbl] *adj.* inflamabil; irascibil.

inflammatory [in'flæmətri] *adj.* inflamator; aţîţător.

inflate [in'fleit] *vt.* a umfla.

inflation [in'fleiʃn] *s.* inflaţie; umflare.

inflect [in'flekt] *vt.* a îndoi; a supune flexiunii.

inflexible [in'fleksəbl] *adj.* neclintit.

inflexion [in'flekʃn] *s.* îndoire; inflexiune; intonaţie.

inflict [͵in'flikt] *vt.* a da (o lovitură, o pedeapsă).

influence ['influəns] *s.* influenţă. *vt.* a influenţa.

influential [͵influ'enʃl] *adj.* influent; important.

influenza [͵influ'enzə] *s.* gripă.

influx ['inflʌks] *s.* aflux.

inform [in'fɔ:m] *vt.* a informa. *vi.*: *to ~ against* a denunţa.

informal [in'fɔ:ml] *adj.* fără ceremonie; neoficial; de mică ţinută.

informality [͵infɔ:'mæliti] *s.* lipsă de ceremonie.

information [͵infə'meiʃn] *s.* informaţii.

informer [in'fɔ:mə] *s.* informator.

infrequent [in'fri:kwənt] *adj.* rar.

infringe [in'frindʒ] *vt.* a încălca.. *vi.*: *to ~ upon* a încălca.

infuse [in'fju:z] *vt.* a turna; *fig.* a imprima.

infusion [in'fju:ʒn] *s.* infuzie.

ingenuous [in'dʒenjuəs] *adj.* sincer; nevinovat.

inglorious [in'glɔ:riəs] *adj.* ruşinos; obscur.

ingot ['iŋgɔt] *s.* lingou.

ingratiate [in'greiʃieit] *vt.*: *to ~ oneself with smb.* a se băga pe sub pielea cuiva.

ingratitude [in'grætitju:d] *s.* nerecunoştinţă.

ingress ['ingres] *s.* intrare; *tehn.* admisie.

inhabit [in'hæbit] *vt.* a locui.

inhabitant [in'hæbitnt] *s.* locuitor.

inhale [in'heil] *vt.*, *vi.* a respira.

inherent [in'hiərnt] *adj.* înnăscut; esenţial.

inherit [in'herit] *vt.*, *vi.* a moşteni.

inheritance [in'heritns] s. moştenire.

inhibit [in'hibit] vt. a inhiba; a opri.

inhospitable [in'hospitəbl] adj. neospitalier; ostil.

inhuman [in'hju:mən] adj. sălbatic; fără inimă.

inimical [i'nimikl] adj. ostil; dăunător.

inimitable [i'nimitəbl] adj. fără seamăn; extraordinar.

iniquity [i'nikwiti] s. nedreptate; ticăloşie.

initial [i'niʃl] s. iniţială. adj. iniţial. vt. a parafa; a aproba.

initiate[1] [i'niʃiit] s., adj. iniţiat.

initiate[2] [i'niʃieit] vt. a iniţia; a începe.

initiative [i'niʃətiv] s. iniţiativă; spirit întreprinzător.

injection [in'dʒekʃn] s. injecţie.

injunction [in'dʒʌŋʃn] s. poruncă; hotărîre judecătorească.

injure ['indʒə] vt. a strica; a jigni; a răni.

injurious [in'dʒuəriəs] adj. dăunător; jignitor.

injury ['indʒri] s. rană; rău; stricăciune; jignire.

injustice [in'dʒʌstis] s. nedreptate.

ink [iŋk] s. cerneală. vt. a scrie cu cerneală; a păta cu cerneală.

inkling ['iŋkliŋ] s. bănuială; idee vagă.

ink-pot ['iŋkpɔt], inkstand ['iŋkstænd], ink-well ['iŋkwel] s. călimară.

inky ['iŋki] adj. întunecos; murdar de cerneală.

inlaid ['in'leid] adj. încrustat. vt. trec. şi part. trec. de la inlay.

inland ['inlænd] adj. intern; interior.

in-law ['in'lɔ:] s. rudă prin alianţă.

inlay ['in lei] vt. a încrusta.

inlet ['inlet] s. golf; intrînd.

inmate ['inmeit] s. pensionar (al unui azil etc.); colocatar.

inmost ['inmoust] adj. profund; ascuns.

inn [in] s. han; birou de avocatură.

innate. [i'neit] adj. înnăscut.

inner ['inə] adj. interior.

innings ['iniŋz] s. repriză (la crichet etc.).

innkeeper ['in ki:pə] s. hangiu.

innocence ['inəsns] s. nevinovăţie.

innocent ['inəsnt] adj. nevinovat; neştiutor.

innocuous [i'nɔkjuəs] adj. inofensiv.

Inns of Court ['inzəv'kɔ:t] s. baroul londonez.

innuendo [,inju'endou] s. aluzie.

innumerable [i'nju:mrəbl] adj. nenumărat.

inoperative [in'ɔprətiv] adj. fără efect.

inordinate [i'nɔ:dinit] adj. neobişnuit; excesiv.

inorganic [,inɔ:'gænik] adj. anorganic; nefiresc.

in-patient ['in,peiʃnt] s. bolnav internat.

inquest ['inkwest] s. anchetă.

inquire [in'kwaiə] vt., vi. a întreba; to ~ after a întreba de; to ~ for a cere; to ~ into a cerceta; a ancheta.

inquirer [in'kwaiərə] s. solicitant; vizitator.

inquiring [in'kwaiəriŋ] *adj.* întrebător ; curios.

inquiry [in'kwaiəri] *s.* întrebare ; cercetare ; anchetă.

inquisition [ˌinkwi'ziʃn] *s.* cercetare ; anchetă ; inchiziție.

inquisitive [in'kwizitiv] *adj.* curios.

inroad ['inroud] *s.* atac ; incursiune.

insane [in'sein] *adj.* nebun, dement ; nesăbuit.

insanity [in'sæniti] *s.* demență.

insatiable [in'seiʃəbl] *adj.* nesătios ; nemulțumit.

inscribe [in'skraib] *vt.* a (în)-scrie ; a imprima.

inscription [in'skripʃn] *s.* inscripție.

inscrutable [in'skru:təbl] *adj.* nebănuit ; indescifrabil.

insect ['insekt] *s.* insectă ; gînganie.

insecure [ˌinsi'kjuə] *adj.* nesigur ; neserios.

insensible [in'sensəbl] *adj.* insensibil ; toropit ; insesizabil.

insensitive [in'sensitiv] *adj.* impalpabil ; insensibil.

inseparable [in'seprəbl] *adj.* nedespărțit.

insert [in'sə:t] *s.* inserție. *vt.* a insera ; a potrivi.

inset[1] ['inset] *s.* inserție ; parte introdusă.

inset[2] ['in'set] *vt.* a insera.

inside ['in'said] *s.* interior ; ~ out întors pe dos. *adj.* lăuntric. *adv., prep.* înăuntru ; ~ of în cursul a.

insight ['insait] *s.* perspicacitate ; pătrundere psihologică.

insignia [in'signiə] *s. pl.* simbol (al autorității etc.).

insignificant [ˌinsig'nifiknt] *adj.* neimportant ; neinteresant.

insincere [ˌinsin'siə] *adj.* nesincer.

insinuate [in sinjueit] *vt.* a insinua. *vr.* a se băga.

insist [in'sist] *vt.* a susține. *vi.* a insista ; *to* ~ *on* a cere.

insistent [in'sistnt] *adj.* insistent ; imperios ; urgent.

insolent ['inslənt] *adj.* obraznic ; insultător.

insoluble [in'sɔljubl] *s., adj.* insolubil; de nerezolvat.

insolvent [in'sɔlvnt] *s., adj.* falit.

insomuch [ˌinso'mʌtʃ] *adv.* în așa măsură.

inspector [in'spektə] *s.* inspector ; ofițer de poliție.

inspiration [ˌinspə'reiʃn] *s.* inspirație.

inspire [in'spaiə] *vt.* a inspira ; a însufleți ; a da aripi la.

inspirit [in'spirit] *vt.* a însufleți.

install [in'stɔ:l] *vt.* a instala ; a instaura.

installation [ˌinstə'leiʃn] *s.* instalare ; instalație ; utilaj.

instal(l)ment [in'stɔ:lmənt] *s.* rată ; acont ; fascicul ; parte dintr-un foileton.

instance ['instəns] *s.* exemplu ; caz ; *for* ~ de exemplu ; *in the first* ~ la început. *vt.* a da ca exemplu.

instant ['instənt] *s.* clipă. *adj.* imediat ; urgent ; curent.

instead [in'sted] *adv.* în schimb ; ~ *of* în loc de.

instep ['instep] *s.* scobitura piciorului.

instil(l) [in'stil] *vt.* a introduce ; a inculca.

instinct¹ ['instiŋt] *s.* instinct.

instinct² [in'stiŋt] *adj.* plin; însufleţit.

institute ['institjuːt] *s.* institut. *vt.* a institui; a numi.

institution [ˌinsti'tjuːʃn] *s.* instituţie; tradiţie; azil.

instruct [in'strʌkt] *vt.* a instrui.

instruction [in'strʌkʃn] *s.* învăţătură; *pl.* instrucţiuni.

instructor [in'strʌktə] *s.* instructor; învăţător; călăuză.

instrument ['instrumənt] *s.* instrument; contract.

instrumental [ˌinstru'mentl] *adj.* folositor; esenţial; instrumental.

instrumentality [ˌinstrumen'tæliti] *s.* mijloc.

insubordinate [insə'bɔːdnit] *adj.* nesupus.

insubordination ['insəˌbɔːdi'neiʃn] *s.* nesupunere.

insufferable [in'sʌfrəbl] *adj.* insuportabil.

insularity [ˌinsju'læriti] *s.* izolare.

insulate ['insjuleit] *vt.* a izola; a separa.

insulator ['insjuleitə] *s.* izolator.

insult¹ ['insʌlt] *s.* insultă.

insult² [in'sʌlt] *vt.* a insulta; a jigni.

insuperable [in'sjuːprəbl] *adj.* de netrecut.

insurance [in'ʃuərns] *s.* asigurări; (poliţă de) asigurare.

insure [in'ʃuə] *vt.* a asigura.

insurgent [in'səːdʒnt] *s., adj.* rebel.

insurmountable [ˌinsə'mauntəbl] *adj.* de netrecut.

intake ['inteik] *s.* înghiţitură; înghiţire; *tehn.* admisie.

intangible [in'tændʒəbl] *adj.* de neatins; abstract; imaterial.

integrate ['intigreit] *vt.* a completa; a integra.

integrity [in'tegriti] *s.* integritate; cinste.

intellect ['intilekt] *s.* minte.

intelligence [in'telidʒns] *s.* inteligenţă; înţelepciune; informaţii; spionaj.

intelligentsia [inˌteli'dʒentsiə] *s.* intelectualitate.

intemperate [in'temprit] *adj.* necumpătat.

intemperance [in'temprns] *s.* abuz; exces.

intend [in'tend] *vt.* a intenţiona.

intense [in'tens] *adj.* puternic; extrem(ist).

intensify [in'tensifai] *vt., vi.* a spori.

intensive [in'tensiv] *adj.* intens; întăritor.

intent [in'tent] *s.* intenţie; scop. *adj.* atent; serios; concentrat.

intention [in'tenʃn] *s.* intenţie; scop.

intentional [in'tenʃənl] *adj.* intenţionat; dorit.

inter [in'təː] *vt.* a îngropa.

intercede [ˌintə'siːd] *vi.* a interveni.

intercession [ˌintə'seʃn] *s.* intervenţie; pilă; pledoarie.

interchange [ˌintə'tʃeindʒ] *vt., vi.* a (se) schimba reciproc.

intercourse ['intəkɔːs] *s.* legătură; comunicaţie; relaţii.

interdict [ˌintə'dikt] *vt.* a interzice; a opri.

interest ['intrist] *s.* interes; scop; întreprindere; trust; dobîndă; profit. *vt.* a interesa.

interfere [ˌintə'fiə] *vi.* a se amesteca ; a se băga ; *to ~ with smth.* a deranja; a împiedica ceva ; *don't ~ with my orders* nu contrazice ordinele mele.

interference [ˌintə'fiərns] *s.* amestec ; opoziţie.

interim ['intərim] *s.* interimat. *adj.* interimar.

interior [in'tiəriə] *s.* interior ; afaceri interne. *adj.* interior ; intern.

interlace [ˌintə'leis] *vt., vi.* a (se) împleti.

interlard [ˌintə'la:d] *vt.* a împăna.

interleave [ˌintə'li:v] *vt.* a ingera ; a împăna (*fig.*).

interline [ˌintə'lain] *vt.* a scrie printre (rînduri).

interlinear [intə'liniə] *adj.* scris printre rînduri.

interloper ['intəloupə] *s.* intrus ; băgăreţ.

interlude ['intəlu:d] *s.* interludiu ; pauză.

intermediate [ˌintə'mi:djət] *s.* lucru intermediar. *adj.* intermediar.

intermingle [ˌintə'miŋgl] *vt., vi.* a (se) amesteca.

intermission [ˌintə'miʃn] *s.* pauză.

intern [in'tə:n] *s.* intern (de spital). *vt.* a interna.

internal [in'tə:nl] *adj.* intern ; interior.

international [ˌintə'næʃənl] *s.* internaţională. *adj.* internaţional.

interplay ['intə'plei] *s.* influenţă reciprocă.

interpolate [in'tə:poleit] *vt.* a interpela ; a insera.

interpose [ˌintə'pouz] *vt., vi.* a (se) interpune.

interpret [in'tə:prit] *vt.* a interpreta ; a traduce. *vi.* a fi interpret.

interrogation [inˌterə'geiʃn] *s.* întrebare ; interogare.

interrupt [ˌintə'rʌpt] *vt.* a întrerupe ; a stînjeni.

intersperse [ˌintə'spə:s] *vt.* a răspîndi ; a presăra.

intertwine [ˌintə'twain] *vt., vi.* a (se) împleti.

interval ['intəvl] *s.* interval ; pauză.

intervene [ˌintə'vi:n] *vi.* a interveni ; a surveni ; a se amesteca.

intervention [ˌintə'venʃn] *s.* intervenţie.

interview ['intəvju:] *s.* întrevedere ; întîlnire ; interviu. *vt.* a intervieva.

interweave [ˌintə'wi:v] *vt., vi.* a se întretese.

intimacy ['intiməsi] *s.* intimitate.

intimate¹ ['intimit] *s.* intim. *adj.* profund ; personal ; familiar.

intimate² ['intimeit] *vt.* a anunţa ; a sugera ; a comunica.

intimation [ˌinti meiʃn] *s.* anunţ(are) ; sesizare ; sugestie ; aluzie.

intimidate [in'timideit] *vt.* a intimida.

into ['intə, 'intu] *prep.* în ; înăuntrul.

intolerable [in'tɔlərəbl] *adj.* insuportabil.

intonation [ˌintə'neiʃn] *s.* intonaţie ; recitare.

intoxicant [in'tɔksikənt] *s., adj.* excitant.

intoxicate [in'tɔksikeit] vt. a
îmbăta ; a excita ; a stîrni.
intoxication [in,tɔksi keiʃn] s.
beţie ; emoţie ; intoxicaţie.
intractable [in'træktəbl] adj
dificil (de mînuit).
intrepid [in'trepid] adj. îndrăzneţ.
intricacy ['intrikəsi] s. complicaţie.
intricate ['intrikit] adj. complicat.
intrigue [in tri:g] s. intrigă. vt.
a intriga. vi. a face intrigi.
intrinsic [in'trinsik] adj. intrin-
sec.
introduce [,intrə'dju:s] vt. a
introduce ; a prezenta.
introduction [,intrə'dʌkʃn] s.
introducere ; prezentare.
introductory [,intrə'dʌktri] adj.
introductiv.
intrude [in'tru:d] vt. a deranja ;
a forţa ; a aduce pe cap. vi.
a fi un intrus ; a se băga ;
a deranja.
intruder [in'tru:də] s. intrus ;
nepoftit.
intrusion [in'tru:ʒn] s. deranj ;
tulburare.
inure [i njuə] vt. a deprinde.
invade [in'veid] vt. a invada ;
a ataca ; a încălca.
invader [in'veidə] s. invadator ;
intrus.
invalid¹ ['invəli:d] s. bolnav ;
infirm ; invalid. adj. bolnav ;
infirm ; invalid ; pentru bolnavi.
invalid² [in'vælid] adj. fără
valoare (legală).
invalidate [in'vælideit] vt. a
anula.
invaluable [in'væljuəbl] adj. nepreţuit.

invariable [in vɛəriəbl] adj. neschimbător ; permanent.
invariably [in'vɛəriəbli] adv.
permanent, mereu.
invasion [in'veiʒn] s. invazie ;
atac ; încălcare.
invective [in'vektiv] s. insultă ;
limbaj violent.
inveigh [in vei] vi. : to ~ against
a ataca ; a critica.
inveigle [in'vi:gl] vt. a ademeni ;
a sili.
invent [in'vent] vt. a inventa.
invention [in'venʃn] s. invenţie ;
imaginaţie ; născocire.
inventory ['in,vəntri] s. inventar. vt. a inventaria.
inversion [in'və:ʃn] s. inversiune ; lucru inversat.
invert [in'və:t] vt. a inversa ;
a răsturna.
invertebrate [in'və:tibrit] s., adj.
nevertebrat ; slăbănog.
inverted commas [in'və:tid
'kɔməz] s. pl. ghilimele.
invest [in vest] vt. a investi ;
a instala. vi. : to ~ in a cumpăra ; a cheltui pe.
investigate [in'vestigeit] vt. a
cerceta ; a ancheta.
investment [in'vestmənt] s. investiţie ; investire.
inveterate [in'vetrit] adj. înrădăcinat ; înrăit.
invigorate [in'vigəreit] vt. a
înviora ; a întări.
invincible [in'vinsəbl] adj. invincibil.
inviolable [in'vaiələbl] adj. sacru ; de neatins.
inviolate [in'vaiəlit] adj. nepîn-
gărit ; sacru.
invisible [in'vizəbl] adj. invizibil.

invisible ink [in'vizəbl 'iŋk] *s.* cerneală simpatică.

invite [in'vait] *vt.* a chema ; a ruga ; a atrage ; a cere.

inviting [in'vaitiŋ] *adj.* ispititor.

invoice ['invɔis] *s.* factură. *vt.* a factura.

invoke [in'vouk] *vt.* a invoca.

involve [in vɔlv] *vt.* a implica ; a atrage ; a cuprinde ; a produce.

inward ['inwəd] *s.* măruntaie ; maţe. *adj.* îndreptat spre interior. *adv.* spre interior.

iodine ['aiədi:n] *s.* iod.

iota [ai'outə] *s.* iotă.

IOU ['aiou'ju:] *s.* chitanţă.

irascible [i'ræsibl] *adj.* irascibil.

irate [ai'reit] *adj.* furios.

iris ['aiəris] *s.* stînjenel.

Irish ['aiəriʃ] *s.* (limba) irlandeză ; *the* ~ irlandezii. *adj.* irlandez.

Irishman ['aiəriʃmən] *s.* irlandez.

irk [ə:k] *vt.* a enerva.

irksome ['ə:ksəm] *adj.* enervant ; plicticos.

iron ['aiən] *s.* fier (de călcat *sau* de coafat) ; *pl.* lanţuri ; *to have ioo many* ~s *in the fire* a fi băgat în prea multe. *vt.* a călca (rufe) ; a înlănţui.

ironic(al) [ai'rɔnik(l)] *adj.* ironic.

ironmonger ['aiən,mʌŋgə] *s.* negustor de fierărie.

ironwork ['aiənwə:k] *s.* armătură ; *pl.* uzină metalurgică.

irony ['aiərəni] *s.* ironie.

irrational [i'ræʃənl] *adj.* iraţional ; prostesc.

irreconcilable [i'rekənsailəbl] *adj.* (de) neîmpăcat.

irrecoverable [,iri'kʌvrəbl] *adj.* iremediabil ; nerecuperabil.

irredeemable [,iri di:məbl] *adj.* nerecuperabil.

irreducible [,iri'dju:səbl] *adj.* ireductibil ; imposibil de mînuit.

irrefutable [i'refjutəbl] *adj.* de netăgăduit.

irregular [i'regjulə] *adj.* neregulat.

irrelevant [i relivnt] *adj.* neinteresant ; nelalocul lui.

irreplaceable [,iri'pleisəbl] *adj.* de neînlocuit.

irrepressible [,iri presəbl] *adj.* nestăpînit.

irresolute [i'rezəlu:t] *adj.* nehotărît ; şovăielnic.

irresolution [i,rezə'lu:ʃn] *s.* nehotărîre ; şovăială.

irrespective [,iris'pektiv] *adj.* neatent ; ~ *of* indifcrent de ; fără a ţine scama de.

irresponsible [iris'pɔnsəbl] *adj.* iresponsabil ; nedemn de încredere.

irretrievable [,iri'tri:vəbl] *adj.* nerecuperabil.

irreverent [i'revrənt] *adj.* lipsit de respect ; nerespectuos.

irrigate ['irigeit] *vt.* a iriga ; a drena.

irritable ['iritəbl] *adj.* iritabil ; nervos ; ţîfnos ; inflamabil.

irritant ['iritnt] *s., adj.* iritant.

irritate ['iriteit] *vt.* a irita ; a enerva.

is [iz] *v. aux., vi. pers.* a III-a *sg. ind. prez.* de la **be.**

isinglass ['aiziŋgla:s] *s.* clei de peşte.

island ['ailənd] *s.* insulă.

islander ['ailəndə] *s.* insular.

isle [ail] s. insulă.
islet ['ailit] s. ostrov.
isolate ['aisəleit] vt. a izola; a separa.
issue ['isju:] s. scurgere; sursă; publicare; ediție; număr (de ziar etc.); problemă; rezultat; progenitură; at ~ în discuție, în joc. vt. a publica; a emite. vi. a se scurge; a țîșni; a curge.
isthmus ['isməs] s. istm.
it [it] pron. el, ea; aceasta; se; ~ is hot e cald; ~ rains plouă.
Italian [i'tæljən] s., adj. italian(ă).
italic [i'tælik] s., adj. cursiv(ă).
itch [itʃ] s. mîncărime; rîie;

nerăbdare; poftă. vi. a avea mîncărime; a fi nerăbdător.
item ['aitem] s. articol; număr. adv. de asemenea.
itemize ['aitəmaiz] vt. a amănunți; a detalia.
iterate ['itəreit] vt. a repeta.
itinerant [i'tinrnt] adj. ambulant.
itinerary [i'tinrəri] s. itinerar; jurnal de călătorie.
its [its] adj. său; sa; lui; ei.
itself [it'self] pron. se; însuși; însăși; singur(ă).
ivory ['aivri] s. fildeș. adj. de fildeș.
ivy ['aivi] s. iederă.

J

J [dʒei] s. J, j.
jab [dʒæb] s. ghiont. vt. a înghionti; a lovi.
jabber ['dʒæbə] s. pălăvrăgeală; babilonie. vi. a pălăvrăgi; a vorbi neclar.
jack, Jack [dʒæk] s. om; bărbat; marinar; lucrător; valet (la cărți); vinci, cric; steag; steagul britanic. vt. a ridica.
jackal ['dʒækɔ:l] s. șacal.
jackanapes ['dʒækəneips] s. ștrengar; obraznic.
jackass ['dʒækæs] s. măgar; tîmpit.
jack-boot ['dʒækbu:t] s. cizmă înaltă.
jacket ['dʒækit] s. jachetă; supracopertă; învelitoare.

Jack Frost ['dʒæk'frɔst] s. Moș Gerilă.
jack-in-office ['dʒækin,ɔfis] s. birocrat încrezut; slujbaș care își dă importanță.
jack-knife ['dʒæknaif] s. briceag.
jack-of-all-trades ['dʒækəv'ɔ:ltreidz] s. om bun la toate; factotum.
jack-o'-lantern ['dʒækə'læntən] s. flăcăruie.
jack tar ['dʒæk'ta:] s. marinar; lup de mare.
jade [dʒeid] s. jad; mîrțoagă; iron. femeie.
jaded ['dʒeidid] adj. istovit; plictisit.
jag [dʒæg] s. colț de stîncă.

jaguar ['dʒægjuə] s. jaguar.

jail [dʒeil] s. temniţă. vt. a întemniţa.

jailbird ['dʒeilbə:d] s. ocnaş; deţinut.

jailer ['dʒeilə] s. temnicer.

jam [dʒæm] s. marmeladă; dulceaţă; gem; aglomeraţie. vt. a strivi; a bloca; a strica; a bruia. vi. a se înţepeni.

jangle ['dʒæŋgl] s. zornăit. vt., vi. a zornăi.

janitor ['dʒænitə] s. portar.

January ['dʒænjuəri] s. ianuarie.

japan [dʒə'pæn] s. obiecte de lac. vt. a lăcui.

Japanese [,dʒæpə'ni:z] s., adj. japonez(ă).

jar [dʒɑ:] s. zgîrietură; ceartă; borcan. vt. a zgîria; a supăra. vi. a nu se împăca; a fi supărător; it ~s on my nerves mă calcă pe nervi.

jargon ['dʒɑ:gən] s. jargon; limbă străină; limbă stricată.

jarring ['dʒɑ:riŋ] adj. aspru; supărător; discordant.

jasmin(e) ['dʒæsmin] s. iasomie.

jaundice ['dʒɔ:ndis] s. icter; gelozie; invidie.

jaunt [dʒɔ:nt] s. plimbare. vt. a se plimba.

jaunty ['dʒɔ:nti] adj. vioi; vesel; nepăsător.

javelin ['dʒævlin] s. sport suliţă.

jaw [dʒɔ:] s. falcă; pl. gură; cleşte.

jay [dʒei] s. gaiţă.

jazz [dʒæz] s. jaz; dans; gălăgie.

jealous ['dʒeləs] adj. gelos; invidios; grijuliu.

jealousy ['dʒeləsi] s. gelozie; invidie.

jean [dʒi:n] s. postav; pl. salopetă; pantaloni (de cowboy).

jeer [dʒiə] s. ironie; batjocură. vi. a-şi bate joc; a rîde.

jelly ['dʒeli] s. gelatină; piftie; peltea.

jelly fish ['dʒelifiʃ] s. moluscă.

jenny ['dʒeni] s. ring de filat.

jeopardize ['dʒepədaiz] vt. a primejdui.

jeopardy ['dʒepədi] s. primejdie.

jerk [dʒə:k] s. smucitură; zguduitură. vt. a zdruncina; a smulge.

jerky ['dʒə:ki] adj. plin de hopuri; smucit.

jerry-built ['dʒeribilt] adj. şubred.

jersey ['dʒə:zi] s. jerseu.

jest [dʒest] s. glumă. vi. a glumi.

jester ['dʒestə] s. bufon; mucalit.

jesting ['dʒestiŋ] adj. glumeţ.

Jesuit ['dʒezjuit] s. iezuit.

jet [dʒet] s. jet; ţîşnitură; bec (de gaz etc.); lignit; avion cu reacţie. adj. negru.

jetsam ['dʒetsəm] s. lest; lucruri aruncate, aduse de apă; vagabond.

jetty ['dʒeti] s. dig; debarcader.

Jew [dʒu:] s. evreu.

jewel ['dʒu:əl] s. juvaer; piatră preţioasă; rubin.

jeweller ['dʒu:ələ] s. giuvaergiu.

jewel(le)ry ['dʒu:əlri] s. bijuterii; nestemate.

Jewess ['dʒuis] s. evreică.

Jewish ['dʒuiʃ] adj. evreiesc.

Jew's harp ['dʒu:z'hɑ:p] s. drîmbă.

jibe [dʒaib] s. glumă. vi. a glumi.

jiffy ['dʒifi] s. moment.

jig [dʒig] s. *muz.* gigă. *vi.* a dănţui.

jilt [dʒilt] s. cochetă ; crai, *vt.* a părăsi (o iubită etc.).

Jim Crow [ˈdʒimˈkrou] s. negru ; discriminare rasială. *adj.* rasist.

jingle [ˈdʒiŋgl] s. clinchet ; zornăit. *vt.* a face să sune (clopotele etc.) ; a zornăi. *vi.* a zornăi ; a clincăni.

jingo [ˈdʒiŋgou] s. şovin ; by ~ ! formidabil !

jingoism [ˈdʒiŋgoizəm] s. şovinism.

jinrik(i)sha [dʒinˈrik(i)ʃə] s. ricşă.

jitters [ˈdʒitəz] *s. pl.* bîţiială.

job [dʒɔb] s. lucrare ; treabă ; slujbă. *vi.* a face afaceri.

jobber [ˈdʒɔbə] s. antreprenor ; agent de bursă ; escroc.

jockey [ˈdʒɔki] s. jocheu.

jocular [ˈdʒɔkjulə] *adj.* glumeţ ; umoristic.

jocund [ˈdʒɔkənd] *adj.* vesel.

jog [dʒɔg] s. ghiont. *vt.* a înghionti ; a stîrni ; a împinge.

John Bull [ˈdʒɔnˈbul] s. englezul (tipic) ; naţiunea britanică.

join [dʒɔin] *vt.* a uni ; a intra în (asociaţie etc.) ; a ajunge din urmă ; a se uni cu. *vi.* a se uni ; a se asocia.

joiner [ˈdʒɔinə] s. tîmplar (de mobilă).

joinery [ˈdʒɔinəri] s. tîmplărie ; mobilă.

joint [dʒɔint] s. articulaţie ; îmbinare; pulpă (de vacă etc.); cîrciumă. *adj.* comun ; unic ; asociat.

jointly [ˈdʒɔintli] *adv.* în comun.

joint-stock company [ˈdʒɔintstɔk ˈkʌmpəni] s. societate pe acţiuni.

joke [dʒouk] s. glumă. *vi.* a glumi.

joker [ˈdʒoukə] s. glumeţ ; individ.

jollification [ˌdʒɔlifiˈkeiʃn] s. petrecere.

jollity [ˈdʒɔliti] s. veselie ; petrecere.

jolly [ˈdʒɔli] *adj.* vesel ; plăcut. *adv.* foarte ; destul de.

jolt [dʒoult] s. zdruncinătură. *vt., vi.* a zdruncina.

jostle [ˈdʒɔsl] s. ghiont. *vt.* a îmbrînci ; a înghionti. *vi.* a se înghesui.

jot [dʒɔt] s. notiţă ; not a ~ nici un pic. *vt.* a nota.

journal [ˈdʒə:nl] s. jurnal ; axă.

journalese [ˌdʒə:nəˈli:z] s. stil gazetăresc.

journalism [ˈdʒə:nəlizəm] s. gazetărie.

journalist [ˈdʒə:nəlist] s. ziarist.

journey [ˈdʒə:ni] s. călătorie. *vi.* a călători.

journeyman [ˈdʒə:nimən] s. calfă ; salahor.

jowl [dʒaul] s. falcă (de jos) ; obraz.

joy [dʒɔi] s. bucurie ; plăcere.

joyful [ˈdʒɔifl] *adj.* vesel ; fericit ; îmbucurător.

joyous [ˈdʒɔiəs] *adj.* vesel.

jubilant [ˈdʒubilənt] *adj.* triumfător.

jubilee [ˈdʒubili:] s. jubileu (de 50 de ani).

judge [dʒʌdʒ] s. judecător ; arbitru. *vt.* a judeca ; a considera ; a presupune.

judg(e)ment [ˈdʒʌdʒmənt] s. judecată ; sentinţă ; părere.

judicial [dʒu(:)ˈdiʃl] *adj.* judecătoresc ; juridic.

judicious [dʒu'diʃəs] *adj.* înţelept; cu judecată.

jug [dʒʌg] *s.* urcior, chiup.

juggle ['dʒʌgl] *vi.* a jongla.

juggler ['dʒʌglə] *s.* jongler; scamator.

juice [dʒuːs] *s.* suc.

juicy ['dʒuːsi] *adj.* zemos; suculent.

juke-box ['dʒuːkbɔks] *s.* tonomat.

July [dʒu'lai] *s.* iulie.

jumble ['dʒʌmbl] *s.* încurcătură; amestec. *vt.*, *vi.* a (se) amesteca; a (se) încurca.

jump [dʒʌmp] *s.* săritură; zdruncinătură. *vt.* a sări (peste); a depăşi; a lăsa la o parte. *vi.* a (tre)sări; a se repezi.

jumper ['dʒʌmpə] *s.* săritor; jerseu.

jumpy ['dʒʌmpi] *adj.* nerăbdător; nervos.

junction ['dʒʌŋʃn] *s.* conjunctură; joncţiune; nod (de cale ferată etc.).

juncture ['dʒʌŋtʃə] *s.* conjunctură; punct, loc.

June [dʒuːn] *s.* iunie.

jungle ['dʒʌŋgl] *s.* junglă.

junior ['dʒuːnjə] *s.* junior; tî-năr; student în primii ani; elev în primele clase. *adj.* mai mic; junior; inferior.

juniper ['dʒuːnipə] *s.* ienupăr.

junk [dʒʌŋk] *s.* gunoi; resturi; fleacuri; joncă.

junket ['dʒʌŋkit] *s.* petrecere; plimbare; banchet.

juror ['dʒuərə] *s.* jurat; membru al unui juriu.

jury ['dʒuəri] *s.* juraţi; juriu.

juryman ['dʒuərimən] *s.* jurat.

just [dʒʌst] *adj.* drept; întemeiat; înţelept. *adv.* chiar; tocmai; abia; cam; ~ *now* adineauri.

justice ['dʒʌstis] *s.* judecată; justiţie; dreptate; judecător.

justification [ˌdʒʌstifi'keiʃn] *s.* justificare; scuză; dreptate.

justify ['dʒʌstifai] *vt.* a îndreptăţi; a scuza.

jut [dʒʌt] *s.* ieşitură, colţ; proeminenţă. *vi.* a ieşi în afară.

jute [dʒuːt] *s.* iută.

juvenile ['dʒuːvinail] *s.* tînăr; *pl.* cărţi pentru tineret. *adj.* tineresc; pentru tineret.

juxtaposition [ˌdʒʌkstəpə'ziʃn] *s.* alăturare.

K

K [kei] *s.* K, k.

kangaroo [ˌkæŋgə'ruː] *s.* cangur.

keel [kiːl] *s.* pîntece de navă, chilă. *vt.*, *vi.* a (se) răsturna.

keen [kiːn] *adj.* ascuţit; ager; puternic; pasionat.

keep [kiːp] *s.* întreţinere. *vt.* a păstra; a ţine; a deţine; a ascunde; a reţine; a întreţine; a respecta; a apăra; a sărbători; *to* ~ *off* a se ţine de o parte; a se feri; *to* ~ *out* a nu se amesteca.

keeper ['ki:pə] s. paznic; portar; îngrijitor.

keeping ['ki:piŋ] s. grijă; protecţie; apărare; înţelegere; conformitate; in ~ with conform cu, după.

keepsake ['ki:pseik] s. suvenir.

keg [keg] s. butoiaş.

ken [ken] s. cunoaştere; posibilităţi.

kennel ['kenl] s. cuşcă de cîine.

kept [kept] vt., vi. trec. şi part. trec. de la keep.

kerb [kə:b] s. refugiu (pentru pietoni).

kerbstone ['kə:bstoun] s. bordură (de trotuar).

kerchief ['kə:tʃif] s. batic, basma.

kernel ['kə:nl] s. sîmbure; miez.

kerosene ['kerəsi:n] s. gaz (lampant); petrol.

ketchup ['ketʃəp] s. sos picant.

kettle ['ketl] s. ceainic; ibric.

kettle drum ['ketl,drʌm] s. toba mare.

key [ki:] s. (poziţie) cheie; ton; clapă (de pian etc.). adj. esenţial, cheie. vt.: to ~ up a aţîţa; muz. a acorda.

keyboard ['ki:bɔ:d] s. claviatură.

keyhole ['ki:houl] s. gaura cheii.

keynote ['ki:nout] s. (notă) dominantă.

keystone ['ki:stoun] s. cheie de boltă.

khaki ['ka:ki] s., adj. kaki.

kick [kik] s. lovitură cu piciorul, şut; plăcere; senzaţie. vt. a lovi cu piciorul; a azvîrli. vi. a da din picioare; a face scandal.

kid [kid] s. (piele de) ied; piele fină; copil. vt. a păcăli. vi. a glumi.

kid glove ['kid,glʌv] s. mănuşă de piele fină; blîndeţe.

kidnap ['kidnæp] vt. a răpi.

kidney ['kidni] s. rinichi.

kill [kil] vt. a omorî; a tăia (animale); a distruge.

kiln [kiln] s. cuptor (de var etc.).

kilo ['ki:lou] s. kilogram.

kilometer, kilometre ['kilə,mi:tə] s. kilometru.

kilowatt ['kiləwɔt] s. kilowatt.

kilt [kilt] s. fustanela scoţienilor.

kin [kin] s. neamuri.

kind [kaind] s. gen, fel; chip; fire. adj. bun; blînd; dulce, prietenos; amabil; binevoitor, drăgăstos.

kindergarten ['kindəga:tn] s. grădiniţă de copii.

kind hearted ['kaind'ha:tid] adj. bun; înţelegător.

kindle ['kindl] vt., vi. a (se) aprinde.

kindly ['kaindli] adj. bun; binevoitor. adv. cu blîndeţe; amabil.

kindness ['kaindnis] s. bunătate; amabilitate.

kindred ['kindrid] s. rude. adj. înrudit.

king [kiŋ] s. rege; magnat.

kingdom ['kiŋdəm] s. regat; regn; ţară; domnie.

kingly ['kiŋli] adj. regesc; strălucitor; bogat.

King's Counsel ['kiŋz'kaunsl] s. avocat al statului.

kink [kiŋk] s. creţ; buclă; întorsătură. vt., vi. a (se) suci; a (se) încreţi.

kinsfolk ['kinzfouk] s. neamuri; familie.

kinship ['kinʃip] s. înrudire; asemănare.

kinsman ['kinzmən] s. neam; rudă.

kinswoman ['kinzwumən] s. rudă.

kiosk, kiosque [ki'ɔsk] s. chioşc.

kipper ['kipə] s. scrumbie afumată; somon.

kiss [kis] s. sărut. vt. a săruta; a atinge. vi. a se săruta.

kit [kit] s. echipament.

kitchen ['kitʃin] s. bucătărie.

kitchen garden ['kitʃin'gɑ:dn] s. grădină de zarzavat.

kitchen-maid ['kitʃin meid] s.ajutoare de bucătăreasă.

kite [kait] s. zmeu (jucărie); uliu.

kitten ['kitn] s. pisic(uţă).

knack [næk] s. pricepere; îndemînare.

knapsack ['næpsæk] s. raniţă; desagă; rucsac.

knave [neiv] s. ticălos; valet (la cărţi).

knavery ['neivəri] s. ticăloşie.

knavish ['neiviʃ] adj. înşelător; ticălos.

knead [ni:d] vt. a frămînta.

knee [ni:] s. genunchi.

knee-cap ['ni:kæp] s. rotulă.

knee-deep ['ni:'di:p] adj., adv. pînă la genunchi.

kneel [ni:l] vi. a îngenunchea.

knell [nel] s. dangăt de clopot (funerar). vt. a anunţa (moartea cuiva). vi. a suna trist.

knelt [nelt] vi. trec. şi part. trec. de la kneel.

knew [nju:] vt.,vi. trec. de la know.

knicker(bocker)s ['nikə(bɔkə)z] s. pantaloni scurţi; chiloţi.

knick-knack['niknæk] s. găteală; bibelou.

knife [naif] s. cuţit. vt. a înjunghea.

knight [nait] s. cavaler; cal (la şah).

knight-errant ['nait'ernt] s. cavaler rătăcitor.

knit [nit] inf., trec. şi part. trec. vt. a împleti; a tricota; a îmbina. vi. a se uni; a se îmbina.

knitting ['nitiŋ] s. împletit; tricotat.

knitwear ['nitwɛə] s. tricotaje.

knives [naivz] s. pl. de la knife.

knob [nɔb] s. mîner rotund; umflătură.

knock [nɔk] s. lovitură; pocnitură. vt. a lovi; a izbi; a trînti; a zdrobi; to ~ out a scoate din luptă; to ~ together a înjgheba; to ~ up a distruge; a istovi; a înjgheba. vi. a bate; a se lovi; to ~ about a vagabonda.

knock-about ['nɔkəbaut] adj. de dîrvală; improvizat.

knocker ['nɔkə] s. ciocănaş.

knock-kneed ['nɔkni:d] s. cu picioarele strîmbe.

knock-out ['nɔkaut] s. scoatere din luptă.

knoll [noul] s. movilă; măgură.

knot [nɔt] s. nod; nucleu; grup. vt., vi. a (se) înnoda.

knotty ['nɔti] adj. noduros; încurcat.

know [nou] vt. a şti; a cunoaşte; a recunoaşte; a înţelege; a trece prin; a suferi. vi. a fi ştiutor; priceput.

know-how ['nouhau] s. pricepere; competenţă.

knowing ['nouiŋ] adj. inteligent; ager; plin de înţeles; informat.

knowingly ['nouiŋli] adv. cu bunăştiinţă; cu (sub)înţeles.

knowledge ['nɔlidʒ] s. cunoaştere; cunoştinţe; ştiinţă; învăţătură; pricepere.

known [noun] vt., vi. part. trec. de la know.

knuckle ['nʌkl] s. încheietură

a degetelor. vi.: to ~ under a se supune, a ceda.

kohlrabi ['koul'rɑːbi] s. gulie.

kotow ['kou'tau], **kowtow** ['kau'tau] s. plecăciune. vi. a se ploconi.

L

L [el] s. L, l.

lab [læb] s. laborator.

label ['leibl] s. etichetă. vt. a eticheta.

laboratory [lə'bɔrətri] s. laborator. adj. de laborator.

laborious [lə'bɔːriəs] adj. greu; complicat; harnic.

labo(u)r ['leibə] s. muncă; activitate; sarcină; muncitori(me); mişcarea laburistă; trudă; chin. vt. a chinui; a elabora. vi. a trudi; a se chinui.

labo(u)rer ['leibərə] s. muncitor necalificat.

labour exchange ['leibəriks'tʃeindʒ] s. oficiu de plasare.

labour saving device ['leibə ˌseiviŋ di'vais] s. dispozitiv care cruţă munca omului; aparat de uz casnic.

laburnum [lə'bəːnəm] s. salcîm galben.

labyrinth ['læbərinθ] s. labirint.

lace [leis] s. dantelă; ornament; şiret; şirag. vt. a încheia; a înnoda; a împodobi cu dantelă.

lacerate ['læsəreit] vt. a tăia; a răni.

lack [læk] s. lipsă. vt. a fi lipsit de; a nu avea. vi. a lipsi.

lackadaisical [ˌlækə'deizikl] adj. sentimental.

lackey ['læki] s. lacheu.

laconic [lə'kɔnik] adj. laconic.

lacquer ['lækə] s. lustru; (obiecte de) lac. vt. a lăcui.

lacy ['leisi] adj. dantelat.

lad [læd] s. flăcău.

ladder ['lædə] s. scară (mobilă); fir dus (la ciorapi).

lade [leid] vt. a încărca.

laden ['leidn] part. trec. de la lade.

ladle ['leidl] s. polonic. vt. a servi (supa); a împărţi.

lady ['leidi] s. doamnă; soţie de lord; femeie.

lady-bird ['leidibəːd] s. vaca domnului; buburuză.

lady-in-waiting ['leidi in'weitiŋ] s. doamnă de onoare.

lady-killer ['leidiˌkilə] s. seducător.

ladyship ['leidiʃip] s. doamnă; soţie de lord.

lag [læg] vi. a rămîne în urmă.

lagoon [lə'guːn] s. lagună.

laid [leid] vt., vi. trec. şi part. trec. de la lay².

lain [lein] vi. part. trec. de la lie².

lair [lεə] s. vizuină.

laity ['leiiti] s. mireni; caracter laic.

lake [leik] s. lac.

lamb [læm] s. miel.

lambskin ['læmskin] s. blană de miel; meşină.

lame [leim] adj. şchiop; neconvingător; nesatisfăcător.

lame duck ['leim'dʌk] s. infirm; prăpădit; nenorocit.

lament [lə'ment] s. bocet. vt. a deplînge. vi. a (se) plînge.

lamentable ['læməntəbl] adj. lamentabil; regretabil.

lamp [læmp] s. lampă.

lamp-black ['læmpblæk] s. negru de fum.

lamp-lighter ['læmplaitə] s. lampagiu.

lampoon [læm'pu:n] s. pamflet. vt. a satiriza.

lamp-shade['læmpʃeid] s. abajur.

lance [lɑ:ns] s. lance.

lancet ['lɑ:nsit] s. bisturiu; lanţetă.

land [lænd] s. pămînt; uscat; teren; ţară; proprietate. vt. a debarca; a prinde; a nimeri; a atinge; a plasa. vi. a debarca; a ateriza; a nimeri.

land agent ['lænd,eidʒnt] s. misit de moşii.

landed ['lændid] adj. funciar; latifundiar.

landing ['lændiŋ] s. debarcare; aterizare; palier.

landing stage ['lændiŋsteidʒ] s. debarcader.

landlady ['læn,leidi] s. moşiereasă; proprietăreasă; hangiţă.

landlord ['lænlɔ:d] s. moşier; proprietar; hangiu; cîrciumar.

landmark ['lænmɑ:k] s. semn vizibil; piatră kilometrică; cotitură (fig).

landowner ['lænd,ounə] s. moşier. adj. moşieresc.

landscape ['lænskeip] s. peisaj.

landslide ['lænslaid], landslip ['lænslip] s. alunecare de teren; schimbare a opiniei publice.

lane [lein] s. uliţă; fundătură; interval.

language ['læŋgwidʒ] s. limbă; limbaj.

languid ['læŋgwid] adj. slab, plăpînd; apatic; plicticos.

languish ['læŋgwiʃ] vi. a lîncezi; a privi galeş.

langour ['læŋgə] s. lîncezeală; apatie.

lank(y) ['læŋk(i)] adj. deşirat.

lantern ['læntən] s. felinar.

lap [læp] s. poală; genunchi; sorbitură; bălăceală; etapă; tur. vt., vi. a lipăi; a sorbi.

lap-dog ['læpdɔg] s. cîine de salon.

lapel [lə'pel] s. rever (de haină).

lapse [læps] s. scurgere; trecere; cădere. vi. a trece; a cădea.

larboard ['lɑ:bəd] s. babord.

larceny ['lɑ:sni] s. furt(işag).

larch [lɑ:tʃ] s. zadă.

lard [lɑ:d] s. unturǎ. vt. a împăna.

larder ['lɑ:də] s. cămară.

large [lɑ:dʒ] adj. mare; întins; larg (la inimă etc.).

largely ['lɑ:dʒli] adv. în mare măsură; cu mărinimie.

lark [lɑ:k] s. ciocîrlie; distracţie.

larkspur ['lɑ:kspə:] s. nemţişor.

lash [læʃ] s. (şfichi de) bici; biciuire; satiră; geană. vt. a biciui; a aţîţa; a lega.

lass [læs] s. fetişcană.

lassitude ['læsitju:d] *s.* oboseală.

last [la:st] *s.* calapod; capăt; încetare. *superl. de la* **late.** *adj.* ultimul; trecut; definitiv. *vi.* a dura; a dăinui; a ajunge. *adv.* la urmă; ultima dată; *at* ~ în sfîrşit.

lasting ['la:stiŋ] *adj.* permanent, trainic.

latch [lætʃ] *s.* zăvor; iale.

last night ['la:stnait] *adv.* aseară.

last straw ['la:ststrɔ:] *s.* picătură care umple paharul.

Last Supper [,la:st'sʌpə] *s.* Cina cea de taină.

late [leit] *adj.* întîrziat; tîrziu; recent; defunct; fost; *of* ~ nu de mult. *adv.* tîrziu; ~*r on* mai tîrziu, pe urmă.

lately ['leitli] *adv.* în ultima vreme; recent.

later ['leitə] *adj., adv. comp. de la* **late** ulterior.

latest ['leitist] *adj. superl. de la* **late** cel mai recent; *at (the)* ~ cel mai tîrziu.

lath [la:θ] *s.* drug; ştachetă.

lathe [leið] *s.* strung. *vt.* a strunji.

lather ['la:ðə] *s.* spumă (de săpun). *vt.* a săpuni. *vi.* a face spume.

Latin ['lætin] *s., adj.* latin(ă).

latitude ['lætitju:d] *s.* latitudine.

latter ['lætə] *adj. comp. de la* **late** al doilea; acesta din urmă.

latterly ['lætəli] *adv.* de curînd.

lattice ['lætis] *s.* grătar de lemn; zăbrele de lemn.

laudable ['lɔ:dəbl] *adj.* lăudabil.

laugh [la:f] *s.* rîs(et). *vi.* a rîde; a hohoti; a-şi bate joc.

laughable ['la:fəbl] *adj.* amuzant; ridicol.

laughing ['la:fiŋ] *s.* rîs. *adj.* vesel; rîzător.

laughing-stock ['la:fiŋstɔk] *s.* obiect de batjocură.

laughter ['la:ftə] *s.* (hohot de) rîs.

launch [lɔ:ntʃ] *s.* lansare; barcă; şalupă. *vt.* a lansa; a arunca.

launder ['lɔ:ndə] *vt., vi.* a spăla şi a călca (rufe).

laundress ['lɔ:ndris] *s.* spălătoreasă.

laundry ['lɔ:ndri] *s.* (rufe date la) spălătorie.

laurel ['lɔrl] *s.* laur.

lavatory ['lævətri] *s.* closet; toaletă.

lavender ['lævində] *s.* levănţică.

lavish ['læviʃ] *adj.* generos; abundent. *vt.* a împărţi; a răspîndi; a acorda.

law [lɔ:] *s.* lege; autorităţi; justiţie; drept.

law-court ['lɔ:kɔ:t] *s.* tribunal.

lawful ['lɔ:fl] *adj.* legal; legitim.

lawless ['lɔ:lis] *adj.* nelegiuit; nelegitim.

lawn [lɔ:n] *s.* peluză; răzor; pajişte.

lawn-mower ['lɔ:n,mo.ə] *s.* maşină de tuns iarba.

lawn-tennis ['lɔ:n'tenis] *s.* tenis pe iarbă; tenis de cîmp.

law suit ['lɔ:sju:t] *s.* proces (civil).

lawyer ['lɔ:jə] *s.* jurist; avocat; jurisconsult.

lax [læks] *adj.* neglijent; liber; lejer.

laxity ['læksiti] *s.* lipsă de stricteţe; neglijenţă.

lay[1] [lei] *vi. trec. de la* **lie**[2].

lay[2] [lei] *adj.* laic; mirean; amator; profan. *vt.* a aşeza;

a pune (la bătaie) ; a întinde ;
a oua ; a impune ; a paria ;
to ~ aside sau by a pune
sau lăsa la o parte ; to ~ down
a depune (armele) ; a formula ;
a hotărî ; a prevedea ; to ~
off a renunţa la ; a lăsa ; amer.
a concedia ; to ~ out a întinde ; a pregăti ; a plănui ;
to ~ up a stoca ; a pune la
pat. vi. a oua. vr. a se aşeza ;
a se întinde etc.

layer [lɛə] s. strat ; parior
(la curse) ; găină ouătoare.

layman ['leimən] s. mirean ;
profan.

lay-off ['lei‚ɔːf] s. amer. concediere ; şomaj.

lay-out ['leiaut] s. aşezare ;
plan ; tehnoredactare.

laze [leiz] vi. a trîndăvi.

laziness ['leizinis] s. lene.

lazy ['leizi] adj. leneş ; trîndav.

lazy bones ['leizibounz] s. trîntor (fig.).

lead[1] [led] s. (fir cu) plumb ;
grafit ; mină de creion.

lead[2] [liːd] s. conducere ; călăuzire ; întîietate ; lesă ; rol principal ; protagonist. vt. a duce ;
a conduce ; a guverna ; a sili ;
a călăuzi ; a influenţa. vi.
a duce ; a conduce ; a fi în
frunte ; to ~ up to a pregăti.

leaden ['ledn] adj. (ca) de plumb.

leader ['liːdə] s. conducător ;
(articol) editorial ; ramură principală.

leadership ['liːdəʃip] s. conducere.

leading ['liːdiŋ] adj. conducător ;
principal.

leading article ['liːdiŋ'ɑːtikl] s.
articol de fond.

leading man ['liːdiŋ‚mæn] s.
protagonist.

leaf [liːf] s. frunză ; foaie.

leafless ['liːflis] adj. desfrunzit.

leaflet ['liːflit] s. manifest.

league [liːg] s. leghe ; ligă ; cîrdăşie ; sport categorie. vt., vi.
a (se) alia.

leak [liːk] s. crăpătură ; scurgere.
vi. a se scurge ; (d. veste etc.)
a se afla.

leakage ['liːkidʒ] s. scurgere.

lean [liːn] s. carne macră ; înclinaţie. adj. slab ; sărac. vt.
a apleca ; a înclina. vi. a se
apleca ; a tinde.

leaning ['liːniŋ] s. înclinaţie.

leant [lent] vt., vi. trec. şi part.
trec. de la **lean**.

lean-to ['liːntuː] s. şopron.

leap [liːp] s. salt ; ţopăială. vt.,
vi. a sări.

leap-frog ['liːpfrɔg] s. (jocul de-a)
capra.

leapt [lept] vt., vi. trec. şı part.
trec. de la **leap**.

leap year ['liːpjə] s. an bisect.

learn [ləːn] vt., vi. a învăţa ;
a afla ; a auzi.

learned ['ləːnid] adj. învăţat.

learner ['ləːnə] s. învăţăcel.

learning ['ləːniŋ] s. învăţătură.

learnt [ləːnt] vt., vi. trec. şi part.
trec. de la **learn**.

lease [liːs] s. contract ; concesiune ; arendă ; drepturi ; perspectivă. vt. a închiria ; a concesiona ; a arenda.

leash [liːʃ] s. lesă ; frîu (fig.).
vt. a lega ; a ţine legat.

least [liːst] s. minimul ; at ~
cel puţin ; ~ of all cîtuşi de
puţin ; not in the ~ de loc. adj.
superl. de la **little** cel mai puţin ;

cel mai mic. *adv. superl. de la little* cel mai puțin.

leather ['leðə] *s.* piele (lucrată).

leave [li:v] *s.* permisie; permisiune; concediu; plecare; *by your* ~ dacă îmi permiteți. *vt.* a părăsi; a încredința; a înmîna; a lăsa (moștenire); *to* ~ *behind* a lăsa în urmă; a uita; *to* ~ *alone* a lăsa în pace; a lăsa la o parte. *vi.* a pleca; a porni; *to* ~ *off* a înceta, a întrerupe.

leaven ['levn] *s.* drojdie; maia; influență. *vt.* a pune la dospit.

leaves [li:vz] *s. pl. de la* **leaf.**

lecherous ['letʃrəs] *adj.* pofticios; lasciv.

lechery ['letʃəri] *s.* poftă; lascivitate.

lectern ['lektən] *s.* strană; pupitru.

lecture ['lektʃə] *s.* prelegere; conferință; lecție. *fig.* morală. *vt.* a ocărî. *vi.* a ține o prelegere *sau* o conferință.

lecturer ['lektʃərə] *s.* conferențiar.

led [led] *vt., vi. trec. și part. trec. de la* **lead².**

ledge [ledʒ] *s.* pervaz; tăpșan.

ledger ['ledʒə] *s.* registru (mare).

lee [li:] *s.* adăpost, protecție. *adj.* apărat (de vînt).

leech [li:tʃ] *s.* lipitoare.

leek [li:k] *s.* praz.

leer [liə] *s.* privire libidinoasă *sau* scîrboasă; rînjet. *vi.* a rînji.

lees [li:z] *s. pl.* drojdie (de cafea etc.).

leeway ['li:wei] *s.* abatere din drum; întîrziere.

left [left] *s.* stînga. *adj.* de (la)

stînga. *vt., vi. trec. și part. trec. de la* **leave.** *adv.* la stînga.

left-hand ['lefthænd] *adj.* din stînga; cu stînga.

left-handed ['left'hændid] *adj.* stîngaci; fals.

leg [leg] *s.* picior; gambă; crac de pantalon; etapă; ajutor.

legacy ['legəsi] *s.* moștenire.

legal ['li:gl] *adj.* legal; juridic.

legal tender ['li:gl'tendə] *s.* monedă oficială.

legation [li'geiʃn] *s.* legație.

legend ['ledʒnd] *s.* legendă; poveste.

legendary ['ledʒndri] *adj.* legendar.

leggings ['leginz] *s. pl.* jambiere.

legible ['ledʒəbl] *adj.* lizibil; clar.

legion ['li:dʒn] *s.* legiune; oaste; mulțime.

legislature ['ledʒisleitʃə] *s.* corpuri legiuitoare.

leisure ['leʒə] *s.* răgaz.

leisurely ['leʒəli] *adj., adv.* fără grabă; încet.

lemon ['lemən] *s.* lămîie.

lend [lend] *vt.* a da cu împrumut; a (acor)da; a adăuga. *vr.* a se preta.

length [leŋθ] *s.* lungime; măsură; întregime; *at arm's* ~ la distanță; *at full* ~ cît e de lung.

lengthen ['leŋθn] *vt., vi.* a (se) lungi.

lengthwise ['leŋθwaiz] *adj., adv.* în lungime.

lengthy ['leŋθi] *adj.* prea lung; plictisitor.

lenient ['li:njənt] *adj.* îngăduitor; blînd.

lenity ['leniti] *s.* blîndețe; îngăduință.

lens [lenz] *s.* lentilă.
lent[1] [lent] *vt., vr. trec. și part. trec. de la* **lend.**
Lent[2] [lent] *s.* postul Paştelui.
lentil ['lentil] *s.* linte.
leopard ['lepəd] *s.* leopard.
leper ['lepə] *s.* lepros.
leprosy ['leprəsi] *s.* lepră.
lesion ['li:ʒn] *s.* leziune; rană.
less [les] *adj. compar. de la* **little** mai puţin; mai mic; mai puţin important. *adv. compar. de la* **little** în mai mică măsură; mai puţin. *prep.* fără, minus; scăzînd.
lessee [le'si:] *s.* arendaş; chiriaş.
lessen ['lesn] *vt., vi.* a (se) micşora.
lesser ['lesə] *adj.* (mai) mic; mai puţin important.
lesson ['lesn] *s.* lecţie.
lest [lest] *conj.* ca nu cumva; ca să nu.
let [let] *inf., trec. şi part. trec. v. aux. pentru imperativ:* ∼'s go să mergem. *vt.* a lăsa; a permite; a da cu chirie; a arenda; *to* ∼ *alone* a lăsa în pace; a lăsa la o parte; *to* ∼ *be* a lăsa în pace; *to* ∼ *down* a coborî; a dezamăgi; a lăsa la ananghie. *vi.* a (se) închiria.
lethal ['li:θl] *adj.* mortal.
letter ['letə] *s.* literă; scrisoare; *pl.* literatură.
letter-box ['letəbɔks] *s.* cutie de scrisori; poştă; curier.
lettered ['letəd] *adj.* învăţat; instruit.
lettuce ['letis] *s.* salată verde; lăptucă.
level ['levl] *s.* întindere; suprafaţă; nivel(ă); *on the* ∼ cinstit. *adj.* întins; orizontal;

egal; **echilibrat**; neted. *vt.* a nivela; a **egaliza**; a aşeza orizontal; a **ochi** cu (puşca etc.).
lever ['li:və] *s.* pîrghie.
levity ['leviti] *s.* uşurinţă; neseriozitate.
levy ['levi] *s.* percepere (a impozitelor **etc.**); taxe; contingent. *vt.* a **percepe**; a strînge.
lewd [lu:d] *adj.* obscen; lasciv.
liability [ˌlaiə'biliti] *s.* obligaţie; posibilitate; susceptibilitate; *pl.* datorii.
liable ['laiəbl] *adj.* supus; susceptibil; **posibil**; dator.
liaison [li'eizɔŋ] *s.* legătură de dragoste.
liar ['laiə] *s.* mincinos.
libel ['laibl] *s.* calomnie. *vt.* a calomnia.
liberal ['librl] *s.* generos; liberal; om progresist. *adj.* cu orizont larg; progresist; generos; liberal.
liberality [ˌlibə'ræliti] *s.* generozitate; concepţii largi, progresiste.
liberation [ˌlibə'reiʃn] *s.* eliberare.
liberty ['libəti] *s.* libertate; îndrăzneală; alegere; *pl.* drepturi.
librarian [lai'brɛəriən] *s.* bibliotecar.
library ['laibrəri] *s.* bibliotecă.
lice [lais] *s. pl. de la* **louse.**
licence ['laisns] *s.* autorizaţie; carnet (de conducere); brevet; patent; licenţă.
license ['laisns] *s. v.* **licence.** *vt.* a autoriza.
lick [lik] *vt.* a linge; a bate.
licking ['likiŋ] *s.* bătaie.
lid [lid] *s.* capac; pleoapă,

lie[1] [lai] s. minciună. vi. a minţi.

lie[2] [lai] vi. a sta întins; a zăcea; a se culca; a se afla; a fi; a consta; to ~ back a se rezema; to ~ down a se întinde; to ~ in a sta culcat; a fi lăuză; to ~ over a rămîne.

liege [li:dʒ] s. vasal; stăpîn.

lieutenant [le(f)'tenənt] s. locotenent; locţiitor.

life [laif] s. viaţă; vioiciune.

life-belt ['laifbelt] s. colac de salvare.

life-boat ['laifbout] s. barcă de salvare.

life-jacket ['laif͵dʒækit] s. vestă de salvare.

life-size ['laif'saiz] s. mărime naturală. adj. în sau de mărime naturală.

life-time ['laiftaim] s. viaţă; timpul vieţii.

life-work ['laif'wəːk] s. operă de o viaţă întreagă.

lift [lift] s. ridicare; lift; ajutor; plimbare (cu maşina). vt. a ridica; a înălţa; a scoate; a şterpeli.

light [lait] s. lumină; vedere; flacără; lumînare; bec; reflector; luminător; celebritate. adj. luminos, deschis; uşor; mic; slab; neserios. vt. a (i)lumina; a aprinde. vi. a arde; a (se) lumina; a se aşeza; a nimeri.

lighten ['laitn] vt. a lumina; a uşura; a înveseli. vi. a (se) lumina; a fulgera; a (se) uşura; a (se) înveseli.

lighter ['laitə] s. lampagiu; brichetă.

light-hand ['laithænd] s. îndemînare; tact.

lighthouse ['laithaus] s. far.

lightning ['laitniŋ] s. fulger.

lightning-rod ['laitniŋ͵rɔd] s. paratrăsnet.

light-weight ['laitweit] s. (boxer de) categoria uşoară.

lignite ['lignait] s. lignit.

likable ['laikəbl] adj. plăcut.

like [laik] s. lucru etc. asemănător; plăcere; înclinaţie; the ~s of you cei de o seamă cu tine; and the ~ şi altele asemenea. adj. asemănător; caracteristic; dispus; I don't feel ~ (drinking) tea n-am chef de ceai. vt. a iubi; a-i plăcea; a ţine la; a prefera. prep. ca (şi).

likelihood ['laiklihud] s. probabilitate.

likely ['laikli] adj. probabil; posibil;. acceptabil; de conceput; potrivit. adv. probabil.

liken ['laikn] vt. a asemui.

likeness ['laiknis] s. asemănare; copie.

likewise ['laikwaiz] adv. la fel; (de) asemenea.

liking ['laikiŋ] s. simpatie.

lilac ['lailək] s. liliac(hiu).

Lilliput ['lilipʌt] s. liliput.

Lilliputian [͵lili pjuʃjən] s., adj. liliputan.

lily ['lili] s. crin.

lily of the valley ['lili əv ðə 'væli] s. lăcrămioară.

limb [lim] s. anat. membru; ramură; odraslă.

limbo ['limbou] s. purgatoriu.

lime [laim] s. var; tei; lămîie.

lime-juice ['laim͵dʒuːs] zeamă de lămîie.

limelight ['laimlait] s. luminile rampei.

limestone ['laimstoun] s. calcar.

limit ['limit] s. limită ; graniță. vt. a limita ; a îngrădi.

limitation [‚limi'teiʃn] s. limită ; limitare.

limp [limp] adj. neputincios ; țeapăn ; amorțit. vi. a șchiopăta.

linden ['lindən] s. tei.

line [lain] s. linie ; fir ; dungă ; rînd ; vers ; limită ; zbîrcitură ; lizieră ; amer. coadă, șir ; undiță ; sfoară ; funie ; direcție ; curent ; ocupație ; familie ; specialitate ; mil. front ; baráci. vt. a căptuși ; a linia ; a alinia.

lineage ['liniidʒ] s. genealogie ; origine.

linen ['linin] s. pînză sau pînzeturi de in ; rufărie.

liner ['lainə] s. (avion) transatlantic.

linesman ['lainzmən] s. picher ; sport arbitru de tușă.

linger ['liŋgə] vt. a continua. vi. a stărui ; a rămîne ; a întîrzia, a zăbovi ; a o lungi.

lingo ['liŋgou] s. jargon.

linguistics [liŋ'gwistiks] s. pl. lingvistică.

lining ['lainiŋ] s. căptușeală.

link [liŋk] s. verigă ; măsură de lungime ; ruletă ; legătură ; pl. pajiște ; pl. teren de golf ; pl. butoni de manșetă. vt. a uni ; a lega. vi. a se lega ; a se îmbina.

linnet ['linit] s. cînepar.

linseed ['linsi:d] s. sămînță de in.

linseed-oil ['linsi:d'ɔil] s. ulei de in.

lint [lint] s. scamă.

lintel ['lintl] s. pragul de sus al ușii.

lion ['laiən] s. leu.

lioness ['laiənis] s. leoaică.

lip [lip] s. buză ; margine ; obrăznicie ; vorbe.

lip-service ['lip‚sə:vis] s. promisiuni nesincere ; vorbe goale ; ipocrizie.

lipstick ['lipstik] s. ruj de buze.

liqueur [li'kjuə] s. lichior.

liquid ['likwid] s. lichid. adj. lichid ; transparent ; clar ; nestatornic.

liquidate ['likwideit] vt. a lichida. vi. a da faliment.

liquor ['likə] s. băutură alcoolică.

lisp [lisp] s. sîsîială. vt., vi. a sîsîi.

lissom(e) ['lisəm] adj. suplu.

list [list] s. listă. vt. a înșira ; a înscrie.

listen ['lisn] vi. a asculta ; to ~ ~ in a asculta la radio.

listener ['lisnə] s. ascultător.

listless ['listlis] adj. placid ; neatent.

lit [lit] vt., vi. trec. și part. trec. de la **light.**

liter ['li:tə] s. litru.

literacy ['litrəsi] s. știință de carte.

literally ['litrəli] adv. exact ; pur și simplu.

literature ['litritʃə] s. literatură.

lithe [laið] adj. suplu.

litotes ['laitoti:z] s. litotă.

litre ['li:tə] s. litru.

litter ['litə] s. litieră ; dezordine ; resturi ; așternut de paie ; pui fătați. vt. a deranja ; a lăsa în dezordine. vi. a făta.

little ['litl] adj. mic(uț) ; puțin (tel) ; neînsemnat ; meschin ; mărunt. pron. puțin ; nimic. adv. puțin ; în mică măsură ; de loc ; nicidecum.

live¹ [laiv] *adj.* viu; arzînd; activ; important.

live² [liv] *vi.* a trăi; a locui; a supravieţui; a rămîne; *to ~ through* a trece prin; *to ~ up to* a corespunde *(cu dat.)*; a fi la înălţimea ... *(cu gen.)*.

livelihood ['laivlihud] *s.* (mijloace de) trai.

liveliness ['laivliniis] *s.* vioiciune; vigoare.

lively ['laivli] *adj.* vioi; activ; vesel; viu; realist.

liver ['livə] *s.* ficat.

livery ['livəri] *s.* livrea; grajd.

livestock ['laivstɔk] *s.* şeptel.

living ['liviŋ] *s.* trai; funcţie. *adj.* viu; activ; veridic.

living-room ['liviŋrum] *s.* cameră de zi.

lizard ['lizəd] *s.* şopîrlă.

llama ['lɑːmə] *s. zool.* lama.

load [loud] *s.* încărcătură; sarcină; *~s of* o mulţime de. *vt.* a încărca; a măslui. *vi.* a se încărca.

loadstar ['loudstɑː] *s.* stea călăuzitoare.

load-stone ['loudstoun] *s.* magnet.

loaf [louf] *s.* (codru de) pîine; căpăţînă de zahăr; plimbare. *vt.* a irosi (timpul). *vi.* a vagabonda; a pierde vremea.

loafer ['loufə] *s.* vagabond; pierde-vară.

loan [loun] *s.* împrumut (de bani).

loath [louθ] *adj.* nedoritor; refractar.

loathe [louð] *vt.* a detesta; a nu putea suferi.

loathsome ['louðsəm] *adj.* dezgustător; nesuferit.

loaves [louvz] *s. pl. de la* loaf.

lobby ['lɔbi] *s.* foaier; hol (la hotel etc.); *pol.* culoar la parlament; influenţarea parlamentarilor.

lobster ['lɔbstə] *s.* homar.

local ['loukl] *s.* tren local; filială; sindicat local. *adj.* local.

locality [lo'kæliti] *s.* aşezare; peisaj; localitate.

locate [lo'keit] *vt.* a localiza; a aşeza, a situa; a găsi (pe hartă).

location [lo'keiʃn] *s.* aşezare; situaţie.

lock [lɔk] *s.* buclă; lacăt; încuietoare; ecluză. *vt.* a închide; a încuia; a păstra (cu sfinţenie); a fixa; a înţepeni; a bloca; *to ~ up* a băga la închisoare *sau* la azil; a închide; a pune la păstrare. *vi.* a se încuia; a se închide.

locker ['lɔkə] *s.* dulăpior (de vestiar).

locket ['lɔkit] *s.* medalion.

lock-out ['lɔkaut] *s.* închidere a unei fabrici.

locksmith ['lɔksmiθ] *s.* lăcătuş.

locomotive ['loukə‚moutiv] *s.* locomotivă.

locust ['loukəst] *s.* lăcustă.

lode [loud] *s.* filon.

lodestar ['loudstɑː] *s.* steaua polară; principiu călăuzitor.

lodestone ['loudstoun] *s.* magnet.

lodge [lɔdʒ] *s.* căsuţa portarului; cabană; lojă (masonică etc.). *vt.* a găzdui; a băga; a investi; a înainta autorităţilor. *vi.* a locui (cu chirie); a intra.

lodger ['lɔdʒə] *s.* chiriaş.

lodging ['lɔdʒiŋ] *s.* locuinţă.

loft [lɔft] *s.* podul casei; galerie; porumbar.

lofty ['lɔfti] *adj.* înalt; trufaş.

log [lɔg] *s.* buştean; jurnal de bord.

logarithm ['lɔgəriθm] *s.* logaritm.

loggerhead ['lɔgəhed] *s.* cretin; *to be at* ~*s (with)* a nu se înţelege cu.

logic ['lɔdʒik] *s.* logică.

loin [lɔin] *s.* muşchi (de oaie etc.); *pl.* şale.

loin-cloth ['lɔinklɔθ] *s.* pînză purtată în jurul şalelor; şorţ.

loiter ['lɔitə] *vi.* a zăbovi.

loll [lɔl] *vi.* a pierde vremea.

lollipop ['lɔlipɔp] *s.* acadea; bomboană.

lone(ly) ['lounli] *adj.* singur(atic); trist; pustiu.

long [lɔŋ] *adj.* lung. *vi.* a dori; a tînji.

long-bow ['lɔŋbou] *s.* arc; poveşti vînătoreşti.

long face ['lɔŋfeis] *s.* mutră plouată.

longing ['lɔŋiŋ] *s.* dor. *adj.* doritor.

long jump ['lɔŋ dʒʌmp] *s.* săritură în lungime.

longshoreman ['lɔŋʃɔ:mən] *s.* docher.

long-sighted [lɔŋ'saitid] *adj.* prezbit; prevăzător.

long-winded ['lɔŋ'windid] *adj.* plicticos.

look [luk] *s.* privire; înfăţişare; *pl.* aspect. *vt.* a privi; *to* ~ *over* a cerceta. *vi.* a privi, a se uita; a arăta; a părea; *to* ~ *after* a îngriji; a se uita în urma; *to* ~ *for* a căuta; *to* ~ *(up)on* a considera; a vedea;

a privi; *to* ~ *forward to* a aştepta cu nerăbdare; *to* ~ *out* a băga de seamă; *to* ~ *round* a chibzui; *to* ~ *through* a străbate; a se ivi; *to* ~ *up* a ridica ochii sau capul; a căuta; a vizita; *to* ~ *up to* a respecta.

looker-on ['lukər'ɔn] *s.* privitor.

looking-glass ['lukiŋglɑ:s] *s.* oglindă.

look-out ['luk'aut] *s.* pază; grijă; perspectivă.

loom [lu:m] *s.* război de ţesut. *vi.* a se ivi; a apărea (neclar); a ameninţa.

loon [lu:n] *s.* cufundar.

loop [lu:p] *s.* laţ; inel; cerc; luping. *vt.* a lega.

loop-hole ['lu:phoul] *s.* deschizătură; scăpare.

loose [lu:s] *adj.* slobod; larg; slab; nefixat; vag; imoral; rar; dezlînat. *vt.* a dezlega; a slăbi; a slobozi.

loosely ['lu:sli] *adv.* slobod; larg; în genere.

loosen ['lu:sn] *vt., vi.* a slăbi.

loot [lu:t] *s.* pradă. *vt., vi.* a prăda.

lop-sided ['lɔp'saidid] *s.* asimetric; strîmb.

loquacious [lo'kweiʃəs] *adj.* vorbăreţ.

lord [lɔ:d] *s.* lord; stăpîn; conducător; aristocrat; *(the) Lord* Dumnezeu. *vt.* a stăpîni; a domni.

lordly ['lɔ:dli] *adj.* magnific; splendid; trufaş.

lordship ['lɔ:dʃip] *s.* stăpînire; moşie, proprietate.

lore [lɔ:] *s.* ştiinţă; înţelepciune.

lorry ['lɔri] *s.* camion.

lose [lu:z] *vt.* a pierde; a scăpa;

a face să se piardă. *vi.* a pierde ;
(d. ceas) a rămîne în urmă.

loser ['lu:zə] *s.* învins.

losing ['lu:ziŋ] *adj.* pierdut ; care
pierde ; nefavorabil.

loss [lɔs] *s.* pierdere ; înfrîngere ;
at a ~ în încurcătură.

lost [lɔst] *vt., vi. trec. şi part.
trec. de la* **lose.**

lot [lɔt] *s.* lot ; mulţime ; grup ;
bandă ; soartă ; *pl.* sorţi ; parcelă ; *a* ~ *of* ; ~*s of* o mulţime
de ; *a* ~ foarte mult *(şi iron.).*

lottery ['lɔtəri] *s.* loterie.

lotus ['loutəs] *s.* lotus.

lotus-eater ['loutəs'i:tə] *s.* pierde-vară ; chefliu.

loud [laud] *adj.* tare ; răsunător ; ţipător. *adv.* (cu voce) tare.

loudly ['laudli] *adv.* (cu voce)
tare.

loud-speaker ['laud'spi:kə] *s.* megafon ; difuzor.

lounge [laundʒ] *s.* trîndăveală ;
hol (de hotel etc.) ; şezlong ;
canapea ; costum de oraş. *vi.*
a pierde vremea ; a se plimba.

lounge-chair ['laundʒˌtʃɛə] *s.*
şezlong ; canapeluţă.

lounge lizard ['laundʒ'lizəd]
s. pierde-vară ; gigolo.

lounge-suit ['laundʒˌsju:t] *s.* costum de oraş.

louse [laus] *s.* păduche.

lousy ['lauzi] *adj.* păduchios ;
împuţit ; nenorocit ; mizerabil.

lout [laut] *s.* mocofan ; huidumă.

love [lʌv] *s.* dragoste, amor ; complimente ; *sport* zero ; scor alb.
vt. a iubi ; a adora ; a savura.

love-affair ['lʌv əˌfɛə] *s.* amor ;
legătură amoroasă.

love-child ['lʌvtʃaild] *s.* copil din
flori.

lovely ['lʌvli] *adj.* frumos ; atrăgător ; încîntător.

lover ['lʌvə] *s.* îndrăgostit ;
amant(ă) ; iubit ; iubitor ; amator.

love-sick ['lʌvsik] *adj.* îndrăgostit.

loving ['lʌviŋ] *adj.* iubitor.

low [lou] *s.* muget (de vacă).
adj. jos ; josnic ; scund ; umil ;
(d. sunete) încet ; înapoiat ; vulgar ; slab ; prost. *vi.* a mugi.
adv. jos ; ieftin ; încet (ca sonoritate) ; ascuns.

lower ['louə] *adj.* inferior ; de
jos. *vt.* a coborî ; a slăbi ; a
ruşina.

lowland ['loulənd] *s.* şes ; regiune de cîmpie.

lowly ['louli] *adj., adv.* modest ;
umil.

loyal ['lɔil] *adj.* credincios.

loyalty ['lɔilti] *s.* credinţă ;
obligaţie ; lealitate.

lozenge ['lɔzindʒ] *s.* romb ; tabletă.

lubberly ['lʌbəli] *adj.* stîngaci ;
mătăhălos.

lubricate ['lu:brikeit] *vt.* a unge.

luck [lʌk] *s.* noroc ; şansă.

luckily ['lʌkili] *adv.* din fericire.

lucky ['lʌki] *adj.* norocos ; fericit.

lucrative ['lu:krətiv] *adj.* rentabil.

lucre ['lu:kə] *s.* profit.

ludicrous ['lu:dikrəs] *adj.* ridicol ; absurd.

lug [lʌg] *vt.* a trage ; a tîrî.

luggage ['lʌgidʒ] *s.* bagaje.

lukewarm ['lu:kwɔ:m] *adj.* călduţ.

lull [lʌl] *s.* linişte ; răgaz. *vt.* a
legăna (un copil) ; a linişti ; a
alina.

lullaby ['lʌləbai] *s.* cîntec de leagăn.

lumber ['lʌmbə] *s.* lemne; cherestea (neprelucrată) ; mobilă veche ; balast.

lumberman ['lʌmbəmən] *s.* muncitor forestier.

lumber yard ['lʌmbə jɑːd] *s.* depozit de lemne.

lump [lʌmp] *s.* bucată ; bulgăr ; umflătură ; om greoi ; *in the* ~ în ansamblu ; *a* ~ *in the throat* un nod în gît. *vt.* a pune laolaltă ; a înghiţi.

lump sugar ['lʌmp͵ʃugə] *s.* zahăr cubic.

lump sum ['lʌmp͵sʌm] *s.* sumă globală.

lunacy ['luːnəsi] *s.* nebunie.

lunatic ['luːnətik] *s., adj.* nebun.

lunch(eon) ['lʌntʃ(n)] *s.* dejun. *vi.* a lua dejunul.

lung [lʌŋ] *s.* plămîn ; parc.

lurch [ləːtʃ] *s.* legănare. *vi.* a se legăna, a se clătina.

lure [ljuə] *s.* momeală ; atracţie. *vt.* a momi.

lurid ['ljuərid] *adj.* strălucitor ; ademenitor ; scandalos.

lurk [ləːk] *vi.* a sta ascuns ; a pîndi.

luscious ['lʌʃəs] *adj.* delicios.

lush [lʌʃ] *adj.* luxuriant.

lust [lʌst] *s.* poftă ; voluptate. *vi.: to* ~ *for* sau *after* a pofti (la).

lustful ['lʌstfl] *adj.* pofticios ; voluptuos ; lasciv.

luster, lustre ['lʌstə] *s.* lustru ; strălucire ; distincţie.

lusty ['lʌsti] *adj.* sănătos ; viguros ; voinic.

luxuriant [lʌg'zjuəriənt] *adj.* bogat ; luxuriant.

luxurious [lʌg'zjuəriəs] *adj.* luxos ; extravagant.

luxury ['lʌkʃəri] *s.* lux.

lye [lai] *s.* leşie.

lynch [lintʃ] *vt.* a linşa.

lyre ['laiə] *s. muz.* liră.

lyric ['lirik] *s.* poezie ; cîntec ; *pl.* text de cîntec.

lyric(al) ['lirik(l)] *adj.* liric ; emotiv ; entuziast.

M

M [em] *s.* M, m.

ma [mɑː] *s.* mămică.

ma'am [mæm] *s.* coniţă ; doamnă.

machination [͵mæki'neiʃn] *s.* maşinaţie ; manevră.

machine [mə'ʃiːn] *s.* maşină ; aparat.

machine-gun [mə'ʃiːngʌn] *s.* mitralieră.

machinery [mə'ʃiːnəri] *s.* maşinărie ; aparat.

machinist [mə'ʃiːnist] *s.* mecanic.

mackerel ['mækrl] *s.* scrumbie.

mack(intosh) ['mæk(intɔʃ)] *s.* haină de ploaie.

mad [mæd] *adj*. nebun; violent; turbat.

madam ['mædəm] *s*. doamnă.

madcap ['mædkæp] *s*., *adj*. trăsnit.

madden ['mædn] *vt*., *vi*. a înnebuni.

made [meid] *adj*. fabricat. *vt*., *vi*. *trec*. *şi part*. *trec*. *de la* make.

madman ['mædmən] *s*. nebun.

magazine [,mægə'zi:n] *s*. revistă ilustrată; magazie.

maggot ['mægət] *s*. larvă; *pl*. gărgăuni.

magic ['mædʒik] *s*. magie; vrajă; amăgire. *adj*. magic; vrăjit.

magistrate ['mædʒistrit] *s*. magistrat; demnitar; funcţionar.

magnanimity [,mægnə'nimiti] *s*. generozitate; orizont larg.

magnanimous [mæg'næniməs] *adj*. generos.

magnate ['mægneit] *s*. magnat.

magnet ['mægnit] *s*. magnet.

magnificent [mæg'nifisnt] *adj*. măreţ; excelent.

magnify ['mægnifai] *vt*. a mări; a exagera.

magnifying-glass ['mægnifaiin'glɑ:s] *s*. lupă.

magnitude ['mægnitju:d] *s*. mărime; importanţă.

magpie ['mægpai] *s*. coţofană; *fig*. gaiţă.

mahogany ['mə'hɔgəni] *s*. (lemn de) mahon.

maid [meid] *s*. fată (în casă).

maiden ['meidn] *s*. fecioară. *adj*. feciorelnic; imaculat; inaugural.

maidenhood ['meidnhud] *s*. feciorie.

maid-in-waiting ['meidin'weitiŋ] *s*. domnişoară de onoare.

mail [meil] *s*. zale; poştă. *vt*. a expedia.

mail-coach ['meil'koutʃ] *s*. diligenţă.

maim [meim] *vt*. a ciopîrţi; a mutila.

main [mein] *s*. conductă; continent; mare, ocean; forţă; *in the* ~ în general. *adj*. principal; puternic.

mainland ['meinlənd] *s*. continent; uscat.

mainly ['meinli] *adv*. în special.

mainspring ['meinspriŋ] *s*. resort principal; motiv de bază.

mainstay ['meinstei] *s*. odgon; *fig*. reazem.

maintain [men'tein] *vt*. a menţine; a susţine.

maintenance ['meintinəns] *s*. întreţinere; susţinere.

maize [meiz] *s*. porumb.

majestic [mə'dʒestik] *adj*. maiestuos; măreţ.

majesty ['mædʒisti] *s*. maiestate.

major ['meidʒə] *s*. maior; major. *adj*. major; principal.

majority [mə'dʒɔriti] *s*. majoritate; majorat.

make [meik] *s*. fabricaţie; marcă; alcătuire. *vt*. a face; a făuri; a căpăta; a sili; a ajunge la; a se ridica la; a se purta ca. *to* ~ *out* a alcătui; a înţelege; a distinge; *to* ~ *over* a transfera; *to* ~ *up* a completa; a machia; a farda; a deghiza; a împăca; a alcătui. *vi*. a porni; a se îndrepta; a se mişca; a curge; a creşte; *to* ~ *for* a se îndrepta către; a promova; a ataca ; *to ~ off* a fugi ; *to ~ up* a se machia ; a se farda ; *to ~ up for* a compensa.

make-believe ['meikbiˌliːv] *s.* prefăcătorie ; joacă.

maker ['meikə] *s.* creator.

makeshift ['meikʃift] *s.* expedient.

make-up ['meikʌp] *s.* machiaj ; deghizare ; fard ; tehnoredactare ; compoziţie ; fire.

making ['meikiŋ] *s.* creare ; *pl.* germeni ; calităţi.

male [meil] *s.* mascul. *adj.* masculin, bărbătesc.

malefactor ['mælifæktə] *s.* răufăcător.

malevolent [mə'levələnt] *adj.* rău ; răuvoitor.

malice ['mælis] *s.* răutate ; pică.

malicious [mə'liʃəs] *adj.* răutăcios.

malign [mə'lain] *adj.* rău ; răutăcios. *vt.* a bîrfi.

malignant [mə'lignənt] *adj.* rău ; malign.

malinger [mə'liŋgə] *vi.* a face pe bolnavul.

mallet ['mælit] *s.* ciocan (mai ales de lemn).

mallow ['mælou] *s.* nalbă.

malnutrition ['mælnju'triʃn] *s.* proastă alimentaţie.

malt [mɔːlt] *s.* malţ.

mam(m)a [mə'mɑː] *s.* mămică.

mammal ['mæml] *s.* mamifer(ă).

mammoth ['mæməθ] *s.* mamut. *adj.* uriaş.

mammy ['mæmi] *s.* mămică ; guvernantă (negresă).

man [mæn] *s.* om ; bărbat ; soldat ; lucrător ; servitor ; piesă de şah etc. *vt.* a furniza echipaj pentru.

manacle ['mænəkl] *s.* cătuşă. *vt.* a încătuşa.

manage ['mænidʒ] *vt.* a conduce ; a administra ; a rezolva ; a izbuti. *vi.* a se descurca.

manager ['mænidʒə] *s.* director ; conducător ; administrator ; gospodar.

mandate ['mændeit] *s.* mandat ; poruncă.

mandrake ['mændreik] *s.* mătrăgună.

mane [mein] *s.* coamă.

man-eater ['mænˌiːtə] *s.* canibal.

manganese [ˌmæŋgə'niːz] *s.* mangan.

manger ['meindʒə] *s.* iesle.

mangle ['mæŋgl] *vt.* a ciopîrţi ; a stîlci.

mangy ['meindʒi] *adj.* rîios ; soios.

man-hole ['mænhoul] *s.* trapă ; deschizătură ; gură de canal.

manhood ['mænhud] *s.* bărbăţie ; bărbaţi.

mania ['meinjə] *s.* manie ; nebunie.

maniac ['meiniæk] *s.* nebun. *adj.* maniac.

manifest ['mænifest] *adj.* clar ; manifest.

manifold ['mænifould] *adj.* variat ; multiplu.

manikin ['mænikin] *s.* manechin ; omuleţ.

mankind[1] [mæn'kaind] *s.* omenire.

mankind[2] ['mænkaind] *s.* sexul tare.

manly ['mænli] *adj.* bărbătesc ; viteaz.

mannequin ['mænikin] *s.* manechin.

manner ['mænə] s. mod; cale; manieră; purtare; pl. bună creştere; stil.

mannerism ['mænərizəm] s. particularitate; manierism.

mannerly ['mænəli] adj. binecrescut.

man(o)euvre [mə'nu:və] s. manevră. vt., vi. a manevra.

man-of-war ['mænəv'wɔ:] s. cuirasat.

manor ['mænə] s. conac; moşie.

mansion ['mænʃn] s. casă mare; amer. bloc.

manslaughter ['mæn͵slɔ:tə] s. omucidere.

mantel(piece) ['mæntl(pi:s)] s. poliţa căminului.

mantle ['mæntl] s. manta; mantie.

man-trap ['mæntræp] s. capcană.

manufactory [͵mænju'fæktri] s. fabrică; atelier.

manufacture [͵mænju'fæktʃə] s. fabricaţie; pl. fabricate. vt. a fabrica.

manufacturer [͵mænju'fæktʃərə] s. fabricant.

manure [mə'njuə] s. bălegar. vt. a îngrăşa (pămîntul).

manuscript ['mænjuskript] s. manuscris.

many ['meni] adj., pron. mulţi, multe.

many-sided ['meni'saidid] adj. multilateral.

map [mæp] s. hartă; plan. vt. a plănui; a trasa.

maple ['meipl] s. arţar.

mar [ma:] vt. a strica; a dăuna.

maraud [mə'rɔ:d] vi. a umbla după pradă.

marble ['ma:bl] s. marmură; pietricică.

March[1] [ma:tʃ] s. martie.

march[2] [ma:tʃ] s. marş; înaintare. vi. a mărşălui; a înainta.

marchioness ['ma:ʃnis] s. marchiză.

mare [mɛə] s. iapă.

mare's nest ['mɛəz'nest] s. cai verzi pe pereţi.

margin ['ma:dʒin] s. margine; chenar.

marigold ['mærigould] s. bot. filimică; gălbenea.

marine [mə'ri:n] adj. marin; maritim.

marjoram ['ma:dʒrəm] s. maghiran.

mark [ma:k] s. semn; particularitate; marcă; notă (la şcoală); ţintă; standard; up to the ~ cum trebuie. vt. a marca; a însemna; a nota (teze etc.); a caracteriza; a asculta cu atenţie.

marked [ma:kt] adj. clar; pronunţat; remarcabil.

market ['ma:kit] s. piaţă; tîrg; afaceri. vt. a vinde; a duce la piaţă.

market-town ['ma:kittaun] s. tîrg; oraş comercial.

marksman ['ma:ksmən] s. ţintaş.

marmalade ['ma:məleid] s. dulceaţă de citrice.

marquee [ma:'ki:] s. constr. marchiză; cort mare.

marquess, marquis ['ma:kwis] s. marchiz.

marriage ['mæridʒ] s. căsătorie; nuntă.

marriage lines ['mæridʒ'lainz] s. certificat de căsătorie.

marrow ['mærou] s. măduvă; dovlecel; *fig.* esenţă.

marry ['mæri] *vt., vi.* a (se) căsători.

Mars [ma:z] s. Marte.

marsh [ma:ʃ] s. mlaştină.

marshal ['ma:ʃl] s. mareşal; maestru de ceremonii; *amer.* şerif.

marshy ['ma:ʃi] *adj.* mlăştinos.

marten ['ma:tin] s. jder.

martin ['ma:tin] s: rîndunică; lăstun.

martyr ['ma:tə] s. martir.

martyrdom ['ma:tədəm] s. calvar.

marvel ['ma:vl] *adj.* minune. *vt., vi.* a (se) minuna.

marvel(l)ous ['ma:viləs] *adj.* minunat; uluitor.

Marxian ['ma:ksjən] *s., adj.* marxist.

Marxism ['ma:ksizəm] s. marxism.

Marxist(-Leninist) ['ma:ksist (-'leninist)] *s., adj.* marxist (-leninist).

masculine ['mæskjulin] *adj.* masculin; bărbătesc.

mash [mæʃ] s. terci; pireu.

mask [ma:sk] s. mască. *vt., vi.* a (se) masca.

mason ['meisn] s. zidar; francmason.

masonry ['meisnri] s. zidărie.

masque [ma:sk] s. dramă medievală.

masquerade [ˌmæskə'reid] s. bal mascat; mascaradă.

mass¹ [mæs] s. mulţime; masă; învălmăşeală. *adj.* de masă. *vt., vi.* a (se) masa, a (se) îngrămădi.

Mass, mass² [ma:s, mæs] s. liturghie, slujbă.

massage ['mæsa:ʒ] s. masaj. *vt.* a masa.

mast [ma:st] s. catarg; stîlp.

master ['ma:stə] s. stăpîn; domn; conducător; căpitan de marină; profesor; învăţător; doctor; maestru. *vt.* a stăpîni; a căpăta.

masterly ['ma:stəli] *adj.* autoritar; măiestru, magistral.

Master of Arts ['ma:stərəv'a:ts] s. doctor în litere.

masterpiece ['ma:stəpi:s] s. capodoperă.

masterstroke ['ma:stəstrouk] s. lovitură de maestru.

mastery ['ma:stri] s. stăpînire; pricepere.

mastiff ['mæstif] s. dulău.

mat [mæt] s. rogojină; ştergător.

match [mætʃ] s. chibrit; joc, meci; rival; pereche; potrivire; partidă, căsătorie. *vt.* a opune; a se potrivi cu, la; a egala. *vi.* a se potrivi.

matchless ['mætʃlis] *adj.* fără pereche.

mate [meit] s. tovarăş; coleg; partener; *mar.* şef de echipă; ajutor; mat *(la şah). vt., vi.* a (se) căsători; a (se) împerechea; a face mat.

material [mə'tiəriəl] s. material. *adj.* material; important.

materialism [mə'tiəriəlizəm] s. materialism.

materialist [mə'tiəriəlist] s. materialist.

materialize [mə'tiəriəlaiz] *vt., vi.* a (se) materializa; a (se) concretiza.

maternal [mə'tə:nl] *adj.* matern; după mamă.

mathematics [ˌmæθiˈmætiks] *s.* matematică.

matriculate [məˈtrikjuleit] *vi.* a intra la facultate.

matrimony [ˈmætrimni] *s.* căsătorie.

matron [ˈmeitrn] *s.* matroană; menajeră; soră șefă.

matter [ˈmætə] *s.* materie; subiect; chesti(un)e (importantă); material(e); substanță; esență; puroi; *as a ~ of fact* de fapt; *no ~ (how)* nu contează (cum); *what's the ~ ?* ce este? *vi.* a conta; *it doesn't ~* nu face nimic.

matter-of-fact [ˈmætərəˈfækt] *adj.* (cu spirit) practic; prozaic; banal.

mattock [ˈmætək] *s.* săpăligă.

mattress [ˈmætris] *s.* saltea; somieră.

mature [məˈtjuə] *adj.* matur. *vt., vi.* a (se) coace.

maudlin [ˈmɔːdlin] *adj.* sentimental.

mawkish [ˈmɔːkiʃ] *adj.* dulceag.

may¹ [mei] *v. mod.* a putea; a avea voie; a fi posibil.

May² [mei] *s.* luna mai.

maybe [ˈmeibi] *adv.* poate.

May Day [ˈmeiˈdei] *s.* Întîi Mai; sărbătoarea primăverii.

mayor [mɛə] *s.* primar.

maypole [ˈmeipoul] *s.* stîlp simbolic în jurul căruia se dansează de 1 Mai.

maze [meiz] *s.* labirint.

me [mi(ː)] *pron.* pe mine, mă; mie, îmi; eu.

meadow [ˈmedou] *s.* pajiște; luncă.

meager, meagre [ˈmiːgə] *adj.* slab; sărac.

meal [miːl] *s.* făină; masă (de prînz etc.).

meal-time [ˈmiːltaim] *s.* ora mesei.

mealy [ˈmiːli] *adj.* făinos; palid.

mean [miːn] *s.* medie; *pl.* mijloc, cale; mijloace; avere; metodă; *by ~s of* prin; cu ajutorul. *adj.* mijlociu; mediocru; meschin; josnic; umil. *vt.* a vrea să spună; a se referi la; a intenționa; a destina.

meander [miˈændə] *s.* meandră; șerpuire. *vi.* a face meandre; a rătăci; a vorbi alandala.

meaning [ˈmiːniŋ] *s.* înțeles.

meant [ment] *vt. trec. și part. trec. de la* **mean.**

meantime [ˈmiːnˈtaim], **meanwhile** [ˈmiːnˈwail] *adv.* între timp.

measles [ˈmiːzlz] *s.* pojar.

measure [ˈmeʒə] *s.* măsură; grad; etalon; cantitate; lege; ritm. *vt.* a măsura; a aprecia.

measurement [ˈmeʒəmənt] *s.* măsură; măsurătoare.

meat [miːt] *s.* carne; mîncare.

mechanic [miˈkænik] *s.* mecanic; *pl.* mecanică.

mechanize [ˈmekənaiz] *vt.* a mecaniza.

medal [ˈmedl] *s.* medalie.

meddle [ˈmedl] *vi.* a se amesteca; a umbla (cu un lucru etc.).

meddler [ˈmedlə] *s.* om băgăreț.

meddlesome [ˈmedlsəm] *adj.* băgăreț.

media *s. pl. de la* **medium.**

mediate¹ [ˈmiːdiit] *adj.* indirect (legat).

mediate² [ˈmiːdieit] *vt., vi.* a media.

medicine ['medsin] s. medicină; medicament.

meditate ['mediteit] vt., vi. a medita; a chibzui.

meditation [,medi'teiʃn] s. meditaţie; contemplare.

medium ['miːdjəm] s. mijloc; mediu; medie. adj. mediu.

medley ['medli] s. amestec; potpuriu.

meek [miːk] adj. supus; cuminte; blînd.

meet [miːt] s. întîlnire; competiţie. vt. a întîlni; a cunoaşte; a întîmpina; a satisface; a acoperi; to ~ smb. half way a face concesii cuiva. vi. a se întîlni; a se cunoaşte.

meeting ['miːtiŋ] s. întîlnire; întrunire.

melancholy ['melənkəli] s. melancolie. adj. melancolic.

mellow ['melou] adj. copt; moale; roditor; vesel. vt., vi. a (se) coace; a (se) muia.

melon ['melən] s. pepene.

melt [melt] vt., vi. a (se) topi; a (se) dizolva; a (se) muia.

member ['membə] s. membru; element.

membership ['membəʃip] s. calitatea de membru; număr de membri.

memento [mi'mentou] s. avertisment.

memoir ['memwɑː] s. memoriu; memorii; proces-verbal.

memorial [mi'mɔːriəl] s. monument comemorativ; memoriu; pl. cronică. adj. comemorativ.

memorize ['meməraiz] vt. a memora; a nota.

memory ['meməri] s. memorie; amintire; reputaţie.

men [men] s. pl. de la man.

menace ['menəs] s. ameninţare; primejdie. vt. a ameninţa.

menacingly ['menəsiŋli] adv. ameninţător.

mend [mend] s. reparaţie; cusătură. vt. a repara; a cîrpi; a corecta. vi. a se îmbunătăţi; a se corija; a se înzdrăveni.

mendacious [men'deiʃəs] adv. mincinos.

menfolk ['menfouk] s. pl. bărbaţii.

menial ['miːnjəl] s. slugă. adj. servil; umil.

menses ['mensiːz] s. pl. menstruaţie.

mental ['mentl] adj. mintal.

mentality [men'tæliti] s. minte; capacitate (intelectuală); stare de spirit.

mention ['menʃn] s. menţiune; referire. vt. a pomeni; a menţiona; don't ~ it! n-aveţi pentru ce.

menu ['menjuː] s. meniu.

mercantile ['məːkntail] adj. comercial.

mercer ['məːsə] s. pînzar.

merchandise ['məːtʃndaiz] s. marfă.

merchant ['məːtʃnt] s. (mare) negustor. adj. comercial.

merchantman ['məːtʃntmən] s. vas comercial.

merciful ['məːsifl] adj. îndurător.

merciless ['məːsilis] adj. neîndurător; sălbatic.

mercurial [məː'kjuəriəl] adj. mercuric; cu mercur; zglobiu, vesel; optimist.

mercury ['məːkjuri] s. mercur.

mercy ['məːsi] s. îndurare; milă. at the ~ of în puterea (cu gen.).

mere [miə] *adj.* simplu ; *a ~ chance* doar o întîmplare.

merely ['miəli] *adv.* numai ; doar; pur şi simplu.

merge [mə:dʒ] *vt., vi.* a (se) uni ; a fuziona.

merger ['mə:dʒə] *s.* fuziune.

merit ['merit] *s.* merit ; valoare. *vt.* a merita.

meritorious [ˌmeri'tɔ:riəs] *adj.* merituos.

mermaid ['mə:meid] *s.* sirenă.

merriment ['merimənt] *s.* distracţie, amuzament ; petrecere.

merry ['meri] *adj.* vesel ; fericit.

merry-go-round ['merigouˌraund] *s.* căluşei ; sens giratoriu.

merry-making ['meriˌmeikiŋ] *s.* veselie ; petrecere.

mesh [meʃ] *s.* (ochi de) plasă. *vt.* a prinde în plasă.

mesmerism ['mezmərizəm] *s.* hipnotism ; letargie.

mess [mes] *s.* încurcătură ; murdărie ; porcărie ; popotă ; sală de mese. *vt.* a strica ; a încurca ; a învălmăşi.

message ['mesidʒ] *s.* mesaj ; anunţ.

messenger ['mesindʒə] *s.* mesager ; curier.

Messrs. ['mesəz] *s. pl. com.* domnii ..., domnilor ... ; firmă.

messy ['mesi] *adj.* murdar ; în dezordine.

met [met] *vt., vi. trec. şi part. trec. de la* meet.

metal ['metl] *s.* metal ; piatră de pavaj *vt.* a pietrui.

metamorphosis [ˌmetə'mɔ:fəsis] *s.* metamorfoză.

metaphor ['metəfə] *s.* metaforă.

metaphysical [ˌmetə'fizikl] *adj.* metafizic ; abstract.

metaphysics [ˌmetə'fiziks] *s.* metafizică ; teorie.

meter ['mi:tə] *s.* aparat de măsură ; contor ; metru.

method ['meθəd] *s.* metodă ; ordine ; aranjament.

methodology [ˌmeθə'dɔlədʒi] *s.* metodică.

Methodism ['meθədizəm] *s. rel.* metodism.

methylated ['meθileitid] *adj.* metilic ; denaturat.

metre ['mi:tə] *s.* metru ; ritm.

metropolis [mi'trɔpəlis] *s.* metropolă ; centru.

metropolitan [ˌmetrə'pɔlitn] *s.* cetăţean al capitalei ; mitropolit. *adj.* metropolitan.

mettle ['metl] *s.* curaj ; bărbăţie.

mettlesome ['metlsəm] *adj.* viguros ; bătăios.

mew [mju:] *s. ornit.* pescar ; pescăruş ; mieunat. *vt., vi.* a mieuna.

Mexican ['meksikən] *s., adj.* mexican(ă).

mica ['maikə] *s.* mică.

mice [mais] *s. pl. de la* mouse.

microbe ['maikroub] *s.* microb.

microphone ['maikrəfoun] *s.* microfon.

midday ['middei] *s.* amiază.

middle ['midl] *s.* mijloc, centru. *adj.* mijlociu.

middle-aged ['midl eidʒd] *adj.* între două vîrste.

Middle Ages ['midl'eidʒiz] *s.* evul mediu.

middle classes ['midl'kla:siz] *s. pl.* burghezie ; clasele de mijloc.

middling ['midliŋ] *adj.* mediocru. *adv.* binişor.

midget ['midʒit] *s.* pitic.

midland ['midlənd] *s.* inima ţării.

midnight ['midnait] *s.* miezul nopţii.

midshipman ['midʃipmən] *s. mar.* aspirant.

midst [midst] *s.* mijloc.

midsummer ['mid‚sʌmə] *s.* miezul verii; Sînziene.

midway ['mid'wei] *adj.* de mijloc. *adv.* la mijloc.

midwife ['midwaif] *s.* moaşă.

mien [miːn] *s.* înfăţişare; mină.

might [mait] *s.* putere; *with ~ and main* cu toată puterea. *v. mod. trec. de la* **may.**

mighty ['maiti] *adj.* puternic; mare. *adv.* foarte.

migrate [mai'greit] *vi.* a emigra; a migra.

mike [maik] *s.* microfon.

milch [miltʃ] *adj.* cu lapte; de lapte.

mild [maild] *adj.* blînd; dulce; slab.

mildew ['mildjuː] *s.* mucegai; *bot.* tăciune. *vt., vi.* a mucegăi.

mildly ['maildli] *adv.* blînd; dulce; uşor.

mile' [mail] *s.* (măsură de o) milă; *it's ~s better* e mult mai bine.

mileage ['mailidʒ] *s.* distanţă; kilometraj.

milestone ['mailstoun] *s.* piatră kilometrică; piatră de hotar.

militant ['militənt] *s.* activist. *adj.* combativ; războinic.

military ['militri] *s.: the ~* armata. *adj.* militar.

militate ['militeit] *vi.* a milita; a activa.

militia [mi'liʃə] *s.* miliţie.

militiaman [mi'liʃəmən] *s.* miliţian.

milk [milk] *s.* lapte. *vt.* a mulge.

milkmaid ['milkmeid] *s.* mulgătoare; lăptăreasă.

milkman ['milkmən] *s.* lăptar.

milksop ['milksɔp] *s.* papă-lapte.

milky ['milki] *adj.* lăptos.

Milky Way ['milki'wei] *s.* Calea Laptelui.

mill [mil] *s.* fabrică (în special textilă); moară; rîşniţă; viaţă grea. *vt.* a măcina; a produce; a lamina. *vi.* a se învîrti.

millennium [mi leniəm] *s.* mileniu; epocă de aur.

miller ['milə] *s.* morar.

millet ['milit] *s.* mei.

milliner ['milinə] *s.* modistă

millinery ['milinri] *s.* magazin de mode.

millionaire [‚miljə'nɛə] *s.* milionar; miliardar.

millstone ['milstoun] *s.* piatră de moară.

mime [maim] *s.* mim(ă). *vt., vi.* a mima.

mimeograph ['mimiəgrɑːf] *s.* şapirograf. *vt.* a şapirografia.

mimic ['mimik] *s.* imitator. *adj.* de mimică; imitativ. *vt.* a imita.

mimicry ['mimikri] *s.* mimică.

mince [mins] *vt.* a toca; *not to ~ matters* ca să spunem lucrurilor pe nume.

mince-meat ['minsmiːt] *s.* umplutură de fructe (la prăjitură); carne tocată.

mincing ['minsiŋ] *adj.* afectat.

mind [maind] *s.* minte; înţelepciune; părere; spirit; hotărîre; *of one ~ sau of a ~* de acord; *to my ~* după părerea mea ; după gustul meu ; *out of one's* ~ descreierat ; *the* ~'s *eyes* imaginaţia ; *absence of* ~ zăpăceală. *vt.* a observa ; a păzi ; a avea grijă de ; a-i păsa de ; a da atenţie la ; a se feri de. *vi.* a se supăra ; a fi atent ; *never* ~ *!* nu face nimic !

mindful ['maindfl] *adj.* atent ; pătruns (de o idee etc.).

mine [main] *s.* mină. *pron.* al meu etc. *vt.* a săpa ; a (sub)mina.

miner ['mainə] *s.* miner. *mil.* pionier.

mingle ['miŋgl] *vt., vi.* a (se) amesteca.

minim ['minim] *s. muz.* doime.

minimize ['minimaiz] *vt.* a minimaliza.

mining ['mainiŋ] *s.* minerit.

minister ['ministə] *s.* ministru ; preot ; agent.

ministerial [ˌminis'tiəriəl] *adj.* ministerial ; guvernamental.

ministry ['ministri] *s.* minister ; guvern ; cler.

mink [miŋk] *s.* nurcă.

minor ['mainər] *s., adj.* minor.

minstrel ['minstrl] *s.* menestrel ; colindător.

mint [mint] *s.* mentă ; monetărie ; sursă. *vt.* a bate (monedă) a născoci.

minuet [ˌminju'et] *s.* menuet.

minus ['mainəs] *s., adj., prep.* minus.

minute[1] ['minit] *s.* clipă ; minut(ă) ; proces-verbal.

minute[2] [mai'njuːt] *adj.* amănunţit ; minuţios ; mărunt.

minute-hand [miuithænd] *s.* minutar.

minx [miŋks] *s.* obrăznicătură ; fetişcană neserioasă.

miracle ['mirəkl] *s.* miracol ; model.

mire ['maiə] *s.* noroi ; mlaştină ; încurcătură.

mirror ['mirə] *s.* oglindă. *vt.* a oglindi.

mirth [məːθ] *s.* veselie ; distracţie.

mirthless ['məːθlis] *adv.* trist.

misadventure ['misəd'ventʃə] *s.* nenorocire ; necaz.

misalliance ['misə'laiəns] *s.* mezalianţă.

misappropriate ['misə'prouprieit] *vt.* a deturna (fonduri).

misapprehension ['misˌæpri'henʃn] *s.* temere ; neînţelegere.

misbehave ['misbi'heiv] *vt., vr.* a se purta rău.

miscalculate ['mis'kælkjuleit] *vt., vi.* a calcula greşit.

miscarriage [mis'kæridʒ] *s.* eşec ; greşeală ; avort.

miscarry [mis'kæri] *vi.* a eşua ; a se pierde ; a avorta.

miscellaneous [ˌmisi'leinjəs] *adj.* amestecat ; variat.

miscellany [mi'seləni] *s.* miscelaneu ; varietate.

mischance [mis'tʃɑːns] *s.* ghinion.

mischief ['mistʃif] *s.* rău ; stricăciune ; ticăloşie ; poznă ; drăcuşor.

mischievous ['mistʃivəs] *adj.* rău ; poznaş.

misconduct[1] [mis'kɔndəkt] *s.* purtare rea ; neglijenţă (în serviciu).

misconduct[2] ['miskən dʌkt] *vt., vr.* a greşi.

misconstruction ['miskəns'trʌkʃn] *s.* neînţelegere.

misconstrue ['miskən'stru:] *vt.*
a interpreta greşit.

misdeed ['mis'di:d] *s.* fărădelege, ticăloşie ; crimă.

misdemeano(u)r [‚misdi'mi:nə]
s. nelegiuire ; contravenţie.

misdoing ['mis'du:iŋ] *s.* ticăloşie ; fărădelege.

miser ['maizə] *s.* zgîrcit.

miserable ['mizərəbl] *adj.* nenorocit ; sărac ; mizerabil.

misery ['mizəri] *s.* mizerie ; sărăcie ; nenorocire ; supărare.

misfit ['misfit] *s.* lucru nepotrivit ; om nepotrivit ; inadaptabil.

misfortune [mis'fɔ:tʃn] *s.* nenorocire.

misgiving [mis'giviŋ]*s.* îndoială ;
presimţire.

mishap ['mishæp] *s.* ghinion.

misinform ['misin'fɔ:m] *vt.* a
dezinforma.

misinterpret ['misin'tə:prit] *vt.*
a interpreta greşit.

misjudge ['mis'dʒʌdʒ] *vt., vi.*
a judeca greşit.

mislaid [mis'leid] *vt. trec. şi
part. trec. de la* mislay.

mislay [mis'lei] *vt.* a pierde ;
a zăpăci.

mislead [mis'li:d] *vt.* a duce pe
o cale greşită ; a înşela.

misled [mis'led] *vt. trec. şi part.
trec. de la* mislead.

mismanage ['mis'mænidʒ] *vt.* a
administra prost.

misplace ['mis'pleis] *vt.* a pune
unde nu trebuie ; a zăpăci.

misprint¹ ['mis'print] *s.* greşeală
de tipar.

misprint² [mis'print] *vt.* a tipări greşit.

mispronounce ['misprə'nauns]
vt. a pronunţa greşit.

misrepresent [mis‚repri'zent] *vt.*
a deforma.

miss¹ [mis] *s.* scăpare ; eşec.
vt. a nu atinge ; a scăpa ; a
pierde ; a-ţi fi dor de ; a omite ;
to ~ fire a nu lua foc ; a nu
porni. *vi.* a greşi ţinta ; a cădea
prost.

Miss² [mis] *s.* domnişoară.

misshapen ['mis'ʃeipn] *adj.* diform.

missile ['misail] *s.* proiectil.

missing ['misiŋ] *s. pl.: the ~*
dispăruţii. *adj.* absent ; lipsă ;
dispărut.

mission ['miʃn] *s.* misiune ; îndatorire.

missis ['misiz] *s.* coniţă ; stăpînă ;
soţie.

mis-spell ['mis'spel] *vt.* a orto-
grafia greşit.

missus ['misəs] *s. v.* missis.

mist [mist] *s.* ceaţă.

mistake [mis'teik] *s.* greşeală ;
confuzie ; accident. *vt.* a greşi ;
a confunda ; a înţelege
greşit.

mistaken [mis'teikn] *adj.* greşit ;
rău înţeles. *vt. part. trec. de la*
mistake.

mister ['mistə] *s.* domnul ...

mistletoe ['misltou] *s.* vîsc.

mistook [mis'tuk] *vt. trec. de la*
mistake.

mistress ['mistris] *s.* doamna... ;
stăpînă ; maestră ; profesoară ;
iubită ; amantă ; metresă.

mistrust ['mis'trʌst] *s.* neîncredere. *vt.* a̕ bănui.

misty ['misti] *adj.* ceţos ; vag.

misunderstand ['misʌndə'stænd]
vt. a înţelege greşit.

misunderstanding ['misʌndə-
'stændiŋ] *s.* neînţelegere.

misuse[1] ['mis'ju:s] *s.* folosire greşită; abuz.

misuse[2] ['mis'ju:z] *vt.* a folosi greşit; a abuza de; a maltrata.

mite [mait] *s.* monedă măruntă; pic; ţînc; gîză; musculiţă.

mitigate ['mitigeit] *vt.* a îmblînzi; a micşora; a înmuia.

mitt(en) ['mit(n)] *s.* mănuşă groasă (de sport), cu un deget; mitenă.

mix [miks] *vt.*, a amesteca, a pune laolaltă. *vi.* a se amesteca; a veni în contact (în societate).

mixed [mikst] *adj.* amestecat; mixt; învălmăşit; confuz.

mixer ['miksə] *s.* malaxor; persoană sociabilă.

mixture ['mikstʃə] *s.* amestec-(ătură).

moan [moun] *s.* geamăt. *vi.* a geme.

moat [mout] *s.* şanţ (cu apă).

mob [mɔb] *s.* gloabă; mulţime. *vt.* a se îngrămădi.

mock [mɔk] *s.* batjocură; satiră. *adj.* comic; simulat. *vt.* a-şi bate joc de; a înfrînge. *vi.: to ~ at* a lua în rîs.

mockery ['mɔkəri] *s.* batjocură; parodie.

mode [moud] *s.* mod; modă.

model ['mɔdl] *s.* model; machetă; tipar. *adj.* model. *vt.* a modela.

moderate[1] ['mɔdrit] *adj.* moderat.

moderate[2] ['mɔdəreit] *vt.*, *vi.* a (se) modera; a (se) stăpîni.

moderation [ˌmɔdə'reiʃn] *s.* moderaţie; cumpătare; modestie.

modern ['mɔdən] *adj.* modern.

modest ['mɔdist] *adj.* modest;

timid; cuminte; decent; moderat.

modesty ['mɔdisti] *s.* modestie; timiditate; delicateţe; decenţă.

modify ['mɔdifai] *vt.* a modifica; a schimba; a modera; a tempera.

mo'dish ['moudiʃ] *adj.* elegant, la modă.

mohair ['mouhɛə] *s.* mohair, păr de capră de angora.

Mohammedan [mo'hæmidn] *s.*, *adj.* mahomedan.

moist [mɔist] *adj.* umed.

moisten ['mɔisn] *vt.*, *vi.* a (se) umezi.

moisture ['mɔistʃə] *s.* umezeală.

molasses [mə'læsiz] *s.* melasă.

mole [moul] *s.* neg; cîrtiţă; dig portuar.

mole-hill ['moulhil] *s.* muşuroi de cîrtiţă.

molest [mo'lest] *vt.* a necăji; a tulbura.

mollify ['mɔlifai] *vt.* a înmuia; a potoli.

molly-coddle ['mɔlikɔdl] *s.* papă-lapte; răsfăţat. *vt.* a răsfăţa.

molten ['moultn] *adj.* topit.

moment ['moumənt] *s.* clipă; moment; importanţă.

momentary ['mouməntri] *adj.* momentan; imediat.

momentous [mo'mentəs] *adj.* foarte important.

momentum [mo'mentəm] *s.* avînt; mişcare; proporţii.

monarch ['mɔnək] *s.* monarh.

monarchy ['mɔnəki] *s.* monarhie.

monastery ['mɔnəstri] *s.* mănăstire.

Monday ['mʌndi] *s.* luni.

money ['mʌni] s. bani; avere.

money-bag ['mʌnibæg] s. avere; bogătaş, magnat.

money-lender ['mʌni‚lendə] s. cămătar.

money-order ['mʌni'ɔ:də] s. mandat.

mongrel ['mʌŋgrl] s., adj. corcitură.

monk [mʌŋk] s. călugăr.

monkey ['mʌŋki] s. maimuţă; maimuţoi; copilaş.

monkey-wrench ['mʌŋki‚rentʃ] s. tehn. cheie universală sau franceză.

monograph ['mɔnəgra:f] s. monografie.

monomania ['mɔno'meinjə] s. idee fixă; nebunie.

monopoly [mə'nɔpəli] s. monopol. adj. monopolist.

monsoon [mɔn'su:n] s. muson.

monster ['mɔnstə] s. monstru.

monstrous ['mɔnstrəs] adj. monstruos; uriaş.

month [mʌnθ] s. lună.

monthly ['mʌnθli] s. publicaţie lunară. adj., adv. lunar.

monument ['mɔnjumənt] s. monument.

moo [mu:] s. muget. vi. a mugi.

mood [mu:d] s. dispoziţie; capriciu; gram. mod.

moody ['mu:di] adj. capricios; prost dispus; morocănos.

moon [mu:n] s. luna; lumina lunii.

moonbeam ['mu:nbi:m] s. rază de lună.

moonlit ['mu:nlit] adj. luminat de lună.

moonshine ['mu:nʃain] s. lumina lunii; aiureală.

moonstruck ['mu:nstrʌk] adj. aiurit.

moor[1] [muə] s. bărăgan; ierburi. vt. a priponi (o barcă etc.).

Moor[2] [muə] s. maur.

moorings ['muəriŋz] s. pl. odgoane.

Moorish ['muəriʃ] adj. maur.

mop [mɔp] s. şomoiog; smoc; pămătuf. vt. a şterge (cu cîrpa etc.); a mătura.

mope [moup] s. morocănos; pl. proastă dispoziţie. vi. a bombăni.

moral ['mɔrl] s. morală. adj. moral; cumpătat.

morale [mɔ'ra:l] s. moral.

morality [mə'ræliti] s. morală; dramă medievală.

moralize ['mɔrəlaiz] vt. a aduce pe calea cea bună; a moraliza. vi. a ţine predici.

more [mɔ:] adj. compar. de la **much** sau **many** mai mult; mai mulţi; în plus; suplimentar; alt. pron. mai mult; mai mulţi. adv. compar. de la **much** mai mult; pe deasupra, iarăşi; no ~ nu mai; niciodată.

moreover [mɔ:'rouvə] adj. pe deasupra, pe lîngă asta.

morning ['mɔ:niŋ] s. dimineaţă.

morocco [mə'rɔkou] s. marochin.

moron ['mɔ:rɔn] s. debil mintal; arierat.

morose [mə'rous] adj. morocănos; sumbru.

morphia ['mɔ:fjə] s. morfină.

morsel ['mɔ:sl] s. bucăţică; îmbucătură; înghiţitură.

mortal ['mɔ:tl] s. muritor. adj. muritor; mortal; de moarte; extrem.

mortar ['mɔ:tə] s. tencuială; mojar; mortieră. vt. a tencui.

mortgage ['mɔ:gidʒ] s. ipotecă. vt. a ipoteca; a angaja. vr. a se angaja.

mortician [mɔ:'tiʃn] s. amer. antreprenor de pompe funebre.

mortification [͵mɔ:tifi keiʃn] s. ruşine; jignire; penitenţă; gangrenă.

mortify ['mɔ:tifai] vt. a jigni; a înfrînge. vi. a se gangrena.

mortuary ['mɔ:tjuəri] s. capelă funerară. adj. mortuar.

Moslem ['mɔzlem] s., adj. musulman.

mosque [mɔsk] s. moschee.

mosquito [məs'ki:tou] s. ţînţar.

moss [mɔs] s. bot. muşchi.

most [moust] adj. superl. de la **much** şi **many** cel mai mult; cei mai mulţi; majoritatea. pron.: ~ of cei mai mulţi din(tre); majoritatea. adv. superl. de la **much** cel mai mult; foarte; cît se poate de.

mostly ['moustli] adv. mai ales, în special; aproape tot.

mote [mout] s. fir (de praf etc.).

motel [mou'tel] s. hotel pentru automobilişti, motel.

moth [mɔθ] s. molie.

mother ['mʌðə] s. mamă. adj. matern.

mother country ['mʌðə͵kʌntri] s. patrie; metropolă.

motherhood ['mʌðəhud] s. maternitate (fig.).

mother-in-law ['mʌðərinlɔ:] s. soacră.

motherly ['mʌðəli] adj. matern.

mother-of-pearl ['mʌðrə'pə:l] s. sidef.

motif [mou'ti:f] s. temă; motiv.

motion ['mouʃn] s. mişcare; gest; moţiune. vi. a face semn (cuiva).

motionless ['mouʃnlis] adj. nemişcat.

motion-picture ['mouʃn'piktʃə] s. film.

motive ['moutiv] s. motiv. adj. motrice.

motley ['mɔtli] adj. bălţat; amestecat; variat.

motor ['moutə] s. motor; automobil.

motor-bicycle ['moutə'baisikl] s. motoretă.

motor-boat ['moutəbout] s. şalupă.

motor-bus ['moutə'bʌs] s. autobuz.

motor-car ['moutəka:] s. automobil.

motor-cycle ['moutə͵saikl] s. motocicletă.

motorist ['moutərist] s. automobilist.

motorman ['moutəmən] s. vatman; şofer.

motto ['mɔtou] s. moto; deviză.

mould [mould] s. mulaj; formă; mucegai. vt. a turna în forme; a modela; a forma. vi. a se mucegăi.

mouldy ['mouldi] adj. mucegăit.

mound [maund] s. movilă; cavou.

mount [maunt] s. munte; cal de călărie; afet; montură. vt. a urca (pe); a încăleca; a monta; a duce.

mountain ['mauntin] s. munte; morman. adj. de munte.

mountaineer [͵maunti'niə] s. muntean; alpinist.

mountaineering [͵maunti'niəriŋ] s. alpinism.

mountainous ['mauntinəs] *adj.* muntos; uriaş.

mountebank ['mauntibæŋk] *s.* şarlatan; jongler.

mounting ['mauntiŋ] *s.* montură; montaj.

mourn [mɔːn] *vt., vi.* a jeli.

mourner ['mɔːnə] *s.* persoană în doliu; bocitoare.

mournful ['mɔːnfl] *adj.* trist; sumbru.

mourning ['mɔːniŋ] *s.* doliu; supărare. *adj.* îndoliat; de doliu.

mouse [maus] *s.* şoarece.

mouse-trap ['maustræp] *s.* cursă (de şoareci).

moustache [məs'tɑːʃ] *s.* mustaţă.

mouth [mauθ] *s.* gură.

mouthful ['mauθful] *s.* îmbucătură.

mouth-organ ['mauθˌɔːgən] *s.* muzicuţă.

mouthpiece ['mauθpiːs] *s.* muştiuc; purtător de cuvînt.

movable ['muːvəbl] *s.* bun mobil. *adj.* mobil; schimbător.

move [muːv] *s.* mişcare; schimbare; măsură; acţiune. *vt.* a mişca; a muta; a propune. *vi.* a se mişca; a se muta; a înainta; a acţiona.

movement ['muːvmənt] *s.* mişcare.

movie ['muːvi] *s.* film; *pl.* cinema.

moving ['muːviŋ] *adj.* mişcător.

moving pictures ['muːviŋ'piktʃəz] *s. pl.* filme; cinema(tograf).

mow [mou] *vt., vi.* a cosi.

mower ['mouə] *s.* cosaş.

mown [moun] *vt., vi. part. trec. de la* **mow**.

M.P. ['em'piː] *s.* deputat.

Mr. ['mistə] *s.* domnul ...

Mrs. [misiz] *s.* doamna ...

MS ['em'es] *s.* manuscris.

much [mʌtʃ] *adj., pron.* mult; *how ~ ?* cît? cu ce preţ? *adv.* mult (mai); în mare măsură; aproape.

mud [mʌd] *s.* noroi; nămol; mîl.

mudguard ['mʌdgɑːd] *s. auto.* aripă.

muddle ['mʌdl] *s.* învălmăşeală. *vt.* a încurca; a zăpăci.

muddle-headed ['mʌdl'hedid] *adj.* cu mintea încîlcită.

muddy ['mʌdi] *adj.* noroios; mîlos; murdar; întunecat; învălmăşit.

muff [mʌf] *s.* manşon.

muffin ['mʌfin] *s.* biscuit; turtă.

muffle ['mʌfl] *vt.* a înfofoli; a înfăşura; a acoperi (sunetele).

muffler ['mʌflə] *s.* fular; înveliş.

mufti ['mʌfti] *s.* haine civile.

mug [mʌg] *s.* cană; mutră; ageamiu.

mulatto [mju'lætou] *s.* mulatru.

mulberry ['mʌlbri] *s.* dud; dudă.

mule [mjuːl] *s.* catîr; papuc.

mulish ['mjuːliʃ] *adj.* încăpăţînat.

multifarious [ˌmʌlti'fɛəriəs] *adj.* multiplu.

multiple ['mʌltipl] *s., adj.* multiplu.

multiple shop ['mʌltiplˌʃɔp] *s.* magazin cu sucursale.

multiplication [ˌmʌltipli'keiʃn] *s.* înmulţire.

multiply ['mʌltiplai] *vt., vi.* a (se) înmulţi.

multi-stage ['mʌlti'steidʒ] *adj.* cu mai multe trepte.

multitude ['mʌltitjuːd] s. mulţime.

mum [mʌm] adj. tăcut. interj. sst!

mumble ['mʌmbl] s. mormăit. vt., vi. a mormăi; a molfăi.

mummer ['mʌmə] s. mim; actor.

mummery ['mʌməri] s. mimă; caraghioslîc.

mummy ['mʌmi] s. mămică; mumie.

mumps [mʌmps] s. oreion.

munch [mʌntʃ] vt., vi. a molfăi.

mundane ['mʌndein] adj. lumesc.

municipality [mjuˌnisi'pæliti] s. municipiu.

munificent [mju'nifisnt] adj. foarte generos.

munition [mju'niʃn] s. armament. vt. a înarma.

mural ['mjuərl] s. pictură murală. adj. mural.

murder ['məːdə] s. omor. vt. a omorî; a strica.

murderer ['məːdərə] s. ucigaş.

murderous ['məːdərəs] adj. ucigător.

murky ['məːki] adj. întunecos; întunecat; sinistru.

murmur ['məːmə] s. murmur. vt., vi. a murmura.

muscle ['mʌsl] s. muşchi; forţă.

Muse[1] [mjuːz] s. muză.

muse[2] [mjuːz] vi. a medita; a fi dus pe gînduri.

museum [mju'ziəm] s. muzeu.

mush [mʌʃ] s. fiertură; terci.

mushroom ['mʌʃrum] s. ciupercă. vi. a culege ciuperci.

music ['mjuːzik] s. muzică.

musical ['mjuːzikl] adj. muzical; meloman.

music-hall ['mjuːzikhɔːl] s. teatru de revistă, varieteu.

musician [mju'ziʃn] s. muzicant; compozitor; muzician.

music-stand ['mjuːzikstænd] s. pupitru pentru note.

musk [mʌsk] s. mosc.

musket ['mʌskit] s. flintă.

musketeer [ˌmʌski'tiə] s. muşchetar.

musketry ['mʌskitri] s. tir.

muslin ['mʌzlin] s. muselină.

must [mʌst] s. necesitate (imperioasă); must. v. mod. a trebui; a fi foarte probabil; a fi logic.

mustang ['mʌstæŋ] s. cal sălbatic.

mustard ['mʌstəd] s. muştar.

muster ['mʌstə] s. adunare; trecere în revistă. vt., vi. a (se) aduna; a (se) mobiliza.

musty ['mʌsti] adj. mucegăit.

mutability [ˌmjuːtə'biliti] s. nestatornicie.

mute [mjuːt] s. mut; surdină; figurant. adj. mut. vt. a pune surdină la.

mutinous ['mjuːtinəs] adj. rebel.

mutiny ['mjuːtini] s. rebeliune. vi. a se răscula.

mutter ['mʌtə] s. mormăială. vt. a mormăi. vi. a mormăi; a bombăni.

mutton ['mʌtn] s. carne de oaie sau de berbec.

mutual ['mjuːtjuəl] adj. reciproc; comun.

muzzle ['mʌzl] s. botniţă; gură de ţeavă. vt. a pune botniţă la.

my [mai] adj. meu. interj. vai!

myrrh [məː] s. smirnă.

myrtle ['məːtl] s. bot. mirt.

myself [mai'self] *pron.* pe mine ; mă ; însumi ; eu.

mysterious [mis'tiəriəs] *adj.* misterios ; obscur.

mystery ['mistri] *s.* mister.

mystification [ˌmistifi'keiʃn] *s.* înşelătorie ; enigmă.

myth [miθ] *s.* mit.

mythic (al) ['miθik(l)] *adj.* mit(olog)ic ; imaginar ; legendar.

N

N [en] *s.* N, n.

nag [næg] *s.* mîrţoagă ; ponei ; nevastă. *vt.* a necăji ; a cicăli.

nail [neil] *s.* unghie ; cui ; piron. *vt.* a fixa (în cuie) ; a înţepeni.

naive [nɑː'iːv, neiv] *adj.* naiv.

naïveté [nɑː'iːvtei] *s.* naivitate ; nevinovăţie.

naked ['neikid] *adj.* despuiat, gol ; (*d. ochi*) liber.

name [neim] *s.* nume ; reputaţie ; insultă. *vt.* a numi ; a boteza ; a stabili ; a alege.

nameless ['neimlis] *adj.* necunoscut ; anonim.

namely ['neimli] *adv.* adică, şi anume.

namesake ['neimseik] *s.* tiz.

nap [næp] *s.* pui de somn ; *text.* puf. *vi.* a aţipi.

nape [neip] *s.* ceafă.

napkin ['næpkin] *s.* şerveţel.

narrate [næ'reit] *vt.* a povesti.

narrative ['nærətiv] *s.* naraţiune ; relatare. *adj.* narativ.

narrow ['nærou] *adj.* îngust ; limitat ; zgîrcit ; strict ; pe muchie de cuţit. *vt., vi* a (se) strîmba.

narrow-minded ['nærou'maindid] *adj.* limitat ;. îngust la minte.

nasturtium [nəs'təːʃəm] *s. bot.* condurul-doamnei.

nasty ['nɑːsti] *adj.* scîrbos ; ticălos ; greu.

nation ['neiʃn] *s.* naţiune ; popor ; ţară.

national ['næʃənl] *s.* cetăţean. *adj.* naţional.

native ['neitiv] *s.* băştinaş ; localnic. *adj.* băştinaş ; autohton ; înnăscut.

nativity [nə'tiviti] *s.* naştere ; *the Nativity* Crăciunul.

natural ['nætʃrl] *s. muz.* becar ; notă naturală. *adj.* natural ; original ; veridic ; obişnuit ; înnăscut ; *muz.* natural ; becar.

naturalize ['nætʃrəlaiz] *vt., vi.* a (se) naturaliza ; a (se) aclimatiza.

naturally ['nætʃrəli] *adv.* fireşte ; în mod natural.

nature ['neitʃə] *s.* natură ; fire ; caracter.

naught [nɔːt] *s.* nimic.

naughty ['nɔːti] *adj.* rău ; obraznic.

nausea ['nɔːsjə] *s.* greaţă.

nauseate ['nɔːsieit] *vt.* a îngreţoşa.

naval ['neivl] *adj.* naval.

nave [neiv] s. naos.

navel ['neivl] s. buric.

navigate ['nævigeit] vi. a naviga.

navigation [nævi'geiʃn] s. navigaţie ; flotă ; trafic.

navvy ['nævi] s. săpător ; salahor ; excavator.

navy ['neivi] s. marină.

navy blue ['neiviblu:] s., adj. bleumarin.

nay [nei] adv. ba chiar.

Nazi ['nɑ:tsi] s. nazist.

N.C.O. ['en'si:'ou] s. subofiţer.

near [niə] adj. apropiat ; econom. vt. a (se) apropia (de). vi. a se apropia. adv. aproape ; în apropiere. prep. aproape de.

nearly ['niəli] adv. aproape ; foarte ; cît pe-aci ; not ~ cîtuşi de puţin.

nearness ['niənis] s. apropiere.

neat [ni:t] adj. curat ; plăcut ; net ; elegant ; as ~ as a new pin nou-nouţ.

necessarily ['nesisrli] adv. neapărat.

necessary ['nesisri] adj. necesar ; esenţial ; obligatoriu.

necessity [ni'sesiti] s. necesitate ; obligaţie ; sărăcie ; of ~ neapărat.

neck [nek] s. gît ; guler ; istm. ~ or nothing cu toate riscurile ; pe viaţă şi pe moarte.

neckerchief ['nekətʃif] s. batic.

necklace ['neklis] s. colier.

necktie ['nektai] s. cravată.

need [ni:d] s. nevoie ; necesitate. v. mod. a trebui ; a fi obligat să. vt. a avea nevoie de ; a-i lipsi.

needful ['ni:dfl] adj. necesar.

needle ['ni:dl] s. ac.

needless ['ni:dlis] adj. inutil.

needs [ni:dz] adv. neapărat.

needy ['ni:di] adj. sărac.

ne'er-do-well ['nɛə du͵wel] s. neisprăvit ; mişel.

nefarious [ni'fɛəriəs] adj. nefast ; nelegiuit.

negative ['negətiv] s., adj. negativ.

neglect [ni'glekt] s. neglijare ; neglijenţă. vt. a neglija.

neglectful [ni'glektfl] adj. neglijent ; uituc ; lăsător.

negligence ['neglidʒns] s. neglijenţă.

negligible ['neglidʒibl] adj. neglijabil ; infim.

negotiate [ni'gouʃieit] vt. a negocia ; a trece (peste).

negress ['ni:gris] s. negresă.

negro, Negro ['ni:grou] s. negru.

neigh [nei] s. nechezat. vi. a necheza.

neighbo(u)r ['neibə] s. vecin ; seamăn. vi. a se învecina.

neighbo(u)rhood ['neibəhud] s. vecinătate ; vecini ; (oamenii din) cartier.

neighbo(u)rly ['neibəli] adj. bun, prietenos ; amabil.

neither ['naiðə] adj. nici un, nici o. pron. nici unul (din doi). conj. nici.

neon ['ni:ən] s. neon.

nephew ['nevju:] s. nepot (de unchi).

nerve [nə:v] s. nerv ; nervură ; muşchi ; îndrăzneală.

nervous ['nə:vəs] adj. nervos ; speriat.

nest [nest] s. cuib ; cuibar ; sinecură. vi. a se cuibări.

nestle ['nesl] vt. a ţine strîns ; a cocoli. vi. a se cuibări.

net [net] *s.* plasă ; capcană. *adj.* net.

nether ['neðə] *adj.* de jos.

netting ['netiŋ] *s.* plasă.

nettle ['netl] *s.* urzică. *vt.* a urzica ; a aţîţa.

network ['netwə:k] *s.* reţea ; plasă.

neurotic [njuə'rɔtik] *s.* nevropat. *adj.* bolnav de nervi ; cu efect asupra nervilor.

neuter ['nju:tə] *s.*, *adj. gram.* neutru.

neutral ['nju:trl] *s.*, *adj.* neutru.

never ['nevə] *adv.* niciodată ; cîtuşi de puţin. *well I* ~ *!* nemaipomenit !

nevertheless [ˌnevəðə'les] *adv.*, *conj.* totuşi.

new [nju:] *adj.* nou ; modern ; proaspăt ; nepriceput.

new-fangled ['nju:ˌfæŋgld] *adj.* de ultimă oră ; ultrarecent.

newly ['nju:li] *adv.* de curînd ; altfel, într-un chip nou.

newly-weds ['nju:li'wedz] *s. pl.* tineri căsătoriţi.

news [nju:z] *s.* informaţii ; veşti ; radiojurnal ; noutate.

news agent ['nju:zˌeidʒnt] *s.* chioşcar.

newsboy ['nju:zbɔi] *s.* vînzător de ziare.

newspaper ['nju:sˌpeipə] *s.* ziar.

newspaperman ['nju:sˌpeipəmən] *s.* gazetar.

news-reel ['nju:zri:l] *s.* jurnal de actualităţi ; jurnal sonor.

news-room ['nju:zrum] *s.* sală de lectură pentru ziare ; cabina crainicilor.

newt [nju:t] *s.* salamandră de apă.

New Year's Day ['nju:jə:z'dei] *s.* Anul Nou.

next [nekst] *adj. superl. de la* **near** următor, viitor. *adv. superl. de la* **near** mai departe ; la rînd ; data viitoare ; pe urmă ; mai. *prep.:* ~ *to* alături de ; după ; pe lîngă ; aproape.

next door ['nekst'dɔ:] *adj.* de alături ; alăturat. *adv.* alături.

next year ['nekst'jə:] *s.* anul viitor. *adv.* la anul.

nib [nib] *s.* peniţă.

nibble ['nibl] *vt.* a ciuguli. *vi.* a morfoli.

nice [nais] *adj.* drăguţ ; plăcut ; bun ; frumos ; de treabă ; fin ; cinstit.

nicely ['naisli] *adv.* frumos ; exact ; bine.

nicety ['naisiti] *s.* delicateţe ; fineţe ; detaliu ; *to a* ~ perfect ; precis.

niche [nitʃ] *s.* nişă.

nick [nik] *s.* crestătură ; *in the* ~ *of time* tocmai la timp. *vt.* a cresta ; a bifa.

nickel ['nikl] *s.* nichel ; monedă de cinci cenţi ; fisă de telefon.

nickname ['nikneim] *s.* poreclă. *vt.* a porecli.

niece [ni:s] *s.* nepoată (de unchi).

niggard ['nigəd] *s.*, *adj.* zgîrcit ; meschin.

nigger ['nigə] *s. peior.* negru.

night [nait] *s.* noapte ; seară ; întuneric ; *at* sau *by* ~ noaptea.

night-cap ['naitkæp] *s.* scufie ; păhărel băut înainte de culcare.

night club ['naitklʌb] *s.* bar.

night-dress ['naitdres], **night-gown** ['naitgaun] *s.* cămaşă de noapte.

nightmare ['naitmɛə] s. coşmar.

nightingale ['naitiŋgeil] s. privighetoare.

nightwalker ['nait,wɔːkə] s. somnambul.

nil [nil] s. nimic; zero.

nimble ['nimbl] adj. iute; activ; ager (la minte).

nincompoop ['ninkəmpuːp] s. zevzec.

nine [nain] s., num. nouă.

ninepins ['nainpinz] s. pl. popice.

nineteen ['nain'tiːn] s., num. nouăsprezece.

nineteenth ['nain'tiːnθ] s., num. al nouăsprezecelea.

ninetieth ['naintiiθ] s., num. al nouăzecilea.

ninety ['nainti] s., num. nouăzeci; the nineties deceniul al zecelea.

ninny ['nini] s. găgăuţă.

ninth [nainθ] s., num. al nouălea.

nip [nip] s. muscătură; pişcătură; duşcă. vt. a ciupi; a muşca; a distruge; a fura; to ~ off a reteza. vi. a muşca; a ciupi; a fi muşcător.

nipper ['nipə] s. puşti; pl. cleşte.

nipping ['nipiŋ] adj. muşcător; tăios; aspru; îngheţat.

nipple ['nipl] s. ţîţă; sfîrcul sînului; biberon.

no [nou] adj. nici un; nici o; ~ one nimeni. adv. nu; de loc; cîtuşi de puţin.

nobility [no'biliti] s. nobleţe; nobilime.

noble ['noubl] s. nobil. adj. nobil; măreţ; uluitor.

nobody ['noubdi] pron. nimeni.

nod [nɔd] s. încuviinţare (din

cap); salut; aţipeală; somnolenţă. vi. a încuviinţa (din cap); a saluta; a moţăi.

noise [nɔiz] s. zgomot.

noisome ['nɔisəm] adj. supărător; greţos.

noisy ['nɔizi] adj. zgomotos.

nomad ['nɔməd] s. nomad.

nominal ['nɔminl] adj. nominal; simbolic; mic.

nominate ['nɔmineit] vt. a propune (un candidat); a numi.

nomination [,nɔmi'neiʃn] s. numire; propunere (de candidat).

nominee [,nɔmi'niː] s. candidat propus.

nonage ['nounidʒ] s. lipsă de maturitate; copilărie; minoritate.

nonce [nɔns] s.: for the ~ ad-hoc; momentan.

nonchalant ['nɔnʃlənt] adj. placid; nepăsător.

non-commissioned ['nɔnkə'miʃənd] adj. fără gradul de ofiţer.

non-commissioned officer ['nɔnkə'miʃənd'ɔfisə] s. subofiţer.

non-committal ['nɔnkə'mitl] adj. care nu te angajează; vag.

nonconformist ['nɔnkən'fɔːmist] s., adj. rebel; eretic.

nonconformity ['nɔnkən'fɔːmiti] s. nepotrivire; dezacord; erezie.

nondescript ['nɔndiskript] s. ciudăţenie; om ciudat. adj. ciudat; greu de definit.

none [nʌn] pron. nici unul; nimic; ~ of that! încetează!; ~ but numai. adv. nu prea; de loc; ~ the less cu toate acestea; he is ~ the worse for it asta i-a folosit.

nonentity [nɔ'nentiti] s. nefiinţă ; neisprăvit.

nonplus ['nɔn plʌs] vt. a ului ; a încurca.

nonsense ['nɔnsns] s. prostii ; fleacuri ; nonsens.

nonsensical [nɔn'sensikl] adj. fără sens ; aiurit.

non-stop ['nɔn'stɔp] adj., adv. fără oprire.

noodle ['nu:dl] s. găgăuţă ; pl. tăiţei.

nook [nuk] s. colţ ; cotlon.

noon [nu:n] s. amiază.

noose [nu:s] s. laţ ; ştreang.

nor [nɔ:] conj. nici ; neither ... ~ nici ... nici.

norm [nɔ:m] s. normă ; tipar.

Norman ['nɔ:mən] s., adj. normand.

Norse [nɔ:s] s., adj. norvegian(ă).

north [nɔ:θ] s. nord. adj. nordic ; de nord. adv. spre nord.

northerly ['nɔ:ðəli] adj. nordic ; de nord.

northern ['nɔ:ðən] adj. nordic.

northerner ['nɔ:ðnə] s. nordic.

northern lights ['nɔ:ðən'laits] s. auroră boreală.

Northman ['nɔ:θmən] s. nordic ; scandinav ; norvegian ; viking.

northward ['nɔ:θwəd] adj., adv. spre nord.

Norwegian [nɔ:'wi:dʒn] s., adj. norvegian(ă).

nose [nouz] s. nas ; vîrf ; bot. vt. a mirosi ; a adulmeca ; a căuta. vi a adulmeca ; a se amesteca.

nose-dive ['nouzdaiv] s. picaj.

nosegay ['nouzgei] s. buchet.

nostril ['nɔstrl] s. nară.

not [nɔt] adv. nu ; ~ half bad bun.

notable ['noutəbl] s. persoană importantă. adj. remarcabil ; memorabil.

notation [no'teiʃn] s. notaţie ; notare ; notă.

notch [nɔtʃ] s. crestătură. vt. a cresta.

note [nout] s. not(iţ)ă ; însemnare ; bilet ; clapă ; bancnotă ; poliţă ; urmă ; faimă ; atenţie ; semn. vt. a nota ; a observa ; a da atenţie la.

note-book ['noutbuk] s. caiet sau carnet de note.

note-case ['noutkeis] s. portofel.

note-paper ['nout,peipə] s. hîrtie de scrisori.

noted ['noutid] adj. celebru.

note of interrogation ['noutəvin,terə'geiʃn] s. semn de întrebare.

noteworthy ['noutwə:ði] adj. remarcabil.

nothing ['nʌθiŋ] pron. nimic ; for ~ gratis, degeaba ; inutil.

notice ['noutis] s. anunţ ; avertisment ; observaţie ; (pre)aviz ; notiţă ; recenzie etc. vt. a observa ; a remarca ; a lua în seamă.

noticeable ['noutisəbl] adj. remarcabil ; perceptibil.

notify ['noutifai] vt. a anunţa ; a declara (o naştere etc.).

notion ['nouʃn] s. noţiune ; idee ; habar ; pl. amer. mercerie.

notwithstanding [,nɔtwið'stændiŋ] adv. totuşi. prep. în ciuda.

nought [nɔ:t] s. nimic ; zero.

noun [naun] s. substantiv.

nourish ['nʌriʃ] vt. a hrăni ; fig. a nutri.

nourishment ['nʌriʃmənt] s. hrană.

novel ['nɔvl] s. roman. adj. nou ; neobişnuit.

novelist ['nɔvəlist] s. romancier.

novelty ['nɔvlti] s. noutate.

November [no'vembə] s. noiembrie.

now [nau] adv. acum ; imediat ; apoi ; (every) ~ and then sau again din cînd în cînd.

nowadays ['nauədeiz] adv. în zilele noastre.

nowhere ['nouwɛə] adv. nicăieri.

noxious ['nɔkʃəs] adj. dăunător ; otrăvit.

nozzle ['nɔzl] s. gura furtunului.

nuance [nju'ɑ:ns] s. nuanţă.

nuclear ['nju:kliə] adj. nuclear ; atomic.

nucleus ['njukliəs] s. nucleu.

nude [nju:d] s., adj. nud.

nudge [nʌdʒ] s. ghiont. vt. a înghionti.

nugget ['nʌgit] s. pepită (de aur).

nuisance ['nju:sns] s. supărare ; pacoste.

null [nʌl] adj. nul ; demodat.

nullify ['nʌlifai] vt. a anula.

numb [nʌm] adj. amorţit ; ţeapăn. vt. a amorţi ; a copleşi ; a împietri.

number ['nʌmbə] s. număr. vt. a numără ; a se ridica la ; a socoti.

numberless ['nʌmbəlis] adj. nenumărat.

number one ['nʌmbə'wʌn] s. subsemnatul ; interesul personal.

numerator ['nju:məreitə] s. numărător.

numskull ['nʌmskʌl] s. tîmpit.

nun [nʌn] s. călugăriţă.

nunnery ['nʌnəri] s. (mănăstire de) maici.

nurse [nə:s] s. dădacă ; guvernantă ; doică ; infirmieră. vt. a alăpta ; a îngriji ; a cocoli ; fig. a nutri ; a da atenţie la.

nursery ['nə:sri] s. camera copiilor ; creşă ; crescătorie ; pepinieră.

nursery rhymes ['nə:sriraimz] s. pl. poezii pentru copii.

nurture ['nə:tʃə] vt. a hrăni ; a îngriji ; a educa ; a creşte.

nut [nʌt] s. nucă ; alună ; piuliţă ; cap ; filfizon ; pl. nebun ; spărgător de nuci.

nut crackers ['nʌt‚krækəz] s. pl. spărgător de nuci.

nutrition [nju'triʃn] s. hrană ; hrănire.

nutritious [nju'triʃəs] adj. hrănitor.

nutshell ['nʌt-ʃel] s. coajă de nucă.

nylon ['nailən] s. nailon.

O

O [ou] s. O, o. interj. o(h) ; vai.

oak [ouk] s. stejar.

oaken ['oukn] adj. de stejar.

oakum ['oukəm] s. cîlţi.

oar [ɔ:] s. vîslă ; vîslaş.

oasis [o'eisis] s. oază.

oat(s) [out(s)] *s.* ovăz.

oath [ouθ] *s.* jurămînt; promisiune; înjurătură; blestem.

oatmeal ['outmi:l] *s.* fiertură; fulgi de ovăz.

obdurate ['ɔbdjurit] *adj.* încăpăţînat; împietrit.

obedience [ə'bi:djəns] *s.* supunere; ascultare.

obeisance [o'beisns] *s.* plecăciune; omagiu.

obey [ə'bei] *vt.* a asculta de; a se supune la; a executa. *vi.* a fi supus.

obituary [ɔ'bitjuəri] *s.* necrolog. *adj.* necrologic.

object[1] ['ɔbdʒikt] *s.* obiect; subiect; scop; *gram.* complement.

object[2] [əb'dʒekt] *vt.* a obiecta. *vi.* a obiecta; a protesta; a se revolta.

objection [əb'dʒekʃn] *s.* obiecţie; supărare; împotrivire.

objectionable [əb'dʒekʃnəbl] *adj.* neplăcut; condamnabil.

objective [əb'dʒektiv] *s.* (cazul) obiectiv, acuzativ. *adj.* obiectiv; real; impersonal.

obligation [ɔbli'geiʃn] *s.* obligaţie.

oblige [ə'blaidʒ] *vt.* a obliga; a îndatora.

obliging [ə'blaidʒiŋ] *adj.* îndatoritor.

obliterate [ə'blitəreit] *vt.* a distruge; a şterge.

oblivion [ə'bliviən] *s.* uitare.

oblivious [ə'bliviəs] *adj.* neatent; uituc.

oblong ['ɔblɔŋ] *s.* patrulater. *adj.* alungit.

obnoxious [əb'nɔkʃəs] *adj.* nesuferit; supărător.

oboe ['oubou] *s.* oboi.

obscene [ɔb'si:n] *adj.* obscen; imoral.

obscure [əb'skjuə] *adj.* neclar; întunecos; obscur; umil. *vt.* a întuneca; a ascunde; a eclipsa.

obscurity [əb'skjuəriti] *s.* întuneric; neclaritate.

obsequies ['ɔbsikwiz] *s. pl.* funeralii, înmormîntare.

obsequious [əb'si:kwiəs] *adj.* servil.

observance [əb'zə:vns] *s.* respectare; sărbătorire; ceremonie.

observant [əb'zə:vnt] *adj.* atent; cu respect pentru legi.

observation [ɔbzə'veiʃn] *s.* observaţie; remarcă.

observatory [əb'zə:vətri] *s.* observator (astronomic etc.).

observe [əb'zə:v] *vt.* a respecta; a sărbători; a observa; a studia. *vi.* a contempla.

observer [əb'zə:və] *s.* observator *(persoană)*; cel care respectă (legea).

obsess [əb'ses] *vt.* a obseda.

obsession [əb'seʃn] *s.* obsesie.

obsolescent [ɔbsə'lesnt] *adj.* pe cale de dispariţie; desuet.

obsolete ['ɔbsəli:t] *adj.* demodat, învechit.

obstinacy ['ɔbstinəsi] *s.* încăpăţînare; perseverenţă.

obstinate ['ɔbstinit] *adj.* încăpăţînat; perseverent.

obstruct [əb'strʌkt] *vt.* a bloca; a împiedica; a opri.

obtain [əb'tein] *vt.* a obţine. *vi.* a fi la modă; a se menţine.

obtrude [əb'tru:d] *vt.* a forţa; a băga pe gît.

obtrusive [əb'truːsiv] *adj.* băgăreţ.

obtuse [əb'tjuːs] *adj.* obtuz.

obviate ['ɔbvieit] *vt.* a îndepărta ; a eluda.

obvious ['ɔbviəs] *adj.* evident.

occasion [ə'keiʒn] *s.* prilej ; motiv. *vt.* a prilejui ; a produce.

occasional [ə'keiʒənl] *adj* întîmplător ; ocazional.

occasionally [ə'keiʒənli] *adv.* din cînd în cînd ; uneori.

occult [ɔ'kʌlt] *adj.* ascuns ; misterios ; supranatural.

occupy ['ɔkjupai] *vt.* a ocupa.

occur [ə'kəː] *vi.* a se întîmpla, a se produce ; a surveni ; a se afla ; a-i trece prin minte.

occurrence [ə'kʌrns] *s.* întîmplare ; eveniment.

ocean ['ouʃn] *s.* ocean.

o'clock [ə'klɔk] *adv.: four, etc.* ∼ ora patru etc.

octagon ['ɔktəgən] *s.* octogon.

octave ['ɔktiv] *s.* octavă.

October [ɔk'toubə] *s.* octombrie.

octopus ['ɔktəpəs] *s.* caracatiţă.

odd [ɔd] *adj.* impar ; desperecheat ; în plus ; întîmplător ; ciudat ; *thirty* ∼ *years* peste 30 de ani.

oddity ['ɔditi] *s.* ciudăţenie.

oddly ['ɔdli] *adv.* ciudat.

odds [ɔdz] *s. pl.* şanse ; raport de forţe ; diferenţă ; handicap. *what's the* ∼? ce contează ? ; *at* ∼ certat ; ∼ *and ends* resturi, fleacuri ; amestecătură.

ode [oud] *s.* odă.

odo(u)r ['oudə] *s.* miros ; reputaţie.

of [əv, ɔv] *prep.* al, a, ai, ale ; de (la) ; din (partea) ; despre.

off [ɔ(ː)f] *adj.* dinafară ; în plus ; gata ; stins ; plecat ; improbabil ; liber ; liniştit. *adv.* deoparte ; la o parte ; desprins. *prep.* de pe ; de la ; alături de ; mai puţin de ; ∼ *duty* (în timpul) liber ; ∼ *the mark* alături de ţintă ; ∼ *one's head* ţicnit.

offals ['ɔflz] *s.* gunoi ; deşeuri ; resturi.

off-colour ['ɔːf'kʌlə] *adj.* ofilit, veştejit ; decolorat.

offence [ə'fens] *s.* infracţiune ; ofensă ; supărare ; atac.

offend [ə'fend] *vt.* a supăra ; a jigni ; a necăji. *vi.* a greşi ; a comite o infracţiune.

offender [ə'fendə] *s.* infractor.

offense [ə'fens] *s. v.* offence.

offensive [ə'fensiv] *s.* ofensivă ; atac. *adj.* supărător ; jignitor ; ofensiv.

offer ['ɔfə] *s.* ofertă ; propunere. *vt.* a oferi ; a propune ; a întinde ; a (acor)da. *vi.* a se produce ; a se prezenta. *vr.* a se oferi.

offering ['ɔfriŋ] *s.* dar ; pomană ; jertfă.

offhand ['ɔːf'hænd] *adj.* improvizat ; repezit. *adv.* pe nepregătite ; repezit.

office ['ɔfis] *s.* serviciu ; instituţie ; birou ; guvernămînt.

office-boy ['ɔfisbɔi] *s.* băiat de serviciu.

office-holder ['ɔfis,houldə] *s.* funcţionar.

officer ['ɔfisə] *s.* funcţionar ; demnitar ; ofiţer.

official [ə'fiʃl] *s.* demnitar ; funcţionar. *adj.* oficial ; ceremonios.

officious [ə'fiʃəs] adj. (ultra)-serviabil; servil; aferat.

offing ['ɔfiŋ] s. largul mării; in the ~ aproape (de ţărm); în perspectivă.

offset ['ɔːfset] vt. a compensa; a contrabalansa.

offshoot ['ɔːfʃuːt] s. mlădiţă.

off-shore ['ɔːfʃɔː] adj., adv. dinspre ţărm; departe de ţărm; peste ocean.

offside ['ɔːf'said] adj., adv. sport dincolo de apărători; în sau din ofsaid.

offspring ['ɔːfspriŋ] s. odraslă; progenitură; copii.

often ['ɔːfn] adv. adesea.

ogle ['ougl] vt. a sorbi din ochi; a ochi. vi. a face ochi dulci.

ogre ['ougə] s. căpcăun.

oho [o'hou] interj. aha.

oil [ɔil] s. ulei; untdelemn; ţiţei; petrol. vt. a unge (cu ulei).

oil-cake ['ɔilkeik] s. turtă de floarea-soarelui.

oil-can ['ɔilkæn] s. bidon de ulei; pompă de ulei.

oil-cloth ['ɔilklɔθ] s. muşama; linoleum.

oil-colours ['ɔil͵kʌləz] s. pl. artă ulei.

oiler ['ɔilə] s. tanc petrolier; pompă de ulei.

oil-field ['ɔilfiːld] s. teren petrolifer; schelă.

oil-painting ['ɔil'peintiŋ] s. pictură în ulei.

oilskin ['ɔilskin] s. muşama; haine impermeabile.

oil-well ['ɔilwel] s. puţ petrolifer.

oily ['ɔili] adj. uleios; murdar; mieros.

ointment, ['ɔintmənt] s. unsoare; alifie.

O.K. ['ou'kei] interj. bine; în regulă.

old [ould] adj. vechi; bătrîn; trecut; demodat; înrăit.

old-fashioned ['ould'fæʃnd] adj. demodat; conservator.

old soldier [ould 'souldʒə] s. fig. vulpe bătrînă; sticlă goală; chiştoc de trabuc.

old wives'tale ['ould waivz'teil] s. superstiţie; legendă prostească.

olive ['ɔliv] s. măslin(ă); culoarea oliv. adj. măsliniu, oliv.

omen ['oumen] s. semn (mai ales rău); prevestire.

ominous ['ɔminəs] adj. ameninţător; prevestitor de rele; semnificativ.

omission [o'miʃn] s. omisiune.

omit [o'mit] vt. a omite; a uita.

omnibus ['ɔmnibəs] s. omnibuz; autobuz.

omnipotence [ɔm'nipətns] s. atotputernicie.

omniscient [ɔm'nisiənt] adj. atotştiutor.

omnivorous [ɔm'nivrəs] adj. omnivor; ultrareceptiv.

on [ɔn] adv. înainte; în continuare; mai departe; aprins. prep. pe; asupra; deasupra; la (data de); despre; lîngă; împotriva; în.

once [wʌns] adv. o dată; odinioară; cîndva; at ~ imediat; ~ more sau again din nou. conj. îndată ce.

one [wʌn] pron. cineva; unul, una; acelaşi; se.

oneself [wʌn'self] pron. se; însuşi.

one-sided ['wʌn'saidid] *adj.* unilateral.

onion ['ʌnjən] *s.* ceapă.

onlooker ['ɔn,lukə] *s.* spectator ; privitor.

only ['ounli] *adj.* singur ; unic. *adv.* numai ; pur şi simplu; chiar. *conj.* numai că ; afară doar de faptul că.

onomatopoeia [,ɔnomæto'pi:ə] *s.* onomatopee.

onrush ['ɔnrʌʃ] *s.* năvălire ; năvală.

onset ['ɔnset] *s.* invazie ; atac ; năvală.

onslaught ['ɔnslɔ:t] *s.* atac.

onto ['ɔntu] *prep.* pe.

onward ['ɔnwəd] *adj., adv.* înainte.

ooze [u:z] *s.* mîl. *vt.* a scoate. *vi.* a se scurge.

opaque [o'peik] *adj.* opac ; întunecos ; tîmpit.

open ['oupn] *s.* deschidere ; *in the* ~ în aer liber. *adj.* deschis ; liber ; neacoperit ; expus ; desfăcut ; gol ; public ; nerezolvat. *vt.* a deschide ; a iniţia ; a întinde ; a începe. *vi.* a se deschide ; a da (înspre) ; a începe ; a se zări.

open-handed ['oupn'hændid] *adj.* mărinimos.

open-hearted ['oupn,ha:tid] *adj.* sincer ; generos.

open-minded ['oupn'maindid] *adj.* lipsit de prejudecăţi ; cu un orizont larg.

opener ['oupnə] *s.* deschizător ; instrument de deschis.

opening ['oupniŋ] *s.* deschidere ; deschizătură ; introducere ; poziţie iniţială ; început.

opera ['ɔprə] *s.* operă (lirică).

opera-glasses ['ɔprəgla:siz] *s. pl.* binoclu de teatru.

opera-hat ['ɔprəhæt] *s.* joben, clac.

opera-house ['ɔprəhaus] *s.* (teatru de) operă.

operate ['ɔpəreit] *vt.* a mînui ; a conduce ; a pune în funcţiune. *vi.* a opera ; a funcţiona ; a lucra ; a conlucra.

operatic [ɔpə'rætik] *adj.* de operă.

operating-theatre ['ɔpəreitiŋ,θiətə] *s.* sală de operaţie.

operation [,ɔpə'reiʃn] *s.* operaţie ; funcţionare ; vigoare.

operative ['ɔprətiv] *s.* muncitor ; mecanic. *adj.* operativ ; eficient ; în vigoare ; operatoriu.

opiate ['oupiit] *s.* sedativ ; somnifer.

opinion [ə'pinjən] *s.* opinie (publică) ; apreciere.

opium ['oupjəm] *s.* opiu.

opium den ['oupjəmden] *s.* tavernă de fumători de opiu.

opponent [ə'pounənt] *s.* adversar.

opportunity [,ɔpə'tju:niti] *s.* prilej favorabil ; şansă ; posibilitate.

oppose [ə'pouz] *vt.* a se împotrivi la ; a compensa ; a pune împotrivă.

opposite ['ɔpəzit] *s., adj.* opus ; de vizavi.

opposition [,ɔpə'ziʃn] *s.* împotrivire ; opoziţie.

oppress [ə'pres] *vt.* a asupri ; a apăsa ; a chinui.

oppression [ə'preʃn] *s.* asuprire ; nedreptate ; apăsare.

oppressive [ə'presiv] *adj.* apăsător ; aspru ; chinuitor ; asupritor.

oppressor [ə'presə] s. asupritor ; tiran.

optics ['ɔptiks] s. pl. optică.

optimistic [ˌɔpti'mistik] adj. optimist ; încurajator.

option ['ɔpʃn] s. opţiune ; drept de preferinţă.

optional ['ɔpʃənl] adj. facultativ.

opulence ['ɔpjuləns] s. bogăţie ; abundenţă.

or [ɔ:] conj. sau ; whether ... ~ dacă ... sau ...; ~ else căci altfel.

oracle ['ɔrəkl] s. oracol.

oral ['ɔ:rl] adj. oral ; verbal ; referitor la gură.

orange ['ɔrindʒ] s. portocal(ă) ; portocaliu.

orang-outang ['ɔ:rəŋ'u:tæŋ] s. urangutan.

orb(it) ['ɔ:b(it)] s. orbită.

orchard ['ɔ:tʃəd] s. livadă.

orchestra ['ɔ:kistrə] s. (fosă pentru) orchestră ; fotolii de orchestră.

orchestra stall ['ɔ:kistrə stɔ:l] s. fotoliu de orchestră.

orchid ['ɔ:kid], **orchis** ['ɔ:kis] s. orhidee.

ordain [ɔ:'dein] vt. a hirotonisi ; a hotărî ; a predestina.

ordeal [ɔ:'di:l] s. chin ; calvar ; tortură inchizitorială.

order ['ɔ:də] s. ordin ; ordine ; aranjament ; sistem ; (o)rînduire ; comandă ; cerere ; mandat ; haina preoţiei etc. ; on ~ la cerere ; in ~ to pentru a ; in ~ that ca să. vt. a comanda ; a cere ; a ordona ; a conduce.

orderly ['ɔ:dəli] s. sanitar ; mil. ordonanţă ; ofiţer de ordonanţă. adj. ordonat ; liniştit ; disciplinat.

orderly officer ['ɔ:dəli'ɔfisə] s. ofiţer de serviciu.

ordinal ['ɔ:dinl] s. numeral ordinal. adj. ordinal.

ordinarily ['ɔ:dnərili] adv. normal ; de obicei.

ordinary ['ɔ:dnəri] adj. obişnuit ; normal ; ordinar ; mediu.

ordination [ˌɔ:di'neiʃn] s. hirotonisire.

ordnance ['ɔ:dnəns] s. artilerie (grea) ; arsenal.

ore [ɔ:] s. minereu.

organ ['ɔ:gən] s. organ ; instrument ; orgă.

organ-grinder ['ɔ:gən'graində] s. flaşnetar.

organization [ˌɔ:gənai'zeiʃn] s. organizare ; organizaţie.

organize ['ɔ:gənaiz] vt., vi. a (se) organiza.

orient ['ɔ:riənt] s. orient. vt. a orienta.

orientate ['ɔ:rienteit] vt. a orienta (către est). vr. a se orienta.

orifice ['ɔrifis] s. orificiu, gaură.

origin ['ɔridʒin] s. origine.

original [ə'ridʒənl] s., adj. original.

originally [ə'ridʒənli] adv. în mod original ; la origine.

originate [ə'ridʒineit] vt. a iniţia ; a inventa ; a lansa ; a produce. vi. a începe ; to ~ in sau from a se trage din ; a decurge sau a proveni din.

ornate ['ɔ:neit] adj. împodobit.

orphan ['ɔ:fn] s., adj. orfan. vt. a lăsa orfan.

orphanage ['ɔ:fənidʒ] s. orfelinat.

orthodox ['ɔ:θədɔks] adj. ortodox ; convenţional ; aprobat ; obişnuit.

orthodoxy ['ɔ:θədɔksi] *s.* ortodoxie; conformism.

orthography [ɔ:'θɔgrəfi] *s.* ortografie.

oscillate ['ɔsileit] *vi.* a oscila.

osier ['ouʒə] *s.* răchită.

ossify ['ɔsifai] *vt.* a osifica. *vi.* a se osifica; a se împietri; *fig.* a se anchiloza.

ostensible [ɔs'tensəbl] *adj.* aparent; prefăcut; de ochii lumii.

ostentation [,ɔsten'teiʃn] *s.* ostentaţie; prefăcătorie.

ostentatious [,ɔsten'teiʃəs] *adj.* ostentativ; ţipător.

ostler ['ɔslə] *s.* grăjdar.

ostrich ['ɔstritʃ] *s.* struţ.

other ['ʌðə] *adj.* alt; diferit; suplimentar; *the ~ one* celălalt; *the ~ day* deunăzi; *on the ~ hand* pe de altă parte. *pron.: the ~* celălalt; *one after the ~* pe rînd; *each ~* unul pe altul, reciproc. *adv.* altfel.

otherwise ['ʌðəwaiz] *adv.* altfel; în caz contrar; în alte privinţe.

otter ['ɔtə] *s.* vidră.

ouch [autʃ] *interj.* au.

ought [ɔ:t] *v. mod.: ~ to* a se cuveni să; a fi probabil să.

ounce [auns] *s.* uncie; *fig.* dram.

our ['auə] *adj.* nostru etc.

ours ['auəz] *pron.* al nostru etc.

ourselves [auə'selvz] *pron.* ne; înşine; noi; *by ~* singuri.

oust [aust] *vt.* a izgoni.

out [aut] *adv.* afară; pe sfîrşite; în relief; departe; dispărut; răspicat; departe; greşit; *~ and away* de departe; *~ and ~* complet; extrem; *~ of* din; din pricina.

outbreak ['autbreik] *s.* izbucnire; acces.

outbuildings ['aut,bildiŋz] *s.* acareturi.

outburst ['autbə:st] *s.* izbucnire; explozie.

outcast ['autkɑ:st] *s.* surghiunit; paria; apatrid.

outcome ['autkʌm] *s.* rezultat.

outdated ['aut'deitid] *adj.* demodat.

outdistance [aut'distəns] *vt.* a lăsa în urmă.

outdo [aut'du:] *vt.* a întrece.

outdoor ['autdɔ:] *adj.* exterior; în aer liber.

ourdoors ['aut'dɔ:z] *adv.* afară.

outer ['autə] *adj.* exterior.

outfit ['autfit] *s.* echipament; instrumentar; instalaţie.

outflow ['autflou] *s.* scurgere; izbucnire.

outgoing ['aut,gouiŋ] *adj.* fost; demisionar.

outgrow [aut'grou] *vt.* a depăşi; a se dezbăra de.

outgrowth ['autgrouθ] *s.* dezvoltare; **consecinţă**; **excrescenţă**; produs.

outhouse ['authaus] *s.* acaret; dependinţă.

outing ['autiŋ] *s.* plimbare.

outlandish [aut'lændiʃ] *adj.* ciudat; exotic.

outlast ['aut'lɑ:st] *vt.* a depăşi; a supravieţui (cuiva).

outlaw ['autlɔ:] *s.* haiduc. *vt.* a scoate în afara legii.

outlawry ['autlɔ:ri] *s.* haiducie.

outlay ['autlei] *s.* cheltuială.

outlet ['autlet] *s.* ieşire; scăpare; debuşeu.

outline ['autlain] *s.* contur; punctaj; schiță. *vt.* a schița; a contura.

outlive [aut'liv] *vt.* a supraviețui (cuiva).

outlook ['autluk] *s.* concepție (generală); perspectivă.

outlying ['aut͵laiiŋ] *adj.* periferic.

outnumber [aut'nʌmbə] *vt.* a covîrși.

out-of-date ['autəv'deit] *adj.* demodat.

out-of-door(s) ['autəv'dɔ:(z)] *adj.* în aer liber.

out-of-the-way ['autəvðə'wei] *adj.* îndepărtat; ciudat.

outpost ['autpoust] *s.* avanpost.

output ['autput] *s.* producție.

outrage ['autreidʒ] *s.* insultă; atac; crimă; izbucnire. *vt.* a răni; a încălca.

outrageous [aut'reidʒəs] *adj.* scandalos.

outright ['aut'rait] *adj.* total; clar; deschis. *adv.* direct; pe față; total.

outrun [aut'rʌn] *vt.* a întrece.

outset ['autset] *s.* început.

outside ['aut'said] *s.* exterior; înfățișare; extremă; extremitate; limită. *adj.* exterior; extrem; larg; generos; suplimentar. *adv.* (pe din)afară; în aer liber; *prep.* dincolo de; afară din; în afară de.

outsider ['aut'saidə] *s.* persoană dinafară; intrus.

outskirts ['autskə:ts] *s. pl.* periferie; suburbii; margine.

outspoken [aut'spoukn] *adj.* deschis; sincer; fără ascunzișuri.

outspread ['aut'spred] *adj.* întins.

outstanding [aut'stændiŋ] *adj.* remarcabil; restant; nerezolvat.

outstretched [aut'stretʃt] *adj.* întins.

outstrip [aut'strip] *vt.* a depăși.

outward ['autwəd] *adj.* exterior; din străinătate. *adv.* în afară.

outwardly ['autwədli] *adv.* aparent; superficial.

outweigh [aut'wei] *vt.* a depăși.

outwit [aut'wit] *vt.* a fi mai deștept decît.

oven ['ʌvn] *s.* cuptor.

over ['ouvə] *adj.* terminat; încheiat; gata. *adv.* răsturnat; (pe) deasupra; mai sus; dincolo; încă o dată; foarte; prea; ~ *again* iarăși. *prep.* peste; deasupra; mai sus de; mai tîrziu de; ~ *and above* peste; în plus față de.

overall ['ouvərɔ:l] *s.* halat; *pl.* salopetă. *adj.* general; global.

overbearing [͵ouvə'bɛəriŋ] *adj.* arogant; tiran.

overboard ['ouvəbɔ:d] *adv.* peste bord.

overburden [͵ouvə'bə:dn] *vt.* a supraîncărca; a copleși.

overcame [͵ouvə'keim] *vt. trec. de la* **overcome.**

overcast ['ouvəka:st] *adj.* întunecat; noros; trist.

overcharge ['ouvə'tʃa:dʒ] *s.* suprasarcină; suprataxă; preț piperat. *vi.* a supraîncărca; a specula.

overcoat ['ouvəkout] *s.* pardesiu; demi; palton.

overcome [͵ouvə'kʌm] *inf. și part. trec. vt.* a învinge; a covîrși.

overcrowd [͵ouvə'kraud] *vt.* a supraaglomera.

overdo [ˌouvə'du:] vt. a exagera ; a frige prea tare.

overdraw ['ouvə'drɔ:] vt. a exagera ; a depăşi (contul la bancă).

overdress ['ouvə'dres] vt., vi. a (se) împopoţona.

overdue ['ouvə'dju:] adj. întîrziat ; datorat de mult.

overflow[1] ['ouvəflou] s. surplus ; abundenţă ; inundaţie.

overflow[2] [ˌouvə'flou] vt. a inunda ; a trece dincolo de. vi. a da pe dinafară ; a se revărsa ; a abunda.

overfulfilment ['ouvəful'filmənt] s. îndeplinire înainte de termen.

overgrow ['ouvə'grou] vt. a umple ; a acoperi. vi. a creşte exagerat.

overgrowth ['ouvə'grouθ] s. creştere exagerată ; bălării.

overhand ['ouvəhænd] adj., adv. peste umăr.

overhang ['ouvəhæŋ] vi. a atîrna (ameninţător).

overhaul[1] ['ouvəhɔ:l] s. revizie generală ; cercetare.

overhaul[2] [ˌouvə'hɔ:l] vt. a revizui ; a ajunge din urmă.

overhead ['ouvəhed] adj. aerian ; deasupra capului ; com. de regie. adv. (deasupra) capului.

overhear [ˌouvə'hiə] vt. a (sur)prinde (o conversaţie)

over-indulge ['ouvrin'dʌldʒ] vt., vi. a(-şi) permite prea multe. vr. a se desfăta.

over-indulgence [ˌouvrin'dʌldʒns] s. destrăbălare.

overjoyed [ˌouvə'dʒɔid] adj. încîntat.

overland ['ouvə'lænd] adj., adv. pe uscat.

overlap [ˌouvə'læp] vi. a se suprapune.

overload ['ouvə'loud] vt. a supraîncărca.

overlook [ˌouvə'luk] vt. a scăpa din vedere ; a trece cu vederea ; a supraveghea ; a domina (cu privirea).

overnight ['ouvə'nait] adj., adv. peste noapte.

overpower [ˌouvə'pauə] vt. a covîrşi.

overproduction ['ouvəprə'dʌkʃn] s. supraproducţie.

overrate ['ouvə'reit] vt. a supraestima.

overreach [ˌouvə'ri:tʃ] vt. a depăşi.

overrule [ˌouvə'ru:l] vt. a anula ; a respinge.

overrun [ˌouvə'rʌn] vt. a invada ; a covîrşi ; a depăşi.

oversea(s) [ouvə'si:(z)] adj., adv. în străinătate ; (de) peste mări şi ţări.

oversee ['ouvə'si:] vt. a supraveghea.

overseer ['ouvəsiə] s. supraveghetor ; contramaistru.

overshadow ['ouvə'ʃædou] vt. a (ad)umbri.

overshoe ['ouvəʃu:] s. şoşon ; galoş.

overshoot ['ouvə'ʃu:t] vt. a trage sau a ţinti prea departe.

oversight ['ouvəsait] s. neglijenţă ; scăpare ; supraveghere.

oversleep ['ouvə'sli:p] vi., vr. a dormi prea mult.

overstate ['ouvə'steit] vt. a exagera.

overstrain ['ouvə'strein] s. efórt prea mare ; istovire.

overt ['ouvə:t] *adj.* deschis ; public.

overtake [ˌouvə'teik] *vt.* a ajunge din urmă ; a surprinde ; a covîrși.

overtax ['ouvə'tæks] *vt.* a suprasolicita ; *fin.* a impune la o sumă exagerată.

overthrow[1] ['ouvəθrou] *s.* răsturnare ; înfrîngere ; nimicire.

overthrow[2] [ouvə'θrou] *vt.* a răsturna ; a înfrînge.

overtime ['ouvətaim·] *s.* ore suplimentare ; plată suplimentară. *adv.* suplimentar.

overture ['ouvətjuə] *s.* uvertură ; *pl.* ofertă ; avansuri ; propuneri.

overturn [ˌouvə'tə:n] *vt., vi.* a (se) răsturna.

overweight ['ouvə'weit] *s.* greutate suplimentară.

overwhelm [ˌouvə'welm] *vt.* a covîrși ; a nimici ; a stăpîni ; a copleși.

overwhelming [ˌouvə'welmiŋ] *adj.* covîrșitor, copleșitor.

overwork[1] ['ouvəwə:k] *s.* suprasolicitare ; istovire.

overwork[2] ['ouvə'wə:k] *vt., vi.* a (se) istovi.

overwrought ['ouvə'rɔ:t] *adj.* istovit ; nervos ; surescitat.

owe [ou] *vt.* a datora. *vi.* a avea datorii.

owing ['ouiŋ] *adj.* datorat ; restant ; ∼ to din pricina.

owl [aul] *s.* bufniță.

own [oun] *adj.* propriu. *vt.* a mărturisi ; a recunoaște ; a poseda. *vi.* a se recunoaște vinovat.

owner ['ounə] *s.* proprietar.

ownership ['ounəʃip] *s.* proprietate.

ox [oks] *s.* bou ; mascul.

oxen ['ɔksn] *s. pl. de la* **ox.**

Oxonian [ɔk'sounian] *s., adj.* (student) de la Oxford.

oyster ['ɔistə] *s.* stridie.

oz ['aunsiz] *s. pl.* uncii.

P

P [pi:] *s.* P, p.

pa [pɑ:] *s.* tăticu.

pace [peis] *s.* pas ; ritm. *vt.* a măsura ; a regla. *vi.* a păși ; a se plimba.

pacify ['pæsifai] *vt.* a liniști ; a pacifica.

pack [pæk] *s.* pachet (de cărți) ; legătură ; haită ; bandă. *vt.* a împacheta ; a pune în geamantan ; a umple ; a îngrămădi ; a căptuși ; *to* ∼ *off* a expedia ; *to* ∼ *up* a pune în geamantan. *vi.* a face bagajele ; a împacheta ; a se îngrămădi.

package ['pækidʒ] *s.* pachet.

packet ['pækit] *s.* pachet ; pachebot.

packet-boat ['pækitbout] *s.* pachebot.

pact [pækt] *s.* pact.

pad [pæd] *s.* căptușeală (matlasată) ; umplutură ; teanc (de hîrtii) ; tușieră ; perniță (a la-

bei). *vt.* a căptuşi ; a matlasa ;
a umple.

padding ['pædiŋ] *s.* căptuşeală
groasă ; molton ; umplutură.

paddle ['pædl] *s.* vîslă ; padelă ;
lopăţică. *vt.* a împinge cu vîs-
lele. *vi.* a vîsli.

paddock ['pædək] *s.* ţarc ; padoc.

paddy ['pædi] *s.* orez.

padlock ['pædlɔk] *s.* lacăt. *vt.*
a încuia.

paean ['piːən] *s.* imn•de laudă.

pagan ['peigən] *s., adj.* păgîn.

page [peidʒ] *s.* pagină ; paj ;
băiat de serviciu. *vt.* a pagina ;
a căuta ; a anunţa.

pageant ['pædʒnt] *s.* procesiune ; car alegoric ; spectacol
(medieval) în aer liber.

paid [peid] *vt., vi. trec. şi part.
trec. de la* **pay.**

pail [peil] *s.* găleată.

pain [pein] *s.* durere ; efort ;
pedeapsă. *vt.* a chinui.

painful ['peinfl] *adj.* dureros ;
neplăcut.

painstaking ['peinz‚teikiŋ] *adj.*
silitor, harnic ; grijuliu.

paint [peint] *s.* culoare ; vopsea.
vt. a vopsi ; a picta ; a descrie ;
to ~ *the town red* a-şi face de
cap. *vi.* a picta.

painter ['peintə] *s.* pictor ; zugrav.

painting ['peintiŋ] *s.* pictură ;
vopsitorie.

pair [pɛə] *s.* pereche ; *in* ~*s*
perechi-perechi. *vt., vi.* a (se)
împerechea ; a se căsători.

pajamas [pə'dʒɑːməz] *s.* pijama.

pal [pæl] *s.* tovarăş ; prieten bun.

palace ['pælis] *s.* palat.

palatable ['pælətəbl] *adj.* bun
la gust ; acceptabil.

palate ['pælit] *s.* cerul gurii ;
gust.

palaver [pə'lɑːvə] *s.* vorbărie ;
tratative. *vi.* a flecări.

pale [peil] *s.* scîndură ; limită.
adj. palid. *vi.* a păli.

palette ['pælit] *s. artă* paletă.

palfrey ['pɔːlfri] *s.* armăsar ;
cal de paradă.

paling ['peiliŋ] *s.* gard.

palisade [‚pæli'seid] *s.* palisadă ;
gard.

pall [pɔːl] *s.* linţoliu ; văl.

pallet ['pælit] *s.* saltea de paie.

palliate ['pælieit] *vt.* a îmblînzi ;
a scuza.

palm [pɑːm] *s.* palmă ; mînă ;
(frunză de) palmier ; lauri. *vt.*
a trece, a înmîna ; a strecura.

palmist ['pɑːmist] *s.* ghicitor în
palmă.

palmistry ['pɑːmistri] *s.* chiro-
manţie.

palpitate ['pælpiteit] *vi.* a palpita.

palsy ['pɔːlzi] *s.* paralizie.

paltry ['pɔːltri] *adj.* mic ; meschin ; mizerabil.

pamper ['pæmpə] *vt.* a răsfăţa ;
a îndopa.

pamphlet ['pæmflit] *s.* broşură.

pan [pæn] *s.* tigaie (cu coadă).

pancake ['pænkeik] *s.* clătită.

pandemonium [‚pændi'mounjəm]
s. iad ; măcel.

pander ['pændə] *s.* codoş.

pane [pein] *s.* (ochi de) geam.

panel ['pænl] *s.* panou ; lambriu ;
ochi de geam ; listă ; juriu. *vt.*
a îmbrăca în panouri.

pang [pæŋ] *s.* junghi.

panic ['pænic] *s.* panică.

panic-stricken ['pænik‚strikn]
adj. înspăimîntat.

panoply ['pænəpli] s. panoplie; *fig.* arsenal.

panpipe(s) ['pænpaip(s)] s. nai.

pansy ['pænzi] s. panseluţă; homosexual.

pant [pænt] *vt., vi.* a gîfîi.

pantaloon [,pæntə'lu:n] s. clovn; *pl.* pantaloni.

panther ['pænθə] s. pantеră.

pantry ['pæntri] s. cămară.

pants [pænts] s. *pl.* indispensabili; chiloţi; *amer.* pantaloni.

pap [pæp] s. terci.

papa [pə'pɑ:] s. tăticu.

papacy ['peipəsi] s. papalitate.

paper ['peipə] s. hîrtie; document; act (de identitate); ziar; bancnotă; lucrare; teză; *pol.* carte (albă etc.).

paper-hanger ['peipə,hæŋgə] s. tapetar.

paper-knife ['peipənaif] s. coupe-papier, cuţit pentru tăiat hîrtie.

paper-mill ['peipəmil] s. fabrică de hîrtie.

paper-weight ['peipəweit] s. presпапier.

papist ['peipist] s. papistaş.

par [pɑ:] s. egalitate; paritate.

parable ['pærəbl] s. parabolă.

parachute ['pærəʃu:t] s. paraşută. *vt.* a paraşuta.

parachuter ['pærəʃu:tə], **parachutist** ['pærəʃu:tist] s. paraşutist.

parade [pə'reid] s. demonstraţie; (teren de) paradă; promеnadă. *vi.* a face pe grozavul; a mărşălui.

paradise ['pærədaiz] s. paradis.

paraffin ['pærəfin] s. parafină; gaz lampant.

paragon ['pærəgən] s. model.

parallel ['pærəlel] s. paralelă; corespondent; comparaţie. *adj.* paralel; corespunzător; identic. *vt.* a face o paralelă cu.

paralysis [pə'rælisis] s. paralizie; inerţie.

paramount ['pærəmaunt] *adj.* suprem; cel mai înalt.

paramour ['pærəmuə] s. concubină; amantă.

paraphernalia [,pærəfə'neiljə] s. *pl.* catrafuse; accesorii; avere; mărunţişuri.

parasite ['pærəsait] s. parazit.

parasol [,pærə'sɔl] s. umbreluţă de soare.

parcel ['pɑ:sl] s. pachet; parcelă. *vt.* a parcela.

parch [pɑ:tʃ] *vt., vi.* a (se) usca; a (se) prăji.

parchment ['pɑ:tʃmənt] s. (hîrtie) pergament.

pardon ['pɑ:dn] s. iertare; graţiere; îngăduinţă; *I beg your* ~ scuzaţi; poftim? *vt.* a ierta; a graţia; a trece cu vederea.

pardoner ['pɑ:dnə] s. vînzător de indulgenţe.

pare [pɛə] *vt.* a tăia (unghiile etc.).

parent ['pɛərnt] s. părinte; strămoş.

parentage ['pɛərntidʒ] s. paternitate; origine.

parental [pə'rentl] *adj.* părintesc.

parenthesis [pə'renθisis] s. paranteză.

parenthetic(al) [,pærn'θetik(l)] *adj.* între paranteze; incident(al).

parish ['pæriʃ] s. parohie; district; cartier; enoriaş; ~ *register* registrul stării civile.

parishioner [pəˈriʃənə] s. enoriaş; locuitor din cartier.

parity [ˈpæriti] s. paritate; asemănare.

park [pɑːk] s. parc. vt. a parca.

parley [ˈpɑːli] s. negocieri. vi. a negocia.

parliament [ˈpɑːləmənt] s. parlament.

parlo(u)r [ˈpɑːlə] s. salonaş; hol; vorbitor.

parlourmaid [ˈpɑːləmeid] s. servitoare.

parochial [pəˈroukjəl] adj. parohial; limitat; îngust.

parole [pəˈroul] s. cuvînt de onoare; on ~ eliberat condiţionat.

parquet [ˈpɑːkei] s. parchet.

parrot [ˈpærət] s. papagal.

parry [ˈpæri] vt. a para.

parse [pɑːz] vt. a analiza gramatical.

parsimonious [ˌpɑːsiˈmounjəs] adj. zgîrcit.

parsimony [ˈpɑːsiməni] s. zgîrcenie; economie.

parsley [ˈpɑːsli] s. pătrunjel.

parsnip [ˈpɑːsnip] s. păstîrnac.

parson [ˈpɑːsn] s. popă.

part [pɑːt] s. parte; fragment; cotă; merit; fascicul; piesă; rol; in ~ parţial; printre altele; în amănunt. vt. a despărţi; a separa; a pieptăna cu cărare. vi. a se despărţi.

partake [pɑːˈteik] vt. a împărtăşi. vi.: to ~ of a se înfrupta din.

partaken [pɑːˈteikn] vt., part. trec. de la **partake.**

partial [ˈpɑːʃl] adj. parţial; fragmentar; părtinitor; to be ~ to a ţine la.

partiality [ˌpɑːʃiˈæliti] s. părtinire; prejudecată; înclinaţie.

partially [ˈpɑːʃəli] adv. parţial; cu părtinire.

participate [pɑːˈtisipeit] vi. a participa.

participation [pɑːˌtisiˈpeiʃn] s. participare.

particle [ˈpɑːtikl] s. particulă.

parti-colo(u)red [ˈpɑːtikʌləd] adj. bălţat; multicolor.

particular [pəˈtikjulə] s. detaliu; articol. adj. specific; distinct; special; exact; dificil.

particularity [pəˌtikjuˈlæriti] s. exactitate; particularitate; minuţiozitate.

particularize [pəˈtikjuləraiz] vt., vi. a enumera.

particularly [pəˈtikjuləli] adv. în special; în amănunt.

parting [ˈpɑːtiŋ] s. despărţire; (pieptănătură cu) cărare.

partition [pɑːˈtiʃn] s. despărţitură; compartiment; glasvand. vt. a despărţi; a separa; a împărţi.

partly [ˈpɑːtli] adv. parţial; în oarecare măsură.

partner [ˈpɑːtnə] s. partener; tovarăş; părtaş. vt. a se întovărăşi cu.

partnership [ˈpɑːtnəʃip] s. tovărăşie; întovărăşire.

partook [pɑːˈtuk] vt., vi. trec. de la **partake.**

partridge [ˈpɑːtridʒ] s. potîrniche.

part-time [ˈpɑːtˈtaim] adj., adv. temporar; parţial; extrabugetar.

party [ˈpɑːti] s. partid; grup; petrecere; partidă; parte (la un contract etc.); detaşament;

echipă ; persoană. *adj.* partinic, de partid.

pass [pɑːs] *s.* trecere ; succes (la un examen) ; situaţie ; pasă ; permis ; trecătoare ; atac ; a- vans. *vt.* a trece (pe lîngă, din- colo de) ; a petrece ; a răspîndi ; a aproba ; a întrece. *vi.* a trece ; a se strecura ; a se scurge ; a circula ; a fi aprobat ; a dis- părea ; a se întîmpla ; a pasa ; *to ~ away* a trece în lumea drepţilor ; a dispărea ; *to ~ by* a nu observa ; a trece cu vede- rea ; *to ~ for* a trece drept ; *to ~ over* a nesocoti.

passable ['pɑːsəbl] *adj.* pasabil ; acceptabil ; mediocru.

passage ['pæsidʒ] *s.* trecere ; călătorie ; pasaj ; trecătoare ; coridor ; întîmpinare.

passenger ['pæsindʒə] *s.* pasager.

passer-by ['pɑːsə'bai] *s.* trecător.

passing ['pɑːsiŋ] *s.* trecere. *adj.* trecător ; întîmplător.

passion ['pæʃn] *s.* patimă, pa- siune.

passionate ['pæʃənit] *adj.* păti- maş ; pasionat ; fierbinte ; iras- cibil.

passport ['pɑːspɔːt] *s.* paşaport ; cheia succesului.

password ['pɑːswəːd] *s.* cuvînt de ordine ; parolă.

past [pɑːst] *s.* trecut. *adj.* tre- cut ; incapabil de. *adv.* pe ală- turi. *prep.* mai presus ; dincolo de ; *~ bearing* insuportabil.

paste [peist] *s.* pastă ; lipici ; pap. *vt.* a lipi ; a afişa.

pasteboard ['peistbɔːd] *s.* car- ton. *adj.* de carton ; *fig.* şubred.

pastel [pæs'tel] *s.* (culori) pas- tel. *adj.* (în) pastel.

pastime ['pɑːstaim] *s.* distracţie ; joc.

past master ['pɑːst'mɑːstə] *s.* maestru neîntrecut.

pastry ['peistri] *s.* patiserie ; plăcintă.

pasture ['pɑːstʃə] *s.* păşune. *vt.,* *vi.* a paşte.

pasty ['peisti] *adj.* păstos.

pat [pæt] *s.* mîngîiere ; atingere. *adj.* clar ; şablon. *vt.* a mîngîia ; a bate uşurel. *adv.* la ţanc.

patch [pætʃ] *s.* petic ; pată ; răzor. *vt.* a cîrpi ; a împăca.

patchwork ['pætʃwəːk] *s.* cîr- peală.

pate [peit] *s.* căpăţînă.

patent ['peitnt] *s.* patent ; li- cenţă ; autorizaţie ; privilegiu. *adj.* clar ; patentat ; *(d. pantofi etc.)* de lac.

patent leather ['peitnt‚leðə] *s.* piele de lac.

paternal [pə'təːnl] *adj.* părin- tesc ; după tată.

path [pɑːθ] *s.* potecă ; cale.

pathetic [pə'θetik] *adj.* patetic ; emoţional.

pathos ['peiθɔs] *s.* patos ; pa- siune.

pathway ['pɑːθwei] *s.* potecă ; cale.

patience ['peiʃns] *s.* răbdare ; rezistenţă ; perseverenţă ; silin- ţă ; ştevie.

patient ['peiʃnt] *s.* pacient ; bol- nav. *adj.* răbdător.

patriot ['peitriət] *s.* patriot.

patriotism ['pætriətizəm] *s.* pa- triotism.

patrol [pə'troul] *s.* patrulă. *vi.* a patrula.

patron ['peitrn] *s.* patron ; sus- ţinător ; (client) obişnuit.

patronage ['pætrənidʒ] s. patronaj ; aer protector ; clientelă.

patronize ['pætrənaiz] vt. a patrona ; a trata de sus ; a frecventa.

patter ['pætə] s. ciocănit ; repetiţie ; replici ; jargon. vt. a repeta ; a recita. vi. a vorbi repede ; a ciocăni.

pattern ['pætən] s. model ; şablon.

Paul Pry ['pɔːl 'prai] s. om băgăreţ.

paunch [pɔːntʃ] s. burtă ; burduhan.

pauper ['pɔːpə] s. sărac ; cerşetor.

pause [pɔːz] s. pauză ; răgaz. vi. a face o pauză.

pave [peiv] vt. a pava ; a acoperi.

pavement ['peivmənt] s. pavaj ; trotuar.

paving ['peiviŋ] s. pavaj.

paw [pɔː] s. labă.

pawn [pɔːn] s. pion ; amanet. vt. a amaneta ; a pune chezaş.

pawn broker ['pɔːnˌbroukə] s. cămătar (care ţine un magazin de amanet).

pawn shop ['pɔːnʃɔp] s. munte de pietate.

pay [pei] s. leafă ; onorariu ; plată ; răsplată ; soldă. vt. a (răs)plăti ; a achita ; a (acor)da ; a face (curte, vizite, complimente) ; to ~ off a concedia ; to ~ back a achita. vi. a plăti ; a renta.

payable ['peiəbl] adj. plătibil ; profitabil ; scadent.

pay-day ['peidei] s. ziua salariului.

pay-master ['peiˌmɑːstə] s. casier,

payment ['peimənt] s. (răs)-plată ; recompensă.

pay-roll ['peiroul] s. stat de plată.

pay-sheet ['peiʃiːt] s. stat de salarii ; fond de salarii.

pea [piː] s. (bob de) mazăre.

peace [piːs] s. (tratat de) pace ; linişte ; tihnă.

peaceable ['piːsəbl] adj. paşnic ; liniştit.

peaceful ['piːsfl] adj. paşnic ; tihnit.

peach [piːtʃ] s. piersică ; fată frumoasă.

peacock ['piːkɔk] s. păun.

peahen ['piːhen] s. păuniţă.

peak [piːk] s. vîrf ; culme ; cozoroc.

peaked [piːkt] adj. cu vîrf sau cozoroc ; slab ; prăpădit.

peaky ['piːki] adj. ofilit.

peal [piːl] s. zvon de clopote ; bubuitură (de tunet) ; hohot. vi. (d. clopote) a răsuna.

peanut ['piːnʌt] s. (alună) arahidă. adj. mărunt.

pear [pɛə] s. bot. pară ; păr.

pearl [pəːl] s. perlă ; nestemată ; lacrimă.

pearl-barley ['pəːl bɑːli] s. arpacaş.

pearl-diver ['pəːlˌdaivə] s. pescuitor de perle.

peasant ['peznt] s. ţăran. adj. ţărănesc.

peasantry ['pezntri] s. ţărănime.

pease [piːz] s. mazăre.

peat [piːt] s. turbă.

peat-bog ['piːtbɔg] s. turbărie.

pebble ['pebl] s. pietricică ; pl. prundiş.

peck [pek] s. baniţă ; ciocănit

(cu ciocul) ; sărutare. *vt.*, *vi.*
a lovi cu ciocul ; a ciuguli.

pecker ['pekə] *s.* ciocănitoare.

peculiar [pi'kju:ljə] *adj.* specific ; individual ; special ; ciudat.

peculiarity [pi‚kju:li æriti] *s.* particularitate ; ciudăţenie.

pedagogue ['pedəgɔg] *s.* profesor ; învăţător ; pedagog.

pedal ['pedl] *s.* pedală. *vt.* a împinge cu pedalele. *vi.* a pedala.

peddle ['pedl] *vt.* a vinde cu amănuntul ; a colporta.

pedestrian [pi'destriən] *s.* pieton. *adj.* pedestru.

pedigree ['pedigri:] *s.* genealogie ; origine.

pedlar ['pedlə] *s.* vînzător ambulant ; telal.

peel [pi:l] *s.* coajă. *vt.*, *vi.* a se coji.

peelings ['pi:liŋz] *s. pl.* coji.

peep [pi:p] *s.* ochire ; ocheadă ; chiţăit ; ciripit ; ivire. *vi.* a iscodi ; a-şi băga nasul ; a se ivi ; a se iţi ; a chiţăi ; a ciripi.

peer [piə] *s.* egal ; nobil ; pair ; membru al Camerei Lorzilor. *vi.* a străpunge (întunericul etc.) cu privirea ; a se iţi ; a se ivi.

peerage ['piərid3] *s.* Camera Lorzilor ; rangul de pair ; arhondologie.

peerless ['piəlis] *adj.* neasemuit, fără pereche.

peevish ['pi:viʃ] *adj.* ţîfnos ; plîngăreţ.

peg [peg] *s.* ţăruş ; scoabă ; cui ; cuier. *vt.* a fixa.

pekin(g)ese [‚pi:kiŋ'i:z] *s.* pechinez.

pellet ['pelit] *s.* ghemotoc de hîrtie ; bobiţă de pîine etc. ; alică ; pilulă.

pell-mell ['pel'mel] *adj.*, *adv.* claie peste grămadă.

pellucid [pe'lju:sid] *adj.* transparent.

pelt [pelt] *s.* blană, piele ; (ploaie de) lovituri. *vt.* a bombarda. *vi.* a cădea (ca grindina).

pemmican ['pemikən] *s.* pastramă.

pen [pen] *s.* ţarc ; curte ; stînă ; peniţă ; pană ; condei ; stilou. *vt.* a închide (în ţarc) ; a împrejmui ; a scrie.

penal ['pi:nl] *adj.* penal.

penalize ['pi:nəlaiz] *vt.* a pedepsi ; a penaliza.

penal servitude ['pi:nl'sə:vitju:d] *s.* temniţă grea.

penalty ['penlti] *s.* pedeapsă.

penance ['penəns] *s.* pocăinţă ; penitenţă.

pence [pens] *s. pl. de la* **penny.**

pencil ['pensl] *s.* creion. *vt.* a scrie cu creionul.

pencil-case ['penslkeis] *s.* penar.

pencilled ['pensld] *adj.* frumos desenat ; arcuit.

pendant ['pendənt] *s.* pandantiv ; steag. *adj.* care atîrnă ; nerezolvat ; pendinte.

pending ['pendiŋ] *adj.* nehotărît ; nerezolvat ; pendinte. *prep.* în timpul ; pînă la.

penetrate ['penitreit] *vt.* a străpunge ; a înţelege ; a răspîndi în. *vi.* a pătrunde ; a se răspîndi.

penetrating ['penitreitiŋ] *adj.* pătrunzător ; subtil ; ascuţit ; ager.

penetration [‚peni'treiʃn] *s.* pătrundere ; perspicacitate ; agerime.

penguin ['peŋgwin] s. pinguin.

pen-holder ['pen‚houldə] s. toc.

penicillin [‚peni'silin] s. penicilină.

penitence ['penitns] s. (po)căință.

penitent ['penitnt] s., adj. pocăit.

penitentiary [‚peni'tenʃəri] s. şcoală de corecţie ; amer. închisoare.

pen-knife ['pennaif] s. briceag.

penman ['penmən] s. scriitor ; caligraf.

penmanship ['penmənʃip] s. caligrafie ; literatură.

pen-name ['penneim] s. pseudonim (literar).

pennant ['penənt] s. fanion.

penniless ['penilis] adj. lefter.

pennon ['penən] s. fanion ; steag.

penny ['peni] s. (monedă de un) penny ; a douăsprezecea parte dintr-un şiling.

pennyworth ['penəθ] s. marfă de un penny.

pension[1] ['penʃn] s. pensie. vt. a pensiona.

pension[2] ['pɑːŋsiɔŋ] s. pensiune.

pensioner ['penʃənə] s. pensionar.

pensive ['pensiv] adj. gînditor ; melancolic.

pentagon ['pentəgən] s. pentagon ; The P~ Ministerul de Război al S.U.A.

penthouse ['penthaus] s. şopron ; mansardă.

penurious [pi'njuəriəs] adj. sărăcăcios ; meschin ; zgîrcit.

penury ['penjuri] s. lipsă ; sărăcie.

peony ['piəni] s. bujor.

people ['piːpl] s. oameni ; popor ; naţiune ; plebe ; familie ; ~'s popular. vt. a popula.

pep [pep] s. energie ; vioiciune.

pepper ['pepə] s. piper ; ardei. vt. a pipera.

pepper-box ['pepəbɔks] s. solniţă de piper.

peppermint ['pepəmint] s. mentă.

peppery ['pepəri] adj. piperat ; nervos.

perambulator ['præmbjuleitə] s. cărucior de copil.

perceive [pə'siːv] vt. a observa ; a zări ; a înţelege ; a percepe.

per cent [pə 'sent] adv. la sută.

percentage [pə'sentidʒ] s. procentaj ; proporţie.

perceptible [pə'septəbl] adj. perceptibil ; sensibil.

perception [pə'sepʃn] s. pătrundere ; percepţie.

perch [pəːtʃ] s. cocoţare ; loc de cocoţat ; poziţie sigură ; (măsură de o) prăjină ; biban. vt., vi. a (se) cocoţa.

percolator ['pəːkəleitə] s. strecurătoare ; filtru.

percussion [pə'kʌʃn] s. percuţie ; instrumente de percuţie.

perdition [pə'diʃn] s. perdiţie ; osîndă.

peregrination [‚perigri'neiʃn] s. călătorie.

perennial [pə'renjəl] s. plantă perenă. adj. peren ; etern.

perfect[1] [pəːfikt] s. perfect. adj. perfect ; exact ; total.

perfect[2] [pə'fekt] vt. a îmbunătăţi ; a perfecţiona.

perforce [pə'fɔːs] adv. neapărat ; cu forţa.

perform [pə'fɔːm] *vt.* a îndeplini; a (de)săvîrşi; a prezenta; a executa. *vi.* a da spectacole.

performance [pə'fɔːməns] *s.* îndeplinire; spectacol.

perfume¹ ['pəːfjuːm] *s.* parfum.

perfume² [pə'fjuːm] *vt.* a parfuma.

perfunctory [pə'fʌŋtri] *adj.* superficial; de ochii lumii; maşinal.

perhaps [præps, pə'hæps] *adv.* (se prea) poate.

peril ['peril] *s.* primejdie. *vt.* a primejdui.

perilous ['periləs] *adj.* periculos.

period ['piəriəd] *s.* perioadă; propoziţie (lungă); frază; punct; menstruaţie.

perish ['periʃ] *vt.* a ucide. *vi.* a pieri.

periwig ['periwig] *s.* perucă.

perjure ['pəːdʒə] *vt.* a jura strîmb.

perjury ['pəːdʒri] *s.* sperjur.

perky ['pəːki] *adj.* obraznic.

perm [pəːm] *s.* permanent *(coafură)*.

permeate ['pəːmieit] *vt.* a pătrunde; a se infiltra în. *vi.* a se infiltra.

permissible [pə'misəbl] *adj.* permis.

permit¹ ['pəːmit] *s.* autorizaţie.

permit² [pə'mit] *vt., vi.* a permite.

pernicious [pə'niʃəs] *adj.* periculos; dăunător.

peroxide [pə'rɔksaid] *s.* apă oxigenată. *adj.* oxigenat.

perpetrate ['pəːpitreit] *vt.* a săvîrşi.

perpetrator ['pəːpitreitə] *s.* autor (al unei crime).

perpetual [pə'petjuəl] *vt.* neîncetat; etern.

perpetuate [pə'petjueit] *vt.* a perpetua; a imortaliza.

perplex [pə'pleks] *vt.* a încurca; a ului; a zăpăci.

persecute ['pəːsikjuːt] *vt.* a persecuta.

persevere [ˌpəːsi'viə] *vi.* a persevera.

persevering [ˌpəːsi'viəriŋ] *adj.* perseverent.

Persian ['pəːʃn] *s.* persan(ă); pisică persană. *adj.* persan(ă).

persist [pə'sist] *vi.* a continua; a stărui.

persistent [pə'sistnt] *adj.* persistent.

person ['pəːsn] *s.* persoană.

personal ['pəːsnl] *s.* articol biografic. *adj.* personal.

personality [ˌpəːsə'næliti] *s.* personalitate; *pl.* atacuri personale.

personify [pə'sɔnifai] *vt.* a personifica; a întruchipa.

personnel [ˌpəːsə'nel] *s.* personal; cadre.

perspective [pə'spektiv] *s.* perspectivă.

perspicuous [pə'spikjuəs] *adj.* limpede.

perspiration [ˌpəːspə'reiʃn] *s.* transpiraţie.

perspire [pəs'paiə] *vi.* a transpira.

persuade [pə'sweid] *vt.* a convinge; a determina.

persuasion [pə'sweiʒn] *s.* (putere de) convingere.

pert [pəːt] *adj.* obraznic.

pertain [pəː'tein] *vi.: to ~ to* a corespunde la; a fi legat de.

pertinacious [ˌpəːti'neiʃəs] *adj.* hotărît; persistent.

pertinent ['pə:tinənt] *adj*. potrivit ; util.

perturb [pə'tə:b] *vt*. a tulbura.

peruse [pə'ru:z] *vt*. a citi *sau* a cerceta cu atenţie.

pervade [pə'veid] *vt*. a cuprinde ; a umple ; a pătrunde.

perverse [pə'və:s] *adj*. pervers ; afurisit ; potrivnic.

perversion [pə'və:ʃn] *s*. perversiune.

pervert[1] ['pə:və:t] *s*. pervers ; renegat.

pervert[2] [pə:'və:t] *vt*. a perverti ; a corupe ; a deforma.

pessimism ['pesimizəm] *s*. pesimism.

pest [pest] *s*. ciumă ; pacoste.

pester ['pestə] *vt*. a necăji ; a deranja.

pestilence ['pestiləns] *s*. ciumă ; molimă.

pestilent ['pestilənt] *adj*. molipsitor ; mortal ; supărător ; imoral.

pestilential [,pesti'lenʃl] *adj*. corupător ; insuportabil.

pestle ['pesl] *s*. pisălog ; pistil. *vt*. a pisa (în mojar).

pet [pet] *s*. animal de casă ; favorit ; ţîfnă. *vt*. a giugiuli.

petal ['petl] *s*. petală.

peter ['pi:tə] *vi*. a înceta, a fi pe sfîrşite ; a se slei.

petition [pi'tiʃn] *s*. petiţie ; cerere ; rugăminte. *vt*. a solicita. *vi*. a face o petiţie.

pet-name ['petneim] *s*. diminutiv.

petrel ['petrl] *s*. petrel.

petrify ['petrifai] *vt*. a împietri ; a paraliza. *vi*. a se împietri.

petrifaction [,petri'fækʃn] *s*. pietrificare ; împietrire ; uluială.

petrol [petrl] *s*. benzină auto.

petroleum [pi trouljəm] *s*. ţiţei.

petticoat ['petikout] *s*. jupon.

pettifogger ['petifɔgə] *s*. (avocat) chiţibuşar.

pettifogging ['petifɔgiŋ] *adj*. şicanator ; meschin.

petty ['peti] *adj*. mic ; mărunt ; meschin.

petty bourgeois ['peti buəʒwa:] *s*., *adj*. mic-burghez.

petulant ['petjulənt] *adj*. irascibil ; cîrcotaş.

pew [pju:] *s*. strană ; jilţ.

pewter ['pju:tə] *s*. (vase din) aliaj de cositor şi plumb.

phantasy ['fæntəsi] *s*. fantezie.

phantom ['fæntəm] *s*. fantomă.

pharaoh ['feərou] *s*. faraon.

pharmacy ['fa:rməsi] *s*. farmacie.

phase [feiz] *s*. fază.

pheasant ['feznt] *s*. fazan.

phenomenon [fi nɔminən] *s*. fenomen.

phial ['faiəl] *s*. sticluţă ; fiolă.

philander [fi'lændə] *vi*. a flirta ; a umbla după femei.

philanderer [fi'lændərə] *s*. crai (don).

philanthropist [fi'lænθrəpist] *s*. filantrop.

philanthropy [fi'lænθrəpi] *s*. (instituţie de) binefacere.

Philistine ['filistain] *s*. filistin ; duşman al culturii.

philosopher [fi'lɔsəfə] *s*. filozof.

philosophy [fi'lɔsəfi] *s*. filozofie ; stoicism.

phlegmatic [fleg'mætik] *adj*. calm ; placid.

phone [foun] *s*. telefon. *vt*., *vi*. a telefona.

phonetics [fo'netiks] *s*. fonetică

phoney ['founi] *adj.* fals ; prefăcut ; şarlatanesc.

phonograph ['founəgrɑ:f] *s.* fonograf. *amer.* patefon ; picup.

phosphorus ['fɔsfərəs] *s.* fosfor.

photo ['foutou] *s.* fotografie. *vt.* a fotografia.

photograph ['foutəgrɑ:f] *s.* fotografie. *vt.* a fotografia.

photographer [fə'tɔgrəfə] *s.* fotograf (profesionist).

phrase [freiz] *s.* expresie ; locuţiune ; *muz.* frază. *vt.* a exprima.

phthisis ['θaisis] *s.* tuberculoză (pulmonară).

physic ['fizik] *s.* doctorie ; *pl.* fizică. *vt.* a doctorici.

physician [fi'ziʃn] *s.* doctor.

physicist ['fizisist] *s.* fizician.

physics ['fiziks] *s.* fizică.

physique [fi'zi:k] *s.* fizic ; înfăţişare.

piano ['pjænou] *s.* pian.

piccolo ['pikəlou] *s.* piculină.

pick [pik] *s.* tîrnăcop ; sulă ; scobitoare ; alegere ; elită. *vt.* a culege ; a alege ; a nimeri ; a căuta ; a desface ; a fura ; a ciuguli ; *to ~ up* a ridica. *vi.* a ciuguli ; a şterpeli ; *to ~ up* a se întrema ; *to ~ up with* a se împrieteni cu.

pickax(e) ['pikæks] *s.* tîrnăcop.

picket ['pikit] *s.* ţăruş ; stîlp (de gard) ; pichet. *vt.* a bate în ţăruşi ; a fixa ; a păzi. *vi.* a forma pichete.

picking ['pikiŋ] *s.* culegere ; furtişag ; *pl.* pradă ; *pl.* firimituri ; rămăşiţe.

pickle ['pikl] *s.* saramură ; murături ; încurcătură. *vt.* a mura.

pickpocket ['pik,pɔkit] *s.* hoţ de buzunare.

pick-up ['pikʌp] *s.* (braţ de) picup ; *el.* doză ; camionetă ; întremare.

picnic ['piknik] *s.* picnic. *vi.* a petrece la un picnic.

pictorial [pik'tɔ:riəl] *s.* magazin ilustrat. *adj.* pictural ; ilustrat.

picture ['piktʃə] *s.* tablou ; poză ; ilustraţie ; pictură ; imagine ; descriere ; film.

picture-book ['piktʃəbuk] *s.* carte cu poze.

picture-(post)card ['piktʃə'(pous)kɑ:d] *s.* (carte poştală) ilustrată.

picturesque [,piktʃə'resk] *adj* pitoresc ; original ; expresiv.

pidgin English ['pidʒin 'ingliʃ] *s.* engleză stricată vorbită în porturile Asiei.

pie [pai] *s.* plăcintă ; budincă ; pateu.

piebald ['paibɔ:ld] *s., adj.* (cal) bălţat.

piece [pi:s] *s.* bucată ; element ; articol ; armă de foc ; cantitate ; *a ~ of news* o ştire. *vt.* a îmbina ; a înjgheba.

piecemeal ['pi:smi:l] *adj., adv.* treptat.

piece-work ['pi:swə:k] *s.* (muncă în) acord.

pied [paid] *adj.* bălţat.

pier [piə] *s.* dig ; picior de pod ; stîlp.

pierce [piəs] *vt.* a străpunge ; a pătrunde (în) ; a găuri. *vi.* a fi pătrunzător ; a pătrunde.

piety ['paiəti] *s.* pietate ; smerenie ; credinţă.

pig [pig] *s.* (carne de) porc ; mitocan ; lingou de fontă.

pigeon ['pidʒin] *s.* porumbel; fraier; *sport* talèr. *vt.* a trage pe sfoară.

pigeonhole ['pidʒinhoul] *s.* firidă; casetă. *vt.* a sorta; a pune la dosar.

piggish ['pigiʃ] *adj.* porcesc; murdar; lacom.

pig-headed ['pig'hedid] *adj.* căpăţînos.

pig iron ['pig₁aiən] *s.* fontă brută.

pigmy ['pigmi] *s.* pigmeu.

pigsty ['pigstai] *s.* cocină.

pigtail ['pigteil] *s.* codiţă (*pieptănătură*).

pike [paik] *s.* ştiucă; suliţă; barieră.

pile [pail] *s.* stîlp; pilon; morman; rug; ansamblu arhitectonic; *el.* pilă; părul stofei. *vt.* a bate în ţăruşi; a îngrămădi; a încărca. *vi.* a se îngrămădi.

piles [pailz] *s. pl.* hemoroizi.

pilfer ['pilfə] *vt., vi.* a şterpeli.

pilgrim ['pilgrim] *s.* pelerin; călător.

pill [pil] *s.* pilulă; hap; minge.

pillage ['pilidʒ] *s.* jaf; pradă. *vt., vi.* a prăda.

pillar ['pilə] *s.* stîlp; pilon.

pillar-box ['piləbɔks] *s.* cutie poştală.

pill-box ['pilbɔks] *s.* cutie cu medicamente; cazemată.

pillory ['piləri] *s.* stîlpul infamiei.

pillow ['pilou] *s.* pernă de dormit.

pillow-case ['piloukeis], **pillow-slip** ['pilouslip] *s.* faţă de pernă.

pilot ['pailət] *s.* pilot; călăuză. *vt.* a pilota.

pimento [pi'mentou] *s.* ardei (iute).

pimp [pimp] *s.* proxenet; peşte *(fig.)*.

pimpernel ['pimpənel] *s. bot.* scînteiuţă; ochişor.

pimple ['pimpl] *s.* coş (pe faţă).

pin [pin] *s.* ac (cu gămălie, podoabă etc.); bigudiu; ţăruş; popic; *pl.* picioare; ~s and needles amorţeală. *vt.* a fixa; a ţintui · a înţepeni.

pinafore ['pinəfɔ:] *s.* şorţ(uleţ).

pincers ['pinsəz] *s. pl.* cleşte.

pinch [pintʃ] *s.* ciupit(ură); o ·mînă (de tutun etc.); strînsoare. *vt.* a ciupi; a strînge; a apăsa; a aresta. *vi.* a strînge; a fi zgîrcit.

pine [pain] *s.* pin. *vi.* a se ofili; a tînji.

pineapple ['pain₁æpl] *s.* ananas.

ping-pong ['piŋpɔŋ] *s.* tenis de masă.

pinion ['pinjən] *s.* pinion; încheietură; pană; aripă. *vt.* a înţepeni; a tăia aripile (*cu dat.*).

pink [piŋk] *s.* roz; splendoare; garoafă. *adj.* roz.

pinnacle ['pinəkl] *s.* turnuleţ; culme.

pint [paint] *s.* jumătate de litru; halbă.

pioneer [₁paiə'niə] *s.* pionier. *vi.* a face pionierat.

pious ['paiəs] *adj.* pios; cucernic; religios.

pip [pip] *s.* sîmbure de măr, de portocală *sau* de strugure.

pipe [paip] *s.* ţeavă; conductă; fluier; flaut; pipă; cimpoi. *vt.* a cînta din fluier; a rosti cu glas subţirel. *vi.* a cînta

din fluier; a vorbi subțirel;
a șuiera.

piper ['paipə] *s.* fluierar; cimpo-
ier.

piping ['paipiŋ] *s.* fluierat; țevă-
rie; instalații; podoabe. *adj.*
subțirel.

piquant ['pi:kənt] *adj.* picant.

pique [pi:k] *s.* pică; supărare.
vt. a ațîța; a supăra. *vr.* a
se mîndri.

piracy ['paiərəsi] *s.* piraterie.

pirate ['paiərit] *s.* pirat.

pistol ['pistl] *s.* pistol.

piston ['pistn] *s.* piston.

pit [pit] *s.* groapă; gaură;
mină; *teatru* parter; stal II.

pit-a-pat ['pitə'pæt] *s., adv.*
tic-tac.

pitch [pitʃ] *s.* așezare; loc; înăl-
țime; aruncare; intensitate;
pantă; legănat; smoală. *vt.*
a fixa; a înțepeni; a arunca;
muz. a acorda; a smoli. *vi.* a
cădea la pămînt; a arunca;
a se legăna; a se rostogoli;
to ~ in a se apuca serios de
treabă; *to ~ into* a se năpusti
asupra.

pitch and toss [,pitʃən'tɔs] *s.*
rișcă.

pitch dark ['pitʃda:k] *s.* întuneric beznă.

pitcher ['pitʃə] *s.* cană; urcior.

pitchfork ['pitʃfɔ:k] *s.* furcă.

piteous ['pitiəs] *adj.* jalnic.

pitfall ['pitfɔ:l] *s.* capcană; primejdie.

pith [piθ] *s.* măduvă; șira
spinării; esență; vigoare.

pitiable ['pitiəbl] *adj.* jalnic.

pitiful ['pitifl] *adj.* milos; jalnic.

pitiless ['pitilis] *adj.* neîndurător; nemilos.

pittance ['pitns] *s.* cîștig minim.

pity ['piti] *s.* milă; păcat;
jale; *it's a ~* păcat. *vt.* a
compătimi.

placard ['plækɑ:d] *s.* afiș; placardă. *vt.* a afișa.

placate [plə'keit] *vt.* a împăca;
a liniști.

place [pleis] *s.* loc; locaș; poziție; local; localitate; casă;
serviciu; rang; clasificare; spațiu; piață; *out of ~* deplasat.
vt. a pune; a aranja; a numi;
a instala; a situa; a clasifica.

plagiarism ['pleidʒiərizəm] *s.*
plagiat.

plagiarize ['pleidʒiəraiz] *vt.* a
plagia.

plague [pleig] *s.* ciumă; pacoste.
vt. a necăji.

plaice [pleis] *s.* cambulă.

plaid [plæd] *s.* pled.

plain [plein] *s.* cîmpie. *adj.*
limpede; simplu; cinstit; sincer; neatrăgător.

plaint [pleint] *s.* plîngere; acuzație.

plaintiff ['pleintif] *s.* reclamant.

plaintive ['pleintiv] *adj.* plîngăreț; trist.

plait [plæt] *s.* coadă *(coafură)*;
împletitură. *vt.* a împleti (părul).

plan [plæn] *s.* plan; hartă. *vt.*
a plănui; a planifica.

plane [plein] *s.* plan (geometric,
general etc.); nivel; suprafață
dreaptă; *bot.* platan; rindea;
(aripă de) avion. *vt.* a da la
rindea. *vi.* a plana.

planet ['plænit] *s.* planetă.

plank [plæŋk] *s.* scîndură (groasă). *vt.* a podi.

planking ['plæŋkiŋ] s. duşumea.

plant [plɑːnt] s. plantă; răsad; instalaţii tehnice; uzină. vt. a planta; a înfige; a stabili.

plantain ['plæntin] s. bananier; pătlagină.

planter ['plɑːntə] s. plantator; maşină de plantat.

plash [plæʃ] s. plescăit. vt. a stropi. vi. a plescăi.

plaster ['plɑːstə] s. tencuială; plasture; oblojeală; ghips. vt. a tencui; a acoperi; a obloji; a pune în ghips.

plaster of Paris ['plɑːstərəv'pæris] s. ghips; alabastru.

plastic ['plæstik] s. material plastic. adj. plastic; maleabil.

plasticine ['plæstisiːn] s. plastilină.

plate [pleit], s. farfurie (întinsă); tavă; tacîmuri; platoşă; foaie de metal; planşă; placă (fotografică, dentară etc.). vt. a acoperi cu plăci, platoşă, blindaj; a sufla (cu aur, argint).

plateau ['plætou] s. platou, podiş.

plateful ['pleitful] s. conţinutul unei farfurii.

platform ['plætfɔːm] s. platformă (comună); estradă; peron.

plating ['pleitiŋ] s. galvanoplastie; aur dublé.

platoon [plə'tuːn] s. pluton.

plausible ['plɔːzəbl] adj. demn de crezare; verosimil.

play [plei] s. distracţie; joc (de noroc); piesă; libertate de mişcare; acţiune; rîndul la joc. vi. a (se) juca; a se distra; a se preface; a juca jocuri de noroc; a fi actor; a cînta la un instrument.

play-bill ['pleibil] s. afiş teatral.

player ['pleiə] s. jucător; instrumentist; actor.

playful ['pleifl] adj. jucăuş; glumeţ.

playgoer ['pleiˌgouə] s. teatru spectator pasionat.

playground ['pleigraund] s. teren de joacă.

playhouse ['pleihaus] s. teatru; amer. casă a păpuşilor.

playing-card ['pleiiŋkɑːd] s. carte de joc.

playmate ['pleimeit] s. tovarăş de joacă.

plaything ['pleiθiŋ] s. jucărie.

playwright ['pleirait] s. dramaturg.

plea [pliː] s. pledoarie; rugăminte; scuză.

plead [pliːd] vt. a susţine; a aduce (o scuză). vi. a pleda; a se apăra; a se ruga.

pleading ['pliːdiŋ] s. pledoarie. adj. rugător.

pleasant ['pleznt] adj. plăcut; încîntător.

please [pliːz] vt. a încînta; a face pe plac la; ~ yourself! fă cum vrei! vi. a fi dispus; a dori; (if you) ~ vă rog.

pleased [pliːzd] adj. încîntat; mulţumit.

pleasing ['pliːziŋ] adj. încîntător; agreabil.

pleasure ['pleʒə] s. plăcere; dorinţă.

pleasure-ground ['pleʒəgraund] s. parc de distracţii.

pleat [pliːt] s. cută; pliseu. vt. a plisa.

plebeian [pli'biːən] s. plebeu. adj. ordinar, de rînd.

pledge [pledʒ] *s.* gaj; angajament; garanție. *vt.* a pune chezășie; a angaja; a amaneta; a toasta pentru.

plentiful ['plentifl] *adj.* abundent; vast.

plenty ['plenti] *s.* mulțime; abundență; *in* ∼ din abundență. *pron.* mulți, multe. *adv.* foarte; mult.

plenum ['pli:nəm] *s.* plenară.

pliable ['plaiəbl] *adj.* flexibil; influențabil.

pliant ['plaiənt] *adj.* flexibil; docil.

pliers ['plaiəz] *s.* clește; pensă.

plight [plait] *s.* situație grea; mizerie; angajament.

plod [plɔd] *vi.* a înainta cu greu; a trudi; *to* ∼ *one's way* a merge greu.

plot [plɔt] *s.* parcelă; teren; lot; complot; plan; subiect; poveste. *vt.* a plănui; a complota; a parcela.

plough [plau] *s.* plug; ogor. *vt.* a ara; a-și croi (drum); a trînti (un candidat); *to* ∼ *up* a desțeleni. *vi.* a ara; a cădea la examen; a-și croi drum.

ploughman ['plaumən] *s.* plugar.

ploughshare ['plauʃɛə] *s.* fier de plug.

plover ['plʌvə] *s.* fluierar.

plow [plau] etc. *amer. v.* **plough** etc.

pluck [plʌk] *s.* curaj; tărie de caracter. *vt.* a smulge; a trage; a culege; a jecmăni; a trînti (un candidat); *to* ∼ *up courage* a-și lua inima în dinți. *vi.: to* ∼ *at* a apuca; a trage.

plug [plʌg] *s.* dop; priză; *el.*

fișă. *vt.* a astupa; a pune în priză; a omorî.

plum [plʌm] *s.* prun(ă); stafidă; *fig.* floare, boboc; sinecură.

plumage ['plu:midʒ] *s.* penaj.

plumb ['plʌm] *s.* fir cu plumb. *adj.* vertical; adevărat; drept; total. *vt.* a măsura; a sonda; a înțelege. *adv.* vertical; exact; drept.

plumbago [plʌm'beigou] *s.* grafit; plombagină.

plumber ['plʌmə] *s.* instalator de apă și canal.

plumbing ['plʌmiŋ] *s.* instalații tehnico-sanitare.

plum-cake ['plʌmkeik] *s.* budincă cu stafide.

plume [plu:m] *s.* pană (de pălărie). *vt.* a împodobi cu pene. *vr.* a se împăuna.

plump [plʌmp] *adj.* dolofan; direct. *vt.* a rotunji; a trînti. *adv.* direct.

plum pudding ['plʌm'pudiŋ] *s.* budincă cu stafide.

plunder ['plʌndə] *s.* jaf; pradă. *vt., vi.* a prăda, a jefui.

plunge [plʌndʒ] *s.* plonjon; atac; încercare. *vt.* a arunca; a băga. *vi.* a se arunca; a plonja.

plural ['pluərl] *s.* plural.

pluralism ['pluərəlizəm] *s.* cumul.

plurality [pluə'ræliti] *s.* pluralitate; majoritate; cumul (de funcții).

plus [plʌs] *s.* plus. *adj.* suplimentar; în plus; *el.* pozitiv. *prep.* plus.

plus-fours ['plʌs'fɔ:z] *s.* pantaloni (de) golf.

plush [plʌʃ] *s.* pluș.

ply [plai] *s.* pliu; mănunchi de

fire. *vt.* a trudi la.; a asalta *(fig.)* ; a aproviziona (cu) ; a oferi ; a folosi. *vi.* a face naveta ; a circula.

ply-wood ['plaiwud] *s.* placaj.

pneumatic [nju'mætik] *adj.* pneumatic.

pneumonia [nju'mounjə] *s.* pneumonie.

poach [poutʃ] *vt.* a vîna fără voie. *vi.* a face braconaj.

poached eggs ['poutʃt'egz] *s. pl.* ochiuri fierte în apă, ochiuri românești.

poacher ['poutʃə] *s.* braconier.

pock [pɔk] *s.* ciupitură de vărsat.

pocket ['pɔkit] *s.* buzunar ; pungă ; bani. *vt.* a băga în buzunar.

pocket-book ['pɔkitbuk] *s.* agendă (de buzunar) ; portmoneu.

pock-marked ['pɔkmɑːkt] *adj.* ciupit de vărsat.

pod [pɔd] *s.* păstaie.

podgy ('pɔdʒi] *s.* îndesat ; gras.

poem ['poim] *s.* poezie ; poem.

poet ['poit] *s.* poet.

poetic(al) [po'etik(l)] *adj.* poetic.

poetic diction [po'etik'dikʃn] *s.* limbaj poetic.

poetry ['poitri] *s.* versuri ; lirică.

poignant ['pɔinənt] *adj.* ascuțit ; picant ; mușcător ; caustic.

point [pɔint] *s.* vîrf ; ascuțiș ; punct ; chestiune ; element ; esență ; poantă ; scop ; rost ; măsură ; macaz ; *beside the* ~ fără legătură ; inutil ; *in* ~ *of fact* de fapt ; *at all* ~*s* total ; în toate privințele. *vt.* a indica ; a îndrepta ; a ascuți ; a sublinia ; *to* ~ *out* a sublinia, a scoate în relief. *vi.* a atrage atenția ; a arăta (către).

point-blank ['pɔint'blæŋk] *adj., adv.* direct.

pointed ['pɔintid] *adj.* ascuțit.

pointer ['pɔintə] *s.* cîine de vînătoare ; indicator ; băț pentru indicarea pe hartă etc.

pointless ['pɔintlis] *adj.* tocit ; fără sens.

pointsman ['pɔintsmən] *s.* acar ; sergent de stradă.

poise [pɔiz] *s.* echilibru ; stăpînire ; ținută. *vt.* a echilibra ; a ține. *vi.* a sta în echilibru.

poison ['pɔizn] *s.* otravă. *vt.* a otrăvi.

poisonous ['pɔiznəs] *adj.* otrăvitor ; imoral.

poke [pouk] *s.* ghiont ; împunsătură. *vt.* a împinge ; a înghionti ; a băga. *vi.* a se băga ; a bîjbîi.

poker ['poukə] *s.* vătrai ; pocher.

poker-work ['poukəwəːk] *s.* gofraj ; pirogravură.

polar ['poulə] *adj.* polar.

polar bear ['poulə'bɛə] *s.* urs alb.

pole[1] [poul] *s.* pol (opus) ; prăjină.

Pole[2] [poul] *s.* polonez(ă).

pole-axe ['poulæks] *s.* topor. *vt.* a doborî.

pole-star ['poulstɑː] *s.* steaua polară ; stea călăuzitoare.

pole-vault ['poulvɔːlt] *s.* săritură cu prăjina.

police [pə'liːs] *s.* poliție ; polițiști.

police court [pə'liːs,kɔːt] *s.* judecătorie de instrucție.

policeman [pə'lismn] *s.* polițist.

police station [pə'liːs,steiʃn] *s.* secție de poliție.

policy ['pɔlisi] *s.* politică; tactică; poliţă de asigurare.

polio ['pouliou] *s.* poliomielită.

polish[1] ['pɔliʃ] *s.* lustru; luciu; cremă de ghete; pastă de lustruit. *vt., vi.* a lustrui.

Polish[2] ['pouliʃ] *adj.* polonez.

polite [pə'lait] *adj.* politicos; binecrescut; rafinat.

politeness [pə'laitnis] *s.* politeţe.

politic ['pɔlitik] *adj.* prudent; înţelept; diplomat; viclean.

political [pə'litikl] *adj.* politic.

politician [,pɔli'tiʃn] *s.* om politic.

politics ['pɔlitiks] *s.* viaţă *sau* arenă politică.

poll [poul] *s.* (cap de) om; listă electorală; voturi; alegeri; urnă. *vt.* a primi (voturi); a pune la vot. *vi.* a vota.

pollen ['pɔlin] *s.* polen.

pollination [,pɔli'neiʃn] *s.* polenizare.

pollute [pə'lu:t] *vt.* a murdări; *fig.* a corupe; a pîngări.

poltroon [pɔl'tru:n] *s.* laş.

polygamist [pɔ'ligəmist] *s.* poligam.

pomatum [pə'meitəm] *s.* pomadă; alifie.

pomegranate ['pɔm,grænit] *s.* rodie.

pommel ['pʌml] *s.* mîner de sabie; oblînc. *vt.* a bate.

pomp [pɔmp] *s.* pompă; splendoare; paradă.

pond [pɔnd] *s.* eleşteu.

ponder ['pɔndə] *vt., vi.* a chibzui; a considera.

ponderous ['pɔndrəs] *adj.* greoi; apăsător; obositor.

pony ['pouni] *s.* ponei; căluţ; hîrtie de 25 lire.

poodle ['pu:dl] *s.* pudel.

pooh [pu:] *vt.* a respinge. *interj.* pfui.

pool [pu:l] *s.* baltă; fond comun; cartel; pariuri sportive. *vt.* a uni, a pune laolaltă.

poop [pu:p] *s. mar.* pupă.

poor [puə] *s.: the* ~ săracii, sărăcimea. *adj.* sărac; umil; modest; slab; de proastă calitate.

poorly ['puəli] *adj.* prost. *adv.* sărăcăcios.

pop [pɔp] *s.* pocnitură; băutură efervescentă. *vt.* a pocni (din); a băga; a pune (amanet); a coace (porumb). *vi.* a pocni; a crăpa; a se băga; *to* ~ *off* a o şterge; a muri. *adv.* hodoronc-tronc.

pop-corn ['pɔpkɔ:n] *s.* floricele.

pop-gun ['pɔpgʌn] *s.* puşcoci.

pope [poup] *s.* papă; popă.

popery ['poupəri] *s.* papalitate.

pop-eyed ['pɔp,aid] *adj.* holbat; cu ochii ieşiţi din orbite.

popinjay ['pɔpindʒei] *s.* papagal; *fig.* pupăză.

poplar ['pɔplə] *s.* plop.

poppy ['pɔpi] *s.* mac.

populace ['pɔpjuləs] *s.* gloată; norod.

popular ['pɔpjulə] *adj.* popular; simpatizat; admirat.

population [,pɔpju'leiʃn] *s.* populaţie.

populous ['pɔpjuləs] *adj.* aglomerat; populat.

porcelain ['pɔ:slin] *s.* porţelan.

porch [pɔ:tʃ] *s.* pridvor; verandă.

porcupine ['pɔ:kjupain] *s.* porc spinos.

pore [pɔ:] *s.* por. *vi.* a medita; *to* ~ *over* a studia.

pork [pɔːk] s. carne de porc.
porker ['pɔːkə] s. porc (de tăiat).
porous ['pɔrəs] adj. poros.
porphyry ['pɔːfiri] s. porfir.
porpoise ['pɔːpəs] s. delfin.
porridge ['pɔridʒ] s. terci (de ovăz).
porringer ['pɔrindʒə] s. bol; blid.
port [pɔːt] s. port (la mare); *fig.* liman; hublou; ferestruică; babord; vin de Porto; ţinută; *any ~ in a storm* foamea n-alege.
portend [pɔ:'tend] vt. a prevesti.
portent ['pɔːtent] s. semn rău.
portentous [pɔ:'tentəs] adj. prevestitor de rău.
porter ['pɔːtə] s. hamal; conductor de tren; portar; bere ordinară (tare).
portfolio [pɔ:t'fouljou] s. servietă; portofoliu.
porthole ['pɔːthoul] s. hublou; ferestruică.
portion ['pɔːʃn] s. porţi(un)e; soartă. vt. a împărţi; a parcela.
portly ['pɔːtli] adj. corpolent.
portmanteau [pɔ:t'mæntou] s. valiză cu două părţi; hibrid.
portrait ['pɔːtrit] s. portret; imagine.
portray [pɔ:'trei] vt. a portretiza; a descrie; a picta.
portrayal [pɔ:'treəl] s. portretizare.
Portuguese [,pɔ:tju'giːz] s., adj. portughez(ă).
pose [pouz] s. atitudine; poză. vt. a pune; a supune. vi. a poza.
posh [pɔʃ] adj. elegant; modern; după ultimul răcnet.

position [pə ziʃn] s. poziţie; situaţie; atitudine; slujbă; rang. vt. a situa.
positive ['pɔzətiv] s. pozitiv. adj. pozitiv; precis; sigur (de sine).
possess [pə'zes] vt. a poseda; a stăpîni; *to be ~ed of* a deţine.
possession [pə'zeʃn] s. posesie; proprietate; *pl.* avere; stăpînire.
possibility [,pɔsə'biliti] s. posibilitate; ocazie.
possible ['pɔsəbl] s. posibil; eventualitate. adj. posibil; previzibil; normal.
possibly ['pɔsəbli] adv. eventual; cumva.
post [poust] s. stîlp; prăjină; bară; post; trîmbiţă; poştă. vt. a fixa; a afişa; a anunţa; a posta; a plasa; a expedia.
postage ['poustidʒ] s. taxă poştală.
postage-stamp ['poustidʒˌstæmp] s. timbru poştal.
postal ['poustl] adj. poştal.
post-card ['pouskɑːd] s. carte poştală.
poster ['poustə] s. afiş.
posterior [pɔs'tiəriə] s. spate; dos. adj. posterior.
posterity [pɔs'teriti] s. progenitură; posteritate.
postern ['poustəːn] s. uşa din dos.
post-free ['poust'friː] adj. scutit de taxe poştale; inclusiv taxa poştală.
post-graduate ['pous'grædjuit] s. doctorand.
post-graduate course ['pous'grædjuit'kɔːs] s. curs(uri) post-universitar(e).

post-haste ['poust'heist] *adj.* re-pede ; expres.

posthumous ['pɔstjuməs] *adj.* postum.

postman ['pousmən] *s.* poştaş.

post-master ['pous͵mɑːstə] _ *s.* diriginte de poştă.

Post-Master General ['pous͵mɑːs-tə'dʒenərl] *s.* Ministrul Poş-telor.

post-mortem ['pous'mɔːtem] *s.* autopsie. *adj.* post-mortem.

post-office ['poust͵ɔfis] *s.* oficiul poştal ; poştă.

postpone [pous'poun] *vt.* a amîna.

postscript ['pousskript] *s.* post-scriptum.

postulate ['pɔstjuleit] *vt.* a cere ; a presupune ; a necesita.

posture ['pɔstʃə] *s.* atitudine ; situaţie.

post-war ['poust'wɔː] *adj.* post-belic.

pot [pɔt] *s.* oală ; cratiţă ; ceai-nic ; premiu ; sumă mare.

potash ['pɔtæʃ] *s.* potasiu ; po-tasă ; leşie.

potato [pə'teitou] *s.* cartof.

pot-belly ['pɔt͵beli] *s.* (persoa-nă cu) burtă mare.

potent ['poutnt] *adj.* puternic ; convingător.

pot-hat ['pɔt'hæt] *s.* pălărie me-lon ; gambetă.

pot-hole ['pɔthoul] *s.* gaură ; groapă.

pot-house ['pɔthaus] *s.* cîrciumă.

potion ['pouʃn] *s.* poţiune.

pot-luck ['pɔtlʌk] *s.* mîncare.

potsherd ['pɔtʃəːd] *s.* ciob.

potshot ['pɔt'ʃɔt] *s.* foc tras la întîmplare.

potter ['pɔtə] *s.* olar. *vt.* a irosi. *vi.* a se învîrti fără rost.

pottery ['pɔtəri] *s.* olărit ; olă-rie ; oale.

potty ['pɔti] *adj.* mic ; neînsem-nat ; trăsnit.

pouch [pautʃ] *s.* pungă ; buzu-nar. *vt.* a face pungă ; a pune în buzunar. *vi.* a se umfla.

poulterer ['poultrə] *s.* avicultor.

poultice ['poultis] *s.* cataplas-mă. *vt.* a obloji.

poultry ['poultri] *s.* păsări do-mestice.

pounce [pauns] *s.* atac brusc. *vi.* a se năpusti.

pound [paund] *s.* funt, livră (453 gr.) ; liră sterlină. *vt.* a zdrobi ; a pisa ; a măcina ; a băga în ţarc. *vi.* a tropăi.

pour [pɔː] *s.* ploaie torenţială. *vt.* a turna ; a scoate. *vi.* a curge ; a ploua cu găleata.

pout [paut] *s.* bot ; strîmbă-tură. *vi.* a face bot.

poverty ['pɔvəti] *s.* sărăcie ; lipsă.

poverty-stricken ['pɔvəti͵strikn] *adj.* sărac (lipit pămîntului).

powder ['paudə] *s.* pudră ; praf (de puşcă). *vt.*, *vi.* a (se) pudra.

powdery ['paudəri] *adj.* prăfuit ; pudrat.

power ['pauə] *s.* putere ; capaci-tate ; energie (electrică) ; auto-ritate.

powerful ['pauəfl] *adj.* puternic.

powerless ['pauəlis] *adj.* neputin-cios.

power-station ['pauə͵steiʃn] *s.* centrală electrică.

pox [pɔks] *s.* vărsat (de vînt, negru etc.).

practicable ['præktikəbl] *adj.* realizabil.

practical ['præktikl] *adj.* practic.

practical joke ['præktikl'djouk] *s.* festă, farsă.

practically ['præktikəli] *adv.* practic ; într-adevăr ; aproape ; ca şi.

practice ['præktis] *s.* practică ; clientelă ; antrenament.

practise ['præktis] *vt.*, *vi.* a practica ; a profesa ; a exersa ; a experimenta.

practitioner [præk'tiʃnə] *s.* profesionist ; medic.

prairie ['prɛəri] *s.* prerie ; stepă.

praise [preiz] *s.* laudă ; cult. *vt.* a lăuda ; a adora ; *to ~ to the skies* a ridica în slăvi.

praiseworthy ['preizwə:ði] *adj.* merituos.

pram [præm] *s.* cărucior de copil.

prance [prɑ:ns] *s.* cabrare. *vi.* a se cabra ; a face pe grozavul ; a se zbengui.

prank [præŋk] *s.* joc ; capriciu ; zbenguială. *vt.* a se grozăvi.

prate [preit] *s.* vorbărie. *vt.*, *vi.* a flecări.

prattle ['prætl] *s.* vorbe goale. *vt.*, *vi.* a flecări ; a ciripi.

pray [prei] *vt.*, *vi.* a (se) ruga.

prayer ['prɛə] *s.* rugăciune ; rugăminte ; petiţie.

preach [pri:tʃ] *vt.* a propovădui. *vi.* a ţine predici.

preacher ['pri:tʃə] *s.* predicator.

preamble [pri: æmbl] *s.* preambul ; prefaţă.

precarious [pri'kɛəriəs] *adj.* nesigur ; riscant ; primejdios.

precaution [pri'kɔ:ʃn] *s.* precauţie.

precede [pri'si:d] *vt.* a preceda ; a depăşi.

precedence [pri'si:dns] *s.* întîietate.

precincts ['pri:siŋts] *s.* incintă ; zonă.

precious ['preʃəs] *adj.* preţios ; straşnic.

precipice ['presipis] *s.* prăpastie.

precipitate[1] [pri'sipitit] *s.*, *adj.* precipitat.

precipitate[2] [pri'sipiteit] *vt.*, *vr.* a (se) precipita.

precipitous [pri'sipitəs] *adj.* abrupt.

précis ['preisis] *s.* rezumat ; analiză ; conspect.

precise [pri'sais] *adj.* precis ; corect ; minuţios.

precision [pri'siʒn] *s.* precizie ; corectitudine.

preclude [pri klu:d] *vt.* a exclude ; a împiedica.

precocious [pri'kouʃəs] *adj.* precoce.

preconceived ['pri:kən'si:vd] *adj.* preconceput.

predatory ['predətri] *adj.* prădalnic.

predecessor ['pri:disesə] *s.* predecesor ; antecedent.

predestination [pri:,desti'neiʃn] *s.* predestinare.

predestine [pri:'destin] *vt.* a predestina.

predetermine ['pri:di'tə:min] *vt.* a predestina ; a determina.

predicament [pri'dikəmənt] *vt.* situaţie grea ; încurcătură.

predicate ['predikit] *s.* predicat.

predict [pri'dikt] *vt.* a prezice.

predilection [,pri:di'lekʃn] *s.* predilecţie.

predispose ['pri:dis'pouz] *vt.* a predispune.

predisposition ['pri:,dispə'ziʃn] *s* predispoziţie.

predominant [pri'dɔminənt] *adj.* predominant.

preeminent [pri'eminənt] *adj.* superior ; predominant.

pre-emption [pri'emʃən] *s.* prioritate.

preen [priːn] *vt.* a aranja. *vi.* a se făli.

prefab ['priːfæb] *s.* (element) prefabricat.

preface ['prefis] *s.* prefață. *vt.* a prefața ; a precede.

prefer [pri'fəː] *vt.* a prefera ; a întinde ; a înainta.

preference ['prefrns] *s.* preferință ; prioritate.

preferment [pri'fəːmənt] *s.* promovare, înaintare.

prefigure [pri'figə] *vt.* a prevedea ; a prezice.

prefix ['priːfiks] *s.* prefix.

pregnancy ['pregnənsi] *s.* graviditate ; semnificație.

pregnant ['pregnənt] *adj.* gravidă ; important.

prehistoric ['priːhis'tɔrik] *adj.* preistoric.

prejudice ['predʒudis] *s.* prejudecată ; prejudiciu ; *to the* ~ *of* în dauna. *vt.* a prejudicia.

prejudicial [ˌpredʒu'diʃl] *adj.* dăunător.

preliminary [pri'limnəri] *adj.* preliminar.

prelude ['preljuːd] *s.* preludiu. *vt.* a precede.

premature [ˌpremə'tjuə] *adj.* prematur.

premier ['premjə] *s.* premier.

premise ['premis] *s.* premisă ; *pl.* local ; incintă ; sediu.

premium ['priːmjəm] *s.* primă ; premiu ; onorariu.

premonition [ˌpriːmə'niʃn] *s.* presimțire.

preoccupied [pri'ɔkjupaid] *adj.* preocupat.

preordain ['priːɔː'dein] *vt.* a stabili dinainte.

prep [prep] *s.* (cursuri de) pregătire.

preparation [ˌprepə'reiʃn] *s.* pregătire ; preparat.

preparatory [pri'pærətri] *adj.* pregătitor ; ~ *to* înaintea ; în vederea.

prepare [pri'pɛə] *vt., vi.* a (se) prepara.

preparedness [pri'pɛədnis] *s.* pregătire.

preposition [ˌprepə'ziʃn] *s.* prepoziție.

prepossess [ˌpriːpə'zes] *vt.* a influența ; a impresiona ; a inspira.

prepossessing [ˌpriːpə'zesiŋ] *adj.* atrăgător ; plăcut.

prepossession [ˌpriːpə'zeʃn] *s.* impresie bună ; predilecție.

preposterous [pri'pɔstrəs] *adj.* nefiresc ; stupid ; ridicol.

prerequisite ['priː'rekwizit] *s.* condiție esențială.

prerogative [pri'rɔgətiv] *s.* privilegiu ; atribut.

presbytery ['prezbitri] *s.* sanctuar ; prezbiteriu.

prescient ['presiənt] *adj.* prevăzător.

prescribe [pris'kraib] *vt.* a prescrie ; a porunci ; a dicta.

prescription [pris'kripʃn] *s.* poruncă ; rețetă (medicală).

presence ['prezns] *s.* prezență ; înfățișare.

present[1] ['preznt] *s.* prezent ; persoană prezentă ; cadou ; *for* *the* ~ deocamdată. *adj.* prezent ; actual ; de față.

present[2] [pri'zent] *vt.* a dărui ; a prezenta ; a oferi, a arăta ; a ținti.

presentation [,prezen'teiʃn] *s.* prezentare ; expoziție ; spectacol.

presentation copy [,prezen-'teiʃn'kɔpi] *s.* exemplar gratuit.

presently ['prezntli] *adv.* îndată.

presentment [pri'zentmənt] *s.* prezentare ; dăruire.

preservation [,prezə'veiʃn] *s.* păstrare ; ocrotire.

preserve [pri'zə:v] *s.* conservă ; *pl.* dulcețuri ; rezervație. *vt.* a păstra ; a apăra.

preside [pri'zaid] *vi.* a lucra ; a acționa ; a oficia ; a cînta (la un instrument) ; *to* ~ *over* a prezida.

presidency ['prezidnsi] *s.* prezidență.

president ['prezidnt] *s.* președinte ; șef ; ministru.

press [pres] *s.* presă ; dulap ; tipar(niță) ; *in the* ~ sub tipar. *vt.* a presa ; a stoarce ; a strînge ; a forța ; a pune cu insistență ; a incorpora ; a rechiziționa ; *to* ~ *an argument home* a dovedi valoarea unui argument ; *to be* ~*ed for time* a nu avea timp. *vi.* a insista ; a fi urgent ; a se grăbi ; a se îngrămădi.

press clippings ['pres'klipiŋz], **press cuttings** ['pres'kʌtiŋz] *s.* tăieturi din ziare.

pressing ['presiŋ] *adj.* urgent ; presant ; insistent.

pressman ['presmən] *s.* tipograf ; reporter ; ziarist.

pressure ['preʃə] *s.* presiune ; apăsare ; influență.

pressure gauge ['preʃəgeidʒ] *s.* manometru.

prestige [pres'ti:ʒ] *s.* prestigiu.

presumable [pri'zju:məbl] *adj.* rezonabil ; probabil.

presumably [pri'zju:məbli] *adv.* după cît se pare.

presume [pri'zju:m] *vt.* a presupune ; a lua drept bună ; a îndrăzni. *vi.* : *to* ~ *upon smb.* a profita de amabilitatea cuiva.

presuming [pri'zju:miŋ] *adj.* îndrăzneț.

presumption [pri'zʌmʃn] *s.* presupunere ; îndrăzneală.

presumptuous [pri'zʌmtjuəs] *adj.* îndrăzneț ; arogant ; încrezut.

presuppose [,pri:sə'pouz] *vt.* a necesita ; a presupune.

pretence [pri'tens] *s.* pretenție ; ostentație ; pretenții ; aere ; înșelătorie ; prefăcătorie.

pretend [pri'tend] *vt.* a pretinde ; a simula ; a se juca de-a. *vi.* a se preface ; a simula ; a se juca.

pretender [pri'tendə] *s.* pretendent.

pretense [pri'tens] *s. amer. v.* **pretence.**

pretension [pri'tenʃn] *s.* pretenție.

pretentious [pri'tenʃəs] *adj.* pretențios.

preterite ['pretrit] *s.* preterit, trecut (simplu).

preternatural [,pri:tə'nætʃrəl] *adj.* supranatural ; nefiresc ; extraordinar.

pretext ['pri:tekst] *s.* pretext.

prettiness ['pritinis] s. drăgălăşenie.

pretty ['priti] s. drăguţ(ă). adj. drăguţ ; mărişor ; bunişor. adv. bine ; destul de ; cam.

prevail [pri veil] vi. a triumfa ; a fi predominant ; to ~ on smb. a convinge pe cineva.

prevalent ['prevələnt] adj. predominant ; obişnuit ; curent.

prevaricate [pri'værikeit] vt. a vorbi evaziv.

prevent [pri'vent] vt. a împiedica.

prevention [pri'venʃn] s. împiedicare.

preventive [pri'ventiv] adj. preventiv.

preview ['pri:'vju:] s. avanpremieră.

previous ['pri:vjəs] adj. anterior ; precedent ; ~ to înainte de.

prevision [pri'viʒn] s. previziune.

pre-war ['pri:'wɔ:] adj. antebelic.

prey [prei] s. pradă ; victimă. vt. a prăda ; a jefui ; a obseda ; a afecta. vi.: to ~ upon a chinui ; a se năpusti asupra.

price [prais] s. preţ ; sacrificiu ; valoare ; cotă (la pariuri). vt. a preţălui.

priceless ['praislis] adj. nepreţuit ; nostim.

prick [prik] s. ţeapă ; înţepătură. vt. a înţepa ; a găuri ; a ciuli ; to ~ up a ciuli. vi. a înţepa.

prickle ['prikl] s. spin ; ţeapă ; înţepătură ; mîncărime. vt. a înţepa. vi. a simţi mîncărime.

prickly ['prikli] adj. plin de ţepi ; înţepător.

pride [praid] s. mîndrie ; dem-

nitate ; splendoare. vr. a se mîndri.

priest [pri:st] s. preot.

priestess ['pri:stis] s. preoteasă.

priesthood ['pri:sthud] s. preoţie ; cler.

prig [prig] s. pedant.

priggish ['prigiʃ] adj. pedant ; încîntat de sine.

prim [prim] adj. curat ; decent ; politicos. vt. a aranja.

primarily ['praimərili] adv. în primul rînd.

primary ['praiməri] adj. primar ; fundamental.

prime [praim] s. început ; tinereţe ; (perioadă de) înflorire ; floare ; număr prim. adj. prim ; principal ; primar ; fundamental.

prime cost ['praim'kɔst] s. preţ de cost ; cost de producţie.

primer ['praimə] s. abecedar ; manual elementar.

primeval [prai'mi:vl] adj. antic ; preistoric ; neexplorat.

primitive ['primitiv] adj. primitiv.

primrose ['primrouz] s. primulă.

prince ['prins] s. prinţ ; domnitor ; rege.

princely ['prinsli] adj. princiar.

princess [prin'ses] s. prinţesă.

principal ['prinsəpl] s. director ; şef ; partener principal ; autor ; capital (iniţial). adj. principal.

principle ['prinsəpl] s. principiu ; principialitate ; esenţă ; bază.

print [print] s. tipar ; tipărituri ; urmă ; ştampilă ; gravură ; foto. copie ; (hîrtie de) ziar ; out of ~ epuizat ; in ~ publicat ;

disponibil. *vt.* a tipări, a publica ; a imprima ; a copia.

printer ['printə] *s.* tipograf.

printing ['printiŋ] *s.* tipar ; tipăritură.

printing-press ['printiŋ ˌpres] *s.* tipografie ; maşină de imprimat.

prior ['praiə] *s.* stareţ. *adj.* anterior ; mai important ; ~ *to* înainte de.

prioress ['praiəris] *s.* stareţă.

prism ['prizəm] *s.* prismă.

prison ['prizn] *s.* închisoare ; detenţiune ; constrîngere.

prisoner ['priznə] *s.* deţinut ; prizonier.

privacy ['praivəsi] *s.* intimitate ; singurătate ; secret.

private ['praivit] *s.* soldat. *adj.* personal ; particular ; intim ; secret ; intrarea oprită!

privately ['praivitli] *adv.* în taină ; la ureche.

privateer [ˌpraivə'tiə] *s.* pirat ; vas de piraţi. *vi.* a face piraterie.

privation [prai'veiʃn] *s.* privaţiune ; lipsă.

privet ['privit] *s. bot.* lemncîinesc.

privy ['privi] *adj.* secret ; personal ; *to be* ~ *to smth.* a fi informat de ceva.

Privy Council ['privi'kaunsl] *s.* Consiliu de Coroană.

privy parts ['priviˌpɑːts] *s. pl.* organe genitale.

prize [praiz] *s.* premiu ; primă ; răsplată ; pradă (de război). *vt.* a preţui ; a stima.

pro [prou] *s.* : ~*s and cons* (argumente) pentru şi contra.

probability [ˌprobə'biliti] *s.* probabilitate ; posibilitate ; *in all* ~ după toate probabilităţile.

probable ['probəbl] *adj.* probabil.

probably ['probəbli] *adv.* probabil.

probation [prə'beiʃn] *s.* verificare ; stagiu (de candidat) ; eliberare provizorie.

probationer [prə'beiʃnə] *s.* practicant ; candidat.

probe [proub] *s. med.* sondă. *vt.* a sonda.

probity ['proubiti] *s.* cinste ; bunătate.

problem ['probləm] *s.* problemă.

procedure [prə'siːdʒə] *s.* procedeu ; procedură.

proceed [prə'siːd] *vt.* a înainta ; a continua ; a face proces.

proceeding [prə'siːdiŋ] *s.* purtare ; *pl. jur.* acţiune în justiţie ; *pl.* dezbateri ; procese-verbale.

proceeds ['prousiːdz] *s. pl.* profit.

process ['prouses] *s.* proces ; procedeu. *vt.* a prelucra ; a da în judecată.

procession [prə'seʃn] *s.* procesiune.

proclaim [prə'kleim] *vt.* a proclama ; a dezvălui.

proclamation [ˌproklə'meiʃn] *s.* proclamaţie.

proclivity ['prə'kliviti] *s.* înclinaţie.

procrastinate [pro'kræstineit] *vi.* a amîna.

proctor ['proktə] *s.* cestor.

procurator ['prokjureitə] *s.* procuror ; magistrat.

procure [prə'kjuə] *vt.* a procura.

prod [prod] *s.* ghiont. *vt.* a înghionti ; a aţîţa.

prodigal ['prɔdigl] s., adj. risipitor.

prodigality [,prɔdi'gæliti] s. abundenţă ; mărinimie ; risipă.

prodigious [prə'didʒəs] adj. uriaş ; uluitor.

prodigy ['prɔdidʒi] s. minune ; raritate.

produce[1] ['prɔdju:s] s. produs ; rezultat.

produce[2] [prə'dju:s] vt. a produce ; a scoate ; a arăta. vi. a crea ; a produce.

producer [prə'dju:sə] s. producător ; regizor (principal).

product ['prɔdəkt] s. produs ; rezultat.

production [prə'dʌkʃn] s. producţie.

productive [prə'dʌktiv] adj. productiv.

profess [prə'fes] vt. a declara ; a susţine ; a profesa.

profession [prə'feʃn] s. profesi(un)e ; declaraţie ; jurămînt.

professional [prə'feʃənl] s. (liber-)profesionist. adj. profesional ; profesionist.

professor [prə'fesə] s. profesor (universitar).

proffer ['prɔfə] vt. a oferi ; a întinde.

proficient [prə'fiʃnt] s., adj. expert.

profile ['proufi:l] s. profil. vt. a arăta din profil.

profit ['prɔfit] s. profit ; cîştig. vt. a cîştiga ; a aduce (ca profit). vi. a profita.

profitable ['prɔfitəbl] adj. rentabil ; util.

profiteer [,prɔfi'tiə] s. profitor. vi. a stoarce profituri.

profitless ['prɔfitlis] adj. inutil.

profligate ['prɔfligit] s., adj. risipitor ; destrăbălat.

profound [prə'faund] adj. profund ; intens ; serios.

profuse [prə'fju:s] adj. abundent ; generos.

profusion [prə'fju:ʒn] s. abundenţă ; risipă.

progeny ['prɔdʒini] s. progenitură ; odraslă ; descendenţi.

prognosticate [prɔg'nɔstikeit] vt. a prezice.

program(me) ['prougræm] s. program ; spectacol ; plan. vt. a programa ; a plănui.

progress[1] ['prougres] s. progres ; dezvoltare ; înaintare.

progress[2] [prɤ'gres] vi. a progresa ; a se dezvolta.

progression [prə'greʃn] s. progres(ie).

progressive [prə'gresiv] s. progresist. adj. progresist ; progresiv.

prohibit [prə'hibit] vt. a interzice.

prohibition [,proui'biʃn] s. interzicere ; prohibiţie (alcoolică).

project[1] ['prɔdʒekt] s. proiect ; plan ; lucrare ; construcţie.

project[2] [prə'dʒekt] vt. a proiecta ; a plănui. vi. a ieşi în afară.

projection [prə'dʒekʃn] s. proiectare ; proiecţie ; proeminenţă.

projector [prə'dʒektə] s. proiectant ; proiector.

proletarian [,proule'tɛəriən] s., adj. proletar.

proletariat [,proule'tɛəriət] s. proletariat.

prologue ['proulɔg] s. prolog.

prolong [prə'lɔŋ] vt. a prelungi; a extinde.

prolongation [ˌproulɔŋ'geiʃn] s. prelungire; prelungitor.

prom [prɔm] s. concert de promenadă.

promenade [prɔmi'nɑːd] s. promenadă. vi. a se plimba.

prominence ['prɔminəns] s. proeminenţă; ridicătură.

prominent ['prɔminənt] adj. proeminent; remarcabil.

promiscuous [prə'miskjuəs] adj. amestecat; dezordonat.

promise ['prɔmis] s. făgăduială; perspectivă. vt., vi. a promite.

promising ['prɔmisiŋ] adj. promiţător.

promissory note ['prɔmisəri nout] s. cambie.

promote [prə'mout] vt. a promova; a susţine.

promotion [prə'mouʃn] s. înaintare; promovare.

prompt [prɔmt] s. teatru replică suflată. adj. prompt. vt. a sufla (cuvinte); a îndemna.

prompter ['prɔmtə] s. sufler.

prone [proun] adj. înclinat; cu faţa în jos.

prong [prɔŋ] s. (dinte de) furcă.

pronoun ['prounaun] s. pronume.

pronounce [prə'nauns] vt. a pronunţa; a rosti; a anunţa; a declara. vi. a se declara; a se pronunţa.

pronunciation [prəˌnʌnsi'eiʃn] s. pronunţare.

proof [pruːf] s. probă; şpalt. adj. impermeabil; de netrecut; refractar.

proof-reader ['pruːfˌriːdə] s. poligr. corector.

prop [prɔp] s. proptea; reazem. vt. a sprijini; a propti.

propaganda [ˌprɔpə'gændə] s. propagandă. adj. propagandistic.

propagate ['prɔpəgeit] vt., vr. a (se) propaga.

propel [prə'pel] vt. a împinge; a mîna înainte.

propeller [prə'pelə] s. elice.

propensity [prə'pensiti] s. înclinaţie; tendinţă.

proper ['prɔpə] adj. corespunzător; corect; decent; propriu(-zis).

properly ['prɔpəli] adv. cum se cuvine; serios; complet.

propertied ['prɔpətid] adj. înstărit; avut.

property ['prɔpəti] s. proprietate; avere; pl. recuzită.

property man ['prɔpətiˌmæn] s. recuziter.

prophecy ['prɔfisi] s. profeţie.

prophesy ['prɔfisai] vt., vi. a proroci.

prophet ['prɔfit] s. profet.

propitiate [prə'piʃieit] vt. a linişti; a linguşi.

propitiatory [prə'piʃiətri] adj. împăciuitor; linguşitor.

propitious [prə'piʃəs] adj. favorabil.

proportion [prə'pɔːʃn] s. proporţie; măsură. vt. a proporţiona; a împărţi egal.

proposal [prə'pouzl] s. propunere; plan; cerere în căsătorie.

propose [prə'pouz] vt. a propune; a oferi; a intenţiona. vi. a cere mîna (cuiva).

proposition [ˌprɔpə'ziʃn] s. afirmaţie; propunere; teoremă.

proprietary [prə'praiətri] adj. de proprietate; brevetat.

proprietor [prə'praiətə] s. proprietar ; deţinătorul unui patent.

propriety [prə'praiəti] s. decenţă; convenţii (morale) ; corectitudine.

props [prɔps] s. recuzită.

prorogue [prə'roug] vt. a proroga.

proscenium [pro'si:njəm] s. avanscenă.

proscribe [pros'kraib] vt. a proscrie.

prose [prouz] s. proză ; parte prozaică. vi. a ţine predici.

prosecute ['prɔsikju:t] vt. a urmări în justiţie.

prosecution [,prɔsi'kju:ʃn] s. urmărire în justiţie ; acuzare ; procuror ; ministerul public.

prosecutor ['prɔsikju:tə] s. acuzator ; procuror.

proselyte ['prɔsilait] s. prozelit.

prospect¹ ['prɔspekt] s. perspectivă.

prospect² [prəs'pekt] vt., vi. a prospecta.

prospective [prəs'pektiv] adj. viitor ; probabil.

prospectus [prəs'pektəs] s. prospect.

prosper ['prɔspə] vi. a prospera.

prosperous ['prɔsprəs] adj. prosper ; înfloritor.

prostitute ['prɔstitju:t] s. prostituată. vt. a prostitua.

prostitution [,prɔsti'tju:ʃn] s. prostituţie ; prostituare.

prostrate¹ ['prɔstreit] s. prosternat ; culcat pe burtă ; fig. învins ; istovit ; toropit ; abătut.

prostrate² [pros'treit] vt. a trînti la pămînt ; a înfrînge ; a zdrobi. vr. a se trînti la pămînt ; a se ploconi.

prostration [prɔs'treiʃn] s. prostraţie ; deprimare ; istovire.

prosy ['prouzi] adj. plicticos ; monoton ; fără haz.

protect [prə'tekt] vt. a apăra ; a proteja.

protection [prə'tekʃn] s. protecţie ; apărător ; protecţionism (vamal).

protective [prə'tektiv] adj. protector.

protégé ['proutezei] s. protejat.

protein ['prouti:n] s. proteină.

protest¹ ['proutest] s. protest.

protest² [prə'test] vt. a afirma ; a susţine. vi. a protesta.

protestant ['prɔtistənt] s., adj. protestant.

protestation [,proutes'teiʃn] s. afirmaţie ; protest.

proton ['proutɔn] s. proton.

protract [prə'trækt] vt. a prelungi ; a tergiversa.

protractor [prə'træktə] s. raportor (pentru unghiuri).

protrude [prə'tru:d] vi. a ieşi în afară.

protuberant [prə'tju:brnt] adj. holbat ; umflat.

proud [praud] adj. mîndru ; orgolios ; trufaş ; splendid. adv. cu mîndrie.

prove [pru:v] vt. a dovedi ; a verifica. vi., vr. a se dovedi.

proverb ['prɔvəb] s. proverb.

provide [prə'vaid] vt. a furniza ; a aduce ; a prevedea. vi.: to ~ for a întreţine; a susţine.

provided [prə'vaidid] conj.: ~ that cu condiţia ca.

providence ['prɔvidns] s. cumpătare ; providenţă.

provident ['prɔvidnt] adj. prevăzător.

province ['prɔvins] s. provincie ; domeniu ; competenţă.

provision [prə'viʒn] s. prevedere; grijă ; pregătire ; clauză ; pl. provizii. vt. a aproviziona. ⌣

provisional [prə'viʒənl] adj. provizoriu.

proviso [prə'vaizou] s. clauză.

provocation [‚prɔvə'keiʃn] s. provocare ; supărare ; pacoste.

provocative [prə'vɔkətiv] adj. provocător ; supărător ; aţîţător.

provoke [prə'vouk] vt. a stîrni ; a aţîţa ; a enerva ; a provoca.

provoking [prə'voukiŋ] adj. enervant ; supărător.

provost ['prɔvəst] s. director ; magistrat.

prow [prau] s. proră.

prowess ['prauis] s. curaj ; îndemînare ; faptă de arme.

prowl [praul] s. pîndă. vi. a sta la pîndă ; a se învîrti după pradă.

proximate ['prɔksimit] adj. proxim ; următor.

proxy ['prɔksi] s. procurist ; delegat ; procură.

prude [pru:d] s. persoană (de o moralitate) afectată.

prudence ['pru:dns] s. prudenţă.

prudent ['pru:dnt] adj. prudent ; circumspect ; înţelept.

prudery ['pru:dəri] s. moralitate exagerată.

prudish ['pru:diʃ] adj. ultramoralist ; prefăcut.

prune [pru:n] s. prună uscată. vt. a reteza ramurile (la copaci) ; a curăţa (de balast).

prurient ['pruəriənt] adj. obscen; lasciv.

Prussian ['prʌʃn] s., adj. prusac(ă).

pry [prai] vt. a ridica ; a sparge. vi. a se amesteca.

psalm [sɑ:m] s. psalm.

pshaw [pʃɔ:] interj. pfui.

psychiatrist [sai kaiətrist] s. psihiatru.

psychology [sai'kɔlədʒi] s. psihologie.

psychopath ['saikopæθ] s. bolnav de nervi.

pub [pʌb] s. cîrciumă ; cafenea.

public ['pʌblik] s. public ; naţiune. adj. public ; naţional ; social ; obştesc.

publican ['pʌblikən] s. cîrciumar.

publication [‚pʌbli'keiʃn] s. publicare ; publicaţie.

public house ['pʌblik'haus] s. berărie ; cîrciumă.

publicity [pʌb'lisiti] s. reclamă ; publicitate.

public school ['pʌblik'sku:l] s. liceu (cu caracter) aristocratic.

public servant ['pʌblik'sə:vnt] s. funcţionar de Stat.

publish ['pʌbliʃ] vt. a publica ; a anunţa.

publisher ['pʌbliʃə] s. editor.

puck [pʌk] s. spiriduş.

pucker ['pʌkə] s. creţ. vt. a încreţi. vi. a se zbîrci.

pudding ['pudiŋ] s. budincă ; cîrnaţi.

puddle ['pʌdl] s. băltoacă ; noroi ; lut. vi. a frămînta ; a acoperi cu lut. vr. a se bălăci.

pudgy ['pʌdʒi] adj. scurt şi îndesat.

puff [pʌf] s. pufăit ; (ră)suflare ; puf ; reclamă deşănţată. vt. a pufăi ; a sufla ; a face reclamă la ; a supralicita ; to ~ up

a umfla; a face să se îngîmfe.
vi. a sufla; a respira greu;
a pufăi; a se înălţa.
puff box ['pʌfbɔks] *s.* pudrieră.
puffy ['pʌfi] *adj.* umflat; gîfî-
ind; pufăitor.
pug [pʌg] *s.* mops.
pugnacious [pʌg'neiʃəs] *adj.* combativ.
pull [pul] *vt.* a trage; a tîrî;
a împinge; *to ~ down* a dărîma; a slăbi; a deprima;
to ~ out a smulge; *to ~ up*
a trage la scară. *vi.* a trage;
a vîsli; *to ~ round* a-şi reveni
după boală; *to ~ through* a o
scoate la capăt; a se face
bine; *to ~ together* a-şi uni
forţele; *to ~ up* a se opri;
a trage la scară. *vr.: to ~
oneself together* a-şi veni în fire.
pulley ['puli] *s.* scripete.
pull-over ['pul,ouvə] *s.* pulover.
pulp [pʌlp] *s.* pulpă de fructe;
carne (moale). *vt.* a zdrobi.
pulpit ['pulpit] *s.* amvon; cler;
carieră preoţească.
pulsate [pʌl'seit] *vt.* a zgudui.
vi. a pulsa; a vibra.
pulse [pʌls] *s.* puls; păstăi. *vi.*
a pulsa.
pumice (stone) ['pʌmis (stoun)]
s. piatră ponce.
pummel ['pʌml] *vt.* a bate cu
pumnii.
pump [pʌmp] *s.* pompă; cişmea;
pantof fără toc. *vt.* a pompa;
a smulge; a stoarce (informaţii); *to ~ smb.'s hand*
a scutura mîna cuiva. *vi.* a
pompa.
pumpkin ['pʌmkin] *s.* dovleac.
pun [pʌn] *s.* joc de cuvinte.
vi. a face jocuri de cuvinte.

punch [pʌntʃ] *s.* punci; energie;
cleşte de perforat; pumn
(puternic). *vt.* a perfora; a
lovi puternic cu pumnul.
Punch [pʌntʃ] *s.* marionetă;
ziar umoristic englez.
Punch and Judy show ['pʌntʃ
ən'dʒuːdi,ʃou] *s.* teatru de păpuşi.
punctilious [pʌŋ'tiljəs] *adj.* meticulos; ceremonios.
punctual ['pʌŋtjuəl] *adj.* punctual; scrupulos.
punctuate ['pʌŋtjueit] *vt.* a
puncta; a pune punctuaţia
la (un text)
punctuation [,pʌŋtju'eiʃn] *s.*
punctuaţie.
punctuation marks [,pʌŋtju'eiʃn
'maːks] *s. pl.* semne de punctuaţie.
puncture ['pʌŋktʃə] *s.* înţepătură; gaură; pană de cauciuc.
vt. a înţepa; a găuri; a strica.
pungent ['pʌndʒnt] *adj.* picant;
înţepător; ascuţit.
punish ['pʌniʃ] *vt.* a pedepsi;
a bate.
punishment ['pʌniʃmənt] *s.* pedeapsă; înfrîngere.
punitive ['pjuːnitiv] *adj.* de
pedeapsă.
punt [pʌnt] *s.* ponton; barcă
cu fundul lat.
puny ['pjuːni] *adj.* slab; pirpiriu; prăpădit.
pup [pʌp] *s.* căţeluş; pui de
lup etc.
pupil ['pjuːpl] *s.* elev; *anat.*
pupilă.
puppet ['pʌpit] *s.* marionetă,
puppet show ['pʌpit,ʃou] *s.*
teatru de marionete.
puppy ['pʌpi] *s.* căţeluş; pui

de vulpe, de lup etc.; tînăr obraznic.

purblind ['pə:blaind] *adj.* atins de orbul găinilor.

purchase ['pə:tʃəs] *s.* achiziţie; cumpărătură. *vt.* a cumpăra; a obţine.

purchasing power ['pə:tʃəsiŋ 'pauə] *s.* putere de cumpărare.

pure [pjuə] *adj.* pur; distinct; curat (la suflet); simplu; perfect.

purely ['pjuəli] *adv.* curat; total; pur şi simplu.

purge [pə:dʒ] *s.* purgativ; epurare. *vt.* a curăţi; a epura.

purity ['pjuəriti] *s.* puritate; nevinovăţie.

purl [pə:l] *s.* gîlgîit; murmur. *vi.* a gîlgîi; a murmura.

purlieus ['pə:lju:z] *s. pl.* periferie.

purloin [pə:'lɔin] *vt.* a şterpeli.

purple ['pə:pl] *s.* vineţiu; purpuriu; purpură. *adj.* vînăt; purpuriu; roşu.

purport ['pə:pət] *s.* sens; scop; semnificaţie. *vt.* a susţine; a sugera.

purpose ['pə:pəs] *s.* scop; folos; *on ~* anume; *to the ~* folositor; la chestiune; *to no ~* inutil. *vt.* a intenţiona; a-şi propune.

purposeful ['pə:pəsfl] *adj.* hotărît; semnificativ.

purposely ['pə:pəsli] *adj.* intenţionat.

purr [pə:] *vi.* a murmura; *(d. pisică)* a toarce.

purse [pə:s] *s.* pungă; bani; răsplată. *vt.* a pungi; a increţi.

purse strings ['pə:s'striŋz] *s. pl.* baierele pungii.

pursuance [pə'sjuəns] *s.* urmărire; îndeplinire.

pursue [pə'sju:] *vt.* a urma; a urmări; a continua.

pursuer [pə'sjuə] *s.* urmăritor.

pursuit [pə'sju:t] *s.* urmărire; ocupaţie.

purvey [pə:'vei] *vt.* a furniza.

purveyor [pə:'vɛə] *s.* furnizor.

pus [pʌs] *s.* puroi.

push [puʃ] *s.* împingere; energie; hotărîre. *vt.* a împinge; a forţa. *vi.: to ~ along* sau *off* a porni; a pleca.

push-cart ['puʃkɑ:t] *s.* cărucior (de copil).

pusher ['puʃə] *s.* arivist.

pusillanimous [,pju:si'læniməs] *adj.* timid; slab; fricos.

puss [pus] *s.* pisică.

puss-in-boots ['pusin'bu:ts] *s.* motanul încălţat.

pussy ['pusi] *s.* pisicuţă; mîţişor (de salcie etc.).

put [put] *inf., trec. şi part. trec. vt.* a pune; a aşeza; a scrie; a exprima; a duce; a arunca; a evalua; *to ~ across* a duce la bun sfîrşit; *to ~ aside* sau *away* sau *by* a strînge (bani); *to ~ back* a pune la loc; a da înapoi (ceasul); *to ~ down fig.* a înăbuşi; a scrie; a înscrie; a micşora; *to ~ forth* a scoate, a publica; *to ~ forward* a propune, a înainta; *to ~ off* a amîna; a împiedica; *to ~ on* a se îmbrăca cu; a adopta; a căpăta; *to ~ out* a stinge; a scoate; a tulbura; a manifesta; a întinde; a produce; *to ~ through* a îndeplini; a da legătura; *to ~ together*

a alcătui; a aduna; *to ~ up*
a ridica; a găzdui; a manifesta; a născoci; *to ~ smb.
up to* a aţîţa pe cineva la.
vi.: to ~ about a schimba
direcţia; *to ~ off, to ~ out*
a porni; *to ~ up* a se acomoda;
a se instala; a rămîne (peste
noapte etc.); *to ~ up with*
a suporta; a se deprinde cu.
putrid ['pju:trid] *adj.* descom-
pus; scîrbos.

puttee ['pʌti:] *s.* moletieră.
putty ['pʌti] *s.* chit; liant. *vt.*
a chitui.
puzzle ['pʌzl] *s.* enigmă; joc
distractiv. *vt.* a zăpăci; *to ~
out* a rezolva.
pygmy ['pigmi] *s.* pigmeu. *adj.*
neînsemnat.
pyjamas [pə'dʒɑ:məz] *s.* pijama.
pyramid ['pirəmid] *s.* piramidă.
pyre ['paiə] *s.* rug.

Q

Q [kju:] *s.* Q, q.
quack [kwæk] *s.* măcăit; şarlatan; vraci. *adj.* (de) şarlatan;
fals; ignorant. *vi.* a măcăi;
a flecări.
quackery ['kwækəri] *s.* şarlatanie.
quadrangle ['kwɔ,dræŋgl] *s.* dreptunghi.
quadrant ['kwɔdrnt] *s.* cadran.
quadrilateral [,kwɔdri'lætrl] *s.*
patrulater. *adj.* cu patru laturi.
quadrille [kwə'dril] *s.* cadril.
quadruped ['kwɔdruped] *s.* patruped.
quadruple ['kwɔdrupl] *s.* cva-
druplu. *adj.* împătrit. *vt., vi.*
a (se) împătri.
quadruplet ['kwɔdruplit] *s.* grup
de patru; *pl.* patru gemeni.
quaff [kwɑ:f] *vt.* a sorbi.
quagmire ['kwægmaiə] *s.* mlaştină; marasm.
quail [kweil *s.* prepeliţă; pitpalac.
quaint [kweint] *adj.* ciudat;
nostim.

quake [kweik] *s.* (cu)tremur
vi. a tremura.
quaker ['kweikə] *s. rel.* quaker;
tremurător. *adj.* sobru, simplu.
qualify ['kwɔlifai] *vt.* a califica; a modifica. *vi.* a se califica; a reuşi.
qualitative ['kwɔlitətiv] *adj.* calitativ.
quality ['kwɔliti] *s.* calitate;
valoare.
qualm [kwɔ:m] *s.* remuşcare.
quandary ['kwɔndəri] *s.* îndoială; dilemă.
quantitative ['kwɔntitətiv] *adj.*
cantitativ.
quantity ['kwɔntiti] *s.* cantitate;
mărime; *pl.* abundenţă.
quarantine ['kwɔrnti:n] *s.* carantină. *vt.* a pune la carantină.
quarrel ['kwɔrl] *s.* ceartă; plîngere. *vi.* a se certa.
quarrelsome ['kwɔrlsəm] *adj.*
certăreţ; nervos.
quarry ['kwɔri] *s.* pradă; cari-

eră; mină. *vt.* a exploata
(un zăcămînt etc.); a dezgropa.

quart [kwɔ:t] *s.* (măsură de
un) litru; quart.

quarter ['kwɔ:tə] *s.* sfert; trimestru; punct cardinal; *amer.*
25 de cenți; sursă (de infor-
mație etc.); cartier; *pl.* locuință; cantonament; *mar.* pupă; *at close ~s* foarte aproape.
vt. a împărți în patru; a
încartirui.

quarterday ['kwɔ:tədei] *s.* ziua
cîștiurilor; scadență.

quarterly ['kwɔ:təli] *s., adj.,
adv.* trimestrial.

quartermaster ['kwɔ:tə͵mɑ:stə] *s.*
ofițer de administrație; intendent.

quartet(te) [kwɔ:'tet] *s.* cvartet;
grup de patru persoane.

quarto ['kwɔ:tou] *s.* format
sau ediție in cvarto.

quash [kwɔʃ] *vt.* a anula; a
nimici; a stinge.

quaver ['kweivə] *s.* tremur;
tremolo; *muz.* optime. *vt.* a
zgudui. *vi.* a tremura; a vorbi
sau a cînta tremurat; a fremăta.

quay [ki:] *s.* chei.

queasy ['kwi:zi] *adj.* grețos;
prea delicat.

queen [kwi:n] *s.* regină; zeiță;
damă (la cărți).

queenly ['kwi:nli] *adj.* maiestuos;
generos.

queer [kwiə] *adj.* ciudat; dubios;
trăsnit. *vt.* a strica.

quell [kwel] *vt.* a înăbuși.

quench [kwentʃ] *vt.* a stinge;
a potoli; a răci; a distruge;
a nărui.

querulous ['kweruləs] *adj.* plîngăreț; neliniștit.

query ['kwiəri] *s* (semn de)
întrebare; problemă. *vt.* a întreba; a chestiona.

quest [kwest] *s* căutare; cercetare; lucru căutat; *in ~
of* în căutare de. *vi.* a căuta.

question ['kwestʃn] *s.* problemă;
(semn de) întrebare; anchetă;
obiecție; îndoială. *vt.* a întreba; a interoga; a pune la
îndoială. *vi.* a se întreba.

questionable ['kwestʃənəbl] *adj.*
îndoielnic; dubios.

questioningly ['kwestʃəniŋli] *adv.*
întrebător.

question-mark ['kwestʃnmɑ:k] *s.*
semn de întrebare.

queue [kju:] *s.* coadă. *vi.* a
face coadă.

quibble ['kwibl] *s.* joc de cuvinte; eschivare de la un
răspuns. *vi.* a se eschiva de
la un răspuns; a glumi.

quick [kwik] *s.* carne vie;
fig. inimă; *the ~ and the
dead* viii și morții. *adj.* iute;
vioi; prompt; ager; pripit;
viu.

quicken ['kwikn] *vt., vi.* a (se)
grăbi.

quick-lime ['kwiklaim] *s.* var
nestins.

quick march ['kwik'mɑ:tʃ] *s.*
pas alergător.

quicksand ['kwiksænd] *s.* nisip
mișcător; capcană.

quicksilver ['kwik͵silvə] *s.* mercur.

quid [kwid] *s.* tutun de mestecat;
liră sterlină.

quiescent [kwai'esnt] *adj.* pasiv;
tăcut; nemișcat; liniștit.

quiet ['kwaiət] *s.* liniște; tăcere;

calm ; *on the* ~ în taină.
adj. liniştit ; sobru ; tăcut ;
fără zgomot ; paşnic; tainic. *vt.,*
vi. a (se) linişti.

quieten ['kwaiətən] *vt., vi.* a
(se) linişti.

quietude ['kwaiitju:d] *s.* calm ;
tihnă.

quietus [kwai'i:təs] *s.* moarte.

quill [kwil] *s.* pană de gîscă ;
ţeapă.

quill-driver ['kwil'draivə] *s.* conţopist ; scrib ; gazetar.

quilt [kwilt] *s.* plapumă ; cuvertură. *vt.* a matlasa.

quince [kwins] *s.* gutui(e).

quip [kwip] *s.* glumă ; remarcă
caustică. *vi.* a glumi (sarcastic).

quire ['kwaiə] *s.* testea (de
hîrtie) ; fascicul ; două duzini ;
cor.

quit [kwit] *adj.* liber ; chit.
vt. a părăsi ; a lăsa; ~ *doing*
that nu mai fă aşa. *vi.* a pleca.

quite [kwait] *adv.* complet ;
foarte ; destul de ; ~ *a few*
destui. *interj.* chiar aşa.

quits [kwits] *adj.* chit ; egal.

quiver ['kwivə] *s.* tolbă de
săgeţi ; tremur. *vt.* a face să
tremure. *vi.* a tremura.

quixotic [kwik'sɔtik] *adj.* utopic ;
donchişotesc.

quiz [kwiz] *s.* întrebare ; interogatoriu ; concurs. *vt.* a interoga ; a necăji ; a tachina.

quizzical ['kwizikl] *adj.* ciudat ;
comic ; ironic ; întrebător.

quod [kwɔd] *s.* închisoare.

quota ['kwoutə] *s.* cotă ; normă.

quotation [kwo'teiʃn] *s.* citat ;
fin. cotă ; deviz.

quotation marks [kwo'teiʃn mɑ:ks]
s. pl. ghilimele.

quote [kwout] *vt.* a cita ; a
deschide ghilimelele ; a menţiona.

quoth [kwouθ] *inv. vt. pers.*
a III-a. *sg.* zice.

quotient ['kwouʃnt] *s.* cît.

R

R [ɑ:] *s.* R, r.

rabbi ['ræbai] *s.* rabin.

rabbit ['ræbit] *s.* iepure (de
casă).

rabble ['ræbl] *s.* gloată.

rabid ['ræbid] *adj.* turbat ; nebunesc.

rabies ['reibi:z] *s.* turbare.

race [reis] *s.* cursă ; întrecere ;
rasă ; neam ; canal ; şanţ. *vt.*
a goni. *vi.* a alerga (într-o
cursă).

racer ['reisə] *s.* cal ; barcă ;
maşină de curse.

racial ['reiʃl] *adj.* rasial.

racialism ['reiʃəlizəm] *s.* ra-
sism.

racing ['reisiŋ] *s.* curse· (de
cai). *adj.* de (la) curse.

rack [ræk] *s.* grătar ; cuier ;
plasă (pentru bagaje) ; roată
(pentru tortură) ; distrugere.
vt. a tortura ; *to* ~ *one's*
brains a-şi stoarce creierii.

racket ['rækit] *s.* rachetă (de tenis) ; zarvă ; escrocherii.

racketeer [‚ræki'tiə] *s. amer.* profitor ; afacerist.

racquet ['rækit] *s.* rachetă (de tenis).

racy ['reisi] *adj.* intens ; picant ; vioi.

radiance ['reidjəns] *s.* strălucire.

radiant ['reidjənt] *adj.* strălucit(or).

radiate ['reidieit] *adj.* radial ; iradiant. *vt.* a iradia. *vi.* a radia ; a străluci.

radical ['rædikl] *s., adj.* radical ; progresist.

radii ['reidiai] *s. pl. de la* **radius.**

radio ['reidiou] *s., adj.* radio.

radiogram ['reidiogræm] *s.* radiografie ; telegramă-radio ; radio cu picup.

radio set ['reidioset] ᴧ (aparat de) radio ; emiţător.

radish ['rædiʃ] *s.* ridiche.

radius ['reidjəs] *s.* rază (de acţiune)

R.A.F. ['ɑːrei'ef] *s.* aviaţia militară britanică.

raffish ['ræfiʃ] *adj.* depravat.

raft [rɑːft] *s.* plută (pe rîu). *vi.* a merge cu pluta.

rafter ['rɑːftə] *s.* plutaş ; grindă.

rag [ræg] *s.* cîrpă ; zdreanţă ; *fig.* fiţuică ; gălăgie.

ragamuffin ['rægə‚mᴧfin] *s.* zdrenţăros ; golan.

rage [reidʒ] *s.* furie ; modă ; pasiune. *vt.* a urla ; a bîntui.

ragged ['rægid] *adj.* colţuros ; neţesălat ; zdrenţăros.

ragtag and bobtail ['rægtægən 'bɔbteil] *s.* drojdia societăţii.

ragtime ['rægtaim] *s.* jaz sincopat.

raid [reid] *s.* incursiune ; raid ; jaf. *vt.* a bîntui ; a invada.

rail [reil] *s.* balustradă ; şină ; suport (pentru prosop etc.) ; *by* ~ cu trenul ; *off the* ~s deraiat. *vt.* a critica ; a batjocori.

railing ['reiliŋ] *s.* gard ; ocară ; batjocură.

raillery ['reiləri] *s.* ironie ; tachinerie.

railroad ['reilroud], **railway** ['reilwei] *s.* cale ferată.

rain [rein] *s.* ploaie ; ~ *or shine* pe orice vreme. *vt.* a turna. *vi.* a ploua; *it never* ~s *out it pours aprox.* o nenorocire nu vine niciodată singură.

rainbow ['reinbou] *s.* curcubeu.

raincoat ['reinkout] *s.* fulgarin.

rainfall ['reinfɔːl] *s.* (cantitate de) ploaie.

rain-gauge ['reingeidʒ] *s.* pluviometru.

rainy ['reini] *adj.* ploios.

raise [reiz] *s.* spor de salariu. *vt.* a înălţa ; a ridica ; a clădi ; a stîrni ; a spori ; a creşte ; a înjgheba ; a aduna.

raisin ['reizn] *s.* stafidă.

rake [reik] *s.* greblă ; depravat ; don juan. *vt.* a grebla ; a strînge ; *to* ~ *up* a stîrni ; a reînvia.

rakish ['reikiʃ] *adj.* arătos ; elegant ; imoral ; stricat.

rally ['ræli] *s.* strîngere ; adunare ; miting ; revenire. *vt.* a strînge ; a aduna ; *fig.* a mobiliza ; a ironiza ; a tachina. *vi.* a se aduna ; a se însănătoşi ; a-şi reveni.

ram [ræm] *s.* berbec. *vt.* a zdrobi; a izbi; a înfige; a băga.

ramble ['ræmbl] *s.* hoinăreală. *vi.* a hoinări; a bate cîmpii.

rambling ['ræmbliŋ] *s.* hoinăreală; divagație. *adj.* hoinar; dezlînat.

ramp [ræmp] *s.* rampă. *vi.* a se ridica; a se agita.

rampant ['ræmpənt] *adj.* furios; răspîndit; în floare.

rampart ['ræmpɑːt] *s.* meterez.

ramshackle ['ræm͵ʃækl] *adj.* șubred.

ran [ræn] *vt., vi. trec. de la* **run.**

ranch [rɑːntʃ] *s.* fermă de animale.

rancher ['rɑːntʃə] *s.* proprietarul unei ferme de animale.

rancid ['rænsid] *adj.* rînced.

ranco(u)r ['ræŋkə] *s.* ranchiună; pică.

random ['rændəm] *s.: at ∼* la întîmplare. *adj.* făcut la întîmplare.

rang [ræŋ] *vt., vi. trec. de la* **ring.**

range [reindʒ] *s.* rînd; șir; distanță; bătaie (a unei arme); întindere; domeniu; limite; sortiment; *mil.* poligon; mașină de gătit; plită. *vt.* a aranja; a colinda. *vi.* a hoinări; a se întinde; a varia.

ranger ['reindʒə] *s.* paznic de păduri; jandarm.

rank [ræŋk] *s.* rînd; șir; rang; *mil.* grad; categorie; *the ∼s* oamenii de rînd; *mil.* trupa. *adj.* încîlcit; grosolan. *vt.* a rîndui; a categorisi; a considera. *vi.* a se plasa. a fi considerat.

rank and file ['ræŋkən'fail] *s.* oamenii de rînd; *mil.* trupa.

rankle ['ræŋkl] *vi.* a supura; a nu se vindeca.

ransack ['rænsæk] *vt.* a scotoci; a jefui.

ransom ['rænsəm] *s.* (preț pentru) răscumpărare; plată. *vt.* a răscumpăra; a elibera (pe bani).

rant [rænt] *s.* retorică; perorație. *vt., vi.* a perora.

rap [ræp] *s.* bătaie ușoară (cu încheieturile degetelor). *vi.* a bate (cu încheieturile degetelor).

rapacious [rə'peiʃəs] *adj.* rapace.

rape [reip] *s.* rapiță; viol; răpire. *vt.* a viola; a răpi.

rapid ['ræpid] *s. geogr.* cataractă. *adj.* rapid; abrupt.

rapier ['reipjə] *s.* pumnal. *adj.* ascuțit.

rapprochement [ræ'prɔʃmɑːŋ] *s.* apropiere.

rapt [ræpt] *adj.* vrăjit; cufundat.

rapture ['ræptʃə] *s.* încîntare; extaz.

rapturous ['ræptʃərəs] *adj.* entuziast.

rare [reə] *adj.* rar; puțin(tel); prețios; minunat. *adv.* strașnic.

rarely ['reəli] *adv.* rar; rareori; teribil.

rascal ['rɑːskəl] *s.* ticălos.

rash [ræʃ] *s.* urticarie. *adj.* pripit; nesăbuit.

rasher ['ræʃə] *s.* feliuță.

rasp [rɑːsp] *s.* pilă; rașpilă; sunet aspru. *vt.* a pili; a aspri; a ʾenerva.

raspberry ['rɑːzbri] *s.* zmeură.

rat [ræt] *s.* șobolan; laș.

rate [reit] *s.* ritm; proporție; viteză; raport; valoare; taxă, grad; categorie; *at any* ~ în orice caz. *vt.* a aprecia; a ocărî; a evalua. *vi.* a valora`; a vorbi urît.

rate-setter ['reit¸setə] *s.* normator.

rather ['rɑːðə] *adv.* mai degrabă; destul (de). *interj.* oho (şi încă cum).

ratify ['rætifai] *vt.* a ratifica.

rating ['reitiŋ] *s.* evaluare; clasificaţie; categorie; valoare; ocară.

ratio ['reiʃiou] *s.* raport; proporţie.

ratiocination [¸rætiɔsi'neiʃn] *s.* raţionament.

ration ['ræʃn] *s.* raţie; *on* ~*s* raţiona(liza)t.*vt.* a raţiona(liza).

rational ['ræʃənl] *adj.* raţional; înţelept.

rationalist ['ræʃnəlist] *s., adj.* raţionalist.

rationalize ['ræʃnəlaiz] *vt.* a judeca raţional; a raţiona-(liza).

ratsbane ['rætsbein] *s.* otravă.

rattle ['rætl] *s.* sunătoare; cîrîitoare; zbîrnîitoare; clopoţei (ai şarpelui); horcăit; hîrîit; zornăit; gălăgie. *vt., vi.* a zornăi; a trăncăni; a hîrîi.

rattle-box ['rætlbɔks] *s.* sunătoare.

rattle-snake ['rætlsneik] *s.* şarpe cu clopoţei.

rattling ['rætliŋ] *adj.* zbîrnîitor; rapid; grozav. *adv.* straşnic; foarte.

raucous ['rɔːkəs] *adj.* răguşit; aspru.

ravage ['rævidʒ] *s.* distrugere; *pl.* ravagii. *vt.* a jefui; a distruge. *vi.* a face ravagii.

rave [reiv] *vi.* a aiura; a bîntui cu furie; a vorbi entuziast.

ravel ['rævl] *s.* nod; încurcătură. *vt.* a încurca; a deznoda.

raven ['reivn] *s.* corb. *adj.* negru.

ravenous ['rævinəs] *adj.* flămînd (ca un lup).

ravine [rə'viːn] *s.* rîpă; vîlcea.

raving ['reiviŋ] *s.* aiureală; *pl.* elucubraţii. *adj.* nebun. *adv.* nebuneşte.

ravish ['ræviʃ] *vt.* a răpi; a viola; a vrăji.

raw [rɔː] *s.* carne vie. *adj.* necopt; nepriceput; *(d. piele)* nelucrată; jupuită; *(d. rană)* nevindecată.

raw-boned ['rɔː'bound] *adj.* numai pielea şi oasele.

ray [rei] *s.* rază; *iht.* calcan. *vi.* a radia.

rayon ['reiɔn] *s.* mătase artificială.

raze [reiz] *vt.* a rade (de pe faţa pămîntului).

razor ['reizə] *s.* brici.

razor-blade ['reizəbleid] *s.* lamă de ras.

reach [riːtʃ] *s.* atingere; întindere; rază de acţiune; meandră. *vt.* a atinge; a sosi *sau* a ajunge la; a da de. *vi.* a se întinde; a ajunge.

reach-me-downs ['riːtʃmi'daunz] *s.pl.* haine (de) gata.

react [ri'ækt] *vi.* a reacţiona.

reaction [ri'ækʃn] *s.* reacţi(un)e.

read[1] [riːd] *s.* citire. *vt.* a citi; a studia; a ghici; a indica; a interpreta; *to* ~ *out* a citi (cu glas) tare. *vi.* a citi; a studia; a afla; a se citi.

read² [red] *adj.* citit. *vt.*, *vi. trec. şi part. trec. de la* **read.**

readable['ri:dəbl] *adj.* interesant; lizibil.

reader ['ri:də] *s.* cititor; lector (universitar); redactor (la editură); manual; antologie.

readily ['redili] *adv.* uşor; cu dragă inimă; imediat.

readiness ['redinis] *s.* pregătire; promptitudine; bunăvoinţă.

reading ['ri:diŋ] *s.* lectură; citire; cultură; interpretare. *adj.* studios; amator de lectură.

reading-lamp ['ri:diŋlæmp] *s.* lampă de masă.

reading-room ['ri:diŋrum] *s.* sală de lectură.

readjust ['ri:ə'dʒʌst] *vt.* a rearanja; a reprofila; a (re)-adapta.

ready ['redi] *adj.* pregătit; gata; rapid; prompt.

ready-made ['redi'meid] *adj.* (de) gata; copiat.

ready money ['redi'mʌni] *s.* bani gheaţă.

reagent [ri:'eidʒnt] *s.* reactiv; reacţie.

real [riəl] *adj.* real; *jur.* funciar; imobiliar. *adv.* adevărat; straşnic.

realism ['riəlizəm] *s.* realism.

realist ['riəlist] *s.*, *adj.* realist.

realistic [riə'listik] *adj.* realist.

reality [ri'æliti] *s.* realitate; veridicitate.

realization [ˌriəlai'zeiʃn] *s.* înţelegere; îndeplinire.

realize ['riəlaiz] *vt.* a înţelege; a îndeplini. *vi.* a-şi da seama.

really ['riəli]] *adv.* într-adevăr; *interog.* oare? zău?

realm [relm] *s.* regat; tărîm.

ream [ri:m] *s.* top de hîrtie.

reap [ri:p] *vt.* a secera; a recolta; *fig.* a culege. *vi.* a secera.

reaper ['ri:pə] *s.* secerător; secerătoare; combină.

reappear ['ri:ə'piə] *vi.* a reapărea.

reappraisal ['ri:ə'preizl] *s.* reconsiderare; realizare.

rear [riə] *s.* spate, urmă, dos. *vt.* a creşte; a hrăni. *vi.* a se cabra.

rear-admiral ['riə'ædmrl] *s.* contraamiral.

rear-guard ['riəga:d] *s.* ariergardă.

rearmament ['ri:'a:məmənt] *s.* reînarmare.

rearmost ['riəmoust] *adj.* cel de la urmă; cel din spate.

rearrange ['ri:ə'reindʒ] *vt.* a rearanja; a restabili.

reason ['ri:zn] *s.* judecată; raţiune; cauză; *in* ~ rezonabil. *vt.* a raţiona; a convinge. *vi.* a raţiona, a gîndi; a argumenta.

reasonable ['ri:znəbl] *adj.* rezonabil; chibzuit; raţional.

reasoning ['ri:zniŋ] *s.* judecată; argumente.

reassure [ˌri:ə'ʃuə] *vt.* **a** linişti.

rebate ['ri:beit] *s.* rabat, reducere.

rebel¹ ['rebl] *s.* rebel; răzvrătit.

rebel² [ri bel] *vi.* a se răzvrăti; a protesta.

rebellion [ri'beljən] *s.* răzvrătire.

rebellious [ri'beljəs] *adj.* rebel; nesupus.

rebirth ['ri:'bə:θ] *s.* renaştere.

rebound [ri'baund] *s.* ricoşeu. *vi.* a ricoşa; a sări din nou.

rebuff [ri'bʌf] s. ripostă; refuz. vt. a respinge.

rebuke [ri'bjuːk] s. reproş; admonestare. vt. a ocărî; a admonesta.

rebut [ri'bʌt] vt. a respinge.

recall [ri'kɔːl] s. rechemare. vt. a rechema; a evoca; a (-şi) aminti.

recapture ['riː'kæptʃə] s. prindere. vt. a recăpăta; a prinde (din nou).

recast ['riː'kɑːst] s. remodelare. vt. a remodela; a preface. vi. a se retrage; a da înapoi; a scădea; a se şterge.

recede [ri'siːd] vi. a se retrage; a da înapoi; a scădea; a se estompa.

receipt [ri'siːt] s. chitanţă; primire; reţetă (culinară); pl. încasări. vi. a da chitanţă pentru.

receive [ri'siːv] vt., vi. a primi; a cuprinde; a accepta.

receiver [ri'siːvə] s. primitor; receptor; tăinuitor.

recent ['riːsnt] adj. recent.

reception [ri'sepʃn] s. primire; recepţie.

recess [ri'ses] s. pauză; răgaz; sărbătoare; cotlon. vt. a ascunde; a împinge înapoi.

recession [ri'seʃn] s. retragere; amînare; econ. criză.

recipe ['resipi] s. reţetă.

recipient [ri'sipiənt] s. primitor; premiat.

reciprocate [ri'siprəkeit] vt. a răspunde la. vi. a fi complementar.

recital [ri'saitl] s. recital; recitare; povestire.

recitation [ˌresi'teiʃn] s. recitare; povestire.

recite [ri'sait] vt., vi. a recita; a povesti.

reckless ['reklis] adj. nepăsător; nesăbuit.

reckon ['rekn] vt. a socoti; a număra. vi. a socoti; a se bizui; to ~ on a se baza pe; to ~ with a ţine seama de; a se socoti cu.

reckoning ['rekəniŋ] s. socoteală; calcul; răfuială.

reclaim [ri'kleim] vt. a recupera; a îndrepta; a revendica.

recline [ri'klain] vt. a se bizui pe. vi. a se apleca; a se lăsa pe spate; a se culca.

recluse [ri'kluːs] s. pustnic.

recognition [ˌrekəg'niʃn] s. recunoaştere; consideraţie.

recognizance [ri'kɔgnizns] s. obligaţie; amendă.

recognize ['rekəgnaiz] vt. a recunoaşte.

recoil [ri'kɔil] s. recul; oroare. vi. a (se) da înapoi; a avea recul.

recollect [ˌrekə'lekt] vt., vi. a(-şi) aminti.

recollection [ˌrekə'lekʃn] s. amintire.

recommend [ˌrekə'mend] vt. a recomanda; a încredinţa; a lăuda; a face cinste (cu dat.).

recompense ['rekəmpens] s. răsplată. vt. a răsplăti.

reconcile ['rekənsail] vt. a împăca. vr. a se împăca.

reconciliation [ˌrekənsili'eiʃn] s. împăcare; împăciuire.

recondite [ri'kɔndait] adj. ascuns; obscur; modest.

reconnaissance [ri'kɔnisns] s. mil. recunoaştere.

reconnoitre [ˌrekə'nɔitə] vt. a

inspecta. *vi.* a face o recunoaştere.

reconsider ['riːkən'sidə] *vt.* a analiza din nou; a chibzui din nou.

reconstruct ['riːkən'strʌkt] *vt.* a reconstrui.

record[1] ['rekɔːd] *s.* proces-verbal; arhivă; document; urmă; dosar; record; disc (de patefon).

record[2] [ri'kɔːd] *vt.* a înregistra; a nota; a indica; a înscrie.

recorder [ri'kɔːdə] *s.* secretar; magnetofon.

recording [ri'kɔːdiŋ] *s.* înregistrare.

record-player ['rekɔːd͵plɛə] *s.* picup.

recourse [ri'kɔːs] *s.* apel; resursă.

recover [ri'kʌvə] *vt.* a recăpăta; a(-şi) regăsi. *vi.* a se reface; a-şi reveni.

recovery [ri'kʌvəri] *s.* însănătoşire; recăpătare; recuperare.

recreation [͵rekri'eiʃn] *s.* distracţie; recreaţie.

recrimination [ri͵krimi'neiʃn] *s.* acuzaţie; contraacuzaţie.

recruit [ri'kruːt] *s.* recrut; acolit. *vt.* a recruta; a reface. *vi.* a se reface.

rectangle ['rek͵tæŋgl] *s.* dreptunghi.

rectify ['rektifai] *vt.* a îndrepta; a rectifica.

rectitude ['rektitjuːd] *s.* cinste.

rector ['rektə] *s.* preot (anglican); paroh; rector.

recumbent [ri'kʌmbənt] *adj.* aplecat; culcat.

recuperate [ri'kjuːpreit] *vt.* a recupera; a(-şi) reface; a recăpăta. *vi.* a-şi reveni; a se reface.

recur [ri'kəː] *vi.* a reveni; a se repeta.

recurrence [ri'kʌrns] *s.* revenire; repetiţie.

recurrent [ri'kʌrnt] *adj.* recurent; care revine.

red [red] *s., adj.* roşu.

redbreast ['redbrest] *s.* măcăleandru.

redcoat ['redkout] *s. ist.* soldat britanic.

redden ['redn] *vt., vi.* a (se) înroşi.

reddish ['rediʃ] *adj.* roşiatic.

redeem [ri'diːm] *vt.* a răscumpăra; a recupera; a izbăvi.

redemption [ri'demʃn] *s.* izbăvire; răscumpărare.

red-handed ['red'hændid] *adj., adv.* (prins) asupra faptului.

red herring ['red'heriŋ] *s.* scrumbie afumată; *fig.* (mijloc de) diversiune.

red-hot ['red'hɔt] *adj.* înroşit în foc; fierbinte.

red-letter day ['red'letə͵dei] *s.* zi de sărbătoare.

red light ['red'lait] *s.* stop; semnal de primejdie.

redolent ['redolnt] *adj.* parfumat; evocator.

redouble [ri'dʌbl] *vt.* a îndoi; a înzeci.

redoubt [ri'daut] *s.* redută.

redoubtable [ri'dautəbl] *adj.* de temut; viteaz.

redress [ri'dres] *s.* compensare; îndreptare; răscumpărare. *vt.* a îndrepta; a răscumpăra; a redresa.

redskin ['redskin] *s.* (indian) piele-roşie.

red tape ['red'teip] *s.* birocraţie.

reduce [ri'dju:s] vt. a reduce; a micşora; a coborî. vi. a face cură de slăbire.

reduced circumstances [ri'dju:st'sə:kmstnsiz] s. pl. sărăcie; strîmtorare; scăpătare.

reduction [ri'dʌkʃn] s. reducere, micşorare.

redundance [ri'dʌndəns] s. surplus.

redundant [ri'dʌndənt] adj. supraabundent; suplimentar; inutil.

reduplication [ri,dju:pli'keiʃn] s. dublare; repetiţie.

reed [ri:d] s. stuf; trestie; muz. ancie; fluier.

reedy ['ri:di] adj. subţire ca o trestie; plin de stuf.

reef [ri:f] s. recif; stîncă; filon.

reek [ri:k] s. iz; miros. vi. a mirosi; a duhni.

reel [ri:l] s. bobină; rolă; rilă; dans scoţian; legănare. vi. a dansa; a se legăna; a fi ameţit; a se învîrti.

refectory [ri'fektri] s. sală de mese.

refer [ri'fə:] vt. a atribui; a trimite; a îndrepta. vi. a se referi; a face aluzie; a recurge.

referee [,refə'ri:] s. arbitru. vt., vi. a arbitra.

reference ['refrns] s. referire; referinţă; indicaţie; legătură.

reference book ['refrns,buk] s. carte documentară (dicţionar, enciclopedie etc.).

reference library ['refrns'laibrəri] s. bibliotecă de referinţă.

refill¹ ['ri:fil] s. rezervă (de creion etc.).

refill² ['ri:'fil] vt., vr. a (se) umple.

refine [ri'fain] vt., vi. a (se) rafina.

refinement [ri'fainmənt] s. rafinament; subtilitate.

refinery [ri'fainəri] s. rafinărie.

reflect [ri'flekt] vt. a reflecta; a ilustra; a exprima.

reflection [ri'flekʃn] s. reflecţie; răsfrîngere.

reflex ['ri:fleks] s. reflecţie; reflex. adj. reflex.

reflexion [ri'flekʃn] s. reflecţie; răsfrîngere.

reform [ri'fɔ:m] s. reformă; îndreptare. vt., vi. a (se) reforma; a (se) îndrepta.

reformation [,refə'meiʃn] s. reformă; reformare.

reformatory [ri'fɔ:mətri] s. şcoală de corecţie. adj. reformator.

reformer [ri'fɔ:mə] s. reformator.

refractory [ri'fræktri] adj. refractar.

refrain [ri'frein] s. refren. vt. a înfrîna. vi. a se stăpîni; a se opri.

refresh [ri'freʃ] vt. a întări; a întrema; a răcori; a reîmprospăta.

refreshment [ri'freʃmənt] s. întărire; întremare; trataţie; pl. de-ale gurii.

refreshment-room [ri'freʃmənt-rum] s. bufet.

refrigerate [ri'fridʒəreit] vt. a răci; a îngheţa.

refrigerator [ri'fridʒəreitə] s. frigider.

refuge ['refju:dʒ] s. refugiu.

refugee [,refju:'dʒi:] s. refugiat.

refund ['ri:'fʌnd] vt. a rambursa; a acoperi; a plăti.

refusal [ri'fju:zl] s. refuz; respingere.

refuse[1] ['refju:s] *s.* gunoi; resturi; deşeuri.

refuse[2] [ri'fju:z] *vt., vi.* a refuza.

refute [ri'fju:t] *vt.* a respinge; a infirma.

regain [ri'gein] *vt.* a recîştiga; a recăpăta; a ajunge din nou la.

regard [ri'gɑ:d] *s.* atenţie; stimă; simpatie; legătură; privinţă; privire; *pl.* complimente. *vt.* a privi; a considera; a da atenţie la; *as ~s* în ceea ce priveşte, cît despre.

regardful [ri'gɑ:dfl] *adj.* atent; plin de consideraţie.

regarding [ri'gɑ:diŋ] *prep.* cu privire la.

regardless [ri'gɑ:dlis] *adj.* neatent; neglijent; *~ of* indiferent de.

regency ['ri:dʒnsi] *s.* regenţă.

regenerate[1] [ri'dʒenərit] *adj.* renăscut; regenerat; îmbunătăţit.

regenerate[2] [ri'dʒenəreit] *vt.* a regenera. *vi.* a se regenera.

regime [rei'ʒi:m] *s.* regim.

regimen ['redʒimen] *s.* dietă, regim.

regiment ['redʒmənt] *s.* regiment. *vt.* a disciplina; a organiza.

regimental [,redʒi'mentl] *s.* uniformă. *adj.* regimental.

region ['ri:dʒn] *s.* regiune; domeniu.

register ['redʒistə] *s.* registru; *com.* totalizator, aparat care înregistrează bonurile la casă. *vt.* a înregistra; a nota; a indica; a trimite recomandat. *vi.* a (se) înregistra.

registrar [,redʒis'trɑ:] *s.* arhivar; ofiţerul stării civile.

registration [,redʒis'treiʃn] *s.* înregistrare; înscriere.

registry ['redʒistri] *s.* arhivă; oficiul stării civile; înregistrare.

regressive [ri'gresiv] *adj.* regresiv; reacţionar.

regret [ri'gret] *s.* regret. *vt.* a regreta.

regretful [ri gretfl] *adj.* trist; plin de regret *sau* de căinţă.

regular ['regjulə] *s.* soldat. *adj.* regulat; obişnuit; cum se cuvine; total.

regularize ['regjuləraiz] *vt.* a regulariza.

regularly ['regjuləli] *adv.* regulat; mereu; cum trebuie; complet.

regulate ['regjuleit] *vt.* a reg(u)la.

regulation [,regju'leiʃn] *s.* reglare; aranjare; reglementare; dispoziţie (legală).

rehabilitate [,ri:ə'biliteit] *vt.* a restabili; a reface; a reabilita.

rehash ['ri:'hæʃ] *s.* cîrpăceală. *vt.* a reface *(şi fig.).*

rehearsal [ri'hə:sl] *s.* repetiţie.

rehearse [ri hə:s] *vt.* a repeta (o piesă etc.). *vi.* a face repetiţii.

reign [rein] *s.* domnie; stăpînire; putere. *vi.* a domni.

reimburse [,ri:im'bə:s] *vt.* a rambursa; a plăti.

rein [rein] *s.* frîu. *vt.* a înfrîna; a ţine în frîu.

reindeer ['reindiə] *s.* ren.

reinforce [,ri:in'fɔ:s] *vt.* a întări.

reinforced concrete [,ri:in'fɔ:st 'kɔnkri:t] *s.* beton armat.

reinforcement [,ri:in'fɔ:smənt] *s.* întărire.

reinstate ['ri:in'steit] *vt.* a restabili; a restaura.

reissue ['riː'isjuː] s. retipărire ; ediţie nouă. vt. a retipări.

reiterate [riˈitəreit] vt. a repeta.

reject [riˈdʒekt] s. rebut. vt. a respinge ; a arunca.

rejoice [riˈdʒɔis] vt. a înveseli ; a bucura. vi. a se bucura ; a fi încîntat ; to ~ in sau at a se bucura de ; a savura.

rejoicing [riˈdʒɔisiŋ] s. fericire ; veselie ; pl. chef ; petrecere.

rejoin [riˈdʒɔin] vt. a reveni la. vi. a reveni ; a răspunde ; a replica.

rejoinder [riˈdʒɔində] s. răspuns ; replică.

rejuvenate [riˈdʒuːvineit] vt., vi. a întineri.

relapse [riˈlæps] s. (re)cădere ; revenire (a unui rău). vi. a recădea ; a se apuca din nou (de un nărav etc.).

relate [riˈleit] vt. a relata ; a lega ; to be ~d to a se înrudi cu.

relation [riˈleiʃn] s. relatare ; legătură ; ru(be)denie ; relaţie.

relationship [riˈleiʃnʃip] s. înrudire ; relaţie ; legătură.

relative [ˈrelətiv] s. rudă. adj. relativ ; reciproc.

relativity [ˌreləˈtiviti] s. caracter relativ ; relativitate.

relax [riˈlæks] vt. a slăbi ; a relaxa; a micşora (exigenţa etc.). vi. a se destinde ; a slăbi ; a se îmblînzi.

relay [ˈriːˈlei] s. ştafetă ; schimb (de lucrători etc.) ; rezervă ; tehn. releu. vt., vi. a retransmite.

release [riˈliːs] s. eliberare ; izbăvire ; slobozire ; producţie (cinematografică etc.). vt. a

elibera ; a comunica ; a da în vileag ; a produce (un film etc.).

relegate [ˈreligeit] vt. a arunca ; a împinge ; a trimite.

relent [riˈlent] vi. a se îmblînzi.

relentless [riˈlentlis] adj. neîndurător.

relevant [ˈrelivənt] adj. important ; interesant.

reliable [riˈlaiəbl] adj. de încredere ; de nădejde.

reliance [riˈlaiəns] s. încredere ; bazare.

relic [ˈrelik] s. relicvă ; moaşte.

relief [riˈliːf] s. uşurare ; alinare ; bucurie ; schimbare (în bine) ; ajutor(are) ; eliberare ; izbăvire ; schimb (de muncitori etc.) ; relief.

relieve [riˈliːv] vt. a uşura ; a alina ; a elibera ; a schimba (garda) ; a concedia ; to ~ nature a se uşura.

religion [riˈlidʒn] s. religie.

religious [riˈlidʒəs] adj. religios.

relinquish [riˈliŋkwiʃ] vt. a părăsi ; a renunţa la.

relish [ˈreliʃ] s. plăcere ; savoare ; poftă ; stimulent ; entuziasm ; gust. vt. a savura. vi. a mirosi ; a avea gust.

reluctance [riˈlʌktəns] s. aversiune ; opoziţie ; şovăială.

reluctant [riˈlʌktənt] adj. plin de aversiune ; şovăitor ; refractar ; fără tragere de inimă.

reluctantly [riˈlʌktəntli] adv. în silă.

rely [riˈlai] vi. a se bizui ; a avea încredere.

remain [riˈmein] s. rămăşiţă. vi. a rămîne ; a continua.

remainder [riˈmeində] s. rest ; rămăşiţă.

remake [riːˈmeik] vt. a reface.

remand [riˈmɑːnd] s. jur. prevenţie. vt. a reţine preventiv.

remark [riˈmɑːk] s. observaţie; comentariu. vt., vi. a remarca.

remarkable [riˈmɑːkəbl] adj. remarcabil.

remarry [riːˈmæri] vt., vi. a se recăsători.

remedy [ˈremidi] s. remediu. vt. a remedia.

remember [riˈmembə] vt. a nu uita; a ţine minte; a-şi aminti; ~ me to your wife transmite-i complimente soţiei. vi. a ţine minte; a avea memorie bună; a-şi aminti.

remembrance [riˈmembrıs] s. amintire; suvenir; memorie; pl. salutări, complimente.

remind [riˈmaind] vt. a aminti.

reminder [riˈmaində] s. memorandum; lucru evocator.

reminiscent [ˌremiˈnisnt] adj. evocator.

remiss [riˈmis] adj. neglijent; neatent.

remission [riˈmiʃn] s. iertare; achitare.

remit [riˈmit] vt. a remite; a transmite; a amîna; a ierta; a anula.

remittance [riˈmitns] s. plată; stipendiu.

remnant [ˈremnənt] s. rămăşiţă; rest.

remonstrance [riˈmɔnstrns] s. reproş; admonestare; protest.

remonstrate [riˈmɔnstreit] vi. a protesta; to ~ with smb. a ocărî pe cineva.

remorse [riˈmɔːs] s. remuşcare.

remorseful [riˈmɔːsfl] adj. pocăit.

remote [riˈmout] adj. îndepăr-

tat; izolat; fig. străin; puţin probabil.

removable [riˈmuːvəbl] adj. mobil.

removal [riˈmuːvl] s. îndepărtare; mutare.

remove [riˈmuːv] s. distanţă; grad de rudenie. vt. a îndepărta; a muta; a lua; a(-şi) scoate; to ~ mountains a face minuni. vi. a pleca; a se muta. vr. a pleca.

remunerative [riˈmjuːnrətiv] adj. rentabil.

renaissance [rəˈneisns], renascence [riˈnæsns] s. renaştere.

rend [rend] vt. a smulge; a sfîşia; a despica.

render [ˈrendə] vt. a (re)da; a transmite; a face; a interpreta.

rendering [ˈrendriŋ], rendition [renˈdiʃn] s. redare, interpretare.

renegade [ˈrenigeid] s. renegat.

renew [riˈnjuː] vt. a reînnoi; a relua; a continua; a spori.

renewal [riˈnjuəl] s. reînnoire.

rennet [ˈrenit] s. cheag.

renounce [riˈnauns] vt. a renunţa la; a abandona; a abdica de la.

renovate [ˈrenoveit] vt. a reînnoi; a renova.

renown [riˈnaun] s. renume.

rent¹ [rent] s. ruptură; spărtură; fisură; rentă; chirie. vt., vi. a (se) închiria.

rent² [rent] vt. trec. şi part. trec. de la rend.

renunciation [riˌnʌnsiˈeiʃn] s. renunţare; abnegaţie.

reopen [ˈriːˈoupn] vt., vi. a (se) redeschide.

rep [rep] s. teatru cu repertoriu variat; ticălos.

repair [ri'pɛə] s. stare (bună); reparaţie; posibilitate de folosire; out of ~ stricat; under ~ în reparaţie. vt. a repara; a îndrepta.

reparation [‚repə'reiʃn] s. reparaţie; compensaţie; pl. despăgubiri.

repartee [‚repɑ:'ti:] s. replică (spirituală).

repast [ri'pɑ:st] s. banchet.

repay [ri:'pei] vt., vi. a răsplăti; a restitui.

repeal [ri'pi:l] s. anulare; abrogare; retragere. vt. a abroga; a anula; a revoca; a retrage.

repeat [ri'pi:t] s. repetiţie. vt., vi. a (se) repeta. adv. muz. da capo.

repeatedly [ri'pi:tidli] adv. adesea; regulat; (în mod) repetat.

repel [ri pel] vt. a respinge; a scîrbi.

repellent [ri'pelənt] adj. respingător; scîrbos.

repent [ri'pent] vt. a regreta. vi. a se căi; a regreta.

repentance [ri'pentəns] s. regret; (po)căinţă.

reparation [‚repə'reiʃn] s. îndreptare; reparaţie (morală).

repertory ['repətri] s. repertoriu.

repertory theatre ['repətri 'θiətə] s. teatru cu mai multe piese în repertoriu.

repetition [‚repi'tiʃn] s. repetare; repetiţie.

repine [ri'pain] vi. a plînge; a suspina.

replace [ri'pleis] vt. a înlocui.

replenish [ri'pleniʃ] vt. a umple; a aproviziona.

replete [ri'pli:t] adj. plin; bine aprovizionat.

replica ['replikə] s. copie; replică.

reply [ri'plai] s. răspuns. vt. a răspunde la. vi. a răspunde; a fi responsabil.

report [ri'pɔ:t] s. relatare; zvon; declaraţie; raport; ştire; pocnet. vt. a relata; a raporta; a nota. vi. a raporta; a se prezenta.

reported speech [ri'pɔ:tid 'spi:tʃ] s. vorbire indirectă.

repose [ri'pouz] s. odihnă; repaus. vt. a odihni; a sprijini. vi. a se odihni; a se întinde; a se bizui.

repository [ri'pɔzitri] s. loc; local; depozit.

reprehensible [‚repri'hensəbl] adj. condamnabil.

represent [‚repri'zent] vt. a reprezenta; a înfăţişa.

representative [‚repri'zentətiv] s. reprezentant. adj. reprezentativ; tipic.

repress [ri'pres] vt. a stăpîni; a reprima.

reprieve [ri'pri:v] s. amînare; suspendare; răgaz. vt. a suspenda execuţia (cuiva); a elibera (de o ameninţare etc.).

reprimand ['reprimɑ:nd] s. admonestare. vt. a mustra.

reprint ['ri:'print] vt. a retipări; a reedita.

reprisals [ri'praizlz] s. pl. represalii.

reproach [ri'proutʃ] s. reproş; blam; ruşine. vt. a reproşa.

reproachful [ri'proutʃfl] adj. plin de reproş; blamabil; ruşinos.

reprobate ['reprobeit] s., adj. destrăbălat.

reprobation [ˌreproˈbeiʃn] s. dezaprobare ; osîndă.
reproduce [ˌriːprəˈdjuːs] vt., vi.
a (se) reproduce.
reproduction [ˌriːprəˈdʌkʃn] s.
reproducere.
reproof [riˈpruːf] s. ocară ; reproş ; admonestare.
reprove [riˈpruːv] vt. a ocărî ;
a admonesta.
reptile [ˈreptail] s. reptilă.
republic [riˈpʌblik] s. republică ; asociaţie.
repudiate [riˈpjuːdieit] vt. a respinge ; a renega.
repugnant [riˈpʌgnənt] adj. respingător ; potrivnic.
repulse [riˈpʌls] s. respingere ;
ripostă ; ocară. vt. a respinge.
repulsion [riˈpʌlʃn] s. repulsie.
repulsive [riˈpʌlsiv] adj. respingător ; contrar.
repute [riˈpjuːt] s. faimă.
reputed [riˈpjuːtid] adj. celebru.
reputedly [riˈpjuːtidli] adv. după
cum se spune.
request [riˈkwest] s. cerere ; rugăminte ; in great ~ foarte
căutat. vt. a cere ; a solicita.
require [riˈkwaiə] vt. a cere ; a
porunci ; a solicita ; a necesita.
requirement [riˈkwaiəmənt] s.
cerinţă ; necesitate.
requisite [ˈrekwizit] s. lucru necesar. adj. necesar.
requisition [ˌrekwiˈziʃn] s. cerere ;
necesitate ; rechiziţie. vt. a necesita ; a rechiziţiona.
requital [riˈkwaitl] s. plată ;
răsplată ; răzbunare.
requite [riˈkwait] vt. a plăti ;
a răsplăti ; a se răzbuna pe.
rescind [riˈsind] vt. a respinge ;
a anula.

rescue [ˈreskjuː] s. salvare ; ajutor ; victimă salvată. vt. a elibera ; a salva.
research [riˈsəːtʃ] s. cercetare.
vi. a face cercetări.
resemblance [riˈzembləns] s. asemănare.
resemble [riˈzembl] vt. a semăna
cu.
resent [riˈzent] vt. a detesta ;
a nu putea suporta.
resentful [riˈzentfl] adj. refractar ; scîrbit.
resentment [riˈzentmənt] s. re-
sentiment ; pică.
reservation [ˌrezəˈveiʃn] s. rezervă ; ţarc ; bilet ; cameră.
reserve [riˈzəːv] s. rezervă ; re-
zervaţie. vt. a rezerva ; a reţine.
reservoir [ˈrezəvwɑː] s. rezervor ;
sursă.
re-set [ˈriːˈset] vt. inf., trec. şi
part. trec. a repune.
reshuffle [ˈriːˈʃʌfl] s. rearanjare
(a cărţilor).
reside [riˈzaid] vi. a locui ; a se
afla ; a se găsi ; a consta. vt.
a rearanja.
residence [ˈrezidns] s. locuinţă ;
domiciliu ; domiciliere ; reşedinţă.
resident [ˈrezidnt] s. locuitor ;
rezident. adj. localnic ; care lo-
cuieşte (în instituţie).
residential [ˌreziˈdenʃl] adj. de
locuit ; domiciliar.
residual [riˈzidjuəl] s. reziduu.
adj. rămas ; restant.
residue [ˈrezidjuː] s. reziduu ;
rămăşiţă.
resign [riˈzain] vt. a părăsi ; a
demisiona din. vi. a demisiona
vr. a se resemna.

resignation [‚rezig'neiʃn] s. demisie ; resemnare.

resilient [ri'ziliənt] adj. elastic ; ager ; activ.

resin ['rezin] s. răşină.

resist [ri'zist] vt. a se împotrivi la ; a refuza. vi. a rezista.

resistance [ri'zistns] s. rezistenţă.

resistless [ri'zistlis] adj. implacabil ; inevitabil.

resolute ['rezəlu:t] adj. hotărît ; neclintit.

resolution [‚rezə'lu:ʃn] s. hotărîre ; rezoluţie.

resolve [ri'zɔlv] s. fermitate. vt. a hotărî ; a rezolva; a dizolva. vi. a se hotărî ; a se dizolva.

resonant ['reznənt] adj. răsunător ; de rezonanţă.

resort [ri'zɔ:t] s. recurgere ; resursă ; adăpost ; staţiune climaterică. vi.: to ~ to a recurge la ; a se duce la (mare, munte).

resound [ri'zaund] vi. a răsuna ; a avea răsunet.

resource [ri'sɔ:s] s. resursă.

resourceful [ri'sɔ:sfl] adj. plin de resurse ; inventiv.

respect [ris'pekt] s. respect ; pl. complimente ; omagii ; atenţie ; privinţă ; with ~ to, in ~ of în legătură cu. vt. a respecta ; a trata cuviincios.

respectable [ris'pektəbl] adj. respectabil ; onorabil ; convenţional.

respectful [ris'pektfl] adj. respectuos.

respecting [ris'pektiŋ] prep. în privinţa.

respective [ris'pektiv] adj. respectiv.

respectively [ris'pektĭvli] adv. respectiv.

respite ['respait] s. răgaz. vt. a da răgaz (cuiva) ; a alina.

resplendent [ris'plendənt] adj. strălucit(or).

respond [ris'pɔnd] vi. a răspunde ; a reacţiona ; a suferi o influenţă.

response [ris'pɔns] s. răspuns ; ecou ; refren ; reacţie.

responsibility [ris‚pɔnsə'biliti] s. răspundere ; obligaţie.

responsible [ris'pɔnsəbl] adj. responsabil ; demn de încredere.

responsive [ris'pɔnsiv] adj. corespunzător ; înţelegător ; afectuos ; receptiv.

rest [rest] s. tihnă ; odihnă (de veci) ; pauză ; răgaz ; adăpost ; loc de şezut ; rest. vt. a opri ; a odihni ; a sprijini. vi. a se opri ; a se odihni ; a rămîne ; a rezida ; a se încrede ; to ~ on a se sprijini pe ; a se opri asupra.

rest-cure ['restkjuə] s. cură de odihnă.

restful ['restfl] adj. odihnitor.

restitution [‚resti'tju:ʃn] s. restituire ; compensaţie ; despăgubire ; reintegrare.

restive ['restiv] adj. nărăvaş.

restless ['restlis] adj. neastîmpărat ; nestatornic ; fără odihnă ; (d. noapte etc.) de nesomn.

restoration [‚restə'reiʃn] s. refacere ; restaurare ; restauraţie.

restore [ris'tɔ:] vt. a înapoia ; a reda ; a restaura ; a reintegra ; a relua ; a reface ; a întări.

restrain [ris'trein] vt. a restrînge , a ţine în frîu ; a închide (un nebun etc.).

restraint [ris'treint] s. restricţie; recluziune; stăpînire; încorsetare.

restrict [ris'trikt] vt. a limita; a restrînge.

result [ri'zʌlt] s. rezultat. vi. a rezulta; to ~ in a avea drept rezultat.

resultant [ri'zʌltnt] s. rezultantă. adj. care rezultă; derivat.

resume [ri'zju:m] vt. a(şi) relua; a rezuma; a reîncepe.

résumé ['rezjumei] s. rezumat.

resumption [ri'zʌmʃn] s. reluare; reîncepere.

resurrect [ˌrezə'rekt] vt. a reînvia; a dezgropa. vi. a reînvia.

resurrection [ˌrezə'rekʃn] s. înviere; reînviere; dezgropare.

resuscitate [ri'sʌsiteit] vt. a reînvia.

retail¹ ['ri:teil] s. comerţ cu amănuntul. adj., adv. cu amănuntul.

retail² [ri:'teil] vt. a vinde cu amănuntul; a colporta.

retain [ri'tein] vt. a reţine; a opri.

retainer [ri'teinə] s. slujitor.

retaliate [ri'tælieit] vi. a se răzbuna; a replica; a contra-ataca.

retch [ri:tʃ] vi. a rîgîi; a vărsa.

retention [ri'tenʃn] s. reţinere; oprire; înfrînare.

reticence ['retisns] s. reticenţă; tăcere.

reticent ['retisnt] adj. reticent; rezervat; tăcut; secretos.

retinue ['retinju:] s. suită; alai.

retire [ri'taiə] vt., vi. a (se) retrage.

retired [ri'taiəd] adj. retras; izolat; la pensie.

retired pay [ri'taiəd'pei] s. pensie.

retirement [ri'taiəmənt] s. retragere; pensie; izolare.

retiring [ri'taiəriŋ] adj. retras; modest; de pensionar.

retort [ri'tɔ:t] s. replică (promptă); retortă. vt. a răspunde (la); a riposta (la).

retrace [ri'treis] vt. a urmări; a relua; a(-şi) reaminti; a parcurge din nou.

retract [ri'trækt] vt., vi. a retrage; a retracta.

retreat [ri'tri:t] s. (semnal, loc de) retragere. vi. a se retrage.

retrievable [ri'tri:vəbl] adj. recuperabil.

retrieve [ri'tri:v] vt. a recupera; a îndrepta; a salva; (d. cîini) a aporta.

retriever [ri'tri:və] s. cîine de aport.

retrogressive [ˌretro'gresiv] adj. retrograd; înapoiat; reacţionar.

retrogression [ˌretro'greʃn] s. regres.

retrospect ['retrospekt], retrospection [ˌretro'spekʃn] s. retrospectivă.

retrospective [ˌretro'spektiv] adj. retrospectiv.

return [ri'tə:n] s. întoarcere; răsplată; beneficiu; raport; pl. rezultate (electorale); by ~ cu poşta următoare; in ~ for drept compensaţie pentru. adj. de înapoiere; revanşă; dus şi întors. vt. a înapoia; a declara; a produce; a aduce; a vota.

reunion ['ri:'ju:njən] s. reunire; reuniune.

reveal [ri'vi:l] vt. a dezvălui.

reveille [ri'vælı] *s. mil.* deşteptare.

revel ['revl] *s.* petrecere; orgie; distracţie. *vi.* a chefui; *to ~ in* a savura.

revelation [ˌrevi'leiʃn] *s.* revelaţie; dezvăluire; *rel.* apocalips.

revelry ['revlri] *s.* chef(uri); orgie.

revenge [ri'vendʒ] *s.* răzbunare; revanşă. *vt., vr.* a (se) răzbuna.

revengeful [ri'vendʒfl] *adj.* răzbunător.

revenue ['revinju:] *s.* venit; percepţie.

reverberate [ri'və:breit] *vt.* a răsfrînge; a reflecta. *vi.* a reverbera.

revere [ri'viə] *vt.* a respecta; a adora.

reverence ['revrns] *s.* reverenţă; respect; preot. *vt.* a respecta.

reverend ['revrnd] *s.* preot. *adj.* venerabil.

reverent ['revrnt] *adj.* respectuos.

reversal [ri'və:sl] *s.* întoarcere; răsturnare.

reverse [ri'və:s] *s.* revers; opus; răsturnare; înfrîngere; necaz; marşarier. *adj.* opus. *vt.* a inversa; a anula; a da înapoi. *vi.* a merge înapoi (cu spatele).

reversion [ri'və:ʃn] *s.* restituire; lucru înapoiat; revenire.

revert [ri'və:t] *vi.* a reveni; a se întoarce.

review [ri'vju:] *s.* revedere; (trecere în) revistă; recenzie; *under ~* în cauză; în discuţie. *vt.* a revedea; a inspecta; a recenza; a analiza.

reviewer [ri'vju:ə] *s.* recenzent.

revile [ri'vail] *vt.* a ocărî.

revise [ri'vaiz] *s.* copie corectată; pagină. *vt.* a revizui.

revision [ri'viʒn] *s.* revizie; revizuire.

revival [ri'vaivl] *s.* înviere; reînviere; renaştere.

revive [ri'vaiv] *vt.* a învia; a reînvia; a (re)aduce la viaţă; *fig.* a dezgropa. *vi.* a învia; a reînvia; a renaşte.

revoke [ri'vouk] *vt.* a revoca; a anula.

revolt [ri'voult] *s.* răscoală; revoltă. *vt., vi.* a (se) revolta.

revolting [ri'voultiŋ] *adj.* revoltător.

revolution [ˌrevə'lu:ʃn] *s.* revoluţie.

revolutionary [ˌrevə'lu:ʃnəri] *s., adj.* revoluţionar.

revolutionist [ˌrevə'lu:ʃnist] *s.* revoluţionar.

revolutionize [ˌrevə'lu:ʃnaiz] *vt.* a revoluţiona.

revolve [ri'vɔlv] *vt.* a învîrti; a chibzui. *vi.* a se învîrti; a se schimba prin rotaţie.

revolver [ri'vɔlvə] *s.* revolver.

revue [ri'vju:] *s.* (teatru de) revistă.

revulsion [ri'vʌlʃn] *s.* schimbare totală (a sentimentelor etc.).

reward [ri'wɔ:d] *s.* răsplată. *vt.* a răsplăti.

rhetorical [ri'tɔrikl] *adj.* retoric.

rheumatic [ru'mætik] *s.* reumatic; *pl.* reumatism. *adj.* reumatic.

rhinestone ['rainstoun] *s.* cristal de stîncă; bijuterii false; imitaţie.

rhinoceros [rai'nɔsərəs] *s.* rinocer.

rhubarb ['ru:bɑ:b] *s. bot.* rabarb(ur)ă, revent.

rhyme [raim] *s.* rimă; vers; poezie. *vt., vi.* a rima.

rhythm ['riðəm] *s.* ritm.

rib [rib] *s. anat.* coastă; nervură; dungă. *vt.* a dunga; a cresta.

ribald ['ribld] *s.* gură spurcată. *adj.* obscen; scîrbos.

ribaldry ['ribldri] *s.* porcării.

riband ['ribənd] *s.* panglică.

ribbon ['ribən] *s.* panglică; bandă; şiret.

rice [rais] *s.* orez.

rich [ritʃ] *s.: the ~* bogaţii; *~es* bogăţii. *adj.* bogat; costisitor; generos; fertil; abundent; plin; săţios; plăcut; amuzant.

rick [rik] *s.* căpiţă.

rickets ['rikits] *s.* rahitism.

rickety ['rikiti] *adj.* rahitic; şubred.

ricksha(w) ['rikʃɔ:] *s.* ricşă.

rid [rid] *inf., trec. şi part. trec. vt.* a elibera; *to get ~ of* a scăpa de; a îndepărta; a elimina. *vr.* a scăpa.

riddance ['ridns] *s.* scăpare.

ridden ['ridn] *adj.* asuprit; dominat. *vt., vi. part. trec. de la* **ride.**

riddle ['ridl] *s.* ghicitoare; enigmă; sită mare. *vt.* a rezolva (o enigmă); a cerne; a ciurui. *vi.* a vorbi în cimilituri.

ride [raid] *s.* călătorie; plimbare; alee. *vt.* a călări (pe); a mîna; a duce; a pluti pe; a alerga; a face; a străbate; a duce în spinare; *to ~ down*

a urmări; *to ~ to death* a obosi; a istovi; a epuiza; *to ~ the high horse* a face pe grozavul. *vi.* a călă(to)ri; a pluti.

rider ['raidə] *s.* călăreţ; codicil.

ridge [ridʒ] *s.* creastă; cumpăna apelor.

ridicule ['ridikju:l] *s.* ridicol; batjocură. *vt.* a ridiculiza.

ridiculous [ri'dikjuləs] *adj.* ridicol; absurd.

riding ['raidiŋ] *s.* călărie; district.

riding-coat ['raidiŋ,kout], **riding-habit** ['raidiŋ,hæbit] *s.* costum de călărie.

rife [raif] *adj.* răspîndit; în floare.

riff-raff ['rifræf] *s.* gloată; drojdia societăţii.

rifle ['raifl] *s.* carabină; puşcă; ghint; *pl.* puşcaşi. *vt.* a scotoci; a jefui; a ghintui.

rifleman ['raiflmən] *s.* puşcaş (de elită).

rifle range ['raiflreindʒ] *s.* bătaia puştii; poligon.

rift [rift] *s.* spărtură; despicătură. *vt.* a despica.

rig [rig] *s.* velatură; înfăţişare; echipament; înşelătorie. *vt. mar.* a arma; a echipa; a aranja; a îmbrăca; a măslui.

rigging ['rigiŋ] *s.* velatură.

right [rait] *s.* drept; dreptate; dreapta; *by ~s* pe bună dreptate; *by ~ of* datorită. *adj.* drept; just; îndreptăţit; **exact**; corespunzător; bine; din dreapta; de deasupra; *~ oh! all ~!* bine; în regulă; bravo. *vt.* a îndrepta; a corecta. *adv.* drept; direct; just; complet; perfect;

foarte; la dreapta împrejur; complet; ~ *away* sau *off* chiar acum; direct.

righteous ['raitʃəs] *adj.* just; justificat; cinstit.

rightful ['raitfl] *adj.* îndreptăţit; just; legal; cuvenit; bun.

right-hand ['raithænd] *adj.* de dreapta; din dreapta; spre dreapta.

right honourable ['rait'ɔnrəbl] *s.* deputat.

rightly ['raitli] *adv.* după cum se cuvine; pe drept; corect.

right-wing ['raitwiŋ] *adj. pol.* de dreapta.

rigid ['ridʒid] *adj.* rigid; ţeapăn; sever; strict.

rigmarole ['rigməroul] *s.* aiureală.

rigorous ['rigrəs] *s.* sever; riguros.

rigo(u)r ['rigə] *s.* rigoare; asprime.

rile [rail] *vt.* a supăra.

rill [ril] *s.* pîrîu, pîrîiaş.

rim [rim] *s.* obadă; jantă. *vt.* a obăda.

rime [raim] *s.* vers; poezie; promoroacă.

rind [raind] *s.* coajă; piele; suprafaţă.

ring [riŋ] *s.* inel; cerc; belciug; ring; ţarc; bandă; sunet; răsunet; sonerie. *vt.* a încercui; a înconjura; a suna din; a suna (la sonerie, telefon); *to* ~ *down* a coborî cortina; *to* ~ *in* a saluta (Anul nou); a anunţa; *to* ~ *off* a închide telefonul; *to* ~ *out* a anunţa plecarea; *to* ~ *up* a suna la telefon; a ridica (cortina).

ring-finger ['riŋ₁fiŋgə] *s.* inelar.

ringleader ['riŋ₁liːdə] *s.* căpetenie.

ringlet ['riŋlit] *s.* ineluş; zuluf.

rink [riŋk] *s.* patinoar.

rinse [rins] *s* clătire. *vt.* a clăti; a spăla; a înghiţi.

riot ['raiət] *s.* dezordine; tulburare; abundenţă; izbucnire; destrăbălare. *vi.* a-şi face de cap; a participa la tulburări.

riotous ['raiətəs] *adj.* turbulent; destrăbălat.

rip [rip] *s.* sfîşiere; tăietură; mîrţoagă; javră *(fig.)*. *vt.* a spinteca; a tăia. *vi.* a se sfîşia; a se rupe.

ripe [raip] *adj.* copt; matur; gata.

ripen ['raipn] *vt., vi.* a (se) coace; a (se) maturiza.

ripping ['ripiŋ] *adj., adv.* straşnic.

ripple ['ripl] *s.* val mic; ondulaţie; *pl.* vălurele. *vt., vi.* a undui.

rise [raiz] *s.* ridicare; spor; creştere; naştere; sursă; ridicătură.· *vi.* a se ridica (la luptă); a se ivi; a se scula; a răsări; a izvorî.

risen [rizn] *vi. part. trec. de la* **rise.**

riser ['raizə] *s.: an early* ~ un om harnic.

rising ['raiziŋ] *s.* ridicare; creştere; răscoală; (re)înviere. *adj.* crescînd; în dezvoltare; ascendent; de viitor.

risk [risk] *s.* risc. *vt., vi.* a risca.

risky ['riski] *adj.* risca(n)t.

rite [rait] *s.* rit(ual).

rival ['raivl] *s.* rival. *vt.* a concura.

rivalry ['raivlri] *s.* rivalitate; concurenţă.

rive [raiv] *vt.* a despica; a desprinde; a desface. *vi.* a se sfîşia; a se desface.

riven ['rivn] *vt., vi. part. trec. de la* **rive**.

river ['rivə] *s.* rîu; fluviu *(şi fig.).*

river bed ['rivəbed] *s.* albie de rîu.

riverside ['rivəsaid] *s.* luncă; malul rîului. *adj.* riveran.

rivet ['rivit] *s.* nit. *vt.* a nitui; *fig.* a ţintui; a atrage.

rivulet ['rivjulit] *s.* pîrîiaş.

roach [routʃ] *s. iht.* babuşcă; gîndac (de bucătărie).

road [roud] *s.* drum; cale; şosea; *by* ~ pe şosea.

road house ['roudhaus] *s.* han.

road metal [roud'metl] *s.* piatră de pavaj.

roadside ['roudsaid] *s.* (cărarea din) marginea drumului. *adj.* (de) pe drum.

roadstead ['roudsted] *s. mar.* radă.

roadster ['roudstə] *s.* automobil sport.

roadway ['roudwei] *s. mar.* radă.

roam [roum] *vt.* a străbate. *vi.* a hoinări.

roar [rɔ:] *s.* urlet; uruit; hohot. *vt.* a urla. *vi.* a urla; a mugi; a hohoti.

roaring ['rɔ:riŋ] *s.* urlet; muget; uruit. *adj.* zgomotos; furtunos; vioi; activ; *the* ~ *20s* deceniul prohibiţiei (1920—1930).

roast [roust] *s.* friptură. *vt., vi.* a (se) 'frige; a (se) prăji.

rob [rɔb] *vt.* a jefui; a fura; a răpi.

robber ['rɔbə] *s.* tîlhar; bandit.

robbery ['rɔbəri] *s.* tîlhărie.

robe [roub] *s.* robă; rochie; rochiţă. *vt., vi.* a (se) îmbrăca.

robin ['rɔbin] *s.* prihor; măcăleandru.

robust [rə'bʌst] *adj.* robust; viguros.

rock [rɔk] *s.* rocă; stîncă; piatră; legănat; tangaj. *vt.* a legăna. *vi.* a se legăna; a face tangaj.

rocker ['rɔkə] *s.* balansoar.

rocket ['rɔkit] *s.* rachetă.

rocking-chair ['rɔkiŋtʃɛə] *s.* balansoar.

rocking-horse ['rɔkiŋhɔ:s] *s.* căluţ de lemn.

rocky ['rɔki] *adj.* stîncos; tare; şubred.

rod [rɔd] *s.* nuia; mănunchi de vergi; baghetă; bătaie; măsură de 5 m; prăjină; tijă.

rode [roud] *vt., vi. trec. de la* **ride**.

rodent ['roudnt] *s., adj.* rozător.

roe [rou] *s.* icre; căprioară.

rogue [roug] *s.* pungaş; ticălos.

roguery ['rougəri] *s.* ticăloşie; pungăşie; farsă.

roguish ['rougiʃ] *adj.* viclean; ştrengar.

role [roul] *s.* rol.

roll [roul] *s.* rolă; sul; ruliu; bubuit; listă; catalog; chiflă; corn. *vt.* a rula; a învîrti; a suci; a răsuci; a rostogoli; a sufleca; a lamina. *vi.* a se desfăşura; a se rostogoli; a veni; a se răsuci; a undui; *to* ~ *in* a veni (în puhoi); a se bălăci.

roll-call ['roul'kɔ:l] *s.* strigarea catalogului; *mil.* etc. apel.

roller ['roulə] *s.* rulou; compresor.

roller skates ['roulə͵skeits] s. pl. patine cu rotile.

rollick ['rɔlik] s. veselie. vi. a se distra; a petrece.

rolling ['roulin] s. sucire; rulare; bubuit. adj. sucit; răsucit; unduitor.

rolling-mill ['roulinmil] s. laminor.

rolling-pin ['roulinpin] s. sucitor.

rolling-stock ['roulinstɔk] s. material rulant.

Roman ['roumən] s., adj. roman.

romance[1] [rə'mæns] s. roman cavaleresc, sentimental, exotic sau de aventuri; idilă; feerie; romantism; aventură; exagerare.

Romance[2] [rə'mæns] adj. romanic.

Romanian [ro'meinjən] s. român(că); (limba) română; adj. român(ă).

Romanian Communist Party [rou'meinjən 'kɔmjunist 'pɑːti] s. Partidul Comunist Român.

romantic [rə'mæntik] s., adj. romantic.

romanticism [rə'mæntisizəm] s. romantism.

romanticist [rə'mæntisist] s. romantic.

Romany ['rɔməni] s. țigan; țigănime; limba țigănească.

romp [rɔmp] s. ștrengar; ștrengărie. vi. a zburda.

roof [ruːf] s. acoperiș; cupolă; cerul gurii. vt. a acoperi.

roofless ['ruːflis] adj. fără acoperămînt sau adăpost.

rook [ruk] s. corb; tură (la șah).

rookie ['ruki] s. recrut.

room [ru(ː)m] s. cameră (mobilată); spațiu; prilej; posibilitate.

room-mate ['rummeit] s. tovarăș sau coleg de cameră.

roomy ['rumi] adj. spațios.

roost [ruːst] s. băț pe care dorm găinile; coteț. vi. a se culca.

rooster ['ruːstə] s. cocoș.

root [ruːt] s. rădăcină; origine. vt. a sădi; a planta; a înrădăcina; a stabili; a fixa; to ~ out sau up a dezrădăcina; a smulge. vi. a prinde rădăcini; a scormoni.

rooted ['ruːtid] adj. înrădăcinat; întemeiat.

rope [roup] s. funie; frînghie; șirag; ștreang; the ~s ringul; situația; chițibușurile. vt. a lega; a înlănțui.

rope-dancer ['roup͵dɑːnsə] s. dansator pe sîrmă.

rosary ['rouzəri] s. mătănii; parc de trandafiri.

rose [rouz] s. trandafir; roz; under the ~ în taină; nelegitim. adj. roz; trandafiriu. vi. trec. de la rise.

rosebud ['rouzbʌd] s. boboc de trandafir.

rosemary ['rouzmri] s. rozmarin.

rosette ['rozet] s. cocardă; rozetă.

rosin ['rɔzin] s. saciz.

rostrum ['rɔstrəm] s. tribună (pentru orator).

rosy ['rouzi] adj. trandafiriu.

rot [rɔt] s. putreziciune; stricăciune; putregai; prostii. vt. a face să putrezească. vi. a putrezi; a spune prostii.

rotary ['routəri] adj. rotitor.

rotate [ro'teit] vt., vi. a se roti

rotation [ro'teiʃn] s. rotire ; învîrtire ; rotaţie.

rotation of crops [ro'teiʃn əv 'krɔps] s. asolament.

rote [rout] s.: by ~ pe de rost.

rotten ['rɔtn] adj. putred ; stricat ; nenorocit ; prăpădit.

rotten borough ['rɔtn 'bʌrə] s. ist. tîrg părăsit.

rotter ['rɔtə] s. nenorocit ; ticălos.

rotund [ro'tʌnd] adj. rotofei ; rotund ; amplu ; înflorit.

rouble ['ru:bl] s. rublă.

rouge [ru:ʒ] s. ruj. vt., vi. a (se) ruja.

rough [rʌf] s. asprime ; dificultate ; golan ; huligan ; stare brută ; ciornă. adj. brut ; aproximativ ; stîngaci ; nepoliticos. vt. a aspri ; to ~ it a o scoate (cu greu) la capăt. adv. aspru.

rough and tumble [ˌrʌf ən'tʌmbl] s. dîrvală. adj. de dîrvală.

rough copy ['rʌf'kɔpi] s. ciornă.

rough customer ['rʌf'kʌstəmə] s. zurbagiu.

rough diamond ['rʌf'daiəmənd] s. brînză bună în burduf de cîine.

roughly ['rʌfli] adv. aspru ; aproximativ ; ~ speaking în linii mari.

roughness ['rʌfnis] s. asprime.

roughshod ['rʌfʃɔd] adj. brutal.

rough-spoken ['rʌf'spoukn] adj. sincer ; brutal.

rough tongue ['rʌf'tʌŋ] s. limbă ascuţită (fig.).

Roumanian [ru'meinjən] v. Romanian.

round [raund] s. bucată rotundă ; rotunjime ; rundă ; şir ; cerc ; ciclu ; rond(ă) ; dans ; horă ; salvă. adj. rotund ; în cerc ; ciclic ; complet. vt. a rotunji ; a înconjura ; a vizita ; a inspecta ; to ~ off sau out a rotunji ; a termina ; to ~ up a aduna laolaltă ; a rezuma. vi. a se rotunji. adv. de jur împrejur ; în cerc ; încoace ; all the year ~ tot anul ; ~ and ~ de mai multe ori în şir. prep. în jurul ; de jur împrejurul.

roundabout ['raundəbaut] s. căluşei ; sens giratoriu. adj. ocolit, indirect.

rounders ['raundəz] s. oină.

roundly ['raundli] adv. rotund ; în cerc ; tare ; sever ; clar.

roundness ['raundnis] s. rotunjime.

rouse [rauz] vt. a stîrni ; a trezi ; a aţîţa. vi. a se trezi ; a se stîrni.

rout [raut] s. ceată ; gloată (zgomotoasă) ; dezordine. vt. a înfrînge ; a pune pe fugă ; a stîrni.

route [ru:t] s. rută ; cale.

routine [ru:'ti:n] s. obişnuinţă ; rutină ; monotonie ; regularitate. adj. monoton ; regulat ; obişnuit ; banal.

rove [rouv] vt. a străbate. vi. a rătăci ; a se împrăştia.

rover ['rouvə] s. călător ; cercetaş ; pirat.

row[1] [rou] s. şir ; rînd ; linie ; vîslit ; plimbare cu barca. vt. a împinge (vîslind). vi. a vîsli.

row[2] [rau] s. scandal ; ceartă. vt. a ocărî. vi. a face gălăgie.

rowdy ['raudi] s., adj. scandalagiu.

rowlock ['rɔlək] s. furchet.

royal ['rɔi(ə)l] *adj.* regesc ; regal.

royalty ['rɔilti] *s.* regalitate ; monarhie ; familia regală ; drept(uri) de autor.

rub [rʌb] *s.* frecare ; frecuş ; dificultate. *vt.* a freca ; a lustrui ; a spăla ; *to ~ in* a masa cu o unsoare ; *fig.* a băga pe gît ; *to ~ off* sau *out* a şterge. *vi.* a (se) freca.

rubber ['rʌbə] *s.* cauciuc ; gumă ; *pl.* galoşi. *vt.* a cauciuca.

rubberneck ['rʌbənek] *s.* băgăreţ ; turist ; vizitator.

rubbish ['rʌbiʃ] *s.* resturi ; gunoi ; prostii.

rubble ['rʌbl] *s.* dărîmături ; moloz.

ruby ['ru:bi] *s.* rubin. *adj.* rubiniu.

ruck-sack ['ruksæk] *s.* rucsac.

rudder ['rʌdə] *s.* cîrmă.

ruddy ['rʌdi] *adj.* roşu ; rotofei ; plesnind de sănătate.

rude [ru:d] *adj.* nepoliticos ; aspru ; violent ; imperfect ; primitiv ; colţuros ; neţesălat.

rudely ['ru:dli] *adv.* nepoliticos ; violent ; aspru ; grosolan.

rudiment ['ru:dimənt] *s.* rudiment ; *pl.* baze.

rue [ru:] *s.* regret ; milă. *vt.* a regreta ; a se căi pentru.

rueful ['ru:fl] *adj.* trist ; plin de regret.

ruffian ['rʌfjən] *s.* bandit.

ruffle ['rʌfl] *s.* dantelă ; volan ; vălurele ; agitaţie. *vt.* a încreţi ; a tulbura. *vi.* a se tulbura ; a face vălurele.

rug [rʌg] *s.* carpetă ; pătură ; ţol.

rugby (football) ['rʌgbi'futbɔ:l] *s.* rugbi.

rugged ['rʌgid] *adj.* aspru ; colţuros ; necioplit ; sincer.

rugger ['rʌgə] *s.* rugbi.

ruin [ruin] *s.* ruină ; decădere ; nenorocire. *vt.* a ruina ; a deprava.

ruinous ['ruinəs] *adj.* ruinător ; dezastruos.

rule [ru:l] *s.* regulă ; lege ; domnie ; regim ; hotărîre judecătorească ; riglă ; *as a ~* în general. *vt.* a stăpîni ; a guverna ; a conduce ; *jur.* a hotărî ; a declara ; a linia ; *to .~ out* a exclude. *vi.* a fi stăpîn.

ruler ['ru:lə] *s.* conducător ; stăpînitor ; riglă.

ruling ['ru:liŋ] *s.* conducere ; guvernare ; hotărîre judecătorească. *adj.* conducător ; dominant ; la putere.

rum [rʌm] *s.* rom ; *amer.* băutură. *adj.* ciudat.

Rumanian [ru'meinjən] *s., adj. v.* Romanian.

rumble ['rʌmbl] *s.* duduit ; bubuit. *vi.* a dudui ; a bubui ; a hurui.

ruminant ['ru:minənt] *s. adj.* rumegător.

ruminate ['ru:mineit] *vt., vi.* a rumega.

rummage ['rʌmidʒ] *s.* răvăşeală ; scormoneală ; vechituri. *vt., vi.* a scormoni ; a răvăşi.

rummy ['rʌmi] *s.* remi. *adj.* ciudat.

rumo(u)r ['ru:mə] *s.* zvon. *vt.* a lansa (un zvon) ; a şopti.

rump [rʌmp] *s.* tîrtiţă ; fund, spate.

rumple ['rʌmpl] *vt.* a încreţi.

rumpus ['rʌmpəs] *s.* gălăgie.

run [rʌn] *s.* alergare ; plimbare ;

fermă; stînă; curent; conducere; scurgere; *in the long ~* în cele din urmă. *inf. şi part. trec. vt.* a conduce; a administra; a risca; a face; a duce; *to ~ down* a defăima; a găsi; *(d. vehicule)* a călca. *vi.* a alerga; a face curse; a se mişca; a se învîrti; a curge; a deveni; a se întinde; a (se pe)trece; a ajunge; a candida; a suna; *to ~ about* a umbla de colo, colo; *to ~ across* a întîlni; *to ~ against* a se ciocni de; a întîlni; *to ~ away with* a fura; a fugi cu; *(d. gură etc.)* a-l lua pe dinainte; a se pripi (cu o concluzie etc.); *to ~ down* a se opri; a fi istovit; *to ~ high* a fi în floare *sau* în fierbere; *to ~ in* a veni; *to ~ into* a se ciocni de; *to ~ low* a scădea; *to ~ off* a pleca (repede); a curge; a (se s)curge; *to ~ out* a fi insuficient; *to ~ over* a da pe dinafară; a parcurge; a trece în revistă; *to ~ through* a termina; a parcurge; *to ~ up* a se urca; *to ~ up against* a se ciocni de; *to ~ upon* a nimeri; a lovi.

runaway ['rʌnəwei] *s., adj.* fugar.

rung [rʌŋ] *s.* bară; treaptă; spiţă. *vt., vi. part. trec. de la* **ring.**

runner ['rʌnə] *s.* alergător; fugar; mesager; talpă (de sanie); mlădiţă; plantă agăţătoare.

runner-up ['rʌnər'ʌp] *s.* cîştigător ex-aequo, concurent care împarte locul I cu învingătorul.

running ['rʌniŋ] *s.* fugă. *adj.* fugar; în fugă; neîntrerupt;

curgător; purulent. *adv.* la rînd; una după alta.

running-board ['rʌniŋbɔ:d] *s. auto.* scară.

running-knot ['rʌniŋnɔt] *s.* nod marinăresc.

runway ['rʌnwei] *s.* pistă; potecă; drum.

rupee [ru:'pi:] *s.* rupie.

rupture ['rʌptʃə] *s.* ruptură; hernie.

rush [rʌʃ] *s.* goană; alergătură; modă; aflux; pipirig; papură. *vt.* a repezi; a trimite în grabă; a grăbi; a lua cu asalt; a face repede. *vi.* a alerga; a se repezi; a se pripi.

rush hours ['rʌʃauəz] *s. pl.* ore de vîrf; ore de aglomeraţie.

russet ['rʌsit] *s.* roşu; (măr) roşu. *adj.* roşiatic.

Russian ['rʌʃn] *s.* rus(oaică); (limba) rusă. *adj.* rus(esc).

rust [rʌst] *s.* rugină; ramoleală; lipsă de antrenament. *vt.* a (se) rugini.

rustic ['rʌstik] *s.* ţăran; ţărănoi. *adj.* rustic; rural; simplu; grosolan.

rustle ['rʌsl] *s.* fîşîit; foşnet; vîjîit. *vt.* a foşni; a fîşîi; a vîjîi.

rustless ['rʌstlis] *adj.* inoxidabil; care nu rugineşte.

rustling ['rʌsliŋ] *s.* foşnet; fîşîit; vîjîit.

rusty ['rʌsti] *adj.* ruginit; ruginiu; demodat; uzat; arţăgos.

rut [rʌt] *s.* făgaş; urmă; închistare. *vt.* a brăzda.

ruth [ru:θ] *s.* îndurare; compătimire; tristeţe.

ruthless ['ru:θlis] *adj.* neîndurător.

rye [rai] *s.* (rachiu de) secară.

S

S [es] *s*. S, s.

sable ['seibl] *s*. samur.

saboteur ['sæbətə:] *s*. sabotor.

sabre ['seibə] *s*. sabie.

sack [sæk] *s*. sac ; concediere ; jaf. *vt*. a concedia ; a jefui.

sack-coat ['sækkout] *s*. sacou.

sacred ['seikrid] *adj*. sacru.

sacrifice ['sækrifais] *s*. jertfă. *vt.*, *vi.*, *vr.* a (se) jertfi.

sad [sæd] *adj*. trist.

sadden ['sædn] *vt.*, *vi.* a (se) întrista.

saddle ['sædl] *s*. şa ; spinare. *vt*. a înşeua ; a încărca.

saddler ['sædlə] *s*. şelar.

sadness ['sædnis] *s*. tristeţe.

safe [seif] *s*. se(i)f ; casă de bani. *adj*. sigur ; neprimejdios ; în siguranţă ; liniştit.

safeguard ['seifgɑ:d] *s*. garanţie. *vt*. a apăra.

safety ['seifti] *s*. siguranţă ; protecţie.

safety match ['seiftimætʃ] *s*. chibrit (fără fosfor).

safety-pin ['seiftipin] *s*. ac de siguranţă.

safety-razor ['seifti‚reizə] *s*. aparat de ras.

saffron ['sæfrn] *s*. şafran. *adj*. galben.

sag [sæg] *s*. scobitură ; (s)cădere. *vi*. a scădea ; a atîrna.

saga ['sɑ:gə] *s*. saga.

sagacious [sə'geiʃəs] *adj*. înţelept.

sagacity [sə'gæsiti] *s*. înţelepciune (practică).

sage [seidʒ] *s*. înţelept ; *bot*. salvie. *adj*. înţelept.

sago ['seigou] *s*. sago.

said [sed] *vt.*, *vi. trec. şi part. trec. de la* **say.**

sail [seil] *s*. pînză (de corabie) ; (călătorie pe) vas ; *in full* ~ cu toate pînzele sus ; *under* ~ în plină cursă. *vi*. a naviga ; a se mişca.

sailing ['seiliŋ] *s*. navigaţie ; plecare.

sailing boat ['seiliŋbout] *s*. corabie cu pînze.

sailor ['seilə] *s*. marinar.

saint [snt, seint] *s*. sfînt(ă).

saintly ['seintli] *adj*. sfînt.

sake [seik] *s.: for my* ~ de dragul *sau* hatîrul meu ; *for goodness* ~ *!* pentru numele lui Dumnezeu !

salad ['sæləd] *s*. salată ; lăptucă.

salary ['sæləri] *s*. salariu (de funcţionar).

sale [seil] *s*. vînzare.

salesman ['seilzmən] *s*. vînzător ; *amer*. comis-voiajor.

salient ['seiljənt] *adj*. izbitor.

saline ['seilain] *adj*. salin ; sărat.

sallow ['sælou] *adj*. smead ; palid.

sally ['sæli] *s*. glumă ; atac. *vi*. a ataca ; a ieşi.

salmon ['sæmən] *s*. somon.

salon ['sælɔŋ] *s*. salon (literar) ; expoziţie.

saloon [sə'lu:n] *s*. cîrciumă ; *amer*. prăvălie.

salt [sɔ:lt] *s*. sare. *vt*. a săra.

salt-cellar ['sɔ:lt‚selə] *s*. solniţă.

saltpeter, saltpetre ['sɔ:lt‚pi:tə] *s*. salpetru.

salty ['sɔːlti] *adj.* sărat.

salute [sə'luːt] *s.* salut; salutare; *mil.* onor. *vt.*, *vi.* a saluta.

salvage ['sælvidʒ] *s.'* salvare; obiecte recuperate.

salvation [sæl'veiʃn] *s.* salvare.

salve [sælv] *s.* alifie; balsam.

salver ['sælvə] *s.* tăviţă.

salvo ['sælvou] *s.* salvă; ropot.

same [seim] *s.* acest lucru. *adj.* acelaşi; *it is all the* ~ *to me* puţin îmi pasă; *all the* ~ în orice caz; totuşi. *pron.* acesta; acelaşi. *adv.* la fel.

sample ['saːmpl] *s.* mostră. *vt.* a degusta.

sampler ['saːmplə] *s.* mostră; degustător.

sanatorium [ˌsænə'tɔːriəm] *s.* sanatoriu.

sanctify ['sæŋtifai] *vt.* a sfinţi.

sanctimonious [ˌsæŋti'mounjəs] *adj.* ipocrit.

sanction ['sæŋʃn] *s.* permisiune; sancţiune. *vt.* a aproba.

sanctity ['sæŋtiti] *s.* sfinţenie; religiozitate.

sanctuary ['sæŋtjuəri] *s.* sanctuar; altar.

sanctum ['sæŋtəm] *s.* sanctuar; birou.

sand [sænd] *s.* nisip; *pl.* plajă. *vt.* a sabla.

sandal ['sændl] *s.* sandală; *bot.* santal.

sand-bar ['sænbaː] *s.* banc de nisip.

sandglass ['sæŋglaːs] *s.* ceas de nisip.

sandpaper ['sænpeipə] *s.* glaspapir.

sandstone ['sænstoun] *s.* gresie.

sandstorm ['sænstɔːm] *s.* simun.

sandwich ['sænwidʒ] *s.* sandviş.

sandwich man ['sænwidʒmæn] *s.* om-afiş, reclamă vie.

sandy ['sændi] *adj.* nisipos; gălbui.

sane [sein] *adj.* sănătos; înţelept.

sang [sæŋ] *vt.*, *vi. trec. de la* sing.

sanguinary ['sæŋgwinəri] *adj.* sîngeros; sălbatic.

sanguine ['sæŋgwin] *adj.* roşu (la faţă); optimist; vesel.

sanitation [ˌsæni'teiʃn] *s.* salubritate.

sanity ['sæniti] *s.* înţelepciune.

sank [sæŋk] *vt.*, *vi. trec. de la* sink.

sap [sæp] *s.* sevă; vigoare. *vt.* a săpa; a submina; a slăbi.

sapling ['sæpliŋ] *s.* puiet; răsad; tînăr.

sapper ['sæpə] *s. mil.* pionier.

sapphire ['sæfaiə] *s.* safir.

sappy ['sæpi] *adj.* plin de sevă; energic.

sarcasm ['saːkæzəm] *s.* sarcasm.

sardine [saː'diːn] *s.* sardea.

sash [sæʃ] *s.* eşarfă; şal; cercevea.

sat [sæt] *vi. trec. şi part. trec. de la* sit.

satchel ['sætʃl] *s.* ghiozdan.

sate [seit] *vt.* a sătura.

satiate ['seiʃieit] *vt.* a sătura; a satisface; a umple.

satiety [sə'taiəti] *s.* saţ.

satire ['sætaiə] *s.* satiră.

satisfactory [ˌsætis'fæktri] *adj.* mulţumitor.

satisfy ['sætisfai] *vt.* a satisface; a convinge.

Saturday ['sætədi] *s.* sîmbătă.

saturnine ['sætəːnain] *adj.* sumbru; grav.

sauce [sɔːs] s. sos; obrăznicie.

saucepan ['sɔːspən] s. sosieră.

saucer ['sɔːsə] s. farfurioară.

saucy ['sɔːsi] adj. obraznic; neserios.

saunter ['sɔːntə] s. plimbare. vi. a umbla agale.

sausage ['sɔsidʒ] s. cîrnat; salam.

savage ['sævidʒ] s., adj. sălbatic.

savagery ['sævidʒri] s. sălbăticie.

savanna(h) [sə'vænə] s. savană, prerie.

save [seiv] vt. a salva; a cruța; a economisi. vi. a economisi. prep. fără. conj. în afară de cazul cînd.

saving ['seiviŋ] s. economie; scăpare. adj. econom. prep. fără; ~ your presence iertat să-mi fie. conj. în afară de cazul cînd.

saviour ['seivjə] s. mîntuitor.

savo(u)r ['seivə] s. gust; savoare. vt. a gusta; a savura. vi. a mirosi.

savo(u)ry ['seivri] adj. gustos.

saw[1] [sɔː] s. ferăstrău; zicală; fig. clişeu. vt. a tăia cu ferăstrăul. vi. a ferestrui.

saw[2] [sɔː] vt., vi. trec. de la see.

sawdust ['sɔːdʌst] s. rumeguş; talaş.

sawn [sɔːn] vt., vi. part. trec. de la saw.[1]

say [sei] s. cuvînt; influență. vt. a zice; a afirma. vi. a spune; I ~ ! ascultă!

saying ['seiiŋ] s. zicală.

scab [skæb] s. crustă; rîie; spărgător de grevă; trădător.

vi. a acţiona ca spărgător de grevă.

scabbard ['skæbəd] s. teacă.

scaffold ['skæfld] s. spînzurătoare; schelă.

scaffolding ['skæfldiŋ] s. schelărie; eşafodaj.

scald [skɔːld] s. arsură. vt. a opări; a frige.

scale [skeil] s. solz; crustă; gamă; scară; sortiment; pl. cîntar. vt. a cîntări; a urca.

scallawag, scallywag ['skæliwæg] s. vagabond.

scalp [skælp] s. scalp; trofeu. vt. a scalpa.

scalpel ['skælpl] s. bisturiu.

scamp [skæmp] s. ştrengar. vt. a rasoli.

scamper ['skæmpə] vi. a o şterge.

scan [skæn] vt. a scruta; a scanda.

scandal ['skændl] s. scandal; scandalizare; bîrfeală.

scandalmonger ['skændl,mʌŋgə] s. colportor de calomnii, bîrfeli etc.

scandalmongering ['skændl,mʌŋgəriŋ] s. (colportare de) calomnii sau bîrfeli.

scansion ['skænʃn] s. scandare.

scant(y) ['skænt(i)] adj. insuficient; sărac; puţin(tel).

scapegoat ['skeipgout] s. ţap ispăşitor.

scapegrace ['skeipgreis] s. ştrengar; păcală.

scar [skɑː] s. cicatrice; urmă nefastă. vt. a lăsa urme adînci în; a însemna.

scarce [skɛəs] adj. puţin(tel); sărac; rar.

scarcely ['skɛəsli] adv. abia.

scarcity ['skɛəsiti] s. criză.

scare [skɛə] s. spaimă. vt. a speria.

scarecrow ['skɛəkrou] s. sperie-toare (de ciori).

scarf [skɑːf] s. eşarfă; şal.

scarlet ['skɑːlit] s., adj. staco-jiu.

scarlet fever ['skɑːlit'fiːvə] s. scarlatină.

scarves [skɑːvz] s. pl. de la scarf.

scatheless ['skeiðlis] adj. nea-tins; nepedepsit.

scathing ['skeiðiŋ] adj. sever.

scatter ['skætə] vt., vi. a (se) împrăştia.

scatter-brained ['skætə,breind] adj. zăpăcit.

scavenger ['skævindʒə] s. gu-noier.

scene [siːn] s. scenă; tablou; vedere; decor; behind the ~s în culise.

scenery ['siːnəri] s. decor; peisaj.

scent [sent] s. parfum; mıros; pistă. vt. a mirosi; a parfuma.

sceptic ['skeptik] s., adj. sceptic.

scepticism ['skeptisizəm] s. ne-încredere; scepticism.

sceptre ['septə] s. sceptru.

schedule ['ʃedjuːl] s. program; orar; plan; ahead of ~ înainte de termen. vt. a programa; a stabili.

scheme [skiːm] s. plan (rău); schemă; maşinaţie; complot. vt. a cloci (o ticăloşie). vi. a maşina.

scholar ['skɔlə] s. cărturar; şcolar.

scholarship ['skɔləʃip] s. bursă.

scholastic [skə'læstik] adj. sco-lastic.

school [skuːl] s. şcoală; învăţă-tură. vt. a educa.

schoolbook ['skuːlbuk] s. manual şcolar.

school-boy ['skuːlbɔi] s. elev.

school-fellow ['skuːl,felou] s. co-leg de şcoală.

school-girl ['skuːlgəːl] s. elevă.

schooling ['skuːliŋ] s. şcolari-zare; învăţătură.

school-ma'am ['skuːlmɑːm] s. în-văţătoare.

schoolmaster ['skuːl,mɑːstə] s. învăţător.

schoolmistress ['skuːl,mistris] s. învăţătoare.

schoolteacher ['skuːl,tiːtʃə] s. învăţător.

schooner ['skuːnə] s. goeletă; amer. căruţă cu coviltir.

science ['saiəns] s. ştiinţă; în-demînare.

scientific [,saiən'tifik] adj. ştiin-ţific; raţional.

scientist ['saiəntist] s. savant.

scintillate ['sintileit] vi. a scîn-teia.

scion ['saiən] s. (v)lăstar.

scissors ['sizəz] s. pl. foarfece.

scoff [skɔf] s. (obiect de) bat-jocură. vi. a-şi bate joc.

scold [skould] s. gură rea, caţă. vt., vi. a ocărî.

scoop [skuːp] s. linguroi; căuş; reportaj senzaţional. vt. a scoa-te; a găsi.

scooter ['skuːtə] s. trotinetă; scuter.

scope [skoup] s. proporţii; do-meniu; competenţă.

scorch [skɔːtʃ] s. arsură. vt. a arde; a jigni. vi. a merge ca fulgerul.

score [skɔː] s. (însemnare pe)

răboj; scor; situaţie; motiv; privinţă; *pl.* douăzeci; *pl.* zeci; partitură. *vt.* a înregistra; a nota; a marca (un punct); a orchestra.

scorn [skɔːn] *s.* (obiect de) dispreţ. *vt.* a dispreţui.

scornful ['skɔːnfl] *adj.* dispreţuitor; batjocoritor.

Scot [skɔt] *s.* scoţian(ă).

Scotch [skɔtʃ] *s.* (limba) scoţiană; whisky (scoţian); *the* ~ scoţienii. *adj.* scoţian(ă).

scot-free ['skɔt'friː] *adj.* cu faţa curată; fără pedeapsă.

Scotsman ['skɔtsmən] *s.* scoţian.

Scottish ['skɔtiʃ] *s.* (limba) scoţiană. *adj.* scoţian(ă).

scoundrel ['skaundrl] *s.* ticălos.

scour ['skauə] *s.* curăţire. *vt.* a curăţa; a alunga; a cutreiera.

scourge [skəːdʒ] *s.* bici; flagel. *vt.* a chinui.

scout [skaut] *s.* cercetaş; avion de recunoaştere. *vi.* a cerceta.

scowl [skaul] *s.* căutătură urîtă. *vt.*, *vi.* a privi urît.

scrag [skræg] *s.* os; slăbătură.

scraggy ['skrægi] *adj.* osos; slăbănog.

scramble ['skræmbl] *s.* tîrîş; bătaie; ceartă; învălmăşeală. *vi.* a se căţăra; a se tîrî; a se bate.

scrambled ['skræmbld] *adj.* (d. ouă) jumări.

scrap [skræp] *s.* bucăţică; rest; resturi; bătaie; tăieturi din ziare. *vt.* a arunca la gunoi. *vi.* a se bate.

scrape [skreip] *s.* hîrîit; hîrşiit; zgîrietură; strat subţire. *vt.* a curăţa; a freca; a zgîria; a face să hîrşîie, să scîrţîie; a aduna (cu greu). *vi.* a se freca; a hîrşîi; *to* ~ *along* a o scoate cu greu la capăt.

scraper ['skreipə] *s.* răzătoare.

scrapings ['skreipiŋz] *s. pl.* resturi; răzături.

scrap iron ['skræpˌaiən] *s.* fier vechi.

scratch [skrætʃ] *s.* zgîrietură; mîncărime; nimic. *vt.* a zgîria; a scărpina; a mîzgăli. *vi.* a scîrţîi; a se scărpina.

scrawl [skrɔːl] *s.* mîzgăleală. *vt.*, *vi.* a mîzgăli.

scrawny ['skrɔːni] *adj.* slab; deşirat.

scream [skriːm] *s.* ţipăt; grozăvie; veselie. *vt.*, *vi.* a ţipa.

screech [skriːtʃ] *s.* ţipăt (sinistru). *vi.* a ţipa (sinistru).

screen [skriːn] *s.* paravan; ecran; plasă; ciur. *vt.* a apăra; a ascunde; a ecraniza; a cerne; a alege.

screw [skruː] *s.* şurub; elice; stringere; constringere; zgîrcit. *vt.* a înşuruba; a fixa; a stoarce; a răsuci; *to* ~ *up one's courage* a-şi lua inima în dinţi. *vi.* a se răsuci; a fi zgîrcit.

scribble ['skribl] *s.* mîzgăleală; însemnare grăbită. *vt.*, *vi.* a mîzgăli; a nota în grabă.

scribbler ['skriblə] *s.* conţopist; scrib.

scribe [skraib] *s.* conţopist; autor.

scrimmage ['skrimidʒ] *s.* învălmăşeală; *sport* grămadă.

script [skript] *s.* scris; scenariu.

scroll [skroul] *s.* sul.

scrounge [skraundʒ] vt. a stoarce (fig.).

scrub [skrʌb] s. frecare; spălare. vt. a freca (cu peria).

scruff [skrʌf] s. ceafă.

scruple ['skru:pl] s. scrupul; greutate infimă.

scrupulous ['skru:pjuləs] adj. scrupulos; grijuliu; ireproşabil.

scrutinize ['skru:tinaiz] vt. a scruta.

scrutiny ['skru:tini] s. scrutare; scrutin.

scuffle ['skʌfl] s. încăierare.

scullery ['skʌləri] s. bucătărie din dos; bucătărioară.

sculptor ['skʌlptə] s. sculptor.

sculpture ['skʌlptʃə] s. sculptură. vt. a sculpta.

scum [skʌm] s. spumă (la supă); murdărie; fig. drojdia societăţii.

scurrilous ['skʌriləs] adj. batjocoritor; grosolan; obscen.

scurry ['skʌri] s. grabă. vi. a se grăbi.

scurvy ['skə:vi] s. scorbut. adj. scîrbos.

scutcheon ['skʌtʃn] s. blazon; scut.

scuttle ['skʌtl] s. căldare de cărbuni. vi. a pleca.

scythe [saið] s. coasă. vt., vi. a cosi.

sea [si:] s. mare; ocean; valuri; at ~ pe mare; fig. în încurcătură.

sea-cow ['si:'kau] s. morsă.

sea-dog ['si:dɔg] s. marinar; focă.

sea-going ['si: goiŋ] adj. maritim.

sea-gull ['si:gʌl] s. pescăruş.

seal [si:l] (piele de) focă; pecete; gir. vt. a pecetlui; a rezolva.

seam [si:m] s. cusătură; dungă (la ciorap); filon. vt. a brăzda.

seaman ['si:mən] s. marinar.

seamstress ['semstris] s. lenjereasă; cusătoreasă.

seaplane ['si:plein] s. hidroavion.

seaport ['si:pɔ:t] s. port maritim.

sear [siə] adj. uscat, ofilit; istovit. vt. a ofili; a arde.

search [sə:tʃ] s. cercetare; căutare; percheziţie. vt. a cerceta; a percheziţiona.

searching ['sə:tʃiŋ] adj. pătrunzător; cercetător; iscoditor.

searchlight ['sə:tʃlait] s. reflector.

searchparty ['sə:tʃ,pa:ti] s. echipă de salvare.

search-warrant ['sə:tʃ,wɔrnt] s. ordin de percheziţie.

seascape ['si:skeip] . s. peisaj marin.

seashore ['si:ʃɔ:] s. litoral.

seasick ['si:sik] adj. care suferă de rău de mare.

seasickness ['si:siknis] s. rău de mare.

seaside ['si:said] s. litoral.

season ['si:zn] s. timp; anotimp; sezon; stagiune; moment potrivit. vt. a potrivi; a condimenta.

seasonable ['si:znəbl] adj. plăcut; nimerit.

seasonal ['si:zənl] adj. sezonier.

seasoning ['si:zniŋ] s. condiment; condimentare.

season-ticket ['si:zn'tikit] s. abonament.

seat [si:t] s. scaun; bancă; (loc de) şezut; turul pantalonilor; reşedinţă; mandat (parlamentar). vt. a aşeza; (d.

săli etc.) a cuprinde (spectatori); *be ~ed!* ia loc! *vr.* a
se aşeza.

seaweed ['si:wi:d] *s.* algă.

seaworthy ['si:ˌwə:ði] *adj.* apt
pentru navigaţie.

secession [si seʃn] *s.* despărţire.

seclude [si:'klu:d] *vt.* a izola.

secluded [si'klu:did] *adj.* singuratic; de pustnic.

seclusion [si'klu:ʒn] *s.* izolare.

second ['seknd] *s.* secund; secundă; al doilea; ziua de doi.
adj. al doilea; de calitatea a
doua; secundar;ˈsuplimentar;
upon ~ thoughts răzgîndindu-
mă; *~ to none* fără rival.
num. al doilea. *vt.* a ajuta;
a secunda; a sprijini. *adv.* în
al doilea rînd; pe locul doi.

secondary ['sekndri] *adj.* secundar.

second best ['sekndbest] *adj.* de
mîna a doua.

seconder ['sekndə] *s.* ajutor;
secund.

second-hand ['sekndhænd] *s.* secundar. *adj., adv.* de ocazie;
din auzite.

second lieutenant ['seknd-
lef'tenənt] *s.* sublocotenent.

second rate ['seknd'reit] *adj.* de
calitatea a doua; inferior.

secrecy ['si:krisi] *s.* taină; discreţie; *in ~* pe ascuns.

secret ['si:krit] *s., adj.* secret.

secretary ['sekrətri] *s.* secre-
tar(ă); ministru.

Secretary of State ['sekrətri əv-
'steit] *s.* secretar de stat; *amer.*
ministru de externe.

secrete [si'kri:t] *vt.* a secreta.

secretion [si kri:ʃn] *s.* ascun-
dere; secreţie.

secretive [si'kri:tiv] *adj.* secretos.

sect [sekt] *s.* sectă.

sectarian [sek'tɛəriən] *adj.* sectar.

section ['sekʃn] *s.* secţie, secţi-
une; parte; categorie; capitol.

sector ['sektə] *s.* sector.

secure [si kjuə] *adj.* sigur; liniştit; în siguranţă; bine fixat.
vt. a(-şi) asigura; a apăra; a
fixa bine.

security [si'kjuəriti] *s.* siguranţă; securitate; garanţie; titlu
de proprietate.

sedan [si dæn] *s.* lectică; limuzină.

sedate [si'deit] *adj.* liniştit,
grav; aşezat.

sedentary ['sedntri] *adj.* seden-
tar.

sediment ['sedimənt] *s.* sedi
ment.

sedition [si'diʃn] *s.* rebeliune;
agitaţie publică.

seditious [si diʃəs] *adj.* aţîţător.

seduce [si'dju:s] *vt.* a seduce; a
atrage.

seduction [si'dʌkʃn] *s.* seducţie.

sedulous ['sedjuləs] *adj.* perseverent; muncitor.

see [si:] *vt.* a vedea; a zări;
a înţelege; a cunoaşte, a trece
prin; a primi; a vizita; a
consulta; a conduce; *to ~ off*
a conduce (la gară); *to ~ over*
a cerceta; a inspecta. *vi.* a
vedea; a avea văz (bun); a
înţelege; *~ !* priveşte!; *to
~ about* sau *after* a avea grijă
de; *to ~ into* a verifica; *to
~ to* a se ocupa de; a repara.

seed [si:d] *s.* sămînţă; sîmbure;
moştenitori.

seeder ['si:də] s. semănătoare.
seedling ['si:dliŋ] s. răsad ; puiet.
seedy ['si:di] adj. plin de seminţe ; ofilit.
seeing ['si:iŋ] conj. avînd în vedere.
seek [si:k] vt. a căuta ; a cerceta ; a cere ; a încerca ; to ~ out a descoperi. vi. a face cercetări ; a căuta.
seem [si:m] vi. a părea.
seeming ['si:miŋ] adj. aparent.
seemly ['si:mli] adj. cuvenit ; cuviincios.
seen [si:n] vt., vi. part. trec. de la see.
seer [siə] s. profet.
seesaw ['si:sɔ:] s. leagăn ; legănare. vi. a se da în leagăn.
seethe [si:ð] vi. a fierbe.
segment ['segmənt] s. segment ; bucată. vt., vi. a (se) segmenta ; a· (se) fracţiona.
segregate ['segrigeit] vt. a separa. vi. a face discriminări ; a se despărţi.
segregation [ˌsegri'geiʃn] s. segregaţie ; discriminare.
seize [si:z] vt. a prinde ; a cuprinde ; a apuca ; a confisca ; a profita de ; a se repezi la. vi.: to ~ upon a se agăţa de.
seizure ['si:ʒə] s. confiscare ; apucare ; acces.
seldom ['seldəm] adv. rar(eori).
select [si'lekt] adj. select ; snob ; exclusivist ; foarte bun. vt. a alege.
selection [si'lekʃn] s. selecţie ; culegere.
self [self] s. persoană ; fiinţă ; fire ; interese personale. adj. de sine ; auto…

self-abuse ['selfə'bju:s] s. masturbare ; înjosire de sine.
self-assertion ['selfə'sə:ʃn] s. îndrăzneală ; insistenţă.
self-assertive ['selfə'sə:tiv] adj. băgăreţ ; înfipt.
self-complacency ['selfkəm'pleisnsi] s. automulţumire.
self-confidence ['self'kɔnfidns] s. încredere în sine.
self-conscious ['self'kɔnʃəs] adj. timid ; şovăielnic ; cu complexe.
self-contained ['selfkən'teind] adj. stăpînit ; suficient.
self-control ['selfkən'troul] s. stăpînire de sine.
self-defence ['selfdi'fens] s. legitimă apărare.
self-denial ['selfdi'nail] s. jertfă de sine ; abnegaţie.
self-denying ['selfdi'naiiŋ] adj. altruist ; plin de abnegaţie.
self-determination ['selfdiˌtə:mi'neiʃn] s. autodeterminare.
self-educated ['self'edjukeitid] adj. autodidact.
self-evident ['self'evidnt] adj. de la sine înţeles.
self-government ['self'gʌvnmənt] s. autoguvernare ; stăpînire de sine.
self-help ['self'help] s. independenţă morală ; renunţare la ajutor din afară.
self-important ['selfim'pɔ:tnt] adj. îngîmfat, care-şi dă aere.
self-indulgence ['selfin'dʌldʒns] s. viaţă de plăceri ; destrăbălare.
selfish ['selfiʃ] adj. egoist ; egocentric.
selfishness ['selfiʃnis] s. egoism.
selfless ['selflis] adj. altruist ; plin de abnegaţie.

self-made ['self'meid] *adj*. cu caracter de autodidact ; ridicat prin propriile puteri ; parvenit ; făcut cu mîna lui.

self-possessed ['selfpə'zest] *adj*. calm.

self-preservation ['selfprezə-'veiʃn] *s*. instinct de conservare ; autoconservare.

self-reliance ['selfri'lains] *s*. încredere în mijloacele proprii.

self-respect ['selfris'pekt] *s*. demnitate.

self-sacrifice ['self'sækrifais] *s*. sacrificiu de sine ; abnegaţie ; altruism.

self-sacrificing ['self'sækrifaisiŋ] *adj*. care se jertfeşte pe ·sine ; plin de devotament ; altruist.

selfsame ['selfseim] *adj*. identic ; acelaşi.

self-satisfaction ['self‚sætis'fækʃn] *s*. automulţumire ; suficienţă ; înfumurare.

self-seeker ['self'siːkə] *s*. egoist ; carierist ; ciocoi.

self-seeking ['self'siːkiŋ] *s*. arivism ; carierism ; egoism.

self-service ['self'səːvis] *s*. autoservire. *adj*. cu autoservire.

self-styled ['self'staild] *adj*. pretins ; aşa-zis.

self-sufficient ['selfsə'fiʃnt] *adj*. îndestulător.

self-supporting ['selfsə'pɔːtiŋ] *adj*. independent din punct de vedere material.

self-taught ['self'tɔːt] *adj*. autodidact.

self-willed ['self'wild] *adj*. încăpăţînat ; capricios.

sell [sel] *s*. dezamăgire ; înşelăciune. *vt*. a vinde ; a escroca cu ; (*d. cărţi etc.*) *to be sold out*

a fi epuizat ; *to ~ up* a vinde la licitaţie ; *he is sold on music* e mare meloman. *vi*. a (se) vinde.

seller ['selə] *s*. vînzător ; lucru care se vinde.

selvage, selvedge ['selvidʒ] *s*. tiv.

selves [selvz] *s*. *pl*. de la **self**.

semblance ['semblns] *s*. asemănare ; aparenţă.

semibreve ['semi‚briːv] *s*. *muz*. notă întreagă.

semicolon ['semikoulən] *s*. punct şi virgulă.

seminar ['seminɑː] *s*. seminar (universitar).

seminary ['seminəri] *s*. seminar catolic.

semiquaver ['semi‚kweivə] *s*. *muz*. şaisprezecime.

semolina [semə'liːnə] *s*. griş.

sempstress ['semstris] *s*. lenjereasă ; cusătoreasă.

send [send] *vt*. a trimite ; a emite. *vi*. : *to ~ for the doctor* a chema doctorul.

sender ['sendə] *s*. expeditor.

send-off ['send'ɔːf] *s*. rămas bun.

senile ['siːnail] *adj*. senil.

senior ['siːnjə] *s*. persoană mai în vîrstă ; superior ; elev mai mare. *adj*. senior ; superior.

seniority [‚siːni'ɔriti] *s*. bătrîneţe ; vechime (în muncă) ; grad superior.

sensation [sen'seiʃn] *s*. senzaţie.

sense [sens] *s*. simţ ; sentiment ; înţelegere ; înţelepciune ; sens ; *to make ~* a (se) înţelege. *vt*. a-şi da seama de ; a simti ; a presimţi.

senseless ['senslis] ‾*adj*. inconştient ; fără sens.

sensibility [ˌsensiˈbiliti] s. sensibilitate ; înţelegere.

sensible [ˈsensəbl] adj. înţelept ; practic ; sensibil.

sensitive [ˈsensitiv] adj. sensibil ; firav.

sensitive plant [ˈsensitivˈplɑːnt] s. mimoză ; persoană hipersensibilă.

sensitivity [ˌsensiˈtiviti] s. sensibilitate.

sensory [ˈsensəri] adj. senzorial.

sensuous [ˈsensjuəs] adj. senzorial ; senzual.

sent [sent] vt., vi. trec. şi part. trec. de la send.

sentence [ˈsentəns] s. sentinţă ; osîndă ; propoziţie ; frază. vt. a condamna.

sentient [ˈsenʃnt] adj. sensibil.

sentiment [ˈsentimənt] s. sentiment(alism) ; părere.

sentimental [ˌsentiˈmentl] adj. sentimental.

sentimentality [ˌsentimenˈtæliti] s. sentimentalism.

sentry [ˈsentri] s. santinelă.

separate [ˈseprit] adj. separat ; despărţit.

separate [ˈsepəreit] vt., vi. a (se) separa.

separation [ˌsepəˈreiʃn] s. separaţie ; separare ; despărţire.

September [səpˈtembə] s. septembrie.

sepulchre [ˈseplkə] s. mormînt ; cavou.

sepulture [ˈseplt∫ə] s. înmormîntare.

sequel [ˈsiːkwl] s. urmare, continuare.

sequence [ˈsiːkwəns] s. succesiune ; secvenţă ; gram. corespondenţă.

sequester [siˈkwestə] vt. a sechestra.

seraglio [seˈrɑːliou] s. serai.

seraph [ˈserəf] s. serafim.

Serbian [ˈsəːbjən] s. sîrb(oaică) ; (limba) sîrbă.

serene [siˈriːn] adj. calm ; senin ; tihnit.

serf [səːf] s. iobag ; rob.

serfdom [ˈsəːfdəm] s. iobăgie ; feudalism.

serge [səːdʒ] s. gabardină ; serj.

sergeant [ˈsɑːdʒnt] s. sergent ; plutonier major; ofiţer de poliţie.

serial [ˈsiəriəl] s. roman foileton. adj. în serie ; foileton.

series [ˈsiəriːz] s. serie ; serii.

serious [ˈsiəriəs] adj. grav ; serios.

seriousness [ˈsiəriəsnis] s. seriozitate ; gravitate.

serjeant (at-arms) [ˈsɑːdʒnt (ətˈɑːmz)] s. cestor ; agent de ordine.

sermon [ˈsəːmən] s. predică.

serpent [ˈsəːpnt] s. şarpe.

serpentine [ˈsəːpntain] adj. viclean ; în serpentină.

serried [ˈserid] adj. înghesuit.

serum [ˈsiərəm] s. ser.

servant [ˈsəːvnt] s. servitor ; slugă ; fată în casă ; angajat.

serve [səːv] vt. a servi ; a sluji (la, pe) ; a asculta (de) ; a furniza ; a aproviziona ; a trata ; a îndeplini ; a ispăşi ; a înmîna ; a transmite. vi. a servi ; a fi în serviciu.

service [ˈsəːvis] s. serviciu. vt. a servi ; auto. a întreţine.

serviceable [ˈsəːvisəbl] adj. folositor ; serviabil ; durabil.

serviette [ˌsəːviˈet] s. şerveţel.

servile ['sə:vail] *adj.* slugarnic.
servitude ['sə:vitju:d] *s.* robie.
sesame ['sesəmi] *s.* susan.
session ['seʃn] *s.* sesiune ; şedinţă.
set [set] *s.* serviciu ; garnitură ; set ; echipament ; grup ; agregat ; decor ; platou ; apus. *adj.* aşezat ; fix(at) ; bine stabilit, decis. *inf., trec. şi part. trec. vt.* a pune ; a aţîţa ; a aranja ; a stabili ; a monta ; a transpune ; *to ~ about* sau *afloat* a lansa ; *to ~ back* a da înapoi ; *to ~ by* a pune la o parte ; *to ~ forth* a explica ; a face cunoscut ; *to ~ free* a elibera ; a descătuşa ; *to ~ off* a face să explodeze ; a porni ; a reliefa ; a separa ; *to ~ up* a înfiinţa ; a instala ; a instaura ; *to ~ right* sau *to rights* a îndrepta ; a aranja. *vi.* a apune ; a porni ; a se apuca ; a se înţepeni.
set-back ['setbæk] *s.* piedică ; eşec.
settee [se'ti:] *s.* canapea.
setter ['setə] *s.* rasă de cîini de vînătoare ; fixator.
setting ['setiŋ] *s.* cadru ; decor ; montură.
settle ['setl] *vt.* a rezolva ; a stabili ; a achita ; a coloniza ; a linişti ; a lăsa moştenire. *vi.* a se stabili ; a se linişti ; a-şi plăti datoriile ; *to ~ upon* a alege.
settlement ['setlmənt] *s.* aşezare ; dotă ; colonizare ; aşezămînt ; *fin.* achitare.
settler ['setlə] *s.* colonist.
seven ['sevn] *s., num.* şapte.
sevenfold ['sevnfould] *adv.* înşeptit.

seventeen ['sevn'ti:n] *s., num.* şaptesprezece.
seventeenth ['sevn'ti:nθ] *s., num.* al şaptesprezecelea.
seventh ['sevnθ] *s.* şeptime. *num.* al şaptelea ; *in the ~ heaven* în al nouălea cer.
seventieth ['sevntiiθ] *s., num.* al şaptezecilea.
seventy ['sevnti] *s.* vîrsta de şaptezeci de ani ; *pl.* deceniul al optulea. *num.* şaptezeci.
sever ['sevə] *vt.* a despica ; a despărţi. *vi.* a se despărţi.
several ['sevrl] *adj., pron.* mai mulţi.
severally ['sevrəli] *adv.* separat ; individual.
severance ['sevərns] *s.* despărţire ; separaţie.
severe [si'viə] *adj.* aspru ; sever ; auster.
sew [sou] *vt., vi.* a (se) coase.
sewage ['sju:idʒ] *s.* canalizare ; murdărie.
sewer¹ ['sjuə] *s.* canal (colector).
sewer² ['souə] *s.* cel care coase.
sewerage ['sjuəridʒ] *s.* canalizare.
sewing ['souiŋ] *s.* (haine de) cusut.
sewing-machine ['souiŋmə'ʃi:n] *s.* maşină de cusut.
sewn [soun] *vt., vi. part. trec.* de la sew.
sex [seks] *s.* sex ; sexualitate ; viaţă sexuală ; probleme sexuale.
sex appeal ['seks ə'pi:l] *s.* nuri, vino-ncoace ; farmec.
sexless ['sekslis] *adj.* fără sex ; insensibil.
sexton ['sekstn] *s.* paracliser ; cioclu.

shabby ['ʃæbi] adj. sărăcăcios ; ponosit ; meschin.

shack [ʃæk] s. colibă ; baracă.

shackle ['ʃækl] vt. a înlănţui ; a încătuşa.

shackles ['ʃæklz] s. pl. lanţuri ; cătuşe.

shade [ʃeid] s. (loc cu) umbră ; răcoare ; nuanţă ; abajur ; jaluzea. vt. a umbri ; a nuanţa.

shading ['ʃeidiŋ] s. nuanţă ; umbră.

shadow ['ʃædou] s. umbră (a cuiva) ; urmă. vt. a întuneca ; a fila.

shadowy ['ʃædoui] adj. umbros ; neclar ; întunecat.

shady ['ʃeidi] adj. umbros ; dubios.

shaft [ʃɑːft] s. săgeată ; puţ (de mină) ; horn; tehn. arbore, vilbrochen ; tijă.

shaggy ['ʃægi] adj. aspru ; lăţos ; neţesălat.

shah [ʃɑː] s. şahul Persiei.

shake [ʃeik] s. zguduire ; strîngere de mînă ; pl. folos. vt. a zgudui ; a clătina ; a cutremura ; to ~ hands with smb. a da mîna cu cineva. vi., vr. a se zgudui ; a (se cu)tremura.

shakedown ['ʃeikdaun] s. pat improvizat.

shaken ['ʃeikn] vt., vi. part. trec. de la shake.

shaky ['ʃeiki] adj. şubred ; tremurător.

shall [ʃl, 'ʃæl] v. aux. pentru pers. I sg. şi pl. ind. prez. v. mod. a trebui ; a fi obligat ; a avea ordin.

shallow ['ʃælou] s. vad. adj. puţin adînc ; fig. superficial.

shalt [ʃəlt, ʃælt] v. aux., v. mod.

pers. a II-a sing. ind. prez. de la shall. (inv.)

sham [ʃæm] s. imitaţie ; înşelătorie ; prefăcătorie ; fals. adj. fals ; prefăcut. vt. a simula. vi. a se preface.

shambles ['ʃæmblz] s. pl. abator ; masacru.

shame [ʃeim] s. ruşine ; nenorocire ; ~ on you ! for ~ ! să-ţi fie ruşine ! vt. a ruşina ; a face de rîs.

shamefaced ['ʃeimfeist] adj. ruşinos ; ruşinat.

shameful ['ʃeimfl] adj. ruşinos ; nemaipomenit.

shameless ['ʃeimlis] adj. neruşinat.

shampoo [ʃæm'puː] s. şampon ; spălat la cap. vt. a spăla părul.

shamrock ['ʃæmrɔk] s. trifoi ; emblema Irlandei.

shank [ʃæŋk] s. gambă.

shanty ['ʃænti] s. cocioabă ; cîntec marinăresc.

shape [ʃeip] s. formă ; figură ; siluetă. vt. a modela ; a forma. vi. a prinde formă.

shapeless ['ʃeiplis] adj. inform ; dezordonat.

shapely ['ʃeipli] adj. arătos ; bine format ; sculptural.

shard [ʃɑːd] s. ciob.

share [ʃɛə] s. porţie ; cotă ; fin. acţiune ; fier de plug. vt. a împărţi ; a împărtăşi ; a distribui.

shareholder ['ʃɛəˌhouldə] s. acţionar.

shark [ʃɑːk] s. rechin ; escroc.

sharp [ʃɑːp] s. diez. adj. diez ; ascuţit ; abrupt ; aspru ; acru ; intens ; isteţ ; necinstit. adv. brusc ;

muz. prea înalt ; punctual ; fix.

sharpen ['ʃɑːpn] *vt.*, *vi.* a (se) as-cuţi ; a (se) intensifica.

sharpener ['ʃɑːpnə] *s.* ascuţitor ; ascuţitoare.

sharper ['ʃɑːpə] *s.* trişor ; escroc.

shatter ['ʃætə] *vt.* a sfărîma ; a zdruncina. *vi.* a se sfărîma.

shave [ʃeiv] *s.* bărbierit ; scăpare ca prin urechile acului. *vt.*, *vi.* a (se) rade.

shaven ['ʃeivn] *adj.* bărbierit.

shaver ['ʃeivə] *s.* client al bărbierului ; flăcău.

Shavian ['ʃeivjən] *adj.* ca George Bernard Shaw *sau* referitor la el.

shaving ['ʃeiviŋ] *s.* bărbierit ; talaş.

shaving-brush ['ʃeiviŋ brʌʃ] *s.* pă-mătuf, pensulă de bărbierit.

shawl [ʃɔːl] *s.* şal.

she [ʃi(ː)] *adj.* femelă. *pron.* ea.

sheaf [ʃiːf] *s.* snop ; teanc.

shear [ʃiə] *vt.* a tunde ; a păcăli.

shears [ʃiəz] *s. pl.* foarfece mari.

sheath [ʃiːθ] *s.* teacă.

sheathe [ʃiːð] *vt.* a pune în teacă ; a acoperi.

sheaves [ʃiːvz] *s. pl. de la* sheaf.

shed [ʃed] *s.* adăpost ; şopron. *vt. inf.*, *trec.*, *part. trec.* a vărsa ; a scutura.

sheen [ʃiːn] *s.* lustru ; strălu-cire.

sheep [ʃiːp] *s.* oaie ; oi ; prosto-van ; enoriaşi.

sheep dog ['ʃiːpdɔg] *s.* cîine ciobănesc.

sheep fold ['ʃiːpfould] *s.* stînă, ocol.

sheepish ['ʃiːpiʃ] *adj* timid ; încurcat ; stîngaci.

sheep run ['ʃiːp rʌn] *s.* stînă, ocol.

sheepskin ['ʃiːpskin] *s.* blană de oaie.

sheer [ʃiə] *adj.* pur ; total.

sheet [ʃiːt] *s.* cearşaf ; foaie ; ziar.

shelf [ʃelf] *s.* poliţă ; raft *on the* ~ la index. *(fig.)*

shell [ʃel] *s.* coajă ; găoace ; carapace ; scoică ; obuz. *vt.* a coji ; a bombarda.

shellac [ʃə'læk] *s.* şerlac.

shellfish ['ʃelfiʃ] *s.* moluscă.

shelter. ['ʃeltə] *s.* adăpost. *vt.*, *vi.* a (se) adăposti.

shelve [ʃelv] *vt.* a pune la o parte ; a concedia.

shelves ['ʃelvz] *s. pl. de la* shelf.

shepherd ['ʃepəd] *s.* păstor. *vt.* a călăuzi ; a conduce.

shepherdess ['ʃepədis] *s.* păs-toriţă.

sherbet ['ʃəːbət] *s.* suc de fructe.

sheriff ['ʃerif] *s.* şerif.

sherry ['ʃeri] *s.* vin de Xeres.

Shetland horse ['ʃetləndhɔːs], **Shetland pony** ['ʃetlənd'pouni] *s.* ponei.

she-wolf ['ʃiː'wulf] *s.* lupoaică.

shibboleth ['ʃibəleθ] *s.* prin-cipiu fundamental ; piatră de încercare.

shield [ʃiːld] *s.* scut ; apărătoare. *vt.* a apăra.

shift [ʃift] *s.* schimb(are) ; expe-dient ; şmecherie. *vt.* a schim-ba, *vi.* a o scoate la capăt.

shiftless ['ʃiftlis] *adj.* neprevă-zător ; leneş.

shifty ['ʃifti] *adj.* înşelător ; nestatornic.

shilling ['ʃiliŋ] *s.* şiling.

shilly-shally ['ʃili͵ʃæli] *s.* şovăială; zăbavă. *vi.* a şovăi; a zăbovi.

shimmer ['ʃimə] *s.* licărire. *vi.* a licări; a străluci.

shin [ʃin] *s.* tibie, fluierul piciorului. *vi.* a se căţăra.

shindy ['ʃindi] *s.* scandal.

shine [ʃain] *s.* luciu; strălucire. *vt.* a lustrui. *vi.* a străluci.

shingle ['ʃiŋgl] *s.* pietriş; şindrilă; păr tăiat scurt.

shiny ['ʃaini] *adj.* strălucitor; lucios.

ship [ʃip] *s.* (aero)navă. *vt.* a expedia; a transporta.

ship-biscuit ['ʃip'biskit] *s.* pesmet marinăresc.

ship-broker ['ʃip͵broukə] *s.* agent de navlosire.

ship-canal ['ʃipkə͵næl] *s.* canal navigabil.

ship-chandler ['ʃip͵tʃɑ:ndlə] *s.* agent de aprovizionare a vaselor.

shipmate ['ʃipmeit] *s.* tovarăş din echipaj.

shipment ['ʃipmənt] *s.* transport; expediere.

shipowner ['ʃip͵ounə] *s.* armator.

shipping ['ʃipiŋ] *s.* expediere; transport (pe apă).

shipshape ['ʃipʃeip] *adj., adv.* pus la punct.

shipwreck ['ʃiprek] *s.* naufragiu; epavă. *vt.* a face să naufragieze; a ruina; *to be ~ed* a naufragia.

shipyard ['ʃip'jɑ:d] *s.* şantier naval.

shire ['ʃaiə] *s.* comitat.

shirk [ʃə:k] *vt.* a evita. *vi.* a se eschiva.

shirker ['ʃə:kə] *s.* chiulangiu.

shirt [ʃə:t] *s.* cămaşă; bluză.

shirt-front ['ʃə:tfrʌnt] *s.* plastron.

shiver ['ʃivə] *s.* tremur; fior. *vi.* a tremura. –

shoal [ʃoul] *s.* vad; apă mică; banc de nisip; cîrd de peşti.

shock [ʃɔk] *s.* lovitură; şoc (nervos etc.); *a ~ of hair* un păr zburlit. *vt.* a lovi; a şoca.

shocker ['ʃɔkə] *s.* lucru izbitor; roman poliţist.

shocking ['ʃɔkiŋ] *adj.* scandalos; dezgustător; îngrozitor.

shod [ʃɔd] *vt. trec. şi part. trec. de la* **shoe**.

shoddy ['ʃɔdi] *adj.* grosolan.

shoe [ʃu:] *s.* pantof; potcoavă. *vt.* a potcovi; a încălţa.

shoe-black ['ʃu:blæk] *s.* lustragiu.

shoehorn ['ʃu:hɔ:n] *s.* limbă de pantof.

shoe-lace ['ʃu:leis] *s.* şiret de pantof.

shoe-maker ['ʃu: meikə] *s.* pantofar.

shoe-string ['ʃu:striŋ] *s.* şiret de pantof.

shone [ʃɔn] *vt., vi. trec. şi part. trec. de la* **shine**.

shoo [ʃu:] *vt.* a alunga. *interj.* hîş.

shook [ʃuk] *vt., vi. trec. de la* **shake**.

shoot [ʃu:t] *s.* lăstar; lăstăriş; grup de vînători; jgheab. *vt.* a împuşca; a trage cu (arcul, arma); a trece (o cataractă); a fotografia; a filma. *vi.* a trage (cu o armă); a împuşca; a ţîşni; a şuta; a filma; a fotografia.

shooting ['ʃuːtiŋ] s. împuşcare; vînătoare; tir.

shooting-range ['ʃuːtiŋˌreindʒ] s. poligon de tragere.

shooting star ['ʃuːtiŋˌstɑː] s. stea căzătoare.

shooting yard ['ʃuːtiŋˌjɑːd] s. poligon de tir.

shop [ʃɔp] s. magazin, atelier.

shop assistant ['ʃɔpəˌsistnt] s. vînzător sau vînzătoare în magazin.

shop-hours ['ʃɔpauəz] s. orarul magazinelor.

shopkeeper ['ʃɔpˌkiːpə] s. negustor.

shopman ['ʃɔpmən] s. negustor; vînzător.

shopper ['ʃɔpə] s. cumpărător.

shopping ['ʃɔpiŋ] s. tîrguieli.

shop-steward ['ʃɔpstjuəd] s. delegat de atelier.

shop-stewards' committee ['ʃɔp stjuədzkə'miti] s. comitet de întreprindere.

shopwindow ['ʃɔp'windou] s. vitrină.

shore [ʃɔː] s. ţărm. vt. trec. de la shear.

shorn [ʃɔːn] vt. part. trec. de la shear.

short [ʃɔːt] s. film de scurt metraj; pl. şort, pantaloni scurţi. adj. scurt; ~ of insuficient; afară de; cît pe-aci să; for sau in ~ în două vorbe. adv. deodată, brusc; imediat.

shortage ['ʃɔːtidʒ] s. criză, lipsă.

short-circuit ['ʃɔːt'səːkit] s. scurtcircuit. vt. a scurtcircuita.

shortcoming [ʃɔːt'kʌmiŋ] s. deficienţă.

short cut ['ʃɔːt'kʌt] s. scurtătură.

shorten ['ʃɔːtn] vt., vi. a (se) scurta.

shorter short story ['ʃɔːtəˌʃɔːt 'stɔːri] s. schiţă; povestire.

short hand ['ʃɔːthænd] s. stenografie.

short-lived ['ʃɔːt'livd] adj. efemer.

shortly [ʃɔːtli] adv. curînd; pe scurt; brusc.

short-sighted ['ʃɔːt'saitid] adj. miop.

short-story ['ʃɔːt'stɔːri] s. nuvelă.

short-tempered ['ʃɔːt'tempəd] adj. nervos.

short time ['ʃɔːt'taim] s. scurt timp; şomaj parţial.

short-winded ['ʃɔːt'windid] adj. fără suflare.

shot [ʃɔt] s. împuşcătură; şut; lovitură; săgeată; ţintaş; bătaia puştii etc.; alice; sport greutate; încercare; fotografie; secvenţă; injecţie; doză. vt., vi. trec. şi part. trec. de la shoot.

shotgun ['ʃɔtgʌn] s. puşcă de vînătoare (cu ţeava scurtă).

should [ʃəd, ʃud] v. aux. pentru pers. I sing. şi pl., v. mod. trec. de la shall.

shoulder ['ʃouldə] s. umăr. vt. a încărca în spinare; a-şi asuma.

shoulder blade ['ʃouldəbleid] s. omoplat.

shoulder strap ['ʃouldəstræp] s. bridă, bretea; tresă.

shout [ʃaut] s. strigăt. vt., vi. a striga.

shove [ʃʌv] s. împingere; ghiont. vt. a împinge. vi. a (se) împinge; a-şi croi drum.

shovel ['ʃʌvl] s. lopată; lopăţică. vt. a lua sau a încărca cu lopata; a curăţa (zăpada) show [ʃou] s. manifestare; expoziţie; spectacol; ostentaţie; on ~ etalat. vt. a arăta; a manifesta; a dovedi; a conduce; to ~ up a demasca. vi. a se arăta; a se vedea; to ~ off a face pe grozavul.

show-down ['ʃoudaun] s. discuţie lămuritoare, explicaţie (între două persoane).

shower ['ʃauə] s. (aversă de) ploaie; duş; izbucnire; abundenţă.

shown [ʃoun] vt., vi. part. trec. de la show.

showy ['ʃoui] adj. arătos; împopoţonat; ostentativ.

shrank [ʃræŋk] vt., vi. trec. de la shrink.

shred [ʃred] s. zdreanţă; fărîmă. vt. inf., trec. şi part. trec. a zdrenţui.

shrew [ʃruː] s. scorpie (fig.).

shrewd [ʃruːd] adj. isteţ.

shriek [ʃriːk] s. ţipăt. vt., vi. a ţipa.

shrill [ʃril] adj. ascuţit.

shrimp [ʃrimp] s. crevetă.

shrine [ʃrain] s. chivot; altar.

shrink [ʃriŋk] vt. a face să se strîngă. vi. a se strînge; a se micşora; a intra la apă; a se da înapoi.

shrinkage ['ʃriŋkidʒ] s. micşorare; intrare la apă.

shrivelled ['ʃrivld] adj. zbîrcit.

shroud [ʃraud] s. linţoliu. vt. a înfăşura.

Shrove-Tuesday ['ʃrouv'tjuːzdi] s. ziua spovedaniei; lăsata secului.

shrub [ʃrʌb] s. arbust; tufiş.

shrubbery ['ʃrʌbəri] s. tufişuri; boschete.

shrug [ʃrʌg] s. ridicare din umeri. vi. a da din umeri.

shrunk [ʃrʌŋk] vt., vi. trec. şi part. trec de la shrink.

shrunken ['ʃrʌnkn] adj. strîns; scofîlcit.

shudder ['ʃʌdə] s. tremur; fior. vi. a tremura; a se înfiora.

shuffle ['ʃʌfl] s. tîrşîit; împărţirea cărţilor de joc. vt. a (-şi) tîrî (picioarele); a amesteca. vi. a merg egreu; a se eschiva; a face cărţile.

shun [ʃʌn] vt. a evita.

'shun [ʃən] interj. mil. drepţi!

shunt [ʃʌnt] vt. a muta; a schimba. vi. a se muta.

shut [ʃʌt] inf., trec. part. trec. vt. a închide; a prinde; to ~ up a fereca; a face să tacă. vi. a se închide; to ~ up a tăcea.

shutter ['ʃʌtə] s. oblon; jaluzele; foto. diafragmă.

shuttle ['ʃʌtl] s. suveică. vi. a merge încolo şi încoace.

shy [ʃai] adj. timid; fricos; şovăielnic.

sibilant ['sibilənt] s. consoană şuierătoare. adj. şuierător.

sick [sik] s.:the ~ bolnavii. adj. bolnav; indispus; on the ~ list bolnav; I'm going to be ~ îmi vine să vărs.

sickbed ['sikbed] s. patul bolnavului.

sicken ['sikn] vt. a scîrbi. vi. a boli; a se scîrbi.

sickle ['sikl] s. seceră.

sick-leave ['sikliːv] s. concediu de boală.

sickly ['sikli] adj. bolnăvicios; slab; greţos.

sickness ['siknis] s. boală; indispoziţie; greaţă.

side [said] s. parte; latură; faţ(et)ă; partid(ă); *on the wrong ~ of fifty* trecut (bine) de cincizeci de ani; *~ by ~* alături, umăr la umăr; *on the off ~ sport* dincolo de fundaşi. *adj.* lateral; lăturalnic; secundar. *vi.: to ~ with smb.* a fi de partea cuiva; a sprijini pe cineva.

side-board ['saidbɔ:d] s. bufet; servantă.

side-car ['saidkɑ:] s. ataş.

sidelong ['saidlɔŋ] *adj., adv.* pieziş, oblic; lateral.

side-track ['saidtræk] s. linie laterală. *vt.* a abate.

side-view ['saidvju:] s. (vedere din) profil.

side-walk ['saidwɔ:k] s. *amer.* trotuar; marginea drumului.

sideways ['saidweiz] *adj., adv.* lateral.

siding ['saidiŋ] s. linie secundară *sau* moartă.

sidle ['saidl] *vi.* a merge ferindu-se; a se furişa.

siege [si:dʒ] s. asediu.

sieve [si:v] s. sită.

sift [sift] *vt., vi.* a (se) cerne.

sigh [sai] s. oftat; suspin; foşnetul vîntului. *vt.* a spune oftînd. *vi.* a ofta; a suspina; *to ~ for* a tînji după.

sight [sait] s. vedere; văz; privelişte; părere; judecată; obiectiv turistic; *mil.* cătare; cantitate (mare); *by ~* din vedere; *in ~ of* aproape; *out of ~* departe; *within ~* cît vezi cu ochii; la vedere. *vt.* a zări; a da cu ochii de; a observa.

sightless ['saitlis] *adj.* orb.

sightly ['saitli] *adj.* plăcut la vedere.

sightseeing ['saitˌsi:iŋ] s. plimbare; vizită turistică.

sign [sain] s. semn; indicaţie; firmă; tăbliţă. *vt.* a semna(liza). *vi.* a se iscăli; a face semne; *to ~ on* sau *up* a se angaja; a se înrola; *to ~ off* a închide emisiunea.

signal ['signl] s. semnal. *adj.* important; remarcabil. *vt., vi.* a semnaliza.

signatory ['signətri] s., *adj.* semnatar.

signature ['signətʃə] s. autograf; semnătură.

sign-board ['sainbɔ:d] s. firmă.

signet ['signit] s. pecete.

significance [sig'nifikəns] s. semnificaţie.

significant [sig'nifikənt] *adj.* important.

signification [ˌsignifi'keiʃn] s. semnificaţie.

signify ['signifai] *vt.* a anunţa; a însemna. *vi.* a avea importanţă.

sign-post ['sainpoust] s. indicator de circulaţie.

silence ['sailəns] s. tăcere; linişte. *vt.* a linişti; a alina; a reduce la tăcere.

silent ['sailənt] *adj.* tăcut; liniştit; mut.

silhouette [ˌsilu'et] s. siluetă.

silica ['silikə] s. silice; cuarţ.

silicon ['silikən] s. siliciu.

silk [silk] s. mătase. *adj.* de mătase.

silken ['silkn] *adj.* de mătase; mătăsos.

silk hat ['silk'hæt] s. joben.

silkworm ['silkwə:m] s. vierme de mătase.

silky ['silki] adj. mătăsos; mieros.

sill [sil] s. pervaz; prag.

silly ['sili] s., adj. prost.

silo ['sailou] s. siloz.

silt [silt] s. mîl. vt. a (se) mîli.

silver ['silvə] s. argint. adj. argintiu. vt. a arginta. 'vi. a încărunţi.

silver-plate ['silvə'pleit] s. argintărie.

silversmith ['silvəsmiθ] s. argintar.

silvery ['silvri] adj. argintiu.

similar ['similə] adj. similar.

similarity [,simi'læriti] s. asemănare.

simile ['simili] s. comparaţie (figură de stil).

similitude [si'militju:d] s. asemănare; comparaţie.

simmer ['simə] vt., vi. a fierbe la foc mic.

simper ['simpə] s. zîmbet prostesc. vi. a zîmbi prosteşte; a face pe mironosiţa.

simple ['simpl] adj. simplu; simplist; sincer; deschis; umil.

simpleton ['simpltn] s. prostovan.

simplicity [sim'plisiti] s. simplitate; prostie.

simply ['simpli] adv. (pur şi) simplu; doar.

simulate ['simjuleit] vt. a simula; a imita.

simultaneous [,siməl'teinjəs] s. simultan.

sin [sin] s. păcat; imoralitate. vi. a păcătui.

since [sins] adv. de atunci încoace; între timp; long ~ cu mult timp în urmă. prep. (începînd) de la; din. conj. de cînd; întrucît.

sincere [sin'siə] adj. sincer; simplu.

sine [sain] s. mat. sinus.

sinew ['sinju:] s. tendon; muşchi; nerv.

sinewy ['sinju·i] adj. vîn(j)os; viguros; tare.

sinful ['sinfl] adj. păcătos.

sing [siŋ] vt. a cînta (din gură, în versuri); to ~ smb.'s praises a ridica pe cineva în slavă. vi. a cînta (din gură).

singe [sindʒ] s. arsură. vt., vi. a (se) arde; a (se) pîrli.

singer ['siŋə]´s. cîntăreţ; cîntăreaţă.

singing ['siŋiŋ] s. cînt; cîntare.

single ['siŋgl] adj. singur; simplu; direct. vt. a alege; a izola; a scoate în relief.

single combat ['siŋgl'kombət] s. duel.

single-handed ['siŋgl'hændid] adj. singur, fără ajutor.

singleness ['siŋglnis] s. unitate.

singly ['siŋgli] adv. separat; (de unul) singur.

sinless ['sinlis] adj. nevinovat; neprihănit.

sinner ['sinə] s. păcătos.

sing-song ['siŋsɔŋ] s. cîntare monotonă; ison.

singular ['siŋgjulə] s. singular. adj. singular; deosebit; ciudat.

singularity [,siŋgju'læriti] s. singularitate; ciudăţenie.

sink [siŋk] s. chiuvetă. vt. a scufunda; a săpa; a ascunde; a da uitării; a investi (capital). vi. a se cufunda; a coborî; a se prăbuşi; a pătrunde.

Sinn Fein ['ʃin'fein] s. mişcarea irlandeză de eliberare.

sip [sip] s. sorbitură. vt., vi. a sorbi pe încetul.

sir [sə:] s. domnule ; baronet ; cavaler.

sire ['saiə] s. sire ; tată ; strămoş.

sirloin ['sə:lɔin] s. file de muşchi.

sirup ['sirəp] s. sirop.

sister ['sistə] s. soră ; maică.

sisterhood ['sistəhud] s. dragoste de soră ; asociaţie feminină.

sister-in-law ['sistrinlɔ:] s. cumnată.

sit [sit] vi. a şedea ; a sta ; a cloci ; a se potrivi ; a face parte ; a fi membru ; to ~ down a se aşeza ; to ~ up a sta în capul oaselor.

site [sait] s. aşezare, loc ; şantier.

sitting ['sitiŋ] s. şedere ; şedinţă ; pozare (pentru un pictor).

sitting-room ['sitiŋrum] s. cameră de şedere, cameră de zi.

situation [ˌsitjuˈeiʃn] s. situaţie ; slujbă.

six [siks] s. şase ; at ~es and sevens talmeş-balmeş. num. şase ; ~ of one and half a dozen of the others ce mi-e baba Rada, ce mi-e Rada baba.

sixfold ['siksfould] adv. înşesit.

sixpence ['sikspns] s. (monedă de) şase penny.

sixteen ['siks'ti:n] s., num. şaisprezece.

sixteenth ['siks'ti:nθ] s. şaisprezecime. num. al şaisprezecelea.

sixth [siksθ] s. şesime. num. al şaselea.

sixtieth ['sikstiiθ] s., num. al şaizecilea.

sixty ['siksti] s. şaizeci ; deceniul al şaptelea. num. şaizeci.

sizable ['saizəbl] adj. mărişor.

size [saiz] s. mărime ; număr. vt. a aranja după mărime ; to ~ up a cîntări din ochi.

sizzle ['sizl] s. sfîrîit. vi. a sfîrîi.

skate [skeit] s. patină. vi. a patina.

skating-rink ['skeitiŋriŋk] s. patinoar.

skedaddle [ski'dædl] vi. a o şterge.

skein [skein] s. jurubiţă ; scul (de lînă).

skeleton ['skelitn] s. schelet ; schiţă ; secret.

skeleton key ['skelitn'ki:] s. speraclu.

skeptic ['skeptik] s., adj. sceptic.

sketch [sketʃ] s. schiţă. vt. a schiţa. vi. a face schiţe.

sketchy ['sketʃi] adj. schiţat ; incomplet.

skewer ['skjuə] s. frigare. vt. a pune în frigare.

ski [ski:, ʃi:] s. schiu. vi. a schia.

skid [skid] s. derapaj ; piedica roţii. vi. a derapa.

skier [ski:ə, ʃi:ə] s. schior.

skilful ['skilfl] adj. abil.

skill [skil] s. îndemînare ; pricepere.

skilled [skild] adj. priceput ; calificat.

skilly ['skili] s. zeamă lungă.

skim [skim] vt. a smîntîni ; a trece uşor peste ; a frunzări. vi. a trece ca gîsca pe apă.

skimp [skimp] vt., vi. a da cu zgîrcenie.

skimpy ['skimpi] *adj.* insuficient; scurt; calic; mic.

skin [skin] *s.* piele (netăbăcită); ten; burduf; coajă de măr etc. *vt.* a jupui. *vi.* a face caimac.

skinflint ['skinflint] *s.* avar.

skinny ['skini] *adj.* numai pielea şi oasele.

skip [skip] *s.* săritură; ţopăială. *vt.* a sări (peste); a trece cu vederea; a omite; a lăsa la o parte. *vi.* a sări; a ţopăi; a fugi; a face o călătorie fulger.

skipper ['skipə] *s.* căpitan.

skipping-rope ['skipiŋroup] *s.* coardă (de sărit).

skirmish ['skə:miʃ] *s.* încăierare; ambuscadă. *vi.* a duce lupte de hărţuială.

skirt [skə:t] *s.* fustă; *fig.* femeie; *pl.* margine. *vt.* a înconjura.

skit [skit] *s.* satiră.

skittle ['skitl] *s.* popic.

skulk [skʌlk] *vi.* a se furişa.

skull [skʌl] *s.* craniu.

skunk [skʌŋk] *s.* sconcs; păcătos.

sky [skai] *s.* cer; bolta cerului; *pl.* atmosferă; climă;

sky-high ['skai,hai] *s.* succes; victorie; noroc; prosperitate.

skylark ['skailɑ:k] *s.* ciocîrlie.

skylight ['skailait] *s.* lucarnă.

sky-line ['skailain] *s.* linia orizontului; siluetă.

sky-scraper ['skai,skreipə] *s.* zgîrie-nori.

skyward(s) ['skaiwəd(z)] *adj.*, *adv.* către cer.

slab [slæb] *s.* lespede.

slack [slæk] *s.* parte liberă; *pl.* pantaloni largi. *adj.* încet; leneş; moale; lejer, liber; pasiv. *vi.* a lenevi.

slacken ['slækn] *vt.* a încetini; a slăbi. *vi.* a o lăsa mai moale; a se destinde.

slacker ['slækə] *s.* chiulangiu; leneş; codaş.

slag [slæg] *s.* zgură.

slain [slein] *vt. part. trec. de la* **slay.**

slake [sleik] *vt.* a potoli; a stinge (varul).

slam [slæm] *s.* bufnitură; pocnitură; lovitură. *vt.* a trînti (uşa etc.); a bufni; a lovi. *vi.* a se trînti; a bufni.

slander ['slɑ:ndə] *s.* calomnie. *vt.* a calomnia.

slanderous ['slɑ:ndrəs] *adj.* calomnios.

slang [slæŋ] *s.* argou.

slangy ['slæŋi] *adj.* argotic.

slant [slɑ:nt] *s.* pantă; *amer.* concepţie. *vt., vi.* a se înclina.

slanting ['slɑ:ntiŋ] *adj.* oblic.

slap [slæp] *s.* palmă; lovitură. *vt.* a pălmui.

slap-dash ['slæp,dæʃ] *adj.* improvizat; neglijent.

slapstick ['slæpstik] *s.* comedie ieftină; umor grosolan.

slap-up ['slæp,ʌp] *adj.* straşnic; la modă.

slash [slæʃ] *s.* rană. *vt.* a tăia; a biciui.

slate [sleit] *s.* placă (de ardezie); tăbliţă; *amer.* listă de candidaţi. *vt.* a acoperi cu ţiglă; a ocărî; *amer.* a propune candidat.

slatepencil ['sleit,pensl] *s.* creion *sau* plumb pentru tăbliţe.

slattern ['slætən] *s.* femeie şleampătă.

slatternly ['slætənli] *adj.* şleampăt; neglijent.

slaughter ['slɔːtə] s. masacru; măcelărire. vt. a tăia; a masacra.

slaughterer ['slɔːtərə] s. parlagiu.

slaughter-house ['slɔːtəhaus] s. abator.

Slav [slɑːv] s., adj. slav(ă).

slave [sleiv] s. rob. vi. a robi; a trudi.

slave-driver ['sleiv‚draivə] s. paznic de sclavi.

slaver ['sleivə] s. proprietar sau negustor de sclavi; bale. vi. a-i curge balele.

slavery ['sleivəri] s. robie; sclavagism.

slavish ['sleiviʃ] adj. servil.

Slavonic [slə'vɔnik] s. (limba) slavă. adj. slav.

slay [slei] vt. a ucide.

sled(ge) [sled(ʒ)] s. sanie. vi. a se da cu sania.

sledge (hammer) ['sledʒ(‚hæmə)] s. baros.

sleek [sliːk] adj. lucios; alunecos; mieros.

sleep [sliːp] s. somn. vt. a găzdui; a alunga (oboseala etc.) dormind. vi. a dormi.

sleeper ['sliːpə] s. traversă de cale ferată; vagon de dormit.

sleeping ['sliːpiŋ] adj. adormit.

Sleeping Beauty ['sliːpiŋ'bjuːti] s. Frumoasa din Pădurea Adormită.

sleeping-ear ['sliːpiŋ kɑː] s. vagon de dormit.

sleeping-partner ['sliːpiŋ'pɑːtnə] s. comanditar.

sleeping-sickness ['sliːpiŋ'siknis] s. boala somnului.

sleepless ['sliːplis] adj. neodihnit; neobosit; fără somn; de nesomn.

sleeplesness ['sliːplisnis] s. insomnie.

sleep walker ['sliːp‚wɔːkə] s. somnambul(ă).

sleepy ['sliːpi] adj. somnoros; adormit.

sleet [sliːt] s. măzăriche; lapoviță.

sleeve [sliːv] s. mînecă.

sleigh [slei] s. sanie (cu cai).

sleight [slait] s. îndemînare; prestidigitație.

slender ['slendə]ˈ adj. subțire(l); puțintel.

slept [slept] vt., vi. trec. și part. trec. de la **sleep**.

sleuth (hound) ['sluːθ ('haund)] s. copoi.

slew [sluː] vt. trec. de la **slay**.

slice [slais] s. felie; bucată. vt. a tăia (felii).

slick [slik] adj. lucios; fățarnic; îndemînatic.

slid [slid] vt., vi. trec. și part. trec. de la **slide**.

slide [slaid] s. lunecuș; alunecare; tobogan; fotografie; diapozitiv; lamelă; tehn. sertar. vt. a face să alunece; a strecura. vi. a aluneca; a se da pe gheață.

slide-rule ['slaidruːl] s. riglă de calcul.

slight [slait] s. mojicie; desconsiderare. adj. ușurel; subțirel; fără importanță; not the ~est idea nici cea mai mică idee; cîtuși de puțin. vt. a desconsidera; a ofensa.

slightly ['slaitli] adv. ușor; oarecum.

slightingly ['slaitiŋli] adv. disprețuitor.

slim [slim] adj. subțirel; mic; viclean.

slime [slaim] *s.* clisă; noroi.

slimy ['slaimi] *adj.* murdar; perfid.

sling [slin] *s.* laţ; bandaj; praştie. *vt.* a arunca; a împroşca.

slink [slink] *vi.* a se furişa.

slip [slip] *s.* alunecare; scăpare; faţă de pernă; mlădiţă; fiţuică; bilet; fişă; *amer.* combinezon. *vt.* a îmbrăca în grabă; a strecura. *vi.* a aluneca; a scăpa; a cădea; a se strecura; a trece.

slip-knot ['slipnɔt] *s.* nod marinăresc.

slipper ['slipə] *s.* papuc de casă.

slippery ['slipəri] *adj.* alunecos; dubios.

slipshod ['slipʃɔd] *adj.* neglijent.

slit [slit] *s.* deschizătură; şliţ. *vt. inf., trec. şi part. trec.* a despica.

slobber ['slɔbə] *s.* bale; dulcegărie. *vt.* a îmbăla. *vi.* a-i curge balele; a plînge.

sloe [slou] *s. bot.* porumbă; porumbar.

slogan ['slougən] *s.* lozincă.

sloop [slu:p] *s.* cuter.

slop [slɔp] *s.* poliţist; *pl.* mîncare lichidă; lături.

slope [sloup] *s.* pantă; povîrniş. *vi.* a se povîrni; a fi în pantă; a atîrna.

sloppy ['slɔpi] *adj.* umed; apos; murdar; plîngăreţ.

slot [slɔt] *s.* deschizătură; şanţ. *vt.* a face o deschizătură în.

sloth [slouθ] *s.* lene; trîndăvie.

slothful ['slouθfl] *adj.* leneş; trîndav.

slot-machine ['slɔtmə‚ʃi:n] *s.* automat (pt. bomboane etc).

slouch [slautʃ] *s.* şedere într-o rînă; leneş. *vi.* a se bălăbăni.

slouch hat ['slautʃ'hæt] *s.* pălărie cu borurile mari.

slough¹ [slau] *s.* mlaştină.

slough² [slʌf] *s.* pielea şarpelui (care a năpîrlit); nărav părăsit.

slovenly ['slʌvnli] *adj.* şleampăt; neglijent.

slow [slou] *adj.* lent; greoi; *to be ~* a rămîne în urmă; *vt., vi.* a încetini. *adv.* încet.

slow fox ['slou fɔks] *s.* slow.

slowly ['slouli] *adv.* încet; lent.

slow train ['slou trein] *s.* (tren) personal.

sludge [slʌdʒ] *s.* moină; noroi.

slug [slʌg] *s.* limax; melc; glonţ.

sluggard ['slʌgəd] *s.* leneş.

sluggish ['slʌgiʃ] *adj.* trîndav; greoi.

sluice [slu:s] *s.* scurgere; ecluză. *vt.* a spăla.

slum [slʌm] *s.* locuinţă sărăcăcioasă; mahala.

slumber ['slʌmbə] *s.* somn; toropeală. *vi.* a dormi.

slump [slʌmp] *s.* criză; declin. *vi.* a cădea; a se lăsa moale.

slung [slʌn] *vt., vi. trec. şi part. trec. de la* sling.

slunk [slʌnk] *vi. trec. şi part. trec. de la* slink.

slur [slə:] *s.* reproş; mormăială; pronunţare neclară. *vt.* a mormăi; a trece repede peste. *vi.* a mormăi.

slush [slʌʃ] *s.* noroi; moină; dulcegărie.

slut [slʌt] *s.* femeie şleampătă *sau* stricată.

sly [slai] *s.: on the ~* în taină. *adj.* viclean.

smack [smæk] s. iz ; lovitură ; plescăit ; ţocăit. vt. a pocni ; a plescăi. vi. a avea iz ; a mirosi (a ceva).

small [smɔ:l] s.: the ~ of the back şale ; the ~ of the hand căuşul palmei. adj. (prea) mic ; slab.

small fry ['smɔ:l'frai] s. oameni mărunţi ; om neînsemnat, nimic.

smallpox ['smɔ:lpɔks] s. med. variolă.

smart [smɑ:t] s. durere. adj. dureros ; deştept ; obraznic ; elegant. vi. a simţi o durere ; a ustura ; a ~ alec(k) unul care face pe deşteptul ; the ~ set bogaţii ; protipendada.

smarten ['smɑ:tn] vt., vi. şi vr. a (se) face elegant ; a (se) împopoţona.

smash [smæʃ] s. ruină ; accident ; sport bombă. vt. a sfărîma.

smashing ['smæʃiŋ] adj. grozav ; uluitor.

smattering ['smætriŋ] s. fig. spoială.

smear [smiə] s. pată. vt., vi. a (se) păta.

smell [smel] s. miros(ire). vt., vi. a mirosi ; a adulmeca ; to ~ a rat a simţi ceva dubios.

smelling-salts ['smeliŋ‚sɔ:lts] s. pl. săruri (de amoniac) .

smelt [smelt] vt., vi. trec. şi part. trec. de la **smell.**

smile [smail] s. zîmbet. vi. a zîmbi.

smirch [smə:tʃ] s. pată. vt. a păta.

smirk [smə:k] s. zîmbet afectat. vi. a zîmbi afectat.

smite [smait] vt. a izbi ; a afecta ; a vrăji.

smith [smiθ] s. fierar ; potcovar.

smithereens ['smiðə'ri:nz] s. pl. bucăţele.

smithy ['smiθi] s. fierărie ; potcovărie.

smitten ['smitn] vt. trec. şi part. trec. de la **smite.**

smock (frock) ['smɔk ('frɔk)] s. salopetă ; barboteză.

smog [smɔg] s. ceaţă deasă (amestecată cu fum).

smoke [smouk] s. fum(at) ; ţigară. vt. a (a)fuma ; a înnegri ; a alunga cu fum. vi. a afuma ; a scoate fum.

smoke-dried ['smoukdraid] adj. (d. alimente) afumat.

smoker ['smoukə] s. fumător ; compartiment pentru fumători.

smoking ['smoukiŋ] s. fumat.

smoking-jacket ['smoukiŋ‚ʒdækit] s. smoching.

smoking-room ['smokiŋ‚rum] s. fumoar ; salonaş pentru fumat.

smoky ['smouki] adj. afumat ; plin de fum ; care scoate mult fum.

smooth [smu:ð] adj. neted ; lucios ; uşor ; nesincer ; fără zdruncinături. vt. a netezi ; a întinde ; a uşura. vi. a se linişti.

smooth-bore ['smu:ð'bɔ:] s. ţeavă neghintuită. adj. cu ţeava neghintuită ; neghintuit.

smooth-faced ['smu:ðfeist] adj. fără riduri ; nesincer.

smooth-spoken ['smu:ð‚spoukn] adj. mieros.

smooth-tempered ['smu:ð‚tempəd] adj. calm.

smooth-tongued ['smu:ð‚tʌŋd] adj. mieros ; blînd.

smote [smout] *vt. trec. de la* **smite**.

smother ['smʌðə] *vt.* a înăbuşi; a atinge. *vi.* a se sufoca.

smoulder ['smouldə] *s.* foc mocnit. *vi.* a mocni.

smudge [smʌdʒ] *s.* pată; murdărie. *vt., vi.* a (se) păta; a (se) mînji.

smug [smʌg] *adj.* mulţumit (de sine).

smuggle ['smʌgl] *vt.* a strecura (prin contrabandă).

smuggler ['smʌglə] *s.* contrabandist.

smugness ['smʌgnis] *s.* automulţumire; satisfacţie (de sine).

smut [smʌt] *s.* porcărie; pată. *bot.* tăciune; mălură. *vt.* a păta.

smutty ['smʌti] *adj.* murdar; obscen.

snack [snæk] *s.* gustare.

snack-bar ['snækbɑ:] *s.* bufet expres.

snag [snæg] *s.* colţ de stîncă; ciot.

snail [sneil] *s.* melc.

snake [sneik] *s.* şarpe.

snap [snæp] *s.* muşcătură; trosnet; instantaneu. *vt.* a muşca; a hăpăi; a pocni; a fotografia instantaneu. *vi.* a da să muşte; a pocni; a trosni.

snap dragon ['snæp drægn] *s. bot.* gura leului.

snappish ['snæpiʃ] *adj.* muşcător.

snappy ['snæpi] *adj.* muşcător; iute.

snapshot ['snæpʃɔt] *s.* instantaneu.

snare [snɛə] *s.* capcană. *vt.* a ispiti

snarl [snɑ:l] *s.* mîrîit. *vi.* a mîrîi; a-şi arăta colţii.

snatch [snætʃ] *s.* apucare; smulgere; fragment; crîmpei; asalt. *vt.* a apuca; a smulge. *vi.:* to ~ at a da să apuci.

sneak [sni:k] *s.* laş; om de nimic; pîrîtor. *vt.* a şterpeli. *vi.* a se furişa; a pîrî.

sneaking ['sni:kiŋ] *adj.* secret; furiş.

sneer [sniə] *s.* zîmbet dispreţuitor; ironie. *vi.* a rînji; a vorbi ironic.

sneeze [sni:z] *s.* strănut. *vi.* a strănuta.

snicker ['snikə] *s.* chicot. *vi.* a chicoti.

sniff [snif] *s.* pufăit; adulmecare. *vt.* a mirosi; a adulmeca. *vi.* a pufni; a adulmeca; a mirosi; a trage pe nas; a batjocori.

snigger ['snigə] *s.* chicotit. *vi.* a chicoti.

snipe [snaip] *s.* becaţă. *vt.* a împuşca pe la spate. *vi.* a trage cu puşca pe furiş.

sniper ['snaipə] *s.* franctiror.

snivel ['snivl] *s.* miorlăială; scîncet. *vi.* a scînci; a se miorlăi.

snob [snɔb] *s.* snob.

snobbish ['snɔbiʃ] *adj.* snob.

snobbery ['snɔbəri] *s.* snobism.

snoop [snu:p] *vi.* a spiona.

snooze [snu:z] *s.* aţipeală. *vi.* a aţipi.

snore [snɔ:] *s.* sforăit. *vi.* a sforăi.

snort [snɔ:t] *s.* forăială. *vi.* a forăi; a vorbi dispreţuitor.

snot [snɔt] *s.* muci.

snotty ['snɔti] *adj.* mucos; ţîfnos.

snout [snaut] *s.* rît; bot; nas.

snow [snou] *s.* zăpadă; ninsoare; cocaină. *vi.* a ninge;
a veni în valuri.

snow-ball ['snoubɔ:l] *s.* bulgăre
de zăpadă.

snow-boot ['snoubu:t] *s.* şoşon.

snowbound ['snoubaund] *adj.*
înzăpezit.

snow-clad ['snouklæd] *adj.* acoperit de zăpadă.

snowdrift ['snoudrift] *s.* troian.

snowdrop ['snoudrɔp] *s.* ghiocel.

snowflake ['snoufleik] *s.* fulg de
nea.

snowman ['snoumæn] *s.* om de
zăpadă.

snowshoe ['snouʃu:] *s.* rachetă
(de mers pe zăpadă).

snowstorm ['snoustɔ:m] *s.* viscol.

snowy ['snoui] *adj.* înzăpezit;
nins; imaculat.

snub [snʌb] *s.* ripostă; punere
la punct. *adj.* cîrn. *vt.* a jigni.

snuff [snʌf] *s.* tabac (de pri-
zat); muc de lumînare. *vt.* a
mucări; a stinge; a priza
(tabac). *vi.* a priza tabac; a
muri.

snuffers ['snʌfəz] *s. pl.* mucar-
niţă.

snuffle ['snʌfl] *s.* fornăit. *vi.*
a (se) fîrnîi.

snug [snʌg] *adj.* confortabil;
călduros.

snuggle ['snʌgl] *vt.* a strînge
în braţe. *vi.* a se cuibări.

snugness ['snʌgnis] *s.* (sentiment
de) confort.

so [sou] *adv.* astfel, aşa (de);
Mr. ~ *and* ~ domnul cutare;
~ *far* deocamdată; ~ *long*
la revedere; ~ *long as* atîta
vreme cît; *not* ~ *much as*
nici măcar; ~ *many* atîtea,

atîţia; ~ *much* ~ ... *that*
în aşa măsură încît; *and* ~
on, and ~ *forth* şi aşa mai
departe. *conj.* aşadar; de aceea;
vasăzică; ~ *that's that* şi cu
asta basta; ~ *that* ca să; ~ *as
to* pentru a.

soak [souk] *s.* muiere, înmu-
iere; udare. *vt.* a uda; a muia;
a înmuia; a pocni. *vi.* a se
uda; a trage la măsea; *to* ~
through a pătrunde.

soaker ['soukə] *s.* aversă; u-
deală; beţivan.

soap [soup] *s.* săpun. *vt.* a săpuni; a flata.

soap opera ['soup'ɔprə] *s.* pro-
grame (comerciale) proaste la
radio etc.

soap suds ['soupsʌdz] *s. pl.*
clăbuci de săpun.

soapy ['soupi] *adj.* plin de săpun; unsuros; mieros.

soar [sɔ:] *vi.* a se înălţa (spre
cer); a creşte.

sob [sɔb] *s.* suspin; oftat. *vt.*
a spune printre suspine. *vi.* a
suspina; a ofta; a plînge.

sober ['soubə] *adj.* treaz; sobru;
calm; prudent. *vt., vi.* a (se)
linişti; a se trezi.

sober-minded ['soubə,maindid]
adj. înţelept.

so-called ['so'kɔ:ld] *adj.* aşa-zis;
pretins.

soccer ['sɔkə] *s.* fotbal.

sociable ['souʃəbl] *adj.* sociabil;
prietenos.

social ['souʃl] *s.* reuniune; şezătoare. *adj.* social; prietenos.

socialism ['souʃəlizəm] *s.* socialism.

socialist ['souʃəlist] *s., adj.* socialist.

socialize ['souʃəlaiz] *vt.* a socializa ; a naţionaliza.

socially ['souʃəli] *adv.* în societate ; social.

society [sə'saiəti] *s.* societate
(aleasă) ; tovărăşie.

sock [sɔk] *s.* şosetă ; ciorap
bărbătesc ; lovitură. *vt.* a pocni.

socket ['sɔkit] *s.* dulie ; găvan ;
gaură ; orbită.

sod [sɔd] *s.* gazon ; iarbă.

soda ['soudə] *s.* sodă ; sodiu ;
sifon.

soda-fountain ['soudə‚fauntin] *s.*
chioşc, stand *sau* raion de răcoritoare.

soda-water ['soudə‚wɔ:tə] *s.* sifon.

sodden ['sɔdn] *adj.* ud (pînă
la piele) ; beat turtă ; moale.

sofa ['soufə] *s.* canapea, divan.

soft [sɔft] *adj.* moale ; neted ;
dulce ; blînd ; prostuţ ; slab ;
uşor.

soften ['sɔfn] *vt., vi.* a (se) muia.

soft-headed ['sɔft‚hedid] *adj.*
prostuţ ; ramolit.

soft-hearted ['sɔft‚hɑ:tid] *adj.*
cu inima blîndă ; sentimental.

softness ['sɔfnis] *s.* moliciune ;
blîndeţe.

soft-soap ['sɔft‚soup] *s.* săpun
lichid ; linguşire. *vt.* a linguşi.

soft-spoken ['sɔft‚spoukn] *adj.*
(cu glas) blînd.

soft-wood ['sɔft‚wud] *s.* (lemn
de) esenţă moale.

soggy ['sɔgi] *adj.* ud leoarcă.

soil [sɔil] *s.* sol, pămînt. *vt.,
vi.* a (se) murdări *sau* mînji.

soiree ['swɑ:rei] *s.* serată.

sojourn ['sɔ:dʒə:n] *s.* şedere ;
vizită. *vi.* a sta ; a rămîne.

solace ['sɔlis] *s.* consolare. *vt.*
a consola.

sold [sould] *vt., vi. trec. şi part.
trec. de la* **sell.**

solder ['sɔldə] *s.* cositor de lipit. *vt.* a lipi (metale).

soldier ['souldʒə] *s.* soldat ; militar. *vi.* a servi în armată.

soldiery ['souldʒəri] *s. mil.*
trupă.

sole [soul] *s.* talpă ; *iht.* limbă-
de-mare. *adj.* singur ; unic. *vt.*
a tălpui.

soleeism ['sɔlisizəm] *s.* greşeală
(în vorbire).

solely ['soulli] *adv.* numai.

solemn ['sɔləm] *adj.* solemn,
grav ; important.

solemnity [sə'lemniti] *s.* solemnitate ; ceremonie ; gravitate.

solemnize ['sɔləmnaiz] *vt.* a
sfinţi ; a celebra.

solicitor [sə'lisitə] *s.* jurisconsult.

solicitous [sə'lisitəs] *adj.* atent ;
grijuliu.

solid ['sɔlid] *s.* solid ; *pl.* hrană
solidă. *adj.* solid ; solidar ; masiv ; unanim ; neîntrerupt.

solidarity [‚sɔli'dæriti] *s.* solidaritate.

soliloquize [sə'liləkwaiz] *vi.* a
vorbi singur.

soliloquy [sə'liləkwi] *s.* monolog.

solitaire [‚sɔli'tɛə] *s.* pasienţă.

solitary ['sɔlitri] *adj.* singur ;
singuratic ; izolat.

solitary confinement ['sɔlitri-
kən'fainmənt] *s.* regim de carceră.

solitude ['sɔlitju:d] *s.* singurătate.

soloist ['souloist] *s.* solist.

solstice ['sɔlstis] *s.* solstiţiu.

soluble ['sɔljubl] *adj.* solubil ;
rezolvabil.

solution [sə'lu:ʃn] *s.* soluţie; rezolvare; dizolvare.

solve [sɔlv] *vt.* a rezolva.

solvent ['sɔlvnt] *s.* solvent. *adj.* solvabil; solvent.

somber, sombre ['sɔmbə] *adj.* sumbru; întunecos; trist.

some [sʌm] *adj.* nişte; oarecare; puţin(ă); straşnic; ~ *day* într-o bună zi. *pron.* cîţiva; unii. *adv.* vreo, circa.

somebody ['sʌmbədi] *pron.* cineva.

somehow ['sʌmhau] *adv.* cumva.

someone ['sʌmwʌn] *pron.* cineva.

somersault ['sʌməsɔ:lt] *s.* tumbă. *vi.* a se da tumba.

something ['sʌmθiŋ] *pron.* ceva. *adv.* oarecum.

sometime ['sʌmtaim] *adj.* fost. *adv.* cîndva.

sometimes ['sʌmtaimz] *adv.* uneori.

somewhat ['sʌmwɔt] *pron.* ceva. *adv.* oarecum.

somewhere ['sʌmwɛə] *adv.* undeva.

son [sʌn] *s.* fiu, băiat.

song [sɔŋ] *s.* cîntec; poezie; cîntare; cînt.

song-bird ['sɔŋbə:d] *s.* pasăre cîntătoare.

song-book ['sɔŋbuk] *s.* carte de cîntece.

songster ['sɔŋstə] *s.* cîntăreţ; poet; pasăre cîntătoare.

son-in-law ['sʌninˌlɔ:] *s.* ginere.

sonny ['sʌni] *s.* băiete.

sonorous [sə'nɔ:rəs] *adj.* sonor; răsunător; strălucitor.

soon [su:n] *adv.* curînd; devreme; *as* ~ *as* de îndată ce; *no* ~*er* ... *than* nici ... că; *I'd* ~*er* prefer.

soot [su:t] *s.* funingine. *vt.* a murdări.

soothe [su:ð] *vt.* a linişti; a împăca; a alina.

soothingly ['su:ðiŋli] *adv.* blînd; dulce.

soothsayer ['su:θˌsɛə] *s.* ghicitoare.

sooty ['su:ti] *adj.* negru; murdar.

sop [sɔp] *s.* pîine muiată. *vt.* a muia; a şterge (apa).

sophisticated [sə'fistikeitid] *adj.* complicat; rafinat.

sophistry ['sɔfistri] *s.* sofism.

sophomore ['sɔfəmɔ:] *s.* student în anul al II-lea.

sopping ['sɔpiŋ] *adj.* (ud) leoarcă.

soppy ['sɔpi] *adj.* ud leoarcă; siropos.

sorcerer ['sɔ:srə] *s.* vrăjitor.

sorcery ['sɔ:sri] *s.* vrăjitorie; vrăji.

sordid ['sɔ:did] *adj.* murdar; josnic.

sore [sɔ:] *s.* bubă; punct dureros. *adj.* dureros; trist; supărat; cumplit; *to be* ~ *a durea*; a fi furios.

sorely ['sɔ:li] *adv.* groaznic; foarte.

sorrel ['sɔrl] *s.* măcriş; roib. *adj.* roib; roşiatic.

sorrow ['sɔrou] *s.* supărare; necaz. *vi.* a se necăji.

sorrowful ['sɔrəfl] *adj.* trist; nefericit.

sorry ['sɔri] *adj.* supărat; trist; *I am* ~ scuzaţi; îmi pare rău.

sort [sɔ:t] *s.* fel; gen; *all of a* ~ toţi o apă; *after a* ~ într-o oarecare măsură; ~ *of* oarecum; *out of* ~*s* indispus.

vt. a sorta; a alege. *vi.* a se potrivi.

SOS ['es'ou'es] *s.* apel desperat.

so-so ['sousou] *adj.* aşa şi aşa.

sot [sɔt] *s.* beţivan.

sough [sau] *s.* foşnet; şoaptă. *vi.* a foşni.

sought [sɔ:t] *vt., vi. trec. şi part. trec. de la* **seek**.

soul [soul] *s.* suflet.

soulful ['soulfl] *adj.* sentimental.

soulless ['soullis] *adj.* egoist; hain.

sound [saund] *s.* sunet; *med.* sondă. *adj.* sănătos; solid; înţelept. *vt.* a face să răsune; a verifica; a sonda. *vi.* a (ră)-suna; a sonda. *adv.* profund; *he is ~ asleep* doarme dus.

sound-film ['saundfilm] *s.* film sonor.

sounding ['saundiŋ] *s.* sondare; măsurătoare.

soundly ['saundli] *adv.* sănătos; profund.

soundness ['saundnis] *s.* sănătate; soliditate.

sound-proof ['saundpru:f] *adj.* capitonat.

soup [su:p] *s.* supă; *in the ~* la ananghie.

sour ['sauə] *adj.* acru. *vt., vi.* a (se) acri.

sourness ['sauənis] *s.* acritură; ţîfnă.

source [sɔ:s] *s.* izvor.

souse [saus] *vt.* a uda; a îmbăta.

south [sauθ] *s.* sud. *adj.* sudic. *adv.* spre sud.

southerly ['sʌðəli] *adj.* sudic; din sud. *adv.* spre sud.

southern ['sʌðən] *adj.* sudic.

southerner ['sʌðənə] *s.* locuitor din sud(ul S.U.A.).

southward ['sauθwəd] *adj.* sudic. *adv.* spre sud.

southwester [sau(θ)'westə] *s.* vînt din sud-vest; *mar.* pălărie impermeabilă.

sovereign ['sɔvrin] *s.* suveran; *fin.* liră de aur. *adj.* suveran; suprem.

sovereignty ['sɔvrnti] *s.* suveranitate; autoritate.

soviet ['souviet] *s.* soviet. *adj.* sovietic.

sow[1] [sou] *vt.* a însămînţa; a planta; *fig.* a răspîndi; *to ~ one's wild oats* a-şi face de cap (în tinereţe). *vi.* a semăna.

sow[2] [sau] *s.* scroafă.

sown [soun] *vt., vi. part. trec. de la* **sow**[1].

soy(a) ['sɔi(ə)] *s.* soia.

soybean ['sɔibi:n] *s.* (păstaie de) soia.

spa [spɑ:] *s.* izvor mineral; staţiune balneoclimaterică.

space [speis] *s.* spaţiu; perioadă. *vt.* a spaţia.

spaceman ['speismən] *s.* cosmonaut.

spaceship ['speisʃip] *s.* navă cosmică.

spacious ['speiʃəs] *adj.* spaţios; întins.

spade [speid] *s.* cazma; **pică** (*la cărţi*). *vt.* a săpa.

span[1] [spæn] *s.* (distanţă de o) palmă, şchioapă; anvergură; deschidere. *vt.* a traversa.

span[2] [spæn] *vt., vi. trec. de la* **spin**.

spangle ['spæŋl] *s.* podoabă; *pl.* paiete. *vt.* a înstela.

Spaniard ['spænjəd] *s.* spaniol(ă)

spaniel ['spænjəl] s. prepelicar.

Spanish ['spæniʃ] s. (limba) spaniolă; *the* ~ spaniolii. *adj.* spaniol.

spank [spæŋk] s. scatoalcă. *vt.* a bate.

spanking [spæŋkiŋ] s. chelfăneală.

span of life ['spænəv'laif] s. durata medie a vieţii.

spar [spɑ:] s. ceartă; **box**; *fig.* duel. *vi.* a boxa.

spare [spɛə] s. piesă *sau* roată de rezervă. *adj.* suplimentar; de rezervă; liber; subţirel. *vt.* a cruţa; a economisi; a avea disponibil.

sparing ['spɛəriŋ] *adj.* econom; cumpătat.

spark [spɑ:k] s. scînteie; urmă. *vi.* a scînteia.

spark(ing)-plug ['spɑ:k(iŋ)plʌg] s. bujie.

sparkle [spɑ:kl] s. licărire; scînteiere. *vi.* a scînteia; a licări; a străluci; a face spumă.

sparrow ['spærou] s. vrabie.

sparrow-hawk ['spærouhɔ:k] s. erete.

sparse [spɑ:s] *adj.* rar; răspîndit; subţire.

spasm ['spæzəm] s. spasm.

spat [spæt] s. lovitură; *pl.* ghetre. *vt.*, *vi.* *trec. şi part. trec. de la* **spit**.

spatial ['speiʃl] *adj.* spaţial; cosmic.

spatter ['spætə] s. plescăit; ploaie scurtă; ploaie (de gloanţe). *vt.* a stropi. *vi.* a cădea ca o ploaie.

spawn [spɔ:n] s. icre; spori; *iron.* odrasle. *vi.* a-şi depune icrele.

speak [spi:k] *vt.* a spune; a enunţa. *vi.* a vorbi; a ţine cuvîntări; a fi expresiv; a suna; *to* ~ *out* sau *up* a vorbi răspicat; a-şi spune cuvîntul.

speak-easy ['spi:k,i:zi] s. tavernă.

speaker ['spi:kə] s. vorbitor; preşedinte (al Camerei Comunelor etc.).

speaking-tube ['spi:kiŋtju:b] s. portavoce.

spear [spiə] s. suliţă.

spear-head ['spiəhed] s. vîrf de suliţă; *fig.* ascuţiş; lovitură principală. *vt.* a îndrepta (un atac).

special ['speʃl] *adj.* special.

specially ['speʃəli] *adv.* anume.

specialty ['speʃlti] s. specialitate.

specie [spi:ʃi:] s. monezi.

species ['spi:ʃi:z] s. specie; specii.

specifically [spi sifikəli] *adv.* specific; precis; şi anume.

specify ['spesifai] *vt.* a specifica.

specimen ['spesimən] s. specimen; mostră; exemplu.

specious ['spi:ʃəs] *adj.* aparent veridic; înşelător; dubios.

speck [spek] s. fir (de praf); fărîmiţă; pată. *vt.* a păta.

speckled ['spekld] *adj.* bălţat; pătat.

specs [speks] s. *pl.* ochelari.

spectacle ['spektəkl] s. spectacol; privelişte; *pl.* ochelari.

spectacular [spek'tækjulə] *adj.* spectaculos.

spectator [spek'teitə] s. spectator.

specter, **spectre** ['spektə] s. strigoi; spectru.

spectrum ['spektrəm] s. *fiz.* spectru.

speculate ['spekjuleit] *vt.* a face speculaţii; a medita.

speculation [ˌspekju'leiʃn] *s.* speculaţie; meditaţie; presupunere.

speculative ['spekjulətiv] *adj.* speculativ; meditativ; bazat pe presupuneri.

sped [sped] *vt., vi. trec. şi part. trec. de la* **speed.**

speech [spi:tʃ] *s.* cuvîntare; vorbire; limbaj; limbă.

speechify ['spi:tʃifai] *vi.* a ţine discursuri.

speechless ['spi:tʃlis] *adj.* mut; uluit.

speed [spi:d] *s.* viteză; rapiditate. *vt.* a grăbi; (*to wish smb.*) *God* ~ (a ura cuiva) succes. *vi.* a (se) grăbi; a merge în viteză.

speed-boat ['spi:dbout] *s.* vedetă rapidă.

speed limit ['spi:dˌlimit] *s.* viteză maximă.

speedometer [spi:'dɔmitə] *s.* vitezometru.

speed-up ['spi:dʌp] *s.* accelerarea ritmului de muncă.

speedway ['spi:dwei] *s.* pistă; autostradă.

speedy ['spi:di] *adj.* grabnic; rapid.

spell [spel] *s.* farmec; vrajă; perioadă. *vt.* a vrăji; a citi literă cu literă; a însemna. *vi.* a silabisi.

spellbound ['spelbaund] *adj.* vrăjit.

spelling ['speliŋ] *s.* ortografie; citire literă cu literă.

spelt [spelt] *vt., vi. trec. şi part. trec. de la* **spell.**

spend [spend] *vt.* a cheltui; a consuma; a petrece (timpul). *vi.* a cheltui.

spender ['spendə] *s.* risipitor.

spendthrift ['spendθrift] *s., adj.* risipitor.

spent [spent] *adj.* istovit; uzat. *vt., vi. trec. şi part. trec. de la* **spend.**

sperm [spə:m] *s.* spermă.

spermaceti [ˌspə:mə'seti] *s.* spermanţet.

sperm whale ['spə:mweil] *s.* caşalot.

sphere [sfiə] *s.* sferă; glob; domeniu.

spice [spais] *s.* condiment, mirodenie. *vt.* a condimenta.

spick and span ['spikən'spæn] *adj.* curat; ca scos din cutie.

spicy ['spaisi] *adj.* picant.

spider ['spaidə] *s.* păianjen.

spigot ['spigət] *s.* cep.

spike [spaik] *s.* ţintă; cui; ţeapă; spic. *vt.* a înţepa.

spiked boots ['spaiktbu:ts] *s. pl.* bocanci cu ţinte.

spiky ['spaiki] *adj.* ţepos.

spill [spil] *vt.* a vărsa; a răsturna. *vi.* a da pe dinafară.

spilt [spilt] *vt., vi. trec. şi part. trec. de la* **spill.**

spin [spin] *s.* răsucire. *vt.* a răsuci; a toarce; a învîrti; *to* ~ *a coin* a da cu banul. *vi.* a se învîrti; a toarce.

spinach ['spinidʒ] *s.* spanac.

spinal ['spainl] *adj.* dorsal.

spinal cord ['spainl'kɔ:d] *s.* şira spinării.

spindle ['spindl] *s.* fus; axă; osie.

spine [spain] *s.* spinare; ac; ţeapă.

spineless ['spainlis] *adj.* fără şira spinării.

spinet ['spinet] s. claveciu.

spinner ['spinə] s. filator; torcătoare.

spinning-mill ['spíniŋ mil] s. filatură.

spinning-wheel ['spiniŋwi:l] s. vîrtelniţă.

spinster ['spinstə] s. fată bătrînă; torcătoare.

spire ['spaiə] s. turlă.

spirit ['spirit] s. spirit; suflet; fantomă; însufleţire; pl. băuturi spirtoase; spirt; in high ~s bine dispus; entuziast.

spirited ['spiritid] adj. vioi; curajos.

spiritless ['spiritlis] adj. fără vlagă; neinteresant.

spiritual ['spiritjuəl] adj. sufletesc; spiritual; religios.

spirituous ['spiritjuəs] adj. spirtos.

spit [spit] s. scuipat; scuipare; frigare. vt. a scuipa; a rosti; a ţipa; a pune în frigare. vi. a scuipa.

spite [spait] s. pică; duşmănie; răutate; in ~ of în ciuda. vt. a supăra; a necăji; a face în ciudă (cuiva).

spiteful ['spaitfl] adj. ranchiunos; duşmănos.

spittle ['spitl] s. scuipat.

spittoon [spi'tu:n] s. scuipătoare.

spiv [spiv] s. escroc; traficant; parazit.

splash [splæʃ] s. plescăială; împroşcare. vt., vi. a împroşca.

spleen [spli:n] s. splină; proastă dispoziţie; plictis.

splendid ['splendid] adj. splendid; minunat.

splendo(u)r ['splendə] s. splendoare; glorie.

splice [splais] s. îmbinare; nod. vt. a îmbina; a înnoda; a lipi; a căsători.

splint [splint] s. lopăţică.

splinter ['splintə] s. aşchie; schijă. vt. a despica; a tăia.

split [split] s. ruptură; sciziune; băutură răcoritoare. vt. inf., trec. şi part. trec. a despica; a dezbina; a se scinda; to ~ on a denunţa.

splutter ['splʌtə] s. bolboroseală; plescăială. vt., vi. a bolborosi.

spoil [spɔil] s. pradă; pl. profit. vt. a strica; a răsfăţa. vi. a se strica.

spoilt [spɔilt] adj. răsfăţat; neastîmpărat. vt. part. trec. de la spoil.

spoke [spouk] s. spiţă. vt., vi. trec. de la speak.

spoken ['spoukn] vt., vi. part. trec. de la speak.

spokesman ['spouksmən] s. purtător de cuvînt; reprezentant.

sponge [spʌndʒ] s. burete; fig. parazit. vi.: to ~ on smb. a trăi pe socoteala cuiva.

sponger. ['spʌndʒə] s. parazit (fig.).

sponsor ['spɔnsə] s. epitrop; patron (fig.); naş; iniţiator. vt. a sprijini; a finanţa.

spontaneous [spən'teinjəs] adj. spontan.

spook [spu:k] s. fantomă.

spool [spu:l] s. mosor; rolfilm.

spoon [spu:n] s. lingură.

spoonful ['spu:nfl] s. (cît încape într-o) lingură.

spore [spɔ:] s. bot. spor.

sport [spɔ:t] s. distracţie; vînătoare; călărie; pl. sport(uri); glumă; jucărie; persoană veselă, serviabilă, care nu se supără. *vi.* a se distra ; a glumi.

sporting ['spɔ:tiŋ] *adj.* sportiv ; serviabil; generos; nobil *(fig.)*.

sportive ['spɔ:tiv] *adj.* jucăuş ; vesel.

sportsman ['spɔ:tsmən] *s.* sportiv ; vînător ; ţintaş ; caracter bun ; om de treabă, serviabil.

sportsmanlike ['spɔ:tsmənlaik] *adj.* generos ; elegant ; amabil.

sportsmanship ['spɔ:tsmənʃip] *s.* îndemînare sportivă ; caracter elegant ; spirit sportiv.

spot [spɔt] *s.* loc ; urmă ; pată ; picătură ; pic ; *on the ~* imediat ; pe teren ; la locul respectiv. *vt.* a păta ; a strica ; a identifica.

spotless ['spɔtlis] *adj.* nepătat.

spotlight ['spɔtlait] *s.* reflector ; atenţie.

spotted ['spɔtid] *adj.* bălţat ; cu picăţele.

spouse [spauz] *s.* soţ(ie).

spout [spaut] *s.* (gură de) ţeavă ; jgheab ; *up the ~* amanetat. *vt.* a scuipa ; a arunca. *vi.* a ţîşni.

sprain [sprein] *s.* luxaţie. *vi.* a luxa.

sprang [spræŋ] *vt., vi. trec. de la* **spring.**

sprat [spræt] *s. iht.* şprot.

sprawl [sprɔ:l] *s.* tolănire. *vt.* a întinde ; a împrăştia. *vi.* a se tolăni ; a se întinde.

spray [sprei] *s.* crenguţă ; picături ; stropeală ; duş. *vt.* a stropi ; a pulveriza.

sprayer ['spreiə] *s.* vaporizator ; pompă de flit.

spread [spred] *s.* întindere ; răspîndire ; expansiune ; ospăţ ;

cuvertură. *vt., vi. inf., trec. şi part. trec.* a (se) întinde ; a (se) răspîndi.

spree [spri:] *s.* veselie ; chef.

sprightly ['spraitli] *adj.* vesel ; vioi.

spring [spriŋ] *s.* primăvară ; săritură ; izvor ; resort. *vt.* a deschide ; a arunca (în aer). *vi.* a sări ; a ţîşni ; a apărea ; a se naşte ; a se trage.

spring bed ['spriŋ'bed] *s.* somieră.

spring board ['spriŋbɔ:d] *s.* trambulină.

spring mattress ['spriŋ'mætris] *s.* somieră.

springtime ['spriŋtaim] *s.* primăvară.

sprinkle ['spriŋkl] *s.* presărare. *vt.* a stropi ; a presăra.

sprint [sprint] *s.* cursă de viteză. *vi.* a alerga repede.

sprite [sprait] *s.* spiriduş ; zînă.

sprocket ['sprɔkit] *s.* roată dinţată ; dinte de roată.

sprout [spraut] *s.* mugure ; mlădiţă ; *pl.* varză de Bruxelles. *vt.* a produce ; a da naştere la. *vi.* a ţîşni.

spruce [spru:s] *s.* molid. *adj.* curat ; dichisit. *vt., vi.* a (se) dichisi.

sprung [sprʌŋ] *vt., vi. part. trec. de la* **spring.**

spun [spʌn] *vt., vi. part. trec. de la* **spin.**

spur [spə:] *s.* pinten ; imbold ; îndemn. *vt.* a îndemna ; a da pinteni la ; *fig.* a împinge.

spurious ['spjuriəs] *adj.* fals ; prefăcut.

spurn [spə:n] *vt.* a refuza cu dispreţ ; a lua de sus.

spurt [spə:t] s. jet, ţîşnitură; izbucnire; efort. vt. a arunca. vi. a ţîşni; a face un efort; a se încorda.

sputter ['spʌtə] s. izbucnire; bolboroseală. vt., vi. a bolborosi.

spy [spai] s. spion; iscoadă. vt. a spiona; a iscodi. vi. a face spionaj; a pîndi.

spy-glass ['spaiglɑ:s] s. ochean.

squabble ['skwɔbl] s. sfadă. vi. a se ciondăni.

squad [skwɔd] s. detaşament; escadron.

squadron ['skwɔdrn] s. escadron; escadr(il)ă.

squalid ['skuɔlid] adj. sordid; jalnic.

squall [skwɔ:l] s. ţipăt; rafală (de vînt). vt., vi. a ţipa.

squalor ['skwɔlə] s. murdărie; mizerie (cumplită).

squander ['skwɔndə] vt. a risipi; a irosi.

squanderer ['skwɔndrə] s. mînă spartă. ˋ

square [skwɛə] s. pătrat; piaţă; echer; teu. adj. pătrat; (în unghi) drept; corect; total; răspicat. vt. a ridica la pătrat; a îndrepta; a echilibra; a achita.

squash [skwɔʃ] s. terci; aglomeraţie; dovleac. vt. a zdrobi; a terciui; a înăbuşi.

squat [skwɔt] adj. îndesat; turtit. vi. a sta pe vine; a ocupa un teren.

squatter ['skwɔtə] s. primul ocupant al unui teren; fermier.

squaw [skwɔ:] s. soţie de pielerosie.

squeak [skwi:k] s. chiţăit; gui-ţat; primejdie. vi. a chiţăi; a guiţa; a trăda un secret.

squeaker ['skwi:kə] s. denunţător.

squeal [skwi:l] s. ţipăt; chelălăit. vi. a chelălăi; a-şi denunţa complicii; a se plînge.

squeamish ['skwi:miʃ] adj. fandosit; mofturos; pretenţios.

squeeze [skwi:z] s. strînsoare; înghesuială; mită. vt. a strînge; a stoarce; a înghesui; a-şi croi drum. vi. a se strecura.

squint [skwint] s. strabism; ocheadă. vi. a se uita strîmb.

squint-eyed ['skwintaid] adj. saşiu.

squire ['skwaiə] s. boiernaş; (tînăr) cavaler.

squirrel ['skwirl] s. veveriţă.

squirt [skwə:t] s. ţîşnitură. vt. a arunca. vi. a ţîşni.

stab [stæb] s. înjunghiere; junghi; mişelie. vt. a înjunghea; a străpunge; a răni. vi. a simţi junghiuri.

stable ['steibl] s. grajd. adj. stabil; ferm. vt. a băga sau a ţine în grajd.

stable-boy ['steiblbɔi] s. grăjdar.

stack [stæk] s. teanc; căpiţă; morman; coş (de vapor etc.).

stadium ['steidjəm] s. stadion.

staff [stɑ:f] s. prăjină; băţ; cîrjă; redacţie; personal; statmajor; linie de portativ; on the ~ pe schemă. vt. a înzestra cu personal.

stag [stæg] s. cerb; amer. bărbat. adj. pentru bărbaţi.

stage [steidʒ] s. scenă; estradă; teatru; etapă; stadiu; diligenţă. vt. a pune în scenă; a înscena; a juca (o piesă).

stage coach ['steidʒ koutʃ] s. diligenţă.

stage-craft ['steidʒkrɑːft] s. artă scenică; simţ dramatic.

stage-directions ['steidʒdi'rekʃnz] s. pl. indicaţii de regie.

stage-fright ['steidʒfrait] s. trac.

stage-manager ['steidʒˌmænidʒə] s. director de scenă; regizor (secund).

stagger ['stægə] s. mers nesigur; bălăbăneală. vt. a speria. vi. a se bălăbăni.

staging ['steidʒiŋ] s. montare; înscenare.

stagnant ['stægnənt] adj. stătător; static; mort.

staid [steid] adj. liniştit; aşezat.

stain [stein] s. pată; colorare; culoare; colorant. vt. a păta; a colora. vi. a se colora.

stained glass window ['steind 'glɑːs windou] s. pl. vitralii.

stainless ['steinlis] adj. imaculat; inoxidabil.

stair(case) ['stɛə(keis)] s. scară.

stake [steik] s. par; stîlp; rug; miză; interes; at ~ în joc. vt. a miza; a marca; to ~ out sau off one's claim a-şi revendica drepturile.

stale [steil] adj. stătut; vechi; răsuflat.

stalemate ['steilmeit] s. pat (la şah); impas.

stalk [stɔːk] s. tulpină; pai. vt. a urmări; a cutreiera; a străbate. vi. a umbla semeţ.

stall [stɔːl] s. grajd; tarabă; stand; chioşc; stal; strană. vt. a opri. vi. a se opri; a se împotmoli; a tergiversa.

stallion ['stæljən] s. armăsar (de prăsilă).

stalwart ['stɔːlwət] s., adj. viteaz; voinic.

stamen ['steimən] s. stamină.

stamina ['stæminə] s. vigoare; rezistenţă.

stammer ['stæmə] s. bîlbîială. vt., vi. a (se) bîlbîi.

stamp [stæmp] s. pecete; semn; marcă; matriţă; tipar; şteamp; tip; bătaie (din picior). vt. a ştampila; a însemna; a marca; a franca; a lovi cu piciorul; a zdrobi (minereul); a ştanţa; to ~ down a turti; a zdrobi; to ~ out a distruge. vi. a bate din picior.

stamp-collector ['stæmpkəˌlektə] s. filatelist.

stampede [stæm'piːd] s. panică; învălmăşeală. vt., vi. a (se) speria.

stanchion ['stɑːnʃn] s. stîlp de susţinere.

stand [stænd] s. suport; pupitru; stand; chioşc; staţie; tribună; poziţie; loc. vt. a aşeza; a suporta; a plăti; to ~ one's ground a se menţine pe poziţie. vi. a sta în picioare; a se ridica; a rămîne; a se afla (într-o situaţie); a fi valabil; it ~s to reason e la mintea omului; to ~ smb. in good stead a folosi cuiva; to ~ alone a nu avea pereche; to ~ by a sta în preajmă; a ajuta; a(-şi) menţine (o opinie etc.); to ~ for a reprezenta; a însemna; a înlocui; a susţine; a candida pentru; to ~ off a se ţine deoparte; he ~s on ceremony e foarte ceremonios;

to ~ *out* a fi proeminent; a se distinge; a rezista; *to* ~ *to win smth.* a fi în situaţia de a cîştiga ceva; *to* ~ *up for* a apăra; a sprijini; *to* ~ *up to* a înfrunta.

standard ['stændəd] *s.* drapel; stindard; emblemă; principiu; etalon; standard; nivel.

standard-bearer ['stændəd‚bɛərə] *s.* stegar; portdrapel.

standard-time ['stændəd‚taim] *s.* ora oficială.

stand-in ['stænd'in] *s. cin.* cascador, înlocuitor al unui actor.

standing ['stændiŋ] *s.* durată; poziţie; rang. *adj.* din picioare; de pe loc; permanent; drept.

stand-offish ['stænd'ɔ:fiʃ] *adj.* semeţ, înţepat.

standpoint ['stænpɔint] *s.* punct de vedere; atitudine; poziţie.

standstill ['stænstil] *s.* oprire; impas.

stank [stæŋk] *vt., vi. trec. de la* **stink.**

stanza ['stænzə] *s.* strofă.

staple ['steipl] *s.* belciug; capsă (pentru hîrtie); marfă de larg consum; esenţă; materie primă. *adj.* principal; cel mai răspîndit.

staple-fibre ['steipl'faibə] *s.* celofibră.

star [sta:] *s.* stea; corp ceresc; asterisc. *vt.* a însemna cu asteriscuri; a prezenta ca vedetă. *vi.* a juca rolul principal.

starboard ['sta:bəd] *s.* tribord.

starch [sta:tʃ] *s.* scrobeală; amidon; îngîmfare. *vt.* a scrobi.

stare [stɛə] *s.* privire fixă; privire în gol. *vt.* a privi fix. *vi.* a privi lung; a privi în gol.

starfish ['sta:fiʃ] *s.* stea de mare.

star-gazer ['sta:‚geizə] *s.* astrolog; visător.

stark [sta:k] *adj.* ţeapăn; curat; complet. *adv.* complet.

starlight ['sta:lait] *s.* lumina stelelor.

starling ['sta:liŋ] *s.* graur.

starlit ['sta:lit] *adj.* înstelat.

starry ['sta:ri] *adj.* înstelat; luminos; strălucitor.

stars and stripes ['sta:zən'straips], **star-spangled banner** ['sta:‚spæŋld'bænə] *s.* drapelul american.

start [sta:t] *s.* început; începere; start; avantaj; tresărire; smucitură. *vt.* a începe, a porni; a iniţia; a lansa; a da drumul la; a stîrni. *vi.* a (se) porni; a începe; a se stîrni; a tresări; a ieşi.

starting point ['sta:tiŋ pɔint] *s.* început; start.

startle ['sta:tl] *vt.* a surprinde; a speria.

starvation [sta:'veiʃn] *s.* foame(te); inaniţie.

starve [sta:v] *vt.* a înfometa. *vi.* a muri de foame.

starveling ['sta:vliŋ] *s.* flămînd; muritor de foame.

state [steit] *s.* stare; situaţie; rang; pompă; ceremonie; demnitate; stat; guvern. *adj.* de stat; oficial; statal. *vt.* a declara; a exprima; a stabili.

State Department ['steit‚dipa:tmənt] *s.* Ministerul de externe (al S.U.A.).

stately ['steitli] *adj.* maiestuos.

statement ['steitmənt] *s.* declaraţie.

statesman ['steitsmən] *s.* politician; om de stat.

static ['stætik] *s. radio* parazit. *pl.* statică. *adj.* static; pasiv.

station ['steiʃn] *s.* loc; staţie; gară; local; bază militară; rang. *vt. mil.* a staţiona; a disloca.

stationary ['steiʃnəri] *adj.* staţionar.

stationer ['steiʃnə] *s.* corsetier; librar; papetar.

stationery ['steiʃnəri] *s.* papetărie.

statistics [stə'tistiks] *s. pl.* statistică.

statue ['stætju:] *s.* statuie.

statuesque [ˌstætju'esk] *adj.* sculptural.

stature ['stætʃə] *s.* statură; valoare; importanţă.

status ['steitəs] *s.* situaţie; rang; *jur.* statut.

statute ['stætju:t] *s.* lege; statut.

staunch [stɔ:ntʃ] *adj.* fidel; neclintit. *vt.* a opri (sîngele).

stave [steiv] *s.* prăjină; doagă; linie de portativ; strofă. *vt.* a sparge, a zdrobi.

stay [stei] *s.* şedere; oprire; întîrziere; amînare; odgon; sprijin; *pl.* corset. *vt.* a susţine; a potoli; a reţine. *vi.* a sta; a rămîne; a rezista.

stead [sted] *s.: in smb.'s* ~ în locul cuiva.

steadfast ['stedfəst] *adj.* neclintit; fidel; credincios.

steadfastness ['stedfəstnis] *s.* fermitate; credinţă; neclintire.

steadily ['stedili] *adv.* constant; ferm; regulat; mereu.

steady ['stedi] *adj.* ferm; sigur; regulat; serios; harnic. *vt., vi.* a (se) linişti.

steak [steik] *s.* friptură, fleică.

steal [sti:l] *vt.* a fura; a smulge. *vi.* a se strecura; a se furişa; a fura.

stealth [stelθ] *s.* secret; *by* ~ pe furiş.

stealthy ['stelθi] *adj.* furiş; prudent.

steam [sti:m] *s.* aburi; vapori; energie.

steamboat ['sti:mbout] *s.* vapor.

steam-engine ['sti:mˌendʒin] *s.* maşină cu vapori; locomotivă.

steamer ['sti:mə] *s.* vapor; etuvă.

steam-roller ['sti:mˌroulə] *s.* compresor; putere zdrobitoare.

steamship ['sti:mʃip] *s.* vapor.

steed [sti:d] *s.* armăsar.

steel [sti:l] *s.* (instrument de) oţel; armă. *vt.* a oţeli.

steel-works ['sti:lwə:ks] *s.* oţelărie.

steely ['sti:li] *adj.* de oţel; ca oţelul; de culoarea oţelului.

steelyard ['stiljɑ:d] *s.* balanţă romană.

steep [sti:p] *adj.* abrupt; exorbitant; exagerat. *vt.* a cufunda; a înmuia.

steeple ['sti:pl] *s.* clopotniţă; turn.

steeple-chase ['sti:pltʃeis] *s.* cursă cu obstacole.

steer [stiə] *s.* juncan. *vt.* a cîrmi; a călăuzi. *vi.* a sta la cîrmă; a cîrmi.

steering-wheel ['stiəriŋwi:l] *s.* roata cîrmei; *auto.* volan.

steersman ['stiəzmən] *s.* cîrmaci.

stem [stem] *s.* tulpină; origine;

arbore genealogic; picior de pahar; proră. *vt.* a stăvili; a opri; a înfrunta. *vi.* a se naşte; a fi provocat.

stench [stentʃ] *s.* duhoare.

stencil ['stensl] *s.* matriţă; tipar. *vt.* a matriţa; a copia.

step[1] [step] *s.* (urmă de) pas; ritm; măsură; procedeu; treaptă; grad; rang; *muz.* interval; *in* ~ în ritm. *vt.* a măsura cu pasul; *to* ~ *up* a spori; a ridica. *vi.* a păşi; *to* ~ *in* a intra; a interveni; *to* ~ *aside* a se da la o parte.

step[2] [step] *adj.* vitreg.

step-brother ['step brʌðə] *s.* frate vitreg.

step-ladder ['step,lædə] *s.* scăriţă.

steppe [step] *s.* stepă.

sterile ['sterail] *adj.* steril.

sterling ['stə:liŋ] *adj.* curat, veritabil; credincios; de bună calitate; sterlină.

stern [stə:n] *s. mar.* pupă; coadă. *adj.* sever; aspru; cumplit.

stertorous ['stə:tərəs] *adj.* sforăitor.

stevedore ['sti:vidɔ:] *s.* docher.

stew [stju:] *s.* ostropel; mîncare fiartă înăbuşit; bucluc. *vt.* a fierbe la foc mic *sau* înăbuşit.

steward ['stjuəd] *s.* steward; chelner; administrator; intendent.

stick [stik] *s.* băţ; baston; baghetă. *vt.* a sprijini; a propti; a înfige; a băga; a lipi; a fixa; a suporta; *to* ~ *out* a scoate (limba etc.). *vi.* a intra; a înţepa; a se lipi; a se înţepeni; *to* ~ *at* a se da înapoi de la; *to* ~ *out* a ieşi afară.

stick-in-the-mud [stiknðəmʌd] *s., adj.* conservator; reacţionar; retrograd; închistat.

stickler ['stiklə] *s.* maniac.

sticky ['stiki] *adj.* lipicios; umed.

stiff [stif] *s.* cadavru. *adj.* ţeapăn; crispat; tare; glacial; dificil.

stiffen ['stifn] *vt., vi.* a (se) înţepeni; a (se) întări.

stifle ['staifl] *vt., vi.* a (se) înăbuşi.

stigma ['stigmə] *s.* stigmat.

stile [stail] *s.* pîrleaz.

stiletto heel [sti'letou,hi:l] *s.* toc cui.

still [stil] *s.* linişte; alambic; fotografie; secvenţă. *adj.* liniştit; tăcut; tihnit; fără viaţă. *vt.* a linişti; a potoli. *adv.* încă (şi mai); ba chiar; (şi) totuşi.

stillborn ['stilbɔ:n] *adj.* născut mort.

still-life ['stil'laif] *s.* natură moartă *sau* statică.

stilted ['stiltid] *adj.* artificial; pretenţios; afectat.

stilts [stilts] *s. pl.* catalige.

stimulus ['stimjuləs] *s.* stimulent.

sting [stiŋ] *s.* înţepătură; pişcătură; imbold. *vt.* a înţepa; *fig:* a răni.

stinging-nettle ['stiŋiŋ,netl] *s.* urzică.

stingy ['stindʒi] *adj.* cărpănos.

stink [stiŋk] *s.* duhoare, putoare. *vt.* a alunga prin fum, miros urît etc. *vi.* a puţi.

stint [stint] *s.* cruţare; economie (de forţe); porţie; limită. *vt.* a economisi; a priva. *vi.* a se zgîrci.

stintless ['stintlis] *adj.* altruist; plin de abnegaţie.

stipulate ['stipjuleit] *vt.* a stipula, a prevedea. *vi.*: *to* ~ *for* a stipula, a prevedea.

stir [stə:] *s.* agitaţie; senzaţie; mişcare. *vt.* a agita; a mişca; a învîrti; a stîrni. *vi.* a se mişca; a se agita; a se stîrni.

stirring ['stə:riŋ] *adj.* emoţionant; înălţător; aţiţător.

stirrup ['stirəp] *s.* scară (la şa).

stirrup-cup ['stirəpkʌp] *s.* păhărel băut la botul calului.

stitch [stitʃ] *s.* însăilare; saia; cusut; cusătură; junghi. *vt.*, *vi.* a însăila.

stock [stɔk] *s.* tulpină; trunchi; ciot; butuc; portaltoi; pat (de puşcă); origine; stoc; sursă; şeptel; capital; (pachete de) acţiuni; *pl.* obezi; *out of* ~ *com.* epuizat. *adj.* obişnuit; la îndemînă; banal. *vt.* a aproviziona; a stoca.

stock-breeder ['stɔk,bri:də] *s.* crescător de animale.

stock-broker ['stɔk,broukə] *s.* agent de schimb (pentru acţiuni).

stock-exchange [stɔkiks'tʃeindʒ] *s.* bursă de acţiuni.

stock-holder ['stɔk,houldə] *s.* (mare) acţionar.

stocking ['stɔkiŋ] *s.* ciorap lung.

stock-in-trade ['stɔkin'treid] *s.* cele necesare meseriei.

stock-jobber ['stɔk,dʒɔbə] *s.* speculant (de bursă).

stockpile ['stɔkpail] *vt.* a stoca.

stocky ['stɔki] *adj.* îndesat; voinic.

stock-yard ['stɔkjɑːd] *s.* ocol de vite.

stodgy ['stɔdʒi] *adj.* greoi.

stoke [stouk] *vt.* a alimenta cu cărbuni; a înfuleca.

stoker ['stoukə] *s.* fochist.

stole [stoul] *s.* etolă; patrafir. *vt.*, *vi. trec. de la* **steal.**

stolen ['stouln] *vt.*, *vi. part. trec. de la* **steal.**

stolid ['stɔlid] *adj.* placid.

stomach ['stʌmək] *s.* stomac; burtă; poftă. *vt.* a suporta.

stone [stoun] *s.* piatră; bolovan; piatră preţioasă; sîmbure (de drupă); bob de grindină; măsură de greutate (6,350 kg).

stone-deaf ['stoun'def] *adj.* surd ca masa.

stone-fruit ['stounfruːt] *s.* drupă.

stone-mason ['stoun,meisn] *s.* pietrar.

stone-ware ['stounwɛə] *s.* ceramică smălţuită.

stonework ['stounwə:k] *s.* zidărie.

stony ['stouni] *adj.* pietros; tare.

stood [stud] *vt.*, *vi. trec. şi part. trec. de la* **stand.**

stooge [stuːdʒ] *s.* slugă; agent; cirac.

stool [stuːl] *s.* scaun (fără spetează); taburet; scăunel; *med.* scaun.

stool-pigeon ['stuːl pidʒin] *s.* porumbel folosit ca momeală; *fig.* agent plătit, unealtă; informator, provocator.

stoop [stuːp] *s.* încovoiere a umerilor. *vt.* a apleca. *vi.* a se apleca; a se încovoia; *fig.* a se coborî, a se înjosi.

stop [stɔp] *s.* oprire; staţie:

punct; opritoare. *vt.* a opri; a reţine; a astupa; *vi.* a se opri.

stoplight ['stɔplait] *s.* stop; semafor.

stop-news ['stɔpnjuːz] *s.* ultima oră.

stop-over ['stɔpouvə] *s.* escală.

stoppage ['stɔpidʒ] *s.* întrerupere; grevă.

stopper ['stɔpə] *s.* dop. *vt.* a astupa.

stop-watch ['stɔpwɔtʃ] *s.* cronometru.

storage ['stɔːridʒ] *s.* stocare; acumulare; depozitare; taxă de locaţie.

storage battery ['stɔːridʒ'bætri] *s.* acumulator.

store [stɔː] *s.* depozit; aprovizionare; antrepozit; *pl.* magazin universal; *amer.* magazin. *vt.* a aproviziona; a echipa.

store-house ['stɔːhaus] *s.* depozit.

store-keeper ['stɔːˌkiːpə] *s.* magazioner; *amer.* negustor.

store-room ['stɔːrum] *s.* magazie; depozit; cămară.

storey ['stɔːri] *s.* etaj.

storied ['stɔːrid] *adj.* celebru; legendar; cu (două, trei etc.) etaje.

stork [stɔːk] *s.* barză.

storm [stɔːm] *s.* furtună; ropot (de aplauze). *vt.* a lua cu asalt. *vi.* a izbucni.

stormy ['stɔːmi] *adj.* furtunos; violent.

stormy petrel ['stɔːmi'petrl] *s.* pasărea furtunii.

story ['stɔːri] *s.* etaj; povest(ir)e; basm; reportaj; relatare; minciună.

story teller ['stɔːriˌtelə] *s.* povestitor.

stout [staut] *s.* bere tare (neagră). *adj.* gras; voinic; viteaz; tare.

stove [stouv] *s.* sobă; plită; maşină de gătit.

stove pipe ['stouvpaip] *s.* burlan; coş.

stow [stou] *vt.* a depozita; a ascunde.

stowaway ['stouəwei] *s.* pasager clandestin.

straddle ['strædl] *s.* poziţie călare. *vt.* a încăleca. *vi.* a sta călare; *fig.* a şovăi.

strafe [strɑːf] *vt.* a bombarda.

straggle ['strægl] *vi.* a se împrăştia; a se rătăci.

straight [streit] *adj.* drept; direct; neted; cum trebuie; în ordine; cinstit; sincer; demn de încredere. *adv.* direct; imediat.

straighten ['streitn] *vt., vi.* a (se) îndrepta.

straightforward [streit'fɔːwəd] *adj.* cinstit; sincer.

straight-jacket ['streit'dʒækit] *s.* cămaşă de forţă. *vt.* a pune în cămaşă de forţă; a încorseta.

straightway ['streitwei] *adv.* imediat; direct.

strain [strein] *s.* încordare; efort; luxaţie; rasă; dispoziţie. *pl. muz.* acorduri. *vt.* a încorda; a trage; a forţa; a strîmba; a exagera; a strecura. *vi.* a se strădui; *to ~ at smth.* a trage de ceva; a se opinti în ceva; a exagera într-o privinţă.

strainer ['streinə] *s.* strecurătoare.

strait [streit] s. strîmto(r)are. adj. strîmt.

straiten ['streitn] vt. a restrînge; a strîmtora.

strait-jacket ['streit'dʒækit] v. straight-jacket.

strand [strænd] s. ţărm; şuviţă. vt. a lăsa la 'ananghie. vi. a eşua.

strange [streindʒ] adj. ciudat; straniu; neobişnuit.

stranger ['streindʒə] s. străin, necunoscut.

strangle ['stræŋl] vt. a strangula. .

strap [stræp] s. bretea; panglică; curea. vt. a prinde; a bate cu cureaua. vi. a ascuţi (briciul).

strapping ['stræpíŋ] adj. voinic; zdravăn.

strata ['strɑːtə] s. pl. straturi.

stratum ['strɑːtəm] s. strat, pătură.

straw [strɔː] s. (pălărie de) pai(e). adj. de pai; gălbui.

strawberry ['strɔːbri] s. căpşună; frag(ă).

stray [strei] s. om sau animal fără adăpost. adj. rătăcit; sporadic. vi. a (se) rătăci; a se abate.

streak [striːk] s. dungă; umbră; undă; perioadă. vt. a vărga. vi. a ţîşni.

stream [striːm] s. pîrîu; şuvoi; curent (general). vi. a curge; a flutura.

streamer ['striːmə] s. panglică (colorată); flamură.

streamline ['striːmlain] s. şuvoi neîntrerupt. vt. a moderniza.

street [striːt] s. stradă; uliţă; the man in the ~ omul de rînd.

street arab ['striːt'ærəb] s. golan; vagabond; copil al străzil.

streetcar ['striːtkɑː] s. amer. tramvai.

streetdoor ['striːt'dɔː] s. uşa de la stradă.

streetwalker ['striːt'wɔːkə] s. femeie de stradă.

strength [streŋθ] s. tărie; forţă; putere; forţă numerică.

strengthen ['streŋθn] vt., vi. a (se) întări.

strenous ['strenjuəs] adj. dificil; harnic; încordat.

stress [stres] s. presiune; încordare; tensiune; accent; importanţă. vt. a accentua.

stretch [stretʃ] s. întindere; perioadă sau distanţă neîntreruptă; exagerare. vt. a întinde; a exagera; a forţa. vi. a se întinde.

stretcher ['stretʃə] s. targă; brancardă.

stretcher-bearer ['stretʃəˌbɛərə] s. brancardier.

strewn ˌ[struːn] adj. întins; acoperit; împrăştiat.

stricken ['strikn] adj. lovit; speriat; chinuit.

strict [strikt] adj. sever; rigid; strict.

stridden ['stridn] vt., vi. part. trec. de la stride.

stride [straid] s. pas (mare); pas înainte; progres. vt. a încăleca. vi. a păşi; a face paşi mari; a sări.

strife [straif] s. ceartă; conflict; luptă.

strike [straik] s. grevă. vt. a lovi; a izbi; a aprinde (un chibrit); a nimeri; a descoperi; a bate (monedă, orele);

a atinge (o coardă etc.) ; a impresiona ; a mira ; a veni în mintea (cuiva) ; a pătrunde ; a prinde ; to ~ off sau through a şterge ; a tăia ; a tipări ; to ~ up a începe (o melodie). vi. a lovi ; a intra ; a se băga ; (d. ceas) a bate ; a pătrunde ; a se pune în grevă ; to ~ at a încerca să loveşti ; to ~ up a începe să cînte ; to ~ upon a nimeri ; to ~ into smth. a se apuca de ceva.

strike-breaker [straik͵breikə] s. spărgător de grevă.

strike-pay ['straikpei] s. indemnizaţie de grevă.

striker ['straikə] s. grevist.

striking ['straikiŋ] adj. izbitor.

string [striŋ] s. sfoară ; coardă ; şiret ; panglică ; şirag ; aţă. vt. a înşira ; a atîrna ; a pune coarde noi la (vioară etc.). vi. a se înşira.

stringent ['strindʒnt] adj. strict.

strip [strip] s. dungă ; panglică. vt. a dezbrăca ; a dezgoli ; a smulge (masca etc.). vi. a se dezbrăca.

stripe [straip] s. dungă ; tresă. vt. a dunga.

stripling ['stripliŋ] s. adolescent ; tînăr.

strip-tease [strip͵tiːz] s. dezbrăcare treptată (la varieteu).

strive [straiv] vi. a se strădui ; a se lupta.

striven ['strivn] vi. part. trec. de la **strive**.

strode [stroud] vt., vi. trec. de la **stride**.

stroke [strouk] s. lovitură ; mişcare ; atac ; acces ; congestie (cerebrală) ; efort ; trăsătură

(de condei) ; bătaie (a ceasului). vt. a mîngîia ; a atinge.

stroll [stroul] s. plimbare. vi. a se plimba ; a hoinări.

strolling ['strouliŋ] adj. ambulant ; hoinar.

strong [strɔŋ] adj. tare ; puternic ; înrădăcinat ; profund ; 20 ~ (alcătuit) din 20 de oameni. adv. tare ; puternic.

strong-box ['strɔŋbɔks] s. casă de bani, seif.

stronghold ['strɔŋhould] s. fortăreaţă.

strongly ['strɔŋli] adv. puternic ; viguros.

strong-minded ͵['strɔŋ'maindid] adj. decis ; voluntar.

strop [strɔp] s. curea de ascuţit briciul. vt. a ascuţi (briciul).

strove [strouv] vi. trec. de la **strive**.

struck [strʌk] vt., vi. trec. şi part. trec. de la **strike**.

structure ['strʌktʃə] s. structură ; clădire ; eşafodaj.

struggle ['strʌgl] s. luptă ; competiţie ; efort. vi. a se lupta ; a se zbate.

strum [strʌm] s. zdrăngăneală. vt., vi. a zdrăngăni.

strumpet ['strʌmpit] s. prostituată.

strung [strʌŋ] adj.: ~ up încordat ; pregătit. vt., vi. trec. şi part. trec. de la **string**.

strut [strʌt] s. proptea ; suport ; mers trufaş. vt. a sprijini ; a propti. vi. a merge fudul.

stub [stʌb] s. cotor ; ciot ; muc (de ţigară). vt. a se împiedica de.

stubble ['stʌbl] s. mirişte ; barbă ţepoasă.

stubborn ['stʌbən] *adj.* încăpăţînat; dificil; persistent; ferm.

stubby ['stʌbi] *adj.* bont; gros.

stucco ['stʌkou] *s.* stuc.

stuck [stʌk] *vt., vi. trec. şi part. trec. de la* stick.

stuck-up ['stʌkʌp] *adj.* îngîmfat; înţepat.

stud [stʌd] *s.* buton de guler; ţintă; herghelie de armăsari. *vt.* a bate în ţinte; a presăra.

student ['stju:dnt] *s.* student; cercetător; învăţăcel; învăţat.

stud horse ['stʌdhɔ:s] *s.* armăsar (de prăsilă).

studied ['stʌdid] *adj.* intenţionat; studiat.

studio ['stju:diou] *s.* atelier (de artist); (divan-)studio.

studious ['stju:djəs] *adj.* studios; serios.

study ['stʌdi] *s.* învăţătură; examinare; (materie de) studiu; reverie; cameră de lucru. *vt., vi.* a studia; a cerceta.

stuff [stʌf] *s.* material; materie; stofă; ţesătură. *vt.* a umple; a îmbîcsi; a îndesa; a îndopa cu; a împăia; a toci, a învăţa; a împăna. *vi.* a se îndopa.

stuffing ['stʌfiŋ] *s.* umplutură.

stuffy ['stʌfi] *adj.* îmbîcsit; stricat; stupid.

stultify ['stʌltifai] *vt* a ridiculiza; a infirma.

stumble ['stʌmbl] *s.* împleticeală. *vi.* a se împletici; a se împiedica; a merge greu; *to ~ upon* sau *across smth.* a descoperi ceva din întîmplare.

stumbling-block ['stʌmbliŋ blɔk] *s.* obstacol; împiedicare.

stump [stʌmp] *s.* ciot; rădăcină; rest; *pl.* picioare. *vt.* a ului.

stumpy ['stʌmpi] *adj.* greoi; îndesat; bont.

stun [stʌn] *vt.* a şoca; a ameţi, a zăpăci.

stung [stʌŋ] *vt., vi. trec. şi part. trec. de la* sting.

stunk [stʌŋk] *vt., vi. trec. şi part. trec. de la* stink.

stunning ['stʌniŋ] *adj.* grozav; splendid.

stunt [stʌnt] *s.* efort deosebit; performanţă (ostentativă). *vt.* a opri din creştere.

stupefy ['stju:pifai] *vt.* a ului; a abrutiza.

stupendous [stju(:)'pendəs] *adj.* uluitor; fantastic.

stupid ['stju:pid] *s., adj.* tîmpit.

stupidity [stju:'piditi] *s.* prostie.

stupor ['stju:pə] *s.* toropeală.

sturdy ['stə:di] *adj.* viguros, robust; solid; neclintit.

sturgeon ['stə:dʒn] *s.* nisetru; sturion.

stutter ['stʌtə] *s.* bîlbîială. *vt., vi.* a (se) bîlbîi.

sty [stai] *s.* cocină; *med.* urcior.

style [stail] *s.* stil; titlu; stilet. *vt.* a numi; a desemna.

stylish ['stailiʃ] *adj.* elegant; rafinat.

stylus ['stailəs] *s.* stilet; ac de picup.

stymie ['staimi] *vt.* a pune în încurcătură.

subdivide ['sʌbdi'vaid] *vt., vi.* a (se) subîmpărţi.

subdue [səb'dju:] *vt.* a supune; a potoli.

subhuman ['sʌb'hju:mən] *adj.* inferior; animalic.

subject[1] ['sʌbdʒikt] *s.* subiect; obiect de studiu; motiv; pacient; supus. *adj.* supus.

subject² [səb'dʒekt] *vt.* a supune ; a subjuga ; a expune. *vr.* a se supune ; a se expune.

subjection [səb'dʒekʃn] *s.* supunere ; dependenţă ; aservire.

subject-matter ['sʌbdʒikt,mætə] *s.* obiect de studiu, disciplină ; subiect.

subjugate ['sʌbdʒigeit] *vt,* a cuceri ; a subjuga.

subjunctive [səb'dʒʌŋtiv] *s., adj.* subjonctiv.

sublet ['sʌb'let] *vt., vi.* a subînchiria (cuiva).

sublime [sə'blaim] *s., adj.* sublim.

sublimity [sə'blimiti] *s.* splendoare ; sublim.

submarine ['sʌbməri:n] *s., adj.* submarin.

submerge [səb'mə:dʒ] *vt.* a inunda ; a scufunda.

submission [səb'miʃn] *s.* supunere.

submissive [səb'misiv] *adj.* supus.

submit [səb'mit] *vt., vi., vr.* a (se) supune.

subordinate¹ [sə'bɔ:dnit] *s.* inferior ; subordonat. *adj.* supus ; subordonat ; *gram.* secundar.

subordinate² [sə'bɔ:dineit] *vt.* a supune ; a subordona.

suborn [sə'bɔ:n] *vt.* a instiga ; a mitui.

subpoena [səb'pi:nə] *s. jur.* citaţie. *vt. jur.* a cita.

subscribe [səb'skraib] *vt.* a subscrie ; a semna. *vi.* a se abona ; a subscrie.

subscriber [səb'skraibə] *s.* abonat ; filantrop.

subscription [səb'skripʃn] *s.* subscripţie ; abonament (la un ziar). *adj.* în abonament.

subsequent ['sʌbsikwənt] *adj.* ulterior.

subservience [səb'sə:vjəns] *s.* aservire.

subservient [səb'sə:vjənt] *adj.* servil ; amabil.

subside [səb'said] *vi.* a scădea ; a se lăsa.

subsidize ['sʌbsidaiz] *vt.* a subvenţiona.

subsidy ['sʌbsidi] *s.* subvenţie.

subsoil ['sʌbsɔil] *s.* subsol.

substance ['sʌbstns] *s.* substanţă ; materie ; material ; tărie ; avere.

substantial [səb'stænʃl] *adj.* substanţial ; important.

substantiate [səb'stænʃieit] *vt.* a dovedi ; a corobora.

substitute ['sʌbstitju:t] *s.* înlocuitor ; suplinitor. *vt.* a înlocui. *vi.* a ţine locul.

subtle ['sʌtl] *adj.* subtil ; viclean.

subtlety ['sʌtlti] *s.* subtilitate ; viclenie.

subtract [səb'trækt] *vt., vi.* a scădea.

subtraction [səb'trækʃn] *s. mat.* scădere.

suburb ['sʌbə:b] *s.* suburbie.

subversion [səb'və:ʃn] *s.* răsturnare ; subminare ; complot.

subvert [səb'və:t] *vt.* a submina ; a răsturna.

subway ['sʌbwei] *s.* pasaj subteran ; *amer.* metro.

succeed [sək'si:d] *vt.* a moşteni ; a urma (cuiva). *vi.:* to ~ in a reuşi să.

success [sək'ses] *s.* succes ; victorie ; noroc ; prosperitate.

successful [sək'sesfl] *adj.* victorios ; reuşit ; prosper.

succession [sək'seʃn] s. şir.

succo(u)r ['sʌkə] s. ajutor(are). *vt.* a ajuta.

succumb [sə'kʌm] *vi.* a ceda; a muri.

such [sʌtʃ] *adj.* asemenea; similar; ~ *being the case* aşa stînd lucrurile. *pron.* anume; unii; nişte; aceştia; acestea; ~ *as* ca de pildă; *and* ~ (*like*) şi altele asemenea. *adv.* asemenea; astfel; ~ *that* încît; ~ *as to* aşa încît să; *as* ~ ca atare.

suchlike ['sʌtʃlaik] *adj.* similar; de acest fel.

suck [sʌk] s. supt; alăptare. *vt.* a suge; a sorbi; a absorbi. *vi.* a suge.

sucker ['sʌkə] s. sugaci; ventuză; lăstar; *amer.* fraier.

suckle ['sʌkl] *vt.* a alăpta.

suckling ['sʌkliŋ] s. copil de ţîţă.

suction ['sʌkʃr] s. sugere; absorbire.

sudden ['sʌdṇ] *adj.* brusc; neprevăzut; *all of a* ~ dintr-o dată.

suddenly ['sʌdnli] *adv.* brusc.

sue [sju:] *vt.* a da în judecată; a implora. *vi.*: *to* ~ *for* a cere; a urmări în justiţie.

suède [sweid] s. piele fină; velur.

suet ['sjuit] s. seu.

suffer ['sʌfə] *vt.* a suferi; a tolera. *vi.* a suferi.

suffering ['sʌfriŋ] s. suferinţă.

suffice [sə'fais] *vt.* a mulţumi. *vi.* a fi suficient.

sufficiency [sə'fiʃnsi] s. îndestulare; îngîmfare.

suffocate ['sʌfəkeit] *vt., vi.* a (se) sufoca.

suffrage ['sʌfridʒ] s. (drept de) vot; aprobare.

suffuse [sə'fju:z] *vt.* a acoperi; a astupa; a îneca.

sugar ['ʃugə] s. zahăr. *vt.* a îndulci; a presăra cu zahăr.

sugar-basin ['ʃugə,beisn] s. zaharniţă.

sugar-cane ['ʃugəkein] s. trestie de zahăr.

sugar-loaf ['ʃugəlouf] s. căpăţînă de zahăr.

sugary ['ʃugəri] *adj.* dulce; zaharos; mieros; măgulitor.

suggest [sə'dʒest] *vt.* a propune; a sugera; a aminti de (*fig.*).

suicide ['sjuisaid] s. sinucidere; sinucigaş.

suit [sju:t] s. costum; petiţie; cerere; acţiune judiciară; suită. *vt.* a mulţumi; a se potrivi cu; a asorta; a şedea bine (cuiva); a potrivi. *vi.* a corespunde. *vr.* a face ce doreşti.

suitable ['sju:təbl] *adj.* potrivit; corespunzător; favorabil.

suit-case ['sju:tkeis] s. geamantan, valiză.

suite [swi:t] s. suită; garnitură (de mobilă); şir de camere; apartament.

suitor ['sju:tə] s. pretendent; *jur.* reclamant.

sulk [sʌlk] *vi.* a bombăni; a fi morocănos.

sulks [sʌlks] s. *pl.* ţîfnă; tristeţe; supărare.

sulky ['sʌlki] s. şaretă. *adj.* morocănos; mohorît.

sullen ['sʌln] *adj.* mohorît; supărat; ţîfnos.

sully ['sʌli] *vt.* a pîngări; a murdări.

sulphur ['sʌlfə] s. sulf.

sultana [səl'tɑːnə] s. stafidă; sultană.

sultry ['sʌltri] adj. zăpuşitor.

sum [sʌm] s. sumă; total; adunare; rezumat; pl. aritmetică. vt. a aduna; a rezuma.

summarize ['sʌməraiz] vt. a rezuma.

summary ['sʌməri] s. rezumat; sumar. adj. sumar; rapid.

summer ['sʌmə] s. vară; pl. ani. vi. a petrece vara.

summer-house ['sʌməhaus] s. pavilion (de grădină), chioşc.

summer-time ['sʌmətaim] s. (orar de) vară.

summing-up ['sʌmiŋ'ʌp] s. bilanţ; trecere în revistă; rezumat.

summit ['sʌmit] s. vîrf; culme. adj. la cel mai înalt nivel; maxim.

summon ['sʌmən] vt. a chema; a cita (în faţa curţii); a convoca; a mobiliza.

summons ['sʌmənz] s. jur. citaţie. vt. a cita (la judecată).

sumptuous ['sʌmtjuəs] adj. somptuos; abundent.

sun [sʌn] s. soare; lumină.

sun-bath ['sʌnbɑːθ] s. baie de soare.

sun beam ['sʌnbiːm] s. rază de soare.

sun-blind ['sʌnblaind] s. stor; jaluzea.

sun burn ['sʌnbəːn] s. bronzare; arsură.

Sunday ['sʌndi] s. duminică; one's ~ best hainele de sărbătoare.

sundial ['sʌndail] s. cadran solar.

sun-down ['sʌndaun] s. asfinţit.

sundries ['sʌndriz] s. pl. diverse; resturi; fleacuri.

sundry ['sʌndri] adj. divers; variat.

sun-flower ['sʌnˌflauə] s. floarea soarelui.

sung [sʌŋ] vt., vi. part. trec. de la sing.

sun-glasses ['sʌnˌglɑːsiz] s. pl. ochelari de soare.

sunk [sʌŋk] vt., vi. trec. şi part. trec. de la sink.

sunken ['sʌŋkn] adj. scofîlcit; scobit; supt; înfundat; (d. ochi) în fundul capului.

sunless ['sʌnlis] adj. fără soare.

sunlight ['sʌnlait] s. lumina soarelui; soare.

sunlit ['sʌnlit] adj. însorit.

sunny ['sʌni] adj. însorit; luminos; vesel.

sunrise ['sʌnraiz] s. zori, răsăritul soarelui.

sunset ['sʌnset] s. asfinţit.

sunshade ['sʌnʃeid] s. umbrelă de soare.

sunshine ['sʌnʃain] s. lumina soarelui.

sunstroke ['sʌnstrouk] s. insolaţie.

sun-up ['sʌnʌp] s. răsăritul soarelui.

sup [sʌp] s. înghiţitură. vi. a lua cina; a supa.

super ['sjuːpə] s. figurant. adj. straşnic.

superannuated [ˌsjuːpə'rænjueitid] adj. bătrîn; pensionat; depăşit; demodat.

supercilious [ˌsjuːpə'siliəs] adj. dispreţuitor; trufaş.

superfluous [sjuː'pəːfluəs] adj. inutil.

superhuman [ˌsjuːpəˈhjuːmən] *adj.* supraomenesc.

superimpose [ˈsjuːpərimˈpouz] *vt.* a suprapune.

superintend [ˌsjuːprinˈtend] *vt., vi.* a supraveghea; a dirija.

superintendent [ˌsjuːprinˈtendənt] *s.* supraveghetor; administrator.

superior [sjuːˈpiəriə] *s.* superior. *adj.* superior; excepţional.

superman [ˈsjuːpəmæn] *s.* supraom.

supermarket [ˈsjuːpəmɑːkit] *s.* mare magazin (cu autoservire).

supernatural [ˌsjuːpəˈnætʃrl] *s., adj.* supranatural.

supernumerary [ˌsjuːpəˈnjuːmrəri] *s.* figurant. *adj.* supranumerar.

supersede [ˌsjuːpəˈsiːd] *vt.* a înlocui.

superstition [ˌsjuːpəˈstiʃn] *s.* superstiţie.

superstructure [ˈsjuːpəˌstrʌkʃə] *s.* suprastructură; construcţie.

supervene [ˌsjuːpəˈviːn] *vt.* a surveni; a coincide.

supervise [ˈsjuːpəvaiz] *vt.* a supraveghea; a dirija.

supervision [ˌsjuːpəˈviʒn] *s.* supraveghere; conducere; îngrijire.

supervisor [ˈsjuːpəvaizə] *s.* supraveghere; conducător.

supine [sjuːˈpain] *adj.* culcat pe spate; pasiv.

supper [ˈsʌpə] *s.* cină; supeu.

supple [ˈsʌpl] *adj.* suplu; maleabil; influenţabil; servil.

supplement[1] [ˈsʌplimənt] *s.* supliment.

supplement[2] [ˈsʌpliment] *vt.* a adăugi; a completa; a suplimenta.

suppliant [ˈsʌpliənt] *s.* solicitant; petiţionar. *adj.* rugător.

supplicant [ˈsʌpliknt] *s. v.* **suppliant**.

supplicate [ˈsʌplikeit] *vt., vi.* a implora.

supply [səˈplai] *s.* transport; stoc; aprovizionare; *econ.* ofertă; suplinitor; *pl.* fonduri. *vt.* a furniza; a acoperi (necesităţile).

support [səˈpɔːt] *s.* sprijin; susţinere; ajutor; suport. *vt.* a sprijini; a suporta.

supporter [səˈpɔːtə] *s.* susţinător; suporter.

suppose [səˈpouz] *vt.* a presupune; *he is ~d to go* se bănuieşte că va merge; trebuie să meargă; *~ we went?* ce-ar fi să mergem?

supposing [səˈpouziŋ] *conj.* (dar) dacă.

suppress [səˈpres] *vt.* a înăbuşi.

supremacy [sjuːˈpreməsi] *s.* supremaţie.

supreme [sjuːˈpriːm] *adj.* suprem.

surcharge [ˈsəːtʃɑːdʒ] *s.* supraîncărcare; suprataxă.

sure [ʃuə] *adj.* sigur; fix; *as ~ as fate* cum te văd şi cum mă vezi; *well, I'm ~!* ei, asta e bună; *be ~ to come* să vii negreşit; *to be ~* fără doar şi poate; nemaipomenit!

sure-footed [ˈʃuəˈfutid] *adj.* solid; sigur; implacabil.

surely [ˈʃuəli] *adv.* fără doar şi poate.

surety [ˈʃuəti] *s.* siguranţă; garanţie; chezaş.

surf [səːf] *s.* valuri care se sparg de ţărm, resac.

surface ['sə:fis] s. suprafaţă; înfăţişare. adj. superficial.

surfeit ['sə:fit] s. ghiftuială. vt., vr. a (se) ghiftui.

surge [sə:dʒ] s. val; răbufnire; potop. vi. a se ridica; a se năpusti (ca valul).

surgeon ['sə:dʒn] s. chirurg; doctor militar.

surgery ['sə:dʒri] s. chirurgie; cabinet medical.

surgical ['sə:dʒikl] adj. chirurgical.

surly ['sə:li] adj. ursuz.

surmise[1] ['sə:maiz] s. presupunere; ghiceală.

surmise[2] [sə:'maiz] vt., vi. a presupune; a ghici.

surmount [sə:'maunt] vt. a învinge; a rezolva; a trece peste.

surname ['sə:neim] s. nume de familie; poreclă.

surpass [sə:'pɑ:s] vt. a depăşi; a întrece.

surplice ['sə:pləs] s. odăjdii.

surprise [sə'praiz] s. surpriză; surprindere. adj. surpriză; neaşteptat. vt. a surprinde; a ului.

surprisingly [sə'praiziŋli] adv. (în mod cu totul) neaşteptat.

surrealism [sə'riəlizəm] s. suprarealism.

surrender [sə'rendə] s. capitulare. vt. a preda; a ceda. vi. a capitula.

surreptitious [ˌsʌrep'tiʃəs] adj. clandestin; tainic; furiş.

surround [sə'raund] vt. a înconjura.

surroundings [sə'raundiŋz] s. pl. mediu; împrejurimi.

survey[1] ['sə:vei] s. privire generală; (trecere în) revistă; rezumat; cadastru.

survey[2] [sə:'vei] vt. a supraveghea; a trece în revistă; a măsura.

surveying [sə:'veiiŋ] s. cadastru.

surveyor [sə: veiə] s. topograf.

survival [sə:'vaivl] s. supravieţuire; rămăşiţă; urmă.

survive [sə:'vaiv] vt. a supravieţui (cu dat.); a depăşi. vi. a supravieţui.

survivor [sə:'vaivə] s. supravieţuitor.

susceptible [sə'septəbl] adj. susceptibil; influenţabil; slab de înger; ~ of capabil de.

suspect [səs'pekt] s., adj. suspect. vt. a bănui; a suspecta.

suspend [səs'pend] vt. a suspenda; a atîrna.

suspender [səs'pendə] s. jartieră; pl. bretele.

suspense [səs'pens] s. aşteptare; încordare.

suspension [səs'penʃn] s. suspendare; suspensie.

suspicion [səs'piʃn] s. bănuială; suspiciune; idee; urmă; undă.

suspicious [səs'piʃəs] adj. bănuitor; neîncrezător; suspect; dubios.

sustain [səs'tein] vt. a susţine; a aproba; a confirma; a suferi (o lovitură).

sustenance ['sʌstinəns] s. hrană; susţinere.

swab [swɔb] s. şomoiog. vt. a tampona; a freca; a spăla.

swaddle ['swɔdl] vt. a bandaja; a înfăşa.

swadling-clothes ['swɔdliŋklouðz] s. pl. scutece; piedici.

swag [swæg] s. pradă.

swagger ['swægə] s. mers fudul. vi. a se fuduli.

swain [swein] s. țăran; iubit.

swallow ['swɔlou] s. rîndunică; înghițire; îmbucătură. vt., vi. a înghiți.

swallow-tailed ['swɔlouteild] adj. cu coadă de rîndunică.

swallow-tailed coat [swɔlouteild kout] s. frac.

swam [swæm] vt., vi. trec. de la **swim.**

swamp [swɔmp] s. mlaștină. vt. a inunda; a covîrși.

swampy ['swɔmpi] adj. mlăștinos.

swan [swɔn] s. lebădă.

swan dive ['swɔndaiv] s. săritură de la trambulină.

swan song ['swɔnsɔŋ] s. cîntecul lebedei; ultima operă.

swap [swɔp] s. schimb. vt. a schimba; a face schimb de.

sward [swɔ:d] s. pajiște; gazon.

swarm [swɔ:m] s. roi. vi. a roi; to ~ with a fi plin de.

swarthy ['swɔ:ði] adj. oacheș.

swashbuckler ['swɔʃˌbʌklə] s. fanfaron; om bătăios.

swath [swɔ:θ] s. brazdă (cosită).

swathe [sweið] vt. a înfofoli; a bandaja.

sway [swei] s. putere; stăpînire; legănat; to hold ~ over a stăpîni. vt. a stăpîni; a influența; a legăna. vi. a se legăna.

swear [swɛə] vt. a jura; a pune să jure; to ~ an oath a face jurămînt; a înjura. vi. a (în-) jura; to ~ at smb. a înjura pe cineva; to ~ by smth. a jura pe ceva.

sweat [swet] s. sudoare, transpirație; efort; umezeală; in a cold ~; all of a ~ scăldat în sudoare; înspăimîntat. vt. a face să transpire; a elimina sub formă de sudoare; a exploata. vi. a transpira; a se aburi; a munci din greu.

sweater ['swetə] s. truditor; exploatator; jerseu.

Swede [swi:d] s. suedez(ă).

Swedish ['swi:diʃ] s. (limba) suedeză. adj. suedez(ă).

sweep [swi:p] s. măturare; curățenie; măturător; coșar; mișcare; cumpăna fîntînii; (cîștig la) joc de noroc. vt. a mătura; a străbate. vi. a mătura; a se năpusti; a trece.

sweeper ['swi:pə] s. măturător.

sweeping ['swi:piŋ] adj. general; dominant; larg; zdrobitor.

sweepings ['swi:piŋz] s. pl. gunoi.

sweepstake(s) ['swi:psteik(s)] s. (potul la) joc de noroc.

sweet [swi:t] s. bomboană; iubit(ă); pl. dulciuri. adj. dulce; parfumat; plăcut; blînd; încîntător; frumos.

sweeten ['swi:tn] vt., vi. a (se) îndulci.

sweetheart ['swi:tha:t] s. iubit(ă); logodnic(ă).

sweetish ['swi:tiʃ] adj. dulceag.

sweetmeat ['swi:tmi:t] s. bomboană; dulceață; pl. zaharicale.

sweetness ['swi:tnis] s. gust dulce; dulceață (fig.).

sweet-pea ['swi:tpi:] s. bot. sîngele-voinicului.

sweet-william ['swi:tˌwiljəm] s. garofiță-de-grădină.

swell [swel] s. umflătură; umflare; val; filfizon. adj. elegant; pus la punct; strașnic. vt., vi. a (se) umfla.

swelling ['sweliŋ] s. umflătură; umflare; creştere.

swelter ['sweltə] vi. a fi zăpuşeală.

swept [swept] vt., vi. trec. şi part. trec. de la sweep.

swerve [swə:v] vt., vi. a (se) abate.

swift [swift] adj. rapid; repede; prompt; iute.

swiftly ['swiftli] adv. repede; prompt.

swill [swil] s. spălătură; lături; poşircă. vt. a spăla; a bea (repede), a da pe gît. vi. a bea (mult).

swim [swim] s. înot; scăldat. vt. a traversa înot. vi. a înota; a pluti; a se înceţoşa; a ameţi; a se clătina (în faţa ochilor).

swimmer ['swimə] s. înotător.

swimming ['swimiŋ] s. înot. adj. înecat; plutitor.

swim-suit ['swimsju:t] s. costum de baie sau de înot.

swindle ['swindl] s. escrocherie; înşelăciune; păcăleală. vt. a escroca. vi. a face escrocherii.

swindler ['swindlə] s. escroc.

swine [swain] s. porc(i).

swine-herd ['swainhə:d] s. porcar.

swing [swiŋ] s. leagăn; legănare; pendulă; pendulare; oscilaţie; ritm; dans legănat; swing; in full ~ în plin avînt; în floare; în desfăşurare. vt. a legăna; a întoarce; a clătina. vi. a se legăna; a se întoarce; a se clătina; a se da în leagăn.

swinging ['swiŋiŋ] adj. legănat; oscilant; ritmat.

swipe [swaip] s. lovitură. vt. a lovi; a fura.

swirl [swə:l] s. vîrtej. vt., vi. a (se) învolbura.

swish [swiʃ] s. fîşîit; foşnet; vîjîit. vt. a foşni din; a plesni. vi. a foşni; a fîşîi; a vîjîi.

Swiss [swis] s., adj. elveţian(ă); the ~ elveţienii.

switch [switʃ] s. nuia; cravaşă; şaltăr, întrerupător; macaz. vt. a cravaşa; a mişca în sus şi în jos; a întrerupe (curentul); a trece pe altă linie; a schimba. vi. a trece pe altă linie; a se muta.

switch-board ['switʃbɔ:d] s. tablou de comandă; centrală telefonică.

swivel ['swivl] vt., vi. a (se) învîrti.

swivel-chair ['swivl'tʃɛə] s. scaun turnant.

swivel-eyed ['swivlaid] adj. saşiu.

swollen ['swouln] adj. umflat. vt., vi. part. trec. de la swell.

swoon [swu:n] s. leşin. vi. a leşina.

swoop [swu:p] s. atac; năpustire. vi. a se năpusti.

swop [swɔp] s., vt. v. swap.

sword [sɔ:d] s. sabie; militărie; război.

swordsman ['sɔ:dzmən] s. spadasin; scrimer.

swore [swɔ:] vt., vi. trec. de la swear.

sworn [swɔ:n] vt., vi. part. trec. de la swear.

swot [swɔt] s. fig. tocilar. vi. fig. a toci.

swum [swʌm] vt., vi. part. trec. de la swim.

swung [swʌŋ] vt., vi. trec. şi part. trec. de la swing.

swung dash ['swʌŋdæʃ] s. tildă.

sycamore ['sikəmɔ:] s. sicomor ; smochin ; paltin.

sycophant ['sikəfənt] s. lingu- şitor ; parazit.

syllabify [si'læbifai] vt. a îm- părţi în silabe.

syllable ['siləbl] s. silabă.

syllabus ['siləbəs] s. programă analitică ; plan ; conspect.

sylph [silf] s. zînă ; silfidă.

symbol ['simbl] s. simbol.

sympathetic [ˌsimpə'θetik] adj. înţelegător ; plin de compăti- mire ; milos ; simpatic.

sympathize ['simpəθaiz] vt. a fi înţelegător ; a fi milos ; to ~ with a compătimi ; a agrea ; a înţelege.

sympathizer ['simpəθaizə] s. simpatizant.

sympathy ['simpəθi] s. înţele- gere ; milă, compătimire ; sim- patie ; pl. condoleanţe.

symphony ['simfəni] s. simfonie. adj. simfonic.

symposia [sim'pouziə] s. pl. de la symposium.

symposium [sim'pouziəm] s. sim- pozion ; banchet.

symptom ['simtəm] s. simp- tom ; semn.

syncope ['sinkəpi] s. sincopă ; leşin.

syndicate ['sindikit] s. cartel ; concern.

synopsis [si'nɔpsis] s. rezumat ; tablou sinoptic.

synthesis ['sinθisis] s. sinte- ză.

synthesize ['sinθisaiz], synthe- tize ['sinθitaiz] vt. a sinte- tiza.

syringe ['sirindʒ] s. seringă.

system ['sistim] s. sistem(ă) ; regim (social) ; ordine.

system(at)ize ['sistim(ət)aiz] vt. a sistematiza.

T

T [ti:] s. T, t.

tab [tæb] s. apendice, anexă ; cotor, contramarcă ; atîrnă- toare, acăţătoare.

table ['teibl] s. masă ; tabel ; tablă. vt. a pune pe masă ; a propune ; a pune pe un tabel.

tableau ['tæblou] s. tablou ; cortină.

table cloth ['teiblklɔθ] s. faţă de masă.

table-land ['teibllænd] s. podiş, platou.

tablet ['tæblit] s. tabletă.

table-talk ['teiblto:k] s. conver- saţie.

table-tennis ['teiblˌtenis] s. te- nis de masă, ping-pong.

table waters ['teibl wɔ:təz] s. pl. apă minerală.

tabloid ['tæbloid] s. tabletă. adj. concentrat.

taboo [tə'bu:] s. tabu.

tabular ['tæbjulə] adj. în formă de tabel ; neted.

tack [tæk] s. ţintă ; cui ; piu- neză ; tighel.

tackle ['tækl] s. scripete ; odgon ;

instalaţie; echipament; *sport*
placaj. *vt.* a aborda, a ataca;
sport a placa. *vi.* a placa.

tact [tækt] *s.* tact, abilitate.

tactful ['tæktfl] *adj.* abil; plin
de tact.

tactics ['tæktiks] *s.* tactică.

tactless ['tæktlis]' *adj.* lipsit de
tact; greşit.

tadpole ['tædpoul] *s. zool.* mormoloc.

tag [tæg] *s.* etichetă; stampilă; repetiţie. *vt.* a eticheta;
a se ţine după (cineva).

tail [teil] *s.* coadă; spate; pajură; coroană (la o monedă);
pl. frac. *vt.* a pune coadă la
(un obiect). *vi.: to ~ after*
a se ţine după (cineva).

tail-coat ['teilkout] *s.* frac.

tailor ['teilə] *s.* croitor. *vt.* a
croi; a face (haine). *vi.* a face
haine.

tailoring ['teiləriŋ] *s.* croitorie
(*profesie*).

tailor-made ['teiləmeid] *adj.* făcut de croitor.

tailor-made suit ['teiləmeid͵sju:t]
s. taior.

taint [teint] *s.* pată; molipsire;
pîngărire; atingere. *vt.* a pîngări; a strica; a infecta.

taintless ['teintlis] *adj.* nepătat;
imaculat.

take [teik] *vt.* a lua; a primi;
a accepta; a obţine; a (con)-
duce; a fura; a răpi; a simţi;
a mînca; a consuma; a bea;
a alege; a prinde; a ataca;
a' folosi; a atrage; a necesita;
a înregistra; a presupune; a
socoti; a adopta; *to ~ French
leave* a o şterge englezeşte;
to ~ off a scoate; *to ~ on*

a întreprinde; a-şi asuma; a
angaja; *to ~ out* a scoate, a
smulge; a obţine; *to ~ over*
a prelua; *to ~ up* a ridica;
a ocupa; a primi; a se ocupa
de. *vi.* a fi atrăgător; **a face
impresie**; *to ~ after smb.* a
semăna cu cineva; *to ~ off*
a sări;. a decola; *to ~ on* a
fi emoţionat; a se supăra;
to ~ over a intra în funcţie.

taken ['teikn] *vt., vi. part. trec.
de la* **take.**

take-off ['teikɔ:f] *s.* decolare.

tale [teil] *s.* poveste; basm.

talent ['tælənt] *s.* talent; capacitate.

talk [tɔ:k] *s.* conversaţie; discuţie; cozerie; conferinţă; tratative; subiect (al bîrfelilor).
vt. a discuta, a vorbi; a convinge; *to ~ round* a duce cu
vorba; *to ~ over* a discuta pe
îndelete. *vi.* a vorbi; a conversa; a bîrfi.

talkative ['tɔ:kətiv] *adj.* flecar.

talker ['tɔ:kə] *s.* vorbitor; orator; lăudăros.

talkie ['tɔ:ki] *s.* film sonor.

talking-picture ['tɔ:kiŋ'piktʃə] *s.*
film sonor.

tall [tɔ:l] *adj.* mare, înalt;
riscat; exagerat.

tallow ['tælou] *s.* seu.

tally ['tæli] *s.* răboj; etichetă.
vt. a socoti. *vi.* a corespunde,
a se potrivi.

talon ['tælən] *s.* gheară; unghie
lungă.

tame [teim] *adj.* îmblînzit;
blînd; inofensiv; neinteresant.
vt. a îmblînzi; a supune.

tamer ['teimə] *s.* îmblînzitor.

tamper ['tæmpə] *vt.: to ~*

with a umbla la; a falsifica; a strica; a corupe.

tan [tæn] *s.* argăseală; tanin; bronzare. *adj.* gălbui. *vt.* a argăsi; a bronza; a bate.

tangerine [ˌtændʒəˈriːn] *s.* mandarină.

tangible [ˈtændʒəbl] *s.* palpabil; clar.

tangle [ˈtæŋgl] *s.* încureătură. *vt., vi.* a (se) încurca.

tank [tæŋk] *s.* rezervor; tanc.

tankard [ˈtæŋkəd] *s.* cană.

tanker [ˈtæŋkə] *s.* tanc petrolier.

tanner [ˈtænə] *s.* tăbăcar; monedă de şase penny.

tannery [ˈtænəri] *s.* tăbăcărie.

tantalize [ˈtæntəlaiz] *vt.* a chinui; a necăji.

tantamount [ˈtæntəmaunt] *adj.* *to be* ~ *to* a se ridica la; a însemna; a fi egal cu.

tap [tæp] *s.* robinet; (vin de la) canea; bătaie uşoară (în geam, pe umăr etc.); ·bocănit; *pl. mil.* stingerea. *vt.* a da cep la; a deschide; a aborda; a bate (uşor); a tapa; a supraveghea (un telefon).

tape [teip] *s.* panglică; bandă; *vt.* a prinde cu panglici.

taper [ˈteipə] *s.* lumînare subţire. *vi.* a se ascuţi către vîrf.

tape-recorder [ˈteipriˌkɔːdə] *s.* magnetofon.

tapering [ˈteipəriŋ] *adj.* conic; ascuţit.

tapestry [ˈtæpistri] *s.* tapet; tapiserie.

tapeworm [ˈteipwəːm] *s.* tenie.

tap-room [ˈtæprum] *s.* bar, tejghea; bufet.

tar [tɑː] *s.* gudron; catran; marinar. *vt.* a da cu catran.

ta-ra [ˈtɑːrɑː] *interj.* pa, la revedere.

tardy [ˈtɑːdi] *adj.* întîrziat; încet.

tare [tɛə] *s.* tară, dara.

target [ˈtɑːgit] *s.* ţintă; sarcină; normă.

tariff [ˈtærif] *s.* tarif; listă de preţuri.

tarnish [ˈtɑːniʃ] *s.* întunecare. *vt.* a întuneca.

tarpaulin [tɑːˈpɔːlin] *s.* prelată; îmbrăcăminte marinărească (impermeabilă).

tarragon [ˈtærəgən] *s.* tarhon.

tarry [ˈtæri] *vi.* a zăbovi; a rămîne; a aştepta.

tart [tɑːt] *s.* tartă; tîrfă. *adj.* acru; obraznic.

tartan [ˈtɑːtn] *s.* pled; stofă ecosez. *adj.* ecosez.

Tartar[1] [ˈtɑːtə] *s.* tătar; om nervos. *adj.* tătăresc.

tartar[2] [ˈtɑːtə] *s.* tartru.

task [tɑːsk] *s.* sarcină; temă. *vt.* a încărca; (*fig.*) a pune la (grea) încercare.

taskmaster [ˈtɑːskmɑːstə] *s.* şef.

tassel [ˈtæsl] *s.* franjuri.

taste [teist] *s.* gust; gură, muşcătură, înghiţitură; preferinţă. *vt.* a gusta; a simţi; a atinge; a se bucura de. *vi.* a gusta; a simţi un gust; a avea gust (bun, rău etc.); *to* ~ *of* a avea gust de.

tasteful [ˈteistfl] *adj.* gustos; plin de (bun) gust.

tasteless [ˈteistlis] *adj.* fără gust; fără haz; de prost gust.

tasty [ˈteisti] *adj.* gustos.

ta-ta [ˈtɑːtɑː] *interj.* pa, la revedere.

tatter [ˈtætə] *s.* zdreanţă.

tattered ['tætəd] *adj.* zdrenţuit; zdrenţăros.

tatterdemalion [ˌtætədə'meiljən] *s.* zdrenţăros, calic.

tattle ['tætl] *s.* vorbărie (goală); flecăreală. *vt., vi.* a trăncăni; a bîrfi.

tattoo [tə'tu:] *s.* tatuaj; tamtam. *vt.* a tatua.

taught [tɔ:t] *vt., vi. trec. şi part. trec. de la* teach.

taunt [tɔ:nt] *s.* ironie, înţepătură. *vt.* a ironiza, a înţepa.

taut [tɔ:t] *adj.* întins, încordat.

tavern ['tævən] *s.* cîrciumă; han.

tawny ['tɔ:ni] *adj.* roib; maro deschis.

tax [tæks] *s.* impozit; taxă; povară. *vt.* a impune, a taxa; a împovăra; a acuza.

taxation [tæk'seiʃn] *s.* impozite; fisc.

tax-collector ['tækskəˌlektə] *s.* perceptor.

tax-free ['tæks'fri:] *adj.* scutit de impozite *sau* taxe (vamale).

taxi ['tæksi] *s.* taxi. *vi.* a merge cu taxiul; a rula, a merge.

taxicab ['tæksikæb] *s.* taxi.

taximeter ['tæksiˌmi:tə] *s.* aparat de taxat.

taxpayer ['tæksˌpeiə] *s.* contribuabil.

t.b. ['ti:'bi] *s.* tuberculoză.

tea [ti:] *s.* ceai.

teach [ti:tʃ] *vt.* a preda, a învăţa (pe alţii). *vi.* a fi profesor.

teacher ['ti:tʃə] *s.* profesor.

teaching ['ti:tʃiŋ] *s.* învăţătură; profesorat.

tea house ['ti:haus] *s.* ceainărie.

team [ti:m] *s.* echipă; pereche (de boi, cai). *vi.: to ~ up with* a se uni cu.

teamster ['ti:mstə] *s.* conducător de turmă; vizitiu.

tea-party ['ti:ˌpɑ:ti] *s.* petrecere, ceai.

tear[1] [tiə] *s.* lacrimă; *in ~s* plîngînd.

tear[2] [tɛə] *s.* ruptură. *vt.* a sfîşia, a rupe, a tăia; a răni; a smulge; a chinui. *vi.* a se rupe, a se sfîşia; a se repezi; a trece ca fulgerul; *to ~ at smth.* a trage de ceva.

tearful ['tiəfl] *adj.* plîngăreţ; scăldat în lacrimi.

tear-gas ['tiə'gæs] *s.* gaz lacrimogen.

tease [ti:z] *s.* om ironic; mucalit. *vt.* a tachina, a ironiza; a necăji; a pisa, a bate la cap; a desface.

tea spoon ['ti:spu:n] *s.* linguriţă.

teat [ti:t] *s.* mamelon; ţîţă.

tea-things ['ti:θiŋz] *s. pl.* serviciu de ceai.

tea-time ['ti:taim] *s.* ora ceaiului *(patru, cinci după-amiază).*

technical ['teknikl] *adj.* tehnic.

technicality [ˌtekni'kæliti] *s.* chiţibuş; chestiune de specialitate.

technique [tek'ni:k] *s.* tehnică.

technology [tek'nɔlədʒi] *s.* tehnologie; tehnică.

teddy-bear ['tedibɛə] *s.* ursuleţ *(jucărie).*

teddy-boy ['tedibɔi] *s.* huligan; marţafoi.

tedious ['ti:djəs] *adj.* plicticos, lung.

teem [ti:m] *vi.* a mişuna; a roi; *to ~ with* a fi plin de.

teen-ager ['ti:nˌeidʒə] *s.* adolescent(ă) *(13—19 ani).*

teens [ti:nz] *s. pl.* adolescenţă
(*13—19 ani*).

teeth [ti:θ] *s. pl. de la* **tooth.**

teetotal [ti:'toutl] *adj.* cumpătat; nealcoolic.

teetotal(l)er [ti:'toutlə] *s.* abstinent; antialcoolic.

telecast ['telikɑ:st] *s.* emisiune de televiziune.

telegram ['teligræm] *s.* telegramă.

telegraph ['teligrɑ:f] *s.* telegraf.

telephone ['telifoun] *s.* telefon. *vt., vi.* a telefona.

telescope ['teliskoup] *s.* telescop; lunetă. *vt.* a strînge; a ciocni. *vi.* a se ciocni.

television ['teli͵viʒn] *s.* televiziune.

tell [tel] *vt.* a relata, a spune; a distinge; a recunoaşte. *vi.* a povesti, a spune poveşti; *to ~ on smb.* a trăda; a pîrî pe cineva; *it ~s on one's health* are un efect negativ asupra sănătăţii.

teller ['telə] *s.* povestitor; cel ce numără (voturile, banii etc.).

telling ['teliŋ] *adj.* eficient; impresionant, elocvent.

tell-tale ['telteil] *s.* gură spartă. *adj.* trădător.

telly ['teli] *s.* televiziune; televizor.

temerity [ti'meriti] *s.* îndrăzneală (exagerată).

temper ['tempə] *s.* temperament; stăpînire de sine; furie; tărie; *out of ~ (with)* supărat (pe). *vt.* a căli; a înmuia; a tempera. *vi.* a se căli; a se întări.

temperamental [͵temprə'mentl] *adj.* temperamental; nervos; capricios.

temperance ['temprns] *s.* temperanţă; cumpătare; antialcoolism.

temperature ['tempritʃə] *s.* temperatură.

tempest ['tempist] *s.* furtună.

tempestuous [tem'pestjuəs] *adj.* furtunos.

temple ['templ] *s.* templu; tîmplă.

templet ['templit] *s.* şablon.

tempo ['tempou] *s.* ritm.

temporize ['tempəraiz] *vi.* a zăbovi; a căuta să cîştigi timp.

tempt [temt] *vt.* a ispiti; a atrage.

temptation [tem'teiʃn] *s.* ispită.

ten [ten] *s., num.* zece.

tenacious [ti'neiʃəs] *adj.* tenace; unit; lipicios.

tenancy ['tenənsi] *s.* situaţia de chiriaş; perioada închirierii; pămînt pentru care se plăteşte arendă.

tenant ['tenənt] *s.* chiriaş; arendaş; dijmaş; ţăran (de pe o moşie). *vt.* a lua în arendă; a lucra în dijmă; a închiria; a ocupa.

tench [tentʃ] *s. iht.* lin.

tend [tend] *vt.* a păzi; a paşte (vitele). *vi.* a tinde.

tendency ['tendənsi] *s.* tendinţă.

tender ['tendə] *s.* ofertant; ofertă. *fin.* monedă; tender; vas auxiliar. *adj.* moale; delicat; fraged; tandru; necopt; nevîrstnic; dureros; sensibil; milos.

tenderfoot ['tendəfut] *s.* nou-venit; ageamiu.

tendon ['tendən] *s.* tendon.

tendril ['tendril] *s.* cîrcel; cîrlionţ.

tenement ['tenimənt] s. închiriere ; local închiriat.

tenement-house ['tenimənthaus] s. casă de raport.

tenet ['ti:net] s. principiu ; credinţă.

tenfold ['tenfould] adj., adv. înzecit.

tenner ['tenə] s. hîrtie de zece lire.

tenon ['tenən] s. cui de lemn ; îmbucătură. vt. a îmbuca.

tenor ['tenə] s. tenor ; direcţie generală ; sens general.

tense [tens] s. timp al verbului. adj. încordat ; întins.

tensile ['tensail] adj. extensibil ; ductil ; de încordare.

tension ['tenʃn] s. tensiune ; încordare.

tent [tent] s. cort.

tentacle ['tentəkl] s. tentacul.

tentative ['tentətiv] s. ipoteză. adj. experïmental ; făcut la noroc, într-o doară.

tenter-hook ['tentəhuk] s. cîrlig de rufe ; to be on ~s a sta ca pe ghimpi sau jăratic.

tenth [tenθ] s. zecime. num. al zecelea.

tenure ['tenjuə] s. posesiune ; stăpînire.

tepid ['tepid] adj. călduţ.

term [tə:m] s. termen ; limită ; pl. învoială. vt. a numi.

termagant ['tə:məgənt] s. fig. vrăjitoare ; scorpie.

terminal ['tə:minl] s. terminus ; capăt. adj. final ; de la capăt.

termination [ˌtə:mi'neiʃn] s. terminaţie ; încheiere.

terminology [ˌtə:mi'nɔlədʒi] s. terminologie ; nomenclatură.

terminus ['tə:minəs] s. terminus ; capăt.

terrace ['terəs] s. terasă ; parc (de locuinţe).

terrible ['terəbl] s. teribil ; înspăimîntător ; straşnic.

terribly ['terəbli] adv. teribil ; straşnic ; foarte; groaznic (de).

terrier ['teriə] s. (cîine) terier.

terrific [tə'rifik] adj. teribil ; straşnic.

terrify ['terifai] vt. a înspăimînta.

territory ['teritri] s. teritoriu.

terror ['terə] s. teroare ; spaimă.

terror stricken ['terəstrikn], terror-struck ['terəstrʌk] adj. îngrozit, înspăimîntat.

terse [tə:s] adj. concis ; scurt.

test [test] s. încercare ; experienţă ; examen ; analiză, test. adj. de încercare, experimental. vt. a încerca ; a examina ; a analiza ; a pune la grea încercare.

testament ['testəmənt] s. testament.

testify ['testifai] vt. a declara ; a dovedi. vi. a depune mărturie ; to ~ to a afirma ; a dovedi.

testimonial [ˌtesti'mounjəl] s. mărturie ; mărturisire ; semn.

testimony ['testiməni] s. mărturie ; declaraţie.

test-tube ['testju:b] s. eprubetă.

testy ['testi] adj. supărăcios, ţîfnos.

tetchy ['tetʃi] adj. ţîfnos.

tether ['teðə] s. pripon. vt. a priponi.

text [tekst] s. text ; manuscris ; subiect.

text-book ['teksbuk] s. manual.

textile ['tekstail] *s.* textilă. *adj.* textil.

texture ['tekstʃə] *s.* ţesătură; structură.

than [ðən, ðæn] *conj.* decît.

thank [θæŋk] *s.* mulţumire; ~s! mulţumesc; ~s *to* datorită. *vt.* a mulţumi (cuiva); ~ *you* mulţumesc.

thankful ['θæŋkfl] *adj.* recunoscător.

thankfulness ['θæŋkflnis] *s.* recunoştinţă.

thankless ['θæŋklis] *adj.* ingrat.

thanksgiving ['θæŋks,giviŋ] *s.* (rugăciune de) recunoştinţă.

that [ðət, ðæt] *adj.* acel, acea. *pron.* [ðæt] acela, aceea; (pe care). *adv.* [ðæt] atîta; aşa de. *conj.* [ðət] că; încît; pentru că.

thatch [θætʃ] *s.* acoperiş de paie, de stuf; paie. *vt.* a acoperi cu paie *sau* stuf.

thaw [θɔ:] *s.* dezgheţ, moină. *vt., vi.* a (se) topi; a (se) dezgheţa.

the [ðə], înaintea vocalelor [ði] *art. hot.* : ~ *moon* luna; *most beautiful.* cea mai frumoasă. *adv.:* ~ *more* ~ *better* cu cît mai mult, cu atît mai bine.

theater, theatre ['θiətə] *s.* teatru; amfiteatru; *fig.* scenă.

theatergoer, theatregoer ['θiətə-goə] *s.* (mare) amator de teatru.

theatrical [θi'ætrikl] *adj.* teatral.

thee [ði:] *pron. înv.* pe tine.

theft [θeft] *s.* furt; hoţie.

their [ðɛə] *adj.* lor.

theirs [ðɛəz] *pron.* al lor.

them [ðəm] *pron.* pe ei, pe ele; lor.

theme [θi:m] *s.* temă, subiect.

themselves [ðəm'selvz] *pron.* se; înşişi, însele; ei, ele; *by* ~ singuri, fără (alt) ajutor.

then [ðen] *adj.* de atunci. *adv.* atunci; apoi; *now* ~ ei. *conj.* atunci, deci.

theorem ['θiərəm] *s.* teoremă

theorist ['θiərist] *s.* teoretician.

theorize ['θiəraiz] *vt., vi.* a teoretiza.

theory ['θiəri] *s.* teorie.

therapy ['θerəpi] *s.* terapie.

there [ðɛə] *adv.* acolo; atunci; ~ *is* [ðəz, ðə riz] este; ~ *are* [ðərə, ðə'ra:] sînt, se află; ~ *and then* (atunci pe) loc. *interj.* iată.

thereabout(s) ['ðɛərəbaut(s)] *adv.* (cam) pe acolo.

thereby ['ðɛə'bai] *adv.* prin aceasta.

therefore ['ðɛəfɔ:] *adv.* deci, de aceea.

therein [ðɛər'in] *pron.* din care; din ea, din el; din asta. *adv.* acolo (înăuntru); în această privinţă.

thermometer, thermometre [θə'mɔmitə] *s.* termometru.

thermos (flask) ['θə:mɔs (fla:sk)] *s.* termos.

thesaurus [θi'sɔ:rəs] *s.* dicţionar; tezaur.

these [ði:z] *adj.* aceşti, aceste. *pron.* aceştia, acestea.

thesis ['θi:sis] *s.* teză, principiu; eseu.

they [ðei] *pron.* ei, ele; lumea.

thick [θik] *adj.* gros, dens; intim; răguşit; greoi; ~ *with* plin de.

thicken ['θikn] *vt., vi.* a (se) îngroşa.

thickening ['θiknin] s. îngro-
şare; grosime.
thicket ['θikit] s. crîng; tufiş.
thickhead ['θikhed] s. tîmpit.
thickness ['θiknis] s. grosime;
strat.
thickset ['θik'set] adj. solid,
îndesat; des.
thick-skinned ['θik'skind] adj.
cu pielea groasă; gros la
obraz.
thief [θi:f] s. hoţ.
thieve [θi:v] vt., vi. a fura.
thievish ['θi:viʃ] adj. hoţesc.
thigh [θai] s. coapsă, pulpă.
thimble ['θimbl] s. degetar.
thin [θin] s. parte subţire. adj.
subţire; mic; slab; răsfirat;
rar; prost; de necrezut. vt.,
vi. a (se) subţia.
thine [ðain] inv. adj. tău. pron.
al tău.
thing [θiŋ] s. lucru, obiect;
subiect; fiinţă; amănunt; împrejurare; pl. situaţie; the ~
is ... problema este ...; first
~ in the morning primul lucru
ce trebuie făcut.
think [θiŋk] vt. a gîndi, a socoti;
a crede; a-şi închipui; to ~
out a elabora; a chibzui; to
~ over a chibzui. vi. a se
gîndi; a medita; a fi dus pe
gînduri; a născoci.
thinking ['θiŋkiŋ] s. gîndire;
meditaţie. adj. care gîndeşte.
thinker ['θiŋkə] s. gînditor; cugetător.
thinness ['θinnis] s. subţirime;
slăbiciune; rarişte.
third [θə:d] s. treime. num. al
treilea.
third-degree ['θə:d di'gri:] s. brutalitate a poliţiei.

third-rate ['θə:d'reit] adj. foarte
prost.
thirst [θə:st] s. sete; dor. vi.
a fi însetat.
thirsty ['θə:sti] adj. însetat;
care face sete; uscat.
thirteen ['θə:'ti:n] s., num. treisprezece.
thirteenth ['θə:'ti:nθ] s., num.
al treisprezecelea.
thirtieth ['θə:tiiθ] s., num. al
treizecilea.
thirty ['θə:ti] s., num. treizeci;
the thirties deceniul al patrulea.
this [ðis] adj. acest, această.
pron. acesta, aceasta.
thistle ['θisl] s. scai, ciulin.
thither ['ðiðə] adv. într-acolo.
tho' [ðou] conj. deşi.
thorn [θɔ:n] s. spin; ciulin.
thorny ['θɔ:ni] adj. ţepos; spinos.
thorough ['θʌrə] adj. complet;
profund; exact; meticulos.
thoroughbred ['θʌrəbrəd] s. aristocrat; cal pursînge. adj. aristocratic; pursînge.
thoroughfare ['θʌrəfɛə] s. magistrală.
thoroughgoing ['θʌrəgoiŋ] adj.
complet; profund; extrem; meticulos, amănunţit; temeinic.
thoroughly ['θʌrəli] adv. temeinic; complet.
thoroughness ['θʌrənis] s. seriozitate; meticulozitate.
those [ðouz] adj. acei, acele.
pron. aceia, acelea.
thou [ðau] pron. inv. tu.
though [ðou] adv. totuşi. conj.
deşi; totuşi.
thought [θɔ:t] s. gînd; idee;
grijă; nuanţă. vt., vi. trec. şi
part. trec. de la think.

thoughtful ['θɔːtfl] *adj.* serios; gînditor; amabil; atent, grijuliu.

thoughtless ['θɔːtlis] *adj.* aiurit; neatent; egoist.

thoughtlessness ['θɔːtlisnis] *s.* zăpăceală; nechibzuinţă.

thousand ['θauznd] *s.*, *num.* o mie.

thousandfold ['θauznfould] *adj.*, *adv.* înmiit.

thousandth ['θauzənθ] *s.* miime. *num.* al o mielea.

thraldom ['θrɔːldəm] *s.* sclavie.

thrall [θrɔːl] *s.* sclav; rob.

thrash [θræʃ] *vt.* a bate; a treiera; *to ~ out* a discuta pe îndelete; a lămuri. *vi.* a treiera.

thrasher ['θræʃə] *s.* batoză.

thrashing ['θræʃiŋ] *s.* bătaie; treierat.

thread [θred] *s.* aţă; fir (conducător etc.); filet (la şurub). *vt.* a înşira pe aţă.

threadbare ['θredbɛə] *adj.* uzat, ros; ponosit; învechit.

threat [θret] *s.* ameninţare.

threaten ['θretn] *vt.* a ameninţa.

three [θriː] *s.*, *num.* trei.

three-cornered ['θriː'kɔːnəd] *adj.* în trei colţuri.

threefold ['θriːfould] *adj.*, *adv.* întreit.

threepence ['θrepns] *s.* trei penny.

three score ['θriːˌskɔː] *s.*, *num.* şaizeci.

thresh [θreʃ] *vt.*, *vi.* a treiera.

thresher ['θreʃə] *s.* batoză.

threshing-floor ['θreʃiŋflɔː] *s.* arie de treierat.

threshing-machine ['θreʃiŋməˌʃiːn] *s.* batoză.

threshold ['θreʃould] *s.* prag;

threw [θruː] *vt.*, *vi. trec. de la* **throw.**

thrice [θrais] *adv.* de trei ori.

thrift [θrift] *s.* economie; chibzuială.

thriftless ['θriftlis] *adj.* risipitor.

thrifty ['θrifti] *adj.* econom; prosper.

thrill [θril] *s.* fior (de plăcere); emoţie. *vt.* a emoţiona; a captiva; a face să palpite. *vi.* a se înfiora (de plăcere); a palpita; a vibra.

thriller ['θrilə] *s.* roman *sau* film poliţist *sau* de groază.

thrilling ['θriliŋ] *adj.* palpitant; captivant; emoţionant.

thrive [θraiv] *vi.* a prospera; a reuşi; a-i merge bine.

thriven ['θrivn] *vi. part. trec. de la* **thrive.**

thro' [θruː] *prep.* prin.

throat [θrout] *s.* gît(lej).

throaty ['θrouti] *adj.* gutural; din gît.

throb [θrɔb] *s.* puls; vibraţie; duduit; emoţie. *vi.* a pulsa; a dudui; a vibra; (*d. inimă*) a bate.

throes [θrouz] *s. pl.* dureri (ale facerii); chinuri.

throne [θroun] *s.* tron; rege; monarhie.

throng [θrɔŋ] *s.* mulţime, aglomeraţie. *vt.*, *vi.* a (se) aglomera.

throttle ['θrɔtl] *s.* gît, beregată; *auto.* accelerator. *vt.* a strînge de gît; a înăbuşi. *vi.* a încetini viteza.

through [θruː] *adj.* direct; gata. *adv.* de la un capăt la celălalt; complet; gata. *prep.* prin; datorită, din cauza.

throughout [θru'aut] *adv.* întru totul ; peste tot. *prep.* de la un capăt la celălalt ; peste tot cuprinsul.

throve [θrouv] *vi. trec. de la* **thrive.**

throw [θrou] *s.* aruncare. *vt.* a arunca, a azvîrli ; a îndrepta ; a trimite ; a lăsa deoparte ; a făta ; a juca (zaruri) ; a pune ; *to ~ about* a împrăştia ; a mişca (braţele) ; *to ~ away, to ~ to the dogs* a irosi, a da cu piciorul la ; *to ~ down* a răsturna ; a trînti la pămînt ; *to ~ in* a pune la bătaie ; a băga ; a face (o remarcă) ; *to ~ off* a dezbrăca ; a scăpa de ; a arunca (la o parte) ; *to ~ open* a deschide (larg) ; *to ~ out* a respinge ; a arunca (la întîmplare) ; a clădi ; *to ~ over* a părăsi ; a renunţa la ; *to ~ up* a ridica ; a vomita ; a renunţa la. *vi.* a arunca (în lături) ; *to ~ back* a se întoarce. *vr.* a se arunca ; a se trînti.

thrown [θroun] *vt., vi. part. trec. de la* **throw.**

thru [θru:] *prep. amer.* prin ; pînă (la).

thrum [θrʌm] *vt., vi.* a zdrăngăni.

thrush [θrʌʃ] *s.* sturz ; afte.

thrust [θrʌst] *s.* împingere ; împunsătură, înţepătură ; atac ; aluzie (răutăcioasă). *inf., trec. şi part. trec. vt.* a împinge ; a înfige ; a înjunghia. *vi.* a împinge ; a ţîşni.

thud [θʌd] *s.* bubuitură ; dupăit.

thug [θʌg] *s.* criminal ; apaş.

thumb [θʌm] *s.* degetul mare ; *under the ~ of* în puterea cuiva. *vt.* a foileta, a frunzări.

thumb-index ['θʌm,indeks] *s.* litere tipărite pe marginea paginilor cărţii.

thumb-screw ['θʌmskru:] *s.* instrument de tortură ; şurub.

thumb-tack ['θʌmtæk] *s.* piuneză.

thump [θʌmp] *s.* lovitură cu pumnul. *vt., vi.* a lovi ; a bate.

thumping ['θʌmpiŋ] *adj., adv.* straşnic ; teribil.

thunder ['θʌndə] *s.* tunet ; trăsnet ; fulger. *vt.* a urla. *vi.* a trăsni ; a fulgera ; a bubui ; a se năpusti.

thunderbolt ['θʌndəboult] *s.* (lovitură de) trăsnet ; fulger.

thunder-clap ['θʌndəklæp] *s.* (bubuit de) tunet.

thunder-cloud ['θʌndəklaud] *s.* nor de furtună.

thunder-storm ['θʌndəstɔ:m] *s.* furtună cu descărcări electrice.

thunder-struck ['θʌndəstrʌk] *adj.* trăsnit ; uluit.

Thursday ['θə:zdi] *s.* joi.

thus [ðʌs] *adv.* astfel ; aşa ; atîta ; *~ far* deocamdată.

thwart [θwɔ:t] *vt.* a contrazice ; a zădărnici ; a pune beţe în roate la (sau cu dat.).

thy [ðai] *adj. inv.* tău, ta.

thyme [taim] *s.* cimbru.

thyself [ðai'self] *pron. inv.* tu însuţi ; te ; tu.

tiara [ti'a:rə] *s.* tiară.

tick [tik] *s.* ticăit, tic-tac ; semn, bifare ; căpuşă ; faţă de saltea ; credit, veresie. *vt.* a bifa, a însemna. *vi.* a ticăi.

ticker ['tikə] *s.* ceas.

ticket ['tikit] *s.* bilet ; tichet ; *amer.* listă de candidaţi ; notă ; autorizaţie ; *that's the ~* aşa e (bine).

ticking ['tikiŋ] s. ticăit; faţă de saltea.

tickle ['tikl] s. gîdilat. vt. a gîdila; a amuza; a incînta. vi. a gîdila.

ticklish ['tikliʃ] adj. gîdilos; fig. spinos.

tidal ['taidl] adj. legat de flux.

tidbit ['tidbit] s. v. **titbit**.

tide [taid] s. flux (şi reflux); fig. tendinţă (generală), curent; perioadă.

tidiness ['taidinis] s. fire ordonată.

tidings ['taidiŋz] s. pl. veşti.

tidy ['taidi] adj. ordonat; curat; mare. vt. a aranja; a pune în ordine. vi. a face ordine (prin casă).

tie [tai] s. legătură; funie; cravată; amer. traversă; încurcătură; meci nul; muz. legato. vt. a lega, a fixa; a îngrădi. vi. a se lega; sport a face meci nul.

tier [tiə] s. rînd de loji, rafturi sau scaune.

tiff [tif] s. ceartă.

tiger ['taigə] s. tigru.

tight [tait] adj. (bine) închis; strîns; strîmt; etanş; plin (ochi); încordat; beat; zgîrcit. adv. strîns, încordat.

tighten ['taitn] vt. a încorda, a întinde, a întări; a închide; a strînge.

tight-fisted ['tait'fistid] adj. zgîrcit; strîns la pungă.

tight-rope ['taitroup] s. funie întinsă (pentru acrobaţii).

tights [taits] s. pl. pantaloni de balet.

tigress ['taigris] s. tigroaică.

tile [tail] s. ţiglă, olan. vt. a acoperi cu ţiglă.

till [til] s. sertar (la tejghea). vt. a cultiva, a lucra (pămîntul). prep. pînă la. conj. pînă (ce).

tillage ['tilidʒ] s. agricultură; pămînt lucrat.

tiller ['tilə] s. ţăran; muncitor agricol; mînerul cîrmei.

tilt [tilt] s. luptă cavalerească, turnir; înclinare. vt. a înclina; a întoarce, a răsturna; to ~ at a ataca.

timber ['timbə] s. cherestea; lemne; pădure.

timbered ['timbəd] adj. lucrat în lemnărie; împădurit.

timber yard ['timbə‚jaːd] s. depozit de cherestea.

timbre ['tæmbə] s. muz. timbru.

time [taim] s. timp; perioadă; dată; ocazie; epocă; oră; muz. măsură; in no ~ imediat; at one ~ cîndva (în trecut); ~ and again de nenumărate ori; at ~s cînd şi cînd; many a ~, many ~s adesea. vt. a potrivi (în timp); a programa; a cronometra.

time-bomb ['taimbɔm] s. bombă cu întîrziere; maşină infernală.

time-keeper ['taim‚kiːpə] s. normator; cronometru.

timely ['taimli] adj. potrivit, oportun.

time-piece ['taimpiːs] s. ceasornic.

time-serving ['taim‚səːviŋ] adj. oportunist; conformist.

time-table ['taim‚teibl] s. orar; program.

timid ['timid] adj. timid; fricos.

timorous ['timərəs] adj. fricos; timid.

tin [tin] s. cositor; tinichea; cutie (de conserve); bani. vt.

a conserva (în cutii); a cositori.

tinder ['tində] s. iască.

tinfoil ['tinfɔil] s. staniol.

tinge [tindʒ] s. nuanţă, tentă;
urmă. vt. a colora (uşor); fig.
a umbri.

tingle ['tiŋgl] s. furnicătură;
ţiuială. vi. a furnica; a ţiui.

tinker ['tiŋkə] s. tinichigiu;
meseriaş prost. vt., vi. a cîrpăci.

tinkle ['tiŋkl] s. clinchet; zăngănit. vt. a suna din (clopoţel).

tinman ['tinmən] s. tinichigiu;
meseriaş care lipeşte şi cosito-
reşte vasele.

tinned food ['tind'fu:d], **tinned
goods** ['tind'gudz] s. conserve.

tinsel ['tinsl] s. beteală; pole-
ială.

tint [tint] s. nuanţă, culoare,
tentă. vt. a colora.

tiny ['taini] adj. mititel.

tip [tip] s. vîrf; bacşiş; sfat;
răsturnare. vt. a răsturna; a da
bacşiş la.

tip-cart ['tipkɑ:t] s. camion sau
vagon(et) basculant.

tipple [tipl] s. băutură. vt., vi.
a bea; a (se) îmbăta.

tipsy ['tipsi] adj. beat; cherchelit.

tiptoe ['tiptou] s. vîrful picioarelor. vi. a merge în vîrful
picioarelor.

tiptop ['tip'tɔp] s. vîrful cei
mai înalt. adj. straşnic; de
prima calitate.

tire ['taiə] s. anvelopă; cauciuc
de roată. vt. a obosi. vi. a se
obosi; a se plictisi.

tired ['taiəd] adj. obosit; istovit; plictisit.

tiredness ['taiədnis] s. oboseală.

tireless ['taiəlis] adj. neobosit;
energic; neîncetat.

tiresome ['taiəsəm] adj. obositor; supărător; plicticos.

tiro ['taiərou] s. începător, ageamiu.

tissue ['tisju:] s. ţesătură; pînză,
material; ţesut; plasă.

tit [tit] s. piţigoi; ~ for tat
dinte pentru dinte.

titanic [tai'tænik] adj. uriaş;
imens; titanic.

titbit ['titbit] s. bucăţică bună;
delicatese; veste mare.

tithe [taið] s. dijmă; fracţiune.

titillate ['titileit] vt. a gîdila;
a încînta.

titivate ['titiveit] vt., vi. a (se)
împopoţona.

title ['taitl] s. titlu; drept.
adj. de titlu; titular.

titled ['taitld] adj. înnobilat.

titmouse ['titmaus] s. piţigoi.

titter ['titə] s. chicotit. vi. a
chicoti.

title-tattle ['titl,tætl] s. bîrfeală,
flecăreală; zvon. vi. a bîrfi;
a răspîndi zvonuri.

titubation [,titju'beiʃn] s. agitaţie, nervozitate.

to [tə, tu(:)] prep. la; spre;
înainte de; pînă la; pe(ntru).
particulă a inf. (pentru) a.

toad [toud] s. broască rîioasă;
parazit; linguşitor.

toad-eater ['toud,i:tə] s. linguşitor; sicofant.

toadstool ['toudstu:l] s. ciupercă
(otrăvitoare).

toady ['toudi] s. linguşitor. vi.
a linguşi.

toast [toust] s. pîine prăjită;
toast; sărbătorit. vt. a prăji;

a încălzi; a toasta pentru. *vi.*
a se prăji; a se încălzi.

toaster ['toustə] *s.* grătar pentru
prăjit piinea.

tobacco [tə'bækou] *s.* tutuń.

tobacconist [tə'bækənist] *s.* tutungiu; tutungerie.

tobacco-plant [tə'bæko͵plɑ:nt] *s.*
tutun; regina nopţii.

toboggan [tə'bɔgən] *s.* sanie
(lungă).

tocsin ['tɔksin] *s.* (clopot de)
alarmă.

today [tə'dei] *s.* (ziua de) astăzi;
zilele noastre. *adv.* azi.

toddle ['tɔdl] *s.* bălăbăneală. *vi.*
a se bălăbăni; a umbla hai-hui.

toddler ['tɔdlə] *s.* copilaş, pici.

to-do [tə'du:] *s.* zarvă; agitaţie.

toe [tou] *s.* deget de la picior;
bombeu.

toe-cap ['toukæp] *s.* bombeu.

toffee ['tɔfi] *s.* caramelă.

tog [tɔg] *s.* haină. *vt.* a se îmbrăca (elegant).

together [tə'geðə] *adv.* împreună; laolaltă; alături; neîntrerupt.

toil [tɔil] *s.* trudă. *vi.* a trudi;
a merge greu.

toiler ['tɔilə] *s.* truditor.

toilet ['tɔilit] *s.* toaletă.

toilet-paper ['tɔilit͵peipə] *s.* hîrtie igienică.

toilet-table ['tɔilit͵teibl] *s.* măsuţă de toaletă.

toilsome ['tɔilsəm] *adj.* obositor;
laborios.

token ['toukn] *s.* semn; simbol.

token strike ['touknstraik] *s.*
grevă de solidaritate *sau* de
protest.

told [tould] *vt., vi.* trec. şi *part.*
trec. de la **tell.**

tolerable ['tɔlərəbl] *adj.* suportabil; acceptabil.

tolerance ['tɔlərns] *s.* îngăduinţă; toleranţă.

tolerate ['tɔləreit] *vt.* a tolera;
a îngădui.

toll ['toul] *s.* dangăt de clopot;
jertfă. *vt.* a suna (din clopot).
vi. a (ră)suna jalnic.

tomahawk ['tɔməhɔ:k] *s.* secure
a pieilor-roşii.

tomato [tə'mɑ:tou] *s.* (pătlăgică) roşie.

tomb [tu:m] *s.* cavou; mormînt.

tomboy ['tɔmbɔi] *s.* fată băie-
ţoasă.

tombstone ['tu:mstoun] *s.* piatră
funerară.

tomcat ['tɔm'kæt] *s.* motan.

tome [toum] *s.* volum (gros).

tomfool ['tɔm'fu:l] *s.* prostănac.

tomfoolery [tɔm'fu:ləri] *s.* aiureală, prostii.

tommy ['tɔmi] *s.* soldat britanic.

tommy-gun ['tɔmigʌn] *s. mil.*
automat.

tommy rot ['tɔmirɔt] *s.* prostii.

tomorrow [tə'mɔrou] *s.* (ziua
de) mîine. *adv.* mîine.

tomtit ['tɔm'tit] *s.* piţigoi.

ton [tʌn] *s.* tonă.

tone [toun] *s.* ton, glas, intonaţie; spirit, esenţă; nuanţă;
culoare. *vt.* a intona; a colora;
to ~ down a potoli; *to ~ up*
a întări. *vi.* a se îmbina, a se
potrivi.

toneless ['tounlis] *adj.* mort,
fără viaţă; fără culoare.

tongs [tɔŋz] *s. pl.* cleşte.

tongue [tʌŋ] *s.* limbă; limbaj;
flacără.

tongue-tied ['tʌŋ taid] *adj.* amu-
ţit, mut.

tonic ['tɔnik] s. tonic; *muz.* to-
nică. *adj.* tonic; înviorător.

tonight [tə'nait] *adv.* deseară;
la noapte.

tonnage ['tʌnidʒ] s. tonaj.

tonsil ['tɔnsl] s. amigdală.

tonsil(l)itis [ˌtɔnsi'laitis] s. amigdalită.

tonsure ['tɔnʃə] s. tonsură; tunsoare.

too [tu:] *adv.* de asemenea, şi;
prea, foarte.

took [tuk] *vt., vi. trec. de la*
take.

tool [tu:l] s. unealtă.

tooth [tu:θ] s. dinte.

tooth ache ['tu:θeik] s. durere
de dinţi.

tooth brush ['tu:θbrʌʃ] s. periuţă
de dinţi.

toothless ['tu:θlis] *adj.* ştirb,
fără dinţi.

tooth paste ['tu:θpeist] s. pastă
de dinţi.

tooth pick ['tu:θpik] s. scobitoare.

toothsome ['tu:θsəm] *adj.* gustos.

top [tɔp] s. vîrf; culme; partea
de sus; înălţime; sfîrlează;
on ~ deasupra, sus; *on* ~ *of*
deasupra, peste, pe lîngă. *adj.*
maxim. *vt.* a acoperi; a reteza
vîrful la; a depăşi.

top boot ['tɔp'bu:t] s. cizmă.

top coat ['tɔp'kout] s. pardesiu;
demiu.

tope [toup] *vt., vi.* a bea (zdravăn).

toper ['toupə] s. beţivan(că).

top-hat ['tɔp'hæt] s. joben.

topic ['tɔpik] s. subiect.

topical ['tɔpikl] *adj.* interesant;
actual, curent; de actualitate.

topmost ['tɔpmoust] *adj.* cel
mai de sus.

topography [tə'pɔgrəfi] s. topografie.

topper ['tɔpə] s. joben; băiat
bun.

topping ['tɔpiŋ] *adj.* grozav.

topple ['tɔpl] *vt.* a răsturna.
vi. a se bălăbăni; a se răsturna.

top secret ['tɔpˌsi:krit] *adj.*
ultrasecret.

topsy-turvy ['tɔpsi'tə:vi] *adj.,*
adv. cu susul în jos; talmeş-
balmeş.

torch [tɔ:tʃ] s. torţă; flacără;
(şi *electric* ~) lanternă.

torchlight ['tɔ:tʃlait] s. (lumină de) torţă.

torchlight procession ['tɔ:tʃlait
prə'seʃn] s. retragere cu torţe.

tore [tɔ:] *vt., vi. trec. de la*
tear².

torment¹ ['tɔ:mənt] s. chin;
durere; necaz.

torment² [tɔ:'ment] *vt.* a chinui;
a necăji; a nelinişti.

torn [tɔ:n] *vt., vi. part. trec.*
de la **tear².**

tornado [tɔ:'neidou] s. uragan;
trombă.

torpedo [tɔ:'pi:dou] s. torpilă.
vt. a torpila.

torpedo-boat [tɔ:'pi:doubout] s.
torpilor; vedetă torpiloare.

torpid ['tɔ:pid] *adj.* pasiv; toropit; trîndav.

torpor ['tɔ:pə] s. torpoare; toropeală; lene.

torrid ['tɔrid] *adj.* torid, tropical.

torsion ['tɔ:ʃn] s. răsucire; tor-
siune.

torso ['tɔ:sou] s. *anat.* tors,
trunchi.

tortoise ['tɔːtəs] s. broască ţestoasă.

tortoise-shell ['tɔːtəʃel] s. carapace (de broască ţestoasă); baga.

tortuous ['tɔːtjuəs] adj. răsucit; încurcat; necinstit.

torture ['tɔːtʃə] s. tortură, chin. vt. a tortura; a răstălmăci.

Tory ['tɔːri] s., adj. conservator.

toss [tɔs] s. clătinare; prăbuşire; aruncare. vt. a clătina; a răsturna; a arunca de colocolo; to ~ (up) a coin a da cu banul; to ~ off a da pe gît. vi. a se clătina; a se răsuci; a se zbuciuma.

tot [tɔt] s. copilaş; păhărel; coloană de cifre. vt. a aduna. vi.: to ~ up a se ridica la.

total ['toutl] s., adj. total. vt. a totaliza; a se ridica la.

tote [tout] s. maşină de calculat.

totter ['tɔtə] vt. a se clătina (pe picioare).

touch [tʌtʃ] s. atingere; pipăit; tuşeu; încercare; contact; urmă. vt. a atinge; a pune în contact; a mînca; a enerva; a tapa. vi. a se atinge; a fi în contact.

touch-and-go ['tʌtʃən'gou] adj. risca(n)t; nesigur.

touched [tʌtʃt] adj. ţicnit; mişcat (fig.); atins.

touching ['tʌtʃiŋ] adj. mişcător, emoţionant.

touch-line ['tʌtʃlain] s. sport tuşă.

touchstone ['tʌtʃstoun] s. (piatră de) încercare.

touchy ['tʌtʃi] adj. ultrasensibil; iritabil.

tough [tʌf] adj. tare, aspru; încăpăţînat; dificil.

toughen ['tʌfn] vt. a întări; a înăspri.

tour [tuə] s. turneu, tur. vt. a face un turneu prin. vi. a face turism.

touring-car ['tuəriŋkɑː] s. autocar.

tournament ['tuənəmənt] s. competiţie, turneu; ist. turnir.

tousle ['tauzl] vt. a zbîrli; a încurca.

tout [taut] s. agent de publicitate, şleper. vi. a face reclamă zgomotoasă.

tow [tou] s. remorcare, tragere; cîlţi.

toward(s) [tə'wɔːd(z)] prep. către; aproape de; faţă de; pentru.

towel ['tauəl] s. prosop.

tower ['tauə] s. turn. vi. a domina; a se înălţa.

towering ['tauəriŋ] adj. înalt; dominant; violent.

tow-line ['toulain] s. edec.

town [taun] s. oraş; orăşeni.

town clerk ['taunklɑːk] s. arhivar.

town council ['taun‚kaunsl] s. consiliu municipal.

town crier ['taun‚kraiə] s. crainicul oraşului.

town hall ['taun'hɔːl] s. primărie.

townsfolk ['taunzfouk] s. orăşeni.

township ['taunʃip] s. amer. municipalitate; district.

townsman ['taunzmən] s. orăşean; concetăţean.

toy [tɔi] s. jucărie. adj. de jucărie

trace [treis] *s.* urmă. *adj.* trasor. *vt.* a trasa, a schiţa; a copia; a da de urmă; a desluşi.

traceable ['treisəbl] *adj.* identificabil; de găsit.

track [træk] *s.* urmă; pistă; drum, potecă; linie (ferată); teren de sport; drum bătut; şenilă; *off the* ~ aiurea. *vt.* a urmări.

tract [trækt] *s.* teren; întindere; canal, tub; broşură, tratat.

tractable ['træktəbl] *adj.* docil, maleabil.

traction ['trækʃn] *s.* tracţiune.

tractor ['træktə] *s.* tractor.

trade [treid] *s.* meserie, ocupaţie; comerţ; *by* ~ de meserie. *adj.* comercial. *vt.* a schimba (mărfuri), a face negoţ cu. *vi.* a face negoţ; *to* ~ *upon* a profita de.

trade mark ['treidma:k], **trade name** ['treidneim] *s.* marca fabricii.

trader ['treidə] *s.* comerciant; vas comercial.

tradesfolk ['treidzfouk], **tradespeople** ['treidz͵pi:pl] *s. pl.* comercianţi; furnizori.

trade union ['treid'ju:njən] *s.* sindicat. *adj.* sindical.

trade unionist ['treid'ju:njənist] *s.* membru de sindicat.

trade winds ['treidwindz] *s. pl.* alizee.

tradition [trə'diʃn] *s.* tradiţie, datină.

traditional [trə'diʃənl] *adj.* tradiţional; popular; anonim.

traduce [trə'dju:s] *vt.* a defăima.

traffic ['træfik] *s.* trafic, circulaţie; comerţ. *vi.* a trafica.

trafficker ['træfikə] *s.* traficant.

traffic lights ['træfik'laits] *s. pl.* semafor, stop.

tragedy ['trædʒidi] *s.* tragedie.

tragi-comedy ['trædʒi'kɔmidi] *s.* melodramă.

trail [treil] *s.* dîră, urmă; potecă. *vt.* a da de urmă la; a tîrî; a remorca.

trailer ['treilə] *s.* remorcă; urmăritor; plantă tîrîtoare; forşpan.

train [trein] *s.* tren; trenă; suită; alai; şir (de idei). *vt.* a educa, a instrui; a antrena; a ţinti. *vi.* a se antrena.

trainer ['treinə] *s.* antrenor.

training [treiniŋ] *s.* instrucţie, instruire; antrenament; pregătire.

traipse [treips] *vi.* a hoinări; a pierde vremea.

trait [trei] *s.* trăsătură (caracteristică).

traitor ['treitə] *s.* trădător.

traitress ['treitris] *s.* trădătoare.

tram(car) ['træm(ka:)] *s.* tramvai; vagon.

tram-line ['træmlain] *s.* linie de tramvai; şină.

trammel ['træml] *s.* piedică; *pl.* încurcătură. *vt.* a împiedica, a încurca.

tramp [træmp] *s.* vagabond; cerşetor; drum lung; tropăit. *vt.* a cutreiera (pe jos). *vi.* a tropăi; a umbla (haihui).

trample ['træmpl] *s.* tropăit. *vt.* a călca în picioare; a zdrobi. *vi.* a tropăi; a călca apăsat; *to* ~ *on* a călca în picioare.

tramway ['træmwei] *s.* tramvai.

trance [tra:ns] *s.* transă.

tranquil ['træŋkwil] *adj.* liniştit.

tranquil(l)ity [træŋ'kwiliti] s. linişte, calm.

transact [træn'zækt] vt. a încheia, a face (afaceri).

transaction [træn'zækʃn] s. tranzacţie, afacere ; pl. proceseverbale ; arhivă.

transcend [træn'send] vt. a depăşi ; a trece peste.

transcribe [træns'kraib] vt. a transcrie.

transcript ['trænskript] s. copie.

transcription [træns'kripʃn] s. transcriere ; copie.

transfer¹ ['trænsfə] s. trecere ; (act de) transfer ; copie pe indigo.

transfer² [træns'fə:] vi. a se transfera ; a schimba trenul, tramvaiul etc.

transferable [træns'fə:rəbl] adj. care poate fi transferat ; alienabil.

transfiguration [trænsfigju'reiʃn] s. transfigurare.

transfix [træns'fiks] vt. a străpunge ; a paraliza.

transform [træns'fɔ:m] vt. a transforma ; a schimba.

transformation [ˌtrænsfə'meiʃn] s. transformare ; perucă.

transformer [træns'fɔ:mə] s. transformator.

transfuse [træns'fju:z] vt. a face o transfuzie de.

transfusion [træns'fju:ʒn] s. transfuzie.

transgress [træns'gres] vt. a depăşi ; a încălca. vi. a păcătui ; a greşi.

transgression [træns'greʃn] s. încălcare ; păcat.

transgressor [træns'gresə] s. infractor ; păcătos.

transient ['trænziənt] s. pasager ; musafir trecător. adj. trecător, efemer.

transition [træn'siʒn] s. tranziţie. adj. de tranziţie.

transitive ['trænsitiv] adj. tranzitiv.

transitory ['trænsitri] adj. scurt ; efemer.

translatable [træns'leitəbl] adj. traductibil.

translate [træns'leit] vt. a traduce ; a muta.

translation [træns'leiʃn] s. traducere ; translaţie ; mutare.

translator [træns'leitə] s. traducător.

transliterate [trænz'litəreit] vt. a recopia.

translucent [trænz'lu:snt] adj. transparent.

transmigration[ˌtrænzmai'greiʃn] s. migraţie, transhumanţă.

transmission [trænz'miʃn] s. transmisie ; emisie.

transmit [trænz'mit] vt. a transmite ; a emite.

transmitter [trænz'mitə] s. transmiţător ; emiţător.

transmute [trænz'mju:t] vt. a transmuta ; a preface.

transom ['trænsəm] s. oberliht.

transparency [træns'pɛərnsi] s. transparenţă.

transpire [træns'paiə] vt. a degaja (vapori) ; a elimina. vi. a transpira, a se afla.

transplant [træns'plɑ:nt] s. răsad. vt. a răsădi ; a transplanta.

transport¹ ['trænspɔt] s. (vas de) transport ; pl. entuziasm.

transport² [træns'pɔ:t] vt. a transporta ; a deporta ; a entuziasma.

transportation [ˌtrænspɔ:ˈteiʃn] s. transport; deportare.

transpose [trænsˈpouz] vt. a transpune.

transposition [ˌtrænspəˈziʃn] s. transpunere.

trans-ship [trænsˈʃip] vt. a transborda.

transverse [ˈtrænzvə:s] adj. transversal.

trap [træp] s. capcană, cursă; trapă. vt. a prinde în cursă. vi. a pune capcane (pentru animale).

trapeze [trəˈpi:z] s. trapezul acrobatului.

trapezium [trəˈpi:zjəm] s. geom. trapez.

trapper [ˈtræpə] s. vînător care foloseşte capcanele.

trappings [ˈtræpiŋz] s. pl. ornamente; fig. abţibilduri.

trash [træʃ] s. gunoi; prostii.

trashy [ˈtræʃi] adj. fără valoare.

travel [ˈtrævl] s. călătorie. vt. a străbate. vi. a călători, a umbla; a se mişca; a trece.

travel(l)ed [ˈtrævld] adj. umblat.

travel(l)er [ˈtrævlə] s. călător.

travelogue [ˈtrævəloug] s. conferinţă (geografică) cu proiecţii.

traverse [ˈtrævəs] s. traversă; piedică. adj. transversal, cruciş. vt. a traversa; a contrazice; a discuta; a străbate.

travesty [ˈtrævisti] s. travestire; imitaţie; simulacru; parodie. vt. a parodia; a imita (prost).

trawl [trɔ:l] s. plasă (mare) de pescuit. vt. a tîrî (pe fundul mării). vi. a pescui (cu plasa mare).

trawler [ˈtrɔ:lə] s. vas de pescari, trauler.

tray [trei] s. tabla, tavă; tăviţă.

treacherous [ˈtretʃrəs] adj. trădător; înşelător.

treachery [ˈtretʃri] s. trădare; înşelăciune.

treacle [ˈtri:kl] s. melasă.

tread [tred] s. pas; mers; treaptă. vt. a călca; a zdrobi; a bătători; a bate (un drum).

treadle [ˈtredl] s. pedală. vi. a pedala.

treadmill [ˈtredmil] s roată învîrtită de paşii oamenilor; instrument de tortură (şi fig.).

treason [ˈtri:zn] s. trădare.

treasonable [ˈtri:znəbl] adj. trădător.

treasure [ˈtreʒə] s. comoară; bijuterie; avere. vt. a păstra; a colecţiona; a iubi ca ochii din cap; a preţui.

treasure-house [ˈtreʒəhaus] s. vistierie.

treasurer [ˈtreʒrə] s. vistiernic; casier.

treasure trove [ˈtreʒətrouv] s. comoară găsită; obiect fără stăpîn.

treasury [ˈtreʒri] s. vistierie tezaur; antologie.

treasury note [ˈtreʒrinout] s. bon de tezaur; bancnotă.

treat [tri:t] s. încîntare; trataţie. vt., vi. a trata.

treatise [ˈtri:tiz] s. tratat (ştiinţific).

treatment [ˈtri:tmənt] s. tratament.

treaty [ˈtri:ti] s. tratat (comercial, cultural etc.); negociere.

treble [ˈtrebl] s. voce subţire, înaltă; notă acută. adj. întreit; muz. înalt. vt., vi. a (se) tripla.

tree [tri:] s. arbore.
treeless ['tri:lis] adj. despădurit.
trefoil ['trefɔil] s. trifoi.
trellis ['trelis] s. plasă, grătar ;
spalier.
tremble ['trembl] s. tremur. vi.
a tremura.
trembling ['trembliŋ] s. tre-
mur(at). adj. tremurător ; tremurat.
tremendous [tri'mendəs] adj.
uriaş ; nemaipomenit ; teribil ;
straşnic ; fantastic.
tremendously [tri'mendəsli] adv.
extraordinar ; foarte mult.
tremor ['tremə] s. tremur(at) ;
fior, emoţie.
tremulous ['tremjuləs] adj. tremurător ; fricos.
trench [trentʃ] s. tranşee ; şanţ.
trenchant ['trentʃnt] adj. tăios
(fig.) ; hotărît.
trencher ['trentʃə] s. tocător,
fund de lemn.
trend [trend] s. tendinţă, curent.
trepidation [‚trepi'deiʃn] s. tremur ; panică.
trespass ['trespəs] s. încălcare ;
braconaj ; păcat. vi. : to ~ on
a încălca ; a abuza de ; to ~
against a păcătui împotriva ;
a lovi ; no ~ing trecerea oprită ;
intrarea interzisă.
trespasser ['trespəsə] s. infractor.
tress [tres] s. şuviţă ; pl. bucle.
trestle ['tresl] s. constr. capră.
trial ['trail] s. proces ; necaz ;
încercare grea ; experienţă.
triangle ['traiæŋgl] s. triunghi.
triangular [trai'æŋgjulə] adj.
triunghiular.
tribal ['traibl] adj. tribal.

tribe [traib] s. trib ; familie ; clică.
tribesman ['traibzmən] s. membru al tribului.
tribulation [‚tribju'leiʃn] s. necaz ; supărare ; chin.
tribunal [trai'bju:nl] s. tribunal.
tribune ['tribju:n] s. tribun ;
tribună.
tributary ['tribjutri] s. afluent.
adj. tributar ; afluent.
tribute ['tribju:t] s. tribut ;
impozit ; omagiu.
trice [trais] s. clipă, moment.
trick [trik] s. şmecherie ; truc ;
farsă ; acţiune ; scamatorie ; o-
bicei ; levată (la cărţi). vt. a
păcăli.
trickle ['trikl] s. scurgere ; dîră ;
picătură. vt., vi. a picura.
trickster ['trikstə] s. trişor ;
escroc.
tricky ['triki] adj. înşelător ;
complicat.
tricycle ['traisikl] s. triciclu.
tried [traid] adj. încercat ; de
nădejde.
trifle ['traifl] s. fleac, bagatelă ;
pic(ătură). vt. : to ~ away a
irosi. vi. a se juca (fig.).
trifling ['traifliŋ] adj. neînsemnat.
trigger ['trigə] s. trăgaci.
trilby ['trilbi] s. pălărie moale.
trill [tril] s. tril. vi. a face
triluri.
trillion ['triljən] s. trilion ; amer.
bilion.
trim [trim] adj. pus la punct ;
curat ; elegant. vt. a aranja ;
a curăţi ; a netezi ; a tunde ;
a împodobi, a garnisi.
trimming ['trimiŋ] s. aranjare,
potrivire ; ornament(aţie) ; pl.
garnitură, înflorituri.

trinket ['triŋkit] s. podoabă, fleac.

trio ['triou] s. trio; térţet.

trip [trip] s. călătorie (scurtă); excursie; împiedicare; pas greşit. vt. a sări peste; to ~ up a pune piedică (cuiva). vi. a topăi; a se împiedica.

tripe [traip] s. burduf, burtă de vacă; prostii.

triple ['tripl] adj. triplu. vt., vi. a (se) tripla.

triplet ['triplit] s. tripletă; unul din trei gemeni.

tripod ['traipɔd] s. trepied.

trite [trait] adj. banal; banalizat.

triteness ['traitnis] s. banalitate.

triumph ['traiəmf] s. triumf, victorie; entuziasm. vi. a triumfa; a se bucura; to ~ over a triumfa asupra, a învinge.

triumphant [trai'ʌmfənt] adj. triumfal; triumfător.

trivial ['triviəl] adj. neînsemnat; meschin; banal.

triviality [ˌtrivi'æliti] s. fleac; lipsă de importanţă; banalitate.

trochee ['trouki:] s. troheu.

trod [trɔd] vt., vi. trec. de la tread.

trodden ['trɔdn] vt., vi. part. trec. de la tread.

trojan ['troudʒn] s. troian.

trolley ['trɔli] s. cărucior; vagonet; troleu; amer. tramvai.

trolleybus ['trɔlibʌs] s. troleibuz.

trollop ['trɔləp] s. tîrîtură, tîrfă.

troop [tru:p] s. trupă; detaşament; pl. armată, soldaţi. vi. a merge în grup.

trooper ['tru:pə] s. soldat; cavalerist.

trope [troup] s. figură de stil; metaforă; sens figurat.

trophy ['troufi] s. trofeu.

tropical ['trɔpikl] adj. tropical.

trot [trɔt] s. fugă; trap; plimbare. vt. a duce la trap; a plimba. vi. a merge în trap; a se grăbi.

trotter ['trɔtə] s. trăpaş; pl. (răcituri de) picioare de porc.

trouble ['trʌbl] s. necaz; bucluc; încurcătură; dificultate; efort; tulburare; med. afecţiune. vt. a tulbura; a deranja; a necăji. vi. a se necăji; a se agita; a se deranja. vr. a se deranja; a se agita.

troublesome ['trʌblsəm] adj. supărător; chinuitor.

trough [trɔf] s. troacă.

troupe [tru:p] s. trupă (artistică).

trousers ['trauzəz] s. pl. pantaloni (lungi).

trout [traut] s. păstrăv.

trowel ['traul] s. mistrie.

troy [trɔi] s. sistem de greutăţi pentru metale preţioase.

truancy ['truənsi] s. chiul; absenţă.

truant ['truənt] s. chiulangiu; absent. adj. chiulangiu; haimana.

truce [tru:s] s. armistiţiu; răgaz.

truck [trʌk] s. vagon de marfă; vagonet; amer. camion; comerţ; troc; relaţie. vt. a căra; a face troc cu.

truculent ['trʌkjulənt] adj. agresiv; feroce.

trudge [trʌdʒ] s. drum greu. vi. a merge cu greu, a se tîrî.

true [tru:] adj. adevărat; credincios.

true blue ['tru:͵blu:] s., adj. conservator; fanatic.

truffle ['trʌfl] s. trufă.

truism ['truizəm] s. platitudine.

truly ['tru:li] adv. cu adevărat; sincer.

trump [trʌmp] s. trîmbiţă; atu; om săritor. vt. a folosi ca atu; to ~ up a inventa; a înscena.

trumpery ['trʌmpəri] s. bijuterii false.

trumpet ['trʌmpit] s. trompetă; cornet. vt. a trîmbiţa.

trumpeter ['trʌmpitə] s. trompetist, trîmbiţaş.

truncate ['trʌŋkeit] vt. a trunchea.

truncheon ['trʌntʃn] s. bîtă; matracă.

trundle ['trʌndl] vt., vi. a (se) rostogoli.

trunk [trʌŋk] s. trunchi; parte principală, trup; cufăr; trompă; pl. chiloţi de baie. adj. principal.

trunk-call ['trʌŋk͵kɔ:l] s. convorbire telefonică interurbană.

truss [trʌs] s. snop; bandaj. vt. a lega; a sprijini.

trust [trʌst] s. încredere; tutelă; trust. vt. a avea încredere în, a crede; a încredinţa; a nădăjdui. vi. a avea încredere.

trustee [trʌs'ti:] s. tutore; girant.

trusteeship [trʌs'ti:ʃip] s. tutelă; girare.

trustful ['trʌstfl] adj. încrezător.

trustworthy ['trʌst͵wə:ði] adj. demn de încredere; de nădejde.

truth [tru:θ] s. adevăr.

truthful ['tru:θfl] adj. sincer; corect; adevărat.

truthfulness ['tru:θflnis] s. sinceritate; adevăr.

try [trai] s. încercare. vt. a încerca; a judeca; a chinui. vi. a încerca.

trying ['traiiŋ] adj. supărător.

tryst [trist] s. (loc de) întîlnire.

tsar [za:] s. ţar.

tub [tʌb] s. albie, cadă.

tube [tju:b] s. tub; lampă de radio; metrou.

tubercular [tju'bə:kjulə] adj. tuberculos.

tuberculosis [tju:͵bə:kju'lousis] s. tuberculoză.

tubing ['tju:biŋ] s. tub(aj).

tuck [tʌk] s. pliu; mîncare. vt. a băga, a înveli; a sufleca; to ~ away a mînca. vi.: to ~ in(to) a înfuleca.

tuck-in ['tʌk'in] s. gustare, masă; mîncare.

Tuesday ['tju:zdi] s. marţi.

tuft [tʌft] s. smoc; moţ.

tug [tʌg] s. tragere; tracţiune; remorcher. vt. a trage; a remorca. vi.: to ~ at a trage (de).

tuition [tju'iʃn] s. învăţătură; predare; taxe şcolare.

tulip ['tju:lip] s. lalea.

tumble ['tʌmbl] s. cădere; tumbă; încurcătură, dezordine. vt. a răsturna; a trînti la pămînt; a tulbura; a răvăşi. vi. a cădea; a se răsturna; a face tumbe, a se rostogoli.

tumble-down ['tʌmbldaun] adj. dărăpănat.

tumbler ['tʌmblə] s. pahar (fără picior); acrobat.

tummy ['tʌmi] s. stomac; burtică.

tumult ['tjuːmʌlt] s. agitaţie; zarvă.

tun [tʌn] s. butoi.

tune [tjuːn] s. melodie; ton; armonie; to the ~ of la suma de. vt. a acorda (un pian etc.); a potrivi (postul); to ~ up a pune la punct, a repara. vi.: to ~ up a-şi acorda instrumentele; a începe să cînte.

tuneful ['tjuːnfl] adj. muzical; melodios.

tuning-fork ['tjuːniŋfɔːk] s. diapazon.

tunny ['tʌni] s. iht. ton.

tuppence ['tʌpəns] s. doi penny.

turbid ['təːbid] adj. tulbure; murdar; învălmăşit.

turbine ['təːbin] s. turbină.

turbo-jet ['təːbo'dʒet] s. turboreactor.

turbot ['təːbət] s. iht. calcan.

tureen [təˈriːn] s. supieră; sosieră.

turf [təːf] s. (brazdă de) iarbă; turf, curse de cai.

turgid ['təːdʒid] adj. umflat; congestionat; pompos.

Turk [təːk] s. turc.

turkey ['təːki] s. curcan; curcă.

turkey-cock ['təːkikɔk] s. curcan.

turkey-hen ['təːkihen] s. curcă.

Turkish ['təːkiʃ] s. (limba) turcă. adj. turc(esc).

Turkish delight ['təːkiʃ diˈlait] s. rahat.

turmoil ['təːmɔil] s. învălmăşeală; agitaţie; tumult; tulburare.

turn [təːn] s. întoarcere; tur; rotire; cotitură; ocazie; amabilitate; dispoziţie; scop; exprimare; soc. vt. a învîrti, a

(ră)suci, a roti; a schimba; a strunji; a împlini; to ~ away a alunga; to ~ down a respinge; a da în jos; a micşora; to ~ off a stinge, a închide; a concedia; to ~ out a da afară; a produce; to ~ over a învîrti; a preda; a produce; to ~ up a întoarce; a sufleca; a răsuci; a deşteleni; a ara; a scoate la iveală. vi. a se întoarce; a se roti, a se învîrti; a se (ră)suci); to ~ about a se răsuci (cu totul); a face la stînga împrejur; to ~ against smb. a se năpusti asupra cuiva; to ~ aside a se întoarce într-o parte; to ~ away a pleca (dezgustat); to ~ back a se întoarce (cu spatele); to ~ in a se culca; to ~ off a o lua pe alt drum; a se bifurca; to ~ out a apărea; a se ivi; a se dovedi; to ~ over a se învîrti, a se rostogoli; a se răsuci; to ~ round a se răsuci; a schimba politica; to ~ to smb. a se adresa cuiva; a veni la cineva; to ~ to smth. a se apuca de ceva; to ~ up a apărea, a se ivi.

turncoat ['təːnkout] s. apostat; trădător.

turner ['təːnə] s. strungar.

turning ['təːniŋ] s. cotitură.

turning-point ['təːniŋpɔint] s. cotitură, moment decisiv.

turnip ['təːnip] s. nap; gulie.

turnkey ['təːnkiː] s. temnicer.

turnover ['təːnˌouvə] s. dever; profit.

turnpike ['təːnpaik] s. barieră.

turnstile ['təːnstail] s. cruce de barieră, portiţă rotitoare.

turntable ['tə:n‚teibl] *s.* placă turnantă; platan.

turpentine ['tə:pntain] *s.* terebentină.

turquoise ['tə:kwɑ:z] *s.* peruzea.

turret ['tʌrit] *s.* turnuleţ; turelă.

turtle ['tə:tl] *s.* broască ţestoasă; turturea.

turtle-dove ['tə:tldʌv] *s.* turturică.

tusk [tʌsk] *s.* fildeş, colţi.

tussle ['tʌsl] *s.* încăierare. *vi.* a se încăiera.

tut [tʌt] *interj.* aş; mtţ.

tutor ['tju:tə] *s.* profesor, meditator; asistent universitar. *vt.* a medita.

tutorial class [tju'tɔ:riəl'klɑ:s] *s.* seminar; oră practică.

tuxedo [tʌk'si:dou] *s.* smoching.

twaddle ['twɔdl] *s.* vorbărie, aiureală. *vi.* a pălăvrăgi.

twang [twæŋ] *s.* zbîrnîit; vorbire nazală; fîrnîială. *vi.* a zbîrnîi; a se fîrnîi.

tweak [twi:k] *s.* ciupitură. *vt.* a ciupi.

tweed [twi:d] *s.* stofă cu picăţele; *pl.* costum de tuid, costum de golf.

tweezers ['twi:zəz] *s. pl.* pensetă.

twelfth [twelfθ] *s.* doisprezecime. *num.* al doisprezecelea.

twelfth night ['twelfθ'nait] *s.* ajunul Bobotezei.

twelve [twelv] *s., num.* doisprezece.

twelvemonth ['twelvmʌnθ] *s.* an.

twentieth ['twentiiθ] *s., num.* al douăzecilea.

twenty ['twenti] *s.* douăzeci; *pl.* deceniul al treilea. *num.* douăzeci.

twice [twais] *adv.* de două ori, dublu.

twice-told tale ['twaistould'teil] *s.* poveste bine cunoscută.

twiddle ['twidl] *vt.* a învîrti de pomană; *to ~ one's thumbs* a pierde vremea. *vi.* a se juca.

twig [twig] *s.* rămurică.

twilight ['twailait] *s.* amurg, crepuscul; zori.

twill [twil] *s.* postav cu dungi.

twilled ['twild] *adj.* răsucit.

twin [twin] *s.* frate geamăn. *adj.* geamăn; îngemănat.

twine [twain] *s.* fir, şuviţă. *vt.* a împleti; a întinde; a încolăci. *vi.* a se împleti; a se încolăci.

twinge [twindʒ] *s.* junghi; înţepătură; străfulgerare; remuşcare.

twinkle ['twiŋkl] *s.* scînteiere; licărire; lumină. *vi.* a licări; a scînteia.

twinkling ['twiŋkliŋ] *s.* clipă; clipire, clipit; licărire; *in the ~ of an eye* cît a clipi din ochi.

twin set ['twin‚set] *s.* set (de pulovere).

twirl [twə:l] *s.* răsucire; rotocol. *vt., vi.* a (se) răsuci; a (se) învîrti.

twist [twist] *s.* răsucire; întoarcere; ocol; cot(itură); împletitură; întorsătură; twist. *vt.* a (ră)suci; a învîrti; a stoarce; a deforma. *vi.* a se răsuci; a se contorsiona; a face meandre; a fi în serpentină; a face escrocherii.

twister ['twistə] *s.* escroc; dificultate.

twitch [twitʃ] *s.* smucitură; tic nervos. *vt.* a trage, a smulge. *vi.* a se răsuci; a se contracta; a avea un tic.

twitter ['twitə] *s.* ciripit; flecăreală; agitaţie. *vi.* a ciripi.

two [tu:] *s.* doi; pereche. *num.* doi; *one or* ~ vreo doi; *to put* ~ *and* ~ *together* a pune lucrurile în legătură.

two-edged ['tu:edʒd] *adj.* cu două tăişuri; ambiguu.

two-faced ['tu:feist] *adj.* cu două feţe, făţarnic.

twofold ['tu:fould] *adj., adv.* dublu.

twopence ['tʌpəns] *s.* doi penny.

twopenny ['tʌpni] *s.* (monedă de) doi penny. *adj.* de doi penny.

tycoon [tai'ku:n] *s.* magnat.

tympanum ['timpənəm] *s. anat.* timpan.

type [taip] *s.* tip, categorie; persoană; (literă de) tipar. *vt., vi.* a bate la maşină.

type-setter ['taip,setə] *s. poligr.* culegător.

typewrite ['taiprait] *vt., vi.* a dactilografia.

typewriter ['taip,raitə] *s.* maşină de scris.

typhoid ['taifɔid] *s.* febră tifoidă.

typhoon [tai'fu:n] *s.* taifun.

typhus ['taifəs] *s.* tifos exantematic.

typical ['tipikl] *adj.* tipic; caracteristic.

typify ['tipifai] *vt.* a exemplifica; a ilustra; a simboliza; a tipiza.

typist ['taipist] *s.* dactilograf(ă).

tyrannize ['tirənaiz] *vt.: to* ~ *over* a asupri.

tyranny ['tirəni] *s.* tiranie; asuprire.

tyrant ['taiərnt] *s.* tiran.

tyre ['taiə] *s.* cauciuc de automobil.

tyro ['taiərou] *s.* începător.

tzar [zɑ:] *s.* ţar.

U

U [ju:] *s.* U. u.

udder ['ʌdə] *s.* uger.

ugh [uh] *interj.* uf; fui.

uglify ['ʌglifai] *vt.* a urîţi.

ugly ['ʌgli] *adj.* urît; hidos; neplăcut; ameninţător.

ukulele [,ju:kə'leili] *s.* chitară havaiană.

ulcer ['ʌlsə] *s.* bubă; ulcer; corupţie.

ulcerate ['ʌlsəreit] *vt.* a răni.

ulster ['ʌlstə] *s.* raglan.

ultimate ['ʌltimit] *adj.* ultim, final; fundamental.

ultramarine [,ʌltrəmə'ri:n] *s., adj.* bleumarin.

umbrage ['ʌmbridʒ] *s.* jignire.

umbrella [ʌm'brelə] *s.* umbrelă.

umpire ['ʌmpaiə] *s.* arbitru. *vt., vi.* a arbitra.

umpteen ['ʌmti:n] *adj.* mulţi; mult.

'un [ən] *pron.* cineva ; unul, una.

unabashed ['ʌnə'bæʃt] *adj.* mîndru ; nerușinat.

unabated ['ʌnə'beitid] *adj.* neabătut ; nedomolit ; neclintit.

unable ['ʌn'eibl] *adj.* incapabil.

unabridged ['ʌnə'bridʒd] *adj.* întreg ; neprescurtat.

unacceptable ['ʌnək'septəbl] *adj.* inacceptabil.

unaccountable ['ʌnə'kauntəbl] *adj.* inexplicabil.

unaffected ['ʌnə'fektid] *adj.* sincer ; neafectat.

unalterable [ʌn'ɔːltrəbl] *adj.* (de) neschimbat, consecvent ; constant.

unanimity [ˌjuːnə'nimiti] *s.* unanimitate.

unanimous [ju'næniməs] *adj.* unanim.

unassuming ['ʌnə'sjuːmiŋ] *adj.* modest.

unavailing ['ʌnə'veiliŋ] *adj.* inutil, zadarnic.

unavoidable [ˌʌnə'vɔidəbl] *adj.* inevitabil.

unaware ['ʌnə'wɛə] *adj.* surprins.

unawares ['ʌnə'wɛəz] *adv.* pe neașteptate ; fără voie.

unbalanced ['ʌn'bælənst] *adj.* dezechilibrat ; lipsit de echilibru.

unbearable [ʌn'bɛərəbl] *adj.* insuportabil.

unbecoming ['ʌnbi'kʌmiŋ] *adj.* indecent ; rușinos ; degradant.

unbend ['ʌn'bend] *vt., vi.* a (se) dezdoi.

unbending ['ʌn'bendiŋ] *adj.* țeapăn ; încăpățînat.

unbind ['ʌn'baind] *vt.* a dezlega ; a dezlănțui ; a elibera.

unblemished ['ʌn'blemiʃt] *adj.* nepătat, imaculat.

unblushing ['ʌn'blʌʃiŋ] *adj.* nerușinat ; îndrăzneț.

unborn ['ʌn'bɔːn] *adj.* care nu s-a născut ; așteptat.

unbosom [ʌn'buːzəm] *vt., vi.* a (se) destăinui.

unbound ['ʌn'baund] *vt. trec. și part. trec. de la* unbind.

unbounded [ʌn'baundid] *adj.* nemărginit ; uriaș.

unbridled [ʌn'braidld] *adj.* nestrunit ; nestăpînit.

unbroken ['ʌn'broukn] *adj.* întreg ; neîntrerupt ; nesupus ; nedomesticit.

unburden [ʌn'bəːdn] *vt.* a descărca ; a ușura. *vr.* a se destăinui.

unbutton ['ʌn'bʌtn] *vt.* a descheia.

uncalled-for [ʌn'kɔːldfɔː] *adj.* nedorit.

uncanny [ʌn'kæni] *adj.* straniu ; nefiresc.

uncertain [ʌn'səːtn] *adj.* nesigur ; dubios ; schimbător.

uncertainty [ʌn'səːtnti] *s.* nesiguranță ; lucru nesigur.

unchallenged 'ʌn'tʃælindʒd] *adj.* incontestabil, indiscutabil ; necontestat.

unchanged [ʌn'tʃeindʒd] *adj.* neschimbat.

unchaste ['ʌn'tʃeist] *adj.* desfrînat, stricat ; imoral ; nerușinat ; indecent.

uncivil ['ʌn'sivl] *adj.* nepoliticos.

uncle ['ʌŋkl] *s.* unchi, nene.

unclean ['ʌn'kliːn] *adj.* murdar ; prihănit ; obscen.

Uncle Sam ['ʌŋkl'sæm] *s.* unchiul Sam ; S.U.A.

unclothed ['ʌn'klouðd] adj. dezbrăcat ; gol.

unclouded ['ʌn'klaudid] adj. senin, fără nori.

uncollected ['ʌnkə'lektid] adj. neadunat ; lipsit de calm, nestăpînit.

uncomfortable ['ʌn'kʌmftəbl] adj. stînjenit ; penibil ; incomod(at).

uncommon [ʌn'kɔmən] adj. neobişnuit ; extraordinar.

uncomplimentary ['ʌn‚kɔmpli'mentri] adj. ireverenţios.

uncompromising [ʌn'kɔmprəmaiziŋ] adj. intransigent.

unconcern ['ʌnkən'sə:n] s. nepăsare.

unconclusive ['ʌnkən'klu:siv] adj. neconcludent.

unconditional ['ʌnkən'diʃənl] adj. necondiţionat.

unconnected ['ʌnkə'nektid] adj. fără legătură ; irelevant.

unconquerable [ʌn'kɔŋkrəbl] adj. invincibil ; (de) nestăpînit.

unconscious [ʌn'kɔnʃəs] s. subconştient. adj. inconştient ; neintenţionat.

uncooked ['ʌn'kukt] adj. crud.

uncork ['ʌn'kɔ:k] vt. a destupa.

uncouth [ʌn'ku:θ] adj. stîngaci ; necivilizat ; zurbagiu ; sălbatic.

uncover [ʌn'kʌvə] vt., vi., vr. a (se) descoperi.

unction ['ʌŋʃn] s. miruire, ungere ; glas mieros.

unctuous ['ʌŋtjuəs] adj. unsuros ; mieros.

uncultured ['ʌn'kʌltʃəd] adj. necultivat ; incult.

uncurbed ['ʌn'kə:bd] adj. nestăvilit ; nestăpînit.

undamaged ['ʌn'dæmidʒd] adj. intact ; neatins ; în perfectă stare.

undaunted [ʌn'dɔ:ntid] adj. neîmpăcat.

undeceive ['ʌndi'si:v] vt. a trezi la realitate ; a lumina.

undeniable [‚ʌndi'naiəbl] adj. (de) netăgăduit.

under ['ʌndə] adj. inferior, de jos ; subordonat ; supus (la). adv. jos, dedesubt. prep. sub, dedesubtul.

under age ['ʌndər'eidʒ] adj. minor ; necopt (fig.).

underbrush ['ʌndəbrʌʃ] s. cătină.

under carriage ['ʌndə‚kæridʒ] s. tren de aterizare.

underclothes ['ʌndəklouðz] s. pl. lenjerie (de corp).

undercurrent ['ʌndə‚kʌrnt] s. curent subteran.

under-developed ['ʌndədi'veləpt] adj. slab dezvoltat ; subdezvoltat.

underdog ['ʌndədɔg] s. subordonat, supus umil.

underdone ['ʌndə'dʌn] adj. nefript ; nefiert.

underestimate ['ʌndər'estimeit] vt. a subevalua.

underfed ['ʌndə'fed] adj. prost hrănit ; subnutrit.

underfoot [‚ʌndə'fut] adv. sub sau în picioare.

undergarment ['ʌndə‚gɑ:mənt] s. lenjerie de corp.

undergo [‚ʌndə'gou] vt. a suferi ; a păţi ; a trece prin.

undergone [‚ʌndə'gɔn] vt. part. trec. de la undergo.

undergraduate [‚ʌndə'grædjuit] s. student (în ulţimii ani).

underground¹ ['ʌndəgraund] s.
metrou ; ilegalitate ; subteran.
adj. subteran ; secret ; ilegal.
underground² [,ʌndə'graund]
adv. sub pămînt, în subteran ;
pe ascuns.
undergrown ['ʌndə'groun] *adj.*
neisprăvit ; pitic.
undergrowth ['ʌndəgrouθ] s. pădure tînără, (sub)arboret.
underhand ['ʌndəhænd] *adj.* ascuns ; viclean ; necinstit. *adv.*
în secret ; pe furiş, pe ascuns.
underlain [,ʌndə'lein] *vt. part.
trec. de la* **underlie.**
underlay [,ʌndə'lei] *vt. trec.
de la* **underlie.**
underlie [,ʌndə'lai] *vt.* a fundamenta, a susţine ; a se afla
dedesubtul *sau* la baza (unui
lucru).
underline [,ʌndə'lain] *vt.* a sublinia.
underling ['ʌndəliŋ] s. lacheu,
agent ; subaltern.
underlying [,ʌndə'laiiŋ] *adj.* fundamental ; de dedesubt.
undermine [,ʌndə'main] *vt.* a
submina.
underneath [,ʌndə'ni:θ] *adv.* dedesubt. *prep.* sub.
underrate [,ʌndə'reit] *vt.* a sub-
aprecia.
underscore [,ʌndə'skɔ:] *vt.* a
sublinia.
undersecretary ['ʌndə'sekrətri]
s. subsecretar.
undersigned ['ʌndəsaind] s. sub-
semnatul, subsemnaţii.
undersized ['ʌndə'saizd] *adj.* mic,
pitic ; necrescut.
understand [,ʌndə'stænd] *vt.* a
înţelege ; a afla ; a deduce ;
a subînţelege ; *to ~ one another*

a se înţelege (reciproc). *vi.* a
înţelege.
understandable [,ʌndə'stændəbl]
adj. de înţeles ; inteligibil.
understanding [,ʌndə'stændiŋ] s.
înţelegere ; acord ; *on this ~*
cu condiţia asta. *adj.* înţelept ;
înţelegător ; perspicace.
understate ['ʌndə'steit] *vt.* a
atenua, a diminua.
understatement ['ʌndə'steit-
mənt] s. adevăr spus numai
pe jumătate.
understood [,ʌndə'stud] *vt., vi.
trec. şi part. trec. de la*
understand.
understudy ['ʌndə,stʌdi] s. *teatru*
dublură. *vt.* a dubla (un actor,
un rol).
undertake ['ʌndə'teik] *vt.* a întreprinde ; a încerca ; a (pre)-
lua ; a presupune ; a afirma.
undertaken [,ʌndə'teikn] *vt. part.
trec. de la* **undertake.**
undertaker [,ʌndə'teikə] s. antreprenor (de pompe funebre).
undertaking [,ʌndə'teikiŋ] s. sarcină ; antrepriză ; pompe funebre.
undertone ['ʌndətoun] s. glas
scăzut ; nuanţă estompată.
undertook [,ʌndə'tuk] *vt. trec.
de la* **undertake.**
undervalue ['ʌndə'vælju] *vt.* a
nu aprecia suficient.
underwear ['ʌndəwɛə] s. lenjerie
de corp ; indispensabili.
underwent [,ʌndə'went] *vt. trec.
de la* **undergo.**
underworld ['ʌndəwə:ld] s. lumea cealaltă ; iad ; lumea in-
terlopă.
undeserving ['ʌndi'zə:viŋ] *adj.*
nemernic.

undesirable ['ʌndi'zaiərəbl] s., adj. indezirabil.

undesirous ['ʌndi'zaiərəs] adj. refractar; lipsit de entuziasm, de dorință.

undeterred ['ʌndi'tə:d], **undeviating** [ʌn'di:vieitiŋ] adj. neabătut.

undid ['ʌn'did] vt. trec. de la **undo**.

undies ['ʌndiz] s. pl. lenjerie de corp (de damă).

undignified [ʌn'dignifaid] adj. lipsit de demnitate; nedemn; rușinos.

undiminished ['ʌndi'miniʃt] adj. întreg, plin; neabătut.

undisclosed ['ʌndis'klouzd] adj. (ținut) secret.

undiscovered ['ʌndis'kʌvəd] adj. nedescoperit; inedit.

undisguised ['ʌndis'gaizd] adj. sincer; deschis; fățiș.

undisturbed ['ʌndis'tə:bd] adj. netulburat.

undivided ['ʌndi'vaidid] adj. întreg.

undo ['ʌn'du:] vt. a desface; a dezlega; a nimici; a ruina.

undoing ['ʌn'duiŋ] s. desfacere; nimicire; ruină; nenorocire.

undone ['ʌn'dʌn] adj. desfăcut; nenorocit; distrus; neterminat.

undoubted [ʌn'dautid] adj. indiscutabil.

undoubtedly [ʌn'dautidli] adv. fără doar și poate.

undreamed [ʌn'dremt] adj.: ~ of nevisat.

undue ['ʌn'dju:] adj. nepotrivit; exagerat.

undulate ['ʌndjuleit] vt., vi. a (se) undui; a (se) ondula.

unduly [ʌn'dju:li] adv. în mod nejust(ificat).

undutiful ['ʌn'dju:tifl] adj. ingrat.

undying [ʌn'daiiŋ] adj. nemuritor; nepieritor.

unearth ['ʌn'ə:θ] vt. a dezgropa.

unearthly [ʌn'ə:θli] adj. nefiresc; supranatural.

uneasy ['ʌn'i:zi] adj. neliniștit; tulburat; încurcat.

uneducated ['ʌn'edjukeitid] adj. incult; fără școală.

unemotional ['ʌni'mouʃənl] adj. lipsit de afecțiune, rece.

unemployed ['ʌnim'plɔid] s.: the ~ șomerii. adj. șomer; nefolosit.

unemployment ['ʌnim'plɔimənt] s. șomaj; nefolosire. adj. de șomaj.

unending [ʌn'endiŋ] adj. nesfîrșit.

unequalled ['ʌn'i:kwəld] adj. fără seamăn; neegalat.

unerring ['ʌn'ə:riŋ] adj. infailibil; exact.

uneven ['ʌn'i:vn] adj. inegal; accidentat, neregulat; zgrunțuros.

uneventful ['ʌni'ventfl] adj. calm, tihnit; lipsit de senzație.

unexpected ['ʌniks'pektid] adj. neașteptat; surprinzător.

unexplained ['ʌniks'pleind] adj. neexplicat; inexplicabil.

unexpurgated ['ʌn'ekspə:geitid] adj. integral; fără tăieturi.

unfailing [ʌn'feiliŋ] adj. credincios, constant; neabătut.

unfaithful ['ʌn'feiθfl] adj. necredincios.

unfaltering [ʌn'fɔ:ltriŋ] adj. neșovăielnic.

unfamiliar ['ʌnfə'miljə] *adj.* neobişnuit ; nefamiliar.

unfashionable ['ʌn'fæʃnəbl] *adj.* demodat ; lipsit de eleganţă.

unfasten ['ʌn'faːsn] *vt.* a deschide ; a descuia ; a dezlega.

unfathomable [ʌn'fæðəməbl] *adj.* (prea) adînc ; de neînţeles, nepătruns.

unfavourable [ʌn'feivrəbl] *adj.* nefavorabil.

unfeeling [ʌn'fiːliŋ] *adj.* fără inimă, nesimţitor ; crunt.

unfetter ['ʌn'fetə] *vt.* a slobozi ; a elibera ; a dezlega (din lanţuri) ; a descătuşa.

unfinished ['ʌn'finiʃt] *adj.* neterminat.

unfit ['ʌn'fit] *adj.* nepotrivit ; necorespunzător.

unflagging [ʌn'flægiŋ] *adj.* neabătut ; constant.

unfledged ['ʌn'fledʒd] *adj.* imatur.

unflinching [ʌn'flintʃiŋ] *adj.* neclintit, neabătut ; neşovăitor.

unfold ['ʌn'fould] *vt., vi.* a (se) desfăşura ; a (se) dezvălui.

unforeseeable ['ʌnfɔ:'si:əbl] *adj.* imprevizibil, de neprevăzut.

unforgettable ['ʌnfə'getəbl] *adj.* de neuitat.

unforgivable ['ʌnfə'givəbl] *adj.* de neiertat ; nepermis.

unforgotten ['ʌnfə'gɔtn] *adj.* (de) neuitat.

unfortunate [ʌn'fɔ:tʃnit] *s.* nenorocit ; prostituată. *adj.* nefericit.

unfounded ['ʌn'faundid] *adj.* neîntemeiat.

unfriendly ['ʌn'friendli] *adj.* neprietenos, ostil ; glacial, rece.

unfrock ['ʌn'frɔk] *vt.* a răspopi.

unfruitful ['ʌn'fru:tfl] *adj.* steril ; inutil, van.

unfurl [ʌn'fə:l] *vt.* a desfăşura ; a desface.

unfurnished ['ʌn'fə:niʃt] *adj.* nemobilat.

ungainly [ʌn'geinli] *adj.* greoi ; diform.

ungentlemanly [ʌn'dʒentlmənli] *adj.* nedemn de un gentleman, lipsit de eleganţă ; ruşinos.

ungrateful [ʌn'greitfl] *adj.* ingrat, nerecunoscător.

ungrounded ['ʌn'graundid] *adj.* nefondat ; fără învăţătură.

ungrudging ['ʌn'grʌdʒiŋ] *adj.* generos ; fără meschinărie ; (făcut) din toată inima.

unguarded ['ʌn'gaːdid] *adj.* nepăzit ; luat prin surprindere.

unguided ['ʌn'gaidid] *adj.* lipsit de îndrumare *sau* călăuză.

unhampered ['ʌn'hæmpəd] *adj.* nestînjenit.

unhappy [ʌn'hæpi] *adj.* nefericit ; nenorocit ; regretabil ; trist.

unharmed ['ʌn'haːmd] *adj.* nevătămat ; neatins ; intact ; scăpat cu bine.

unhealthy [ʌn'helθi] *adj.* nesănătos ; insalubru.

unheard ['ʌn'hə:d] *adj.* ne(mai)-auzit ; ~ *of* nemaipomenit.

unheeded ['ʌn'hi:did] *adj.* nebăgat în seamă.

unhesitating [ʌn'heziteitiŋ] *adj.* sigur (pe sine) ; fără rezerve ; neşovăitor.

unholy [ʌn'houli] *adj.* profan.

unhoped for [ʌn'houpt fɔ:] *adj.* nesperat.

unhospitable [ʌn'hɔspitəbl] *adj.* neospitalier ; ostil.

uniform ['ju:nifɔ:m] *s.* uniformă. *adj.* uniform.

unify ['ju:nifai] *vt.* a uni(fica) ; a uniformiza.

unilateral ['ju:ni'lætrl] *adj.* unilateral.

unimaginable [ˌʌni'mædʒnəbl] *adj.* (de) neînchipuit.

unimaginative ['ʌni'mædʒnətiv] *adj.* lipsit de imaginaţie.

unimpaired ['ʌnim'pɛəd] *adj.* nevătămat ; neatins, intact.

unimpeachable [ˌʌnim'pi:tʃəbl] *adj.* mai presus de bănuială.

unimportant ['ʌnim'pɔ:tnt] *adj.* neînsemnat ; lipsit de importanţă.

uninhabited ['ʌnin'hæbitid] *adj.* nelocuit ; pustiu ; părăsit.

unintentional ['ʌnin'tenʃənl] *adj.* (făcut) fără voie, neintenţionat ; involuntar.

uninteresting ['ʌn'intristiŋ] *adj.* neinteresant.

union ['ju:njən] *s.* unire ; uniune ; asociaţie ; sindicat; mariaj; *the Union* S.U.A.

unionist ['ju:njənist] *s.* federalist ; sindicalist.

Union Jack [ju:njən dʒæk] *s.* steagul *sau* pavilionul britanic.

unique [ju:'ni:k] *adj.* unic, fără pereche ; ciudat.

unison ['ju:nizn] *s.* unison.

unit ['ju:nit] *s.* unitate ; element.

unite [ju:'nait] *vt.* a uni ; a îmbina. *vi.* a se uni ; a se asocia ; a colabora,

united [ju:'naitid] *adj.* unit ; comun ; unic.

unity ['ju:niti] *s.* unitate, unire ; armonie.

universal [ˌju:ni'və:sl] *adj.* universal.

universe ['ju:nivə:s] *s.* univers.

university [ˌju:ni'və:sti] *s.* universitate.

univocal ['juni'voukl] *adj.* unanim ; într-un singur glas.

unjust ['ʌn'dʒʌst] *adj.* nedrept.

unjustifiable [ʌn'dʒʌstifaiəbl] *adj.* de neiertat ; nejustificat.

unkempt ['ʌn'kemt] *adj.* neţesălat ; zbîrlit ; neîngrijit.

unkind [ʌn'kaind] *adj.* hain ; crud ; rău ; neomenos.

unknown ['ʌn'noun] *adj.* necunoscut, obscur.

unlawful ['ʌn'lɔ:fl] *adj.* ilegal, ilicit ; nedrept.

unless [ən'les] *conj.* dacă nu ; în afară de cazul cînd.

unlettered ['ʌn'letəd] *adj.* analfabet.

unlike ['ʌn'laik] *prep.* spre deosebire de.

unlikely [ʌn'laikli] *adj.* improbabil ; puţin probabil ; neverosimil.

unload ['ʌn'loud] *vt.* a descărca ; a scăpa de. *vi.* a descărca.

unlucky [ʌn'lʌki] *adj.* nenorocos ; ghinionist ; nefericit.

unman ['ʌn'mæn] *vt.* a descuraja ; a deprima ; a lipsi de vlagă.

unmanageable [ʌn'mænidʒəbl] *adj.* refractar ; nărăvaş ; dificil.

unmannerly [ʌn'mænəli] *adj.* lipsit de manieră ; prost crescut,

unmarried ['ʌn'mærid] adj. necăsătorit ; celibatar.

unmask ['ʌn'mɑːsk] vt., vi a (se) demasca.

unmatched ['ʌn'mætʃt] adj. fără rival.

unmeasured [ʌn'meʒəd] adj. nemăsurat ; scandalos.

unmentionable [ʌn'menʃnəbl] adj. nedemn de a fi pomenit.

unmerciful [ʌn'məːsifl] adj. nemilos ; neîndurător.

unmindful [ʌn'mainfl] adj. nepăsător ; neatent.

unmingled [ʌn'miŋgld] adj. pur ; nealterat.

unmistakable ['ʌnmis'teikəbl] adj. sigur ; clar ; evident.

unmitigated [ʌn'mitigeitid] adj. total ; neabătut.

unmixed ['ʌn'mikst] adj. pur neamestecat ; neprefăcut.

unmodified ['ʌn'mɔdifaid] adj. neschimbat.

unmolested ['ʌnmo'lestid] adj. nevătămat, neatins ; ferit de primejdie.

unmoved ['ʌn'muːvd] adj. nepăsător, neafectat ; rece, impasibil.

unnatural [ʌn'nætʃrl] adj. nefiresc ; inuman ; monstruos.

unnecessary [ʌn'nesisri] adj. superfluu ; inutil, zadarnic.

unnerve ['ʌn'nəːv] vt. a slăbi ; a descuraja ; a deprima.

unobjectionable ['ʌnəb'dʒekʃnəbl] adj. ireproşabil.

unobserved ['ʌnəb'zəːvd] adj. neobservat.

unobtrusive ['ʌnəb'truːsiv] adj. modest, umil ; neştiut.

unofficial ['ʌnə'fiʃl] adj. neoficial.

unorthodox [ʌn'ɔːθədɔks] adj. eretic, neortodox.

unostentatious ['ʌn,ɔstən'teiʃəs] adj. simplu ; fără ostentaţie.

unpack ['ʌn'pæk] vt. a despacheta. vi. a despacheta ; a desface bagajele.

unpalatable [ʌn'pælətəbl] adj. de nemîncat, nedigerabil ; insuportabil ; fără haz.

unparalleled ['ʌnpærəleld] adj. incomparabil.

unpardonable [ʌn'pɑːdnəbl] adj. de neiertat ; inadmisibil.

unpaved ['ʌn'peivd] adj. nepietruit, nepavat.

unperturbed ['ʌnpə'təːbd] adj. neturburat.

unplait ['ʌn'plæt] vt. a despleti, a desface.

unpleasant [ʌn'pleznt] adj. neplăcut.

unpolished ['ʌn'pɔliʃt] adj. nelustruit ; neşlefuit ; necioplit.

unpopular ['ʌn'pɔpjulə] adj. nepopular ; antipatizat.

unpractical ['ʌn'præktikl] adj. nepractic.

unprecedented [ʌn'presidntid] adj. nemaipomenit.

unprejudiced [ʌn'predʒudist] adj. lipsit de prejudecăţi ; nepărtinitor ; echitabil.

unprepared ['ʌnpri'pɛəd] adj. nepregătit.

unprepossessing ['ʌn,priːpə'zesiŋ] adj. neatrăgător.

unpresuming ['ʌnpri'zjuːmiŋ] adj. la locul lui ; modest.

unpretending ['ʌnpri'tendiŋ] adj. modest.

unpretentious ['ʌnpri'tenʃəs] adj. fără pretenţii ; modest.

unprincipled [ʌn prinsəpld] adj. neprincipial ; fără scrupule.

unprintable ['ʌn'printəbl] adj. indecent.

unproductive ['ʌnprə'dʌktiv] adj. neproductiv ; arid ; steril.

unprofessional ['ʌnprə'feʃənl] adj. neprofesionist ; amator.

unprofitable [ʌn'prɔfitəbl] adj. nerentabil.

unpropitious ['ʌnprə'piʃəs] adj. nefavorabil, ostil.

unpublished ['ʌn'pʌbliʃt] adj. inedit.

unpunctual ['ʌn'pʌŋtjuəl] adj. nepunctual.

unqualified ['ʌn'kwɔlifaid] adj. necalificat ; incompetent.

unquestionable [ʌn'kwestʃənəbl], unquestioned [ʌn'kwestʃənd] adj. indiscutabil ; mai presus de orice îndoială.

unquote ['ʌn'kwout] vi. a închide ghilimelele.

unravel [ʌn'rævl] vt. a descurca, a descîlci ; a rezolva ; a lămuri.

unreadable ['ʌn'riːdəbl] adj. de necitit, ilizibil.

unreal ['ʌn'riəl] adj. ireal.

unreasonable [ʌn'riːznəbl] adj. fără rațiune, irațional ; de neînțeles, inexplicabil.

unrecognizable ['ʌn'rekəgnaizəbl] adj. de nerecunoscut.

unreconcilable ['ʌn'rekənsailəbl] adj. ireconciliabil, de neîmpăcat.

unrefined ['ʌnri'faind] adj. necioplit, vulgar, grosolan.

unrelated ['ʌnri'leitid] adj. fără legătură.

unrelenting ['ʌnri'lentiŋ] adj. necruțător ; neîmpăcat ; sever.

unreliable ['ʌnri'laiəbl] adj. neserios ; nesigur.

unrelieved ['ʌnri'liːvd] adj. sever ; fără alinare.

unremitting [ˌʌnri'mitiŋ] adj. perseverent.

unrequited ['ʌnri'kwaitid] adj. neîmpărtăşit ; nerăsplătit ; nerăzbunat.´

unreserved ['ʌnri'zəːvd] adj. fără rezerve ; expansiv.

unresisting ['ʌnri'zistiŋ] adj. docil, supus ; care nu opune rezistență.

unresponsive ['ʌnris'pɔnsiv] adj. indiferent ; placid, rece.

unrest ['ʌn'rest] s. neliniște, agitație ; tulburare.

unrewarded ['ʌnri'wɔːdid] adj. nerăsplătit.

unrighteous [ʌn'raitʃəs] adj. nedrept ; injust ; incorect.

unrightful ['ʌn'raitfl] adj. injust, nedrept ; nejustificat ; ilegal.

unripe ['ʌn'raip] adj. necopt ; imatur.

unrival(l)ed [ʌn'raivld] adj. fără rival ; inegalabil.

unromantic ['ʌnrə'mæntik] adj. prozaic ; lipsit de romantism sau imaginație.

unruffled ['ʌn'rʌfld] adj. neturburat.

unruly [ʌn'ruːli] adj. neascultător ; dezordonat ; nestăpînit ; destrăbălat.

unsafe ['ʌn'seif] adj. nesigur ; periculos.

unsaid ['ʌn'sed] adj. nespus ; nedestăinuit.

unsatisfactory ['ʌn sætis'fæktri] adj. nesatisfăcător ; necorespunzător.

unsavo(u)ry ['ʌn'seivri] *adj.* fără gust ; greţos, dezgustător.

unscathed [ʌn'skeiôd] *adj.* (viu şi) nevătămat ; neatins ; scăpat cu bine.

unscrew ['ʌn skru:] *vt.* a deşuruba.

unscrupulous [ʌn'skru:pjuləs] *adj.* fără scrupule, ticălos ; imoral.

unseasonable [ʌn'si:znəbl] *adj.* inoportun ; nepotrivit, deplasat.

unseemly [ʌn'si:mli] *adj.* dizgraţios ; ruşinos ; indecent ; neconvenabil.

unseen ['ʌn'si:n] *adj.* **nevăzut** ; invizibil.

unselfish ['ʌn'selfiʃ] *adj.* altruist ; ferit de egoism ; dezinteresat.

unsettle ['ʌn'setl] *vt.* a tulbura ; a dezorganiza.

unshak(e)able [ʌn'ʃeikəbl] *adj.* neclintit ; (de) nezdruncinat.

unshaken ['ʌn'ʃeikn] *adj.* ferm ; nezdruncinat.

unshapely ['ʌn'ʃeipli] *adj.* diform.

unsightly [ʌn'saitli] *adj.* urît ; urîcios.

unskilful ['ʌn'skilfl] *adj.* neîndemînatic ; stîngaci ; greoi ; nepriceput.

unskilled ['ʌn'skild] *adj.* nepriceput ; necalificat.

unsociable [ʌn'souʃəbl] *adj.* nesociabil ; sălbatic.

unsolved ['ʌn sɔlvd] *adj.* nerezolvat ; nedezlegat.

unsophisticated ['ʌnsə'fistikeitid] *adj.* simplu ; nevinovat.

unsound ['ʌn'saund] *adj.* lipsit de înţelepciune ; nesănătos ; greşit (concept).

unsparing [ʌn'spɛəriŋ] *adj.* neçrutător ; generos,

unspeakable [ʌn'spi:kəbl] *adj.* nespus ; cumplit.

unspoiled ['ʌn'spɔilt] *adj.* nealterat, nestricat ; ferit de răsfăţ ; neprihănit.

unspoken ['ʌn'spoukn] *adj.* nespus, negrăit ; tăinuit, (ţinut) ascuns.

unsportsmanlike ['ʌn'pɔ:tsmənlaik] *adj.* lipsit de sportivitate.

unspotted ['ʌn'spɔtid] *adj.* imaculat.

unstable ['ʌn'steibl] *adj.* instabil ; nestatornic ; şubred.

unsteady ['ʌn'stedi] *adj.* inconstant ; inconsecvent ; nesigur (pe picioare) ; instabil.

unstinted [ʌn'stintid] *adj.* neprecupeţit.

unstrung ['ʌn'strʌŋ] *adj.* slăbit ; destins ; pierdut.

unsubstantial ['ʌnsəb'stænʃl] *adj.* firav ; şubred ; subţiratic.

unsuccessful ['ʌnsək'sesfl] *adj.* neizbutit.

unsuitable ['ʌn'sju:təbl] *adj.* nepotrivit.

unsuited ['ʌn'sju:tid] *adj.* neasortat ; necorespunzător.

unsurmountable ['ʌnsə'mauntəbl] *adj.* de netrecut.

unsuspected ['ʌnsəs'pektid] *adj.* nebănuit.

unsuspecting ['ʌnsəs'pektiŋ], **unsuspicious** ['ʌnsəs'piʃəs] *adj.* încrezător ; care nu bănuieşte nimic.

unswerving [ʌn'swə:viŋ] *adj.* neabătut, neclintit ; credincios.

unsympathetic ['ʌn₁simpə'θetik] *adj.* lipsit de înţelegere *sau* compătimire ; neînţelegător ; rece.

untainted ['ʌn'teintid] *adj.* nealterat ; neprihănit,

unthinkable [ʌn'θiŋkəbl] *adj.* de neconceput.

unthinking ['ʌn'θiŋkiŋ], **unthoughtful** ['ʌn'θɔːtfl] *adj.* nechibzuit; zăpăcit.

untidy [ʌn'taidi] *adj.* neglijent; dezordonat; şleampăt.

untie ['ʌn'tai] *vt.* a dezlega, a desface.

until [ən'til] *prep.* pînă la, în. *conj.* pînă (ce).

untimely [ʌn'taimli] *adj.* inoportun; nepotrivit.

untiring [ʌn'taiəriŋ] *adj.* neobosit.

unto ['ʌntu] *prep.* la; (în)spre; către; aproape de; faţă de.

untold ['ʌn'tould] *adj.* nespus; secret.

untouchable [ʌn'tʌtʃəbl] *s.* paria. *adj.* de neatins; nevrednic.

untoward [ʌn'toəd] *adj.* nenorocit; nefericit; supărător.

untranslatable ['ʌntræns'leitəbl] *adj.* intraductibil.

untrodden ['ʌn'trɔdn] *adj.* nebătut; necălcat.

untroubled ['ʌn'trʌbld] *adj.* netulburat.

untrue ['ʌn'truː] *adj.* neadevărat; mincinos.

untrustworthy ['ʌn'trʌst͵wəːði] *adj.* neserios, care nu merită încredere.

untruth ['ʌn'truːθ] *s.* minciună; falsitate.

untruthful ['ʌn'truːθfl] *adj.* neadevărat; mincinos.

unturned ['ʌn'təːnd] *adj.* neatins; neabordat, neîncercat.

unused *adj.* ['ʌn'juːzd] neuzitat; ['ʌn'juːst] nedeprins, neobişnuit.

unusual [ʌn'juːʒuəl] *adj.* neobişnuit.

unutterable [ʌn'ʌtrəbl] *adj.* nespus.

unwanted ['ʌn'wɔntid] *adj.* nedorit; indezirabil.

unwarrantable [ʌn'wɔrntəbl] *adj.* inexplicabil; nejustificabil; surprinzător.

unwarranted ['ʌn'wɔrntid] *adj.* nejustificat; nemotivat, gratuit; care nu prezintă garanţie.

unwavering [ʌn'weivriŋ] *adj.* neşovăielnic; neclintit.

unwelcome [ʌn'welkəm] *adj.* nedorit; nepoftit; indezirabil.

unwell ['ʌn'wel] *adj.* bolnav; indispus.

unwholesome ['ʌn'houlsəm] *adj.* nesănătos; insalubru.

unwieldy [ʌn'wiːldi] *adj.* greoi; masiv; stîngaci.

unwilling ['ʌn'wiliŋ] *adj.* refractar; ostil; fără chef *sau* poftă.

unwillingly [ʌn'wiliŋli] *adv.* fără voie; din greşeală; cu neplăcere; în duşmănie.

unwise ['ʌn'waiz] *adj.* nechibzuit; lipsit de înţelepciune; imprudent; greşit.

unwittingly [ʌn'witiŋli] *adv.* fără voie; pe neştiute.

unwomanly [ʌn'wumənli] *adj.* lipsit de feminitate.

unwonted [ʌn'wountid] *adj.* neobişnuit; neuzitat; insolit.

unworkable ['ʌn'wəːkəbl] *adj.* nepractic; impracticabil.

unworthy [ʌn'wəːði] *adj.* nedemn; ruşinos.

unwritten ['ʌn'ritn] *adj.* nescris.

unyielding [ʌn'jiːldiŋ] *adj.* ferm; inflexibil; încăpăţînat; inebranlabil.

up [ʌp] *adj.* (care merge) în sus;
ascendent. *vt.* a ridica, a spori.
adv. (în) sus; la centru;
pe picioare; lîngă, alături;
în faţă; complet; ~ *and down*
încolo şi încoace; în sus şi în
jos; peste tot. *prep.* în susul.

upbraid [ʌp'breid] *vt.* a ocărî.

upbringing ['ʌpˌbriɲiŋ] *s.* creştere, educaţie.

upgrade ['ʌp'greid] *s.* urcuş;
progres; îmbunătăţire. *vt.* a
ameliora; a înnobila.

upheaval [ʌp'hiːvl] *s.* prefacere,
schimbare; răsturnare; mişcare
(socială).

upheld [ʌp'held] *vt. trec. şi part.
trec. de la* **uphold.**

uphill ['ʌp'hil] *adj.* ascendent;
dificil. *adv.* în sus(ul dealului).

uphold [ʌp'hould] *vt.* a susţine;
a sprijini; a încuraja; a aproba;
a confirma.

upholder [ʌp'houldə] *s.* susţinător.

upholster [ʌp'houⁱstə] *vt.* a
tapisa.

upholstery [ʌp'houlstri] *s.* tapiserie.

upkeep ['ʌpkiːp] *s.* întreţinere.

uplift [ʌp'lift] *vt.* a ridica; a
înnobila.

upon [ə'pɔn] *prep.* pe.

upper ['ʌpə] *adj.* superior, de
sus.

upper circle ['ʌpə'səːkl] *s. teatru*
balcon doi.

uppercut ['ʌpəkʌt] *s.* upercut,
lovitură de jos în sus.

uppermost ['ʌpəmoust] *adj.* superior; cel mai înalt; deosebit; predominant. *adv.* cel
mai sus; în vîrf,

upper stor(e)y ['ʌpə'stɔːri] *s.*
ultimul etaj, mansardă; *fig.*
creier.

upper ten (thousand) ['ʌpə
'ten(θauznd)] *s.* aristocraţie;
clase sus puse.

uppish ['ʌpiʃ] *adj.* băgăreţ;
încrezut; obraznic.

upright ['ʌprait] *adj.* drept,
vertical; cinstit. *adv.* drept (ca
luminarea).

uprightness ['ʌpˌraitnis] *s.* corectitudine; integritate.

uprising [ʌp'raiziŋ] *s.* răscoală.

uproar ['ʌpˌrɔː] *s.* gălăgie, rumoare; tumult.

uproarious [ʌp'rɔːriəs] *adj.* zgomotos; turbulent.

uproot [ʌp'ruːt] *vt.* a dezrădăcina;
a desfiinţa.

ups and downs ['ʌpsən'daunz] *s.
pl.* valurile vieţii; capricii (ale
soartei etc.).

upset [ʌp'set] *vt., vi., inf.,
trec. şi part. trec.* a (se) răsturna; a (se) tulbura.

upshot ['ʌpʃɔt] *s.* rezultat.

upside-down ['ʌpsai'daun] *adv.*
cu susul în jos; în dezordine.

upstage [ʌp'steidʒ] *adj., adv.*
(din)spre fundul scenei.

upstairs ['ʌp'stɛəz] *adv.* sus
(pe scări); la etaj.

upstanding ['ʌp'stændiŋ] *adj.*
drept (ca luminarea); voinic.

upstart ['ʌpstɑːt] *s., adj.* parvenit; obraznic.

upstream [ʌp'striːm] *adj., adv.*
contra curentului; în susul apei.

upsurge ['ʌpˌsəːdʒ] *s.* avînt;
elan; înălţare.

uptake ['ʌpteik] *s.* înţelegere.

up-to-date ['ʌptə'deit] *adj., adv.*
modern; la modă,

uptown ['ʌp'taun] *adv*. în centru;
amer. la periferie.

up train ['ʌp'trein] *s*. tren pentru
Londra.

upward ['ʌpwəd] *adj*. ascendent ; îndreptat în sus. *adv*. în
sus.

upwards ['ʌpwədz] *adv*. în sus ;
and ~ şi (chiar) mai mult ;
~ *of* peste, mai bine de.

urbane [ə: bein] *adj*. politicos ;
civilizat ; rafinat.

urbanity [ə:'bæniti] *s*. politeţe.

urchin ['ə:tʃin] *s*. copil (neastîmpărat) ; ştrengar.

urge [ə:dʒ] *s*. îndemn ; stimulent. *vt*. a îndemna ; a sili.

urgency ['ə:dʒnsi] *s*. urgenţă ;
presiune ; caracter imperios.

urgent ['ə:dʒnt] *adj*. important ;
absolut necesar ; imperios ; insistent ; urgent.

urn [ə:n] *s*. urnă.

us [əs, ʌs] *pron*. pe noi, ne ;
nouă, ne.

usage ['ju:zidʒ] *s*. folosire, uti-
lizare ; uz(aj) ; obicei.

use¹ [ju:s] *s*. folos ; folosire ;
scop ; valoare.; datină.

use² [ju:z] *vt*. a folosi ; a consuma ; a trata, a se purta cu ;
a obişnui ; *he* ~*d* [ju:st] *to*
come every day venea în fiecare zi.

used [ju:zd] *adj*. uzat ; deformat,
[ju:st] deprins ; obişnuit.

useful ['ju:sfi] *adj*. util ; capabil ;
bun.

useless ['ju:slis] *adj*. inutil ; fără
valoare ; fără efect.

usher ['ʌʃə] *s*. aprod ; plasator.
vt. a conduce ; a anunţa ;
fig. a deschide.

usherette [ˌʌʃə'ret] *s*. plasatoare.

usual ['ju:ʒuəl] *adj*. obişnuit ;
as ~ ca de obicei.

usually ['ju:ʒuəli] *adv*. de obicei.

usurer ['ju:ʒrə] *s*. cămătar.

usurious [ju:'zjuəriəs] *adj*. cămătăresc.

usurp [ju:'zə:p] *vt*. a uzurpa.

usurper [ju:'zə:pə] *s*. uzurpator.

usury ['ju:ʒuri] *s*. dobîndă cămătărească ; speculă cu bani.

utensil [ju'tensl] *s*. unealtă,
ustensil.

utility [ju: tiliti] *s*. utilitate ;
lucru folositor ; serviciu public.

utmost ['ʌtmoust] *s*. (efort)
extrem ; maxim. *adj*. extrem ;
maxim.

utopian [ju:'toupjən] *adj*. utopic.

utter ['ʌtə] *adj*. total ; cumplit.
vt. a rosti ; a exprima, a fabrica.

utterance ['ʌtrns *s*. exprimare ;
glas ; rostire ; declaraţie.

utterly ['ʌtəli] *adv*. total, complet ; groaznic (de).

uttermost ['ʌtəmoust] *s*. extrem,
maxim. *adj*. extrem ; cumplit.

uvula ['ju:vjulə] *s*. vălul palatului ; omuşor.

V

V [vi:] *s*. V, v.

vacancy ['veiknsi] *s*. loc liber ;
vacanţă ; spaţiu gol ; lapsus.

vacant ['veiknt] *adj*. gol ; liber, neocupat ; neatent ; uituc.

vacate [vəˈkeit] *vt.* a elibera, a lăsa vacant ; a anula.

vacation [vəˈkeiʃn] *s.* eliberare ; vacanţă.

vaccine [ˈvæksiːn] *s.* vaccin.

vacillate [ˈvæsileit] *vt.* a şovăi, a se clătina ; a oscila.

vacillation [ˌvæsiˈleiʃn] *s.* şovăială, oscilaţie.

vacuity [væˈkjuiti] *s.* loc liber ; absenţă ; gol ; neatenţie.

vacuous [ˈvækjuəs] *adj.* neatent ; stupid ; gol *(fig.)*.

vacuum [ˈvækjuəm] *s.* vid ; gol ; lapsus ; aspirator de praf.

vacuum-cleaner [ˈvækjuəm ˌkliːnə] *s.* aspirator de praf.

vacuum-flask [vækjuəmˌflɑːsk] *s.* termos.

vade-mecum [ˈveidiˈmiːkəm] *s.* agendă ; ghid.

vagabond [ˈvægəbənd] *s., adj.* vagabond.

vagary [ˈveigəri] *s.* capriciu ; *pl.* gărgăuni.

vagrancy [ˈveigrnsi] *s.* vagabondaj.

vagrant [ˈveigrnt] *s., adj.* vagabond ; rătăcitor.

vague [veig] *adj.* vag ; nelămurit ; nehotărît.

vain [vein] *adj.* inutil ; steril ; încrezut ; *in* ~ degeaba.

vainglorious [veinˈglɔːriəs] *adj.* îngîmfat (la culme) ; lăudăros.

vainglory [veinˈglɔːri] *s.* orgoliu ; lăudăroşenie.

vainly [ˈveinli] *adj.* inutil, zadarnic ; orgolios.

vale [veil] *s.* vale.

valentine [ˈvæləntain] *s.* felicitare (de 14 februarie, Sf. Valentin) ; iubit *sau* iubită proclamată în această zi.

valetudinarian [ˈvæliˌtjudiˌnɛəriən] *s.* om bolnăvicios.

valiant [ˈvæljənt] *adj.* viteaz.

valid [ˈvælid] *adj.* valabil ; serios, întemeiat.

validate [ˈvælideit] *vt.* a valida, a confirma.

validity [vəˈliditi] *s.* valabilitate.

valley [ˈvæli] *s.* vale.

valo(u)r [ˈvælə] *s.* vitejie.

valuable [ˈvæljuəbl] *s.* lucru de valoare. *adj.* valoros, preţios.

valuation [ˌvæljuˈeiʃn] *s.* evaluare.

value [ˈvæljuː] *s.* valoare ; apreciere ; deviz ; preţ ; sens ; *mat.* cantitate. *vt.* a aprecia ; a evalua.

valve [vælv] *s.* supapă, valvă ; lampă de radio.

vamp [væmp] *s.* căpută, petic ; vampă. *vt.* a încăputa ; a repara ; *fig.* a petici ; a stoarce de bani. *vi.* a stoarce bani de la bărbaţi.

van [væn] *s.* camion de mobilă ; dubă ; căruţă cu coviltir ; vagon de marfă (acoperit) ; avangardă ; partea din faţă.

vane [vein] *s.* morişcă de vînt.

vanguard [ˈvængɑːd] *s.* avangardă.

vanish [ˈvæniʃ] *vi.* a dispărea ; a se şterge.

vanity [ˈvæniti] *s.* îngîmfare ; inutilitate ; neseriozitate ; capriciu.

vanity bag [ˈvænitibæg] *s.* poşetă ; pudrieră.

vanquish [ˈvæŋkwiʃ] *vt.* a înfrînge ; a supune.

vantage [ˈvɑːntidʒ] *s.* avantaj.

vantage ground [ˈvɑːntidʒgraund] *s.* poziţie dominantă.

vapid ['væpid] adj. fără gust, insipid; şters; nesărat.

vapo(u)r ['veipə] s. abur(eală); beţie; nebunie; pl. mahmureală.

variable ['vɛəriəbl] adj. variabil.

variance ['vɛəriəns] s. variaţie; diversitate; dihonie; at ~ în duşmănie; în contradicţie.

variant [ˌvɛəri'ənt] s. variantă.

variation [ˌvɛəri'eiʃn] s. variaţie.

varied ['vɛərid] adj. variat; schimbător.

variegated ['vɛərigeitid] adj. variat; multicolor.

variety [və'raiəti] s. diversitate; varieteu.

various ['vɛəriəs] adj. divers; mulţi.

varmint ['vɑːmint] s. ticălos, lepră (fig.).

varnish ['vɑːniʃ] s. lac, verniu; email; fig. spoială. vt. a vernisa; fig. a spoi.

varsity ['vɑːsiti] s. universitate.

vary ['vɛəri] vt., vi. a varia; a (se) modifica.

vase [vɑːz] s. vază, vas.

vassalage ['væsəlidʒ] s. vasalitate; aservire.

vast [vɑːst] adj. vast; mare; uriaş; întins.

vat [væt] s. cuvă, butoi; cadă.

vaudeville ['voudəvil] s. operetă; music-hall, revistă.

vault [vɔːlt] s. boltă; pivniţă; criptă, vistierie; salt. vt. a bolti; a sări. vi. a sări cu voltă.

vaulting-horse ['vɔːltiŋhɔːs] s. capră pentru gimnastică.

vaunt [vɔːnt] s. laudă, lăudăroşenie. vt. a se lăuda cu, a etala. vi. a se lăuda.

veal [viːl] s. carne de viţel.

veer [viə] vi. a vira, a coti.

vegetable ['vedʒtəbl] s. plantă; legumă. adj. vegetal.

vegetable marrow ['vedʒtəbl 'mærou] s. dovlecel.

vegetation [ˌvedʒi'teiʃn] s. vegetaţie.

vehemence ['viːiməns] s. vehemenţă.

vehicle ['viːikl] s. vehicul.

veil [veil] s. văl, voal; fig. paravan. vt. a învălui; a ascunde.

vein [vein] s. vînă; ton.

velocity [vi'lɔsiti] s. viteză.

velvet ['velvit] s. catifea. adj. de catifea.

velvety ['velviti] adj. catifelat; onctuos.

vendor ['vendɔː] s. vînzător.

veneer [vi'niə] s. furnir; fig. spoială. vt. a furnirui; fig. a spoi.

veneering [vi'niəriŋ] s. furnir; furniruire.

venerable ['venrəbl] adj. onorabil, venerabil; respectabil.

venereal [vi'niəriəl] adj. veneric.

veneration [ˌvenə'reiʃn] s. veneraţie; adoraţie.

Venetian [vi niː:ʃn] s., adj. veneţian.

Venetian blind [vi'niːʃn ˌblaind] s. jaluzea.

vengeance ['vendʒns] s. răzbunare; with a ~ straşnic; din plin.

venison ['venzn] s. carne de căprioară.

venom ['venəm] s. venin.

venomous ['venəməs] adj. veninos; otrăvitor; rău.

vent [vent] s. ieşire, supapă; eşapament; uşurare. vt. a slobozi.

venture ['ventʃə] s. aventură; risc; speculaţie; *at a* ~ la întîmplare. *vt.* a risca; a îndrăzni; a exprima. *vi.* a îndrăzni; a se aventura.

venturesome ['ventʃəsəm] *adj.* riscant; aventuros.

venue ['venju:] s. loc de judecată *sau* întîlnire.

verb [və:b] s. verb.

veracious [ve'reiʃəs] *adj.* demn de încredere; adevărat.

veracity [ve'ræsiti] s. sinceritate; adevăr.

verbatim [və:'beitim] *adj., adv.* cuvînt cu cuvînt.

verbose [və: bous] *adj.* înflorit; prolix.

verbosity [və:'bɔsiti] s. limbuţie; vorbărie.

verdant ['və:dnt] *adj.* verde; proaspăt; nevinovat.

verdict [və:dikt] s. verdict.

verdigris ['və:digris] s. cocleală.

verdure ['və:dʒə] s. verdeaţă; tinereţe, prospeţime.

verge [və:dʒ] s. margine; limită. *vi.* a se îndoi; a se apropia.

verger ['və:dʒə] s. paracliser.

verify ['verifai] *vt.* a verifica; a dovedi.

verisimilitude [‚verisi'militju:d] s. probabilitate; caracter verosimil.

verity ['veriti] s. adevăr.

vermicelli [‚və:mi'seli] s. fidea.

vermilion [və'miljən] s., *adj.* purpuriu. *vt.* a împurpura.

vermin ['və:min] s. paraziţi; drojdia societăţii.

verminous ['və:minəs] *adj.* infestat de paraziţi.

vernacular [və'nækjulə] s. limbă naţională; dialect. *adj.* neaoş.

vernal ['və:nl] *adj.* primăvăratic.

versatile ['və:sətail] *adj.* multilateral; elastic; nestatornic.

verse [və:s] s. vers(uri); poezie; strofă; verset.

versed [və:st] *adj.* versat, priceput.

version ['və:ʃn] s. traducere; versiune.

versus ['və:səs] *prep.* contra.

vertex ['və:teks] s. vîrf, culme.

vertical ['və:tikl] s. verticală. *adj.* vertical; suprem.

vertices ['və:tisi:z] s. *pl.* de la **vertex**.

vertigo ['və:tigou] s. ameţeală.

very ['veri] *adj.* adevărat; tocmai acela *sau* aceea; precis; aidoma. *adv.* foarte; tocmai, aidoma; chiar.

vesper ['vespə] s. luceafăr; seară *pl.* vecernie.

vessel ['vesl] s. vas.

vest [vest] s. vestă; maiou. *vt.* a îmbrăca; a învesti.

vested ['vestid] *adj.* îmbrăcat. înveşmîntat; asigurat; stabilit.

vested interests ['vestid'intrists] s. *pl.* investiţii; monopoluri.

vestige ['vestidʒ] s. vestigiu.

vestment ['vesmənt] s. veşmînt.

vestry ['vestri] s. consiliu parohial; (sală pentru) enoriaşi.

vet [vet] s. (medic) veterinar.

vetch [vetʃ] s. *bot.* măzăriche; borceag.

veteran ['vetrn] s. veteran.

veterinary ['vetrinəri] *adj.* veterinar.

veterinary surgeon ['vetrinəri ‚sə:dʒn] s. (medic) veterinar.

veto ['vi:tou] s. veto; interzicere. *vt.* a opune veto la; a interzice.

vex [veks] *vt.* a supăra ; a necăji; a irita.

vexation [vek'seiʃn] *s.* supărare ; necăjire ; pacoste.

vexatious [vek'seiʃəs] *adj.* supărător ; iritant.

via [vaiə] *prep.* prin.

vial ['vaiəl] *s.* sticluță de doctorie ; fiolă.

vibrate [vai'breit] *vt.* a face să vibreze. *vi.* a vibra ; a palpita.

vibration [vai'breiʃn] *s.* vibrație.

vicar ['vikə] *s.* protopop ; preot.

vicarage ['vikəridʒ] *s.* parohie.

vicarious [vai'kɛəriəs] *adj.* (prin) delegat ; locțiitor.

vice [vais] *s.* viciu ; menghină.

viceroy ['vaisrɔi] *s.* vicerege.

vicinity [vi'siniti] *s.* vecinătate, apropiere ; cartier.

vicious ['viʃəs] *adj.* vicios ; nărăvaș ; greșit ; rău(tăcios).

victim ['viktim] *s.* victimă ; jertfă.

victimize ['viktimaiz] *vt.* a persecuta ; a chinui.

victor ['viktə] *s., adj.,* învingător ; cuceritor.

Victorian [vik'tɔːriən] *s., adj.* victorian ; puritan.

victory [viktəri] *s.* victorie ; succes.

victrola [vik'troulə] *s.* picup ; patefon.

victual ['vitl] *s.* mîncare ; *pl.* merinde ; provizii. *vt., vi.* a (se) aproviziona.

victualler ['vitlə] *s.* furnizor ; vas de aprovizionare.

videlicet [vi'diːliset]. *adv.* adică.

vie [vai] *vi.* a rivaliza ; a se întrece.

view [vjuː] *s.* vedere ; privire ; vizionare ; părere ; intenție ; *on* ~ la vedere ; *in* ~ *of* dat(ă) fiind ; din cauza ; *with a* ~ *to, with the* ~ *of* în vederea ; pentru (a). *vt.* a privi ; a cerceta.

viewpoint ['vjuːpɔint] *s.* punct de vedere ; priveliște.

vigil ['vidʒil] *s.* veghe.

vigilance ['vidʒiləns] *s.* vigilență ; pază ; precauție.

vigilant ['vidʒilənt] *adj.* vigilent.

vigorous ['vigərəs] *adj.* viguros ; vioi.

vigour ['vigə] *s.* vigoare ; energie ; forță.

vile [vail] *adj.* stricat ; josnic ; rușinos ; scîrbos.

vilify ['vilifai] *vt.* a defăima ; a calomnia.

village [vilidʒ] *s.* sat.

villager ['vilidʒə] *s.* sătean.

villain ['vilən] *s.* ticălos ; ștrengar ; iobag ; slugă.

villainous ['vilənəs] *adj.* ticălos ; mîrșav ; groaznic.

villainy ['viləni] *s.* ticăloșie ; mîrșăvie.

villein ['vilin] *s.* iobag.

vim [vim] *s.* energie ; vigoare ; zel.

vindicate ['vindikeit] *vt.* a dovedi ; a verifica ; a apăra.

vindication [,vindi'keiʃn] *s.* apărare ; justificare ; dovedire.

vindictive [vin'diktiv] *adj.* răzbunător.

vine [vain] *s.* viță (de vie).

vinegar ['vinigə] *s.* oțet.

vinegary ['vinigəri] *adj.* oțetit ; acru.

vineyard ['vinjəd] *s.* vie ; podgorie.

vintage ['vintidʒ] *s.* culesul viei ; recoltă de vin.

vintner ['vintnə] s. podgorean.
viola [vi'oulə] s. violă.
violate ['vaiəleit] vt. a viola;
a tulbura.
violence ['vaiələns]·s. violenţă;
vehemenţă; jignire.
violent ['vaiələnt] adj. violent;
aprig; puternic.
violet ['vaiəlit] s. violetă, topo-
raş; violet. adj. violet.
violin [ˌvaiə'lin] s. vioară.
violinist ['vaiəlinist] s. violonist.
V.I.P. ['vi: ai'pi:] s. persoană
însemnată, grangur.
viper ['vaipə] s. viperă.
virago [vi'rɑ:gou] s. scorpie.
virgin ['və:dʒin] s. fecioară.
adj. feciorelnic; virgin; neatins.
virginal ['və:dʒinl] s. clavecin.
adj. feciorelnic; nevinovat.
virile ['virail adj. viril; energic;
viguros.
virtual ['və:tjuəl] adj. virtual;
practic; de fapt.
virtually ['və:tjuəli] adv. în
fapt; de fapt.
virtue ['və:tju:] s. virtute; eficacitate; putere; by ~ of
prin; in ~ of pe baza.
visa ['vi:zə] s. viză.
viscount ['vaikaunt] s. viconte.
vise [vais] s. amer. menghină.
visé ['vi:zei] s. viză. vt. a viza.
visible ['vizəbl] adj. vizibil.
vision ['viʒn] s. vedere; viziune; concepţie; vis; privelişte; fantomă.
visit ['vizit] s. vizită (lungă);
şedere. vt. a vizita; a frecventa;
a pedepsi; a răzbuna; a năpăstui. vi. a face vizite.
visitation [ˌvizi'teiʃn] s. vizită
(oficială); pedeapsă; răzbunare;
răsplată.

visiting ['vizitiŋ] adj. de vizită.
visiting-card ['vizitiŋˌkɑ:d] s.
carte de vizită.
visitor ['vizitə] s. vizitator;
client (al unui hotel).
vista ['vistə] s. vedere, privelişte; perspectivă.
visualize ['vizjuəlaiz] vt. a întrezări.
vital ['vaitl] adj. vital; viu,
vioi.
vitals ['vaitlz] s. pl. măruntaie;
centru.
vitamin ['vitəmin] s. vitamină.
vitiate ['viʃieit] vt. a vicia; a
strica; a pîngări.
vitrify ['vitrifai] vt., vi. a (se)
face ca sticla.
vitriol ['vitriəl] s. vitriol.
vituperate [vi'tju:pəreit] vt. a
ocărî.
viva voce ['vaivə'vousi] s., adj.,
adv. oral.
vivid ['vivid] adj. vioi; viu;
strălucitor.
vixen ['viksn] s. vulpe; fig.
scorpie.
viz. [vi'di:liset; 'neimli] adv.
(şi) anume.
vocabulary [və'kæbjuləri] s. vocabular.
vocal ['voukl] adj. vocal.
vocalist ['voukəlist] s. cîntăreţ,
cîntăreaţă.
vocation [vo'keiʃn] s. vocaţie;
profesie.
vocational [vo'keiʃənl] adj. profesional; de meserie.
vocative ['vɔkətiv] s., adj. vocativ.
vogue [voug] s. vogă; modă;
popularitate.
voice [vɔis] s. glas; voce;
sonoritate; exprimare; rostire;

părere ; vot ; *gram* diateză. *vt.* a exprima ; a rosti.

voiceless ['vɔislis] *adj.* fără glas ; mut ; (*d. consoană*) surdă.

void [vɔid] *s.* gol, vid ; lipsă. *adj.* gol ; nul, fără valoare ; ~ *of* lipsit de. *vt.* a goli ; a anula.

volcano [vɔl'keinou] *s.* vulcan.

volition [vo'liʃn] *s.* voinţă ; liber-arbitru.

volley ['vɔli] *s.* salvă ; *fig.* torent ; voleu. *vt.* a trage (o salvă) ; a arunca (în zbor).

volley ball ['vɔli͵bɔːl] *s.* volei.

voluble ['vɔljubl] *adj.* volubil.

volume ['vɔljum] *s.* volum ; tom ; mulţime ; cantitate.

voluntary ['vɔləntri] *s.* solo (de orgă). *adj.* voluntar ; intenţionat.

volunteer [͵vɔlən'tiə] *s.* voluntar. *vt.* a rosti ; a face ; a oferi. *vr.* a se oferi ca voluntar.

voluptuousness [və'lʌptjuəsnis] *s.* voluptate.

vomit ['vɔmit] *s.* vărsătură. *vi.* a vărsa.

voracious [və'reiʃəs] *adj.* lacom.

vortex ['vɔːteks] *s.* vîrtej, bulboană.

votary ['voutəri] *s.* adept ; sus-

ţinător ; credincios ; fanatic.

vote [vout] *s.* vot(are) ; drept de vot. *vt.* a vota (pentru) ; a aproba ; a propune. *vi.* a vota.

voter ['voutə] *s.* alegător.

votive ['voutiv] *adj.* oferit ca jertfă.

votive light ['voutiv͵lait] *s.* candelă.

vouch [vautʃ] *vi.* : *to* ~ *for* a garanta ; a confirma.

voucher ['vautʃə] *s.* chitanţă ; bon ; garanţie ; garant.

vouchsafe [vautʃ'seif] *vt.* a acorda ; a catadicsi să dea.

vow [vau] *s.* jurămînt ; promisiune. *vt.* a promite, a jura.

vowel ['vauəl] *s.* vocală.

voyage [vɔidʒ] *s.* călătorie pe apă. *vt.* a străbate.

voyager ['vɔiədʒə] *s.* călător ; explorator.

vulcanite ['vʌlkənait] *s.* ebonit.

vulgar ['vʌlgə] *adj.* vulgar ; ordinar ; grosolan.

vulgarism ['vʌlgərizəm] *s.* expresie vulgară ; cuvînt vulgar ; vulgarism.

vulgarize ['vʌlgəraiz] *vt.* a vulgariza ; a populariza.

vulture ['vʌltʃə] *s.* vultur (mîncător de cadavre) ; *fig.* corb.

W

W ['dʌbl͵juː] *s.* W, w.

wad [wɔd] *s.* teanc ; tampon (de vată, bandaj). *vt.* a face teanc ; a căptuşi, a moltona.

wadding ['wɔdiŋ] *s.* molton.

wade [weid] *s.* trecere prin vad. *vt.* a trece prin vad. *vi.* a-şi croi drum.

wafer ['weifə] s. tabletă ; foaie de plăcintă ; scoică de înghețată ; limbi de pisică ; anafură.

waft [wɑːft] s. adiere. vt. a purta prin aer.

wag [wæg] s. mucalit; legănare. vt. a legăna. vi. a da din coadă.

wage [weidʒ] s. (și pl.) salariu ; pl. recompensă, plată. vt. a duce, a purta (un război).

wage-earner ['weidʒ,əːnə] s. salariat.

wage-freeze ['weidʒ'friːz] s. înghețarea salariilor.

wager ['weidʒə] s. rămășag. vt., vi. a paria.

waggish ['wægiʃ] adj. comic ; strengăresc.

wag(g)on ['wægən] s. căruță ; vagon de marfă.

wag(g)oner ['wægənə] s. căruțaș.

wag(g)onette [,wægə'net] s. landou.

wagtail ['wægteil] s. codobatură.

waif [weif] s. persoană sau cîine fără adăpost ; de pripas.

waifs and strays ['weifs ən streiz] s. pl. copiii nimănui.

wail [weil] s. bocet ; plîngere. vt., vi. a boci ; a plînge.

wain [wein] s. car.

wainscot(ing) ['weinskət(iŋ)] s. lambriuri.

waist [weist] s. talie ; centură ; amer. pieptăraș.

waist band ['weisbænd] s. betelie ; talie.

waist-coat ['weiskout] s. vestă.

waist line ['weistlain] s. măsura taliei.

wait [weit] s. așteptare ; pîndă ; pl. colindători. vt. a aștepta ;

a pîndi. vi. a aștepta ; to ~ on smb. a servi pe cineva. **waiter** ['weitə] s. ospătar, chelner ; servantă, măsuță.

waiting ['weitiŋ] s. așteptare.

waiting-maid ['weitiŋ meid] s. cameristă ; servitoare.

waiting-room ['weitiŋ rum] s. sală de așteptare.

waitress ['weitris] s. ospătărița, chelnărița.

waive [weiv] vt. a respinge ; a renunța la ; a alunga.

wake [weik] s. veghe, priveghi ; festival ; dîră ; in the ~ of pe urmele. vt. a trezi ; a stîrni ; a evoca. vi. a se trezi ; a veghea.

wakeful ['weikfl] adj. ne(a)dormit ; treaz.

wakefulness ['weikflnis] s. nesomn, insomnie.

waken ['weikn] vt., vi. a (se) trezi.

walk [wɔːk] s. plimbare ; mers pe jos ; pas ; marș ; strat social ; potecă, promenadă. vt. a cutreiera ; a plimba. vi. a se plimba ; a merge (la pas) ; a umbla ; to ~ into a se năpusti asupra ; to ~ up a merge ; a se apropia.

walker ['wɔːkə] s. amator de plimbare ; pieton.

walkie-talkie ['wɔːki 'tɔːki] s. radio portativ.

walking [wɔːkiŋ] s. plimbare ; mers pe jos.

walking-stick ['wɔːkiŋstik] s. baston.

wall [wɔːl] s. zid, perete ; gard. vt. a fortifica ; a îngrădi ; a zidi.

wallet ['wɔːlit] s. portvizit ; portofel ; trusă ; desagă.

wallflower ['wɔːl,flauə] s. bot.

micşunea ruginită ; fată ne-invitată la dans.

wallop ['wɔləp] s. bătaie ; lovi-tură. vt. a bate ; a lovi.

wallow ['wɔlou] vt. a se bălăci.

wallpaper ['wɔ:l‚peipə] s. tapet.

walnut ['wɔ:lnət] s. nuc(ă).

walrus ['wɔ:lrəs] s. zool. morsă.

waltz [wɔ:ls] s. vals. vi. a valsa.

wan [wɔn] adj. pal(id) ; istovit ; supt.

wand [wɔnd] s. baghetă.

wander ['wɔndə] vt. a cutreiera. vi. a umbla, a hoinări ; a se abate.

wanderer ['wɔndərə] s. rătăci-tor, hoinar.

wangle ['wæŋgl] vi. a face intervenţii sau matrapazlîcuri.

wane [wein] s. descreştere, de-clin. vi. a fi în declin.

want [wɔnt] s. nevoie, lipsă ; necesitate ; sărăcie ; dorinţă. vt. a dori ; a necesita ; a cere ; a avea nevoie de ; a voi. vi. a lipsi, a nu se găsi.

wanting ['wɔntiŋ] adj. deficient (mintal) ; prost crescut. prep. fără.

wanton ['wɔntən] s. femeie uşoară. adj. neserios ; nestator-nic ; destrăbălat.

wantonly ['wɔntənli] adv. nese-rios ; fără chibzuinţă.

war [wɔ:] s. război ; militărie ; luptă. vi. a se război.

warble ['wɔ:bl] s. ciripit. vt., vi. a ciripi.

warbler ['wɔ:blə] s. pitulice ; privighetoare.

war clouds ['wɔ:klaudz] s. pl. ameninţarea războiului.

war cry ['wɔ:krai] s. strigăt de luptă.

ward [wɔ:d] s. pază ; tutelă ; pupil(ă) ; cartier ; rezervă, secţie (la spital). vt. a păzi ; to ~ off a evita, a abate (o lovitură).

warden ['wɔ:dn] s. păzitor ; custode ; paznic.

warder ['wɔ:də] s. temnicer.

wardrobe ['wɔ:droub] s. garde-rob(ă) ; dulap.

ward-room ['wɔ:drum] s. came-ră de gardă.

ware [wɛə] s. marfă.

warehouse ['wɛəhaus] s. depozit ; antrepozit.

warfare ['wɔ:fɛə] s. beligeranţă ; strategie ; luptă.

warily ['wɛərili] adv. cu grijă ; prudent.

warlike ['wɔ:laik] adj. războinic belicos.

warlord ['wɔ:lɔ:d] s. mandarin , militarist.

warm [wɔ:m] s. încălzire. adj. cald ; călduros ; entuziast ; proas-păt. vt., vi. a (se) încălzi.

warming-pan ['wɔ:miŋpæn] s. tigaie de încălzit aşternutul.

warmint v. **varmint.**

warmly ['wɔ:mli] adv. cu căl-dură ; călduros ; entuziast.

warmonger ['wɔ:‚mʌŋgə] s. aţî-ţător la război.

warmth [wɔ:mθ] s. căldură entuziasm ; pasiune.

warn [wɔ:n] vt. a avertiza.

warning ['wɔ:niŋ] s. avertis-ment ; avertizare ; (pre)aviz.

War Office ['wɔ:r‚ɔfis] s. Minis-terul de război.

warp [wɔ:p] s. ţesătură, urzeală. vt., vi. a (se) întreţese.

warrant ['wɔrnt] s. autorizaţie ; garanţie ; procură ; certificat. vt. a justifica ; a garanta.

warren ['wɔrin] *s.* crescătorie de iepuri de casă.

warrior ['wɔriə] *s.* războinic.

warship ['wɔ:ʃip] *s.* vas de război.

wart [wɔ:t] *s.* neg.

wary ['wɛəri] *adj.* precaut; şiret; *to be* ～ a avea grijă.

was [wəz, wɔz] *v. aux., vi. pers. I şi a III-a sing. ind. trec. de la* **be.**

wash [wɔʃ] *s.* spălare; spălătură; rufe de spălat; val; lături; loţiune. *vt.* a spăla; a mătura; *to* ～ *one's hands* a se spăla pe mîini; *to* ～ *down* a spăla; a înghiţi; *to* ～ *up* a spăla vasele.

washable ['wɔʃəbl] *adj.* lavabil.

wash basin ['wɔʃˌbeisn] *s.* lighean; chiuvetă.

washed out ['wɔʃtaut] *adj.* istovit; distrus.

washer ['wɔʃə] *s.* spălător; spălătoreasă; şaibă.

washerwoman ['wɔʃəˌwumən] *s.* spălătoreasă.

wash-hand stand ['wɔʃhənd 'stænd] *s.* lavoar.

wash house ['wɔʃhaus] *s.* spălătorie.

washing ['wɔʃiŋ] *s.* spălare; spălătură; rufe pentru spălat *sau* spălate.

wash-out ['wɔʃaut] *s.* şuvoi; eşec; ratat.

wash-stand ['wɔʃstænd] *s.* lavoar.

wash-tub ['wɔʃtʌb] *s.* albie de spălat rufe.

washy ['wɔʃi] *adj.* apos; palid; şters; spălăcit.

wasp [wɔsp] *s.* viespe.

wassail ['wɔseil] *s.* punci; chef. *vi.* a chefui; a toasta.

wastage ['weistidʒ] *s.* risipă; pierderi.

waste [weist] *s.* risipă, irosire; deşeuri; gunoi; pustiu. *adj.* pustiu; înţelenit; nefolositor; aruncat. *vt.* a irosi; a pustii; *to* ～ *one's breath* a strica vorba de pomană. *vi.* a se irosi; a fi în declin; a se pierde.

wasteful ['weistfl] *adj.* risipitor.

waste-paper basket [weis'peipə ba:skit] *s.* coş de hîrtii.

wastrel ['weistrl] *s.* trîntor *(fig.).*

watch [wɔtʃ] *s.* pază; gardă; paznic; cart; ceas (de mînă sau de buzunar). *vt.* a păzi; a privi; a urmări (cu privirea). *vi.* a sta treaz; a veghea; a fi atent; a sta de pază.

watchdog ['wɔtʃdɔg] *s.* cîine de pază.

watcher ['wɔtʃə] *s.* paznic; spectator.

watchful ['wɔtʃfl] *adj.* treaz; atent; precaut.

watchfulness ['wɔtʃflnis] *s.* trezie; veghe.

watchmaker ['wɔtʃmeikə] *s.* ceasornicar.

watchman ['wɔtʃmən] *s.* paznic.

watch-tower ['wɔtʃ'tauə] *s.* turn de pază.

watchword ['wɔtʃwə:d] *s.* cuvînt de ordine; lozincă; parolă.

water ['wɔ:tə] *s.* apă; soluţie apoasă. *vt.* a uda, a stropi; a adăpa; a dilua.

water bottle ['wɔ:təˌbɔtl] *s.* ploscă; bidon.

water cart ['wɔ:təka:t] *s.* saca; (auto)stropitoare.

water closet ['wɔ:təˌklɔzit] *s.* closet (cu apă).

water colo(u)r ['wɔ:təˌkʌlə] *s.* acuarelă.

watercress ['wɔ:təkres] s. bot. năsturel; bobîlnic.

waterfall ['wɔ:təfɔ:l] s. cascadă.

water front ['wɔ:tə,frʌnt] s. malul mării; docherii.

watering-can ['wɔ:trɪŋkæn] s. stropitoare.

watering-cart ['wɔ:trɪŋkɑ:t] s. autostropitoare; saca.

watering-place ['wɔ:trɪŋ pleis] s. staţiune balneară.

water-lily ['wɔ:tə,lili] s. nufăr.

watermark ['wɔ:təmɑ:k] s. nivelul apei; filigran.

water-melon ['wɔ:tə,melən] s. pepene verde.

waterproof ['wɔ:təpru:f] s. fulgarin. adj. impermeabil. vi. a impermeabiliza.

watershed ['wɔ:təʃed] s. cumpăna apelor.

waterside ['wɔ:təsaid] s. mal; docuri.

waterspout ['wɔ:təspaut] s. gură de burlan; trombă marină.

water-supply ['wɔ:təsə,plai] s. reţea de apă potabilă.

watertight ['wɔ:tətait] adj. etanş; invulnerabil.

waterway ['wɔ:təwei] s. cale navigabilă.

waterworks ['wɔ:təwə:ks] s. uzină de apă; instalaţie de apă; fîntîni decorative.

watery ['wɔ:təri] adj. apos; plîns; insipid.

watt [wɔt] s. watt.

wattle ['wɔtl] s. împletitură de nuiele; chirpici; moţul-curcanului. vt. a împleti (nuiele).

wave [weiv] s. val; unduire; gest cu mîna; ondulaţie; încreţire; undă. vt. a face semn cu; a încreţi. vi. a se undui.

wave length ['weivleŋθ] s. lungime de undă.

waver ['weivə] vi. a şovăi; a se clătina; a fîlfîi.

wavy ['weivi] adj. ondulat; încreţit.

wax [wæks] s. ceară. vt. a cerui. vi. a creşte; a deveni.

wax-cloth [wæksklɔθ] s. pînză cerată.

wax-paper ['wæks,peipə] s. hîrtie pergament.

waxy [wæksi] adj. ca ceara; lustruit.

way [wei] s. drum; cale; rută; metodă, mod; progres; obicei; out of the ~ la o parte; ascuns; îndepărtat; by ~ of prin; by the ~ pe drum; apropo; to be under ~ a fi pe drum; a fi aşteptat.

waylay [wei lei] vt. a ţine calea (cuiva).

ways and means ['weizən'mi:nz] s. pl. căi şi mijloace.

wayside ['weisaid] s. marginea drumului; potecă.

wayward ['weiwəd] adj. încăpăţînat; greu de mînuit.

we [wi(:)] pron. noi.

weak [wi:k] adj. slab; firav; insuficient.

weaken ['wi:kn] vt., vi. a slăbi.

weakling ['wi:kliŋ] s. slăbănog.

weakly ['wi:kli] adj. slăbănog; plăpînd. adv. (cu glas) slab, fără vlagă.

weak-minded ['wi:k'maindid] adj. slab de minte.

weakness ['wi:knis] s. slăbiciune.

weal [wi:l] s. bunăstare; dungă, vrîstă.

wealth [welθ] s. avere; bogăţie; abundenţă; prosperitate.

wealthy ['welθi] *adj.* bogat.
wean [wi:n] *vt.* a înţărca ; a dezbăra.
weapon ['wepən] *s.* armă.
wear [wɛə] *s.* îmbrăcăminte ; uzură ; (posibilitate de) folosire ; purtare. *vt.* a purta, a îmbrăca ; a manifesta ; a uza, a roade ; a scîlcia ; a slăbi ; *to ~ out* a uza ; a istovi ; *to ~ the breeches* a-şi ţine bărbatul sub papuc. *vi.* a se purta ; a rezista ; a ţine ; a se uza ; *to ~ away* a se uza ; a se roade ; a se şterge ; a slăbi ; *to ~ on* a trece (încet) ; *to ~ out* a se uza ; a se epuiza.
wear and tear ['wɛərən'tɛə] *s.* uzură.
wearer ['wɛərə] *s.* purtător.
weariness ['wiərinis] *s.* oboseală ; plictiseală.
wearisome ['wiərisəm] *adj.* obositor ; plicticos.
weary ['wiəri] *adj.* obosit ; obositor ; plictisit. *vt., vi.* a (se) obosi ; a (se) plictisi.
weasel ['wi:zl] *s. zool.* nevăstuică.
weather ['weðə] *s.* vreme ; meteorologie ; climă ; *under stress of ~* din cauza vremii proaste ; *~ permitting* dacă e vreme bună. *vt.* a trece cu bine, a înfrunta ; a expune (intemperiilor) ; a decolora ; a roade.
weather beaten ['weðə‚bi:tn] *adj.* asprit de vînturi şi ploi.
weather bound ['weðəbaund] *adj.* blocat de vremea nefavorabilă.
weathercock ['weðəkɔk] *s.* morişcă de vînt.
weave [wi:v] *s.* ţesătură. *vt.* a

ţese ; a urzi. *vi.* a se ţese ; a se împleti.
weaver ['wi:və] *s.* ţesător.
web [web] *s.* plasă, ţesătură ; laba gîştei (raţei etc.).
wed [wed] *vt.* a căsători ; a uni ; *~ded to smth.* ataşat de ceva. *vi.* a se căsători ; a nunti.
wedding ['wediŋ] *s.* nuntă ; căsătorie.
wedding cake ['wediŋkeik] *s.* tort de nuntă.
wedding-ring ['wediŋriŋ] *s.* verighetă.
wedge [wedʒ] *s.* pană ; despicătură. *vt.* a despica.
wedlock ['wedlɔk] *s.* căsătorie.
Wednesday ['wenzdi] *s.* miercuri.
wee [wi:] *adj.* mititel, micuţ ; *a ~ bit* un pic.
weed [wi:d] *s.* buruiană ; iarbă ; *fig.* om plăpînd. *vt.* a plivi ; *to ~ out* a înlătura.
weed-killer ['wi:d‚kilə] *s.* ierbicid.
weeds [wi:dz] *s. pl.* haine de doliu.
weedy ['wi:di] *adj.* plin de buruieni ; slăbănog.
week [wi:k] *s.* săptămînă.
week day ['wi:kdei] *s.* zi lucrătoare, zi de lucru.
week-end [wi:k'end] *s.* răgazul de la sfîrşitul săptămînii. *vi.* a pleca în excursie (sîmbăta şi duminica).
weekly ['wi:kli] *s., adj., adv.* săptămînal.
weep [wi:p] *vt.* a vărsa (lacrimi) ; a deplînge. *vi.* a plînge ; a se umezi.
weevil ['wi:vil] *s.* gărgăriţă.
weft [weft] *s.* băteală ; ţesătură.

weigh [wei] vt. a cîntări; a chibzui; a ridica; to ~ anchor a porni la drum; to ~ down a trage în jos; a împila; to ~ out a împărţi. vi. a cîntări, a trage în balanţă.

weighing-machine ['weiiŋmə‚ʃi:n] s. cîntar decimal.

weight [weit] s. greutate; pondere; influenţă; importanţă; to put on ~ a se îngrăşa; under ~ sub greutatea normală. vt. a îngreuia.

weighty ['weiti] adj. greu; greoi; apăsător; important; convingător.

weir [wiə] s. stăvilar.

weird [wiəd] adj. fatal; supranatural; sinistru; ciudat.

welcome ['welkəm] s. bun venit; primire bună. adj. binevenit; încîntător. vt. a saluta; a primi cu bucurie.

weld [weld] s. sudură. vt., vi. a (se) suda.

welfare ['welfɛə] s. bunăstare.

welfare work ['welfɛə‚wə:k] s. opere caritabile.

well [wel] s. puţ; izvor; sondă. adj. sănătos; bun; mulţumitor. vi. a ţîşni; a izvorî; a curge. adv. bine; complet; cum trebuie; pe bună dreptate; as ~ de asemenea; as ~ as precum şi. interj. ei; vai; în sfîrşit; ei şi? mă rog; prea bine; precum spuneam.

well-balanced ['wel'bælənst] adj. echilibrat; înţelept.

well-being ['wel'bi:iŋ] s. bunăstare, prosperitate.

well-bred ['wel'bred] adj. binecrescut; pur sînge.

well-founded [wel'faundid] adj. (bine) întemeiat.

well-grounded ['wel'graundid] adj. (bine) întemeiat; profund; serios.

well-knit ['wel'nit] adj. solid, bine făcut.

well-nigh ['welnai] adv. aproape; cît pe-aci să.

well-off ['wel ɔ:f] adj. înstărit; bogat.

well-read ['wel'red] adj. citit, cult.

well-to-do ['weltədu:] adj. înstărit.

Welsh [welʃ] s. limba galeză (din Wales); the ~ velşii, locuitorii din Ţara Galilor. adj. velş; galez.

Welshman ['welʃmən] s. velş.

welsh rabbit ['welʃ'ræbit] s. plăcintă cu brînză topită.

welt [welt] s. cureluşă; dungă, vrîstă.

welter ['weltə] s. încurcătură; talmeş-balmeş. vi. a se învălmăşi; a se rostogoli.

welter-weight ['weltə‚weit] s. (boxer de) categoria semimijlocie.

wen [wen] s. gîlcă, bolfă.

wench [wentʃ] s. fată, fetişcană; femeie uşoară.

went [went] vi. trec. de la go.

wept [wept] vt., vi. trec. şi part. trec. de la weep.

were [wə(:)] v. aux., vi. pers. a II-a sg. şi I, a II-a, a III-a pl. trec. de la be.

wert [wə:t] înv. v. aux., vi. pers. a II-a sing. trec. de la be.

west [west] s. vest, apus; Occident. adj. vestic, occidental; de vest. adv. spre vest.

West End ['west'end] s. cartierul elegant al Londrei.

westerly ['westəli] adj. dinspre vest. adv. spre vest.

western ['westən] adj. apusean, occidental.

Westminster ['wesminstə] s. catedrala Westminster; Parlamentul britanic.

westward ['westwəd] adj., adv. spre apus.

wet [wet] adj. ud, umed; ploios; amer. contra prohibiției. vt. a uda, a umezi.

wether ['weðə] s. batal, berbec.

wet nurse ['wet'nə:s] s. doică.

wet through ['wet'θru:] adj. ud leoarcă.

whack [wæk] s. pocnitură; lovitură; porție. vt. a pocni.

whacking ['wækiŋ] s. bătaie. adj. strașnic; groaznic. adv. foarte.

whale [weil] s. balenă. vi. a vîna balene.

whale-boat ['weilbout] s. balenieră.

whalebone ['weilboun] s. os de balenă; balene (de guler, corset etc.).

whaler ['weilə] s. balenieră; vînător de balene.

wharf [wɔ:f] s. debarcader, chei; doc.

what [wɔt] pron. ce? care? cît; ceea ce; ~ for? pentru ce? ~ is it like? cum e? ~ next? la ce ne mai putem aștepta? ~ if? și dacă?

whatever [wɔ'tevə] pron. orice, oricare; indiferent ce; (cu neg.) nici un, de loc.

wheat [wi:t] s. grîu.

wheaten ['wi:tn] adj. de grîu.

wheedle ['wi:dl] vt. a păcăli; a convinge prin lingușeli; a smulge.

wheel [wi:l] s. roată; rotire; volan; ~s within ~s complicații; intrigărie. vt., vi. a (se) răsuci, a (se) roti.

wheelbarrow ['wi:l₁bærou] s. roabă, tărăboanță.

wheelwright ['wi:lrait] s. rotar.

wheeze [wi:z] s. șuierat; vîjiit; glumă; șiretenie. vt. a rosti cu greu. vi. a gîjîi, a vîjîi.

whelp [welp] s. cățel; pui de tigru, lup etc.; golăneț. vt., vi. a făta.

when [wen] adv. cînd. conj. cînd; deși; ori de cîte ori; după ce.

whence [wens] adv. de unde; de la care.

whenever [wen'evə] adv., conj. oricînd; ori de cîte ori.

where [wɛə] adv. unde. conj. unde; în care; oriunde.

whereabouts ['wɛərəbauts] s. loc (unde se află cineva). adv. (pe) unde, cam pe unde.

whereas [wɛər'æz] conj. pe cînd; întrucît.

whereby [wɛə'bai] adv. cum; prin ce.

wherefore ['wɛəfɔ:] s. motiv, rațiune. conj. pentru ce.

wherein [wɛər'in] adv. unde; cum.

whereof [wɛər'ɔv] pron. din care; despre care.

whereto [wɛə'tu:] adv. încotro; în care scop.

whereupon [₁wɛərə'pɔn] adv. la care; drept care.

wherever [wɛər'evə] adv. oriunde; pretutindeni.

wherewithal ['wɛəwiðɔ:l] s. cele necesare.

whet '[wet] vt. a ascuţi; a stimula; a stîrni.

whether [weðə] conj. (indiferent) dacă; ~ or no(t) în orice caz.

whetstone ['wetstoun] s. (piatră de) tocilă.

whey [wei] s. zer.

which [witʃ] adj. care; ~ way? în ce fel? pe unde? pron. care (din ei); pe care; ceea ce.

whichever [witʃ'evə] adj., pron. oricare.

whiff [wif] s. răbufneală; ţigară; fum (de ţigară). vt. a pufăi; a mirosi (a ceva).

Whig [wig] s., adj. liberal; amer. republican.

while [wail] s. perioadă; once in a ~ din cînd în cînd; between ~s pe apucate; the ~ între timp; tot timpul; it was worth your ~ a meritat efortul. vt. a face să treacă (timpul). conj. în timp ce; pe cînd.

whilst [wailst] inv. conj. în timp ce; pe cînd.

whim [wim] s. capriciu, poftă.

whimper ['wimpə] s. scîncet. vi. a scînci; a scheuna.

whimsical ['wimzikl] adj. capricios; ciudat.

whine [wain] s. scîncet; scheunat. vt. a cere cu glas plîngăreţ. vi. a (se) scînci; a se miorlăi; a scheuna.

whinny ['wini] s. nechezat. vi. a necheza.

whip [wip] s. bici; cravaşă; vizitiu; chestor; convocare. vt. a biciui; a bate; a smulge; a înfrînge; to ~ eggs a bate ouăle.

whipped cream ['wipt'kri:m] s. frişcă bătută.

whipping ['wipiŋ] s. bătaie (cu biciul); înfrîngere.

whipper-snapper ['wipə‚snæpə] s. mucos (obraznic).

whip-poor-will ['wippuə‚wil] s. ornit. păpăludă.

whir(r) [wə:] s. vîjîit; fîlfîit; foşnet. vi. a fîlfîi; a vîjîi.

whirl [wə:l] s. vîrtej; bulboană. vt. a lua pe sus. vi. a se învîrti, a se învîrteji; a ameţi; a se învălmăşi.

whirligig ['wə:ligig] s. titirez; căluşei; vîrtej.

whirlpool ['wə:lpu:l] s. bulboană.

whirlwind ['wə:lwind] s. vîrtej; furtună; trombă.

whisk [wisk] s. smoc; canaf; mişcare rapidă, smucitură; bătător (de ouă). vt. a lua pe sus; a bate (frişcă etc.). vi. a se mişca iute; a ţîşni.

whiskers ['wiskəz] s. pl. favoriţi; zool. mustăţi.

whisk(e)y ['wiski] s. whisky.

whisper ['wispə] s. şoaptă; murmur; zvon. vt., vi. a şopti; a susura.

whist [wist] s. jocul de vist. interj. sst.

whistle ['wisl] s. fluier(at). vt., vi. a fluiera, a şuiera; to ~ for smth. a-şi pune pofta în cui.

whit [wit] s. bucăţică, pic(ătură).

white [wait] s. alb(uş). adj. alb.

white coffee ['wait'kɔfi] s. cafea cu lapte.

white collar ['wait'kɔlə] adj. funcţionăresc; de funcţionar(i).

white elephant ['wait'elifənt] s. podoabă inutilă (care te în-curcă).

white frost ['wait'frɔst] s. chi-ciură ; promoróacă.

Whitehall ['wait'hɔ:l] s. guver-nul britanic.

white lie ['wait'lai] s. minciună nevinovată.

white-livered ['wait͵livəd] adj. fricos ; laş.

whiten ['waitn] vt., vi. a (se) albi.

white paper ['wait'peipə] pol. carte albă.

white slave ['wait'sleiv] s. pros-tituată (luată cu forţa).

whitewash ['waitwɔʃ] s. var ; văruială, văruit. vt. a vărui ; fig. a ascunde.

whither ['wiðə] adv. încotro.

whitlow ['witlou] s. panariţiu.

Whitsunday ['wit'sʌndi] s. Rusalii.

Whitsuntide ['witsntaid] s. săp-tămîna Rusaliilor.

whittle ['witl] vt. a ciopîrţi ; a reduce treptat.

whiz(z) [wiz] s. bîzîit ; vîjîit. vi. a vîjîi ; a bîzîi.

who [hu(:)] pron. cine(?); care(?); (acela) care ; pe care.

whodun(n)it [hu'dʌnit] s. ro-man poliţist.

whoever [hu'evə] pron. oricine ; oricare.

whole [houl] s. întreg ; unitate ; as a ~ în ansamblu ; on the ~ dacă ţinem seama de toate. adj. întreg ; complet ; sănătos ; nevătămat.

whole-hearted ['houl'hɑ:tid] adj. sincer ; cordial.

whole length ['houl'leŋθ] adj. în mărime naturală.

wholemeal ['houlmi:l] adj. (din făină) integrală.

wholesale ['houlseil] s. toptan. adj., adv. cu toptanul.

wholesaler ['houl͵seilə] s. angro-sist.

wholesome ['houlsəm] adj. să-nătos ; salubru ; moral.

wholly ['houlli] adv. pe de-a-ntregul ; complet.

whom [hu:m] pron. pe cine (?)͵ pe care (?), cui (?); căruia (?) etc.

whoop [hu:p] s. chiot, strigăt (de bucurie) ; acces de tuse. vi. a ţipa, a chiui.

whooping cough ['hu:piŋ kɔf] s. tuse convulsivă, măgărească.

whopper ['wɔpə] s. lucru uriaş ; minciună gogonată.

whopping ['wɔpiŋ] adj. uriaş ; gogonat. adv. foarte.

whore [hɔ:] s. tîrfă, prostituată.

whorl [wə:l] s. spirală ; bul-boană.

whose [hu:z] pron. al cui(?) ; al cărui (?) etc.

why [wai] s. motiv ; explicaţie. adv. de ce. conj. pentru care ; that is ~ iată de ce. interj. hei ; vai.

wick [wik] s. muc de lumînare.

wicked ['wikid] adj. ticălos, bles-temat ; rău ; dăunător ; rău-tăcios.

wickedness ['wikidnis] s. rău-tate ; ticăloşie.

wicker ['wikə] s. (împletitură de) răchită.

wickerwork ['wikəwə:k] s. îm-pletitură de răchită, de nuiele.

wicket ['wikit] s. portiţă; intrare ; ghişeu ; sport poartă ; punct.

wide [waid] adj. larg, lat ; în-

tins; lejer; larg deschis. *adv.*
peste tot; în lung şi în lat;
departe (de ţintă).

wide awake ['waid ə'weik] *adj.*
treaz (de-a binelea); ager; precaut.

widely ['waidli] *adv.* departe;
în mare măsură; larg.

widen ['waidn] *vt., vi.* a (se)
lărgi.

widespread ['waidspred] *adj.* răspîndit; întins.

widow ['widou] *s.* văduvă.

widowed ['widoud] *adj.* vădu-
vit.

widower ['widoə] *s.* văduv.

widowhood ['widohud] *s.* văduvie.

width [widθ] *s.* lărgime; lăţime; orizont larg; bucată (de
stofă).

wield [wi:ld] *vt.* a mînui; a
stăpîni.

wife [waif] *s.* soţie.

wig [wig] *s.* perucă.

wiggle ['wigl] *s.* legănare (din
şolduri). *vt.* a (ră)suci. *vi.* a se
mişca; a legăna din şolduri.

wigwam ['wigwæm] *s.* cort *sau*
colibă indiană.

wild [waild] *s.* pustiu; sălbăticie. *adj.* sălbatic; nedomesticit; sperios; pustiu; destrăbălat; furtunos; nesăbuit. *adv.*
sălbatic; aspru; aiurea.

wild beast ['waild 'bi:st] *s.* fiară
sălbatică.

wild cat ['waild kæt] *s.* pisică
sălbatică (*şi fig.*). *adj.* neau-
torizat; iresponsabil; nesăbuit.

wilderness ['wildənis] *s.* pustiu;
sălbătăcie; încurcătură; labirint.

wildfire ['waildfaiə] *s.* praf de
puşcă; foc grecesc; flăcăruie;
like ~ ca fulgerul.

wild goose ['waild gu:s] *s.* gîscă
sălbatică; *to go on a* ~ *chase*
a umbla după cai verzi pe pereţi.

wildly ['waildli] *adv.* nebuneşte;
aiurea; nesăbuit.

wildness ['waildnis] *s.* nebunie;
barbarie; furie; frenezie; delir;
nesăbuinţă.

wile [wail] *s.* viclenie. *vt.* a prinde
în cursă; a ademeni.

wilful ['wilfl] *adj.* încăpăţînat;
voluntar; intenţionat.

will¹ [wil] *s.* voinţă; hotărîre;
intenţie; testament; *at* ~ după
bunul său plac. *v. aux. pentru
viit.* voi, vei, va etc. *v. mod.*
a voi.

will² *vt.* a hotărî; a dori; a
lăsa moştenire. *vi.* a avea voinţă.

willing ['wiliŋ] *adj.* doritor; săritor la nevoie; serviabil; voluntar.

willingly 'wiliŋli adv. cu plăcere; bucuros; cu bunăvoinţă.

will-o'-the-whisp ['wiləðwisp] *s.*
flăcăruie (rătăcitoare); miraj.

willow ['wilou] *s.* salcie.

will-power ['wil,pauə] *s.* voinţă;
hotărîre.

willy-nilly ['wili'nili] *adv.* vrînd-
nevrînd.

wilt [wilt] *v. aux., v. mod. înv.
pers. a II-a sing. prez. de la
will¹. vt., vi.* a (se) ofili.

wily ['waili] *adj.* viclean.

win [win] *vt.* a cîştiga; a cuceri; a atinge. *vi.* a cîştiga;
a fi învingător.

wince [wins] *s.* tresărire. *vi.* a
tresări; a se cutremura.

winch [wintʃ] *s.* scripet; vinci.

wind[1] [wind] s. vînt; suflare, adiere; zvon; vorbe goale; *muz.* instrument de suflat; *pl.* suflători. *vt.* a adulmeca; a obosi; a lăsa să răsufle.

wind[2] [waind] s. serpentină, cot; cotitură; meandră. *vt.* a (ră)suci, a învîrti (ceasul); a bobina; a ridica (cu scripetele); *to ~ up* a încheia; a lichida. *vi.* a şerpui; a se răsuci; *to ~ up* a încheia.

wind-bag ['winbæg] s. lăudăros, fanfaron.

windfall ['winfɔːl] s. pară mălăiaţă.

winding ['waindiŋ] s. răsucire; bobinare. *adj.* şerpuitor.

winding up ['waindiŋ'ʌp] s. încheiere; lichidare.

windlass ['windləs] s. scripete.

windmill ['winmil] s. moară de vînt.

window ['windou] s. fereastră.

window-pane ['windopein] s. (ochi de) geam.

windpipe ['winpaip] s. beregată.

wind-screen ['windskriːn], windshield ['windʃiːld] s. parbriz.

wind-swept ['windswept] *adj.* bătut de vînturi.

windy ['windi] *adj.* vîntos; speriat.

wine [wain] s. vin.

winepress ['wainpres] s. teasc.

wing [wiŋ] s. aripă; escadrilă; *pl.* culise. *vt.* a înaripa; a grăbi.

wink [wiŋk] s. clipit; semn din ochi; clipă. *vt.* a închide (ochii). *vi.* a (s)clipi; a face cu ochiul.

winner ['winə] s. cîştigător; învingător.

winning ['winiŋ] s. cîştig. *adj.*

cîştigător; atrăgător; convingător.

winning-post ['winiŋpoust] s. potou.

winnow ['winou] *vt.* a vîntura; a alege.

winsome ['winsəm] *adj.* atrăgător.

winter ['wintə] s. iarnă. *vi.* a ierna.

wintry ['wintri] *adj.* iernatic; rece.

wipe [waip] s. ştergere, şters; lustru. *vt.* a şterge; a mătura; a nimici.

wire ['waiə] s. sîrmă; fir; telegramă. *vt.* a prinde, a lega cu sîrme; a telegrafia; a instala electricitate (în). *vi.* a telegrafia.

wireless ['waiəlis] s. radio; telegrafie fără fir. *adj.* fără fir. *vt., vi.* a transmite prin radio.

wiring ['waiəriŋ] s. instalaţie electrică.

wiry ['waiəri] *adj.* tare, oţelit; musculos.

wisdom ['wizdəm] s. înţelepciune; învăţătură.

wisdom-tooth ['wizdəmˌtuːθ] s. măsea de minte.

wise [waiz] s. fel. *adj.* înţelept.

wiseacre ['waizˌeikə] s. pedant.

wisecrack ['waizkræk] s. glumă.

wise man ['waizmən] s. înţelept; mag.

wish [wiʃ] s. dor; dorinţă; rugăminte; urare. *vt.* a nădăjdui; a ruga; a cere; a ura. *vi.* a spera; *to ~ foː* a dori.

wishful ['wiʃfl] *adj.* doritor; visător.

wishing-bone ['wiʃiŋboun] s. iadeş.

wishy-washy ['wiʃi'wɔʃi] *adj*. a-pos ; slab (de înger) ; neinteresant.

wisp [wisp] *s*. şuviţă.

wistful ['wistfl] *adj*. plin de dor ; visător.

wit [wit] *s*. spirit, inteligenţă ; minte ; înţelepciune ; om spiritual ; *out of one's* ∼*s* înnebunit ; *to have one's* ∼*s about one* a fi cu mintea trează ; *at one's* ∼*s' end* în mare încurcătură ; la ananghie ; *to live by one's* ∼*s* a trăi din expediente.

witch [witʃ] *s*. vrăjitoare ; divă.

witchcraft ['witʃkrɑːft] *s*. vrăjitorie ; fascinaţie.

witchery ['witʃəri] *s*. vrăjitorie ; fascinaţie.

witchhunt ['witʃhʌnt] *s*. vînătoare de vrăjitoare.

with [wið] *prep*. (împreună) cu ; şi la ; asupra ; împotriva, faţă de ; în ciuda.

withal [wi'ðɔːl] *adv*. totodată ; în plus ; pe lîngă toate.

withdraw [wið'drɔː] *vt.*, *vi.* a (se) retrage ; a (se) îndepărta.

withdrawal [wið'drɔːl] *s*. retragere ; retractare.

withdrawn [wið'drɔːn] *vt.*, *vi. part. trec. de la* **withdraw**.

withdrew [wið'druː] *vt.*, *vi. trec. de la* **withdraw**.

wither ['wiðə] *vt.*, *vi.* a (se) veşteji.

withering ['wiðəriŋ] *adj*. dispreţuitor ; distrugător.

withheld [wið'held] *vt. trec. şi part. trec. de la* **withhold**.

withhold [wið'hould] *vt.* a reţine, a opri ; a refuza.

within [wi'ðin] *adv*. înăuntru ; în interior. *prep*. înăuntrul ;

nu mai departe de ; în cadrul ; ∼ *an hour* pînă într-un ceas ; ∼ *an inch of* cît pe-aci să ; ∼ *call* sau *hearing* destul de aproape ca să audă ; ∼ *shot* în bătaia puştii.

without [wi'ðaut] *adv*. (pe) din-afară. *prep*. fără ; în afară ; *to do* sau *go* ∼ a se lipsi de ; *it goes* ∼ *saying* e de la sine înţeles.

withstand [wið'stænd] *vt.* a se împotrivi *sau* a rezista la.

withstood [wið'stud] *vt. trec. şi part. trec. de la* **withstand**.

witless ['witlis] *adj*. prost ; imbecil ; zevzec ; nevinovat.

witness ['witnis] *s*. martor ; mărturie ; dovadă ; *to call to* ∼ a chema ca martor. *vt.* a asista la, a vedea ; a depune mărturie despre ; a trăda. *vi.* a depune mărturie.

witness box ['witnis͵bɔks] *s*. boxa martorilor.

witticism ['witisizəm] *s*. spirit, glumă.

wittingly ['witiŋli] *adv*. cu bună ştiinţă.

witty [witi] *adj*. spiritual, amuzant.

wives [waivz] *s. pl. de la* **wife.**

wizard ['wizəd] *s*. vrăjitor.

wizened ['wiznd] *adj*. zbîrcit ; îmbătrînit.

wobble ['wɔbl] *vt.* a legăna ; a clătina. *vi.* a se clătina, a se legăna ; a şovăi.

wobbler ['wɔblə] *s*. om şovăitor.

wobbly ['wɔbli] *adj*. şubred.

woe [wou] *s*. supărare.; durere ; necaz ; ∼ *is me !* vai de capul meu !

woe-begone ['woubi͵gɔn] adj. nenorocit.

woeful ['woufl] adj. trist ; regretabil ; nenorocit.

woke [wouk] vt., vi. trec. şi part. trec. de la wake.

woken ['woukn] part. trec. de la wake.

wolf [wulf] s. lup ; crai.

wolfish ['wulfiʃ]adj. lacom; de lup.

woman ['wumən] s. femeie ; pl. sexul slab ; feminitate ; sentimentalism.

woman-hater ['wumən͵heitə] s. misogin, duşman al femeilor.

womanhood ['wumənhud] s. feminitate ; sexul slab.

womanish ['wuməniʃ] adj. de femeie ; efeminat, muieratic.

womankind ['wumən'kaind] s. femeile ; sexul feminin.

womanlike ['wumənlaik] adj. femeiesc ; feciorelnic.

womb [wu:m] s. uter ; matrice. fig. sîn.

women(folk) ['wimin(fouk)] s. pl. femei.

won [wʌn] vt., vi. trec. şi part. trec. de la win.

wonder ['wʌndə] s. minune ; mirare ; surprindere ; (it is) no ~ (that) nu e de mirare (că). vt. a se întreba (ceva). vi. a se mira ; a se întreba.

wonderful ['wʌndəfl] adj. minunat ; uluitor ; excepţional.

wonderingly ['wʌndriŋli] adv. cu mirare.

wonderland ['wʌndelænd] s. ţara minunilor.

wonderstruck ['wʌndəstrʌk] adj. uluit.

wondrous ['wʌndrəs] adj. uluitor ; prodigios ; de necrezut.

wont [wount] s. obişnuinţă, obicei. adj. obişnuit ; to be ~ (to) a obişnui (să).

wonted ['wountid] adj. obişnuit, tradiţional.

woo [wu:] vt. a curta ; a cere în căsătorie ; a cuceri ; a implora. vi. a face curte.

wood [wud] s. pădure ; lemn.

woodcock ['wudkɔk] s. sitar.

woodcut ['wudkʌt] s. gravură (în lemn).

woodcutter ['wud͵kʌtə] s. tăietor de lemne.

wooded ['wudid] adj. împădurit.

wooden ['wudn] adj. de lemn ; înţepenit ; greoi.

woodland ['wudlənd] s. păduri.

woodman ['wudmən] s. pădurar.

woodpecker ['wud͵pekə] s. ciocănitoare.

woodsman ['wudzmən] s. pădurar.

woodwind ['wudwind] s. instrument de suflat din lemn.

woodwork ['wudwə:k] s. lemnărie, tîmplărie.

woody ['wudi] adj. păduros ; lemnos.

wooer ['wu:ə] s. curtezan.

woof [wu:f] s. băteală.

wool [wul] s. lînă ; păr creţ ; cîlţi ; vată.

wool gathering ['wul͵gæðriŋ] adj. aiurit ; visător ; dus pe gînduri.

wool(l)en ['wulin] adj. de lînă.

woolly ['wuli] adj. lînos ; ca lîna ; ca un caier.

word [wə:d] s. vorbă ; cuvînt ; cuvîntare ; observaţie ; discuţie ; veste ; cuvînt de onoare ; poruncă, semnal ; ~ for ~

cuvînt cu cuvînt; *by ~ of mouth* oral. *vt.* a exprima, a formula.

wordiness ['wə:dinis] *s.* limbuție; prolixitate.

wording ['wə:diŋ] *s.* formulare, exprimare.

wordless ['wə:dlis] *adj.* mut; fără cuvinte.

wordy ['wə:di] *adj.* prea lung; prolix.

wore [wɔ:] *vt., vi. trec. de la* **wear**.

work [wə:k] *s.* muncă; treabă; slujbă; ocupație; lucrare; lucru; operă; *pl.* uzină; ateliere; *pl.* lucrări publice; *pl.* opere de binefacere. *vt.* a lucra; a prelucra; a acționa; a pune în mișcare; a conduce; a administra; a pune la treabă; a face, a produce; a borda; a plăti cu munca proprie; *to ~ out* a produce; a elabora; a calcula; *to ~ off* a rezolva; *to ~ up* a alcătui; a crea; a stîrni; a ațîța. *vi.* a lucra; a munci; a acționa; a funcționa; a merge, a avea succes; a se strecura, a trece; a se agita; *to ~ out* a ieși (la socoteală); *to ~ up* a crește.

workable ['wə:kəbl] *adj.* practic(abil); care poate fi prelucrat.

workaday ['wə:kədei] *adj.* de lucru; obișnuit, banal.

work-basket ['wə:k͵ba:skit] *s.* coșuleț cu lucru de mînă.

work-day ['wə:kdei] *s.* zi de lucru; zi de muncă.

worker ['wə:kə] *s.* muncitor.

workers' movement ['wə:kəz mu:vmənt] *s.* mișcare muncitorească

workers' party ['wə:kəz͵pa:ti] *s.* partid muncitoresc.

workhouse ['wə:khaus] *s.* azil de muncă; casă de corecție.

working ['wə:kiŋ] *s.* muncă; funcționare; exploatare minieră; abataj. *adj.* muncitor; de lucru.

working-class ['wə:kiŋkla:s] *s.* clasă muncitoare. *adj.* muncitoresc, al clasei muncitoare.

working-day ['wə:kiŋ͵dei] *adj.* zi lucrătoare; zi de lucru.

workman ['wə:kmən] *s.* lucrător; meșteșugar.

workmanship ['wə:kmənʃip] *s.* lucrătură; artizanat.

workshop ['wə:kʃɔp] *s.* atelier.

world [wə:ld] *s.* lume; pămînt; societate; domeniu; planetă; mulțime. *adj.* mondial, internațional.

worldly ['wə:ldli] *adj.* lumesc; profan; trupesc.

world-wide ['wə:ldwaid] *adj.* mondial.

worm [wə:m] *s.* vierme; filet de șurub. *vt.* a-și croi drum; a smulge, a obține.

worm-eaten ['wə:m͵i:tn] *adj.* viermănos; ros de molii; demodat.

wormwood ['wə:mwud] *s.* pelin.

worn [wɔ:n] *vt., vi. part. trec. de la* **wear**.

worn-out ['wɔ:n'aut] *adj.* istovit; uzat; tocit.

worried ['wʌrid] *adj.* necăjit; speriat; tulburat.

worry ['wʌri] *s.* neliniște; tulburare; necaz; grijă. *vt.* a necăji; a chinui; a neliniști, a agita; a hărțui. *vi.* a se necăji; a se agita; a-și face griji.

worse [wə:s] *adj. compar. de la* **bad** mai rău ; mai bolnav. *adv.* mai rău ; ~ *off* într-o situaţie mai proastă.

worsen ['wə:sn] *vt., vi.* a (se) înrăutăţi ; a (se) agrava ; a (se) ascuţi.

worship ['wə:ʃip] *s.* cult ; adoraţie ; religiozitate. *vt.* a se închina la ; a adora. *vi.* a practica cultul (religios).

worshipper ['wə:ʃipə] *s.* adorator ; credincios.

worst [wə:st] *s.* situaţie foarte proastă ; partea cea mai rea ; *at (the)* ~ în cel mai rău caz. *adj., adv. superl. de la* **bad(ly).** cel mai rău ; cel mai prost.

worsted ['wustid] *s.* lînă răsucită ; postav.

worth [wə:θ] *s.* valoare ; merite ; marfă în valoare de (o anumită sumă). *adj.* în valoare de ; merituos ; valoros ; *to be* ~ *a* valora ; a costa ; a merita.

worthless ['wə:θlis] *adj.* fără valoare ; nefolositor.

worthy ['wə:ði] *s.* celebritate, somitate. *adj.* merituos ; onorabil ; demn (de respect etc.).

would [wəd, wud] *v. aux., v. mod., trec. de la* **will**[1].

would-be ['wud bi:] *adj.* aşa-zis, pretins.

wound[1] [wu:nd] *s.* rană ; avarie ; stricăciune ; dăunare ; jignire. *vt.* a răni ; a strica, a dăuna (cuiva) ; a jigni.

wound[2] [waund] *vt., vi. trec. şi part. trec. de la* **wind**[2].

wove [wouv] *vt., vi. trec. de la* **weave.**

woven ['wouvn] *vt., vi. part. trec. de la* **weave.**

wove-paper ['wouv,peipə] *s.* hîrtie velină.

wrangle ['ræŋgl] *s.* ceartă ; hărmălaie. *vi.* a se certa (zgomotos).

wrap [ræp] *s.* şal ; mantie ; haină de blană. *vt.* a înfăşura ; a ambala ; a învălui. *vi.* a se înfăşura, a se înfofoli ; a se învălui.

wrapper ['ræpə] *s.* bandă (de hîrtie) ; supracopertă ; capot (subţire).

wrapping ['ræpiŋ] *s.* înveliş ; ambalaj.

wrath [rɔ:θ] *s.* mînie.

wrathful ['rɔ:θfl] *adj.* mînios.

wreak [ri:k] *vt.* a-şi vărsa, a-şi descărca (furia etc.).

wreath [ri:θ] *s.* ghirlandă ; coroană funerară ; sul ; colac (de fum etc.).

wreck [rek] *s.* epavă ; ruină ; distrugere, năruire ; rămăşiţe aruncate de valuri. *vt.* a distruge ; a nărui ; a face să naufragieze.

wreckage ['rekidʒ] *s.* rămăşiţe (ale unei distrugeri) ; resturi.

wrecker ['rekə] *s.* sabotor ; diversionist.

wren [ren] *s.* pitulice.

wrench [rentʃ] *s.* smulgere ; smucitură ; *fig.* chin ; cheie franceză. *vt.* a smulge ; *fig.* a deforma.

wrest [rest] *vt.* a smulge ; a scoate ; a deforma.

wrestle ['resl] *s.* luptă (corp la corp) ; trîntă. *vi.* a se lupta.

wrestler ['reslə] *s. sport* luptător.

wrestling ['resliŋ} *s. sport* lupte.

wretch [retʃ] s. nenorocit; mizerabil.

wretched ['retʃid] adj. nenorocit; mizerabil; trist; ticălos.

wriggle ['rigl] s. contorsiune; zvîrcoleală. vt. a suci; a agita. vi. a se zvîrcoli; a se zbate.

wring [riŋ] s. strînsoare. vt. a răsuci; a stoarce; a smulge.

wringing wet ['wriŋiŋ‚wet] adj. ud leoarcă.

wrinkle ['riŋkl] s. zbîrcitură; creţ. vt., vi. a (se) zbîrci; a (se) încreţi.

wrist [rist] s. încheietura mîinii.

wristband ['risbænd] s. manşetă.

wristlet ['ristlit] s. brăţară.

wristwatch ['ristwɔtʃ] s. ceas de mînă.

writ [rit] s. document, act; jur. mandat; scriptură.

write [rait] vt. a scrie; a aşterne pe hîrtie; to ~ down a nota; to ~ off a compune; a anula; to ~ up a elabora. vi. a scrie; a se ocupa cu scrisul.

writer ['raitə] s. scriitor; conţopist.

writhe [raið] s. zvîrcoleală. vi. a se zvîrcoli; a se zbate; a se chinui; a suferi.

writing ['raitiŋ] s. scris, scriere.

writing-desk ['raitiŋdesk] s. pupitru.

written ['ritn] vt., vi. part. trec. de la write.

wrong [rɔŋ] s. greşeală; păcat; nedreptate; ticăloşie; to be (in the) ~ a greşi. adj. greşit; păcătos; imoral; incorect; nedrept; on the ~ side of fifty trecut de cincizeci de ani; to take the ~ train a lua un alt tren. vi. a nedreptăţi; a judeca greşit. adv. greşit; rău; incorect; to go ~ a apuca pe un drum greşit; a se duce de rîpă.

wrongdoer ['rɔŋ'duə] s. răufăcător; ticălos.

wrongful ['rɔŋfl] adj. greşit; nedrept; ilegal.

wrongly ['rɔŋli] adv. greşit; prost; incorect.

wrote [rout] vt., vi. trec. de la write.

wrought [rɔ:t] vt., vi. trec. şi part. trec. de la work; lucrat; creat; forjat.

wrung [rʌŋ] vt. trec. şi part. trec. de la wring.

wry [rai] adj. strîmb; deformat; pus greşit; to make a ~ face sau mouth a face o strîmbătură.

X

X [eks] s. X, x.

Xmas ['krismes] s. Crăciun.

X-ray ['eks'rei] s. rază X, radiografie; radioscopie.

xilophone ['zailəfoun] s. xilofon.

Y

Y [wai] s. Y, y.

yacht [jɔt] s. iaht.

yahoo [jə'hu:] s. fiinţă inferioară.

yank [jæŋk] vt. a smuci.

Yankee ['jæŋki:] s. iancheu.

yap [jæp] s. lătrat. vi: a lătra.

yard [jɑ:d] s. iard (90 cm); metru de stofă; mar. vargă de vîntrea; curte; fabrică; şantier; depou de cale ferată; the Yard poliţia londoneză.

yarn [jɑ:n] s. fir tors; poveste (vînătorească). vi. a spune poveşti; a sta la taifas.

yawl [jɔ:l] s. iolă; şalupă.

yawn [jɔ:n] s. căscat. vi. a (se) căsca.

ye [ji:] pron. înv. voi.

yea [jei] s., adv., interj. da.

year [jə:] s. an; pl. vîrstă.

year-book ['jə:buk] s. anuar.

yearling ['jə:liŋ] s. animal de un an.

yearly ['jə:li] adj., adv. anual.

yearn [jə:n] vi. a tînji; a· se ofili de dor.

yearning ['jə:niŋ] s. dor; dorinţă. adj. doritor; care tînjeşte.

yeast [ji:st] s. drojdie (de bere).

yeasty ['ji:sti] adj. spumos; înspumat.

yell [jel] s. ţipăt; strigăt. vt., vi. a ţipa.

yellow ['jelou] s. galben. adj. galben; fricos; invidios; bănuitor, gelos; laş. vt., vi. a îngălbeni.

yellow press ['jeloupres] s. ziare de scandal.

yelp [jelp] s. lătrat. vi. a lătra; a chelălăi.

yeoman ['joumən] s. răzeş; fermier; ţăran; cavalerist.

yeomanry ['joumənri] s. răzeşi(me); cavalerie.

yes [jes] s. da; încuviinţare; vot pentru. adv., interj. da.

yesman [jesmən] s. oportunist; slugă plecată; conformist.

yesterday ['jestədi] s. ieri; trecut. adj. de ieri. adv. ieri.

yet [jet] adv. încă; pînă acum; acum; în plus; cîndva; şi mai; şi totuşi. conj. totuşi.

yew [ju:] s. tisă.

Yiddish ['jidiʃ] s., adj. idiş.

yield [ji:ld] s. producţie (la hectar); pl. produse. vt. a produce; a ceda; a lăsa. vi. a ceda; a se da bătut.

yielding ['ji:ldiŋ] adj. docil; supus; moale.

yoghourt ['jougət] s. iaurt.

yoke [jouk] s. jug; pereche de boi; cobiliţă. vt. a înjuga; a uni.

yokel ['joukl] s. ţărănoi.

yolk [jouk] s. gălbenuş.

yon(der) ['jɔn(də) adv. colo. adj. de colo.

yore [jɔ:] s.: of ~ de demult.

you [ju(:)] pron. tu; mata; dumneata; voi; dumneavoastră.

young [jʌŋ] s. pui; the ~ tinerii. adj. tînăr; tineresc; nou; nepriceput.

young lady ['jʌŋˌleidi] s. domnişoară; tînără.

young man ['jʌŋˌmæn] s. tînăr.

youngster ['jʌŋstə] s. băiat; flăcău.

young woman ['jʌŋˌwumən] s. tînără; domnişoară.

your [jɔ:] *adj.* tău, ta etc.
yours [jɔ:z] *pron.* al tău, a ta etc.
yourself [jɔ:'self] *pron.* ţu însuţi; te; tu; *all by* ~ singur; chiar tu.
yours truly [jɔ:z'tru:lĭ] *s.* sub-semnatul; al dvs. *sau* al tău prieten.

youth [ju:θ] *s.* tinereţe; tînăr; tineret.
youthful ['ju:θfl] *adj.* tînăr; tineresc.

Z

Z [zed] *s.* Z, z.
zeal [zi:l] *s.* zel; entuziasm.
zealot ['zelət] *s.* fanatic (religios).
zebra ['zi:brə] *s.* zebră. *adj.* în dungi.
zebra crossing ['zi:brə'krɔsiŋ] *s.* trecere pentru pietoni (marcată cu dungi).
zenith ['zeniθ] *s.* zenit; *fig.* culme.
zero ['ziərou] *s.* zero.
zest [zest] *s.* gust picant; condiment; entuziasm; zel; interes.

zinc [ziŋk] *s.* zinc.
zinnia ['zinjə] *s. bot.* cîrciumăreasă.
Zionism ['zaiənizəm] *s.* sionism.
zip [zip] *s.* ţiuit; fermoar.
zip fastener [zip'fɑ:snə] *s.* fermoar.
zipper ['zipə] *s.* fermoar.
zither ['ziθə] *s.* ţiteră.
zone [zoun] *s.* zonă; regiune.
zoo [zu:] *s.* grădină zoologică.
zoological [ˌzoə'lɔdʒikl] *adj.* zoologic.
zoologist [zo'ɔlədʒist] *s.* zoolog.